HOUGHTON MIFFLIN

English

D1478017

Portland Christian School
2500 Portland Avenue
Louisville, Kentucky 40212

Authors
Robert Rueda
Tina Saldivar
Lynne Shapiro
Shane Templeton
C. Ann Terry
Catherine Valentino
Shelby A. Wolf

Consultants
Jeanneine P. Jones
Monette Coleman McIver
Rojulene Norris

HOUGHTON MIFFLIN BOSTON

Teacher Advisory Panel

Karen Brohaugh
Scandia Elementary School
Scandia, MN

Sybil Bynum-Williams
Bonaire Middle School
Bonaire, GA

Ann Clayton
Rockway Middle School
Miami, FL

Yvette Colyer
Bel-Air Elementary School
Albuquerque, NM

Charlene Cook
Belair Elementary School
Jefferson City, MO

Brenda Dukes
Aycock Middle School
Greensboro, NC

Sharon Fiske
Meadowlark School
Great Falls, MT

Peggy Gallo
Upper Dublin School District
Dresher, PA

Ann Hoffmeister
Verona Public Schools
Verona, IL

Gerri McManus
Stanley School
Swampscott, MA

Sissy Othicke
Los Ranchos Elementary School
Albuquerque, NM

Rosa Maria Peña
Rodriguez Elementary School
Austin, TX

Connie Rupp
Stukey Elementary School
Northglen, CO

Marge Segal
Holcomb Bridge Middle School
Apharetta, GA

Judy Thomas
Meadowview Elementary School
Meadowview, VA

Carolyn Tucker
Dixon Elementary School
Dixon, KY

Alfie Turner
Colton Elementary School
Spring Valley, NY

Ginger Verrill
Bush Elementary School
Idaho Falls, ID

Linda Wallis
Madison Elementary School
Riverside, CA

Acknowledgments/Credits

For each of the selections listed below, grateful acknowledgment is made for permission to excerpt and/or reprint original or copyrighted material, as follows:

From *Bees Dance and Whales Sing: The Mysteries of Animal Communication* by Margery Facklam, illustrated by Pamela Johnson. Text copyright ©1992 by Margery Facklam. Illustrations copyright 1992 by Pamela Johnson. Reprinted by permission of Sierra Club Books for Children.

"Just a Sunday Drive in the Country" by Pete Hendley from *Cricket* Magazine, May 1999 issue, Volume 26, Number 9. Text copyright ©1996 by Pete Hendley. Cover ©1999 by Carus Publishing Company. Reprinted by permission of the author and *Cricket* Magazine.

Special Character *Sal, the Writing Pal* by LeeLee Brazeal.

Copyright © 2006 by Houghton Mifflin Company. All rights reserved.

No part of this work may be reproduced or transmitted in any form or by any means, electronic or mechanical, including photocopying and recording, or by any information storage or retrieval system without the prior written permission of the copyright owner, unless such copying is expressly permitted by federal copyright law. With the exception of nonprofit transcription in Braille, Houghton Mifflin is not authorized to grant permission for further uses of copyrighted selections reprinted in this text without the permission of their owners as identified herein. Address requests for permission to make copies of Houghton Mifflin material to School Permissions, Houghton Mifflin Company, 222 Berkeley Street, Boston, MA 02116.

Printed in the U.S.A.

ISBN-13: 978-0-618-61127-0 ISBN-10: 0-618-61127-4

5 6 7 8 9 10-B-11 10 09 08 07

Grade 4

HOUGHTON MIFFLIN

English

Authors
Robert Rueda
Tina Saldivar
Lynne Shapiro
Shane Templeton
C. Ann Terry
Catherine Valentino
Shelby A. Wolf

Consultants
Jeanneine P. Jones
Monette Coleman McIver
Rojulene Norris

HOUGHTON MIFFLIN BOSTON

Acknowledgments

For each of the selections listed below, grateful acknowledgment is made for permission to excerpt and/or reprint original or copyrighted material as follows:

Published Models

From *Bats: Night Fliers* by Betsy Maestro, illustrated by Giulio Maestro. Text copyright ©1994 by Betsy Maestro. Illustrations copyright ©1994 by Giulio Maestro. Reprinted by permission of Scholastic Inc.

From *The Changing World: Jungles & Rainforests* by John A. Burton. Copyright ©1996 by Dragon's World Ltd. Reprinted by permission of Belitha Press Ltd.

From *Charlotte's Web* by E.B. White, illustrated by Garth Williams. Text copyright 1952 and renewed ©1980 by E.B. White. Illustrations copyright 1952 and renewed ©1980 by Garth Williams. Used by permission of HarperCollins Publishers.

"Crows" from *Legends of the Seminoles* as told by Betty Mae Jumper, illustrated by Guy LaBree. Text copyright ©1994 by Betty Mae Jumper and Peter B. Gallagher. Illustrations copyright © by Guy LaBree. Used by permission of Pineapple Press, Inc.

Acknowledgments are continued at the back of the book following the last page of the Index.

Copyright © 2006 by Houghton Mifflin Company. All rights reserved.

No part of this work may be reproduced or transmitted in any form or by any means, electronic or mechanical, including photocopying and recording, or by any information storage or retrieval system without the prior written permission of the copyright owner, unless such copying is expressly permitted by federal copyright law. With the exception of nonprofit transcription in Braille, Houghton Mifflin is not authorized to grant permission for further uses of copyrighted selections reprinted in this text without the permission of their owners as identified herein. Address requests for permission to make copies of Houghton Mifflin material to School Permissions, Houghton Mifflin Company, 222 Berkeley Street, Boston, MA 02116.

Printed in the U.S.A.

ISBN: 0-618-61120-7

1 2 3 4 5 6 7 8 9 10-DW-11 10 09 08 07 06 05

HOUGHTON MIFFLIN

English

Just follow the colors . . .

Part 1 **Grammar, Usage, and Mechanics**

Part 2 **Writing, Listening, Speaking, and Viewing**

Part 3 **Tools and Tips**

Part 1

Grammar, Usage, and Mechanics

In the blue grammar units, look for these ways to make your writing stronger.

Proofreading

Revising

Revising Strategies

Writing Wrap-Up

Part 2

Writing, Listening, Speaking, and Viewing

In the green writing units, look for these grammar links for help as you write.

GRAMMAR CHECK

GRAMMAR TIP

GRAMMAR LINK

Revising Strategies

Proofreading Checklist

Grammar and Spelling Connections

Look for these parts, too!

Special Focus

COMMUNICATION LINK

Part 3 Tools and Tips

Use these Tools and Tips whenever you need them.

- Listening and Speaking Strategies
- Building Vocabulary
- Research and Study Strategies
- Test-Taking Strategies
- Using Technology
- Writer's Tools
- Guide to Capitalization, Punctuation, and Usage
- Spelling Guide
- Diagramming Guide
- Thesaurus Plus
- Glossary of Language Arts Terms
- Index

Visit Kids' Place for Houghton Mifflin English at www.eduplace.com/kids/hme for activities like these.

- Bright Ideas for Writing
- Grammar Blast
- Evaluation Station
- Net's Best for Research
- Authors and Illustrators
- Graphic Organizers
- Writers' Showcase

TABLE OF CONTENTS

Getting Started

Part 1 Grammar, Usage, and Mechanics

Table of Contents

Lesson Objective

Students will:

• use a table of contents

Focus on Instruction

- Tell students that a table of contents helps a reader preview a book by showing the organization as well as by providing general information about the book's contents.
- Explain that some tables of contents, such as those for novels, are a simple list of the numbers and titles of the chapters. If the organization of the book is more complex, the table of contents will give more information and may be several pages long.
- Explain that one way to use the contents is by noting the largest sections of the book and then looking at the subsections of each one. Ask students how a table of contents might help them in using this book.
- Have students find the answers to these questions.

1. How many main parts are in this book? (three) What are they? (Part 1 is Grammar, Usage, and Mechanics. Part 2 is Writing, Listening, Speaking, and Viewing. Part 3 is Tools and Tips.)
2. How many units are in Part 1? (seven) What is the title of Unit 2? (Nouns) How many lessons are in this unit? (seven) What other materials are in this unit? (Revising Strategies: Sentence Fluency, Revising Strategies: Vocabulary, Enrichment, Checkup, Test Practice, Cumulative Review, and Extra Practice)
3. How many units are in Part 2? (six) Which unit would you use to find help with writing a story? (Unit 9) How many models of stories are listed? (two) What kinds are they? (published and student) What are the focus skills in this unit? (Planning Characters, Planning Setting and Plot, Developing Characters, Developing the Plot, and Writing with Voice)
4. Each unit in Part 2 includes subsections called Special Focus and Communication Links. Which unit includes the Special Focus on writing a book report? (Unit 12) Which unit includes the Communication Link Comparing Visual Information? (Unit 10)
5. How many sections are in the Tools and Tips? (eleven) Which section would help you use a computer in your writing? (Using Technology) Which section could help you study for an exam? (Test-Taking Strategies)

Part 1

WRITING TRAITS

Unit 2 Nouns 63

WRITING TRAITS

Unit 3 Verbs 95

WRITING TRAITS

Unit 4 Adjectives 135

Table of Contents xiii

Part 1

WRITING TRAITS

Unit 5 Capitalization and Punctuation 165

WRITING TRAITS

Unit 6 Pronouns 203

xiv Table of Contents

WRITING TRAITS

Unit 7 Adverbs and Prepositions 233

Table of Contents xv

Part 2

Writing, Listening, Speaking, and Viewing

SECTION 1 Narrating and Entertaining

Getting Started

WRITING TRAITS

Unit 8 Writing a Personal Narrative 274

WRITING TRAITS

Unit 9 Writing a Story 297

Table of Contents xvii

Part 2

SECTION 2 Explaining and Informing

Getting Started

Unit 10 Writing Instructions 338

WRITING TRAITS

Unit 11 Writing a Research Report 368

Table of Contents xix

Part 2

SECTION 3 Expressing and Influencing

Getting Started

Unit 12 Writing to Express an Opinion 412

Unit 13 Writing to Persuade 446

Table of Contents xxi

Part 3

Tools and Tips

xxii Table of Contents

Getting Started Planning Guide

2 weeks

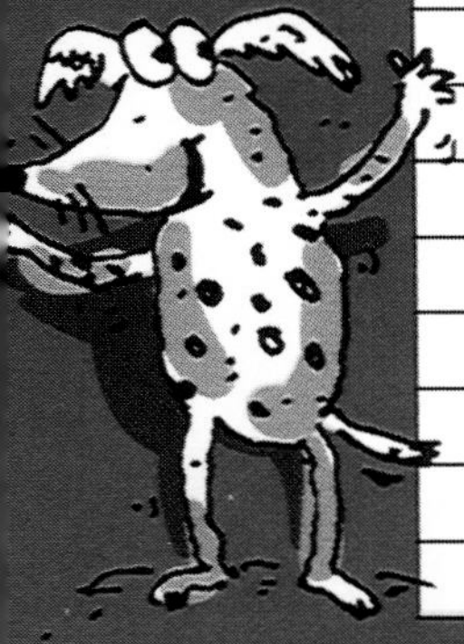

Tools and Tips

- **Listening and Speaking Strategies,** *pp. H4–H10*
- **Building Vocabulary,** *pp. H11–H17*
- **Using Technology,** *pp. H35–H47*
- **Writer's Tools,** *pp. H48–H54*
- **Spelling Guide,** *pp. H65–H69*
- **Guide to Capitalization, Punctuation, and Usage,** *pp. H55–H64*
- **Thesaurus Plus,** *pp. H79–H100*

All audiotape recordings are also available on CD.

Additional Resources

Teacher's Resource Book
Transparencies, Getting Started
Posters, Getting Started
Audiotapes

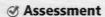

Technology Tools

CD-ROM: *EasyBook Deluxe
MediaWeaver™, Sunburst/Humanities software
*Type to Learn™

*©Sunburst Technology Corporation, a Houghton Mifflin Company. All rights reserved.

INTERNET: http://www.eduplace.com/kids/hme/ *or* http://www.eduplace.com/rdg/hme/

Visit Education Place for these additional support materials and activities:

- author biographies
- student writing models
- graphic organizers
- proofreading practice
- writing prompts
- benchmark papers

Assessment

Test Booklet, Getting Started

Meeting Individual Needs

▶ **FOR SPECIAL NEEDS/INCLUSION:** *Houghton Mifflin English* Audiotape

▶ **FOR STUDENTS ACQUIRING ENGLISH:**

- Notes and activities are included in this Teacher's Edition throughout the unit to help you adapt or use pupil book activities with students acquiring English.
- Students acquiring English can listen to the published and student models on audiotape.
- MediaWeaver™, Sunburst/Humanities software, offers bilingual features, including Spanish menus, a Spanish spelling tool, and a Spanish thesaurus.

▶ **ENRICHMENT:** See *Teacher's Resource Book.*

School-Home Connection

Suggestions for informing or involving family members in classroom activities and learning related to this unit are included in the Teacher's Edition throughout the unit.

Keeping a Journal

Discuss with students the value of keeping a journal as a way of promoting self-expression and fluency. Encourage students to record their thoughts and ideas in a private book or, if you prefer, in a notebook that can be reviewed periodically as a way of measuring each individual's growth. You may wish to use any of the following prompts to help students generate ideas.

Journal Prompts

- What do you do for fun after school and on weekends?
- What is your favorite thing to do? What is your least favorite thing to do?
- Whom do you like to do things with?

Getting Started

Listening, Speaking, and Viewing

A Day in the Life of a Student
If we order pizza at my sleepover party, it might cost less than a home-cooked meal.
Hmm, Mom looks doubtful.
You won't have to cook!
Where is one vertex on this pyramid?
Can you explain *vertex*?
No, it's not very far away at all. In fact, it's right behind you!
Gym
Buy our sneakers, and you'll rule the school!
I don't need those sneakers to be cool!
As the clock struck twelve, a dark cloud of bats burst from the old bell tower . . .

Listening, Speaking, and Viewing

Lesson Objective

Students will:

- identify and discuss everyday activities that involve listening, speaking, and viewing

Focus on Instruction

- Direct students' attention to the pictures, and ask volunteers to read the dialogue in the thought or speech balloons.
- Discuss with students what information is communicated in each scene and how it is conveyed—through listening, speaking, or viewing.
- Ask students which pictures show informal speaking situations, such as talking casually with friends or family. (pictures of mother and daughter, two students) Explain that in these kinds of situations, people may use slang and other informal language and not worry about whether their sentences are grammatically correct. However, in school or in other more formal situations, students may need to use more formal language and follow the rules of English grammar.
- Point out that listening, speaking, and viewing are important means of communication.

Learning from Each Other

Lesson Objectives

Students will:
- identify purposes for listening, speaking, and viewing in daily activities
- cite occasions for using listening, speaking, and viewing to communicate in their lives

Focus on Instruction

- Have a volunteer read the first paragraph aloud. Ask students what special skills, experiences, interests, and opinions they have and how that information might help others.
- Have students look at the pictured students and identify what special skills, experiences, interests, and opinions they could share.
- Ask a volunteer to read the next paragraph aloud. Then review and discuss the purposes and examples in the chart. Ask volunteers to share examples from their own experiences for each purpose.
- Be aware that some students prefer to work alone and might resist the idea of working together. Reassure these students that while they will be asked to collaborate occasionally, they will not have to work this way exclusively.

Think and Discuss

- The people in pictures 1 and 4 are listening to form an opinion and are speaking to persuade. The people in pictures 2 and 3 are listening to get information and are speaking to inform. The people in picture 5 are listening for enjoyment and are speaking to entertain. The people in picture 2 are viewing to get information. The people in picture 4 are viewing to form an opinion.
- Answers will vary. Students might enjoy keeping a communication log for one day. Encourage them to record times during that day when they found themselves listening, speaking, and viewing. Have them share their results with the class.

Learning from Each Other

Each one of you has your own skills, experiences, interests, and opinions. As a boy or a girl, you're like a book full of great information and ideas to share. Together as a class, you're a whole encyclopedia!

Together, we can find
the Big Dipper, tell a stegosaurus from a pterodactyl, juggle oranges, and cook tamales!

By learning from each other, you can make school—and life—easier and much more fun. You will be able to rely on one another to solve problems, to think of new ideas, and to offer encouragement. How can you best learn from each other? SPEAK, LISTEN, and VIEW! Speaking lets you share what you know. Listening and looking, or viewing, help you learn from others. Here are some of the most common reasons for speaking, listening, and viewing.

Speaking	Listening and Viewing	Examples
to entertain	for enjoyment	telling a joke or a story, attending an art exhibit, a movie, or the circus
to inform	to get information	listening to a weather report, explaining a math problem to a friend, reading someone's body language
to persuade	to form an opinion	asking parents for permission to stay up late, selecting a movie at the video store

Think and Discuss See TE margin for answers.

- Look back at the pictures on page 1. What reason does each person have for listening? for speaking? for viewing?
- At what other times do you listen, speak, and view during the day?

Discussion Breakdown

These students are trying to choose a class pet, but they are not using good listening and speaking skills. What's wrong?

Think and Discuss See TE margin for answers.

- What is each student doing wrong in this discussion?
- What could the students do to improve their discussion?

Getting Started: Discussion Breakdown 3

Discussion Breakdown

Lesson Objectives

Students will:

- identify communication problems in a discussion
- suggest ways to improve communication in a discussion

Focus on Instruction

- Have volunteers describe what each character is doing and read aloud what each is saying or thinking.
- Ask students to reflect on the characters pictured. Have them privately acknowledge whether they see themselves and their own behavior in this scene. (Don't make students share this information with the class!) Ask them to pay extra-close attention to their behavior in future discussions and, if necessary, to improve on it.

Think and Discuss

- Starting with the boy at the top center and moving clockwise: Student 1 is controlling the conversation; Student 2 is interrupting; Student 3 is disagreeing impolitely; Student 4 is having a side conversation; Student 5 is not asking for help; Student 6 is not participating; Student 7 is creating distraction; Student 8 is daydreaming and not doing her job.
- You might want to assign each student character to a small group of students.
- Student 1 should give others a chance to speak; Student 2 should wait her turn; Student 3 should disagree politely; Student 4 should share his idea with the group; Student 5 should ask for help; Student 6 should participate; Student 7 should be quiet; Student 8 should pay attention.

Discussion Breakthrough

Lesson Objectives

Students will:

- identify and discuss behavior that promotes good listening and speaking skills
- generate guidelines for being a good listener and speaker

Focus on Instruction

Have volunteers describe what each pictured character is doing and read aloud what each is saying. Ask students how the discussion on this page differs from the one on the previous page. (The students in the picture on this page are all engaged in the discussion. All students are being respectful and contributing their ideas.)

Think and Discuss

- Have students describe the change in each character's behavior. (Student 1 asks others for ideas; Student 2 waits turn; Student 3 expresses an opinion politely; Student 4 shares idea with group; Student 5 asks for help; Student 6 participates; Student 7 stops fidgeting; Student 8 pays attention and takes notes.)
- Have students use what they learned from their demonstrations and the model discussion in this lesson to generate guidelines for being a good listener and speaker.

Discussion Breakthrough

The students are still trying to choose a class pet. How have they improved their listening and speaking skills?

Think and Discuss See TE margin for answers.

- What has each student done to improve his or her listening or speaking skills?

Being a Good Listener and Speaker

Here are some basic guidelines for listening and speaking with others. They will help you communicate at school, on the soccer field, in the mall, or around the dinner table!

When You Listen

- Face the speaker. Look him or her in the eye.
- Listen carefully. Don't daydream.
- Don't create distractions—no foot-tapping, whistling, or waving!
- If you get confused, repeat in your own words what was said. Ask if you've understood.

When You Speak

- Share your ideas with the group, not just your neighbor.
- Look at your listeners.
- Ask others what they think of your ideas. Say what you think about theirs.
- If you disagree, politely explain why.
- Stick to the subject being discussed.
- Don't interrupt or try to take over the conversation.
- Speak loudly and clearly enough for your listeners to hear and understand your words.

Try It Out Read the statements below. Choose one that interests you. Decide whether or not you agree with the statement. Discuss your opinions in small groups.

- Kids today watch too much TV.
- Summer is the best season.
- Animals are happy living in zoos.

Being a Good Listener and Speaker

Lesson Objectives

Students will:

- discuss guidelines for good listening and speaking
- use the guidelines to evaluate their listening and speaking abilities during a discussion

Focus on Instruction

Discuss the guidelines on this page with students. Ask them to compare these guidelines with the ones they created. Were there other guidelines they should add to theirs?

Try It Out

- Remind students that listening, speaking, and viewing really work together. Tell students to keep the listening and speaking guidelines in mind as they discuss their topics. Have students use the self-assessment checklists on Blackline Master GS–1 to evaluate their listening and speaking abilities.
- Help students to select another topic if the ones suggested do not appeal to them. Try to find a topic that is meaningful to your students, and about which they share a variety of opinions. Here are some additional categories you could consider: bedtimes, allowances, computers, sports salaries, food, movie ratings, wild animals as pets, and the length of the school year.
- Circulate among the groups to observe students' skills and to reinforce positive behavior.

Looking Ahead Tell students that this book includes Communication Link lessons that will help them develop good listening and speaking skills for various purposes, such as to give an oral presentation, to persuade, or to dramatize a story. Have them locate some of these lessons in Part 2 of the Contents. In addition, draw their attention to the Listening and Speaking Strategies in Part 3, Tools and Tips.

The guidelines on this page are also available as a poster.

Being a Good Viewer

Lesson Objectives

Students will:
- identify ways in which they learn by viewing
- identify ways to be a good observer

Focus on Instruction

Have students work in small groups to generate lists of things, places, and situations from which people gather information visually (maps, diagrams, signs, body language, company logos, flags, and so on). Challenge students to say what kind of information can be learned by viewing each.

Looking Ahead Draw students' attention to the Communication Link lessons in Part 2 of the Contents. Tell students that these lessons will help them develop their critical viewing skills so that they will be better able to understand and evaluate information acquired through visual sources.

Try It Out

Students can use the self-assessment viewing checklist on Blackline Master GS–2 to evaluate their viewing abilities during the Try It Out activity or with the following additional suggested activities.

- To support the points under Viewing the World Around You, have students imagine spotting a nest in a tree. Tell them to imagine climbing into the tree to get a closer look at the nest. Ask them to close their eyes and share what they see. (As students look inside, they might spy a piece of an eggshell. This clue would tell them that chicks had hatched. Upon examining the materials the nest is woven from, they might find scraps taken from their own houses!) Encourage students to share what other kinds of information they could gather.
- To support Viewing Others, have volunteers pantomime different nonverbal cues, such as an expressionless face, rolling eyes, and crossed arms. Ask students to interpret the meaning of each cue. Then have volunteers pantomime impatience, sympathy, and boredom, and ask students to decide what message they are giving. Discuss the importance of using and interpreting nonverbal cues when communicating. For a lesson on nonverbal cues, see page H7.
- To support Viewing Images, provide students with several magazine advertisements so that they can practice identifying audience, purpose, techniques, and messages. Try doing this activity as a class before asking students to work independently.

Being a Good Viewer

When you view, you look carefully and learn from what you see. What are these students learning by viewing?

When You View

Viewing the World Around You
- ▶ First, open your eyes wide! Notice all that you can.
- ▶ Then focus. What is the most important part of what you see?
- ▶ Then refocus. What interesting or important details do you see?

Viewing Others
- ▶ Watch for hand gestures that help explain what someone is saying.
- ▶ Watch people's faces for clues to how they feel.
- ▶ When you speak, watch your listeners' body language to see how they are reacting.

Viewing Still or Moving Images
- ▶ Notice the main focus of the image. What catches your eye?
- ▶ Look more closely. What details are important? Why?
- ▶ Look for the purpose of the image. Is it to entertain? inform? persuade?
- ▶ Who is the audience? How do you know?
- ▶ Does the image send the audience a message? What message?

Try It Out Using books and other materials in your classroom, look for images whose purpose is to entertain, inform, and persuade. Try to find one of each. Discuss your images with a small group. How can you tell the purpose? What is the main focus? What details are important? Answers will vary.

- Show students examples of images where different techniques such as color, bold type, large type size, and close-up camera shots have been used to get the viewer's attention. Encourage students to find their own images that use these and other techniques.

The guidelines on this page are also available as a poster.

Getting Started

The Writing Process

The Writing Process

Lesson Objective

Students will:

- identify and discuss everyday activities that involve writing

Focus on Instruction

- Ask students what kind of writing each pictured character is doing. (a thank-you note, interview notes, lab notes, a story, a sign)
- Explain to students that people write for different purposes and that not all writing requires complete accuracy. Explain that the writing people do for themselves, such as lists, notes, and diary entries, does not have to be checked for spelling, punctuation, capitalization, and other rules. However, in messages people write to others, they should always check the accuracy of names, dates, times, and other facts. Ask students which picture on this page shows writing done for oneself. (the interview notes)
- Explain to students that they need to pay attention to accuracy and to clarity of content and organization in more formal writing, such as school papers, letters, and writing for publication.

Looking Ahead Tell students that in this section they will learn how to use a series of steps known as the writing process that will help them write effectively for any audience or purpose.

What Is the Writing Process?

Lesson Objective

Students will:
- discuss the steps of the writing process

Focus on Instruction

- Explain that even professional authors use the writing process because, although they are very skillful, they still have to go back to their writing to review and improve it before they consider it final for their audience.
- Explain that the cartoon dog, Sal, will be their writing pal throughout the writing portions of this book. He will help them make their writing the best that it can be.
- Review the graphics that illustrate the different stages of the writing process. Discuss with students that the writing process is not a lockstep approach and that a writer moves back and forth between different stages as necessary, especially among prewriting, drafting, and revising.

Looking Ahead Tell students that first they will read a published model of a description. Then they will learn about the steps of the writing process one at a time as they write their own description.

This page is available as a poster.

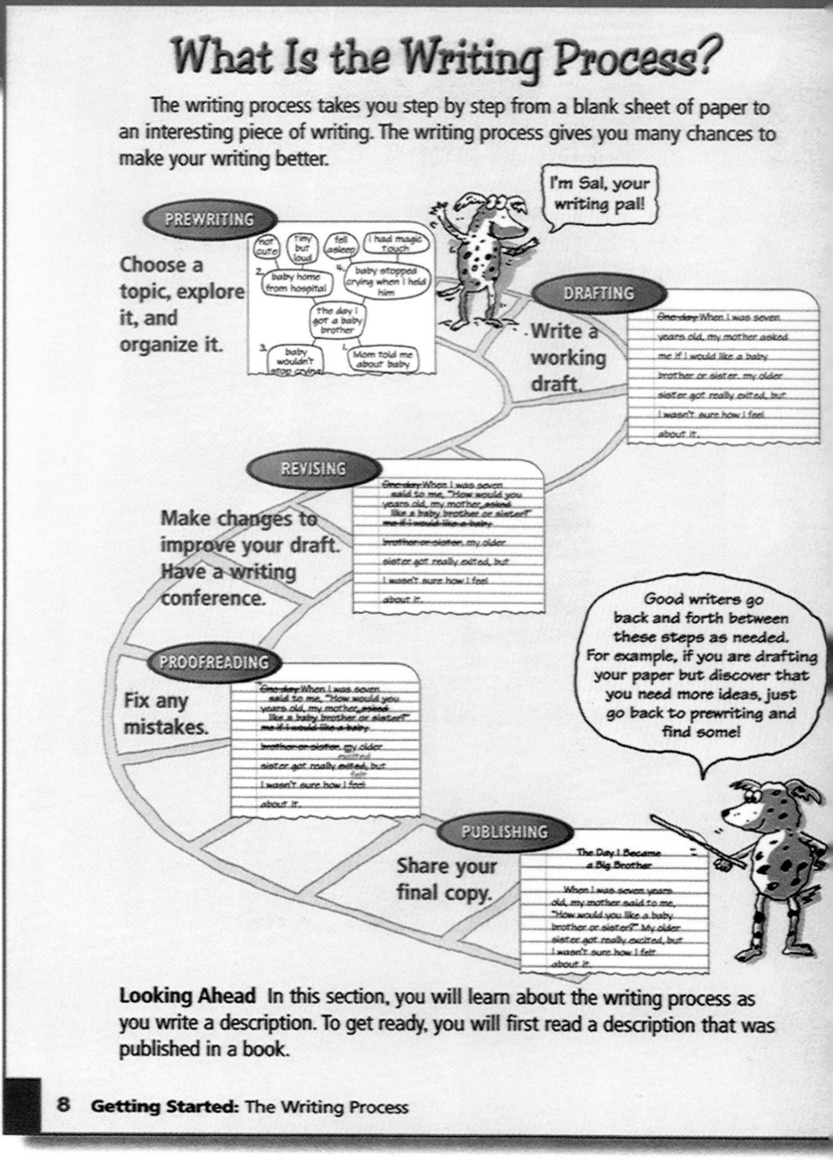

What Is the Writing Process?

The writing process takes you step by step from a blank sheet of paper to an interesting piece of writing. The writing process gives you many chances to make your writing better.

Looking Ahead In this section, you will learn about the writing process as you write a description. To get ready, you will first read a description that was published in a book.

8 **Getting Started:** The Writing Process

A Published Model

Read the following description of a barn from *Charlotte's Web*. As you read, try to imagine yourself standing inside this barn. What would you see, smell, and feel?

The Barn

from *Charlotte's Web*, by E. B. White

The barn was very large. It was very old. It smelled of hay and it smelled of manure. It smelled of the perspiration of tired horses and the wonderful sweet breath of patient cows. It often had a sort of peaceful smell—as though nothing bad could happen ever again in the world. It smelled of grain and of harness dressing and of axle grease and of rubber boots and of new rope. And whenever the cat was given a fish-head to eat, the barn would smell of fish. But mostly it smelled of hay, for there was always hay in the great loft up overhead. And there was always hay being pitched down to the cows and the horses and the sheep.

sory
ails

more ▶

Go to www.eduplace.com/kids/ for information about E. B. White.

A Published Model 9

About the Author

INTERNET CONNECTION Send your students to www.eduplace.com/kids/ for information about E. B. White.

Resources

Both fiction and nonfiction texts include excellent descriptions of characters, animals, scenes, and events. Encourage students to look for strong descriptive passages that appeal to the senses when they read and to share some of these passages with the class.

"The Barn"

Lesson Objectives

Students will:

- read a published model of a description
- identify characteristics of a description
- identify sentences listing items in a series
- describe how the illustrator's choice of content helps to extend the text's meaning

Focus on the Model

Building Background

Ask students to raise their hands if they have ever been inside a barn. Ask volunteers to describe what they saw, heard, smelled, and touched in the barn. Explain that they will read one writer's description of a barn. Tell them to pay close attention to how the writer uses sensory words to describe the barn.

Introducing Vocabulary

Introduce key vocabulary words by writing these sentences on the chalkboard.

We shoveled the **manure** out of the horse stalls and used it for fertilizer.

The farmer swung his **scythe** to cut down the tall grass.

Grandpa sharpened his knife on the spinning **grindstone**.

Reading the Selection

- Have students read the introduction to "The Barn." The purpose-setting question focuses on a characteristic of a description, the use of sensory words.

Have students read the selection as a class, independently, or with partners, or they can listen to the selection on audiotape.

- The call outs highlight key characteristics of a description that are addressed in the Think About the Description questions at the end of this selection.

A Published Model

The barn was pleasantly warm in winter when the animals spent most of their time indoors, and it was pleasantly cool in summer when the big doors stood wide open to the breeze. The barn had stalls on the main floor for the work horses, tie-ups on the main floor for the cows, a sheepfold down below for the sheep, a pigpen down below for Wilbur, and it was full of all sorts of things that you find in barns: ladders, grindstones, pitch forks, monkey wrenches, scythes, lawn mowers, snow shovels, ax handles, milk pails, water buckets, empty grain sacks, and rusty rat traps. It was the kind of barn that swallows like to build their nests in. It was the kind of barn that children like to play in. And the whole thing was owned by Fern's uncle, Mr. Homer L. Zuckerman.

touch

sight

Reading As a Writer

See TE margin for answers.

Think About the Description

- What sense—sight, sound, or smell—does E. B. White use to describe the barn in the paragraph on page 9?
- What are four smells that the writer describes?
- What does the barn feel like during the winter? during the summer?
- Where are the stalls, the sheepfold, and the pigpen found in the barn?

Think About Writer's Craft

- In the paragraph on page 10, which sentence names the most things found in the barn? What mark separates each thing listed in this sentence?

Think About the Picture

- Look at the picture on page 10. What shows you that the girl and the animals are friends?

Looking Ahead

Now you are ready to write your own description. Starting on the next page, you will find many ideas to help you. You will see how one student, Jack Welch, used the writing process to write a description of his oboe.

Mapping the Selection

Mapping helps students visualize how a piece of writing is organized. After students have read the description, draw the following chart on the board. Have students list details that the writer used to describe how the barn looks, smells, and feels. Then have students number each column of the chart to show the sequence in which the writer presents each category of details.

How It Looks	How It Smells	How It Feels

Answers to Reading As a Writer

Think About the Description

- E. B. White used smell to describe the barn.
- Sample response: The writer describes hay, the breath of cows, grain, new rope, and fish.
- The barn feels warm in winter and cool in summer.
- The stalls are found on the main floor. The sheepfold and pigpen are found beneath the main floor.

Think About Writer's Craft

- The second sentence names the most things found in the barn. A comma separates each thing.

Think About the Picture

- The animals and girl are comfortable being close to each other.

More About Writer's Craft

- Discuss with students how commas are used in a series in the second paragraph. Explain that using commas is a way to name many things in one sentence.
- This selection uses prepositional phrases to elaborate the details. Have students locate the words *of* and *in* and the words following them to see how the writer uses these phrases to add information. (Examples: *perspiration of tired horses, breath of patient cows; in the great loft, in winter*) Students might also locate prepositional phrases beginning with *to, on,* and *for*. Point out that these phrases often answer the questions *What kind?* and *Where?* Encourage students to use prepositional phrases to add detail to their own writing.

MEETING INDIVIDUAL NEEDS

FOR STUDENTS ACQUIRING ENGLISH

This story includes vocabulary that will be unfamiliar to many students. Begin by showing photos of a typical barn in the U. S. Next, help students name the five senses: sight, hearing, smell, taste, touch. Ask students to name sights, sounds, and smells in a barn; list ideas on the board. In addition to words for farm animals, ensure that selection words such as *hay, manure, grain, loft, stalls,* and *pigpen* are listed and explained. Explain that it is not necessary to know every word to understand the description. Direct students' attention to the list of things found in the barn, and suggest that they simply imagine the kinds of things that might be in an old barn.

Using the Writing Process

Lesson Objective

Students will:

- discuss prewriting strategies for choosing a topic

What Is Prewriting?

Focus on Instruction

- Ask students why knowing their audience and their purpose before they begin writing is important. (They can determine what tone and language will be most effective.)
- **Audience** Ask students whom E. B. White probably expected would read "The Barn." (Sample answer: children) Then ask how the description might have been written differently if he had written it for a group of farmers. (Sample answer: might be more about the structure and dimensions of the barn)
- **Purpose** Discuss with students what E. B. White's purpose in writing his description might have been. (Sample answer: to help readers appreciate the fascinating environment inside a barn) Ask how the description might have been different if he had wanted to frighten his readers. (Sample answer: focus more on details such as the rats, spiders, and bats that live in the barn)
- **Format** Ask students how E. B. White might have written the text differently if it were being published as a newspaper article. (Sample answer: less description, more facts) Suggest that students think about their purpose, audience, and publishing format throughout their writing.
- Review and discuss the strategies in the chart. Point out that these strategies can be used for any type of writing. Note that most topic ideas spring from everyday thoughts or events.
- Tell students that many writers—even adults who get paid to write—think finding a topic is the hardest part of writing.
- Tell students that not every topic will be right for the piece of writing they are doing.
- Remind students to choose a topic they want to write about. Explain that they will not grab their readers if their topic does not grab them.
- When discussing the Ways to Think of Topics chart, emphasize that each way of finding a topic can work for many different kinds of writing. Tell students, for example, that experiences are not just for personal narratives, and imagination is not just for stories.
- Tell students to refer to this page any time they need to think of different ways to find a topic.

Using the Writing Process

What Is Prewriting?

Prewriting has three parts. First, you choose your topic. Next, you explore your topic. Then you organize, or plan, your writing.

Start thinking about **audience** and **purpose**. Who will read or listen to your writing? What kind of paper will you write?

Think about how you are going to **publish** or **share** your paper. This may make a difference in how you write your paper.

How Do I Choose a Topic?

Here are a few ways to find an idea to write about.

Ways to Think of Topics

Try this!	Here's how.	
Remember your experiences or those of others.	You fell off your bike into a huge, deep puddle of mud.	• Write a **personal narrative** about what happened. • Add this event to a **story**. • **Describe** how you looked when you stood up out of the puddle.
Read a book.	You enjoyed reading about the life of a baseball player.	• Write a **research report** about an athlete you like. • **Persuade** your classmates to play baseball.
Reread your journal.	You wrote a journal entry about your summer vacation.	• Write an **opinion essay** about why summer is the best season. • **Compare and contrast** summer and winter.
Use your imagination.	What would it be like to be a pioneer?	• Write a **story** about a pioneer family. • Write a **research report** about pioneer life.

Write a Description

Choosing a Description Topic

Learning from a Model Jack's school newspaper has a section called "My Favorite Things." Jack wanted to write a description for this section of the paper. First, he made a list of ideas and thought about each idea.

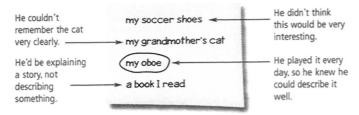

- my soccer shoes ← He didn't think this would be very interesting.
- He couldn't remember the cat very clearly. → my grandmother's cat
- (my oboe) ← He played it every day, so he knew he could describe it well.
- He'd be explaining a story, not describing something. → a book I read

Choose Your Topic

As you choose your topic, think about your **purpose**, your **audience**, and how you will **publish** or **share** your description.

1. **List** five topics that you would like to describe, such as a special person, a pet, or a place you love. Use the chart on page 12 to think of ideas.
2. **Discuss** your topics with a partner. Which ideas does your partner like? Why?
3. **Ask** yourself these questions about each topic.
   - Can I observe it before I write about it?
   - Can I use at least three senses to describe it?
   - Which topic would I most like to write about?
4. **Circle** the topic you will write about.

Keep all your work for your description in one place, such as a writing folder.

Tech Tip
See page H39 for ideas for using a computer at each stage of the writing process.

Help with Choosing a Topic

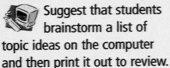

SOURCES OF TOPIC IDEAS
Suggest these description topics.
- a treasured object
- a family member or friend
- a pet
- a favorite food
- a flower or tree
- an article of clothing
- a favorite room

TECH TIP
Suggest that students brainstorm a list of topic ideas on the computer and then print it out to review.

SCHOOL-HOME CONNECTION
Suggest that students discuss their topic ideas with someone at home.

Write a Description

Lesson Objectives

Students will:
- evaluate a modeled list of description topics
- list their ideas for audience, purpose, and publishing and sharing formats
- list possible topics for a description
- discuss their ideas with a partner
- choose an appropriate topic to write about

Choosing a Description Topic

Focus on the Model

- Ask students to identify Jack's audience, purpose, and format for sharing or publishing his description. (students at his school, to share information about a favorite thing, a section of his school newspaper)
- Ask students why they think Jack chose his oboe as his topic. (Sample response: because he can look at it as he writes, he can use several senses to describe it, and it's interesting)

Choose Your Topic

- Discuss with students possible audiences, purposes, and forms of publishing or sharing their description.
- Provide students with these specific questions about audience, purpose, and publishing or sharing.

  Will you write for a friend? the general public?

  Do you want to tell how complicated, delicate, or silly something is?

  Will you publish it in a newspaper? a poster?
- Encourage students to select topics that they can observe as they write or that they can clearly remember.
- Review each student's final topic choice. Be sure that the student can describe it by using at least three of the five senses.
- If students are not sure whether they can describe an object using three senses, suggest creating a chart with a column for each sense. Then have students write their details to see if they have enough.
- Point out the Tech Tip and refer students to page H39.

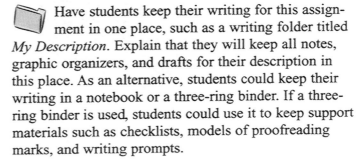

Have students keep their writing for this assignment in one place, such as a writing folder titled *My Description*. Explain that they will keep all notes, graphic organizers, and drafts for their description in this place. As an alternative, students could keep their writing in a notebook or a three-ring binder. If a three-ring binder is used, students could use it to keep support materials such as checklists, models of proofreading marks, and writing prompts.

Lesson Objective

Students will:

- discuss prewriting strategies for exploring and elaborating on a topic

What Is Exploring?

Focus on Instruction

- Explain to students that as they explore their topic and list details related to it, they may discover that they have more information than they can use in a short description. If this happens, tell students to narrow their topic further. Tell students that exploring may instead show them that a topic is too small. If this happens, they should go back to their list of ideas and start with another topic. Note that a modified sense chart is also used for organizing on page 17.
- Review and discuss the Exploring Strategies chart with students. Explain that they can use any of the six strategies for any kind of writing, but some strategies may be more helpful than others for a specific topic or kind of writing. Suggest that students refer to this page whenever they need to explore a writing topic.
- As students review the chart, emphasize that clustering and making a chart are also brainstorming tools.
- During exploring, encourage students to ask themselves *What do my readers need to know?* Students should brainstorm details that elaborate, or tell more, about their topic. Good writers think about the questions their readers will have. Now have students ask themselves *Is my topic still too big to write about all of it?* Students should narrow their topic further. They might focus on one part and leave out the other parts.
- Remind students to let their ideas flow freely when they explore. Students should not stop to evaluate their ideas—the more the better!
- Tell students that as they explore their topic they should continue to consider their audience and purpose.

FOR STUDENTS ACQUIRING ENGLISH

Give students extra practice with the exploring strategies, using topics familiar to all. Have students work with partners or in groups. Students can, for example, brainstorm words and ideas associated with a relative's house. For clustering, use a common animal such as a dog or cat. Have students make a chart of the senses for a day at the beach. Students can draw and label a bicycle. For oral interviewing, partners can ask about a pet. Questioning can relate to a brother or sister.

What Is Exploring?

The second part of prewriting is exploring. You remember events, collect facts, and think of details to elaborate, or tell more, about your topic.

How Do I Explore My Topic?

This chart shows different strategies you can use to explore a topic.

Exploring Strategies

Try this!	Here's how.
Brainstorming a list	My Grandmother's Farm barn, goat, cows, mosquitoes stream, tractor, hay, barbecues
Clustering	GRIZZLY BEARS — what they eat; where they live; what they look like
Making a chart	Snowstorm Touch: cold snow on my face Sound: whistling wind
Drawing and labeling	 We spent all day paddling around!
Interviewing with a partner	 How long was your dog lost? 
Asking *Who? What? When? Where? Why? How?*	Hitting the Winning Run What? last baseball game of the season When? the bottom of the last inning

See page H50 for more graphic organizers.

Exploring a Description Topic

Learning from a Model Jack drew a picture of his oboe. Then he wrote words to describe how it looked, felt, and sounded.

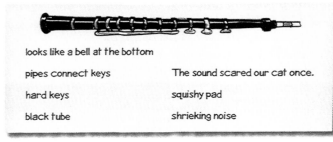

looks like a bell at the bottom
pipes connect keys
hard keys
black tube
The sound scared our cat once.
squishy pad
shrieking noise

▲ Jack's picture and list

Explore Your Topic

1. **Think** about what you are describing.
2. **Draw** a picture of your topic.
3. **Use your five senses** to brainstorm sense words and details to write beneath your picture. Use words from the chart below, or think of your own.

Sight	Sound	Smell	Touch	Taste
fluffy	buzz	fruity	squishy	oily
teal	chirp	fishy	slimy	sweet
oval	grunt	nutty	damp	tart
dull	bellow	rotten	lumpy	tangy
enormous	thump	musty	prickly	bitter
glossy	rattle	fresh	scalding	spicy
pointed	crash	burnt	silky	buttery
muddy	honk	moldy	fuzzy	sour
dusty	whimper	flowery	sticky	peppery
foamy	croak	vinegary	crisp	sugary

If you can't think of details for three senses, try describing something else.

Help with Exploring the Topic

EXPLORING WITH PARTNERS

Having students talk about their topics helps them use their oral language as a foundation for writing. See the following ideas.

- Have students ask questions about their partner's topic as if playing a guessing game to identify it. Questions should focus on the sensory details of the topic. Have partners write down the answers and use them in their description.
- Have students orally describe their topic as their partner tries to draw it. Inaccuracies in the drawing should indicate where the writer needs to add details or describe them more specifically.

RESOURCE

Refer students to the Thesaurus Plus on page H79 for more help choosing sensory words.

TECH TIP

Suggest that students use the thesaurus function in their word-processing program to find other, more creative, ways to describe their topic.

Lesson Objectives

Students will:

- draw pictures of their topics
- brainstorm sensory words and detail

Exploring a Description Topic

Focus on the Model

- Ask students which exploring strategy Jack used. (drawing)
- Ask students which three senses Jack used to describe his oboe. (sight—*looks like a bell at the bottom, pipes connect keys, black tube*; sound—*scared our cat once, shrieking noise*; touch—*squishy pad, hard keys*)

Explore Your Topic

- Students should choose the exploring strategy that works best for their topic. They can draw a picture and write words that tell about it, or they can choose another exploring strategy from page 14. Point out that all of the strategies except questioning work well when exploring a topic for a description.
- Discuss with students the meanings of any unfamiliar words in the chart. Ask volunteers to suggest sensory words that describe their topics and tell in which column each word belongs. Point out that some words, such as *burnt,* can describe several senses.
- Review students' lists of sensory words and details. If a list is very short or includes only one or two senses, help the student elaborate by asking these questions.

  What else can you tell me about how your topic looks?

  How does it sound, smell, taste, or feel?

  If there are still not enough details, encourage the student to choose another topic.
- If a student has chosen a topic that is too broad, help him or her focus on only one part of it.

Lesson Objective

Students will:

- discuss prewriting strategies for organizing writing

What Is Organizing?

Focus on Instruction

- Explain that organizing one's notes and details before writing makes the writing stage much easier. The organizational plan provides a map for what information goes together and in what order. Writing that is not clearly planned often lacks a sense of purpose and is difficult to understand. If the writer does not carefully plan beforehand, he or she will have to spend much more time revising.
- Explain to students that in the organizing stage they should plan the order of their description and choose which details to include. Tell students to decide how to group and sequence their facts, events, ideas, and details. What will they tell first? second? third? Students must also decide which events, facts, or ideas are important to the topic and leave out the others.
- Tell students that in the process of organizing their topic they may decide that they need more details or that their topic is too big. Remind students that the writing process allows them to move back to exploring to expand their topic or narrow it further.
- Discuss with students the organizational options in the chart. Remind them of the published model, "The Barn" from *Charlotte's Web,* and ask how E. B. White organized his description. (logical order)
- Discuss with students possible ways to organize details for the following topics. (Sample responses are shown.)

Topic	Ways to Organize
a person	• place order (i.e., top to bottom) • logical order (by sense)
a favorite place	• place order (i.e., near-to-far or far-to-near) • order of importance (most important to least important)
riding a roller coaster	• time order • order of importance (most important to least important) • logical order (by sense)

What Is Organizing?

The third part of prewriting is organizing, or planning. You choose what ideas and details to include. Then you group them and put the groups in order.

How Do I Organize My Writing?

Group facts, events, or ideas. Put related details into separate groups, such as how two things are alike and how they are different.

Choose an organization. Put the groups of details in an order that fits your purpose. It often helps to chart, diagram, or outline your plan.

Ways to Organize

Try this!	Here's how.
Time order First Next Last	Tell events in the order they happen.
Place order	Describe things from top to bottom, bottom to top, right to left, left to right, near to far, or far to near.
Comparison and contrast	Describe how two subjects are alike. Then describe how they are different. You can also tell the differences first and the likenesses next.
Order of importance LEAST → MOST MOST → LEAST	Tell the least important reason first, or tell the most important reason first.
Question and answer Q? A . . . Q? A . . .	Ask a question and tell the answer. Then ask another question and answer that.
Logical order	Group details that belong together. Present the groups in an order that makes sense.

Organizing a Description

Learning from a Model Jack needed to group the details he had listed. He decided to group them by sense.

- First, he circled details about each sense with a different colored pen.
- Next, he made an Observation Chart showing each group of details.
- Then he numbered the groups in a logical order.
- Finally, he added more details.

① How It Looks	③ How It Sounds	② How It Feels
looks like a bell at the bottom	The sound scared our cat once.	squishy pad
pipes connect keys	like an elephant's cry ^ shrieking noise	cold, ^ hard keys
about two feet long ^ black tube		

▲ Jack's Observation Chart

Organize Your Description

1. **Group** the details about your topic that belong together.
2. **Organize** your details. Make an Observation Chart.
3. **Number** your details in the order you will write about them.
4. **Add** any more details you think of. Use exact words.

Go to www.eduplace.com/kids/hme/ for graphic organizers.

Help with Organizing

CODING TECHNIQUES
Once students have listed details about their topic, have them code the details with letters or numbers rather than colors. Then have students think of a category that describes each group and use the categories to create an organizer.

EVALUATION TIP
Review students' graphic organizers before they draft to troubleshoot any problems.

MANAGEMENT TIP
Suggest that students color-code their details the way Jack did. Remind students that each group of details they create will become a paragraph in their paper.

Lesson Objectives

Students will:
- analyze a modeled organizational plan for a description
- group details into appropriate categories for their description
- organize their groups of details into a logical plan

Organizing a Description

Focus on the Model

- Explain that Jack grouped his details in the way that made the most sense to write about them.
- Point out Jack's method of organizing details with a different colored pen. Help students see that those items circled in one color are in the same column of the Observation Chart. Explain that the information in each column appears in a separate paragraph of Jack's description.
- Ask volunteers to identify details Jack added when he made his chart. Reinforce that writers add new ideas and details at any point in the writing process.

Organize Your Description

- Blackline Master GS–3 is a graphic organizer for students to use. If students' topics require a different kind of organizer, refer them to pages H50–H54.
- Reassure students that their notes can be messy as long as they are readable.
- Explain that the organizational structure students choose might depend on their purpose or the impression they want to create. Suggest that students discuss the possibilities with a partner.
- Tell students to use only details that support the point of view or the impression that they want to create.
- If students need extra support identifying categories, suggest that they first try to group their details by sense. If this approach does not work, help them try using place order, order of importance, and logical order.

Looking Ahead Tell students that this prewriting work will make writing their descriptions easier.

MEETING INDIVIDUAL NEEDS — FOR STUDENTS ACQUIRING ENGLISH
Provide a variety of small objects for partners to group in different ways. Students should describe the grouping as, for example, things that are round or blue. Ask how this activity relates to grouping in writing. Then review time words, place words, prepositional phrases, and words for comparing.

Lesson Objectives

Students will:

- discuss drafting strategies
- discuss the use of transitional words for different purposes

What Is Drafting?

Focus on Instruction

- Explain that the goal of a working draft is to get thoughts and ideas on paper. Later, students can revise and correct any mistakes.
- Explain that a beginning introduces the topic and makes the reader want to read more. Write the examples below on the board. Ask which beginnings simply state the topic and which add interest. (The first in each pair just states the topic.) Point out that beginning with a question or an interesting comment gets the reader's interest.

  Here's what my room looks like.
  Walking into my room is like stepping into paradise.

  Let me tell you about rocks.
  Have you ever looked really closely at a rock?

- Explain that an ending should summarize the paper, give an overall impression, or make a final comment. Write these endings on the board. Point out that the second ending in each pair is better. Ask students why.

  So that's my room.
  I can't imagine a better place to spend my time.

  That's what I know about rocks.
  Rocks tell one of the most fascinating stories on earth.

- Lessons about topic sentences are in the Getting Started segments that open each major writing section in Part 2. However, you can introduce topic sentences by writing these examples on the board.

  Chipmunks are good pets. (topic—chipmunks; main idea—good pets)

  Regular exercise makes you feel good. (topic—exercise regularly; main idea—feel good)

  Once the door slammed shut, I knew there was no escaping the scariest ride of all. (topic—scariest ride; main idea—no escaping)

- Explain that a topic sentence tells what the paragraph will be about. In paragraphs that explain or persuade, it states the main idea. In stories or narratives, the topic sentence often leads into the events in the paragraph.

What Is Drafting?

When you draft, you just write. Don't worry about mistakes. You can fix them later because this is a **working draft**.

- Keep your audience and purpose in mind.
- Keep adding details. A new idea can come at any time.
- Write on every other line to leave room for changes.
- If you decide you don't like something, just cross it out. Don't start over. Keep writing!

How Do I Draft My Paper?

Write sentences and paragraphs. Use the plan you made when you organized your ideas. Turn the words and phrases into sentences. Each part of your plan should make at least one paragraph. Most paragraphs will need a topic sentence. The **topic sentence** tells the main idea of the paragraph.

Write a beginning and an ending. Write an interesting beginning that introduces your topic. Write an ending that finishes your paper by making a final comment about your topic.

Make connections. Use connecting words to tie your sentences and paragraphs together.

Ways to Make Connections	
Try this!	**Look at these examples.**
Use time clues.	finally, until, often, first, tomorrow, Friday, during the day, before, then, after, next, when
Link causes and effects.	because, as a result, so that, therefore, if ... then
Use place clues.	above, around, down, here, there, beside, inside, outside, over, under
Signal likenesses and differences.	however, although, in contrast, similarly
Signal another idea.	also, too, another, in addition

- Explain that transitional words connect ideas. Review the types of transitional words in the chart. Explain that they often appear at the beginning of a sentence but that they can also appear elsewhere. Explain that they are positioned to make the text flow more smoothly.
- Encourage students to write passionately about their topic, using appropriate words and phrases that fully express their feelings. Tell them that this is called "writing with voice."

MEETING INDIVIDUAL NEEDS

FOR STUDENTS ACQUIRING ENGLISH

Write the word *draft;* show how it is used as a noun and as a verb. Discuss what a draft is; concentrate on the bulleted items that tell how to handle a working draft. Make sure students understand that what they write in the draft is not meant to be perfect. Then work with words and phrases used to make different connections.

Drafting a Description

Learning from a Model Jack wrote his working draft. He introduced his topic in an interesting way. Then he started with the part he had numbered *1* on his Observation Chart: *How It Looks.* He wrote a topic sentence and used details from his chart to write his other sentences.

The Oboe is an old instrument that was played in faraway countries ~~I wonder what old~~

I like to look at my oboe. It is a tube about two feet long, and it looks like a Bell at the bottom. it is black with pipes conecting ~~a whole bunch of~~ the diffrent keys

The pad ~~under~~ on the thumbrest feels squishy, and the keys are cold and hard.

My oboe can make a shrieking noise, like the cry of an elephant. Once I played a bad low D, and you should have seen what our cat did!

▲ Jack's working draft

Draft Your Description

1. **Write** an interesting beginning.
2. **Use** your Observation Chart to help you write the main part of your paper. Skip every other line. Don't worry about mistakes yet.
3. **Think** about the main idea of each paragraph, and write a topic sentence. Write other sentences that fill in the details about the main idea.
4. **Write** an ending that makes a final comment about your topic.

Help with Choosing a Topic

MORE DRAFTING TIPS

- Suggest that students first write the body paragraphs and then write the beginning and the ending.
- Suggest that students write on only one side of their paper so they can cut apart the sentences and rearrange them.

TECH TIP

Suggest that students type their details in sentences on separate lines. Then have them use the Cut and Paste functions to rearrange their sentences and see how their description reads.

Lesson Objectives

Students will:

- evaluate a model working draft
- draft their description

Drafting a Description

Focus on the Model

- Have a volunteer read the model aloud.

  As an alternative, students can listen to this draft read by a student (although not the student writer) on audiotape.
- Have students match the sentences in Jack's draft to details in his chart on page 17.
- If students notice the mistakes in Jack's draft, explain that he did not worry about fixing them while drafting because he just wanted to get his ideas on paper. Explain that it is important for the writer to focus first on content and then to fix mistakes later.

Reading As a Writer

Ask the following questions about the model.

- Why did Jack cross out some words? (He decided not to include some information; he decided to use different words.)
- Why is Jack's beginning a good one? (He creates interest by stating some history about the oboe.)
- What topic sentence did Jack write to open his first paragraph? *(I like to look at my oboe.)* Why is this a good topic sentence? (because it tells the main idea of the paragraph—what the oboe looks like)
- Which paragraph needs a topic sentence? (the second)
- What does Jack need to add to the draft? (an ending that makes a final comment)
- What questions would you like to ask Jack? What suggestions would you offer? (Answers will vary.)

Draft Your Description

- Tell students that their description may be one or more paragraphs, depending on details and organization. Remind students to write at least one paragraph from each section of their organizer.
- Remind students to let their voice come through in their description.
- Remind students not to agonize over every word or sentence. They can make revisions and corrections later.
- Tell students to spell words as best they can, circle any spellings they are unsure of, and move on.

Lesson Objective

Students will:
- discuss revising strategies

What Is Revising?

Focus on Instruction

- Emphasize to students that when they revise, they will focus on making their writing clearer and more interesting. Tell them that at the next stage, the proofreading stage (sometimes referred to as editing), they will fix any mistakes in their writing.
- Explain to students that they may do some additional drafting during the revising stage. For example, they might add new paragraphs, rewrite sentences or paragraphs for smoothness or clarity, or reorganize the information in several paragraphs. Students might also decide to rework the order of their paragraphs or write a different beginning or ending.
- Discuss with students the revision strategies shown in the chart. Then write the following sentences on the board for practice. Have volunteers make the corrections noted in parentheses as the other students copy and revise the sentences at their desks.

  One day I found a coin in the sand. (Use a caret to insert *valuable, old* in front of *coin*.)

  Our group cannot hardly finish the project on time. (Cross out *hardly*.)

  Cara planned an outdoor party, hoping it would be sunny. (Move *hoping it would be sunny* in front of *Cara,* capitalize *Hoping,* and follow the phrase with a comma.)

What Is Revising?

When you revise, you change your writing to make it clearer or more interesting. Ask yourself the Big Questions. Don't worry about fixing mistakes yet.

Revising: The Big Questions
- Did I say what I wanted to say?
- Did I elaborate and use details?
- Did I organize the facts, events, or ideas clearly?
- Did I write in an interesting way that suits my audience?

How Do I Make Revisions?

Make changes on the draft. Don't erase! Your paper might look messy, but that's okay. You can make a clean copy later. Here are ways to make your changes.

Ways to Mark Your Revisions

Try this!	Look at these examples.
Cross out parts that you want to change or take out.	The costumes were ~~yellow~~, red ^ orange, yellow, and purple.
Use carets to add new words or sentences.	The clown had on ^ baggy yellow pants and a flowered hat.
Draw circles and arrows to move words, sentences, or paragraphs.	(Don't forget clothes for both warm and cold weather.) Be sure to pack carefully for the trip.
Use numbers to show how sentences should be ordered.	② Draw a picture on heavy paper. ③ Then cut it into puzzle pieces. ① This is how you make a puzzle.
Add wings to add sentences that won't fit on your paper.	Last night I couldn't sleep. ^ Could a tiny animal be scampering between the walls? — I kept hearing a scratching sound behind my bed.

Revising a Description

Learning from a Model Jack reread his working draft. To help his readers picture his oboe, he added details and more exact words. He added a topic sentence. He also added a comparison to make his description more vivid.

The Oboe is an old ^musical^ instrument that was played in faraway countries ~~I wonder what old~~

I like to look at my oboe. It is a ^slender^ tube about two feet long, and it looks like a Bell at the bottom. it is black with pipes conecting ~~a whole bunch of~~ the diffrent keys ^The keys look like little manhole covers.^

^When I pick it up, my oboe feels both soft and hard.^ The pad ~~under~~ on the thumbrest feels squishy, and the keys are ^as^ cold and hard ^as marbles^.

▲ Part of Jack's revised draft

Revise Your Description

Reread your description. Use the Revising Checklist to help you make changes. Think about what you meant to say. Use a thesaurus to find exact, descriptive words. Don't worry about fixing any mistakes yet!

Revising Checklist

- ✓ Did I write clear topic sentences?
- ✓ Did I use details that support the topic sentences in each paragraph?
- ✓ Did I order the details so my readers can follow them easily?
- ✓ Where do I need to add sense words or details?
- ✓ Did I make a final comment about my topic in my ending?

See the Thesaurus Plus on page H79.

Don't be afraid to mark up your paper!

Help with Revising

LOOKING AGAIN
Suggest that students look again at their subject to help them think of more details to add to their description.

HIGHLIGHTING
Suggest that students use a highlighter to mark all nouns and verbs in their description. Have them focus on each one to see if they can think of more exact words to replace them.

TECH TIP
Suggest that students put their topic sentences in bold type to help them see whether each paragraph focuses on its main idea.

Lesson Objectives

Students will:
- evaluate a revised model draft
- revise their draft, using a revising checklist

Revising a Description

Focus on the Model

Have a volunteer read the model aloud, incorporating the revisions. Discuss the meaning of the revision marks, if necessary.

Reading As a Writer

- Ask the following questions about the model.

  What new comparisons did Jack add? (He compared the appearance of the keys to manhole covers and their cold, hard touch to marbles.)

  Why did Jack add the sentence about the oboe feeling both soft and hard? (He made it the topic sentence for that paragraph.)

  What other details did he add? (old *musical* instrument; a *slender* tube)

- Ask students how the changes Jack made improve the description. (They make it more interesting, better organized, and easier to visualize.)

Revise Your Description

Review the questions on the Revising Checklist with students. Use the following questions to discuss with students how to use the checklist questions to evaluate their description.

Good topic sentences Does the first sentence of each paragraph tell the main idea of that paragraph?

Order of details Are the details that go together grouped in the same paragraph? Are they in an order that is easy to follow?

Sensory words and details Did I use exact words to describe how this looks, sounds, smells, feels, or tastes?

Ending Does the ending tell what I think or feel about this topic?

MEETING INDIVIDUAL NEEDS

FOR STUDENTS ACQUIRING ENGLISH

Make sure students understand the verbs *revise, elaborate,* and *organize*. Give examples of each by showing how you would change a sentence, add to a sentence, and organize sentences in a paragraph. Use the conventions noted in the book. Then ask students for their own examples.

Lesson Objective

Students will:

- discuss guidelines for a writing conference

What Is a Writing Conference?

Focus on Instruction

- Review and discuss the Guides for a Writing Conference with students. If students have no experience with writing conferences, assure them that the purpose of the conference is to be helpful, not critical.
- Discuss how to word questions and comments politely. Explain that students should never use the following comments: "This is boring," "This is stupid," "You don't write very well," or "I can't follow your writing." Explain that these comments are critical, not helpful. Advise students instead to use questions or suggestions that help the writer solve a problem, such as "I didn't understand this part. Could you add some details to make it clearer?" or "Why did you include this part? How does it go with your topic?"

Writing Conference Tips

- Explain to students that reading their paper aloud allows their partners to focus on the content rather than on any mistakes or unclear handwriting.
- Emphasize that it is important for the listener to first compliment the writer about his or her paper. Compliments might resemble the following: "The details about your raft trip really make your story exciting" or "The reasons you give for building a community center are very convincing."
- Explain that when the listener retells what he or she heard, the writer knows whether or not the writing clearly communicates his or her ideas.
- Suggest that writers list questions to ask their partners about problems they are having with their papers or aspects they want to be sure are effective.
- Reinforce that writers should listen carefully to their partners' comments but that they should decide for themselves what changes to make.

What Is a Writing Conference?

In a writing conference, a writer reads his or her paper to a partner or a group. The listeners tell what they like, ask questions, and make suggestions. Your conference partners might be a classmate, a small group, your teacher, or someone who knows about your topic.

How Do I Have a Writing Conference?

In a writing conference, you will be either the writer or the listener. The following guides can help you.

Guides for a Writing Conference

When You're the Writer . . .	When You're the Listener . . .
• Read your paper aloud. • Pay attention to your listeners' comments and suggestions. Keep an open mind. • Take notes to remember any compliments, questions, or suggestions. • Reread your paper after the conference. • Use your notes. Make any other changes you want.	• Look at the writer. • Listen carefully. Don't let your thoughts wander. • Retell what you have heard. • Then tell two things that you like about the paper. • Next, ask questions about things you don't understand. • Finally, give one or two suggestions to help the writer. • Always be positive and polite.

Having a Writing Conference

Learning from a Model Jack had a conference with a partner, Jorge.

Have Your Writing Conference

1. **Find** a partner or a small group, and have a writing conference. Use the guides on page 22.
2. **Use** your conference notes to make any other changes you want.

Help with Conferencing

CONFERENCING QUESTIONS

Share these questions with students as samples, or use them in teacher-student conferences.

- Can you tell more about how ________ looks [or sounds, smells, feels, or tastes]?
- How could you sum up what you've said?
- Can you state the main idea of this paragraph and put it into a topic sentence?
- What could you say in the beginning to grab my attention?

EVALUATION TIP

Read the notes that student writers took during the conference to see if they benefited from the experience.

Lesson Objectives

Students will:

- evaluate a sample part of a writing conference
- discuss their draft in a writing conference
- make additional revisions to their draft

Having a Writing Conference

Focus on the Model

Have two volunteers role-play Jack and Jorges having a writing conference. Remind the actors to maintain a positive and helpful tone of voice during the role-playing. Then ask the following questions about the conference.

What three compliments did Jorges give Jack? (He liked the beginning and the comparison between the oboe keys and manhole covers, and he found the order of details easy to follow.)

What questions or suggestions did Jorges have? (Jorges asked about the color of the keys and the sound and whether Jack could add a final comment.)

Why is Jack's question a good one for a writer to ask? (It encourages the conferencing partner to make a helpful suggestion.)

Have Your Conference

- Students can use Blackline Master GS–4 during their conferences.
- Model a conference for the class with a student volunteer. Read the student's paper in advance so that you can be prepared with compliments, questions, and suggestions.
- Conferencing can occur in small groups or in pairs. For students who need extra support, you can participate in the conference.
- Share the following sample compliments that students can use during the conference.

  Your use of sensory words and details makes it easy to picture your topic.

  Your description is easy to follow.

- After each conference, review students' notes and discuss which changes they plan to make and why.

MEETING INDIVIDUAL NEEDS — FOR STUDENTS ACQUIRING ENGLISH

Write the word *conference* on the board; explain what it means. Students may find the concept somewhat easier to grasp if you also explain the meaning of the verb *confer*. Work with students on ways to be a polite listener, including body language; ways to give polite feedback; and ways to ask polite questions.

Lesson Objectives

Students will:

- discuss the purpose of and methods for proofreading
- learn how to use proofreading marks

What Is Proofreading?

Focus on Instruction

- To reinforce what it means to proofread for usage mistakes, write these examples on the board. Discuss the errors in verb, pronoun, and adjective usage and why the answers are correct.

  My best friend live around the corner. (lives)

  Josh invited Kyle and I to his party. (me)

  Keeva seems more happy since she returned from vacation. (happier)

- Encourage students to use proofreading marks and try one of the other ideas each time they proofread. Explain that they will eventually discover which techniques work best for them.
- Have volunteers write on the board each sentence from the right-hand column of the chart of proofreading marks, showing how the sentence would appear after the writer makes the changes that are marked.

Proofreading Tips

- Suggest that students mark their proofreading corrections with a pen or a pencil that is a different color from the one they used for their revisions.
- Explain to students that reading their paper aloud will help them hear words that are repeated too often. Have them underline these words and look them up in a thesaurus to find other words they can use that mean the same thing.

What Is Proofreading?

When you proofread, you correct any mistakes. You check spelling, capitalization, and punctuation. You also check that you have used words correctly, written complete sentences, and indented paragraphs.

How Do I Proofread?

Choose from these ideas to help you.

- Use proofreading marks.
- Proofread for one skill at a time.
- Read one line at a time. Hold a ruler or a strip of cardboard under the line to help you focus on the spelling of each word.
- Say each word aloud to yourself.
- Read your paper aloud. You may notice mistakes when you hear them.
- Circle any word that might be misspelled. Check spellings in a dictionary.

Proofreading Tip

Remember **CUPS** when proofreading.
Capitalization
Usage
Punctuation
Spelling

Proofreading Marks

Try this!	Here's when.	Look at these examples.
¶	to begin a new paragraph; to indent the paragraph	¶ All eyes were looking up. Everyone was begging the kitten to come down. The frightened animal wouldn't budge.
∧	to add letters, words, or sentences	Bring your scissors ∧ glue to class. (and)
⌐	to take out words, sentences, and punctuation marks; to correct spelling	Mrs. Jones asked, me to work at the book sail. (sale)
/	to change a capital letter to a small letter	We pitched our tent near a small Stream.
≡	to change a small letter to a capital letter	Last summer we went to Yellowstone national Park.

Proofreading a Description

Learning from a Model Jack made more changes to his description after talking to Jorge. Then he proofread it.

musical
¶ The Øboe is an old instrument that was played in faraway
countries. ~~I wonder what old~~
slender
I like to look at my oboe. It is a tube about two feet long.
a dull, sooty shiny silver connecting
and it looks like a Ɓell at the bottom. it is black with pipes ~~conecting~~
different
~~a whole bunch of the diffrent~~ keys. The keys look like little manhole covers.
When I pick it up, my oboe feels both soft and hard.
The pad ~~under~~ on the thumbrest feels squishy, and the
as as marbles
keys are cold and hard.

▲ Part of Jack's proofread draft

Proofread Your Description

Proofread your description, using the Proofreading Checklist. Use the proofreading marks shown on page 24.

Proofreading Checklist

Did I

- ✓ indent all paragraphs?
- ✓ use complete sentences?
- ✓ use capital letters and punctuation correctly?
- ✓ use the correct form of adjectives when comparing?
- ✓ use nouns and verbs correctly?
- ✓ correct any spelling errors?

Use the Guide to Capitalization, Punctuation, and Usage on page H55 and the Spelling Guide on page H65 for help.

Help with Proofreading

MANAGEMENT TIP

Have each student start a personal checklist of skills that he or she needs to proofread for. Attach the list to the student's writing folder.

TECH TIP

Suggest that students use the spelling tool on their computer to find and correct misspelled words. Have them refer to Using a Spelling Tool on page H38.

RESOURCES

Identify atlases, almanacs, encyclopedias, and biographical dictionaries for students to use in checking names, dates, or other facts in their descriptions. The index of the pupil book can help students find specific rules and examples of correct usage and mechanics.

Lesson Objectives

Students will:

- review a proofread model to determine how and why corrections were made
- proofread their description

Proofreading a Description

Focus on the Model

- Point out to students that Jack did not recopy his revised working draft before proofreading it. Explain to students that as long as they are able to read their working draft, it's okay if the draft gets messy. Remind students that their working draft is for them alone; no one else will be reading it.
- Ask how Jack separated his proofreading corrections from his revisions. (used a different color)
- Ask students to find any new revisions that Jack made after the writing conference. If necessary, have students compare this proofread draft with the revised draft on page 21. Ask them to review comments in the writing conference that prompted each change. (*What color are those keys?* prompted the addition of *shiny silver* and *dull, sooty.*)
- See Jack's complete working draft with all revisions and proofreading corrections on Blackline Master GS–5.

Reading As a Writer

Ask the following questions about the model.

- Which words are incorrectly capitalized? Why? (*oboe, bell;* not proper nouns, do not begin a sentence) How did Jack show this? (with a slash)
- Which word begins with a small letter that should begin with a capital letter? Why? (*It;* begins a sentence) What mark did he use to show this? (three underscores)
- What punctuation mark did Jack add? (added a period to the end of two statements)
- What adjective did Jack add to the first sentence? Why? (*musical;* to add details) What mark did he use to show this? (a caret)

Proofread Your Description

- Review and discuss the Proofreading Checklist. Remind students to try some of the proofreading ideas on page 24.
- Students can refer to page H18 at the back of the book for help in using a dictionary.
- Help students locate the Guide to Capitalization, Punctuation, and Usage and the Spelling Guide. Encourage students to use them as they proofread.

Lesson Objectives

Students will:
- discuss ideas for publishing and sharing
- discuss the purpose of reflecting on writing

What Is Publishing?

Focus on Instruction

- Explain that there are many ways to share one's writing. Students should think about which way would best convey their message and most appeal to their audience.
- Tell students that they can improve their writing by reflecting on what they learned about writing after they finish their papers. Discuss the points for reflection in the text.

Creating a Writing Portfolio

A writing portfolio is a selective collection of a student's writing, compiled over the school year, to determine writing strengths and weaknesses, to monitor growth, to inform instruction, and to set goals. It should *not* be a place to store all of the student's writing.

Selection A paper might be selected because it is generally noteworthy, a good example of a particular aspect of writing, an example of a particular kind of writing, representative work at a particular point in the school year, or a typical example of the student's work.

Appearance and format The portfolio can be an expandable file folder, or it can be more elaborate, such as a three-ring binder with multiple sections. If the portfolio will be passed on to next year's teacher, it may include a table of contents that lists the papers in the order they were written or groups them by type or special quality, such as good examples of word choice.

Use Students select papers for their portfolios, often completing a form for each paper, explaining why they chose it. Students periodically review their portfolios to determine strengths and weaknesses and to set goals as writers.

What Is Publishing?

When you publish your writing, you prepare to share it with your audience.

How Do I Publish My Writing?

Here are some ideas for sharing your writing.

Write It
- Turn your paper into a book. Add pictures and a cover.
- Send your paper as a letter or an e-mail.
- Create a class book of writing with your classmates.
- Post your paper on the Internet.
- Send your paper to a magazine or a newspaper that publishes student writing.

Say It
- Record your paper on tape. Add sound effects.
- Read your paper aloud from the Author's Chair.
- Read your paper as a speech.

Show It
- Add photographs or drawings to your paper.
- Make a diorama and attach your paper to it.
- Act out your writing with a small group. Have a teacher or other adult videotape your performance.
- Show slides about your topic to the class while reading your paper aloud.

Tech Tip
Make a multimedia presentation. See page H45 for ideas.

How Do I Reflect on My Writing?

When you reflect, you think about what you have written. You can think about what you did well, what you could do better next time, and what your goals are for your next writing assignment.

You might want to keep a collection of some of your writing, such as favorite or unusual pieces.

Publishing a Description

Learning from a Model Jack made a neat, correct final copy of his description. He sent it to the editor of his school newspaper.

Jack Welch

My Oboe
by Jack Welch

The oboe is an old musical instrument that was played in faraway countries.

I like to look at my oboe. It is a slender tube about two feet long, and it looks like a bell at the bottom. It is a dull, sooty black with shiny silver pipes connecting the different keys. The keys look like little manhole covers.

When I pick it up, my oboe feels both soft and hard. The pad on the thumbrest feels squishy, and the keys are as cold and hard as marbles.

My oboe makes a smooth, clear sound, like someone singing. It also can make a shrieking noise, like the cry of an elephant. Once I played a bad low D, and you should have seen what our cat did! Even when I play badly, I like to play my oboe.

I love all your comparisons!

I can almost hear it!

Great! You end by making a final comment about your oboe.

Publish Your Description

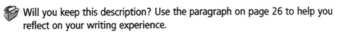

1. **Check** that you fixed all mistakes. Make a neat final copy of your description. Give your description a title.
2. **Publish or share** your description. Look at page 26 for ideas.

Will you keep this description? Use the paragraph on page 26 to help you reflect on your writing experience.

See www.eduplace.com/kids/hme/ for more examples of student writing. Publishing 27

Help with Publishing

TECH TIP
Suggest that students print out their description on decorative paper.

AUTHOR'S CHAIR
Students can sit in the Author's Chair and read aloud their published pieces or works in progress that they need help with. Have a student read from the Author's Chair every day if time permits.

MANAGEMENT TIP
Suggest that students plan the steps they need to take in publishing their description. If necessary, they could write down the steps and check off each one as they complete it.

SCHOOL-HOME CONNECTION
Have students post their description with illustrations on the bulletin board for Family Night.

Lesson Objectives

Students will:
- review and evaluate a published model
- choose a way to publish their description
- make a neat final copy of their description
- reflect on their writing experience

Publishing a Description

Focus on the Model

Have volunteers read the final copy aloud.

As an alternative, students can listen to the final copy read by a student (although not the student writer) on audiotape.

Reading As a Writer

Ask the following questions about the model.

- What does Sal like about the final copy? (the comparisons, the description of the oboe's sound, the ending)
- What do you like about it? (Answers will vary.)

Publish Your Description

- If students discover mistakes after making their final copy, suggest that they make neat corrections instead of making another copy. Suggest that students erase cleanly, use white tape to cover their error and then write over it, or cross out an error carefully and write the correction above it.
- Tell students they can use one of the publishing ideas that they thought of before they began writing, or they can think of alternative ideas.
- Help students reflect on their writing, perhaps by sharing your thoughts about a piece of writing you have done. Ask students the following questions to help them reflect on writing a description.

  What have you learned about writing descriptions?

  Which part of your description do you like best? Why?

  Which part could be stronger? Why?

  Which was easier—thinking of sensory details or writing about them clearly? Why?

  What might you do differently the next time you write a description?

If students create writing portfolios, help them decide whether to include their description.

INTERNET CONNECTION Students can read more models of student writing at www.eduplace.com/kids/hme/. You can also find and print these models at www.eduplace.com/rdg/hme/.

About Part 1

Part 1 includes all units that provide instruction and practice for grammar, usage, and mechanics skills. Each unit provides basic skill lessons, a unit Checkup that reviews all basic skills, Test Practice using multiple-choice formats found on national tests, and Extra Practice at three levels of difficulty for every basic skill lesson. Cumulative Reviews occur in every other or every third unit and provide additional practice to review basic skills taught in that unit and all prior units up to that point.

Each unit also includes Revising Strategy feature lessons and Enrichment activities. Revising Strategies: Sentence Fluency features show students how to apply basic skills to promote sentence fluency by elaborating and combining sentences. Revising Strategies: Vocabulary lessons appear in units focused on parts of speech and tie in with the unit part of speech to develop vocabulary knowledge.

Using Part 1

The Part 1 units are grouped together for ease of use but are intended to be used flexibly with the units and features in Part 2. Units and lessons in Part 1 may be used in sequence or alternated with units and lessons in Part 2. Part 1 can provide instruction and/or serve as a resource while using Part 2. If desired, selected lessons in Part 1 can be taught on an as-needed basis.

Choose among these units and lessons to address the curriculum requirements in your school and to meet the needs of your students.

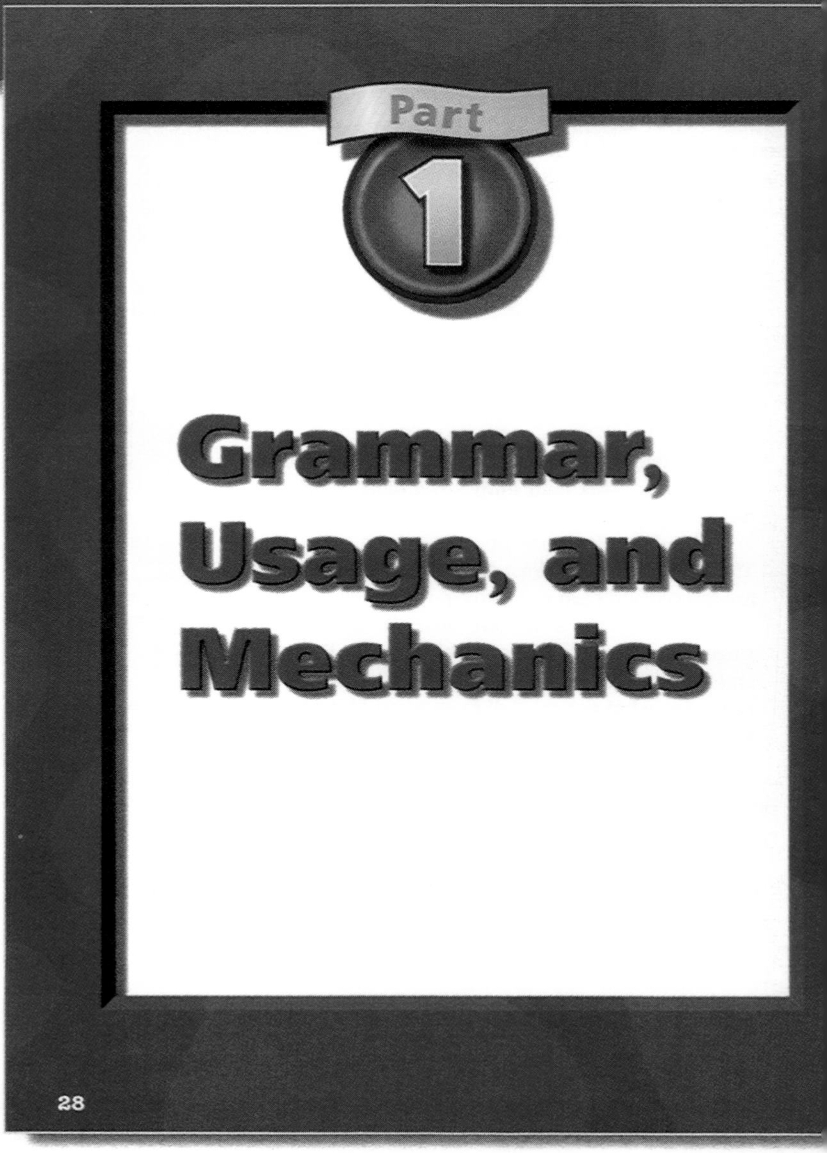
Part 1

Grammar, Usage, and Mechanics

28

What You Will Find in This Part:

Planning Part 1

The planning chart below suggests an approximate time allocation for completing the lessons in Part 1.

Unit 1	The Sentence *2 weeks*
Unit 2	Nouns *2 weeks*
Unit 3	Verbs *$2\frac{1}{2}$ weeks*
Unit 4	Adjectives *$1\frac{1}{2}$ weeks*
Unit 5	Capitalization and Punctuation *$2\frac{1}{2}$ weeks*
Unit 6	Pronouns *2 weeks*
Unit 7	Adverbs and Prepositions *$1\frac{1}{2}$ weeks*

Why Learn Grammar?

Introducing Part 1

- Read the following words aloud.

  lunch after we journals write will our in

  Ask students what message you just told them. When they cannot answer, tell them the message. (After lunch we will write in our journals.) Point out that word order is important in English in order to communicate meaning.

- Read these sentences aloud.

  Cam runs across the street.

  Cam ran across the street.

  Cam will run across the street.

  Cam chased the ball. Cam chased the balls.

  Ask students how the sentences in each group differed. (The verbs *runs, ran,* and *will run* tell when; the nouns *ball* and *balls* tell how many.) Explain that the correct forms of words also communicate meaning.

- Write these sentences on the board.

  Maria found a quarter in her pocket she found a nickel after school she bought some crackers.

  Ask students to find the three sentences. (There are several possible combinations.) When they suggest different ideas, point out that without capital letters and punctuation, it is hard to determine the intended meaning.

- Have students summarize that the rules for speaking and writing a language enable people to communicate clearly with each other.

- Have volunteers read the page aloud. Discuss with students why it is important to use language correctly when speaking and writing in school and in more formal situations with people outside of school. Ask students to cite some situations in their lives when they should use more formal language.

Why Learn Grammar?

Informal Language

When you're with your friends or in other informal situations, you may not worry about using every word correctly. That's fine.

When you write in your diary or do other personal writing, it doesn't matter if every word or punctuation mark is correct. YOU know what you mean.

Formal Language

In school and in many situations outside of school, though, you need to use more formal language, for both speaking and writing. This section of the book will help you develop your ability to use formal language when you need it.

Unit 1 Planning Guide

The Sentence

2 weeks

	Lesson	Checkup (PE)	Extra Practice (PE)	Graphic Organizer (BLM)	Writing Wrap-Up (BLM)	More Practice (TE)	Workbook Plus	Reteaching Workbook	Students Acquiring English Practice Book
1	What Is a Sentence? *(32–33)*	51	56	1–1	1–4	56	1–2	1	1+
	Revising Strategies: Sentence Fluency Writing Good Sentences *(34–35)*						3–4	2–3	
2	Statements and Questions *(36–37)*	51	57	1–1	1–4	57	5–6	4	3+
3	Commands and Exclamations *(38–39)*	51	58	1–1	1–4	58	7–8	5	5+
4	Subjects and Predicates *(40–41)*	51	59	1–2	1–4	59	9–10	6	7+
5	Simple Subjects *(42–43)*	51	60	1–2	1–5	60	11–12	7	9+
6	Simple Predicates *(44–45)*	52	61	1–2	1–5	61	13–14	8	11+
7	Correcting Run-on Sentences *(46–47)*	52	62	1–3	1–5	62	15–16	9	13+
	Revising Strategies: Sentence Fluency Writing Good Sentences *(48–49)*						17–18	10–11	
	Enrichment *(50)*								
	Test Practice *(53–55)*								15+

Unit 1

Tools and Tips

- **Diagramming Guide,** *pp. H70–H78*
- **Guide to Capitalization, Punctuation, and Usage,** *pp. H55–H64*

School-Home Connection

Suggestions for informing or involving family members in classroom activities and learning related to this unit are included in the Teacher's Edition throughout the unit.

Meeting Individual Needs

- **FOR SPECIAL NEEDS/INCLUSION:** *Houghton Mifflin English* Audiotape. See also Reteaching.
- **FOR STUDENTS ACQUIRING ENGLISH:**
  - Notes and activities are included in this Teacher's Edition throughout the unit to help you adapt or use pupil book activities with students acquiring English.
  - Additional support is available for students at various stages of English proficiency: **Beginning/Preproduction**, **Early Production/Speech Emergence**, and **Intermediate/Advanced**. See Students Acquiring English Practice Book.
  - Students can listen to the Try It Out activities on audiotape.
- **ENRICHMENT:** *p. 50*

All audiotape recordings are also available on CD.

Daily Language Practice

Each sentence includes one error based on skills taught in this Grammar unit. Each day write one sentence on the chalkboard. Have students find the error and write the sentence correctly on a sheet of paper. To make the activity easier, identify the kind of error.

1. Do you have enough money to buy three tickets Do you have enough money to buy three tickets? (end punctuation)
2. the pilot flew her plane above the storm. The pilot flew her plane above the storm. (capitalization)
3. How beautiful the garden looks. How beautiful the garden looks! (end punctuation)
4. Keisha is ready for the race she has practiced for weeks. Sample: Keisha is ready for the race. She has practiced for weeks. (run-on sentences)
5. Please take an umbrella along! Please take an umbrella along. (end punctuation)
6. José found a wallet it was full of money. Sample: José found a wallet. It was full of money. (run-on sentences)
7. You should be more careful on your bicycle? You should be more careful on your bicycle. (end punctuation)
8. are you expecting someone for dinner? Are you expecting someone for dinner? (capitalization)
9. My soup has not cooled yet? My soup has not cooled yet. (end punctuation)
10. The students did not know the answer, they had not read the chapter. Sample: The students did not know the answer. They had not read the chapter. (run-on sentences)

Additional Resources

Workbook Plus, Unit 1
Reteaching Workbook, Unit 1
Students Acquiring English Practice Book, Unit 1
Transparencies, Unit 1
Teacher's Resource Book
Audiotapes

Technology Tools

INTERNET: http://www.eduplace.com/kids/hme/ *or* http://www.eduplace.com/rdg/hme/

Visit Education Place for these additional support materials and activities:

- tricky usage question
- Wacky Web Tales®
- interactive quizzes
- a proofreading game

Assessment

Test Booklet, Unit 1

Keeping a Journal

Discuss with students the value of keeping a journal as a way of promoting self-expression and fluency. Encourage students to record their thoughts and ideas in a notebook. Inform students whether the journal will be private or will be reviewed periodically as a way of assessing growth. The following prompts may be useful for generating writing ideas.

Journal Prompts

- If you could have any pet, what would it be? Why?
- What do you like most about bedtime?
- Who would you most like to spend a day with? What would you do together?

Unit 1

The Sentence

Where else can a kid have this much fun going this fast? What a blast you can have on a corkscrew coaster! The first ride is always the best. Promise that you'll come with me.

Introducing the Unit

Using the Photograph

- Have volunteers look at the photograph and tell about the roller coaster. (Sample response: The roller coaster turns upside down.) Emphasize that most descriptions of a roller coaster will include not just what it looks like, but also what is happening to it.
- Tell students that a **sentence** is a group of words that tells a complete thought. Explain to students that in order to tell a complete thought, a sentence must tell *who* or *what*. It must also tell *what is* or *what happens*.
- Have a volunteer read the caption aloud, and ask students to count the number of sentences. Point out to students the purpose each sentence serves. (asks a question, expresses strong feeling, makes a statement, gives a command) Tell students that they will learn about all four kinds of sentences (question, exclamation, statement, command) in this unit.

Grammar Song

See Blackline Master G–1 for a song to help students remember some of the concepts and rules taught in this unit.

Students can also listen to this song on audiotape.

Shared Writing Activity

Work with students to write a paragraph about a day at an amusement park, highlighted by a ride on a roller coaster.

1. Have students suggest various activities at an amusement park. (Sample responses: rides, eating, games) Write students' responses on the board or on an overhead transparency.
   - Help students decide which activities to write about by asking such questions as "Who have you gone to the amusement park with? Are you at a big amusement park or a local carnival? Do you want to visit the fun house or haunted house?"
   - For the description of the roller coaster ride, students may use their previous observations.
2. Discuss with students the order in which to tell the events. Should the most or least important event come first? Have students number the events in the proper order.
3. Have students suggest sentences to write the paragraph.
   - Help students fix fragments and run-on sentences. As you write, ask students to tell you the correct punctuation and capitalization to use.
4. Have a volunteer read the paragraph aloud to the class. Have students add, modify, or delete sentences depending on how they feel the paragraph fits together.

What Is a Sentence?

Lesson Objectives

Students will:

- distinguish between complete sentences and sentence fragments
- write a journal entry describing the weather, using complete sentences

One-Minute Warm-Up Have volunteers write the sentence on the board. Have them underline once the part that tells *who* or *what* the sentence is about. (The hottest flames) Have them underline twice the part that tells *what happens*. (clawed up the trunks of large trees)

Focus on Instruction

Point out that just because a group of words begins with a capital letter and ends with a period doesn't necessarily mean it is a sentence. The real test is whether a group of words tells *who* or *what* and also *what is* or *what happens*.

Try It Out

VIEWING Have students suggest sentences about the photograph. Record students' suggestions in a chart. Ask volunteers to supply any missing sentence parts. (Sample responses are shown.)

Who or What	What Is or What Happens
Parks	are a great place to visit.
Many parks	have bike and hiking trails.
Some parks	have camping grounds too.

FOR STUDENTS ACQUIRING ENGLISH

- Have students listen to the Try It Out sentences on the audiotape. Distribute SAE Practice pages for Unit 1, Lesson 1, to support listening.
- Ask volunteers to explain the photo of the geyser at Yellowstone National Park. Briefly discuss camping trips; on the board, write vocabulary from sentences and explain as needed. Help students suggest sentences to fit the photo. Students listen to words or sentences about the park. Students tell you if what they heard is a sentence or not by saying "sentence" or "not." Remind students that each sentence should tell *who* or *what*, and also *what is* or *what happens*. Revise nonsentences with students. Example: Is a geyser. (not; This is a geyser.)

Grammar 1

What Is a Sentence?

One-Minute Warm-Up

Read the sentence below. Whom or what is the sentence about? What happened? Whom or what underlined once; what happened, twice.

The hottest flames clawed up the trunks of large trees.

—from *The Great Yellowstone Fire*, by Carole G. Vogel and Kathryn A. Goldner

A sentence is a group of words that tells a complete thought. In order to tell a complete thought, a sentence must tell *who* or *what*. It must also tell *what is* or *what happens*.

Who or What	What Is or What Happens
Mr. Nolan	rolled up the sleeping bags.
Your backpack	is too heavy!

Sentences	Not Sentences
Jason likes camping.	Likes camping by the lake.
Our new tent leaks.	Our new green tent.

Try It Out

Speak Up Which groups of words are sentences? Which are not sentences?

1. At Yellowstone National Park. not
2. The park has famous hot springs. sentence
3. The first national park in the world. not
4. Flows through the park into the canyon. not
5. Many different kinds of wildlife. not
6. Jason's family camped at Yellowstone. sentence
7. They saw a fossil forest. sentence
8. Hot springs, waterfalls, and canyons. not

Old Faithful erupts.

Meeting Individual Needs

RETEACHING
ALTERNATIVE STRATEGY

- Write this sentence on a paper strip: *A brown bear stood by the lake.*
- Tell students that a sentence expresses a complete thought and has two parts. One part tells *who* or *what;* the other part tells *what is* or *what happens.* Ask students which part of the sentence tells *who* or *what.* (A brown bear) Then ask which part tells *what happens.* (stood by the lake)
- Follow the same procedure for the sentences *A deer hid among the trees* and *A silver fox ran across the path.*

CHALLENGE
Have each student list the titles of five favorite traditional or popular songs, such as "Take Me Out to the Ball Game." Have students exchange titles and identify each as either a fragment or a sentence. Have them add words to make the fragments sentences. Students can say or sing their sentences.

FOR STUDENTS ACQUIRING ENGLISH
Write a sentence about something in class: *This is a science book.* Circle the subject while saying "what;" circle the predicate while saying "what it is." Continue. Include some nonsentences, indicating that a part is missing.

On Your Own

For each pair, write the group of words that is a sentence.

Example: Lisa visited a national park. Camping in a park last summer.
Lisa visited a national park.

9. Planned the trip ahead of time.
   Lisa's family planned the trip.
10. Her parents sent for information.
    Maps about the park.
11. The family camped in a meadow.
    Enjoyed the mountain view.
12. Hiked together along the trail.
    They admired the rocks.
13. Over sixty kinds of animals.
    The hikers saw deer and bears.
14. Skiing in winter.
    The park is open all year.

15–20. Read these notes from a science journal. Write each group of words that is a sentence. Sentences are underlined.

Example: March 1 Snow flurries this morning. I saw many deer tracks.
I saw many deer tracks.

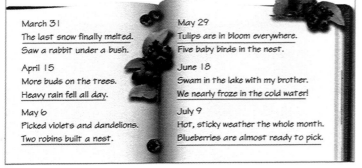

March 31
The last snow finally melted.
Saw a rabbit under a bush.

April 15
More buds on the trees.
Heavy rain fell all day.

May 6
Picked violets and dandelions.
Two robins built a nest.

May 29
Tulips are in bloom everywhere.
Five baby birds in the nest.

June 18
Swam in the lake with my brother.
We nearly froze in the cold water!

July 9
Hot, sticky weather the whole month.
Blueberries are almost ready to pick.

Writing Wrap-Up

WRITING • THINKING • LISTENING • SPEAKING

DESCRIBING

Write a Journal Entry

Write an entry describing today's weather for a science journal. Write complete sentences. Find a partner and read your descriptions to each other. Listen for any sentences that are not complete.

For Extra Practice see page 56.

Summing Up Help students summarize these key points about the lesson:

> A **sentence** is a group of words that tells a complete thought. It tells *who* or *what* and *what is* or *what happens.*

You may want to have students complete the parts related to this lesson on Blackline Master 1–1.

On Your Own

Suggest that students test each group of words by asking:

> Does the word group have two parts—one part that tells who or what and another part that tells what is or what happens?

MEETING INDIVIDUAL NEEDS

FOR STUDENTS ACQUIRING ENGLISH

Distribute SAE Practice pages for Unit 1, Lesson 1. Have students cut up the strips on the page and sort them into sentence and nonsentence piles. Students can work with partners or in groups, reading the strips aloud and identifying *who* or *what* and *what happens.*

Writing Wrap-Up

Writing Tip: Suggest that students first create a list of words or phrases that describe the day's weather, such as *breezy, blowing leaves,* and *sunny but crisp.* See Blackline Master 1–4 for a sample journal entry.

TECHNOLOGY CONNECTION

Students may wish to use a word-processing program to keep an electronic weather journal.

● RETEACHING WORKBOOK, page 1

1 What Is a Sentence?

- A **sentence** is a group of words that tells a complete thought. A sentence always tells *who* or *what* and *what is* or *what happens.*

Sentences	Pet shops sell many kinds of animals. People like the playful kittens.
Not sentences	Many pet shops. Like the playful kittens.

Write *sentence* if the group of words is a sentence. Write *not a sentence* if it is not a sentence.

Example: Beautiful fish swim in tanks. — sentence

1. Pet shops are busy places. — sentence
2. Can hear a dog howl. — not a sentence
3. There are colorful birds in cages. — sentence
4. Parrots repeat words. — sentence
5. Flutter their feathers. — not a sentence
6. A bunny wiggles its nose. — sentence
7. Wants carrots from visitors. — not a sentence
8. Drinks water from a bottle. — not a sentence
9. A hamster plays in a cage. — sentence
10. Runs in a wheel. — not a sentence
11. A pup plays with a toy bone. — sentence
12. A beautiful poodle with curly hair. — not a sentence
13. Looks like a ball of fur. — not a sentence
14. The salespeople are very helpful. — sentence
15. Answer questions. — not a sentence
16. Information about the pets. — not a sentence
17. The pets need lots of love. — sentence
18. Love pets. — not a sentence

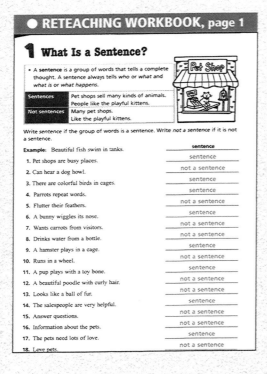

▲■ WORKBOOK PLUS, pages 1–2

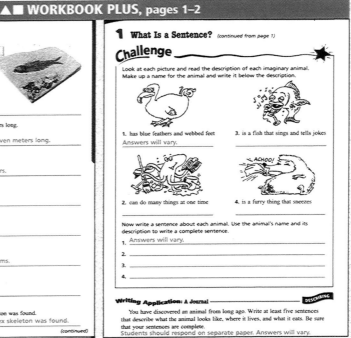

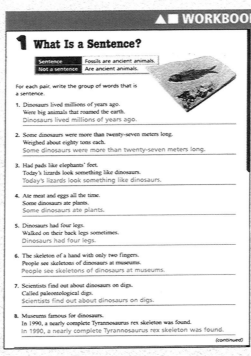

1 What Is a Sentence?

Sentence	Fossils are ancient animals.
Not a sentence	Are ancient animals.

For each pair, write the group of words that is a sentence.

1. Dinosaurs lived millions of years ago.
   Were big animals that roamed the earth.
   Dinosaurs lived millions of years ago.
2. Some dinosaurs were more than twenty-seven meters long.
   Weighed about eighty tons each.
   Some dinosaurs were more than twenty-seven meters long.
3. Had pads like elephants' feet.
   Today's lizards look something like dinosaurs.
   Today's lizards look something like dinosaurs.
4. Ate meat and eggs all the time.
   Some dinosaurs ate plants.
   Some dinosaurs ate plants.
5. Dinosaurs had four legs.
   Walked on their back legs sometimes.
   Dinosaurs had four legs.
6. The skeleton of a hand with only two fingers.
   People see skeletons of dinosaurs at museums.
   People see skeletons of dinosaurs at museums.
7. Scientists find out about dinosaurs on digs.
   Called paleontological digs.
   Scientists find out about dinosaurs on digs.
8. Museums famous for dinosaurs.
   In 1990, a nearly complete Tyrannosaurus rex skeleton was found.
   In 1990, a nearly complete Tyrannosaurus rex skeleton was found.

(continued)

1 What Is a Sentence? (continued from page 1)

Challenge

Look at each picture and read the description of each imaginary animal. Make up a name for the animal and write it below the description.

1. has blue feathers and webbed feet
   Answers will vary.

3. is a fish that sings and tells jokes

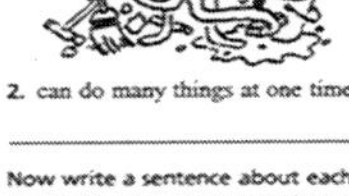

2. can do many things at one time

4. is a furry thing that sneezes

Now write a sentence about each animal. Use the animal's name and its description to write a complete sentence.

1. Answers will vary.
2.
3.
4.

Writing Application: A Journal DESCRIBING

You have discovered an animal from long ago. Write at least five sentences that describe what the animal looks like, where it lives, and what it eats. Be sure that your sentences are complete.
Students should respond on separate paper. Answers will vary.

Writing Good Sentences

Lesson Objectives

Students will:
- correct incomplete sentences by adding them to complete sentences
- correct two incomplete sentences by combining them

Focus on Instruction

Have students read the introductory information and the examples. Have students identify the incomplete sentences by asking which group of words doesn't tell a complete thought. *(In old shipwrecks.)* Tell students that an incomplete sentence is called a fragment. Point out that a fragment may be missing a subject or a predicate or both. It does not form a complete idea.

Apply It

Have students complete the revising activity independently. Point out that when a fragment is combined with a sentence or another fragment, there should be only one end mark and one initial capitalized word in the final sentence.

Have students look in their writing in progress to find incomplete sentences that they can correct by combining.

Sample Answers to Apply It

1. The saguaro cactus can survive in the Arizona desert because it can hold two tons of water.
2. A national park ranger explores a historical underwater site.
3. Have you ever seen caribou grazing near Alaska's tallest mountain?
4. A river inside Mammoth Cave flows 360 feet underground.

FOR STUDENTS ACQUIRING ENGLISH

Write the following phrases on the board: *Deep sea divers,* and *can be found in shipwrecks.* Then write the examples below on the board. Have students use the phrases to make complete sentences.

1. Lost treasure _______. (can be found in shipwrecks)
2. _______ dive for treasure. (Deep sea divers)

Have the students read the completed sentences aloud with you.

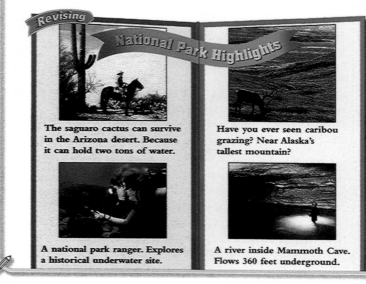

Revising Strategies

Writing Good Sentences

Writing Complete Sentences You have learned that a group of words is not a sentence unless it tells a complete thought. Sometimes you can fix an incomplete sentence by adding it to a complete sentence.

Many clues to American history lie buried underwater. In old shipwrecks.	Many clues to American history lie buried underwater in old shipwrecks.

Sometimes you can fix two incomplete sentences by combining them.

Many amazing sights. Are found in national parks.	Many amazing sights are found in national parks.

Apply It

1–4. Rewrite the picture captions below to make complete sentences.
See TE margin for answers.

Revising

National Park Highlights

The saguaro cactus can survive in the Arizona desert. Because it can hold two tons of water.

Have you ever seen caribou grazing? Near Alaska's tallest mountain?

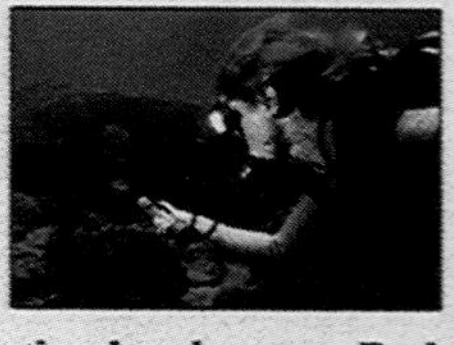

A national park ranger. Explores a historical underwater site.

A river inside Mammoth Cave. Flows 360 feet underground.

34 Unit 1: The Sentence

Meeting Individual Needs

● RETEACHING WORKBOOK, page 2

Writing Good Sentences

- A sentence is a group of words that states a complete thought.
- You can sometimes fix an incomplete sentence by adding it to a complete sentence.

Complete sentence	All living things are made up of tiny units of life.
Incomplete sentence	Called cells.
Sentences combined	All living things are made up of tiny units of life called cells.

Writing Complete Sentences Rewrite each set of sentences below to make a complete sentence.

Example: Did you know that we use algae to make paint? And ice cream too?
Did you know that we use algae to make paint and ice cream too?

Revising

1. Algae are the simplest plants. And some of the oldest living things on Earth.
Algae are the simplest plants and some of the oldest living things on Earth.
2. I thought algae were a slimy mystery the first time I saw some. On the beach.
I thought algae were a slimy mystery the first time I saw some on the beach.
3. Now I know all kinds of interesting things. About algae.
Now I know all kinds of interesting things about algae.
4. The first algae grew in and near water. About three billion years ago.
The first algae grew in and near water about three billion years ago.
5. The first land plant did not appear. Until two and a half billion years later!
The first land plant did not appear until two and a half billion years later!
6. Some scientists believe. Algae will be the perfect food of the future.
Some scientists believe algae will be the perfect food of the future.

(continued)

▲■ WORKBOOK PLUS, page 3

Writing Good Sentences

Complete sentence	Sacajawea helped Lewis and Clark explore western America.
Incomplete sentence	In 1805.
Sentences combined	Sacajawea helped Lewis and Clark explore western America in 1805.
Two incomplete sentences	Explorers Meriwether Lewis and William Clark. Traveled 8,000 miles in 28 months.
Sentences combined	Explorers Meriwether Lewis and William Clark traveled 8,000 miles in 28 months.

Writing Complete Sentences 1–5. Rewrite this paragraph from an essay. Fix the incomplete sentences by combining them or adding each to a complete sentence.

Revising

Sacajawea helped Lewis and Clark in many ways. When they explored the American West. She could translate Native American languages for the explorers. Because she was the daughter of a Shoshone chief. Sacajawea had grown up in the territory Lewis and Clark were exploring. Along the Missouri River. Sacajawea helped the explorers build a friendship with a Shoshone chief. The chief became very helpful. When he found out that Sacajawea was his long-lost little sister! The generous Shoshone. Provided horses, supplies, and information needed by the explorers for crossing the Rocky Mountains.

Sacajawea helped Lewis and Clark in many ways when they explored the American West. She could translate Native American languages for the explorers because she was the daughter of a Shoshone chief. Sacajawea had grown up in the territory Lewis and Clark were exploring along the Missouri River. Sacajawea helped the explorers build a friendship with a Shoshone chief. The chief became very helpful when he found out that Sacajawea was his long-lost little sister! The generous Shoshone provided horses, supplies, and information needed by the explorers for crossing the Rocky Mountains.

(continued)

Sentence Fluency

When you write, make sure your sentences state a complete thought. Incomplete sentences can confuse your reader.

The saguaro produces white flowers. In May and June. Its juicy red fruits are good to eat.

The incomplete sentence above makes the meaning unclear. Does the saguaro produce white flowers or good fruit in May and June? The writer can revise by adding the incomplete sentence to the first sentence.

The saguaro produces white flowers in May and June.

Be sure your new sentences make sense.

Apply It

5–10. Rewrite this part of a report. Fix each incomplete sentence by adding it to a complete sentence or to another incomplete sentence.
See TE margin for answers.

Revising — Cactus

Desert Survival

How does a cactus survive in the desert? With so little water? It can usually find enough water because its roots are very long. Cactus stems are hollow or spongy inside. For storing the water. A waxy coating. Makes them waterproof. The stems may also have sharp thorns that keep thirsty animals away.

One fascinating kind of cactus. Is the giant saguaro. Don't expect to see the saguaro's lovely blossoms. Until it is at least fifty years old! The saguaro may still be less than an inch tall. When it is ten years old. However, it reaches a height of at least thirty feet when it is about one hundred years old! The largest saguaros live to be 200 years old. They can reach fifty feet in height. This is as tall as a five-story building!

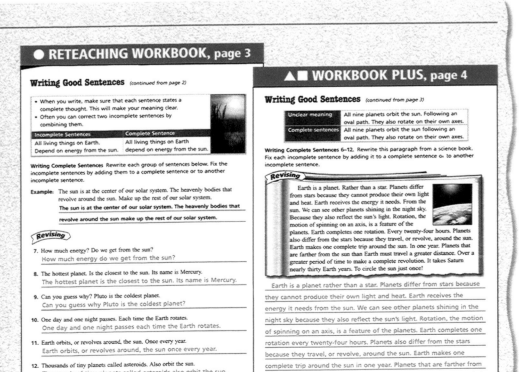

● RETEACHING WORKBOOK, page 3

Writing Good Sentences *(continued from page 2)*

- When you write, make sure that each sentence states a complete thought. This will make your meaning clear.
- Often you can correct two incomplete sentences by combining them.

Incomplete Sentences	Complete Sentence
All living things on Earth. Depend on energy from the sun.	All living things on Earth depend on energy from the sun.

Writing Complete Sentences Rewrite each group of sentences below. Fix the incomplete sentences by adding them to a complete sentence or to another incomplete sentence.

Example: The sun is at the center of our solar system. The heavenly bodies that revolve around the sun. Make up the rest of our solar system.
The sun is at the center of our solar system. The heavenly bodies that revolve around the sun make up the rest of our solar system.

Revising

7. How much energy? Do we get from the sun?
How much energy do we get from the sun?
8. The hottest planet. Is the closest to the sun. Its name is Mercury.
The hottest planet is the closest to the sun. Its name is Mercury.
9. Can you guess why? Pluto is the coldest planet.
Can you guess why Pluto is the coldest planet?
10. One day and one night passes. Each time the Earth rotates.
One day and one night passes each time the Earth rotates.
11. Earth orbits, or revolves around, the sun. Once every year.
Earth orbits, or revolves around, the sun once every year.
12. Thousands of tiny planets called asteroids. Also orbit the sun.
Thousands of tiny planets called asteroids also orbit the sun.

▲■ WORKBOOK PLUS, page 4

Writing Good Sentences *(continued from page 3)*

Unclear meaning	All nine planets orbit the sun. Following an oval path. They also rotate on their own axes.
Complete sentences	All nine planets orbit the sun following an oval path. They also rotate on their own axes.

Writing Complete Sentences 6–12. Rewrite this paragraph from a science book. Fix each incomplete sentence by adding it to a complete sentence or to another incomplete sentence.

Revising

Earth is a planet. Rather than a star. Planets differ from stars because they cannot produce their own light and heat. Earth receives the energy it needs. From the sun. We can see other planets shining in the night sky. Because they also reflect the sun's light. Rotation, the motion of spinning on an axis, is a feature of the planets. Earth completes one rotation. Every twenty-four hours. Planets also differ from the stars because they travel, or revolve, around the sun. Earth makes one complete trip around the sun. In one year. Planets that are farther from the sun than Earth must travel a greater distance. Over a greater period of time to make a complete revolution. It takes Saturn nearly thirty Earth years. To circle the sun just once!

Earth is a planet rather than a star. Planets differ from stars because they cannot produce their own light and heat. Earth receives the energy it needs from the sun. We can see other planets shining in the night sky because they also reflect the sun's light. Rotation, the motion of spinning on an axis, is a feature of the planets. Earth completes one rotation every twenty-four hours. Planets also differ from the stars because they travel, or revolve, around the sun. Earth makes one complete trip around the sun in one year. Planets that are farther from the sun than Earth must travel a greater distance over a greater period of time to make a complete revolution. It takes Saturn nearly thirty Earth years to circle the sun just once!

Lesson Objective

Students will:

- combine fragments with appropriate sentences

Focus on Instruction

- Have volunteers read the example sentences aloud, first adding *In May and June* to the first sentence and then to the last sentence. Ask how the meaning of the sentences changes as the position of the phrase changes.
- Tell students that when they add a fragment to a sentence, they should select the sentence in which the addition makes the most sense. Point out that students should also be careful when deciding how fragments should be combined to form a complete sentence. Tell students to read aloud each sentence formed by combining fragments to make sure that it makes complete sense.

Apply It

Have students complete the revising activity independently. Tell students to first determine if each word group has both a subject and a verb. If it doesn't, students should add the word group to a nearby word group that completes its thought.

Have students find places in their own writing in progress where they can combine fragments with appropriate sentences and with other fragments.

Answers to Apply It

5. How does a cactus survive in the desert with so little water?
6. Cactus stems are hollow or spongy inside for storing the water.
7. A waxy coating makes them waterproof.
8. One fascinating kind of cactus is the giant saguaro.
9. Don't expect to see the saguaro's lovely blossoms until it is at least fifty years old!
10. The saguaro still may be less than an inch tall when it is ten years old.

Statements and Questions

Lesson Objectives

Students will:

- identify statements and questions
- proofread for correct end marks and capital letters
- create a persuasive ad, writing statements and questions correctly

One-Minute Warm-Up Have volunteers write their riddles on the board. Ask students what mark ends each sentence and have them explain why.

Focus on Instruction

Point out that a person's voice will rise on the final words of a question. Explain that in writing, the question mark represents this rise.

Try It Out

VIEWING Have students make up questions and statements about the airline passengers in the picture. Have students write their sentences in a two-column chart. Use the second column for students to name the correct end mark for each sentence. (Sample responses are shown.)

Sentence	End Mark
The girl looks out the window.	period
Where is the plane going?	question mark

FOR STUDENTS ACQUIRING ENGLISH

- Have students listen to the Try It Out sentences on the audiotape. Distribute SAE Practice pages for Unit 1, Lesson 2, to support listening.
- Help students suggest statements and questions about the photograph. Write *statement* and *question* on the board and ask students what the first letter of each is called. First, students listen to the audio and respond by saying "S" for statement or "Q" for question. Remind students to listen for rising intonation on yes or no questions. Then students add the correct punctuation.
  1. Do you like to fly? (Q)
  2. My sister flew to Saigon. (S)
  3. No, I don't. (S)
  4. What time did the plane leave (?)
  5. We went to the airport (.)

Grammar/Mechanics

2 Statements and Questions

One-Minute Warm-Up

Riddle: Why was the plane so tired in the morning?
Answer: It stayed up all night. Answers will vary.
Think of a riddle to try out on your classmates. Use a question to ask and a statement to answer the riddle.

- Different kinds of sentences have different jobs. **A sentence that tells something is a statement.** A statement ends with a period (.).
- **A sentence that asks something is a question.** A question ends with a question mark (?).
- A sentence always begins with a capital letter.

Statements	Questions
The airport was crowded.	Was the airport crowded?
Her plane landed on time.	When did her plane land?
Carlos bought a ticket.	Did Carlos buy a ticket?

Try It Out

Speak Up Is each sentence a statement or a question? What end mark should follow each sentence?

1. The flight attendant welcomed the passengers. S
2. I pushed my small brown bag under the seat. S
3. Have you fastened your seat belts? Q
4. Can you see out the window? Q
5. What city is below? Q
6. The cars look like ants. S
7. Now everything looks foggy. S
8. Are we flying through a cloud? Q
9. How high will the plane climb? Q
10. We will land in about an hour. S
11. Is this your first flight? Q

Meeting Individual Needs

RETEACHING
ALTERNATIVE STRATEGY

- Have students write questions they might ask to get to know a new student. Write the questions on the board, and point out the initial capital letters and question marks.
- Have volunteers write answers to the questions on the board.
- Tell students that statements are different from questions. Questions end with a question mark and ask something, but statements end with a period and tell something.

CHALLENGE
Have students write statements that answer riddles, such as *It has a long neck.* Have students exchange papers and write a question for each statement. For example, *What is a giraffe?*

FOR STUDENTS ACQUIRING ENGLISH
Model the rising intonation of yes or no questions. Present examples; have students repeat. Then present more examples as you model falling intonation in information questions—*who, what, where* questions. Have students repeat. Then contrast the two types, using a chart on the board.

On Your Own

Write *statement* if the sentence is a statement. Write *question* if it is a question.

Example: Who made the first flight alone across the Atlantic? *question*

12. Charles Lindbergh was the pilot's name. S
13. A prize of $25,000 was offered. S
14. What kind of plane did he fly? Q
15. His plane was called the *Spirit of St. Louis*. S
16. Lindbergh flew from New York to Paris. S
17. How long did the flight take? Q
18. The flight took thirty-three and one-half hours. S
19. Have you ever seen Lindbergh's plane? Q
20. His plane is in the Smithsonian Institution. S

21–28. This ad has three missing capital letters and five missing or incorrect end marks. Write the ad correctly. Underlined letters should be capitalized.

Example: can anyone learn to fly *Can anyone learn to fly?*

Proofreading

LEARN TO FLY!

Did you ever dream of flying like a bird? Would you like to see the world? the Ace Pilot School is the answer to your dreams. Our teachers are experts. You will learn the skills of safe flying. lessons are half-price in January. you cannot afford to wait? Isn't it time to make your dream come true?

Writing Wrap-Up WRITING • THINKING • LISTENING • SPEAKING

PERSUADING

Write an Ad

Write an ad that would convince people to learn to juggle, use a yo-yo, or learn some other fun or unusual skill. Include questions and statements in your ad. Then read it to a partner. Is your ad convincing? Work together to check for capital letters and end marks.

For Extra Practice see page 57.

Summing Up Help students summarize these key points about the lesson:

> A **statement** is a sentence that tells something. It ends with a period (.). A **question** is a sentence that asks something. It ends with a question mark (?). Every sentence begins with a capital letter.

You may want to have students complete the parts related to this lesson on Blackline Master 1–1.

On Your Own

Tell students that many sentences starting with *what, who, when, why,* or *how* are questions.

MEETING INDIVIDUAL NEEDS

FOR STUDENTS ACQUIRING ENGLISH

Distribute SAE Practice pages for Unit 1, Lesson 2. Have students cut up the strips of questions and answers on the page. Then have students match questions and answers. Students can work with partners, alternating reading the questions and answers aloud. Example: Was Charles Lindbergh the pilot? Yes, he was.

Writing Wrap-Up

Writing Tip: Point out that a good way to begin an ad like this is to start with a question. See Blackline Master 1–4 for a sample ad.

TECHNOLOGY CONNECTION

Students may wish to use available software to create colorful print ads.

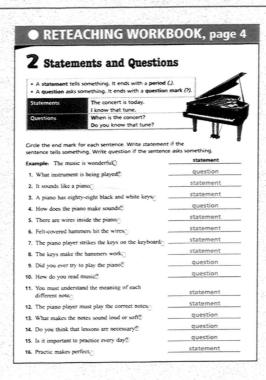

● RETEACHING WORKBOOK, page 4

2 Statements and Questions

- A **statement** tells something. It ends with a **period** (.).
- A **question** asks something. It ends with a **question mark** (?).

Statements	The concert is today. I know that tune.
Questions	When is the concert? Do you know that tune?

Circle the end mark for each sentence. Write *statement* if the sentence tells something. Write *question* if the sentence asks something.

Example: The music is wonderful. statement

1. What instrument is being played? question
2. It sounds like a piano. statement
3. A piano has eighty-eight black and white keys. statement
4. How does the piano make sounds? question
5. There are wires inside the piano. statement
6. Felt-covered hammers hit the wires. statement
7. The piano player strikes the keys on the keyboard. statement
8. The keys make the hammers work. statement
9. Did you ever try to play the piano? question
10. How do you read music? question
11. You must understand the meaning of each different note. statement
12. The piano player must play the correct notes. statement
13. What makes the notes sound loud or soft? question
14. Do you think that lessons are necessary? question
15. Is it important to practice every day? question
16. Practic makes perfect. statement

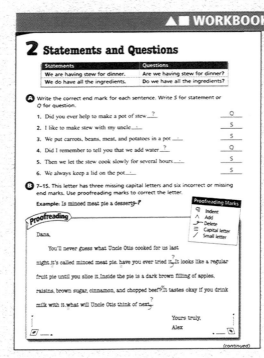

▲■ WORKBOOK PLUS, pages 5–6

2 Statements and Questions

Statements	Questions
We are having stew for dinner.	Are we having stew for dinner?
We do have all the ingredients.	Do we have all the ingredients?

A Write the correct end mark for each sentence. Write *S* for statement or *Q* for question.

1. Did you ever help to make a pot of stew ? Q
2. I like to make stew with my uncle . S
3. We put carrots, beans, meat, and potatoes in a pot . S
4. Did I remember to tell you that we add water ? Q
5. Then we let the stew cook slowly for several hours . S
6. We always keep a lid on the pot . S

B 7–15. This letter has three missing capital letters and six incorrect or missing end marks. Use proofreading marks to correct the letter.

Example: Is minced meat pie a dessert. ?

Proofreading Marks
- ¶ Indent
- ^ Add
- Delete
- ≡ Capital letter
- / Small letter

Proofreading

Dana,

You'll never guess what Uncle Otis cooked for us last night.it's called minced meat pie. have you ever tried it. ? It looks like a regular fruit pie until you slice it.Inside the pie is a dark brown filling of apples, raisins, brown sugar, cinnamon, and chopped beef?.It tastes okay if you drink milk with it.what will Uncle Otis think of next. ?

Yours truly,
Alex

(continued)

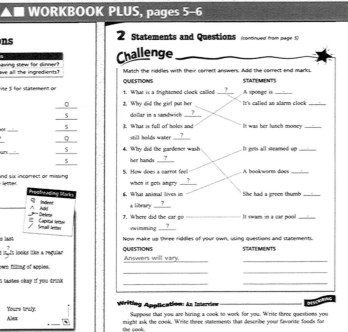

2 Statements and Questions (continued from page 5)

Challenge

Match the riddles with their correct answers. Add the correct end marks.

QUESTIONS	STATEMENTS
1. What is a frightened clock called ?	A sponge is .
2. Why did the girl put her dollar in a sandwich ?	It's called an alarm clock .
3. What is full of holes and still holds water ?	It was her lunch money .
4. Why did the gardener wash her hands ?	It gets all steamed up .
5. How does a carrot feel when it gets angry ?	A bookworm does .
6. What animal lives in a library ?	She had a green thumb .
7. Where did the car go swimming ?	It swam in a car pool .

Now make up three riddles of your own, using questions and statements.

QUESTIONS	STATEMENTS
Answers will vary.	

Writing Application: An Interview DESCRIBING

Suppose that you are hiring a cook to work for you. Write three questions you might ask the cook. Write three statements that describe your favorite foods for the cook.

Commands and Exclamations

Lesson Objectives

Students will:
- identify commands and exclamations
- proofread for correct end marks and capital letters
- write a paragraph for a travel brochure, using commands and exclamations

One-Minute Warm-Up Have volunteers take turns reading each sentence aloud, using voice cues to signal its end punctuation. Ask how reading the second sentence with strong expression affects the end punctuation.

Focus on Instruction

Explain to students that in a command, such as *Give your ticket to the conductor,* the *who* or *what* of the sentence is understood to be *you.* Also point out that an exclamation is a sentence and, as such, should tell *who* or *what* and *what is* or *what happens.*

Try It Out

VIEWING Have students create commands and exclamations telling about applying for a passport. Record the sentences on a chart. (Sample responses are shown.)

Commands	Exclamations
Wait in that line.	How long the line is!
Sign your name.	My passport photo is so funny!

FOR STUDENTS ACQUIRING ENGLISH

- Have students listen to the Try It Out sentences on the audiotape. Distribute SAE Practice pages for Unit 1, Lesson 3, to support listening.
- First, invite students to talk about the passport in the photograph. Write the word *passport* on the board and explain that a passport is used for travel. Next, review the differences between an exclamation and a command. Tell students that *you* is understood but not stated in a command. Demonstrate strong stress on a sample exclamation. Remind students that all sentences must begin with a capital letter. Then have students listen and choose a period or exclamation point as punctuation.
  1. Let's leave for the airport early (.)
  2. I forgot my passport (!)
  3. The plane has already left (!)
  4. Wait for me, please (.) or (!)

Grammar/Mechanics

3 Commands and Exclamations

One-Minute Warm-Up

Read these sentences about the picture aloud. Use your voice to express the meaning of each sentence.

The bus is going to leave!
Get on now.

You have learned about two kinds of sentences called statements and questions. Now you will learn about two other kinds of sentences.

- **A sentence that tells someone to do something is a command.** A command ends with a period.
- **A sentence that shows strong feeling such as surprise, excitement, or fear is an exclamation.** It ends with an exclamation point (!).
- Remember to begin every sentence with a capital letter.

Commands	Exclamations
Please wait at the bus stop.	The bus finally arrived!
Meet me at Paige's Bookstore.	What a huge store it is!
Take the subway home.	How fast the train travels!

Try It Out

Speak Up Is each sentence a command or an exclamation? What end mark should be put at the end of each sentence?

1. Plan your trip carefully. C
2. Apply for your passport. C
3. Please bring a photo of yourself. C
4. How excited I am! E
5. My dream is coming true! E
6. We're leaving at last! E
7. Lock the door. C

Meeting Individual Needs

RETEACHING
ALTERNATIVE STRATEGY

- Surprise students by dropping a book on a desk. Have them suggest sentences that describe their reactions. Write these sentences on the board.
- Explain that a sentence that expresses strong feeling is called an exclamation. It ends with an exclamation point.
- Have students suggest sentences that tell what to do, such as *Open your books.* List these commands on the board.
- Explain that a sentence that tells someone to do something is a command and ends with a period.

CHALLENGE
Have students write a paragraph about an imaginary trip they would like to take, such as to the moon. They should include statements, questions, commands, and exclamations. Have groups of students combine their paragraphs into a wacky travel brochure.

FOR STUDENTS ACQUIRING ENGLISH
Write the word *command* on the board. Then give students a series of simple commands to follow, such as *sit down, stand up, pat your heads, touch your ears.* Students perform these actions in unison, and then they give some themselves.

On Your Own

Write *command* if the sentence tells someone to do something. Write *exclamation* if it shows strong feeling.

Example: What a perfect day it is to fly to England! *exclamation*

8. Be at the airport early. C
9. Show your ticket at the gate. C
10. How hard it is to stay calm! E
11. I can't wait to fly! E
12. Find your seat quickly. C
13. Let me fasten your seat belt. C
14. What a smooth takeoff that was! E
15. How tiny everything looks! E
16. Please stay in your seat. C
17. We have arrived at last! E

18–24. This page from a travel brochure has two missing capital letters and five missing end marks. Each sentence is a command or an exclamation. Write the page correctly. Underlined letters should be capitalized.

Example: what delicious food Mexico has *What delicious food Mexico has!*

Proofreading

Unforgettable Mexico

How exciting it is to visit Mexico!

- Explore Aztec temples.
- swim in the warm Pacific Ocean.
- Shop for handmade jewelry.
- Enjoy lively festivals.

what a land of surprises Mexico is! It is a place you will never forget!

Writing Wrap-Up
WRITING • THINKING • LISTENING • SPEAKING

DESCRIBING

Write a Travel Brochure

Write a paragraph about your city or town for a travel brochure. What will you say to make people want to visit? Include commands and exclamations. Add pictures. Read your paragraph to a partner. Make your voice show the types of sentences you used. Ask your partner to supply the end marks.

For Extra Practice see page 58.

Summing Up Help students summarize these key points about the lesson:

A **command** is a sentence that tells someone to do something. It ends with a period (.). An **exclamation** is a sentence that shows strong feeling. It ends with an exclamation point (!).

You may want to have students complete the parts related to this lesson on Blackline Master 1–1.

On Your Own

Suggest that students test for an exclamation by asking whether a sentence expresses strong feeling.

MEETING INDIVIDUAL NEEDS

FOR STUDENTS ACQUIRING ENGLISH

Distribute SAE Practice pages for Unit 1, Lesson 3. Discuss airports and plane travel; list new vocabulary on the board and explain as needed. Students add a period or an exclamation point to each sentence. Then they say "command" or "exclamation." Students read sentences aloud; check for strong stress on exclamations.

Writing Wrap-Up

Writing Tip: Tell students to use details that will help readers see, hear, smell, or feel the place they are describing. See Blackline Master 1–4 for a sample travel brochure paragraph.

TECHNOLOGY CONNECTION

Suggest that students boldface particularly enticing words and phrases in their brochure descriptions.

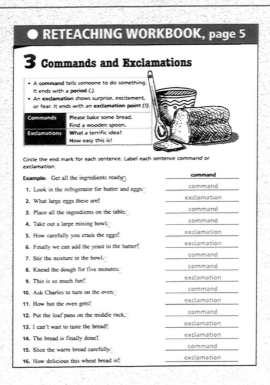

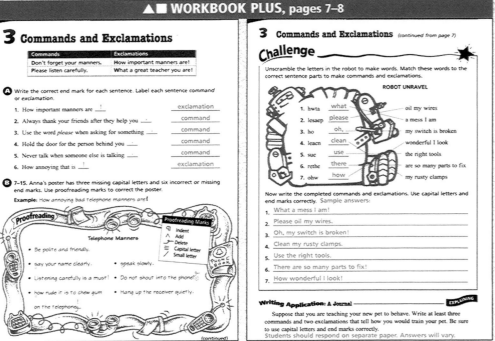

● RETEACHING WORKBOOK, page 5

3 Commands and Exclamations

- A **command** tells someone to do something. It ends with a **period** (.).
- An **exclamation** shows surprise, excitement, or fear. It ends with an **exclamation point** (!).

Commands	Please bake some bread. Find a wooden spoon.
Exclamations	What a terrific idea! How easy this is!

Circle the end mark for each sentence. Label each sentence *command* or *exclamation*.

Example: Get all the ingredients ready. **command**

1. Look in the refrigerator for butter and eggs. command
2. What large eggs these are! exclamation
3. Place all the ingredients on the table. command
4. Take out a large mixing bowl. command
5. How carefully you crack the eggs! exclamation
6. Finally we can add the yeast to the batter! exclamation
7. Stir the mixture in the bowl. command
8. Knead the dough for five minutes. command
9. This is so much fun! exclamation
10. Ask Charles to turn on the oven. command
11. How hot the oven gets! exclamation
12. Put the loaf pans on the middle rack. command
13. I can't wait to taste the bread! exclamation
14. The bread is finally done! exclamation
15. Slice the warm bread carefully. command
16. How delicious this wheat bread is! exclamation

▲■ WORKBOOK PLUS, pages 7–8

3 Commands and Exclamations

Commands	Exclamations
Don't forget your manners.	How important manners are!
Please listen carefully.	What a great teacher you are!

A Write the correct end mark for each sentence. Label each sentence *command* or *exclamation*.

1. How important manners are ! exclamation
2. Always thank your friends after they help you . command
3. Use the word *please* when asking for something . command
4. Hold the door for the person behind you . command
5. Never talk when someone else is talking . command
6. How annoying that is ! exclamation

B 7–15. Anna's poster has three missing capital letters and six incorrect or missing end marks. Use proofreading marks to correct the poster.

Example: *How annoying bad telephone manners are!*

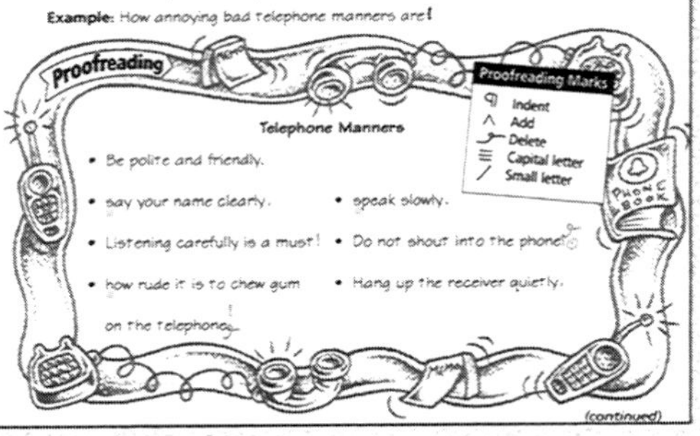

(continued)

3 Commands and Exclamations *(continued from page 7)*

Challenge

Unscramble the letters in the robot to make words. Match these words to the correct sentence parts to make commands and exclamations.

ROBOT UNRAVEL

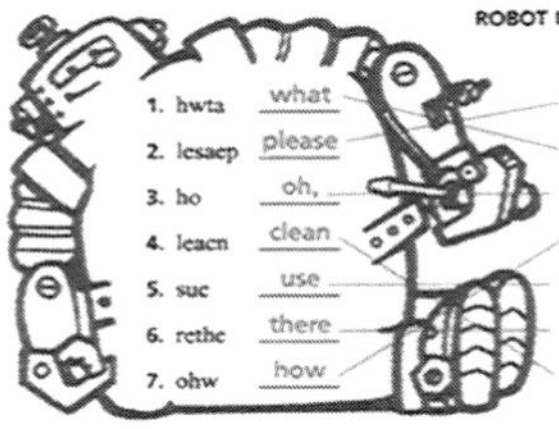

Now write the completed commands and exclamations. Use capital letters and end marks correctly. Sample answers:

1. What a mess I am!
2. Please oil my wires.
3. Oh, my switch is broken!
4. Clean my rusty clamps.
5. Use the right tools.
6. There are so many parts to fix!
7. How wonderful I look!

Writing Application: A Journal EXPLAINING

Suppose that you are teaching your new pet to behave. Write at least three commands and two exclamations that tell how you would train your pet. Be sure to use capital letters and end marks correctly.
Students should respond on separate paper. Answers will vary.

Subjects and Predicates

Lesson Objectives

Students will:
- identify the complete subjects of sentences
- identify the complete predicates of sentences
- write a poem containing complete subjects and complete predicates

One-Minute Warm-Up Have volunteers write the sentence on the board. Tell them to underline once the part that tells *whom* or *what* the sentence is about. Have them underline twice the part that tells *what happened.*

Focus on Instruction

Point out to students that either the complete subject or the complete predicate can be one word or many words. The key to finding the complete subject is to ask *whom* or *what* the sentence is about; the key to finding the complete predicate is to ask what the subject *is* or *does*.

Try It Out

VIEWING Make a chart on the board with two columns, one headed *Who/What* and the other *Is/Does*. Have students name people and objects they see in the fishing scene. Record their responses in the *Who/What* column. Then list their suggestions telling what each person or object is or does in the *Is/Does* column. Have students combine their suggestions to make complete sentences.

Who/What	Is/Does
The boy	caught a fish.
The waves	crashed against the shore.

FOR STUDENTS ACQUIRING ENGLISH

- Have students listen to the Try It Out sentences on the audiotape. Distribute SAE Practice pages for Unit 1, Lesson 4, to support listening.
- Help students suggest sentences about the photograph. Remind students that the subject tells *who* or *what* and the predicate tells what the subject *is* or *does.* Also remind them that each part can be more than one word long. Students listen and then underline the complete subject once and the complete predicate twice.

1. Henry likes to fish.
2. My little sister doesn't like to fish.
3. She doesn't like to eat fish either.
4. All my brothers do.
5. The ocean is calm today.

Grammar

4 Subjects and Predicates

One-Minute Warm-Up

Read the sentence below. Whom or what is the sentence about? What happened? Whom or what underlined once; what happened, twice.

A large trout leapt in the air.

—from *A River Dream*, by Allen Say

- **The subject tells whom or what the sentence is about. The predicate tells what the subject does or is.**
- All the words in the subject make up the **complete subject**. All the words in the predicate make up the **complete predicate**. A complete subject or a complete predicate may be one word.

Complete Subjects	Complete Predicates
Angela Kelly	is the captain of the boat.
We	waited at the dock.
The red ferryboat	stops.
Passengers	get off the boat.

- Ask whom or what the sentence is about to find the subject. Ask what the subject does or is to find the predicate.

Try It Out

Speak Up What are the complete subject and the complete predicate of each sentence? Subject underlined once; predicate, twice.

1. Henry Delgado fished from the wharf.
2. The ocean was calm.
3. Several gulls flew overhead.
4. The gulls squawked noisily.
5. Henry cast his line into the sea.
6. He waited.
7. A large fish tugged on his line.

Meeting Individual Needs

RETEACHING

ALTERNATIVE STRATEGY

- Write this sentence on the board: *An orange gorilla paddles a canoe.* Ask students *who* or *what* paddles a canoe. (An orange gorilla) Explain that this is the complete subject of the sentence.
- Ask *what* the gorilla does. (paddles a canoe) Explain that this is the complete predicate of the sentence. Explain that every sentence has a subject and a predicate.
- Have students create zany sentences about other animals. For each sentence, help students identify the complete subject and the complete predicate.

CHALLENGE

Have students choose sentences from a story. Have them rewrite each sentence, using a different complete subject. Then have them rewrite the original sentence, using a different complete predicate. *(A crab walks on the sand. A man walks on the sand. A crab bit my foot.)*

FOR STUDENTS ACQUIRING ENGLISH

Write a sentence about something in class: *My book is new.* Underline the complete subject while saying "what;" underline the complete predicate twice while saying "what it is." Continue with other sentences.

On Your Own

Write each sentence. Draw a line between the complete subject and the complete predicate.

Example: Many people enjoy the ocean. *Many people | enjoy the ocean.*

8. Children | splash in the waves.
9. Two older children | swim to the raft.
10. Geneva Simpson | works at the beach.
11. She | is a lifeguard.
12. Lifeguards | watch the swimmers carefully.
13. Mr. Mota | runs the snack bar.
14. His children | help.

15–22. Write this poem. Draw a line between the complete subject and the complete predicate in each sentence.

Example: Bright pebbles tumble on the shore.
Bright pebbles | tumble on the shore.

The Beach

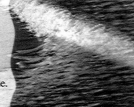

Green waves | toss their foamy heads.
Clams | sleep in their sandy beds.
A lonely man | wades. A girl | skips by.
They | look at clouds up in the sky.
The wind | is cool. Big white birds | glide.
Footprints | wash away in the tide.

Writing Wrap-Up

WRITING • THINKING • LISTENING • SPEAKING

CREATING

Write a Poem

Write a poem made up of sentences. The poem does not have to rhyme, but each sentence should have a complete subject and a complete predicate. With a small group, take turns reading your poems aloud. Which poems did you like the best? Why?

For Extra Practice see page 59.

Summing Up Help students summarize these key points about the lesson:

The **complete subject** of a sentence includes all the words that tell *whom* or *what* the sentence is about. The **complete predicate** includes all the words that tell what the subject *does* or *is*.

You may want to have students complete the parts related to this lesson on Blackline Master 1–2.

On Your Own

Remind students that a complete subject or a complete predicate may be only one word.

MEETING INDIVIDUAL NEEDS

FOR STUDENTS ACQUIRING ENGLISH

Distribute SAE Practice pages for Unit 1, Lesson 4. Discuss the illustration of the beach. List vocabulary on the board and define as needed. Then have students draw a line between the complete subject and the complete predicate. Example: *The ocean/is large.* Before they begin, ask students how many words each can have.

Writing Wrap-Up

Writing Tip: Remind students to use exact, interesting words in their poems. See Blackline Master 1–4 for a sample poem.

SCHOOL-HOME CONNECTION

Encourage students to read their poems to family members.

● RETEACHING WORKBOOK, page 6

4 Subjects and Predicates

- The **complete subject** includes all the words that tell *whom or what* the sentence is about.
- The **complete predicate** includes all the words that tell what the subject *does* or *is*.

Complete Subjects	Complete Predicates
Many people	listen to the radio.
People	enjoy different kinds of shows.

Tell what is underlined in each sentence.
Write *CS* for the complete subject or *CP* for the complete predicate.

Example: Many children <u>like cartoons.</u> CP

1. Cartoons are exciting for people of all ages. CP
2. Television offers many kinds of programs. CS
3. Many adults like evening comedy shows. CS
4. Movies are very popular. CP
5. Walt Disney made many fine films. CS
6. Children of all ages enjoy his adventure films. CS
7. My family attends concerts. CP
8. We like concerts in the park. CP
9. The sound of violins is beautiful. CS
10. Grandmother goes to many plays in the city. CS
11. *My Fair Lady* is her favorite musical. CP
12. The circus is made up of many acts. CP
13. A happy audience cheers. CP
14. Other people attend operas. CS
15. They listen to the trained voices of the singers. CS
16. Good shows are an important part of life. CP

▲■ WORKBOOK PLUS, pages 9–10

4 Subjects and Predicates

Complete Subjects	Complete Predicates
Many inventors	lived in Philadelphia, Pennsylvania.
Some inventors	became famous.

Draw a line to divide the complete subject and the complete predicate of each sentence. Write *CS* above the complete subject and *CP* above the complete predicate.

1. Thomas Edison (CS) | invented the light bulb. (CP)
2. Some inventions (CS) | are practical. (CP)
3. Other inventions (CS) | are fun. (CP)
4. The first bicycle (CS) | was built over one hundred years ago. (CP)
5. A man from England (CS) | built the first modern bicycle. (CP)
6. Television (CS) | became popular in the United States. (CP)
7. This invention (CS) | is over eighty years old. (CP)
8. People (CS) | bought their first frozen foods in 1925. (CP)
9. Levi Strauss (CS) | made the first denim pants in 1847. (CP)
10. Many people (CS) | call them jeans. (CP)
11. Gold miners (CS) | were Levi's best customers. (CP)
12. The telephone (CS) | is not a new invention. (CP)
13. Many inventions (CS) | change over the years. (CP)
14. A cellular telephone (CS) | is one example of this change. (CP)
15. The computer (CS) | is another example. (CP)
16. Computers (CS) | have become smaller and more powerful. (CP)
17. Scientists (CS) | are not the only inventors. (CP)
18. Many ordinary people (CS) | invent. (CP)
19. We (CS) | hear of new inventions all the time. (CP)
20. New products (CS) | help many people. (CP)

(continued)

4 Subjects and Predicates *(continued from page 9)*

Challenge

Look at the lists of inventions for the future. Write a sentence that describes what each invention will do. Underline the complete subject and circle the complete predicate of each sentence.

Outdoor Inventions	Indoor Inventions
1. Way Finder	4. Dish Swisher
2. Power Center	5. Floor Crawler
3. Star Searcher	6. Sweeper Beeper

1. Answers will vary.
2.
3.
4.
5.
6.

Draw a picture that shows one or two of the inventions above.

Writing Application: An Advertisement CREATING

Suppose that you are an inventor. Write an advertisement for one of your inventions. Write the name of your invention. Then write five sentences that describe what it looks like and what it does. Draw a line between the complete subject and the complete predicate of each sentence.
Students should respond on separate paper. Answers will vary.

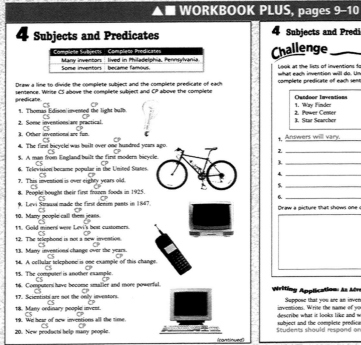

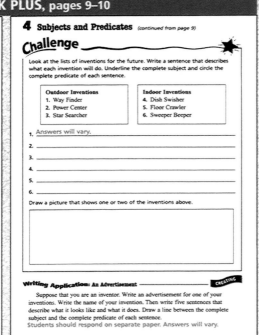

Simple Subjects

Lesson Objectives

Students will:
- identify the simple subject of a sentence
- write interview questions and answers

One-Minute Warm-Up Write the headline on the board. Have volunteers complete the sentence. Record their words in ladder-like fashion in, above, and below the blank. Point out that their words tell exactly whom or what the sentence is about because they tell exactly who or what "broke the record."

Focus on Instruction

Point out that the simple subject is usually one word. If the simple subject is the name of a particular person or place, it may contain two or more words—for example, *Martin Johnson, New Mexico,* or *Golden Gate Bridge.*

Try It Out

VIEWING Have students name people and objects they might see if they were playing basketball, like the child in the photograph. List their suggestions in a chart like the one shown. Then have students use each word as the simple subject of a sentence.

Who/What	Sentence
basket	The basket was too high.
basketball	The basketball goes through the hoop.

FOR STUDENTS ACQUIRING ENGLISH
- Have students listen to the Try It Out sentences on the audiotape. Distribute SAE Practice pages for Unit 1, Lesson 5, to support listening.
- Help students describe the photo. Assist with vocabulary as needed for basketball as well as baseball. Remind students that the simple subject is one word or one name. Contrast the simple subject with the complete subject by writing this sentence on the board: *My big brother plays baseball.* Underline *My big brother* once and then draw students' attention to it as you underline *brother* a second time.

1. James plays baseball well.
2. Our parents like to watch him play.
3. His team is not very good.

Grammar

5 Simple Subjects

One-Minute Warm-Up

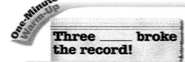

Three ____ broke the record!

How many different ways can you complete this headline?
Sample answer: Three swimmers broke the record!

- You have learned that the complete subject includes all the words that tell whom or what the sentence is about. In every complete subject, there is one main word that is the simple subject. **The simple subject tells exactly whom or what the sentence is about.**
- Sometimes the complete subject and the simple subject are the same. The simple subjects below are shown in yellow.

Complete Subjects	Complete Predicates
Many people	watch ball games at the park.
Marcus Johnson	slides into third base.
He	pitched five innings.
The palm of his glove	is torn.

Try It Out

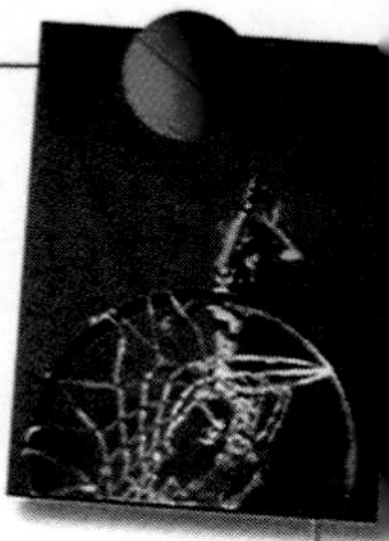

Speak Up The complete subject of each sentence is underlined. What is the simple subject?

1. James Naismith invented basketball in 1891.
2. He was a teacher in Springfield, Massachusetts.
3. The head of the school wanted a winter game.
4. Naismith tacked peach baskets to the walls of the gym.
5. He called the game "basket ball."
6. The first players used soccer balls.
7. Each team had nine players.
8. The new players scored only one basket in the first game.
9. The members of the teams loved the game anyway.
10. A clever player cut the bottoms out of the baskets fifteen years later.

Meeting Individual Needs

RETEACHING
ALTERNATIVE STRATEGY
- Display this sentence: *The ______ watched an exciting basketball game.* Then ask students to fill in the blank to tell who watched the game.
- Write the noun in the blank. Explain that it is the simple subject of the sentence. Tell students that the simple subject is usually one word; it tells exactly whom or what the sentence is about.
- Follow a similar procedure to help students identify the simple subject in other sentences.

CHALLENGE
Have partners work together to write sentences about a favorite sport or activity. Tell them to use long, complete subjects. Have each pair share its best and longest sentence and challenge the group to identify its simple subject.

FOR STUDENTS ACQUIRING ENGLISH
Present sentences about students' and classroom objects: *The green sweater is on the chair.* Underline the complete subject once; catch students' attention as you underline the simple subject a second time. Continue.

On Your Own

The complete subject of each sentence is underlined. Write the simple subject.

Example: People all over the world play basketball. *People*

11. A high basket hangs at each end of the court.
12. A toss of the ball starts the game.
13. Players pass, dribble, and shoot the ball.
14. The team with the ball tries to put it into the basket.
15. The other team tries to stop them.
16. The five players on a team try to score points.
17. Michael Jordan scored a lot of points.
18. He was one of the best players in history.

19–28. The complete subject of each sentence is underlined in this online magazine article. Write the article, and circle the simple subjects.

Example: Modern baseball is fun. *Modern (baseball) is fun.*

Web site

Home | Back | Forward | Stop | Images | Reload | Help | Mail

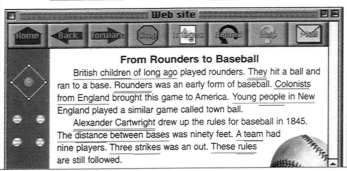

From Rounders to Baseball

British children of long ago played rounders. They hit a ball and ran to a base. Rounders was an early form of baseball. Colonists from England brought this game to America. Young people in New England played a similar game called town ball.

Alexander Cartwright drew up the rules for baseball in 1845. The distance between bases was ninety feet. A team had nine players. Three strikes was an out. These rules are still followed.

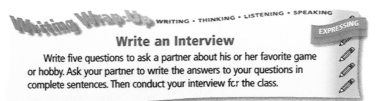

Writing Wrap-Up — WRITING • THINKING • LISTENING • SPEAKING — EXPRESSING

Write an Interview

Write five questions to ask a partner about his or her favorite game or hobby. Ask your partner to write the answers to your questions in complete sentences. Then conduct your interview for the class.

For Extra Practice see page 60.

Summing Up Help students summarize these key points about the lesson:

The **simple subject** is the main word in the complete subject. It tells exactly whom or what the sentence is about.

You might want to have students complete the parts related to this lesson on Blackline Master 1–2.

On Your Own

Remind students that the words *a, and,* and *the* are not part of the simple subject but belong to a special word group that they will study later.

MEETING INDIVIDUAL NEEDS

FOR STUDENTS ACQUIRING ENGLISH

Distribute SAE Practice pages for Unit 1, Lesson 5. Write an example from the page on the board, underline the complete subject once, and then ask a student to go to the board to underline the simple subject a second time. Example: My sister plays basketball.

Writing Wrap-Up

Writing Tip: Tell students to use words such as *what, when, who, why,* and *how* to begin their interview questions. See Blackline Master 1–5 for sample interview questions and answers.

SCHOOL-HOME CONNECTION

Suggest that students use their questions to interview family members or friends about their hobbies.

● RETEACHING WORKBOOK, page 7

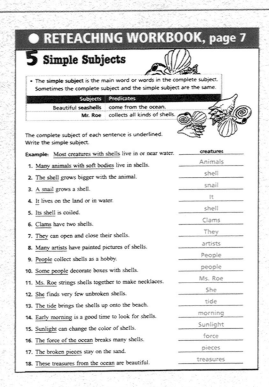

5 Simple Subjects

- The **simple subject** is the main word or words in the complete subject. Sometimes the complete subject and the simple subject are the same.

Subjects	Predicates
Beautiful **seashells**	come from the ocean.
Mr. Roe	collects all kinds of shells.

The complete subject of each sentence is underlined. Write the simple subject.

Example: Most creatures with shells live in or near water. creatures

1. Many animals with soft bodies live in shells. Animals
2. The shell grows bigger with the animal. shell
3. A snail grows a shell. snail
4. It lives on the land or in water. It
5. Its shell is coiled. shell
6. Clams have two shells. Clams
7. They can open and close their shells. They
8. Many artists have painted pictures of shells. artists
9. People collect shells as a hobby. People
10. Some people decorate boxes with shells. people
11. Ms. Roe strings shells together to make necklaces. Ms. Roe
12. She finds very few unbroken shells. She
13. The tide brings the shells up onto the beach. tide
14. Early morning is a good time to look for shells. morning
15. Sunlight can change the color of shells. Sunlight
16. The force of the ocean breaks many shells. force
17. The broken pieces stay on the sand. pieces
18. These treasures from the ocean are beautiful. treasures

▲■ WORKBOOK PLUS, pages 11–12

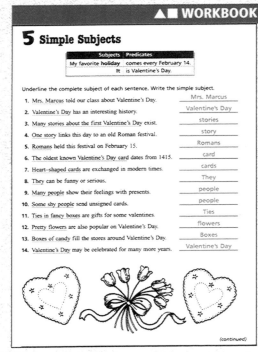

5 Simple Subjects

Subjects	Predicates
My favorite **holiday**	comes every February 14.
It	is Valentine's Day.

Underline the complete subject of each sentence. Write the simple subject.

1. Mrs. Marcus told our class about Valentine's Day. Mrs. Marcus
2. Valentine's Day has an interesting history. Valentine's Day
3. Many stories about the first Valentine's Day exist. stories
4. One story links this day to an old Roman festival. story
5. Romans held this festival on February 15. Romans
6. The oldest known Valentine's Day card dates from 1415. card
7. Heart-shaped cards are exchanged in modern times. cards
8. They can be funny or serious. They
9. Many people show their feelings with presents. people
10. Some shy people send unsigned cards. people
11. Ties in fancy boxes are gifts for some valentines. Ties
12. Pretty flowers are also popular on Valentine's Day. flowers
13. Boxes of candy fill the stores around Valentine's Day. Boxes
14. Valentine's Day may be celebrated for many more years. Valentine's Day

(continued)

5 Simple Subjects *(continued from page 11)*

Challenge

Underline the simple subjects in the sentences below. Use them to complete the puzzle.

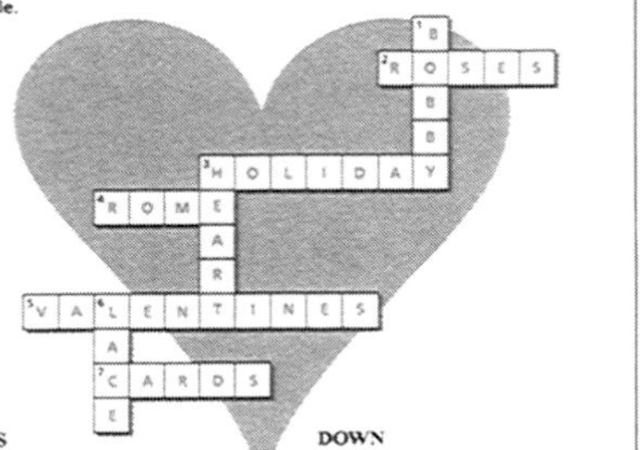

ACROSS

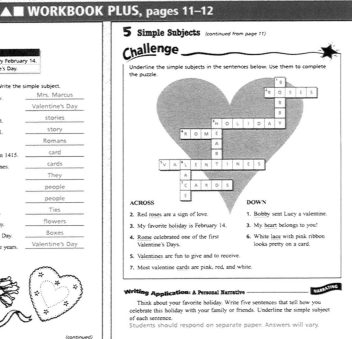

2. Red roses are a sign of love.
3. My favorite holiday is February 14.
4. Rome celebrated one of the first Valentine's Days.
5. Valentines are fun to give and to receive.
7. Most valentine cards are pink, red, and white.

DOWN

1. Bobby sent Lucy a valentine.
3. My heart belongs to you!
6. White lace with pink ribbon looks pretty on a card.

Writing Application: A Personal Narrative — NARRATING

Think about your favorite holiday. Write five sentences that tell how you celebrate this holiday with your family or friends. Underline the simple subject of each sentence.

Students should respond on separate paper. Answers will vary.

Simple Predicates

Lesson Objectives

Students will:

- identify the simple predicate of a sentence
- write a list of tips in sentence form

One-Minute Warm-Up Write the sentence on the board. Have volunteers suggest words to complete it. Record their suggestions. Explain that each suggestion is the simple predicate of the sentence because it tells exactly what the astronauts did in space.

Focus on Instruction

Tell students that the simple predicate is easier to find if they first find the simple subject, the whom or what the sentence is about. Then they can ask what word tells exactly what the subject is or does.

Try It Out

VIEWING Have students generate a list of action words suggested by the space camp scene in the photograph. Record students' words in a chart like the one shown. Then suggest that students make up sentences, using each word as a simple predicate.

Action Words	Sentences
watch	The students watch the screens.
sit	Several students sit at computers.

FOR STUDENTS ACQUIRING ENGLISH

- Have students listen to the Try It Out sentences on the audiotape. Distribute SAE Practice pages for Unit 1, Lesson 6, to support listening.
- Explain that the children in the photo are at a special space camp that is held by NASA—the U.S. space organization. Brainstorm vocabulary relating to space. Then help students suggest sentences about the children in the photograph. Have students listen and underline the complete predicate once. Have them listen again and underline the simple predicate a second time. Remind students that the simple predicate is the main word in the predicate; it tells what something *is* or what it *does*.

1. The children are at space camp.
2. NASA runs this camp for children.

Grammar

6 Simple Predicates

One-Minute Warm-Up

How many different ways can you complete this sentence? Sample answer: did

The astronauts _____ amazing things in space!

The complete predicate includes all the words that tell what the subject does or is. In every complete predicate, there is one main word that is the simple predicate. **The simple predicate tells exactly what the subject does or is.** In each sentence below, the simple predicate is shown in yellow.

Complete Subjects	Complete Predicates
Some students	go to space camp.
The camp	is in Alabama.
Campers	build rockets.
They	wear real space suits.

Try It Out

Space Camp in Huntsville, Alabama

Speak Up The complete predicate of each sentence is underlined. What is the simple predicate?

1. Campers are astronauts for a week.
2. They work in teams of ten.
3. The members name their teams after planets.
4. Some of the teams launch rockets into the air.
5. Other teams take a make-believe space flight.
6. Campers run a control center on the ground.
7. Team members work together to solve problems on the flight.
8. They use headphones to hear and talk to the astronauts.
9. Teams help the astronauts land safely.

Meeting Individual Needs

RETEACHING

ALTERNATIVE STRATEGY

- Display these sentences:
  The purple banana _____ from a peach tree.
  A red mouse _____ on a blue camel.
- Have volunteers suggest words to complete each sentence. Write students' responses in the blanks.
- Tell students that each of their words is the main word in the predicate and tells exactly what the subject *is* or *does*. This main word is called the simple predicate.

CHALLENGE

Give students a list of interesting and unusual verbs such as *extol, careen, bobble, hoist,* and *prevaricate.* Have them use a dictionary to find the word meanings. Then have them create sentences, using the verbs as simple predicates.

FOR STUDENTS ACQUIRING ENGLISH

Present sentences about classroom objects and activities: *We do math problems every day.* Underline the complete predicate once; catch students' attention as you underline the simple predicate a second time. Continue.

On Your Own

The complete predicate of each sentence is underlined. Write the simple predicate.

Example: Hundreds of boys and girls attend space camp. *attend*

10. One camp is in Huntsville, Alabama.
11. Trained leaders help the campers.
12. The campers do different activities each day.
13. These activities teach them about an astronaut's job.
14. Campers visit the U.S. Space and Rocket Center.
15. It has special exhibits from the space program.
16. Campers taste freeze-dried space food.
17. They use spacecraft computers.
18. Special equipment imitates the feeling of a space walk.

19–26. The complete predicate of each sentence is underlined in these tips. Write the tips, and circle the simple predicates. Simple predicates are underlined.

Example: People need advice for a trip. *People (need) advice for a trip.*

These tips are for new space travelers.

- Most travelers avoid crumbly foods. The crumbs float all over the spacecraft.
- Muscles lose strength in outer space. Exercise is very important. Space travelers use exercise machines to stay fit.
- Some people suffer from space sickness. Light meals help sometimes.

Writing Wrap-Up

WRITING • THINKING • LISTENING • SPEAKING

INFORMING

Write a List

Write five helpful tips for new students in your school. Make sure each sentence has a subject and a predicate. Read your tips to a classmate. Have you left out anything important?

For Extra Practice see page 61.

Summing Up Help students summarize these key points about the lesson:

The **simple predicate** is the main word in the complete predicate. It tells exactly what the subject *does* or *is*.

You may wish to have students complete the parts related to this lesson on Blackline Master 1–2.

On Your Own

Remind students that simple predicates are words that do one of two things: (1) show action, such as the words *go, travel,* and *giggle;* or (2) tell what someone or something is or is like, such as *am, is,* and *were.*

MEETING INDIVIDUAL NEEDS

FOR STUDENTS ACQUIRING ENGLISH

Distribute SAE Practice pages for Unit 1, Lesson 6. Students complete cloze sentences by choosing the best verb as the simple predicate.

1. My friend ______ to space camp last year. (went)
2. The camp ______ in Alabama. (is)
3. The campers ______ many things. (do)

Writing Wrap-Up

Writing Tip: Tell students to begin a new paragraph for each new tip and its related sentences. See Blackline Master 1–5 for sample tips.

TECHNOLOGY CONNECTION

Students might use available software to write their tips, which can be updated as things change.

● RETEACHING WORKBOOK, page 8

6 Simple Predicates

- The **simple predicate** is the main word in the predicate.

Subjects	Predicates
Most dogs	**make** great pets.
They	**are** good friends for children.

The complete predicate of each sentence is underlined. Write the simple predicate.

Example: People teach dogs different kinds of tricks. teach

1. Puppies catch newspapers in their mouths. catch
2. Other dogs beg for food. beg
3. Many dogs play quietly inside the house. play
4. Some pets do important jobs. do
5. Guide dogs help blind people. help
6. Watchdogs guard people's homes. guard
7. These dogs bark at strangers. bark
8. Other dogs watch sheep and cows. watch
9. Dogs depend on their owners for daily care. depend
10. These animals need exercise every day. need
11. Most dogs like outdoor exercise. like
12. Meat and chicken are good foods for them. are
13. Some children feed vitamins to their dogs. feed
14. Some owners enter their dogs in shows. enter
15. Judges vote for the best dogs. vote
16. The most obedient dog wins a blue ribbon. wins
17. The prettiest dog gets a prize at some shows. gets
18. Dogs make good pets indeed! make

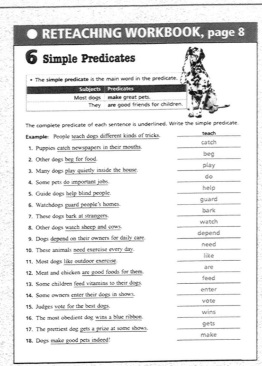

▲■ WORKBOOK PLUS, pages 13–14

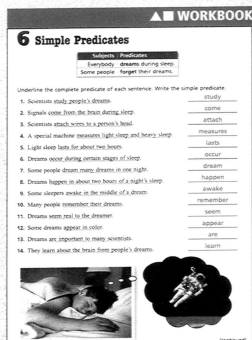

6 Simple Predicates

Subjects	Predicates
Everybody	**dreams** during sleep.
Some people	**forget** their dreams.

Underline the complete predicate of each sentence. Write the simple predicate.

1. Scientists study people's dreams. study
2. Signals come from the brain during sleep. come
3. Scientists attach wires to a person's head. attach
4. A special machine measures light sleep and heavy sleep. measures
5. Light sleep lasts for about two hours. lasts
6. Dreams occur during certain stages of sleep. occur
7. Some people dream many dreams in one night. dream
8. Dreams happen in about two hours of a night's sleep. happen
9. Some sleepers awake in the middle of a dream. awake
10. Many people remember their dreams. remember
11. Dreams seem real to the dreamer. seem
12. Some dreams appear in color. appear
13. Dreams are important to many scientists. are
14. They learn about the brain from people's dreams. learn

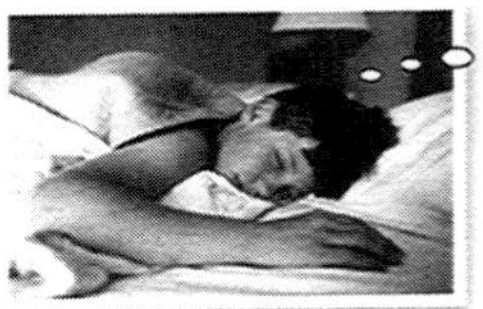

(continued)

6 Simple Predicates (continued from page 13)

Challenge

The children below have dreams for the future. Write a sentence about each child, following the directions below.

1. Katya loves animals. Write a sentence about Katya, using the simple predicate *dreams.* Answers will vary.

2. Wesley loves airplanes. Write a sentence about Wesley, using the simple predicate *hopes.* ______

3. Tokie loves working with clay. Write a sentence about Tokie, using the simple predicate *wants.* ______

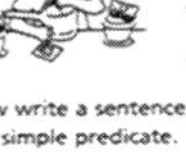

4. Rico loves growing flowers. Write a sentence about Rico, using the simple predicate *wishes.* ______

Now write a sentence about a dream that you have for your future. Underline the simple predicate.

Writing Application: A Journal EXPRESSING

Suppose that you have come from another country to live in the United States. What are your dreams for a new life? Write at least five sentences that describe your feelings on your first day in the United States. Underline the simple predicate of each sentence.

Students should respond on separate paper. Answers will vary.

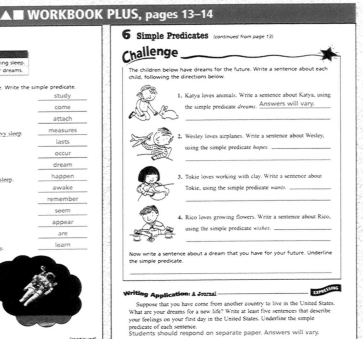

Correcting Run-on Sentences

Lesson Objectives

Students will:

- identify run-on sentences
- proofread for run-on sentences
- write an exhibit sign, using correctly written sentences

One-Minute Warm-Up Have volunteers write the two sentences correctly on the board. Have them circle the capital letter that begins each sentence and draw a box around each end mark. Discuss how they know where one sentence ends and the other begins.

Focus on Instruction

Suggest that students check for run-on sentences by reading a sentence aloud. If it is so long that they can't catch their breath before they reach the end mark, it could be a run-on sentence.

Try It Out

LISTENING AND SPEAKING Have students listen as volunteers read each of the sentences aloud, not stopping until they reach the final period. Ask why Sentences 1, 4, and 5 are confusing. (The ideas or thoughts in each sentence run together.) Have volunteers reread each sentence, telling where they think one thought ends and another begins.

FOR STUDENTS ACQUIRING ENGLISH

- Have students listen to the Try It Out sentences on the audiotape. Distribute SAE Practice pages for Unit 1, Lesson 7, to support listening.
- Explain that this photo shows what life was like in the United States in the past. Ask students to describe what they see. Then have them listen to sentences and circle *correct* or *run-on.* Then have them listen again and mark the place where the run-ons should be separated. Tell them to listen for clues in the intonation they hear. Remind students that each sentence must begin with a capital letter and must have its own end mark. Example: This is a history museum it is very interesting. (run-on—separate between *museum* and *it*)

Usage/Mechanics

7 Correcting Run-on Sentences

One-Minute Warm-Up Can you find two sentences in this sign? Where should an end mark and a capital letter be added?

This is a picture of a famous ship. it is a whaling vessel.

- **When two sentences run into each other, they make a run-on sentence.** Do not use run-on sentences in your writing.
- A run-on sentence can be corrected by writing each complete thought as a separate sentence. Remember to use capital letters and end marks correctly. Do not separate the two sentences with a comma.

Incorrect:	Our class visited a museum we saw whaling ships.
Incorrect:	Our class visited a museum, we saw whaling ships.
Correct:	Our class visited a museum. We saw whaling ships.

Try It Out

Speak Up Which of the following sentences are run-on sentences, and which sentences are correct? What are the two complete thoughts in each run-on sentence?

Colonial Williamsburg in Virginia

1. History museums are fun|they teach about the past. run-on
2. A whaling museum is one kind of history museum. correct
3. A whole village can sometimes be a museum. correct
4. People dress in costumes,|visitors can ask them questions. run-on
5. Some famous people's homes become museums|you can visit Paul Revere's house in Boston. run-on
6. Natural history museums show animals and their habitats. correct
7. The Smithsonian Institution is the world's largest museum complex,|it has fourteen museums and a zoo. run-on

Meeting Individual Needs

RETEACHING

Alternative Strategy

- On the board, write these instructions: *Go to the palm tree open the box. Follow the directions on the map in the box. They will lead you to a discovery.*
- Read the first sentence aloud without pausing. Explain that it is a run-on sentence because two complete thoughts run together. Then reread the sentence, pausing after *tree.* Have students add a period after *tree* and capitalize *open.* Have them read aloud the corrected sentences.

CHALLENGE

Have students rewrite the following exhibit sign, correcting the run-on sentences: This glass slipper belonged to Cinderella it fell from her foot as she ran down the steps of the palace the slipper was given to the museum by her fairy godmother.

FOR STUDENTS ACQUIRING ENGLISH

To practice capital and lowercase letters, present random paired letters, some with the capital letter first, some with lowercase first, and have students circle the capital letter. Also review end marks.

On Your Own

Rewrite each sentence correctly. Underlined portions are rewritten.

Example: Our class went to the museum it is at Science Park.
Our class went to the museum. It is at Science Park.

8. Nick had never been there he was eager to go. there. He
9. There was a special show it was about China. show. It
10. Jamie had read about China, she was prepared. China. She
11. People were doing crafts we could watch them work. crafts. We
12. There was a huge loom two men were weaving silk. loom. Two
13. Kites are important in China we watched a kite maker. China. We
14. He made a dragon kite it had a long tail. kite. It
15. Jamie bought a dragon kite Nick bought a book about China. kite. Nick

16–20. The information on this exhibit sign has five run-on sentences. Write the information correctly. Underlined portions are rewritten.

Example: Amber is a kind of fossil most amber is yellow.
Amber is a kind of fossil. Most amber is yellow.

Proofreading

Amber

jewelry. Some

Artists use amber to make jewelry some beads are amber. Amber is not a stone it is tree sap. The stone. It sap dripped from trees long ago, then it hardened. ago. Then
Scientists use amber, it helps them study amber. It animals that lived long ago. Sometimes insects were trapped in the sap as it dripped down trees trees. Their their bodies can still be seen today in amber.

Writing Wrap-Up

WRITING • THINKING • LISTENING • SPEAKING

INFORMING

Write an Exhibit Sign

In the future, something of yours may be in a museum. Write several sentences about the object for an exhibit sign. Read your notes to a partner. Work together to check for run-on sentences.

For Extra Practice see page 62.

Summing Up Help students summarize these key points about the lesson:

> A **run-on sentence** has two complete thoughts that run together. To correct a run-on sentence, write each complete thought as a separate sentence.

You may wish to have students complete the parts related to this lesson on Blackline Master 1–3.

On Your Own

If students are unable to find the location of the second sentence, have them read the words aloud, pausing at various points until the two thoughts—and sentences—make sense.

MEETING INDIVIDUAL NEEDS

FOR STUDENTS ACQUIRING ENGLISH

Distribute SAE Practice pages for Unit 1, Lesson 7. Help students brainstorm vocabulary relating to museums. Define words as needed. Then have students rewrite run-on sentences to correct them. Example: We went to the museum last week everyone learned a lot. (week. Everyone)

Writing Wrap-Up

Writing Tip: Suggest to students that they tell where they got their object and why it was special. See Blackline Master 1–5 for a sample sign.

TECHNOLOGY CONNECTION

Students may want to use a scanner to scan photographs into their exhibit sign.

● RETEACHING WORKBOOK, page 9

7 Correcting Run-on Sentences

- A run-on sentence has two complete thoughts that run into each other. Correct a run-on sentence by writing each complete thought as a separate sentence.

Incorrect	They went on a trip the three of them took the train.
Correct	They went on a trip. The three of them took the train.

Correct each run-on sentence by writing it as two separate sentences.

Example: Cora and Theo visited Seaside Farm Mr. Li went with them.
Cora and Theo visited Seaside Farm. Mr. Li went with them.

1. Seaside Farm is very old it's the oldest farm in the state.
Seaside Farm is very old. It's the oldest farm in the state.
2. Seaside is two hundred years old it is a very large farm.
Seaside is two hundred years old. It is a very large farm.
3. There are seventy chickens there they lay sixty eggs a day.
There are seventy chickens there. They lay sixty eggs a day.
4. On some days there are hay rides many visitors enjoy them.
On some days there are hay rides. Many visitors enjoy them.
5. People ride in a wagon of hay everybody brings picnic lunches.
People ride in a wagon of hay. Everybody brings picnic lunches.
6. The owner lets visitors milk the cows this job isn't for everyone.
The owner lets visitors milk the cows. This job isn't for everyone.
7. Farmers wake up early it takes all day to get the chores done.
Farmers wake up early. It takes all day to get the chores done.
8. Everyone enjoys the trip to Seaside people learn a lot there.
Everyone enjoys the trip to Seaside. People learn a lot there.

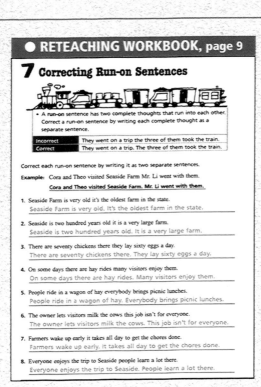

▲■ WORKBOOK PLUS, pages 15–16

7 Correcting Run-on Sentences

Incorrect	Storms bring rain and snow they can also bring hail.
Correct	Storms bring rain and snow. They can also bring hail.

A Write each run-on sentence correctly. Write *correct* if the sentence is not a run-on.

1. Some storms cause problems the effects depend on where you live.
Some storms cause problems. The effects depend on where you live.
2. Strong winds blow during a storm thunder booms sometimes.
Strong winds blow during a storm. Thunder booms sometimes.
3. Winds above the Earth's surface can reach more than 75 miles per hour.
correct
4. A rainstorm can be very dangerous to crops and farm animals.
correct

B 5–10. Use proofreading marks to correct the six run-on sentences in this report.
Example: Some storms bring plenty of rain. heavy rain can damage land.

Proofreading

BULLETIN!

You can keep yourself safe in a tornado. follow some important rules. Listen to a radio when the weather is bad. go to a safe place when you hear a warning. Stay away from windows. go to an inside room or hallway. Basements are safe places. getting under a heavy table or the stairs gives you extra protection. Bathrooms are good. you can even get into an empty bathtub. If you are outside, stay away from power lines. Go to a ditch or other low ground. Plan ahead what you will do. have a tornado drill every year.

Proofreading Marks
¶ Indent
∧ Add
Delete
≡ Capital letter
/ Small letter

(continued)

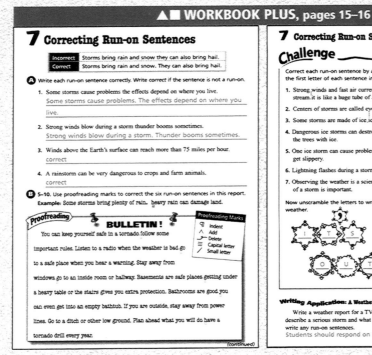

7 Correcting Run-on Sentences *(continued from page 15)*

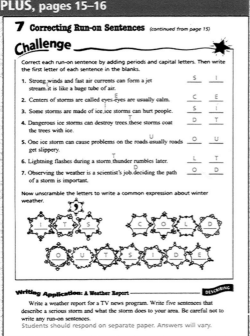

Challenge

Correct each run-on sentence by adding periods and capital letters. Then write the first letter of each sentence in the blanks.

1. Strong winds and fast air currents can form a jet stream. it is like a huge tube of air. S I
2. Centers of storms are called eyes. eyes are usually calm. C E
3. Some storms are made of ice. ice storms can hurt people. S I
4. Dangerous ice storms can destroy trees. these storms coat the trees with ice. D T
5. One ice storm can cause problems on the roads. usually roads get slippery. O U
6. Lightning flashes during a storm. thunder rumbles later. L T
7. Observing the weather is a scientist's job. deciding the path of a storm is important. O D

Now unscramble the letters to write a common expression about winter weather.

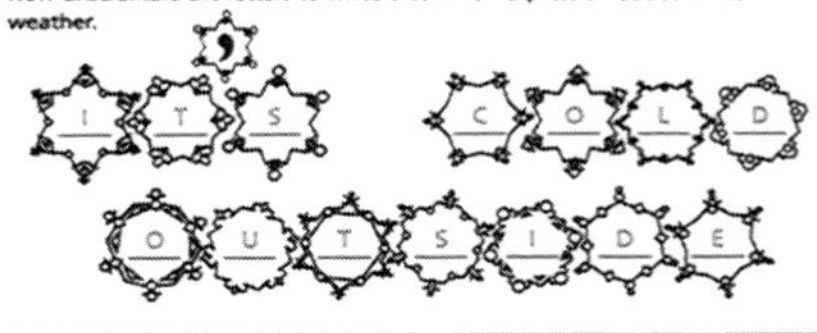

Writing Application: A Weather Report DESCRIBING

Write a weather report for a TV news program. Write five sentences that describe a serious storm and what the storm does to your area. Be careful not to write any run-on sentences.
Students should respond on separate paper. Answers will vary.

Writing Good Sentences

Lesson Objective

Students will:

- correct run-on sentences by adding a comma and the word *and* between the two sentences

Focus on Instruction

Ask a volunteer to read the incorrect sentence aloud. Have students identify the subject and predicate of each of the sentences that have been incorrectly run together. (first sentence—potter, pressed; second sentence—bowl, took)

Apply It

Have students complete the revising activity independently.

If some students need extra support, have them work with partners to identify the subjects and predicates of the sentences that have been incorrectly run together. (A sample run-on is shown.)

S: The potter / P: puts a ball of clay on the wheel / S: he / P: starts turning the wheel.

Have students look in their writing in progress to find run-on sentences that they can correct by adding a comma and the word *and*.

Sample Answers to Apply It

1. The potter puts a ball of clay on the wheel, and he starts turning the wheel.
2. His hands shape the spinning clay, and it begins to look like a vase.
3. He fires the vase in a hot kiln, and the clay becomes dry and hard.
4. The potter decides on a color for the vase, and he glazes the vase.
5. The vase is fired again, and the glaze melts.
6. It forms a smooth, shiny surface, and it makes the vase waterproof.

FOR STUDENTS ACQUIRING ENGLISH

Show students two ways to fix the run-on sentence. Example: The potter got some clay he made a pot. (The potter got some clay. He made a pot.) (The potter got some clay, and he made a pot.)

Revising Strategies

Writing Good Sentences

Combining Sentences When two sentences run into each other, they make a run-on sentence. Good writers can fix run-on sentences by making two separate sentences. Another good way to fix run-on sentences is to add a comma (,) and the word *and* between the two sentences.

Incorrect: The potter pressed the clay with his thumbs a small bowl took shape.
Correct: The potter pressed the clay with his thumbs, and a small bowl took shape.

Apply It

1–6. Revise these captions for a poster. Correct each run-on sentence by adding a comma and the word *and* between the two sentences. See TE margin for answers.

Revising

Making a Vase

1. The potter puts a ball of clay on the wheel he starts turning the wheel.
2. His hands shape the spinning clay it begins to look like a vase.
3. He fires the vase in a hot kiln the clay becomes dry and hard.
4. The potter decides on a color for the vase he glazes the vase.
5. The vase is fired again the glaze melts.
6. It forms a smooth, shiny surface it makes the vase waterproof.

48 **Unit 1:** The Sentence

Meeting Individual Needs

● RETEACHING WORKBOOK, page 10

Combining Sentences

- Good writers can fix run-on sentences by making two separate sentences.
- Another way to correct a run-on sentence is to add a comma (,) and the word *and* between the two sentences.

Run-on sentence	Balloons are colorful you can do many things with them.
Corrected sentence	Balloons are colorful, and you can do many things with them.

Combining Sentences Correct each run-on sentence by adding a comma and the word *and* between the two sentences.

Example: Balloons can be used to play games they can also be decorations.
Balloons can be used to play games, and they can also be decorations.

Revising

1. Painting balloons is easy to do it is lots of fun too.
Painting balloons is easy to do, and it is lots of fun too.
2. All it takes is imagination you'll also need a few supplies.
All it takes is imagination, and you'll also need a few supplies.
3. Be sure to put some water in a cup have some paper towels handy.
Be sure to put some water in a cup, and have some paper towels handy.
4. Blow up your balloon start painting your picture.
Blow up your balloon, and start painting your picture.
5. Let the balloon dry repeat the steps with another balloon.
Let the balloon dry, and repeat the steps with another balloon.

(continued)

▲■ WORKBOOK PLUS, page 17

Writing Good Sentences

Run-on sentence	On the Fourth of July, Americans celebrate their independence they observe the birthday of their nation.
Corrected sentence	On the Fourth of July, Americans celebrate their independence, and they observe the birthday of their nation.

Combining Sentences 1–6. Rewrite the following letter describing Sam's favorite holiday. Correct each run-on sentence by adding a comma and the word *and*.

Revising

Dear Tony,
The Fourth of July is my favorite holiday our town always has such a wonderful party! The celebration begins with a parade. Marching bands come from all over the state they play lively music. A barbecue follows the parade everyone eats hot dogs and watermelon. Kids compete in sack races many people play softball. After sunset, bright colors explode across the sky the day ends with an awesome display of fireworks. I wish you could be here to join in the fun!
Sincerely,
Sam

Dear Tony,
The Fourth of July is my favorite holiday, and our town always has such a wonderful party! The celebration begins with a parade. Marching bands come from all over the state, and they play lively music. A barbecue follows the parade, and everyone eats hot dogs and watermelon. Kids compete in sack races, and many people play softball. After sunset, bright colors explode across the sky, and the day ends with an awesome display of fireworks. I wish you could be here to join in the fun!
Sincerely,
Sam

(continued)

Sentence Fluency

Good writers use sentences of different lengths. Too many short sentences can make your writing sound boring and choppy. If two short sentences are about the same idea, sometimes you can join them to make a **compound sentence**. Use a comma and the word *and*, *but*, or *or* to join the sentences.

Most murals are wall paintings. Many are outdoors.	Most murals are wall paintings, and many are outdoors.
Our mural is only half painted. It already looks great!	Our mural is only half painted, but it already looks great!
Did one student paint the mural? Did a group paint it?	Did one student paint the mural, or did a group paint it?

Apply It

7–12. Rewrite this part of a letter. Combine each underlined pair of sentences into a compound sentence. Use the word in ( ). See TE margin for answers.

Revising

Dear Mayor Stevens,

I am in fourth grade. I go to Washington School. My art teacher is Mr. Mori. (and) Last week Mr. Mori showed us slides of fantastic outdoor murals. Our neighborhood doesn't have a mural. We think it needs one. (but)

We would like to create a mural on the playground wall. Mr. Mori would design it for free. His students would paint it. (and) The mural would not cost the city anything. We would raise the money for supplies. Maybe a paint store would donate them. (or)

Will you support this project? People can see art in museums. Art should be part of their everyday lives too. (but) The students would be proud of their mural. Everyone would enjoy it! (and)

Lesson Objective

Students will:

- use the conjunctions *and, but,* and *or* to combine two short sentences to form compound sentences

Focus on Instruction

- Point out to students that when two short sentences are combined to form a compound sentence, there should be only one end mark and one initial capitalized word.
- Explain that the words used to join two short sentences (*and, but, or*) are called *conjunctions.* Tell students that the relationship between the sentences being joined will determine which conjunction to use. Write the information below on the board.

  And shows equal importance.
  Or shows an alternative.
  But shows contrast or an exception.

  Then write each of the pairs of sentences below on the board. Have students discuss which conjunction should be used to connect each pair.

  People enjoy murals in public buildings.
  Some have them in their own homes.

  You could paint a mural on a wall somewhere.
  First you should get permission.

  You could paint a scene from nature.
  You could create an urban landscape.

Apply It

Have students complete the revising activity independently. Remind them that a comma precedes the conjunction in a compound sentence.

Have students find places in their own writing in progress where they can combine sentences with conjunctions.

Answers to Apply It

7. I go to Washington School, and my art teacher is Mr. Mori.
8. Our neighborhood doesn't have a mural, but we think it needs one.
9. Mr. Mori would design it for free, and his students would paint it.
10. We would raise the money for supplies, or maybe a paint store would donate them.
11. People can see art in museums, but art should be part of their everyday lives too.
12. The students would be proud of their mural, and everyone would enjoy it.

● RETEACHING WORKBOOK, page 11

Combining Sentences *(continued from page 10)*

Too many short sentences can make your writing sound choppy.
- You can join two short, related sentences to make a compound sentence.
- Use a comma (,) and the connecting word *and, but,* or *or* to join the sentences.

Two sentences	Running is great exercise. Many children run just for fun.
Compound sentence	Running is great exercise, but many children run just for fun.

Combining Sentences Rewrite each pair of short sentences, combining them to make a compound sentence. Use a comma and the connecting word in parentheses. Write the new compound sentence.

Example: Josh runs every day. He never runs at night. **(but)**
Josh runs every day, but he never runs at night.

Revising

6. Josh runs in good weather. He runs in the rain. **(and)**
Josh runs in good weather, and he runs in the rain.
7. Many runners must pace themselves. They tire easily. **(or)**
Many runners must pace themselves, or they tire easily.
8. Josh runs far. He can't run a mile yet. **(but)**
Josh runs far, but he can't run a mile yet.
9. Should Josh run on a track? Should he run in the street? **(or)**
Should Josh run on a track, or should he run in the street?
10. Some people run on the street. An indoor track is better. **(but)**
Some people run on the street, but an indoor track is better.
11. Some companies make running shoes. They make running clothes. **(and)**
Some companies make running shoes, and they make running clothes.
12. Josh wore his running shoes in a race. They felt great! **(and)**
Josh wore his running shoes in a race, and they felt great!

▲■ WORKBOOK PLUS, page 18

Writing Good Sentences *(continued from page 17)*

Short, choppy sentences	Many coin tricks look hard. They are actually easy to do.
Compound sentence	Many coin tricks look hard, but they are actually easy to do.

Combining Sentences 7–12. Rewrite the following paragraph from a book about magic tricks. Combine the underlined pairs of short sentences by adding a comma (,) and the word that is in parentheses.

Revising

Many people enjoy magic shows. Few people understand how tricks are done. (but) Most magicians practice their skills for hours. They perform tricks to entertain. (and) Much of their magic is based on illusion. One thing seems to be happening. Something different actually occurs. (but) A good magician can misdirect the attention of the audience. Spectators are led to focus on a magic wand or on one of the magician's hands. They do not notice the movement of the other hand. (and) Did the coin really disappear? Did the magician simply hide it in her palm? (or) People are curious about how tricks work. Magicians do not tell their secrets. (but)

Many people enjoy magic shows, but few people understand how tricks are done. Most magicians practice their skills for hours, and they perform tricks to entertain. Much of their magic is based on illusion. One thing seems to be happening, but something different actually occurs. A good magician can misdirect the attention of the audience. Spectators are led to focus on a magic wand or on one of the magician's hands, and they do not notice the movement of the other hand. Did the coin really disappear, or did the magician simply hide it in her palm? People are curious about how tricks work, but magicians do not tell their secrets.

Enrichment

Objectives

Students will:
- generate compound sentences, forming rhyming couplets
- provide appropriate end marks for sentences

Using the Activities

The Enrichment page provides fun, creative activities that reinforce students' understanding and use of sentences. The activities are designed to be enjoyed by all students. Here are some ideas for using the activities.

- Pair students who need extra support with more capable classmates.
- Students can work with these activities in class after they have completed other assignments.
- Activities that can be completed individually can be assigned as homework.

Focus on the Activities

RHYMING COUPLETS

- This is a good activity to put in a learning center. Provide thesauruses, dictionaries, and drawing materials.
- Students can make two lists of rhyming words—one that tells *who* or *what* and a second that tells *what happens*. Then they can select words from the rhyming word lists to make their rhyming couplets.

MIXED-UP MESSAGES

After students provide the proper punctuation, have them determine whether each sentence is a statement, a question, a command, or an exclamation.

MEETING INDIVIDUAL NEEDS **CHALLENGE** Tell students that they must include all four types of sentences in their messages.

MEETING INDIVIDUAL NEEDS **FOR STUDENTS ACQUIRING ENGLISH**

Brainstorm with students the names of famous people. Explain the meaning of *famous* as necessary. Write the names that the students suggest on the board and have them use an encyclopedia or other reference book to find out *a)* what made the person famous, and *b)* when the person was famous. Choose two names suggested by students and have them combine the information into sentences.

Enrichment

Rhyming Couplets

Write some two-line poems, called couplets. Use one compound sentence for each poem. Choose words that rhyme with each other for the two subjects. The two predicates should also rhyme with each other. Draw pictures to go with your couplets.

The train roars,
and the plane soars.

The dog flops,
and the frog hops.

Mixed-up Messages

Go to Pirate's Cove at sunset How beautiful the sky is Stand on the beach facing the sun On your right is a big tree Do you see its shadow The shadow falls over a large rock The treasure is buried six feet below the rock Do you have a shovel Start digging now What a lot of work this is

Pirate Redbeard wrote this message. He forgot to use end marks. Write the message so that it makes sense. Add periods, question marks, and exclamation points.

Challenge Write your own message for a friend to solve.

Checkup: Unit 1

See TE margin for answers.

1 What Is a Sentence? *(p. 32)* If a group of words below is a sentence, copy it. If not, write *not a sentence.*

1. Many people visit parks.
2. The high mountains.
3. We slept in a tent.
4. Bears visit the campsites.
5. Looking for food.

2 Statements and Questions *(p. 36)* Write *statement* or *question* to tell what kind of sentence each one is.

6. Airliners carry passengers, baggage, and mail.
7. Would you like to be a flight attendant?
8. My cousin is training to be an airplane pilot.
9. Have you ever flown in a plane?
10. Are you sending your package by air mail?

3 Commands and Exclamations *(p. 38)* Write each command or exclamation correctly.

11. the buses in London are certainly wonderful
12. take a ride on one of these double-decker buses
13. what a strange bus this is
14. give your money to the collector
15. please sit in the top of the bus
16. how high we are

4 Subjects and Predicates *(p. 40)* Write each sentence. Draw a line between the complete subject and the complete predicate.

17. My entire family entered the sandcastle contest.
18. I used my pail and my shovel.
19. We packed the pail with wet sand.
20. My brother shaped a tower at the top.
21. Many beautiful castles were in the contest.
22. Three judges chose the winner of the contest.
23. Our sandcastle won first prize.

5 Simple Subjects *(p. 42)* The complete subject of each sentence is underlined. Write the simple subject.

24. My older brother plays in a wheelchair basketball league.
25. His teammates play the game in wheelchairs too.
26. Their wheelchairs move quickly and easily.
27. The players on his team practice twice a week.
28. They make some very difficult shots.
29. The game on Friday was quite exciting!
30. That game was the first game of the new season.

Test?

Go to www.eduplace.com/tales/ for more fun with parts of speech.

Checkup 51

Checkup

Objectives

Students will:
- distinguish sentences from non-sentences
- identify statements, questions, commands, and exclamations
- identify the subject and predicate of a sentence
- identify the simple subject of a sentence

Using the Checkup

Use the Checkup exercises as assessment, as review for the unit test, as extra practice, or as a diagnostic aid to help determine those students who need reteaching.

INTERNET CONNECTION Students can take an interactive quiz for this unit at www.eduplace.com/kids/hme/ and then get immediate feedback.

Answers

What Is a Sentence?

1. Many people visit parks.
2. not a sentence
3. We slept in a tent.
4. Bears visit the campsites.
5. not a sentence

Statements and Questions

6. statement
7. question
8. statement
9. question
10. question

Commands and Exclamations

11. The buses in London are certainly wonderful!
12. Take a ride on one of these double-decker buses.
13. What a strange bus this is!
14. Give your money to the collector.
15. Please sit in the top of the bus.
16. How high we are!

Subjects and Predicates

17. My entire family | entered the sandcastle contest.
18. I | used my pail and my shovel.
19. We | packed the pail with wet sand.
20. My brother | shaped a tower at the top.
21. Many beautiful castles | were in the contest.
22. Three judges | chose the winner of the contest.
23. Our sandcastle | won first prize.

Simple Subjects

24. brother
25. teammates
26. wheelchairs
27. players
28. They
29. game
30. game

Objectives

Students will:

- identify the simple predicate of a sentence
- rewrite run-on sentences correctly
- proofread for incorrect capitalization and punctuation

Answers *continued*

Simple Predicates

31. is
32. travel
33. leaves
34. blaze
35. explode
36. hear

Correcting Run-on Sentences

37. The museum had many old cars. My friend liked that exhibit.
38. The whale looked huge. Sara was amazed at the sharks.
39. The mummies were in a special room. We wanted to see them.
40. The museum had an old airplane. It looked small.
41. We saw a spacecraft. It had two model astronauts.
42. There are fossils in this museum. Let's find the dinosaur bones.

6 Simple Predicates *(p. 44)* The complete predicate of each sentence below is underlined. Write the simple predicate.

31. A meteor is a bright streak of light in the sky.
32. Meteors travel through space at very great speeds.
33. A meteor leaves behind a trail of hot gas.
34. Meteors blaze in the sky for a few seconds.
35. Sometimes they explode into small pieces.
36. People hear the noise for miles.

7 Correcting Run-on Sentences *(p. 46)* Rewrite each of these run-on sentences correctly.

37. The museum had many old cars my friend liked that exhibit.
38. The whale looked huge Sara was amazed at the sharks.
39. The mummies were in a special room we wanted to see them.
40. The museum had an old airplane it looked small.
41. We saw a spacecraft it had two model astronauts.
42. There are fossils in this museum let's find the dinosaur bones.

Mixed Review 43–50. This announcement has three missing capital letters and five missing or incorrect end marks. Write the announcement correctly.

Proofreading Checklist

Did you write these correctly?

✓ capital letters
✓ end marks

Proofreading

Sign Up for the School Play!

Do you remember last year's school play? fifty students took part in *The Wizard of Oz*. What a success it was! This year's play will be even better. we are putting on the musical *Cats*.

Can you act, sing, or dance? Come and try out for a part. tryouts will be held on Friday in the cafeteria. Would you like to help with the scenery or costumes? Sign up for one of these jobs. Plenty of jobs are left. We need you.

DRAMA CLUB

See www.eduplace.com/kids/hme/ for an online quiz.

Assessment Link

Test Practice

Write the numbers 1–8 on a sheet of paper. For items 1–4, read each sentence. Choose the underlined word that is the simple subject of the sentence. Write the letter for that answer.

1 A major earthquake struck the city around midnight.
A (B) C D

2 The weary umpire took a rest after the game.
F (G) H J

3 That pumpkin weighs three hundred pounds!
A (B) C D

4 Ashley peeled some carrots for the salad.
(F) G H J

For items 5–8, read each sentence. Choose the underlined word that is the simple predicate of the sentence. Write the letter for that answer.

5 The ship moved quickly through the water.
A (B) C D

6 A castle in a forest is the setting for the play.
F G (H) J

7 The driver honked at his friend in the truck.
A (B) C D

8 The salesperson sold Darius some laces for his boots.
(F) G H J

Test Practice

Test Practice

Objective

Students will:

- practice completing a test format that requires them to choose the correct sentence part among four

Using the Test Practice

These Test Practice pages provide practice with common formats used in standardized or multiple-choice tests.

All three pages work with skills taught in the basic lessons in Unit 1.

Focus on the Test Format

- Have a volunteer read the test directions aloud. Ask another volunteer to explain what the directions ask students to do.
- Then have students evaluate each sentence to choose the simple subject or simple predicate. Tell students that only words with underlines are allowable choices.
- After students choose their answer, have them find the letter that appears below the word. Tell them that they should write this letter as their answer.

FOR STUDENTS ACQUIRING ENGLISH

Begin by reviewing subjects, predicates, and word order in English. Next, review the end points that correspond to the three types of sentences. Discuss how to recognize and fix run-on sentences. Distribute the SAE Test Practice pages for Unit 1. Point out that there are two parts to each page. Have a volunteer read the directions aloud for each part; make sure students know how to circle the answers they choose. Remind students that all sentences must begin with capital letters and must have some type of end punctuation.

Test Practice *continued*

Objective

Students will:

- practice completing a test format that requires them to select the correct end mark among four

Focus on the Test Format

- Have a volunteer read the test directions aloud. Ask another volunteer to explain what the directions ask students to do.
- Then have students evaluate each sentence to choose the end mark. Tell students that they will choose among a question mark, a period, an exclamation point, and a comma.
- After students choose their answer, have them find the letter that appears next to the correct end mark. Tell them that they should write this letter as their answer.

Test Practice *continued*

Now write the numbers 9–18 on your paper. Choose the correct end mark for each sentence. Write the letter for that answer.

9 The airplane soared above the clouds
A ? (B) . C ! D ,

10 What is your favorite summer sport
(F) ? G . H ! J ,

11 Please put this letter in the mailbox
A ? (B) . C ! D ,

12 What a dreadful movie that was
F ? G . (H) ! J ,

13 Kirsten is making cocoa in the microwave
A ? (B) . C ! D ,

14 Did the clown really juggle all of those balls
(F) ? G . H ! J ,

15 Find the Amazon River on your map of South America
A ? (B) . C ! D ,

16 How terrified the dog is of lightning
F ? G . (H) ! J ,

17 Have you remembered to turn off the faucet
(A) ? B . C ! D ,

18 Take those muddy shoes down to the basement
F ? (G) . H ! J ,

54 Unit 1: The Sentence

Now write the numbers 19–24 on your paper. Read the passage and find the numbered, underlined parts. Choose the answer that shows the best way to capitalize and punctuate each part. Write the letter for that answer.

There are at least one million kinds of insects in the world. Some insects are pests other (19) insects are very helpful to people. A spider is not an insect. Do you know why. Insects (20) have six legs. Spiders (21) have eight legs.

Have you heard about the time Derek decided to make himself a really special sandwich. He (22) started with two thick slices of rye bread. He spread strawberry jam on the bread then (23) he put pepperoni on top of the jam. He added some mustard. What a disgusting creation it was? (24)

19 A Pests. Other
B pests. other
(C) pests. Other
D Correct as it is

20 (F) why? Insects
G why. insects
H why? insects
J Correct as it is

21 A legs? Spiders
B legs! spiders
C legs spiders
(D) Correct as it is

22 F sandwich! he
(G) sandwich? He
H sandwich? he
J Correct as it is

23 A bread Then
B bread? Then
(C) bread. Then
D Correct as it is

24 (F) it was!
G it was
H it. Was
J Correct as it is

Objective

Students will:
- practice completing a test format that requires them to select the correct item among four

Focus on the Test Format

- Have a volunteer read the test directions aloud. Ask another volunteer to explain what the directions ask students to do.
- Point out the vertical line that runs down the center of the page and breaks the text into columns. Tell students to read the left-hand column first and the right-hand column second.
- Then have students read each passage and find the numbered, underlined parts. Have students evaluate each underlined part to choose the correct capitalization and punctuation.
- After students choose their answer, have them find the letter that appears next to the correct capitalization and end mark. Tell them that they should write this letter as their answer.

What Is a Sentence?

Objectives

Students will:
- identify complete sentences
- add words to sentence fragments to form complete sentences

Using the Extra Practice

The Extra Practice activities provide additional practice for the basic lesson at three levels of difficulty: Easy (●), Average (▲), and Challenging (■).

The Extra Practice activities can be used in the following ways.

- Assign activities according to students' needs and abilities as homework after students have completed the basic lesson.
- Assign the Easy activities after using the lesson Reteaching instruction.
- Assign the Average activities to prepare students for the Checkup.
- Assign the Easy and/or Average activities to students who had difficulty with specific lessons on the Checkup.
- Assign the Challenging exercises as a Bonus activity.

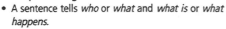

Extra Practice

(pages 32–33)

1 What Is a Sentence? Remember

- A sentence is a group of words that tells a complete thought.
- A sentence tells *who* or *what* and *what is* or *what happens.*

● Write *sentence* if the group of words is a sentence. Write *not a sentence* if it is not a sentence.

Example: Our camp was near a lake. *sentence*

1. My brother John. not sent.
2. We went fishing. sent.
3. Caught a huge fish. not sent.
4. Dad cooked the fish. sent.
5. The fish was very tasty. sent.

▲ For each pair, write the group of words that is a sentence.

Example: Enjoyed driving to California.
The Lams drove to California.
The Lams drove to California.

6. They visited the national parks.
Had very beautiful scenery.
7. Oldest and largest giant trees.
Many giant trees are very old.
8. Wanted to see some of the giant trees.
One giant tree is named General Grant.
9. Another tree is named General Lee.
Were named for famous generals.

■ Write one sentence for each group of words. Sentences will vary.

Example: Saw wild animals. *Tim and Jasmine saw wild animals.*

10. A deer. A deer stood nearby.
11. Hiked through the woods. Malcolm hiked through the woods.
12. A small black bear. We saw a small black bear.
13. Alone in the woods. I do not like to be alone in the woods.
14. Strange sounds. Do you hear strange sounds?
15. Swam in the cool lake. Paulette swam in the cool lake.

Meeting Individual Needs — More Practice for Lesson 1

● EASY

Underline each group of words that is a sentence.

1. Our tent was beside a stream.
2. Rain fell all night.
3. Comfortable inside the tent.
4. In the morning, the sun.
5. Dan cooked fish for breakfast.

▲ AVERAGE

Fill in the blank to make the words a sentence. Write the sentence. (Sample answers are given.)

1. _______ went swimming at noon. (I)
2. After lunch, everyone _______. (slept)
3. _______ climbed Lookout Point. (We)
4. Then a _______ began. (storm)
5. _______ had to run for shelter. (Everyone)

■ CHALLENGING

Add words to make each group of words a sentence. Write the sentence. (Answers will vary.)

1. hiked almost twenty miles
2. a fat old porcupine
3. under a tall oak tree
4. a peaceful trail
5. the stars overhead

Extra Practice

(pages 36–37)

2 Statements and Questions

Remember

- A statement is a sentence that tells something. It ends with a period (.).
- A question is a sentence that asks something. It ends with a question mark (?).
- Every sentence begins with a capital letter.

● Write *statement* if the sentence is a statement. Write *question* if it is a question.

Example: How did the Wright brothers become famous? *question*

1. They began to build gliders in the early 1900s. S
2. Where did they test the gliders? Q
3. Kitty Hawk, North Carolina, was a good place to test gliders. S
4. When did they begin to build airplanes? Q
5. They built their first plane in 1903. S

▲ Write each sentence correctly. Underlined letters should be capitalized.

Example: did you read about the hot-air balloon
Did you read about the hot-air balloon?

6. two brothers in France invented the balloon.
7. it carried a duck, a rooster, and a sheep.
8. when was that flight?
9. the flight took place in 1783.
10. how long were the animals in the air?
11. they landed safely after eight minutes.

■ Change each statement to a question. Change each question to a statement. Write the new sentences correctly.

Example: was Richard Byrd in the United States Navy
Richard Byrd was in the United States Navy.

12. he was a pilot Was he a pilot?
13. was he also an explorer He was also an explorer.
14. He traveled to Antarctica in 1928 Did he travel to Antarctica in 1928?
15. did Byrd set up a camp Byrd set up a camp.

Extra Practice 57

Statements and Questions

Objectives

Students will:

- distinguish statements from questions
- identify the end marks for statements and questions
- write statements and questions correctly

Using the Extra Practice

The Extra Practice activities provide additional practice for the basic lesson at three levels of difficulty: Easy (●), Average (▲), and Challenging (■).

Meeting Individual Needs

More Practice for Lesson 2

● **EASY**

Underline the end mark of punctuation after each sentence. Then write *S* after each statement and *Q* after each question.

1. This is my favorite lake. (S)
2. May I ride in your canoe? (Q)
3. Is your fishing rod new? (Q)
4. What kind of bait is that? (Q)
5. I caught trout last year. (S)
6. Do you fish very often? (Q)
7. Fish nibble at my hook. (S)
8. Have you hooked one? (Q)

▲ **AVERAGE**

Add the correct end mark to each sentence to show whether it is a statement or a question.

1. Is that an ostrich(?)
2. Some birds cannot fly(.)
3. Birds always have feathers(.)
4. Do birds hatch from eggs(?)
5. What do eagles eat(?)
6. Some hummingbirds fly thousands of miles each year(.)
7. Have you ever seen one(?)

■ **CHALLENGING**

Imagine that you are a park ranger. Write five questions that you think visitors to the park might ask. Write five statements telling how you would answer these questions. (Answers will vary.)

Commands and Exclamations

Objectives

Students will:

- distinguish commands from exclamations
- identify the end marks for commands and exclamations
- write exclamations and commands correctly

Using the Extra Practice

The Extra Practice activities provide additional practice for the basic lesson at three levels of difficulty: Easy (●), Average (▲), and Challenging (■).

Extra Practice

3 Commands and Exclamations (pages 38–39) Remember

- A command is a sentence that tells someone to do something. It ends with a period.
- An exclamation is a sentence that shows strong feeling. It ends with an exclamation point (!).
- Every sentence begins with a capital letter.

● Write *command* if the sentence is a command. Write *exclamation* if it is an exclamation.

Example: Here comes the train at last! *exclamation*

1. Give your tickets to the conductor. C
2. Let me show you to your seat. C
3. What a loud noise the train makes! E
4. I can't wait to eat in the dining car! E
5. Please get me something to eat. C
6. How fast we are moving! E

▲ Write each command or exclamation correctly.
Underlined letters should be capitalized.

Example: be ready for the bike trip at eight o'clock
Be ready for the bike trip at eight o'clock.

7. let me help you pump up your tires.
8. be sure to bring a water bottle.
9. don't forget your helmet.
10. how tired I am!
11. what a huge blister I have!
12. this bike trip was so much fun!

■ Write each sentence correctly. Underlined letters should be capitalized.

Example: wait in line to board the ferry. *Wait in line to board the ferry.*

13. what a lot of cars there are!
14. please come to the upper deck.
15. why does the ferry open at both ends?
16. it can be loaded from either end.
17. it does not have to turn around.
18. what a good idea that is!

58 **Unit 1:** The Sentence

Meeting Individual Needs — More Practice for Lesson 3

● EASY

Underline the end mark of punctuation after each sentence. Then write *E* after each exclamation and *C* after each command.

1. We've reached the top! (E)
2. Look over there. (C)
3. What a beautiful view! (E)
4. Follow me back to camp. (C)
5. Climbing down is easy! (E)

▲ AVERAGE

Complete each sentence with the correct end punctuation.

1. Light the campfire(.)
2. Boy, am I hungry(!)
3. Get some firewood(.)
4. How great breakfast smells(!)

■ CHALLENGING

Write a command and an exclamation for each situation.

1. During the storm, rain starts to leak through the roof.
2. Your dog runs away and you need help finding him.
3. A child is riding a bike in the garden you just planted.

Sample answers:

1. Get out a bucket. The water is rising!
2. My dog is lost! Look in the alley.
3. My tomatoes are ruined! Don't ride here again.

Extra Practice

4 Subjects and Predicates

(pages 40–41)

Remember

- Every sentence has a subject and a predicate.
- The complete subject includes all the words that tell *whom* or *what* the sentence is about.
- The complete predicate includes all the words that tell what the subject *does* or *is*.

● For each sentence, write *subject* if the subject is underlined or *predicate* if the predicate is underlined.

Example: Ina went swimming in the ocean. *predicate*

1. Eric stayed on the beach. S
2. Their mother called Ina. S
3. The waves were too high. P
4. The sun shone. P
5. The whole family enjoyed the beach. S

▲ Write each sentence. Draw a line between the subject and the predicate.

Example: A fluffy white cloud drifted across the sky.
A fluffy white cloud | drifted across the sky.

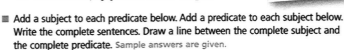

6. Luis|watched the cloud.
7. It|looked like a huge white elephant.
8. Then the cloud's shape|changed.
9. An enormous white train|was now in the sky.
10. The children|enjoyed the clouds' shapes.

■ Add a subject to each predicate below. Add a predicate to each subject below. Write the complete sentences. Draw a line between the complete subject and the complete predicate. Sample answers are given.

Example: Streaks of lightning. *Streaks of lightning | flashed across the sky.*

11. A strong wind. A strong wind | blew at dawn.
12. Pounded on the rocks. Waves | pounded on the rocks.
13. Towering waves. Towering waves | crashed on the beach.
14. The lifeguards. The lifeguards | saved some people.
15. Roared like a lion. The surf | roared like a lion.
16. Small boats. Small boats | sailed past.

Extra Practice 59

Subjects and Predicates

Objectives

Students will:

- identify the complete subjects of sentences
- identify the complete predicates of sentences
- write sentences with subjects and predicates

Using the Extra Practice

The Extra Practice activities provide additional practice for the basic lesson at three levels of difficulty: Easy (●), Average (▲), and Challenging (■).

Meeting Individual Needs — More Practice for Lesson 4

● **EASY**

Match each complete subject with a complete predicate to finish a line from a rhyme.

1. Jack and Jill (B)
2. Old Mother Hubbard (D)
3. Humpty Dumpty (A)
4. Yankee Doodle (C)

A. sat on a wall
B. went up the hill
C. went to town
D. went to her cupboard

▲ **AVERAGE**

Write these sentences. Underline the complete subject once and the complete predicate twice.

1. A big cat played in the tree.
2. A funny dog chased its tail.
3. An angry bee stung the dog.
4. An old horse led the way.
5. A gray goose honked noisily.

■ **CHALLENGING**

Write *S* or *P* to tell whether each word group is missing a subject or predicate. Add the needed part and write a complete sentence. (Answers will vary.)

1. The elephant at the zoo (P)
2. Swung madly in the cages (S)
3. Were growling angrily (S)
4. Three seals in a tank (P)
5. Slithered over hot sand (S)

Simple Subjects

Objectives

Students will:

- identify the simple subject of a sentence
- distinguish the simple subject from the complete subject and the complete predicate
- write sentences and identify their simple subjects

Using the Extra Practice

The Extra Practice activities provide additional practice for the basic lesson at three levels of difficulty: Easy (●), Average (▲), and Challenging (■).

Extra Practice

(pages 42–43)

5 Simple Subjects — Remember

- The simple subject is the main word in the complete subject. It tells exactly *whom* or *what* the sentence is about.

● Choose a simple subject from the box to complete each sentence. Write the sentence. Use each subject once.

name
Babe Ruth
games
sport
players
He
series

Example: My favorite _____ is baseball.
My favorite sport is baseball.

1. The most exciting _____ are the World Series. games
2. This _____ is played in October. series
3. Some baseball _____ become famous. players
4. _____ was a famous player. Babe Ruth
5. His real _____ was George. name
6. _____ became a hero to many young people. He

▲ The complete subject of each sentence is underlined. Write the simple subject.

Example: The game of baseball comes from an old English sport. *game*

7. Children in colonial times played a game with two bases. children
8. Abner Doubleday did not invent the game of baseball. Abner Doubleday
9. It developed from the English game of rounders. It
10. The first professional baseball team was formed in 1869. team
11. The name of the team was the Cincinnati Red Stockings. name
12. Eight teams formed the National League in 1876. teams

■ Write the complete subject of each sentence. Then underline the simple subject.
Complete subject underlined once; simple subject, twice.

Example: Outstanding athletes are honored in halls of fame.
Outstanding athletes

13. Baseball has its own Hall of Fame.
14. It opened in Cooperstown, New York, in 1939.
15. A candidate for the Hall of Fame must be retired.
16. Ten years in the major leagues is also necessary.
17. Many famous players are listed in the Hall of Fame.
18. Babe Ruth was elected to the Hall of Fame.

Meeting Individual Needs — More Practice for Lesson 5

● EASY

Complete each sentence with a simple subject. (Sample answers are given.)

1. Of all games, (baseball) is probably my favorite.
2. At the stadium, (people) cheer for their favorite team.
3. The necessary (equipment) for baseball includes bats, gloves, and balls.
4. To play football, (players) must be strong and fast.
5. The (crowd) at a ball game adds to the excitement.

▲ AVERAGE

Draw a line between each complete subject and complete predicate. Then underline the simple subject.

1. Our best pitcher | threw a high fast ball.
2. The crack of the bat | echoed loudly.
3. The speedy outfielder | jumped for the ball.
4. The smiling batter | rounded the bases proudly.

■ CHALLENGING

Write ten sentences about a sport you enjoy. Underline the simple subject of each sentence. (Answers will vary.)

6 Simple Predicates

(pages 44–45)

Remember

- The simple predicate is the main word in the complete predicate. It tells exactly what the subject does or is.

● Choose a simple predicate from the box to complete each sentence. Write the sentence. Use each predicate once.

collected
have
learned
move
means
is
landed
shines

Example: Earth ______ a planet. *Earth is a planet.*

1. Planets ______ around the sun. move
2. The word *planet* ______ "wanderer." means
3. Some planets ______ one or more moons. have
4. Earth's moon ______ in the sky at night. shines
5. Astronauts ______ on our moon in 1969. landed
6. They ______ moon rocks and soil. collected
7. Scientists ______ more about the moon. learned

▲ The complete predicate of each sentence is underlined. Write the simple predicate.

Example: Comets are balls of dust and ice. *are*

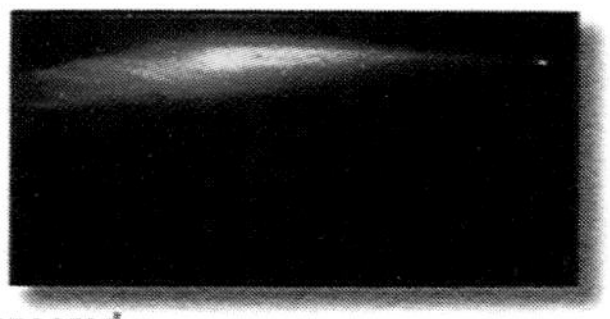

8. Early people called them "hairy stars." called
9. A comet has a tail. has
10. Comets travel around the Sun. travel
11. Halley's Comet is a very brilliant comet. is
12. People saw this comet long ago. saw
13. Halley's Comet appeared in 1985 and 1986. appeared

■ Write the complete predicate of each sentence. Then underline the simple predicate. Complete predicate underlined once; simple predicate, twice.

Example: Early people studied the sky. *studied the sky*

14. They named groups of stars after heroes or animals.
15. We see these same star groups today.
16. The Big Dipper has seven stars.
17. It is part of the Great Bear group.
18. The handle of the dipper forms the tail of the bear.

Extra Practice 61

Simple Predicates

Objectives

Students will:

- identify the simple predicate of a sentence
- distinguish the simple predicate from the complete subject and complete predicate of a sentence
- write sentences and identify their simple predicates

Using the Extra Practice

The Extra Practice activities provide additional practice for the basic lesson at three levels of difficulty: Easy (●), Average (▲), and Challenging (■).

Meeting Individual Needs — More Practice for Lesson 6

● EASY

Complete each sentence with a simple predicate. (Sample answers are given.)

1. A rocket (zoomed) through space toward Mars.
2. Scientists on Earth (watched).
3. Cameras on board (took) photographs of Mars.
4. The craft (landed) on Mars.
5. It (sent) information to Earth.

▲ AVERAGE

Draw a line between the complete subject and the complete predicate of each sentence. Underline the simple predicate.

1. People | call Mars "the red planet."
2. A dry red dust | gives Mars this color.
3. Little water | exists on Mars.
4. Temperatures | stay well below freezing on the planet.
5. Mars | circles the sun between Earth and Jupiter.

■ CHALLENGING

Imagine your spaceship has landed on Mars. Write ten sentences that describe what you see. Underline the complete predicate of each sentence once. Underline the simple predicate twice. (Answers will vary.)

Compound Sentences

Objectives

Students will:
- identify run-on sentences
- correct run-on sentences

Using the Extra Practice

The Extra Practice activities provide additional practice for the basic lesson at three levels of difficulty: Easy (●), Average (▲), and Challenging (■).

Extra Practice

(pages 46–47)

7 Correcting Run-on Sentences

Remember

- A run-on sentence has two complete thoughts that run into each other. Correct a run-on sentence by writing each thought as a separate sentence.

● Write *run-on* if the group of words is a run-on sentence. Write *correct* if it is correct.

Example: The White House is in Washington it is the President's home. *run-on*

1. It was not always white it was once gray. run-on
2. Theodore Roosevelt had the walls painted white. correct
3. Roosevelt changed the name it became the White House. run-on
4. Every President except George Washington has lived there. correct
5. The White House has more than 140 rooms you can visit five. run-on

▲ Write each run-on sentence correctly. Underlined portions are rewritten.

Example: Mount Vernon is a famous house it was George Washington's home. *Mount Vernon is a famous house. It was George Washington's home.*

6. Washington's father built Mount Vernon it was a farm. Vernon. It
7. Mount Vernon is on a hill trees surround the house. hill. Trees
8. Washington planted trees many of them are still there. trees. Many
9. Each year over a million people come they visit the graves of George and Martha Washington. come. They
10. They see Washington's furniture his books are in the study. furniture. His

■ 11–14. Rewrite the following paragraph. Correct each run-on sentence. Underlined portions are rewritten.

Example: Congress meets in the United States Capitol it is a building in Washington. *Congress meets in the United States Capitol. It is a building in Washington.*

parts. There The Capitol has two parts there is a huge dome over the center. One part is for the House of Representatives the other is for the Senate. There is Representa The dome. It a statue on top of the dome it is called the Statue of Freedom. Each year about ten million people visit the Capitol. People may watch a meeting of Congress these visitors need a special pass. Congress. These

62 **Unit 1:** The Sentence

Meeting Individual Needs — More Practice for Lesson 7

● EASY

If a sentence is a run-on, draw a line to show where it can be divided. If a sentence is correct, write *C*.

1. The hare dared the animals to race | the tortoise accepted.
2. The hare ran fast at first. (C)
3. Then he got tired | he rested.
4. The tortoise did not stop | he walked slowly past the sleeping hare.

▲ AVERAGE

Correct each run-on sentence in two ways. First, write it as two sentences. Then use a comma with *and* to combine them correctly.

1. The fox saw some grapes on a vine he tried to get them. (vine. He) (vine, and)
2. But the grapes were too high the fox could not reach them. (high. The) (high, and)
3. The fox told himself, "I don't really like grapes those were probably sour anyway," (grapes. Those) (grapes, and)

■ CHALLENGING

Copy a passage from a favorite story. Leave out some capital letters and punctuation marks to make some of the sentences into run-ons. Then exchange papers with another student. Find and correct the run-ons in the passage that your partner gives you.

Unit 2 Planning Guide

Nouns

2 weeks

		Checkup (PE)	Extra Practice (PE)	Graphic Organizer (BLM)	Writing Wrap-Up (BLM)	More Practice (TE)	Workbook Plus	Reteaching Workbook	Students Acquiring English Practice Book
1	What Is a Noun? *(64–65)*	82	88	2–1	2–4	88	19–20	12	17+
2	Common and Proper Nouns *(66–67)*	82	89	2–1	2–4	89	21–22	13	19+
	Revising Strategies: Sentence Fluency Writing with Nouns *(68–69)*						23–24	14–15	
3	Singular and Plural Nouns *(70–71)*	82	90	2–1, 2–2	2–4	90	25–26	16	21+
4	Nouns Ending with *y (72–73)*	82	91	2–2	2–4	91	27–28	17	23+
5	More Plural Nouns *(74–75)*	82	92	2–2	2–5	92	29–30	18	25+
6	Singular Possessive Nouns *(76–77)*	83	93	2–3	2–5	93	31–32	19	27+
7	Plural Possessive Nouns *(78–79)*	83	94	2–3	2–5	94	33–34	20	29+
	Revising Strategies: Vocabulary Using Exact Nouns *(80)*						35	21	
	Enrichment *(81)*								
	Test Practice *(84–85)*								31+
	Cumulative Review *(86–87)*								

Tools and Tips

- **Diagramming Guide,** *pp. H70–H78*
- **Guide to Capitalization, Punctuation, and Usage,** *pp. H55–H64*

School-Home Connection

Suggestions for informing or involving family members in classroom activities and learning related to this unit are included in the Teacher's Edition throughout the unit.

Meeting Individual Needs

- **FOR SPECIAL NEEDS/INCLUSION:** *Houghton Mifflin English* Audiotape See also Reteaching.
- **FOR STUDENTS ACQUIRING ENGLISH:**
  - Notes and activities are included in this Teacher's Edition throughout the unit to help you adapt or use pupil book activities with students acquiring English.
  - Additional support is available for students at various stages of English proficiency: **Beginning/Preproduction, Early Production/Speech Emergence,** and **Intermediate/Advanced.** See Students Acquiring English Practice Book.
  - Students can listen to the Try It Out activities on audiotape.
- **ENRICHMENT:** *p. 81*

All audiotape recordings are also available on CD.

Daily Language Practice

Each sentence includes two errors based on skills taught in this or previous Grammar units. Each day write one sentence on the chalkboard. Have students find the errors and write the sentence correctly on a sheet of paper. To make the activity easier, identify the kinds of errors.

1. New York city is an exciting place it can also be quite noisy. Sample: New York City is an exciting place. It can also be quite noisy. **(proper nouns; run-on sentences)**
2. Those movers will pack and ship the boxs Those movers will pack and ship the boxes. **(plural nouns; end punctuation)**
3. How the rubys and other jewels sparkle. How the rubies and other jewels sparkle! **(plural nouns; end punctuation)**
4. we tracked rabbits, foxes, and deers through the snow. We tracked rabbits, foxes, and deer through the snow. **(capitalization; plural nouns)**
5. Has the nurse checked that childs temperature. Has the nurse checked that child's temperature? **(possessive nouns; end punctuation)**
6. Three students paintings are hanging in the hall they are tied for first place. Sample: Three students' paintings are hanging in the hall. They are tied for first place. **(possessive nouns; run-on sentences)**
7. The Baseball hall of Fame is located in Cooperstown, New York? The Baseball Hall of Fame is located in Cooperstown, New York. **(proper nouns; end punctuation)**
8. How many inchs have you grown this year! How many inches have you grown this year? **(plural nouns; end punctuation)**
9. Listen carefully to each notes sound! Listen carefully to each note's sound. **(possessive nouns; end punctuation)**
10. Two mooses locked horns in battle Two moose locked horns in battle. **(plural nouns; end punctuation)**

Additional Resources

Workbook Plus, Unit 2
Reteaching Workbook, Unit 2
Students Acquiring English Practice Book, Unit 2
Transparencies, Unit 2
Teacher's Resource Book
Audiotapes

Technology Tools

INTERNET: http://www.eduplace.com/kids/hme/ *or* http://www.eduplace.com/rdg/hme/

Visit Education Place for these additional support materials and activities:

- tricky usage question
- Wacky Web Tales®
- interactive quizzes
- a proofreading game

Assessment

Test Booklet, Unit 2

Keeping a Journal

Discuss with students the value of keeping a journal as a way of promoting self-expression and fluency. Encourage students to record their thoughts and ideas in a notebook. Inform students whether the journal will be private or will be reviewed periodically as a way of assessing growth. The following prompts may be useful for generating writing ideas.

Journal Prompts

- Where in the world would you most like to visit? Why?
- What is a best friend like? What does he or she do?
- Which room in your house is your favorite? Why?

Unit 2

...uns

Taking a shortcut th...
the coral, this squir...
dashes ahead of th...

Noah I
Kendal O

63

Introducing the Unit

Using the Photograph

Note on the Photograph The photo shows a diver and a squirrelfish. Squirrelfish live in coral reefs throughout the tropics.

- Have students look at the photograph and name the things they see. (Sample responses: diver, squirrelfish, coral, water)
- Have a volunteer read the caption aloud. Ask students to repeat the words that name people, places, or things. Write the word *diver* on the board or on an overhead transparency. Ask students how they would write this word if it referred to more than one diver. *(divers)* Explain to students that although many words can be made to refer to two or more by adding *-s* or *-es*, other words are treated differently to do so. Ask students if they can name any such words. (Sample responses: *knives, loaves, feet, teeth*) Point out that *squirrelfish* appears the same whether it refers to one or more than one.
- Explain to students that a **noun** is a word that names a person, a place, or a thing. Tell students that they will learn about nouns in this unit.

Grammar Song

See Blackline Master G–1 for a song to help students remember some of the concepts and rules taught in this unit.

Students can also listen to this song on audiotape.

Shared Writing Activity

Work with students to write a paragraph that contains the three types of nouns presented in the lesson: person, place, and thing.

1. Have students think of a place to write about. (Sample responses: a ballpark, the beach, the city, a farm, a desert)
2. Have students next choose the people they will include. (Sample responses: themselves, family members, friends, celebrities)
3. Ask students what things the people will be using in the place. (Sample response: At the ballpark, Tara will hit the ball with the bat.)
4. Have students generate sentences using their people, place, and things.
   - Help students fix fragments and run-on sentences. As you write, ask students to tell you the correct punctuation and capitalization to use.
   - Have students pay extra attention to how each noun's plural is formed. Make sure students realize that all proper nouns are capitalized.
5. Have a volunteer read the paragraph aloud, emphasizing the nouns.

What Is a Noun?

Lesson Objectives

Students will:

- identify nouns in sentences
- write sentences and identify the nouns in them
- write a fact sheet about a place, using nouns to identify its special or interesting features

One-Minute Warm-Up Write the sentence on the board. Have volunteers put a single line under the name of any persons (none), two lines under the names of places *(fields)*, and three lines under the names of things *(horses, plow, sun)*. Tell students the underlined words are nouns. Have them suggest other nouns to replace those in the sentence.

Focus on Instruction

Suggest that students check their dictionary when they are unsure if a word is a noun. Explain that their dictionary uses the abbreviation *n.* to indicate that a word is a noun.

Try It Out

VIEWING Have students suggest nouns that name persons, places, and things in the photograph. Place the nouns in a chart. (Sample responses are shown.) Then have students use the nouns in sentences that tell about the photograph.

Persons	man, fisherman
Places	ocean, sea
Things	lobster, birds, trap, shirt

FOR STUDENTS ACQUIRING ENGLISH

- Have students listen to the Try It Out sentences on the audiotape. Distribute SAE Practice page for Unit 2, Lesson 1, to support listening.
- Begin by brainstorming vocabulary relating to fishing and life by the sea, especially along the New England coast. Use a map and additional photos of fish, lobsters, and the New England seacoast. List vocabulary on the board and explain as needed. Students listen to sentences and decide whether the underlined nouns are persons, places, or things.

1. My friend is a fisherman. (person; person)
2. John lives in Maine. (person; place)
3. The state of Maine is large. (thing; place)
4. John catches fish. (person; thing)

Grammar

1 What Is a Noun?

One-Minute Warm-Up

Read the sentence below. What words name persons, places, or things?

In the fields, the horses pulled the plow up and down under the hot summer sun.

—from *Sarah, Plain and Tall*, by Patricia MacLachlan

A noun is a word that names a person, a place, or a thing.

Persons	Cheryl brother dentists	Cheryl and her brother are dentists.
Places	Waterville park zoo	Waterville has a park and a zoo.
Things	pears plums bag	Some pears and plums are in the bag.

Try It Out

Speak Up What are the two nouns in each sentence? Does each noun name a person, a place, or a thing?

1. Jeff lives on an island. person; place
2. The house faces the dark blue ocean. thing; thing
3. Fishing boats enter the harbor daily. thing; place
4. Many people catch lobsters. person; thing
5. Workers lift the heavy traps. person; thing
6. Gulls fly over the town. thing; place
7. Alicia stands on the shore. person; place
8. The coast of Maine looks far away. place; place
9. A ferry arrives from Portland. thing; place
10. Passengers step onto the dock. person; thing

Meeting Individual Needs

RETEACHING

ALTERNATIVE STRATEGY

- On the board, draw a large ticket for an imaginary vacation. On the ticket write these headings: *Places I Will Visit, Things I Will Pack, People I Will See.*
- Have students suggest words for each heading. List the words under the headings.
- Explain that the words in the lists are nouns and that nouns name people, places, and things.
- Say each noun at random; have students tell whether it names a person, place, or thing.

CHALLENGE

Show students a photo that includes a variety of objects. Have students list places, people, and things shown in the picture. Have students see who can list the most nouns.

FOR STUDENTS ACQUIRING ENGLISH

Point to various people and objects in the room, saying whether they are persons or things. Then point to various cities, states, and countries on a map and say "place." Next point to people, places, and objects and have students respond with the appropriate term.

On Your Own

Write the nouns in these sentences.

Example: Jamal and Lewis stepped off the airplane. *Jamal Lewis airplane*

11. The boys were excited about their vacation in Hawaii.
12. They stayed with their parents in a big hotel.
13. Their room opened onto a beautiful beach.
14. Some people rode surfboards over the waves.
15. Jamal found beautiful shells along the shore.
16. Lewis found a piece of pink coral.
17. The family traveled the twisting highways together.
18. Their car passed by valleys and mountains.
19. Jamal took many pictures with his new camera.

20–32. This part of a social studies report has thirteen nouns. Write the report. Underline the nouns.

Example: Many beautiful flowers grow in Hawaii.
Many beautiful flowers grow in Hawaii.

Hawaii

Hawaii is made up of many islands. The islands were formed by volcanoes. The state is famous for its beautiful scenery. Waikiki is a famous beach there. Swimmers enjoy the warm water. Tourists visit the many shops and big hotels.

Writing Wrap-Up

WRITING • THINKING • LISTENING • SPEAKING

INFORMING

Write a Fact Sheet

Write several sentences that describe your city, town, or state. Include any special features or interesting places to see. Use as many nouns as you can. Then read your sentences to a small group. Have the group list all of the nouns you used.

For Extra Practice see page 88.

Summing Up Help students summarize this key point about the lesson:

A **noun** is a word that names a person, a place, or a thing.

You may want to have students complete the parts related to this lesson on Blackline Master 2–1.

On Your Own

Suggest that students identify nouns by asking:

Which words refer to people, places, or things?

MEETING INDIVIDUAL NEEDS

FOR STUDENTS ACQUIRING ENGLISH

Distribute SAE Practice page for Unit 2, Lesson 1. First, talk about the state of Hawaii. Use a map and photos. Then students write down all the nouns in the sentences. Review the answers by asking students if the noun names a person, a place, or a thing. Example: *Hawaii is an island in the Pacific. (Hawaii; island; Pacific)* (place) (place) (place)

Writing Wrap-Up

Writing Tip: Suggest that, before they begin writing their sentences, students brainstorm a list of interesting places or things, such as city hall, forest preserves, old church on Cedar Street. See Blackline Master 2–4 for a sample fact sheet.

SCHOOL-HOME CONNECTION

Before they write, invite students to talk with their families about interesting places in their town.

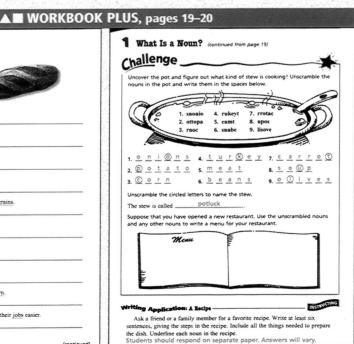

● RETEACHING WORKBOOK, page 12

1 What Is a Noun?

• A noun is a naming word. It names a person, a place, or a thing.

Persons	Sara is riding. A **woman** sits beside her.
Places	She goes to **Smithville**. She visits a big **city**.
Things	Her **suitcase** is heavy. It is full of **clothes**.

Write *person, place,* or *thing* for each underlined noun.

Example: The ride will be one hour long. **thing**

1. Sara pays for her ticket. thing
2. The conductor gives her the change. person
3. Food and drinks are served on one car. thing
4. Sara always buys a snack during the ride. thing
5. This train goes to the city. place
6. People travel there for different reasons. person
7. One woman carries a leather case. thing
8. She is going to work at an office. place
9. Many workers use the train each day. person
10. Sometimes Sara rides with her friend Anika. person
11. The girls like to read books during the trip. thing
12. The train always stops at Easton. place
13. Anika's uncle gets on the train there. person
14. Then the train crosses a river. place
15. There's only one more stop before Smithville. place
16. Sara can't wait to see her grandma. person

▲■ WORKBOOK PLUS, pages 19–20

1 What Is a Noun?

person — thing — place
My **uncle** sells **bread** in his **store**.

Underline the nouns in each sentence.
Write these nouns.

1. Becky and Pedro visited a factory in Ohio.
   Becky, Pedro, factory, Ohio
2. This place made many different breads.
   place, breads
3. A guide told the children stories about bread.
   guide, children, stories, bread
4. Bread is an important food in many lands.
   Bread, food, lands
5. People long ago made flat loaves from different grains.
   People, loaves, grains
6. Bakers in Scotland often used oats.
   Bakers, Scotland, oats
7. The loaves were baked on hot stones.
   loaves, stones
8. Men and women explored our country long ago.
   Men, women, country
9. Many pioneers ate "journeycakes" made from corn.
   pioneers, journeycakes, corn
10. Now workers in bakeries have machines to make their jobs easier.
    workers, bakeries, machines, jobs

(continued)

1 What Is a Noun? (continued from page 19)

Challenge

Uncover the pot and figure out what kind of stew is cooking! Unscramble the nouns in the pot and write them in the spaces below.

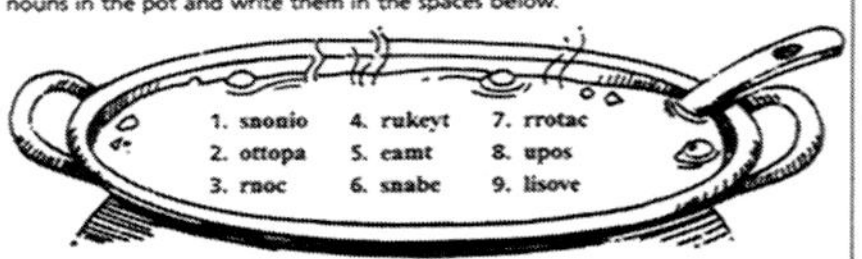

1. o n i ⓞ n s
2. ⓟ o t a t o
3. ⓒ o r n
4. t u r ⓚ e y
5. m e a t
6. b e a n s
7. c a r r o ⓣ
8. s o ⓤ p
9. o ⓛ i v e s

Unscramble the circled letters to name the stew.

The stew is called potluck.

Suppose that you have opened a new restaurant. Use the unscrambled nouns and any other nouns to write a menu for your restaurant.

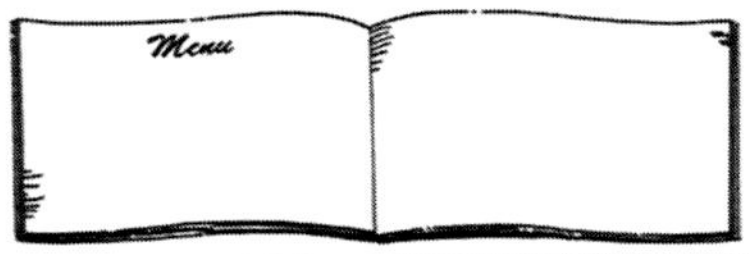

Writing Application: A Recipe INSTRUCTING

Ask a friend or a family member for a favorite recipe. Write at least six sentences, giving the steps in the recipe. Include all the things needed to prepare the dish. Underline each noun in the recipe.

Students should respond on separate paper. Answers will vary.

Common and Proper Nouns

Lesson Objectives

Students will:

- distinguish between common and proper nouns
- capitalize proper nouns
- proofread for proper nouns
- write a biographical sketch using common and proper nouns

One-Minute Warm-Up Students may be unfamiliar with the word *corner* as used in the excerpt. Explain that in this case *corner* refers to "the area enclosed by the intersection of two lines, edges, or surfaces."

Focus on Instruction

Point out that proper nouns are often made up of more than one word, such as *Gulf of Mexico*. Stress that all of the important words in a proper noun are capitalized but that a word like *of* usually is not.

Try it Out

VIEWING Have students suggest nouns associated with the alligator in the photograph, identifying each as a common or proper noun. Record students' responses in a chart. (Sample responses are shown.)

Common Nouns	Proper Nouns
swamp	Florida
animal	Everglades National Park
reptile	

FOR STUDENTS ACQUIRING ENGLISH

- Have students listen to the Try It Out sentences on the audiotape. Distribute SAE Practice page for Unit 2, Lesson 2, to support listening.
- Write *Florida* on the board. Help students locate Florida on a map; show photos. Find out what students know about the state. List ideas on the board, pointing out the capital letters as you write any place names they mention. Students listen and underline all the nouns. Then they listen again and underline proper nouns a second time. Remind students that a common noun at the beginning of a sentence would have a capital letter.
  1. Florida is a state.
  2. Disney World is in Florida.
  3. Ana Flores is from Tampa.

Grammar/Mechanics

2 Common and Proper Nouns

One-Minute Warm-Up

Read the sentence below. Name the nouns. What nouns name special persons, places, or things? CN underlined once; PN, twice.

Florida is a state in the southeastern corner of the United States.

—from *Florida*, by Dennis Brindell Fradin

- **A noun that names any person, place, or thing is called a common noun. A noun that names a particular person, place, or thing is called a proper noun.**

Common and Proper Nouns

Common	Proper	Common	Proper
girl	Maria	bay	Bay of Fundy
uncle	Uncle George	park	Glacier National Park
queen	Queen Elizabeth	pet	Patches
state	Kansas	day	Saturday
country	Canada	holiday	Fourth of July

- Begin a proper noun with a capital letter. If a proper noun is more than one word, capitalize the first letter of each important word.

Try It Out

CN underlined once; PN, twice. PN should be capitalized.

Speak Up Find the common noun and the proper noun in each sentence. Which nouns should begin with capital letters?

1. tanya is an explorer.
2. Her kitten magellan is too!
3. Their trips to florida are always exciting.
4. Do the alligators in everglades national park look scary?
5. The guides at cape canaveral are helpful.

Meeting Individual Needs

RETEACHING

ALTERNATIVE STRATEGY

- Tell students that a noun that names any person, place, or thing is a common noun. Write examples on the board, such as *student, city, country,* and *school*.
- Ask students to name particular examples of the first common noun. (Chris, Roberto)
- Point out that the particular examples are proper nouns; they always begin with a capital letter.
- Follow the same procedure with the other common nouns.

CHALLENGE

Have students list on a sheet of paper fifteen common nouns for which proper nouns can be substituted. Have students exchange papers and write proper nouns to correspond with each common noun on their partner's list.

FOR STUDENTS ACQUIRING ENGLISH

Review capital and lower case letters. Gather objects; have students make and attach labels. Gather several students; make and attach name cards. Make sure capital letters are correct. Sort objects and people into common and proper nouns.

On Your Own

List the common nouns and the proper nouns in these sentences. Begin the proper nouns with capital letters. CN underlined once; PN, twice. PN should be capitalized.

Example: The explorer christopher columbus made several voyages.
common: *explorer* ***proper:*** *Christopher Columbus*

6. On tuesday timmy brought in a book about famous explorers.
7. The book told about brave sailors from europe.
8. Was columbus looking for gold and spices?
9. His ship got lost and landed off the coast of north america in 1492.
10. Now columbus day is celebrated in october.
11. Our class also learned about later explorers.
12. maria mitchell discovered a comet in 1847.
13. In 1969 neil armstrong walked on the moon.

14–20. This page from a biography has seven nouns that should have capital letters. Write the biography correctly. Underlined letters should be capitalized.

Example: The explorer matthew henson made a daring journey.
The explorer Matthew Henson made a daring journey.

Proofreading

Polar Explorer

Matthew Henson was born in maryland in 1866. When he was a boy, Henson worked on a ship. Years later an explorer named robert peary hired Henson as an assistant. In 1909 the two men traveled northward on the arctic ocean. Their goal was to reach the north pole.

Writing Wrap-Up

WRITING • THINKING • LISTENING • SPEAKING

INFORMING

Write a Biographical Sketch

Find out some interesting things about a classmate. Take notes. Then write a paragraph about the person. Read the biography to some classmates. Have them identify proper nouns.

For Extra Practice see page 89.

Summing Up Help students summarize these key points about the lesson:

A **common noun** names any person, place, or thing. A **proper noun** names a particular person, place, or thing. Proper nouns are capitalized.

You may want to have students complete the parts related to this lesson on Blackline Master 2–1.

On Your Own

Suggest that students identify the common and proper nouns by asking:

Does the noun name any person, place, or thing or a particular person, place, or thing?

MEETING INDIVIDUAL NEEDS

FOR STUDENTS ACQUIRING ENGLISH

Distribute SAE Practice page for Unit 2, Lesson 2. Students mark common nouns and proper nouns and add capital letters. Example: On monday our class read about explorers. *(Monday; class; explorers)*

Writing Wrap-Up

Writing Tip: Suggest that students begin by making a list of questions to ask their classmates. See Blackline Master 2–4 for a sample biography.

TECHNOLOGY CONNECTION

Students may want to scan photos or pictures to illustrate their biography.

● RETEACHING WORKBOOK, page 13

2 Common and Proper Nouns

- A **common noun** names any person, place, or thing.
- A **proper noun** names a particular person, place, or thing.
- Capitalize each important word in a proper noun.

proper noun — common noun — common noun
The **Sahara** is the largest **desert** in the **world**.

Write *C* for each underlined common noun and *P* for each underlined proper noun. Then write the proper nouns correctly.

Example: At its longest, the sahara is about 3,200 miles. **P—Sahara**

1. The desert is located in northern africa. P—Africa
2. It stretches from the Atlantic Ocean to the red sea. P—Red Sea
3. Only about four inches of rain fall there each year. C
4. Very few people live there. C
5. Most of the sahara is made up of rock, not sand. P—Sahara
6. Some of the sand dunes rise over two hundred feet. C
7. The namib is in southwestern Africa. P—Namib
8. It is along the atlantic ocean. P—Atlantic Ocean
9. The orange river is south of the desert. P—Orange River
10. Two large rivers flow north of the desert. C
11. The cape of good hope is also in Africa. P—Cape of Good Hope
12. It is located at the southern tip of Africa. C
13. An explorer first sailed around the cape in 1487. C
14. His name was dias. P—Dias
15. After that, sailors used this route for trade. C

▲■ WORKBOOK PLUS, pages 21–22

2 Common and Proper Nouns

proper noun — common noun
Janet Guthrie drives a race **car**.

A Write the nouns in each sentence. Be sure to write each proper noun correctly.

1. janet guthrie was born in iowa city, iowa.
   Janet Guthrie, Iowa City, Iowa
2. The young woman bought a special automobile.
   woman, automobile
3. Her first race at watkins glen in new york lasted six hours.
   race, Watkins Glen, New York, hours
4. This bold driver entered the indianapolis 500.
   driver, Indianapolis 500
5. Her car was called the texaco star.
   car, Texaco Star

B 6–16. This part of a research report has eleven capitalization errors. Use proofreading marks to correct the report.

Example: In this contest, ms. guthrie finished near the top.

Proofreading Marks
¶ Indent
∧ Add
Delete
≡ Capital letter
/ Small letter

Proofreading

In 1977, janet guthrie became the first woman driver to compete in the Indianapolis 500. That year she also won an award, Top rookie, at the Daytona 500 race. Because of her accomplishments, ms. guthrie was one of the first women chosen to be in the women's sports hall of fame. Her driving helmet and suit are in the smithsonian institution.

(continued)

2 Common and Proper Nouns *(continued from page 21)*

Challenge

Richmond County holds a road rally each year. The map below shows the race route and all the checkpoints where the drivers must stop. The map is incorrect because the proper nouns are not capitalized. Write each proper noun correctly on the lines below.

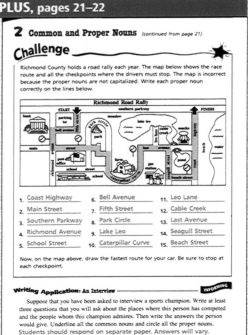

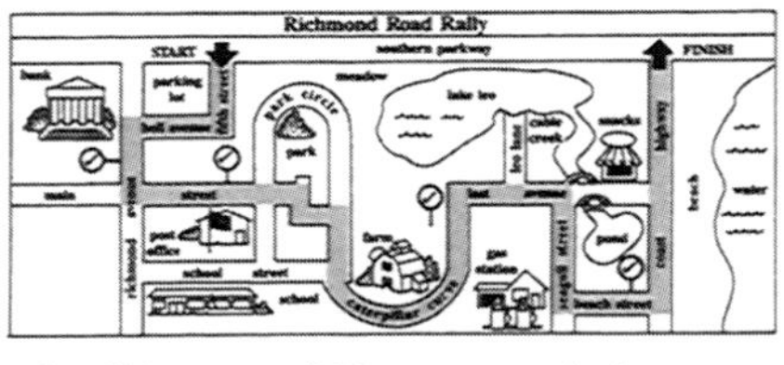

1. Coast Highway	6. Bell Avenue	11. Leo Lane
2. Main Street	7. Fifth Street	12. Cable Creek
3. Southern Parkway	8. Park Circle	13. Last Avenue
4. Richmond Avenue	9. Lake Leo	14. Seagull Street
5. School Street	10. Caterpillar Curve	15. Beach Street

Now, on the map above, draw the fastest route for your car. Be sure to stop at each checkpoint.

Writing Application: An Interview INFORMING

Suppose that you have been asked to interview a sports champion. Write at least three questions that you will ask about the places where this person has competed and the people whom this champion admires. Then write the answers the person would give. Underline all the common nouns and circle all the proper nouns. Students should respond on separate paper. Answers will vary.

Writing with Nouns

Lesson Objective

Students will:

- combine two short sentences with the same predicate to create a sentence with a compound subject

Focus on Instruction

- Point out that changing a singular subject to a compound subject will change the verb from singular to plural unless the verb is in the past tense.
- Write the sentences below on the board.

Present Tense
One canoe *holds* everything for the journey.
One canoe and a large raft *hold* everything for the journey.
Past Tense
One canoe *held* everything for the journey.
One canoe and a large raft *held* everything for the journey.

- Remind students to check for subject-verb agreement when they combine sentences and form compound subjects.

Apply It

Have students complete the revising activity independently.

MEETING INDIVIDUAL NEEDS: If some students need extra support, have them work with partners to identify the similar predicate in both underlined sentences. Have them first write the common predicate and then write the two subjects connected with an *and* to the left of the predicate.

Have students look in their writing in progress to find sentences with the same predicate that can be combined to form a sentence with a compound subject.

Sample Answers to Apply It

1. Meriwether Lewis and William Clark led the expedition.
2. A large boat and two canoes had been packed for the journey.
3. Sacajawea and her husband joined them.
4. Wild animals and harsh weather threatened them.
5. Lewis and Clark reached the Pacific Ocean safely.

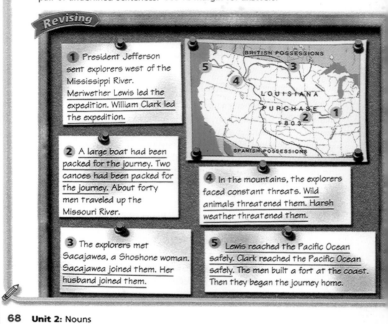

Revising Strategies

Writing with Nouns

Combining Sentences You know that too many short sentences can make your writing sound choppy. If two short sentences have the same predicate, you can combine them by joining the subjects with the word *and*. Your new sentence will have a **compound subject**.

	Compound Subject
Meriwether Lewis explored the West. William Clark explored the West.	Meriwether Lewis and William Clark explored the West.

Apply It

1–5. Revise these facts about the journey of Lewis and Clark. Combine each pair of underlined sentences. See TE margin for answers.

Revising

1 President Jefferson sent explorers west of the Mississippi River. Meriwether Lewis led the expedition. William Clark led the expedition.

2 A large boat had been packed for the journey. Two canoes had been packed for the journey. About forty men traveled up the Missouri River.

3 The explorers met Sacajawea, a Shoshone woman. Sacajawea joined them. Her husband joined them.

4 In the mountains, the explorers faced constant threats. Wild animals threatened them. Harsh weather threatened them.

5 Lewis reached the Pacific Ocean safely. Clark reached the Pacific Ocean safely. The men built a fort at the coast. Then they began the journey home.

68 **Unit 2:** Nouns

Meeting Individual Needs

● RETEACHING WORKBOOK, page 14

Writing with Nouns

- Too many short sentences can make your writing sound choppy.
- If two short sentences have the same predicate, you can combine them by joining the subjects with the word *and*. Your new sentence will have a **compound subject**.

Two sentences	Tracy knelt in the starting block. The other runners knelt in the starting block.
Combined sentence	**Tracy and the other runners** knelt in the starting block.

Combining Sentences Combine each pair of sentences by joining the subjects with the word *and*. Write the revised sentences on the lines.

Example: Swimming relays are exciting to watch.
Gymnastics competitions are exciting to watch.
Swimming relays and gymnastics competitions are exciting to watch.

Revising

1. Legends describe early Olympic competitions. Greek poems describe early Olympic competitions.
Legends and Greek poems describe early Olympic competitions.
2. Displays of strength were part of the Olympics. Athletic contests were part of the Olympics.
Displays of strength and athletic contests were part of the Olympics.
3. Footraces provided excitement for spectators. Chariot races provided excitement for spectators.
Footraces and chariot races provided excitement for spectators.
4. Enthusiasm for sports competition brought back the Olympic Games in 1896. A need for world friendship brought back the Olympic Games in 1896.
Enthusiasm for sports competition and a need for world friendship brought back the Olympic Games in 1896.

(continued)

▲■ WORKBOOK PLUS, page 23

Writing with Nouns

Two sentences	Jessica trained for the figure skating championship. Eve trained for the figure skating championship.
Combined sentence	**Jessica and Eve** trained for the figure skating championship.

Combining Sentences 1–5. Rewrite the following paragraph from this first draft of a newspaper article. Combine each pair of underlined sentences to form one sentence with a compound subject.

Revising

Document 1

Elizabeth skated in the All-Star Competition. Mark skated in the All-Star Competition. They are partners on the ice. Graceful lifts make their performances exciting to watch. Energetic jumps make their performances exciting to watch. They spend hours each week perfecting their routine. Elizabeth's sprained ankle made practicing difficult. Mark's broken toe made practicing difficult. When it was time to compete, however, the young pair skated beautifully. Their coaches encourage them to do their best. Their parents encourage them to do their best. The judges know that these skaters are champions. The fans know that these skaters are champions.

Elizabeth and Mark skated in the All-Star Competition. They are partners on the ice. Graceful lifts and energetic jumps make their performances exciting to watch. They spend hours each week perfecting their routine. Elizabeth's sprained ankle and Mark's broken toe made practicing difficult. When it was time to compete, however, the young pair skated beautifully. Their coaches and their parents encourage them to do their best. The judges and the fans know that these skaters are champions.

(continued)

Sentence Fluency

When one sentence gives details about a subject in a previous sentence, you can combine the two sentences. Put the details from one sentence directly after the noun in the other sentence.

The Omaha have lived in Nebraska since the 1600s. They are a Native American people.	The Omaha, a Native American people, have lived in Nebraska since the 1600s.

Use commas to set apart the added words.

Apply It

6–10. Rewrite the underlined sentences in this first draft of a biography. The first pair of sentences has been done for you.

Revising

Second Draft

Susan La Flesche, an Omaha Indian, was a determined woman from Nebraska. La Flesche

First Draft

Susan La Flesche

Susan La Flesche was a determined woman from Nebraska. She was an Omaha Indian. La Flesche dreamed of becoming a medical doctor. She was a caring and smart woman.

Two people helped her with this goal. These people were her father and her friend. Her father made sure La Flesche had an excellent education. Her father sent her to a famous school in Virginia. Her father was an Omaha chief.

A friend helped La Flesche to enroll in medical school. The friend was Alice Cunningham Fletcher. The determined young woman was about to realize her childhood dream. La Flesche succeeded in her goal. She was an excellent student. She became the first Native American woman to graduate from medical school and practice medicine.

Lesson Objective

Students will:
- combine two sentences by using an appositive

Focus on Instruction

- Tell students that the details they move from one sentence to another should define or explain the subject of the final sentence. These details, called an appositive, are not just any group of descriptive words. They must contain a noun.
- Point out that an appositive placed in the middle of a sentence must be surrounded by commas.
- Write these sentences on the board. Ask students how to use an appositive to combine them.

  Susan La Flesche was determined to become a medical doctor. She was an Omaha Indian.

Apply It

Have students complete the revising activity independently.

Have students find places in their own writing in progress where they can combine sentences by using appositives.

Answers to Apply It

6. La Flesche, a caring and smart woman, dreamed of becoming a medical doctor.
7. Two people, her father and her friend, helped her with this goal.
8. Her father, an Omaha chief, sent her to a famous school in Virginia.
9. A friend, Alice Cunningham Fletcher, helped La Flesche to enroll in medical school.
10. La Flesche, an excellent student, succeeded in her goal.

● RETEACHING WORKBOOK, page 15

Writing with Nouns *(continued from page 14)*

- When one sentence gives details about a subject in a previous sentence, you can combine the two sentences.
- Put the details from one sentence directly after the noun in the other sentence. Use commas to set apart the added words.

First sentence	The Olympic Games are held every four years.
Sentence with details	The Olympics are an international sports competition.
Combined sentence	The Olympic Games, **an international sports competition,** are held every four years.

Combining Sentences Combine the following sentence pairs by moving details from the second sentence into the first. Rewrite the revised sentences.

Example: Evelyn Ashford ran the 100-meter dash. She was an American athlete.
Evelyn Ashford, an American athlete, ran the 100-meter dash.

Revising

5. The first Olympic games honored the Greek god Zeus. These games were contests of physical power and skill.
   The first Olympic games, contests of physical power and skill, honored the Greek god Zeus.
6. Mount Olympus was the site of the earliest Olympic games. Mount Olympus was a sacred spot in Greece.
   Mount Olympus, a sacred spot in Greece, was the site of the earliest Olympic games.
7. Spiridon Loues won the marathon in 1896. He was a Greek water carrier.
   Spiridon Loues, a Greek water carrier, won the marathon in 1896.
8. Babe Didrikson set two world records at the 1932 Olympics. Didrikson was a determined competitor.
   Babe Didrikson, a determined competitor, set two world records at the 1932 Olympics.

▲■ WORKBOOK PLUS, page 24

Writing with Nouns *(continued from page 23)*

Two sentences	Joseph Merlin designed the first pair of roller skates. Joseph Merlin was a creative inventor.
Combined sentence	Joseph Merlin, **a creative inventor,** designed the first pair of roller skates.

Combining Sentences 6–10. Rewrite these paragraphs from a book about inventions by combining the underlined sentence pairs. Move details from the second sentence into the first sentence.

Revising

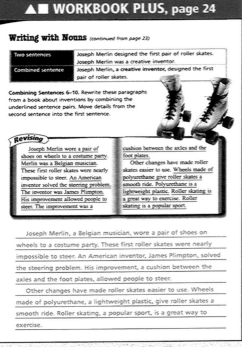

Joseph Merlin wore a pair of shoes on wheels to a costume party. Merlin was a Belgian musician. These first roller skates were nearly impossible to steer. An American inventor solved the steering problem. The inventor was James Plimpton. His improvement allowed people to steer. The improvement was a cushion between the axles and the foot plates.

Other changes have made roller skates easier to use. Wheels made of polyurethane give roller skates a smooth ride. Polyurethane is a lightweight plastic. Roller skating is a great way to exercise. Roller skating is a popular sport.

Joseph Merlin, a Belgian musician, wore a pair of shoes on wheels to a costume party. These first roller skates were nearly impossible to steer. An American inventor, James Plimpton, solved the steering problem. His improvement, a cushion between the axles and the foot plates, allowed people to steer.

Other changes have made roller skates easier to use. Wheels made of polyurethane, a lightweight plastic, give roller skates a smooth ride. Roller skating, a popular sport, is a great way to exercise.

Singular and Plural Nouns

Lesson Objectives

Students will:

- identify singular and plural nouns
- write the plural forms of nouns correctly
- proofread for plural nouns
- use singular and plural nouns to create a list of chores

One-Minute Warm-Up Have volunteers write their responses on the board so students can see how each word is spelled.

Focus on Instruction

Tell students to use context clues to decide if a noun is singular or plural. Words such as *many* and *all* precede plural nouns. The word *a* precedes singular nouns.

Try It Out

LISTENING AND SPEAKING Randomly use the listed words in sentences, sometimes using the singular, sometimes the plural. Use context clues such as *some, many,* or *three* for plural forms of a noun. Ask students to raise their hands when they hear a plural noun.

FOR STUDENTS ACQUIRING ENGLISH

- Have students listen to the Try It Out sentences on the audiotape. Distribute SAE Practice page for Unit 2, Lesson 3, to support listening.
- First, have students look at the singular nouns in the labeled drawings in the left column. Have students listen to the words on tape and then repeat. Next, have students look at the drawings on the right, listen to the plurals on tape, and repeat. Check pronunciation of endings. Then students write in the plural form of the noun.
  1. (drawing of two girls) *(girls)*
  2. (drawing of three brushes) *(brushes)*
  3. (drawing of two foxes) *(foxes)*
  4. (drawing of two desks) *(desks)*

Grammar/Mechanics

3 Singular and Plural Nouns

One-Minute Warm-Up

Look around the classroom. What objects do you see? Complete these sentences by filling in the blanks with different objects.

There is one ______. There are several ______.

A noun can name one or more than one. **A noun that names only one person, place, or thing is called a singular noun. A noun that names more than one is called a plural noun.**

Singular Nouns	Plural Nouns
One goat is in the barn.	Many goats are in those barns.
This hen laid one egg.	These hens laid a dozen eggs.

How to Form Plurals

Rules	Singular	Plural
Add *-s* to most singular nouns.	one boy one puddle a rose	two boys both puddles ten roses
Add *-es* to singular nouns that end with *s, x, ch,* or *sh.*	one bus this box one bunch a wish	three buses some boxes six bunches many wishes

Try It Out

Speak Up What is the plural form of each of the following singular nouns?

1. brush*es*
2. gift*s*
3. class*es*
4. patch*es*
5. prize*s*
6. circus*es*
7. inch*es*
8. fox*es*

70 **Unit 2:** Nouns

Meeting Individual Needs

RETEACHING

ALTERNATIVE STRATEGY

- Display the following poem: *I only went shopping to buy a few boxes, / But I got a hen, two bears, a seal, and three foxes.*
- Have volunteers underline each noun that names one thing. *(seal, hen)* Tell students these are singular nouns.
- Tell students that a noun that names more than one thing is a plural noun. Invite volunteers to circle the plural nouns. (*boxes, bears, foxes*) Point out that many plural nouns end in *-s* or *-es.*

CHALLENGE

Have students write an ad for a movie, leaving a blank space for each noun they intend to use. Have pairs of students exchange ads and fill in the blanks with the singular and plural nouns that best complete their partner's paragraph.

FOR STUDENTS ACQUIRING ENGLISH

Write *singular* and *plural* on the board. Have students pronounce both words. Move about the room naming single or multiple objects that take *-s* or *-es* and saying "singular" or "plural," accordingly. Students repeat after you. Check for correct pronunciation of the endings.

On Your Own

Write the correct noun to complete each sentence. Label the noun *singular* or *plural.*

Example: My family works in many (business, businesses).
businesses plural

9. Cousin Woody makes many (toolbox, toolboxes). P
10. Grandmother Hooper is a basketball (coaches, coach). S
11. Uncle Sandy is a lifeguard at a (beach, beaches). S
12. My sister grows bushels of (radishes, radish). P
13. Grandpa Taylor makes some wedding (dress, dresses). P
14. Aunt Fern owns a plant (store, stores). S
15. I rest in the kitchen and eat lots of (sandwich, sandwiches)! P

16–22. This list of tasks has seven incorrect plural nouns. Write the list correctly.
Incorrect words are underlined.
Example: Peel two bunchs of banana. *Peel two bunches of bananas.*

Proofreading

The Cozy Kitchen

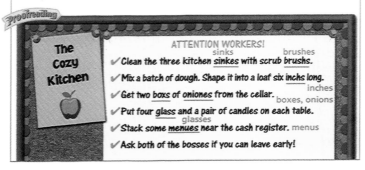

ATTENTION WORKERS!
- Clean the three kitchen sinkes with scrub brushs. (sinks, brushes)
- Mix a batch of dough. Shape it into a loaf six inchs long. (inches)
- Get two boxs of oniones from the cellar. (boxes, onions)
- Put four glass and a pair of candles on each table. (glasses)
- Stack some menues near the cash register. (menus)
- Ask both of the bosses if you can leave early!

Writing Wrap-Up

WRITING • THINKING • LISTENING • SPEAKING

CREATING

Write a List

Years from now the chores you do at home might be very different. Write a list of chores for the year 2050. Use the plural form of four of these nouns: *box, house, dress, computer, batch, brush.* Read your list to a small group. Have them raise their hands when they hear a plural noun.

For Extra Practice see page 90.

Summing Up Help students summarize these key points about the lesson:

A **singular noun** names one person, place, or thing. A **plural noun** names more than one person, place, or thing. To form plural nouns, add *-s* to most singular nouns. Add *-es* to singular nouns that end with *s, x, ch,* or *sh.*

You may want to have students complete the parts related to this lesson on Blackline Masters 2–1 and 2–2.

On Your Own

Remind students to look for context clues to decide if a noun should be singular or plural.

MEETING INDIVIDUAL NEEDS

FOR STUDENTS ACQUIRING ENGLISH

Distribute SAE Practice page for Unit 2, Lesson 3. Ask students to talk about what they see in the drawing. Then have them write the correct form of the noun.

1. These ______ make many things. *(business/businesses)*
2. The store on the left sells ______. *(dress/dresses)*

Writing Wrap-Up

Writing Tip: Suggest that students use short phrases to describe their chores. See Blackline Master 2–4 for a sample list.

SCHOOL-HOME CONNECTION

Invite students to look at their list with a family member and identify the singular and plural nouns.

RETEACHING WORKBOOK, page 16

3 Singular and Plural Nouns

- A **singular noun** names one person, place, or thing.
- A **plural noun** names more than one person, place, or thing.
- To form plural nouns, add *-s* to most singular nouns. Add *-es* to singular nouns that end with *s, x, ch,* or *sh.*

Singular	toy	store	glass	fox	lunch	dish
Plural	toys	stores	glasses	foxes	lunches	dishes

ball

balls

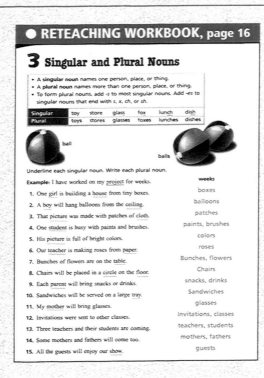

Underline each singular noun. Write each plural noun.

Example: I have worked on my project for weeks. **weeks**

1. One girl is building a house from tiny boxes. boxes
2. A boy will hang balloons from the ceiling. balloons
3. That picture was made with patches of cloth. patches
4. One student is busy with paints and brushes. paints, brushes
5. His picture is full of bright colors. colors
6. Our teacher is making roses from paper. roses
7. Bunches of flowers are on the table. Bunches, flowers
8. Chairs will be placed in a circle on the floor. Chairs
9. Each parent will bring snacks or drinks. snacks, drinks
10. Sandwiches will be served on a large tray. Sandwiches
11. My mother will bring glasses. glasses
12. Invitations were sent to other classes. Invitations, classes
13. Three teachers and their students are coming. teachers, students
14. Some mothers and fathers will come too. mothers, fathers
15. All the guests will enjoy our show. guests

WORKBOOK PLUS, pages 25–26

3 Singular and Plural Nouns

Singular	apple	day	class	box	lunch	brush
Plural	apples	days	classes	boxes	lunches	brushes

A Write the plural form of the noun in parentheses to complete each sentence.

1. Many clubs take part in the county fair. **(club)**
2. Last year our club won a lot of awards. **(award)**
3. We grew fifty perfect peaches. **(peach)**
4. We took them to the fair in five boxes. **(box)**
5. Two judges thought that our fruit was the best. **(judge)**
6. Several cash prizes were given for the best quilts. **(prize)**
7. The winners made their quilts from patches of cloth. **(patch)**
8. Our neighbor won a prize for the six largest radishes. **(radish)**
9. Aunt Lou entered two dresses in the sewing contest. **(dress)**

B 10–14. Use proofreading marks to correct five plural nouns in this list of county fair expenses.

Example: 4 ~~ride~~ rides on the Giant Wheel......... $6.00

Proofreading Marks
- ¶ Indent
- ∧ Add
- Delete
- ≡ Capital letter
- / Small letter

Proofreading

- 8 game-booth ~~ticket~~ tickets $8.00
- 2 tickets for the Cyclone Roller Coaster $3.00
- 2 cheese ~~sandwich~~ sandwiches $2.50
- 3 helium ~~balloon~~ balloons $3.00
- 5 ~~glass~~ glasses of pink lemonade $3.00
- Basket of fresh ~~peach~~ peaches for Granddad. $5.50

TOTAL $25.00

(continued)

3 Singular and Plural Nouns *(continued from page 25)*

Challenge

Carver County is having a fair. There will be contests and games. Make three signs for the fair, using the plural form of each noun listed below. Decorate the signs with drawings or fancy lettering. Answers will vary.

GARDENING CONTEST

cucumber	peach
radish	apple
box	berry

SEWING CONTEST

patch	blanket
quilt	shirt
dress	stitch

REFRESHMENT STAND

egg	glass
sandwich	plate
juice	salad
cheese	dish
lunch	snack

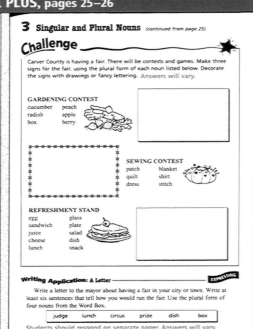

Writing Application: A Letter EXPRESSING

Write a letter to the mayor about having a fair in your city or town. Write at least six sentences that tell how you would run the fair. Use the plural form of four nouns from the Word Box.

judge	lunch	circus	prize	dish	box

Students should respond on separate paper. Answers will vary.

Nouns Ending with *y*

Lesson Objectives

Students will:

- write the plural forms of nouns ending with *y*
- proofread for plural forms of nouns ending with *y*
- write a persuasive speech, using nouns ending with *y*

One-Minute Warm-Up After students identify *countries,* write it on the board. Ask what its singular form is (country) and write it beside the plural form. Have a volunteer explain how the plural was formed. Then ask students to tell other nouns that form their plural in the same way.

Focus on Instruction

If necessary, review that the five vowels are *a, e, i, o,* and *u.*

Try It Out

VIEWING Have students tell about a visit to the ponies in the photograph, using singular nouns that end with *y.* (The boy walked across the valley to see the pony.) Have volunteers identify each noun that ends with a *y* and write it in the first column of a two-column chart. Have students complete the chart by writing the plural of each noun in the second column.

Nouns Ending with *y*	Plural
boy	boys
valley	valleys
pony	ponies

FOR STUDENTS ACQUIRING ENGLISH

- Have students listen to the Try It Out sentences on the audiotape. Distribute SAE Practice page for Unit 2, Lesson 4, to support listening.
- First, have students look at the drawings to see how many of these nouns they can identify on their own. Call on students to tell you what the drawings are. Write students' ideas on the board. Continue until someone gives you the noun ending with *y*. Ask what they think the plural will be. Then have students listen to the tape and circle the drawing in the pair that corresponds to what they hear on tape.

1. pony ponies (drawing of 2 ponies)
2. turkey turkeys (drawing of 2 turkeys)
3. baby babies (drawing of 1 baby)

Grammar

4 Nouns Ending with *y*

One-Minute Warm-Up

Read the sentences below. Can you name the plural noun?

In Europe the main area for drilling gas is the North Sea. The area is shared by several countries.

—from *Natural Resources,* by Damian Randle

You have already learned some rules for making nouns plural. Here are two special rules for making the plural forms of nouns that end with *y.*

How to Form Plurals

Rules	Singular	Plural
If the noun ends with a vowel and *y,* add *-s.*	one toy a monkey	many toys five monkeys
If the noun ends with a consonant and *y,* change the *y* to *i* and add *-es.*	one family this city a baby	some families six cities two babies

Tip If you forget these rules, you can use a dictionary to find the plural spelling of a noun.

Try It Out

Speak Up What is the plural form of each noun?

1. berry ies
2. holidays
3. turkeys
4. boys
5. pony ies
6. party ies
7. lady ies
8. donkeys
9. puppy ies
10. sky ies
11. hobby ies
12. keys
13. bluejays
14. bunny ies
15. firefly ies
16. rays

72 Unit 2: Nouns

Meeting Individual Needs

RETEACHING
ALTERNATIVE STRATEGY

- Write *boy* on the board. Add an *-s* to the end of the word. Explain that to form the plural of a noun that ends with a vowel and *y,* add an *-s.*
- Have students form the plural of *toy, day, donkey.* (toys, days, donkeys)
- Write the word *party.* Point out that the word ends with a consonant and *y.* Form the plural by changing the *y* to *i* and adding *-es.*
- Have students form the plural of *puppy, city, body.* (puppies, cities, bodies)

CHALLENGE

Have students write a list of eight singular nouns that end with *y.* Have them exchange papers with a partner and write the plural form of each noun on the partner's list. Then have students use the eight plural nouns in a poem or song.

FOR STUDENTS ACQUIRING ENGLISH

Write the following on the board: *baby, puppy, bunny, donkey, key, day.* Say the plural, cross out the *y,* and add *-ies* to the first three. Add *-s* to the last three. Then ask what the difference is. Mark the vowels before the *y* with colored chalk.

On Your Own

Write the plural form of the noun in ( ) to complete each sentence.

Example: People are finding ______ to save energy. (way) *ways*

17. Drivers save gas by driving slower on ______. (highway) highways
18. We save gas by taking buses or ______ to work. (subway) subways
19. In some ______, workers travel by boat. (city) cities
20. Many ______ help by turning off air conditioners. (company) companies
21. How can all the ______ in your town help? (family) families
22. All ______ and girls can turn off extra lights. (boy) boys
23. People can make sure that their ______ are working properly. (chimney) chimneys

24–30. This speech has seven incorrect plural nouns. Write the speech correctly. Incorrect words are underlined.

Example: Large bodys of water can be used to make energy.
Large bodies of water can be used to make energy.

Proofreading

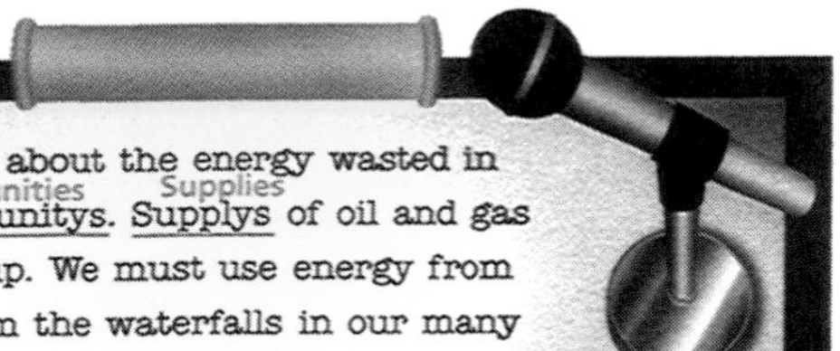

We all worry about the energy wasted in American communitys (communities). Supplys (Supplies) of oil and gas are being used up. We must use energy from the sun and from the waterfalls in our many valleyes (valleys). We must turn the garbage in alleyies (alleys) into fuel for factorys (factories). Leave your cars at home, ladys (ladies) and gentlemen. Find other wayes (ways) to travel. Saving energy now will make a better future for everyone!

Writing Wrap-Up

WRITING • THINKING • LISTENING • SPEAKING

PERSUADING

Write a Speech

Your town is working on an ad campaign to discourage littering. Write a speech to give at a rally. Include reasons why people should dispose of trash properly. Use the plural form of *lady, highway, family, sky,* and *company*. Present your speech. Was it convincing?

For Extra Practice see page 91.

Summing Up Help students summarize these key points about the lesson:

If a noun ends with a vowel and *y*, add *-s*. If a noun ends with a consonant and *y*, change the *y* to *i* and add *-es*.

You may want to have students complete the parts related to this lesson on Blackline Master 2–2.

On Your Own

Tell students that if they aren't sure whether the plural form of the noun is correct, they should first determine its singular form and then use the rules.

MEETING INDIVIDUAL NEEDS

FOR STUDENTS ACQUIRING ENGLISH

Distribute SAE Practice page for Unit 2, Lesson 4. Write *energy* on the board. Brainstorm things that use energy and what type (for example, gas and electricity) and ways to save energy. Then have students complete the sentences with the plural form of the noun. Example: _____ save energy. *(Subway)* (Subways)

Writing Wrap-Up

Writing Tip: Suggest that students use a catchy opening to their speech to capture their audience. See Blackline Master 2–4 for a sample speech.

SCHOOL-HOME CONNECTION

Encourage students to present their speech to family members and then discuss whether it convinced them to avoid littering.

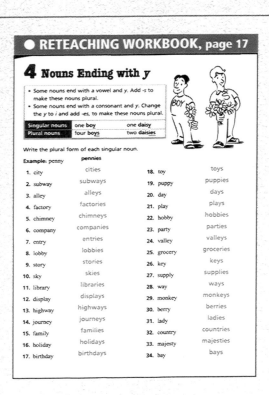

● RETEACHING WORKBOOK, page 17

4 Nouns Ending with *y*

- Some nouns end with a vowel and *y*. Add *-s* to make these nouns plural.
- Some nouns end with a consonant and *y*. Change the *y* to *i* and add *-es*, to make these nouns plural.

Singular nouns	one boy	one daisy
Plural nouns	four boys	two daisies

Write the plural form of each singular noun.

Example: penny **pennies**

1. city cities
2. subway subways
3. alley alleys
4. factory factories
5. chimney chimneys
6. company companies
7. entry entries
8. lobby lobbies
9. story stories
10. sky skies
11. library libraries
12. display displays
13. highway highways
14. journey journeys
15. family families
16. holiday holidays
17. birthday birthdays
18. toy toys
19. puppy puppies
20. day days
21. play plays
22. hobby hobbies
23. party parties
24. valley valleys
25. grocery groceries
26. key keys
27. supply supplies
28. way ways
29. monkey monkeys
30. berry berries
31. lady ladies
32. country countries
33. majesty majesties
34. bay bays

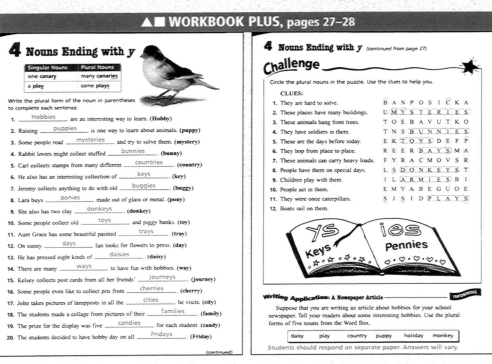

▲■ WORKBOOK PLUS, pages 27–28

4 Nouns Ending with *y*

Singular Nouns	Plural Nouns
one canary	many canaries
a play	some plays

Write the plural form of the noun in parentheses to complete each sentence.

1. Hobbies are an interesting way to learn. **(Hobby)**
2. Raising puppies is one way to learn about animals. **(puppy)**
3. Some people read mysteries and try to solve them. **(mystery)**
4. Rabbit lovers might collect stuffed bunnies. **(bunny)**
5. Carl collects stamps from many different countries. **(country)**
6. He also has an interesting collection of keys. **(key)**
7. Jeremy collects anything to do with old buggies. **(buggy)**
8. Lara buys ponies made out of glass or metal. **(pony)**
9. She also has two clay donkeys. **(donkey)**
10. Some people collect old toys and piggy banks. **(toy)**
11. Aunt Grace has some beautiful painted trays. **(tray)**
12. On sunny days Ian looks for flowers to press. **(day)**
13. He has pressed eight kinds of daisies. **(daisy)**
14. There are many ways to have fun with hobbies. **(way)**
15. Kelsey collects post cards from all her friends' journeys. **(journey)**
16. Some people even like to collect pits from cherries. **(cherry)**
17. John takes pictures of lampposts in all the cities he visits. **(city)**
18. The students made a collage from pictures of their families. **(family)**
19. The prize for the display was five candies for each student. **(candy)**
20. The students decided to have hobby day on all Fridays. **(Friday)**

(continued)

4 Nouns Ending with *y* *(continued from page 27)*

Challenge

Circle the plural nouns in the puzzle. Use the clues to help you.

CLUES:

1. They are hard to solve.
2. These places have many buildings.
3. These animals hang from trees.
4. They have soldiers in them.
5. These are the days before today.
6. They hop from place to place.
7. These animals can carry heavy loads.
8. People have them on special days.
9. Children play with them.
10. People act in them.
11. They were once caterpillars.
12. Boats sail on them.

B	A	N	P	O	S	I	C	K	A
U	M	Y	S	T	E	R	I	E	S
T	O	E	B	A	V	U	T	K	O
T	N	S	B	U	N	N	I	E	S
E	K	T	O	Y	S	D	E	F	P
R	E	E	R	B	A	Y	S	M	A
F	Y	R	A	C	M	O	V	S	R
L	S	D	O	N	K	E	Y	S	T
I	L	A	R	M	I	E	S	B	I
E	M	Y	A	B	E	G	U	O	E
S	J	S	I	D	P	L	A	Y	S

Writing Application: A Newspaper Article INFORMING

Suppose that you are writing an article about hobbies for your school newspaper. Tell your readers about some interesting hobbies. Use the plural forms of five nouns from the Word Box.

daisy	play	country	puppy	holiday	monkey

Students should respond on separate paper. Answers will vary.

More Plural Nouns

Lesson Objectives

Students will:

- write the plural form of irregular nouns
- identify nouns as singular or plural
- proofread for plural nouns
- use plural nouns to write a paragraph describing a story idea

One-Minute Warm-Up Ask students to write their silly sentences on the board. Have volunteers identify the singular and plural nouns.

Focus on Instruction

Tell students that they can use their dictionary to check the spelling of any plural noun that is formed in a special way.

Try It Out

VIEWING Have students suggest sentences about the moose in the photograph, using singular and plural nouns from this lesson. Have students write the sentence and the singular and plural nouns on a chart. (Sample responses are shown.)

Sentence	Singular Nouns	Plural Nouns
The moose sees four geese.	moose	geese

FOR STUDENTS ACQUIRING ENGLISH

- Have students listen to the Try It Out sentences on the audiotape. Distribute SAE Practice page for Unit 2, Lesson 5, to support listening.
- First, have students look at the drawings on the left to see how many of these nouns they can identify on their own. Then call on students to read the labels. Ask if anyone knows the plural for any of these. Write correct responses on the board. Have students listen to the tape and say the singular forms. Then students listen again and fill in the plural form.

1. child ______ (children)
2. foot ______ (feet)
3. mouse ______ (mice)
4. sheep ______ (sheep)

Grammar

5 More Plural Nouns

One-Minute Warm-Up

Can you make your own silly sentences using the words below?

foot goose mice feet mouse teeth geese tooth

Be careful when you peek at a crocodile's teeth!

- Some nouns have special plural forms. Since these words follow no spelling pattern, you must remember them.

Singular and Plural Nouns

Singular	Plural	Singular	Plural
one child	two children	each tooth	five teeth
a man	many men	one goose	both geese
this woman	three women	an ox	nine oxen
that foot	these feet	a mouse	some mice

- Other nouns are the same in both the singular and the plural forms.

Singular Nouns	Plural Nouns
One deer nibbled the bark	Several deer ate quietly.
Did you see a moose?	Two moose crossed a stream.
I have a pet sheep.	These sheep have soft wool.

Try It Out

Speak Up Complete each sentence with the plural form of the underlined noun.

1. One child helped two smaller ______ tie their shoes. children
2. That man sang while two other ______ played guitars. men
3. This sheep is my pet, and those ______ belong to Dan. sheep
4. Mai hopped on one foot and then jumped with both ______. feet
5. Ana saw one moose in Maine and four ______ in Canada. moose

74 **Unit 2:** Nouns

Meeting Individual Needs

RETEACHING

ALTERNATIVE STRATEGY

- On the board, write *tooth.* Erase the *oo* and replace it with *ee.* Repeat the procedure with *foot/feet* and *goose/geese.* Point out that these nouns have special plural forms. Ask volunteers to use each word in a sentence.
- Write these word pairs: *child/children, woman/women,* and *man/men.* Explain that these words also have special plural forms. Randomly point to the words. Have students identify each word as singular or plural and use it in a sentence.

CHALLENGE

Have students unscramble the plural form of each noun and then write its singular form.

nem (men, man)
enchdlir (children, child)
soome (moose, moose)
rede (deer, deer)
ciem (mice, mouse)
hetet (teeth, tooth)
etef (feet, foot)

FOR STUDENTS ACQUIRING ENGLISH

Show drawings and write the following on the board: *child, man, woman, foot, tooth.* Say the word. Then write and say the plural. Repeat with *sheep, deer, moose.* Then have students come to the board to write the plural as you spell it.

On Your Own

Write each underlined noun. Label it *singular* or *plural*.

Example: The child and his grandfather stared out the window.
child singular

6. Their train sped past many sheep grazing in a field. P
7. Nearby, two oxen slowly pulled a plow. P
8. A woman wearing overalls followed the animals. S
9. In the distance, two men were cutting down trees. P
10. The teeth of their saws gleamed in the sunlight. P
11. Several deer watched from the edge of the forest. P

12–18. This story beginning has seven incorrect plural nouns. Write the story beginning correctly. Incorrect words are underlined.

Example: Papa whistled through his two front tooths.
Papa whistled through his two front teeth.

Proofreading

LIFE ON THE FRONTIER

oxen Papa tied the four oxes to the wagon. Several men and
women womans from nearby farms helped him load it. The five
geese gooses would ride in the back of the wagon. All of the
sheep sheeps would walk beside the wagon. Our dog stood on
feet his hind feets and looked longingly into the wagon. He
children would have to walk too. Both childs took a last peek into
mice the house. It was empty except for a family of mouses.

Writing Wrap-Up WRITING • THINKING • LISTENING • SPEAKING

DESCRIBING

Write a Story Idea

Write a paragraph describing an idea for a story. Use the plural form of *child, man, woman, foot,* and *mouse*. Compare your paragraph with a partner's. How are your story ideas alike and different?

For Extra Practice see page 92.

Summing Up Help students summarize these key points about the lesson:

Some nouns have special plural forms. Some nouns have the same singular and plural forms.

You may want to have students complete the parts related to this lesson on Blackline Master 2–2.

On Your Own

Suggest that students look for context clues that will help them figure out if a noun is plural or singular.

MEETING INDIVIDUAL NEEDS

FOR STUDENTS ACQUIRING ENGLISH

Distribute SAE Practice page for Unit 2, Lesson 5. Students choose the correct form of the noun or circle *singular* or *plural*.

1. The ______ took a train trip with their grandfather. *(child/children)* (children)
2. They saw some deer in a forest. SINGULAR PLURAL (plural)

Writing Wrap-Up

Writing Tip: Suggest that students figure out a simple plot for their story before they begin writing. See Blackline Master 2–5 for a sample paragraph.

SCHOOL-HOME CONNECTION

Encourage students to share their story idea with family members. Afterwards, family members might discuss ways to improve the plot, for the student to consider.

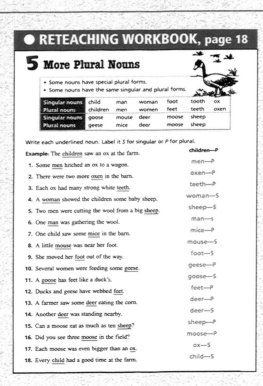

● RETEACHING WORKBOOK, page 18

5 More Plural Nouns

- Some nouns have special plural forms.
- Some nouns have the same singular and plural forms.

Singular nouns	child	man	woman	foot	tooth	ox
Plural nouns	children	men	women	feet	teeth	oxen
Singular nouns	goose	mouse	deer	moose	sheep	
Plural nouns	geese	mice	deer	moose	sheep	

Write each underlined noun. Label it *S* for singular or *P* for plural.

Example: The children saw an ox at the farm. children—P

1. Some men hitched an ox to a wagon. men—P
2. There were two more oxen in the barn. oxen—P
3. Each ox had many strong white teeth. teeth—P
4. A woman showed the children some baby sheep. woman—S
5. Two men were cutting the wool from a big sheep. sheep—S
6. One man was gathering the wool. man—s
7. One child saw some mice in the barn. mice—P
8. A little mouse was near her foot. mouse—S
9. She moved her foot out of the way. foot—S
10. Several women were feeding some geese. geese—P
11. A goose has feet like a duck's. goose—S
12. Ducks and geese have webbed feet. feet—P
13. A farmer saw some deer eating the corn. deer—P
14. Another deer was standing nearby. deer—S
15. Can a moose eat as much as ten sheep? sheep—P
16. Did you see three moose in the field? moose—P
17. Each moose was even bigger than an ox. ox—S
18. Every child had a good time at the farm. child—S

▲■ WORKBOOK PLUS, pages 29–30

5 More Plural Nouns

Singular Nouns	Plural Nouns	Singular Nouns	Plural Nouns
this **woman**	some **women**	one **sheep**	eight **sheep**
each **foot**	both **feet**	a **moose**	both **moose**
a **mouse**	several **mice**	that **deer**	these **deer**

Write the plural form of the noun in parentheses to complete each sentence.

1. All the ___geese___ honked as they flew by. **(goose)**
2. The farmer bought some ___oxen___ for his farm. **(ox)**
3. My yard is filled with ___mice___. **(mouse)**
4. Look out the window at the flock of ___sheep___. **(sheep)**
5. Three ___women___ are in the play. **(woman)**
6. The dentist has to fill two holes in my ___teeth___. **(tooth)**
7. My ___feet___ hurt after hiking for an hour. **(foot)**
8. At eight o'clock, the ___children___ go to sleep. **(child)**
9. There are two ___moose___ in the woods. **(moose)**
10. Some ___deer___ are crossing the road. **(deer)**
11. A few ___men___ refused the prize money. **(man)**
12. The child has lost two ___teeth___. **(tooth)**
13. All the ___sheep___ have left the pasture. **(sheep)**
14. Are four ___women___ sitting at the table? **(woman)**
15. How many ___feet___ are between the floor and the loft? **(foot)**
16. Many ___deer___ ran through the woods that day. **(deer)**
17. How are ___oxen___ like cattle? **(ox)**
18. It is fun to watch the ___geese___ fly. **(goose)**
19. Will the ___children___ help in the barn? **(child)**
20. Five ___men___ had to haul the broken tractor. **(man)**

(continued)

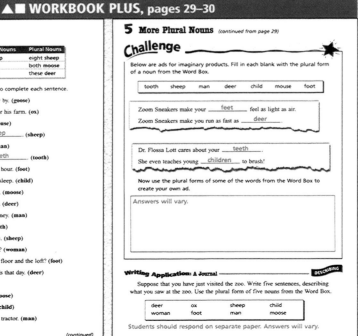

5 More Plural Nouns *(continued from page 29)*

Challenge

Below are ads for imaginary products. Fill in each blank with the plural form of a noun from the Word Box.

tooth	sheep	man	deer	child	mouse	foot

Zoom Sneakers make your ___feet___ feel as light as air.
Zoom Sneakers make you run as fast as ___deer___.

Dr. Flossa Lott cares about your ___teeth___.
She even teaches young ___children___ to brush!

Now use the plural forms of some of the words from the Word Box to create your own ad.

Answers will vary.

Writing Application: A Journal DESCRIBING

Suppose that you have just visited the zoo. Write five sentences, describing what you saw at the zoo. Use the plural form of five nouns from the Word Box.

deer	ox	sheep	child
woman	foot	man	moose

Students should respond on separate paper. Answers will vary.

Singular Possessive Nouns

Lesson Objectives

Students will:

- form singular possessive nouns
- proofread for singular possessive nouns
- write a review evaluating a school event, using possessive nouns

One-Minute Warm-Up Have students write the identifying word on the board. Ask how the word shows ownership. (The name has an apostrophe and *-s*.)

Focus on Instruction

Remind students that a singular noun names one person, place, or thing. Stress that even if a singular noun ends with *s* or *ss*, an apostrophe and *-s* must be added to form the possessive, as in *princess's*.

Try It Out

VIEWING Have volunteers make up sentences about the mask in the picture using singular possessive nouns. Have students write the sentence and the possessive noun on a chart. (Sample responses are shown.)

Sentence	Possessive Noun
The mask's color is yellow.	mask's
Carlos's mask has whiskers.	Carlos's

FOR STUDENTS ACQUIRING ENGLISH

- Have students listen to the Try It Out sentences on the audiotape..Distribute SAE Practice page for Unit 2, Lesson 6, to support listening.
- Display various objects belonging to students and ask incorrectly about ownership. Call on students to give the real ownership. For example, *Is this Tran's soccer ball? No, this is Ana's soccer ball.* To avoid first language interference, discourage students from using *of,* as in *the nose of the rabbit,* instead of the possessive. Next have students listen and write the possessive form in the blank. Explain that *y* does not change to *i* in singulars and the number of the noun does not affect the possessive.

1. the girl ______ books ('s)
2. the puppy ______ tail ('s)
3. the child ______ toys ('s)
4. the rabbit ______ nose ('s)

Grammar/Mechanics

6 Singular Possessive Nouns

One-Minute Warm-Up

Read the sentences below. Which noun shows ownership? How do you know? Matthew's; 's at the end

Matthew's room had pictures of great home run hitters of the past, like Babe Ruth, the Sultan of Swat.

—from *Yang the Youngest and His Terrible Ear,* by Lensey Namioka

Sometimes you may want to tell what someone or something has or owns. **A noun that shows ownership is called a possessive noun.** Add an apostrophe and an *-s* (*'s*) to a singular noun to make it possessive.

Singular Nouns	Singular Possessive Nouns
The football belongs to Bob.	This is Bob's football.
The bike the girl owns is new.	The girl's bike is new.
These poems by Wes are funny.	Wes's poems are funny.
The tail of the beaver is flat.	The beaver's tail is flat.

Try It Out

Speak Up What is another way to make each group of words show ownership? Use the possessive form of the underlined noun.

1. balloon of one child one child's balloon
2. nose of the rabbit the rabbit's nose
3. mask of Carlos Carlos's mask
4. computer of this man this man's computer
5. den of one fox one fox's den
6. collar of our puppy our puppy's collar
7. basketball of a friend a friend's basketball
8. drawings by an artist an artist's drawings

Meeting Individual Needs

RETEACHING
ALTERNATIVE STRATEGY

- Ask students to suggest items to fill a time capsule that would show future generations what their school is like now. Write these examples on the board: *Ms. Lamont's books, Tony Pierson's science fair exhibit.* Explain that the apostrophe and *-s* in the phrases shows ownership.
- Distribute strips of paper on which students can write items they own. Remind them to use an apostrophe and *-s* to show ownership. Collect the papers in a box. Have volunteers select papers at random and read them aloud.

CHALLENGE

Have students write silly sentences containing possessive phrases made of words that rhyme, such as *The cat's hat is green* or *The hog's dog ran away.*

FOR STUDENTS ACQUIRING ENGLISH

Move about the room identifying objects that belong to students. For example, say, "Maria's homework, Tom's backpack, Carlos's desk." Have students repeat each as you write it on the board. Ask what is the same in each case; show how to make the apostrophe.

On Your Own

Write each phrase another way. Use the possessive form of each underlined noun.

Example: science projects of my class *my class's science projects*

9. eyes of the dinosaur — the dinosaur's eyes
10. posters drawn by Pervis — Pervis's posters
11. magnets owned by Marita — Marita's magnets
12. rocks owned by Chan — Chan's rocks
13. telescope belonging to a teacher — a teacher's telescope
14. hamsters owned by my sister — my sister's hamsters
15. fur of one hamster — one hamster's fur
16. volcano made by Chris — Chris's volcano

17–24. This review for a school newspaper has eight incorrect singular possessive nouns. Write the review correctly. Incorrect words are underlined.

Example: A monkeys tricks caused giggles.
A monkey's tricks caused giggles.

Proofreading

Central School News Volume 8, Number 4

Class's Circus Is a Hit

Mrs. Green [Mrs. Green's] class put on a circus show last week. Charles Owens was a clown. Charles [Charles's] jokes kept everyone laughing. He squirted one boys [boy's] face with water from a fake flower and tickled the principal with a foxs [fox's] tail. The audience also admired an elephant's dance and an acrobats [acrobat's] skill. They cheered a lion tamer [tamer's] courage in handling a roaring lion (played by Josh Eng) and joined in the ringmasters [ringmaster's] song. The students made each performer's costume, with help from Sonia Perez [Sonia Perez's] mother.

Class Clown

Writing Wrap-Up

WRITING • THINKING • LISTENING • SPEAKING

EVALUATING

Write a Review

Think of a school event you have attended, such as a class play or a special assembly. Write a review of it for the school paper. Describe the event. Was anyone's performance particularly good or funny? Include singular possessive nouns. When you are done, read your review to a partner. Does your partner agree with your review?

For Extra Practice see page 93.

Summing Up Help students summarize these key points about the lesson:

A noun that shows ownership is called a **possessive noun**. To form the possessive of a singular noun, add an apostrophe and *-s*.

You may want to have students complete the parts related to this lesson on Blackline Master 2–3.

On Your Own

Remind students that they should add an apostrophe and an *s* only if they are showing ownership, not to form the plural form of a noun.

MEETING INDIVIDUAL NEEDS

FOR STUDENTS ACQUIRING ENGLISH

Distribute SAE Practice page for Unit 2, Lesson 6. First, students change phrases to possessives. Then they correct errors in possessives.

1. project done by Luis (Luis's project)
2. snake owned by Ann (Ann's snake)
3. Mrs. Smith class put on a science fair. (Mrs. Smith's)

Writing Wrap-Up

Writing Tip: Explain that reviews are often read by people who weren't at the event. Have students use enough details so readers will get a clear picture of the event. See Blackline Master 2–5 for a sample review.

TECHNOLOGY CONNECTION

Students may want to use a prepared news article format on available software to write their review.

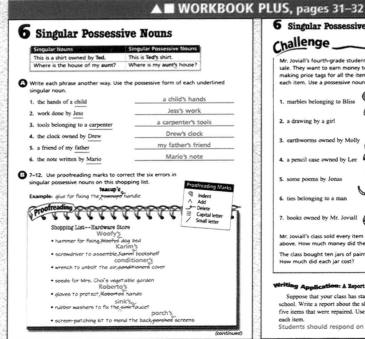

● RETEACHING WORKBOOK, page 19

6 Singular Possessive Nouns

- A **possessive** noun is a noun that shows ownership.
- To form the possessive of a singular noun, add an apostrophe and *-s* ('s).

Singular Nouns	Singular Possessive Nouns
This book belongs to **Joan**.	This is **Joan's** book.
The dog the **boy** owns is here.	The **boy's** dog is here.
These drawings by **Tim** are pretty.	**Tim's** drawings are pretty.
The voice of the **singer** boomed.	The **singer's** voice boomed.

Write the possessive form of each underlined singular noun to complete each group of words.

Example: the garden of a man — a **man's** garden

1. the song of the canary — the canary's song
2. the den of a fox — a fox's den
3. the apple tree owned by my neighbor — my neighbor's apple tree
4. the horses owned by Grandmother — Grandmother's horses
5. the smile of this child — this child's smile
6. the shadow of Donna — Donna's shadow
7. a bowling trophy won by my father — my father's bowling trophy
8. the secretary of Mrs. Sheen — Mrs. Sheen's secretary
9. a wing of that bird — that bird's wing
10. the computer owned by Chris — Chris's computer
11. the tail of a donkey — a donkey's tail
12. a tractor belonging to the farmer — the farmer's tractor
13. the brown eyes of the puppy — the puppy's brown eyes
14. the palace of a princess — a princess's palace
15. the science project owned by Zina — Zina's science project
16. the office of Dr. Lee — Dr. Lee's office

▲■ WORKBOOK PLUS, pages 31–32

6 Singular Possessive Nouns

Singular Nouns	Singular Possessive Nouns
This is a shirt owned by **Ted**.	This is **Ted's** shirt.
Where is the house of my **aunt**?	Where is my **aunt's** house?

A Write each phrase another way. Use the possessive form of each underlined singular noun.

1. the hands of a child — a child's hands
2. work done by Jess — Jess's work
3. tools belonging to a carpenter — a carpenter's tools
4. the clock owned by Drew — Drew's clock
5. a friend of my father — my father's friend
6. the note written by Mario — Mario's note

B 7–12. Use proofreading marks to correct the six errors in singular possessive nouns on this shopping list.

Example: *glue for fixing the ~~teacups~~ teacup's handle*

Proofreading Marks
- ¶ Indent
- ∧ Add
- Delete
- ≡ Capital letter
- / Small letter

Proofreading

Shopping List--Hardware Store
- hammer for fixing ~~Woofys~~ Woofy's dog bed
- screwdriver to assemble ~~Karim~~ Karim's bookshelf
- wrench to unbolt the air ~~conditioners~~ conditioner's cover
- seeds for Mrs. Choi's vegetable garden
- gloves to protect ~~Robertos~~ Roberto's hands
- rubber washers to fix the ~~sink~~ sink's faucet
- screen-patching kit to mend the back ~~porches~~ porch's screens

(continued)

6 Singular Possessive Nouns *(continued from page 31)*

Challenge

Mr. Joviall's fourth-grade students at the Perdie Smart School are holding a tag sale. They want to earn money to buy paints for their class. Today they are making price tags for all the items. Help the class by writing a price tag for each item. Use a possessive noun for each tag.

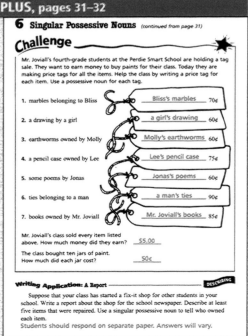

1. marbles belonging to Bliss — Bliss's marbles 70¢
2. a drawing by a girl — a girl's drawing 60¢
3. earthworms owned by Molly — Molly's earthworms 60¢
4. a pencil case owned by Lee — Lee's pencil case 75¢
5. some poems by Jonas — Jonas's poems 60¢
6. ties belonging to a man — a man's ties 90¢
7. books owned by Mr. Joviall — Mr. Joviall's books 85¢

Mr. Joviall's class sold every item listed above. How much money did they earn? $5.00

The class bought ten jars of paint. How much did each jar cost? 50¢

Writing Application: A Report DESCRIBING

Suppose that your class has started a fix-it shop for other students in your school. Write a report about the shop for the school newspaper. Describe at least five items that were repaired. Use a singular possessive noun to tell who owned each item.
Students should respond on separate paper. Answers will vary.

Plural Possessive Nouns

Lesson Objectives

Students will:

- form plural possessive nouns
- proofread for plural possessive nouns
- write a program of events, using plural possessive nouns

One-Minute Warm-Up Have a volunteer write the sentences on the board, showing the correct placement of the apostrophe. Ask how students decided where to place the apostrophe.

Focus on Instruction

Remind students that some nouns are spelled the same in the singular and plural, such as *deer* and *moose*. Emphasize that in these cases, the singular possessive form and the plural possessive form are the same.

Try It Out

LISTENING AND SPEAKING Have volunteers read the phrases, first as written and then using possessive nouns. Have students pause at the end of each phrase, allowing time for volunteers to write the possessive noun they hear. Have students check the possessive nouns for proper spelling and punctuation.

FOR STUDENTS ACQUIRING ENGLISH

- Have students listen to the Try It Out sentences on the audiotape. Distribute SAE Practice page for Unit 2, Lesson 7, to support listening.
- Review plurals, including irregulars and those that change from *y* to *-ies* by having teams of students generate lists and quiz each other. The tape asks "Whose ______ are these?" and students write the answer. Again, discourage students from using *of* instead of the possessive. In the second part, students listen and add the apostrophe.
  1. (drawing of 2 girls in soccer uniforms) (the girls' uniforms)
  2. (drawing of 2 puppies with long ears) (the puppies' ears)
  3. the two coaches rules (coaches')
  4. my four cousins house (cousins')

Grammar/Mechanics

7 Plural Possessive Nouns

One-Minute Warm-Up This lost-and-found ad is missing an apostrophe. Where should the apostrophe go?

My kittens are lost. If you see them please call the kittens owner at 555-4072.

Sometimes you may want to show ownership by more than one person or thing.

- When a plural noun ends with *-s*, add an apostrophe (').

pumpkins owned by the boys	the boys' pumpkins
eyes of the puppies	the puppies' eyes

- When a plural noun does not end with *-s*, add an apostrophe and *-s* ('s).

antlers of both deer	both deer's antlers
reports by these men	these men's reports

Singular	Singular Possessive	Plural	Plural Possessive
animal	animal's	animals	animals'
pony	pony's	ponies	ponies'
class	class's	classes	classes'
mouse	mouse's	mice	mice's
deer	deer's	deer	deer's

Try It Out

Speak Up What is another way to make each group of words show ownership? Use the possessive form of the underlined noun.

1. canoe of two <u>women</u>
2. tails of some <u>deer</u>
3. poems by four <u>authors</u>
4. saddles of these <u>ponies</u>
5. cage of both <u>mice</u>
6. rules of many <u>coaches</u>

1. two women's canoe 2. some deer's tails 3. four authors' poems 4. these ponies' saddles 5. both mice's cage 6. many coaches' rules

Meeting Individual Needs

RETEACHING
Alternative Strategy

- Write this recipe on the board:
  Party Crunch
  10 lions' claws
  5 bats' wings.
- Point out that *lions'* and *bats'* are nouns that show ownership. Circle the apostrophe in each word. Tell students that plural nouns ending in *-s* add an apostrophe to show ownership.
- Ask volunteers to suggest other ingredients for the recipe. As you write responses, have students tell where to place the apostrophe.

CHALLENGE

Ask students to write a poem using four plural nouns. Have them exchange poems and revise their partner's poem by changing the plural nouns to plural possessive nouns.

FOR STUDENTS ACQUIRING ENGLISH

Use gestures to indicate multiple girls and write *the girls' books* on the board. Continue with *boys', friends'*, and *students'* and then with *children's, men's*, and *women's*. Ask what is different.

On Your Own

Write each phrase, using the possessive form of the underlined noun.

Example: reports by three students *three students' reports*

7. horns of several oxen oxen's horns
8. duties of both pilots pilots' duties
9. trucks belonging to these women women's trucks
10. reports by three students students' reports
11. antlers of some moose moose's antlers
12. tents owned by two families families' tents
13. awards of two actresses actresses' awards

14–18. This program for a pet show has five incorrect plural possessive nouns. Write the program correctly. Incorrect words are underlined.

Example: The two judges tables faced the ring.
The two judges' tables faced the ring.

Proofreading

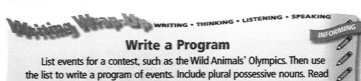

PET COMPETITION
Order of Events

2:00 The judges announce the finalists. Several childrens' pets will compete in each event. children's

2:15 Four dogs's barks are judged for the Most Annoying award. dogs'

2:30 Five mices' skills are tested in the Run the Maze contest. mice's

2:45 Three canaries's songs are judged for the Most Musical award. canaries'

3:00 The winning pets' prizes are presented. Their owners pictures will be taken with their pets. owners'

Writing Wrap-Up
WRITING • THINKING • LISTENING • SPEAKING

INFORMING

Write a Program

List events for a contest, such as the Wild Animals' Olympics. Then use the list to write a program of events. Include plural possessive nouns. Read your program to a partner. Check the possessive nouns together.

For Extra Practice see page 94.

Summing Up Help students summarize these key points about the lesson:

To form the possessive of a plural noun that ends with *-s,* add only an apostrophe. To form the possessive of a plural noun that does not end with *-s,* add an apostrophe and *-s.*

You may want to have students complete the parts related to this lesson on Blackline Master 2–3.

On Your Own

Remind students that they can often determine how to make a noun plural by asking whether or not it ends with an *s*.

MEETING INDIVIDUAL NEEDS

FOR STUDENTS ACQUIRING ENGLISH

Distribute SAE Practice page for Unit 2, Lesson 7. First, students write the possessive form of the plural nouns. Then they correct errors.

1. cars belonging to both families (both families' cars)
2. The sheeps' tails were moving. (sheep's)

Writing Wrap-Up

Writing Tip: Suggest that students close their eyes and visualize events in their contest before they write. See Blackline Master 2–5 for a sample program.

TECHNOLOGY CONNECTION

Students may want to use available software to create columns in their programs for the event, time, and so on.

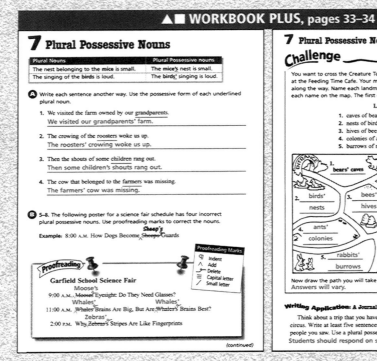

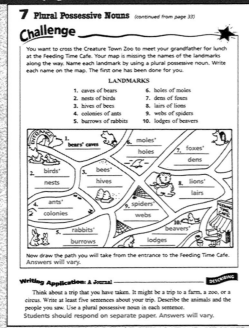

● RETEACHING WORKBOOK, page 20

7 Plural Possessive Nouns

- When a plural noun ends with *s,* add an apostrophe (') to form the possessive.
- When a plural noun does not end with *s,* add an apostrophe and *-s* ('s) to form the possessive.

Plural Nouns	Plural Possessive Nouns
books of these **children**	these **children's** books
chickens owned by **farmers**	**farmers'** chickens

Write the possessive form of each underlined plural noun to complete each group of words.

Example: hats owned by the clowns — the clowns' hats

1. the eyes of men — the men's eyes
2. teachers of our classes — our classes' teachers
3. the cries of many babies — many babies' cries
4. the gray fur of mice — the mice's gray fur
5. new shoes belonging to these girls — these girls' new shoes
6. the clucking of the hens — the hens' clucking
7. a toy owned by the children — the children's toy
8. the den of those foxes — those foxes' den
9. loud honks made by these geese — these geese's loud honks
10. the gloves owned by both boys — both boys' gloves
11. tails of some calves — some calves' tails
12. recipes made by my uncles — my uncles' recipes
13. notebooks belonging to the women — the women's notebooks
14. lovely wings of the butterflies — the butterflies' lovely wings
15. mother of these deer — these deer's mother
16. the wool of those sheep — those sheep's wool

▲■ WORKBOOK PLUS, pages 33–34

7 Plural Possessive Nouns

Plural Nouns	Plural Possessive nouns
The nest belonging to the **mice** is small.	The **mice's** nest is small.
The singing of the **birds** is loud.	The **birds'** singing is loud.

A Write each sentence another way. Use the possessive form of each underlined plural noun.

1. We visited the farm owned by our grandparents.
We visited our grandparents' farm.
2. The crowing of the roosters woke us up.
The roosters' crowing woke us up.
3. Then the shouts of some children rang out.
Then some children's shouts rang out.
4. The cow that belonged to the farmers was missing.
The farmers' cow was missing.

B 5–8. The following poster for a science fair schedule has four incorrect plural possessive nouns. Use proofreading marks to correct the nouns.

Example: 8:00 A.M. How Dogs Become ~~Sheeps'~~ Sheep's Guards

Proofreading Marks
¶ Indent
∧ Add
Delete
≡ Capital letter
/ Small letter

Proofreading

Garfield School Science Fair

9:00 A.M. ~~Mooses'~~ Moose's Eyesight: Do They Need Glasses?

11:00 A.M. ~~Whales~~ Whales' Brains Are Big, But Are ~~Whales's~~ Whales' Brains Best?

2:00 P.M. Why ~~Zebras's~~ Zebras' Stripes Are Like Fingerprints

(continued)

7 Plural Possessive Nouns *(continued from page 33)*

Challenge

You want to cross the Creature Town Zoo to meet your grandfather for lunch at the Feeding Time Cafe. Your map is missing the names of the landmarks along the way. Name each landmark by using a plural possessive noun. Write each name on the map. The first one has been done for you.

LANDMARKS

1. caves of bears
2. nests of birds
3. hives of bees
4. colonies of ants
5. burrows of rabbits
6. holes of moles
7. dens of foxes
8. lairs of lions
9. webs of spiders
10. lodges of beavers

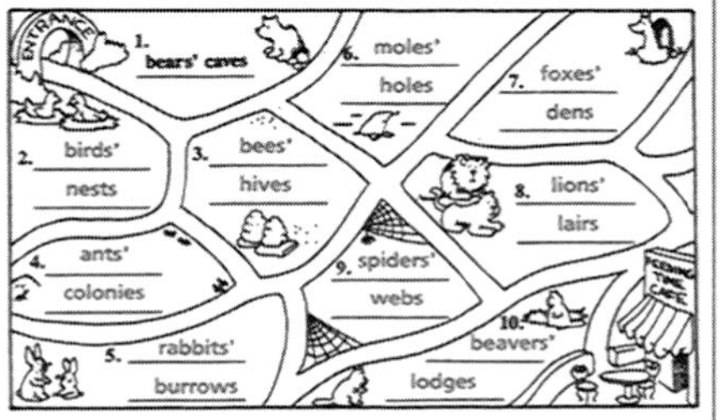

Now draw the path you will take from the entrance to the Feeding Time Cafe.
Answers will vary.

Writing Application: A Journal DESCRIBING

Think about a trip that you have taken. It might be a trip to a farm, a zoo, or a circus. Write at least five sentences about your trip. Describe the animals and the people you saw. Use a plural possessive noun in each sentence.
Students should respond on separate paper. Answers will vary.

Using Exact Nouns

Lesson Objective

Students will:

- replace weak nouns with exact nouns

Focus on Instruction

- Have students read the introductory paragraph and the examples. Point out that *frog* replaces *pet* in the second example sentence.
- Discuss with students what information the noun *frog* conveys that *pet* does not. (*Frog* describes a particular kind of pet.) Ask students how the exact noun improves the sentence. (It gives the reader a better picture of what is happening.)

Apply It

Have students complete the activity independently. Remind students to choose words that fit the sentence context. Have volunteers read their revised journal entry. Ask students how the new entry makes the writing clearer and easier to understand.

If students have difficulty thinking of more exact words to use in the journal entry, have them work with partners to brainstorm possible words they might use.

Have students find places in their own writing where they can use more exact nouns.

Sample Answers to Apply It

1. house
2. parents
3. spaghetti
4. shirt
5. yo-yo
6. dogs
7. tulips
8. table

FOR STUDENTS ACQUIRING ENGLISH

Write these nouns on the board: *dog, roses.* Have the students use them to replace the underlined words in the following sentence: *My pet dug up my aunt's plants.* (dog, roses)

Revising Strategies — Vocabulary

Using Exact Nouns

When you write, it is important to use exact nouns. Using exact nouns will make your writing clearer and easier to understand.

Less exact noun: My pet likes to sit on my shoulder.

More exact noun: My frog likes to sit on my shoulder.

Apply It

1–8. Rewrite this journal entry. Change the underlined nouns to more exact nouns. See TE margin for sample answers.

Revising

July 6

My aunt has a big place on top of a hill. My family and I went there for dinner to celebrate my cousin Jeff's birthday. The food was delicious. I got sauce on my clothes. My aunt brought out a birthday cake for Jeff. He cut pieces for everyone. I gave Jeff a great new toy.

Afterward, Jeff and I went outside to play with his three animals. They ran into the garden and ruined some of my aunt's flowers. They also knocked down my aunt's outdoor furniture. Boy, were we in trouble!

80 Unit 2: Nouns

Meeting Individual Needs

● RETEACHING WORKBOOK, page 21

Using Exact Nouns

- Use exact nouns to make your writing clearer, more interesting, and easier to understand.

The ~~vegetables~~ tomatoes are ripe.

tales	nature
essays	poems
speeches	adventures
novel	poet
author	

Replace each underlined noun with a more exact noun from the box. Be sure the meaning of the word fits the meaning of the sentence.

Example: Jean reads things to her little sister.
Jean reads fairy tales to her little sister.

Revising

1. Jack London wrote works about the outdoors.
Jack London wrote tales about the outdoors.
2. Emily Dickinson wrote short rhymes about familiar subjects.
Emily Dickinson wrote short poems about familiar subjects.
3. Gwendolyn Brooks is a writer who is known for her vivid rhymes.
Gwendolyn Brooks is a poet who is known for her vivid rhymes.
4. Abraham Lincoln gave many talks.
Abraham Lincoln gave many speeches.
5. Sandra Cisneros is a talented writer of stories about Mexico.
Sandra Cisneros is a talented author of stories about Mexico.
6. Robert Frost's poems reflect his interest in the outdoors.
Robert Frost's poems reflect his interest in nature.
7. Ralph Waldo Emerson wrote poetry and works.
Ralph Waldo Emerson wrote poetry and essays.
8. Early American explorers often wrote about their trips.
Early American explorers often wrote about their adventures.

▲■ WORKBOOK PLUS, page 35

Using Exact Nouns

Vibrant red ~~flowers~~ poppies carpeted the field.

1–10. Replace each underlined noun in this journal entry with a more exact noun from each pair of words in the box. Be sure the meaning of the noun you choose fits the meaning of the sentence.

friends	kids	jackets	shoes
Mount Pine	Lake Vista	breeze	oxygen
songs	adventures	deer	camel
canoe	sailboat	cliff	riverbank
ocean	creek	apples	carrots

Revising

Every summer some ~~children~~ friends and I go to camp at ~~the lake~~ Lake Vista. We look forward to many exciting ~~things~~ adventures every summer. Paddling a ~~boat~~ canoe on the ~~water~~ creek is a real challenge. The morning air is chilly, so everyone wears warm ~~clothes~~ jackets. The ~~air~~ breeze feels cool and refreshing as we race along the rapids. From time to time someone spots ~~animals~~ deer on the shore. At noontime we make our way to the ~~edge~~ riverbank and climb ashore. We listen to the song of a cardinal as we munch on the ~~fruit~~ apples that we brought for lunch. I can't think of a more perfect summer day!

Enrichment

Plan Your Own Mall

Plan a new shopping mall for young people. First, write the name of the mall on a sheet of paper. Then list the names of the stores in alphabetical order. Use some singular and plural possessive nouns in the store names, such as Bob's Bikes or Girls' Sneakers. List some things that will be sold in each store. Finally, make a map of an imaginary town. Show where your mall will be located.

A Biographical Dictionary

A biographical dictionary lists famous people and tells what they are known for. Make your own biographical dictionary. Think of at least five famous people. List their names in alphabetical order as in the example below. Write a sentence explaining why each person is famous.

Jackie Robinson

Robinson, Jackie. He was an outstanding baseball player who opened up major-league baseball to African Americans.

Washington, George. He was the first president of the United States.

Challenge Find out more about one of the people in your dictionary who especially interests you. Write a paragraph about the person and add it to your dictionary as a special feature.

Enrichment 81

FOR STUDENTS ACQUIRING ENGLISH

- Have students write these store names in alphabetical order: *Bob's Boots, Cathy's Cats, Annie's Albums, Doug's Dogs*. Have them make up a name for their own store and use it in this sentence: *My store is called* ______.
- Have them illustrate their sentences, encouraging them to add as many words as possible in a caption.

Enrichment

Objectives

Students will:

- use singular and plural possessive nouns as they plan their mall
- use proper nouns in a list of names for a biographical dictionary

Using the Activities

The Enrichment page provides fun, creative activities that reinforce students' understanding and use of nouns. The activities are designed to be enjoyed by all students. Here are some ideas for using the activities.

- Pair students who need extra support with more capable classmates.
- Students can work with these activities in class after they have completed other assignments.
- Activities that can be completed individually can be assigned as homework.

Focus on the Activities

PLAN YOUR OWN MALL

- This activity can be carried out by several small groups working in sequence. One group can design the layout of the mall, another can plan the names of the shops, and a third group can compile the alphabetical listing to be displayed in the mall.
- You might want to plan a bulletin board that brings together all the groups' work on the mall.

A BIOGRAPHICAL DICTIONARY

- Students might compile a class biographical dictionary. Provide students with note cards and reference materials, such as biographies and encyclopedias. If the Internet is available to your students, they can search it for information. Refer students to page H43 for help with using the Internet.
- Tell students to describe one person per note card. Once the note cards are completed, students can combine all cards, alphabetize them, and use binder rings to attach them.

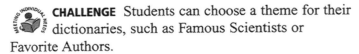

CHALLENGE Students can choose a theme for their dictionaries, such as Famous Scientists or Favorite Authors.

Unit 2 Checkup Lessons 1–7

Checkup

Objectives

Students will:
- identify and correctly write nouns, common nouns, and proper nouns
- identify and correctly write singular and plural nouns

Using the Checkup

Use the Checkup exercises as assessment, as review for the unit test, as extra practice, or as a diagnostic aid to help determine those students who need reteaching.

INTERNET CONNECTION The Wacky Web Tales® at www.eduplace.com/tales/ are cloze stories that students complete, using designated parts of speech. Students may choose any word to fill in a blank as long as it is the correct part of speech. As a result, the completed stories are often amusing, even "wacky," depending on the specific words chosen. Most of the stories at this Web site are student submissions.

INTERNET CONNECTION Students can take an interactive quiz for this unit at www.eduplace.com/kids/hme/ and then get immediate feedback.

Answers

What Is a Noun?

1. Greenland, island, world
2. part, miles, Canada
3. weather, island
4. people, fish, seals, food
5. Women, clothes, holidays

Common and Proper Nouns

6. C.N.—report
   P.N.—Pam, Robbie, Gulf of Mexico
7. C.N.—library, books
   P.N.—Kara
8. C.N.—class
   P.N.—Gulf Stream
9. C.N.—stream
   P.N.—Benjamin Franklin
10. C.N.—water, sun
    P.N.—Gulf Stream

Singular and Plural Nouns

11. ranger—sing.
12. jobs—pl.
13. fires—pl.
14. branches—pl.
15. axes—pl.
16. pass—sing.

Nouns Ending with *y*

17. hobbies
18. plays
19. stories
20. trolleys
21. delays

More Plural Nouns

22. men
23. feet
24. oxen
25. deer
26. mice
27. sheep

Checkup: Unit 2

See TE margin for answers.

1 What Is a Noun? *(p. 64)* Write the nouns in each sentence.

1. Greenland is the largest island in the world.
2. One part is only ten miles from Canada.
3. The weather is usually cold on the island.
4. The people catch fish and seals for food.
5. Women wear traditional clothes on holidays.

2 Common and Proper Nouns *(p. 66)* Write the common nouns in these sentences in one list. Write the proper nouns in another list.

6. Pam and Robbie wrote a report about the Gulf of Mexico.
7. Kara went to the library to get some books.
8. Her class is learning about the Gulf Stream.
9. This stream was named by Benjamin Franklin.
10. The water in the Gulf Stream is warmed by the hot sun.

3 Singular and Plural Nouns *(p. 70)* Write the correct form of the noun in ( ) to complete each sentence. Label the noun *singular* or *plural*.

11. Mr. Graves is a forest ____. (ranger)
12. Reporting forest fires is one of the ____ of a ranger. (job)
13. Mr. Graves reports all forest ____ quickly. (fire)
14. Rangers clear away lots of dead ____. (branch)
15. Many bulldozers and ____ are used to clear forests. (ax)
16. People get a ____ to some special sights from the rangers. (pass)

4 Nouns Ending with *y* *(p. 72)* Write the plural form of the noun in ( ) to complete each sentence.

17. Acting is one of my favorite ____. (hobby)
18. I was in two school ____ last year. (play)
19. One play is made from three short ____. (story)
20. Two people in one story ride ____ to work. (trolley)
21. They talk during ____ on the trolley. (delay)

5 More Plural Nouns *(p. 74)* Write the plural form of the noun in ( ) to complete each sentence.

22. In 1850 some ____ were looking for gold. (man)
23. They walked until their ____ were very sore. (foot)
24. Sometimes ____ pulled the wagons. (ox)
25. Often they saw ____ in the distance. (deer)
26. Some field ____ nibbled the supplies of flour and cornmeal. (mouse)
27. Jake kept some ____ near his mine. (sheep)

82 **Unit 2:** Nouns

Go to www.eduplace.com/tales/ for more fun with parts of speech.

28. The ____ shared the work. (woman)
29. The ____ played a simple game with a string and a button. (child)

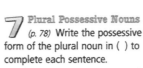

6 Singular Possessive Nouns

(p. 76) Write each group of words another way. Use the possessive forms of each underlined noun.

30. brown horse belonging to Sara
31. shiny saddle on the horse
32. first horse show for Mike
33. cheers of my brother
34. voice of the announcer
35. horse the rider has
36. instructions of the trainer
37. starting point of the jumper
38. notebook of the judge
39. trophy belonging to the winner

Mixed Review 48–54. This newspaper article has two missing capital letters, three incorrect plural nouns, and two incorrect possessive nouns. Write the article correctly.
Incorrect words are underlined.

7 Plural Possessive Nouns

(p. 78) Write the possessive form of the plural noun in ( ) to complete each sentence.

40. Katie and Tyler enjoyed visiting my ____ farm. (grandparents)
41. Grandfather let us pat the ____ noses. (sheep)
42. The ____ coats are brushed every day. (horses)
43. The ____ chores take all day long. (workers)
44. The ____ lunch is hearty. (men)
45. Grandmother gathers the ____ eggs each morning. (chickens)
46. Some ____ nest is underneath the coop. (mice)
47. The ____ honking was heard all over the farm. (geese)

Proofreading Checklist

Did you write these words correctly?
- ✔ proper nouns
- ✔ plural nouns
- ✔ singular possessive nouns
- ✔ plural possessive nouns

Proofreading

Students' Plan Brings Cheer

This year a group of students in the town of waterville [Waterville] decided to make their thanksgiving [Thanksgiving] more meaningful. Mrs. Brown [Mrs. Brown's] fourth graders came up with a plan. The childrens' [children's] idea was to provide holiday meals for people in need.

The students collected twenty-five boxs [boxes] of groceries from men and women in their neighborhoods. Local stores also donated twelve frozen turkies [turkeys]. All of the students' efforts made the holiday a happier one for many familys [families].

See www.eduplace.com/kids/hme/ for an online quiz.

Objectives

Students will:
- write the correct form of singular and plural possessive nouns
- proofread for correct noun usage

Answers *continued*

28. women
29. children

Singular Possessive Nouns

30. Sara's brown horse
31. the horse's shiny saddle
32. Mike's first horse show
33. my brother's cheers
34. the announcer's voice
35. the rider's horse
36. the trainer's instructions
37. the jumper's starting point
38. the judge's notebook
39. the winner's trophy

Plural Possessive Nouns

40. grandparents'
41. sheep's
42. horses'
43. workers'
44. men's
45. chickens'
46. mice's
47. geese's

Test Practice

Objective

Students will:

- practice completing a test format that requires them to choose the correct item among four

Using the Test Practice

These Test Practice pages provide practice with common formats used in standardized or multiple-choice tests.

The first page works with skills taught in the basic lessons in Unit 2. The second page works with skills taught in Units 1 and 2.

Focus on the Test Format

- Have a volunteer read the test directions aloud. Ask another volunteer to explain what the directions ask students to do.
- Point out that each sentence contains an underlined word or group of words. Explain that the words below the sentences are choices for word substitutions.
- Tell students to read each sentence, then read it three more times substituting each choice of words. After they have reviewed each choice, have them choose the correct sentence.
- After students choose their answer, have them find the letter that appears next to the correct word choice. Tell them that they should write this letter as their answer.

FOR STUDENTS ACQUIRING ENGLISH

Review common and proper nouns, endings for plurals, and irregulars. Then review singular and plural possessives. Distribute the SAE Test Practice pages for Unit 2. Have a volunteer read the directions aloud for each section. In the first section, students circle the answer that is the best way to fix the underlined part, or if the sentence is correct, they circle the last answer. In the second section, they find the sentence that corresponds to each number and circle the best way to fix the sentence. If the sentence on the page is correct, they circle the last answer.

Assessment Link

Test Practice

Write the numbers 1–8 on a sheet of paper. Choose the best way to write the underlined part of each sentence. Write the letter for that answer. If there is no mistake, write the letter for the last answer.

1 My little sister loves frilly dressies.
A dresses
B dresss
C dress's
D (No mistakes)

2 Uncle Kevin tells the best storys!
F story
G story's
H stories
J (No mistakes)

3 That carpenter's belt holds lots of tools.
A carpenters
B carpenteres
C carpenters'
D (No mistakes)

4 The dentist carefully checked all of Morgan's tooth.
F tooths
G teeth
H teeths
J (No mistakes)

5 All of the actors' costumes are too big for them.
A actor's
B actors
C actor
D (No mistakes)

6 You wouldn't want to swim in the icy waters of crater lake!
F Crater lake
G crater Lake
H Crater Lake
J (No mistakes)

7 The store sells mattresses.
A mattress's
B mattressies
C mattress
D (No mistakes)

8 Marcos stared at the Statue of liberty.
F Statue of Liberty
G statue of liberty
H statue of Liberty
J (No mistakes)

84 Unit 2: Nouns

Now write the numbers 9–14 on your paper. Write the letter of the best way to write each sentence.

[9]Deer were becoming a real problem in our town. [10]They wandered into peoples yards and ate the flowers. [11]One day aunt jane got an idea from a gardening magazine. [12]She hung many bar of soap around her garden. [13]Her plan worked the deer are staying away. [14]Now mooses are her only problem.

9 **A** Deers were becoming a real problem in our town.
B Deers was becoming a real problem in our town.
C Deer was becoming a real problem in our town.
(D) Best as it is

10 **(F)** They wandered into people's yards and ate the flowers.
G They wandered into people yards and ate the flowers.
H They wandered into peoples' yards and ate the flowers.
J Best as it is

11 **A** One day Aunt jane got an idea from a gardening magazine.
(B) One day Aunt Jane got an idea from a gardening magazine.
C One day aunt Jane got an idea from a gardening magazine.
D Best as it is

12 **(F)** She hung many bars of soap around her garden.
G She hung many bar's of soap around her garden.
H She hung many Bars of Soap around her garden.
J Best as it is

13 **A** Her plan worked. the deer are staying away.
B Her plan worked? The deer are staying away.
(C) Her plan worked. The deer are staying away.
D Best as it is

14 **F** Now meese are her only problem.
(G) Now moose are her only problem.
H Now moose is her only problem.
J Best as it is

Test Practice

Objective

Students will:

- practice completing a test format that requires them to choose the correct sentence among four

Focus on the Test Format

- Have a volunteer read the test directions aloud. Ask another volunteer to explain what the directions ask students to do.
- Have students read the paragraph. Point out that each sentence in the paragraph is numbered, and that the numbers correspond to the items below.
- Remind students that the vertical line breaks the text into columns, and to read the left-hand column before reading the right-hand column.
- Point out that each numbered item gives three possible ways to word each sentence in the paragraph, and that the last choice is always "Best as it is."
- After students choose their answer, have them find the letter that appears next to the correct sentence. Tell them that they should write this letter as their answer.

Cumulative Review

Objectives

Students will:
- distinguish sentences from sentence fragments
- distinguish between statements, questions, commands, and exclamations
- identify subjects, predicates, simple subjects, and simple predicates
- write sentences with correct punctuation
- distinguish between common and proper nouns

Using the Cumulative Review

This Cumulative Review provides cumulative practice with basic grammar, usage, and mechanics skills taught in Units 1 and 2. You can use these pages for assessment, as a review for a test, as extra practice, or as a diagnostic aid to determine those students who may need reteaching.

INTERNET CONNECTION Send your students to www.eduplace.com/kids/hme/ for a tricky question related to usage or spelling.

Answers

Sentences

1. My family and I ski each winter.—statement
2. not a sentence
3. Cross-country skiing is hard work.—statement
4. How thirsty you get!—exclamation
5. Have you ever skied downhill?—question
6. What a thrill it is!—exclamation
7. not a sentence
8. Practice on the small hill.—command
9. Would you like some help?—question
10. Watch the instructor.—command

Subjects and Predicates

11. This book | is about insects.
12. Most bees | are social insects.
13. They | live in groups.
14. The bees | live on food from plants.
15. Colorful flowers | attract the bees.
16. Beekeepers | raise bees for honey.

Cumulative Review

See TE margin for answers.

Unit 1: The Sentence

Sentences *(pp. 32, 36, 38)* If a group of words below is a sentence, copy it correctly. If not, write *not a sentence.* Label each sentence *statement, question, command,* or *exclamation.*

1. my family and I ski each winter
2. my skis, boots, and poles
3. cross-country skiing is hard work
4. how thirsty you get
5. have you ever skied downhill
6. what a thrill it is
7. near the trees
8. practice on the small hill
9. would you like some help
10. watch the instructor

Subjects and Predicates *(pp. 40, 42, 44)* Write each sentence. Draw a line between the complete subject and the complete predicate. Then underline each simple subject once. Underline each simple predicate twice.

11. This book is about insects.
12. Most bees are social insects.
13. They live in groups.
14. The bees live on food from plants.
15. Colorful flowers attract the bees.
16. Beekeepers raise bees for honey.

Run-on Sentences *(p. 46)* Rewrite each run-on sentence correctly.

17. Our class visited a museum it is on Oak Street.
18. The museum is in the heart of the city I had never been there.
19. Some teachers went to the museum they liked the Navajo art.
20. The paintings were very old we had learned about them in class.
21. The blankets were colorful Robin liked their beautiful patterns.

Unit 2: Nouns

Kinds of Nouns *(pp. 64, 66)* Write the fifteen nouns in these sentences. Label each noun *common* or *proper.*

22. Mr. Grasso and his family flew over the Rocky Mountains.
23. David and Jessica saw rivers, plains, and cities.
24. Their grandparents live in San Francisco.

86 **Unit 2:** Nouns   See www.eduplace.com/kids/hme/ for a tricky usage or spelling question.

Run-on Sentences

17. Our class visited a museum. It is on Oak Street.
18. The museum is in the heart of the city. I had never been there.
19. Some teachers went to the museum. They liked the Navajo art.
20. The paintings were very old. We had learned about them in class.
21. The blankets were colorful. Robin liked their beautiful patterns.

Kinds of Nouns

22. Mr. Grasso—p., family—c., Rocky Mountains—p.
23. David—p., Jessica—p., rivers—c., plains—c., cities—c.
24. grandparents—c., San Francisco—p.

25. Grandpa was at the airport.
26. The children and their parents enjoyed California.

Singular and Plural Nouns *(pp. 70, 72, 74)* Write the plural form of each singular noun.

27. joke
28. child
29. hunch
30. wax
31. journey
32. tooth
33. hobby
34. woman

Singular Possessive Nouns *(p. 76)* Write the possessive form of the noun in ( ) for each sentence.

35. My ______ drama club put on a play. (sister)
36. ______ scenery was great. (Kim)
37. The ______ costumes were terrific. (cast)
38. The ______ helper collected the props. (director)
39. I laughed at the ______ entrance. (captain)
40. His voice sounded like a ______ roar. (lion)
41. That ______ song was the best in the show. (man)

Plural Possessive Nouns *(p. 78)* Write the possessive form of the noun in ( ) for each sentence.

42. My twin ______ birthday party was yesterday. (brothers)
43. Everyone went to our ______ house to ride the ponies. (neighbors)
44. The ______ manes were tied with ribbons. (ponies)
45. The ______ games were fun! (children)
46. We made ______ tails out of colored paper. (donkeys)
47. Adam tied on the ______ blindfolds. (girls)
48. My ______ friend made the birthday cake. (parents)

Objectives

Students will:

- write the correct plural form for singular nouns
- write the correct possessive form for singular nouns
- write the correct possessive form for plural nouns

Answers *continued*

25. Grandpa—p., airport—c.
26. children—c., parents—c., California—p.

Singular and Plural Nouns

27. jokes
28. children
29. hunches
30. waxes
31. journeys
32. teeth
33. hobbies
34. women

Singular Possessive Nouns

35. sister's
36. Kim's
37. cast's
38. director's
39. captain's
40. lion's
41. man's

Plural Possessive Nouns

42. brothers'
43. neighbors'
44. ponies'
45. children's
46. donkeys'
47. girls'
48. parents'

What Is a Noun?

Objectives

Students will:

- supply the missing nouns for sentences
- identify the nouns in a sentence
- write sentences, identifying the nouns in them

Using the Extra Practice

The Extra Practice activities provide additional practice for the basic lesson at three levels of difficulty: Easy (●), Average (▲), and Challenging (■).

The Extra Practice activities can be used in the following ways.

- Assign activities according to students' needs and abilities as homework after students have completed the basic lesson.
- Assign the Easy activities after using the lesson Reteaching instruction.
- Assign the Average activities to prepare students for the Checkup.
- Assign the Easy and/or Average activities to students who had difficulty with specific lessons on the Checkup.
- Assign the Challenging exercises as a Bonus activity.

Extra Practice

(pages 64–65)

1 What Is a Noun?

- A noun is a word that names a person, a place, or a thing.

Remember

● One of the underlined words in each sentence is a noun. Write each underlined noun.

Example: Justin learned about underwater volcanoes. *Justin*

1. First, the floor of the ocean shakes. floor
2. Then a long crack appears. crack
3. Melted rock pushes up through the crack. rock
4. It comes from deep inside the earth. earth
5. The volcano gets larger and larger. volcano
6. Finally, the tip pushes through the water. tip

▲ Write the two nouns in each sentence.

Example: The students are reading about Indonesia.
students Indonesia

7. The country is located in Asia.
8. Its many islands are on the equator.
9. Many of its great mountains are volcanoes.
10. Tigers live in some of the dark, green jungles.
11. Rice is an important food.
12. Explorers once came searching for valuable spices.

■ Write the nouns in these sentences. Write *person, place,* or *thing* beside each noun.

Example: The Collinses flew to Bermuda in a jet.
Collinses—person Bermuda—place jet—thing

13. Then a taxi took the family to an inn. th., per., pl.
14. Their room had a window facing the ocean. pl., th., pl.
15. Michael noticed that the beach had pink sand! per., pl., th.
16. Sarah read from a magazine for tourists. per., th., per.
17. One story explained how some settlers came to the island. th., per., pl.
18. Their ship crashed on the rocks during a bad storm. th., th., th.

88 **Unit 2:** Nouns

Meeting Individual Needs — More Practice for Lesson 1

● EASY

Write each sentence, using nouns in the blanks. (Sample answers are given.)

1. A (fish) dived into the (sea).
2. An old (man) sold (pies).
3. (Roy) climbed the (hill).
4. Two (keys) were in a (box).
5. The (girl) ran for the (bus).
6. Red (ink) marked the (paper).

▲ AVERAGE

Underline the nouns in each sentence.

1. The workers used a bulldozer to tear down the old building.
2. Is your house on that street?
3. Two boys, three girls, and a man watched the workers.
4. They used tools, cement, and trucks.
5. A park and a pool will be built there.
6. The town will plant trees, flowers, and grass.

■ CHALLENGING

Write a paragraph that tells how you would like your town or neighborhood to change. Tell how the change might take place. When you have finished, underline each noun in your paragraph. Above each noun write *person, place,* or *thing* to show what the noun names.

2 Common and Proper Nouns

(pages 66–67)

Remember

- A common noun names any person, place, or thing.
- A proper noun names a particular person, place, or thing.
- Capitalize proper nouns.

● Write each noun correctly. Next to it, write *common* or *proper*.
Underlined words should be capitalized.

Example: aunt betty *Aunt Betty—proper*

1. africa P
2. maps C
3. henry hudson P
4. statue of liberty P
5. sailor C
6. forest C
7. october P
8. mississippi river P

▲ List the common nouns and the proper nouns. Use capital letters correctly.
CN underlined once, PN twice; PN should be capitalized.

Example: Hikers follow trails through the grand canyon.
common: Hikers proper: Grand Canyon

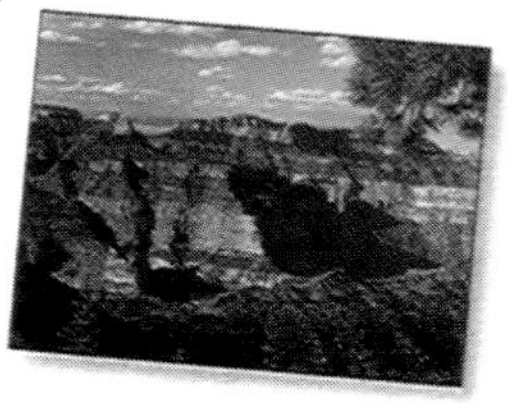

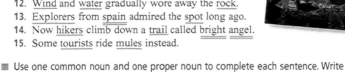

9. Visitors from many states go there daily.
10. The spectacular canyon is located in arizona.
11. Its steep walls were formed by the colorado river.
12. Wind and water gradually wore away the rock.
13. Explorers from spain admired the spot long ago.
14. Now hikers climb down a trail called bright angel.
15. Some tourists ride mules instead.

■ Use one common noun and one proper noun to complete each sentence. Write the sentence correctly. You may add or remove words such as *a, an,* and *the.*
Sample answers are given.

Example: ______ and his ______ are brave explorers!
Henry and his sister are brave explorers!

16. They took a trip with ______ to explore the ______. Paul, valley
17. Henry carefully packed the ______ that ______ gave him. supplies, Serena
18. On ______ they finally arrived at the ______. Monday, trail
19. According to their map, they had to cross ______ to reach ______. a creek, the Grand River
20. They walked along ______ until they saw ______. the riverbank, Mount Blake
21. Henry quickly discovered ______ beside ______. a fossil, the Grand River
22. After climbing ______ they finally reached ______! the Blue Devil Trail, the campground

Common and Proper Nouns

Objectives

Students will:

- distinguish common nouns from proper nouns
- capitalize proper nouns correctly
- name proper nouns that specify common nouns

Using the Extra Practice

The Extra Practice activities provide additional practice for the basic lesson at three levels of difficulty: Easy (●), Average (▲), and Challenging (■).

Meeting Individual Needs

More Practice for Lesson 2

● EASY

Draw one line under each common noun and two lines under each proper noun.

1. The tour visited Philadelphia.
2. The city is the largest in Pennsylvania.
3. It is called the birthplace of the United States.
4. During the Revolutionary War, it was the capital.
5. The Liberty Bell is located in the city.
6. The Declaration of Independence was written in a nearby building.

▲ AVERAGE

Underline the proper nouns and rewrite them correctly.

1. ocean
2. monday (M)
3. july (J)
4. lake erie (L, E)
5. river
6. chicago (C)
7. dan (D)
8. woman

■ CHALLENGING

Write a proper noun for each common noun. Use a social studies textbook or map, if necessary. (Answers will vary.)

1. continent
2. country
3. state
4. city
5. ocean
6. bridge
7. desert
8. island
9. dam
10. river

Singular and Plural Nouns

Objectives

Students will:

- identify singular and plural nouns
- write the plural forms of nouns correctly
- write sentences, using plural nouns as subjects

Using the Extra Practice

The Extra Practice activities provide additional practice for the basic lesson at three levels of difficulty: Easy (●), Average (▲), and Challenging (■).

Extra Practice

(pages 70–71)

3 Singular and Plural Nouns

Remember

- A singular noun names one person, place, or thing.
- A plural noun names more than one person, place, or thing.
- To form plural nouns, add *-s* to most singular nouns. Add *-es* to singular nouns that end with *s, x, ch,* or *sh.*

● Write each underlined noun. Beside it, write *singular* or *plural.*

Example: Mr. Okawa sells peaches at his farm. *peaches—plural*

1. He puts the peaches in large wooden boxes. P
2. Mr. Okawa sells pears too. P
3. My bus passes the farm stand every day. S
4. We often see Mrs. Okawa out trimming her flower bushes. P
5. She has a basket of beautiful pink roses beside her. S
6. Once she gave two bunches of flowers to our bus driver. P

▲ Write the plural form of the noun in ( ) to complete each sentence.

Example: Kayla went to work with her two ______. (uncle) *uncles*

skyscrapers 7. They build ______ in the city. (skyscraper)
sandwiches 8. Kayla took two ______ and a pear for lunch. (sandwich)
bosses 9. Uncle Carl introduced Kayla to both of his ______. (boss)
carpenters 10. Next, Kayla met several ______. (carpenter)
toolboxes 11. They explained how the tools in two ______ worked. (toolbox)
12. A woman hurried by with a box of ______. (paintbrush) paintbrushes

■ If the underlined noun is singular, make it plural. If it is plural, make it singular. Write the new sentence.

Example: Grandmother had her own clothing store in Italy.
Grandmother had her own clothing stores in Italy.

13. She made dresses for Italy's most famous actresses. actress
14. I hoped Grandmother would leave her business in Italy. businesses
15. I wanted her to live with my cousin and me in New York. cousins
16. My wish finally came true! wishes
17. Grandmother arrived with her boxes of beautiful cloth. box
18. Soon she opened her new dress shop downtown. shops

Meeting Individual Needs — More Practice for Lesson 3

● EASY

Write *S* next to singular nouns and *P* next to plural nouns.

1. bunches (P)
2. glass (S)
3. fox (S)
4. faces (P)
5. wish (S)
6. boxes (P)
7. bus (S)
8. classes (P)
9. shovels (P)
10. bush (S)

▲ AVERAGE

Write the plural nouns in each sentence.

1. Branches of the old oak rub against the windows of my room.
2. A family of squirrels lives near the top of the old tree.
3. Their nest is filled with acorns and other nuts.
4. A robin, some wrens, and other birds call back and forth.
5. Two foxes once had a hole underneath the big roots.
6. My dog sleeps in the bushes near their old den.

■ CHALLENGING

Write the plural form of each noun. Then make each plural form the subject of a sentence. (Sentences will vary.)

1. bench (benches)
2. dish (dishes)
3. business (businesses)
4. raccoon (raccoons)
5. ax (axes)
6. customer (customers)

Extra Practice

(pages 72–73)

4 Nouns Ending with *y*

Remember

- If a singular noun ends with a vowel and *y*, add *-s* to make the noun plural.
- If a singular noun ends with a consonant and *y*, make it plural by changing the *y* to *i* and adding *-es*.

● Write the plural nouns in these sentences.

Example: The libraries in our city are closed on holidays.
libraries holidays

1. All the factories are closed as well.
2. Some companies remain open.
3. We can still buy groceries at the corner store.
4. The drugstores will not make any deliveries.
5. The subways do not run very often.
6. The airport runways are busier than usual.

▲ Write each sentence. Use the plural form of the noun in ( ).

Example: Two Presidents have ______ in February. (birthday)
Two Presidents have birthdays in February.

7. Our class performed two short ______ about them. (play) plays
8. Miss Moran read us ______ about both men. (story) stories
9. We learned many facts in just a few ______. (day) days
10. Washington's army had very few ______. (supply) supplies
11. Lincoln carried out his many ______ honestly. (duty) duties
12. He didn't want the northern and southern states to become ______. (enemy) enemies

■ Find the noun in each sentence that should be plural. Write the noun correctly.

Example: Of all the holiday, Thanksgiving is my favorite. *holidays*

13. Dad gets up very early and puts two turkey in the oven. turkeys
14. I watch puffy smoke rise from all the chimney in town. chimneys
15. My sisters and both of their family arrive early. families
16. Then Aunt Rita arrives with two large tray of fruit and cheese. trays
17. Uncle Nate tells long story of when he was a boy. stories
18. My favorite is about the time he lost his three pet donkey. donkeys

Extra Practice 91

Nouns Ending with *y*

Objective

Students will:

- write the plural forms of nouns ending with *y* correctly

Using the Extra Practice

The Extra Practice activities provide additional practice for the basic lesson at three levels of difficulty: Easy (●), Average (▲), and Challenging (■).

Meeting Individual Needs

More Practice for Lesson 4

● EASY

Underline the correct spelling of the word in parentheses.

1. I picked (cherrys, cherries).
2. Both (valleys, vallies) are covered in snow.
3. Three (donkeys, donkies) passed.
4. Both (companys, companies) had offices here.
5. Rock collecting is one of her favorite (hobbys, hobbies).

▲ AVERAGE

Write the plural form of the word in parentheses.

1. We'll need more (berry) to make jam. (berries)
2. (Story) about the past are fun to hear. (Stories)
3. Those (holiday) come in the fall. (holidays)
4. In the end, the two (enemy) became friends. (enemies)
5. Two new (highway) will connect the cities. (highways)

■ CHALLENGING

Write correctly the misspelled noun in each sentence.

1. Three families had partys. (parties)
2. At one party, we told storys and put on plays. (stories)
3. At another, people ate strawberrys and tasted several trays of desserts. (strawberries)
4. At the third party, we rode carts pulled by donkies and ponies. (donkeys)

More Plural Nouns

Objectives

Students will:
- identify the singular form of irregular plural nouns
- identify nouns as either singular or plural
- write the correct plural form of a noun

Using the Extra Practice

The Extra Practice activities provide additional practice for the basic lesson at three levels of difficulty: Easy (●), Average (▲), and Challenging (■).

Extra Practice

(pages 74–75)

5 More Plural Nouns

Remember

- Some nouns have special plural forms.
- Some nouns have the same singular and plural forms.

● Write each underlined noun. Beside it, write *singular* or *plural.*

Example: Some deer are good swimmers. *deer—plural*

1. The farmer uses two oxen to pull his cart. P
2. Six sheep grazed quietly in the meadow. P
3. The men drove tractors through the fields. P
4. The goose honked loudly at some chickens. S
5. Are the children awake yet? P
6. My little pet mouse eats seeds and nuts. S
7. A duck has webbed feet to help it swim. P

▲ Write each sentence correctly. Use the plural form of the noun in ( ).

Example: Two _____ showed us the pioneer village. (woman)
Two women showed us the pioneer village.

8. We saw some _____ working at spinning wheels. (child) children
9. They made thread from the wool of many _____. (sheep) sheep
10. Several _____ were repairing the roof of a barn. (man) men
11. Some surprised _____ hurried across the barnyard. (mouse) mice
12. Two _____ pulled a wagon filled with hay. (ox) oxen
13. A boy gathered eggs that all his _____ had laid. (goose) geese
14. A blacksmith put new shoes on a horse's front _____. (foot) feet

■ Write the correct form of the noun in ( ) for each sentence.

Example: A painting of a _____ was on the wall. (deer) *deer*

15. A picture of some _____ was next to it. (moose) moose
16. Two small _____ played by the fire. (child) children
17. They sat on pillows stuffed with feathers from _____. (goose) geese
18. One child played with a pet white _____. (mouse) mouse
19. Near the window, two _____ played fiddles. (woman) women
20. They tapped their _____ to the music. (foot) feet

Meeting Individual Needs — More Practice for Lesson 5

● EASY

Rewrite each sentence, using the singular form of the noun in parentheses.

1. Do you know a (women) who works in the zoo? (woman)
2. Today she must care for a sick (deer). (deer)
3. It broke its (teeth). (tooth)
4. The zookeeper also cares for the (oxen). (ox)
5. She must not let it step on her (feet)! (foot)

▲ AVERAGE

If a noun below is singular, write *S* and its plural form. If it is plural, write *P* and its singular form.

1. child (S children)
2. men (P man)
3. mice (P mouse)
4. goose (S geese)
5. ox (S oxen)

■ CHALLENGING

If the underlined plural noun is correct, write *C*. If it is not correct, write the correct plural form.

1. Oxes are in the barn. (oxen)
2. A family of mices live in the hay nearby. (mice)
3. Sheeps chew hay happily. (sheep)
4. They have wide flat teeth. (C)
5. Two gooses honk in the barnyard. (geese)

Singular Possessive Nouns

Objectives

Students will:
- identify singular possessive nouns
- form singular possessive nouns correctly
- rewrite sentences, substituting singular possessive nouns for phrases

Using the Extra Practice

The Extra Practice activities provide additional practice for the basic lesson at three levels of difficulty: Easy (●), Average (▲), and Challenging (■).

Extra Practice

6 Singular Possessive Nouns

(pages 76–77)

Remember

- A possessive noun is a noun that shows ownership.
- To form the possessive of a singular noun, add an apostrophe and a *-s* (*'s*).

● Write the possessive form of each singular noun.

Example: brother *brother's*

1. Monica's
2. tiger's
3. singer's
4. Carlos's
5. panda's
6. Chris's
7. mouse's
8. principal's
9. Kenny's
10. coach's
11. Jess's
12. boy's

▲ Write each group of words another way. Use the possessive form of the underlined noun.

Example: paintings by one student
one student's paintings

13. picture painted by Isabel Isabel's picture
14. paintbrushes belonging to Li Li's paintbrushes
15. mask drawn by Julio Julio's mask
16. face of the gorilla the gorilla's face
17. wings of the clay dragon the clay dragon's wings
18. art show of the whole class the whole class's art show

■ Write each sentence another way. Use a possessive noun to take the place of the underlined words.

Example: The club of Jess had a neighborhood circus.
Jess's club had a neighborhood circus.

19. They held their circus in the yard belonging to Mr. Wong. Mr. Wong's yard
20. Posters made by Chris announced the circus. Chris's posters
21. Tickets were designed on a computer owned by Marcus. Marcus's computer
22. Julia made the nose of the elephant from a hose. the elephant's nose
23. The roar of the lion came from a tape recorder. lion's roar
24. The hat belonging to one clown had tin cans on it. One clown's hat
25. A goat owned by Marcy pulled the circus wagon. Marcy's goat

Extra Practice 93

Meeting Individual Needs — More Practice for Lesson 6

● EASY

Write the five possessive nouns in this paragraph.

Donald's garden is a lovely place. Each flower's bright colors are beautiful. Donald grows the family's vegetables. He dug a small goldfish pool near the garden's center. He also has his rabbit's cage in the garden.

▲ AVERAGE

Complete the paragraph by writing the singular possessive form of each noun in parentheses.

Many things are stored in (grandmother) attic. (Uncle Gus) roller skates sit in a corner. Even the (canary) old cage is there. Looking around one day, I found my (dad) old baseball mitt. But the best thing I found was the (family) first radio.

(grandmother's, Uncle Gus's, canary's, dad's, family's)

■ CHALLENGING

Rewrite each sentence, using a possessive noun.

1. The dog belonging to the clown did a flip. (The clown's dog)
2. The plumes on the pony bob up and down. (The pony's plumes)
3. The growl made by the tiger scared me. (The tiger's growl)
4. The dance done by the elephant was amazing! (The elephant's dance)

Plural Possessive Nouns

Objectives

Students will:

- distinguish singular possessive nouns from plural possessive nouns
- use plural possessive nouns in sentences

Using the Extra Practice

The Extra Practice activities provide additional practice for the basic lesson at three levels of difficulty: Easy (●), Average (▲), and Challenging (■).

Extra Practice

(pages 78–79)

7 Plural Possessive Nouns

Remember

- To form the possessive of a plural noun that ends with *-s,* add only an apostrophe (').
- To form the possessive of a plural noun that does not end with *-s,* add an apostrophe and *-s* ('*s*).

● For each pair, write the group of words that has a plural possessive noun.

Example: my teacher's dictionaries
my teachers' dictionaries *my teachers' dictionaries*

1. the butterflies' wings / the butterfly's wings
2. our bosses' notebook / our boss's notebook
3. her brother's snowshoes / her brothers' snowshoes
4. the woman's cameras / the women's cameras

▲ Write the possessive form of the noun in ( ) for each sentence.

Example: The Young ______ Club meets after school. (Farmers) *Farmers'*

5. Everyone learns a lot about ______ habits. (animals) animals'
6. Each year the ______ entries win prizes at the fair. (children) children's
7. Their ______ eggs are the largest in the county! (geese) geese's
8. People always admire the ______ dairy cows. (girls) girls'
9. The ______ ponies win many ribbons. (boys) boys'
10. Judges carefully check the ______ coats. (ponies) ponies'

■ Write the plural possessive form of the singular noun in ( ) to complete each sentence.

Example: Our ______ farm is next to ours. (neighbor)
Our neighbors' farm is next to ours.

11. Their ______ goats often wander onto our lawn. (son) sons'
12. The goats have taken over my ______ job of cutting the grass. (sister) sister
13. Who would like my job of collecting the ______ eggs? (chicken) chickens'
14. Amy makes sweaters from the ______ wool. (sheep) sheep's
15. She makes all the ______ sweaters for the family. (child) children's

94 Unit 2: Nouns

Meeting Individual Needs — More Practice for Lesson 7

● EASY

Write *SP* if a group of words has a singular possessive noun. Write *PP* if a group has a plural possessive noun.

1. the ox's feet (SP)
2. the strawberry's color (SP)
3. the women's club (PP)
4. the neighbors' garden (PP)
5. the bus's seats (SP)
6. the chickens' eggs (PP)

▲ AVERAGE

Rewrite each phrase, using the possessive form of each underlined noun.

1. the boots owned by children (the children's boots)
2. the lunchroom of the teachers (the teachers' lunchroom)
3. the honking made by geese (the geese's honking)
4. the land the people have (the people's land)
5. the trails of many deer (many deer's trails)
6. the smoke from the factories (the factories' smoke)

■ CHALLENGING

Write five sentences that tell about things your class, family, or friends own or have. Use a plural possessive noun in each sentence.

Unit 3 Planning Guide

Verbs

2 1/2 weeks

	Lesson	Checkup (PE)	Extra Practice (PE)	Graphic Organizer (BLM)	Writing Wrap-Up (BLM)	More Practice (TE)	Workbook Plus	Reteaching Workbook	Students Acquiring English Practice Book
1	Action Verbs *(96–97)*	120	125	3–1	3–7	125	36–37	22	33+
2	Main Verbs and Helping Verbs *(98–99)*	120	126	3–1	3–7	126	38–39	23	35+
3	Present, Past, and Future *(100–101)*	120	127	3–2	3–7	127	40–41	24	37+
	Revising Strategies: Sentence Fluency Writing with Verbs *(102–103)*						42–43	25–26	
4	Subject-Verb Agreement *(104–105)*	120	128	3–1	3–7	128	44–45	27	39+
5	Spelling the Present Tense *(106–107)*	120	129	3–3	3–8	129	46–47	28	41+
6	Spelling the Past Tense *(108–109)*	120	130	3–3	3–8	130	48–49	29	43+
7	The Past with Helping Verbs *(110–111)*	120	131	3–2	3–8	131	50–51	30	45+
8	Irregular Verbs *(112–113)*	121	132	3–4	3–8	132	52–53	31	47+
9	The Special Verb *be (114–115)*	121	133	3–5	3–9	133	54–55	32	49+
10	Contractions with *not (116–117)*	121	134	3–6	3–9	134	56–57	33	51+
	Revising Strategies: Vocabulary Using Exact Verbs *(118)*						58	34	
	Enrichment *(119)*								
	Test Practice *(122–124)*								53+

Unit 3

Tools and Tips

- **Diagramming Guide,** *pp. H70–H78*
- **Guide to Capitalization, Punctuation, and Usage,** *pp. H55–H64*

School-Home Connection

Suggestions for informing or involving family members in classroom activities and learning related to this unit are included in the Teacher's Edition throughout the unit.

Meeting Individual Needs

- **FOR SPECIAL NEEDS/INCLUSION:** *Houghton Mifflin English* Audiotape See also Reteaching.
- **FOR STUDENTS ACQUIRING ENGLISH:**
  - Notes and activities are included in this Teacher's Edition throughout the unit to help you adapt or use pupil book activities with students acquiring English.
  - Additional support is available for students at various stages of English proficiency: **Beginning/Preproduction**, **Early Production/Speech Emergence**, and **Intermediate/ Advanced**. See Students Acquiring English Practice Book.
  - Students can listen to the Try It Out activities on audiotape.
- **ENRICHMENT:** *p. 119*

All audiotape recordings are also available on CD.

Daily Language Practice

Each sentence includes two errors based on skills taught in this or previous Grammar units. Each day write one sentence on the chalkboard. Have students find the errors and write the sentence correctly on a sheet of paper. To make the activity easier, identify the kinds of errors.

1. The puppies wants to play in the bushs. The puppies want to play in the bushes. (subject-verb agreement; plural nouns)
2. Zach studys at the Dallas Public library every weekend. Zach studies at the Dallas Public Library every weekend. (present tense; proper nouns)
3. Our dog buryed its dish somewhere in the back yard Our dog buried its dish somewhere in the back yard. (past tense; end punctuation)
4. The coach have listed the players for Saturdays game. Sample: The coach has listed the players for Saturday's game. (subject-verb agreement; possessive nouns)
5. Mark throwed the runner out at first base? Mark threw the runner out at first base. (irregular verbs; end punctuation)
6. The children was eager to put their tooths under their pillows. The children were eager to put their teeth under their pillows. (subject-verb agreement; plural nouns)
7. Haven'nt you opened the jar of cherries yet. Haven't you opened the jar of cherries yet? (contractions; end punctuation)
8. Please dont pick the daisys. Please don't pick the daisies. (contractions; plural nouns)
9. Olivia taked Charles' advice and tried out for the play. Olivia took Charles's advice and tried out for the play. (irregular verbs; possessive nouns)
10. The choir has sang its last song now the band will play. Sample: The choir has sung its last song. Now the band will play. (irregular verbs; run-on sentences)

Additional Resources

Workbook Plus, Unit 3
Reteaching Workbook, Unit 3
Students Acquiring English Practice Book, Unit 3
Transparencies, Unit 3
Teacher's Resource Book
Audiotapes

Technology Tools

INTERNET: http://www.eduplace.com/kids/hme/ *or* http://www.eduplace.com/rdg/hme/

Visit Education Place for these additional support materials and activities:

- tricky usage question
- Wacky Web Tales®
- interactive quizzes
- a proofreading game

Assessment

Test Booklet, Unit 3

Keeping a Journal

Discuss with students the value of keeping a journal as a way of promoting self-expression and fluency. Encourage students to record their thoughts and ideas in a notebook. Inform students whether the journal will be private or will be reviewed periodically as a way of assessing growth. The following prompts may be useful for generating writing ideas.

Journal Prompts

- What is your favorite game or carnival ride? Why?
- Describe how your ideal bedroom would look.
- If you could be any character in a book, who would you be? Why?

Unit 3

Verbs

She raced to the ball, bent her knee, and kicked the ball solidly.

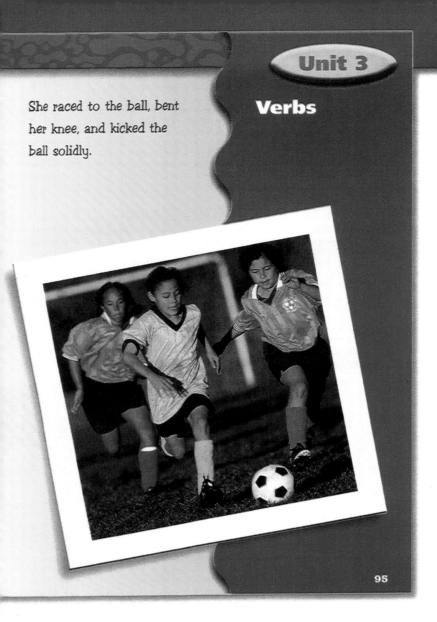

95

Introducing the Unit

Using the Photograph

- Direct students' attention to the photograph and have a volunteer read the caption aloud. Ask students to identify the words that show action. *(raced, bent, kicked)*
- Write *kick* on the board or on an overhead transparency. Ask students how they would describe this action if it had taken place last week. *(kicked)* Ask students how they would describe the action if it were going to take place next week. *(will kick* or *shall kick)*
- Explain to students that words that can show action are called **verbs**. Tell students they will learn about verbs and verb tenses in this unit.

Grammar Song

See Blackline Master G–1 for a song to help students remember some of the concepts and rules taught in this unit.

Students can also listen to this song on audiotape.

Shared Writing Activity

Work with students to write a paragraph describing the soccer game in the photograph before, during, and after the moment the photograph was taken.

1. Write the words *Past, Present,* and *Future* on the board or on an overhead transparency.
2. Ask students to list verbs describing the actions they see in the photograph. (Sample responses: *run, chase, roll*) Write the words under *Present.*
3. Ask students for verbs telling what might have happened just before this photograph was taken. (Sample responses: *stole, kicked, bounced*) Write the verbs under *Past.*
4. Have students suggest verbs to predict what might happen after the scene in the photograph. (Sample responses: *will shoot, will score, will fall)* Write these verbs under *Future.*
5. Have students use these verbs to suggest sentences for the paragraph. Write the sentences on the board or on an overhead transparency.
   - As you write the sentences, call students' attention to the proper tense of the verb. You may want to underline the main verb and any helping verbs.
   - Help students fix fragments and run-on sentences. As you write, ask students to tell you the correct punctuation and capitalization.
6. Have a volunteer read the paragraph aloud, emphasizing the verb in each sentence. Have students add, modify, or delete sentences depending on how they feel the paragraph fits together.

Action Verbs

Lesson Objectives

Students will:

- identify and use action verbs in sentences
- write instructions, using action verbs

One-Minute Warm-Up Have a volunteer act out the actions in the sentences as other volunteers read the sentences. Encourage volunteer actors to be creative.

Focus on Instruction

Remind students that a sentence is made up of a complete subject and a complete predicate. The subject tells *who* or *what*. The predicate tells *what is* or *what happens*. The main word in the predicate is called the simple predicate. When the simple predicate tells what happens, it is an action verb.

Try It Out

VIEWING Have students use action verbs to describe some things that the students in the photograph are doing. Ask students to create a concept web similar to the one below. Ask volunteers to supply details to make complete sentences out of the subject and action verbs. (Sample answers are shown.)

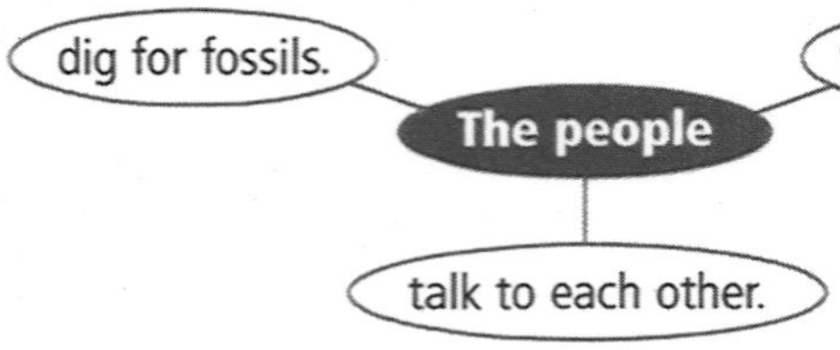
dig for fossils.
write notes.
The people
talk to each other.

FOR STUDENTS ACQUIRING ENGLISH

- Have students listen to the Try It Out sentences on the audiotape. Distribute SAE Practice page for Unit 3, Lesson 1, to support listening.
- Ask students if they've had any experience with archaeological sites that they could share. Help students suggest sentences about the photo. List vocabulary such as *dig, study, search, look, uncover,* and *find* on the board. Then have students brainstorm what they think a scientist would do to remove artifacts buried in the ground. Then students listen to sentences and underline the action verbs.
  1. Scientists study ancient civilizations. (study)
  2. Sometimes they find clues. (find)
  3. Students dig for pottery. (dig)

Grammar

1 Action Verbs

One-Minute Warm-Up

Radio Man
Arthur Dorros

Read the sentences below. Which word in each sentence shows action?

Diego sang. David tapped a rhythm on the side of the truck. . . .
The family drove through forests and through dry country.

—from *Radio Man/Don Radio*, by Arthur Dorros

You know that every sentence has a subject and a predicate. The main word in the predicate is the verb. **A verb is a word that can show action. When a verb tells what people or things do, it is called an action verb.**

Subjects	Predicates
Rita and Eric	dig slowly and carefully.
The students	helped the scientists.
Rita	uncovered some pottery.
The pieces of pottery	provide clues about the past.

Try It Out

Speak Up What is the action verb in each sentence?

1. Rita cleaned the pieces of pottery.
2. Two students stand in the water.
3. They hold a tub with a screen in the bottom.
4. Water fills the tub.
5. Eric pours dirt into the tub.
6. Light objects float in the water.
7. Dirt goes through the screen.
8. The students attach labels to the objects.
9. The scientists take the objects to their lab.
10. They learn many things about early people.

Meeting Individual Needs

RETEACHING
ALTERNATIVE STRATEGY

- Write this sentence on the board: *The archaeologists found a skeleton.*
- Tell students that the main word in the predicate of a sentence is always a verb. The verb may show action. Action verbs tell what people or things do. Ask students to identify the action verb that tells what archaeologists did. *(found)*
- Follow the same procedure for the sentences *They cleaned the bones* and *Stephanie spotted a gold ring. (cleaned, spotted)*

CHALLENGE

Write the name of a sport on the board and challenge teams of students to list as many action verbs associated with the sport as they can in one minute. Give one point for each action verb. The winning team chooses another sport and repeats the process.

FOR STUDENTS ACQUIRING ENGLISH

Write the sentence stems *She is* ______. and *He is* ______. on the board. Have volunteers mime actions while other students guess what they are doing. List the action verbs on the board under the appropriate sentence stem. Review subjects and predicates.

On Your Own

Write each action verb.

Example: Deserts cover a large part of the American Southwest. *cover*

11. Spanish explorers crossed these deserts long ago.
12. They noticed tall, steep rocks with flat tops.
13. The explorers named these rocks *mesas*.
14. They called smaller mesas *buttes*.
15. Early people settled on Mesa Verde in Colorado.
16. They built homes on the flat tops of the mesas.
17. These people disappeared long ago.
18. People tell stories about a famous mesa, Weaver's Needle.
19. Hundreds of people still search for a gold mine there.

20–30. This part of an online encyclopedia article has eleven action verbs. Write the article. Underline the verbs.

Example: Winds blow across the mesas. *Winds blow across the mesas.*

Web site

Back Forward

Mesas

Wind and water make a mesa. It takes millions of years. The wind and water carve the rock. The softer part of the rock disappears first. The harder part forms a mesa. The hot sun beats down on it.

A few plants grow on mesas. Flowers open only at night. They protect themselves from the daytime sun. Only small animals live on mesas. Lizards and pack rats make their homes there.

Writing Wrap-Up

WRITING • THINKING • LISTENING • SPEAKING

EXPLAINING

Write Instructions

Think of a real rock, tree, building, or other object. Write instructions explaining how to get to the object from your school. Use action verbs in your sentences. Read your instructions to a partner. Have your partner identify the verbs.

For Extra Practice see page 125.

Summing Up Help students summarize these key points about the lesson:

An **action verb** is a word in a sentence that can show action. It tells what people or things do.

You may want to have students complete the parts related to this lesson on Blackline Master 3–1.

On Your Own

Suggest that students identify action verbs by asking:

What does or did the subject do?

MEETING INDIVIDUAL NEEDS

FOR STUDENTS ACQUIRING ENGLISH

Distribute SAE Practice page for Unit 3, Lesson 1. Provide photos of the Southwest; briefly discuss the history and geography of that area. Then students fill in blanks with action verbs from a list.

1. The Spanish ______ the Southwest. (explored)
2. Explorers ______ many beautiful places. (found)
3. Miners ______ for gold and silver. (looked)

Writing Wrap-Up

Writing Tip: Suggest that students draw a map of the area being described. They can show the starting place, landmarks or streets, and the goal. See Blackline Master 3–7 for sample instructions.

SCHOOL-HOME CONNECTION

Ask students to have a family member test the instructions to see if they can find the place or object described in the Writing Wrap-Up.

● RETEACHING WORKBOOK, page 22

1 Action Verbs

- An **action verb** is a word that tells what people or things do.

verb
The ships **sailed** away weeks ago.
predicate

verb
Bill **looks** for the ships every day.
predicate

Write the action verb in each underlined predicate.

Example: Bill stood on the dock. — stood

1. Bill watched the workers on the dock. — watched
2. The workers loaded boxes onto a large ship. — loaded
3. Bill's father works on this ship. — works
4. Some people boarded the ship. — boarded
5. The crew checked their names on a list. — checked
6. The captain blew the whistle. — blew
7. Bill heard three loud blasts. — heard
8. Tugboats towed the ship into deep water. — towed
9. The ship left the harbor after that. — left
10. Bill watches it for a long time. — watches
11. He walks home slowly. — walks
12. He misses his father already. — misses
13. Bill's father sends letters from far away. — sends
14. Bill goes to the docks again. — goes
15. The big ship arrives home at last! — arrives

▲■ WORKBOOK PLUS, pages 36–37

1 Action Verbs

verb
A news reporter **announces** the news on television or radio.
predicate

verb
A news event **happened** only an hour ago.
predicate

Write the action verb in each sentence.

1. Reporters travel to the scene of a news event. — travel
2. They interview people about these events. — interview
3. Reporters discover the important facts in the story. — discover
4. Most reporters work many hours a day. — work
5. They write about fairs, parades, and meetings. — write
6. Some reporters type their stories on paper. — type
7. Other reporters put their stories onto computers. — put
8. Television cameras film some news stories. — film
9. TV reporters wear microphones on their clothes. — wear
10. These microphones catch every word. — catch
11. Cameras record their movements and expressions. — record
12. Many newspeople studied this business in school. — studied
13. Others learned at work. — learned
14. They watched other reporters. — watched
15. They chose an interesting career. — chose
16. Many schools offer courses in reporting. — offer
17. Reporters often spend much time out of the office. — spend
18. Newspapers take pride in reporting news accurately. — take

(continued)

1 Action Verbs *(continued from page 36)*

Challenge

Choose the correct action verbs from the box to complete the sentences below. Then write the action verbs in the crossword puzzle.

collects	raises	discovers	decides
mends	explores	solves	steers
prepares	manages	operates	lends
grooms	plants	teaches	leads

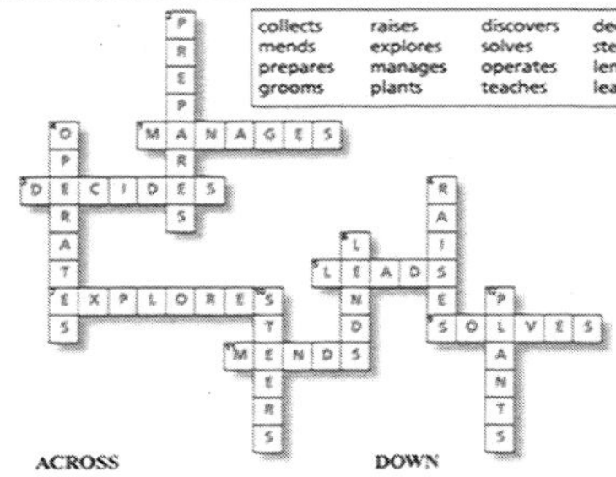

ACROSS

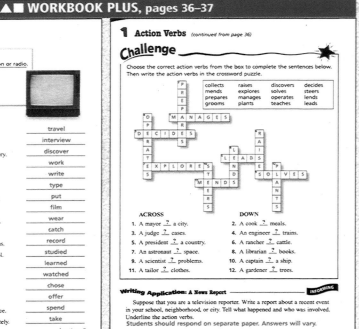

1. A mayor ? a city.
3. A judge ? cases.
5. A president ? a country.
7. An astronaut ? space.
9. A scientist ? problems.
11. A tailor ? clothes.

DOWN

2. A cook ? meals.
4. An engineer ? trains.
6. A rancher ? cattle.
8. A librarian ? books.
10. A captain ? a ship.
12. A gardener ? trees.

Writing Application: A News Report INFORMING

Suppose that you are a television reporter. Write a report about a recent event in your school, neighborhood, or city. Tell what happened and who was involved. Underline the action verbs.

Students should respond on separate paper. Answers will vary.

Main Verbs and Helping Verbs

Lesson Objectives

Students will:

- identify the main verb and the helping verb in a sentence
- write an informative announcement about an event, using main verbs and helping verbs

One-Minute Warm-Up After students identify the two words that make up the verb *(had put),* write them on the board. Ask which word is more important. Explain that *put* is the main verb because it shows the action and that *had* is a helping verb. Ask volunteers to make up other sentences using *had* with an action verb.

Focus on Instruction

Point out that different forms of the main verb are used with different helping verbs. For example, a main verb ends in *-ing* when it is used with the words *am, is, are, was,* and *were.*

Try It Out

VIEWING Have students suggest action words about the racers in the photograph. Record these words in a chart. Ask other students to use the action words with helping verbs to make complete sentences. (Sample responses are shown.)

Subject	Helping Verbs	Main Verbs
The racers	are	racing in wheelchairs.
Only one racer	will	win the race.

FOR STUDENTS ACQUIRING ENGLISH

- Have students listen to the Try It Out sentences on the audiotape. Distribute SAE Practice page for Unit 3, Lesson 2, to support listening.
- Help students suggest sentences about the wheelchair racers in the photograph. Then invite students to create a word web relating to Junior Olympics. Briefly review some of the simpler verb tenses that use helping verbs: the present progressive, present perfect, and future with *will.* Also include *do* and *does* in present tense negatives and questions and *did* for past. Students listen and underline the complete verb once; then they underline the main verb a second time.
  1. The girl is racing in a wheelchair.
  2. The racers have trained for many months.

Grammar

2 Main Verbs and Helping Verbs

One-Minute Warm-Up

The verb in the sentence below is made up of two words. What are they? Which word shows the action? **had, put; put**

Jim Thorpe had put the Olympics on the world map.

—from *The Story of the Olympics,* by Dave Anderson

A verb may be more than one word. **The main verb is the most important verb. The helping verb comes before it.**

Some Common Helping Verbs		
am	was	has
is	were	have
are	will	had

The main verbs below are in yellow. Helping verbs are in blue.

Alberto is training for a marathon.
He has run five miles each day.
His coach will help him next week.

Try It Out

Speak Up Find each helping verb and main verb. **HV is underlined once; MV, twice.**

1. Sara was racing in a wheelchair race.
2. She had joined the Wheelchair Athlete Club.
3. The racers were using special racing wheelchairs.
4. They are training several times a week.
5. They have lifted weights too.
6. Sara has raced for several years.
7. She will race many more times.
8. She is practicing for the Olympics.

Meeting Individual Needs

RETEACHING
ALTERNATIVE STRATEGY

- Write this sentence on the board: *Todd will run in the Junior Olympics.* Have students identify the two words that tell what Todd does. *(will run)*
- Underline *run* and explain that it is the main verb because it shows the action.
- Circle *will.* Tell students that *will* helps the main verb show action and is called a helping verb.

CHALLENGE

Have students write five sentences to describe five actions that they have done today, leaving a blank for the helping verbs in their sentences. Tell students to exchange papers with a partner and fill in the blanks with the correct helping verbs.

FOR STUDENTS ACQUIRING ENGLISH

Write the following on the board: *Do you know Ana? Ana is playing soccer. She has played soccer for one year. She will go to soccer camp next summer.* Volunteers underline main verbs in yellow and helping verbs in blue.

On Your Own

Write the sentences. Underline helping verbs once and main verbs twice.

Example: I am reading about the Junior Olympics.
I am reading about the Junior Olympics.

9. The Junior Olympics were started in 1967.
10. The games are held every summer.
11. The annual event has included twenty-four sports.
12. Each young athlete was dreaming of a gold medal.
13. All of the competitors had won other contests.
14. They have earned a place in the Junior Olympics.
15. The athletes will remember the games all their lives.
16. I am practicing for the next Junior Olympics.

17–24. This announcement has eight verbs. Write the announcement. Underline each helping verb once and each main verb twice.

Example: The fans are holding their breath.
The fans are holding their breath.

The Murray School

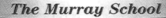

The Murray School Olympic Games have started with a bang. The Red Team has claimed the gold for the sack relay. No one was expecting such a fast race. Last year's event had lasted twice as long. Now, which children will win the medals for the somersault race? A moment ago the teams were taking their places. The suspense is growing. Now they are rolling!

Writing Wrap-Up WRITING • THINKING • LISTENING • SPEAKING

INFORMING

Write an Announcement

Write an announcement about an event for the Goofy Olympic Games. Use helping verbs. Read your announcement to a partner. Listen for the verbs. How many helping verbs did you use?

For Extra Practice see page 126.

Summing Up Help students summarize these key points about the lesson:

A verb may be more than one word. The **main verb** is the most important verb. The **helping verb** comes before it.

You may want to have students complete the parts related to this lesson on Blackline Master 3–1.

On Your Own

Remind students that the helping verb always comes before the main verb.

MEETING INDIVIDUAL NEEDS

FOR STUDENTS ACQUIRING ENGLISH

Distribute SAE Practice page for Unit 3, Lesson 2. Invite comments on the Olympics; ask what students know about the Junior Olympics. Students underline helping verbs once, main verbs twice.

1. Many young people have competed.
2. Where will the next Junior Olympics be?

Writing Wrap-Up

Writing Tip: Suggest that students begin by answering these questions: What is the event? Where and when is it to take place? Who can participate in the event? See Blackline Master 3–7 for a sample announcement.

TECHNOLOGY CONNECTION
Students may want to use available word processing or page layout software to decorate their announcements.

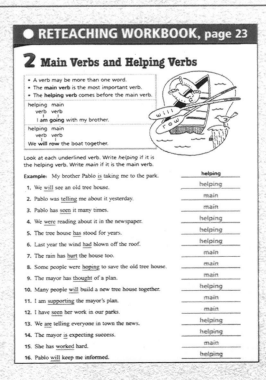

● RETEACHING WORKBOOK, page 23

2 Main Verbs and Helping Verbs

- A verb may be more than one word.
- The **main verb** is the most important verb.
- The **helping verb** comes before the main verb.

helping verb, main verb: I **am going** with my brother.

helping verb, main verb: We **will row** the boat together.

Look at each underlined verb. Write *helping* if it is the helping verb. Write *main* if it is the main verb.

Example: My brother Pablo is taking me to the park. helping

1. We will see an old tree house. helping
2. Pablo was telling me about it yesterday. main
3. Pablo has seen it many times. main
4. We were reading about it in the newspaper. helping
5. The tree house has stood for years. helping
6. Last year the wind had blown off the roof. helping
7. The rain has hurt the house too. main
8. Some people were hoping to save the old tree house. main
9. The mayor has thought of a plan. main
10. Many people will build a new tree house together. helping
11. I am supporting the mayor's plan. main
12. I have seen her work in our parks. main
13. We are telling everyone in town the news. helping
14. The mayor is expecting success. helping
15. She has worked hard. main
16. Pablo will keep me informed. helping

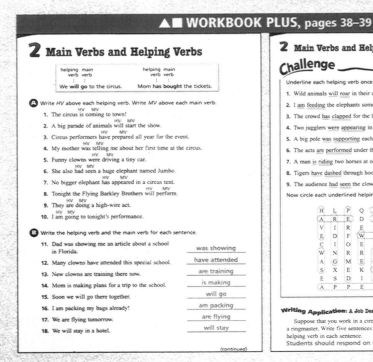

▲■ WORKBOOK PLUS, pages 38–39

2 Main Verbs and Helping Verbs

helping verb, main verb: We **will go** to the circus. helping verb, main verb: Mom **has bought** the tickets.

A Write *HV* above each helping verb. Write *MV* above each main verb.

1. The circus is (HV) coming (MV) to town!
2. A big parade of animals will (HV) start (MV) the show.
3. Circus performers have (HV) prepared (MV) all year for the event.
4. My mother was (HV) telling (MV) me about her first time at the circus.
5. Funny clowns were (HV) driving (MV) a tiny car.
6. She also had (HV) seen (MV) a huge elephant named Jumbo.
7. No bigger elephant has (HV) appeared (MV) in a circus tent.
8. Tonight the Flying Barkley Brothers will (HV) perform (MV).
9. They are (HV) doing (MV) a high-wire act.
10. I am (HV) going (MV) to tonight's performance.

B Write the helping verb and the main verb for each sentence.

11. Dad was showing me an article about a school in Florida. was showing
12. Many clowns have attended this special school. have attended
13. New clowns are training there now. are training
14. Mom is making plans for a trip to the school. is making
15. Soon we will go there together. will go
16. I am packing my bags already! am packing
17. We are flying tomorrow. are flying
18. We will stay in a hotel. will stay

(continued)

2 Main Verbs and Helping Verbs *(continued from page 38)*

Challenge

Underline each helping verb once and each main verb twice.

1. Wild animals will roar in their cages.
2. I am feeding the elephants some peanuts.
3. The crowd has clapped for the high-wire act.
4. Two jugglers were appearing in the sideshow.
5. A big pole was supporting each tent.
6. The acts are performed under the big top.
7. A man is riding two horses at once.
8. Tigers have dashed through hoops.
9. The audience had seen the clown act already.

Now circle each underlined helping verb and main verb in the puzzle.

H	L	P	Q	H	A	D	I	S	W
A	R	E	D	S	E	E	N	U	F
V	I	R	E	B	N	C	D	P	E
E	D	F	W	I	L	L	A	P	E
C	I	O	E	P	H	A	S	O	D
W	N	R	R	R	Y	P	H	R	I
A	G	M	E	O	L	P	E	T	N
S	X	E	K	A	M	E	D	I	G
E	S	D	I	R	U	D	G	N	W
A	P	P	E	A	R	I	N	G	E

Writing Application: A Job Description EXPLAINING

Suppose that you work in a circus as an animal trainer, a clown, an acrobat, or a ringmaster. Write five sentences about your circus job. Use a main verb and a helping verb in each sentence.
Students should respond on separate paper. Answers will vary.

Present, Past, and Future

Lesson Objectives

Students will:

- identify and correctly use present, past, and future tense verbs
- write a cause-and-effect paragraph, using present, past, and future tense verbs correctly

One-Minute Warm-Up Tell students that each label has something to do with time and that the words following each label are clues. Have students explain how each label relates to the group of words following it.

Focus on Instruction

Tell students that the word *tense* means "time." Explain that choosing the right verb tense depends on the time of the action. For example, a verb in the present tense shows action that is occurring in the present.

Try It Out

LISTENING AND SPEAKING Have students listen as volunteers read the sentences. Ask them if they hear any clues other than the verbs that help identify verb tense. (Sentence 3: *yesterday;* Sentence 4: *tomorrow*) Point out that words such as *today, next,* and *yesterday* are clues that help the reader tell when the action is happening. Have volunteers add a clue to Sentence 5 that helps the reader know that the verb is in the future tense.

FOR STUDENTS ACQUIRING ENGLISH

- Have students listen to the Try It Out sentences on the audiotape. Distribute SAE Practice page for Unit 3, Lesson 3, to support listening.
- Write the headings *Past, Present,* and *Future* on the board. Elicit examples of each tense; list suggestions on the board under each heading. Students may use forms with *going to* instead of *will;* both are acceptable, but check for correct use of the helping verb and infinitive with *going to.* Students listen and underline the verb. They listen again and circle *present, past,* or *future.*
  1. My brother <u>likes</u> animals. (*present/past/future*) (present)
  2. He <u>bought</u> a book about birds. (*present/past/future*) (past)

Grammar

3 Present, Past, and Future

One-Minute Warm-Up

Unscramble the label that goes with each group of words below.

repents: swoop, find, screech, land, hide present
spat: ate, searched, collected, slept, soared past
rufute: will clean, will go, will rest, will feed, will chase future

A verb tells when something happens. **The tense of a verb lets you know whether something happens in the present, in the past, or in the future.**

Verb Tenses

Rules	Examples
A verb in the **present tense** shows action that is happening now.	Bats hunt at night. Now the bat rests.
A verb in the **past tense** shows action that has already happened. Many verbs in the past tense end with *-ed.*	It hunted last night. The bats rested.
A verb in the **future tense** shows action that will happen. Verbs in the future tense use the helping verb *will.*	They will hunt tonight. The bat will rest.

Try It Out

Speak Up What is the verb in each sentence? Is it in the present tense, the past tense, or the future tense?

1. Michael <u>likes</u> many kinds of animals. pres.
2. He <u>collects</u> facts about animals. pres.
3. I <u>finished</u> a book about birds yesterday. past
4. We <u>will go</u> to the library tomorrow. fut.
5. Michael <u>will look</u> for books about bats. fut.
6. The librarian <u>will help</u> him. fut.

Meeting Individual Needs

RETEACHING
ALTERNATIVE STRATEGY

- Write these words on the board: *today, yesterday, tomorrow.*
- Have a volunteer perform a particular task, such as lifting a book. Write a sentence that tells what the volunteer is doing. (Today, Tim lifts the book.) Underline the verb. Explain that it is the present tense. Point out that a verb's tense tells whether something happens in the present, in the past, or in the future.
- Explain the use of the past tense and the future tense of the same verb, and have students make sentences about the same action in these tenses.

CHALLENGE

Have students make an "I'm Proud" display. Have each student write three sentences on a sheet of paper telling about personal accomplishments they are proud of: one current, one past, and one anticipated in the future. Display accomplishments in an interesting manner.

FOR STUDENTS ACQUIRING ENGLISH

Write *oobk, eskd,* and *pma* on the board. Tell students the letters are in the wrong order. Have partners unscramble the letters. Then help students unscramble the words in the lesson. Then ask what *present, past,* and *future* refer to.

On Your Own

Write the verb in each sentence. Beside it write *present, past,* or *future.*

Example: Bats help people a great deal. *help present*

7. Most bats will eat insects. fut.
8. They help gardeners a great deal. pres.
9. A flying bat makes sounds. pres.
10. The sounds send echoes to the bat's ears. pres.
11. The echoes direct the bat. pres.
12. One scientist studied bats. past
13. Then he trained some of them. past
14. The bats will fly to him on command. fut.
15. Someday he will write a book about them. fut.

16–24. This ad has nine verbs. Write each verb. Then write *past, present,* or *future* beside it.

Example: Every gardener needs a Cozy Bat House! *needs present*

For years insects spoiled my past flowers. They chewed every petal. Now past I grow flowers with no trouble. I simply purchased a Cozy Bat House. Then I attached it to a tree. Bats sleep there pres. during the day. At night they gobble up insects. A Cozy Bat House will keep fut. your garden beautiful. You will thank fut. your friends the bats.

pres.
past
past
pres.

Writing Wrap-Up

WRITING • THINKING • LISTENING • SPEAKING

EXPLAINING

Write a Cause-and-Effect Paragraph

Write a paragraph about what might happen if a bat got into your school. Use verbs in the past, present, and future tenses. Read your ideas to a partner. Can your partner add anything else?

For Extra Practice see page 127.

Summing Up Help students summarize these key points about the lesson:

Verbs in the **present tense** show action that is happening now. **Past tense** verbs show action that has already happened. **Future tense** verbs show action that will happen.

You may want to have students complete the parts related to this lesson on Blackline Master 3–2.

On Your Own

Suggest that students find verb tense by asking:

Does the verb end in *-ed?* Does the verb use the helping verb *will?*

MEETING INDIVIDUAL NEEDS

FOR STUDENTS ACQUIRING ENGLISH

Distribute SAE Practice page for Unit 3, Lesson 3. List what students know about bats on a concept map. Students cut up sentence strips and match them to complete sentences. Then they decide the verb tense.

Writing Wrap-Up

Writing Tip: Have students consider these questions before they write: How did the bats get into the school? What did the bats do in the school? What did people do when they saw the bats? See Blackline Master 3–7 for a sample cause-and-effect paragraph.

SCHOOL-HOME CONNECTION

Before they begin writing, students might ask family members about their experiences with bats.

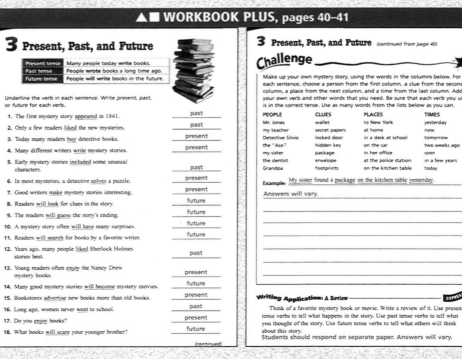

● RETEACHING WORKBOOK, page 24

3 Present, Past, and Future

- A **present tense** verb shows action that is happening now.
- A **past tense** verb shows action that has already happened.
- A **future tense** verb shows action that will happen.

Present tense	The Kamals **live** here now.
Past tense	The Kamals **lived** here last year.
Future tense	The Kamals **will live** here for many years.

Write *present, past,* or *future* for each underlined verb.

Example: The Kamals will leave early in the morning. **future**

1. Kate Kamal's family moved to Los Angeles a few years ago. past
2. Mrs. Kamal works in Long Beach. present
3. She rides a long way to her job every day. present
4. Tomorrow the Kamal family will move to Long Beach. future
5. Then Mrs. Kamal will travel only a few miles to work. future
6. The Kamal family prepares everything for the move. present
7. Last week Mr. Kamal found many empty boxes. past
8. He saved them for moving day. past
9. Now the Kamals pack books and records into boxes. present
10. The Kamals will pack the pots and pans next. future
11. Tonight they will eat dinner at a restaurant. future
12. Kate gave her new address to all her friends. past
13. She will give us her new phone number soon. future
14. Everyone wished Kate good luck. past
15. Now the Kamals wave good-bye to us. present

▲■ WORKBOOK PLUS, pages 40–41

3 Present, Past, and Future

Present tense	Many people today **write** books.
Past tense	People **wrote** books a long time ago.
Future tense	People **will write** books in the future.

Underline the verb in each sentence. Write *present, past,* or *future* for each verb.

1. The first mystery story appeared in 1841. past
2. Only a few readers liked the new mysteries. past
3. Today many readers buy detective books. present
4. Many different writers write mystery stories. present
5. Early mystery stories included some unusual characters. past
6. In most mysteries, a detective solves a puzzle. present
7. Good writers make mystery stories interesting. present
8. Readers will look for clues in the story. future
9. The readers will guess the story's ending. future
10. A mystery story often will have many surprises. future
11. Readers will search for books by a favorite writer. future
12. Years ago, many people liked Sherlock Holmes stories best. past
13. Young readers often enjoy the Nancy Drew mystery books. present
14. Many good mystery stories will become mystery movies. future
15. Bookstores advertise new books more than old books. present
16. Long ago, women never went to school. past
17. Do you enjoy books? present
18. What books will scare your younger brother? future

(continued)

3 Present, Past, and Future *(continued from page 40)*

Challenge

Make up your own mystery story, using the words in the columns below. For each sentence, choose a person from the first column, a clue from the second column, a place from the next column, and a time from the last column. Add your own verb and other words that you need. Be sure that each verb you use is in the correct tense. Use as many words from the lists below as you can.

PEOPLE	CLUES	PLACES	TIMES
Mr. Jones	wallet	to New York	yesterday
my teacher	secret papers	at home	now
Detective Silvio	locked door	in a desk at school	tomorrow
the "Ace"	hidden key	on the car	two weeks ago
my sister	package	in her office	soon
the dentist	envelope	at the police station	in a few years
Grandpa	footprints	on the kitchen table	today

Example: My sister found a package on the kitchen table yesterday.

Answers will vary.

Writing Application: A Review EXPRESSING

Think of a favorite mystery book or movie. Write a review of it. Use present tense verbs to tell what happens in the story. Use past tense verbs to tell what you thought of the story. Use future tense verbs to tell what others will think about this story.

Students should respond on separate paper. Answers will vary.

Writing with Verbs

Lesson Objective

Students will:

- rewrite sentences to make verb tenses consistent

Focus on Instruction

- Review with students how to form the present, past, and future tenses of some common regular and irregular verbs. Suggest that they pair the word *today, yesterday,* or *tomorrow* with each subject-verb combination to help them remember the present, past, or future tense of these verbs.
- Tell students to keep all the verbs in a paragraph in the same tense unless a change in time is indicated.

Apply It

Have students complete the revising activity independently.

If some students need extra support, have them work with partners to identify the subject and verb in each sentence. Because the social studies report tells about a time long ago, suggest that students say the word *yesterday* before each subject-verb combination.

Have students look at their writing in progress to find verbs that might be written in the wrong tense.

Answers to Apply It

1. Long ago, millions of bison roamed the American West.
2. They lived in towns and on farms and ranches.
3. They built railroads.
4. Huge numbers of bison were killed.
5. By 1885 the bison were nearly extinct.

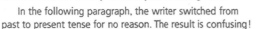

Revising Strategies

Writing with Verbs

Change tense only to show a change in time.

Keeping Verbs in the Same Tense You know that verb tense tells when an event happened. Verb tenses show past, present, and future time. When you write, use verb tenses carefully to make your meaning clear.

In the following paragraph, the writer switched from past to present tense for no reason. The result is confusing!

In the 1800s, large herds of bison crossed railroad tracks in the Great Plains. They cause long delays for the trains. Railroad companies then encouraged bison hunting as a sport.

In the paragraph above, the verb *cause* should be changed to the past tense.

Apply It

1–5. Rewrite these two paragraphs from a social studies report so that every verb is in the same tense. See TE margin for answers.

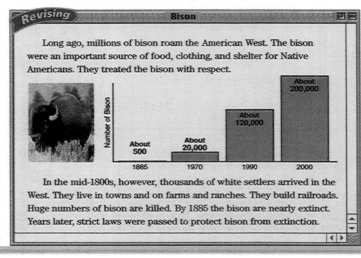

Revising — Bison

Long ago, millions of bison roam the American West. The bison were an important source of food, clothing, and shelter for Native Americans. They treated the bison with respect.

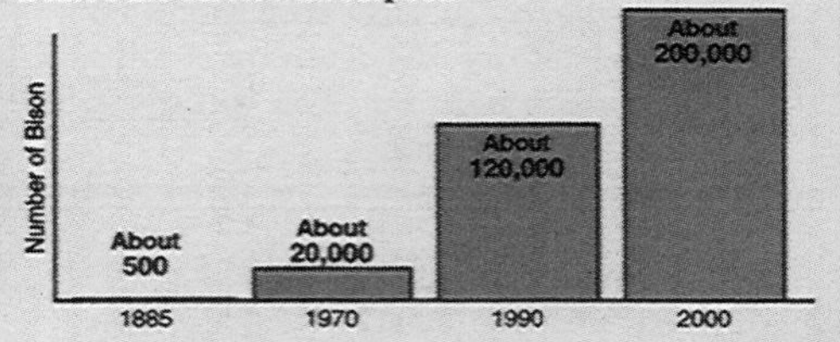

In the mid-1800s, however, thousands of white settlers arrived in the West. They live in towns and on farms and ranches. They build railroads. Huge numbers of bison are killed. By 1885 the bison are nearly extinct. Years later, strict laws were passed to protect bison from extinction.

102 **Unit 3:** Verbs

Meeting Individual Needs

● RETEACHING WORKBOOK, page 25

Writing with Verbs

- Verb tenses tell when an event happens or happened.
- Change tense only to show a change in time.

Mixed tenses	Last summer, I picked our vacation. I choose camping.
Same tense	Last summer, I picked our vacation. I chose camping.

Keeping Verbs in the Same Tense Rewrite each pair of sentences so that both underlined verbs are in the tense shown in parentheses.

Example: We find a great campsite. It was by a lake. **(past)**
We found a great campsite. It was by a lake.

Revising

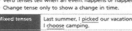

1. My family went camping. We get a brand-new tent. **(past)**
   My family went camping. We got a brand-new tent.
2. We camp by a lake. We fished every day. **(past)**
   We camped by a lake. We fished every day.
3. Dad cooks fish for dinner. It smelled good. **(past)**
   Dad cooked fish for dinner. It smelled good.
4. At night, we look at the stars. We sang songs. **(past)**
   At night, we looked at the stars. We sang songs.
5. Next winter we will ski. We stayed in a cabin. **(future)**
   Next winter we will ski. We will stay in a cabin.
6. Winter is my favorite season. I liked snow. **(present)**
   Winter is my favorite season. I like snow.
7. Now I take cross-country skiing lessons. I fell down a lot. **(present)**
   Now I take cross-country skiing lessons. I fall down a lot.
8. My teacher was good. My skiing improves every day. **(present)**
   My teacher is good. My skiing improves every day.

(continued)

▲■ WORKBOOK PLUS, page 42

Writing with Verbs

Mixed tenses	Benjamin Franklin was a great statesman and inventor. He travels to France to get help for the American colonies during the Revolutionary War.
Same tense	Benjamin Franklin was a great statesman and inventor. He **traveled** to France to get help for the American colonies during the Revolutionary War.

Keeping Verbs in the Same Tense 1–8. Rewrite this part of an article about Benjamin Franklin so that every verb is in the same tense.

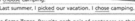

Revising

Benjamin Franklin was involved in many businesses in his life, but he is always reading and writing. He learns to read at an early age. He became an apprentice printer in 1718, when he reaches the age of twelve. At sixteen, Franklin is in charge of his brother's newspaper.

Franklin's most famous work is *Poor Richard's Almanack*, a yearly calendar that includes wise sayings by "Poor Richard." These sayings encourage good habits such as honesty and hard work. Many colonists respect Benjamin Franklin and his writing.

Benjamin Franklin was involved in many businesses in his life, but he was always reading and writing. He learned to read at an early age. He became an apprentice printer in 1718, when he reached the age of twelve. At sixteen, Franklin was in charge of his brother's newspaper.

Franklin's most famous work was Poor Richard's Almanack, a yearly calendar that included wise sayings by "Poor Richard." These sayings encouraged good habits such as honesty and hard work. Many colonists respected Benjamin Franklin and his writing.

(continued)

Sentence Fluency

Combining Sentences Sometimes you can make your writing flow more smoothly by combining short sentences to form a longer sentence. If two short sentences have the same subject, you can combine them by joining the predicates with *and*. Your new sentence will have a **compound predicate**.

She was the smartest buffalo.
She had many friends.
} She was the smartest buffalo and had many friends.

Apply It

6–10. Rewrite these paragraphs from part of a story. Combine each pair of underlined sentences. See TE margin for sample answers.

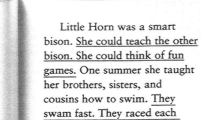

Revising

Little Horn was a smart bison. She could teach the other bison. She could think of fun games. One summer she taught her brothers, sisters, and cousins how to swim. They swam fast. They raced each other.

One day a hungry cougar crept down a nearby mountain. It saw the herd. It hid in the grass. Little Horn spotted the cougar. She didn't want to scare the others, so she started a game.

Little Horn ran to the river. She began a race with everyone. They all swam across to safety. Meanwhile, the cougar came to a sudden stop at the riverbank. It couldn't swim. The big cat had been tricked. It looked silly. The bison cheered.

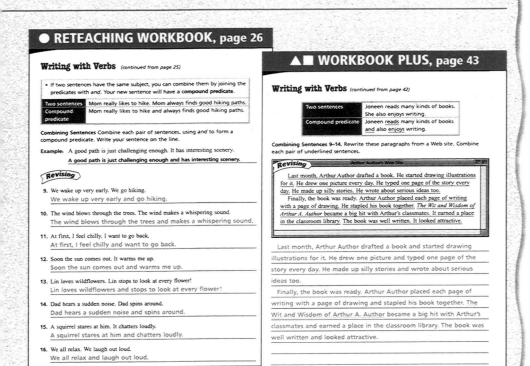

● RETEACHING WORKBOOK, page 26

Writing with Verbs *(continued from page 25)*

- If two sentences have the same subject, you can combine them by joining the predicates with *and*. Your new sentence will have a **compound predicate**.

Two sentences	Mom really likes to hike. Mom always finds good hiking paths.
Compound predicate	Mom really likes to hike and always finds good hiking paths.

Combining Sentences Combine each pair of sentences, using *and* to form a compound predicate. Write your sentence on the line.

Example: A good path is just challenging enough. It has interesting scenery.
A good path is just challenging enough and has interesting scenery.

Revising

9. We wake up very early. We go hiking.
We wake up very early and go hiking.

10. The wind blows through the trees. The wind makes a whispering sound.
The wind blows through the trees and makes a whispering sound.

11. At first, I feel chilly. I want to go back.
At first, I feel chilly and want to go back.

12. Soon the sun comes out. It warms me up.
Soon the sun comes out and warms me up.

13. Lin loves wildflowers. Lin stops to look at every flower!
Lin loves wildflowers and stops to look at every flower!

14. Dad hears a sudden noise. Dad spins around.
Dad hears a sudden noise and spins around.

15. A squirrel stares at him. It chatters loudly.
A squirrel stares at him and chatters loudly.

16. We all relax. We laugh out loud.
We all relax and laugh out loud.

▲■ WORKBOOK PLUS, page 43

Writing with Verbs *(continued from page 42)*

Two sentences	Joneen reads many kinds of books. She also enjoys writing.
Compound predicate	Joneen reads many kinds of books and also enjoys writing.

Combining Sentences 9–14. Rewrite these paragraphs from a Web site. Combine each pair of underlined sentences.

Revising — Arthur Author's Web Site

Last month, Arthur Author drafted a book. He started drawing illustrations for it. He drew one picture every day. He typed one page of the story every day. He made up silly stories. He wrote about serious ideas too.

Finally, the book was ready. Arthur Author placed each page of writing with a page of drawing. He stapled his book together. *The Wit and Wisdom of Arthur A. Author* became a big hit with Arthur's classmates. It earned a place in the classroom library. The book was well written. It looked attractive.

Last month, Arthur Author drafted a book and started drawing illustrations for it. He drew one picture and typed one page of the story every day. He made up silly stories and wrote about serious ideas too.

Finally, the book was ready. Arthur Author placed each page of writing with a page of drawing and stapled his book together. The Wit and Wisdom of Arthur A. Author became a big hit with Arthur's classmates and earned a place in the classroom library. The book was well written and looked attractive.

Lesson Objective

Students will:
- combine two short sentences with the same subject to create a sentence with a compound predicate

Focus on Instruction

- Point out that a compound predicate must contain two verbs, not just two objects of the same verb. Write the two sentences below on the board and discuss why the first one has a compound predicate, but the second one does not.

  Bison once roamed the prairies in the West and provided food, shelter, and clothing for the Native Americans.

  Native Americans made warm clothing and durable shoes out of bison hides.

- Explain that when two sentences have subjects that refer to the same person, place, or thing, they can often be combined to form a sentence with a compound predicate. Ask a volunteer to read the first two sentences in the first paragraph. Point out that *Little Horn* and *She* refer to the same character. Have students tell how to combine the two sentences to form a sentence with a compound predicate. (Little Horn was smart and could teach the other bison.)

Apply It

Have students complete the revising activity independently. Remind them that each revised sentence will have one subject and two predicates. Suggest that students label the subject and verbs in each revised sentence.

Have students find places in their own writing in progress where they can combine sentences with the same subject to form a sentence with a compound predicate.

Answers to Apply It

6. She could teach and think of fun games.
7. They swam fast and raced each other.
8. It saw the herd and hid in the grass.
9. Little Horn ran to the river and began a race with everyone.
10. The big cat had been tricked and looked silly.

Subject-Verb Agreement

Lesson Objectives

Students will:

- choose correct present tense verbs for singular and plural subjects
- proofread for subject-verb agreement
- write a thank-you note, using singular and plural verbs correctly.

One-Minute Warm-Up Ask students what clues they used to figure out if the subject was singular or plural. (Possible answer: *An* refers to one.) Point out the *s* in *fits* and explain that verbs that are used with singular nouns often end in *-s*. Tell students that both the subject and the verb in the sentence are singular.

Focus on Instruction

Remind students that an action verb tells what people or things do in a sentence. Also remind students that a present tense verb shows action that is happening now.

Try It Out

VIEWING Have students suggest sentences about the girl in the picture, using present tense verbs. Record the sentences in a chart. For each sentence have volunteers underline the subject and verb and tell whether they are singular or plural.

Sentence	Singular or Plural?
The girl looks at the computer.	S
The computers have color monitors.	P

FOR STUDENTS ACQUIRING ENGLISH

- Have students listen to the Try It Out sentences on the audiotape. Distribute SAE Practice page for Unit 3, Lesson 4, to support listening.
- Review the subject pronouns. Ask which ones take an *-s* ending on the present tense verb and which do not. Remind students that *he* and *she* are normally used only for people and animals. Review the verb *be*. Also make sure students understand that negatives and questions in the present use the helping verbs *do* and *does;* it is often helpful to point out the *s* in *does*. Then students listen and underline the correct form of the verb to complete the sentence.

1. My brother (has, have) a computer.
2. I (want, wants) a computer too.
3. Our little sister doesn't (use, uses) the computer.

Grammar/Usage

4 Subject-Verb Agreement

One-Minute Warm-Up

What is the subject of the sentence below? Is it singular or plural? What is the verb?

An internal modem fits into a special slot inside your computer. **modem; sing.; fits**

—from *Why Doesn't My Floppy Disk Flop?* by Peter Cook and Scott Manning

A verb in the present tense must **agree** with the subject of the sentence. This means that the subject and the verb must work together. They must both be singular or both be plural.

Subject-Verb Agreement	
Singular subjects	When the subject is a singular noun or *he, she,* or *it,* add *-s* to the verb. A computer helps people. It solves problems.
Plural subjects	When the subject is a plural noun or *I, we, you,* or *they,* do not add *-s* to the verb. Computers help people. They solve problems.

Try It Out

Speak Up Which verb correctly completes each sentence?

1. Marta (test, tests) her new computer program.
2. Marta (own, owns) a computer.
3. She (use, uses) it to do her homework.
4. The computer (help, helps) her parents too.
5. Her brothers (play, plays) games on it.
6. Computers (work, works) very rapidly.
7. Many people (use, uses) computers at work.
8. They (store, stores) a great deal of information.
9. I (want, wants) to learn more about computers.

Meeting Individual Needs

RETEACHING

ALTERNATIVE STRATEGY

- Write these sentences on the board:
  1. *A computer stores data.*
  2. *Computers store data.*
- Ask which sentence tells about one computer. (Sentence 1) Underline the verb. Explain that the *-s* ending makes the verb agree with the singular subject. Explain that singular verbs often end with an *-s*.
- Underline *store* in Sentence 2. Ask how it differs from the verb in Sentence 1. (It lacks an *-s* ending.) Ask which word the verb agrees with *(Computers)* and whether the word is singular or plural. (plural)

CHALLENGE

Have students write five test sentences about how they use computers. Have them write the singular and plural forms of the verb in parentheses, just as they appear in the On Your Own sentences. Ask students to exchange papers and complete each other's tests.

FOR STUDENTS ACQUIRING ENGLISH

Review subject pronouns. Write *he, she, it* on 25–30 stick-on labels. (1) Have students take turns attaching a label to a person or an object. (2) Attach labels, some incorrectly. Students find and correct the mistakes.

On Your Own

Choose the verb that correctly completes each sentence. Write the sentence.

Example: Computers (produce, produces) pictures called graphics.
Computers produce pictures called graphics.

10. Computer pictures (help, helps) people in many ways.
11. They (assist, assists) pilots like my uncle.
12. Special graphics (imitate, imitates) a real flight.
13. People (send, sends) computers into space.
14. A camera (take, takes) a picture on Mars.
15. It (send, sends) signals to a computer on Earth.
16. Many other workers (use, uses) computers in their jobs.
17. A doctor (look, looks) deep inside the human body.
18. An engineer (design, designs) new cars.

19–26. This part of a note has eight incorrect verbs. Write the note correctly.
Incorrect words are underlined.
Example: The game get harder. *The game gets harder.*

Proofreading — THANK YOU THANK YOU THANK YOU THANK YOU THANK YOU

Dear Grandpa,
I loves [love] my new computer game. You give the best gifts! The computer graphics looks [look] so real. First, you follows [follow] a river through a tropical forest. A jungle animal ask [asks] you questions along the way. Correct answers brings [bring] you to the next level. Steven enjoy [enjoys] the game too. He stays on Level 2 all the time. It make [makes] him so angry! We all plays [play] the game a lot.

Writing Wrap-Up

WRITING • THINKING • LISTENING • SPEAKING

EXPRESSING

Write a Thank-You Note

Write your name and the name of a gift on a piece of paper. Put the paper in a class "gift" bag. Pick a gift from the bag, and write a thank-you note to the person whose name you drew. Use present tense verbs. Read your note to a partner. Do subjects and verbs agree?

For Extra Practice see page 128.

Summing Up Help students summarize these key points about the lesson:

When the subject is a singular noun or *he, she,* or *it,* add *-s* to the verb to make subject and verb agree. When the subject is a plural noun or *I, we, you,* or *they,* do not add *-s* to the verb.

You may want to have students complete the parts related to this lesson on Blackline Master 3–1.

On Your Own

Remind students that plural nouns often end in *-s;* plural verbs usually do not.

MEETING INDIVIDUAL NEEDS

FOR STUDENTS ACQUIRING ENGLISH

Distribute SAE Practice page for Unit 3, Lesson 4. Brainstorm some of the things computers can do. Assist with vocabulary as needed. Students choose a logical verb from pairs of verbs in a box.

1. Computers ______ expensive. (are)
2. People ______ computers for many things. (use)

Writing Wrap-Up

Writing Tip: Remind students that thank-you notes, like letters, begin with a greeting and end with a closing. Tell students to be sure to name the gift in the note. See Blackline Master 3–7 for a sample thank-you note.

SCHOOL-HOME CONNECTION

Students may want to write notes to family members, thanking them for a recent gift or favor.

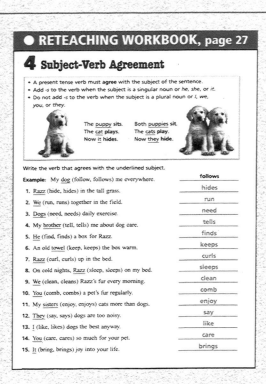

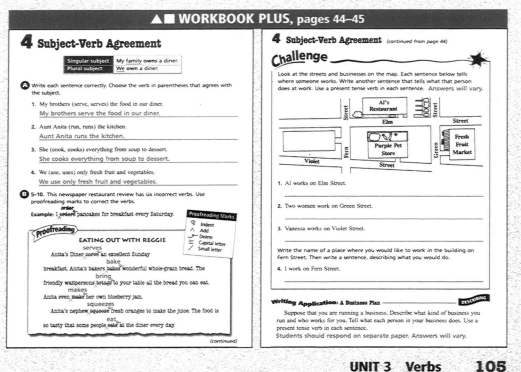

● RETEACHING WORKBOOK, page 27

4 Subject-Verb Agreement

- A present tense verb must **agree** with the subject of the sentence.
- Add -s to the verb when the subject is a singular noun or *he, she,* or *it.*
- Do not add -s to the verb when the subject is a plural noun or *I, we, you,* or *they.*

The puppy **sits.** Both puppies **sit.**
The cat **plays.** The cats **play.**
Now it **hides.** Now they **hide.**

Write the verb that agrees with the underlined subject.

Example: My dog (follow, follows) me everywhere. **follows**

1. Razz (hide, hides) in the tall grass. hides
2. We (run, runs) together in the field. run
3. Dogs (need, needs) daily exercise. need
4. My brother (tell, tells) me about dog care. tells
5. He (find, finds) a box for Razz. finds
6. An old towel (keep, keeps) the box warm. keeps
7. Razz (curl, curls) up in the bed. curls
8. On cold nights, Razz (sleep, sleeps) on my bed. sleeps
9. We (clean, cleans) Razz's fur every morning. clean
10. You (comb, combs) a pet's fur regularly. comb
11. My sisters (enjoy, enjoys) cats more than dogs. enjoy
12. They (say, says) dogs are too noisy. say
13. I (like, likes) dogs the best anyway. like
14. You (care, cares) so much for your pet. care
15. It (bring, brings) joy into your life. brings

▲■ WORKBOOK PLUS, pages 44–45

4 Subject-Verb Agreement

Singular subject	My family owns a diner.
Plural subject	We own a diner.

A Write each sentence correctly. Choose the verb in parentheses that agrees with the subject.

1. My brothers (serve, serves) the food in our diner.
   My brothers serve the food in our diner.
2. Aunt Anita (run, runs) the kitchen.
   Aunt Anita runs the kitchen.
3. She (cook, cooks) everything from soup to dessert.
   She cooks everything from soup to dessert.
4. We (use, uses) only fresh fruit and vegetables.
   We use only fresh fruit and vegetables.

B 5–10. This newspaper restaurant review has six incorrect verbs. Use proofreading marks to correct the verbs.

Example: I orders [order] pancakes for breakfast every Saturday.

Proofreading Marks
¶ Indent
∧ Add
Delete
≡ Capital letter
/ Small letter

Proofreading

EATING OUT WITH REGGIE

Anita's Diner serve [serves] an excellent Sunday breakfast. Anita's bakers bakes [bake] wonderful whole-grain bread. The friendly waitpersons brings [bring] to your table all the bread you can eat. Anita even make [makes] her own blueberry jam.

Anita's nephew squeeze [squeezes] fresh oranges to make the juice. The food is so tasty that some people eats [eat] at the diner every day.

(continued)

4 Subject-Verb Agreement *(continued from page 44)*

Challenge

Look at the streets and businesses on the map. Each sentence below tells where someone works. Write another sentence that tells what that person does at work. Use a present tense verb in each sentence. Answers will vary.

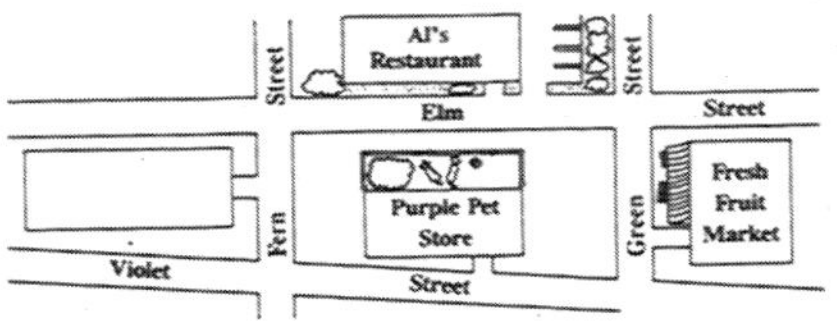

1. Al works on Elm Street.
2. Two women work on Green Street.
3. Vanessa works on Violet Street.

Write the name of a place where you would like to work in the building on Fern Street. Then write a sentence, describing what you would do.

4. I work on Fern Street.

Writing Application: A Business Plan — DESCRIBING

Suppose that you are running a business. Describe what kind of business you run and who works for you. Tell what each person in your business does. Use a present tense verb in each sentence.
Students should respond on separate paper. Answers will vary.

Spelling the Present Tense

Lesson Objectives

Students will:

- form the present tense of verbs
- proofread for spelling of present tense verbs
- write a compare-contrast sports report, using present tense verbs

One-Minute Warm-Up Write the corrected answer sentence on the board. Underline *makes* and tell students that it is a singular verb that ends with *-s*. Write the sentence *The coach fixes breakfast.* Point out that the singular form of the verb *fix* ends with *-es*.

Focus on Instruction

Point out that the spelling rules for forming present tense verbs are the same as those for forming the plurals of nouns with the same ending.

Try It Out

LISTENING AND SPEAKING Tell students to listen as volunteers read the sentences aloud, saying the verbs correctly. Have students use sound clues to decide how to correctly spell the present tense verbs.

FOR STUDENTS ACQUIRING ENGLISH

- Have students listen to the Try It Out sentences on the audiotape. Distribute SAE Practice page for Unit 3, Lesson 5, to support listening.
- Review regular *-s* verb endings. Explain that adding *-es* instead of *-s* is a pronunciation rule, but changing *y* to *-ies* after a consonant is a spelling rule. Say and write pairs such as *watch-watches, fix-fixes, miss-misses,* and have students repeat after you. Contrast these words with pairs such as *fly-flies, study-studies, cry-cries.* Have students pronounce these word pairs. Elicit more examples of each type. Then students listen and complete the sentence with the correct form of the verb.
  1. James ______ baseball after school. *(play)* (plays)
  2. We ______ him play. *(watch)* (watch)

Grammar/Usage

5 Spelling the Present Tense

One-Minute Warm-Up What's wrong with this riddle? How can you fix it?

Question: Why does the baseball coach fix a pancake breakfast for his team?

Answer: His batter make a hit!
makes

You add *-s* to most present tense verbs to make them agree with a singular subject. Some other verbs, however, add *-es* when they are used with a singular noun subject or with *he, she,* or *it.*

Present Tense with Singular Subjects		
1. **For most verbs:** Add *-s*.	sing + -s stay + -s	Corey sings. He stays.
2. **For verbs that end with *s, x, z, ch,* or *sh*:** Add *-es*.	pitch + -es buzz + -es	She pitches. A bee buzzes.
3. **For a verb that ends with a consonant and *y*:** Change the *y* to *i* and add *-es*.	study + -es fly + -es	Marisa studies. The bird flies.

Try It Out

Speak Up How should you spell the verb in the present tense to complete each sentence correctly?

1. Ben ______ tennis at the park. (play) plays
2. His friend Lin often ______ him. (watch) watches
3. Sometimes Ben ______ the ball. (miss) misses
4. Lin ______ his strokes carefully. (study) studies
5. Ben ______ his mistakes. (fix) fixes
6. Ben ______ tennis. (enjoy) enjoys
7. He ______ to get better. (want) wants

106 **Unit 3:** Verbs

Meeting Individual Needs

RETEACHING
ALTERNATIVE STRATEGY

- Write these sentences on the board: *Carlos plays football. Anita watches the game. The coach studies the game.*
- Have a volunteer read the first sentence and circle the *-s* ending. Explain that most verbs form the singular in this way.
- Next, ask a volunteer to circle the *-es* ending in the second sentence. Explain that verbs ending in *s, x, z, ch,* or *sh* form the present tense by adding *-es*.
- Repeat the procedure for the final sentence, explaining that verbs that end in a consonant and *y* form their plurals this way.

CHALLENGE

Have groups of students divide a sheet of paper into two columns: *Verbs ending in* s, x, z, ch, *or* sh; *Verbs ending in a consonant and* y. Have groups compete to see how many verbs they can list in each column in ten minutes.

FOR STUDENTS ACQUIRING ENGLISH

Review the rules for adding *-es* and changing *y* to *-ies* for plural nouns. Have students compare the rules for plurals with those for present tense verb endings.

On Your Own

Write each sentence with the correct verb.

Example: Nicole (love, loves) the game of softball.
Nicole loves the game of softball.

8. Every afternoon Nicole (hurry, hurries) to the field.
9. First, she (dress, dresses) in the locker room.
10. Then the players (toss, tosses) the ball around.
11. Nicole (throw, throws) the ball to Ashley.
12. The ball (fly, flies) high over her head.
13. Some more players (arrive, arrives) at the field.
14. The coach (teach, teaches) them some new plays.

15–22. This journal entry has eight incorrect verb forms. Write the entry correctly. Incorrect words are underlined.

Example: My swing improve every day.
My swing improves every day.

Proofreading

July

Wednesday, July 25

like I likes the mornings best at baseball camp. Our counselors practice practices with us every day after breakfast. One counselor pitches pitchs extremely fast. The ball buzzes buzzies right past the batter! shows He showes us all his tricks. The other counselor watches watch us at bat. Sometimes he copies copys everyone's mistakes. We laugh at ourselves a lot. Then each camper tries tryes harder.

Writing Wrap-Up

WRITING • THINKING • LISTENING • SPEAKING

COMPARING / CONTRASTING

Write a Sports Report

Choose two sports that you like. Write one paragraph comparing the two sports and one paragraph contrasting them. Use verbs in the present tense. Find a partner, and read your reports to each other. Compare your choices.

For Extra Practice see page 129.

Summing Up Help students summarize these key points about the lesson:

For spelling present tense verbs used with singular subjects, add *-es* to verbs that end with *s, x, z, ch,* or *sh*. For a verb ending with a consonant and *y,* change the *y* to *i* and add *-es*.

You may want to have students complete the parts related to this lesson on Blackline Master 3–3.

On Your Own

Remind students that they can find whether the subject is singular or plural by determining if it names one or more than one person, place, or thing.

MEETING INDIVIDUAL NEEDS

FOR STUDENTS ACQUIRING ENGLISH

Distribute SAE Practice page for Unit 3, Lesson 5. Help students describe the art; list vocabulary on the board. Have students identify verbs from the list. Then students choose the correct form of the verb.

1. Mary ______ soccer well. (plays)

2. She ______ the ball to the goal. (kicks)

Writing Wrap-Up

Writing Tip: Have students first list how the sports are alike and then how they are different. See Blackline Master 3–8 for a sample sports report.

TECHNOLOGY CONNECTION

Students can use the computer software's column feature to design their report as a newspaper article.

● RETEACHING WORKBOOK, page 28

5 Spelling the Present Tense

- Some present tense verbs change their spellings when used with singular subjects.
- Add -s to most verbs.
- Add -es to verbs that end with *s, x, z, ch,* or *sh*.
- If a verb ends with a consonant and *y,* change the *y* to *i* and add -es.

jump + -s	The cat **jumps**.
catch + -es	She **catches** the baseball.
try + -es	My sister **tries** to play the piano.

Write the form of the verb in parentheses to complete each sentence. The underlined letters are spelling clues.

Example: Kim ___studies___ the piano. (**study**)

1. Mr. Morales ___teaches___ Kim. (**teach**)
2. He also ___fixes___ her piano sometimes. (**fix**)
3. He ___carries___ music books in his bag. (**carry**)
4. Kim's brother Don ___watches___ her at the piano. (**watch**)
5. He ___wishes___ for a lesson too. (**wish**)
6. Don ___stretches___ his fingers. (**stretch**)
7. Kim ___passes___ him a music book. (**pass**)
8. Don ___tries___ to play a song. (**try**)
9. He ___touches___ the keys carefully. (**touch**)
10. Kim ___presses___ the pedal for him. (**press**)
11. She ___sings___ along. (**sing**)
12. Don___finishes___ the whole song. (**finish**)
13. Mr. Morales ___praises___ Don and Kim. (**praise**)
14. A timer ___buzzes___ after an hour. (**buzz**)
15. Then the lesson ___ends___. (**end**)

▲■ WORKBOOK PLUS, pages 46–47

5 Spelling the Present Tense

The girls **wish** for parts in the play.	Elena **wishes** for a part in the play.
The boys **try** out for the play.	She **tries** out for the play.

A Write each sentence correctly. Use the verb in parentheses that agrees with the subject.

1. Ramon (sell, sells) tickets for the show.
   Ramon sells tickets for the show.
2. Ingrid (search, searches) for the props.
   Ingrid searches for the props.
3. They both (dash, dashes) to the store for make-up.
   They both dash to the store for make-up.
4. Luisa (paint, paints) the sets for the stage.
   Luisa paints the sets for the stage.
5. The boys (fix, fixes) the lighting equipment.
   The boys fix the lighting equipment.

B 6–12. These instructions to the actors in the school play have seven incorrect verb forms. Use proofreading marks to correct the message.

Example: The play finishes with a loud trumpet call.

Proofreading Marks
- ¶ Indent
- ∧ Add
- Delete
- ≡ Capital letter
- / Small letter

Proofreading

Attention, Actors!

Each actor relies on others during a performance. Jerry makes sure your costume fits. The actors wait until Director Li presses a button to call you on-stage. A signal buzzes. The script runner rushes to help actors who forget their lines. All the actors try to do their best. Good luck!

(continued)

5 Spelling the Present Tense (continued from page 46)

Challenge

Suppose that you write reviews of plays for your school newspaper. You have seen the five new plays listed below. Write a short description of each play so that other students can decide which ones to see. In each description, use the verb in parentheses with a singular subject.

1. *Catch a Magic Star*
   (**catch**) Answers will vary.
2. *The Wish*
   (**wish**) ______
3. *Try, Try Again*
   (**try**) ______
4. *The Case of the Buzzing Bee*
   (**buzz**) ______
5. *The Fix-It Kid*
   (**fix**) ______

Writing Application: Instructions EXPLAINING

Suppose that you are the stage manager for the school play. It has six actors. The director has asked you to write notes that explain what each actor does on-stage. Use forms of some verbs from the Word Box.

watch	cross	relax	try	push	catch	hurry	buzz

Students should respond on separate paper. Answers will vary.

Spelling the Past Tense

Lesson Objectives

Students will:

- form the past tense of verbs, including those ending with *e*, those ending with a single vowel and a consonant, and those ending with a consonant and *y*
- proofread for spelling of past tense verbs
- write a descriptive letter, using the past tense forms of verbs

One-Minute Warm-Up Have a volunteer read the tongue twister aloud. Have students identify the words that are confused (mopped/moped) and suggest the change that would correct the confusion. Then write *mope* and *mop* on the board and have students explain how the past tense of each verb is formed.

Focus on Instruction

Point out to students that the past tense form of a verb is the same for both singular and plural subjects. Give examples such as *The family camped* and *The families camped.*

Try It Out

VIEWING Have students write in a chart on the board both the present and the past tense of verbs suggested by the picture, and have them tell which rule from the chart above helped them spell the past tense. (Sample responses are shown.) Ask volunteers to use the past tense verbs in sentences about the picture.

Present Tense	Past Tense	Spelling Rule
float	floated	1.
tip	tipped	3.
gaze	gazed	2.

FOR STUDENTS ACQUIRING ENGLISH

- Have students listen to the Try It Out sentences on the audiotape. Distribute SAE Practice page for Unit 3, Lesson 6, to support listening.
- Begin by calling out a common regular verb. Have a volunteer come to the board to write the verb. Then have small groups say the verb and decide what the past tense ending should be. Possible examples include *talk, study, laugh, fix, hop, watch, want.* Students listen to verbs and locate the verbs on the page. Then students decide what the past tense for each verb should be. Check for correct pronunciation of verb plus ending.
  1. walk (walked)
  2. fill (filled)

Grammar

6 Spelling the Past Tense

This tongue twister doesn't match the picture. Fix it by moving one letter to a different word.

Molly mopped and mooed to be milked, but Marty merely moped. **Molly moped and mooed to be milked, but Marty merely mopped.**

The past tense is usually formed by adding *-ed* to the verb.

Rules for Spelling the Past Tense		
1. **Most verbs:** Add *-ed.*	play + -ed call + -ed	We played. Dad called us.
2. **Verbs ending with *e*:** Drop the *e* and add *-ed.*	graze + -ed rope + -ed	The cattle grazed. He roped a calf.
3. **Verbs ending with a single vowel and a consonant:** Double the consonant and add *-ed.*	stop + -ed tug + -ed	The horse stopped. I tugged the rope.
4. **Verbs ending with a consonant and *y*:** Change the *y* to *i* and add *-ed.*	carry + -ed hurry + -ed	Men carried ropes. They hurried out.

Try It Out

Speak Up What is the past tense of each verb?

1. splash splashed
2. hum hummed
3. bake baked
4. fry fried
5. watch watched
6. save saved
7. drop dropped
8. study studied
9. slip slipped
10. talk talked
11. divide divided
12. worry worried
13. hop hopped
14. trip tripped
15. spray sprayed
16. look looked

Meeting Individual Needs

RETEACHING
ALTERNATIVE STRATEGY

- Write these sentences on the board in a column: *I talk to friends; I hurry home; I plan my schedule.* Point out that the verbs are present tense.
- Change *talk* in the first sentence by adding *-ed.*
- Have a volunteer change *y* to *i* in *hurry* in the second sentence and add *-ed.*
- Ask another volunteer to add an *n* and *-ed* to *plan* in the third sentence.
- Explain that these changes are examples of ways in which verbs form their past tense.

CHALLENGE

Have students create tongue twisters using the past tense of the verbs *wash, jog, bake, toss, race, skip, pull,* and *paste.* Encourage them to use words that begin with the same sound. For example, *Walter washed whales on Wednesday.* Ask students to read each other's tongue twisters aloud.

FOR STUDENTS ACQUIRING ENGLISH

Explain what a tongue twister is. Then write and say *mopped* and *moped.* Have students repeat. Describe the difference in meaning; have students identify the difference in spelling. Then have them locate the words in the book.

On Your Own

Use the past tense of the verb in ( ) to complete each sentence. Write the sentence.

Example: Luis and Cristina ______ on a cattle drive. (help)
Luis and Cristina helped on a cattle drive.

17. Their grandparents owned a cattle ranch. (own)
18. The whole family planned the summer drive. (plan)
19. They moved the cattle to new pastures. (move)
20. At night they stopped at a water hole. (stop)
21. The adults cooked dinner over a campfire. (cook)
22. Luis carried buckets of water. (carry)
23. After dinner he washed the dishes. (wash)
24. Cristina dried them. (dry)

25–30. This part of an e-mail message has six misspelled verbs in the past tense. Write the message correctly. Incorrect words are underlined.

Example: I hoped onto the saddle.
I hopped onto the saddle.

Proofreading

e-mail

Dear Jarrod,
We startted (started) the third day of the cattle drive today. It turnned exciting! One cow walked away from the herd. Luis and I hurryed after the stray. Luis troted (trotted) up behind it on his horse. Then both of us guided the cow back. Mom and Dad claped (clapped) their hands. Grandpa praiseed (praised) us for our good work.

Writing Wrap-Up
WRITING • THINKING • LISTENING • SPEAKING

DESCRIBING

Write a Letter

Write a letter to a pen pal in another country. Describe something interesting, such as a town parade or a family event. Use verbs in the past tense. Then read your letter to a partner. Did your partner describe a similar experience?

For Extra Practice see page 130.

Summing Up Help students summarize these key points about the lesson:

Add *-ed* to most verbs to form the past tense. For verbs ending with *e,* drop the *e* and add *-ed.* For verbs ending with a single vowel and a consonant, double the consonant and add *-ed.* For verbs ending with a consonant and *y,* change the *y* to *i* and add *-ed.*

You may want to have students complete the parts related to this lesson on Blackline Master 3–3.

On Your Own

Remind students to look at the ending of each verb and then use the chart on page 108 to form the past tense.

MEETING INDIVIDUAL NEEDS

FOR STUDENTS ACQUIRING ENGLISH

Distribute SAE Practice page for Unit 3, Lesson 6. Show students photos of large cattle ranches; help students describe what they see. Refer to a map of the West. List vocabulary on the board. Students complete sentences with the correct past form. Example: John's grandparents ______ a ranch in Texas. *(own)* (owned)

Writing Wrap-Up

Writing Tip: Suggest that students first jot down notes about the event, arranging them in chronological order. See Blackline Master 3–8 for a sample letter.

SCHOOL-HOME CONNECTION

Students may want to consult family members for additional details about a family event.

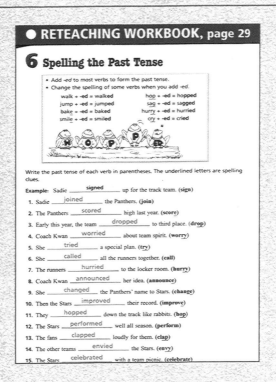

● RETEACHING WORKBOOK, page 29

6 Spelling the Past Tense

- Add *-ed* to most verbs to form the past tense.
- Change the spelling of some verbs when you add *-ed.*

walk + -ed = walked
jump + -ed = jumped
bake + -ed = baked
smile + -ed = smiled
hop + -ed = hopped
sag + -ed = sagged
hurry + -ed = hurried
cry + -ed = cried

Write the past tense of each verb in parentheses. The underlined letters are spelling clues.

Example: Sadie signed up for the track team. **(sign)**

1. Sadie joined the Panthers. **(join)**
2. The Panthers scored high last year. **(score)**
3. Early this year, the team dropped to third place. **(drop)**
4. Coach Kwan worried about team spirit. **(worry)**
5. She tried a special plan. **(try)**
6. She called all the runners together. **(call)**
7. The runners hurried to the locker room. **(hurry)**
8. Coach Kwan announced her idea. **(announce)**
9. She changed the Panthers' name to Stars. **(change)**
10. Then the Stars improved their record. **(improve)**
11. They hopped down the track like rabbits. **(hop)**
12. The Stars performed well all season. **(perform)**
13. The fans clapped loudly for them. **(clap)**
14. The other teams envied the Stars. **(envy)**
15. The Stars celebrated with a team picnic. **(celebrate)**

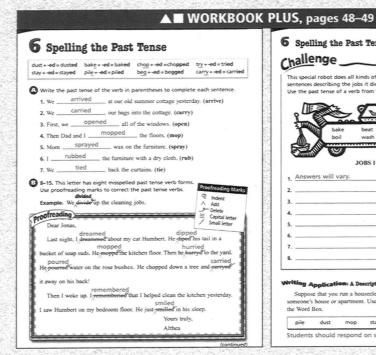

▲■ WORKBOOK PLUS, pages 48–49

6 Spelling the Past Tense

dust + -ed = dusted	bake + -ed = baked	chop + -ed = chopped	try + -ed = tried
stay + -ed = stayed	pile + -ed = piled	beg + -ed = begged	carry + -ed = carried

A Write the past tense of the verb in parentheses to complete each sentence.

1. We arrived at our old summer cottage yesterday. **(arrive)**
2. We carried our bags into the cottage. **(carry)**
3. First, we opened all of the windows. **(open)**
4. Then Dad and I mopped the floors. **(mop)**
5. Mom sprayed wax on the furniture. **(spray)**
6. I rubbed the furniture with a dry cloth. **(rub)**
7. We tied back the curtains. **(tie)**

B 8–15. This letter has eight misspelled past tense verb forms. Use proofreading marks to correct the past tense verbs.

Example: We ~~divide~~ divided up the cleaning jobs.

Proofreading Marks
¶ Indent
∧ Add
Delete
≡ Capital letter
/ Small letter

Proofreading

Dear Jonas,

Last night, I ~~dreammed~~ dreamed about my cat Humbert. He ~~diped~~ dipped his tail in a bucket of soap suds. He ~~moppd~~ mopped the kitchen floor. Then he ~~hurryd~~ hurried to the yard. He ~~pourred~~ poured water on the rose bushes. He chopped down a tree and ~~carryed~~ carried it away on his back!

Then I woke up. I ~~rememberied~~ remembered that I helped clean the kitchen yesterday. I saw Humbert on my bedroom floor. He just ~~smilled~~ smiled in his sleep.

Yours truly,
Althea

(continued)

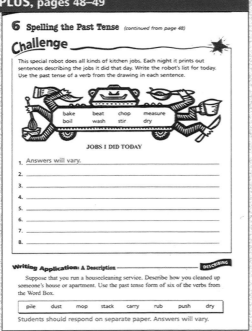

6 Spelling the Past Tense (continued from page 48)

Challenge

This special robot does all kinds of kitchen jobs. Each night it prints out sentences describing the jobs it did that day. Write the robot's list for today. Use the past tense of a verb from the drawing in each sentence.

JOBS I DID TODAY

1. Answers will vary.
2.
3.
4.
5.
6.
7.
8.

Writing Application: A Description DESCRIBING

Suppose that you run a housecleaning service. Describe how you cleaned up someone's house or apartment. Use the past tense form of six of the verbs from the Word Box.

pile	dust	mop	stack	carry	rub	push	dry

Students should respond on separate paper. Answers will vary.

The Past with Helping Verbs

Lesson Objectives

Students will:

- identify and write past tense verbs with the helping verbs *has, have,* or *had,* with singular or plural subjects
- proofread a poem for helping verbs with past tense verbs
- write a creative poem, using helping verbs with past tense verbs

One-Minute Warm-Up Have students make up additional sentences about Aunt Molly's travels, using the helping verb *had* to show the past tense. Record the sentences on the board and have students underline the verbs. Point out that *had* helps the main verb.

Focus on Instruction

Review subject-verb agreement, which means that the subject and verb must both be singular or both be plural.

Try It Out

LISTENING AND SPEAKING Have students listen as volunteers read each sentence aloud. For each sentence, have students identify the subject and indicate whether it is singular or plural. Ask students what they can tell about the helping verbs in sentences 3 and 5 based on what they have heard. (The helping verbs are singular to agree with the singular subjects.)

FOR STUDENTS ACQUIRING ENGLISH

- Have students listen to the Try It Out sentences on the audiotape. Distribute SAE Practice page Unit 3, Lesson 7, to support listening.
- Before they listen, ask several students, "Have you ever been to the circus? When/How long ago did you go? Had you been to the circus before you came to the United States?" Explain that often an earlier event is stated or implied by using the helping verb *has, have,* or *had* with the past form of most verbs. Tell students to imagine they are waiting at home, ready to go to the circus for the first time. As they listen, they underline the verbs. Then, as a group, discuss the sequence of events.

  I have never been to the circus. This will be the first time. John had invited me two weeks ago. I am worried. My bus had been late. Maybe John has already left.

Grammar/Usage

7 The Past with Helping Verbs

One-Minute Warm-Up

Read the sentences below. Are the verbs in the present tense, the past tense, or the future tense? Which sentence has a helping verb? **past; second sentence**

Aunt Molly worked for an airline. She had traveled all over the world.

—from *Cam Jansen and the Mystery of the Circus Clown,* by David A. Adler

You know that you can add *-ed* to most verbs to show action that happened in the past. There is another way to show that something has already happened.

- Use the helping verb *has, have,* or *had* with the past form of most verbs.
- The helping verb must agree with the subject of the sentence.

Agreement with Helping Verbs	
1. With singular subjects: Use *has.*	Jillian has joined a circus. She has traveled all over.
2. With plural subjects and *I* or *you*: Use *have.*	Horses have learned tricks. You have dropped your ticket.
3. With either singular or plural subjects: Use *had.*	Bears had danced. A clown had hurried into the ring.

Try It Out

Speak Up What are the helping verb and the main verb in each sentence? **HV is underlined once; MV, twice.**

1. We have watched the circus with Aunt Millie.
2. She had invited us two weeks ago.
3. Ray has hurried to the circus grounds.
4. The first act had started.
5. The ringmaster has stepped into the ring.

Meeting Individual Needs

RETEACHING
ALTERNATIVE STRATEGY

- On the board, write *We have enjoyed our stay in Florida.*
- Explain that *enjoyed* is the main verb and that a helping verb can help the main verb show action in the past. Tell students that helping verbs come before main verbs. Have students circle the helping verb in the sentence. *(have)*
- Then have students dictate their own sentences about a stay in Florida, using these verbs: *have watched, had played,* and *has returned.*

CHALLENGE

Have pairs of students write a short dialogue between a circus trainer and one of the circus animals. Tell students they must use past tense verbs with helping verbs in each sentence. Have students present their dialogues to the class.

FOR STUDENTS ACQUIRING ENGLISH

The contrast between the present perfect and simple past is challenging. Practice these verb forms before working with the past perfect. Explain that *for, since, already,* and *yet* are clues for present perfect; *in* and *ago* are clues for past.

On Your Own

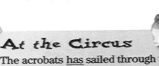

Write each sentence. Underline each helping verb once and each main verb twice.

Example: I have enjoyed the circus. *I have enjoyed the circus.*

6. You have liked it too.
7. The ringmaster has cracked her whip.
8. The elephants had paraded in a circle.
9. They have walked right in front of me.
10. One chimp has grinned at the audience.
11. We have clapped loudly for the performers.

12–18. This poem has seven incorrect helping verbs. Write the poem correctly.
Incorrect words are underlined.

Example: A dog have jumped through a hoop.
A dog has jumped through a hoop.

Proofreading

At the Circus

The acrobats has sailed through the air. have
They has dangled on ropes without a care. have
One clown have balanced a chair on his nose. has
The others has sprayed the crowd with a hose. have
A monkey have carried off the ringmaster's hat. has
Nobody had planned on that.
The lions has settled down at last. have
The show have ended much too fast! has

Writing Wrap-Up WRITING • THINKING • LISTENING • SPEAKING

CREATING

Write a Poem

Can you fly a kite or do a handstand? Did you ever watch a fireworks show? Write a poem about something you like to do or see. Use verbs in the past with helping verbs. With a small group, take turns reading your poems aloud. Listen for any incorrect helping verbs.

For Extra Practice see page 131.

Summing Up Help students summarize these key points about the lesson:

> The helping verbs *has, have,* and *had* can be used with the past form of most verbs to show action that has already happened. The helping verb must agree with the subject.

You may want to have students complete the parts related to this lesson on Blackline Master 3–2.

On Your Own

Point out that the verb that ends in *-ed* is the main verb.

MEETING INDIVIDUAL NEEDS

FOR STUDENTS ACQUIRING ENGLISH

Distribute SAE Practice page for Unit 3, Lesson 7. Use the art to practice verbs; students describe what is happening now or what happened last night, for example. Students correct errors in helping verbs. If the helping verb is correct, they mark a ✓.

1. We has always liked the clowns. (has→have)
2. They have made us laugh. ✓

Writing Wrap-Up

Writing Tip: Remind students that poems do not have to rhyme. See Blackline Master 3–8 for a sample poem.

SCHOOL-HOME CONNECTION

Suggest that students and their families read poems together. Students can point out the helping verbs in the poems.

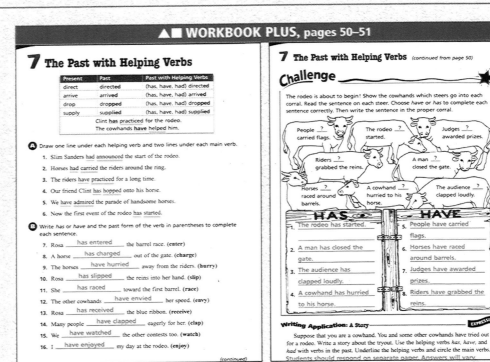

● RETEACHING WORKBOOK, page 30

7 The Past with Helping Verbs

- The helping verbs *has, have,* and *had* can be used with the past form of a verb to show action that has already happened.

Present	Past	Past with Helping Verbs
bake	baked	(has, had, have) baked
wish	wished	(has, had, have) wished
swap	swapped	(has, had, have) swapped
try	tried	(has, had, have) tried

Underline the helping verb in each sentence.
Write the main verb.

Example: We had learned about inventors. **learned**

1. Our class had visited a museum last week. visited
2. This museum had displayed a huge windmill. displayed
3. Robert Johnson had created it. created
4. Robert Johnson has tried many things. tried
5. Machines have interested him since his youth. interested
6. He had fixed clocks as a boy. fixed
7. Different inventors had delighted him. delighted
8. Mr. Johnson has copied old machines. copied
9. The new ones have looked just like the old ones. looked
10. He has collected rare books also. collected
11. He has swapped the books for more machines. swapped
12. Famous museums have traded books with him. traded
13. Judges have awarded him different prizes. awarded
14. They have praised his work. praised
15. Robert Johnson's interesting life has amazed us. amazed

▲■ WORKBOOK PLUS, pages 50–51

7 The Past with Helping Verbs

Present	Past	Past with Helping Verbs
direct	directed	(has, have, had) directed
arrive	arrived	(has, have, had) arrived
drop	dropped	(has, have, had) dropped
supply	supplied	(has, have, had) supplied

Clint **has** practiced for the rodeo.
The cowhands **have** helped him.

A Draw one line under each helping verb and two lines under each main verb.

1. Slim Sanders had announced the start of the rodeo.
2. Horses had carried the riders around the ring.
3. The riders have practiced for a long time.
4. Our friend Clint has hopped onto his horse.
5. We have admired the parade of handsome horses.
6. Now the first event of the rodeo has started.

B Write *has* or *have* and the past form of the verb in parentheses to complete each sentence.

7. Rosa has entered the barrel race. **(enter)**
8. A horse has charged out of the gate. **(charge)**
9. The horses have hurried away from the riders. **(hurry)**
10. Rosa has slipped the reins into her hand. **(slip)**
11. She has raced toward the first barrel. **(race)**
12. The other cowhands have envied her speed. **(envy)**
13. Rosa has received the blue ribbon. **(receive)**
14. Many people have clapped eagerly for her. **(clap)**
15. We have watched the other contests too. **(watch)**
16. I have enjoyed my day at the rodeo. **(enjoy)**

(continued)

7 The Past with Helping Verbs *(continued from page 50)*

Challenge

The rodeo is about to begin! Show the cowhands which steers go into each corral. Read the sentence on each steer. Choose *have* or *has* to complete each sentence correctly. Then write the sentence in the proper corral.

People ? carried flags.
The rodeo ? started.
Judges ? awarded prizes.
Riders ? grabbed the reins.
A man ? closed the gate.
Horses ? raced around barrels.
A cowhand ? hurried to his horse.
The audience ? clapped loudly.

HAS	HAVE
1. The rodeo has started.	5. People have carried flags.
2. A man has closed the gate.	6. Horses have raced around barrels.
3. The audience has clapped loudly.	7. Judges have awarded prizes.
4. A cowhand has hurried to his horse.	8. Riders have grabbed the reins.

Writing Application: A Story EXPRESSING

Suppose that you are a cowhand. You and some other cowhands have tried out for a rodeo. Write a story about the tryout. Use the helping verbs *has, have,* and *had* with verbs in the past. Underline the helping verbs and circle the main verbs. Students should respond on separate paper. Answers will vary.

Irregular Verbs

Lesson Objectives

Students will:

- write past tense forms of irregular verbs
- proofread for forms of irregular verbs
- write a narrative using irregular verbs

One-Minute Warm-Up Write the corrected sentence on the board. Point out that *took* is a verb that does not form its past tense by adding *-ed.* Have students identify other verbs that do not form their past tense by adding *-ed.* Tell students that these verbs and the ones in the chart are called irregular verbs.

Focus on Instruction

Point out to students that they already use many of the verbs they will learn about in this lesson. If, however, students are unsure of the different verb forms, they can always check a dictionary. They can find the irregular forms listed under the entry for the verb's present tense form.

Try It Out

LISTENING AND SPEAKING Have volunteers give the past tense of the verbs by using short sentences, such as *I sing, Yesterday I sang,* and *I have sung many times.* As students listen, have them raise their hand when they hear an incorrect answer. If students cannot agree on an answer, have them look up the verb in a dictionary.

FOR STUDENTS ACQUIRING ENGLISH

- Have students listen to the Try It Out sentences on the audiotape. Distribute SAE Practice page for Unit 3, Lesson 8, to support listening.
- Write *memorize* on the board. Ask students what this means; then ask for examples of things they have had to memorize. Explain that there are many irregular verbs in English and that all of us have to memorize what they are and how they are spelled. Practice chanting the verb sets in a rhythmic way. Also have students describe what in each set changes. Is it just one letter? Are two of the forms the same? Are the three quite different? Then as students listen, they write in the missing form(s).

1. begin		(has, have, had)	begun	(began)
2. throw	threw	(has, have, had)		(thrown)

Grammar/Usage

8 Irregular Verbs

One-Minute Warm-Up One of the verbs in the sentences below is incorrect. Do you know how to fix it? Incorrect verb is underlined.

Someone has eaten my lunch! The sea gull has took it!
has taken or took

Verbs that do not add *-ed* to show past action are called irregular verbs. You must remember the spellings of irregular verbs.

I eat now. I ate earlier. I have eaten already.

Irregular Verbs

Present	Past	Past with helping verb
begin	began	(has, have, had) begun
break	broke	(has, have, had) broken
bring	brought	(has, have, had) brought
come	came	(has, have, had) come
drive	drove	(has, have, had) driven
eat	ate	(has, have, had) eaten
give	gave	(has, have, had) given
grow	grew	(has, have, had) grown
know	knew	(has, have, had) known
make	made	(has, have, had) made
say	said	(has, have, had) said
sing	sang	(has, have, had) sung
take	took	(has, have, had) taken
tell	told	(has, have, had) told
throw	threw	(has, have, had) thrown
wear	wore	(has, have, had) worn

Try It Out

Speak Up What are the past tense and the past with a helping verb for each irregular verb below?

1. sing sang, sung
2. begin began, begun
3. come came, come
4. know knew, known
5. eat ate, eaten
6. tell told, told

Meeting Individual Needs

RETEACHING
ALTERNATIVE STRATEGY

- Write on the board *Yesterday I _______ a train ride.* (take)
- Ask a volunteer to add *-ed* to the end of the verb *take* and then say the sentence aloud, using the verb in the blank space. Ask students to explain what is wrong with the sentence. (*Taked* is not a correct word.)
- Explain that such verbs as *take* are irregular, which means that *-ed* cannot be added to them to show past action. The spellings of these verbs must be memorized.
- Have students use other irregular verbs in sentences.

CHALLENGE

Divide the class into small groups. Challenge small groups of students to list on paper the present and past tense of as many irregular verbs beginning with the letter *r* as they can in three minutes. The group with the most words gets to choose the initial letter for the next group of irregular verbs.

FOR STUDENTS ACQUIRING ENGLISH

Work first with the irregular past. On the board, write and say partial statements; call on students to complete them logically. For example, *I drove _______. James broke _______. Sinae ate _______.* Have students mark the verbs.

On Your Own

Write each sentence, using the correct form of the verb to show past action.

Example: His uncle had ______ Matthew sailing lessons. (give)
His uncle had given Matthew sailing lessons.

7. They had ______ many sailing trips together. (take) taken
8. Matthew ______ his friend Tyler to join them one day. (tell) told
9. Tyler's father ______ him to the boat. (drive) drove
10. Tyler ______ good-bye to his father. (say) said
11. Matthew's uncle ______ how to handle the boat. (know) knew
12. The boat had ______ to a pleasant island. (come) come
13. Everyone ______ a big lunch on the island. (eat) ate

14–20. This part of an adventure story has seven incorrect irregular verb forms. Write the story. Correct the underlined verbs. Incorrect words are underlined.

Example: Mr. Williams had taked Buster for a boat ride.
Mr. Williams had taken Buster for a boat ride.

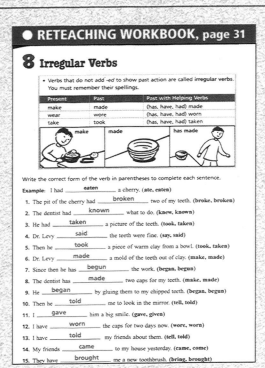

Proofreading

Buster the Superdog

begun The trip had began calmly. Suddenly, the grew weather grown worse. Huge waves broked broke over the small boat. One wave pushed Mr. Williams overboard. Fortunately, he had wore a life jacket. worn Buster the Superdog had make a strict rule about that. made Buster thrown Mr. Williams a rope. The clever pet threw bringed him safely back onboard. brought

Writing Wrap-Up

WRITING • THINKING • LISTENING • SPEAKING

NARRATING

Write a Story

Write the beginning of an adventure story. The setting might be the darkest jungle or the hottest desert or any place else you want. Use verbs from the chart on page 112. Then read your story to a partner. Ask your partner to listen for the verbs. Did you use the correct verb forms?

For Extra Practice see page 132.

Summing Up Help students summarize these key points about the lesson:

Verbs that do not add *-ed* to show the past action are called **irregular verbs**. The spellings of irregular verbs must be remembered.

You may want to have students complete the parts related to this lesson on Blackline Master 3–4.

On Your Own

Suggest that students read each sentence aloud. They might find that they automatically say the irregular verbs correctly in their past tenses.

MEETING INDIVIDUAL NEEDS

FOR STUDENTS ACQUIRING ENGLISH

Distribute SAE Practice page for Unit 3, Lesson 8. Discuss the art. List vocabulary on the board; explain as needed. Then students choose the correct form of the verb.

1. We ______ a song last night. *(sang/sung)* (sang)
2. We had ______ a big dinner. *(ate/eaten)* (eaten)

Writing Wrap-Up

Writing Tip: Remind students that the beginning of a story introduces the characters and tells where and when the story takes place. See Blackline Master 3–8 for a sample adventure story beginning.

SCHOOL-HOME CONNECTION

Encourage students to read their stories to family members and then discuss ideas for the next part of it.

● RETEACHING WORKBOOK, page 31

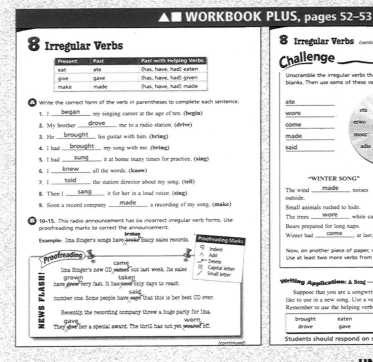

8 Irregular Verbs

- Verbs that do not add *-ed* to show past action are called **irregular verbs**. You must remember their spellings.

Present	Past	Past with Helping Verbs
make	made	(has, have, had) made
wear	wore	(has, have, had) worn
take	took	(has, have, had) taken

Write the correct form of the verb in parentheses to complete each sentence.

Example: I had ___eaten___ a cherry. **(ate, eaten)**

1. The pit of the cherry had ___broken___ two of my teeth. **(broke, broken)**
2. The dentist had ___known___ what to do. **(knew, known)**
3. He had ___taken___ a picture of the teeth. **(took, taken)**
4. Dr. Levy ___said___ the teeth were fine. **(say, said)**
5. Then he ___took___ a piece of warm clay from a bowl. **(took, taken)**
6. Dr. Levy ___made___ a mold of the teeth out of clay. **(make, made)**
7. Since then he has ___begun___ the work. **(began, begun)**
8. The dentist has ___made___ two caps for my teeth. **(make, made)**
9. He ___began___ by gluing them to my chipped teeth. **(began, begun)**
10. Then he ___told___ me to look in the mirror. **(tell, told)**
11. I ___gave___ him a big smile. **(gave, given)**
12. I have ___worn___ the caps for two days now. **(wore, worn)**
13. I have ___told___ my friends about them. **(tell, told)**
14. My friends ___came___ to my house yesterday. **(came, come)**
15. They have ___brought___ me a new toothbrush. **(bring, brought)**

▲■ WORKBOOK PLUS, pages 52–53

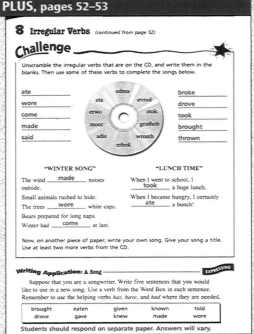

8 Irregular Verbs

Present	Past	Past with Helping Verbs
eat	ate	(has, have, had) eaten
give	gave	(has, have, had) given
make	made	(has, have, had) made

A Write the correct form of the verb in parentheses to complete each sentence.

1. I ___began___ my singing career at the age of ten. **(begin)**
2. My brother ___drove___ me to a radio station. **(drive)**
3. He ___brought___ his guitar with him. **(bring)**
4. I had ___brought___ my song with me. **(bring)**
5. I had ___sung___ it at home many times for practice. **(sing)**
6. I ___knew___ all the words. **(know)**
7. I ___told___ the station director about my song. **(tell)**
8. Then I ___sang___ it for her in a loud voice. **(sing)**
9. Soon a record company ___made___ a recording of my song. **(make)**

B 10–15. This radio announcement has six incorrect irregular verb forms. Use proofreading marks to correct the announcement.

Example: Ima Singer's songs have ~~broke~~ broken many sales records.

Proofreading Marks
- ¶ Indent
- ^ Add
- Delete
- ≡ Capital letter
- / Small letter

Proofreading

NEWS FLASH!

Ima Singer's new CD ~~camed~~ came out last week. Its sales have ~~grew~~ grown very fast. It has ~~took~~ taken only days to reach number one. Some people have ~~says~~ said that this is her best CD ever.

Recently, the recording company threw a huge party for Ima. They ~~give~~ gave her a special award. The thrill has not yet ~~weared~~ worn off.

(continued)

8 Irregular Verbs *(continued from page 52)*

Challenge

Unscramble the irregular verbs that are on the CD, and write them in the blanks. Then use some of these verbs to complete the songs below.

ate		broke
wore		drove
come		took
made		brought
said		thrown

"WINTER SONG"

The wind ___made___ noises outside.
Small animals rushed to hide.
The trees ___wore___ white caps.
Bears prepared for long naps.
Winter had ___come___ at last.

"LUNCH TIME"

When I went to school, I ___took___ a huge lunch.
When I became hungry, I certainly ___ate___ a bunch!

Now, on another piece of paper, write your own song. Give your song a title. Use at least two more verbs from the CD.

Writing Application: A Song EXPRESSING

Suppose that you are a songwriter. Write five sentences that you would like to use in a new song. Use a verb from the Word Box in each sentence. Remember to use the helping verbs *has*, *have*, and *had* where they are needed.

brought	eaten	given	known	told
drove	gave	knew	made	wore

Students should respond on separate paper. Answers will vary.

The Special Verb *be*

Lesson Objectives

Students will:

- recognize the different forms of the verb *be*
- proofread for forms of *be*
- write an opinion paragraph about fire safety, using the correct forms of *be*

One-Minute Warm-Up Have volunteers read the sentence aloud, using the word on the shirt that correctly completes it. (are) Have students identify the incorrect word. Ask students to rewrite the sentence so that *is* could be used. (Rigsy is glad he forgot his lunch.)

Focus on Instruction

Explain to students that in Lesson 2 they learned how the verb *be* can be used as a helping verb with main verbs to show action. In this lesson, they will learn how to use *be* as the main verb in a sentence.

Try It Out

LISTENING AND SPEAKING Have students listen as volunteers read each sentence aloud, using the correct form of *be*. Ask students to tell the subject of each sentence.

FOR STUDENTS ACQUIRING ENGLISH

- Have students listen to the Try It Out sentences on the audiotape. Distribute SAE Practice page for Unit 3, Lesson 9, to support listening.
- Call out a pronoun or a noun from a list prepared in advance and have students write the correct form of *be*. First they answer just with the present forms. Include some plurals such as *elephants* and a few with possessive adjectives such as *my mother*. Gradually decrease the time you allow. Repeat with *was* and *were*. Have students check answers with partners or in small groups. Then students listen and choose the correct verb to complete each sentence.
  1. Chiara ______ an artist. (is) (am/is/are)
  2. Her brother ______ an artist too. (is) (am/is/are)

Grammar/Usage

9 The Special Verb *be*

Which word on the shirts will *not* complete the sentence below correctly?

Rigsy and Chuckles ______ glad they forgot their lunches. is

The verb *be* has special forms for different subjects.

Subject	Present	Past
I	am	was
you	are	were
he, she, it	is	was
singular noun (Miguel)	is	was
we	are	were
they	are	were
plural noun (stories)	are	were

The verb *be* does not show action. It tells what someone or something is or is like.

I **am** a reporter. You **are** a photographer.
That story **was** long. Those cartoons **were** funny.

Try It Out

Speak Up Which verb correctly completes each sentence? Is it in the present tense or the past tense?

1. I (was, were) a cartoon writer last year. past
2. Kayla (is, are) good at drawing. pres.
3. We (is, are) a great team! pres.
4. Two cartoons (was, were) about the cafeteria food. past
5. The food (is, are) pretty bad! pres.

114 **Unit 3:** Verbs

Meeting Individual Needs

RETEACHING
ALTERNATIVE STRATEGY

- Write these sentences on the board: *Mr. Johnson is a newspaper reporter. These people are reporters too. I am a photographer.*
- Ask when the action in the sentences happens. (in the present) Underline the verbs and explain that each is a present tense form of the verb *be*.
- Explain that *be* has special forms for different subjects and for different tenses.
- Rewrite the sentences, changing the verbs to past tense. Discuss the special forms of *be* in the past tense.

CHALLENGE

Have students write a riddle about a person or an ordinary object. The main verb of each clue should be a form of *be*. Read this riddle as an example: *I am shorter today than I was yesterday. My dark trail is easy to follow. What am I?* (a pencil)

FOR STUDENTS ACQUIRING ENGLISH

Ask students various questions about themselves using the verb *be*, such as *Are you a doctor? Is your name Andrea? Are they your brothers?* (pointing to two boys) Students should respond accurately but may use short or long answers.

On Your Own

Write the verb in each sentence. Then write *past* or *present* to tell the tense of the verb.

Example: The *Scoop* is our school newspaper. *is—present*

6. I am the editor of the *Scoop*. pres.
7. William is a good writer. pres.
8. He was the sports writer. past
9. You are a good writer too. pres.
10. I was happy with your last story. past
11. All the reporters were busy. past
12. The paper is ready for the printers. pres.
13. We are proud of our work. pres.

14–20. This part of a newspaper article has seven incorrect forms of the verb *be*. Write the article correctly. Incorrect words are underlined.

Example: The fire were in an apartment building.
The fire was in an apartment building.

Proofreading

Smoky Blaze Alarms Residents

Chicago, April 12 — Mrs. Allen were [was] at home with her husband when a fire began in the kitchen. "We was [were] so afraid. The smoke were [was] so thick and black," Mrs. Allen said. "The firefighters was [were] there for us in minutes," she added. "They is [are] heroes. I is [am] very grateful."

"Your smoke detector batteries were dead," one firefighter told her later. "You was [were] lucky this time," he warned. "Get new batteries right away."

Writing Wrap-Up

WRITING • THINKING • LISTENING • SPEAKING

EXPRESSING

Write an Opinion

Write a paragraph about fire safety in the home. In your opinion, what are the best ways to protect a home against fire? Use forms of the verb *be*. Then read your paragraph to a small group. Does the group share your opinion? Can anyone suggest other fire safety tips?

For Extra Practice see page 133.

Summing Up Help students summarize these key points about the lesson:

The verb *be* does not show action. It tells what someone or something is or is like. Use *am* or *was* with *I*. Use *is* or *was* with singular nouns and *he, she,* or *it*. Use *are* or *were* with plural nouns and *we, you,* or *they*.

You may want to have students complete the parts related to this lesson on Blackline Master 3–5.

On Your Own

Suggest that, while writing the newspaper article correctly, students ask themselves *What is the subject of the sentence? Is the subject singular or plural?*

MEETING INDIVIDUAL NEEDS

FOR STUDENTS ACQUIRING ENGLISH

Distribute SAE Practice page for Unit 3, Lesson 9. Discuss school newspapers. Show samples if possible. Students decide which pronoun completes each sentence.

1. ______ am a writer on our school paper. (I)
2. That boy works on the paper. ______ is a good writer. (He)

Writing Wrap-Up

Writing Tip: Remind students that they should include several reasons to support their opinion. See Blackline Master 3–9 for a sample opinion.

TECHNOLOGY CONNECTION

Groups of students can use available software to create a class newspaper using the articles they wrote.

● RETEACHING WORKBOOK, page 32

9 The Special Verb *be*

- The special verb *be* does not show action. It tells what someone or something is or is like.
- Use the form of the verb *be* that agrees with the subject of the sentence.

Subject	Present	Past	Sentences
I	am	was	I was near the tree.
he, she, it	is	was	He was surprised.
singular noun	is	was	Silvio is here now.
we, you, they	are	were	We are good friends.
plural noun	are	were	Trees were around us.

Write the verb in parentheses that agrees with each underlined subject.

Example: This tree ___is___ a maple tree. **(is, are)**

1. The branches ___are___ close to the ground. **(is, are)**
2. They ___are___ thick and strong. **(is, are)**
3. I ___am___ up in the tree now. **(am, is)**
4. This tree ___was___ my sister's favorite. **(was, were)**
5. My sister ___is___ a good climber. **(is, are)**
6. She ___is___ away at school now. **(am, is)**
7. Many trees ___were___ here before the storm. **(was, were)**
8. The storm ___was___ a very bad one. **(was, were)**
9. It ___was___ the worst storm in ten years. **(was, were)**
10. I ___was___ afraid of the strong winds. **(was, were)**
11. You ___were___ calm during the storm. **(was, were)**
12. Then we ___were___ not afraid. **(was, were)**
13. Our school ___is___ a safe place. **(is, are)**
14. Our friends ___were___ there during the storm. **(was, were)**
15. We ___are___ happy about that. **(is, are)**

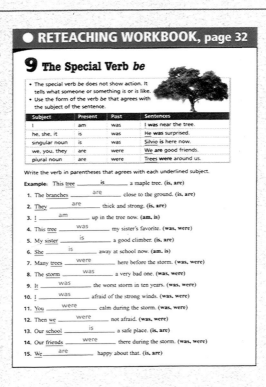

▲■ WORKBOOK PLUS, pages 54–55

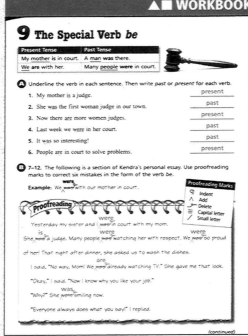

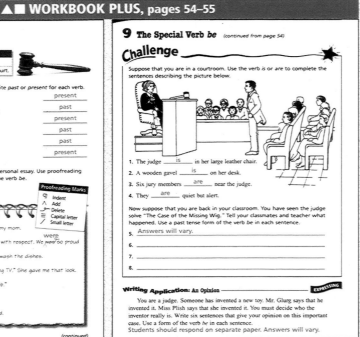

9 The Special Verb *be*

Present Tense	Past Tense
My mother is in court.	A man was there.
We are with her.	Many people were in court.

A Underline the verb in each sentence. Then write *past* or *present* for each verb.

1. My mother is a judge. ___present___
2. She was the first woman judge in our town. ___past___
3. Now there are more women judges. ___present___
4. Last week we were in her court. ___past___
5. It was so interesting! ___past___
6. People are in court to solve problems. ___present___

B 7–12. The following is a section of Kendra's personal essay. Use proofreading marks to correct six mistakes in the form of the verb *be*.

Example: We ~~was~~ were with our mother in court.

Proofreading Marks
¶ Indent
∧ Add
Delete
≡ Capital letter
/ Small letter

Proofreading

Yesterday my sister and I ~~was~~ were in court with my mom. She ~~was~~ is a judge. Many people ~~was~~ were watching her with respect. We ~~was~~ were so proud of her! That night after dinner, she asked us to wash the dishes.

I said, "No way, Mom! We ~~was~~ are already watching TV." She gave me that look.

"Okay," I said. "Now I know why you like your job."

"Why?" She ~~were~~ was smiling now.

"Everyone always does what you say!" I replied.

(continued)

9 The Special Verb *be* (continued from page 54)

Challenge

Suppose that you are in a courtroom. Use the verb *is* or *are* to complete the sentences describing the picture below.

1. The judge ___is___ in her large leather chair.
2. A wooden gavel ___is___ on her desk.
3. Six jury members ___are___ near the judge.
4. They ___are___ quiet but alert.

Now suppose that you are back in your classroom. You have seen the judge solve "The Case of the Missing Wig." Tell your classmates and teacher what happened. Use a past tense form of the verb *be* in each sentence.

5. Answers will vary.
6. ______
7. ______
8. ______

Writing Application: An Opinion EXPRESSING

You are a judge. Someone has invented a new toy. Mr. Glurg says that he invented it. Miss Plish says that she invented it. You must decide who the inventor really is. Write six sentences that give your opinion on this important case. Use a form of the verb *be* in each sentence.
Students should respond on separate paper. Answers will vary.

Contractions with *not*

Lesson Objectives

Students will:

- form contractions using verbs and the word *not*
- determine which words make up a contraction
- proofread for contractions
- create a song using contractions

One-Minute Warm-Up Write the sentence on the board twice, once with the contraction, and once without it. Ask students which sounds more friendly, or less formal. (the sentence with *didn't*) Explain that people often use contractions in everyday language when they combine verbs with the word *not*. Have students suggest situations where they would use contractions, and where they would not.

Focus on Instruction

Explain that the contraction *won't* is unusual because of its spelling change. Encourage students to memorize the spelling of this word.

Try It Out

VIEWING Have students identify the contraction on the sign in the photograph and tell what two words are combined to form it. (don't; do, not) Write the equation below to show how the contraction is formed. Then have students make up their own signs, using contractions. Have them write an equation for each contraction they use.

do + not = don't

FOR STUDENTS ACQUIRING ENGLISH

- Have students listen to the Try It Out sentences on the audiotape. Distribute SAE Practice page for Unit 3, Lesson 10, to support listening.
- With students, practice saying the contractions in the list. Make sure they understand that contractions represent spoken forms. Explore meaning. Explain that contractions on the list all are accepted in writing, but there are many, many words in English that are shortened in speech. Elicit examples students have heard. (for example, *gonna, wanna, dontcha*) Distinguish between accepted contractions they may use in their writing and those that should be used just in conversation. Students listen and match contractions with their unshortened forms. Then they listen and write the complete form or the contraction.

Grammar/Mechanics

10 Contractions with *not*

One-Minute Warm-Up

The Secret Shortcut

Read the sentences below. Which word has an apostrophe? What two words make up this word?

"Shortcut?" asked Floyd. "I didn't know there were any good shortcuts to school." **didn't; did not**

—from *The Secret Shortcut*, by Mark Teague

Sometimes you can join a verb with the word *not*. **The shortened word is called a contraction.** An **apostrophe** (') takes the place of the letter *o* in each contraction with *not*.

Tim is not ready yet. Tim isn't ready yet.

Contractions with *not*

Word Pairs	Contractions	Word Pairs	Contractions
is not	isn't	has not	hasn't
are not	aren't	have not	haven't
was not	wasn't	had not	hadn't
were not	weren't	could not	couldn't
do not	don't	should not	shouldn't
does not	doesn't	would not	wouldn't
did not	didn't	will not	won't
cannot	can't		

Please don't feed the birds!

Try It Out

Speak Up What is the contraction for each word or pair of words?

1. do not **don't**
2. could not **couldn't**
3. were not **weren't**
4. have not **haven't**
5. will not **won't**
6. has not **hasn't**
7. should not **shouldn't**
8. cannot **can't**
9. is not **isn't**

Meeting Individual Needs

RETEACHING
ALTERNATIVE STRATEGY

- Write these sentences on the board: *The car doesn't go very fast. There isn't enough room in the back seat.* Explain that *doesn't* and *isn't* are contractions, two words combined into one.
- Then write the following to show how *doesn't* is formed: *does + not = doesn't.* Point out that the apostrophe replaces the *o* in *not.*
- Repeat the procedure with *don't, aren't, shouldn't,* and *won't.* Be sure students understand that *won't* means "will not."

CHALLENGE

Challenge students to write a riddle describing a common object. The riddle should tell only what the object can't do, doesn't have, and isn't like. For example, *It doesn't leave its home. It hasn't got any fur or hair. You couldn't find a quieter pet. What is it?* (a turtle)

FOR STUDENTS ACQUIRING ENGLISH

Write *contraction* on the board. Then write *is not* and *isn't.* Ask if students have heard the word *isn't* used. Explain what a contraction is; point out the apostrophe. Write *wasn't.* Ask where the apostrophe is and what the contraction is short for. Continue.

On Your Own

Write the contraction for the underlined word or words.

Example: Tim cannot find his gloves. *can't*

10. They are not in his closet. aren't
11. They were not anywhere he looked. weren't
12. He had not started getting ready when I called. hadn't
13. Tim should not wait until the last minute. shouldn't
14. I did not expect him to be ready on time. didn't
15. This was not the first time. wasn't

16–22. This song has seven contractions that are misspelled or that have problems with apostrophes. Write the song correctly. Incorrect words are underlined.

Example: My best friend did'nt call me. *My best friend didn't call me.*

Proofreading

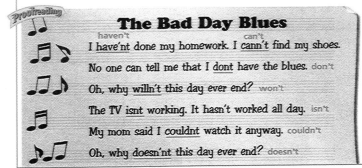

The Bad Day Blues

I have'nt done my homework. I cann't find my shoes. haven't can't
No one can tell me that I dont have the blues. don't
Oh, why willn't this day ever end? won't
The TV isnt working. It hasn't worked all day. isn't
My mom said I couldnt watch it anyway. couldn't
Oh, why doesn'nt this day ever end? doesn't

Writing Wrap-Up

WRITING • THINKING • LISTENING • SPEAKING

CREATING

Write a Song

Write your own song about a bad day. What went wrong? Use contractions from page 116. Then teach your song to a small group. Take turns performing one another's songs. Which song had the most contractions?

For Extra Practice see page 134.

Summing Up Help students summarize these key points about the lesson:

You can form a **contraction** by joining a verb and the word *not*. An **apostrophe** takes the place of the letter or letters that are dropped.

You may want to have students complete the parts related to this lesson on Blackline Master 3–6.

On Your Own

Students can determine where the apostrophe goes in each contraction by asking:

Which letter is dropped to form the contraction?

MEETING INDIVIDUAL NEEDS

FOR STUDENTS ACQUIRING ENGLISH

Distribute SAE Practice page for Unit 3, Lesson 10. Review meaning of challenging contractions such as *wouldn't, couldn't, shouldn't.* Then students write in the contraction for the words next to the sentence.

1. You ______ stay up too late. *(should not)* (shouldn't)
2. We ______ go to the movies. *(cannot)* (can't)

Writing Wrap-Up

Writing Tip: Encourage students to use simple rhymes in their songs. They might borrow the tune from a favorite song. See Blackline Master 3–9 for a sample song.

SCHOOL-HOME CONNECTION
Students can teach their song to family members.

● RETEACHING WORKBOOK, page 33

10 Contractions with *not*

• A **contraction** is the combined form of two words. An **apostrophe** (') takes the place of the missing letter or letters.

Two Words	Contraction
The books **were not** there.	The books **weren't** there.
We **could not** find them.	We **couldn't** find them.
I **will not** look again.	I **won't** look again.

Write the contraction for the word or words in parentheses. Use an apostrophe in place of the underlined letter or letters.

Example: The library ___isn't___ open yet. **(is not)**

1. I ___didn't___ know that the library opens late on Friday. **(did not)**
2. ___Don't___ forget to meet me there later. **(Do not)**
3. I ___can't___ carry all the books home by myself. **(cannot)**
4. The librarian ___wasn't___ at his desk. **(was not)**
5. He ___doesn't___ get back until one o'clock. **(does not)**
6. He ___hasn't___ eaten his lunch yet. **(has not)**
7. The doors ___aren't___ closed now. **(are not)**
8. ___Isn't___ this the right shelf to find cookbooks? **(is not)**
9. The cookbooks ___weren't___ on that shelf. **(were not)**
10. We ___didn't___ know where to look for them. **(did not)**
11. I ___haven't___ found one cookbook yet. **(have not)**
12. You ___hadn't___ seen them either. **(had not)**
13. We ___won't___ stop searching until we find one. **(will not)**
14. The librarian said you ___shouldn't___ look there. **(should not)**
15. Cookbooks ___wouldn't___ be on that shelf. **(would not)**
16. No wonder we ___couldn't___ find them. **(could not)**
17. This ___wasn't___ my best day at the library. **(was not)**
18. I hope it ___doesn't___ happen again. **(does not)**

▲■ WORKBOOK PLUS, pages 56–57

10 Contractions with *not*

Two Words	Contraction
We **do not** have rules.	We **don't** have rules.
It **is not** easy to make them.	It **isn't** easy to make them.
Fred **will not** help.	Fred **won't** help.

A Write a contraction for the word or words in parentheses.

1. My old club ___hadn't___ made any rules. **(had not)**
2. Our new club ___hasn't___ made rules either. **(has not)**
3. I ___don't___ like the club meetings. **(do not)**
4. The members ___aren't___ listening to each other. **(are not)**
5. Several members ___weren't___ even at the last meeting. **(were not)**
6. We ___can't___ get anything done. **(cannot)**
7. We ___haven't___ agreed to anyone's ideas. **(have not)**
8. Club members ___shouldn't___ have to guess the rules. **(should not)**

B Underline the contraction in each sentence. Write the word or words that make up each contraction.

9. You wouldn't like this club. ___would not___
10. Wally and Inga won't join the club. ___will not___
11. They didn't enjoy the first meeting. ___did not___
12. Wally couldn't say his ideas. ___could not___
13. People weren't listening to him. ___were not___
14. Wasn't that a rude way to act? ___Was not___
15. Doesn't anyone else want some rules? ___Does not___
16. It isn't so hard to make them. ___is not___
17. Why shouldn't it work? ___should not___
18. People don't like too many rules. ___do not___

(continued)

10 Contractions with *not* *(continued from page 56)*

Challenge

Clever Cleaver posted the following rules in the lunchroom. Cleaver's rules don't make sense. Rewrite each rule, using a contraction with *not*. Then write three more lunchroom rules. Use a contraction with *not* in each rule.

Sample answers:

LUNCHROOM RULES

1. Trays should be left on tables.
   Trays shouldn't be left on tables.
2. Put your books on the floor.
   Don't put your books on the floor.
3. Children should run in the lunchroom.
   Children shouldn't run in the lunchroom.
4. Your feet belong on the table.
   Your feet don't belong on the table.
5. Children will be allowed to take three desserts.
   Children won't be allowed to take three desserts.
6. Answers will vary.
7. ______
8. ______

Writing Application: Rules EXPLAINING

You and some friends have formed the Bicycle Safety Club. Make up five bicycle safety rules that club members should follow. Use a contraction with *not* in each rule.

Students should respond on separate paper. Answers will vary.

Using Exact Verbs

Lesson Objectives

Students will:

- replace weak verbs with exact verbs
- use a thesaurus

Focus on Instruction

- Have students read the introductory paragraph and the examples. Ask how the two example sentences differ. (The word *screamed* replaces *said.*)
- Ask which sentence gives a clearer picture of how Alicia spoke. (the second sentence) Ask how the exact verb improves the sentence. (*Screamed* tells that Alicia said her words loudly and with fright or excitement.)

Apply It

- Review with students the use of the Thesaurus Plus at the back of the student book.
- Have students complete the activity independently. Remind them to be sure they choose a synonym that fits the meaning of the sentence. Explain that if two or more words work in a sentence, they may choose any that fit. Have students explain their word choices.
- Have small groups of students read and compare their revised stories to see how their choice of words affects the meaning of the story.

Suggest that students who need more support work with partners.

Have students find places for exact verbs in their own writing.

Sample Answers to Apply It

1. noticed, observed, or viewed
2. hurdled, leaped, or sprang
3. hurdled, leaped, or sprang
4. hurdled, leaped, or sprang
5. notice, observe, or view
6. noticed, observed, or viewed
7. yelled, cried, or hollered
8. racing or dashing

FOR STUDENTS ACQUIRING ENGLISH

Pantomime for students the meanings of *leaped, opened,* and *ran.* Write the following sentence on the board: *Joe* ______ (leaped) *to his feet,* ______ (opened) *the door, and* ______ (ran) *to the mailbox.* Have students read it aloud as you pantomime each action.

Using Exact Verbs

A verb is a word that can show action. Use exact verbs in your writing so the reader can imagine the actions you write about.

Less exact verb: Alicia said, "Watch out for the puddle!"
More exact verb: Alicia screamed, "Watch out for the puddle!"

Apply It

1–8. Use your Thesaurus Plus in the Tools and Tips section at the end of your book to find synonyms for each underlined verb. Then rewrite this story. Use a different, more exact verb in place of each underlined word. See TE margin for sample answers.

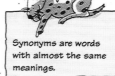

Synonyms are words with almost the same meanings.

Revising

Enzo the Energetic Dog

Toby <u>saw</u> Enzo acting funny. Suddenly, Enzo <u>jumped</u> quickly to his feet and <u>jumped</u> the fence. Toby, who was sitting happily on the porch, <u>jumped</u> from his chair.

Toby got a pair of binoculars so he could <u>see</u> Enzo close up. He <u>saw</u> that Enzo wasn't wearing his collar. Just as Toby started to worry, Mimi came home. When she heard that Enzo was missing, she <u>shouted</u>, "Enzo, come home!" Then Enzo came <u>running</u> back.

Meeting Individual Needs

● RETEACHING WORKBOOK, page 34

Using Exact Verbs

- Using exact verbs helps readers picture the action.

Less exact verb	The driver goes around the track.
More exact verb	The driver zooms around the track.

Replace each underlined verb with a more exact verb from the box. Be sure the meaning of the word fits the meaning of the sentence.

explain	listed	outlined	shout
wondered	invited	waved	divided

Example: Ms. Luc <u>saw</u> an old book of games in the closet.
Ms. Luc discovered an old book of games in the closet.

Revising

1. Everyone began to <u>tell</u> the name of a favorite game.
   Everyone began to shout the name of a favorite game.
2. Rosalba <u>moved</u> her hand and said, "Let's play patty-cake!"
   Rosalba waved her hand and said, "Let's play patty-cake!"
3. "Who remembers how to play jacks?" <u>said</u> Wendy.
   "Who remembers how to play jacks?" wondered Wendy.
4. Miguel wanted to <u>tell</u> how to play with a piñata.
   Miguel wanted to explain how to play with a piñata.
5. The class <u>got</u> into groups to plan a Game Day.
   The class divided into groups to plan a Game Day.
6. All the students <u>said</u> games they remembered.
   All the students listed games they remembered.
7. Then they <u>made</u> a plan for the event.
   Then they outlined a plan for the event.
8. They <u>asked</u> family members to come to Game Day.
   They invited family members to come to Game Day.

▲■ WORKBOOK PLUS, page 58

Using Exact Verbs

The woman and her son ~~had~~ owned only a poor shack and a horse.

1–10. Replace each underlined verb in this story with a more exact one from each pair of words in the box. Be sure the exact verb fits the meaning of the sentence. Cross out the weak verb and write the exact verb over it.

left	returned	demanded	commented
cracked	broke	kicked	poked
strolled	galloped	nurse	teach
exclaimed	sighed	marched	bicycled
earn	grab	won	carried

Revising

A poor young man named Pavel rode his only horse to work every morning and ~~came~~ returned home with supper every night. One day the horse ~~got~~ broke loose and ran away, and the villagers cried, "What bad luck!"

"Maybe it's good. Maybe it's bad," stated Pavel. "Who knows?"

The next day, Pavel's horse ~~came~~ galloped into his yard with four wild horses chasing it, and the villagers ~~said~~ exclaimed, "What good luck! The horses will help you ~~get~~ earn money."

"Maybe it's good. Maybe it's bad," ~~said~~ commented Pavel. "Who knows?"

The next day, one wild horse ~~hit~~ kicked Pavel and broke his leg, and the villagers cried, "What bad luck! Now your mother must ~~help~~ nurse you."

The next day, soldiers ~~came~~ marched into the village and ~~took~~ carried every healthy man off to meet the king, but they did not take Pavel. Was it good luck or bad luck?

Extra Practice

1 Action Verbs

(pages 96–97)

Remember

- An action verb is a word that tells what people or things do.

● The complete predicate of each sentence is underlined. Find the action verb in the predicate. Write the action verb.

Example: Our class read about Mono Lake in California. *read*

1. We visited this unusual lake. visited
2. A park ranger guided us around the lake. guided
3. The lake covers a large area. covers
4. It contains unusual rocks. contains
5. People call these rocks *tufas*. call
6. Tufas grow under the lake. grow

▲ Write the action verb in each of the following sentences.

Example: No fish live in salty Mono Lake. *live*

7. Swimmers float easily in the lake.
8. The very salty water holds them up.
9. The water also stings the swimmers' eyes.
10. Freshwater springs bubble into the lake from the bottom.
11. The fresh water mixes with the salty lake water.
12. This mixture makes the strange-looking tufa rocks.

■ Use an action verb that makes sense to complete each sentence. Write the sentences. Sample answers are given.

Example: Many kinds of birds _____ Mono Lake.
Many kinds of birds visit Mono Lake.

13. The birds _____ in the spring and summer. arrive
14. Some birds _____ for the whole summer. stay
15. Others just _____ for food and rest. come
16. California gulls _____ their nests near the lake. make
17. The eggs _____ sometime in June. hatch
18. Birdwatchers _____ that Mono Lake is a great place for them. know

Extra Practice 125

Action Verbs

Objectives

Students will:
- distinguish action verbs from non-action verbs
- identify action verbs in sentences
- write a paragraph, and identify its action verbs

Using the Extra Practice

The Extra Practice activities provide additional practice for the basic lesson at three levels of difficulty: Easy (●), Average (▲), and Challenging (■).

The Extra Practice activities can be used in the following ways.

- Assign activities according to students' needs and abilities as homework after students have completed the basic lesson.
- Assign the Easy activities after using the lesson Reteaching instruction.
- Assign the Average activities to prepare students for the Checkup.
- Assign the Easy and/or Average activities to students who had difficulty with specific lessons on the Checkup.
- Assign the Challenging exercises as a Bonus activity.

Meeting Individual Needs — More Practice for Lesson 1

● EASY

If the underlined word is an action verb, write *AV*. If it is not an action verb, write *N*.

1. We visited the Grand Canyon National Park. (AV)
2. The park covers more than one million acres. (AV)
3. We hiked down to the bottom. (AV)
4. The canyon is very deep. (N)
5. Others enter by boat or raft on the Colorado River. (AV)

▲ AVERAGE

Underline the action verb in each sentence.

1. The Colorado River formed the canyon long, long ago.
2. It cut through many layers of rock.
3. In some places, the canyon reaches a depth of one mile.
4. About 275 different kinds of birds live in the Grand Canyon.
5. Many unusual animals make their homes here too.

■ CHALLENGING

Write a paragraph about a park or scenic spot that you have visited. In five or more sentences, tell what makes the place special. Underline each action verb that you use in your paragraph.

Main Verb and Helping Verbs

Objectives

Students will:

- identify whole verbs containing a main verb and a helping verb
- identify helping verbs in sentences
- use main verbs and helping verbs in sentences

Using the Extra Practice

The Extra Practice activities provide additional practice for the basic lesson at three levels of difficulty: Easy (●), Average (▲), and Challenging (■).

Extra Practice

(pages 98–99)

2 Main Verbs and Helping Verbs

Remember

- A verb may be more than one word.
- The main verb is the most important verb.
- The helping verb comes before the main verb.

● Copy the underlined verbs in each sentence. Write *helping* or *main* beside each verb.

Example: I am going to soccer practice. *am—helping going—main*

1. Mrs. Martinez has coached our team for three years. has—helping, coached-
2. She has started a new job. has—helping, started—main
3. It is keeping her very busy. is—helping, keeping—main
4. We will play for Mr. Lewis this year. will—helping, play—main
5. He was helping Mrs. Martinez last year. was—helping, helping—main

▲ Write each sentence. Draw one line under the helping verb and two lines under the main verb. HV is underlined once; MV, twice.

Example: Karla is signing up for soccer camp.
Karla is signing up for soccer camp.

6. Cedric and Phong are thinking about it.
7. Susana has made her decision.
8. She will attend the camp for a week in July.
9. Her family had planned a vacation that week.
10. Now they have changed their plans.

■ Use a helping verb that makes sense to complete each sentence. Write the sentence. Sample answers are given.

Example: The students ______ talking about the games.
The students are talking about the games.

11. The school Olympics ______ begin on Friday. will
12. They ______ held at this time every year. are
13. Each class ______ planned a game. has
14. Last week the classes ______ divided into two teams. had
15. Each team ______ play in every game. will

126 Unit 3: Verbs

Meeting Individual Needs — More Practice for Lesson 2

● EASY

Write the whole verb in each sentence.

1. The hobby shop has sold many kites this week.
2. The kite-flying contest will begin today at noon.
3. Twenty boys and girls are flying kites in the contest.
4. I have seen box kites and dragon kites.
5. Luckily, strong winds are blowing.

▲ AVERAGE

Underline the helping verb in each sentence. If there is no helping verb, write *None*.

1. The students have built model airplanes.
2. The plane kits were bought at a hobby shop.
3. The students worked on the planes for days. (None)
4. They are showing their planes today.
5. Many people will see them.

■ CHALLENGING

Make up two sentences for each of the following verbs. Use the verb by itself in one sentence and with a helping verb in another sentence.

Example: I walk slowly. I will walk with you.

walk
run
shout
watch
drive

(pages 100–101)

3 Present, Past, and Future

Remember

- A present tense verb shows action that is happening now.
- A past tense verb shows action that has already happened.
- A future tense verb shows action that will happen.

● Write *present, past,* or *future* to tell the tense of the underlined verb in each sentence.

Example: The birds arrived early last spring. *past*

1. I watched them all summer from my window. past
2. Then the air grew cold. past
3. Winter will come soon. fut.
4. The birds will leave for their winter homes. fut.
5. Scientists call this migration. pres.
6. Some birds travel many miles each year. pres.

▲ Write the verbs in these sentences. Write *present, past,* or *future* to describe the verb in each sentence.

Example: I watch the birds in our yard. *watch—present*

7. Last winter Dad and I built a birdhouse. past
8. In the spring, some wrens made a nest in it. past
9. Now a family of birds lives in the house. pres.
10. The parent birds bring food to the babies. pres.
11. Next spring a new family of birds will nest in our yard. fut.

■ Write these sentences. Write each underlined verb in the tense shown at the end of the sentence.

Example: Jack receive a canary for his birthday. (past)
Jack received a canary for his birthday.

12. Rance names the bird Clarence. (past) named
13. Clarence sang to Rance all day long. (present) sings
14. Rance will read a book about canaries. (past) read
15. He will give Clarence fresh food and water. (present) gives
16. Clarence stays healthy with such good care. (future) will stay

Present, Past, and Future

Objectives

Students will:
- distinguish present tense from past and future tense verbs
- write sentences, using present, past, and future tense verbs correctly

Using the Extra Practice

The Extra Practice activities provide additional practice for the basic lesson at three levels of difficulty: Easy (●), Average (▲), and Challenging (■).

Meeting Individual Needs — More Practice for Lesson 3

● EASY

Write the present tense verb in parentheses.

1. Henry (wanted, wants) to save his money.
2. He (likes, liked) the bicycle in Mrs. Rosen's store.
3. He (calls, will call) Mrs. Rosen about a job.
4. Henry (earned, earns) money cutting Mrs. Rosen's lawn.
5. At last, Henry (will buy, buys) the bicycle.

▲ AVERAGE

Write the past tense and future tense of each verb.

1. laugh (laughed, will laugh)
2. count (counted, will count)
3. pour (poured, will pour)
4. show (showed, will show)
5. push (pushed, will push)

■ CHALLENGING

Choose a verb to complete each sentence. Write it in the tense shown at the end of the sentence. (Sample answers are given.)

1. Henry _______ his new bicycle every day. *(present)* (rides)
2. Last week, he _______ a horn and light to it. *(past)* (added)
3. He also _______ a bicycle club. *(past)* (joined)
4. Next summer, he _______ it in the country. *(future)* (will pedal)
5. Henry _______ bicycle riding. *(present)* (enjoys)

Subject-Verb Agreement

Objectives

Students will:

- select a subject that agrees with the verb in a sentence
- use verbs that agree with their subjects
- write sentences with present tense verbs that agree with their subjects

Using the Extra Practice

The Extra Practice activities provide additional practice for the basic lesson at three levels of difficulty: Easy (●), Average (▲), and Challenging (■).

Extra Practice

(pages 104–105)

4 Subject-Verb Agreement — Remember

- If the subject of a sentence is a singular noun or *he, she, they,* or *it,* add *-s* to a present tense verb.
- If the subject is a plural noun or *I, we, you,* or *they,* do not add *-s* to a present tense verb.

● For each sentence, write *correct* if the underlined verb agrees with the subject. Write *not correct* if it does not agree.

Example: Many schools buys computers. *not correct*

1. A school uses computers in many different ways. C
2. A teacher keeps records on a computer. C
3. A computer help the school librarian. not correct
4. Students practices math skills on a computer. not correct
5. Some computers make writing fun and easy. C
6. Sometimes we play games on the computer. C

▲ Write each sentence with the correct verb.

Example: My sister Julie (work, works) with computers.
My sister Julie works with computers.

7. She (write, writes) programs for computers.
8. The programs (tell, tells) the computer what to do.
9. Computers (change, changes) rapidly.
10. Julie (take, takes) classes to keep up with the changes.
11. I (plan, plans) to work with computers too.
12. I (read, reads) all the computer books I can find.

■ Use the correct form of the verb to complete each sentence. Write the sentences.

Example: Computers ______ people plan the Olympics. (help)
Computers help people plan the Olympics.

13. They ______ the best route for carrying the torch. (show) show
14. A computer ______ places for players to stay. (locate) locates
15. It ______ rooms for thousands of people. (find) finds
16. Computers ______ how much food will be needed. (figure) figure
17. A special computer ______ shoes for runners. (design) designs
18. Computers ______ the modern Olympics possible. (make) make

Meeting Individual Needs — More Practice for Lesson 4

● EASY

Underline the subject in parentheses that agrees with the verb in each sentence.

1. The (puppy, puppies) grow so quickly!
2. My (cat, cats) chases after squirrels.
3. The (bird, birds) sings so beautifully.
4. Your (duck, ducks) follow you everywhere.
5. Our (dog, dogs) leaves the goose alone.

▲ AVERAGE

Complete each newspaper headline with a present tense verb. (Sample answers are given.)

1. Team ______ Big Game (Wins)
2. Doctor ______ New Cure (Finds)
3. Twins ______ Contest (Win)
4. Girls ______ Cat in Tree (Find)
5. School ______ for Summer (Closes)
6. Parrot ______ a Speech! (Gives)

■ CHALLENGING

On one sheet of paper, make a list of ten sentence subjects. On another sheet, list ten action verbs in the present tense. Then exchange your list of verbs with a partner. Write ten sentences, using your subjects and the verbs given to you by your partner.

Extra Practice

(pages 106–107)

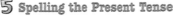

5 Spelling the Present Tense

Remember

For spelling present tense verbs used with singular subjects:
- Add *-es* to verbs that end with *s, x, ch,* or *sh.*
- If a verb ends with a consonant and *y,* change the *y* to *i* and add *-es.*

● Choose the verb that correctly completes each sentence. Write the sentences.

Example: Jon (watch, watches) Keyshawn in a hockey game.
Jon watches Keyshawn in a hockey game.

1. Keyshawn (fix, fixes) his face mask.
2. A signal (buzzes, buzz) loudly.
3. Elsa (score, scores) first.
4. The crowd (cheer, cheers) for her.
5. The puck (flies, fly) toward the net.
6. The goalie (catch, catches) it in his glove.

▲ Use the correct present tense form of the verb to complete each sentence. Write the sentences.

Example: Jill's brother _____ hockey. (play)
Jill's brother plays hockey.

7. Jill _____ to play too. (want) wants
8. Mark _____ her all the rules. (teach) teaches
9. Then Jill _____ out for the hockey team. (try) tries
10. Jill _____ the hockey stick well. (handle) handles
11. She _____ the puck well too. (pass) passes
12. Finally, the coach _____ her the good news. (give) gives

■ Write each sentence, spelling the present tense verb correctly.

Example: Jana love ice skating. *Jana loves ice skating.*

13. She wish for a new pair of skates. wishes
14. She never miss a lesson. misses
15. Jana carry her skates to school every day. carries
16. She rush to the rink right after school. rushes
17. She practice for three hours. practices
18. Her mother pick her up at six o'clock. picks

Extra Practice 129

Spelling the Present Tense

Objectives

Students will:
- spell the present tense of verbs ending in *s, x, z, ch,* or *sh* correctly
- spell the present tense of verbs ending in a consonant and *y* correctly

Using the Extra Practice

The Extra Practice activities provide additional practice for the basic lesson at three levels of difficulty: Easy (●), Average (▲), and Challenging (■).

Meeting Individual Needs — More Practice for Lesson 5

● EASY

Write the present tense of each verb to complete this sentence:
The girl _____.
1. splash, splashes
2. hums, hum
3. try, tries
4. mix, mixes
5. guesses, guess

▲ AVERAGE

Choose the correct present tense form of the verb. Write the complete sentence.
1. Biff (hurry, hurries) up to bat.
2. His team (need, needs) a run.
3. Biff (miss, misses) the first two pitches.
4. Biff (hit, hits) the next pitch hard.
5. The crowds (watch, watches) the ball.
6. "Home run!" Biff (cry, cries).

■ CHALLENGING

If the verb in the sentence is spelled correctly, write *C.* If it is not, write it correctly.
1. Every night, Dad fish from the boat. (fishes)
2. He always catchs at least one big fish. (catches)
3. He carries the fish home. (C)
4. He frys them on a fire. (fries)
5. At the table, he passes fish to all of us. (C)

Spelling the Past Tense

Objectives

Students will:
- identify the present tense form of past tense verbs
- form the past tense of verbs that end with *e*, with a single vowel and a consonant, or with a consonant and *y*

Using the Extra Practice

The Extra Practice activities provide additional practice for the basic lesson at three levels of difficulty: Easy (●), Average (▲), and Challenging (■).

Extra Practice

6 Spelling the Past Tense

(pages 108–109)

Remember
- Add *-ed* to most verbs to form the past tense.
- Remember the rules for spelling the past tense of verbs ending with *e*, with a single vowel and a consonant, and with a consonant and *y*.

● Write the verb in each pair that is in the past tense.

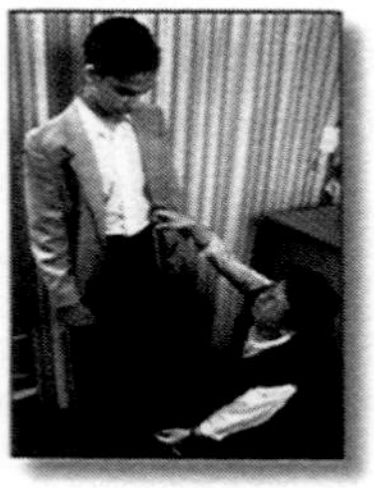

Example: grab—grabbed *grabbed*

1. gulped—gulp
2. hemmed—hem
3. try—tried
4. trip—tripped
5. owed—owe
6. worried—worry

▲ Use the past tense of the verb to complete each sentence. Write the sentence.

Example: Susan _____ sandwiches for the trip. (prepare) *Susan prepared sandwiches for the trip.*

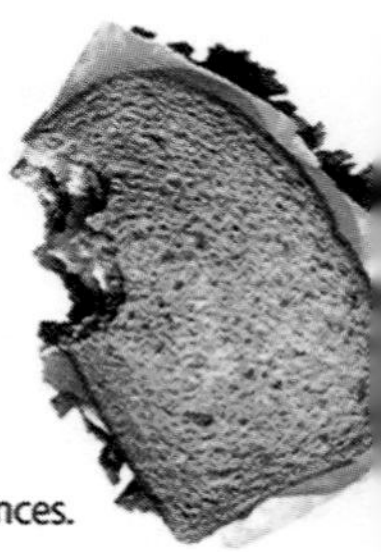

7. She _____ them in waxed paper. (wrap) wrapped
8. Tarika _____ up the backpacks. (zip) zipped
9. Daryl _____ them to the car. (carry) carried
10. Dad _____ his list one more time. (check) checked
11. The children _____ into the back seat. (hop) hopped
12. They all _____ their seat belts. (fasten) fastened

■ Change each present tense verb to past tense. Write the sentences.

Example: Jan's family explores a museum in the desert. *Jan's family explored a museum in the desert.*

13. A guide shows them around the outdoor museum. showed
14. Hats shade their faces from the hot sun. shaded
15. Bobcats and beavers live in the area. lived
16. A new dam stops the river. stopped
17. The streams dry up. dried
18. The animals move to other places. moved

130 Unit 3: Verbs

Meeting Individual Needs — More Practice for Lesson 6

● EASY

Write the present tense verb for each past tense verb below.

1. studied (study)
2. hoped (hope)
3. slipped (slip)
4. tied (tie)
5. planned (plan)

▲ AVERAGE

Rewrite each sentence, changing the underlined verb to the past tense.

1. Our tiny boat bobs up and down at the dock. (bobbed)
2. We all hurry on. (hurried)
3. Mom raises the sail. (raised)
4. We glide out to sea. (glided)
5. The dark clouds worry no one. (worried)

■ CHALLENGING

If the past tense of the verb is correct, write *C*. If it is not correct, write it correctly.

1. Suddenly, the winds whistled wildly. (C)
2. The waves tryed to overturn our sailboat. (tried)
3. Luckily, I spoted a cove. (spotted)
4. We raced towards it. (C)
5. Safe inside it, we droped our anchor. (dropped)
6. Soon the storm dyed down. (died)

Extra Practice

(pages 110–111)

7 The Past with Helping Verbs

Remember

- The helping verbs *has, have,* and *had* can be used with the past form of a verb to show action that has already happened.

● Copy the underlined verbs in each sentence. Write *helping* or *main* beside each verb.

Example: Jim had received tickets to the ice show.
had—helping received—main

1. He has offered me a ticket. has—helping, offered—main
2. I have thanked him for the ticket. have—helping, thanked—main
3. Jim and I had hurried to the show. had—helping, hurried—main
4. An usher had guided us to our seats. had—helping, guided—main
5. Now the lights have dimmed. have—helping, dimmed—main

▲ Write each sentence. Draw one line under the helping verb and two lines under the main verb. HV is underlined once; MV, twice.

Example: Posters had advertised the ice show.
Posters had advertised the ice show.

6. Lin and Dan have hurried ahead for good seats.
7. I had arrived in time for the first act.
8. Ten skaters in mouse costumes had scurried onto the ice.
9. A skater in a cat costume has chased after them.
10. The crowd has clapped for the mice.

■ Rewrite each sentence. Use the helping verb *has, have,* or *had* and the past form of the verb. Sample answers are given.

Example: Two ice skaters dance in the spotlight.
Two ice skaters have danced in the spotlight.

11. Their costumes sparkle in the golden light. had sparkled
12. The man lifts the woman over his head. had lifted
13. They twirl like a top together. had twirled
14. The man trips on something. has tripped
15. The team tries the dance again. has tried

Extra Practice 131

The Past with Helping Verbs

Objectives

Students will:

- write the past with a helping verb to agree with singular and plural subjects
- write sentences, using past tense verbs with helping verbs correctly

Using the Extra Practice

The Extra Practice activities provide additional practice for the basic lesson at three levels of difficulty: Easy (●), Average (▲), and Challenging (■).

Meeting Individual Needs — More Practice for Lesson 7

● EASY

Underline the correct helping verb.

1. Some friends of mine (has, have) planned a picnic.
2. Ralph (has, have) invited friends from Utah to join us.
3. We (has, have) decided to leave early in the morning.
4. I (has, have) made salads.
5. My dad (has, have) promised to make some tasty sandwiches.

▲ AVERAGE

Write *S* if the subject is singular and *P* if it is plural. Then complete the sentence by writing *has* or *have* in the blank.

1. Bill and John _______ planned to go hiking. (P—have)
2. My other friends _______ decided to play baseball. (P—have)
3. The new playground near our building _______ opened. (S—has)
4. Two teams _______ agreed to play a game after school. (P—have)
5. Each team _______ won two games. (S—has)

■ CHALLENGING

Pretend that you have just returned from a trip to a distant planet. Write a letter to a friend about the trip. Describe what you saw and did there. Use the past tense form of verbs with *has, have,* or *had.*

Irregular Verbs

Objectives

Students will:

- identify the present tense form of irregular past tense verbs
- write the past tense forms of irregular verbs
- write sentences, using irregular verbs in the past tense correctly

Using the Extra Practice

The Extra Practice activities provide additional practice for the basic lesson at three levels of difficulty: Easy (●), Average (▲), and Challenging (■).

Extra Practice

(pages 112–113)

8 Irregular Verbs

Remember

- Irregular verbs are changed in special ways to show action that happened in the past. You must remember their spellings.

● Choose the correct verb to complete each sentence. Write the sentences.

Example: Pam's dad had (drove, driven) for three hours.
Pam's dad had driven for three hours.

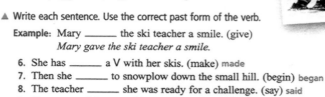

1. The car radio had (break, <u>broken</u>) last week.
2. Pam and Joe (<u>sang</u>, sung) songs to pass the time.
3. Snow had (begin, <u>begun</u>) to fall.
4. Their mother (say, <u>said</u>) that the ski lodge was not far.
5. They (<u>ate</u>, eaten) supper at the lodge later.

▲ Write each sentence. Use the correct past form of the verb.

Example: Mary _____ the ski teacher a smile. (give)
Mary gave the ski teacher a smile.

6. She has _____ a V with her skis. (make) made
7. Then she _____ to snowplow down the small hill. (begin) began
8. The teacher _____ she was ready for a challenge. (say) said
9. She _____ Mary to a bigger hill. (bring) brought
10. Mary _____ she could do it. (know) knew
11. Mary _____ down the hill without falling. (come) came

■ Use the correct past form of the verb from the box to complete each sentence. Write the sentences.

break
know
give
come
make
say

Example: Kris had _____ about winter camping.
Kris had known about winter camping.

12. Eva had _____ that she wanted to learn. said
13. The girls _____ to winter camping school. came
14. An instructor _____ them directions for building a snow shelter. gave
15. Eva _____ the crust of the snow with a shovel. broke
16. Soon they had _____ a good snow shelter. made

Meeting Individual Needs — More Practice for Lesson 8

● EASY

Write the present tense verb for each past tense verb given.

1. gave (give)
2. told (tell)
3. took (take)
4. thought (think)
5. grew (grow)

▲ AVERAGE

Complete Sentence **a** with the past tense of the underlined verb, and Sentence **b** with the past tense and a helping verb.

1. My friends <u>sing</u> in the chorus.
   a. My friends <u>(sang)</u> in the chorus.
   b. My friends <u>(have/had sung)</u> in the chorus.
2. Bonzo <u>eats</u> bananas.
   a. Bonzo <u>(ate)</u> bananas.
   b. Bonzo <u>(has/had eaten)</u> bananas.
3. That plant <u>grows</u> tall.
   a. That plant <u>(grew)</u> tall.
   b. That plant <u>(has/had grown)</u> tall.

■ CHALLENGING

Write five sentences, using the past tense of *take, think, drive, eat,* and *make*. Then write five more sentences, using the past tense of the same verbs with a helping verb.

(Sample answers: He took the tickets. He has taken the tickets all day long.)

(pages 114–115)

9 The Special Verb *be*

Remember

- The special verb *be* does not show action. It tells what someone or something is or is like.
- Use *am* or *was* with the subject *I*.
- Use *is* or *was* with singular nouns and *he, she,* or *it*.
- Use *are* or *were* with plural nouns and *we, you,* or *they*.

● Write each sentence. Underline the form of the verb *be*.

Example: I am Jane's best friend. *I am Jane's best friend.*

1. Jane is in my class.
2. I was at Jane's house yesterday.
3. Her mother was there too.
4. She is a sportswriter.
5. You are in her latest article.

▲ Choose the verb that correctly completes each sentence. Write the sentences.

Example: Kim Wang (is, are) a television reporter.
Kim Wang is a television reporter.

6. She (was, were) at our school last week.
7. You (was, were) not in school that day.
8. We (was, were) in the auditorium.
9. I (was, were) in the front row.
10. I (am, is) a big fan of Ms. Wang.

■ Write each sentence. Use the correct form of the verb *be*. The word in ( ) tells which tense to use.

Example: My father ______ a helicopter pilot. (present)
My father is a helicopter pilot.

11. He ______ also a traffic reporter. (present) is
12. His reports ______ on the radio. (present) are
13. Yesterday I ______ in his helicopter. (past) was
14. It ______ very exciting. (past) was
15. We ______ high above the ground. (past) were

The Special Verb *be*

Objectives

Students will:

- identify the form of *be* that agrees with the subject of a sentence
- use the correct form of *be* in sentences

Using the Extra Practice

The Extra Practice activities provide additional practice for the basic lesson at three levels of difficulty: Easy (●), Average (▲), and Challenging (■).

Meeting Individual Needs

More Practice for Lesson 9

● EASY

Underline the correct form of the verb *be* in parentheses to complete each sentence.

1. Our soccer team (am, is) exhausted.
2. We (are, were) on the field all yesterday afternoon.
3. Our coach (is, are) hard on us.
4. We (are, is) the state champions.
5. I (is, am) team captain this year.

▲ AVERAGE

Write each sentence. Use the correct form of *be*.

1. The video store (was) very busy yesterday.
2. My sister (is) the manager there now.
3. The store (is/was) the busiest in the shopping mall.
4. Now there (are) five video stores in our neighborhood.
5. Videotapes (are) more popular than movies.

■ CHALLENGING

Complete the following sentences, using a form of the verb *be* as the main verb. (Sample answers are given.)

1. I (am an artist).
2. My friend (is a drummer).
3. A girl I know (was a coach).
4. Several buildings near my house (were on fire).
5. Yesterday I (was lazy).
6. Last year we (were at camp).

Contractions with *not*

Objectives

Students will:
- determine the words that make up contractions
- write sentences, substituting contractions for written words

Using the Extra Practice

The Extra Practice activities provide additional practice for the basic lesson at three levels of difficulty: Easy (●), Average (▲), and Challenging (■).

Extra Practice

(pages 116–117)

10 Contractions with *not*

- A contraction is the combined form of two words. An apostrophe (') takes the place of any missing letters.

Remember

● Write the contraction in each sentence.

Example: I can't go out now. *can't*

1. I haven't finished my homework.
2. It won't take long, though.
3. It isn't hard.
4. My sister hasn't come home yet.
5. I don't want to leave without her.

▲ Write each sentence. Use a contraction in place of the underlined words.

Example: We were not able to play softball today.
We weren't able to play softball today.

6. The rain did not stop all afternoon. didn't
7. Our team could not have been luckier. couldn't
8. We did not have a chance against the Gorillas. didn't
9. Now we will not have to play them this year. won't
10. There is not enough time left in the season. isn't

■ Write a sentence to answer each question. Use a contraction made up of the underlined verb and the word *not* in each one. Sample answers are given.

Example: Did you try out for the school musical?
I didn't try out for the school musical.

11. Were Phil and Marita at the tryouts? Phil and Marita weren't at the tryouts.
12. Has the school ever done a musical before? The school hasn't done a musical bef
13. Do you have a good singing voice? I don't have a good singing voice.
14. Does Paul know how to dance? Paul doesn't know how to dance.
15. Can Bob and Winona get the tickets printed? Bob and Winona can't get the tickets printed.
16. Will Rico help build the scenery? Rico won't help build the scenery.

134 **Unit 3:** Verbs

Meeting Individual Needs — More Practice for Lesson 10

● EASY

Match the word or words with the correct contraction.

1. has not (c)	a. isn't
2. cannot (d)	b. doesn't
3. was not (e)	c. hasn't
4. does not (b)	d. can't
5. is not (a)	e. wasn't

▲ AVERAGE

Write each sentence with the contraction made from the words in parentheses.

1. Ann (has not) named her dog yet. (hasn't)
2. She (cannot) think of a good name. (can't)
3. He (does not) have any spots. (doesn't)
4. Sometimes, it (is not) easy to name a pet. (isn't)
5. I (was not) much help. (wasn't)

■ CHALLENGING

Write the paragraph, using contractions for any words that can be made into contractions.

Jeremy has not (hasn't) eaten his spinach. He did not (didn't) want it for dinner. He and his sister Kate do not (don't) like it. Jeremy and Kate do like carrots, but their parents are not (aren't) carrot lovers. Kate made a salad of tomatoes and lettuce. The whole family could not (couldn't) wait to eat it.

Unit 4 Planning Guide

Adjectives

1 1/2 weeks

		Checkup (PE)	Extra Practice (PE)	Graphic Organizer (BLM)	Writing Wrap-Up (BLM)	More Practice (TE)	Workbook Plus	Reteaching Workbook	Students Acquiring English Practice Book
1	What Is an Adjective? *(136–137)*	150	159	4–1	4–4	159	59–60	35	55+
	Revising Strategies: Sentence Fluency Writing with Adjectives *(138–139)*						61–62	36–37	
2	Adjectives After *be (140)*	150	160	4–1	4–4	160	63	38	57+
3	Using *a*, *an*, and *the (141)*	150	161	4–1	4–4	161	64	39	59+
4	Making Comparisons *(142–143)*	150	162	4–2	4–4	162	65–66	40	61+
5	Comparing with *more* and *most (144–145)*	151	163	4–2	4–5	163	67–68	41	63+
6	Comparing with *good* and *bad (146–147)*	151	164	4–3	4–5	164	69–70	42	65+
	Revising Strategies: Vocabulary Using Exact Adjectives *(148)*						71	43	
	Enrichment *(149)*								
	Test Practice *(152–154)*								67+
	Cumulative Review *(155–158)*								

Unit 4

Tools and Tips

- **Diagramming Guide,** *pp. H70–H78*
- **Guide to Capitalization, Punctuation, and Usage,** *pp. H55–H64*

School-Home Connection

Suggestions for informing or involving family members in classroom activities and learning related to this unit are included in the Teacher's Edition throughout the unit.

Meeting Individual Needs

- **FOR SPECIAL NEEDS/INCLUSION:** *Houghton Mifflin English* Audiotape See also Reteaching.
- **FOR STUDENTS ACQUIRING ENGLISH:**
  - Notes and activities are included in this Teacher's Edition throughout the unit to help you adapt or use pupil book activities with students acquiring English.
  - Additional support is available for students at various stages of English proficiency: **Beginning/Preproduction**, **Early Production/Speech Emergence**, and **Intermediate/Advanced**. See Students Acquiring English Practice Book.
  - Students can listen to the Try It Out activities on audiotape.
- **ENRICHMENT:** *p. 149*

All audiotape recordings are also available on CD.

Daily Language Practice

Each sentence includes two errors based on skills taught in this or previous Grammar units. Each day write one sentence on the chalkboard. Have students find the errors and write the sentence correctly on a sheet of paper. To make the activity easier, identify the kinds of errors.

1. Julie planed to make a applesauce cake for her mother's birthday. Julie planned to make an applesauce cake for her mother's birthday. **(past tense; articles)**
2. My brother ted is smartest than he thinks. My brother Ted is smarter than he thinks. **(proper nouns; comparing with adjectives)**
3. Camping in the Smoky Mountains was the enjoyablest part of my familys vacation. Camping in the Smoky Mountains was the most enjoyable part of my family's vacation. **(comparing with adjectives; possessive nouns)**
4. Gargle with salt water to make your throat feel gooder! Gargle with salt water to make your throat feel better. **(comparing with adjectives; end punctuation)**
5. A opossum has ate the seedlings in our garden. An opossum has eaten the seedlings in our garden. **(articles; irregular verbs)**
6. Our cat is happyest chasing mouses. Our cat is happiest chasing mice. **(comparing with adjectives; plural nouns)**
7. The weather is expected to be worser this year than last year? The weather is expected to be worse this year than last year. **(comparing with adjectives; end punctuation)**
8. The front door need the new doorknob. The front door needs a new doorknob. **(subject-verb agreement; articles)**
9. I receiveed the goodest grade in English on my report card. I received the best grade in English on my report card. **(past tense; comparing with adjectives)**
10. The most juiciest peaches come from pennsylvania. The juiciest peaches come from Pennsylvania. **(comparing with adjectives; proper nouns)**

Additional Resources

Workbook Plus, Unit 4
Reteaching Workbook, Unit 4
Students Acquiring English Practice Book, Unit 4
Transparencies, Unit 4
Teacher's Resource Book
Audiotapes

Technology Tools

INTERNET: http://www.eduplace.com/kids/hme/ *or* http://www.eduplace.com/rdg/hme/

Visit Education Place for these additional support materials and activities:

- tricky usage question
- Wacky Web Tales®
- interactive quizzes
- a proofreading game

Assessment

Test Booklet, Unit 4

Keeping a Journal

Discuss with students the value of keeping a journal as a way of promoting self-expression and fluency. Encourage students to record their thoughts and ideas in a notebook. Inform students whether the journal will be private or will be reviewed periodically as a way of assessing growth. The following prompts may be useful for generating writing ideas.

Journal Prompts

- If you could be any animal, what would you be? Why?
- What is the best part about vacations? Explain.
- What is your favorite time of day? Explain.

Unit 4

Adjectives

Although it's boldly dressed in bright reds, blues, greens, and yellows, the flashy toucan still blends with the forest colors.

135

Introducing the Unit

Using the Photograph

Note on the Photograph The photograph shows a chestnut-mandibled toucan *(Ramphastos swainsonii)*. The chestnut-mandibled toucan is native to Costa Rica.

- Have a volunteer read the caption aloud. Ask students which words in the caption help to give a picture of the toucan. *(flashy, reds, greens)*
- Direct students' attention to the photograph. Have students suggest words to describe the toucan, its beak, or the forest in the picture. (Sample responses: toucan—*black, yellow;* beak—*large, curved, colorful;* forest—*green, bright*) Write student responses on the board or on an overhead transparency.
- Explain to students that words that describe nouns are called **adjectives**. Tell students that they will learn about adjectives in this unit.

Grammar Song

See Blackline Master G–2 for a song to help students remember some of the concepts and rules taught in this unit.

Students can also listen to this song on audiotape.

Shared Writing Activity

Work with students to use adjectives to write a paragraph describing a toucan to someone who has never seen one before.

1. Discuss with students in what order they would like to describe the toucan. Ask if the paragraph would be more effective if students described first the most unusual part (the beak) or if they started with an overall view of the bird.
2. Number the listed words to show the order in which they will be used. Encourage students to add new adjectives.
3. Have students suggest sentences, using the listed words in the numbered order. Write the sentences on the board or on the overhead transparency. Help students fix fragments and run-on sentences. As you write, ask students to tell you the correct punctuation and capitalization to use.
4. When finished, have a volunteer read the paragraph aloud. How well does the description match the picture?

What Is an Adjective?

Lesson Objectives

Students will:

- identify adjectives that tell *what kind* or *how many*
- identify the nouns that adjectives describe
- write an ad, using adjectives

One-Minute Warm-Up Read the sentence aloud without the adjectives. Discuss how the adjectives make the sentence more meaningful.

Focus on Instruction

Write the nouns *trees* and *cars* on the board, and have students suggest adjectives to describe each noun. Discuss how using different adjectives can change our understanding of the noun.

Try It Out

VIEWING Have students describe the picture of the dogs. Build a word web using the adjectives that the students provide. Use the adjectives in sentences. (Sample responses are shown.)

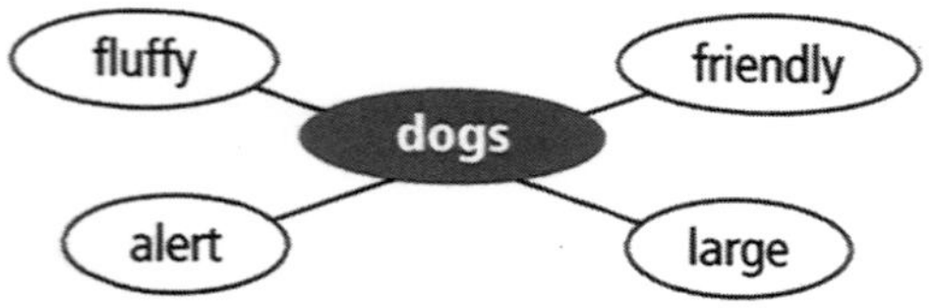

FOR STUDENTS ACQUIRING ENGLISH

- Have students listen to the Try It Out sentences on the audiotape. Distribute the SAE Practice page for Unit 4, Lesson 1, to support listening.
- Help students talk about the dogs in the photograph. Guide the conversation with questions about dogs students have had as pets or have heard about. List vocabulary on the board. Next have students identify any words on the list that are adjectives. Students listen and write the adjectives that describe the underlined nouns. Then students listen again and decide if the adjectives tell *what kind* or *how many*. Example: My uncle has two big dogs. (*two, big*—how many, what kind)

Grammar

1 What Is an Adjective?

One-Minute Warm-Up

How many describing words can you find in this sentence? What are they? Adjectives are underlined.

Through steep climbs and dangerous ascents, icy waters and confusing trails, Akiak always found the safest and fastest way.

—from *Akiak*, by Robert J. Blake

- **An adjective is a word that gives information about a noun.** A noun names a person, a place, a thing, or an idea. Some adjectives tell *what kind* or *how many*. They often appear right before the nouns they describe.

What Kind	How Many
We have a large dog.	Two dogs played in the yard.
The dog has a curly coat.	Many dogs like children.

- You can use more than one adjective to describe a noun.

We have a large, friendly dog.
The brown and white puppy is sleeping.
The dog has five tiny puppies.

Try It Out

Speak Up Find the adjectives that describe the underlined nouns. Does each adjective tell *what kind*, or does it tell *how many*?

1. Early people found that dogs made good hunters. what kind, what kind
2. Strong dogs can pull sleds through deep snow. what kind, what kind
3. One famous dog rescued forty lost people in the mountains. how many, what kind; how many, what kind
4. Clever sheepdogs help farmers with large herds of sheep. what kind, what kind
5. Some smart dogs help people who cannot see. how many, what kind

136 Unit 4: Adjectives

Meeting Individual Needs

RETEACHING
ALTERNATIVE STRATEGY

- Write on the board:
  Monster
  _______ *hair* _______ *teeth*
  _______ *arms* _______ *legs*
- Ask students to imagine a scary monster. Have them describe the creature by telling the color, size, shape, or number of each listed feature. Write the adjectives in the blanks.
- Explain that the words you added are adjectives and that adjectives describe nouns by telling *what kind* or *how many*.

CHALLENGE

Have students draw a picture of a silly animal. Have them exchange pictures with a partner. Students then list as many vivid adjectives about their partner's animal as possible.

FOR STUDENTS ACQUIRING ENGLISH

Display photographs of dogs and have students think of as many words as possible to describe each one. List ideas on the board. Students might say *big, soft, black, happy*. Say that these words are adjectives. Ask for other examples.

On Your Own

Write the adjectives that describe the underlined nouns. Write *what kind* or *how many* for each adjective.

Example: Linda Gunn has an interesting job. *interesting–what kind*

6. Linda trains young dogs. young—what kind
7. The dogs learn to help people with a hearing problem. hearing—what kind
8. Two people in California found a lost dog. two—how many, lost—what kind
9. They took the little white dog to a shelter. little, white—what kind
10. One kind worker at the shelter named the dog Penny. one—how many, kind—what kind
11. Linda found Penny at the shelter two days later. two—how many
12. She could see that Penny was an intelligent dog. intelligent—what kind
13. It took about four months to train Penny. four—how many

14–19. This lost-and-found ad has six adjectives that tell *what kind* or *how many*. Write the ad. Underline each adjective. Do not include *a, an,* and *the.*

Example: Trooper has a wonderful personality.
Trooper has a wonderful personality.

TROOPER IS MISSING!

Please help find Trooper. Trooper is a huge mutt with black spots. He has a large spot around one eye. He has a loud bark, but he does not bite. Trooper likes tasty snacks. Please return the dog to 120 Pleasant Street, and you will receive a reward.

Tim Baker
555-2894

Writing Wrap-Up WRITING • THINKING • LISTENING • SPEAKING

DESCRIBING

Write a Lost-and-Found Ad

Write a lost-and-found ad for something that you have lost. Use adjectives to describe the item clearly. Then read your ad to a partner. Have your partner name the adjectives you used.

For Extra Practice see page 159.

Summing Up Help students summarize these key points about the lesson:

An **adjective** is a word that describes a noun.
An adjective can tell *what kind* or *how many*.

You may want to have students complete the parts related to this lesson on Blackline Master 4–1.

On Your Own

If students have trouble finding the adjectives, have them focus on the nouns first, and then look for words that describe the nouns.

MEETING INDIVIDUAL NEEDS

FOR STUDENTS ACQUIRING ENGLISH

Distribute the SAE Practice page for Unit 4, Lesson 1. Ask students what they would do if they lost a dog. Also discuss work dogs can do to help people. Next, students write the adjectives that describe the underlined nouns. Then students write *what kind* or *how many*. Example: Have you seen a small brown dog? (*small, brown*—what kind, what kind)

Writing Wrap-Up

Writing Tip: Before students write their ads, have them make a list of adjectives that describe the object or its parts. See Blackline Master 4–4 for a sample ad.

TECHNOLOGY CONNECTION

Students may wish to use available software to make their ad into a colorful poster.

● RETEACHING WORKBOOK, page 35

1 What Is an Adjective?

- An **adjective** is a word that describes a noun.
- An adjective can tell *what kind* or *how many*.

What kind	We wanted to make **hot** soup. We like soup on a **cold, rainy** day.
How many	We made **ten** bowls of soup. There are **many** people in my family.

Write the adjective or adjectives that describe each underlined noun.

Example: Soup is a healthy food. **healthy**

1. We cooked homemade soup. homemade
2. We had to buy several things for the soup. several
3. We went to the new market on Brown Street. new
4. I asked for three pounds of chicken. three
5. I bought a few carrots too. few
6. Eli got two fresh peppers. two, fresh
7. We also needed some small onions. some, small
8. Everything fit into one large bag. one, large
9. At home we took out the big, heavy pot. big, heavy
10. There are many ways to make soup. many
11. We put in white rice and a dash of pepper. white
12. A dash of pepper is a tiny bit. tiny
13. Then we cooked it on a low flame. low
14. I like soup that is a golden color. golden
15. We left the soup on the stove for four hours. four
16. Everyone enjoyed the delicious, hot soup. delicious, hot

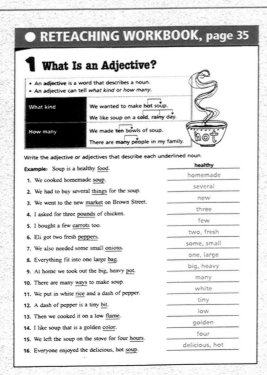

▲■ WORKBOOK PLUS, pages 59–60

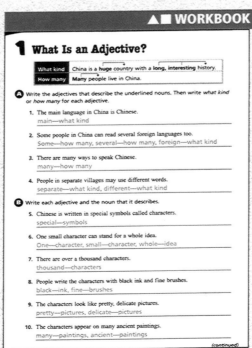

1 What Is an Adjective?

What kind	China is a **huge** country with a **long, interesting** history.
How many	**Many** people live in China.

A Write the adjectives that describe the underlined nouns. Then write *what kind* or *how many* for each adjective.

1. The main language in China is Chinese.
   main—what kind
2. Some people in China can read several foreign languages too.
   Some—how many, several—how many, foreign—what kind
3. There are many ways to speak Chinese.
   many—how many
4. People in separate villages may use different words.
   separate—what kind, different—what kind

B Write each adjective and the noun that it describes.

5. Chinese is written in special symbols called characters.
   special—symbols
6. One small character can stand for a whole idea.
   One—character, small—character, whole—idea
7. There are over a thousand characters.
   thousand—characters
8. People write the characters with black ink and fine brushes.
   black—ink, fine—brushes
9. The characters look like pretty, delicate pictures.
   pretty—pictures, delicate—pictures
10. The characters appear on many ancient paintings.
    many—paintings, ancient—paintings

(continued)

1 What Is an Adjective? (continued from page 59)

Challenge

The Chinese are famous not only for their beautiful writing but also for their beautiful paintings and drawings. Look at these examples of Chinese-style drawings. Then write three sentences to describe each one. Use adjectives that tell *what kind* and *how many*.

1. Answers will vary.
2.
3.
4.
5.
6.

Writing Application: A Journal Entry DESCRIBING

You are traveling in a foreign country. You don't speak the people's language, and they don't speak English. Write five sentences about your first day in this country. Describe the problems that you face and how you solve them. Use adjectives that tell *what kind* or *how many* in each sentence.
Students should respond on separate paper. Answers will vary.

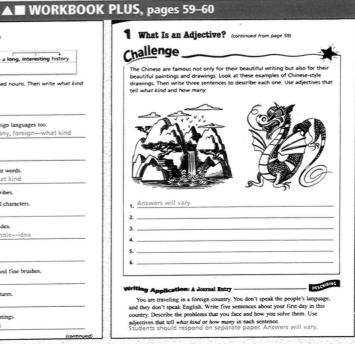

Writing with Adjectives

Lesson Objective

Students will:

- elaborate sentences by adding adjectives

Focus on Instruction

- Remind students that adjectives tell more about a noun by telling *what kind* or *how many.*
- Point out that a comma sometimes separates two adjectives that come before a noun. Tell students to try adding the word *and* between the two adjectives. If the adjectives sound awkward separated by *and,* a comma is not needed.

Apply It

Have students finish the revising activity on their own.

Students who need extra support can work with partners to list adjectives that describe the nouns in each sentence. (Sample chart is shown.)

Adjectives that Describe Nouns				
Noun	Dalmatian	hero	boots	hat
Adjective	sleek	famous	black	red

Have students look in their writing in progress for sentences to elaborate with adjectives.

Sample Answers to Apply It

1. This loyal Dalmatian dreams of being a famous hero.
2. She is wearing polished black boots and a shiny big hat.
3. FooFoo is a clothing designer.
4. She is wearing expensive jewels to a birthday party with her two best friends.
5. Montie prepares for a long, difficult hike.
6. He is filling his big green backpack with hiking gear and delicious treats.
7. This dashing Border collie is "the talk of Doggy Town."
8. All sheep obey this smart dog.

FOR STUDENTS ACQUIRING ENGLISH

Show students pictures of dogs. Have them think of words to describe them. Write their responses on the board. Show students how to move adjectives to combine these sentences: *The dog ran. The dog is spotted.* (The spotted dog ran.) Have students use the adjectives on the board to create new sentences.

Revising Strategies

Writing with Adjectives

Elaborating Sentences Adjectives add information about color, shape, size, and other details. Use adjectives to make your writing more interesting and to create pictures in your reader's mind.

The dogs dressed for the fashion show.

The four charming dogs dressed for the fashion show.

Apply It

1–8. Revise these cartoon captions about a fashion show for dogs. Each caption contains two sentences. Elaborate each one with adjectives.

See TE margin for sample answers.

Revising
This Dalmatian dreams of being a hero. She is wearing boots and a hat.
FooFoo is a designer. She is wearing jewels to a party with her friends.
Montie prepares for a hike. He is filling his backpack with gear and treats.
This Border collie is "the talk of Doggy town." Sheep obey this dog.

138 **Unit 4:** Adjectives

Meeting Individual Needs

● RETEACHING WORKBOOK, page 36

Writing with Adjectives

- Adjectives describe color, size, shape, and other details.
- Use adjectives to make your writing colorful, detailed, and interesting to read.

Without adjectives	We had pie for dessert.
With adjectives	We had delicious hot apple pie for dessert.

Elaborating Sentences Elaborate each sentence by adding adjectives.

Example: We picked apples from the tree.
We picked twelve apples from the big tree.

Revising

1. Dad climbed the ladder.
   Answers will vary.
2. We put the apples in a basket.
3. Jamie and I carried the basket home.
4. Mom put the apples on the table.
5. She cut them into pieces.
6. We helped her make the pie.
7. We put the pie in the oven.
8. The smell of the apples drifted through the house.

(continued)

▲■ WORKBOOK PLUS, page 61

Writing with Adjectives

huge, trumpeting / center
The ^ circus elephants marched into the ^ ring.

Elaborating Sentences 1–8. Rewrite this letter. Use adjectives to elaborate each underlined sentence.

Revising

Dear Aunt Sally,

We went to the circus last night. I laughed when the clown stumbled. He pretended he could not get up. In the middle ring, acrobats rode a bicycle. The tightrope walker was high overhead. She held an umbrella for balance. Next, the ringmaster blew a whistle. Horses raced into the ring. Each horse carried a rider. The riders did tricks while the horses galloped.

Then circus workers put up a safety net. High above, the trapeze artists performed. The most exciting act was next. A daredevil was shot out of a cannon. The circus ended with a parade. What a great time we had!

Your nephew,
Sam

Sentences will vary.

(continued)

Combining Sentences Good writers try new ways to make their writing smooth and clear. You can experiment with your writing, too, by moving adjectives to combine sentences.

The two choppy sentences below are both about a rabbit. You can combine them to make one smooth sentence by placing the adjective *brown* before the noun *rabbit*.

A rabbit hops across the field. The rabbit is brown.	A brown rabbit hops across the field.

The two short sentences below each tell about rabbits' legs. The sentences can be combined by joining the adjectives *long* and *powerful* with the word *and*. Notice that both adjectives follow a form of the verb *be*.

Rabbits' hind legs are long. Rabbits' hind legs are powerful.	Rabbits' hind legs are long and powerful.

Apply It

9–14. Read these paragraphs from a report. Rewrite each underlined pair of sentences by combining them.

Example: A rabbit's tail is short. Its tail is fluffy.
A rabbit's tail is short and fluffy.

Revising — **Rabbit Report**

A rabbit's front teeth are long. The teeth are sharp. Rabbits use their teeth for gnawing plants. In warm weather, rabbits eat green, leafy plants. Rabbits like to nibble clover. Clover is sweet. During the winter a rabbit's diet changes. Rabbits eat twigs during the winter. During the winter rabbits also eat bark.

Rabbits are small. They are also weak. They have many enemies. Foxes are one enemy. Foxes are dangerous. When a fox is near, rabbits usually hide. They may hide in grass. The grass is tall.

Lesson Objective

Students will:

- combine sentences by using adjectives from one or more shorter sentences

Focus on Instruction

- Emphasize that when combining sentences, the meaning of the original sentences should not be changed. Write the sentences below on the board.

  Most rabbits live in burrows.
  The burrows are underground.

  Then write these possible combinations.

  Most underground rabbits live in burrows.
  Rabbits underground live in most burrows.
  Most rabbits live in underground burrows.

- Ask students how the first two combinations change the meaning. (*Underground* should describe *burrows*, not *rabbits*. *Most* should describe *rabbits*.)

Apply It

Have students complete the revising activity independently.

Have students find places in their own writing in progress where they can combine sentences using adjectives.

Answers to Apply It

9. A rabbit's front teeth are long and sharp.
10. Rabbits like to nibble sweet clover.
11. Rabbits eat twigs and bark during the winter.
12. Rabbits are small and weak.
13. Foxes are one dangerous enemy.
14. They may hide in the tall grass.

● RETEACHING WORKBOOK, page 37

Writing with Adjectives *(continued from page 36)*

- Using many short sentences makes writing choppy.
- Combine sentences about the same subject to make your writing smooth and clear.

Two sentences	Oysters use their shells for protection. Oyster shells are hard.
One sentence	Oysters use their hard shells for protection.

Combining Sentences Combine each pair of sentences into one sentence by moving adjectives.

Example: This lizard is small. This lizard is quick.
This lizard is small and quick.

Revising

9. Some animals' tongues are long. The tongues are sticky.
   Some animals' tongues are long and sticky.
10. The giraffe's tongue is long. The giraffe's tongue is dark.
    The giraffe's tongue is long and dark.
11. Have you seen a snake's tongue? It is forked.
    Have you seen a snake's forked tongue?
12. The armadillo is heavy. The armadillo is slow.
    The armadillo is heavy and slow.
13. The snail carries its shell on its back. The shell is coiled.
    The snail carries its coiled shell on its back.
14. Porcupines have quills for protection. The quills are sharp.
    Porcupines have sharp quills for protection.
15. The parrotfish has overlapping scales. The parrotfish is colorful.
    The colorful parrotfish has overlapping scales.
16. The male lion showed his teeth. His teeth are sharp.
    The male lion showed his sharp teeth.

▲■ WORKBOOK PLUS, page 62

Writing with Adjectives *(continued from page 61)*

Not combined	We bought cotton candy at the circus. The cotton candy was pink.
Combined	We bought pink cotton candy at the circus.

Combining Sentences 9–16. Rewrite this e-mail message, combining each pair of underlined sentences.

Revising — e-mail

To: Rena
From: Max
Subject: The Circus

I rode a camel at the circus. The camel was tan. Its legs were long. Its legs were skinny. To get on the camel, I climbed a ladder. The ladder was tall. Then I stepped onto the camel's back. I rode in a saddle. The saddle was leather. A blanket covered the saddle. The blanket was wool.

The camel's name was Whitney. Whitney had big eyes. Her eyes were brown. I rode Whitney around a ring. The ring was small. The ride was bumpy. The ride was fun.

I rode a tan camel at the circus. Its legs were long and skinny. To get on the camel, I climbed a tall ladder. Then I stepped onto the camel's back. I rode in a leather saddle. A wool blanket covered the saddle.

The camel's name was Whitney. Whitney had big brown eyes. I rode Whitney around a small ring. The ride was bumpy and fun.

Adjectives After *be*

Lesson Objectives

Students will:

- identify an adjective that follows the word it describes and a form of the verb *be*, and identify the noun being described
- write a description, using adjectives after the verb *be*

One-Minute Warm-Up Write the adjectives on the board. Have volunteers tell what word each describes.

Focus on Instruction

Review with students the different conjugated forms of *be*: *am*, *is*, *was*, *are*, and *were*.

Try It Out

LISTENING AND SPEAKING Have volunteers read each sentence aloud, replacing the adjective.

FOR STUDENTS ACQUIRING ENGLISH

- Have students listen to the Try It Out sentences on the audiotape. Distribute SAE Practice page for Unit 4, Lesson 2, to support listening.
- Review *be* in the present and past tenses. Ask for sentences with *be;* write suggestions on the board. Help students mark with colored chalk any words in the sentences that are adjectives. Have students underline adjectives once and the noun each adjective describes twice. Example: John is tall.

Summing Up Help students summarize this key point about the lesson:

An **adjective** can follow the word it describes and a form of the verb *be*.

Have students complete the parts related to this lesson on Blackline Master 4–1.

On Your Own

Remind students to look for the adjective *after* a form of the verb *be*.

Writing Wrap-Up

Writing Tip: Tell students to use sensory words that help readers see, taste, touch, and smell the food. See Blackline Master 4–4 for a sample description.

Grammar

2 Adjectives After *be*

One-Minute Warm-Up

Read the sentence below. How many adjectives can you find? What are they?

The next day was rainy and dark.

—from *Charlotte's Web*, by E. B. White

Adjectives describe nouns. They can also describe words like *I*, *it*, and *we*, which take the place of nouns. An adjective can come after the word it describes. This usually happens when an adjective follows a form of the verb *be*.

The project is ready. I am excited.

Try It Out

Speak Up Find each adjective. What word does it describe?
Adj. is underlined once; word it describes, twice.

1. The weather is beautiful.
2. The fair is exciting.
3. We were eager.
4. Jamie is proud.
5. The chicken is fat.
6. The eggs are large.

On Your Own

7–12. This checklist for an apple pie contest has six adjectives. Write each adjective and the word it describes. Adj. is underlined once; word it describes, twice.

Example: The crust is flaky. *flaky crust*

Apple Pie CONTEST Checklist

- ☐ The pie is homemade.
- ☐ It is moist.
- ☐ The crust is delicate.
- ☐ The apples were fresh.
- ☐ They are juicy.
- ☐ I am happy with the taste.

Writing Wrap-Up WRITING • THINKING • LISTENING • SPEAKING

DESCRIBING

Write a Description

Use adjectives to describe your favorite food. Read your description to a partner. Do the descriptions make your mouth water?

140 **Unit 4:** Adjectives For Extra Practice see page 160.

Meeting Individual Needs

● RETEACHING WORKBOOK, page 38

2 Adjectives After *be*

- An adjective can follow the word it describes. It usually follows a form of the verb *be*.

Science is interesting. They were easy.
Experiments are useful. It was fun too.

Write the adjective that follows each underlined word.

Example: The class was busy in science. busy

1. The class was curious about eggs. curious
2. Carmen is familiar with chickens. familiar
3. Carmen's hens are beautiful. beautiful
4. The eggs are brown. brown
5. Carmen is proud of the eggs. proud
6. An experiment was possible. possible
7. Ms. Amato was helpful with the experiment. helpful
8. She is enthusiastic about science. enthusiastic
9. We were excited about it. excited
10. The machine was large. large
11. The eggs were warm in the machine. warm
12. Soon the eggs were open. open
13. The chicks are tiny now. tiny
14. They are weak too. weak
15. Maria is gentle with them. gentle
16. She is careful about the food. careful
17. I am happy about the experiment. happy
18. The results were amazing. amazing

▲■ WORKBOOK PLUS, page 63

2 Adjectives After *be*

The weather was awful. The lakes were frozen.
It is cold. They are slippery now.

Write each adjective and the word that it describes.

1. Finally, the sky was clear. clear—sky
2. The winds are cold on our faces. cold—winds
3. I am chilly. chilly—I
4. The snow is fluffy like cotton. fluffy—snow
5. It is deep everywhere. deep—it
6. Plows were busy on our street. busy—Plows
7. They are noisy. noisy—They
8. Snowstorms are exciting! exciting—Snowstorms

Challenge

You have invented a wonderful new snow shovel called the Super Shovel. Complete this advertisement for the Super Shovel. Use an adjective in each sentence. The adjective must follow a form of the verb *be*.

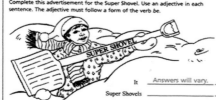

It Answers will vary. .
Super Shovels ______ .
They ______ .

Usage

3 Using *a, an,* and *the*

One-Minute Warm-Up

What mistake can you find in this ad?

For dads or moms a shovel makes a excellent gift!

For dads or moms a shovel makes *an* excellent gift!

The words *a, an,* and *the* are special adjectives called articles. Learn these rules for using articles.

With Singular Nouns:

Use *a* if the next word begins with a consonant sound.	a flower
Use *an* if the next word begins with a vowel sound.	an iris
Use *the* if the noun names a particular person, place, or thing.	the garden

With Plural Nouns:

Use *the*. the flowers the irises

Try It Out

Speak Up Which article or articles could be used before each word?

1. contest 2. award 3. orchids 4. students 5. prize

1. a, the 2. an, the 3. the 4. the 5. a, the

On Your Own

6–10. These tree labels for an Arbor Day poster have five incorrect articles. Write each label correctly. (Some labels can take more than one article.)

Incorrect words are underlined.

Example: a ash *an ash, the ash*

Proofreading

- a dogwood
- an maples the
- a aspen an, the
- an weeping willow a, the
- a oak an, the
- a evergreens the

Writing Wrap-Up WRITING • THINKING • LISTENING • SPEAKING

INFORMING

Write Labels

Write labels for objects in the classroom. Use *a, an,* or *the*. Read your labels to a partner. Are the articles correct?

For Extra Practice see page 161.

Using *a, an,* and *the*

Lesson Objectives

Students will:

- choose correct articles
- proofread for articles
- write labels, using *a, an,* and *the*

One-Minute Warm-Up Ask how changing the article *a* to *the* changes the meaning of the sentence.

Focus on Instruction

Explain that words starting with *h* can begin with a consonant sound, as in *hop,* or a vowel sound, as in *hour.*

Try It Out

LISTENING AND SPEAKING Ask volunteers to read aloud each correct answer and tell other words they could use with each article.

MEETING INDIVIDUAL NEEDS

FOR STUDENTS ACQUIRING ENGLISH

Distribute SAE Practice page for Unit 4, Lesson 3. Explain that *a* and *an* are used for the first mention of something; afterward *the* is used, as in: *I bought a new sweater. The sweater is green. A* and *an* are used before a general group; *the* is used for specific people, places, or things. *I need a pen. I lost the pen I had.* Students listen and fill in the article. Example: My parents bought ______ new car. (a)

Summing Up Help students summarize these key points about the lesson:

Use *an* and *a* with singular nouns.
Use *the* with a particular noun.

Have students complete the parts related to this lesson on Blackline Master 4–1.

On Your Own

Tell students that the meaning changes with the use of different articles.

Writing Wrap-Up

Writing Tip: Tell students to use words that start with both consonants and vowels. See Blackline Master 4–4 for a sample labels.

Meeting Individual Needs

● RETEACHING WORKBOOK, page 39

3 Using *a, an,* and *the*

- *A, an,* and *the* are special adjectives called **articles**.
- Use *a* before a word that begins with a consonant sound.
- Use *an* before a word that begins with a vowel sound.
- Use *the* if the noun names a particular person, place, or thing.

With singular nouns	a coin	an old coin	the coin
With plural nouns	the coins	the old and new coins	

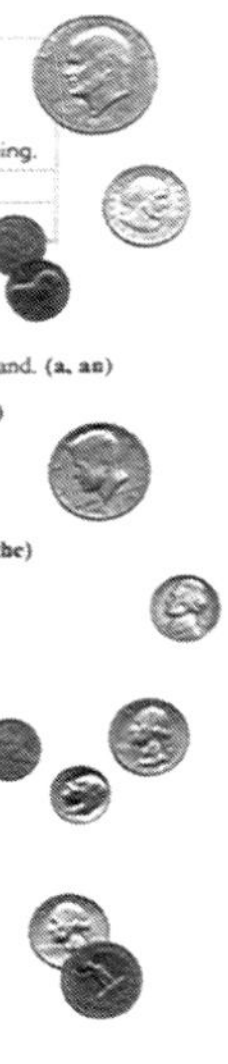

Write the correct article in parentheses to complete each sentence. The underlined letters are clues.

Example: Chang spent last summer on ___an___ island. (a, an)

1. One day Chang took ___a___ long walk. (a, an)
2. ___The___ sun was bright that day. (An, The)
3. Chang passed ___a___ white fence. (a, an)
4. He walked beyond ___the___ small cottages. (a, the)
5. Soon he reached ___the___ water. (an, the)
6. ___The___ high waves were splashing. (A, The)
7. There he saw ___a___ sand castle. (a, an)
8. It was ___an___ enormous castle. (a, an)
9. Did ___a___ child build it? (a, an)
10. Did ___an___ adult do this careful work? (a, an)
11. Chang looked at ___the___ tall towers. (a, the)
12. He peeked into ___an___ opening. (a, an)
13. ___An___ old coin lay inside the castle. (A, An)
14. Who could have left such ___a___ strange coin? (a, an)
15. Chang returned ___the___ next day. (an, the)
16. ___The___ old coin and the castle were gone. (A, The)

▲■ WORKBOOK PLUS, page 64

3 Using *a, an,* and *the*

Jacob is a good student.
He knows how to use an encyclopedia.
He finds the correct volume and the right pages.

Write the correct article in parentheses to complete each sentence.

1. Jacob is writing ___a___ report. (a, an)
2. It is about ___a___ famous inventor. (a, an)
3. Elisha Otis invented ___the___ elevator. (a, the)
4. In Otis's day, ___a___ building could not be very tall. (a, an)
5. Walking up ___the___ stairs was tiring. (a, the)
6. ___The___ elevator changed all that. (A, The)
7. Jacob used ___an___ encyclopedia for his report. (a, an)
8. He took out ___the___ volume marked *O.* (an, the)
9. Jacob found ___an___ article about Otis. (a, an)
10. He also looked for information about ___the___ elevator. (a, the)
11. Jacob made notes on ___a___ piece of paper. (a, an)

Challenge

The elevator is an invention that moves people from one place to another. Think of other inventions that move people from place to place. Write the names of two real inventions and two imaginary inventions below.

REAL INVENTIONS	IMAGINARY INVENTIONS
1. Answers will vary.	3. ______
2. ______	4. ______

Choose one of these inventions. On another piece of paper, draw a picture of the invention. Then describe it, using the articles *a, an,* and *the*.

Making Comparisons

Lesson Objectives

Students will:
- add *-er* to adjectives to compare two persons, places, or things and add *-est* to adjectives to compare three or more persons, places, or things
- proofread for comparative and superlative forms
- write a report, using comparative and superlative forms of adjectives

One-Minute Warm-Up Ask volunteers to read their sentences aloud. Have them identify the adjectives that compare. Write these on the board. Circle the *-er* endings and underline the *-est* endings. Ask which ending is used to compare two objects and which is used to compare more than two objects.

Focus on Instruction

Point out that the word *than* often appears after an adjective with the *-er* ending. The words *of all* often appear after an adjective with the *-est* ending.

Try It Out

LISTENING AND SPEAKING Have students read sentences, using the proper form of the adjective. Ask them to tell what is being compared in each sentence.

FOR STUDENTS ACQUIRING ENGLISH
- Have students listen to the Try It Out sentences on the audiotape. Distribute SAE Practice page for Unit 4, Lesson 4, to support listening.
- Ask students what the image in the book is. Find out what they know about Alaska. Help them locate it on a map. Make sure they know this is one of the states, even though it is next to Canada. Write *Alaska is the biggest state* on the board. Have a student mark the adjective. Then ask what other words double consonants when an ending is added. (verbs) Discuss the doubling rule. Then discuss dropping *e* and changing *y* to *i.* Students listen and fill in adjectives.
  1. Alaska is ______ than Texas. *(big)* (bigger)
  2. Hawaii is the ______ state. *(new)* (newest)

Grammar/Usage

4 Making Comparisons

Samples: Griz is fatter than Kody. Kody is the tallest of the three.

One-Minute Warm-Up

Look at the picture. How many sentences can you make to compare the sizes of the bears? Use words such as *tall, taller, tallest, fat, fatter, fattest.*

Sometimes you may want to tell how things are alike or how they are different. You can use adjectives to compare. You usually add *-er* to an adjective to compare two persons, places, or things, and *-est* to compare three or more.

One trip: William took a long trip.
Two trips: Jason's trip was longer than his.
Three or more: I took the longest trip of all.

Rules for Adding *-er* and *-est*	
1. **Adjectives ending with *e*:** Drop the *e* before adding the ending.	wide wider widest
2. **Adjectives ending with a single vowel and a consonant:** Double the consonant and add the ending.	thin thinner thinnest
3. **Adjectives ending with a consonant and *y*:** Change the *y* to *i* before adding the ending.	tiny tinier tiniest

Try It Out

Speak Up What form of the adjective in ( ) completes each sentence correctly?

1. Alaska is not the ______ state. (new) newest
2. Every state except Hawaii is ______ than Alaska. (old) older
3. Alaska is the ______ of all the states. (big) biggest
4. However, Wyoming has the ______ population. (tiny) tiniest
5. ______ people live there than in my state. (few) Fewer

Alaska's State Flag

Meeting Individual Needs

RETEACHING
ALTERNATIVE STRATEGY
- Write *A bear is big. An elephant is bigger than a bear.* Ask how many animals are being compared (two). Point out that *g* and *-er* were added to *big* to compare two animals.
- Write *The dinosaur was the biggest creature of all.* Ask how many animals are being compared. (more than two) Point out that *g* and *-est* were added to big to compare many animals.
- Review the spelling rules that apply to words with *-er* and *-est* endings.

CHALLENGE
Divide the class into teams. Say an adjective and have the first person in each group compete to correctly write its comparative forms. Continue for each team member. Teams receive a point for each correctly spelled word.

FOR STUDENTS ACQUIRING ENGLISH
Find out what students know about comparatives and superlatives. Set up comparisons and ask questions. For example, arrange three pencils and ask, "Is the red pencil longer than the blue pencil? Which is the longest pencil?"

On Your Own

Write the correct form of the adjective in ( ) to complete each sentence.

Example: We will be visiting the ______ state of all. (large) *largest*

6. It is ______ to get to Alaska than it used to be. (easy) easier
7. We will see the ______ mountains in North America. (tall) tallest
8. Mount McKinley is the ______ peak of all. (high) highest
9. Alaska is ______ than the last place we visited. (wild) wilder
10. It is home to the ______ bears in the world. (big) biggest
11. The Kodiak bear is even ______ than a grizzly bear. (large) larger
12. A Kodiak bear can also be ______ than a grizzly. (fierce) fiercer
13. The ______ thing of all is to keep away from these bears! (safe) safest
14. Don't make the bear any ______ than it already is! (angry) angrier

15–20. This draft of an article for a Web site on Alaska has six incorrect forms of *-er* and *-est*. Write the article correctly. Incorrect words are underlined.

Example: Northern Alaska has the colder climate in the United States.
Northern Alaska has the coldest climate in the United States.

Proofreading — Web site

You Can Wear Shorts in Alaska!

Alaska's climate can be mild than many people think. The city of Anchorage can get hoter than seventy degrees. Southern Alaska has the warmer climate in the state. The south is also the wetter of all the regions. It has the higher average rainfall in Alaska. Northern Alaska is colder and dryer than the southern part of the state.

milder; hotter; warmest; wettest; highest; drier

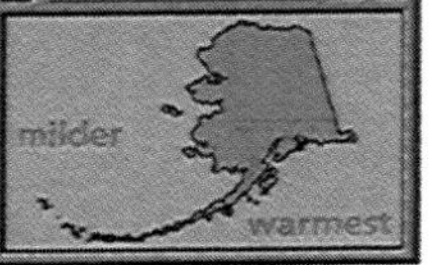

Writing Wrap-Up

WRITING • THINKING • LISTENING • SPEAKING

COMPARING / CONTRASTING

Write a Geography Report

How does your state compare with Alaska or another state? Does it have the same scenery, climate, or animals? Write a paragraph about how the two states are alike. Then write one about how they are different. Use adjectives with *-er* and *-est*. Find a partner and read your reports to each other. Did you make similar comparisons?

For Extra Practice see page 162.

Summing Up Help students summarize these key points about the lesson:

> Add *-er* to most adjectives to compare two persons, places, or things. Add *-est* to most adjectives to compare three or more persons, places, or things.

You may want to have students complete the parts related to this lesson on Blackline Master 4–2.

On Your Own

Advise students to first review the rules for adding *-er* and *-est*.

MEETING INDIVIDUAL NEEDS

FOR STUDENTS ACQUIRING ENGLISH

Distribute SAE Practice page for Unit 4, Lesson 4. Remind students to look for *than* with comparatives and *the* with superlatives. Students fill in the blanks with adjectives.

1. Alaska has the ______ mountain in the United States. *(tall)* (tallest)
2. Alaska has the third ______ population. *(small)* (smallest)

Writing Wrap-Up

Writing Tip: Before students begin, have them make a Venn diagram to compare the two states. See Blackline Master 4–4 for a sample report.

SCHOOL-HOME CONNECTION

Invite students to share their reports with family members and discuss how the two states compare.

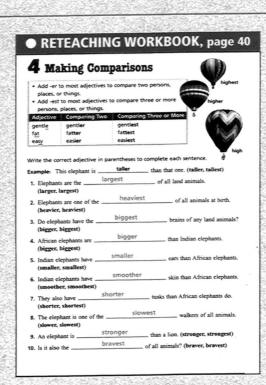

● RETEACHING WORKBOOK, page 40

4 Making Comparisons

- Add -er to most adjectives to compare two persons, places, or things.
- Add -est to most adjectives to compare three or more persons, places, or things.

Adjective	Comparing Two	Comparing Three or More
gentle	gentler	gentlest
fat	fatter	fattest
easy	easier	easiest

Write the correct adjective in parentheses to complete each sentence.

Example: This elephant is ___taller___ than that one. **(taller, tallest)**

1. Elephants are the ___largest___ of all land animals. **(larger, largest)**
2. Elephants are one of the ___heaviest___ of all animals at birth. **(heavier, heaviest)**
3. Do elephants have the ___biggest___ brains of any land animals? **(bigger, biggest)**
4. African elephants are ___bigger___ than Indian elephants. **(bigger, biggest)**
5. Indian elephants have ___smaller___ ears than African elephants. **(smaller, smallest)**
6. Indian elephants have ___smoother___ skin than African elephants. **(smoother, smoothest)**
7. They also have ___shorter___ tusks than African elephants do. **(shorter, shortest)**
8. The elephant is one of the ___slowest___ walkers of all animals. **(slower, slowest)**
9. An elephant is ___stronger___ than a lion. **(stronger, strongest)**
10. Is it also the ___bravest___ of all animals? **(braver, bravest)**

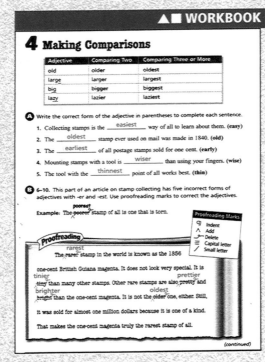

▲■ WORKBOOK PLUS, pages 65–66

4 Making Comparisons

Adjective	Comparing Two	Comparing Three or More
old	older	oldest
large	larger	largest
big	bigger	biggest
lazy	lazier	laziest

A Write the correct form of the adjective in parentheses to complete each sentence.

1. Collecting stamps is the ___easiest___ way of all to learn about them. **(easy)**
2. The ___oldest___ stamp ever used on mail was made in 1840. **(old)**
3. The ___earliest___ of all postage stamps sold for one cent. **(early)**
4. Mounting stamps with a tool is ___wiser___ than using your fingers. **(wise)**
5. The tool with the ___thinnest___ point of all works best. **(thin)**

B 6–10. This part of an article on stamp collecting has five incorrect forms of adjectives with -er and -est. Use proofreading marks to correct the adjectives.

Example: The ~~poorer~~ poorest stamp of all is one that is torn.

Proofreading Marks
- ¶ Indent
- ^ Add
- Delete
- ≡ Capital letter
- / Small letter

Proofreading

The ~~rarer~~ rarest stamp in the world is known as the 1856 one-cent British Guiana magenta. It does not look very special. It is ~~tiny~~ tinier than many other stamps. Other rare stamps are also ~~pretty~~ prettier and ~~bright~~ brighter than the one-cent magenta. It is not the ~~older~~ oldest one, either. Still, it was sold for almost one million dollars because it is one of a kind. That makes the one-cent magenta truly the rarest stamp of all.

(continued)

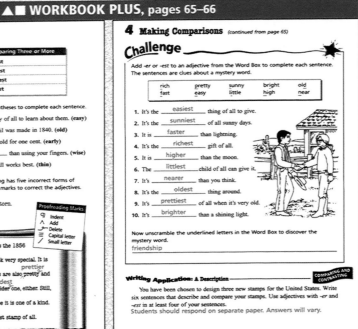

4 Making Comparisons *(continued from page 65)*

Challenge

Add -er or -est to an adjective from the Word Box to complete each sentence. The sentences are clues about a mystery word.

rich	pretty	sunny	bright	old
fast	easy	little	high	near

1. It's the ___easiest___ thing of all to give.
2. It's the ___sunniest___ of all sunny days.
3. It is ___faster___ than lightning.
4. It's the ___richest___ gift of all.
5. It is ___higher___ than the moon.
6. The ___littlest___ child of all can give it.
7. It's ___nearer___ than you think.
8. It's the ___oldest___ thing around.
9. It's ___prettiest___ of all when it's very old.
10. It's ___brighter___ than a shining light.

Now unscramble the underlined letters in the Word Box to discover the mystery word.
friendship

Writing Application: A Description — COMPARING AND CONTRASTING

You have been chosen to design three new stamps for the United States. Write six sentences that describe and compare your stamps. Use adjectives with *-er* and *-est* in at least four of your sentences.
Students should respond on separate paper. Answers will vary.

Comparing with *more* and *most*

Lesson Objectives

Students will:

- use *more* with long adjectives to compare two things, and use *most* with long adjectives to compare three or more things
- proofread sentences for comparisons with *more* and *most*
- write an opinion, using *more* and *most*

One-Minute Warm-Up On the board, write *most* and *popularest,* underlining the *est*. Ask what the *-est* ending tells. (that more than two pets are being compared) Point out that *most* also tells that more than two cats are being compared. Tell students that they can only use *most* or the *-est* ending.

Focus on Instruction

Tell students to check the dictionary if they are unsure whether a word uses *more* and *most* or *-er* and *-est* to make comparisons.

Try It Out

VIEWING Have students list adjectives that describe the cat in the photo. Place the words in the appropriate column of a chart with the headings *more, most* and *-er, -est*. Use the adjectives in the *more, most* column in comparative sentences. (Sample responses are shown.)

more, most	-er, -est
amazing	light
interesting	friendly

FOR STUDENTS ACQUIRING ENGLISH

- Have students listen to the Try It Out sentences on the audiotape. Distribute SAE Practice page for Unit 4, Lesson 5, to support listening.
- Discuss the photo; list vocabulary. Review comparatives with *-er* and superlatives with *-est*. Explain that *more* and *most* are used with longer words. Say several adjectives as students count syllables. Say that adjectives with one syllable use *-er* and *-est*. Those with three or more use *more* and *most;* those with two vary. If it ends in *y,* it adds *-er* and *-est*. Ask for examples. (easy, pretty) Students listen and fill in the adjective.
  1. Birds are ______ than turtles. *(popular)* (more popular)
  2. Dogs are ______ to feed than cats. *(expensive)* (more expensive)

Grammar/Usage

5 Comparing with *more* and *most*

One-Minute Warm-Up

What's wrong with this sentence? How can you fix it?

Did you know that cats are the most popularest pets in the United States?

Did you know that cats are the most popular pets in the United States?

- With long adjectives, use the words *more* and *most* to compare persons, places, or things. Use *more* to compare two. Use *most* to compare three or more.

One	Tiger is a playful cat.
Two	Ginger is a more playful cat than Tiger.
Three or More	Ike is the most playful cat of all.

- Never add *-er* and *more* or *-est* and *most* to the same adjective.

Incorrect: Tiger is more smarter than Ginger.
Tiger is the most intelligentest cat.

Correct: Tiger is smarter than Ginger.
Tiger is the most intelligent cat.

Try It Out

Speak Up What word should you add to the adjective in ( ) to complete each sentence correctly?

1. Cats and dogs are among the ______ of all pets. (common) most common
2. Cats are ______ than dogs, though. (independent) more independent
3. One of the ______ of all breeds of cat is the Siamese. (popular) most popular
4. Some people think that a Persian cat is ______ than any other cat. (beautiful) more beautiful
5. However, a cat from an animal shelter can be the ______ of all. (lovable) most lovable

Meeting Individual Needs

RETEACHING
ALTERNATIVE STRATEGY

- On the board, write *sad.* Ask students to change *sad* to compare two nouns (*sadder*) and three nouns. (*saddest*)
- Next write *sorrowful.* Explain that the *-er* ending isn't used for long adjectives. Write *more sorrowful* and *most sorrowful.* Have students identify words that compare. (*more, most*)
- Explain that *more* and *most* can be used in place of *-er* and *-est.* Have students practice using *more* and *most* with long adjectives of their own choosing.

CHALLENGE

Have students find their favorite ads in magazines or on TV or radio. Have them rewrite the ads, using adjectives that use *more* and *most* to compare.

FOR STUDENTS ACQUIRING ENGLISH

Choose three sweaters, pairs of shoes, or chairs to demonstrate *comfortable,* and three books to demonstrate *interesting.* As you try each one, make comparisons and then express the superlative among the three. Continue by asking students questions.

On Your Own

Add *more* or *most* to the adjective in ( ) to complete each sentence correctly. Write the sentence.

Example: Cats are ______ to train than kittens. (difficult) *more difficult*

6. A cat is one of the ______ kinds of pets. (independent) most independent
7. Cats are among the ______ of all animals. (curious) most curious
8. A cat's tricks can be ______ than a clown's. (amusing) more amusing
9. Cats are the ______ pets for keeping mice away. (useful) most useful
10. Some cats are ______ hunters than others. (skillful) more skillful
11. Some people think that cats are ______ than any other pet. (intelligent) more intelligent
12. Some cats seem to think that they are the ______ animals too. (intelligent) most intelligent

13–18. This part of an article for a cat magazine has six missing or incorrect forms of *more* and *most*. Write the article correctly. Incorrect words are underlined.

Example: The tabby's face is the most sweetest of all.
The tabby's face is the sweetest of all.

Proofreading

Tips Takes Top Honors

It was the excitingest [most exciting] moment of the annual cat show. The prize for the most beautiful cat went to Tips. His fur was even more sleeker [sleeker] than Moe's. His whiskers were even wonderful [more wonderful] than Cleo's. His eyes were the most biggest [biggest] I've ever seen. His tail was the more graceful [most graceful] of all. Never had I given the prize to a cat most deserving [more deserving] than Tips.

Writing Wrap-Up WRITING • THINKING • LISTENING • SPEAKING

EXPRESSING

Write an Opinion

Write a paragraph explaining which animal you think is the most intelligent of all. Use adjectives with *more* and *most*. Read your paragraph to a partner. Does your partner agree with you?

For Extra Practice see page 163.

Summing Up Help students summarize these key points about the lesson:

With long adjectives, use *more* to compare two things and *most* to compare three or more. Never add *-er* and *more* or *-est* and *most* to the same adjective.

You may want to have students complete the parts related to this lesson on Blackline Master 4–2.

On Your Own

Remind students that the adjective itself does not change when adding *more* or *most*.

MEETING INDIVIDUAL NEEDS

FOR STUDENTS ACQUIRING ENGLISH

Distribute SAE Practice page for Unit 4, Lesson 5. Briefly review the forms for both types of comparative and superlative. Write *comparative* and *superlative* on the board. As you say an adjective, point to one or the other and have students call out the form. Then students complete the chart with forms for both short and long adjective.

Writing Wrap-Up

Writing Tip: Remind students to state their opinion in a topic sentence, and then support their opinion. See Blackline Master 4–5 for a sample opinion.

TECHNOLOGY CONNECTION

Students may wish to use the Internet to gather information to support their opinion.

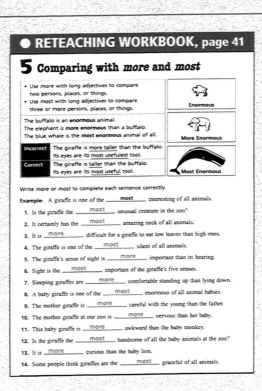

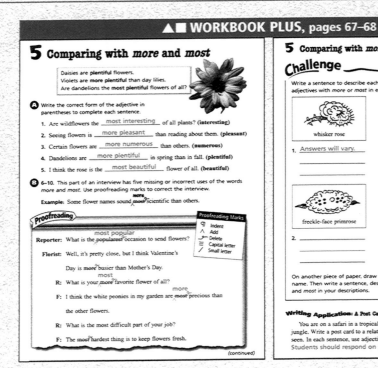

● RETEACHING WORKBOOK, page 41

5 Comparing with *more* and *most*

- Use *more* with long adjectives to compare two persons, places, or things.
- Use *most* with long adjectives to compare three or more persons, places, or things.

The buffalo is an **enormous** animal.
The elephant is **more enormous** than a buffalo.
The blue whale is the **most enormous** animal of all.

Incorrect	The giraffe is more taller than the buffalo. Its eyes are its most usefulest tool.
Correct	The giraffe is taller than the buffalo. Its eyes are its most useful tool.

Enormous

More Enormous

Most Enormous

Write *more* or *most* to complete each sentence correctly.

Example: A giraffe is one of the **most** interesting of all animals.

1. Is the giraffe the __most__ unusual creature in the zoo?
2. It certainly has the __most__ amazing neck of all animals.
3. It is __more__ difficult for a giraffe to eat low leaves than high ones.
4. The giraffe is one of the __most__ silent of all animals.
5. The giraffe's sense of sight is __more__ important than its hearing.
6. Sight is the __most__ important of the giraffe's five senses.
7. Sleeping giraffes are __more__ comfortable standing up than lying down.
8. A baby giraffe is one of the __most__ enormous of all animal babies.
9. The mother giraffe is __more__ careful with the young than the father.
10. The mother giraffe at our zoo is __more__ nervous than her baby.
11. This baby giraffe is __more__ awkward than the baby monkey.
12. Is the giraffe the __most__ handsome of all the baby animals at the zoo?
13. It is __more__ curious than the baby lion.
14. Some people think giraffes are the __most__ graceful of all animals.

▲■ WORKBOOK PLUS, pages 67–68

5 Comparing with *more* and *most*

Daisies are **plentiful** flowers.
Violets are **more plentiful** than day lilies.
Are dandelions the **most plentiful** flowers of all?

A Write the correct form of the adjective in parentheses to complete each sentence.

1. Are wildflowers the __most interesting__ of all plants? **(interesting)**
2. Seeing flowers is __more pleasant__ than reading about them. **(pleasant)**
3. Certain flowers are __more numerous__ than others. **(numerous)**
4. Dandelions are __more plentiful__ in spring than in fall. **(plentiful)**
5. I think the rose is the __most beautiful__ flower of all. **(beautiful)**

B 6–10. This part of an interview has five missing or incorrect uses of the words *more* and *most*. Use proofreading marks to correct the interview.

Example: Some flower names sound ~~most~~ [more] scientific than others.

Proofreading

Proofreading Marks
¶ Indent
∧ Add
Delete
≡ Capital letter
/ Small letter

Reporter: What is the ~~popularest~~ [most popular] occasion to send flowers?

Florist: Well, it's pretty close, but I think Valentine's Day is ~~more~~ busier than Mother's Day.

R: What is your ~~more~~ [most] favorite flower of all?

F: I think the white peonies in my garden are ~~most~~ [more] precious than the other flowers.

R: What is the most difficult part of your job?

F: The ~~most~~ hardest thing is to keep flowers fresh.

(continued)

5 Comparing with *more* and *most* (continued from page 67)

Challenge

Write a sentence to describe each of the imaginary flowers below. Use adjectives with *more* or *most* in each description.

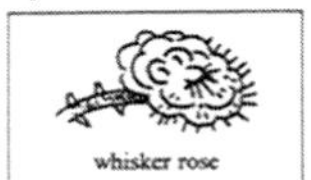
whisker rose

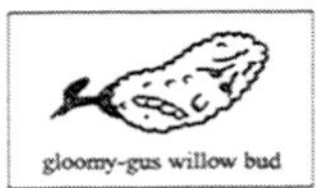
gloomy-gus willow bud

1. Answers will vary.

3. ______

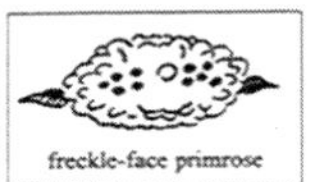
freckle-face primrose

sweet-and-sour lily

2. ______

4. ______

On another piece of paper, draw two imaginary flowers. Give each flower a name. Then write a sentence, describing each flower. Use adjectives with *more* and *most* in your descriptions.

Writing Application: A Post Card DESCRIBING

You are on a safari in a tropical jungle. Unusual flowers bloom all over the jungle. Write a post card to a relative, telling about the flowers that you have seen. In each sentence, use adjectives with *more* or *most*.
Students should respond on separate paper. Answers will vary.

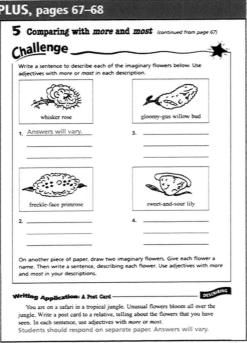

Comparing with *good* and *bad*

Lesson Objectives

Students will:

- use comparative and superlative forms of *good* and *bad*
- proofread for forms of *good* and *bad*
- write a book review, using forms of *good* and *bad*

One-Minute Warm-Up Have volunteers read their sentences. Ask which words are used to compare two things (*better, worse*) and which are used to compare more than two. (*best, worst*)

Focus on Instruction

Tell students not to use *more, most, -er,* or *-est* with *better, best, worse,* and *worst.*

Try It Out

LISTENING AND SPEAKING Have students repeat the exercise, but substitute the opposite form of *good* or *bad* in each blank.

FOR STUDENTS ACQUIRING ENGLISH

- Have students listen to the Try It Out sentences on the audiotape. Distribute the SAE Practice page for Unit 4, Lesson 6, to support listening.
- Help students suggest sentences about the library in the illustration. Ask students to describe your local library and the school library. If students have not been to either, try to plan a visit. Then ask questions about everyday things to prompt use of *good* and *bad* comparatives and superlatives. For example, "Who is a better singer, your mother or your father?" Students listen and fill in the correct word. Remind them that *than* and *the* are clues.
  1. Which is the ______ book about spiders? *(good)* (best)
  2. This picture of spiders is ______ than that one. *(bad)* (worse)

Usage

6 Comparing with *good* and *bad*

One-Minute Warm-Up

I taste better than a lime!

Choose three foods to compare. How many ways can you compare two of them? How many ways can you compare all three? Use the adjectives *good, better, best* and *bad, worse, worst.* Answers will vary.

Hey!

- Change the forms of the adjectives *good* and *bad* when you make comparisons. Change *good* to *better* when comparing two things. Change *good* to *best* when comparing three or more things.

One	I found a good book at the library.
Two	It is better than the last book I read.
Three or More	What is the best book you have ever read?

- Change *bad* to *worse* when comparing two things. Change *bad* to *worst* when comparing three or more things.

One	I read a bad story last night.
Two	It was worse than the story we read yesterday.
Three or More	It may be the worst story I ever read.

Try It Out

CARS

Speak Up What form of the adjective in ( ) completes each sentence correctly?

1. Danny thinks that the ______ thing of all on a rainy Saturday is to visit the library. (good) best
2. Danny's sister had the ______ time ever at the library last Saturday. (bad) worst
3. She wanted a ______ book than her last one. (good) better
4. Every book she looked at was ______ than the one before. (bad) worse
5. The one Danny chose for her was the ______ book of all. (bad) worst

146 **Unit 4:** Adjectives

Meeting Individual Needs

RETEACHING
ALTERNATIVE STRATEGY

- Ask students to name three movies they know about. Ask students to compare the movies and to write their responses on the board. (For example, *Movie A is better than Movie B, but Movie C is the best.*)
- Ask a volunteer to circle the words that are used to compare two movies (*better, worse*) and more than two movies. (*best, worst*) Tell students that these forms of *good* and *bad* are used to make comparisons.

CHALLENGE

Have students write a paragraph comparing several kinds of food. Tell them to leave blanks instead of the words *good, bad, better, worse, best,* and *worst.* Have students exchange papers with a partner who will supply the missing words.

FOR STUDENTS ACQUIRING ENGLISH

Review basic comparisons. Then write the word *good.* Ask what the comparative and superlative forms are. Dictate the forms as needed. Write *bad* and ask again. Then dictate the comparative and superlative forms.

On Your Own

Write the correct form of the adjective in ( ) to complete each sentence.

Example: This is the ______ weather of the week. (bad) *worst*

6. The rain today is much ______ than yesterday's. (bad) worse
7. Today would be the ______ day of the week to visit the library. (good) best
8. I think that animal stories are ______ than science fiction. (good) better
9. The ______ book I ever read was a science fiction book. (bad) worst
10. Pete thinks that this is the ______ library in all the city. (good) best
11. It has a ______ set of Braille books than other libraries do. (good) better
12. The ______ part of the trip will be carrying all the books home! (bad) worst

13–18. This book review has six incorrect forms of *good* and *bad*. Write the book review correctly.

Example: This is one of the worstest books ever published!
This is one of the worst books ever published!

Proofreading

Boring, Boring, Boring!

Book Review

I. M. Dull has published his fourth book, *How to Bore Anyone in Five Minutes*. It is his better book best so far, but that isn't saying much. Dull's first work, *Boring Ways to Dress*, was the worstest book of worst 2001. His new book has better writing, but it's still a snoozer. *How to Bore Anyone in Five Minutes* is not a best good book, but *Boring Ways to Dress* is worser worse. Will Dull ever write something really goodest good? Maybe he needs a best better name.

Writing Wrap-Up

WRITING • THINKING • LISTENING • SPEAKING

EVALUATING

Write a Book Review

Choose a book you have read and design a new cover for it. Write a review of the book for the back cover. Use forms of *good* and *bad*. Use other adjectives too. Share your work in a small group.

For Extra Practice see page 164.

Summing Up Help students summarize these key points about the lesson:

To use the adjectives *good* and *bad* to compare, use *better* or *worse* to compare two things. Use *best* and *worst* to compare three or more things.

You may want to have students complete the parts related to this lesson on Blackline Master 4–3.

On Your Own

Remind students that they can count the number of things being compared in each sentence.

MEETING INDIVIDUAL NEEDS

FOR STUDENTS ACQUIRING ENGLISH

Distribute the SAE Practice page for Unit 4, Lesson 6. Students fill in the correct word. Again remind them to look for *than* and *the* as clues.

1. This is the ______ way to go to the library. *(good)* (best)
2. Which book is ______, this one or that one? *(good)* (better)

Writing Wrap-Up

Writing Tip: Tell students to include some interesting parts of the book. See Blackline Master 4–5 for a sample review.

TECHNOLOGY CONNECTION

Suggest that students use available software to design colorful book covers.

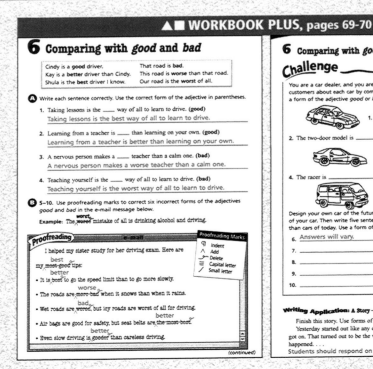

● RETEACHING WORKBOOK, page 42

6 Comparing with *good* and *bad*

- When you use the adjectives *good* and *bad* to compare, you must change their forms.
- Use *better* or *worse* to compare two.
- Use *best* or *worst* to compare three or more.

good better best

Joe is a **good** eater. This sour milk tastes **bad**.
I am a **better** eater than Joe. The juice tastes **worse** than the milk.
Bob is the **best** eater of all. The cheese tastes **worst** of all.

Write the correct adjective in parentheses to complete each sentence.

Example: Some people eat better meals than other people. **(better, best)**

1. Hot cereal is a better breakfast than doughnuts. **(better, best)**
2. Skipping breakfast is the worst way of all to start your day. **(worse, worst)**
3. Missing meals is worse than eating regular meals. **(worse, worst)**
4. Eating large meals is often worse than eating small ones. **(worse, worst)**
5. Eating too much at one time is the worst way to eat. **(worse, worst)**
6. Eating slowly is better for you than eating fast. **(better, best)**
7. Some foods are better for you than other foods. **(better, best)**
8. Fresh vegetables are some of the best foods of all. **(better, best)**
9. Baked potatoes are better for you than potato chips. **(better, best)**
10. Fatty meats are worse for you than lean meats. **(worse, worst)**
11. Fried meats are worse for your heart than broiled meats. **(worse, worst)**
12. Sugary foods are the worst foods of all for your teeth. **(worse, worst)**
13. Apples are one of the best of all fruits for your teeth. **(better, best)**
14. Milk is one of the best drinks of all. **(better, best)**

▲■ WORKBOOK PLUS, pages 69-70

6 Comparing with *good* and *bad*

Cindy is a **good** driver. That road is **bad**.
Kay is a **better** driver than Cindy. This road is **worse** than that road.
Shula is the **best** driver I know. Our road is the **worst** of all.

A Write each sentence correctly. Use the correct form of the adjective in parentheses.

1. Taking lessons is the ____ way of all to learn to drive. **(good)**
   Taking lessons is the best way of all to learn to drive.
2. Learning from a teacher is ____ than learning on your own. **(good)**
   Learning from a teacher is better than learning on your own.
3. A nervous person makes a ____ teacher than a calm one. **(bad)**
   A nervous person makes a worse teacher than a calm one.
4. Teaching yourself is the ____ way of all to learn to drive. **(bad)**
   Teaching yourself is the worst way of all to learn to drive.

B 5–10. Use proofreading marks to correct six incorrect forms of the adjectives *good* and *bad* in the e-mail message below.

Example: The worst ~~worse~~ mistake of all is drinking alcohol and driving.

Proofreading e-mail

I helped my sister study for her driving exam. Here are my best ~~most good~~ tips:

- It is better ~~best~~ to go the speed limit than to go more slowly.
- The roads are worse ~~more bad~~ when it snows than when it rains.
- Wet roads are bad ~~worse~~, but icy roads are worst of all for driving.
- Air bags are good for safety, but seat belts are better ~~the most best~~.
- Even slow driving is better ~~gooder~~ than careless driving.

Proofreading Marks
¶ Indent
∧ Add
Delete
≡ Capital letter
/ Small letter

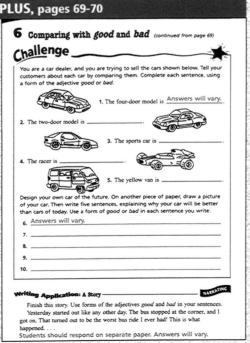

(continued)

6 Comparing with *good* and *bad* *(continued from page 69)*

Challenge

You are a car dealer, and you are trying to sell the cars shown below. Tell your customers about each car by comparing them. Complete each sentence, using a form of the adjective *good* or *bad*.

1. The four-door model is Answers will vary.

2. The two-door model is ______.

3. The sports car is ______.

4. The racer is ______.

5. The yellow van is ______.

Design your own car of the future. On another piece of paper, draw a picture of your car. Then write five sentences, explaining why your car will be better than cars of today. Use a form of *good* or *bad* in each sentence you write.

6. Answers will vary.
7. ______
8. ______
9. ______
10. ______

Writing Application: A Story NARRATING

Finish this story. Use forms of the adjectives *good* and *bad* in your sentences.

Yesterday started out like any other day. The bus stopped at the corner, and I got on. That turned out to be the worst bus ride I ever had! This is what happened. . . .

Students should respond on separate paper. Answers will vary.

Using Exact Adjectives

Lesson Objectives

Students will:
- replace weak adjectives with exact adjectives
- use a thesaurus

Focus on Instruction

- Have students read the introductory paragraph and the examples. Point out that *chilly* replaces *cold* in the second example sentence.
- Ask students how the meaning of the two words differ. (*Chilly* tells that it's not very cold.) Ask how replacing *cold* with *freezing, cool,* or *icy* would change the meaning of the sentence.

Apply It

- Review with students the use of the Thesaurus Plus at the back of the student book.
- Have students complete the activity independently. Remind them to read the definitions to be sure they choose a synonym that fits the meaning of the sentence. Explain that if more than one word works in a sentence, they may choose any that fit. Have students explain their word choices.

MEETING INDIVIDUAL NEEDS: Suggest that students who need more support work with partners.

Have students find places in their own writing where they can use exact adjectives. Remind them to use an online thesaurus if they are working on a computer.

Sample Answers to Apply It

1. moist, damp, dank, dewy, or wettish
2. moist, damp, dank, dewy, or wettish
3. moist, damp, dank, dewy, or wettish
4. soppy, soggy, or sodden
5. drenched, saturated, soaked, water-logged, sopping, or flooded
6. moist, damp, dank, dewy, or wettish

MEETING INDIVIDUAL NEEDS — FOR STUDENTS ACQUIRING ENGLISH

Explain the meanings of *damp, wet,* and *soaked,* gesturing as necessary to emphasize the different meanings. Have students use them to complete these sentences:

1. The mist made me feel ______. (damp)
2. I got ______ in the rain. (wet)
3. I got completely ______ in the ocean! (soaked)

Using Exact Adjectives

Adjectives add important details about people, places, and things. Using exact adjectives in your writing will give your readers a clear picture of what you're writing about.

Less exact adjective: It is cold out today.
More exact adjective: It is chilly out today.

Apply It

1–6. Use your Thesaurus Plus in the Tools and Tips section at the back of your book to find synonyms for *wet*. Then rewrite this e-mail message. Use a different, more exact adjective in place of each underlined word.
See TE margin for sample answers.

Revising — e-mail

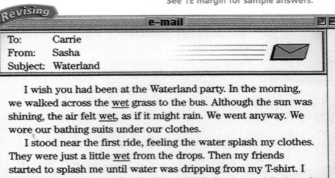

To: Carrie
From: Sasha
Subject: Waterland

I wish you had been at the Waterland party. In the morning, we walked across the wet grass to the bus. Although the sun was shining, the air felt wet, as if it might rain. We went anyway. We wore our bathing suits under our clothes.

I stood near the first ride, feeling the water splash my clothes. They were just a little wet from the drops. Then my friends started to splash me until water was dripping from my T-shirt. I was feeling pretty wet. Finally, I just decided to jump right in and I got completely wet. Even the inside of my ears got wet! We had a blast that day!

Meeting Individual Needs

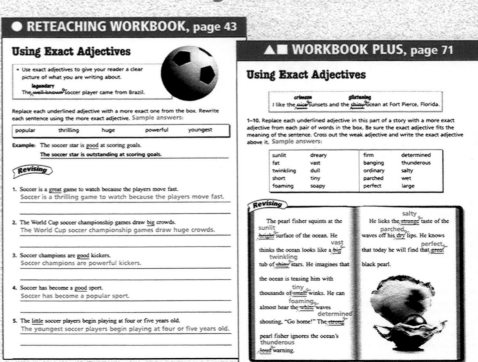

● RETEACHING WORKBOOK, page 43

Using Exact Adjectives

- Use exact adjectives to give your reader a clear picture of what you are writing about.

The ~~well-known~~ legendary soccer player came from Brazil.

Replace each underlined adjective with a more exact one from the box. Rewrite each sentence using the more exact adjective. Sample answers:

popular	thrilling	huge	powerful	youngest

Example: The soccer star is good at scoring goals.
The soccer star is outstanding at scoring goals.

Revising

1. Soccer is a great game to watch because the players move fast.
Soccer is a thrilling game to watch because the players move fast.
2. The World Cup soccer championship games draw big crowds.
The World Cup soccer championship games draw huge crowds.
3. Soccer champions are good kickers.
Soccer champions are powerful kickers.
4. Soccer has become a good sport.
Soccer has become a popular sport.
5. The little soccer players begin playing at four or five years old.
The youngest soccer players begin playing at four or five years old.

▲■ WORKBOOK PLUS, page 71

Using Exact Adjectives

I like the ~~nice~~ crimson sunsets and the ~~shiny~~ glistening ocean at Fort Pierce, Florida.

1–10. Replace each underlined adjective in this part of a story with a more exact adjective from each pair of words in the box. Be sure the exact adjective fits the meaning of the sentence. Cross out the weak adjective and write the exact adjective above it. Sample answers:

sunlit	dreary	firm	determined
fat	vast	banging	thunderous
twinkling	dull	ordinary	salty
short	tiny	parched	wet
foaming	soapy	perfect	large

Revising

The pearl fisher squints at the ~~bright~~ sunlit surface of the ocean. He thinks the ocean looks like a ~~big~~ vast tub of ~~shiny~~ twinkling stars. He imagines that the ocean is teasing him with thousands of ~~small~~ tiny winks. He can almost hear the ~~white~~ foaming waves shouting, "Go home!" The ~~strong~~ determined pearl fisher ignores the ocean's ~~loud~~ thunderous warning.

He licks the ~~strange~~ salty taste of the waves off his ~~dry~~ parched lips. He knows that today he will find that ~~great~~ perfect black pearl.

Enrichment

Adjective Challenge

Players: 3 or more

Materials: Letter tiles or letter cards turned facedown; for each player, a grid with 4 with nouns written across the top

To play: One player draws a letter, and all players write it in the left column of their grid. Players fill each row with as many adjectives as they can in 3 minutes. The adjectives in the row must begin with that letter and must describe the noun in each column. Play as many rounds as there are players.

Scoring: Each different adjective on a player's grid earns 1 point.

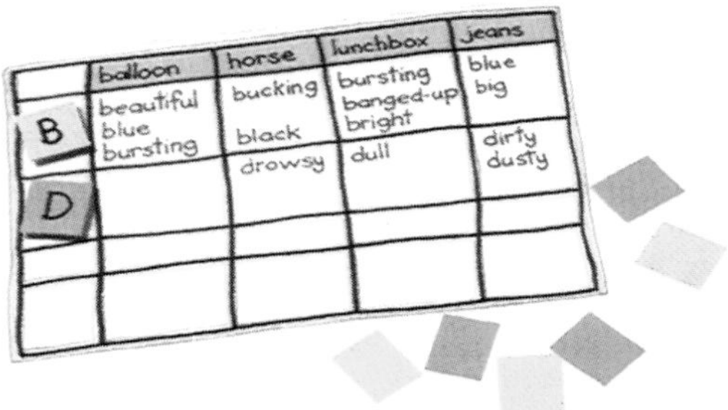
balloon
horse
lunchbox
jeans
B
beautiful
blue
bursting
bucking
black
bursting
banged-up
bright
blue
big
D
drowsy
dull
dirty
dusty

Sneaky Poems

In small groups, list adjectives that describe sneakers. Then copy the poem on paper, leaving blanks where the adjectives belong.

Choose words from your list to complete the poem. Then read your group's poem aloud.

I like sneakers.
_______ sneakers,
_______ sneakers,
_______, _______, _______ sneakers,
Any kind of sneakers.
I like sneakers.

Challenge Write a poem about another object, leaving blanks where the adjectives belong. Have a partner complete your poem with adjectives that all begin with the same letter.

Enrichment

Objectives

Students will:
- generate adjectives to describe nouns by playing a categorizing game
- generate adjectives to complete a poem

Using the Activities

The Enrichment page provides fun, creative activities that reinforce students' understanding and use of adjectives. The activities are designed to be enjoyed by all students. Here are some ideas for using the activities.

- Pair students who need extra support with more capable classmates.
- Students can work with these activities in class after they have completed other assignments.
- Activities that can be completed individually can be assigned as homework.

Focus on the Activities

ADJECTIVE CHALLENGE

- This is a good activity to put in a learning center.
- You can draw reusable grids on large index cards. Write four different nouns across the top and laminate them. Students fill in the blanks with erasable marking pens.
- Students may also copy the grids on their own paper. Even though the game uses the same nouns repeatedly, the game changes as students draw new letters.

SNEAKY POEMS

Encourage students to use a thesaurus to find specific, interesting adjectives to describe the sneakers. After students have written their poems, have them list adjectives that they especially liked on a chart or in their writing notebooks for future reference.

MEETING INDIVIDUAL NEEDS **CHALLENGE** Students can illustrate their poems to reflect the adjectives used and then read their poems aloud to the class or post them on the bulletin board.

MEETING INDIVIDUAL NEEDS **FOR STUDENTS ACQUIRING ENGLISH**

Have students decide where to use the words *funny* and *dirty* in this poem to make it rhyme.

My sneakers are _______. (funny)
My sneakers are _______. (dirty)
I'll wear my sneakers until I'm thirty!

Have students brainstorm other words that can be used to describe their sneakers.

Checkup

Objectives

Students will:

- identify the adjectives that describe specific nouns
- determine whether an adjective tells *what kind* or *how many*
- identify the noun an adjective describes after a form of *be*
- use articles in sentences correctly
- use *-er* and *-est* with adjectives to compare nouns

Using the Checkup

Use the Checkup exercises as assessment, as review for the unit test, as extra practice, or as a diagnostic aid to help determine those students who need reteaching.

INTERNET CONNECTION The Wacky Web Tales® at www.eduplace.com/tales/ are cloze stories that students complete, using designated parts of speech. Students may choose any word to fill in a blank as long as it is the correct part of speech. As a result, the completed stories are often amusing, even "wacky," depending on the specific words chosen. Most of the stories at this Web site are student submissions.

INTERNET CONNECTION Students can take an interactive quiz for this unit at www.eduplace.com/kids/hme/ and then get immediate feedback.

Checkup: Unit 4

See TE margin for answers.

1 What Is an Adjective? (p. 136)

Write the adjectives that describe the underlined nouns. Write *what kind* or *how many* for each adjective.

1. Tara has an interesting hobby.
2. She collects beautiful seashells.
3. She has found thirty different kinds of shells.
4. She keeps them in glass boxes.
5. Liz is a clever artist.
6. She and Tara make lovely jewelry from the shells.
7. Tara and Liz go to sandy beaches to hunt for new shells.
8. Each day brings new treasures.
9. Calm pools are good places to find shells.
10. Most snails have a single, twisted shell.
11. Empty shells may be homes for tiny crabs.
12. Tara found three pink stones.
13. They have unusual markings.
14. Tara will begin a new collection.

2 Adjectives After *be* (p. 140)

Write each sentence. Draw a line under the adjective. Then draw an arrow to the word it describes.

15. Cal is eager to play the game.
16. The game is difficult.
17. It was new last year.
18. We are happy to play with Cal.
19. The questions are clever.
20. They were funny at first.
21. Now I am bored with them.

3 Using *a, an,* and *the* (p. 141)

Write the correct article to complete each sentence.

22. (A, An) trunk was in (a, an) corner of the attic.
23. It held (a, an) old white dress.
24. There was also (a, an) old album.
25. (A, The) pictures show (a, an) young woman.
26. There is (a, an) name on one of (a, the) photos.
27. (An, The) young woman is my grandmother!

4 Making Comparisons (p. 142)

Write each sentence, using the correct form of the adjective in ( ).

28. The sun is the (close) star of all to Earth.
29. However, the sun is not the (big) star of all.
30. The (hot) stars of all look blue.
31. A blue star is (hot) than a yellow star.
32. A red star is (cool) than the sun.
33. It is also (bright) than the sun.
34. Jupiter is (big) than the other planets.
35. Mercury is the (near) planet of all to the sun.
36. The moon is the (bright) object of all in our nighttime sky.
37. Earth's gravity is (strong) than the moon's.
38. This makes objects (heavy) on Earth than they are on the moon.

150 Unit 4: Adjectives

Go to www.eduplace.com/tales/ for more fun with parts of speech.

Answers

What Is an Adjective?

1. interesting—what kind
2. beautiful—what kind
3. thirty—how many
   different—what kind
4. glass—what kind
5. clever—what kind
6. lovely—what kind
7. sandy—what kind
   new—what kind
8. new—what kind
9. Calm—what kind
   good—what kind
10. Most—how many
11. Empty—what kind
12. three—how many
    pink—what kind
13. unusual—what kind
14. new—what kind

Adjectives After *be*

Adjective is underlined once; the word it describes, twice.

15. eager, Cal
16. difficult, game
17. new, It
18. happy, We
19. clever, questions
20. funny, They
21. bored, I

Using *a, an,* and *the*

22. A, a
23. an
24. an
25. The, a
26. a, the
27. The

Making Comparisons

28. closest
29. biggest
30. hottest
31. hotter
32. cooler
33. brighter
34. bigger
35. nearest
36. brightest
37. stronger
38. heavier

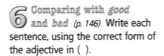

5 Comparing with *more* and *most* (p. 144)

Write each sentence, using the correct form of the adjective in ( ).

39. People think that bear cubs are (lovable) than grown bears.
40. However, all bears are (dangerous) than house pets.
41. The (common) bear of all is the black bear.
42. I think polar bears are (beautiful) than black bears.
43. They are (comfortable) in the cold weather than other bears.
44. Their thick white fur is their (valuable) protection of all.

6 Comparing with *good* and *bad* (p. 146)

Write each sentence, using the correct form of the adjective in ( ).

45. I had a (good) time at summer camp this year than last year.
46. My cabin had the (good) view of all.
47. Insects are (bad) near the lake than in the woods.
48. That is the (bad) place in the whole camp to sleep.
49. The pool is a (good) place to swim than the chilly lake.
50. The weather was (bad) in July than in August.

Mixed Review 51–58. This entertainment report has two mistakes in using articles and six mistakes in comparing adjectives. Write the report correctly.

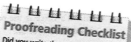

Proofreading Checklist

Did you write these correctly?

- ✓ the articles *a*, *an*, and *the*
- ✓ adjectives with *-er* and *-est*
- ✓ adjectives with *more* and *most*
- ✓ forms of *good* and *bad*

Proofreading

What's Hot?

Movies

Are you looking for an fun weekend activity? Try the movie a
at the Star Theater. It's much gooder than the last movie I saw better
there. It's about a monster. The hairy monster looks scary, but
he is really ~~more~~ gentler than a kitten.

Museums

exciting
The dinosaur exhibit is the most excitingest at the museum.
You can see the tinyest dinosaur ever found. You won't want to tiniest
miss the big dinosaur bone in the world. biggest

Music

Would you enjoy a evening of good music? Then I'd skip the an
concert at the library. The songs are worser than the ones they worse
played last year.

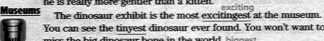

See www.eduplace.com/kids/hme/ for an online quiz.

Objectives

Students will:

- use *more* and *most* with adjectives to compare nouns
- make comparisons with the correct forms of *good* and *bad*
- proofread sentences for correct adjective forms and correct use of articles

Answers *continued*

Comparing with *more* and *most*

39. more lovable
40. more dangerous
41. most common
42. more beautiful
43. more comfortable
44. most valuable

Comparing with *good* and *bad*

45. better
46. best
47. worse
48. worst
49. better
50. worse

Test Practice

Objective

Students will:

- practice completing a test format that requires them to choose the correct sentence among four

Using the Test Practice

These Test Practice pages provide practice with common formats used in standardized or multiple-choice tests.

The first page works with skills taught in the basic lessons in Unit 4. The second and third pages work with skills taught in Units 1–4.

Focus on the Test Format

- Have a volunteer read the test directions aloud. Ask another volunteer to explain what the directions ask students to do.
- Point out the vertical line that runs down the center of the page and breaks the text into columns. Tell students to answer the questions in the first column before proceeding to the second column.
- Call attention to the numbers and letters next to the sentences. Explain that each number corresponds to an item number. Explain that the letters identify each sentence.
- Have students read each sentence and decide whether it is written correctly. After students find the correct sentence, have them look to its left to find the correct letter to write for the answer.

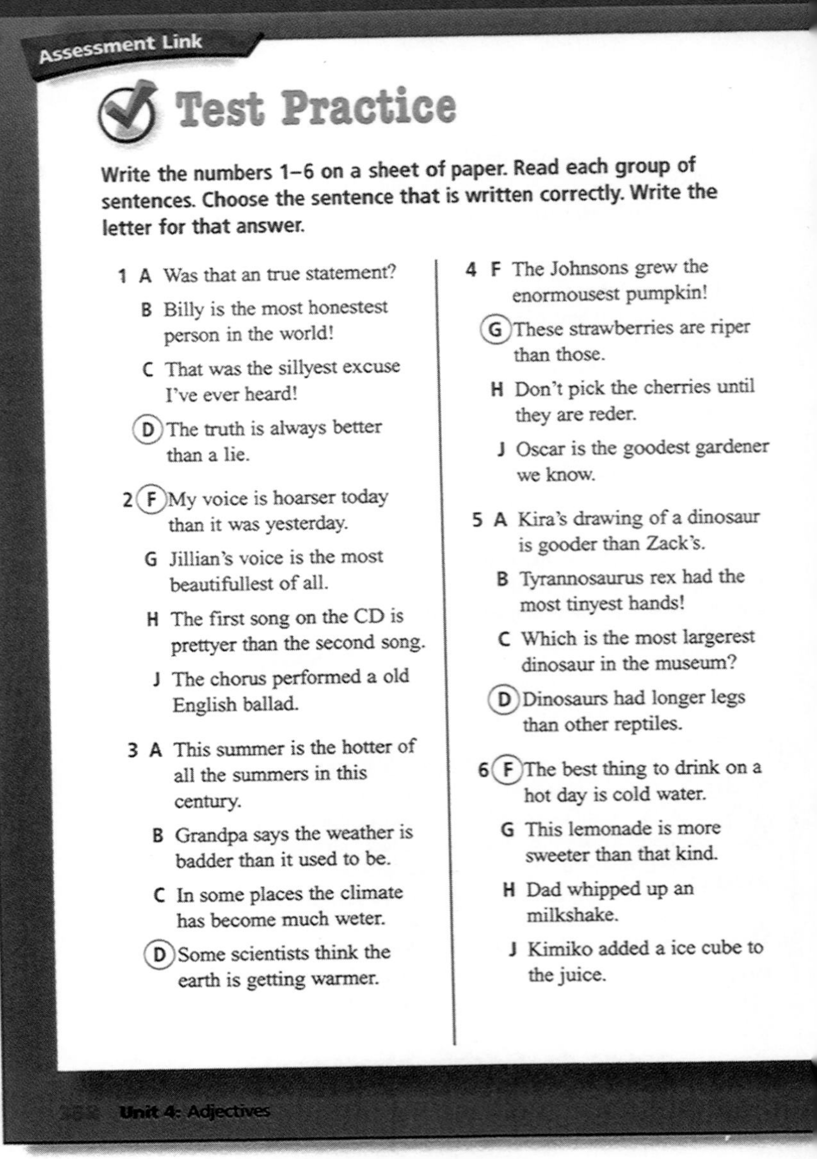

Assessment Link

Test Practice

Write the numbers 1–6 on a sheet of paper. Read each group of sentences. Choose the sentence that is written correctly. Write the letter for that answer.

1 A Was that an true statement?
B Billy is the most honestest person in the world!
C That was the silliest excuse I've ever heard!
(D) The truth is always better than a lie.

2 (F) My voice is hoarser today than it was yesterday.
G Jillian's voice is the most beautifullest of all.
H The first song on the CD is prettyer than the second song.
J The chorus performed a old English ballad.

3 A This summer is the hotter of all the summers in this century.
B Grandpa says the weather is badder than it used to be.
C In some places the climate has become much weter.
(D) Some scientists think the earth is getting warmer.

4 F The Johnsons grew the enormousest pumpkin!
(G) These strawberries are riper than those.
H Don't pick the cherries until they are reder.
J Oscar is the goodest gardener we know.

5 A Kira's drawing of a dinosaur is gooder than Zack's.
B Tyrannosaurus rex had the most tinyest hands!
C Which is the most largerest dinosaur in the museum?
(D) Dinosaurs had longer legs than other reptiles.

6 (F) The best thing to drink on a hot day is cold water.
G This lemonade is more sweeter than that kind.
H Dad whipped up an milkshake.
J Kimiko added a ice cube to the juice.

152 Unit 4: Adjectives

FOR STUDENTS ACQUIRING ENGLISH

Ask for examples of adjectives. Review placement of adjectives. Next, review comparatives and superlatives with *-er, -est,* and *more, most* as well as irregulars. Distribute the SAE Test Practice pages for Unit 4. Have a volunteer read the directions aloud for each section. Make sure students understand that in the first section, only one of the four sentences is correct in each set. In the second section, explain that they are to find the best way to correct the underlined word or words. If the underlined part is correct, they mark the last answer.

Now write the numbers 7–12 on your paper. Look at each underlined part of the paragraph. Find the correct way to write the underlined part in each numbered line. Write the letter for that answer. If the part is already correct, write the letter for the last answer, "Correct as it is."

(7) Nine planets move around our sun. Of these nine
(8) planets, the larger is Jupiter. It has 16 moons, and it is
(9) surrounded by a band of dust. Venus is the hotest of the
(10) nine. This planets temperature is about 896 degrees F.
(11) Spaceships have took pictures of many planets. Uranus
(12) and Neptune are both blue, but Neptune is more darker.

7 **A** moves
B has moved
C will move
D Correct as it is

8 **F** more larger
G large
H largest
J Correct as it is

9 **A** hottest
B most hotest
C hotter
D Correct as it is

10 **F** planets'
G planet's
H planets's
J Correct as it is

11 **A** has took
B has taken
C have taken
D Correct as it is

12 **F** darker
G more dark
H darkest
J Correct as it is

Objective

Students will:

- practice completing a test format that requires them to choose the correct item among four

Focus on the Test Format

- Have a volunteer read the test directions aloud. Ask another volunteer to explain what the directions ask students to do.
- Have students read the paragraph. Point out that each line in the paragraph is numbered, and that the numbers correspond to the item numbers below. Also point out that part of each line is underlined, and this is the portion of the line that students will need to evaluate.
- Explain that each item below gives three choices that substitute for the underlined words in the paragraph. Point out that every item also has a fourth choice—"Correct as it is."
- Tell students to read each line, then read it three more times, substituting the word choices. Have students write the letter of the correct response.

Objective

Students will:

- practice completing a test format that requires them to choose the correct item among four

Focus on the Test Format

The test format on this page is the same as the format on the preceding page.

Test Practice *continued*

Now write the numbers 13–18 on your paper. Look at each underlined part of the paragraph. Find the correct way to write the underlined part in each numbered line. Write the letter for that answer. If the part is already correct, write the letter for the last answer, "Correct as it is."

(13) For my birthday, Mom and Dad <u>gived</u> me a cute little
(14) hamster. I named it <u>chubby cheeks</u>. I saved my money
(15) to buy toys for the <u>hamsters</u> cage. I was for a time the
(16) <u>happyest</u> kid in the world! But now I have a problem.
(17) My pet makes noise all night. It chews on the cage <u>two</u>.
(18) Maybe I should trade it for some quiet little <u>mouses</u>!

13 A given
B gives
(C) gave
D Correct as it is

14 (F) Chubby Cheeks
G chubby Cheeks
H Chubby cheeks
J Correct as it is

15 A hamsters's
(B) hamster's
C hamsters'
D Correct as it is

16 F most happiest
(G) happiest
H happier
J Correct as it is

17 (A) too
B to
C tow
D Correct as it is

18 F mousies
G moose
(H) mice
J Correct as it is

234 Unit 4: Adjectives

Cumulative Review

See TE margin for answers.

Unit 1: The Sentence

The Sentence, Kinds of Sentences
(pp. 32, 36, 38) If a group of words below is a sentence, write it correctly. If not, write *not a sentence*.

1. do you know how to use the computer at school
2. it is a very useful tool
3. would you like to learn
4. stores large amounts of important information
5. the top row of keys
6. how quickly you learn
7. please turn the computer off now
8. makes corrections quickly and easily

Subjects and Predicates
(pp. 40, 42, 44) Write each sentence. Draw a line between the complete subject and the complete predicate. Draw one line under the simple subject and two lines under the simple predicate.

9. Mrs. Consuelo Greene has a solar house.
10. It has metal plates on the roof.
11. These metal plates are collectors.
12. They trap the sun's rays.
13. The heat of the sun warms a liquid inside the collectors.
14. The liquid heats a tank of water.
15. It is in the basement.
16. This water warms the whole solar house.

Run-on Sentences *(p. 46)* Write each run-on sentence correctly as two sentences.

17. Jill and Ted were sailing a big storm suddenly came up.
18. A strong wind blew waves crashed onto the shore.
19. The lake was very rough small boats hurried toward the dock.
20. Then the thunder roared the downpour began.
21. Jill and Ted tied up the boat they had made it just in time.

Unit 2: Nouns

Common and Proper Nouns
(pp. 64, 66) Write each noun. Beside it, write *common* or *proper*. Begin each proper noun with a capital letter.

22. On friday uncle leo brought a newspaper to our house.
23. My mother read the news.
24. One story in the paper was about the fourth of july.
25. Our town will hold a celebration on that day.
26. A big parade will march right down main street.
27. The mayor will give a speech from the grandstand.
28. A band from middletown will play at goss park.
29. People will watch fireworks over the johnstown river.

See www.eduplace.com/kids/hme/ for a tricky usage or spelling question.

Cumulative Review 155

Cumulative Review

Objectives

Students will:

- write sentences correctly, distinguishing sentences from sentence fragments
- distinguish subjects from predicates
- write run-on sentences correctly as two sentences
- identify and correctly write common and proper nouns

Using the Cumulative Review

This Cumulative Review provides cumulative practice with basic grammar, usage, and mechanics skills taught in Units 1 through 4. You can use these pages for assessment, as a review for a test, as extra practice, or as a diagnostic aid to determine those students who may need reteaching.

INTERNET CONNECTION Send your students to www.eduplace.com/kids/hme/ for a tricky question related to usage or spelling.

Answers

The Sentence, Kinds of Sentences

1. Do you know how to use the computer at school?
2. It is a very useful tool.
3. Would you like to learn?
4. not a sentence
5. not a sentence
6. How quickly you learn!
7. Please turn the computer off now.
8. not a sentence

Subjects and Predicates

9. Mrs. Consuelo Greene | has a solar house.
10. It | has metal plates on the roof.
11. These metal plates | are collectors.
12. They | trap the sun's rays.
13. The heat of the sun | warms a liquid inside the collectors.
14. The liquid | heats a tank of water.
15. It | is in the basement.
16. This water | warms the whole solar house.

Run-on Sentences

17. Jill and Ted were sailing. A big storm suddenly came up.
18. A strong wind blew. Waves crashed onto the shore.
19. The lake was very rough. Small boats hurried toward the dock.
20. Then the thunder roared. The downpour began.
21. Jill and Ted tied up the boat. They had made it just in time.

Common and Proper Nouns

22. Friday—p., Uncle Leo—p., newspaper—c., house—c.
23. mother—c., news—c.
24. story—c., paper—c., Fourth of July—p.
25. town—c., celebration—c., day—c.
26. parade—c., Main Street—p.
27. mayor—c., speech—c., grandstand—c.
28. band—c., Middletown—p., Goss Park—p.
29. People—c., fireworks—c., Johnstown River—p.

Objectives

Students will:

- write the plural form of nouns correctly
- write the possessive form of nouns correctly
- identify verbs and distinguish helping verbs from main verbs
- identify verb tense

Answers *continued*

Singular and Plural Nouns

30. dishes
31. masks
32. duties
33. sheep
34. compasses
35. men

Singular and Plural Possessive Nouns

36. family's
37. carpenters'
38. men's
39. women's
40. painters'
41. Bert's
42. mother's
43. children's
44. Dad's
45. animals'
46. horses'
47. Sport's
48. pet's

Action Verbs, Main Verbs, and Helping Verbs

49. was—helping, making—main
50. had—helping, found—main
51. were—helping, helping—main
52. has—helping, glued—main
53. is—helping, drying—main

Past, Present, and Future

54. carry—present
55. haul—present
56. began—past
57. will be—future
58. will steer—future

Cumulative Review *continued*

Singular and Plural Nouns *(pp. 70, 72, 74)* Write the plural form of each singular noun.

30. dish
31. mask
32. duty
33. sheep
34. compass
35. man

Singular and Plural Possessive Nouns *(pp. 76, 78)* Write the possessive form of the noun in ( ).

36. The (family) new house is being built rapidly.
37. The (carpenters) job will be done by the end of next week.
38. The (men) hammers are pounding away busily.
39. The (women) saws are noisy too.
40. Next week the (painters) work will start.
41. (Bert) room is in the back of the new house.
42. His (mother) office is next to it.
43. The other (children) rooms are upstairs.
44. (Dad) workshop will be in the basement.
45. The (animals) big new barn will be built next.
46. The (horses) stalls will be roomy and comfortable.
47. (Sport) new doghouse is not ready.
48. Bert is planning to build his (pet) house himself.

Unit 3: Verbs

Action Verbs, Main Verbs, and Helping Verbs *(pp. 96, 98)* Write the verbs in these sentences. Write *main* or *helping* beside each verb.

49. Heidi was making a collage.
50. She had found magazine pictures.
51. We were helping her.
52. She has glued them onto cardboard.
53. The glue is drying now.

Past, Present, and Future *(p. 100)* Write each verb, and label it *past, present,* or *future.*

54. Some trains carry passengers.
55. Other trains haul products.
56. The first public railroads began in England in the 1820s.
57. Tomorrow's trains will be different.
58. Computers will steer those trains.

156 **Unit 4:** Adjectives

Agreement, Spelling the Present Tense *(pp. 104, 106)* Write the correct present tense form of each verb.

59. Candy (rub) the balloons on the wool rug.
60. Her brother (watch) curiously.
61. She (stick) them to the wall.
62. The balloons (stay) there!
63. Static electricity (make) them stick.

Spelling the Past Tense, The Past with Helping Verbs *(pp. 108, 110)* Write each sentence. Use *have* or *has* with the correct form of the verb.

64. Pete (enjoy) folk dancing.
65. This week he (try) a difficult new dance.
66. Everyone (practice) the steps.
67. The dancers (form) a circle.
68. They (step) to the music.

Irregular Verbs *(p. 112)* Write each sentence, using the correct past form of the verb.

69. The show (begin) at two o'clock.
70. One hundred people had (come).
71. The actors (wear) shiny costumes.
72. Jen and Terrance had (make) them.
73. We (take) our places on-stage.
74. I (grow) more and more nervous.
75. I had (know) my lines earlier!

The Special Verb *be* *(p. 114)* Write the verb that correctly completes each sentence.

76. My cousins (is, are) in Australia.
77. We (was, were) there last year.
78. Australia (is, are) both a country and a continent.
79. You (was, were) in Sydney for a month last winter.
80. It (is, are) the largest city.

Contractions with *not* *(p. 116)* Write the contractions for the following words.

81. is not	85. had not
82. cannot	86. do not
83. was not	87. could not
84. would not	88. did not

Unit 4: Adjectives

Adjectives *(p. 136)* Write each adjective and the noun it describes.

89. A giraffe is a tall animal that lives in dry areas of Africa.
90. It has a long, thin neck and four skinny legs.
91. The neck of a giraffe contains seven bones.
92. That is the same number that a human has.
93. Many people think that a giraffe cannot make a single sound.
94. However, most giraffes do make some low sounds.

Objectives

Students will:

- write verbs to agree with their subjects in the present tense
- spell the past participle of verbs correctly
- write the correct past form for irregular verbs
- use the verb *be* correctly
- write contractions with *not* correctly

Answers *continued*

Agreement, Spelling the Present Tense

59. rubs
60. watches
61. sticks
62. stay
63. makes

Spelling the Past Tense, The Past with Helping Verbs

64. has enjoyed
65. has tried
66. has practiced
67. have formed
68. have stepped

Irregular Verbs

69. The show began at two o'clock.
70. One hundred people had come.
71. The actors wore shiny costumes.
72. Jen and Terrance had made them.
73. We took our places onstage.
74. I grew more and more nervous.
75. I had known my lines earlier!

The Special Verb *be*

76. are
77. were
78. is
79. were
80. is

Contractions with *not*

81. isn't
82. can't
83. wasn't
84. wouldn't
85. hadn't
86. don't
87. couldn't
88. didn't

Adjectives

89. tall—animal, dry—areas
90. long—neck, thin—neck, four—legs, skinny—legs
91. seven—bones
92. same—number
93. Many—people, single—sound
94. most—giraffes, some—sounds, low—sounds

Objectives

Students will:

- identify adjectives and the nouns they describe
- use the articles *a, an,* and *the* in sentences correctly
- compare, using adjectives correctly

Answers *continued*

Adjectives After *be*

Adjective is underlined once; the word it describes twice.

95. interested, I
96. old, art
97. tiny, stitches
98. different, patterns
99. skillful, Grandma
100. beautiful, quilts

Using *a, an,* and *the*

101. The
102. An, an
103. A, an
104. a, a
105. an, a

Comparing with Adjectives

106. saddest
107. sadder
108. best
109. longer
110. better
111. most
112. hardest

Adjectives After *be* (p. 140) Write each adjective and the word it describes.

95. I am interested in quilting.
96. The art is old.
97. The stitches are tiny.
98. The patterns are different.
99. Mother said that Grandma was skillful at quilting.
100. Her quilts were beautiful.

Using *a, an,* and *the* (p. 141) Choose the correct article or articles in ( ) to complete each sentence. Write the sentences.

101. (A, The) names of many young animals are interesting.
102. (A, An) owl's baby is called (a, an) owlet.
103. (A, An) young eagle is called (a, an) eaglet.
104. We know that (a, an) baby cat is (a, an) kitten.
105. Does that mean that (a, an) infant bat is (a, an) bitten?

Comparing with Adjectives (pp. 142, 144, 146) Choose the correct word in ( ) to complete each sentence. Write the sentences.

106. *Stone Fox* is the (sadder, saddest) book I have read.
107. Is it (sadder, saddest) than *Annie and the Old One*?
108. What is the (better, best) mystery you have ever read?
109. Is *Charlotte's Web* (longer, longest) than *Stuart Little*?
110. I think it is a (better, best) story than *Stuart Little*.
111. Peg thinks that nonfiction books are the (more, most) useful kind of all.
112. Sometimes they are also the (harder, hardest) of all to read.

Extra Practice

(pages 136–137)

1 What Is an Adjective?

Remember

- An adjective is a word that describes a noun. An adjective can tell *what kind* or *how many.*

● Write the adjective that describes each underlined noun.

Example: Carlo has a new puppy. *new*

1. Carlo takes good care of the puppy. good
2. He gives it food in a clean dish. clean
3. The puppy always has fresh water. fresh
4. Carlo gives the puppy four meals a day. four
5. He is teaching the puppy to obey simple commands. simple

▲ Write each sentence. Underline each adjective. Then draw an arrow to the noun it describes. Adjectives are underlined once; nouns, twice.

Example: In cold places, many people travel by sled.
In cold places, many people travel by sled.

6. Huskies are strong, sturdy dogs.
7. A husky has two coats of thick fur.
8. Large, hairy feet keep it from sinking in soft snow.
9. There may be eight huskies in a team.
10. The team may travel forty miles in one day.

■ Write each sentence. Use one or two adjectives to replace each blank. Draw one line under adjectives that tell what kind and two lines under adjectives that tell how many. Sample answers are given.

Example: There were ______ dogs in the dog show.
There were fifty excited dogs in the dog show.

11. Jaime's ______ beagle Harry won a prize. handsome
12. Rita's poodle Fifi won ______ ribbons. three
13. The dog did ______ tricks. seven great
14. ______ dogs pulled a ______ wagon. Five; red
15. We all laughed at the ______ sight. funny
16. LeShon's ______ collie was somewhat frightened by the ______ crowd. beautiful; noisy

Extra Practice 159

What Is an Adjective?

Objectives

Students will:

- identify adjectives that tell *what kind* or *how many*
- supply adjectives for sentences and identify the nouns that the adjectives describe
- use adjectives correctly in a sentence

Using the Extra Practice

The Extra Practice activities provide additional practice for the basic lesson at three levels of difficulty: Easy (●), Average (▲), and Challenging (■).

The Extra Practice activities can be used in the following ways.

- Assign activities according to students' needs and abilities as homework after students have completed the basic lesson.
- Assign the Easy activities after using the lesson Reteaching instruction.
- Assign the Average activities to prepare students for the Checkup.
- Assign the Easy and/or Average activities to students who had difficulty with specific lessons on the Checkup.
- Assign the Challenging exercises as a Bonus activity.

Meeting Individual Needs — More Practice for Lesson 1

● EASY

Does the underlined adjective tell *what kind* or *how many?*

1. Jay has a hard-working dog. (WK)
2. It guards fifty sheep. (HM)
3. The intelligent dog moves the sheep from field to field. (WK)
4. The sheep and the dog have become good friends. (WK)
5. Many shepherds have sheepdogs. (HM)

▲ AVERAGE

Complete each sentence with an adjective. Underline the noun it describes. (Adjectives will vary.)

1. Some dogs are a ______ help to blind people.
2. They guide sightless people through busy, ______ streets.
3. Sudden, loud noises do not frighten these ______ dogs.
4. The careful animals protect their masters from ______ things.
5. The ______ dogs usually serve one master an entire lifetime.

■ CHALLENGING

Write eight sentences about a favorite pet or animal. Include at least two adjectives in each sentence. Underline adjectives that tell *what kind* once and adjectives that tell *how many* twice.

Adjectives After *be*

Objectives

Students will:
- identify adjectives after *be* and the nouns they describe
- use adjectives correctly in a sentence after the words they describe and a form of *be*

Using the Extra Practice

The Extra Practice activities provide additional practice for the basic lesson at three levels of difficulty: Easy (●), Average (▲), and Challenging (■).

Extra Practice

(page 140)

2 Adjectives After *be*

Remember
- An adjective can follow the word it describes and a form of the verb *be*.

● Write the adjective that describes the underlined word in each sentence. Adjectives are underlined.

Example: The streets are crowded. *crowded*

1. The sun is bright.
2. The music is loud.
3. The people are happy.
4. Parades are exciting.
5. The food was delicious.
6. The speeches were grand.

▲ Write each sentence. Underline the adjective. Then draw an arrow to the word that it describes. Adjectives are underlined once; nouns, twice.

Example: Dad is thrilled by the show.
Dad is thrilled by the show.

7. Before the show, the performers were nervous.
8. Under the lights, the costumes were beautiful.
9. Up on the stage, the tricks were dazzling.
10. I was amazed at one of the tricks.
11. It was unbelievable.
12. The children were speechless.

■ Write these sentences, supplying an adjective for each blank. Then write the word that the adjective describes. Sample answers are given.

Example: The dancers were ______.
The dancers were graceful. dancers

13. The music was ______. lovely—music
14. This morning's puppet show was ______. funny—show
15. The little puppet was ______. cute—puppet
16. His tricks were ______. unbelievable—tricks
17. After the performance, I was ______. thrilled—I
18. The whole street fair was ______. wonderful—fair

160 **Unit 4:** Adjectives

Meeting Individual Needs — More Practice for Lesson 2

● EASY

Complete each sentence. Write an adjective that describes the underlined noun in each sentence. (Adjectives will vary.)

1. The lion tamer was so ______!
2. The clowns were ______.
3. The tightrope walker is ______.
4. The elephant act is ______.
5. The audience was ______.

▲ AVERAGE

Underline each adjective once. Underline the noun it describes twice.

1. In the ring, the clowns were silly.
2. At the end of the act, the horses were tired.
3. The boy was frightened by the roars of the lions.
4. At the end, the music is louder than ever.
5. I am so sorry the show has ended.

■ CHALLENGING

Write four sentences about an object. Have each sentence give one detail about it. Each sentence should have an adjective after a form of *be* and give a clue to the object's identity. Example: *This animal is gray. Its ears are floppy. Its nose is long. Its feet are dangerous!* Ask a classmate to guess the object's identity.

Extra Practice

(page 141)

3 Using *a, an,* and *the*

Remember

- Use the articles *a* and *an* before singular nouns.
- Use the article *the* with both singular and plural nouns.

● Write each word. Before it, write *a* or *an.*

Example: ______ orange *an orange*

1. ______ bulb a
2. ______ onion an
3. ______ root a
4. ______ stem a
5. ______ edge an
6. ______ carrot a
7. ______ eggplant an
8. ______ vegetable a
9. ______ tomato a
10. ______ apple an
11. ______ inchworm an
12. ______ ice cube an

▲ Write each sentence, using the correct article.

Example: Mushrooms grow in (an, the) woods.
Mushrooms grow in the woods.

13. (A, An) mushroom is (a, an) kind of fungus.
14. It looks like (a, an) umbrella.
15. It does not grow from (a, an) seed.
16. (A, The) fungi grow from tiny cells called spores.
17. They may be blown by (an, the) wind.
18. (A, The) spores land on (an, the) warm, damp earth.

■ The following sentences have no articles. Rewrite the sentences, supplying the correct articles where they belong. Sample answers are given.

Example: Pitcher plant can eat insect.
A pitcher plant can eat an insect.

19. Rainwater collects in plant's leaves. The rainwater collects in the plant's leaves.
20. Thick hairs grow at end of leaf. Thick hairs grow at the end of a leaf.
21. Hairs point downward. The hairs point downward.
22. Sweet smell attracts insects. A sweet smell attracts insects.
23. Insect drowns in rainwater. The insect drowns in the rainwater.
24. Then plant waits for new victim. Then the plant waits for a new victim.

Using *a, an,* and *the*

Objectives

Students will:

- select the correct article to describe a noun
- use *a, an,* and *the* correctly in sentences

Using the Extra Practice

The Extra Practice activities provide additional practice for the basic lesson at three levels of difficulty: Easy (●), Average (▲), and Challenging (■).

Meeting Individual Needs

More Practice for Lesson 3

● **EASY**

Write the correct article for each word.

1. (a, an) maple
2. (an, the) elms
3. (a, an) oak
4. (the, a) pines
5. (a, an) spruce
6. (the, an) willow
7. (the, a) ash

▲ **AVERAGE**

Write *a, an,* or *the* to complete each sentence.

1. I bought ______ fruit trees. (the)
2. One is ______ apple tree. (an/the)
3. Mom dug ______ enormous holes in ______ backyard. (the; the)
4. We put ______ apple tree in ______ hole. (the/an; a/the)
5. Mom filled it in with ______ mixture of rich soil. (a/the)
6. I pour ______ pails of water on the tree every day. (the)

■ **CHALLENGING**

Write a paragraph about a tree, plant, or flower. Leave out *a, an,* and *the* from your writing. Then exchange papers with a classmate, and add *a, an,* and *the* to your partner's paragraph as needed.

Making Comparisons

Objectives

Students will:

- add *-er* to adjectives to compare two persons, places, or things
- add *-est* to adjectives to compare three or more persons, places, or things
- use the correct forms of adjectives in sentences to make comparisons

Using the Extra Practice

The Extra Practice activities provide additional practice for the basic lesson at three levels of difficulty: Easy (●), Average (▲), and Challenging (■).

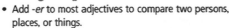

Extra Practice

(pages 142–143)

4 Making Comparisons — Remember

- Add *-er* to most adjectives to compare two persons, places, or things.
- Add *-est* to compare three or more persons, places, or things.

● For each adjective, write the form for comparing two and the form for comparing three or more.

Example: pretty *prettier* *prettiest*

1. late later, latest
2. thick thicker, thickest
3. safe safer, safest
4. lucky luckier, luckiest
5. dark darker, darkest
6. hot hotter, hottest
7. fine finer, finest
8. shiny shinier, shiniest
9. wet wetter, wettest
10. windy windier, windiest

▲ Use the correct form of the adjective in ( ) to complete each sentence. Write the sentences.

Example: The _____ bears of all live in Alaska. (big)
The biggest bears of all live in Alaska.

11. Polar bears live in the _____ part of the state. (cold) coldest
12. The _____ bears of all can weigh 1,700 pounds. (heavy) heaviest
13. Bears are _____ in the fall than in the summer. (fat) fatter
14. They eat _____ amounts of food in the fall than in the winter. (large) larger
15. Bears' food is the _____ of all in the winter. (scarce) scarcest

■ Write each incorrect sentence correctly. If a sentence is already correct, write *correct*. Incorrect words are rewritten.

Example: Bald eagles are America's mightier birds of all.
Bald eagles are America's mightiest birds of all.

16. A bald eagle is no baldest than any other bird. balder
17. In earlier times, *bald* meant "marked with white." correct
18. The eagle's body may be longest than three feet. longer
19. Its wingspan is greatest than six feet. greater
20. The largest eagle's nest ever found weighed two tons. correct

Meeting Individual Needs — More Practice for Lesson 4

● EASY

Write the missing form(s) of the adjective in each group.

1. hungry	(hungrier)	hungriest
2. fine	finer	(finest)
3. mad	(madder)	maddest
4. (skinny)	skinnier	skinniest
5. brave	(braver)	(bravest)
6. (fit)	fitter	(fittest)

▲ AVERAGE

Complete each sentence with an adjective of your own choice, using the ending given. (Adjectives will vary.)

1. *-er:* Bears are _____ than raccoons.
2. *-est:* Ants are the _____ insects in the forest.
3. *-er:* Deer can run _____ than porcupines or beavers.
4. *-est:* Is the eagle the _____ bird?
5. *-er:* This fox is _____ than the other fox.

■ CHALLENGING

Write sentences that include a noun from Column A and an adjective from Column B. Then think of another noun and use it in a sentence with the other form (*-er* or *-est*) of the adjective. Example: The turtle is the slowest animal I've seen. Jacob says the snail is slower.

A	B
1. turtle	scarier
2. wolf	slowest
3. frog	prettier
4. snake	smartest

Extra Practice

(pages 144–145)

5 Comparing with *more* and *most*

Remember

- With long adjectives, use *more* to compare two things and *most* to compare three or more.
- Never add *-er* and *more* or *-est* and *most* to the same adjective.

● Choose the correct word to complete each sentence. Write the sentences.

Example: What is the (more, most) popular zoo animal?
What is the most popular zoo animal?

1. The monkeys are the (more, most) amusing of all.
2. A big cat is (more, most) exciting than a monkey.
3. Leopards are the (more, most) graceful of all big cats.
4. They are also the (more, most) skillful climbers of all.
5. A leopard may be (more, most) dangerous than a lion.

▲ Use *more* or *most* to complete each sentence. Write the sentences.

Example: The lion is ______ social than any other cat.
The lion is more social than any other cat.

6. It is ______ likely than another cat to live in a group. more
7. Lions are the ______ courageous of all animals. most
8. The ______ beautiful part of a lion is its mane. most
9. It makes the male lion ______ attractive than the female. more
10. The female, however, is a ______ skillful hunter than the male. more

■ Use the correct form of the adjective to complete each sentence. Write the sentences.

Example: The ______ of all cats is the tiger. (magnificent)
The most magnificent of all cats is the tiger.

11. A tiger's roar is the ______ of all sounds. (terrifying) most terrifying
12. Tigers are ______ hunters than lions. (fierce) fiercer
13. Tigers are ______ in the water than any other cat. (comfortable) more comfortable
14. Tigers hunt some of the ______ animals in the jungle. (big) biggest
15. White tigers are one of the ______ animals of all. (rare) rarest

Comparing with *more* and *most*

Objectives

Students will:

- use *more* with long adjectives to compare two things
- use *most* with long adjectives to compare three or more things
- use *more* and *most* to make comparisons in sentences correctly

Using the Extra Practice

The Extra Practice activities provide additional practice for the basic lesson at three levels of difficulty: Easy (●), Average (▲), and Challenging (■).

Meeting Individual Needs

More Practice for Lesson 5

● EASY

Complete and write each sentence, using *more* or *most* with the underlined adjective.

1. Only dogs are (more) popular than cats as pets.
2. Do you think that cats are (more) independent than dogs?
3. Many people think that cats are the (most) graceful animals alive.
4. Because they move silently, cats seem (more) mysterious than dogs.
5. A cat's sense of smell is (more) accurate than a person's.
6. Seeing in dim light is probably the cat's (most) famous skill.

▲ AVERAGE

Use each of these adjective forms in a sentence.

1. more important
2. most familiar
3. most amazing
4. more confusing
5. more useful
6. most difficult

■ CHALLENGING

Write eight sentences comparing two or more persons or things. In each sentence, use an adjective with *more* or *most*.

Comparing with *good* and *bad*

Objectives

Students will:

- use the correct comparative and superlative forms of *good* and *bad* in sentences
- write comparison sentences, using comparative and superlative forms of *good* and *bad*

Using the Extra Practice

The Extra Practice activities provide additional practice for the basic lesson at three levels of difficulty: Easy (●), Average (▲), and Challenging (■).

Extra Practice

(pages 146–147)

6 Comparing with *good* and *bad*

Remember

- When you use the adjectives *good* and *bad* to compare, you must change their forms.
- Use *better* or *worse* to compare two.
- Use *best* or *worst* to compare three or more.

● Write the adjective that correctly completes each sentence.

Example: I like mystery books (good, better) than any other kind. *better*

1. The (better, best) part of all is solving the mystery.
2. Michael's father won a special award for the (better, best) local writer.
3. I liked his last book (better, best) than his first.
4. The first one was not the (bad, worst) book I have read.
5. I have read a (worse, worst) book than that.

▲ Use the correct form of the adjective in ( ) to complete each sentence. Write the sentences.

Example: We were the ______ readers in the school. (bad)
We were the worst readers in the school.

6. We wanted to become ______ readers than we were. (good) better
7. Ms. Lee gave us the ______ books in the library to read. (good) best
8. Some of the books were ______ than we had expected. (bad) worse
9. Others were much ______. (good) better
10. After a month, we reported on the ______ book we had read. (good) best
11. The ______ part of all was choosing a favorite book. (bad) worst

■ Rewrite each sentence, using comparisons correctly. Incorrect words are rewritten.

Example: We wanted to be good writers than we were.
We wanted to be better writers than we were.

12. Mr. Diaz said that writing would be the better practice of all. best
13. Our first paper had the worse mistakes of all. worst
14. The second paper was much good than the first. better
15. My first story was not the better work I have done. best
16. In fact, it was the bad thing I have ever written. worst

164 Unit 4: Adjectives

Meeting Individual Needs

More Practice for Lesson 6

● EASY

Write the adjective that correctly completes each sentence.

1. What could be (bad, worse, worst) than not knowing how to read?
2. Reading is the (good, better, best) way to learn.
3. The (bad, worse, worst) reader in my class improved with practice.
4. Will you be a (good, better, best) reader next year than you are now?

▲ AVERAGE

Complete each sentence with the correct form of either *good* or *bad.*

1. This short story was the ______ I've ever read. (worst / best)
2. I can't imagine anything ______. (worse / better)
3. I wonder if there are ______ stories than this to read. (worse / better)
4. This story is the ______ in the library. (worst / best)
5. I wonder if the next story will be a ______ one? (good / bad; better / worse)

■ CHALLENGING

Write three sentences in which you compare kinds of foods, cars, or sports, using three forms of *good.* Then write three more sentences on the same topic, using three forms of *bad.*

Unit 5 Planning Guide

Capitalization and Punctuation

$2\frac{1}{2}$ *weeks*

	Lesson	Checkup (PE)	Extra Practice (PE)	Graphic Organizer (BLM)	Writing Wrap-Up (BLM)	More Practice (TE)	Workbook Plus	Reteaching Workbook	Students Acquiring English Practice Book
1	Correct Sentences *(166–167)*	189	194	5–1, 5–2	5–7	194	72–73	44	69+
	Revising Strategies: Sentence Fluency Writing Good Sentences *(168–169)*						74–75	45–46	
2	Names of People and Pets *(170–171)*	189	195	5–1	5–7	195	76–77	47	71+
3	Names of Places and Things *(172–173)*	189	196	5–1	5–7	196	78–79	48	73+
4	Abbreviations *(174–175)*	189	197	5–3	5–7	197	80–81	49	75+
5	Commas in a Series *(176–177)*	189	198	5–4	5–8	198	82–83	50	77+
	Revising Strategies: Sentence Fluency Writing Good Sentences *(178–179)*						84–85	51–52	
6	More Uses for Commas *(180–181)*	189	199	5–4	5–8	199	86–87	53	79+
7	Quotation Marks *(182–183)*	190	200	5–5	5–9	200	88–89	54	81+
8	Quotations *(184–185)*	190	201	5–5	5–9	201	90–91	55	83+
9	Titles *(186–187)*	190	202	5–6	5–9	202	92–93	56	85+
	Enrichment *(188)*								
	Test Practice *(191–193)*								87+

Tools and Tips

- **Diagramming Guide,** *pp. H70–H78*
- **Guide to Capitalization, Punctuation, and Usage,** *pp. H55–H64*

School-Home Connection

Suggestions for informing or involving family members in classroom activities and learning related to this unit are included in the Teacher's Edition throughout the unit.

Meeting Individual Needs

- **FOR SPECIAL NEEDS/INCLUSION:** *Houghton Mifflin English* Audiotape See also Reteaching.
- **FOR STUDENTS ACQUIRING ENGLISH:**
  - Notes and activities are included in this Teacher's Edition throughout the unit to help you adapt or use pupil book activities with students acquiring English.
  - Additional support is available for students at various stages of English proficiency: **Beginning/Preproduction**, **Early Production/Speech Emergence**, and **Intermediate/Advanced**. See Students Acquiring English Practice Book.
  - Students can listen to the Try It Out activities on audiotape.
- **ENRICHMENT:** *p. 188*

All audiotape recordings are also available on CD.

Daily Language Practice

Each sentence includes two errors based on skills taught in this or previous Grammar units. Each day write one sentence on the chalkboard. Have students find the errors and write the sentence correctly on a sheet of paper. To make the activity easier, identify the kinds of errors.

1. Chang had the baddest cold last week. he had to stay home from school. Chang had the worst cold last week. He had to stay home from school. (comparing with adjectives; capitalization)
2. every morning our dog wake us up. Every morning our dog wakes us up. (capitalization; subject-verb agreement)
3. "Is that the bestest team in the league"? the fan asked. "Is that the best team in the league?" the fan asked. (comparing with adjectives; quotations)
4. In January we celebrates a holiday for Martin Luther King Jnr. In January we celebrate a holiday for Martin Luther King Jr. (subject-verb agreement; abbreviations)
5. I'll bring bread, jam and peanut butter for our sandwichs. I'll bring bread, jam, and peanut butter for our sandwiches. (commas; plural nouns)
6. Yes we studyed the effects of acid rain on our forests. Yes, we studied the effects of acid rain on our forests. (commas; past tense)
7. Tyrone telled us "that more students' poems will be published in the school paper." Sample: Tyrone told us that more students' poems will be published in the school paper. (irregular verbs; quotations)
8. "Is that the bestest this team can do"? the coach asked. "Is that the best this team can do?" the coach asked. (comparing with adjectives; quotations)
9. Gus' favorite book is <u>Jake, the wonder dog.</u> Gus's favorite book is <u>Jake, the Wonder Dog.</u> (possessive nouns; titles)
10. Nadia the girls club will meet Saturday afternoon. Nadia, the girls' club will meet Saturday afternoon. (commas; possessive nouns)

Additional Resources

Workbook Plus, Unit 5
Reteaching Workbook, Unit 5
Students Acquiring English Practice Book, Unit 5
Transparencies, Unit 5
Teacher's Resource Book
Audiotapes

Technology Tools

INTERNET: http://www.eduplace.com/kids/hme/ *or* http://www.eduplace.com/rdg/hme/

Visit Education Place for these additional support materials and activities:

- tricky usage question
- Wacky Web Tales®
- interactive quizzes
- a proofreading game

Assessment

Test Booklet, Unit 5

Keeping a Journal

Discuss with students the value of keeping a journal as a way of promoting self-expression and fluency. Encourage students to record their thoughts and ideas in a notebook. Inform students whether the journal will be private or will be reviewed periodically as a way of assessing growth. The following prompts may be useful for generating writing ideas.

Journal Prompts

- Invent a new kind of ice-cream flavor. Describe it and give it a name.
- What is the most important thing you have learned since you have been in fourth grade? Explain.
- Whom would you like to trade places with for a day? Why?

Unit 5

Capitalization and Punctuation

These ancient, mysterious statues stand on Easter Island in the South Pacific Ocean.

Introducing the Unit

Using the Photograph

Note on the Photograph The photograph is of prehistoric statues along a grassy hillside on Easter Island. Easter Island is an island of Chile and is known locally as Rapa Nui.

- Have students look at the photograph and read the caption. Ask students to identify the words with capital letters and explain why these are capitalized. (They are proper nouns.)
- Suggest to students that Easter Island might be an interesting place to visit. Ask students what other places they might like to visit one day. Write student responses in a row on the board or on an overhead transparency. Ask students which punctuation mark to put between the names. (commas)
- Explain to students that they will be studying these and other rules of **capitalization and punctuation** in this unit.

Grammar Song

See Blackline Master G–2 for a song to help students remember some of the concepts and rules taught in this unit.

Students can also listen to this song on audiotape.

Shared Writing Activity

Work with students to use their understanding of capitalization and punctuation to write a paragraph about three friends who see the carved heads on Easter Island for the first time.

1. Have volunteers provide three names. Write the names on the board or on an overhead transparency. Have students decide what each friend's reaction will be to the carved heads. (Sample responses: fear, laughter, amazement) Write the reaction next to the friend's name.
2. Have students suggest a reason for the three friends to be on Easter Island. (Sample responses: It is their home. They are on vacation. They were shipwrecked.)
3. Work with students to write four or five sentences for the paragraph.
   - The first one or two sentences should set up the story. (For example, *Pedro, Anton, and Camille got shipwrecked in a strange place.*)
   - The remaining sentences should tell what each friend said when he or she first saw the statues. (For example, *"Oh no," Pedro said, "they look like monsters!"*)
   - Encourage students to use quotations when they suggest their sentences.
4. As you record students' suggestions, write slowly and focus on the use of capital letters and the type and placement of punctuation. Help students fix any sentence fragments or run-on sentences.
5. Select three or four students to read the completed paragraph aloud. Have each student take one of the speaking parts, and a fourth can act as the narrator.

Correct Sentences

Lesson Objectives

Students will:

- begin sentences with capital letters and end them with the correct end marks
- proofread for missing capital letters and end marks
- write a food column, including examples of the four types of sentences

One-Minute Warm-Up Have volunteers tell which sentence is a statement *(He jabbed his hands into his pockets and sighed.)* and which is a question *(Why couldn't he get his room straight?)*. Then have volunteers tell about the clues they used to identify each type.

Focus on Instruction

Remind students that an end mark represents their voice in writing. Suggest that to decide whether a sentence is a run-on, students should read the sentence slowly, letting their voices tell them where one idea ends and another begins.

Try It Out

LISTENING AND SPEAKING Write a period, question mark, and exclamation point each on a separate index card. Have volunteers read each of the sentences aloud, not stopping until they reach the end. Then have them read the sentence again while holding up an index card to show the correct punctuation at the end of the sentence.

FOR STUDENTS ACQUIRING ENGLISH

- Have students listen to the Try It Out sentences on the audiotape. Distribute SAE Practice page for Unit 5, Lesson 1, to support listening.
- Write *sentence* on the board. Remind students that the term *sentence* includes statements, questions, commands, and exclamations. Ask how students know where one sentence ends and another begins. Write *What wonderful bread this is!* Ask what type of sentence this is. Make sure they understand this is not a question even though it begins with *what*. Contrast with *What kind of bread is it?* Then students listen and add punctuation. Remind students that the intonation is a clue.
  1. what a great day (What !)
  2. when are we leaving (When ?)

Mechanics 1

Correct Sentences

One-Minute Warm-Up

Read the sentences below. Which sentence is a statement? Which sentence is a question? the first; the second

He jabbed his hands into his pockets and sighed. Why couldn't he get his room straight?

—from *Justin and the Best Biscuits in the World*, by Mildred Pitts Walter

- When you write, you must show where each sentence begins and ends. Use a capital letter to show where each sentence begins, and an end mark to show where it ends.

Run-on:	Something smells good are you baking bread?
Correct:	Something smells good. Are you baking bread?

- Statements and commands end with periods.
- Questions end with question marks.
- Exclamations end with exclamation points.

Statement:	We like warm bread.
Command:	Bake some bread, please.
Question:	Do you like warm bread?
Exclamation:	What wonderful bread this is!

Try It Out

Speak Up How would you write these sentences? Underlined letters should be capitalized.

1. we are making dinner. would you like to help?
2. do you need an apron? please find the large pot.
3. pour in some ketchup.
4. did you remember to add the peanut butter?
5. i'll chop the cabbage. what a great stew this will be!
6. how surprised Mom and Dad will be!
7. what should we have for dessert?
8. do you like strawberries? let's put some on the table.

Meeting Individual Needs

RETEACHING
ALTERNATIVE STRATEGY

- Write these sentences on the board and have students tell what kind each is.
  What a wonderful surprise! (exclamation)
  Who decorated the room? (question)
  Get the camera, please. (command)
  It's time to cut the cake. (statement)
- Point out that each sentence begins with a capital letter and has an end mark. Discuss the end mark for each type of sentence.
- Ask students to provide other examples of each kind of sentence.

CHALLENGE

Have students, as a group, write silly stories using the four types of sentences. Provide an envelope containing slips of paper, each naming a type of sentence. One student chooses a paper and writes the type of sentence identified on the paper. Other students follow the procedure to complete the story together.

FOR STUDENTS ACQUIRING ENGLISH

Write a period, a question mark, and an exclamation point on the board. Ask what these marks are. Ask for sentences as examples. Then write sentences and have students add punctuation.

On Your Own

Write these sentences correctly. Add capital letters and end marks. Write each run-on sentence as two sentences. Underlined letters should be capitalized.

Example: have you ever eaten soup made from a bird's nest
Have you ever eaten soup made from a bird's nest?

9. what a strange dish it must be!
10. tell me how it is made.
11. only the nests of swiftlets are used. these birds are related to hummingbirds.
12. the nests are made of saliva.
13. that is amazing! or .
14. where can I taste bird's-nest soup?
15. try a Chinese restaurant.
16. the soup has been a part of Chinese culture for hundreds of years.
17. it is a special treat in Asia.
18. does collecting the nests harm the birds?
19. laws protect the birds. the nests can be gathered only at certain times.

20–26. This part of an interview has two missing capital letters and five missing end marks. Write the interview correctly. Underlined letters should be capitalized.

Example: is bird's-nest soup expensive *Is bird's-nest soup expensive?*

Proofreading

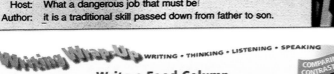

Host: Please welcome the author of *There's a Bird's Nest in My Soup*. What an amazing book this is! Where do swiftlets live?
Author: They live high up on cliffs. people climb to get the nests.
Host: What a dangerous job that must be!
Author: it is a traditional skill passed down from father to son.

Writing Wrap-Up WRITING • THINKING • LISTENING • SPEAKING

COMPARING/CONTRASTING

Write a Food Column

You are a reporter. Compare the best dish in the cafeteria with the worst. Include all four types of sentences. Read aloud your column to a partner. Does your partner agree with you?

For Extra Practice see page 194.

Summing Up Help students summarize these key points about the lesson:

> Begin every sentence with a capital letter. Use a period after a statement or a command. Use a question mark after a question. Use an exclamation point after an exclamation.

You may want to have students complete the parts related to this lesson on Blackline Masters 5–1 and 5–2.

On Your Own

If students are unable to identify run-on sentences, suggest that students read the sentences aloud, listening for natural pauses that might signal a new sentence.

MEETING INDIVIDUAL NEEDS

FOR STUDENTS ACQUIRING ENGLISH

Distribute SAE Practice page for Unit 5, Lesson 1. Ask what the strangest food is that they have eaten. How is it made? Assist with vocabulary as needed. Students add punctuation.
Example: when did you eat this food (When ?)

Writing Wrap-Up

Writing Tip: Suggest that students first choose the best and worst foods they've had in the cafeteria and then list descriptive adjectives to describe each one. See Blackline Master 5–6 for a sample food column.

TECHNOLOGY CONNECTION

Students may wish to desktop publish a newsletter of all their food columns.

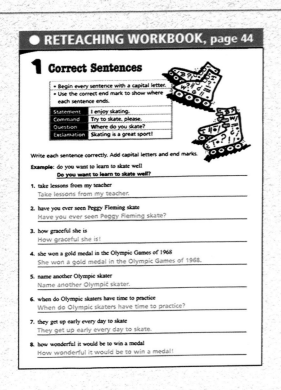

● RETEACHING WORKBOOK, page 44

1 Correct Sentences

- Begin every sentence with a capital letter.
- Use the correct end mark to show where each sentence ends.

Statement	I enjoy skating.
Command	Try to skate, please.
Question	Where do you skate?
Exclamation	Skating is a great sport!

Write each sentence correctly. Add capital letters and end marks.

Example: do you want to learn to skate well
Do you want to learn to skate well?

1. take lessons from my teacher
   Take lessons from my teacher.
2. have you ever seen Peggy Fleming skate
   Have you ever seen Peggy Fleming skate?
3. how graceful she is
   How graceful she is!
4. she won a gold medal in the Olympic Games of 1968
   She won a gold medal in the Olympic Games of 1968.
5. name another Olympic skater
   Name another Olympic skater.
6. when do Olympic skaters have time to practice
   When do Olympic skaters have time to practice?
7. they get up early every day to skate
   They get up early every day to skate.
8. how wonderful it would be to win a medal
   How wonderful it would be to win a medal!

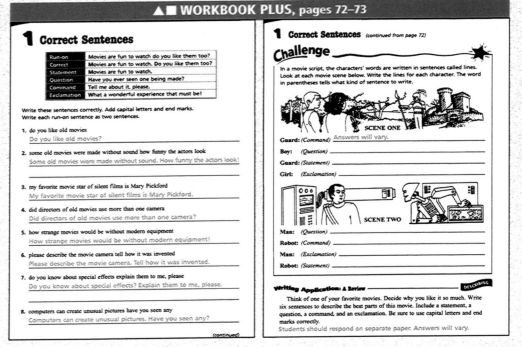

▲■ WORKBOOK PLUS, pages 72–73

1 Correct Sentences

Run-on	Movies are fun to watch do you like them too?
Correct	Movies are fun to watch. Do you like them too?
Statement	Movies are fun to watch.
Question	Have you ever seen one being made?
Command	Tell me about it, please.
Exclamation	What a wonderful experience that must be!

Write these sentences correctly. Add capital letters and end marks.
Write each run-on sentence as two sentences.

1. do you like old movies
   Do you like old movies?
2. some old movies were made without sound how funny the actors look
   Some old movies were made without sound. How funny the actors look!
3. my favorite movie star of silent films is Mary Pickford
   My favorite movie star of silent films is Mary Pickford.
4. did directors of old movies use more than one camera
   Did directors of old movies use more than one camera?
5. how strange movies would be without modern equipment
   How strange movies would be without modern equipment!
6. please describe the movie camera tell how it was invented
   Please describe the movie camera. Tell how it was invented.
7. do you know about special effects explain them to me, please
   Do you know about special effects? Explain them to me, please.
8. computers can create unusual pictures have you seen any
   Computers can create unusual pictures. Have you seen any?

(continued)

1 Correct Sentences (continued from page 72)

Challenge

In a movie script, the characters' words are written in sentences called lines. Look at each movie scene below. Write the lines for each character. The word in parentheses tells what kind of sentence to write.

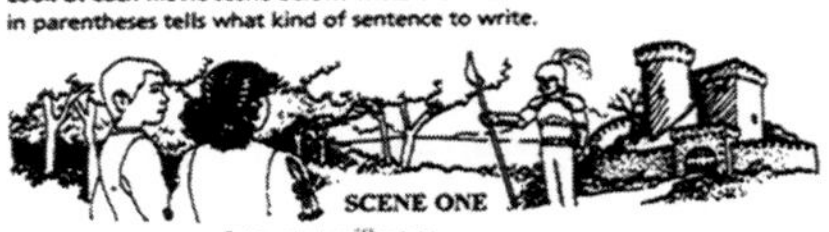

Guard: *(Command)* Answers will vary.
Boy: *(Question)*
Guard: *(Statement)*
Girl: *(Exclamation)*

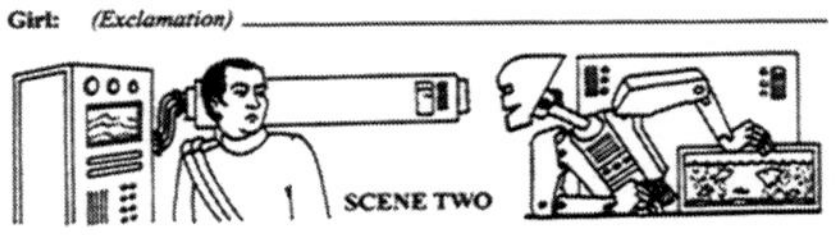

Man: *(Question)*
Robot: *(Command)*
Man: *(Exclamation)*
Robot: *(Statement)*

Writing Application: A Review DESCRIBING

Think of one of your favorite movies. Decide why you like it so much. Write six sentences to describe the best parts of this movie. Include a statement, a question, a command, and an exclamation. Be sure to use capital letters and end marks correctly.
Students should respond on separate paper. Answers will vary.

Writing Good Sentences

Lesson Objective

Students will:
- rewrite statements as questions, commands, or exclamations

Focus on Instruction

- Share these tips on converting statements to other types of sentences.
  1. To create a command, look for statements in which *you* is the subject: *You should go to the concert and enjoy yourself.*
  2. To create an exclamation, look for statements that demonstrate feeling: *We had a great time at the concert.*
- Point out that not every statement can be rewritten as another type of sentence. Explain that statements that provide information cannot usually be written as a different kind of sentence.
- Remind students to avoid writing too many sentences of any one kind. Encourage a variety of sentence types in their writing.

Apply It

Have students complete the revising activity independently. If necessary, review the characteristics of a question, a command, and an exclamation.

Have students look in their writing in progress to find statements that could be rewritten as commands, questions, or exclamations.

Sample Answers to Apply It

1. Can a good meal and a good deed go together?
2. Come to our Small World Picnic at King School.
3. We all had a great meal too!
4. What a great chance to make your favorite food!
5. Bring one of your special dishes for others to try.
6. Can you join us on June 15?

FOR STUDENTS ACQUIRING ENGLISH

Write the following sentence pairs on the board. Show the two ways to combine the first pair. Have the students show two ways to combine the second pair. Example: *The cookies are soft. They are chewy.* (The cookies are soft, and they are chewy. The cookies are soft and chewy.)

Writing Good Sentences

Writing Different Types of Sentences You know how to write statements, questions, commands, and exclamations. Avoid using too many statements when you write. Make your writing livelier by turning some statements into questions, commands, or exclamations.

Compare the first paragraph below to the second paragraph. Notice how questions, commands, and exclamations make the writing more interesting.

My mom makes great burritos. I am learning how to make them myself. You can come over sometime and try them.

My mom makes great burritos! Can you believe that I am learning to make them myself? Come over sometime and try them.

Apply It

1–6. Rewrite this flier. Change each underlined statement to a question, a command, or an exclamation. The word in ( ) will tell you which kind of sentence to write. See TE margin for sample answers.

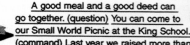

Revising

Small World Picnic

Martin Luther King Jr. School

June 15, 12–2 P.M.

Admission: $3.00

A good meal and a good deed can go together. (question) You can come to our Small World Picnic at the King School. (command) Last year we raised more than two hundred dollars for our town's food bank. We all had a great meal too. (exclamation)

We need volunteers to bring food for the picnic. This is a great chance to make your favorite food. (exclamation) Come share your family traditions. You can bring one of your special dishes for others to try. (command)

You can join us on June 15. (question)

Meeting Individual Needs

● RETEACHING WORKBOOK, page 45

Writing Good Sentences

- Use a mix of statements, questions, commands, and exclamations to make your writing more interesting.

One type of sentence	I just finished reading *Nightbirds on Nantucket*. You may have read this book. You should read it if you haven't. It is an exciting story.
Different types of sentences	I just finished reading *Nightbirds on Nantucket*. Have you read this book? Read it as soon as possible. It is the most exciting story I've ever read!

Writing Different Types of Sentences Rewrite each statement. The word in parentheses will tell you which kind of sentence to write. Sample answers:

Example: It is a good day to go to the library. **(exclamation)**
What a good day to go to the library!

Revising

1. You have a library card. **(question)**
   Do you have a library card?
2. You really should have one. **(exclamation)**
   You really should have one!
3. There is a form to fill out to get your own card. **(command)**
   Fill out a form to get your own card.
4. We can borrow five books right now. **(exclamation)**
   We can borrow five books right now!
5. You have read *Treasure Island*. **(question)**
   Have you read Treasure Island?
6. The best part is the shipwreck. **(exclamation)**
   The best part is the shipwreck!
7. You like other kinds of books. **(question)**
   What other kinds of books do you like?

(continued)

▲■ WORKBOOK PLUS, page 74

Writing Good Sentences

One type of sentence	I like to look at the stars. I always look for the North Star. Once I saw a shooting star. I thought it was beautiful.
Different types of sentences	Have you ever noticed how many brilliant stars you can see? Look for the North Star. Once I saw a shooting star. It was so beautiful!

Writing Different Types of Sentences 1–6. Rewrite this science article. Change each underlined statement to a question, a command, or an exclamation. The word in parentheses will tell you which kind of sentence to write. Sample answers:

Revising

When the sun goes down, the night lights come up. This is a beautiful sight to see. (exclamation) First, you might spend some time looking at the moon. (command) Moonlight is sunlight reflected off the moon. Then you can move on to the twinkling lights in the sky. (command) The twinkling lights are stars. Some of the stars we see are more than 2.5 million light-years away. (exclamation) You may notice pinpoints of light that do not twinkle. (question) They are planets. The night sky is so beautiful. (question)

1. What a beautiful sight to see!
2. First, spend some time looking at the moon.
3. Then move on to the twinkling lights in the sky.
4. Some of the stars we see are more than 2.5 million light-years away!
5. Have you noticed pinpoints of light that do not twinkle?
6. Have you ever seen anything so beautiful?

(continued)

Combining Sentences You know that combining sentences can improve your writing. If two sentences have the same subject, you can combine them in two different ways. You can join the whole sentences with *and* to form a compound sentence.

A compound sentence needs a comma. Do not use a comma with compound predicates.

He makes breakfast. He serves his family.

Compound Sentence: He makes breakfast, and he serves his family.

You can also join just the predicates to form a sentence with a compound predicate.

Compound Predicate: He makes breakfast and serves his family.

Apply It

7–12. Rewrite each underlined pair of sentences in this comic strip in two ways. First, combine the two sentences to form a compound sentence. Then combine them to form a sentence with a compound predicate. The first pair has been done for you. See TE margin for answers.

Revising

It is a mess, and it has a hundred dirty dishes.

It is a mess and has a hundred dirty dishes.

Lesson Objectives

Students will:

- combine two sentences to form a compound sentence
- combine two sentences to form a sentence with a compound predicate

Focus on Instruction

- Point out that a compound sentence contains two complete sentences. Each complete sentence has a subject and a verb. Explain that a comma and the word *and* join the two sentences and also bring a pause into the sentence.
- Write this compound sentence on the board. Have a volunteer read it aloud, label the subject and verb in each sentence and circle the comma and the word *and.*

  He makes breakfast, and he serves his family.
- Tell students that a compound predicate contains two predicates. Only the word *and* is needed to join two predicates. Point out that there is no pause in this kind of sentence. Write this sentence with a compound predicate on the board. Have a volunteer read the sentence and label the subject and two predicates and circle the word *and.*

  He makes breakfast and serves his family.
- Encourage students to use a variety of sentence structures in their writing.

Apply It

Have students complete the revising activity independently. Suggest that students check their sentences by labeling subjects and verbs. Remind them that the reader must pause when two complete sentences are joined.

Have students find places in their own writing in progress where they can combine sentences.

Answers to Apply It

7. I made some biscuits, and I saved one for you.
8. I made some biscuits and saved one for you.
9. They are too dry, and they taste awful!
10. They are too dry and taste awful!
11. Well, I make the best dog biscuits, and I love them!
12. I make the best dog biscuits and love them!

● RETEACHING WORKBOOK, page 46

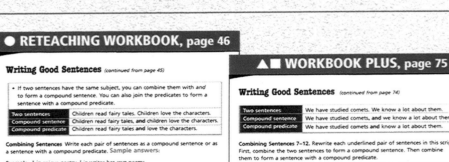

Writing Good Sentences *(continued from page 45)*

- If two sentences have the same subject, you can combine them with *and* to form a compound sentence. You can also join the predicates to form a sentence with a compound predicate.

Two sentences	Children read fairy tales. Children love the characters.
Compound sentence	Children read fairy tales, **and** children love the characters.
Compound predicate	Children read fairy tales **and** love the characters.

Combining Sentences Write each pair of sentences as a compound sentence or as a sentence with a compound predicate. Sample answers:

Example: Liz enjoys poetry. Liz writes her own poems.

Liz enjoys poetry, and Liz writes her own poems.

Liz enjoys poetry and writes her own poems.

Revising

8. I read to my brother. I make him laugh.
   I read to my brother and make him laugh.
9. He found an old book. He brought it to me.
   He found an old book, and he brought it to me.
10. We opened the book. We looked at the pictures.
    We opened the book and looked at the pictures.
11. It was beautiful. It made us think of olden days.
    It was beautiful, and it made us think of olden days.
12. My favorite stories are exciting. My favorite stories have adventure.
    My favorite stories are exciting and have adventure.
13. We rewrote one story. We turned it into a play.
    We rewrote one story, and we turned it into a play.
14. I acted out the story. I rescued the king.
    I acted out the story, and I rescued the king.

▲■ WORKBOOK PLUS, page 75

Writing Good Sentences *(continued from page 74)*

Two sentences	We have studied comets. We know a lot about them.
Compound sentence	We have studied comets, **and** we know a lot about them.
Compound predicate	We have studied comets **and** know a lot about them.

Combining Sentences 7–12. Rewrite each underlined pair of sentences in this script. First, combine the two sentences to form a compound sentence. Then combine them to form a sentence with a compound predicate.

Revising

Professor Starr  I know all about comets. I can tell you about them. Comets appear suddenly in the sky. They are rock-and-ice balls. They have a tail of gas and dust. Reflected sunlight makes the tail of the comet glow.

Professor Knight  Well, do you know what a meteor is? It is a rock from space. It enters Earth's atmosphere at high speed. Most meteors burn up when they hit the atmosphere. Some crash into the ground.

7. Compound Sentence: I know all about comets, and I can tell you about them.
8. Compound Predicate: I know all about comets and can tell you about them.
9. Compound Sentence: They are rock-and-ice balls, and they have a tail of gas and dust.
10. Compound Predicate: They are rock-and-ice balls and have a tail of gas and dust.
11. Compound Sentence: It is a rock from space, and it enters Earth's atmosphere at high speed.
12. Compound Predicate: It is a rock from space and enters Earth's atmosphere at high speed.

Names of People and Pets

Lesson Objectives

Students will:

- capitalize the names of people and pets
- capitalize titles used with names
- proofread for proper capitalization
- write an ad, using the names of people and pets

One-Minute Warm-Up Have a volunteer write the corrected sentence on the board, giving a reason for each letter that is capitalized. Explain that proper nouns begin with a capital letter. Then have volunteers write their own office signs on the board, using silly names.

Focus on Instruction

To make sure that students understand the distinction between a common and a proper noun, ask them to supply some sentences that use a family title, such as *uncle,* as a name and other sentences that do not.

Try It Out

VIEWING Create a chart on the board in which students can list their own silly proper names for the woman and the dog in the picture. (Sample responses are shown.) Then have students use the proper nouns to make up their own newspaper headlines about the picture.

Woman	Dog
Miss Sun E. Face	Puffy
Mrs. Ima Beauty	Pinkie

FOR STUDENTS ACQUIRING ENGLISH

- Have students listen to the Try It Out sentences on the audiotape. Distribute SAE Practice page for Unit 5, Lesson 2, to support listening.
- Ask students how they refer to adults they know. Keep in mind that use of titles varies in different cultures; ask about people students would likely address in English. Ask questions such as "What do you call me? What do you call the principal? Your doctor?" List titles and names. Explain that words for family relationships have capitals only when used as names; a possessive such as *my* is a clue the word is not capitalized. Explain middle initials. Students listen and add capitals.

1. My name is ms. castro. (Ms. Castro)
2. His name is brian p. yeager. (Brian P. Yeager)

Mechanics

2 Names of People and Pets

One-Minute Warm-Up

What's wrong with this sentence? How can you fix it?

dr. belle e. ache cures stomach problems.

Underlined letters should be capitalized.

- A proper noun begins with a capital letter. Always capitalize the names of people and pets because they are proper nouns.
- When titles and initials are used with names, you should capitalize them too.

Mario Gomez	Miss Diane Dawson	Dr. Richard Cohen
U. R. Wright	Mrs. Carol M. Ling	Governor J. Bryant
Mr. Todd Rossi	Ms. E. S. Ryan	Sparky

- Capitalize family titles when they are used as names or as parts of names.

  Today Grandmother arrived.

  Did Uncle Harry bring worms?

- Do not capitalize family titles when the titles are not used as names.

  My grandmother took us fishing.

  Our uncle paddled the canoe.

Try It Out

Dog Island Daily News
Pink Poodle Saves the Day

Speak Up Where should you use capital letters?

1. Every morning mom and aunt helen read the newspaper.
2. Today a photo of mr. derek johnson is on the front page.
3. He and james p. mullen just ran a marathon.
4. Did governor garcia give them a special award?
5. On the next page is a story about miss rosa perez.
6. My aunt read about her amazing poodle named pinky.
7. That smart dog saved the life of mrs. betty bowman!
8. dr. samuel washington wrote a letter to the editor.

Meeting Individual Needs

RETEACHING

ALTERNATIVE STRATEGY

- Write a two-column chart on the board. Ask volunteers to name some family members and their relationship to students, for example, *brother* and *William.* List each common noun in the left column and each proper noun in the right column.
- Explain that the words at the left are common nouns and those at the right are proper nouns; all proper nouns begin with a capital letter. Add headings to the columns.

CHALLENGE

Have students write short paragraphs using only common nouns, such as *mother* and *cat.* Then have students exchange papers and replace all the common nouns with names, such as *Mom* and *Fluffball,* making sure to capitalize as needed.

FOR STUDENTS ACQUIRING ENGLISH

Review capital and lowercase letters. Ask all of the students to write their names, the name of their best friend, and your name. Check for correct use of capital letters and for the correct title with your own name.

On Your Own

Write these sentences correctly. Add capital letters where they are needed.

Example: mr. nye runs the school newspaper.
Mr. Nye runs the school newspaper.

9. This year dillon, sonia, and I are reporters.
10. I wrote about the science fair that ms. chan organized.
11. One of the judges was the science writer dr. d. j. hillman.
12. According to principal schultz, the fair was a big success!
13. I told mom and my friend marcus barnes about my next article.
14. I want to interview grandma winkler.
15. She and granddad moved here many years ago.
16. They started a pet store with mrs. wilma katz.
17. I want to know how my grandma's parrot, cha cha, learned to talk.

18–24. This article from a town newspaper has seven missing or incorrect capital letters. Write the article correctly. Underlined letters should capitalized.

Example: Marie walks frisky for officer joe.
Marie walks Frisky for Officer Joe.

Proofreading

Issue 194 No. 40 — Central Valley Newspaper — Section 2 Page 11

Fourth-Grader Starts Business

Marie frasier has her own business. It all began when her neighbor Alex p. Sloan was planning a trip to visit his Aunt. He said, "Can I hire you to walk brownie while I visit aunt Rachel?"

Since then, miss Lena Chin has hired Marie to walk her dog. dr. Victor Ortiz also hired the girl to care for his cat.

Writing Wrap-Up

WRITING • THINKING • LISTENING • SPEAKING

PERSUADING

Write an Ad

Marie wants to expand her pet business. Write an ad to help her attract new customers. Include the names of people and pets she has worked with. Read your ad to a partner. Check capitalization of names.

For Extra Practice see page 195.

Summing Up Help students summarize these key points about the lesson:

Capitalize the following: (1) the names of people and pets, (2) titles and initials that are parts of names, and (3) family titles when they are used as names or parts of names.

You may want to have students complete the parts related to this lesson on Blackline Master 5–1.

On Your Own

Remind students that they can figure out if a word is a proper noun and needs capitalization by asking if the noun names a particular person, place, or thing.

MEETING INDIVIDUAL NEEDS

FOR STUDENTS ACQUIRING ENGLISH

Distribute SAE Practice page for Unit 5, Lesson 2. Briefly review capital letters on titles and family relationships. Then students add capital letters.

1. We had a party for grandmother. (Grandmother)
2. All of my aunts and uncles came. (correct)

Writing Wrap-Up

Writing Tip: Suggest that, before writing their ads, students brainstorm ideas about how to attract customers. See Blackline Master 5–6 for a sample ad.

SCHOOL-HOME CONNECTION

Have students and family members look up ads for pet services in a telephone directory and talk about those that are persuasive and why.

● RETEACHING WORKBOOK, page 47

2 Names of People and Pets

- Capitalize the names of people and pets.
- Capitalize titles and initials that are parts of names.
- Capitalize family titles when they are used as names.

People and pets	Melissa Stewart took her dog Fluffy for a walk.
Titles and initials	Mr. Jim S. Breen and Dr. Dolores Lopez are here.
Family titles	Aunt Marsha and my uncle live in the city.

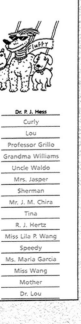

Two nouns in each sentence are underlined. Find the proper noun and write it correctly.

Example: dr. p. j. hess is a talented animal doctor. — Dr. P. J. Hess

1. We take our dog, curly, to her. — Curly
2. My sister lou wants to be a vet also. — Lou
3. The doctor told her to see professor grillo. — Professor Grillo
4. The professor knows grandma williams. — Grandma Williams
5. He and uncle waldo know a pet-shop owner. — Uncle Waldo
6. The owner, mrs. jasper, gave my sister a job. — Mrs. Jasper
7. Lou learned to take care of sherman the bird. — Sherman
8. Our neighbor is mr. j. m. chira. — Mr. J. M. Chira
9. He wants my sister to feed his cat, tina. — Tina
10. My best friend is r. j. hertz. — R. J. Hertz
11. She told miss lila p. wang about my sister. — Miss Lila P. Wang
12. Lila's turtle is named speedy. — Speedy
13. The turtle once belonged to ms. maria garcia. — Ms. Maria Garcia
14. Now my sister takes care of it for miss wang. — Miss Wang
15. The vet and mother are proud of my sister. — Mother
16. Now our mother calls her dr. lou! — Dr. Lou

▲■ WORKBOOK PLUS, pages 76–77

2 Capitalizing Names of People and Pets

People and pets	David Mazur has a bird named Bert.
Titles and initials	R. U. Shure voted for Mayor Rita Day.
Family titles	Uncle Milt and my grandfather are here.

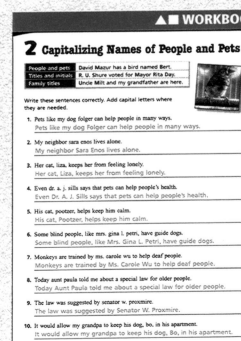

Write these sentences correctly. Add capital letters where they are needed.

1. Pets like my dog folger can help people in many ways.
   Pets like my dog Folger can help people in many ways.
2. My neighbor sara enos lives alone.
   My neighbor Sara Enos lives alone.
3. Her cat, liza, keeps her from feeling lonely.
   Her cat, Liza, keeps her from feeling lonely.
4. Even dr. a. j. sills says that pets can help people's health.
   Even Dr. A. J. Sills says that pets can help people's health.
5. His cat, pootzer, helps keep him calm.
   His cat, Pootzer, helps keep him calm.
6. Some blind people, like mrs. gina l. petri, have guide dogs.
   Some blind people, like Mrs. Gina L. Petri, have guide dogs.
7. Monkeys are trained by ms. carole wu to help deaf people.
   Monkeys are trained by Ms. Carole Wu to help deaf people.
8. Today aunt paula told me about a special law for older people.
   Today Aunt Paula told me about a special law for older people.
9. The law was suggested by senator w. proxmire.
   The law was suggested by Senator W. Proxmire.
10. It would allow my grandpa to keep his dog, bo, in his apartment.
    It would allow my grandpa to keep his dog, Bo, in his apartment.

(continued)

2 Capitalizing Names of People and Pets (continued from page 76)

Challenge

Some people say that dog owners and their dogs look alike. Look at the pictures of these dogs and their owners. Then write a name for each pet owner and pet. The first one has been done for you.

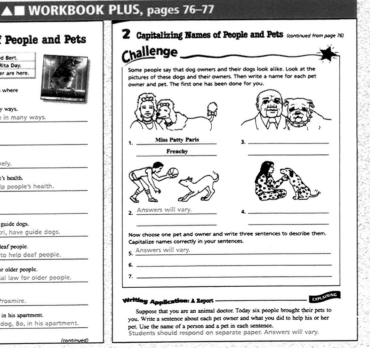

1. Miss Patty Paris
   Frenchy
2. Answers will vary.
3. ______
4. ______

Now choose one pet and owner and write three sentences to describe them. Capitalize names correctly in your sentences.

5. Answers will vary.
6. ______
7. ______

Writing Application: A Report EXPLAINING

Suppose that you are an animal doctor. Today six people brought their pets to you. Write a sentence about each pet owner and what you did to help his or her pet. Use the name of a person and a pet in each sentence.
Students should respond on separate paper. Answers will vary.

Names of Places and Things

Lesson Objectives

Students will:
- capitalize proper nouns that name places and things
- proofread for correct capitalization
- write an opinion, including proper nouns that name places and things

One-Minute Warm-Up Ask volunteers to identify the common nouns from the sentence and write them in a column on the board. Have them identify the proper nouns and list them in a second column. Have students compare the nouns in the two columns. Point out that the proper nouns begin with a capital letter.

Focus on Instruction

Name some "unimportant words" that often appear in titles, such as *of, on, in, and, a,* and *the.* Explain that these words are not capitalized unless they are the first word in the title or proper noun phrase. Mention *Fourth of July* as an example.

Try It Out

VIEWING Under appropriate headings on the board, have students list common nouns and corresponding proper nouns for places and things in the picture. Students can then use some of the proper nouns to write a description that might appear with the picture in a travel brochure.

Common Nouns	Proper Nouns
ocean	Atlantic Ocean
beach	Coral Beach

FOR STUDENTS ACQUIRING ENGLISH

- Have students listen to the Try It Out sentences on the audiotape. Distribute SAE Practice page for Unit 5, Lesson 3, to support listening.
- Have students write the days of the week and months of the year. Check for use of capital letters. Rules for punctuation vary widely across languages, so students will need to be reminded to apply the rules for English, not their first language. Explain that English has somewhat more capital letters than many other languages, and we capitalize not just the first important word but all important words. Students listen and add capital letters.

1. Two of the students are from russia. (Russia)
2. We will go to the movies on saturday. (Saturday)

Mechanics

3 Names of Places and Things

One-Minute Warm-Up

Read the sentence below. Name the common nouns and the proper nouns. Common nouns are underlined once; proper nouns, twice.

One morning in August 1954, Sadako Sasaki looked up at the blue sky over Hiroshima and saw not a cloud in the sky.

—from *Sadako,* by Eleanor Coerr

- Always capitalize the names of particular places and things.
- Whenever a proper noun is more than one word, remember to begin each important word with a capital letter.

Proper Nouns That Name Places and Things

Places	Things
street—Pebble Creek Road	days—Monday
city—Dallas	Thursday
state—Colorado	months—February
country—Mexico	August
building—Museum of Science	holidays—Flag Day
mountain—Pikes Peak	Fourth of July
park—Acadia National Park	groups—Avon Garden Club
water—Indian Ocean	New York Mets

Try It Out

Speak Up Which words need capital letters?

1. My pen pal from japan is coming to visit
2. He plans to arrive in ocean city next tuesday.
3. We'll visit the seaside museum if he isn't too tired.
4. Then we can go to pacific park or rocky road.
5. Afterward we can watch the miami dolphins play football.
6. I'm glad he's staying until columbus day!
7. Many exciting things happen here in september and october.

Meeting Individual Needs

RETEACHING
ALTERNATIVE STRATEGY

- Write this incomplete sentence on the board: *Every ______, my family drives to ______.*
- Have students suggest specific names to complete the sentence. (for example: *January, Florida*) Write their responses on the board.
- Point out that each of the written responses names a particular time or place. Explain that the words are proper nouns and must be capitalized.
- Have volunteers name proper nouns for streets, days, months, and holidays as you write them.

CHALLENGE

Have students select a paragraph in a newspaper or magazine. Tell them to identify all the common nouns and then rewrite the paragraph, replacing each common noun with a proper one. Paragraphs can be serious or zany.

FOR STUDENTS ACQUIRING ENGLISH

Ask students for the name of their favorite museum, zoo, amusement park, make of car, or cereal. Write responses on the board. Call on students to mark the capital letters with colored chalk. Ask why these words have capitals.

On Your Own

Write these sentences correctly. Add capital letters where they are needed. Underlined letters should be capitalized.

Example: Last saturday Heather returned from her trip.
Last Saturday Heather returned from her trip.

8. On friday we saw the slides she took in june and july.
9. They showed highlights of her travels in canada.
10. Her trip began near the bay of fundy.
11. She drove north to forillon national park.
12. There were pictures of the st. lawrence river.
13. Heather was there for canada day!
14. She also visited the canadian museum of man.
15. I visited my uncle in montreal last year.
16. He works in a skyscraper on dorchester boulevard.

17–24. This part of an e-mail message has eight missing or incorrect capital letters. Write the message correctly. Underlined letters should be capitalized.

Example: Will you climb Pikes peak? *Will you climb Pikes Peak?*

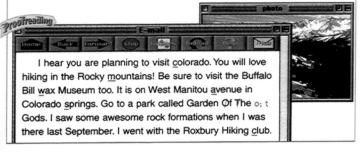

Proofreading

E-mail

I hear you are planning to visit colorado. You will love hiking in the Rocky mountains! Be sure to visit the Buffalo Bill wax Museum too. It is on West Manitou avenue in Colorado springs. Go to a park called Garden Of The o; t Gods. I saw some awesome rock formations when I was there last September. I went with the Roxbury Hiking club.

Writing Wrap-Up

WRITING • THINKING • LISTENING • SPEAKING

EXPRESSING

Write an Opinion

Write an e-mail message to a friend in another state. Tell about the best places to visit in your state. Include names of places and things. Read your message to a partner. Have your partner name the proper nouns.

For Extra Practice see page 196.

Summing Up Help students summarize these key points about the lesson:

> Capitalize the names of particular places and things. If the name has more than two words, capitalize only the important words.

You may want to have students complete the parts related to this lesson on Blackline Master 5–1.

On Your Own

Tell students to identify names that should be capitalized by asking:

> Does the noun name a particular person, place, or thing?

MEETING INDIVIDUAL NEEDS

FOR STUDENTS ACQUIRING ENGLISH

Distribute SAE Practice page for Unit 5, Lesson 3. Review by writing and having students add capital letters to names of local places. Then students add capital letters to sentences.

1. My family is going to new york in july. (New York, July)
2. I want to visit the statue of liberty. (Statue of Liberty)

Writing Wrap-Up

Writing Tip: Tell students to be sure to explain why they think each place is among the best to visit. See Blackline Master 5–6 for a sample opinion.

TECHNOLOGY CONNECTION

Students may wish to e-mail their messages.

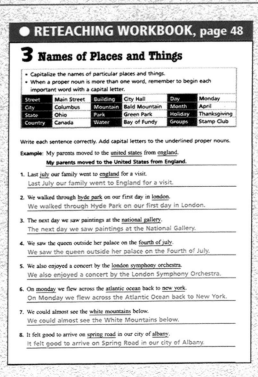

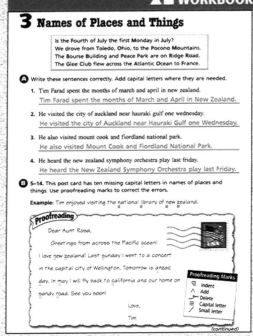

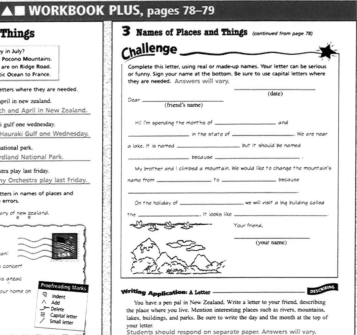

● RETEACHING WORKBOOK, page 48

3 Names of Places and Things

- Capitalize the names of particular places and things.
- When a proper noun is more than one word, remember to begin each important word with a capital letter.

Street	Main Street	Building	City Hall	Day	Monday
City	Columbus	Mountain	Bald Mountain	Month	April
State	Ohio	Park	Green Park	Holiday	Thanksgiving
Country	Canada	Water	Bay of Fundy	Groups	Stamp Club

Write each sentence correctly. Add capital letters to the underlined proper nouns.

Example: My parents moved to the united states from england.
My parents moved to the United States from England.

1. Last july our family went to england for a visit.
Last July our family went to England for a visit.
2. We walked through hyde park on our first day in london.
We walked through Hyde Park on our first day in London.
3. The next day we saw paintings at the national gallery.
The next day we saw paintings at the National Gallery.
4. We saw the queen outside her palace on the fourth of july.
We saw the queen outside her palace on the Fourth of July.
5. We also enjoyed a concert by the london symphony orchestra.
We also enjoyed a concert by the London Symphony Orchestra.
6. On monday we flew across the atlantic ocean back to new york.
On Monday we flew across the Atlantic Ocean back to New York.
7. We could almost see the white mountains below.
We could almost see the White Mountains below.
8. It felt good to arrive on spring road in our city of albany.
It felt good to arrive on Spring Road in our city of Albany.

▲■ WORKBOOK PLUS, pages 78–79

3 Names of Places and Things

Is the Fourth of July the first Monday in July?
We drove from Toledo, Ohio, to the Pocono Mountains.
The Bourse Building and Peace Park are on Ridge Road.
The Glee Club flew across the Atlantic Ocean to France.

A Write these sentences correctly. Add capital letters where they are needed.

1. Tim Farad spent the months of march and april in new zealand.
Tim Farad spent the months of March and April in New Zealand.
2. He visited the city of auckland near hauraki gulf one wednesday.
He visited the city of Auckland near Hauraki Gulf one Wednesday.
3. He also visited mount cook and fiordland national park.
He also visited Mount Cook and Fiordland National Park.
4. He heard the new zealand symphony orchestra play last friday.
He heard the New Zealand Symphony Orchestra play last Friday.

B 5–14. This post card has ten missing capital letters in names of places and things. Use proofreading marks to correct the errors.

Example: Tim enjoyed visiting the national library of new zealand.

Proofreading

Dear Aunt Rosa,

Greetings from across the Pacific ocean! I love new zealand! Last sunday I went to a concert in the capital city of Wellington. Tomorrow is anzac day. In may I will fly back to california and our home on sandy road. See you soon!

Love,
Tim

Proofreading Marks
¶ Indent
∧ Add
Delete
≡ Capital letter
/ Small letter

(continued)

3 Names of Places and Things *(continued from page 78)*

Challenge

Complete this letter, using real or made-up names. Your letter can be serious or funny. Sign your name at the bottom. Be sure to use capital letters where they are needed. Answers will vary.

________ (date)

Dear ________ (friend's name)

Hi! I'm spending the months of ________ and ________ in the state of ________. We are near a lake. It is named ________, but it should be named ________ because ________.

My brother and I climbed a mountain. We would like to change the mountain's name from ________ to ________ because ________.

On the holiday of ________, we will visit a big building called the ________. It looks like ________.

Your friend,

________ (your name)

Writing Application: A Letter DESCRIBING

You have a pen pal in New Zealand. Write a letter to your friend, describing the place where you live. Mention interesting places such as rivers, mountains, lakes, buildings, and parks. Be sure to write the day and the month at the top of your letter.
Students should respond on separate paper. Answers will vary.

Abbreviations

Lesson Objectives

Students will:

- capitalize and punctuate abbreviations for titles, addresses, months, and days
- recognize special two-letter abbreviations used for state names with ZIP Codes
- proofread for incorrect abbreviations
- write an address book, including a title and abbreviation for each entry

One-Minute Warm-Up Have a volunteer write the revised sign on the board. Point out the capital letters and the period in each abbreviation. Explain that *Mr.* and *Co.* are abbreviations. Ask students to write other abbreviations they are familiar with.

Focus on Instruction

Point out that abbreviations for months and days are not usually used in writing compositions, letters, and reports.

Try It Out

VIEWING Have students use abbreviations to write names and addresses for the postcard, which shows a view of Utah. (Sample responses are shown.)

Names	Addresses
Ms. Rita Jones	101 Stone Ave.
Mr. Dan Mack	923 Hilltop Blvd.

FOR STUDENTS ACQUIRING ENGLISH

- Have students listen to the Try It Out sentences on the audiotape. Distribute SAE Practice page for Unit 5, Lesson 4, to support listening.
- Explain that most abbreviations have a period to show the word is shortened. The exception is abbreviations for the states; these have two capitals and no period. Explain that they were developed by the post office so that all state abbreviations would have two letters. (In the past, some had fewer and some more.) Supply the postal abbreviations for states around yours. Help students write their own addresses using abbreviations. Then students listen and rewrite abbreviations.
  1. Thursday (Thurs.)
  2. Walton Company (Co.)

Mechanics

4 Abbreviations

One-Minute Warm-Up

Which words can you shorten to make this sign fit on the truck better?
Mister Bucky Buckette's Cleaning Company
Mr. Bucky Buckette's Cleaning Co.

- **Some words have a shortened form called an abbreviation.** An abbreviation stands for a whole word. Most abbreviations begin with a capital letter and end with a period. Use them only in special kinds of writing, such as addresses and lists.

Some Common Abbreviations

Titles	Mr. Jr.	Mister Junior	Sr. Dr.	Senior Doctor	Mrs. Ms.	married woman any woman
Addresses	Rd. St.	Road Street	Ave. Blvd.	Avenue Boulevard	Co. P. O.	Company Post Office
Months	Jan.	January	Apr.	April	Sept.	September
Days	Sun.	Sunday	Wed.	Wednesday	Thurs.	Thursday

- Special two-letter abbreviations for state names are used with ZIP codes. Both letters are capitals, and no period is used.

AL Alabama UT Utah OH Ohio VT Vermont

Try It Out

Speak Up What is the correct abbreviation for each underlined word?

1. Marina Boat Company Co.
2. Monument Valley, Utah UT
3. A. V. Pyke Junior Jr.
4. Tuesday, April 5 Tues.
5. Doctor Ramon Dr.
6. Grant Road Rd.

Monument Valley, Utah

Meeting Individual Needs

RETEACHING
ALTERNATIVE STRATEGY

- Display several abbreviations. Explain that the abbreviations begin with a capital letter and end with a period. Ask what each abbreviation stands for.
- Have students write a tic-tac-toe grid and place one abbreviation from the chart on the student page in each section of the grid.
- Ask questions that students can answer using words from the grid. As volunteers answer, students can cross off that abbreviation. The first student to cross off all words in a row wins.

CHALLENGE
Have students scan a newspaper for abbreviations, writing each one on an index card and telling on a second card what it stands for. Have students exchange cards with a partner, who then matches words with abbreviations.

FOR STUDENTS ACQUIRING ENGLISH
Write *St.* on the board. Ask what that is. After students correctly respond with *street* or *saint,* write and say *abbreviation.* Have students copy the word and say it themselves.

On Your Own

Write these groups of words using correct abbreviations. Words to be abbreviated are underlined.

Example: Wednesday, November 4 *Wed., Nov. 4*

7. Doctor Ann Chang Dr.
8. Mister John Cliff Senior Mr., Sr.
9. May Lee, a married woman Mrs./Ms.
10. Cooper Copper Company Co.
11. Joseph L. Louis Junior Jr.
12. 19 Seneca Street St.
13. Tuesday, October 28 Tues., Oct.
14. Post Office Box 6 P. O.
15. El Monte Avenue Ave.
16. January 1, 1999 Jan.

17–24. These addresses have eight incorrect abbreviations. Write the addresses correctly. Incorrect abbreviations are underlined.

Example: 33 Forest ST *33 Forest St.*

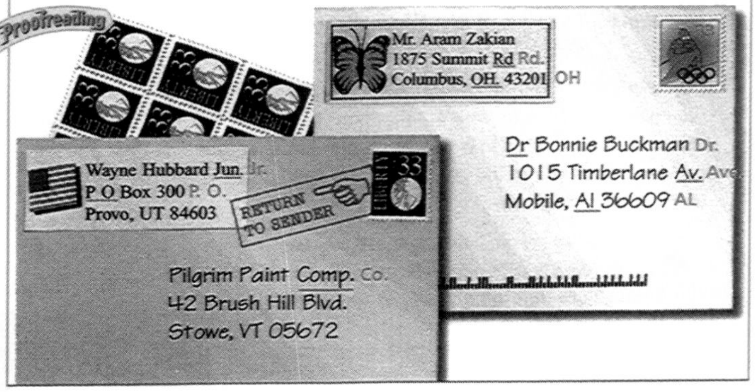

Writing Wrap-Up WRITING • THINKING • LISTENING • SPEAKING — CREATING

Write an Address Book

Make a booklet by folding several sheets of paper in half. Then make up some silly names and addresses to write in the booklet, such as *Mr. Rollin N. Dough, 50 Cash Lane, Richfield, PA.* Include a title and birth month for each person. Use correct abbreviations. Then read your address book to a partner. Check the abbreviations together.

For Extra Practice see page 197.

Summing Up Help students summarize these key points about the lesson:

An **abbreviation** is a short form of a word. Most abbreviations begin with a capital letter and end with a period.

You may want to have students complete the parts related to this lesson on Blackline Master 5–3.

On Your Own

Tell students to check their abbreviations for correct capitalization and use of periods.

MEETING INDIVIDUAL NEEDS

FOR STUDENTS ACQUIRING ENGLISH

Distribute SAE Practice page for Unit 5, Lesson 4. Then students rewrite addresses using abbreviations.
Mister James Brown (Mr.)
44 White Road (Rd.)
Boston, Massachusetts 02116 (MA)

Writing Wrap-Up

Writing Tip: Suggest that students brainstorm a list of phrases, such as *Lightning strikes,* from which they can create names. (Mrs. Light Ning Strikes) See Blackline Master 5–7 for sample address book entries.

TECHNOLOGY CONNECTION

Students may want to use stylistic formats on available software to design their address book.

● RETEACHING WORKBOOK, page 49

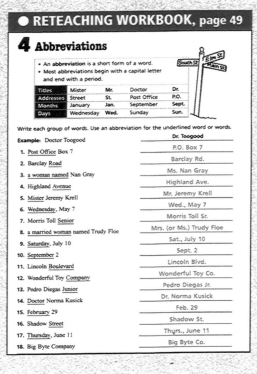

4 Abbreviations

- An **abbreviation** is a short form of a word.
- Most abbreviations begin with a capital letter and end with a period.

Titles	Mister	Mr.	Doctor	Dr.
Addresses	Street	St.	Post Office	P.O.
Months	January	Jan.	September	Sept.
Days	Wednesday	Wed.	Sunday	Sun.

Write each group of words. Use an abbreviation for the underlined word or words.

Example: Doctor Toogood — Dr. Toogood

1. Post Office Box 7 — P.O. Box 7
2. Barclay Road — Barclay Rd.
3. a woman named Nan Gray — Ms. Nan Gray
4. Highland Avenue — Highland Ave.
5. Mister Jeremy Krell — Mr. Jeremy Krell
6. Wednesday, May 7 — Wed., May 7
7. Morris Toll Senior — Morris Toll Sr.
8. a married woman named Trudy Floe — Mrs. (or Ms.) Trudy Floe
9. Saturday, July 10 — Sat., July 10
10. September 2 — Sept. 2
11. Lincoln Boulevard — Lincoln Blvd.
12. Wonderful Toy Company — Wonderful Toy Co.
13. Pedro Diegas Junior — Pedro Diegas Jr.
14. Doctor Norma Kusick — Dr. Norma Kusick
15. February 29 — Feb. 29
16. Shadow Street — Shadow St.
17. Thursday, June 11 — Thurs., June 11
18. Big Byte Company — Big Byte Co.

▲■ WORKBOOK PLUS, pages 80–81

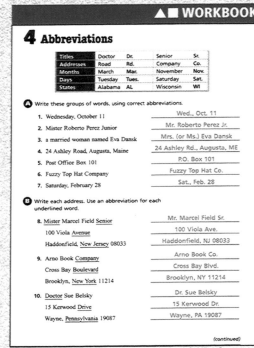

4 Abbreviations

Titles	Doctor	Dr.	Senior	Sr.
Addresses	Road	Rd.	Company	Co.
Months	March	Mar.	November	Nov.
Days	Tuesday	Tues.	Saturday	Sat.
States	Alabama	AL	Wisconsin	WI

A Write these groups of words, using correct abbreviations.

1. Wednesday, October 11 — Wed., Oct. 11
2. Mister Roberto Perez Junior — Mr. Roberto Perez Jr.
3. a married woman named Eva Dansk — Mrs. (or Ms.) Eva Dansk
4. 24 Ashley Road, Augusta, Maine — 24 Ashley Rd., Augusta, ME
5. Post Office Box 101 — P.O. Box 101
6. Fuzzy Top Hat Company — Fuzzy Top Hat Co.
7. Saturday, February 28 — Sat., Feb. 28

B Write each address. Use an abbreviation for each underlined word.

8. Mister Marcel Field Senior / 100 Viola Avenue / Haddonfield, New Jersey 08033 — Mr. Marcel Field Sr. / 100 Viola Ave. / Haddonfield, NJ 08033
9. Arno Book Company / Cross Bay Boulevard / Brooklyn, New York 11214 — Arno Book Co. / Cross Bay Blvd. / Brooklyn, NY 11214
10. Doctor Sue Belsky / 15 Kerwood Drive / Wayne, Pennsylvania 19087 — Dr. Sue Belsky / 15 Kerwood Dr. / Wayne, PA 19087

(continued)

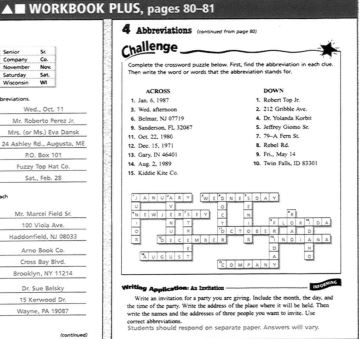

4 Abbreviations (continued from page 80)

Challenge

Complete the crossword puzzle below. First, find the abbreviation in each clue. Then write the word or words that the abbreviation stands for.

ACROSS
1. Jan. 6, 1987
3. Wed. afternoon
6. Belmar, NJ 07719
9. Sanderson, FL 32087
11. Oct. 22, 1980
12. Dec. 15, 1971
13. Gary, IN 46401
14. Aug. 2, 1989
15. Kiddie Kite Co.

DOWN
1. Robert Top Jr.
2. 212 Gribble Ave.
4. Dr. Yolanda Korbit
5. Jeffrey Giomo Sr.
7. 79–A Fern St.
8. Rebel Rd.
9. Fri., May 14
10. Twin Falls, ID 83301

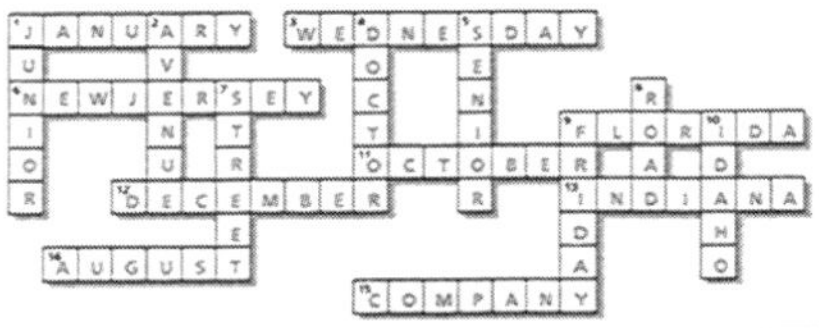

Writing Application: An Invitation — INFORMING

Write an invitation for a party you are giving. Include the month, the day, and the time of the party. Write the address of the place where it will be held. Then write the names and the addresses of three people you want to invite. Use correct abbreviations.

Students should respond on separate paper. Answers will vary.

Commas in a Series

Lesson Objectives

Students will:

- use commas to separate items in a series correctly
- proofread for missing commas or those placed incorrectly
- write a story, using serial commas correctly

One-Minute Warm-Up On the board, write the first part of the sentence: *His mother prepared* ______. Provide volunteers with an index card on which a comma is written. Have volunteers read the sentence part aloud, completing it with a series of nouns. Have them hold up the comma card each time a comma should be inserted after a word.

Focus on Instruction

Point out that each item in a series may be one word or more than one word.

Try It Out

LISTENING AND SPEAKING Have volunteers read the sentences aloud. Instruct students to raise their hand whenever they hear a pause where a comma should be placed.

FOR STUDENTS ACQUIRING ENGLISH

- Have students listen to the Try It Out sentences on the audiotape. Distribute SAE Practice page for Unit 5, Lesson 5, to support listening.
- Help students suggest sentences about the boy in the photograph. Ask what they think he is doing. As needed, explain that he is looking for gold and that this process is called panning. Ask students where they think gold is found in the United States. Briefly discuss the California and Alaska Gold Rushes. List vocabulary; explain as needed. Students listen and add commas to sentences.
  1. Ana Mary and Paula went shopping. (Ana, Mary, Paula)
  2. Mary bought a skirt a blouse and shoes. (a skirt, a blouse, and shoes)

Mechanics

5 Commas in a Series

One-Minute Warm-Up

Read the sentence aloud. When do you pause? Why?

His mother prepared warm flour tortillas, fried eggs, and fresh salsa for breakfast. after the name of each food; the commas tell you to pause

—from *Carlos and the Skunk/Carlos y el zorrillo*, by Jan Romero Stevens

- When you talk, you often pause briefly as you speak. When you write, you must use a comma (,) to tell your reader where to pause. Commas help make the meaning of your sentences clear.

Incorrect: Alexa bought oatmeal bread cheese and nuts.
Colin likes to ski swim or play tennis.

- How many things did Alexa buy? How many sports does Colin enjoy? Commas are needed to separate the items in each sentence. **When you list three or more words in a sentence, the list is called a series.** Use the word *and* or *or* before the last item in the series. Place a comma after each item except the last one.

Correct: Alexa bought oatmeal, bread, cheese, and nuts.
Alexa bought oatmeal bread, cheese, and nuts.
Colin likes to ski, swim, or play tennis.

Try It Out

Speak Up Where are commas needed?

1. Gold is found in California, Idaho, and Georgia.
2. Tim, Kara, and David are learning to pan for gold.
3. Tim watches men, women, and children standing in a stream.
4. They scoop, shovel, or toss dirt into a pan.
5. Then they sift, shake, and slosh the gravel.
6. Pebbles, sand, and gold are left in the pan.
7. Panning for gold is muddy, wet, and tiring work.

Meeting Individual Needs

RETEACHING
ALTERNATIVE STRATEGY

- Write *I see, and,* and two commas, each on a separate index card.
- Display a book and a pen, placing the *I see* card before them and the *and* card between them. Point out the number of items. (two)
- Add a pencil before the *and* card. Add a comma card after the book and after the pencil. Tell students that a comma always appears after every item except the last one in a series of three or more. Have students use other items to make similar displays.

CHALLENGE

Have students create sentences with a series that can be punctuated in more than one way. (macaroni salad; macaroni, salad) Have students exchange papers and determine the other way to punctuate each sentence.

FOR STUDENTS ACQUIRING ENGLISH

Set up groups of three or more objects. Write and say what you have. Ask a student to mark the commas with colored chalk. Show students how to make the comma and point out that it is different from the apostrophe used in contractions (placement next to, but above, letters).

On Your Own

Write these sentences correctly. Add commas where they are needed.

Example: Sarah Andy and Kristin learned about the Gold Rush.
Sarah, Andy, and Kristin learned about the Gold Rush.

8. They read, studied, and took notes.
9. Could anyone get rich with just a shovel, a pan, and a dream?
10. Farmers, teachers, and shopkeepers hoped so!
11. They headed west from Ohio, Virginia, and New York.
12. Many others came from Asia, Europe, and Australia.
13. The students wrote, practiced, and performed a play about the Gold Rush.
14. Their friends, family, and teachers watched the play.
15. They clapped, cheered, and whistled when it was over.

16–22. This part of an encyclopedia article has seven missing or incorrect commas. Write the article correctly.

Example: People left families friends, and jobs, to find gold.
People left families, friends, and jobs to find gold.

Proofreading

THE GOLD RUSH

Newspapers in Boston, New York, and Philadelphia told amazing stories about the gold in California. People sailed, rode, or walked to the region. They lived in tents, huts, and shacks. Few became rich. Some suffered, starved, and died. Others quit, packed up, and left. However, many people stayed. They became storekeepers, farmers, and, teachers.

Writing Wrap-Up

WRITING • THINKING • LISTENING • SPEAKING

NARRATING

Write a Story

Gold has been discovered on the moon. Write about joining the gold rush. Include sentences with a series of three or more words. Read your story to a group. Pause when you come to a comma. Work together to make sure all commas are in the right places.

For Extra Practice see page 198.

Summing Up Help students summarize these key points about the lesson:

> A **series** is a list of three or more items. Use commas to separate the items in a series. Put a comma after each item in the series except the last one.

You may want to have students complete the parts related to this lesson on Blackline Master 5–4.

On Your Own

Have students softly say each sentence to determine where they would pause. Remind them that in writing, each pause would be a comma.

MEETING INDIVIDUAL NEEDS

FOR STUDENTS ACQUIRING ENGLISH

Distribute SAE Practice page Unit 5, Lesson 5. Review vocabulary from the discussion on the Gold Rush. Then students add commas to sentences.
Example: The miners looked for gold silver and copper. (gold, silver, and copper)

Writing Wrap-Up

Writing Tip: Suggest that students tell what they might see on their trip or when they arrive on the moon. See Blackline Master 5–8 for a sample story.

TECHNOLOGY CONNECTION

Students may want to use available software to add clip art to their stories.

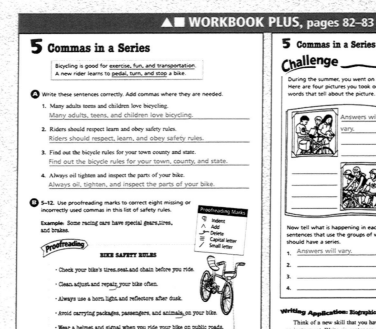

● RETEACHING WORKBOOK, page 50

5 Commas in a Series

- A **series** is a list of three or more items.
- Put a **comma** (,) after each item in a series except the last one.
  Sam packs bread, cheese, and nuts.
  I buy, carry, and load the groceries.

Write each sentence correctly. Add commas to each underlined series.

Example: Terry Helga and Dino work in Powell's grocery store.
Terry, Helga, and Dino work in Powell's grocery store.

1. The children sweep wash and wax the floors.
   The children sweep, wash, and wax the floors.
2. They count unpack and stack boxes of food.
   They count, unpack, and stack boxes of food.
3. They also deliver carry and fill grocery bags.
   They also deliver, carry, and fill grocery bags.
4. Dino rinses sorts and stacks the vegetables.
   Dino rinses, sorts, and stacks the vegetables.
5. Apples oranges and bananas have to be weighed.
   Apples, oranges, and bananas have to be weighed.
6. Crates cans and boxes must be moved into the store.
   Crates, cans, and boxes must be moved into the store.
7. This store sells grain nuts and flour by the pound.
   This store sells grain, nuts, and flour by the pound.
8. Men women and children in the neighborhood like Powell's store.
   Men, women, and children in the neighborhood like Powell's store.

▲■ WORKBOOK PLUS, pages 82–83

5 Commas in a Series

Bicycling is good for exercise, fun, and transportation.
A new rider learns to pedal, turn, and stop a bike.

A Write these sentences correctly. Add commas where they are needed.

1. Many adults teens and children love bicycling.
   Many adults, teens, and children love bicycling.
2. Riders should respect learn and obey safety rules.
   Riders should respect, learn, and obey safety rules.
3. Find out the bicycle rules for your town county and state.
   Find out the bicycle rules for your town, county, and state.
4. Always oil tighten and inspect the parts of your bike.
   Always oil, tighten, and inspect the parts of your bike.

B 5–12. Use proofreading marks to correct eight missing or incorrectly used commas in this list of safety rules.

Example: Some racing cars have special gears, tires, and brakes.

Proofreading Marks
¶ Indent
∧ Add
Delete
≡ Capital letter
/ Small letter

Proofreading

BIKE SAFETY RULES

- Check your bike's tires, seat, and chain before you ride.
- Clean, adjust, and repair, your bike often.
- Always use a horn, light, and reflectors after dusk.
- Avoid carrying packages, passengers, and animals, on your bike.
- Wear a helmet and signal when you ride your bike on public roads.

(continued)

5 Commas in a Series (continued from page 82)

Challenge

During the summer, you went on a bicycle trip with the Bicycle Buzzards Club. Here are four pictures you took on your trip. Beside each picture, write three words that tell about the picture.

Now tell what is happening in each picture in your photo album. Write sentences that use the groups of words you wrote above. Each sentence should have a series.

1. Answers will vary.
2.
3.
4.

Writing Application: Biographical Nonfiction EXPLAINING

Think of a new skill that you have learned, such as fishing, sewing, or playing an instrument. Write six sentences about how you learned this skill. Use a series of three words in each sentence.
Students should respond on separate paper. Answers will vary.

Writing Good Sentences

Lesson Objective

Students will:

- combine sentences by joining single words in a series

Focus on Instruction

- Point out to students that whenever three or more words are listed in a series, they should be the same kind of word—all nouns, all adjectives, all verbs. Write the examples below on the board and discuss.

  We bought apples, grapes, and bananas at the store. (nouns)

  Old, rare, and handmade items are sold at the flea market. (adjectives)

  Zach always smells, squeezes, and examines a piece of fruit before buying it. (verbs)

- Point out that a comma follows each word in the series except the last word, and *and* follows the last comma.

Apply It

Have students do the revising activity independently.

MEETING INDIVIDUAL NEEDS: If some students need extra support, have them work with partners to identify and record the three similar sentences. Then suggest that they cross out the identical words in the sentences and combine the remaining words in a series.

Have students look in their writing in progress to find sentences that can be combined by joining single words in a series.

Sample Answers to Apply It

1. For example, they traded with shells, feathers, and plants.
2. Scarce, beautiful, and useful objects were used as money.
3. Gold can be molded, hammered, and bent.
4. Other metals dulled, darkened, and weathered.

FOR STUDENTS ACQUIRING ENGLISH

Write the sentences below on the board. Show how to join the first set. Have students join the second set. Example: *The mint gets old coins. It melts them. It makes new ones.* (The mint gets old coins, melts them, and makes new ones.)

Revising Strategies

Writing Good Sentences

Combining Sentences to Make a Series You know that a list of three or more words in a sentence is called a series. Sometimes you can combine short, choppy sentences by joining single words in a series.

Since ancient times, money has been earned. It has been spent. It has been saved.	Since ancient times, money has been earned, spent, and saved.

Remember to use a comma after each word in a series, except the last one.

Apply It

1–4. Rewrite the report on this poster. Combine each underlined set of sentences into one new sentence. See TE margin for answers.

Revising

From Feathers to Gold: The History of Money

Long ago, people used objects from nature as money. For example, they traded with shells. They traded with feathers. They traded with plants. They didn't use just any item. Scarce objects were used as money. Beautiful objects were used as money. Useful objects were used as money.

When people made the first coins about 2,700 years ago, they used gold. Gold was rare, and it stayed beautiful forever. Gold can be molded. It can be hammered. It can be bent. Ancient people knew that gold coins would always be valuable. Other metals dulled. They darkened. They weathered.

178 Unit 5: Capitalization and Punctuation

Meeting Individual Needs

● RETEACHING WORKBOOK, page 51

Writing Good Sentences

- Combine short, choppy sentences by joining single words in a series. Use a comma after each word in a series, except the last one.

Choppy sentences	Howard opens the store. He runs the store. He closes the store.
Combined sentence	Howard opens, runs, and closes the store.

Combining Sentences to Make a Series Combine each set of sentences into one new sentence by joining single words in a series.

Example: Howard waited on customers. Danny waited on customers. Keesha waited on customers.
Howard, Danny, and Keesha waited on customers.

Revising

1. Howard stocks the shelves. He cleans the shelves. He orders the shelves.
   Howard stocks, cleans, and orders the shelves.
2. Many people look for tools. Many people look for paint. Many people look for brushes.
   Many people look for tools, paint, and brushes.
3. Howard sells rakes. He sells shovels. He sells plants.
   Howard sells rakes, shovels, and plants.
4. A new worker sweeps the store. He cleans the store. He closes the store.
   A new worker sweeps, cleans, and closes the store.
5. Many tourists buy surfboards. They buy chairs. They buy visors.
   Many tourists buy surfboards, chairs, and visors.
6. In winter, Howard's son fixes shovels. He fixes tires. He fixes windows.
   In winter, Howard's son fixes shovels, tires, and windows.
7. Anya sorts the nails. Danny sorts the nails. Keesha sorts the nails.
   Anya, Danny, and Keesha sort the nails.

(continued)

▲■ WORKBOOK PLUS, page 84

Writing Good Sentences

Choppy sentences	Deer live in fields. Deer live in meadows. Deer live in woods.
Combined sentence	Deer live in fields, meadows, and woods.

Combining Sentences to Make a Series 1–5. Rewrite each underlined set of sentences in this report as one new sentence.

Revising

Bison belong to the same family as sheep. They belong to the same family as goats. Bison belong to the same family as cattle. Bison are also called buffalo. They have large heads and a hump between their shoulders. Bison's heads are covered by long, shaggy fur. Their necks are covered by long, shaggy fur. Their shoulders are covered by long, shaggy fur. Bison eat grass. Bison eat twigs. Bison eat leaves.

In the past, Native Americans hunted bison. They used every part of the animal. They used the bison's hide. They used the bison's meat. They used the bison's bones.

Today, bison are bred in zoos and on ranches. Then they are released into parks and refuges. Buffalo roam in parks in Wyoming. They roam in parks in Montana. They roam in parks in Canada.

1. Bison belong to the same family as sheep, goats, and cattle.
2. Bison's heads, necks, and shoulders are covered by long, shaggy fur.
3. Bison eat grass, twigs, and leaves.
4. They used the bison's hide, meat, and bones.
5. Buffalo roam in parks in Wyoming, Montana, and Canada.

(continued)

You know how to combine sentences by joining single words in a series. You can also join groups of words, or phrases, in a series.

The United States Mint collects worn-out coins. It melts them down. It makes new coins from the metal.	The United States Mint collects worn-out coins, melts them down, and makes new coins from the metal.

Apply It

5–8. Rewrite this part of a book report. Combine each set of underlined sentences into one sentence. See TE margin for answers.

Revising

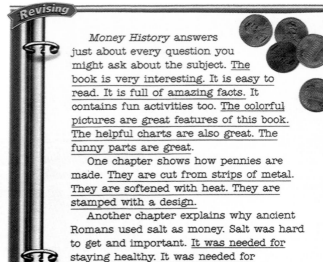

Money History answers just about every question you might ask about the subject. The book is very interesting. It is easy to read. It is full of amazing facts. It contains fun activities too. The colorful pictures are great features of this book. The helpful charts are also great. The funny parts are great.

One chapter shows how pennies are made. They are cut from strips of metal. They are softened with heat. They are stamped with a design.

Another chapter explains why ancient Romans used salt as money. Salt was hard to get and important. It was needed for staying healthy. It was needed for seasoning food. It was needed for keeping food from spoiling.

If you have any interest in money, read this book. It's fascinating!

Lesson Objective

Students will:

- combine sentences by joining phrases in a series

Focus on Instruction

- Point out to students that when three or more phrases are listed in a series, they should have the same structure. Write the examples below on the board and discuss.

  The squirrel dug a hole, found a nut, and ate it. (verb phrases)

  The colorful decorations, lively music, and tasty food made the party fun. (noun phrases)

  Daily exercise is known for improving circulation, for increasing energy levels, and for toning the skin. (prepositional phrases)

- Point out that a comma follows the last word in each phrase except the last phrase. Explain that the word *and* should follow the last comma.

Apply It

Have students complete the revising activity independently.

If some students need extra support, have them work with partners to identify and record the three similar sentences. Then suggest that they cross out the identical words in the sentences and combine the remaining phrases in a series.

Have students find places in their own writing in progress where they can combine sentences by joining phrases in a series.

Answers to Apply It

5. The book is very interesting, easy to read, and full of amazing facts.
6. The colorful pictures, helpful charts, and funny parts are great features of this book.
7. They are cut from strips of metal, softened with heat, and stamped with a design.
8. It was needed for staying healthy, seasoning food, and keeping food from spoiling.

● RETEACHING WORKBOOK, page 52

Writing Good Sentences *(continued from page 51)*

- Combine short, choppy sentences by joining groups of words in a series.

Choppy sentences	Gigi Agnello cooks with apples. Mr. Choi cooks with apples. Ms. Perez cooks with apples.
Combined sentence	Gigi Agnello, Mr. Choi, and Ms. Perez cook with apples.

Combining Sentences to Make a Series Rewrite each group of sentences as one sentence.

Example: Gigi peels the apples. Gigi removes the cores. Gigi slices the fruit.
Gigi peels the apples, removes the cores, and slices the fruit.

Revising

8. Mr. Jones has apple trees. Mr. Jones has peach trees. Mr. Jones has rose bushes.
   Mr. Jones has apple trees, peach trees, and rose bushes.
9. He picks the fruit. He puts it in baskets. He takes it home.
   He picks the fruit, puts it in baskets, and takes it home.
10. Gigi likes to make applesauce. Gigi likes to bake apple pies. Gigi likes to put apples in salads.
    Gigi likes to make applesauce, bake apple pies, and put apples in salads.
11. Mr. Choi bakes apple pies. Mr. Choi bakes bread. Mr. Choi bakes spice cake.
    Mr. Choi bakes apple pies, bread, and spice cake.
12. The Perez children like apples. Their parents like apples. Their cousins like apples.
    The Perez children, their parents, and their cousins like apples.
13. Roadside stands sell fresh apples. They sell apple cider. They sell caramel apples.
    Roadside stands sell fresh apples, apple cider, and caramel apples.
14. Apples grow in the United States. Apples grow in South America. Apples grow in New Zealand.
    Apples grow in the United States, South America, and New Zealand.

▲■ WORKBOOK PLUS, page 85

Writing Good Sentences *(continued from page 84)*

Choppy sentences	Bluestem bunchgrass grows on the plains. Thin needlegrass grows on the plains. Tough wire grass grows on the plains.
Combined sentence	Bluestem bunchgrass, thin needlegrass, **and** tough wire grass grow on the plains.

Combining Sentences to Make a Series 6–10. Rewrite each set of underlined sentences in this video script as one sentence.

Revising

NARRATOR: The bison's habitat is the grassland of the Great Plains, but bison are not the only animals on the grasslands. Pronghorn antelope live there. Prairie dogs live there. Several kinds of rabbit live there too. Don't let the name "grassland" fool you. There are other plants besides grasses. Berry bushes grow in bison country. Small aspen trees grow in bison country. Wild roses grow in bison country. Many species of birds also live on the plains. There are prairie falcons. There are American kestrels. There are two kinds of owl. People have settled there too. Spanish colonists have lived there. Native Americans have lived there. Other settlers have lived there. Nowadays, residents of the Great Plains make a living from grain farming. They make a living from cattle ranching. They make a living from mineral products.

6. Pronghorn antelope, prairie dogs, and several kinds of rabbit live there too.
7. Berry bushes, small aspen trees, and wild roses grow in bison country.
8. There are prairie falcons, American kestrels, and two kinds of owl.
9. Spanish colonists, Native Americans, and other settlers have lived there.
10. Nowadays, residents of the Great Plains make a living from grain farming, cattle ranching, and mineral products.

More Uses for Commas

Lesson Objectives

Students will:
- use commas after the introductory words *yes, no,* and *well*
- use commas to set off names of people being addressed
- proofread for missing commas
- write a persuasive plan, including sentences containing names and introductory words

One-Minute Warm-Up Ask students why it makes sense to set off *Allie* and *Well* with commas. (A speaker naturally pauses after these words.) Then ask where students would place the comma if *Allie* were moved to the beginning of the sentence (after *Allie*) or within the sentence (before and after *Allie*).

Focus on Instruction

Tell students that if they are unsure whether to set off a name or word with a comma, they should read the sentence without the word or name. If the sentence still makes sense, they should use commas.

Try It Out

LISTENING AND SPEAKING Have volunteers read the sentences aloud, clapping their hands to show the placement of commas. Have students explain why they placed the commas where they did.

FOR STUDENTS ACQUIRING ENGLISH
- Have students listen to the Try It Out sentences on the audiotape. Distribute SAE Practice page for Unit 5, Lesson 6, to support listening.
- First, help students understand the humor of the riddle. Write *bridle* and *bridal* on the board. Tell students these are homonyms, words that sound alike but have different meanings and spellings. Have volunteers explain the meanings. Then help students suggest sentences about the covered wagons in the photo. Ask when they think this photo was taken. Find out what students know about horses. Then students listen and add commas to sentences. Remind students to listen for pauses as clues.
  1. Ramón did you find your backpack? (Ramón,)
  2. No I didn't. (No,)

Mechanics

6 More Uses for Commas

One-Minute Warm-Up Read the riddle below. What punctuation mark should you add to the second sentence to make it correct?

Where did the horse get her wedding outfit, Allie?
Well,I guess she got it at the bridle shop.

- When you speak, you pause briefly if you begin the answer to a question with *yes, no,* or *well.* Use a comma after these words to show the pause in your writing.

  Yes, I gave the horse some oats.
  No, I haven't brushed his coat.
  Well, you can clean his hoofs tomorrow.

- Sometimes you use a person's name when you address, or speak directly to, that person. When you write, use a comma or commas to set off the name of the person who is being addressed.

  Mariko, are you going riding with us?
  We wondered, Mariko, which trail we should take.
  We're really happy that you're joining us, Mariko!

Try It Out

Speak Up Where are commas needed?
1. Ryan,have we always had horses in this country?
2. No,explorers brought them in the 1500s.
3. They left some horses here,Christopher.
4. Well,did many people use the horses?
5. Yes,the Plains Indians rode horses.
6. Later,Eric,horses pulled the pioneers' wagons.
7. Did you know,Christopher, that wild mustangs are small, hardy, and smart?
8. No,I didn't know that.
9. Well,they are. They descended from tame horses of settlers and Plains Indians.

Meeting Individual Needs

RETEACHING
ALTERNATIVE STRATEGY
- Display this sentence: *Yes, a comma tells you to pause between words.* Read the sentence, emphasizing the pause with a clap. Explain that a comma is placed after introductory words such as *yes, no,* or *well.*
- Write and read aloud this sentence, having students clap for the pause: *Joe, did you hear the pause?*
- Write other sentences that begin similarly, omitting the commas. As you read each sentence, stress the pause before having a student add the comma.

CHALLENGE
Have volunteers take turns asking a classmate the following question, clapping to show the placement of a comma. *[student name], do you like [item]?* The student addressed answers with a sentence beginning with *Yes, No,* or *Well* and clapping to show the comma.

FOR STUDENTS ACQUIRING ENGLISH
Ask students a series of yes-no questions. Use the student's name, pausing where the comma is placed. Write your question and the student's response on the board. Call on a student to mark the commas with colored chalk. Continue.

On Your Own

Write these sentences correctly. Add commas where they are needed.

Example: Have you heard of Chincoteague John?
Have you heard of Chincoteague, John?

10. Yes,it's an island off the coast of Virginia.
11. Well,herds of wild horses live there.
12. Roberto,have you read the book *Misty of Chincoteague*?
13. No,I haven't read it.
14. The book,Jillian,tells about a pony from that island.
15. Joshua,do you know where the ponies came from?
16. No,where did they come from?
17. Well,some people say a ship was wrecked in a storm.
18. The ship was carrying some ponies,Marcos.
19. Each year,Megan,the ponies are rounded up.
20. Yes,they swim to a nearby island.

21–28. This part of a script has eight missing commas. Write the script correctly.

Example: Dad the wild horses need help! *Dad, the wild horses need help!*

Proofreading — document

Mark: You know, Dad, about the wild horses out West. Well,there isn't enough grass for them to eat.
Dad: That's a serious problem, Mark.
Mark: Yes,I agree. Dad,the government wants people to adopt these horses.
Dad: I know what's coming next,Mark. No,we can't have a horse in the city.
Mark: Wait,Dad,until I tell you my plan!

Writing Wrap-Up

WRITING • THINKING • LISTENING • SPEAKING

PERSUADING

Write a Persuasive Plan

Write a plan to convince Mark's father to adopt a horse. Include names and the words *well, yes,* and *no* in some sentences. Use commas correctly. Share your plan with a partner. Is it convincing?

For Extra Practice see page 199.

Summing Up Help students summarize these key points about the lesson:

> Use a comma to set off the words *yes, no,* and *well* when they are at the beginning of a sentence. Use a comma to set off the names of people who are addressed directly.

You may want to have students complete the parts related to this lesson on Blackline Master 5–4.

On Your Own

Tell students to read the entire sentence through at least once before adding commas.

MEETING INDIVIDUAL NEEDS

FOR STUDENTS ACQUIRING ENGLISH

Distribute SAE Practice page Unit 5, Lesson 6. Have students talk about the drawing. Discuss vocabulary relating to horses. Students may want to label the drawings. Students add commas to a conversation about horses. Example: Sam do you ride horses? (Sam,) Yes I have ridden for six years. (Yes,)

Writing Wrap-Up

Writing Tip: Suggest that students make a list of logical reasons why Mark's father should adopt a horse. See Blackline Master 5–8 for a sample persuasive plan.

TECHNOLOGY CONNECTION

Students might want to use available software to create their plans, using a large font that is easy to read.

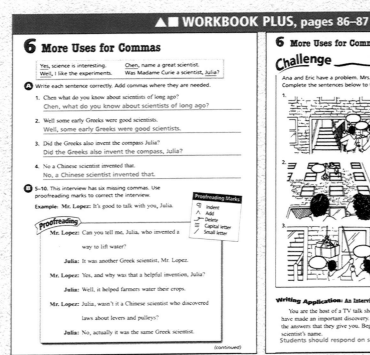

● RETEACHING WORKBOOK, page 53

6 More Uses for Commas

- Use a comma to set off the words *yes, no,* and *well* when they are at the beginning of a sentence.
- Use a comma or commas to set off the name of a person you are speaking to directly.

Yes, the library is open. Aki, will you come too?
Well, we can go inside. I will, Marta, after lunch.

Write each sentence correctly. Use commas to set off the underlined words.

Example: Marta what do you like best about the library?
Marta, what do you like best about the library?

1. It's hard to decide what I like best Aki.
   It's hard to decide what I like best, Aki.
2. Well I guess the books and the records are my favorites.
   Well, I guess the books and the records are my favorites.
3. No I like using the computer best.
   No, I like using the computer best.
4. Yes the computer is fun!
   Yes, the computer is fun!
5. I always find the books I want Marta at the library.
   I always find the books I want, Marta, at the library.
6. There is always someone to help you Aki.
   There is always someone to help you, Aki.
7. Marta do your parents use the library?
   Marta, do your parents use the library?
8. Yes they hear speakers and go to meetings there.
   Yes, they hear speakers and go to meetings there.

▲■ WORKBOOK PLUS, pages 86–87

6 More Uses for Commas

Yes, science is interesting. Chen, name a great scientist.
Well, I like the experiments. Was Madame Curie a scientist, Julia?

A Write each sentence correctly. Add commas where they are needed.

1. Chen what do you know about scientists of long ago?
   Chen, what do you know about scientists of long ago?
2. Well some early Greeks were good scientists.
   Well, some early Greeks were good scientists.
3. Did the Greeks also invent the compass Julia?
   Did the Greeks also invent the compass, Julia?
4. No a Chinese scientist invented that.
   No, a Chinese scientist invented that.

B 5–10. This interview has six missing commas. Use proofreading marks to correct the interview.

Example: **Mr. Lopez:** It's good to talk with you, Julia.

Proofreading Marks
¶ Indent
∧ Add
Delete
≡ Capital letter
/ Small letter

Proofreading

Mr. Lopez: Can you tell me, Julia, who invented a way to lift water?
Julia: It was another Greek scientist, Mr. Lopez.
Mr. Lopez: Yes, and why was that a helpful invention, Julia?
Julia: Well, it helped farmers water their crops.
Mr. Lopez: Julia, wasn't it a Chinese scientist who discovered laws about levers and pulleys?
Julia: No, actually it was the same Greek scientist.

(continued)

6 More Uses for Commas (continued from page 86)

Challenge

Ana and Eric have a problem. Mrs. Blake helps them solve their problem. Complete the sentences below to tell what Ana, Eric, and Mrs. Blake are saying.

1.

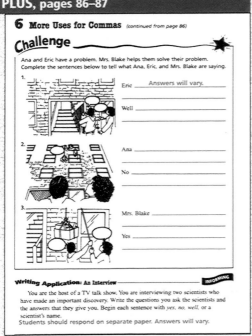

Eric Answers will vary.
Well

2.

Ana
No

3.

Mrs. Blake
Yes

Writing Application: An Interview INFORMING

You are the host of a TV talk show. You are interviewing two scientists who have made an important discovery. Write the questions you ask the scientists and the answers that they give you. Begin each sentence with *yes, no, well,* or a scientist's name.
Students should respond on separate paper. Answers will vary.

Quotation Marks

Lesson Objectives

Students will:

- identify direct quotations in sentences
- use quotation marks before and after a direct quotation
- understand the difference between direct and indirect quotations
- proofread for missing or incorrect quotation marks
- write a conversation, using direct quotations

One-Minute Warm-Up Ask students why it is important to use quotation marks around a direct quotation. (so that the reader knows exactly what the speaker said)

Focus on Instruction

Explain to students that the main point of this lesson is to identify direct quotations in sentences. Further explain that the capitalization and punctuation of direct quotations will be covered in the next lesson.

Try It Out

LISTENING AND SPEAKING Have volunteers read aloud the sentences. Tell students to raise their hands when they hear a sentence that contains a speaker's exact words. Then have students tell which words should be enclosed in quotation marks.

FOR STUDENTS ACQUIRING ENGLISH

- Have students listen to the Try It Out sentences on the audiotape. Distribute SAE Practice page for Unit 5, Lesson 7, to support listening.
- Remind students that quotation marks show a speaker's exact words. Contrast beginning and end quotation marks with the apostrophe. Have each student write a line of dialogue, add punctuation, and mark quotations. Then have them add the speaker's name, *asked* or *said,* and a period. Explain they cannot use *told* unless they also have an object. Number and explain each of the elements; then discuss variations in order of the elements. Students listen and add quotation marks.
  1. John said, Good morning! ("Good morning!")
  2. When can we go? asked Mary. ("When can we go?")

Mechanics 7

Quotation Marks

One-Minute Warm-Up

Read the sentence below. What did the cat say? How can you tell? What a glorious supper. Quotation marks show a speaker's exact words.

"What a glorious supper!" said the Cat.

—from *Fables,* by Arnold Lobel

- Sometimes you may want to write a conversation between two or more people. **When you write the exact words that a speaker says, you are writing a direct quotation.**
- A direct quotation can come at the beginning or at the end of a sentence. Use **quotation marks** (" ") before and after a speaker's exact words. Do not place quotation marks around the words that explain who is talking.

  Ali asked, "Have you read about the fox and the grapes?"
  "That's my favorite fable!" I exclaimed.

- Do not use quotation marks unless you give the exact words of the speaker.

  Mr. Stuart said that we would write fables today.
  Mr. Stuart said, "Today we will write fables."

Try It Out

Speak Up Which sentences need quotation marks? Where should they be placed?

1. Ms. Diaz asked,"Have you read Aesop's fables?"
2. "I've read them all!"Nick exclaimed.
3. James explained that the characters are talking animals. correct
4. Melissa told us that each story teaches a lesson. correct
5. "Aesop lived over two thousand years ago,"Kelly added.
6. "He was captured by pirates and taken to Greece,"she said.
7. Kelly explained that Aesop worked in a court of law. correct
8. "Many of his stories were used to make a point in court,"she said.

182 **Unit 5:** Capitalization and Punctuation

Meeting Individual Needs

RETEACHING
ALTERNATIVE STRATEGY

- Have students use a sentence to name their favorite animal character in a story. Write a response in this form: *Tina said, "I like Tigger."* Ask which words tell exactly what Tina said. *(I like Tigger.)* Point out that quotation marks enclose the speaker's exact words.
- Then write *"I like Tigger," said Tina.* Have a volunteer underline the exact words of the speaker. *(I like Tigger.)* Explain that the exact words of the speaker should be set off with quotation marks regardless of where they appear in the sentence.

CHALLENGE
Have students choose a famous person they would like to meet and write a short, imaginary conversation with that person. Remind students to use quotation marks when appropriate.

FOR STUDENTS ACQUIRING ENGLISH
Pairs of students write a dialogue asking about a homework assignment or planning a weekend event. Use one of the dialogues as a model for punctuation; add quotation marks and *[student name] said.* Help partners revise punctuation.

On Your Own

Write each sentence. Add quotation marks where they are needed. Write *correct* for those sentences that do not need quotation marks.

Example: Who knows the fable of the crow? Kimi asked.
"Who knows the fable of the crow?" Kimi asked.

9. "I remember that one!"exclaimed Ashley.
10. Vanessa asked,"Do you remember what the crow wanted?"
11. "The crow was thirsty and wanted water,"answered Antonio.
12. Henry said,"Some water was at the bottom of the jar."
13. Brandon explained that the crow couldn't push the jar over. correct
14. "The crow filled the jar with pebbles,"Ashley added.
15. "Little by little the level of the water rose,"Ben said.
16. Kimi asked if we knew what lesson the fable teaches. correct

17–24. This part of a fable has eight missing or incorrect quotation marks. Write the fable correctly.

Example: I'll try hard, said the tortoise. *"I'll try hard," said the tortoise.*

Proofreading

"I'll win this race easily!" the hare bragged.
The tortoise replied,"We shall see."
The crowd yelled "that the hare was way ahead."
Then the hare announced, "I think I will stop for a little snooze."
The tortoise kept going until he crossed the finish line.
"Where is the hare?" he asked.
"The hare is still napping!"yelled the crowd.

Writing Wrap-Up

WRITING • THINKING • LISTENING • SPEAKING

NARRATING

Write a Conversation

Write a conversation between your favorite story characters. Use quotation marks correctly. Then read your conversation to a partner. Check that you used quotation marks correctly.

For Extra Practice see page 200.

Summing Up Help students summarize these key points about the lesson:

A **direct quotation** tells a speaker's exact words. Use quotation marks before and after a direct quotation.

You may want to have students complete the parts related to this lesson on Blackline Master 5–5.

On Your Own

Tell students to ask this question when deciding whether words in a sentence are a direct quotation:

Do the words tell exactly what the speaker said?

MEETING INDIVIDUAL NEEDS

FOR STUDENTS ACQUIRING ENGLISH

Distribute SAE Practice page for Unit 5, Lesson 7. Review by writing lines of dialogue and having students add punctuation, a name, and a verb. Then students add quotation marks to sentences as needed. Example: We have to write two paragraphs, John explained. ("We . . . paragraphs,")

Writing Wrap-Up

Writing Tip: Suggest that students write down information about each character before they write their conversation. The information will give clues about what a character might say. See Blackline Master 5–9 for a sample conversation.

TECHNOLOGY CONNECTION

Students may want to use available hardware to scan in pictures of their story characters.

● RETEACHING WORKBOOK, page 54

7 Quotation Marks

- A **direct quotation** tells a speaker's exact words.
- Use **quotation marks** (" ") before and after a direct quotation.

Jon asked, "Where is my butterfly book?"
"Here it is," Ezra said.

Write each sentence correctly. Add quotation marks where they are needed.

Example: Jon asked, Will you tell us about butterflies?
Jon asked, "Will you tell us about butterflies?"

1. Ezra said, Most butterflies have colorful wings.
Ezra said, "Most butterflies have colorful wings."
2. They fly around during the day, he added.
"They fly around during the day," he added.
3. Where do butterflies live? asked Kenya.
"Where do butterflies live?" asked Kenya.
4. They are found all over the world, Lucia answered.
"They are found all over the world," Lucia answered.
5. Ezra added, Some even live high in the mountains.
Ezra added, "Some even live high in the mountains."
6. Lucia said, Look at that black and orange butterfly.
Lucia said, "Look at that black and orange butterfly."
7. How beautiful it is! Jon exclaimed.
"How beautiful it is!" Jon exclaimed.
8. Ezra said, It will fly many miles to its winter home.
Ezra said, "It will fly many miles to its winter home."

▲■ WORKBOOK PLUS, pages 88–89

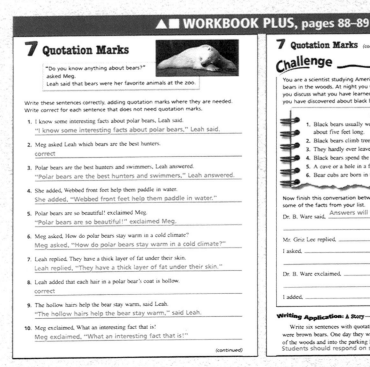

7 Quotation Marks

"Do you know anything about bears?" asked Meg.
Leah said that bears were her favorite animals at the zoo.

Write these sentences correctly, adding quotation marks where they are needed. Write *correct* for each sentence that does not need quotation marks.

1. I know some interesting facts about polar bears, Leah said.
"I know some interesting facts about polar bears," Leah said.
2. Meg asked Leah which bears are the best hunters.
correct
3. Polar bears are the best hunters and swimmers, Leah answered.
"Polar bears are the best hunters and swimmers," Leah answered.
4. She added, Webbed front feet help them paddle in water.
She added, "Webbed front feet help them paddle in water."
5. Polar bears are so beautiful! exclaimed Meg.
"Polar bears are so beautiful!" exclaimed Meg.
6. Meg asked, How do polar bears stay warm in a cold climate?
Meg asked, "How do polar bears stay warm in a cold climate?"
7. Leah replied, They have a thick layer of fat under their skin.
Leah replied, "They have a thick layer of fat under their skin."
8. Leah added that each hair in a polar bear's coat is hollow.
correct
9. The hollow hairs help the bear stay warm, said Leah.
"The hollow hairs help the bear stay warm," said Leah.
10. Meg exclaimed, What an interesting fact that is!
Meg exclaimed, "What an interesting fact that is!"

(continued)

7 Quotation Marks *(continued from page 88)*

Challenge

You are a scientist studying American black bears. Each day you watch the bears in the woods. At night you write notes about what you have seen, and you discuss what you have learned with other scientists. Here is a list of facts you have discovered about black bears.

BEAR FACTS

1. Black bears usually weigh up to three hundred pounds and are about five feet long.
2. Black bears climb trees when they are in danger.
3. They hardly ever leave the forest.
4. Black bears spend the winter in a den.
5. A cave or a hole in a fallen tree serves as a den.
6. Bear cubs are born in the den during the winter.

Now finish this conversation between you and the other scientists. Include some of the facts from your list.

Dr. B. Ware said, Answers will vary. ______.
______? asked Ms. Furr.
Mr. Griz Lee replied, ______.
I asked, ______?
______, Ms. Furr answered.
Dr. B. Ware exclaimed, ______!
______, said Mr. Griz Lee.
I added, ______.

Writing Application: A Story NARRATING

Write six sentences with quotations to finish this story: Bruno and Matilda were brown bears. One day they walked and walked. Suddenly they stepped out of the woods and into the parking lot of a giant mall. Bruno exclaimed, . . .
Students should respond on separate paper. Answers will vary.

Quotations

Lesson Objectives

Students will:

- capitalize the first word of a quotation
- use commas and end marks correctly in quotations
- proofread for missing or incorrect punctuation marks and missing capital letters
- write riddles containing quotations

One-Minute Warm-Up Have a volunteer read the sentence. Ask if what Emily is saying is a statement or a question. (question) Ask what kind of punctuation mark goes at the end of a question. (question mark) Then have students tell how to correct the sentence.

Focus on Instruction

Explain to students that when they write a direct quotation, they should think first about how they would punctuate the quotation before thinking about the entire sentence.

Try It Out

VIEWING Have four students pretend to be the birds in the picture. Have them discuss the food they are eating. Ask four other students to record the conversation on the board, using quotation marks and speaker tags. Then have students read the conversation, correcting any punctuation errors. (Sample responses are shown.)

Quotations
"These are yummy seeds," said Robin.
Jay yelled, "They sure are!"

FOR STUDENTS ACQUIRING ENGLISH

- Have students listen to the Try It Out sentences on the audiotape. Distribute SAE Practice page for Unit 5, Lesson 8, to support listening.
- Model pauses and intonation for quotations as students read along. Repeat, pointing out the pauses associated with commas, the drop in intonation for a period or *wh-* question, the rise for a yes-no question, and the extra stress for an exclamation. Call on students to read quotations aloud. Check for pauses and intonation. Students listen and add punctuation to quotations.
  1. "what time is it" asked Ana. ("What time is it?" asked Ana.)
  2. Richard shouted "give me the ball" (Richard shouted, "Give me the ball!")

Mechanics

8 Quotations

One-Minute Warm-Up

Read the sentence. What two punctuation marks should you switch to make the sentence correct?

"Does Polly want a cracker." Emily asked?
"Does Polly want a cracker?" Emily asked.

Quotation marks show a speaker's exact words. More punctuation marks, as well as capital letters, are needed to write quotations correctly.

- Always capitalize the first word of a quotation. When a quotation comes last in a sentence, use a comma to separate the quotation from the words that tell who is speaking. Put the end mark inside the last quotation marks.

  Brittany said, "All birds have feathers."
  Hideki asked, "Can all birds fly?"
  Lauren said, "Look at the tiny hummingbird."

- When a quotation that is a statement or a command comes first in a sentence, put a comma inside the last quotation marks. If the quotation is a question or an exclamation, put the question mark or the exclamation point inside the last quotation marks. A period always follows the last word in the sentence.

  "Say hello to Pauline," Renee suggested.
  "Pauline is a parrot!" I exclaimed.

Try It Out

Underlined letters should be capitalized.

Speak Up These sentences have quotations. How would you capitalize and punctuate each sentence?

1. Jay shouted, "there must be thirty birds here!"
2. Robin said, "I guess they like our bird feeder."
3. Polly added, "they're eating all the sunflower seeds."
4. "what kind of bird is that?" I asked.
5. "Look it up in our bird book," Robin said.
6. Jay exclaimed, "bird watching is a lot of fun!"

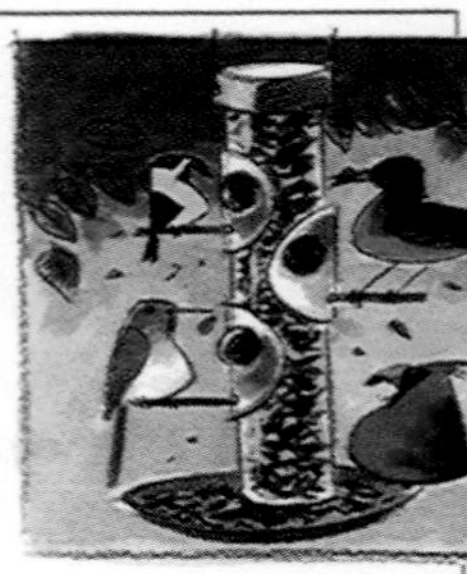

Meeting Individual Needs

RETEACHING
ALTERNATIVE STRATEGY

- Write this on a sentence strip: *"We were looking for you."* (Include the quotation marks.) On another strip write *Maria said.*
- Place the second strip in front of the first one, and add a comma after *said.* Tell students that the first word in a quotation begins with a capital letter and that a comma separates the quotation from the words that tell who is speaking.
- Move the second strip to the right of the first one and exchange the period with the comma. Explain the changes.

CHALLENGE

Have a student write on the board the first sentence of a dialogue, using his or her name in the speaker tag. Have a second student continue the dialogue, using direct quotations and a speaker tag. Have students continue the process until all students have added a sentence.

FOR STUDENTS ACQUIRING ENGLISH

Review by having pairs of students write a dialogue asking about a test, a sporting event, or a party. Remind students to use quotation marks and other punctuation. Have students role-play their dialogues.

On Your Own

These sentences have quotations. Write them correctly. Underlined letters should be capitalized.

Example: Lindsay asked how many kinds of birds are there
Lindsay asked, "How many kinds of birds are there?"

7. "there are over nine thousand kinds," Chan exclaimed.
8. "different birds live in different places," Erin added.
9. "have you seen my list of birds?" Felipe asked.
10. he explained, "I write down each kind of bird I see."
11. Lindsay asked, "why do you put different seeds on the ground?"
12. "all birds don't like the same food," Erin explained.
13. Chan said, "put out a pan of water too."

14–22. These riddles have six missing or incorrect punctuation marks and three missing capital letters. Write the riddles correctly. Underlined letters should be capitalized.

Example: Brian asked "is it an owl"? *Brian asked, "Is it an owl?"*

Proofreading

"what bird is always sad?" asked Heather.

Brian replied, "It's the bluebird, of course."

"Name the bird that writes the best," said Heather.

Brian exclaimed, "it must be the penguin!"

"What bird has an initial in its name?" Heather asked.

Brian responded, "could it be the blue jay?"

Writing Wrap-Up

WRITING • THINKING • LISTENING • SPEAKING

CREATING

Write Riddles

Write questions for two or three riddles about animals, plants, or food. Have a partner write the answers. Then write the riddles as conversations between you and your partner. Use correct punctuation. Then trade places. Read your conversations to the class.

For Extra Practice see page 201.

Summing Up Help students summarize these key points about the lesson:

> Begin a quotation with a capital letter. When a quotation comes at the end of a sentence, use a comma to separate the quotation from the words that tell who is speaking. Put end punctuation marks inside the last quotation marks.

You may want to have students complete the parts related to this lesson on Blackline Master 5–5.

On Your Own

If students are having trouble determining which punctuation marks to use, suggest that they cover up the name of the speaker and look only at the direct quotation.

MEETING INDIVIDUAL NEEDS

FOR STUDENTS ACQUIRING ENGLISH

Distribute SAE Practice page for Unit 5, Lesson 8. Show photos of wild birds common in your area. Have students describe them; assist with vocabulary. Then students add punctuation to quotations. Example: what kind of bird is that asked Jane ("What kind of bird is that?" asked Jane.)

Writing Wrap-Up

Writing Tip: Suggest to students that it is often helpful to think first of the answer to a riddle and then a clever question. See Blackline Master 5–9 for sample riddles.

SCHOOL-HOME CONNECTION

Have students share riddles with their families.

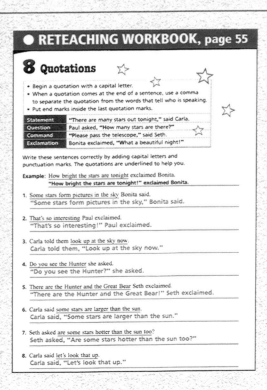

● RETEACHING WORKBOOK, page 55

8 Quotations

- Begin a quotation with a capital letter.
- When a quotation comes at the end of a sentence, use a comma to separate the quotation from the words that tell who is speaking.
- Put end marks inside the last quotation marks.

Statement	"There are many stars out tonight," said Carla.
Question	Paul asked, "How many stars are there?"
Command	"Please pass the telescope," said Seth.
Exclamation	Bonita exclaimed, "What a beautiful night!"

Write these sentences correctly by adding capital letters and punctuation marks. The quotations are underlined to help you.

Example: How bright the stars are tonight exclaimed Bonita.
"How bright the stars are tonight!" exclaimed Bonita.

1. Some stars form pictures in the sky Bonita said.
   "Some stars form pictures in the sky," Bonita said.
2. That's so interesting Paul exclaimed.
   "That's so interesting!" Paul exclaimed.
3. Carla told them look up at the sky now.
   Carla told them, "Look up at the sky now."
4. Do you see the Hunter she asked.
   "Do you see the Hunter?" she asked.
5. There are the Hunter and the Great Bear Seth exclaimed.
   "There are the Hunter and the Great Bear!" Seth exclaimed.
6. Carla said some stars are larger than the sun.
   Carla said, "Some stars are larger than the sun."
7. Seth asked are some stars hotter than the sun too?
   Seth asked, "Are some stars hotter than the sun too?"
8. Carla said let's look that up.
   Carla said, "Let's look that up."

▲■ WORKBOOK PLUS, pages 90–91

8 Quotations

Statement	"I have gone up in a balloon," Faith said.
Question	Dom asked, "What is it like to go up in a balloon?"
Command	Pia said, "Tell us about it."
Exclamation	"I can't wait to hear!" Dom exclaimed.

A These sentences have quotations. Write each sentence correctly.

1. ballooning is such an adventure Faith exclaimed
   "Ballooning is such an adventure!" Faith exclaimed.
2. tell me how the balloon works said Pia
   "Tell me how the balloon works," said Pia.
3. Pia asked do people race balloons
   Pia asked, "Do people race balloons?"
4. Dom exclaimed I think balloon racing would be great
   Dom exclaimed, "I think balloon racing would be great!"

B 5–12. This part of a story based on a historical event has eight errors in punctuation and capitalization. Use proofreading marks to correct the story.

Proofreading

Proofreading Marks: ¶ Indent; ^ Add; Delete; ≡ Capital letter; / Small letter

The True Story of Three Farm Animals

In 1783, two French brothers sent a duck, a rooster, and a sheep up in a hot-air balloon.

"Are we in a giant canopy bed?" asked the sheep.

"What are those flames?" cried the duck.

"we're flying," or ! cried the sheep.

The rooster said, "we must be on a special mission from King Louis XVI. We are teaching humans to fly."

(continued)

8 Quotations (continued from page 90)

Challenge

Boris and Bertha are two hot-air balloons who have just escaped for an adventure of their own. Write a conversation between Boris and Bertha as they float across the countryside. Use a quotation in each sentence.

1. Answers will vary.
2.
3.
4.
5.
6.

Writing Application: A Dialogue NARRATING

You are riding in a balloon with a friend. You don't know exactly where you are. Write a conversation between you and your friend. Use a quotation in each sentence.

Students should respond on separate paper. Answers will vary.

Titles

Lesson Objectives

Students will:
- capitalize the first, last, and important words in a title
- underline a title to indicate italics
- proofread for titles capitalized incorrectly
- write summaries of books and magazines, writing their titles correctly

One-Minute Warm-Up Ask a volunteer to share his or her title. Write it on the board. Point to the first, last, and each important word in the title as you explain that each one is capitalized. Then have volunteers write additional titles, using correct capitalization.

Focus on Instruction

Explain to students that italics are a kind of type used by printers in which the letters slant to the right. Also tell them that underlining or italics set off a title from the other words in a sentence and prevent confusion for readers.

Try It Out

VIEWING Encourage students who are familiar with *Charlotte's Web* to discuss parts of the book they especially liked. Students can then suggest favorite books and list their titles on the board. (Sample responses are shown.) Have each student write the title of a favorite book and a brief paragraph explaining why reading the book was enjoyable.

Our Favorite Books
Charlotte's Web
Little House on the Prairie
Mr. Popper's Penguins

FOR STUDENTS ACQUIRING ENGLISH

- Have students listen to the Try It Out sentences on the audiotape. Distribute SAE Practice page for Unit 5, Lesson 9, to support listening.
- Have partners copy book titles. Remind students to capitalize only important words. (Choose books without capitals added to prepositions for design reasons.) Check correct use of capitals and lowercase. Write *italics* on the board. Show an example. Then make sure they understand why titles are sometimes in italics and sometimes underlined in writing. Students listen and add underlining and capital letters to titles. Example: ranger rick (Ranger Rick)

Mechanics

9 Titles

One-Minute Warm-Up Look at the picture. What do you think this book might be about? Make up an interesting title for the book. Answers will vary.

- When you write the title of a book, a magazine, or a newspaper, capitalize the first, the last, and each important word. Capitalize words like *and, in, of, to, a,* and *the* only when they are the first or last word in the title.

Danger on Midnight River	*Children of the Midnight Sun*	*News and Views*
The Old Man and His Door	*Boys' Life*	*The Fun Times*

- In print the titles of books, magazines, and newspapers are set off by *italics.* Since you cannot write in italics, always underline the title of a book, a magazine, or a newspaper.

Is Tom Sawyer your favorite book? I am reading the magazine Stone Soup.

Try It Out Titles are underlined once; letters to be capitalized, twice.

Speak Up How would you write these titles?

1. tracks in the wild
2. tales of a fourth grade nothing
3. the rooftop reporter
4. sports illustrated for kids
5. the real mcCoy
6. harbor town post
7. national geographic world
8. searching for velociraptor
9. harry potter and the sorcerer's stone
10. aladdin and the wonderful lamp

How would you write these sentences?

11. The chicago sun-times has great comics.
12. Is cricket a magazine?
13. Who wrote king of the wind?
14. Read a wrinkle in time.
15. Get walton weekly.
16. I read charlotte's web.

Meeting Individual Needs

RETEACHING
ALTERNATIVE STRATEGY

- Write this sentence on the board: *My mother reads The New York Times every day.* Explain that the underlined words are the name of a newspaper. Tell students that names of books, newspapers, and magazines must be underlined in writing.
- Ask students what else they notice about the title. (All the words begin with a capital letter.) Tell students that all important words in a title are capitalized, and the first and last words also begin with capitals.

CHALLENGE

Have students write the titles of their five favorite books, making sure to capitalize correctly. Compile a class list of favorite books.

FOR STUDENTS ACQUIRING ENGLISH

Hold up several books and have students point out the title. Discuss which words have capital letters. Keep in mind that rules for capital letters in titles vary in different languages. (For example, in Spanish, only the first word and proper names are capitalized.)

On Your Own

Write these sentences correctly. Titles are underlined once; letters to be capitalized, twice.

Example: An article in this week's village herald praised the new library.
An article in this week's Village Herald praised the new library.

17. The library is giving away the magazine calliope.
18. My little sister is reading jalapeño bagels.
19. It was on a shelf next to tea with milk.
20. I found an article for my report in neighborhood news.
21. I'm also using the book boss of the plains.
22. Did you read a book called poppy and rye?
23. I thought the book by the shores of silver lake was better.
24. Is cobblestone your favorite history magazine?

25–32. This ad has eight errors in titles. Write the ad correctly. Letters underlined twice should be capitalized.

Example: Perhaps you would enjoy Sarah, Plain And Tall.
Perhaps you would enjoy Sarah, Plain and Tall.

Proofreading

Would you like to read the Summer Of the Swans or The life and times of the Peanut? Maybe you'd prefer Arrow To the Sun or Orphan Train Rider. A New York Times report says that Wendy's Bookstore has books for everyone. You can also find magazines like highlights for children and Ranger Rick.

Wendy's Bookstore

Writing Wrap-Up

WRITING • THINKING • LISTENING • SPEAKING

SUMMARIZING

Write Summaries

On index cards, write the titles of books and magazines you like. Include a few sentences about each one. Then work with a partner to make sure your titles are written correctly. Next, decide what category each title belongs in, such as nature, mystery, or adventure, and arrange the cards by categories. File your cards in a class box.

For Extra Practice see page 202.

Summing Up Help students summarize these key points about the lesson:

> Capitalize the first, last, and each important word in the titles of books, magazines, or newspapers. Underline all titles.

You may want to have students complete the parts related to this lesson on Blackline Master 5–6.

On Your Own

Remind students that the first word of any title is capitalized even if the word is not an important one.

MEETING INDIVIDUAL NEEDS

FOR STUDENTS ACQUIRING ENGLISH

Distribute SAE Practice page for Unit 5, Lesson 9. Briefly review the rules for punctuation of book titles. Then students add punctuation to titles in sentences. Example: I loved the book the snowman. (I loved the book The Snowman.)

Writing Wrap-Up

Writing Tip: Remind students that a summary tells about a book in a few sentences; it does not retell the book. See Blackline Master 5–9 for sample summaries.

TECHNOLOGY CONNECTION

Students may want to create a class database to store their information.

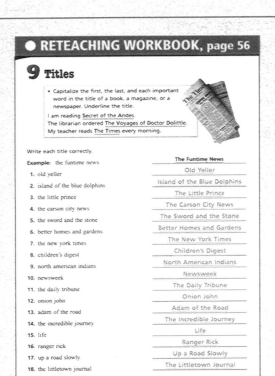

● RETEACHING WORKBOOK, page 56

9 Titles

- Capitalize the first, the last, and each important word in the title of a book, a magazine, or a newspaper. Underline the title.

I am reading Secret of the Andes.
The librarian ordered The Voyages of Doctor Dolittle.
My teacher reads The Times every morning.

Write each title correctly.

Example: the funtime news — The Funtime News

1. old yeller — Old Yeller
2. island of the blue dolphins — Island of the Blue Dolphins
3. the little prince — The Little Prince
4. the carson city news — The Carson City News
5. the sword and the stone — The Sword and the Stone
6. better homes and gardens — Better Homes and Gardens
7. the new york times — The New York Times
8. children's digest — Children's Digest
9. north american indians — North American Indians
10. newsweek — Newsweek
11. the daily tribune — The Daily Tribune
12. onion john — Onion John
13. adam of the road — Adam of the Road
14. the incredible journey — The Incredible Journey
15. life — Life
16. ranger rick — Ranger Rick
17. up a road slowly — Up a Road Slowly
18. the littletown journal — The Littletown Journal

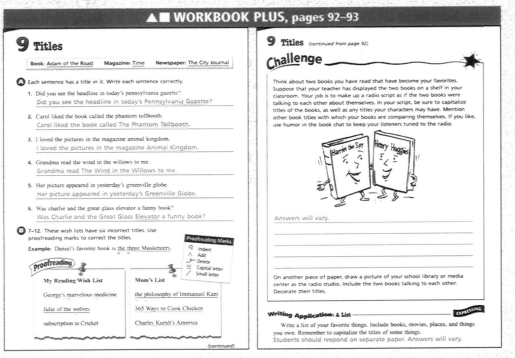

▲■ WORKBOOK PLUS, pages 92–93

9 Titles

Book: Adam of the Road **Magazine:** Time **Newspaper:** The City Journal

A Each sentence has a title in it. Write each sentence correctly.

1. Did you see the headline in today's pennsylvania gazette?
   Did you see the headline in today's Pennsylvania Gazette?
2. Carol liked the book called the phantom tollbooth.
   Carol liked the book called The Phantom Tollbooth.
3. I loved the pictures in the magazine animal kingdom.
   I loved the pictures in the magazine Animal Kingdom.
4. Grandma read the wind in the willows to me.
   Grandma read The Wind in the Willows to me.
5. Her picture appeared in yesterday's greenville globe.
   Her picture appeared in yesterday's Greenville Globe.
6. Was charlie and the great glass elevator a funny book?
   Was Charlie and the Great Glass Elevator a funny book?

B 7–12. These wish lists have six incorrect titles. Use proofreading marks to correct the titles.

Example: Daniel's favorite book is the three Musketeers.

Proofreading Marks
¶ Indent
∧ Add
Delete
≡ Capital letter
/ Small letter

Proofreading

My Reading Wish List

George's marvelous medicine
Julie of the wolves
subscription to Cricket

Mom's List

the philosophy of Immanuel Kant
365 Ways to Cook Chicken
Charles Kuralt's America

(continued)

9 Titles (continued from page 92)

Challenge

Think about two books you have read that have become your favorites. Suppose that your teacher has displayed the two books on a shelf in your classroom. Your job is to make up a radio script as if the two books were talking to each other about themselves. In your script, be sure to capitalize titles of the books, as well as any titles your characters may have. Mention other book titles with which your books are comparing themselves. If you like, use humor in the book chat to keep your listeners tuned to the radio.

Answers will vary.

On another piece of paper, draw a picture of your school library or media center as the radio studio. Include the two books talking to each other. Decorate their titles.

Writing Application: A List EXPRESSING

Write a list of your favorite things. Include books, movies, places, and things you own. Remember to capitalize the titles of some things.
Students should respond on separate paper. Answers will vary.

Enrichment

Objectives

Students will:

- use proper capitalization and punctuation for names, addresses, and dates
- use quotation marks to correctly punctuate quotations

Using the Activities

The Enrichment page provides fun, creative activities that reinforce students' understanding and use of capitalization and punctuation. The activities are designed to be enjoyed by all students. Here are some ideas for using the activities.

- Pair students who need extra support with more capable classmates.
- Students can work with these activities in class after they have completed other assignments.
- Activities that can be completed individually can be assigned as homework.

Focus on the Activities

PET HOTEL

- Direct students' attention to the sample identification card. Point out *Purr St.* and *Furball, MA,* in the Owner's address. Discuss how these words relate to cats. Suggest that students use similar "fun" names and addresses in their cards.
- Encourage students to use their imaginations in writing these cards and to include exotic pets, such as aardvarks, mongooses, kangaroos, and so on.
- Students can add pictures of pets cut from magazines or draw them.

TALKING NUMBERS

- Provide students with this example: *"I am the number of items in a dozen," said number ______.* (12)
- You might use this activity as a class game. Collect all the cards from students. Divide students into teams. Select a card and read the number clue. The first team to correctly identify the number wins a point.

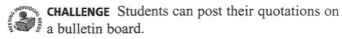

CHALLENGE Students can post their quotations on a bulletin board.

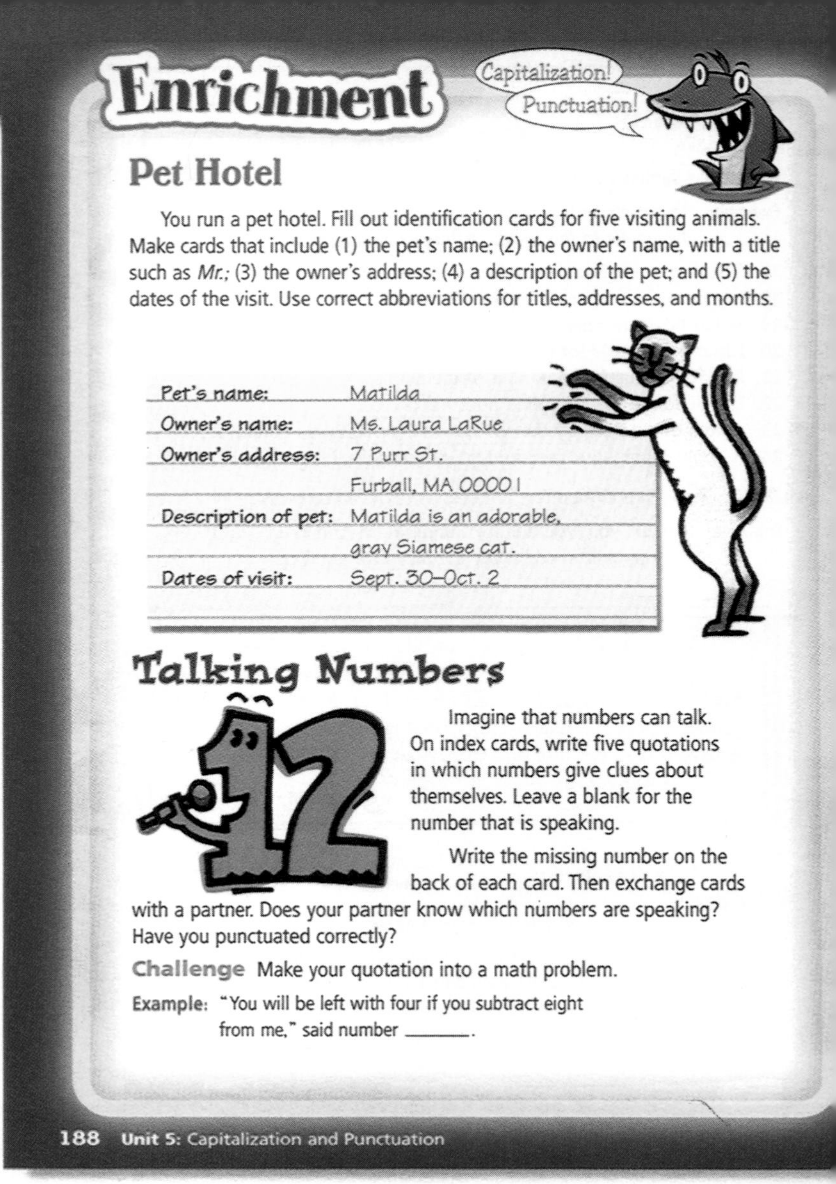

Enrichment

Pet Hotel

You run a pet hotel. Fill out identification cards for five visiting animals. Make cards that include (1) the pet's name; (2) the owner's name, with a title such as *Mr.*; (3) the owner's address; (4) a description of the pet; and (5) the dates of the visit. Use correct abbreviations for titles, addresses, and months.

Pet's name:	Matilda
Owner's name:	Ms. Laura LaRue
Owner's address:	7 Purr St.
	Furball, MA 00001
Description of pet:	Matilda is an adorable,
	gray Siamese cat.
Dates of visit:	Sept. 30–Oct. 2

Talking Numbers

Imagine that numbers can talk. On index cards, write five quotations in which numbers give clues about themselves. Leave a blank for the number that is speaking.

Write the missing number on the back of each card. Then exchange cards with a partner. Does your partner know which numbers are speaking? Have you punctuated correctly?

Challenge Make your quotation into a math problem.

Example: "You will be left with four if you subtract eight from me," said number ______.

188 Unit 5: Capitalization and Punctuation

FOR STUDENTS ACQUIRING ENGLISH

Show pictures of various kinds of pets and discuss them. Show how to make an I.D. tag for a pet. Have the students follow this format to make a pet tag:

Name of pet ______
Owner's name ______
Owner's phone number ______

Checkup: Unit 5

See TE margin for answers.

1 Correct Sentences (p. 166) Write these sentences correctly. Add capital letters and end marks. Separate run-on sentences.

1. this is a lovely new aquarium
2. how long have you had it
3. some fish have unusual shapes other fish are brightly colored
4. how huge that angelfish is
5. can you see the tiny fish they are hiding among the rocks
6. do not give them too much food

2 Names of People and Pets (p. 170) Write these sentences. Add capital letters where they are needed.

7. My uncle has a dog named nomad.
8. He leaves uncle henry very early each morning.
9. First, nomad heads downtown.
10. He visits dr. sarah aaron.
11. Then he stops at central high.
12. My mother and mr. l. m. rowe are teachers there.

3 Names of Places and Things (p. 172) Write these sentences. Add capital letters where they are needed.

13. Cindy will go to cleveland in the middle of august.
14. She will return on labor day.
15. The terminal tower is the name of a tall building in cleveland.
16. Cindy wants to see the cleveland indians play baseball.
17. On monday the family will visit gates mills, a nearby village.
18. It is on the chagrin river.

4 Abbreviations (p. 174) Write each group of words. Use an abbreviation in place of each underlined word.

19. 98 South Main <u>Street</u>
20. <u>Doctor</u> James Asher
21. <u>Wednesday</u>, <u>November</u> 15, 2000
22. 86 Ripley <u>Road</u>
23. T. J. Lamont, <u>Junior</u>
24. <u>Post Office</u> Box 162

5 Commas in a Series (p. 176) Write these sentences. Add commas where they are needed.

25. Cranberries blueberries and Concord grapes grow in the northern United States.
26. Cranberries grow in bogs where there are sand moss and water.
27. They grow in Massachusetts Wisconsin and Washington.
28. Josh Sarah and Liz are going to a bog to see the harvest.
29. Workers will pick inspect and pack the berries for sale.
30. Cranberries are used in sauce juice and baked goods.

6 More Uses for Commas (p. 180) Write these sentences. Use commas correctly.

31. Have you heard about the new contest Chris?
32. No I have not heard about it.

Checkup **189**

Checkup

Objectives

Students will:

- punctuate and capitalize sentences correctly
- capitalize proper nouns correctly
- spell abbreviations correctly
- use commas in a series correctly

Using the Checkup

Use the Checkup exercises as assessment, as review for the unit test, as extra practice, or as a diagnostic aid to help determine those students who need reteaching.

INTERNET CONNECTION Students can take an interactive quiz for this unit at www.eduplace.com/kids/hme/ and then get immediate feedback.

Answers

Correct Sentences

1. This is a lovely new aquarium.
2. How long have you had it?
3. Some fish have unusual shapes. Other fish are brightly colored.
4. How huge that angelfish is!
5. Can you see the tiny fish? They are hiding among the rocks.
6. Do not give them too much food.

Names of People and Pets

7. Nomad
8. Uncle Henry
9. Nomad
10. Dr. Sarah Aaron
11. Central High
12. Mr. L. M. Rowe

Names of Places and Things

13. Cleveland, August
14. Labor Day
15. Terminal Tower, Cleveland
16. Cleveland Indians
17. Monday, Gates Mills
18. Chagrin River

Abbreviations

19. 98 South Main St.
20. Dr. James Asher
21. Wed., Nov. 15, 2000
22. 86 Ripley Rd.
23. T. J. Lamont, Jr.
24. P.O. Box 162

Commas in a Series

25. Cranberries, blueberries, and Concord grapes
26. sand, moss, and water
27. Massachusetts, Wisconsin, and Washington
28. Josh, Sarah, and Liz
29. pick, inspect, and pack
30. sauce, juice, and baked goods

Objectives

Students will:

- use commas to separate introductory words and nouns in direct address
- use quotation marks correctly
- write titles of works with the correct punctuation
- proofread for correct capitalization and punctuation

Answers *continued*

More Uses for Commas

31. Have you heard about the new contest, Chris?
32. No, I have not heard about it.
33. Well, each person must design a stone carving.
34. Yes, the best drawing will win.
35. What will you draw, Lisa?
36. Damon, what do you hope to win?
37. Well, the winning design will be carved in stone.
38. It will be put on the roof, Jon.

Quotations

39. "I love to ice skate," announced Jeff.
40. Rebecca asked, "Is the ice thick?"
41. "Don't be afraid to fall," said Don.
42. correct
43. Molly cried, "Look out for the hole!"
44. "I would much rather go in-line skating," declared June.

Titles

45. A Light in the Attic
46. Sports Illustrated for Kids
47. Island of the Blue Dolphins
48. Rocky Mountain News
49. A Very Important Day

Checkup *continued*

33. Well each person must design a stone carving.
34. Yes the best drawing will win.
35. What will you draw Lisa?
36. Damon what do you hope to win?
37. Well the winning design will be carved in stone.
38. It will be put on the roof Jon.

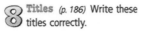

7 Quotations *(pp. 182, 184)* Write these sentences. Use capital letters and punctuation marks correctly. Write *correct* if a sentence is already correct.

39. I love to ice skate announced Jeff
40. Rebecca asked is the ice thick
41. Don't be afraid to fall said Don
42. Luke answered that he wouldn't.
43. Molly cried look out for the hole
44. I would much rather go in-line skating declared June

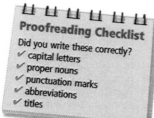

8 Titles *(p. 186)* Write these titles correctly.

45. a light in the attic
46. sports illustrated for kids
47. island of the blue dolphins
48. rocky mountain news
49. a very important day

Mixed Review 50–56. This story beginning has three capitalization errors and four punctuation errors. Write the story correctly.

Underlined letters should be capitalized.

Proofreading Checklist

Did you write these correctly?

- ✓ capital letters
- ✓ proper nouns
- ✓ punctuation marks
- ✓ abbreviations
- ✓ titles

Proofreading

It was a rainy july day. Eric's brother Nigel burst into the room. "Eric, look at this," said Nigel. He shoved a small ad from the magazine Kids in Business under Eric's nose. in

Have you invented a game, puzzle, or toy? You can get rich! Send for a free pamphlet.
Bright Ideas CO. Co.
33 Lilac Blossom Ave.
Canton, OH 44701
Bright Ideas Co.

Nigel announced, "I'm going to send for the pamphlet right away."

See www.eduplace.com/hme/ for an online quiz.

Assessment Link

Test Practice

Write the numbers 1–6 on a sheet of paper. Read the passage and look at the numbered, underlined parts. Choose the answer that shows the best way to write each underlined part. Write the letter for that answer.

Helen keller (1) was born in 1880 in alabama. When (2) she was two years old, she came down with a fever that left her deaf and blind. For the next five years, Helen was silent and unhappy (3) Then miss anne sullivan (4) became Helen's teacher. Sullivan taught Helen how to read words that were spelled into her hand. Helen became a student at Radcliffe College. (5) She even wrote a famous book. It was called the story of my life. (6)

1 (A) Helen Keller
B helen keller
C helen Keller
D Correct as it is

2 F alabama, When
(G) Alabama. When
H Alabama. when
J Correct as it is

3 A silent and unhappy?
(B) silent and unhappy.
C silent and, unhappy.
D Correct as it is

4 F miss Anne Sullivan
G miss anne Sullivan
(H) Miss Anne Sullivan
J Correct as it is

5 A radcliffe College
B Radcliffe college
C radcliffe college
(D) Correct as it is

6 F The story of my life
(G) The Story of My Life
H the Story of My Life
J Correct as it is

Test Practice 191

Test Practice

Objective

Students will:

- practice completing a test format that requires them to choose the correct item among four

Using the Test Practice

These Test Practice pages provide practice with common formats used in standardized or multiple-choice tests.

The first page works with skills taught in the basic lessons in Unit 5. The second and third pages work with skills taught in Units 1–5.

Focus on the Test Format

- Have a volunteer read the test directions aloud. Ask another volunteer to explain what the directions ask students to do.
- Remind students that the vertical line breaks the text into columns, and to answer the items in the first column before proceeding to the second column.
- Have students read the paragraph. Tell students that the numbers below the underlined words correspond to the item numbers below.
- Explain that each item below gives three choices that substitute for the underlined words in the paragraph. Point out that every item also has a fourth choice—"Correct as it is."
- Tell students to read each sentence with underlined words, then read it three more times, substituting the word choices. Have students write the letter of the correct response.

MEETING INDIVIDUAL NEEDS

FOR STUDENTS ACQUIRING ENGLISH

First, review capitalization, including proper names, words for family relationships, and titles such as *Dr.* or *Mrs.* Then review commas, quotes, and underlining for book titles. Discuss which words in titles have capital letters. Distribute the SAE Test Practice page for Unit 5. Have a volunteer read the directions aloud. Explain that students are to circle the answer that best replaces the underlined portion. If there is no mistake, they circle the last answer. For the second section, students choose the best way to rewrite sentences in a paragraph.

Objective

Students will:

- practice completing a test format that requires them to choose the correct sentence among four

Focus on the Test Format

- Have a volunteer read the test directions aloud. Ask another volunteer to explain what the directions ask students to do.
- Have students read the paragraph. Point out that each sentence in the paragraph is numbered, and that the numbers correspond to the items below.
- Remind students that the vertical line breaks the text into columns, and to answer the questions in the first column before proceeding to the second column.
- Point out that each numbered item gives three possible ways to word each sentence in the paragraph, and that the last choice is always "Best as it is."
- Tell students to read each item and compare the choices with the corresponding sentence in the paragraph. Have students write the letter of the correct response.

Test Practice *continued*

Now write the numbers 7–15 on your paper. Use the paragraphs to answer the questions. Write the letter for each answer.

[7]On Tuesday morning, Dorrie throwed on her new red shirt. [8]Would people like it? [9]In class mrs. Pierce stared. [10]Then Dorrie's friend whispered, "Dorrie, your shirt is on backwards! [11]Dorrie felt like the sillyer person in the world.

7 Which is the best way to rewrite Sentence 7?

- **A** On tuesday morning, Dorrie throw on her new red shirt.
- **(B)** On Tuesday morning, Dorrie threw on her new red shirt.
- **C** On Tuesday morning, Dorrie thrown on her new red shirt.
- **D** Best as it is

8 Which is the best way to rewrite Sentence 8?

- **F** Would people like it!
- **G** would people like it?
- **H** Would people like it.
- **(J)** Best as it is

9 Which is the best way to rewrite Sentence 9?

- **(A)** In class Mrs. Pierce stared.
- **B** In class mrs. Pierce stared.
- **C** In class Mrs. pierce stared.
- **D** Best as it is

10 Which is the best way to rewrite Sentence 10?

- **F** Then Dorries friend whispered, "Dorrie, your shirt is on backwards!"
- **G** Then Dorries' friend whispered "Dorrie your shirt is on backwards!"
- **(H)** Then Dorrie's friend whispered, "Dorrie, your shirt is on backwards!"
- **J** Best as it is

11 Which is the best way to rewrite Sentence 11?

- **A** Dorrie felt like the sillyest person in the world.
- **(B)** Dorrie felt like the silliest person in the world.
- **C** Dorrie felt like the most silliest person in the world.
- **D** Best as it is

[12]Mariah went to the ashton public library. [13]She needed facts about swans ducks and geese. [14]The librarian showed Mariah a set of books called The Nature Encyclopedia. [15]"These books have the goodest pictures I have ever seen!" said Mariah.

12 Which is the best way to rewrite Sentence 12?

- **F** Mariah goed to the ashton public library.
- **(G)** Mariah went to the Ashton Public Library.
- **H** Mariah went to the Ashton public library.
- **J** Best as it is

13 Which is the best way to rewrite Sentence 13?

- **A** She needed facts about swans, ducks and geese.
- **(B)** She needed facts about swans, ducks, and geese.
- **C** She needed facts about swans, ducks, and, geese.
- **D** Best as it is

14 Which is the best way to rewrite Sentence 14?

- **F** The librarian showed Mariah a set of books called The nature Encyclopedia.
- **G** The librarian showed Mariah a set of books called The nature encyclopedia.
- **(H)** The librarian showed Mariah a set of books called The Nature Encyclopedia.
- **J** Best as it is

15 Which is the best way to rewrite Sentence 15?

- **(A)** "These books have the best pictures I have ever seen!" said Mariah.
- **B** "These books have the best pictures I have ever seen"! said Mariah.
- **C** "These books have the most bestest pictures I have ever seen!" said Mariah.
- **D** Best as it is

Objective

Students will:

- practice completing a test format that requires them to choose the correct sentence among four

Focus on the Test Format

The test format on this page is the same as the format on the preceding page.

Correct Sentences

Objectives

Students will:

- use capital letters to start sentences and use the correct punctuation marks to end them
- identify statements, questions, commands, and exclamations
- correct run-on sentences
- write a description, including examples of the four types of sentences

Using the Extra Practice

The Extra Practice activities provide additional practice for the basic lesson at three levels of difficulty: Easy (●), Average (▲), and Challenging (■).

The Extra Practice activities can be used in the following ways.

- Assign activities according to students' needs and abilities as homework after students have completed the basic lesson.
- Assign the Easy activities after using the lesson Reteaching instruction.
- Assign the Average activities to prepare students for the Checkup.
- Assign the Easy and/or Average activities to students who had difficulty with specific lessons on the Checkup.
- Assign the Challenging exercises as a Bonus activity.

Extra Practice

(pages 166–167)

1 Correct Sentences Remember

- Begin every sentence with a capital letter.
- Use a period after a statement or a command.
- Use a question mark after a question.
- Use an exclamation point after an exclamation.

● Each sentence is missing a capital letter or an end mark. Write each sentence correctly. Underlined letters should be capitalized.

Example: have you ever seen a dolphin? *Have you ever seen a dolphin?*

1. some scientists were diving near the Bahama Islands.
2. one scientist met a dolphin underwater.
3. How excited she was !
4. What did the dolphin do ?
5. it poked her playfully with its snout.

▲ Write these sentences correctly. Add capital letters and end marks. Separate run-on sentences. Underlined letters should be capitalized.

Example: dolphins breathe air how do they do it
Dolphins breathe air. How do they do it?

6. a dolphin breathes through a blowhole.
7. do you know where this is?it is on top of the head.
8. a dolphin can stay underwater for six minutes.
9. that is a long time.how long can you stay underwater?
10. some scientists think that dolphins can learn to speak.

■ Write these sentences correctly. Then label each sentence *statement, question, command,* or *exclamation.* Underlined letters should be capitalized.

Example: can you name a very large animal
Can you name a very large animal? question

11. the blue whale is the world's largest animal. S
12. is it bigger than a dinosaur? Q
13. this animal is as large as twenty-five elephants. S
14. they have no teeth.they strain food from seawater. S, S
15. what interesting animals they are!please tell me more. E, C

194 **Unit 5:** Capitalization and Punctuation

Meeting Individual Needs — More Practice for Lesson 1

● EASY

Write each sentence. Add a capital letter. Label each sentence as a *statement, question, command,* or *exclamation.*

1. (T)this great barracuda is about six feet long. (statement)
2. (W)why is it called the "tiger of the sea"? (question)
3. (L)look at its teeth. (command)
4. (H)how sharp they are! (exclamation)

▲ AVERAGE

Each sentence is a run-on sentence. Write the sentences correctly, adding capital letters and end marks.

1. A stingray is a flat sea fish(.) (I)it has a poisonous bite.
2. Is a stingray bite dangerous(?) (I)it is almost as bad as a snakebite(.)
3. Some stingrays are fourteen feet long(.) (H)how scary they look!
4. Do you know where a stingray's teeth are(?) (T)they are along its tail(.)

■ CHALLENGING

Write a paragraph describing an imaginary sea monster. Use and label each of the four types of sentences in your description.

Extra Practice

(pages 170–171)

2 Names of People and Pets

Remember

- Capitalize the names of people and pets.
- Capitalize titles and initials that are parts of names.
- Capitalize family titles when they are used as names or as parts of names.

● Write these names of people and pets correctly. Underlined letters should be capitalized.

Example: aunt sally *Aunt Sally*

1. uncle barry
2. fifi
3. queen elizabeth
4. dr. doris cortez
5. mr. joseph b. zaturka
6. betsy chun
7. miss w. r. lin
8. mayor santos
9. porky
10. p. j. levy

▲ Write these sentences. Use capital letters correctly.

Example: My aunt's cat scaredy was in the pet show.
My aunt's cat Scaredy was in the pet show.

11. Her cat's full name is lord summerfield.
12. I heard that dr. jessie jones was very disappointed.
13. The doctor's cat, harvey, climbed a tree and stayed there.
14. Even grandmother tried to get the cat out of the tree.
15. It was too late to enter harvey in the show.

■ Use a noun from the box to complete each sentence. Use each noun once. Write the sentences. Be sure to capitalize the proper nouns.

Example: Show this article to ______. *Show this article to Aunt Jane.*

dr. dan d. lyons	aunt jane	uncle
attorney m. dodd	grandmother	doctor

16. It is about a veterinarian named ______. Dr. Dan D. Lyons
17. The ______ has a new office. doctor
18. It is above the law office of ______. Attorney M. Dodd
19. My aunt and ______ will take our cat to the vet. uncle
20. ______ will take care of the other cats. Grandmother

Names of People and Pets

Objectives

Students will:

- capitalize the names of people and pets
- capitalize titles and initials used with names
- write a story, capitalizing people's and pets' names correctly

Using the Extra Practice

The Extra Practice activities provide additional practice for the basic lesson at three levels of difficulty: Easy (●), Average (▲), and Challenging (■).

Meeting Individual Needs — More Practice for Lesson 2

● EASY

Some words have been capitalized correctly in these sentences. Some have not. Rewrite these sentences correctly.

1. My pony's name is rags. (Rags)
2. The vet, Dr. adams, says he's at least thirty-five years old. (Adams)
3. Our neighbor roger hilton is the same age. (Roger Hilton)
4. It was twenty years ago that grandpa bought Rags. (Grandpa)

▲ AVERAGE

Rewrite each sentence correctly. Some words should be capitalized. Some capitalized words should not be capitalized.

1. At the stadium, we saw governor Hill. (Governor)
2. my Grandfather and uncle Lou were talking to him. (My, grandfather, Uncle)
3. A Horse called lightning, owned by dr. Ling, won first prize. (horse, Lightning, Dr.)
4. A Horse named tripper won the jumping event. (horse, Tripper)

■ CHALLENGING

Imagine that all your family and friends were to have a pet show. Write a paragraph telling what people and pets would be there. Be sure to use capital letters correctly.

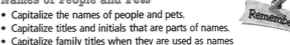

Names of Places and Things

Objectives

Students will:

- provide examples of proper nouns to describe places and things
- capitalize proper nouns that name places and things
- write sentences, capitalizing proper nouns correctly

Using the Extra Practice

The Extra Practice activities provide additional practice for the basic lesson at three levels of difficulty: Easy (●), Average (▲), and Challenging (■).

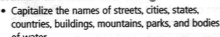

Extra Practice

(pages 172–173)

3 Names of Places and Things

Remember

- Capitalize the names of streets, cities, states, countries, buildings, mountains, parks, and bodies of water.
- Capitalize the names of days, months, holidays, and groups.

● Write these names of places and things correctly. Underlined letters should be capitalized.

Example: washington, d.c. *Washington, D.C.*

1. monday
2. united states
3. potomac river
4. jefferson memorial
5. the white house
6. may 31
7. pennsylvania avenue
8. memorial day
9. rock creek park
10. capitol hill

▲ Write these sentences. Use capital letters correctly. Underlined letters should be capitalized.

Example: The largest city in louisiana is new orleans.
The largest city in Louisiana is New Orleans.

11. This city lies along the mississippi river.
12. It is north of the gulf of mexico.
13. A holiday called mardi gras takes place every year.
14. Tourists come in february or march for this celebration.
15. Jazz fans hear great music at preservation hall.
16. One of the largest indoor stadiums is the louisiana superdome.
17. The new orleans saints play football there.

■ Invent a city. Write a sentence to answer each question about your city. Make up names to answer the questions. Answers will vary, but proper nouns should be capitalized.

Example: What is the name of your city?
The name of my city is Clowntown.

18. Who is the mayor?
19. What is the nearest body of water?
20. In what country is it located?
21. What big holiday is celebrated in your city?
22. When does it take place?

196 **Unit 5:** Capitalization and Punctuation

Meeting Individual Needs — More Practice for Lesson 3

● EASY

Write a proper noun that fits each category, for example, *street—Acorn Avenue.* (Answers will vary.)

1. state
2. park
3. holiday
4. street
5. month
6. city
7. lake
8. building

▲ AVERAGE

Rewrite each sentence correctly. Some words should be capitalized. Some capitalized words should not be capitalized.

1. The guinness Book of World Records contains strange Facts. (Guinness, facts)
2. Plennie L. Wingo walked backward from fort worth, Texas, to istanbul, turkey. (Fort Worth, Istanbul, Turkey)
3. Clinton Shaw roller-skated five thousand Miles on the Trans-canadian Highway. (miles, Canadian)
4. Steve McPeak rode from chicago to Las vegas on a unicycle. (Chicago, Vegas)
5. He crossed the Mississippi river and the rocky Mountains. (River, Rocky)

■ CHALLENGING

Write sentences that tell your favorite day, month, holiday, musical group, team, park, city, and state. Give a reason why you like each item so much.

Extra Practice

(pages 174–175)

4 Abbreviations

Remember

- An abbreviation is a short form of a word.
- Most abbreviations begin with a capital letter and end with a period.

● Write each group of words. Underline the abbreviation.

Example: Oct. 1, 1988 *Oct. 1, 1988*

1. Abbot Travel Co.
2. Sun., March 2, 1986
3. 3456 Fifth Ave.
4. Pots and Pans Co.
5. Ms. Maria Garcia
6. Marvin Hogan Jr.
7. Atlanta, GA 30043
8. Mrs. Monica Cohen
9. Leo Lyons Sr.
10. P. O. Box 567
11. Bennington, VT 05201
12. Jan. 4, 1989

▲ Write the words. Use an abbreviation in place of each underlined word.

Example: Douglas Food Company *Douglas Food Co.*

13. January 12, 1874 Jan.
14. Irving White Senior Sr.
15. Mister Howard Klein Mr.
16. Doctor Harriet Correlli Dr.
17. Cleveland, Ohio 44114 OH
18. Thursday, July 4, 1776 Thurs.
19. Post Office Box 76 P. O.
20. 6710 South Maple Street St.
21. Mobile, Alabama 36609 AL
22. 5110 Clinton Avenue Ave.
23. Sporting Life Company Co.
24. Tuesday, November 1, 2001 Tues., Nov.

■ Write each group of words, using correct abbreviations. Add capital letters where they are needed.

Example: doctor ann mack *Dr. Ann Mack*

25. thursday, january Thurs., Jan.
26. apex shipping company
27. 678 goldrush road Goldrush Rd.
28. post office box 89 P. O. Box
29. mister michael burns
30. salt lake city, utah 84101 Salt Lake City, UT
31. sunday, november 1 Sun., Nov.
32. 450 milford avenue Milford Ave.
33. doctor lorna cook Dr. Lorna Cook
34. hunter boulevard Hunter Blvd.
35. mister john chen senior Mr. John Chen Sr.
36. santora music company Santora Music Co.

Extra Practice 197

Abbreviations

Objectives

Students will:

- recognize the words that abbreviations stand for
- capitalize and punctuate abbreviations for titles, addresses, months, and days
- write a letter, using abbreviations correctly

Using the Extra Practice

The Extra Practice activities provide additional practice for the basic lesson at three levels of difficulty: Easy (●), Average (▲), and Challenging (■).

Meeting Individual Needs — More Practice for Lesson 4

● EASY

Write the word from which each abbreviation is formed.

1. Nov. (November)
2. Mon. (Monday)
3. Jr. (Junior)
4. Ave. (Avenue)
5. P.O. (Post Office)
6. Blvd. (Boulevard)

▲ AVERAGE

Write correct abbreviations for the words and phrases.

1. September (Sept.)
2. Mister Brady (Mr. Brady)
3. Tuesday (Tues.)
4. Rock Road (Rock Rd.)
5. Doctor Green (Dr. Green)
6. Key Company (Key Co.)
7. Maple Avenue (Maple Ave.)

■ CHALLENGING

Write a letter to your favorite character in a book. Include the following information, using as many abbreviations as possible.

- your own name and address
- today's date
- character's name and address
- invitation to a party, giving a person's name and address, and date of party
- a postscript

Commas in a Series

Objectives

Students will:

- identify correct use of commas in a series
- write sentences, using commas in a series correctly

Using the Extra Practice

The Extra Practice activities provide additional practice for the basic lesson at three levels of difficulty: Easy (●), Average (▲), and Challenging (■).

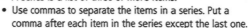

Extra Practice

(pages 176–177)

5 Commas in a Series

Remember

- A series is a list of three or more items.
- Use commas to separate the items in a series. Put a comma after each item in the series except the last one.

● Complete each sentence by adding words to form a series. Write the sentence.

Answers will vary.

Example: Rita's best friends are Kim, ______, and ______.
Rita's best friends are Kim, Tommy, and Ben.

1. They all like to swim, ______, and ______.
2. Rita likes to cook spaghetti, ______, and ______.
3. Last week she invited Kim, ______, and ______ for lunch.
4. She made salad, ______, and ______.
5. After lunch the friends talked, ______, and ______.

▲ Write these sentences. Use commas correctly.

Example: Farmers hunters and trappers became pioneers.
Farmers, hunters, and trappers became pioneers.

6. Pioneers settled in Kansas, Nebraska, and Minnesota.
7. Pioneer women spun, wove, and sewed cloth.
8. The pioneers built shelters, wagons, and boats.
9. At first men, women, and children lived in sod houses.
10. Sod houses were made of grass, mud, and dirt.

■ Write each sentence two different ways. The meaning of each sentence will change depending on where you use commas.

Example: Pioneers ate oatmeal bread and potatoes.
Pioneers ate oatmeal bread and potatoes.
Pioneers ate oatmeal, bread, and potatoes.

11. On the road, they ate cod stew pork and beans. cod, stew, pork, and beans; cod stew, pork, and beans
12. Cows gave them cream cheese and milk. cream, cheese, and milk; cream cheese and milk
13. A good dinner included chicken soup and noodles. chicken, soup, and noodles; chicken soup and noodles
14. They used cornmeal flour and eggs to make pancakes. cornmeal, flour, and eggs; cornmeal flour and eggs
15. Their apple walnut and cherry breads were delicious. apple, walnut, and cherry; apple walnut and cherry

198 **Unit 5:** Capitalization and Punctuation

Meeting Individual Needs

More Practice for Lesson 5

● EASY

Write *correct* if each series is written correctly. If it is not, rewrite it correctly.

1. carrots, beans, and peas (correct)
2. Bill, Jake(,) and Frank
3. dogs(,) cats, and canaries
4. bat, ball, glove, and mitt (correct)
5. apple(,) peach(,) and pears

▲ AVERAGE

Complete each sentence with three examples. Add commas where needed. (Answers will vary.)

1. I like to eat ______.
2. My friends' names are ______.
3. Three kinds of pets are ______.
4. The sports I like are ______.
5. My favorite colors are ______.

■ CHALLENGING

Add commas where they are needed in the story.

Mrs. O'Brien is clever(,) generous(,) and friendly. Each year she organizes a town picnic for the Fourth of July. For it, she makes baked beans and potato salad. Mr. O'Brien directs the chorus(,) the marching band(,) and the orchestra. The band and the chorus perform at the parade. After the picnic, the O'Briens organize baseball(,) softball(,) and volleyball games.

Extra Practice

(pages 180–181)

6 More Uses for Commas

Remember

- Use a comma to set off the words *yes, no,* and *well* when they are at the beginning of a sentence.
- Use a comma or commas to set off the names of people who are addressed directly.

● Write these sentences. Use commas correctly.

Example: Well have you heard about the wild horses?
Well, have you heard about the wild horses?

1. Yes,I read that some people are adopting them.
2. No,the horses are not still wild.
3. Carmen,the horses have been tamed.
4. Well,let's go to see them.
5. Bill,have any wild horses become gentle pets?

▲ Write these sentences. Use commas correctly.

Example: Do you know how tall the first horses were Ann?
Do you know how tall the first horses were, Ann?

6. Yes,this book says they were eleven inches tall.
7. Well,today's horses are much taller.
8. Some horses grow to be seven feet tall,Iris.
9. They are giants,Paul,compared to the early horses.
10. Frank,did people always ride horses?
11. No,the early horses were not tall or strong enough.

■ Write correctly the sentences that need commas. Write *correct* for each sentence that does not need commas.

Example: Can you tell me Marcos who the nomad people were?
Can you tell me, Marcos, who the nomad people were?

12. Nomads,Jeff,wandered from place to place.
13. Pete,were they lost?
14. No,the nomads were looking for food.
15. Nomads were the first people to ride horses. correct
16. They put animal skins on the horses' backs. correct

Extra Practice 199

More Uses for Commas

Objectives

Students will:

- identify nouns used in direct address
- use commas to set off introductory words and nouns in direct address
- write sentences, using commas with introductory words and nouns in direct address

Using the Extra Practice

The Extra Practice activities provide additional practice for the basic lesson at three levels of difficulty: Easy (●), Average (▲), and Challenging (■).

Meeting Individual Needs — More Practice for Lesson 6

● EASY

Write the name of the person addressed in each sentence.

1. Does Sean have a horse named Buddy, Jeff?
2. May, Arnie helps Mr. Diaz train horses.
3. Ron says that Hope is a pony, Tom, because she is less than fifty-eight inches tall.
4. Can Cal ride Hope, Ron?

▲ AVERAGE

A comma is missing from each sentence. Rewrite the sentence correctly.

1. A Fallabella is the world's smallest horse(,) Ann.
2. Yes(,) I understand they are only thirty inches tall. (,)
3. Tara(,) can people ride these Fallabella horses? (,)
4. No(,) Ann, they are kept as pets. (,)

■ CHALLENGING

Write an answer to each question. Begin your answer with *Yes* or *No.* Address your answer to a person in your class. (Answers will vary.)

1. Do you like horses?
2. Have you ever ridden a horse?
3. Have you ever gone to a rodeo?
4. Do your local police use horses?

Quotation Marks

Objectives

Students will:

- identify direct quotations in sentences
- write sentences, using quotation marks before and after a direct quotation

Using the Extra Practice

The Extra Practice activities provide additional practice for the basic lesson at three levels of difficulty: Easy (●), Average (▲), and Challenging (■).

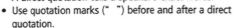

Extra Practice

7 Quotation Marks

(pages 182–183)

Remember

- A direct quotation tells a speaker's exact words.
- Use quotation marks (" ") before and after a direct quotation.

● Copy each sentence. Underline the direct quotation.

Example: "I know a fable," said Alicia. *"I know a fable," said Alicia.*

1. A fox said, "I will invite the stork for dinner."
2. The fox added, "I will serve soup in a shallow dish."
3. Then the stork said to the fox, "Have dinner with me."
4. "What did the stork serve for dinner?" asked Emily.
5. Alicia answered, "It was soup in a tall, narrow jar."
6. "Well, one bad turn deserved another!" laughed Carlos.

▲ Write each sentence correctly, using quotation marks.

Example: Let's hear another fable, begged Jon.
"Let's hear another fable," begged Jon.

7. Carrie said,"A crow found a piece of cheese."
8. A fox exclaimed,"I want that crow's cheese!"
9. "You are a beautiful bird!"the fox told the crow.
10. "Then the fox asked the crow to sing,"replied DeVona.
11. Ned said,"It opened its beak and dropped the cheese."
12. Eric added,"Do not be fooled by too much praise."

■ Write correctly each sentence that needs quotation marks. If a sentence is already correct, write *correct.*

Example: A lion caught a small mouse, said Joey.
"A lion caught a small mouse," said Joey.

13. The mouse squeaked,"Let me go, and I'll never forget it!"
14. The lion declared that a mouse could never help a lion. correct
15. "However, the lion let the mouse go,"said Jason.
16. "Hunters later tied the lion to a tree,"added Leesa.
17. Nick said,"The mouse chewed the rope and freed the lion."
18. May stated that little friends may prove great friends. correct

Meeting Individual Needs — More Practice for Lesson 7

● EASY

Rewrite these sentences. Underline all direct quotations.

1. "Let's go hiking," said Carrie.
2. Lee said she was too tired.
3. "I've been working," Lee added.
4. "I need to relax," Lee moaned.
5. Carrie said they'd hike slowly.

▲ AVERAGE

Write *correct* if the quotation marks are correct. If not, rewrite the sentence, using correct quotation marks.

1. "You bring the food, and I'll bring something to drink for our hike," said Carrie. (correct)
2. (")All right, I'll bring a snack," said Lee.
3. When the girls met, Carrie said, (")I forgot drinks!(")
4. "I brought some oranges," said Lee. "We'll have orange juice." (correct)

■ CHALLENGING

Rewrite each sentence so that it is a direct quotation. (Answers will vary.)

1. Carrie said that she and Lee should get started on their hike.
2. Lee asked Carrie which trail they should take.
3. Carrie wondered what they would find at the hilltop.
4. Lee cried out in surprise that she saw a juice stand.

Extra Practice

(pages 184–185)

8 Quotations

Remember

- Begin a quotation with a capital letter.
- When a quotation comes at the end of a sentence, use a comma to separate the quotation from the words that tell who is speaking. Put end punctuation marks inside the last quotation marks.

● Each sentence is missing a comma or a capital letter. Write each sentence correctly. Underlined letters should be capitalized.

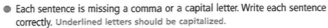

Example: Don asked, "have you ever heard of a snipe?"
Don asked, "Have you ever heard of a snipe?"

1. "Please tell me about it," answered Flora.
2. Don said, "it is a kind of bird."
3. "The snipe is related to the gull," Ann continued.
4. Pat asked, "What kind of bill does it have?"
5. "A snipe has a long, pointed bill," Phuong explained.

▲ Write each sentence correctly. Add capital letters, commas, and end marks where they are needed. Underlined letters should be capitalized.

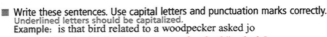

Example: Ellen exclaimed "what a funny-looking bird"
Ellen exclaimed, "What a funny-looking bird!"

6. Oscar explained, "it is called an umbrella bird."
7. "it has a funny hat on its head," laughed Ellen.
8. "those are feathers," explained Lora.
9. Chan said, "it has long feathers hanging from its neck."
10. "they look like an umbrella handle," added Al.

■ Write these sentences. Use capital letters and punctuation marks correctly. Underlined letters should be capitalized.

Example: is that bird related to a woodpecker asked jo
"Is that bird related to a woodpecker?" asked Jo.

11. "yes it is," answered dan.
12. "please show me the picture," begged les.
13. "its bill is almost as big as its body!" exclaimed kim.
14. sue asked, "well, what kind of bird is it?"
15. "it is called a toucan, sue," explained dan.

Extra Practice 201

Quotations

Objectives

Students will:

- use capital letters, commas, and end punctuation marks correctly in quotations
- write dialogue, capitalizing and punctuating quotations correctly

Using the Extra Practice

The Extra Practice activities provide additional practice for the basic lesson at three levels of difficulty: Easy (●), Average (▲), and Challenging (■).

Meeting Individual Needs

More Practice for Lesson 8

● EASY

Add one missing punctuation mark to each sentence.

1. "In this cage we see an emu,(") explained Dr. Brown.
2. I asked (,) "Can it fly?"
3. He replied, "No, but it can run very fast(.)"
4. (")It certainly is big!" Peg remarked.
5. Dr. Brown said, "The only taller bird is an ostrich.(")

▲ AVERAGE

Write *correct* for each correct sentence. If a sentence is not correct, rewrite it, using correct punctuation.

1. Dr. Boe said, "(H)here is the ostrich in this zoo, Paul(.)"
2. "It is seven feet tall and weighs three hundred pounds," he said. (correct)
3. I yelped, ("W)what a giant!"
4. ("H)how can it escape enemies if it can't fly(?") asked Peg.
5. Dr. Boe said (, "I)it uses its speed and fine eyesight(.")

■ CHALLENGING

From one of your books, choose a picture in which there are two or more characters. Write a conversation that the characters in the picture might be having. Use direct quotations and include correct punctuation.

Titles

Objectives

Students will:
- identify correctly written titles
- write the titles of publications correctly

Using the Extra Practice

The Extra Practice activities provide additional practice for the basic lesson at three levels of difficulty: Easy (●), Average (▲), and Challenging (■).

Extra Practice

(pages 186–187)

9 Titles

Remember
- Capitalize the first, the last, and each important word in the titles of books, magazines, or newspapers. Underline them.

● Write each sentence. Underline each title.

Example: This week's Brookland Bugle printed a list of books.
This week's Brookland Bugle printed a list of books.

1. A Cricket in Times Square was on the list.
2. Is Newsweek your dad's favorite magazine?
3. Did The Year of the Panda make you laugh?
4. How to Eat Fried Worms certainly did.
5. Did Kathleen Krull write Wilma Unlimited?
6. Yes, a Belview News critic wrote about that book.

▲ Write these sentences correctly. Letters to be capitalized are underlined twice; titles, once.

Example: I lent stowaway to the mushroom planet to Jan.
I lent Stowaway to the Mushroom Planet to Jan.

7. She is reading the wind in the willows now.
8. There is a review of it in highlights for children.
9. I wrote a story about it for hale school news.
10. Another article was about the book runaway ralph.
11. Wasn't Ralph also in the mouse and the motorcycle?
12. The editor of lee times asked Jim to write a column.
13. This week's column discussed the book lou gehrig: The Luckiest man alive.

■ Make up a title to complete each sentence. Write the sentences correctly. Answers will vary.

Example: ______ is a collection of scary stories. (book)
Terrifying Tales is a collection of scary stories.

14. ______ reports on scientific discoveries. (newspaper)
15. Read ______ to learn how to make a robot. (book)
16. Learn the latest news about musicians in ______. (magazine)
17. ______ is the story of a new pet. (book)
18. Buy a copy of ______ to learn about the zoo. (newspaper)

202 Unit 5: Capitalization and Punctuation

Meeting Individual Needs — More Practice for Lesson 9

● EASY

Write *yes* if a title is written correctly. Write *no* if it is not correct.

1. A Wrinkle in Time (yes)
2. The Spider, The Cave, and The Pottery Bowl (no)
3. Here and there (no)
4. Sasha, My Friend (yes)
5. The Enormous egg (no)
6. On the Banks of Plum Creek (yes)

▲ AVERAGE

Write *correct* if the title is written correctly. If not, rewrite the sentence, writing the title correctly.

1. A Daily Times story told about the author Beverly Cleary. (correct)
2. One of her best books is dear Mr. Henshaw. (Dear Mr. Henshaw)
3. Ramona and her father is another favorite. (Ramona and Her Father)
4. I write reviews of her work for the weekly news. (Weekly News)
5. Look up Beverly Cleary in The World Book Encyclopedia. (correct)

■ CHALLENGING

In a paragraph, describe three books that you would like to write someday. Give the title of each, and tell briefly what it will be about.

Unit 6 Planning Guide

Pronouns

2 weeks

		Checkup (PE)	Extra Practice (PE)	Graphic Organizer (BLM)	Writing Wrap-Up (BLM)	More Practice (TE)	Workbook Plus	Reteaching Workbook	Students Acquiring English Practice Book
1	What Is a Pronoun? *(204–205)*	222	226	6–1	6–5	226	94–95	57	89+
2	Subject Pronouns *(206–207)*	222	227	6–1	6–5	227	96–97	58	91+
3	Object Pronouns *(208–209)*	222	228	6–1	6–5	228	98–99	59	93+
	Revising Strategies: Sentence Fluency Writing with Pronouns *(210–211)*						100–101	60–61	
4	Using I and me *(212–213)*	222	229	6–2	6–6	229	102–103	62	95+
5	Possessive Pronouns *(214–215)*	222	230	6–3	6–6	230	104–105	63	97+
6	Contractions with Pronouns *(216–217)*	223	231	6–4	6–7	231	106–107	64	99+
7	Pronouns and Homophones *(218–219)*	223	232	6–3	6–7	232	108–109	65	101+
	Revising Strategies: Vocabulary Homophones *(220)*						110	66	
	Enrichment *(221)*								
	Test Practice *(224–225)*								103+

Unit 6

Tools and Tips

- **Diagramming Guide,** *pp. H70–H78*
- **Guide to Capitalization, Punctuation, and Usage,** *pp. H55–H64*

School-Home Connection

Suggestions for informing or involving family members in classroom activities and learning related to this unit are included in the Teacher's Edition throughout the unit.

Meeting Individual Needs

- **FOR SPECIAL NEEDS/INCLUSION:** *Houghton Mifflin English* Audiotape See also Reteaching.
- **FOR STUDENTS ACQUIRING ENGLISH:**
  - Notes and activities are included in this Teacher's Edition throughout the unit to help you adapt or use pupil book activities with students acquiring English.
  - Additional support is available for students at various stages of English proficiency: **Beginning/Preproduction**, **Early Production/Speech Emergence**, and **Intermediate/Advanced**. See Students Acquiring English Practice Book.
  - Students can listen to the Try It Out activities on audiotape.
- **ENRICHMENT:** *p. 221*

All audiotape recordings are also available on CD.

Daily Language Practice

Each sentence includes two errors based on skills taught in this or previous Grammar units. Each day write one sentence on the chalkboard. Have students find the errors and write the sentence correctly on a sheet of paper. To make the activity easier, identify the kinds of errors.

1. "Her is my best friend, said Helen." "She is my best friend," said Helen. **(subject pronouns; quotations)**
2. Molly gave the bigest apples to they. Molly gave the biggest apples to them. **(comparing with adjectives; object pronouns)**
3. Nate and me toured the statue of Liberty. Nate and I toured the Statue of Liberty. **(subject pronouns; proper nouns)**
4. Mitch does'nt practice Mitch's piano often enough. Mitch doesn't practice his piano often enough. **(contractions; possessive pronouns)**
5. Youll need to get plenty of sleep tomorrow will be a busy day. Sample: You'll need to get plenty of sleep. Tomorrow will be a busy day. **(contractions; run-on sentences)**
6. Its easy to remember Dctr. Shot's name. It's easy to remember Dr. Shot's name. **(homophones; abbreviations)**
7. Please bring flea soap, towels, and the dog, to Dad and I. Please bring flea soap, towels, and the dog to Dad and me. **(commas; object pronouns)**
8. Brett said that hes making cookys for everyone. Brett said that he's making cookies for everyone. **(contractions; plural nouns)**
9. Joel can you take Kate and I to the store? Joel, can you take Kate and me to the store? **(commas, object pronouns)**
10. The monkies live on that island over their. The monkeys live on that island over there. **(plural nouns; homophones)**

Additional Resources

Workbook Plus, Unit 6
Reteaching Workbook, Unit 6
Students Acquiring English Practice Book, Unit 6
Transparencies, Unit 6
Teacher's Resource Book
Audiotapes

Technology Tools

INTERNET: http://www.eduplace.com/kids/hme/ *or* http://www.eduplace.com/rdg/hme/

Visit Education Place for these additional support materials and activities:

- tricky usage question
- Wacky Web Tales®
- interactive quizzes
- a proofreading game

Assessment

Test Booklet, Unit 6

Keeping a Journal

Discuss with students the value of keeping a journal as a way of promoting self-expression and fluency. Encourage students to record their thoughts and ideas in a notebook. Inform students whether the journal will be private or will be reviewed periodically as a way of assessing growth. The following prompts may be useful for generating writing ideas.

Journal Prompts

- What are the three most important qualities that parents should have? Explain.
- Tell about the funniest thing that ever happened to you.
- Write a poem that describes your pet or a pet you would like to have.

Unit 6

Pronouns

Picnic dinners are Grandpa's specialty. He packs our favorite summer foods in a basket and drives us to the park.

203

Introducing the Unit

Using the Photograph

- Have students describe what the people in the photograph are doing. Have a volunteer read the caption. Ask students to whom *He* (Grandpa) and *us* (the boy, the girl, and the grandmother) refer.
- Explain to students that a word that takes the place of one or more nouns is called a **pronoun**. Tell students that they will learn about different types of pronouns in this unit.

Grammar Song

See Blackline Master G–3 for a song to help students remember some of the concepts and rules taught in this unit.

Students can also listen to this song on audiotape.

Shared Writing Activity

Work with students to use pronouns to write a paragraph telling Grandpa's story from the photo and caption.

1. Have students decide from whose point of view they will tell the story. (Grandpa's, the grandmother's, the boy's, or the girl's)
2. Discuss with students how Grandpa may have prepared for the picnic. (Sample response: He prepared food, packed the basket, and drove to the park.)
3. Encourage students to bring all the characters into Grandpa's story. For example, students can add details such as *The children helped Grandpa pack the picnic basket* or *Grandma set the table while Grandpa hung lanterns.*
4. Remind students to tell the events in the proper order.
5. Have students suggest sentences to tell the story. Write the sentences on the board or on an overhead transparency.
   - Help students fix fragments and run-on sentences. As you write, ask students to tell you the correct punctuation and capitalization to use.
   - Have students pay special attention to make sure readers can tell which noun or nouns are referred to by every pronoun they use.
6. Have a volunteer read the paragraph to the class. Ask students whether they feel pronouns make their story easier to understand.

What Is a Pronoun?

Lesson Objectives

Students will:
- identify pronouns in sentences
- distinguish between singular and plural pronouns
- write informative captions, using pronouns

One-Minute Warm-Up Have volunteers share their rhymes with the class and identify the words the pronouns replace.

Focus on Instruction

Give an example of *you* as a singular pronoun and *you* as a plural pronoun, as in *You are late, John* and *You are all good friends.* Explain that listeners distinguish singular from plural *you* by sentence context.

Try It Out

LISTENING AND SPEAKING After students complete the exercise, have them read the sentences, substituting a pronoun for each person.

FOR STUDENTS ACQUIRING ENGLISH

- Have students listen to the Try It Out sentences on the audiotape. Distribute SAE Practice page for Unit 6, Lesson 1, to support listening.
- Ask students to discuss the art. List vocabulary relating to the beach; assist with vocabulary as needed. Work with subject pronouns first. Students may have difficulty with *he, she,* so try to include extra examples when possible. Plan to help students identify proper names as belonging to males or females; you may want to have a small drawing of a male and a female handy for this purpose. Then work with object pronouns. Students listen and underline the pronouns. Discuss which are singular and which are plural. Example: John and Sam went to the beach. <u>They</u> like the beach.

Grammar/Usage

1 What Is a Pronoun?

One-Minute Warm-Up

Snails leave trails.
They drag their tails.

Make up your own silly rhyme. Begin the first sentence with a noun. Begin the second sentence with a word from the list that can replace the noun. Answers will vary.

he she it we they

- A noun names a person, a place, or a thing. **A pronoun is a word that takes the place of one or more nouns.** When you write, you do not have to keep repeating nouns. Instead, you can replace some of the nouns with pronouns. Compare the two paragraphs below. What pronouns take the place of nouns?

  Sara asked Brett and Leah to go to the seashore with Sara. Sara, Brett, and Leah spoke to Ms. Lanski. Ms. Lanski gave Sara, Brett, and Leah a special book. The book was about sea life.

  Sara asked Brett and Leah to go to the seashore with her. They spoke to Ms. Lanski. She gave them a special book. It was about sea life.

- Like the nouns they replace, pronouns are singular or plural.

Singular Pronouns:	I, me, you, he, him, she, her, it
Plural Pronouns:	we, us, you, they, them

Try It Out

Speak Up Which words in these sentences are pronouns? Is each pronoun singular or plural?

1. Sara said, "Come with <u>us</u> to the seashore." P
2. Leah carried a pail. <u>She</u> wanted to collect shells. S
3. Brett took a notebook. Sara had asked <u>him</u> to take notes. S
4. Leah saw a sea star. Brett wrote about <u>it</u> in the book. S
5. "<u>You</u> are good scientists," Sara told Leah and Brett. P

Meeting Individual Needs

RETEACHING
ALTERNATIVE STRATEGY

- Write these sentences on the board: *Ana speaks French. She speaks French.* Have volunteers underline the words that tell who speaks French. (Ana, She) Tell students that *She* in the second sentence is a pronoun because it stands for *Ana,* a noun.
- Write these sentences: *Sue and Al saw a lion. They saw a lion.* Have students say the words that tell who saw the lion. (Sue and Al, They) and name the pronoun. (They)

CHALLENGE

Write each pronoun from the lesson on an index card. Have students take turns selecting cards and using the pronouns on the cards in rhyming couplets. For example, *He is a boy who looks like me./He always likes to sit on my knee.*

FOR STUDENTS ACQUIRING ENGLISH

Write the subject and object pronouns on index cards. Have students sort the pronouns into singular and plural groups. Later, have the students sort the cards into subject and object pronouns.

On Your Own

Write the pronoun in each sentence that takes the place of the underlined word or words.

Example: Brett said, "I see a large pink shell." *I*

6. "Should we take this shell?" asked Brett and Leah.
7. Sara asked Brett and Leah, "What do you hear inside the shell?"
8. Brett and Leah listened. The noise reminded them of the ocean.
9. Sara told Brett that he had found a queen conch shell.
10. "I see that the shell is empty," said Leah.
11. "This book will tell us about the conch," said Brett and Leah.
12. The conch is a kind of snail. It lives in the sea.
13. Once there were many of these snails. Now they are rare.

14–20. Write the pronouns in this part of a newscast that take the place of the underlined word or words.

Example: Adam watches conch eggs and writes about them. *them*

She Marta Rivera is a young scientist. She is working to save the conch. The job is difficult, but it it is rewarding. Marta collects conch eggs and them puts them in tanks. Adam Caldwell assists Marta. He; her He helps her to feed the young snails. When the snails are they large enough, they will be returned to the sea. Adam and They Marta believe the work they are doing is important.

Writing Wrap-Up

WRITING • THINKING • LISTENING • SPEAKING

INFORMING

Write Captions

Draw pictures of three or four things from nature, such as shells, plants, and animals. Then write a few sentences about each item below its picture. Use pronouns in each caption. Read your captions to a partner. Have your partner name the pronouns you used.

For Extra Practice see page 226.

Summing Up Help students summarize these key points about the lesson:

A **pronoun** is a word that replaces one or more nouns. A pronoun can be singular or plural.

You may want to have students complete the parts related to this lesson on Blackline Master 6–1.

On Your Own

Have students decide if the underlined word or phrase is singular or plural and then write the pronoun in the sentence that matches it in number.

MEETING INDIVIDUAL NEEDS

FOR STUDENTS ACQUIRING ENGLISH

Distribute SAE Practice page for Unit 6, Lesson 1. Discuss the art. Review subject and object pronouns. Students circle the noun to which the underlined pronoun refers. Example: William and Aria found a shell. It was pink. (shell)

Writing Wrap-Up

Writing Tip: Suggest that students choose objects they can draw well. Students should group drawings in ways that will provide opportunities for writing both singular and plural pronouns. See Blackline Master 6–5 for sample captions.

TECHNOLOGY CONNECTION

Students can use available hardware to scan their drawings into a file and then enter their captions.

● RETEACHING WORKBOOK, page 57

1 What Is a Pronoun?

• A **pronoun** is a word that can take the place of one or more nouns.

Singular pronouns: I, me, you, he, him, she, her, it

Plural pronouns: we, us, you, they, them

Nouns	Pronouns
Maya went to the park.	She went to the park.
Maya watched the squirrels.	Maya watched **them**.

Underline the pronoun in each sentence. Then write *singular* or *plural* for each pronoun.

Example: Dennis had a camera. He took some pictures. **singular**

1. He went to the park with Maya. singular
2. She brought a camera along too. singular
3. At the park, they started taking pictures. plural
4. A little squirrel raced past them. plural
5. Maya snapped a picture of it. singular
6. The squirrel ran past her and behind a tree. singular
7. "Don't run away from us," Maya called. plural
8. "We have to be quick," said Dennis. plural
9. Then he heard two soft voices. singular
10. Two little boys walked up to him. singular
11. "Show me how a camera works," a boy said to Dennis. singular
12. He answered, "The camera's eye works like a person's eye." singular
13. "I see the camera's eye open and close," said the boy. singular
14. "Please take pictures of us," said the other boy. plural
15. "Both of you smile at the camera," said Maya. plural
16. She raised the camera, aimed, and clicked. singular

▲■ WORKBOOK PLUS, pages 94–95

1 What Is a Pronoun?

Nouns	Pronouns
Lynn wants to help.	**She** wants to help.
Matt cleans the parks and streets.	Matt cleans **them**.

Write the pronouns in these sentences. Then write the underlined words that they replace.

1. "Let us think of a way to clean up litter," said Matt and Lynn.
   us—Matt and Lynn
2. Lynn told Matt that he could use things over again.
   he—Matt
3. Dora and Ahmed collected bottles. Matt wanted to help them.
   them—Dora and Ahmed
4. Lynn wanted to help too. She had an idea.
   She—Lynn
5. "I have saved newspapers," said Lynn. Lynn wanted to recycle them.
   I—Lynn, them—newspapers
6. "You must take out the papers," Lynn told Matt. "Help me," Lynn said.
   You—Matt, me—Lynn
7. A truck took the newspapers away. It came once a month.
   It—A truck
8. "Now we should clean up the park," said Matt and Lynn.
   we—Matt and Lynn
9. Matt began to pick up paper from the grass. Lynn helped him.
   him—Matt
10. At last Matt and Lynn finished working. They were happy and tired.
    They—Matt and Lynn

(continued)

1 What Is a Pronoun? *(continued from page 94)*

Challenge

Here are four signs about cleaning up litter. Each sign is missing a pronoun. Write the correct pronouns on the signs.

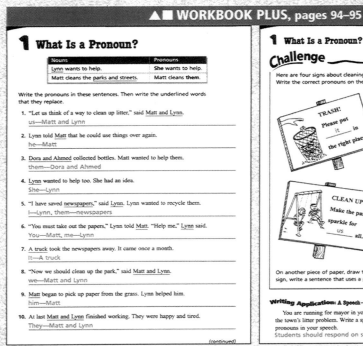

On another piece of paper, draw two signs about cleaning up litter. On each sign, write a sentence that uses a pronoun.

Writing Application: A Speech EXPLAINING

You are running for mayor in your town or city. You have an idea for solving the town's litter problem. Write a speech about your idea. Use at least five pronouns in your speech.

Students should respond on separate paper. Answers will vary.

Subject Pronouns

Lesson Objectives

Students will:
- identify subject pronouns in sentences
- substitute pronouns for nouns as the subjects of sentences
- write an opinion, using subject pronouns

One-Minute Warm-Up On the board write *They have a devoted mother.* Tell students to change the sentence to tell about one earwig. (It has a devoted mother.) Then have students change the sentence to tell about a classmate. (Sample: She has a devoted mother.)

Focus on Instruction

Remind students that the subject of a sentence is the "doer" in an action sentence, such as *Ron washed the dishes.* The subject can also be the person, place or thing that is described by a non-action verb in a sentence, such as *They were dirty.*

Try It Out

VIEWING Have students make up short sentences about the ladybugs in the photo. Record students' suggestions on a chart. Ask volunteers to substitute subject pronouns for nouns in the sentences. (Sample responses are shown.)

Sentences Without Subject Pronouns	Sentences with Subject Pronouns
The ladybug has six legs.	It has six legs.
Many spots dot the bug's back.	They dot the bug's back.

FOR STUDENTS ACQUIRING ENGLISH

- Have students listen to the Try It Out sentences on the audiotape. Distribute SAE Practice page for Unit 6, Lesson 2, to support listening.
- Discuss the art. Help students suggest sentences about the helpful insects in the drawing. Ask what students know about these insects. Students listen and choose the subject pronoun that can replace the underlined noun(s).
  1. Pat and I found a ladybug. (We)
  2. The ladybug was red with black spots. The ladybug had six legs. (It)
  3. Bees produce honey. Bees feed the honey to their young. (They)
  4. Honey tastes very good. Honey is better than sugar. (It)

Grammar/Usage

2 Subject Pronouns

One-Minute Warm-Up

Read the sentences below. What pronoun takes the place of the noun *earwigs*? They

Imagine having thirty brothers and sisters to bug you! Some earwigs do. They also have a devoted mother.

—from *Creepy, Crawly Baby Bugs,* by Sandra Markle

- Like a noun, a pronoun can be used as the subject of a sentence. Remember that the subject tells whom or what the sentence is about.

Nouns	Pronouns
Aki did a project on insects.	She did a project on insects.
Justin worked with Aki.	He worked with Aki.
Aki and Justin gave a report.	They gave a report.
Nakisha and I enjoyed the report.	We enjoyed the report.

- Not all pronouns can be used as subjects. **Only the subject pronouns *I, you, he, she, it, we,* and *they* can be used as the subjects of sentences.**

Subject Pronouns	
Singular	**Plural**
I	we
you	you
he, she, it	they

Try It Out

Speak Up Which subject pronoun could take the place of the underlined word or words in each sentence?

1. Matt said to Selena, "Selena found a ladybug." You
2. Matt and I know that ladybugs are helpful insects. We
3. Ladybugs are not really bugs. Ladybugs are beetles. They
4. This beetle eats insects that destroy plants. It
5. Selena did not disturb the ladybug. She
6. Selena said, "Selena should not hurt such a helpful insect." I

Meeting Individual Needs

RETEACHING
ALTERNATIVE STRATEGY

- Display this incomplete ad on the board:

  FREE KITTENS
  Sassy is my cat. _______ *has five new kittens.* _______ *are cute and cuddly. My mother says that* _______ *cannot keep all five.* _______ *can have one.*
- Tell students that a subject pronoun can be used as the subject of a sentence, just as a noun can.
- Write these subject pronouns on the board: *you, I, she, they,* and *we.* Help students fill in the blanks in the ad with these pronouns.

CHALLENGE

Have students write riddles in which each clue begins with a subject pronoun. Example: *They have hands but no arms. They have faces but no noses. They tell us something. What are they?* (clocks)

FOR STUDENTS ACQUIRING ENGLISH

Write *she, he, it, they* on index cards. Point to people or objects; have students place the correct card with the person or object and say the pronoun. Display cards and have students choose people or objects to fit the pronouns.

On Your Own

Write each sentence. Use a subject pronoun in place of the underlined word or words.

Example: The book is about butterflies. *It is about butterflies.*

7. Holly and Henry read the book. They
8. Henry learned that butterflies start out as eggs. He
9. Then the eggs hatch into caterpillars. they
10. Henry read that the third stage is the pupa. He
11. Holly said that the caterpillar spins a hard shell. She
12. When this shell cracks, a butterfly comes out. it

13–18. Write these jokes. Use a subject pronoun in place of the underlined word or words.

Example: Nikki and Jason practice jokes with each other.
They practice jokes with each other.

Jason, why did the man keep wasps in the closet?

The man had a good reason. The wasps were yellow jackets! Now I will ask one. Can you guess why the fly landed on the toast? He; They

The fly wanted to be a butterfly! I have another joke. Why did the woman call the insect expert? It

The woman was sick with a bug! She

These jokes are funny. My father will love them! They; He

Writing Wrap-Up

WRITING • THINKING • LISTENING • SPEAKING

EXPRESSING

Write an Opinion

Write a paragraph on any kind of insect. Explain why the insect is harmful or helpful. Use as many subject pronouns as you can. Then read your paragraph to a group. Do they agree with you?

For Extra Practice see page 227.

Summing Up Help students summarize these key points about the lesson:

I, you, he, she, it, we, and *they* are **subject pronouns**. Only use subject pronouns as the subjects of sentences.

You may want to have students complete the parts related to this lesson on Blackline Master 6–1.

On Your Own

Suggest that students first look at the underlined word or phrase and decide whether it is singular or plural. Then students can look at the chart of subject pronouns and select the appropriate one.

MEETING INDIVIDUAL NEEDS

FOR STUDENTS ACQUIRING ENGLISH

Distribute SAE Practice page for Unit 6, Lesson 2. Discuss the art. Help students describe and label the stages. Then students replace the underlined nouns with subject pronouns.

1. Sean found a butterfly. (He)
2. Butterflies are beautiful. (They)

Writing Wrap-Up

Writing Tip: Tell students to be sure that they state their opinions clearly and give at least two reasons to support it. See Blackline Master 6–5 for a sample opinion.

SCHOOL-HOME CONNECTION

Suggest that students ask family members to talk about insects they like or don't like. Have students listen for subject pronouns.

● RETEACHING WORKBOOK, page 58

2 Subject Pronouns

• Use only **subject pronouns** as the subjects of sentences.

Singular subject pronouns: I, you, he, she, it

Plural subject pronouns: we, you, they

Nouns	Pronouns
Tara has an exciting new toy.	**She** has an exciting new toy.
Tara and Rico play with the toy.	**They** play with the toy.

Write the subject pronoun in parentheses that can take the place of the underlined word or words.

Example: Aunt Lori bought great toys for Rico. **(She, We)** She

1. Rico is only four years old. **(He, You)** He
2. Aunt Lori has found toys to help Rico learn. **(She, I)** She
3. This toy teaches children to tell time. **(It, They)** It
4. Those toys are for making music. **(We, They)** They
5. Tara showed Rico a brand-new toy. **(You, She)** She
6. "Tara and I will play with the toy," said Rico. **(They, We)** We
7. "Rico will play with this toy all day," said Rico. **(You, I)** I
8. Tara showed Aunt Lori a new puzzle. **(She, They)** She
9. This puzzle was a map of the fifty states. **(It, They)** It
10. "My brother and I also have paints," Tara said. **(We, He)** We
11. Uncle Joe and Aunt Lori had bought these paints. **(She, They)** They
12. Uncle Joe told Tara about toys of long ago. **(He, We)** He
13. The toys were balls made of wood. **(It, They)** They
14. Hoops were also used as toys long ago. **(You, They)** They
15. "Tara will learn more about toys," said Tara. **(I, You)** I
16. Aunt Lori and Uncle Joe love toys too! **(She, They)** They

▲■ WORKBOOK PLUS, pages 96–97

2 Subject Pronouns

Nouns	Pronouns
Simon plays in the band.	**He** plays in the band.
Rachel is in the band too.	**She** is in the band too.
Simon and Rachel help each other.	**They** help each other.
The band is fun.	**It** is fun.

A Write the subject pronoun in each sentence.

1. We play in the music room every day after school. We
2. I play the trumpet in the band. I
3. It is a wonderful instrument. It
4. Have you ever played in a band? you
5. Next week Rachel and I will play at a town dance. I
6. She was asked to play by Mr. Chu. She
7. He and Mrs. Russo had heard the band at a football game. He
8. They will be glad to hear the band play again. They

B Write each sentence. Use a subject pronoun in place of the underlined word or words.

9. Musicians must learn to play the right notes.
They must learn to play the right notes.
10. George can play very high notes on the flute.
He can play very high notes on the flute.
11. Rachel has learned to play the drums.
She has learned to play the drums.
12. Rachel and I keep the beat for the band.
We keep the beat for the band.

(continued)

2 Subject Pronouns (continued from page 96)

Challenge

The musicians below are talking about music and their instruments. First, write a different subject pronoun in each speech balloon. Then, on another piece of paper, write a sentence that tells what each musician is saying. Begin each sentence with the subject pronoun in the balloon. Answers will vary.

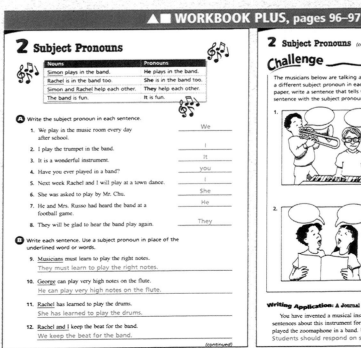

Writing Application: A Journal DESCRIBING

You have invented a musical instrument called a zoomaphone. Write six sentences about this instrument for your journal. Describe the first time you played the zoomaphone in a band. Use a subject pronoun in each sentence. Students should respond on separate paper. Answers will vary.

Object Pronouns

Lesson Objectives

Students will:
- identify object pronouns
- substitute object pronouns for nouns in sentences
- write a story, using object pronouns

One-Minute Warm-Up Introduce the activity by asking, "Would you like a pony ride? Who else among your friends and family would like one?" Write names on the board as students say them. Then have volunteers read the sentence in the book and insert the appropriate pronoun for each name you've written. Make sure someone inserts *me.*

Focus on Instruction

Have volunteers use *you* and *it* in sentences, first as subject pronouns, and then as object pronouns. Examples: *You ring the bell. These are for you. It is my turn. Color it blue.*

Try It Out

VIEWING Have students make up short sentences about the girl and the horse in the photo. Record the sentences on a chart. Then have volunteers substitute the objects with object pronouns. Write the resulting sentences in the second column of the chart. (Sample responses are given.)

Sentences Without Object Pronouns	Sentences with Object Pronouns
The girl grooms the horse.	The girl grooms it.
She likes horses.	She likes them.

FOR STUDENTS ACQUIRING ENGLISH
- Have students listen to the Try It Out sentences on the audiotape. Distribute SAE Practice page for Unit 6, Lesson 3, to support listening.
- Discuss the art. List vocabulary relating to horses and riding. Tell students that people in the United States usually refer to their pets as *he* or *she.* Review prepositions. Say and write examples such as *Mother bought a dress for me. She gave it to me.* Have students mark object pronouns with colored chalk. They may need extra work with *him, her.* Contrast subject and object pronouns. Students listen and write the object pronoun that replaces the underlined noun. Example: Samantha and Alex ride horses. The children brush the horses before they ride. (them)

Grammar/Usage

3 Object Pronouns

One-Minute Warm-Up Complete the sentence below with as many different pronouns as you can. him, her, them, us, you, me

Frisky the pony gave a ride to _____.

- Subject pronouns can be used as the subjects of sentences. **The pronouns *me, you, him, her, it, us,* and *them* are called object pronouns.** Object pronouns follow action verbs and words such as *to, with, for,* and *at.*

Nouns	Pronouns
Mr. Rossi fed the horses.	Mr. Rossi fed them.
James helped Mr. Rossi.	James helped him.
James showed a pony to Rachel and me.	James showed a pony to us.
Then James gave the pony a carrot.	Then James gave it a carrot.

Object Pronouns	
Singular	**Plural**
me	us
you	you
him, her, it	them

- Never use the object pronouns *me, him, her, us,* and *them* as subjects. You can use the pronouns *you* and *it* as either subject or object pronouns.

Try It Out

Speak Up Which object pronoun could take the place of the underlined word or words in each sentence?

1. Rachel rides horses every day. them
2. Cody said to Rachel, "Please teach Cody." me
3. Rachel took Cody to the stable with Rachel. her
4. Rachel told Cody, "I will teach Cody grooming first." you
5. Then Rachel brushed the horse. it
6. Cody said, "The horse likes Rachel and Cody." us

Meeting Individual Needs

RETEACHING
ALTERNATIVE STRATEGY
- Write each of these words on a slip of paper and distribute to students: *I, me, you, she, her, we, us, they,* and *them.*
- List these phrases on the board: *see _____; with _____; hit _____; for _____; tell _____.*
- Read the first phrase. Then have a volunteer read his or her slip. Ask the group whether the word fits in the phrase. Repeat this exercise for all slips of paper.
- Explain that the words that fit are called object pronouns. Object pronouns follow the verb and words such as *to, with, for,* and *at.*

CHALLENGE
Organize teams for a game in which players create sports sentences containing object pronouns. For example, *The pitcher struck me out.* Give three points for a correct sentence and a one-point penalty for a sentence with errors.

FOR STUDENTS ACQUIRING ENGLISH
Have students complete a series of actions delivering objects to people. For example, say, "Pick up that pencil. Give it to Kaya." Include multiple direct and indirect objects. Then have students take turns giving directions to classmates.

On Your Own

Write each sentence. Use an object pronoun in place of the underlined word or words.

Example: Mr. Rossi handed Ernesto and me hard hats.
Mr. Rossi handed us hard hats.

7. He said, "You must wear these hats." them
8. Kendra led a pony into the ring and patted the pony. it
9. Mr. Rossi lifted Kendra onto the pony's back. her
10. Pick up the reins and hold the reins like this. them
11. Mr. Rossi gave Ernesto, Kendra, and me a riding lesson. us
12. We thanked Mr. Rossi for the lesson. him
13. We said that we had enjoyed the lesson. it

14–20. Write this part of a story. Use an object pronoun in place of the underlined word or words.

Example: Tate and I hurried to Cara. *Tate and I hurried to her.*

Mystery on the Mountain

us The horses carried Cara, Tate, and me slowly up the rocky trail. We had been searching since dawn for the missing ponies. My horse stumbled, it and I spoke softly to the horse. Cara was far ahead of Tate and me. We couldn't see Cara. Suddenly, Tate heard Cara us; her call excitedly to Tate. I told Tate to run ahead. He yelled him; him that Cara had found the ponies. At last I reached the top of the trail. Then I too saw the ponies. them

Writing Wrap-Up WRITING • THINKING • LISTENING • SPEAKING — NARRATING

Write a Story

What may happen next in the story above? Write the next paragraph. Use three or four object pronouns. Then read your paragraph to a partner. Does your paragraph make sense?

For Extra Practice see page 228.

Summing Up Help students summarize these key points about the lesson:

> **Object pronouns** include *me, you, him, her, it, us,* and *them.* Use object pronouns after action verbs and words such as *to, with, for,* and *at.*

You may want to have students complete the parts related to this lesson on Blackline Master 6–1.

On Your Own

Suggest that students examine the underlined word or phrase, decide whether it is singular or plural, and then select the appropriate object pronoun from the chart.

MEETING INDIVIDUAL NEEDS

FOR STUDENTS ACQUIRING ENGLISH

Distribute SAE Practice page for Unit 6, Lesson 3. Have students describe what they see in the art. Students replace the underlined words with object pronouns.

1. The two girls ride the horses every day. (them)
2. Samantha helped Alex get on the horse. (him)

Writing Wrap-Up

Writing Tip: Remind students to keep the story moving with action events. See Blackline Master 6–5 for a sample story.

SCHOOL-HOME CONNECTION

Suggest that students read their paragraph to family members and then discuss what each member thinks will happen next.

● RETEACHING WORKBOOK, page 59

3 Object Pronouns

- Use **object pronouns** after action verbs and words such as *to, with, for,* and *at.*

Singular object pronouns: me, you, him, her, it
Plural object pronouns: us, you, them

Noun	Firefighters spoke to the children.
Pronoun	Firefighters spoke to **them.**
Noun	Chief Drake gave Andrea a book.
Pronoun	Chief Drake gave **her** a book.

Write the object pronoun in parentheses that can take the place of the underlined word or words.

Example: "We can help Andrea," said the chief. **(her, she)** **her**

1. One day Andrea smelled smoke in the house. **(it, them)** it
2. She knew what the firefighters had taught Andrea. **(her, she)** her
3. She felt the door before she opened the door. **(them, it)** it
4. The door did not feel hot to Andrea. **(her, she)** her
5. Andrea phoned the firefighters. **(they, them)** them
6. "Give Chief Drake the address," said Chief Drake. **(me, I)** me
7. Andrea gave the address to Chief Tom Drake. **(he, him)** him
8. The fire trucks were ready for the firefighters. **(they, them)** them
9. Soon the firefighters arrived at the house. **(it, you)** it
10. Andrea's mother was outside with Andrea. **(her, she)** her
11. "Can you help Andrea and me?" asked Mrs. Katz. **(we, us)** us
12. The firefighters hooked a hose to the truck. **(it, me)** it
13. Then they aimed the hose at the flames. **(them, they)** them
14. Later, Andrea and Mrs. Katz thanked Chief Drake. **(he, him)** him
15. Chief Drake asked Andrea and Mrs. Katz if there was anything else he could do. **(they, them)** them

▲■ WORKBOOK PLUS, pages 98–99

3 Object Pronouns

Nouns	Pronouns
Jill Waldo writes books.	Jill Waldo writes **them.**
I spoke to Jill.	I spoke to **her.**

A Write the object pronouns in these sentences.

1. I asked Jill to show Russell and me a writer's office. me
2. Jill showed us the desk and the computer. us
3. A history book was on the desk. Jill had written it. it
4. Jill said, "I will tell you how schoolbooks are made." you
5. Writers write the books. Editors correct them. them
6. We listened carefully to her. her

B Write each sentence. Use an object pronoun in place of the underlined word or words.

7. Jill introduced Russell and me to Frank Silvio.
   Jill introduced us to Frank Silvio.
8. Frank is an artist who works with Jill.
   Frank is an artist who works with her.
9. Frank draws maps. We enjoyed looking at the maps.
   Frank draws maps. We enjoyed looking at them.
10. We asked Frank many questions about this work.
    We asked him many questions about this work.
11. He said, "I have to be very careful with the drawings."
    He said, "I have to be very careful with them."
12. Frank gave Russell a drawing. We liked the drawing.
    Frank gave Russell a drawing. We liked it.

(continued)

3 Object Pronouns *(continued from page 98)*

Challenge

Look at the pictures below. They show four steps in writing and publishing a book. Sample answers:

1. 
Rita Lott writes it.

3. 
The editor corrects them.

2. 
The editor thanks her for the book.

4. 
The books are printed by him.

These four sentences tell about the pictures above. Write each sentence under the picture that it describes. Use an object pronoun in place of the underlined word or words.

The editor thanks Rita for the book.
The books are printed by a printer.
Rita Lott writes a book.
The editor corrects the mistakes.

Writing Application: A Report — DESCRIBING

Think of a job or a project that you have worked on with your friends or your family. Write a short description of this project. Use six object pronouns.
Students should respond on separate paper. Answers will vary.

Writing with Pronouns

Lesson Objective

Students will:
- replace confusing pronouns with nouns

Focus on Instruction

- Remind students that a pronoun takes the place of a noun and that pronouns can make writing easier to read. Explain to students that it must be clear which noun a pronoun refers to or that pronoun should not be used. Write the sentences below on the board.

  Jess and his brother Aaron teach young children how to play chess. They completely enjoy the experience.

- Ask students which noun or nouns the word *they* replaces. (It's not clear.)
- Then ask a volunteer to suggest a way to fix the confusion. (Sample answers: *The brothers completely enjoy the experience. The children completely enjoy the experience.*)

Apply It

Have students complete the revising activity independently.

Have students look in their writing in progress to find confusing pronouns that need to be changed to nouns.

Sample Answers to Apply It

1. The sheep were scared, but the clippers didn't hurt them.
2. Later Albert looked so much cooler and happier!
3. The hens frightened me a little, but I stayed anyway.
4. At last the hens ran out the door, and I collected six eggs!

FOR STUDENTS ACQUIRING ENGLISH

Have students write a pronoun to replace the underlined noun in these sentences:
The cow ate grass as ______ walked. (it)
María sang as ______ worked. (she)
Joe read as ______ sat. (he)

Revising Strategies

Writing with Pronouns

Writing Clearly with Pronouns When you use pronouns, be sure their meanings are clear. This will help your reader understand your writing.

Marja had never visited Aunt Shelby before. She ran a dairy farm in Vermont.

Did Marja or Aunt Shelby run a dairy farm? When a pronoun might confuse your reader, simply replace it with a noun.

Marja had never visited Aunt Shelby before. Aunt Shelby ran a dairy farm in Vermont.

Apply It

1–4. Rewrite this journal entry. Replace the underlined pronouns with nouns. Make sure the sentences make sense. See TE margin for sample answers.

Revising

Tuesday, May 4

Yesterday Aunt Shelby and Uncle Patel sheared the sheep with electric clippers. They were scared, but the clippers didn't hurt them. Uncle Patel struggled with one wiggly sheep named Albert. Later he looked so much cooler and happier!

Today I went to the hen house for eggs. The hens were sleeping inside. They woke up when I walked in. They started clucking, and they flew off their nests. They frightened me a little, but I stayed anyway. At last they ran out the door, and I collected six eggs!

210 Unit 6: Pronouns

Meeting Individual Needs

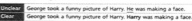

● RETEACHING WORKBOOK, page 60

Writing with Pronouns

- When you use pronouns, be sure their meanings are clear.
- Replace confusing pronouns with nouns.

Unclear	George took a funny picture of Harry. He was making a face.
Clear	George took a funny picture of Harry. **Harry** was making a face.

Writing Clearly with Pronouns Rewrite the sentences below. Replace the underlined pronoun with a noun. You may need to add *a* or *the* before the noun.
Sample answers:
Example: George took a picture with his camera. He gave it to Harry.
George took a picture with his camera. He gave the picture to Harry.

Revising

1. George met Harry in the park. He took pictures.
   George met Harry in the park. George took pictures.
2. The boys found a bird's nest with three eggs. They were blue.
   The boys found a bird's nest with three eggs. The eggs were blue.
3. George photographed a bridge from a hill. It was made of iron.
   George photographed a bridge from a hill. The bridge was made of iron.
4. The boys collected leaves and acorns. They were red and yellow.
   The boys collected leaves and acorns. The leaves were red and yellow.
5. Children played in the leaves. George took pictures of them.
   Children played in the leaves. George took pictures of the children.
6. A squirrel scampered up a tree. It had a bushy tail.
   A squirrel scampered up a tree. The squirrel had a bushy tail.

▲■ WORKBOOK PLUS, page 100

Writing with Pronouns

Unclear pronoun	Mr. Norris smiled as Jeremy entered the elevator. He pressed the button to close the door.
Pronoun replaced with a noun	Mr. Norris smiled as Jeremy entered the elevator. **Mr. Norris** pressed the button to close the door.

Writing Clearly with Pronouns 1–5. Rewrite the sentences within this story that have underlined pronouns. Replace the underlined pronouns with nouns.

Revising

Jenny Mouse lives in the country. One day, Jenny traveled to the city to visit her cousin, Annie Mouse. Annie took Jenny to the tallest building in town. She had never seen anything like it. From the observation deck on the top floor, Annie and Jenny looked at the buildings and cars below. It seemed that they could see for miles. Annie put a coin in the telescope. Then she pointed it at an apartment building across from a park. "I live over there," she told her cousin. Annie flitted from one window to another, trying to see everything, but the view made Jenny dizzy. She couldn't wait to get back on solid ground again.

The next day she went to the train station with Jenny.

"Come again soon!" called Annie, as the train pulled out of the station.

1. Jenny had never seen anything like it.
2. It seemed that Annie and Jenny could see for miles.
3. Then she pointed the telescope at an apartment building across from a park.
4. Jenny couldn't wait to get back on solid ground again.
5. The next day Annie went to the train station with Jenny.

(continued)

Combining Sentences Sometimes you can combine two sentences by joining them with words such as *because, before, when, since,* and *after.* If the two sentences have the same subject, you can change one of the subjects to a pronoun. Your writing will be smoother and more interesting.

The cows are fed. The cows have been milked.

The cows are fed after they have been milked.

Apply It

5–8. Rewrite each picture caption below. Change the subject of the underlined sentence to a pronoun. Then use the word in ( ) to combine the two sentences.
See TE margin for answers.

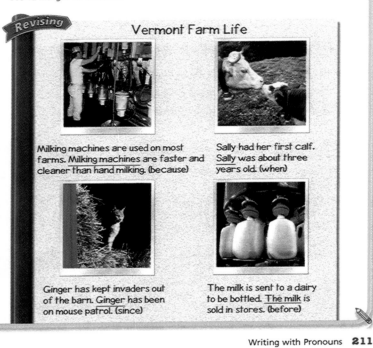

Revising

Vermont Farm Life

Milking machines are used on most farms. Milking machines are faster and cleaner than hand milking. (because)

Sally had her first calf. Sally was about three years old. (when)

Ginger has kept invaders out of the barn. Ginger has been on mouse patrol. (since)

The milk is sent to a dairy to be bottled. The milk is sold in stores. (before)

Lesson Objective

Students will:

- combine sentences by making one sentence a main clause and one a subordinate clause

Focus on Instruction

- Point out that two consecutive sentences often have a relationship. One sentence event may happen before, after, or at the same time as the other, or one may happen as a result of or in spite of the other. This relationship can be demonstrated by combining the two sentences into a complex sentence.
- Tell students that a complex sentence has a main clause and a subordinate clause (one clause that can stand alone as a sentence and one that cannot). The words used to introduce a subordinate clause are called *subordinating conjunctions.* Give these examples: *after, although, before, since, because,* and *when.*
- Write on the board the two simple sentences below and discuss their relationship. Then write the complex sentence. Ask a volunteer to find the subordinating conjunction. (because)

  The baseball game was canceled. A bad storm had flooded the field.

  The baseball game was canceled because a bad storm had flooded the field.

Apply It

Have students complete the revising activity independently. Tell students that when they substitute the second subject with a pronoun, they should be sure to use a subject pronoun that agrees with the first subject in person and number.

Have students find places in their own writing in progress where they can combine simple sentences into complex ones.

Answers to Apply It

5. Milking machines are used on most farms because they are faster and cleaner than hand milking.
6. Sally had her first calf when she was about three years old.
7. Ginger has kept invaders out of the barn since she has been on mouse patrol.
8. The milk is sent to a dairy to be bottled before it is sold in stores.

● RETEACHING WORKBOOK, page 61

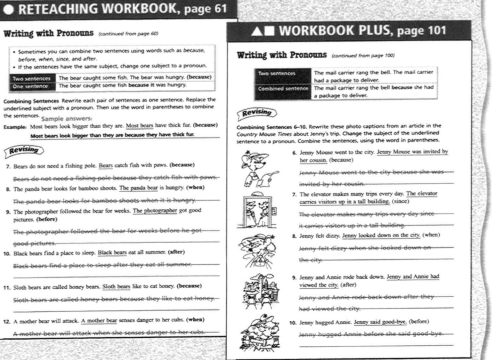

Writing with Pronouns *(continued from page 60)*

- Sometimes you can combine two sentences using words such as *because, before, when, since,* and *after.*
- If the sentences have the same subject, change one subject to a pronoun.

Two sentences	The bear caught some fish. The bear was hungry. **(because)**
One sentence	The bear caught some fish **because it** was hungry.

Combining Sentences Rewrite each pair of sentences as one sentence. Replace the underlined subject with a pronoun. Then use the word in parentheses to combine the sentences. Sample answers:

Example: Most bears look bigger than they are. Most bears have thick fur. **(because)**
Most bears look bigger than they are because they have thick fur.

Revising

7. Bears do not need a fishing pole. Bears catch fish with paws. **(because)**
   Bears do not need a fishing pole because they catch fish with paws.
8. The panda bear looks for bamboo shoots. The panda bear is hungry. **(when)**
   The panda bear looks for bamboo shoots when it is hungry.
9. The photographer followed the bear for weeks. The photographer got good pictures. **(before)**
   The photographer followed the bear for weeks before he got good pictures.
10. Black bears find a place to sleep. Black bears eat all summer. **(after)**
   Black bears find a place to sleep after they eat all summer.
11. Sloth bears are called honey bears. Sloth bears like to eat honey. **(because)**
   Sloth bears are called honey bears because they like to eat honey.
12. A mother bear will attack. A mother bear senses danger to her cubs. **(when)**
   A mother bear will attack when she senses danger to her cubs.

▲■ WORKBOOK PLUS, page 101

Writing with Pronouns *(continued from page 100)*

Two sentences	The mail carrier rang the bell. The mail carrier had a package to deliver.
Combined sentence	The mail carrier rang the bell **because** she had a package to deliver.

Revising

Combining Sentences 6–10. Rewrite these photo captions from an article in the *Country Mouse Times* about Jenny's trip. Change the subject of the underlined sentence to a pronoun. Combine the sentences, using the word in parentheses.

6. Jenny Mouse went to the city. Jenny Mouse was invited by her cousin. (because)
   Jenny Mouse went to the city because she was invited by her cousin.

7. The elevator makes many trips every day. The elevator carries visitors up in a tall building. (since)
   The elevator makes many trips every day since it carries visitors up in a tall building.

8. Jenny felt dizzy. Jenny looked down on the city. (when)
   Jenny felt dizzy when she looked down on the city.

9. Jenny and Annie rode back down. Jenny and Annie had viewed the city. (after)
   Jenny and Annie rode back down after they had viewed the city.

10. Jenny hugged Annie. Jenny said good-bye. (before)
   Jenny hugged Annie before she said good-bye.

Using *I* and *me*

Lesson Objectives

Students will:

- use *I* and *me* correctly
- proofread a thank-you note for correct usage of *I* and *me*
- write a thank-you note, using *I* and *me*

One-Minute Warm-Up Have students read the second sentence twice—once as written and again without *Mom and.* Explain that *me* is incorrect because object pronouns cannot be used as subjects.

Focus on Instruction

Explain that often people mistakenly use *I* after words such as *with* because it "sounds right" to them, as in *Please come with Dee and I.* Tell students to restate the sentence, omitting *Dee and.* (Please come with I.) Point out that it is easy to hear that the object pronoun *me* must be used instead of *I.*

Try It Out

VIEWING Display a two-column chart with the headings *I* and *me*. Have students use *I* and *me* to make up sentences that the boy in the picture might say. Place the sentences in the appropriate column of the chart. (Sample responses are shown.)

I	Me
My family and I made dinner.	They made me laugh.

FOR STUDENTS ACQUIRING ENGLISH

- Have students listen to the Try It Out sentences on the audiotape. Distribute SAE Practice page for Unit 6, Lesson 4, to support listening.
- Tell students that sometimes English speakers forget that it is good manners to mention other people first. Give several examples of prepositions followed by single object pronouns, and then multiple objects. Remind students to think about the object pronoun by itself if they are unsure whether to use *I* or *me.* Students listen and choose the correct pronoun.

1. ______ visited Jaime. *(Jane and I/I and Jane)* (Jane and I)

2. His mother gave ______ milk and cookies. *(Jane and me/me and Jane)* (Jane and me)

Usage

4 Using *I* and *me*

One-Minute Warm-Up

What's wrong with this e-mail message? How can you fix it?
Mom and I will make tacos.

> Please join Ethan and me for dinner. Mom and me will make tacos.

- When you talk or write about yourself, you use the pronoun *I* or *me.* Do you ever have trouble deciding whether to use *I* or *me* with another noun or pronoun? One way to check is to say the sentence to yourself with only *I* or *me.*

Kim and I study.	I study.
Mrs. Ling teaches Kim and me.	Mrs. Ling teaches me.
Aaron studies with Kim and me.	Aaron studies with me.

- Remember to use *I* as the subject of a sentence. Use *me* after action verbs and after words such as *to, with, for,* and *at.*
- When you talk about yourself and another person, always name yourself last.

Incorrect: I and Kim help Aaron. Aaron thanks me and Kim.

Correct: Kim and I help Aaron. Aaron thanks Kim and me.

Try It Out

Speak Up Which words complete each sentence correctly?

1. Reggie invited (me and Jen, **Jen and me**) to his house.
2. (I and Jen, **Jen and I**) walked home with Reggie.
3. Reggie talked to (**Jen and me**, me and Jen) about Barbados.
4. Jen and (**I**, me) were very interested.
5. Jen and (**I**, me) ate with Reggie's family.
6. The food tasted wonderful to Jen and (I, **me**).
7. (I and Jen, **Jen and I**) had never eaten a roti before.
8. A roti is a curried meat pie. Both (I and Jen, **Jen and I**) liked it immensely.

Meeting Individual Needs

RETEACHING
ALTERNATIVE STRATEGY

- On the board, write *My family and I moved to Texas. The Texans welcomed my family and me.*
- Have students identify the subject of the first sentence. (My family and I) Explain that *I* is a subject pronoun. Point out that *me* follows the action verb *welcomed* and is an object pronoun.
- Tell students that when a pronoun is used with a double subject or a double object, the pronoun comes last. Have students make up sentences using *I* and *me* in double subjects and in double objects.

CHALLENGE

Ask each student to write his or her name on a slip of paper and place it in an envelope. In another envelope, put slips of paper on which you have written *I* or *me.* Have students take a slip from each envelope and use the two words with the word *and* in a sentence.

FOR STUDENTS ACQUIRING ENGLISH

Explain that when two or more people are mentioned at the same time, some English speakers have trouble deciding when to use *I* and when to use *me.* Write and say sentences with *me* as an object pronoun. Include a few sentences with a second object.

On Your Own

Write the words that correctly complete each sentence.

Example: (Scott and me, Scott and I) visited Japan. *Scott and I*

9. Scott came with (me and my family, my family and me).
10. (Scott and me, Scott and I) sat together on the plane.
11. (Scott and I, I and Scott) became friends with Michiko.
12. She took (Scott and me, Scott and I) on a tour.
13. (He and me, He and I) learned about the capital city, Tokyo.
14. Michiko taught (Scott and me, Scott and I) Japanese words.

15–20. This thank-you note has six mistakes in using *I* and *me*. Write the note correctly. Underlined words are rewritten.

Example: Me and Becky love our kimonos. *Becky and I love our kimonos.*

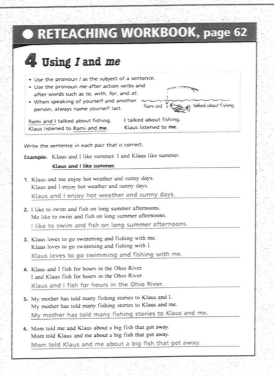

Proofreading

Dear Mrs. Ono,

Thanks for being a great host to my family and I in Japan. (me) You showed my family and me a wonderful time! My family and me (I) will never forget you. Dad is trying all your recipes. He made me and my sister (my sister and me) some bean-curd soup. Me and Mom (Mom and I) were talking about the Bunraku puppets today. They looked so real! Becky and me (I) look at the photos from our trip every day. Will you write to Becky and I (me) soon?

Yours truly,
Katie

Writing Wrap-Up

WRITING • THINKING • LISTENING • SPEAKING

EXPRESSING

Write a Thank-You Note

Write a thank-you note to a friend or relative that you and your family visited recently. Use *I* and *me* in your sentences. Then read your thank-you note to a partner. Work together to make sure you used *I* and *me* correctly.

For Extra Practice see page 229.

Summing Up Help students summarize these key points about the lesson:

Use *I* as the subject of a sentence. Use *me* after action verbs and words such as *to, for,* and *at.* When you use *I* or *me* with another noun or pronoun, always name yourself last.

You may want to have students complete the parts related to this lesson on Blackline Master 6–2.

On Your Own

Suggest that students check their choices by omitting the noun and rereading the sentence with the pronoun only.

MEETING INDIVIDUAL NEEDS

FOR STUDENTS ACQUIRING ENGLISH

Distribute SAE Practice page for Unit 6, Lesson 4. Have students locate Japan on a map or globe. Ask if any of them have been there. Students underline the correct pronouns.

Example: ______ visited Japan. (My father and I) (Me and my father/My father and I)

Writing Wrap-Up

Writing Tip: Suggest that students describe a particular activity or food that they enjoyed while on the visit. See Blackline Master 6–6 for a sample thank-you note.

TECHNOLOGY CONNECTION

Have students use word-processing software to format their note as a friendly letter.

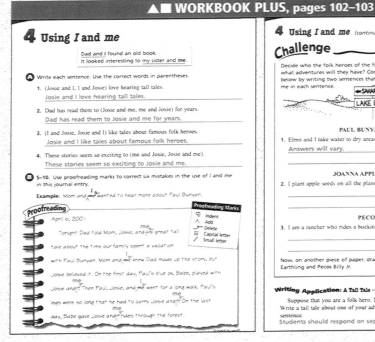

● RETEACHING WORKBOOK, page 62

4 Using *I* and *me*

- Use the pronoun *I* as the subject of a sentence.
- Use the pronoun *me* after action verbs and after words such as *to, with, for,* and *at.*
- When speaking of yourself and another person, always name yourself last.

Rami and I talked about fishing. I talked about fishing.
Klaus listened to Rami and **me**. Klaus listened to **me**.

Write the sentence in each pair that is correct.

Example: Klaus and I like summer. I and Klaus like summer.
Klaus and I like summer.

1. Klaus and me enjoy hot weather and sunny days.
   Klaus and I enjoy hot weather and sunny days.
   Klaus and I enjoy hot weather and sunny days.
2. I like to swim and fish on long summer afternoons.
   Me like to swim and fish on long summer afternoons.
   I like to swim and fish on long summer afternoons.
3. Klaus loves to go swimming and fishing with me.
   Klaus loves to go swimming and fishing with I.
   Klaus loves to go swimming and fishing with me.
4. Klaus and I fish for hours in the Ohio River.
   I and Klaus fish for hours in the Ohio River.
   Klaus and I fish for hours in the Ohio River.
5. My mother has told many fishing stories to Klaus and I.
   My mother has told many fishing stories to Klaus and me.
   My mother has told many fishing stories to Klaus and me.
6. Mom told me and Klaus about a big fish that got away.
   Mom told Klaus and me about a big fish that got away.
   Mom told Klaus and me about a big fish that got away.

▲■ WORKBOOK PLUS, pages 102–103

4 Using *I* and *me*

Dad and I found an old book.
It looked interesting to my sister and **me**.

A Write each sentence. Use the correct words in parentheses.

1. (Josie and I, I and Josie) love hearing tall tales.
   Josie and I love hearing tall tales.
2. Dad has read them to (Josie and me, me and Josie) for years.
   Dad has read them to Josie and me for years.
3. (I and Josie, Josie and I) like tales about famous folk heroes.
   Josie and I like tales about famous folk heroes.
4. These stories seem so exciting to (me and Josie, Josie and me).
   These stories seem so exciting to Josie and me.

B 5–10. Use proofreading marks to correct six mistakes in the use of *I* and *me* in this journal entry.

Example: Mom and ~~me~~ I wanted to hear more about Paul Bunyan.

Proofreading

Proofreading Marks
¶ Indent
∧ Add
Delete
≡ Capital letter
/ Small letter

April 6, 2001

Tonight Dad told Mom, Josie, and ~~I~~ me a great tall tale about the time our family spent a vacation with Paul Bunyan. Mom and ~~me~~ I knew Dad made up the story, but Josie believed it. On the first day, Paul's blue ox, Babe, played with Josie and ~~I~~ me. Then Paul, Josie, and ~~me~~ I went for a long walk. Paul's legs were so long that he had to carry Josie and ~~I~~ me. On the last day, Babe gave Josie and ~~I~~ me rides through the forest.

(continued)

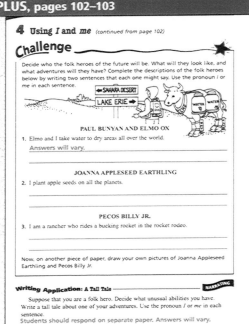

4 Using *I* and *me* (continued from page 102)

Challenge

Decide who the folk heroes of the future will be. What will they look like, and what adventures will they have? Complete the descriptions of the folk heroes below by writing two sentences that each one might say. Use the pronoun *I* or *me* in each sentence.

PAUL BUNYAN AND ELMO OX

1. Elmo and I take water to dry areas all over the world.
   Answers will vary.

JOANNA APPLESEED EARTHLING

2. I plant apple seeds on all the planets.

PECOS BILLY JR.

3. I am a rancher who rides a bucking rocket in the rocket rodeo.

Now, on another piece of paper, draw your own pictures of Joanna Appleseed Earthling and Pecos Billy Jr.

Writing Application: A Tall Tale NARRATING

Suppose that you are a folk hero. Decide what unusual abilities you have. Write a tall tale about one of your adventures. Use the pronoun *I* or *me* in each sentence.
Students should respond on separate paper. Answers will vary.

Possessive Pronouns

Lesson Objectives

Students will:

- identify possessive pronouns in sentences
- substitute possessive pronouns for possessive nouns
- write an interview, using possessive pronouns

One-Minute Warm-Up Make sure that students understand the concept of possession. Ask students how to describe something that belongs to them. Encourage responses such as *my bicycle.* Then ask how they might describe something that belongs to a group. Example: *their boat* or *our house.*

Focus on Instruction

Point out that an apostrophe and *s* are never added to a possessive pronoun as they are to a possessive noun.

Try It Out

VIEWING Direct students' attention to the photo of the boy and the bird. Ask the questions in the chart below and have students answer, using possessive pronouns. Have students identify the possessive pronouns. (Sample answers are shown.)

Question/ Answer	Possessive Pronoun
What is the boy doing? The boy is looking at his parakeet.	his
What kind of bird do you and I have? Our bird is a canary.	our

FOR STUDENTS ACQUIRING ENGLISH

- Have students listen to the Try It Out sentences on the audiotape. Distribute SAE Practice page for Unit 6, Lesson 5, to support listening.
- Have students describe the art. Discuss pet ownership. Assist with vocabulary. Explain that most people in the United States refer to their pets as *he* or *she* rather than *it.* However, *it* is the pronoun that we use when we do not know the gender of the animal. Use students' names and possessions as you briefly review possessives with *'s.* Students listen and replace possessives with pronouns.
  1. Mr. Ling owns a pet shop. Chris went to Mr. Ling's pet shop. (his)
  2. Chris's dog Jake needs a new collar. (Her)
  3. Jake broke the dog's collar. (his)

Grammar/Usage

5 Possessive Pronouns

One-Minute Warm-Up

Read the sentences below. Find the pronouns. Which pronouns show ownership?

"Llamas usually live in South America, in Peru," my mother said. "Their hair is used to make wool and they are good at carrying things." my, Their, they; my, Their

—from *A Llama in the Family,* by Johanna Hurwitz

You have learned that possessive nouns show ownership. You can use pronouns in place of possessive nouns. **A pronoun that shows ownership is a possessive pronoun.**

Possessive Nouns	Possessive Pronouns
Pam feeds Pam's pet.	Pam feeds her pet.
She fills the pet's dish.	She fills its dish.
The boys' gerbil is playful.	Their gerbil is playful.

Possessive Pronouns

Singular	Plural
my	our
your	your
her, his, its	their

Try It Out

Speak Up Which possessive pronoun should you use in place of the underlined word or words?

his 1. Max and I help Mr. Lee at Mr. Lee's pet shop.
their 2. Max gives the puppies the puppies' food.
her 3. Angela is saving Angela's money for a pet.
its 4. She will buy the parakeet and the parakeet's cage.
your 5. Angela, you and Angela's sister will love the parakeet.
its 6. Max watches the parakeet as it sits on the parakeet's perch.
my 7. Angela says, "One day this bird will be Angela's parakeet."

Meeting Individual Needs

RETEACHING
ALTERNATIVE STRATEGY

- Ask these questions and write students' responses on the board. "How would you refer to the radio you own?" (my radio) "How would I refer to Aunt Mae's house when I'm talking to her?" (your house) "How would team members refer to their coach?" (our coach)
- Have volunteers underline the word in the answer that shows ownership. Tell students that these words are possessive pronouns and they take the place of possessive nouns in sentences.
- Have students tell what possessive noun each possessive pronoun replaces.

CHALLENGE

Have students list the seven possessive pronouns. Have them imagine that they are shipwrecked on a desert island. Ask them to list seven possessions they would want to have, one to go with each pronoun. Have them add in parentheses the possessive noun that each pronoun replaces.

FOR STUDENTS ACQUIRING ENGLISH

Write the possessive pronouns on index cards. Have students display the cards in front of appropriate people or objects and say, for example, "his hair; their desks."

On Your Own

Write the possessive pronoun in each sentence.

Example: My favorite animal is the llama. *My*

8. Its close relative is the camel.
9. People in Peru use llamas to carry their packs.
10. A llama will lie down if its pack is too heavy.
11. People in our country are using llamas too.
12. Sheep ranchers use llamas to guard their flocks.
13. One man in Nebraska raises llamas on his ranch.
14. A woman bought one as a pet for her grandchildren.

15–20. Write this letter. Use a possessive pronoun in place of each underlined word or words.

Example: Mr. Cook sold Mr. Cook's ranch. *Mr. Cook sold his ranch.*

Dear Adriana,

My uncle has two llamas on my (his) uncle's ranch. If a coyote comes near, the llamas stamp the llamas' (their) feet, bray, spit, chase, and kick. Coyotes decide to find coyotes' (their) next meal elsewhere.

The llamas will not let a coyote, wolf, or mountain lion near a lamb or a lamb's (its) mother. In Sam's (my) opinion, llamas are the best guards a rancher can have for a rancher's (his/her) flock.

Your friend,
Sam

Writing Wrap-Up

WRITING • THINKING • LISTENING • SPEAKING

EXPRESSING

Write an Interview

You need to hire someone to take care of a pet. What skills will the person need? Write five questions to ask in an interview. Use possessive pronouns. Ask a partner to write answers to the questions. Conduct your interview for the class.

For Extra Practice see page 230.

Summing Up Help students summarize these key points about the lesson:

A **possessive pronoun** may be used in place of a possessive noun to show ownership. Possessive pronouns include *my, your, her, his, its, our,* and *their.*

You may want to have students complete the parts related to this lesson on Blackline Master 6–3.

On Your Own

Remind students to look for a word that takes the place of a noun and shows ownership.

MEETING INDIVIDUAL NEEDS

FOR STUDENTS ACQUIRING ENGLISH

Distribute SAE Practice page for Unit 6, Lesson 5. Write *llama* and *donkey;* ask students what they know about these animals. Students underline the possessive pronouns. Then students identify the nouns to which the pronouns refer.

Example: Llamas and donkeys carry packs. Their packs are heavy. (Llamas and donkeys)

Writing Wrap-Up

Writing Tip: Suggest that students first list five skills a person needs to do the job well. Tell students to write a question about each skill. See Blackline Master 6–6 for a sample interview.

SCHOOL-HOME CONNECTION

Have students ask family members about their experiences in job interviews. What questions were they asked? How could they best prepare for a job interview?

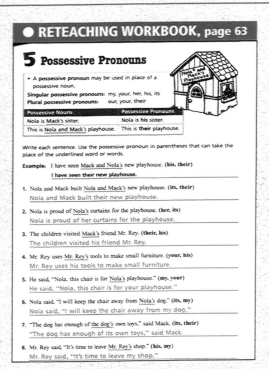

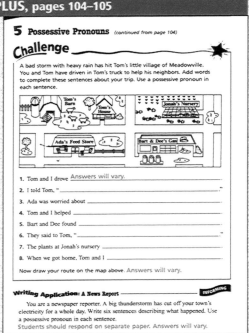

● RETEACHING WORKBOOK, page 63

5 Possessive Pronouns

- A **possessive pronoun** may be used in place of a possessive noun.

Singular possessive pronouns: my, your, her, his, its
Plural possessive pronouns: our, your, their

Possessive Nouns	Possessive Pronouns
Nola is Mack's sister.	Nola is **his** sister.
This is Nola and Mack's playhouse.	This is **their** playhouse.

Write each sentence. Use the possessive pronoun in parentheses that can take the place of the underlined word or words.

Example: I have seen Mack and Nola's new playhouse. **(his, their)**
I have seen their new playhouse.

1. Nola and Mack built Nola and Mack's new playhouse. **(its, their)**
Nola and Mack built their new playhouse.
2. Nola is proud of Nola's curtains for the playhouse. **(her, its)**
Nola is proud of her curtains for the playhouse.
3. The children visited Mack's friend Mr. Rey. **(their, his)**
The children visited his friend Mr. Rey.
4. Mr. Rey uses Mr. Rey's tools to make small furniture. **(your, his)**
Mr. Rey uses his tools to make small furniture.
5. He said, "Nola, this chair is for Nola's playhouse." **(my, your)**
He said, "Nola, this chair is for your playhouse."
6. Nola said, "I will keep the chair away from Nola's dog." **(its, my)**
Nola said, "I will keep the chair away from my dog."
7. "The dog has enough of the dog's own toys," said Mack. **(its, their)**
"The dog has enough of its own toys," said Mack.
8. Mr. Rey said, "It's time to leave Mr. Rey's shop." **(his, my)**
Mr. Rey said, "It's time to leave my shop."

▲■ WORKBOOK PLUS, pages 104–105

5 Possessive Pronouns

Possessive Nouns	Possessive Pronouns
Harry reads Harry's book.	Harry reads **his** book.
The girls did the girls' report.	The girls did **their** report.

A Write the possessive pronoun in each sentence.

1. The students worked together on their report. their
2. Harry told Carla about his book on weather. his
3. "There are many facts about storms in my book," said Harry. my
4. "Its pages have interesting pictures too," said Carla. Its
5. Tai got her information from a science program on TV. her
6. "Your notebook is full of facts now," said Harry. Your

B Write each sentence. Use a possessive pronoun in place of the underlined word or words.

7. The report told the children's classmates about safety in storms.
The report told their classmates about safety in storms.
8. Carla Rossini's part of the report was about lightning.
Her part of the report was about lightning.
9. The Rossinis' house is protected by a lightning rod.
Their house is protected by a lightning rod.
10. A lightning rod's purpose is to lead lightning safely to the ground.
Its purpose is to lead lightning safely to the ground.
11. Harry's section of the report was about safety in floods.
His section of the report was about safety in floods.
12. Mr. Akito gave Mr. Akito's students much praise for the report.
Mr. Akito gave his students much praise for the report.

(continued)

5 Possessive Pronouns *(continued from page 104)*

Challenge

A bad storm with heavy rain has hit Tom's little village of Meadowville. You and Tom have driven in Tom's truck to help his neighbors. Add words to complete these sentences about your trip. Use a possessive pronoun in each sentence.

1. Tom and I drove Answers will vary.
2. I told Tom, "______."
3. Ada was worried about ______.
4. Tom and I helped ______.
5. Bart and Dee found ______.
6. They said to Tom, "______."
7. The plants at Jonah's nursery ______.
8. When we got home, Tom and I ______.

Now draw your route on the map above. Answers will vary.

Writing Application: A News Report INFORMING

You are a newspaper reporter. A big thunderstorm has cut off your town's electricity for a whole day. Write six sentences describing what happened. Use a possessive pronoun in each sentence.
Students should respond on separate paper. Answers will vary.

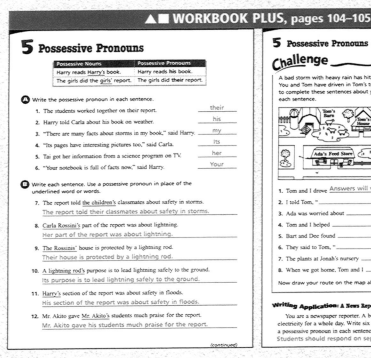

Contractions with Pronouns

Lesson Objectives

Students will:
- combine pronouns and verbs to write contractions
- proofread for contraction errors
- write a set of instructions, using pronoun contractions

One-Minute Warm-Up Ask students how they know which word is a contraction. (It has an apostrophe.) Tell students that an apostrophe takes the place of one or more letters. Ask students what letters were left out in *I'll.* (the *wi* in *will*)

Focus on Instruction

Point out that only subject pronouns are used to form contractions with verbs.

Try It Out

LISTENING AND SPEAKING Have a volunteer say a sentence using the first pair of words (I had). Then have someone repeat the sentence, this time using the contraction. Example: *I had hoped you would come./I'd hoped you would come.* Continue with the remaining word pairs.

FOR STUDENTS ACQUIRING ENGLISH

- Have students listen to the Try It Out sentences on the audiotape. Distribute SAE Practice page for Unit 6, Lesson 6, to support listening.
- Explain that *'s* can stand for *is* or *has* and *'d* can stand for *would* or *had*. Tell students that context will help them figure out which verb it is. Have partners or small groups work together to list as many contractions as they can. Tell students to write the full pronoun-verb phrases next to their contractions. Then pairs or groups can quiz others. Students listen and write the contraction for each pair of words. Practice saying the contractions.
  1. she is (she's)
  2. we will (we'll)
  3. you are (you're)

Grammar/Mechanics

6 Contractions with Pronouns

One-Minute Warm-Up

Read the sentences below. Which word is a contraction?

As the sun set in the western sky, Steven turned to his grandfather. "Thanks, PaPa, I'll never forget this," he said. I'll

—from *Clambake: A Wampanoag Tradition*, by Russell M. Peters

- A **contraction** may be formed by combining a pronoun and a verb. Use an apostrophe (') in place of the letter or letters that are left out.

Pronoun and Verb	Contraction	Pronoun and Verb	Contraction
I am	I'm	I have	I've
he is	he's	he has	he's
she is	she's	she has	she's
it is	it's	it has	it's
you are	you're	you have	you've
we are	we're	we have	we've
they are	they're	they have	they've
I will	I'll	I had	I'd
you will	you'll	you had	you'd
she will	she'll	he had	he'd
they will	they'll	we had	we'd

- Notice that *he's, she's,* and *it's* are listed twice. The contractions for the pronouns *he, she,* and *it* with the verbs *is* and *has* are the same.

Try It Out

Speak Up What is the contraction for each of the following pairs of words?

1. I had I'd
2. she will she'll
3. he had he'd
4. we have we've
5. they will they'll
6. she has she's
7. you have you've
8. it has it's

Meeting Individual Needs

RETEACHING
ALTERNATIVE STRATEGY

- List these pairs of words on the board:

I am	*you'll*
they are	*I'm*
you will	*they're*

- Ask volunteers to draw lines to match the words in column 1 with the contractions in column 2.
- Discuss how each contraction was formed, combining a pronoun with a verb. Help students identify the letter(s) replaced by an apostrophe.
- Continue the activity with other contractions.

CHALLENGE

Write *am, is, are, will, have, has,* and *had* on the board. Then write *I, he, she, it, you, we,* and *they* on individual cards. Have students draw a pronoun card and make sentences, using the pronoun in a contraction with as many of the listed verbs as possible.

FOR STUDENTS ACQUIRING ENGLISH

Have volunteers explain what a contraction is and how it is made. Briefly review contractions such as *isn't, can't, won't.* Alternate asking for full pronoun-verb phrases and their contractions.

On Your Own

Write the contractions for the underlined words.

Example: It is time for our club's dinner. *It's*

9. We are going to have a potluck supper. We're
10. We have each planned to make something different. We've
11. We hope you will bring your famous apple pie. you'll
12. The twins said they will bring chicken soup. they'll
13. They are experts at making chicken soup. They're
14. Lori said she will come early to decorate the hall. she'll
15. She is planning to bring vegetables and dip. She's

16–22. This cooking demonstration has seven incorrect contractions. Write the demonstration correctly. Incorrect words are underlined.

Example: Im going to teach you how to prepare noodles.
I'm going to teach you how to prepare noodles.

Proofreading

They're
The'yre easy to prepare and delicious too. I've Iv'e asked a volunteer to help me today. Hes He's never cooked before. First, sir, you're going to put water in the pot. When its' come it's to a boil, add the noodles. Separate them if they've stuck together. After you've youve done that, stir the noodles well. We'll W'ell let them boil for eight minutes. Then, presto, theyre cooked! they're

Writing Wrap-Up WRITING • THINKING • LISTENING • SPEAKING

EXPLAINING

Write Instructions

Write a paragraph explaining how to make a favorite food. Use at least five contractions. Then have a partner pantomime the instructions as you read them. Do your instructions make sense?

For Extra Practice see page 231.

Summing Up Help students summarize these key points about the lesson:

Pronouns and verbs may be combined to form **contractions**. Use an apostrophe in place of the letters that are left out.

You may want to have students complete the parts related to this lesson on Blackline Master 6–4.

On Your Own

Refer students to the charts on page 216 for help in spelling the contractions.

MEETING INDIVIDUAL NEEDS

FOR STUDENTS ACQUIRING ENGLISH

Distribute SAE Practice page for Unit 6, Lesson 6. Write *potluck* on the board. Ask, "What type of dinner is this?" As needed, explain that everyone brings a favorite dish and shares with the other guests. Students write contractions. Example: Our neighbors invited us to a party. They are having a potluck dinner. (They're)

Writing Wrap-Up

Writing Tip: Tell students to use words such as *first, then, last,* to keep the steps clear. See Blackline Master 6–7 for sample instructions.

SCHOOL-HOME CONNECTION

Before students write their cooking instructions, they might ask a family member to review the procedure to make sure the student has included all the steps.

● RETEACHING WORKBOOK, page 64

6 Contractions with Pronouns

- Pronouns and verbs may be combined to form contractions.
- Use an apostrophe (') in place of letters that are left out.

Pronoun and Verb	Contraction
We are learning about plants.	We're learning about plants.
She is working with me.	She's working with me.

Complete each sentence by writing a contraction for the words in parentheses. Use an apostrophe in place of the underlined letter or letters.

Example: You'll hear what we learned. (You will)

1. Last year we'd seen a film about Luther Burbank. (we had)
2. I've also asked Rita about Burbank. (I have)
3. She's read all about Burbank's work. (She has)
4. He'd developed many new plants. (He had)
5. You've seen some of Burbank's fruits at the market. (You have)
6. They're different kinds of plums and berries. (They are)
7. It's true that he grew plums that tasted like pears. (It is)
8. Now I'll ask Rita to explain Burbank's work. (I will)
9. She'll describe the main kinds of berries he grew. (She will)
10. We've found out more about Burbank. (We have)
11. We'd learned that he grew flowers too. (We had)
12. He's often remembered for developing the Shasta daisy. (He is)
13. You'll certainly enjoy eating Burbank potatoes. (You will)
14. I'm sure Burbank's work has helped other scientists. (I am)
15. They've used Burbank's ways of developing new plants. (They have)
16. They'll try to grow better plants in the future. (They will)
17. We're grateful for Burbank's work. (We are)
18. It's given us some delicious foods. (It has)

▲■ WORKBOOK PLUS, pages 106–107

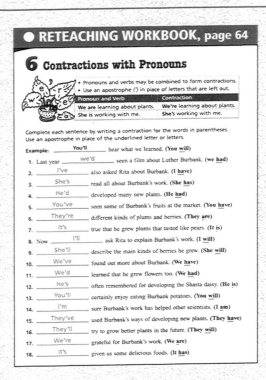

6 Contractions with Pronouns

Pronoun and Verb	Contraction
We are going to the beach.	We're going to the beach.
You will have fun there.	You'll have fun there.
It is a beautiful day.	It's a beautiful day.

A Write the two words that make up each underlined contraction.

1. We've got everything we need. We have
2. I'm bringing the beach blanket. I am
3. Selina said that she's bringing the food. she is
4. Luis said that he'll drive the van. he will
5. He's looked at the map already. He has
6. Don and Helen said that they're going to be late. they are

B 7–12. Use proofreading marks to correct six incorrect contractions in this post card greeting.

Example: They're Theyr'e wearing sun hats and dark glasses.

Proofreading

Dear Don and Helen,

I'm Im happy as a clam at the beach. I hope you'll youll' come with us next time. Selina said that she's shes bringing more food next time because we're wer'e like hungry sharks after we swim. I'll bring more sunblock too. It's Its been no fun having a sunburn. You'd Youd' be surprised at what Selina calls my peeling skin. I'll tell you at the beach!

Your friend,
Luis

Proofreading Marks
¶ Indent
^ Add
Delete
≡ Capital letter
/ Small letter

(continued)

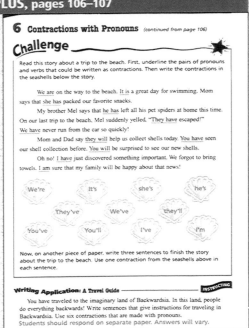

6 Contractions with Pronouns (continued from page 106)

Challenge

Read this story about a trip to the beach. First, underline the pairs of pronouns and verbs that could be written as contractions. Then write the contractions in the seashells below the story.

We are on the way to the beach. It is a great day for swimming. Mom says that she has packed our favorite snacks.

My brother Mel says that he has left all his pet spiders at home this time. On our last trip to the beach, Mel suddenly yelled, "They have escaped!" We have never run from the car so quickly!

Mom and Dad say they will help us collect shells today. You have seen our shell collection before. You will be surprised to see our new shells.

Oh no! I have just discovered something important. We forgot to bring towels. I am sure that my family will be happy about that news!

We're It's she's he's They've We've they'll You've You'll I've I'm

Now, on another piece of paper, write three sentences to finish the story about the trip to the beach. Use one contraction from the seashells above in each sentence.

Writing Application: A Travel Guide INSTRUCTING

You have traveled to the imaginary land of Backwardsia. In this land, people do everything backwards! Write sentences that give instructions for traveling in Backwardsia. Use six contractions that are made with pronouns.
Students should respond on separate paper. Answers will vary.

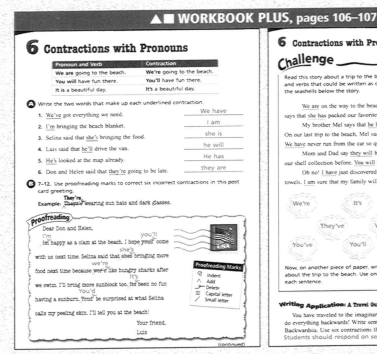

Pronouns and Homophones

Lesson Objectives

Students will:

- distinguish between the homophones *its* and *it's; they're, their,* and *there;* and *you're* and *your*
- proofread for pronoun and homophone usage
- write a nature report, using homophones

One-Minute Warm-Up Ask students why *your* and *you're* should be switched. (Sample answer: *Your*, a possessive pronoun, identifies the album owner, and *you're* is the contraction for *you are*.)

Focus on Instruction

Stress that a contraction uses an apostrophe whereas a possessive pronoun does not.

Try It Out

VIEWING Ask students to look at the photo of the puppies and make up phrases about them using each homophone in the lesson. Record the phrases in webs connecting each word group. (A sample web is shown.) Then have students make a complete sentence with each phrase.

They're adorable.
Their fur is soft.
they're
their
there
There the puppies sat.

FOR STUDENTS ACQUIRING ENGLISH

- Have students listen to the Try It Out sentences on the audiotape. Distribute SAE Practice page for Unit 6, Lesson 7, to support listening.
- Remind students that the context will help them decide which homophone is needed. Guide students in comparing the context for *their* and *they're*. Say, "What follows the word? If it's a noun, the word is probably the possessive *their*." Continue with other homophones from the list; provide sample sentences for context. Then students listen and choose the correct homophone.

1. Put the flowers over ______ on the table. (there) (there/they're)
2. ______ ideas are always good. (Your) (your/you're)

Grammar/Usage

7 Pronouns and Homophones

One-Minute Warm-Up

What two words should you switch to make this sentence correct?

Your going to want this picture in you're photo album. Your and you're

Homophones are words that sound alike but have different spellings and meanings. Writers often confuse some contractions and their homophones because these words sound alike. Study the chart below. Learn the spelling and the meaning of each homophone.

Homophone	Meaning	Sentence
it's its	it is belonging to it; of it	It's a beautiful bird! Take its picture.
they're their there	they are belonging to them in that place	They're odd birds. Their wings are big! There is a black one.
you're your	you are belonging to you	You're very lucky. Get your camera.

Try It Out

Speak Up Which word would you use to complete each sentence correctly?

1. I hear (you're, your) entering the photo contest.
2. Which of (you're, your) pictures will you enter?
3. (They're, There) all so good!
4. The puppies love having (they're, their) picture taken.
5. The picture (their, there) on your desk is interesting.
6. (It's, Its) colors are sharp and clear.
7. (It's, Its) hard to choose the best one!

Meeting Individual Needs

RETEACHING
ALTERNATIVE STRATEGY

- Write these sentences on the board: *You are invited to a party. It is Tuesday at 3:00. They are bringing food.*
- Ask what contractions can replace the underlined words. (*You're, It's,* and *They're*) Write each word and review its spelling.
- Write *Their party was fun. Your gift was unusual. Its wrapping was colorful.* Say that each underlined word is a possessive pronoun.
- Explain that homophones are words that sound alike but have different spellings and meanings. Have students identify the homophone pairs in the sentences.

CHALLENGE

Have teams prepare homophone cards. A member of each team draws a card and writes a sentence, using the homophone, as quickly as possible on the board. Others repeat the procedure until all of the homophones are used correctly. The first team to use all the words correctly wins.

FOR STUDENTS ACQUIRING ENGLISH

Say and write *to, two,* and *too.* Ask what each means. Explain that these words are called homophones; they all sound the same. Write *there.* Ask if students know two more words that sound like this. (they're, their)

On Your Own

Choose the word that completes each sentence correctly. Write the sentences.

Example: They've packed (their, they're) cameras.
They've packed their cameras.

8. (Their, They're) taking pictures in the park.
9. (You're, Your) invited to join them.
10. (There, They're) is a chipmunk.
11. (It's, Its) a member of the squirrel family.
12. You can take (it's, its) picture.
13. The squirrels over (they're, there) are noisy!
14. You should take (their, there) picture.
15. Is the chipmunk still sitting (their, there)?
16. (Your, You're) voice scared it.

17–22. This report has six incorrect pronouns. Write the report correctly.
Incorrect words are underlined.
Example: Squirrels use they're bushy tails like blankets.
Squirrels use their bushy tails like blankets.

Proofreading — Report, draft 2

Treetop Acrobats

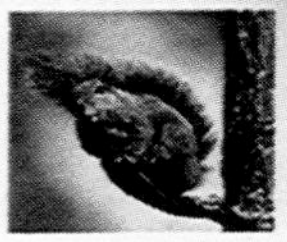

Everyone has seen a gray squirrel making it's way its through the trees. Their a familiar sight in cities and They're towns. Powerful jaws help squirrels remove seeds and nuts from there (their) hard shells. Look out you're window. your You might see a squirrel in your bird feeder!

The shy chipmunk is less common in the city. You probably won't find one they're. This little rodent makes it's home underground. there; its

Writing Wrap-Up

WRITING • THINKING • LISTENING • SPEAKING

COMPARING / CONTRASTING

Write a Nature Report

Use the information on this page and what you already know to write a report about chipmunks and squirrels. Include homophones from the chart on page 218. Read your report out loud. After each sentence with a homophone, pause and ask your classmates to spell it.

For Extra Practice see page 232.

Summing Up Help students summarize this key point about the lesson:

> Don't confuse contractions *it's, they're,* and *you're* with **homophones** *its, their, there,* and *your.* They have different meanings.

You may want to have students complete the parts related to this lesson on Blackline Master 6–3.

On Your Own

If students have trouble deciding when to use *it's, you're,* and *they're,* suggest that they insert *it is, you are,* or *they are* to find out if it makes sense in the sentence.

MEETING INDIVIDUAL NEEDS

FOR STUDENTS ACQUIRING ENGLISH

Distribute SAE Practice page for Unit 6, Lesson 7. Write one homophone on either side of a card. Partners use the cards to quiz each other. Discuss the art; assist with vocabulary. Students pick the correct homophone. Example: Look at the squirrels. _____ so cute! (They're) (There/They're)

Writing Wrap-Up

Writing Tip: Before they write, suggest that students make a Venn diagram to point out similarities and differences between squirrels and chipmunks. See Blackline Master 6–7 for a sample nature report.

SCHOOL-HOME CONNECTION

Invite students to ask family members to share nature observations, such as those about birds.

● RETEACHING WORKBOOK, page 65

7 Pronouns and Homophones

- Do not confuse the contractions *it's, they're,* and *you're* with their homophones *its, their, there,* and *your.*

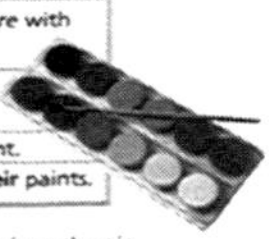

Homophones	
	You're a good painter.
	Your picture is pretty.
	It's a picture of a bird. Its colors are bright.
	They're going to paint too. There are their paints.

Write the words in parentheses to complete the sentences in each pair. Begin each sentence with a capital letter.

Example: All the children brought ___their___ paints. **(they're, their)**
___They're___ going to paint masks.

1. "May I use ___your___ yellow paint?" asked Teresa. **(your, you're)**
"___You're___ welcome to use it," said Nikos.
2. "___It's___ going to be a large mask," said Olive. **(its, it's)**
"I am painting ___its___ eyes yellow," Teresa said.
3. "___They're___ the strangest eyes!" said Nikos. **(they're, there)**
"Paint some black spots right ___there___," he added.
4. "Now ___its___ eyes look better," said Teresa. **(its, it's)**
"___It's___ a wonderful mask!" exclaimed Olive.
5. "___Your___ mask looks like a tiger," said Nikos. **(you're, your)**
"___You're___ right about that," replied Teresa.
6. "Only ___its___ whiskers are missing," said Olive. **(it's, its)**
"___It's___ time to clean up," said Teresa.
7. The children rinsed ___their___ brushes in water. **(they're, their)**
___They're___ drying them now with towels.
8. Now ___they're___ hanging the masks on the wall. **(they're, there)**
The masks are ___there___ for all to see.

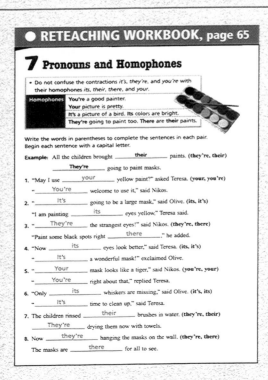

▲■ WORKBOOK PLUS, pages 108–109

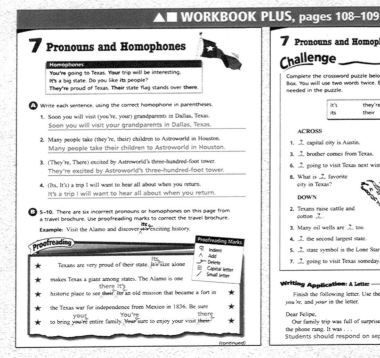

7 Pronouns and Homophones

Homophones
You're going to Texas. **Your** trip will be interesting.
It's a big state. Do you like **its** people?
They're proud of Texas. **Their** state flag stands over **there.**

A Write each sentence, using the correct homophone in parentheses.

1. Soon you will visit (you're, your) grandparents in Dallas, Texas.
Soon you will visit your grandparents in Dallas, Texas.
2. Many people take (they're, their) children to Astroworld in Houston.
Many people take their children to Astroworld in Houston.
3. (They're, There) excited by Astroworld's three-hundred-foot tower.
They're excited by Astroworld's three-hundred-foot tower.
4. (Its, It's) a trip I will want to hear all about when you return.
It's a trip I will want to hear all about when you return.

B 5–10. There are six incorrect pronouns or homophones on this page from a travel brochure. Use proofreading marks to correct the travel brochure.

Example: Visit the Alamo and discover ~~it's~~ its exciting history.

Proofreading

Proofreading Marks: ¶ Indent; ∧ Add; Delete; ≡ Capital letter; / Small letter

★ Texans are very proud of their state. ~~It's~~ Its size alone makes Texas a giant among states. The Alamo is one historic place to see ~~their~~ there. ~~Its~~ It's an old mission that became a fort in the Texas war for independence from Mexico in 1836. Be sure to bring ~~you're~~ your entire family. ~~Your~~ You're sure to enjoy your visit ~~their~~ there.

(continued)

7 Pronouns and Homophones *(continued from page 108)*

Challenge

Complete the crossword puzzle below, using the homophones from the Word Box. You will use two words twice. Be sure to use apostrophes where they are needed in the puzzle.

it's	they're	there	your
its	their	you're	

ACROSS
1. ? capital city is Austin.
3. ? brother comes from Texas.
6. ? going to visit Texas next winter.
8. What is ? favorite city in Texas?

DOWN
2. Texans raise cattle and cotton ?.
3. Many oil wells are ? too.
4. ? the second largest state.
5. ? state symbol is the Lone Star.
7. ? going to visit Texas someday.

Writing Application: A Letter NARRATING

Finish the following letter. Use the words *it's, its, they're, their, there, you're,* and *your* in the letter.

Dear Felipe,
Our family trip was full of surprises. Just before we left on Saturday morning, the phone rang. It was . . .
Students should respond on separate paper. Answers will vary.

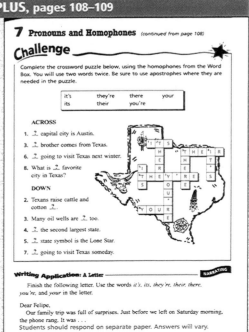

Homophones

Lesson Objective

Students will:
- proofread sentences, using homophones correctly

Focus on Instruction

- Have a volunteer read the introductory paragraph aloud. Discuss the meaning of *it's* and *its*. Have students use each word in a sentence.
- Draw students' attention to the chart. Ask students why some people might confuse the words in the word list. (The words sound the same when spoken.) Ask volunteers to use each homophone in a sentence.

Apply It

Have students complete the activity independently. Point out that the homophones in the word list have very different meanings. Tell students to read the definitions to be sure they are using the correct word. Have students explain how they knew which homophone to use.

Suggest that students who need more support work with partners.

Have students find places in their own writing where they may have confused homophones.

Answers to Apply It

It only took an hour on the plane to get to Austin. We got our luggage right away. We will be at my cousins' house for a week. They have a blue house with a pool. It was stormy tonight, and the wind almost blew over a tree. They are showing us all the neat places. My aunt stays home sometimes because she still feels weak from the flu.

My little cousin is four, and she likes to hear bedtime stories. It's really fun here.

FOR STUDENTS ACQUIRING ENGLISH

Write these homophone pairs on the board: *four/for, here/hear*. Write the following sentences on the board and have students complete them with the appropriate homophone:

1. I have ______ dogs. This present is ______ you. (*four, for*) (for)
2. Come ______! I ______ you. (*here, hear*) (here)

Call on volunteers to make other sentences with these homophones.

Revising Strategies — Vocabulary

Homophones

Words that sound alike but have different spellings and meanings are **homophones**. The words *it's* and *its* are homophones. When you write, make sure that you use the correct homophone. The chart below shows some homophones and their meanings.

Homophone	Meaning	Homophone	Meaning
our	belonging to us	hear	listen to
hour	sixty minutes	here	at this place
weak	not strong	blue	a color
week	seven days	blew	past tense of *blow*

Apply It

1–8. Rewrite this post card, using the correct homophones. Use the chart above to help you. See TE margin for answers.

Revising

Hi, Asa!

It took only an our on the plane to get to Austin. We got hour luggage right away. We will be at our cousins' house for a weak. They have a blew house with a pool. It was stormy tonight and the wind almost blue over a tree. They are showing us all the neat places. My aunt stays home sometimes because she still feels week from the flu.

My little cousin is four, and she likes to here bedtime stories. It's really fun hear.

Place Stamp Here

Your friend,
Ariel

Meeting Individual Needs

● RETEACHING WORKBOOK, page 66

Homophones

- **Homophones** are words that sound alike but have different spellings and different meanings.

Write one of the words in parentheses to complete each sentence.

Homophone	Meaning	Homophone	Meaning
our	belonging to us	hear	listen to
hour	sixty minutes	here	at this place
weak	not strong	blue	a color
week	seven days	blew	past tense of blow

Example: You need an ___oar___ to row a boat. **(or, oar)**

Revising

1. We arrived in Italy last ___week___. **(weak, week)**
2. ___Our___ plane landed in Rome. **(Our, Hour)**
3. An ___hour___ later we decided to have lunch. **(our, hour)**
4. People really eat a lot of spaghetti ___here___! **(hear, here)**
5. One evening we went to a theater to ___hear___ Italian opera. **(here, hear)**
6. How do opera singers hold a note so long without turning ___blue___ in the face? **(blew, blue)**
7. Yesterday, ___our___ tour guide took us to Pisa. **(hour, our)**
8. After we climbed the Leaning Tower of Pisa, we were ___weak___ in the knees. **(week, weak)**
9. When we reached the top, my baseball cap ___blew___ off. **(blue, blew)**
10. I wish you were ___here___ too Alice. **(hear, here)**

▲■ WORKBOOK PLUS, page 110

Homophones

Jeremy had a big ~~roll~~ role in the school play.

Revising

1–10. This journal entry has ten incorrect homophones. Cross out each mistake and write the correct homophone above it. Use the chart below to help you.

November 24

I got up before the ~~son~~ sun rose this morning to help Mom make breakfast for my ~~ant~~ aunt and uncle. They were going ~~two~~ to leave on a long trip at ~~ate~~ eight o'clock. We sliced ~~pairs~~ pears and sifted ~~flower~~ flour. I ~~beet~~ beat eggs and milk together. We ~~maid~~ made the best pancakes with fruit ever ~~scene~~ seen at my house. I ~~no~~ know that everyone enjoyed the delicious meal!

Homophone	Meaning
ant	an insect
aunt	a sister of a parent
ate	past tense of *eat*
eight	the number 8
beat	to mix by stirring
beet	a red root vegetable
flower	a bloom
flour	milled grain
know	to understand
no	opposite of *yes*
made	past tense of *make*
maid	a female servant
pear	a fruit
pair	two of a kind
scene	a setting
seen	viewed
son	a male offspring
sun	a star
to	toward
two	the number 2

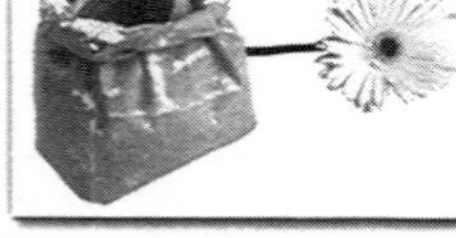

Enrichment

Homophone Book

Use four sheets of paper. On one page, write your name and *Homophone Book*. On the other pages, write a sentence using a set of homophones. Make pages for *it's, its; your, you're;* and *they're, their, there.* Underline the homophones. Then draw a picture for each sentence. Staple the pages together.

Challenge Think of other homophone sets, such as *sea, see* or *meat, meet.* Add these homophones to your book.

I or Me?

Players: 3

Materials: A game board, 3 markers, and 30 index cards; on each of 10 index cards, each player writes a sentence, using *I* in 5 sentences and *me* in the other 5. Leave a blank where *I* or *me* should be.

To play: Mix the cards. Put them facedown. One player picks a card and says *I* or *me* to complete the sentence. If correct with *I*, the player moves to the next space marked *I*. If correct with *me*, the player moves to the next space marked *me*. If incorrect, the player does not move. The first to reach *Finish* wins.

Enrichment 221

Enrichment

Objectives

Students will:
- use homophones correctly
- use the pronouns *I* and *me* correctly

Using the Activities

The Enrichment page provides fun, creative activities that reinforce students' understanding and use of homophones and pronouns. The activities are designed to be enjoyed by all students. Here are some ideas for using the activities.

- Pair students who need extra support with more capable classmates.
- Students can work with these activities in class after they have completed other assignments.
- Activities that can be completed individually can be assigned as homework.

Focus on the Activities

HOMOPHONE BOOK

This is a good activity to put in a learning center. Provide art supplies that students can use.

CHALLENGE Stock the learning center with reading materials so students can search for additional homophones.

***I* OR *ME*?**

- This is a good activity to put in a learning center.
- Make game boards in advance, using poster board and colored markers. Laminate the boards, if possible.
- Students may wish to make additional sentence cards to add variety to the game.

FOR STUDENTS ACQUIRING ENGLISH

Write the following adverbs on the board: *happily, sadly, angrily.* Then read aloud the sentences below, pantomiming the adverb as necessary, and have students complete them with the correct adverb. Have students practice with other made-up sentences.

1. The girl sang ______. (happily)
2. The dog barked ______. (angrily)
3. The baby cried ______. (sadly)

Checkup

Objectives

Students will:

- replace nouns with the correct pronouns
- use the pronouns *I* and *me* correctly
- use possessive pronouns in sentences correctly

Using the Checkup

Use the Checkup exercises as assessment, as review for the unit test, as extra practice, or as a diagnostic aid to help determine those students who need reteaching.

INTERNET CONNECTION The Wacky Web Tales® at www.eduplace.com/tales/ are cloze stories that students complete, using designated parts of speech. Students may choose any word to fill in a blank as long as it is the correct part of speech. As a result, the completed stories are often amusing, even "wacky," depending on the specific words chosen. Most of the stories at this Web site are student submissions.

INTERNET CONNECTION Students can take an interactive quiz for this unit at www.eduplace.com/kids/hme/ and then get immediate feedback.

Checkup: Unit 6

See TE margin for answers.

1 What Is a Pronoun? (p. 204)

Write the pronoun in each sentence that replaces the underlined word or words.

1. Gary and Ana went to the aquarium. They saw many fish.
2. A white shark was swimming in a tank. It is the most dangerous kind of shark.
3. Ana went to another tank. Gary followed her.
4. The penguins had a funny walk. Ana laughed at them.
5. A penguin has short wings. They look like flippers.
6. Gary and Ana said, "We can buy a poster of the penguins."
7. Ana asked Gary, "Do you have enough money for a poster?"

2 Subject Pronouns (p. 206)

Write each sentence. Use a subject pronoun in place of the underlined word or words.

8. Uncle Bill and Aunt Jenny joined a birdwatchers club.
9. Aunt Jenny takes pictures of birds.
10. The camera has a special lens.
11. Uncle Bill and Aunt Jenny bring the pictures to their club meetings.
12. The pictures help other members learn about different birds.
13. Aunt Jenny and I write the names of the birds in a notebook.
14. The notebook is very full now.

3 Object Pronouns (p. 208)

Write each sentence. Use object pronouns for the underlined words.

15. Mark took Megan and me riding.
16. Megan asked Mark for help.
17. Mark gave Megan a saddle.
18. She put a pad under the saddle.
19. The horse suddenly backed away from Megan and Mark.
20. Mark spoke softly to the horse.
21. The horse stood still for Mark.

4 Using *I* and *me* (p. 212)

Choose the word or words that complete each sentence correctly. Then write the sentences.

22. (Jeff and I, I and Jeff) visited Mr. Vega's kitchen.
23. The chef gave a lesson to (Jeff and me, me and Jeff).
24. He taught (him and me, me and him) how to make tortillas.
25. Jeff and (I, me) rolled the dough into pancakes.
26. It was hard for Jeff and (I, me).

5 Possessive Pronouns (p. 214)

Write each sentence. Use a possessive pronoun in place of the underlined word or words.

27. A llama looks like a small camel without the camel's hump.
28. For many years, people have made blankets from the llama's wool.
29. Peru's craft workers sell the workers' colorful woven goods.

222 Unit 6: Pronouns

Answers

What Is a Pronoun?

1. They
2. It
3. She
4. They
5. them
6. They
7. him

Subject Pronouns

8. He
9. She
10. It
11. They
12. They
13. We
14. It

Object Pronouns

15. us
16. him
17. her
18. it
19. them
20. it/him/her
21. him

Using *I* and *me*

22. Jeff and I
23. Jeff and me
24. him and me
25. I
26. me

Possessive Pronouns

27. its
28. its
29. their

30. My brother spent my brother's allowance on a scarf from Peru.
31. He gave the scarf to Alice for Alice's birthday.
32. My brother and sister collected pottery on my brother and sister's trip to Peru.

6 Contractions with Pronouns

(p. 216) Write the contraction for the underlined words in each sentence.

33. We are learning about foods.
34. I am cooking with new foods.
35. I have cooked corn and squash.
36. You will be surprised at what I did with them.
37. I had asked my mother for advice.
38. They will taste better that way.

7 Pronouns and Homophones

(p. 218) Write each sentence. Use the correct word for each sentence.

39. Parrots have many colors in (there, their) feathers.
40. (You're, Your) parrot is so pretty!
41. (It's, Its) name is Hector.
42. A parrot like Hector can repeat (you're, your) words.
43. (You're, Your) speaking like him!
44. Did you ever see parrots do (their, there) tricks?
45. (They're, There) very clever tricks.
46. (It's, Its) fun to talk to parrots.
47. (Their, There) is a sale on parrots at the pet store.

Mixed Review 48–55. This letter has three mistakes in using *I* and *me*, four mistakes in using contractions and their homophones, and one other contraction mistake. Write the letter correctly. Incorrect words are underlined.

Proofreading Checklist

Did you write these words correctly?
- ✓ *I* and *me*
- ✓ pronouns and their homophones
- ✓ contractions

Proofreading

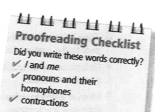

Dear Uncle Ricky,

Carlos and me

Last week Mom took me and Carlos to Apple Acres. Its a huge It's

there orchard. You can pick your own apples their. There much crisper They're

than the ones from the market. Carlos and I picked four big

bagfuls. Were going to be eating apples for a long time! We're

Yesterday, Mom and me made an apple pie for Dad. I had I

never baked before. It was quite an experience for Mom and I. me

How are you and you're family? I hope you're all fine. your

Love,

Anita

Objectives

Students will:
- correctly write contractions that contain pronouns
- identify homophones that contain pronouns
- proofread for correct pronoun use

Answers *continued*

30. his
31. her
32. their

Contractions with Pronouns

33. We're
34. I'm
35. I've
36. You'll
37. I'd
38. They'll

Pronouns and Homophones

39. their
40. Your
41. Its
42. your
43. You're
44. their
45. They're
46. It's
47. There

Test Practice

Objective

Students will:

- practice completing a test format that requires them to choose the correct sentence among four

Using the Test Practice

These Test Practice pages provide practice with common formats used in standardized or multiple-choice tests.

The first page works with skills taught in the basic lessons in Unit 6. The second page works with skills taught in Units 1–6.

Focus on the Test Format

- Have a volunteer read the test directions aloud. Ask another volunteer to explain what the directions ask students to do.
- Point out the vertical line that runs down the center of the page and breaks the text into columns. Tell students to answer the questions in the first column before proceeding to the second column.
- Call attention to the numbers and letters next to the sentences. Explain that each number corresponds to an item number. Explain that the letters identify each sentence.
- Have students read each sentence and decide whether it is written correctly. After students find the correct sentence, have them look to its left to find the letter to write for the answer.

FOR STUDENTS ACQUIRING ENGLISH

Review subject, object, and possessive pronouns. Ask how students can distinguish *its/it's, your/you're, their/they're/there*. Distribute the SAE Test Practice pages for Unit 6. Have a volunteer read the directions aloud for each section. Make sure students understand that in the first section, only one of the four sentences is correct in each set. For the second section, make sure students understand that they are to refer to the sentences lined up to the left of the questions. If the underlined part is correct, they circle the last answer.

Assessment Link

Test Practice

Write the numbers 1–6 on a sheet of paper. Read each group of sentences. Choose the sentence that is written correctly. Write the letter for that answer.

1 (A) I'll send you a post card of a kangaroo from Australia!
B Your going to have a great time on your trip to Kentucky.
C Theyll stop and see the Grand Canyon.
D He'ld better get me a gift from his vacation in Canada.

2 **F** I and Edgar will go skateboarding.
G Their is a cool skateboard park in the center of town.
(H) He's promised to teach me some new moves.
J Mom is going to drive us their in a few minutes.

3 **A** Aunt Pamela gave Reta and I new necklaces.
B Shes the nicest aunt in the world.
(C) I put my necklace on right away.
D Its a sparkling star on a thin silver chain.

4 **F** Is you're house really a log cabin?
G The Wongs built they house in the side of a hill.
H Im making a huge tree house with my cousin.
(J) It's possible to build a house out of old tires!

5 **A** Jon and me will help clean the garage.
B Dad will pay Jon and I five dollars for helping.
C Me and Jon found my old tricycle behind a trunk.
(D) Mom and Dad found their old snowshoes in a box.

6 **F** Isabel and Phil will bring they're pets to school.
(G) His pet is a hairy spider.
H She's pet is a big snake.
J Im afraid to see these creatures up close!

Unit 6: Pronouns

Now write the numbers 7–10 on your paper. Read the passage all the way through once. Then look at the underlined parts. Decide if they need to be changed or if they are fine as they are. Choose the best answer from the choices given. Write the letter for each answer.

My grandmother was not born in the United States. She growed up in Mexico. She moved to this country when she was thirteen.	**7 A** growed up in mexico **B** grow up in Mexico Ⓒ grew up in Mexico **D** (No change)
Her parents wanted a better life for their six children. At first	**8 F** more better life for there six children **G** better life for their six childs **H** better life for they're six children Ⓙ (No change)
my grandmother missed her old home. She cried every night for a month. Then her mother said, "Maria, this is you're home now."	**9 A** said "Maria this is your home now." **B** said, "Maria, this is you're home now." Ⓒ said, "Maria, this is your home now." **D** (No change)
Over time my grandmother began to like her new home. She made new friends their. She learned English, and she did well in school.	**10** Ⓕ She made new friends there. **G** She made new friends they're. **H** She made new friends theyre. **J** (No change)

Objective

Students will:

- practice completing a test format that requires them to choose the correct item among four

Focus on the Test Format

- Have a volunteer read the test directions aloud. Ask another volunteer to explain what the directions ask students to do.
- Have students read the paragraph in the left-hand column. Point out that the underlined portions of the paragraph pertain to the items in the right-hand column.
- Explain that each item gives three choices that substitute for the underlined words in the paragraph. Point out that the fourth choice is used when there are no changes.
- Tell students to read each sentence with underlined words, then read it three more times, substituting the word choices. Have students decide which words fit the paragraph best, then write the letter of the correct response.

What Is a Pronoun?

Objectives

Students will:

- recognize pronouns in sentences
- use singular and plural pronouns correctly in sentences

Using the Extra Practice

The Extra Practice activities provide additional practice for the basic lesson at three levels of difficulty: Easy (●), Average (▲), and Challenging (■).

The Extra Practice activities can be used in the following ways.

- Assign activities according to students' needs and abilities as homework after students have completed the basic lesson.
- Assign the Easy activities after using the lesson Reteaching instruction.
- Assign the Average activities to prepare students for the Checkup.
- Assign the Easy and/or Average activities to students who had difficulty with specific lessons on the Checkup.
- Assign the Challenging exercises as a Bonus activity.

Extra Practice

(pages 204–205)

1 What Is a Pronoun?

- A pronoun is a word that replaces one or more nouns.
- A pronoun can be singular or plural.

Remember

● Write the pronoun in each sentence. Pronouns are underlined.

Example: Jan asked Dad to tell her about walruses. *her*

1. "Daryl and I have never seen a walrus," Jan added.
2. "What would you like to know?" Dad asked.
3. "We want to know what a walrus weighs," said Jan.
4. "A big walrus can weigh a ton," he said.
5. "Please show us a picture," begged Jan.
6. Dad showed them a photograph of a walrus.
7. "It has big teeth called tusks," said Dad.

▲ Write each pronoun. Tell whether it is singular or plural.

Example: Rays are related to sharks, but they look different. *they plural*

8. Here is a picture of a ray. It has a flat body. sing.
9. "Please show me that picture," said Marco. sing.
10. Some rays are dangerous. People get stung by them. pl.
11. "I once saw a stingray at the beach," Kate said. sing.
12. "What do you know about stingrays?" Carlos asked Kate. sing.
13. Kate said she knew that stingrays have poisonous tails. sing.
14. "We would not want to get stung," Carlos and Marco said. pl.
15. "Then you should be careful," Kate told Carlos and Marco. pl.

■ 16–25. Write each pronoun and the word or words that it stands for.

Example: "Dolores and I know about sea horses," said Luis. *I—Luis*

"Sea horses are strange-looking sea animals," he told Pete. he—Luis

"A sea horse has a head like a horse's," Dolores said. "It has a pouch like a kangaroo's," she continued. It—seahorse she—Dolores

"Can you tell me how long a sea horse is?" Pete asked her. you—Dolores me—Pete her—Dolores

"I can tell you," Dolores said to him. "It is about five inches." I—Dolores you—Pete him—Pete It—seahorse

Meeting Individual Needs — More Practice for Lesson 1

● EASY

Find and write the five pronouns in the paragraph.

Lisa reported to the class on the archerfish. She told us how it hunts for food. The archerfish spits drops of water at insects above the water. The insects fall into the water when they are hit. Then the archerfish eats them.

▲ AVERAGE

Write a pronoun to complete each sentence correctly. (Sample answers are given.)

1. Ann asked (me) to go bowling.
2. (We) often go bowling on Saturday.
3. (She) kept score.
4. (I) got two strikes.
5. (It) was the best game ever.

■ CHALLENGING

(Give students sentences 1–5 from the Average level.) Write a singular and a plural pronoun to complete each sentence. Change the verb to match the pronoun if necessary. (A sample answer is given.)

1. Ann asked (me/us) to go bowling.

2 Subject Pronouns

(pages 206–207)

Remember

- *I, you, he, she, it, we,* and *they* are subject pronouns.
- Use only subject pronouns as the subjects of sentences.

● Write the subject pronoun in each sentence.

Example: You must come and see the ant farm. *You*

1. We set up the ant farm with Ms. Walton's help.
2. She has had ant farms before.
3. It is in the classroom near Nadeem's desk.
4. He takes care of the farm.
5. We study the ants every day.
6. They live inside the big plastic case.

▲ Write each sentence. Use a subject pronoun in place of the underlined word or words. Underline the subject pronoun.

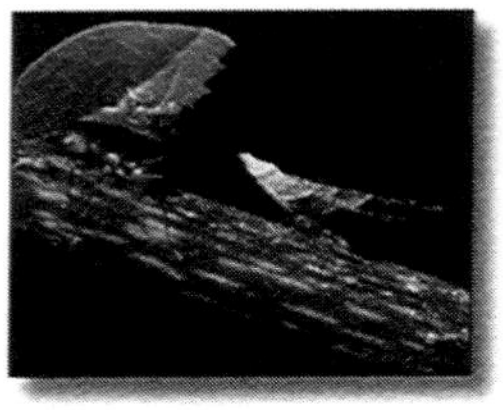

Example: Ants live in nests that the ants build.
Ants live in nests that they build.

7. The nests may be above ground or underground. They
8. Eli and I found an ant's nest. We
9. Eli said that an ant's nest is called a colony. He
10. A colony is a very orderly place. It
11. Eli said to Peg, "Peg will be interested in the nest." You
12. Peg was surprised at how many ants were in the colony. She

■ Write each subject pronoun and tell whether it is singular or plural. Write the word or words that the pronoun stands for.

Example: Jay and Amy were walking. They disturbed some bees.
They plural Jay and Amy

13. "Amy, you almost stepped on a bee's nest," shouted Jay. sing., Amy
14. Amy and Jay said, "We should be more careful." pl., Amy and Jay
15. Later they talked about bees and bees' nests. pl., Amy and Jay
16. "I think bumblebees' nests are in trees," Amy said. sing., Amy
17. She had seen a movie about bumblebees. sing., Amy
18. It showed the bees making nests in tree holes. sing., movie

Subject Pronouns

Objectives

Students will:
- use subject pronouns correctly in sentences
- distinguish subject pronouns from other pronouns

Using the Extra Practice

The Extra Practice activities provide additional practice for the basic lesson at three levels of difficulty: Easy (●), Average (▲), and Challenging (■).

Meeting Individual Needs

More Practice for Lesson 2

● EASY

Write a different subject pronoun to complete each sentence. (Sample answers are shown.)

1. (We) raced with bikes.
2. (I) went on a hike.
3. (He) caught a beautiful butterfly.
4. (They) found a robin's egg.

▲ AVERAGE

Write sentences, using pronouns as subjects. If a pronoun cannot be used as a subject, write *no.* (Sentences will vary.)

1. they
2. me (no)
3. we
4. she
5. you
6. I
7. them (no)
8. her (no)

■ CHALLENGING

Complete the passage with subject pronouns.

"Ann, do (you) have baby pigeons?" asked Bob and Cal.

"Yes, (I) do," said Ann.

"Can (we) hold them?" Bob and Cal asked. Ann said (she) thought it would be all right.

"When (they) first hatch, pigeons are called squabs," Ann told the boys. "(They) are blind and have no feathers at birth."

Object Pronouns

Objectives

Students will:

- use the correct object pronoun in sentences
- use object pronouns to replace nouns in sentences

Using the Extra Practice

The Extra Practice activities provide additional practice for the basic lesson at three levels of difficulty: Easy (●), Average (▲), and Challenging (■).

Extra Practice

3 Object Pronouns

(pages 208–209)

Remember

- *Me, you, him, her, it, us,* and *them* are object pronouns.
- Use object pronouns after action verbs and words such as *to, with, for,* and *at.*

● Write the object pronoun in each sentence.

Example: The Gaos bought the farm next door to us. *us*

1. Sally and Chip visited us yesterday.
2. Chip showed me a beautiful horse.
3. I fed it an apple.
4. The horse ate it in one bite.
5. Chip hitches it to a big sled in the winter.
6. Sally and Chip will take us for a ride sometime.

▲ Write each sentence. Use an object pronoun in place of the underlined word or words. Underline the object pronoun.

Example: Liz asked Dan about horses. *Liz asked him about horses.*

7. Dan knows a lot about horses. them
8. He told Liz that there are about sixty kinds of horses. her
9. Horses have long legs that help the horses run fast. them
10. A horse will run if anything scares the horse. it
11. Dan asked Liz, "What else can I tell Liz about horses?" you
12. Liz told Dan that she wanted to know what horses eat. him

■ Write each pronoun. Write *subject* if it is a subject pronoun and *object* if it is an object pronoun. Subject pronouns underlined once; object pronouns, twice.

Example: Draft horses are very large. Farmers may use them. *them—object*

13. You can also see them in circuses and parades.
14. We went to a parade with draft horses in it.
15. People rode bareback and did tricks on them.
16. One huge horse had a woman on it.
17. It walked along very steadily for her.
18. "She stood on it and did somersaults," Yancy said.

Meeting Individual Needs — More Practice for Lesson 3

● EASY

Write a different object pronoun to complete each sentence. (Sample answers are given.)

1. Tom gave the ball to (me).
2. Mary cleaned (it).
3. Father fed (us).
4. We went with (him).

▲ AVERAGE

Rewrite each sentence. Replace the underlined word or words with an object pronoun.

1. Ron called Jerry and me about the trip to the farm. (us)
2. Marie told Dave and Lynn about the trip. (them)
3. Sy talked Joy into going. (her)
4. Did Julia ask you to get a ticket for Frank? (him)
5. Bess sat next to the lunchbasket on the bus. (it)

■ CHALLENGING

Write each sentence. Use an object pronoun to replace the noun that follows either an action verb or words such as *to, with, for,* or *at.*

1. The horse looked up and spotted the girls. (them)
2. He ran to Rae. (her)
3. Rae gave a carrot to the horse. (it)
4. Ann said, "Look how much he likes Ann." (me)

Extra Practice

(pages 212–213)

4 Using *I* and *me*

Remember

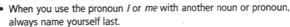

- Use the pronoun *I* as the subject of a sentence.
- Use the pronoun *me* after action verbs and words such as *to, with, for,* and *at.*
- When you use the pronoun *I* or *me* with another noun or pronoun, always name yourself last.

● Copy the sentence that is correct in each pair.

Example: My sister and I have a pen pal. I and my sister have a pen pal.
My sister and I have a pen pal.

1. Ian writes to Kara and me.
   Ian writes to me and Kara.
2. Ian and I are the same age.
   I and Ian are the same age.
3. Ian and me both play soccer.
   Ian and I both play soccer.

▲ Use *I* or *me* to complete each sentence. Write the sentences.

Example: Kara and ______ visited our pen pal.
Kara and I visited our pen pal.

4. Ian met Kara and ______ at the airport in Scotland. me
5. He asked her and ______ what we wanted to do in Scotland. me
6. Kara told Ian and ______ that she wanted to see Loch Ness. me
7. She and ______ had read about this lake's famous monster. I
8. Kara and ______ asked Ian where Loch Ness is. I
9. Ian showed her and ______ a map. me

■ Write each incorrect sentence correctly. Write *correct* for each sentence that has no errors.

Example: Ian took I and Kara fishing on the lake.
Ian took Kara and me fishing on the lake.

10. Kara caught a fish, but Ian and I did not. correct
11. Ian told Kara and I about a nearby castle. Kara and me
12. I and Kara asked him to take us there. Kara and I
13. My sister and me had never seen a real castle. My sister and I
14. Kara and I learned that the castle is now a museum. correct

Extra Practice 229

Using *I* and *me*

Objectives

Students will:
- recognize the correct use of *I* and *me* in sentences
- write sentences, using *I* and *me* correctly

Using the Extra Practice

The Extra Practice activities provide additional practice for the basic lesson at three levels of difficulty: Easy (●), Average (▲), and Challenging (■).

Meeting Individual Needs

More Practice for Lesson 4

● EASY

Write *correct* if *I* and *me* are used correctly. Write *incorrect* if they are not.

1. Do you want to fly kites with me and Jake? (incorrect)
2. Are there enough kites for Jake and me? (correct)
3. You and me can use these flat kites. (incorrect)
4. Tara once let Jake and me fly her dragon kite. (correct)

▲ AVERAGE

Write *correct* if *I* and *me* are used correctly. If they are not used correctly, change the sentence so that it is correct.

1. Rita and I own sailboats. (correct)
2. Bob sails with Rita and I. (me)
3. She and I like fishing too. (correct)
4. Yesterday, Rita and me went fishing. (I)

■ CHALLENGING

Copy the paragraph, correcting pronouns as needed.

Kevin and I visited Rainbow Bridge in Utah. Kevin and me (I) were amazed that a river could carve out a bridge. Kevin and me (I) were told that the bridge is almost three hundred feet long. Kevin made a video of me and his father (his father and me) beside it.

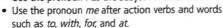

Possessive Pronouns

Objectives

Students will:

- identify possessive pronouns in sentences
- use possessive pronouns in sentences
- write sentences, using possessive pronouns correctly

Using the Extra Practice

The Extra Practice activities provide additional practice for the basic lesson at three levels of difficulty: Easy (●), Average (▲), and Challenging (■).

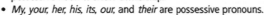

Extra Practice

(pages 214–215)

5 Possessive Pronouns

Remember

- A possessive pronoun may be used in place of a possessive noun to show ownership.
- *My, your, her, his, its, our,* and *their* are possessive pronouns.

● Write the possessive pronoun in each sentence.

Example: Reggie enjoyed his book about llamas. *his*

1. Their soft wool was black and brown.
2. My friend Alma saw a statue of a gold llama in a museum.
3. Her guide said that the Inca people had made the statue.
4. These people made their homes in what is now Peru.
5. Our teacher told Alma how these people used the llama.
6. The Inca people used its wool to make clothing.
7. Llamas carried their heavy loads across the mountains.

▲ Write each sentence. Use a possessive pronoun to take the place of the underlined word or words.

Example: Mark showed us Mark's new alpaca shirt.
Mark showed us his new alpaca shirt.

8. Mark's brother Dom has one just like it. His
9. Cheryl's sister said that alpacas are related to llamas. Her
10. People of ancient Peru wove the alpaca's wool. its
11. Only the people's royal family could wear alpaca cloth. their
12. Mark and Dom's uncle bought the shirts in Peru. Their
13. Uncle George spent Uncle George's vacation there. his

■ 14–18. Copy the paragraph. Replace possessive nouns with possessive pronouns.

Example: Elena wrote Elena's report about the vicuña.
Elena wrote her report about the vicuña.

A vicuña looks like a llama. It is a llama's smaller relative. its The vicuña's home is in South America. Vicuñas' babies are able to run soon after the babies' birth. The vicuña's wool is brownish-red. The animals had almost disappeared from the countries of South America. Then the countries' governments made a law protecting vicuñas.

(Answers: Its; their; Their; their)

Meeting Individual Needs — More Practice for Lesson 5

● EASY

Write these sentences. Underline each possessive pronoun.

1. Luke has a swimming pool in his backyard.
2. His mom and dad said the pool is their dream come true.
3. Luke's sister, Sarah, had her swimming party last week.
4. All of her friends, including my sister, were invited.

▲ AVERAGE

Read each pair of sentences. Write the correct possessive pronoun to complete the second sentence.

1. My friends and I planted a garden. (Our) garden was a success.
2. Jeff planted tomatoes. (His) tomatoes were huge!
3. Alice grew corn. (Her) corn is now over six feet tall.
4. Look at this huge pumpkin. (Its) size is remarkable.

■ CHALLENGING

Find a magazine picture that shows a number of people and objects. Write five sentences that describe some details in the picture. Use five different possessive pronouns in the sentences.

(pages 216–217)

6 Contractions with Pronouns

Remember

- Pronouns and verbs may be combined to form contractions.
- Use an apostrophe (') in place of letters that are left out.

● Write the contraction in each sentence.

Example: I'm having a birthday next week. *I'm*

1. I've invited some friends for dinner.
2. You're invited to come too.
3. You'll love what my sister makes.
4. She's the best cook in our whole family.
5. I hope that she'll make her famous shrimp dish.
6. It's my favorite thing to eat.

▲ Write each sentence. Use a contraction in place of the underlined words.

Example: We are planning a special meal for our parents.
We're planning a special meal for our parents.

7. They are celebrating their fifteenth wedding anniversary. They're
8. Fran and I hope they will be surprised. they'll
9. I am going shopping with Fran now. I'm
10. She is taking a cooking course after school. She's
11. It has helped her learn how to shop for food. It's
12. It is going to be Mom and Dad's best anniversary ever! It's

■ Write each sentence. Use contractions whenever possible.

Example: You are sure to enjoy the farmers' market.
You're sure to enjoy the farmers' market.

13. It is the best place to buy fresh fruits and vegetables. It's
14. We are going with my parents. We're
15. They have been shopping there for years. They've
16. We will be able to buy fresh string beans. We'll
17. I hope that you have brought your camera. you've
18. I am sure that you will get some good shots. I'm; you'll

Contractions with Pronouns

Objectives

Students will:

- write contractions that contain pronouns
- identify the contractions that replace pronouns and verbs in sentences

Using the Extra Practice

The Extra Practice activities provide additional practice for the basic lesson at three levels of difficulty: Easy (●), Average (▲), and Challenging (■).

Meeting Individual Needs — More Practice for Lesson 6

● EASY

Use each pronoun and verb to write a contraction. Use each contraction in a sentence. (Sentences will vary.)

1. she is (she's)
2. I have (I've)
3. you will (you'll)
4. they are (they're)
5. we have (we've)

▲ AVERAGE

Rewrite each sentence. Use a contraction to replace the underlined words.

1. I have known Jack for years. (I've)
2. He is a fine pianist. (He's)
3. It is great to have such talent. (It's)
4. I hear you are taking piano lessons too. (you're)
5. We are all going to your recital. (We're)

■ CHALLENGING

Copy the paragraph. Use contractions when possible.

The audience waits for the recital to start. They are (They're) talking softly. Richard performs first. He is (He's) nervous, but he has (he's) practiced his song often. It is (It's) a song about winter. His teacher said, "You have (You've) learned your song and will do well. Don't worry."

Pronouns and Homophones

Objectives

Students will:

- distinguish the pronoun homophones *its/it's, they're/their/there,* and *you're/your*
- use the correct pronoun homophones in sentences

Using the Extra Practice

The Extra Practice activities provide additional practice for the basic lesson at three levels of difficulty: Easy (●), Average (▲), and Challenging (■).

Extra Practice

(pages 218–219)

7 Pronouns and Homophones

Remember

- Do not confuse the contractions *it's, they're,* and *you're* with their homophones *its, their, there,* and *your.*

● Write the words in each pair of sentences that sound the same but have different spellings and meanings.

Example: I picked up your pictures at the drugstore.
You're in for a real treat. *your You're*

1. They're great pictures of our trip. There are some pictures of our hike in the woods.
2. Look! It's a red fox! How did you ever get its picture?
3. My sister says they're very shy. It is not easy to see them outside their dens.

▲ Write each sentence, using the correct word.

Example: Sean and Ike showed me (your, you're) pictures.
Sean and Ike showed me your pictures.

4. Today (their, they're) taking pictures of beavers.
5. (There, They're) are two beavers making a dam.
6. They use (there, their) sharp teeth to cut trees.
7. The dam is important. (Its, It's) a wall used to hold back water.
8. After a while, a deep pond forms (there, their).
9. A beaver will build (its, it's) home in the pond.

■ Write each incorrect sentence correctly. Write *correct* for each sentence that has no errors.

Example: Quick! Get you're camera. *Quick! Get your camera.*

10. There is a cardinal perched on that branch. correct
11. It's feathers are a beautiful bright red color. Its
12. Your looking at the male bird. You're
13. It's more colorful than the female. correct
14. Cardinals once made their homes only in the Southeast. correct
15. Now its common to see them in the Northeast too. it's

Meeting Individual Needs — More Practice for Lesson 7

● EASY

Choose the correct homophone to complete each sentence. Write the homophone.

1. The dog lost (it's, its) leash.
2. The men put (their, they're) suitcases into the car.
3. (It's, Its) time to leave.
4. (You're, Your) going to be late.

▲ AVERAGE

Use the homophones in parentheses to complete each sentence correctly.

1. (their, they're) (They're) going to bring (their) car with them.
2. (it's, its) (Its) tire is flat, and (it's) out of gas.
3. (your, you're) Remember that (you're) going to return (your) library book.

■ CHALLENGING

Rewrite each sentence below, using the correct homophone.

1. After the boys put down they're blanket, Paul said, "Its going to rain!" (their, It's)
2. As they sat their, the weather took its course and rain fell. (there)
3. "You're soaking wet, Paul," said Jake, "but its too late to take cover now." (it's)

Unit 7 Planning Guide

Adverbs and Prepositions

1 1/2 weeks

		Checkup (PE)	Extra Practice (PE)	Graphic Organizer (BLM)	Writing Wrap-Up (BLM)	More Practice (TE)	Workbook Plus	Reteaching Workbook	Students Acquiring English Practice Book
1	What Is an Adverb? *(234–235)*	250	259	7–1	7–5	259	111–112	67	105+
	Revising Strategies: Sentence Fluency Writing with Adverbs *(236–237)*						113–114	68–69	
2	Comparing with Adverbs *(238–239)*	250	260	7–1	7–5	260	115–116	70	107+
3	Using *good* and *well* *(240–241)*	250	261	7–2	7–5	261	117–118	71	109+
4	Negatives *(242–243)*	250	262	7–3	7–6	262	119–120	72	111+
5	What Is a Preposition? *(244–245)*	250	263	7–4	7–6	263	121–122	73	113+
	Revising Strategies: Sentence Fluency Writing with Prepositions *(246–247)*						123–124	74–75	
	Revising Strategies: Vocabulary Changing Meaning with Adverbs *(248)*						125	76	
	Enrichment *(249)*								
	Test Practice *(252–254)*								115+
	Cumulative Review *(255–258)*								

Unit 7

Tools and Tips

- **Diagramming Guide,** *pp. H70–H78*
- **Guide to Capitalization, Punctuation, and Usage,** *pp. H55–H64*

School-Home Connection

Suggestions for informing or involving family members in classroom activities and learning related to this unit are included in the Teacher's Edition throughout the unit.

Meeting Individual Needs

- **FOR SPECIAL NEEDS/INCLUSION:** *Houghton Mifflin English* Audiotape See also Reteaching.
- **FOR STUDENTS ACQUIRING ENGLISH:**
  - Notes and activities are included in this Teacher's Edition throughout the unit to help you adapt or use pupil book activities with students acquiring English.
  - Additional support is available for students at various stages of English proficiency: **Beginning/Preproduction**, **Early Production/Speech Emergence**, and **Intermediate/Advanced**. See Students Acquiring English Practice Book.
  - Students can listen to the Try It Out activities on audiotape.
- **ENRICHMENT:** *p. 249*

All audiotape recordings are also available on CD.

Daily Language Practice

Each sentence includes two errors based on skills taught in this or previous Grammar units. Each day write one sentence on the chalkboard. Have students find the errors and write the sentence correctly on a sheet of paper. To make the activity easier, identify the kinds of errors.

1. Your kite flew more high than mine Your kite flew higher than mine. (comparing with adverbs; end punctuation)
2. John and me worked good together on our project. John and I worked well together on our project. (subject pronouns; *good/well*)
3. Miguel you can't go nowhere without a bicycle. Sample: Miguel, you can't go anywhere without a bicycle. (commas; negatives)
4. Your supposed to walk carefuller on ice. You're supposed to walk more carefully on ice. (homophones; comparing with adverbs)
5. Jennifers' adventure story is quite well. Jennifer's adventure story is quite good. (possessive nouns; *good/well*)
6. No one never takes time to smell the roses! No one ever takes time to smell the roses. (negatives; end punctuation)
7. He read the book Miss Nelson Is Missing fastest than anyone else. He read the book Miss Nelson Is Missing faster than anyone else. (book titles; comparing with adverbs)
8. That artist can draw people, animals and scenes quite good. That artist can draw people, animals, and scenes quite well. (commas; *good/well*)
9. Carol hasn't wraped none of her friends' gifts yet. Sample: Carol hasn't wrapped any of her friends' gifts yet. (past tense; negatives)
10. Franco worked hardest than anyone they're. Franco worked harder than anyone there. (comparing with adverbs; homophones)

Additional Resources

Workbook Plus, Unit 7
Reteaching Workbook, Unit 7
Students Acquiring English Practice Book, Unit 7
Transparencies, Unit 7
Teacher's Resource Book
Audiotapes

Technology Tools

INTERNET: http://www.eduplace.com/kids/hme/ *or* http://www.eduplace.com/rdg/hme/

Visit Education Place for these additional support materials and activities:

- tricky usage question
- Wacky Web Tales®
- interactive quizzes
- a proofreading game

Assessment

Test Booklet, Unit 7

Keeping a Journal

Discuss with students the value of keeping a journal as a way of promoting self-expression and fluency. Encourage students to record their thoughts and ideas in a notebook. Inform students whether the journal will be private or will be reviewed periodically as a way of assessing growth. The following prompts may be useful for generating writing ideas.

Journal Prompts

- What is your favorite movie? Why?
- What would you like to be when you grow up? Why?
- What circus performer would you most like to be? Why?

Unit 7

Adverbs and Prepositions

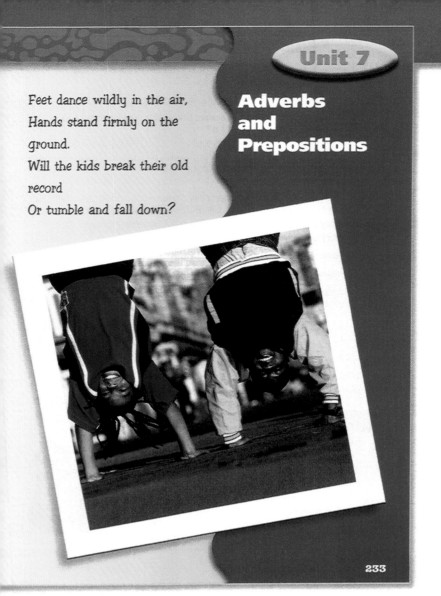

Feet dance wildly in the air,
Hands stand firmly on the ground.
Will the kids break their old record
Or tumble and fall down?

233

Introducing the Unit

Using the Photograph

- Have students look at the photograph and read the caption. Ask how the caption says the children's feet are dancing *(wildly)*, how the children's hands are standing *(firmly)*, and where the children might fall. *(down)*
- Direct students' attention to the phrases *in the air* and *on the ground.* Ask to which words these phrases refer *(dance, stand)*. Emphasize that the words *on* and *in* show relationships. *In* shows the relationship between *dance* and *air,* and *on* shows the relationship between *stand* and *ground*.
- Explain to students that a word that describes a verb is called an **adverb** and that a word that shows a relationship between two words is a **preposition**. Tell students that they will learn about adverbs and prepositions in this unit.

Grammar Song

See Blackline Master G–3 for a song to help students remember some of the concepts and rules taught in this unit.

Students can also listen to this song on audiotape.

Shared Writing Activity

Work with students to use adverbs and prepositions to write a paragraph describing a handstand championship competition.

1. Work with students to come up with verb/adverb pairs describing the actions at a handstand competition. (Sample responses: carefully balance, dance wildly, tumble down) Write these word pairs on the board or on an overhead transparency.
2. Have students describe what steps someone must go through to prepare for a handstand. (Sample response: put hands on the ground, pull legs off the ground, put your weight on your hands) As you list these, help students phrase their responses as prepositional phrases.
3. Ask students to suggest sentences using the listed words and phrases. Write the sentences on the board or on an overhead transparency.
   - Help students fix fragments and run-on sentences. As you write, ask students to tell you the correct punctuation and capitalization to use.
4. Have a volunteer read the paragraph aloud. If any student in the class can do a handstand, ask him or her if the paragraph sounds truthful. (Warning: Do not allow a student to demonstrate a handstand.)

What Is an Adverb?

Lesson Objectives

Students will:
- identify adverbs in sentences
- recognize whether an adverb tells *how, when,* or *where* about the verb
- write a descriptive letter, using adverbs correctly

One-Minute Warm-Up Ask volunteers how they know the word *hugged* is a verb. (It is an action word.) Then ask which words tell how Ernestine hugged. *(tightly)* Ask for other words that can tell *how, when,* or *where* Ernestine hugged.

Focus on Instruction

Tell students that an adverb may come before or after the verb it describes. Have students practice moving the adverb to different spots in a sentence.

Try It Out

VIEWING Have students suggest sentences that describe what the girls in the picture are doing. Ask volunteers to identify the verb in each sentence. Write each verb in the center of a word web. Brainstorm with students adverbs that could describe each verb. Record adverbs on the word web. (Sample responses are shown.) Have students use the verbs and adverbs to make additional sentences.

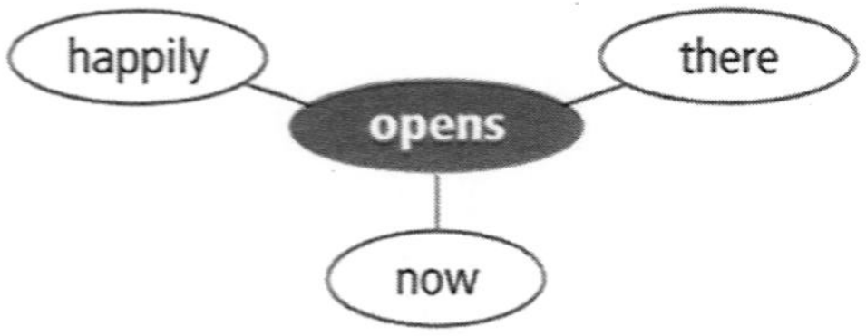

FOR STUDENTS ACQUIRING ENGLISH

- Have students listen to the Try It Out sentences on the audiotape. Distribute SAE Practice page for Unit 7, Lesson 1, to support listening.
- Write *How, When, Where* on the board. Generate an adverb for each. Then have partners list as many adverbs as possible for each category. After ten minutes, bring the group together to compare lists.

Students listen and find the adverbs that describe the underlined verbs. They underline the adverbs twice. They listen again and decide whether the adverb tells how, when, or where.

1. My brother and I ran downstairs. (where)
2. The package had finally come. (when)
3. We quickly opened the box. (how)

Grammar

1 What Is an Adverb?

One-Minute Warm-Up

Read the sentence below. Which two words tell *how*? What are they? *tightly, slowly*

Ernestine hugged everyone tightly, then slowly headed for bed.

—from *The Sunday Outing*, by Gloria Jean Pinkney

An adjective is a word that describes a noun or a pronoun. **An adverb is a word that describes a verb.** Adverbs give us more information about an action verb or a form of the verb *be*. They tell *how, when,* or *where*. Most adverbs telling *how* end with *-ly*.

How: Amanda typed the letter carefully.

When: Then I sealed the envelope.

Where: All the stamps were upstairs.

How	When	Where
angrily	always	downtown
carefully	finally	inside
fast	often	off
loudly	once	out
quickly	sometimes	there
sadly	then	upstairs

Try It Out

Speak Up Find the adverb that describes each underlined verb. Does the adverb tell *how, when,* or *where*?

1. Amanda and I waited inside. where
2. The mail carrier finally arrived. when
3. We ran out to get the mail. where
4. I quickly opened the gold envelope. how
5. Then Amanda read the letter. when
6. "We won the contest!" she shouted proudly. how

Meeting Individual Needs

RETEACHING
ALTERNATIVE STRATEGY
- Push a book from your desk to the floor, making it look like an accident. Then write this sentence on the board: *I accidentally dropped my book.*
- Ask students to find the verb. *(dropped)* Then have them find a word that describes how, when, or where it was dropped. *(accidentally)*
- Explain that *accidentally* is an adverb because it gives more information about the verb. Have students suggest other adverbs that could be added to the sentence.

CHALLENGE
Have small groups of students write short paragraphs about an activity, without using adverbs. Have groups exchange paragraphs and rewrite them, using adverbs to make the paragraphs more interesting or silly.

FOR STUDENTS ACQUIRING ENGLISH
Perform actions as you say *how* you are doing something. "I'm walking slowly. I'm talking loudly." Write the sentences. Ask a student to mark with colored chalk the words that tell *how*. Have students perform actions.

On Your Own

Write each adverb. Label it *how, when,* or *where.*

Example: Brandon always enjoys collecting stamps. *always* *when*

7. He keeps his collection upstairs. where
8. He works on it often. when
9. Sometimes friends send Brandon new stamps. when
10. He buys unusual stamps downtown. where
11. Then Mark Miller trades with Brandon. when
12. Brandon carefully soaks the used stamps. how
13. He gently removes the wet paper. how
14. Brandon arranges the stamps neatly. how

15–22. This encyclopedia article has eight adverbs. Write each adverb and the verb it describes. Adverbs are underlined once; verbs, twice.

Example: Pony express riders once carried the mail. *once* *carried*

The Pony Express

The Pony Express

These horseback riders bravely traveled a long route. They stopped briefly at small stations. There they received fresh horses. The pony express riders changed horses quickly. They continued ahead. The daring riders rode swiftly. People soon received their letters. Later the telegraph system replaced the pony express.

Writing Wrap-Up

WRITING • THINKING • LISTENING • SPEAKING

DESCRIBING

Write a Letter

You have decided to bury a time capsule. Write a letter to the people who will open your time capsule one hundred years from now. Describe ways people communicate with one another. Use adverbs in your letter. Then read your letter to a partner. Have your partner list the adverbs you used.

For Extra Practice see page 259.

Summing Up Help students summarize these key points about the lesson:

An **adverb** is a word that describes a verb. Adverbs tell *how, when,* and *where.*

You may want to have students complete the parts related to this lesson on Blackline Master 7–1.

On Your Own

Remind students that not all adverbs end in *-ly* and that they are not always located next to the verb.

MEETING INDIVIDUAL NEEDS

FOR STUDENTS ACQUIRING ENGLISH

Distribute SAE Practice page for Unit 7, Lesson 1. Discuss what the children in the drawing are doing. Ask if students know anyone who collects any of these things as a hobby. Ask what they collect. Students choose an adverb from the box to complete the sentence. Example: Brian ______ looks at his baseball cards. (often)

Writing Wrap-Up

Writing Tip: Tell students that the descriptions need to be written as if the reader had never known about the ways of communication. See Blackline Master 7–5 for a sample letter.

TECHNOLOGY CONNECTION

Students may want to use available software to illustrate the forms of communication being described.

● RETEACHING WORKBOOK, page 67

1 What Is an Adverb?

- An **adverb** is a word that describes a verb.
- An adverb can tell *how, when,* or *where.*

How	The baby lion's eyes opened **slowly**.
When	**Then** it yawned.
Where	The baby lion looked **around**.

Write the adverb that describes each underlined verb.

Example: A mother lion carries her cubs gently. gently

1. A mother lion sometimes leaves her cubs. sometimes
2. She looks everywhere for food. everywhere
3. The cubs stay inside. inside
4. Patiently they wait for their mother. Patiently
5. They play with each other happily. happily
6. They sleep peacefully. peacefully
7. The mother lion finally returns. finally
8. Soon the cubs grow big and strong. Soon
9. Now they travel with their group. Now
10. Lions always travel as a group. always
11. A young lion learns quickly from the other lions. quickly
12. The older lions carefully guard the younger ones. carefully
13. The big lions roar loudly. loudly
14. Strange lions stay away. away
15. The lions see a zebra there. there
16. Then they chase it. Then

▲■ WORKBOOK PLUS, pages 111–112

1 What Is an Adverb?

How	Jake **quickly** threw the ball. I ran **fast**.
When	**Finally**, I caught the ball. **Then** I felt a pain in my foot.
Where	**Down** I fell. Jake helped me **inside**.

A Write each adverb. Label it *how, when,* or *where.*

1. My foot hurt badly. badly—how
2. My mother quickly called the doctor. quickly—how
3. Soon Dr. Kay answered the phone. Soon—when
4. He works downtown. downtown—where
5. Mother drove me there. there—where
6. A nurse helped me inside. inside—where
7. Then she brought me a wheelchair. Then—when
8. We rode the elevator up. up—where
9. Later, the nurse took my temperature. Later—when
10. Dr. Kay examined me carefully. carefully—how

B Underline each adverb. Write the verb it describes.

11. Dr. Kay often asks important questions. asks
12. He always listens to my heart. listens
13. I breathed slowly for him. breathed
14. He moved my sore foot gently. moved
15. Dr. Kay finally took a picture of my foot. took
16. The picture clearly showed a broken bone. showed
17. He skillfully made a new cast for my foot. made
18. I walked out on a pair of crutches. walked

(continued)

1 What Is an Adverb? *(continued from page 111)*

Challenge

Tom Swift is a character in a book who always speaks in a special way. Read the two examples of Tom's sentences. Notice that the way Tom says something always matches an idea in the sentence. Now complete Tom's sentences below, using the adverbs from the Word Box.

Examples: "I'm not nervous," Tom said **calmly**.

Tom said **smartly**, "I got the highest grade on the test."

sourly	clumsily	firmly	rapidly	pointedly
brightly	coldly	stiffly	sharply	patiently

1. "Turn on the light," Tom said brightly.
2. "Please hand me my coat and gloves," Tom said coldly.
3. "You are going much too fast," Tom replied rapidly.
4. "These scissors will cut anything," Tom announced sharply.
5. Tom said firmly, "You're squeezing my arm."
6. "I'm going to see the doctor," Tom said patiently.
7. "Will you sharpen my pencil?" Tom asked pointedly.
8. Tom said clumsily, "Don't trip over the bucket."
9. "I have to iron a shirt," Tom said stiffly.
10. "Are pickles your favorite snack?" Tom asked sourly.

On another piece of paper, write three more sentences that Tom might say.

Writing Application: Instructions INSTRUCTING

You are a doctor, and one of your patients has asked for instructions on staying healthy. Write six sentences that tell your patient how to stay healthy. Use an adverb in each sentence.

Students should respond on separate paper. Answers will vary.

Writing with Adverbs

Lesson Objective

Students will:
- add adverbs to sentences

Focus on Instruction

- Have students look at the first two sentences. Ask why the second sentence is clearer. (Sample response: The second sentence also tells when the Collector Club met.)
- Have students read the next four sentences. Ask students if these sentences have different meanings. (Students should recognize that all four sentences mean the same thing.) Caution students that, although adverbs can go anywhere in the sentence, it is often a good idea to keep adverbs near the words they modify.

Apply It

Have students complete the revising activity independently. Have them identify whether the adverbs they use tell *how, when,* or *where.*

Have students look in their writing in progress to find places where adverbs can be added.

Sample Answers to Apply It

1. The posters of Asian countries arrived yesterday.
2. I really want to thank you for them.
3. As I mentioned before, I like to collect posters from different countries.
4. I sometimes use them for school projects.
5. Today I went to my friend's house.
6. She excitedly showed me her new posters, and we traded our extra ones.
7. This always makes collecting much more fun.
8. You have truly been a big help to me.
9. I greatly appreciate everything you've done.
10. Because of your help, I now have posters from many countries.

FOR STUDENTS ACQUIRING ENGLISH

Write the sentences below on the board. Have students choose the correct adverb (today, neatly) for each sentence:

1. I got a new poster ______. (today)
2. I will be careful and hang it ______ on my wall. (neatly)

Revising Strategies

Writing with Adverbs

Elaborating Sentences You know that adverbs tell *how, when,* and *where* something happens. You can make your writing clearer and more interesting by adding adverbs to your sentences.

The Collector Club had its meeting.
The Collector Club had its meeting yesterday.

She neatly arranged her posters on the wall.
She arranged her posters neatly on the wall.
Neatly she arranged her posters on the wall.
She arranged her posters on the wall neatly.

Adverbs usually can go in more than one place in a sentence.

Apply It

1–10. Rewrite this part of a letter to a travel agency. Elaborate each sentence with an adverb. Use adverbs from the box, or choose your own.
See TE margin for sample answers.

yesterday	before	sometimes	excitedly	now
badly	always	today	usually	soon

Revising

Dear Mr. Tikit T. Go,

The posters of Asian countries arrived. I want to thank you for them. As I mentioned, I like to collect posters from different countries. I use them for school projects.

I went to my friend's house. She showed me her new posters, and we traded our extra ones. This makes collecting much more fun.

You have been a big help to me. I appreciate everything you've done. Because of your help, I have posters from many countries.

236 **Unit 7:** Adverbs and Prepositions

Meeting Individual Needs

● RETEACHING WORKBOOK, page 68

Writing with Adverbs

- Adverbs are words that describe verbs.
- They tell *how, when,* or *where* something happens.

Without adverbs	I met my new neighbors.
Elaborated with adverb	I met my new neighbors **today**.

Elaborating Sentences Rewrite these sentences. Elaborate each sentence with an adverb from the box, or choose your own. Sample answers:

inside	here	enthusiastically
shyly	politely	today

Example: New families are ______ welcome in our neighborhood.
New families are always welcome in our neighborhood.

Revising

1. The Okasaki family arrived ______.
   The Okasaki family arrived today.
2. Aki and Kim waved ______ before they disappeared into the house.
   Aki and Kim waved shyly before they disappeared into the house.
3. Mother welcomed the new family ______.
   Mother welcomed the new family enthusiastically.
4. I went ______ to meet Aki and Kim.
   I went inside to meet Aki and Kim.
5. Mrs. Okasaki smiled ______ and thanked my mother for the fruit basket.
   Mrs. Okasaki smiled politely and thanked my mother for the fruit basket.
6. We hope that the family will be happy ______.
   We hope that the family will be happy here.

(continued)

▲■ WORKBOOK PLUS, page 113

Writing with Adverbs

Brad displayed his coin collection at a hobby show.
Brad **eagerly** displayed his coin collection at a hobby show.
Eagerly, Brad displayed his coin collection at a hobby show.
Brad displayed his coin collection **eagerly** at a hobby show.

Elaborating Sentences 1–8. Rewrite this paragraph from a school newspaper. Elaborate each sentence with an adverb. Use the adverbs in the box or choose your own. Sample answers:

yesterday	proudly	neatly	now
always	before	finally	carefully

Revising

My brother Pete wanted to be a collector. He had started many collections, but he lost interest. He has found something that is exciting. He collects sand from different places. Pete pours each bag of sand into a glass jar. He labels each bottle with the place where the sand was found. He shows his collection to anyone who is interested. He showed me his newest addition, which is black sand from Italy.

My brother Pete always wanted to be a collector. He had started many collections before, but he lost interest. He has finally found something that is exciting. Now he collects sand from different places. Pete pours each bag of sand carefully into a glass jar. He neatly labels each bottle with the name of the place where the sand was found. He proudly shows his collection to anyone who is interested. Yesterday he showed me his newest addition, which is black sand from Italy.

(continued)

Sentence Fluency

Combining Sentences You know that you can make your writing smoother by combining sentences. Sometimes you can combine them by moving an adverb from one sentence into another.

The first two choppy sentences below both tell about the same action. You can combine the two sentences by moving the adverb *eagerly* to the first sentence.

Our class is collecting one million popcorn kernels. We collect **eagerly**.	Our class is **eagerly** collecting one million popcorn kernels.

Apply It

11–14. Rewrite this Web page. Combine each pair of sentences by moving an adverb from the second sentence into the first sentence.

See TE margin for sample answers.

Revising

Web site

SAVING STUFF!
A WEB SITE FOR COLLECTORS

"These posters changed my bedroom. They changed my room quickly."

"I covered my walls with travel posters. I completely covered the walls."

"We can count the buttons. We can count them easily."

"We put 100 buttons in each jar. We put exactly this number in each jar."

Lesson Objective

Students will:
- combine sentences by moving an adverb

Focus on Instruction

Point out to students that when they combine two sentences by moving an adverb, they need to place the adverb close to the word it modifies. Tell students first to try placing the adverb directly before or after the modified word. Suggest that they then read the sentence aloud to hear how it sounds. Write the sentences below on the board and discuss the adverb placement.

The students raised enough money to buy a computer. They raised it *quickly*.

The students *quickly* raised enough money to buy a computer.

Apply It

Have students complete the revising activity independently.

Have students find places in their own writing in progress where they can combine sentences by moving an adverb.

Answers to Apply It

11. These posters quickly changed my bedroom.
12. I completely covered my walls with travel posters.
13. We can count the buttons easily.
14. We put exactly 100 buttons in each jar.

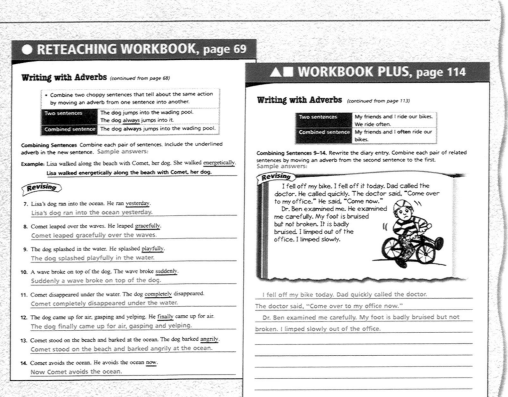

● RETEACHING WORKBOOK, page 69

Writing with Adverbs *(continued from page 68)*

- Combine two choppy sentences that tell about the same action by moving an adverb from one sentence into another.

Two sentences	The dog jumps into the wading pool. The dog always jumps into it.
Combined sentence	The dog **always** jumps into the wading pool.

Combining Sentences Combine each pair of sentences. Include the underlined adverb in the new sentence. Sample answers:

Example: Lisa walked along the beach with Comet, her dog. She walked energetically.
Lisa walked energetically along the beach with Comet, her dog.

Revising

7. Lisa's dog ran into the ocean. He ran yesterday.
Lisa's dog ran into the ocean yesterday.
8. Comet leaped over the waves. He leaped gracefully.
Comet leaped gracefully over the waves.
9. The dog splashed in the water. He splashed playfully.
The dog splashed playfully in the water.
10. A wave broke on top of the dog. The wave broke suddenly.
Suddenly a wave broke on top of the dog.
11. Comet disappeared under the water. The dog completely disappeared.
Comet completely disappeared under the water.
12. The dog came up for air, gasping and yelping. He finally came up for air.
The dog finally came up for air, gasping and yelping.
13. Comet stood on the beach and barked at the ocean. The dog barked angrily.
Comet stood on the beach and barked angrily at the ocean.
14. Comet avoids the ocean. He avoids the ocean now.
Now Comet avoids the ocean.

▲■ WORKBOOK PLUS, page 114

Writing with Adverbs *(continued from page 113)*

Two sentences	My friends and I ride our bikes. We ride often.
Combined sentence	My friends and I **often** ride our bikes.

Combining Sentences 9–14. Rewrite the diary entry. Combine each pair of related sentences by moving an adverb from the second sentence to the first.
Sample answers:

Revising

I fell off my bike. I fell off it today. Dad called the doctor. He called quickly. The doctor said, "Come over to my office." He said, "Come now."

Dr. Ben examined me. He examined me carefully. My foot is bruised but not broken. It is badly bruised. I limped out of the office. I limped slowly.

I fell off my bike today. Dad quickly called the doctor. The doctor said, "Come over to my office now."

Dr. Ben examined me carefully. My foot is badly bruised but not broken. I limped slowly out of the office.

Comparing with Adverbs

Lesson Objectives

Students will:

- add *-er* and *-est* to short adverbs to compare actions
- add *more* and *most* to adverbs that end in *ly* to compare actions
- proofread for adverbs that compare and contrast
- write an expressive sportscast, using adverbs to compare

One-Minute Warm-Up Write the corrected sentence on the board. Have students brainstorm other comparative adverbs or adverbial phrases to replace *faster.* (slower, more quickly)

Focus on Instruction

Explain that adverbs ending in *-ly* already have a suffix, so adding *-er* or *-est* is incorrect. Instead, use *more* or *most* to make comparisons.

Try It Out

LISTENING AND SPEAKING Have students read aloud each sentence, using the correct adverb. Then have students brainstorm other adverbs to replace the one in each sentence. Check each suggested adverb for correct form.

FOR STUDENTS ACQUIRING ENGLISH

- Have students listen to the Try It Out sentences on the audiotape. Distribute SAE Practice page for Unit 7, Lesson 2, to support listening.
- Help students generate comparisons of their own for the art, using adjectives and then adverbs. Remind students to look for *than* as a clue for the comparative and *the* as a clue for the superlative. Explain that many adverbs have two or more syllables, so most, but not all, take *more* and *most.* List vocabulary. Work with adverbs of frequency *always, usually, often,* and so on. Students listen and complete sentences with the correct form.
  1. Fran skates ______ than Amanda does. *(fast)* (faster)
  2. Eric skates the ______ of all the children. *(fast)* (fastest)

Grammar/Usage

2 Comparing with Adverbs

One-Minute Warm-Up

Goldstein runs more faster than Crawford!

What's wrong with this headline? How can you fix it? Goldstein runs faster than Crawford!

- Adjectives are used to compare people, places, and things. You can also use adverbs to make comparisons. Add *-er* to short adverbs to compare two actions. Add *-est* to compare three or more actions.

One Action	Ken skis fast.
Two Actions	LaToya skis faster than Ken does.
Three or More	Katie skis fastest of the three.

- For most adverbs that end with *-ly,* use *more* to compare two actions. Use *most* to compare three or more actions.

One Action	Kristina swam gracefully.
Two Actions	Did Trent swim more gracefully than Kristina?
Three or More	Kevin swam most gracefully of all.

Try It Out

Speak Up What form of the adverb in ( ) correctly completes each sentence?

1. Today we practiced ______ than we did yesterday. (long) longer
2. Of all the team members, Fatima skated ______. (skillfully) most skillfully
3. Does Jackie skate ______ than Shawn? (quickly) more quickly
4. Andrew jumps ______ of us all. (high) highest
5. Of everyone on the team, Tara tries ______! (hard) hardest

Meeting Individual Needs

RETEACHING

ALTERNATIVE STRATEGY

- Display this chart:

Adverb	fast	quickly
Comparing two		
Comparing three		

- Tell students that when they compare two things using a short adverb, they should add *-er* to the adverb. When comparing more than two things, add *-est.*
- Have students complete the first column of the chart. Repeat the procedure, telling students to use the words *more* and *most* when comparing adverbs that end in *-ly.*
- Add columns for other adverbs to the chart.

CHALLENGE

Give teams four cards. Tell them to write one of the following on each: *more, most, -er,* or *-est.* Say an adverb and tell whether you want the form for comparing two actions or more than two actions. The first team to display the correct card gets a point and the privilege of naming the next adverb.

FOR STUDENTS ACQUIRING ENGLISH

Review comparisons for adjectives. Ask questions about the class. "Is Liam taller than Andres? Who is the tallest?" Then have students dance. Ask, "Did Megan dance more beautifully than Felipe? Who danced the most beautifully?" Continue.

On Your Own

Write each sentence. Use the correct form of the adverb in ( ).

Example: These Special Olympics lasted ______ than last year's. (long)
These Special Olympics lasted longer than last year's.

6. Richie's relay team ran ______ than my brother's team. (swiftly) more swiftly
7. Meredith ran ______ of all the students. (fast) fastest
8. I watched her ______ of all the runners. (closely) most closely
9. She crossed the finish line ______ than the rest. (soon) sooner
10. The runners moved ______ than the wheelchair racers. (slowly) more slowly
11. I cheered ______ of all the fans. (loudly) most loudly
12. The broad jump began ______ than the high jump. (late) later
13. Roberto jumped ______ of all the boys. (high) highest

14–20. This part of a sportscast has seven incorrect adverb forms. Write the sportscast correctly. Incorrect words are underlined.

Example: Paul swims more smoother than Jeremy.
Paul swims more smoothly than Jeremy.

Proofreading

Special Olympics

Nicholas swam skillfullier (more skillfully) this year than last. Ross swam the faster (fastest) of anyone. He had practiced longer and more harder (harder) than anyone else. He came nearer (nearest) of all to setting a personal best. David swam only slightly slowest (slower) than Ross. Chris tried the most hardest (hardest) of anyone in the diving event. He performed the backward somersault more expertlier (most expertly) of all.

Writing Wrap-Up WRITING • THINKING • LISTENING • SPEAKING

COMPARING / CONTRASTING

Write a Sportscast

Write a sportscast about a sporting event at your school. Write about the different players, using adverbs to compare and contrast their performances. Then find a partner and read your sportscasts to each other. Work together to make sure you used the correct adverb forms.

For Extra Practice see page 260.

Summing Up Help students summarize these key points about the lesson:

Add *-er* to short adverbs to compare two actions. Add *-est* to compare three or more actions. Use *more* to compare two actions with adverbs ending in *-ly*. Use most to compare three or more adverbs ending in *-ly*. Never use *er* with *more*. Never use *-est* with *most*.

You may want to have students complete the parts related to this lesson on Blackline Master 7–1.

On Your Own

Remind students to ask themselves: *Is the sentence comparing two actions or more than two?*

MEETING INDIVIDUAL NEEDS

FOR STUDENTS ACQUIRING ENGLISH

Distribute SAE Practice page for Unit 7, Lesson 2. Explain that many comparisons with adverbs include structures such as *than . . . does/do* or *of all.* Refer to examples presented. Students complete sentences with adverbs. Example: The parents cheered ______ of all. *(loudly)* (most loudly)

Writing Wrap-Up

Writing Tip: Before students begin writing, have them jot down a few facts about each athlete's performance. See Blackline Master 7–5 for a sample sportscast.

SCHOOL-HOME CONNECTION

Students and their family members may identify their favorite athletes and compare their performances.

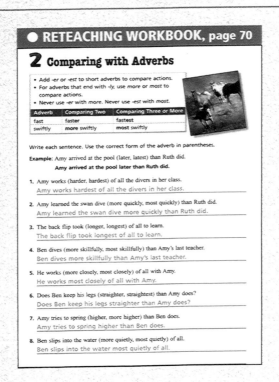

● RETEACHING WORKBOOK, page 70

2 Comparing with Adverbs

- Add *-er* or *-est* to short adverbs to compare actions.
- For adverbs that end with *-ly*, use *more* or *most* to compare actions.
- Never use *-er* with *more*. Never use *-est* with *most*.

Adverb	Comparing Two	Comparing Three or More
fast	faster	fastest
swiftly	more swiftly	most swiftly

Write each sentence. Use the correct form of the adverb in parentheses.

Example: Amy arrived at the pool (later, latest) than Ruth did.
Amy arrived at the pool later than Ruth did.

1. Amy works (harder, hardest) of all the divers in her class.
Amy works hardest of all the divers in her class.
2. Amy learned the swan dive (more quickly, most quickly) than Ruth did.
Amy learned the swan dive more quickly than Ruth did.
3. The back flip took (longer, longest) of all to learn.
The back flip took longest of all to learn.
4. Ben dives (more skillfully, most skillfully) than Amy's last teacher.
Ben dives more skillfully than Amy's last teacher.
5. He works (more closely, most closely) of all with Amy.
He works most closely of all with Amy.
6. Does Ben keep his legs (straighter, straightest) than Amy does?
Does Ben keep his legs straighter than Amy does?
7. Amy tries to spring (higher, more higher) than Ben does.
Amy tries to spring higher than Ben does.
8. Ben slips into the water (more quietly, most quietly) of all.
Ben slips into the water most quietly of all.

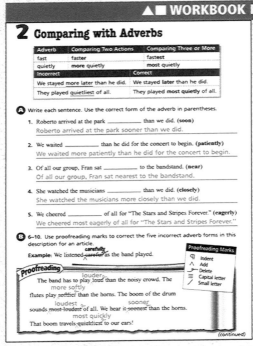

▲■ WORKBOOK PLUS, pages 115–116

2 Comparing with Adverbs

Adverb	Comparing Two Actions	Comparing Three or More
fast	faster	fastest
quietly	more quietly	most quietly

Incorrect	Correct
We stayed more later than he did.	We stayed **later** than he did.
They played quietliest of all.	They played **most quietly** of all.

A Write each sentence. Use the correct form of the adverb in parentheses.

1. Roberto arrived at the park ______ than we did. **(soon)**
Roberto arrived at the park sooner than we did.
2. We waited ______ than he did for the concert to begin. **(patiently)**
We waited more patiently than he did for the concert to begin.
3. Of all our group, Fran sat ______ to the bandstand. **(near)**
Of all our group, Fran sat nearest to the bandstand.
4. She watched the musicians ______ than we did. **(closely)**
She watched the musicians more closely than we did.
5. We cheered ______ of all for "The Stars and Stripes Forever." **(eagerly)**
We cheered most eagerly of all for "The Stars and Stripes Forever."

B 6–10. Use proofreading marks to correct the five incorrect adverb forms in this description for an article.

Example: We listened ~~careful~~ carefully as the band played.

Proofreading Marks
- ¶ Indent
- ∧ Add
- Delete
- ≡ Capital letter
- / Small letter

Proofreading

The band has to play ~~loud~~ louder than the noisy crowd. The flutes play ~~softlier~~ more softly than the horns. The boom of the drum sounds ~~most loudest~~ loudest of all. We hear it ~~soonest~~ sooner than the horns. That boom travels ~~quickliest~~ most quickly to our ears!

(continued)

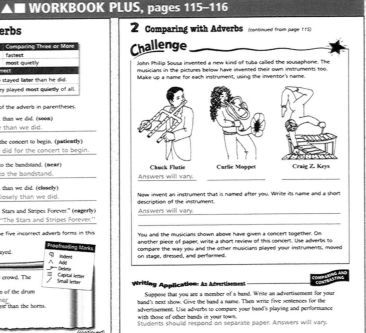

2 Comparing with Adverbs *(continued from page 115)*

Challenge

John Philip Sousa invented a new kind of tuba called the sousaphone. The musicians in the pictures below have invented their own instruments too. Make up a name for each instrument, using the inventor's name.

Chuck Flutie — Answers will vary.
Curlie Moppet
Craig Z. Keys

Now invent an instrument that is named after you. Write its name and a short description of the instrument.
Answers will vary.

You and the musicians shown above have given a concert together. On another piece of paper, write a short review of this concert. Use adverbs to compare the way you and the other musicians played your instruments, moved on stage, dressed, and performed.

Writing Application: An Advertisement COMPARING AND CONTRASTING

Suppose that you are a member of a band. Write an advertisement for your band's next show. Give the band a name. Then write five sentences for the advertisement. Use adverbs to compare your band's playing and performance with those of other bands in your town.
Students should respond on separate paper. Answers will vary.

Using *good* and *well*

Lesson Objectives

Students will:

- use *good* and *well* correctly
- proofread sentences that use *good* and *well*
- write a descriptive travel brochure, using *good* and *well* correctly

One-Minute Warm-Up Have a volunteer write the sign on the board, placing *good* and *well* in their correct positions. Ask which word is an adjective that describes a noun *(good)* and which word is an adverb that describes a verb. *(well)* Explain that since *well* is an adverb, it should always be used with verbs.

Focus on Instruction

Tell students that both *good* and *well* use the word *better* to compare two things and *best* to compare more than two things.

Try It Out

VIEWING Write *good* and *well* on the board and circle each. Direct attention to the picture of the three people. Have students suggest nouns from the picture and write them on a web, surrounding the word *good*. Repeat with verbs and *well*. Then have students use the webs to write sentences about the picture. (A sample web is shown.)

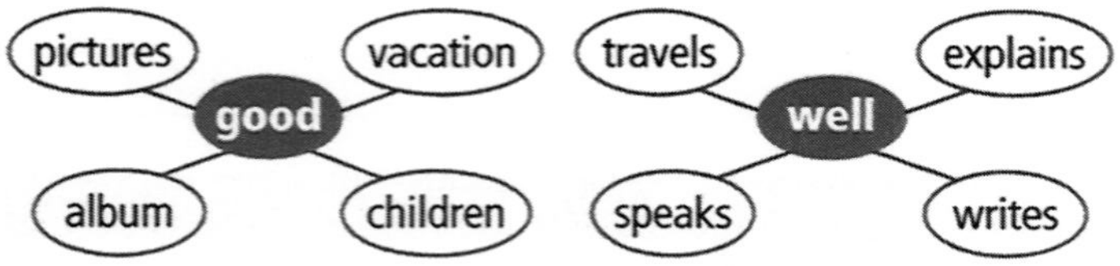

FOR STUDENTS ACQUIRING ENGLISH

- Have students listen to the Try It Out sentences on the audiotape. Distribute SAE Practice page for Unit 7, Lesson 3, to support listening.
- Help students suggest sentences about the family in the drawing. Encourage speculation about what is happening and where they are going. List vocabulary. Explain that *good* is an adjective and *well* is an adverb. Remind students to ask themselves whether the word answers *what kind of* or *how*. Students listen and complete the sentences with *good* or *well*.
  1. Mrs. Ruiz drives ______. (well)
  2. She is a ______ driver. (good)
  3. The children usually behave ______. (well)
  4. Mr. Ruiz is ______ at finding places. (good)

Usage

3 Using *good* and *well*

One-Minute Warm-Up

The words GOOD and WELL fell off this motel sign. Where would you put each word?

Rest well here. Have a good night.

Sometimes it may be hard to decide whether to use *good* or *well*. How can you make sure that you use these words correctly? Remember, *good* is an adjective that describes nouns. *Well* is an adverb that describes verbs.

Marcia is a good guide. She speaks well.

This photo album is good. You chose the pictures well.

Try It Out

Speak Up Which word is correct?

1. Corey's trips are all (good, well).
2. He plans (good, well) for his adventures.
3. Corey's guidebook is (good, well).
4. His road maps are (good, well) too.
5. He has learned to read maps (good, well).
6. Corey speaks several languages (good, well).
7. Talking to people helps him learn (good, well) about other countries.
8. Corey is (good, well) at taking pictures.
9. Photos help him remember his trips (good, well).
10. Corey describes his travels (good, well).
11. Everyone listens (good, well) to his stories.
12. The presents that he brings to his family are always (good, well).
13. Corey is a (good, well) traveler.
14. He is polite to everyone and treats them (good, well).

Meeting Individual Needs

RETEACHING

ALTERNATIVE STRATEGY

- Write these headings on the board: *Things We Like* and *Things We Like to Do.* Then have students contribute words for each heading.
- After the lists are complete, write *good* above the first heading and point out that the list contains nouns. Write *well* above the second heading and point out that the list contains verbs.
- Explain that the adjective *good* describes nouns, and the adverb *well* describes verbs. Have students suggest sentences that use *good* and *well* correctly.

CHALLENGE

Ask students to write a brief review of a favorite TV show or film, using the words *good* and *well*. Then have students copy their reviews, replacing the words *good* or *well* with a blank. Have pairs of students exchange papers and fill in each blank.

FOR STUDENTS ACQUIRING ENGLISH

Display several things that you like, using the adjective *good*. Say, "This is a good book. This orange is good." Then refer to skills, using the adverb *well*. "Diana spells well. Richard plays soccer well." Contrast *good* and *well*. Continue.

On Your Own

Use *good* or *well* to complete each sentence correctly. Write the sentences.

Example: Erika's vacation didn't go ______. *Erika's vacation didn't go well.*

15. The train trip was not ______. good
16. Her hotel room was not very ______ either. good
17. She didn't sleep very ______ that night. well
18. Erika discovered that she hadn't packed ______. well
19. Erika learned her lesson ______. well
20. This year she has prepared ______ for her vacation. well
21. Her decision to stay home was ______. good
22. It will be ______ to relax in the back yard. good

23–28. This part of an online travel brochure has six mistakes in using *good* and *well*. Write the brochure correctly. Underlined words are rewritten.

Example: You'll sleep good on our beds. *You'll sleep well on our beds.*

Proofreading — Web site

Home | Back | forward | Stop | Images | Reload | Help | Mail

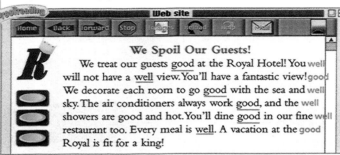

We Spoil Our Guests!

We treat our guests good at the Royal Hotel! You will not have a well view. You'll have a fantastic view! We decorate each room to go good with the sea and sky. The air conditioners always work good, and the showers are good and hot. You'll dine good in our fine restaurant too. Every meal is well. A vacation at the Royal is fit for a king!

(Answers: well; good; well; well; well; good)

Writing Wrap-Up

WRITING • THINKING • LISTENING • SPEAKING

DESCRIBING

Write a Travel Brochure

Where would your "dream vacation" be? Write a travel brochure describing the place, what you eat, and what you do. Use *good* or *well* in each sentence. Then read your brochure to a partner. Have your partner check for the correct use of *good* and *well*.

For Extra Practice see page 261.

Summing Up Help students summarize these key points about the lesson:

Use the adjective *good* to describe nouns and the adverb *well* to describe verbs.

You may want to have students complete the parts related to this lesson on Blackline Master 7–2.

On Your Own

Suggest to students that they choose *good* or *well* based on which word sounds correct, and then check their choice by finding out if it describes a noun or a verb.

MEETING INDIVIDUAL NEEDS

FOR STUDENTS ACQUIRING ENGLISH

Distribute SAE Practice page for Unit 7, Lesson 3. Help students describe the art. Does the family still look happy? Students complete the sentences with *good* or *well*.

1. Mrs. Ruiz did not sleep ______. (well)
2. The bed was not very ______. (good)
3. The children have not behaved ______. (well)

Writing Wrap-Up

Writing Tip: Tell students to picture their dream vacation in their mind before they write. See Blackline Master 7–5 for a sample travel brochure.

TECHNOLOGY CONNECTION

Students may want to use clip art or photographs to create a colorful brochure.

● RETEACHING WORKBOOK, page 71

3 Using *good* and *well*

- Use the adjective *good* to describe nouns.
- Use the adverb *well* to describe verbs.

Adjective	Adverb
Audrey chooses **good** colors.	Audrey paints **well**.
This color is **good**.	Audrey chooses colors **well**.

Write *good* or *well* to complete each sentence correctly. The underlined nouns and verbs are clues.

Example: Audrey had a **good** idea.

1. Audrey wanted to give her room a good paint job.
2. She went to a good store for paint.
3. She knew the store owner well.
4. He showed Audrey a good way of choosing colors.
5. His color wheel showed colors that match well.
6. Red goes well with yellow.
7. Blue is good for a cool look.
8. Light colors are good for making rooms seem larger.
9. A good shade of pink makes a room seem warmer.
10. Audrey planned her paint job well.
11. She thought gray would be good for the windows and the door.
12. Light pink would be a good color for the walls.
13. Audrey painted her room well.
14. Before painting, she covered the furniture well.
15. After painting, she cleaned the paintbrushes well.
16. Audrey showed her brother her good work.

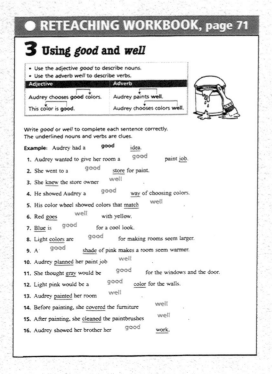

▲■ WORKBOOK PLUS, pages 117–118

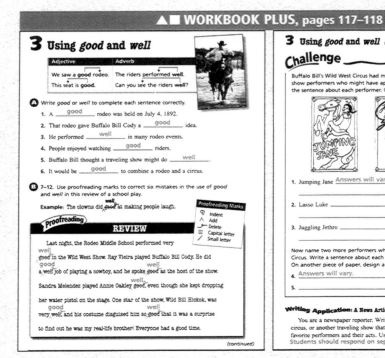

3 Using *good* and *well*

Adjective	Adverb
We saw a **good** rodeo.	The riders performed **well**.
This seat is **good**.	Can you see the riders **well**?

A Write *good* or *well* to complete each sentence correctly.

1. A good rodeo was held on July 4, 1892.
2. That rodeo gave Buffalo Bill Cody a good idea.
3. He performed well in many rodeo events.
4. People enjoyed watching good riders.
5. Buffalo Bill thought a traveling show might do well.
6. It would be good to combine a rodeo and a circus.

B 7–12. Use proofreading marks to correct six mistakes in the use of *good* and *well* in this review of a school play.

Example: The clowns did ~~good~~ **well** at making people laugh.

Proofreading Marks
- ¶ Indent
- ^ Add
- Delete
- ≡ Capital letter
- / Small letter

Proofreading — REVIEW

Last night, the Rodeo Middle School performed very ~~good~~ well in the Wild West Show. Ray Vieira played Buffalo Bill Cody. He did a ~~well~~ good job of playing a cowboy, and he spoke ~~good~~ well as the host of the show. Sandra Melendez played Annie Oakley ~~good~~ well, even though she kept dropping her water pistol on the stage. One star of the show, Wild Bill Hickok, was very ~~well~~ good, and his costume disguised him so ~~good~~ well that it was a surprise to find out he was my real-life brother! Everyone had a good time.

(continued)

3 Using *good* and *well* *(continued from page 117)*

Challenge

Buffalo Bill's Wild West Circus had many exciting performers. The posters below show performers who might have appeared in the Wild West Circus. Complete the sentence about each performer. Use the word *good* or *well* in each sentence.

1. Jumping Jane Answers will vary.
2. Lasso Luke ______
3. Juggling Jethro ______

Now name two more performers who might have appeared in the Wild West Circus. Write a sentence about each performer, using the word *good* or *well*. On another piece of paper, design a poster advertising one performer's act.

4. Answers will vary.
5. ______

Writing Application: A News Article — DESCRIBING

You are a newspaper reporter. Write a short news article about a rodeo, a circus, or another traveling show that has come to your town. Describe your favorite performers and their acts. Use the word *good* or *well* in each sentence. Students should respond on separate paper. Answers will vary.

Negatives

Lesson Objectives

Students will:

- use only one negative word in a sentence
- proofread for correct use of negatives
- write an informative list of rules, using negatives correctly

One-Minute Warm-Up Ask volunteers to write on the board two ways to correctly write the second sentence.

Focus on Instruction

Point out that using two negative words to express a single negative idea is called a double negative.

Try It Out

LISTENING AND SPEAKING Have students change the sentences so they can correctly use the other word choice in the parentheses.

FOR STUDENTS ACQUIRING ENGLISH

- Have students listen to the Try It Out sentences on the audiotape. Distribute SAE Practice page for Unit 7, Lesson 4, to support listening.
- Discuss the photo and art. Many languages use double negatives, so expect interference. Remind students that English uses only one negative at a time. Have partners list as many negatives as they can. Present the following: *never/ever, no/any, none/any, no one/anyone, nowhere/anywhere.* Learning these pairs can help students avoid double negatives. Contrast *I never have enough money* with *I don't ever have enough money.* Keep in mind that the negative verbs can be troublesome. Students listen and choose the correct word.
  Example: Our neighbors don't ______ work in the yard. (ever) (never/ever)

Usage

4 Negatives

One-Minute Warm-Up

What's wrong with this riddle? How can you fix it?

Question: Why didn't the tree travel anywhere?

Answer: It couldn't never carry its trunk!

It couldn't ever (or could never) carry its trunk!

- Sometimes when you write sentences, you use the word *no* or words that mean "no." **A word that makes a sentence mean "no" is called a negative.**

  No one picked the beans. I didn't water the garden.

- The words *no, no one, nobody, none, nothing, nowhere,* and *never* are negatives. The word *not* and contractions made with *not* are also negatives. Never use two negatives together in a sentence.

Incorrect	Correct
There weren't no trees.	There weren't any trees. There were no trees.
I won't never rake leaves!	I won't ever rake leaves! I will never rake leaves.

Try It Out

Speak Up Which word in ( ) is correct?

1. John can't go (nowhere, anywhere) until he has finished raking.
2. He never likes (anything, nothing) about yard work.
3. No one (never, ever) has time to help him.
4. Luckily there (are, aren't) no leaves left on the trees.
5. There won't be (no, any) more leaves to rake until next fall!

Meeting Individual Needs

RETEACHING
ALTERNATIVE STRATEGY

- Write this sentence: *No cats never bark.* Ask students to identify the two words that mean "no." (no, never)
- Explain that a sentence can have only one "no" word. Have students suggest ways to rewrite the sentence correctly.
- Write other sentences that contain double negatives. Have students point out the negatives and suggest ways to correct each sentence.

CHALLENGE

Have students write a skit about a negative character who doesn't like anyone and won't try anything. Tell students to use negatives in their scripts. Have students present their skits to the class.

FOR STUDENTS ACQUIRING ENGLISH

Explain that in English people use only one negative word at a time. Mention that sometimes English speakers make mistakes and use two negative words. Give *not* as an example of a negative. Ask the group to name other negative words.

On Your Own

Write the correct word to complete each sentence.

Example: Aki (hadn't, had) never collected leaves before. *had*

6. Now she never goes (nowhere, anywhere) without finding leaves.
7. Aki didn't find (anything, nothing) new today.
8. Jordan wouldn't show his collection to (no one, anyone).
9. He hasn't pressed (none, any) of his leaves in wax paper.
10. Jordan didn't know (no one, anyone) who could teach him how!
11. Nina couldn't find any red leaves (anywhere, nowhere).
12. She (hasn't, has) found no birch leaves today.
13. Didn't (anybody, nobody) find oak leaves?

14–20. These rules have seven mistakes in using negatives. Write the rules correctly. Answers will vary.

Example: Don't never climb no trees. *Don't ever climb any trees.*

Proofreading

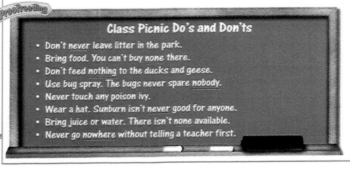

Class Picnic Do's and Don'ts

- Don't never leave litter in the park.
- Bring food. You can't buy none there.
- Don't feed nothing to the ducks and geese.
- Use bug spray. The bugs never spare nobody.
- Never touch any poison ivy.
- Wear a hat. Sunburn isn't never good for anyone.
- Bring juice or water. There isn't none available.
- Never go nowhere without telling a teacher first.

Writing Wrap-Up

WRITING • THINKING • LISTENING • SPEAKING

INFORMING

Write Rules

Write five rules for your school. They can be silly or serious, such as *Don't do cartwheels on the desks!* Use a negative in each rule. Read your rules to a partner. Check that you used negatives correctly.

For Extra Practice see page 262.

Summing Up Help students summarize these key points about the lesson:

> A **negative** is a word that means "no." Do not use two negative words together in a sentence.

You may want to have students complete the parts related to this lesson on Blackline Master 7–3.

On Your Own

Remind students that a contraction is a shortened form of two words. Many contractions are formed from a helping verb and *not.* Remind students to watch for contractions that contain *not* as they read the sentences.

MEETING INDIVIDUAL NEEDS — FOR STUDENTS ACQUIRING ENGLISH

Distribute SAE Practice page for Unit 7, Lesson 4. Ask students what the girls are doing. Explain that one is collecting leaves; the other is birdwatching. Students choose the correct word.

Example: Helena ______ ever seen an eagle. (hasn't)
(hasn't/has)

Writing Wrap-Up

Writing Tip: If students have trouble writing their rules, have them begin their sentences with phrases such as *Don't . . .* or *You shouldn't. . . .* See Blackline Master 7–6 for sample rules.

TECHNOLOGY CONNECTION

Students may wish to use available software to compile the class rules to make colorful banners.

● RETEACHING WORKBOOK, page 72

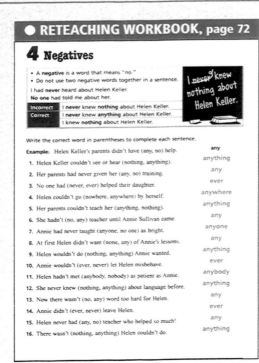

4 Negatives

- A **negative** is a word that means "no."
- Do not use two negative words together in a sentence.

I had **never** heard about Helen Keller.
No one had told me about her.

Incorrect	I **never** knew **nothing** about Helen Keller.
Correct	I **never** knew **anything** about Helen Keller.
	I knew **nothing** about Helen Keller.

I ~~never~~ knew nothing about Helen Keller.

Write the correct word in parentheses to complete each sentence.

Example: Helen Keller's parents didn't have (any, no) help. **any**

1. Helen Keller couldn't see or hear (nothing, anything). anything
2. Her parents had never given her (any, no) training. any
3. No one had (never, ever) helped their daughter. ever
4. Helen couldn't go (nowhere, anywhere) by herself. anywhere
5. Her parents couldn't teach her (anything, nothing). anything
6. She hadn't (no, any) teacher until Annie Sullivan came. any
7. Annie had never taught (anyone, no one) as bright. anyone
8. At first Helen didn't want (none, any) of Annie's lessons. any
9. Helen wouldn't do (nothing, anything) Annie wanted. anything
10. Annie wouldn't (ever, never) let Helen misbehave. ever
11. Helen hadn't met (anybody, nobody) as patient as Annie. anybody
12. She never knew (nothing, anything) about language before. anything
13. Now there wasn't (no, any) word too hard for Helen. any
14. Annie didn't (ever, never) leave Helen. ever
15. Helen never had (any, no) teacher who helped so much! any
16. There wasn't (nothing, anything) Helen couldn't do. anything

▲■ WORKBOOK PLUS, pages 119–120

4 Negatives

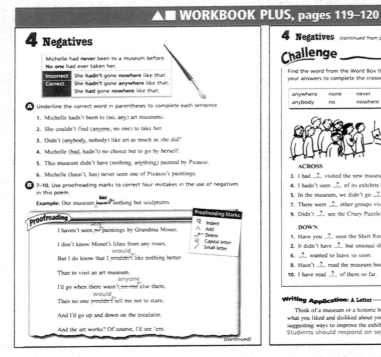

Michelle had **never** been to a museum before.
No one had ever taken her.

Incorrect	She **hadn't** gone **nowhere** like that.
Correct	She **hadn't** gone **anywhere** like that.
	She **had** gone **nowhere** like that.

A Underline the correct word in parentheses to complete each sentence.

1. Michelle hadn't been to (no, any) art museums.
2. She couldn't find (anyone, no one) to take her.
3. Didn't (anybody, nobody) like art as much as she did?
4. Michelle (had, hadn't) no choice but to go by herself.
5. This museum didn't have (nothing, anything) painted by Picasso.
6. Michelle (hasn't, has) never seen one of Picasso's paintings.

B 7–10. Use proofreading marks to correct four mistakes in the use of negatives in this poem.

Example: Our museum ~~hasn't~~ has nothing but sculptures.

Proofreading

I haven't seen ~~no~~ any paintings by Grandma Moses.
I don't know Monet's lilies from any roses,
But I do know that I ~~wouldn't~~ would like nothing better
Than to visit an art museum.
I'd go when there wasn't ~~no one~~ anyone else there,
Then no one ~~wouldn't~~ would tell me not to stare,
And I'd go up and down on the escalator,
And the art works? Of course, I'd see 'em.

Proofreading Marks
- ¶ Indent
- ∧ Add
- Delete
- ≡ Capital letter
- / Small letter

(continued)

4 Negatives *(continued from page 119)*

Challenge

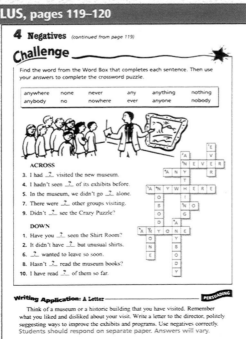

Find the word from the Word Box that completes each sentence. Then use your answers to complete the crossword puzzle.

anywhere	none	never	any	anything	nothing
anybody	no	nowhere	ever	anyone	nobody

ACROSS
3. I had _?_ visited the new museum.
4. I hadn't seen _?_ of its exhibits before.
5. In the museum, we didn't go _?_ alone.
7. There were _?_ other groups visiting.
9. Didn't _?_ see the Crazy Puzzle?

DOWN
1. Have you _?_ seen the Shirt Room?
2. It didn't have _?_ but unusual shirts.
6. _?_ wanted to leave so soon.
8. Hasn't _?_ read the museum books?
10. I have read _?_ of them so far.

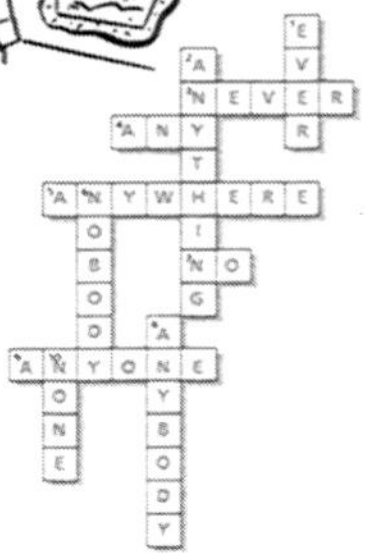

Writing Application: A Letter PERSUADING

Think of a museum or a historic building that you have visited. Remember what you liked and disliked about your visit. Write a letter to the director, politely suggesting ways to improve the exhibits and programs. Use negatives correctly. Students should respond on separate paper. Answers will vary.

What Is a Preposition?

Lesson Objectives

Students will:

- identify prepositions and prepositional phrases
- write and proofread sentences with prepositions
- write a creative comic strip, using prepositional phrases correctly

One-Minute Warm-Up Write students' responses on the board. Ask volunteers to underline the phrase that tells the location of each item. Ask which word in the phrase connects it to other words in the sentence. Circle these words and tell students that the connecting words are called prepositions.

Focus on Instruction

Tell students that the table is an incomplete list of prepositions and that they should identify prepositions by finding the word that connects two words in a sentence.

Try It Out

VIEWING Make a chart on the board in which students can write their own sentences about the picture. Then have them rewrite each sentence, adding a prepositional phrase to elaborate meaning. (Sample responses are shown.)

Sentences	Sentences with Prepositions
Three friends skated.	Three friends skated on a frozen pond.
Sarah enjoys skating.	Sarah enjoys skating during the winter.

FOR STUDENTS ACQUIRING ENGLISH

- Have students listen to the Try It Out sentences on the audiotape. Distribute SAE Practice page for Unit 7, Lesson 5, to support listening.
- Help students describe the picture. List vocabulary; explain as needed. Encourage use of prepositions in the descriptions. Then have partners list as many prepositions as they can. Then students compare lists. Remind students that prepositions are always followed by a noun or pronoun. This is in contrast to phrasal verbs such as *sit down,* but watch for problems with transitive phrasal verbs such as *pick up.* Students listen and mark the preposition twice in the underlined phrase.

1. Heather skated over the wall.
2. The children are playing in the park.

Grammar

5 What Is a Preposition?

One-Minute Warm-Up Look at the picture. Using complete sentences, tell where each item is located.
Sample answer: The ice skates are under the table.

Little words can make a big difference in meaning.

The skate is on the table. The skate is under the table.

- The words *on* and *under* show a different connection between the words *skate* and *table.* **A word that shows the connection between other words in a sentence is a preposition.**

Common Prepositions						
about	around	beside	for	near	outside	under
above	at	by	from	of	over	until
across	before	down	in	off	past	up
after	behind	during	inside	on	through	with
along	below	except	into	out	to	without

- **A prepositional phrase begins with a preposition and ends with a noun or pronoun.** All the words in between are part of the prepositional phrase.

Mike glided easily across the frozen pond. His friends cheered for him.

Try It Out

Speak Up Find the preposition in each underlined prepositional phrase.

1. Jen had never skated until last Tuesday. until
2. At first she wobbled on her new skates. on
3. She clung to the fence. to
4. Then Sofia skated beside her. beside
5. Together they moved around the rink. around
6. Sometimes Jen glided across the rink. across
7. At other times she stumbled ungracefully along the ice. along

Meeting Individual Needs

RETEACHING
ALTERNATIVE STRATEGY

- Write this sentence on the board, underlining the preposition: *He placed the box under the bed.*
- Tell students that the underlined word is called a preposition. Explain that the word *under* connects *box* to where it was placed.
- Write other sentences with prepositional phrases on the board, and have students repeat this exercise.

CHALLENGE
Have students create short poems with a prepositional phrase at the end of each line. For example: *The cat was on the table. / The boy sat on the floor. / The girl ran in the room. / So the cat jumped out the door.*

FOR STUDENTS ACQUIRING ENGLISH
Give a series of commands telling students where to put things. "Put your finger on your nose. Put the book under the table." Call attention to prepositions with contrasting commands. Students take turns giving each other commands.

On Your Own

Write each sentence. Underline the prepositional phrase once and the preposition twice.

Example: Many talented skaters competed for the championship.

8. One skater fell during his performance.
9. Tina finished without a mistake.
10. Joe skated with her.
11. They performed to beautiful music.
12. A reporter wrote about them.
13. Joe flipped Tina over his shoulders.
14. She spun around him.
15. Then she leaped into the air.

16–22. This e-mail message has seven prepositional phrases. Write the message. Underline each prepositional phrase once and each preposition twice.

Example: Beth has skated for years.

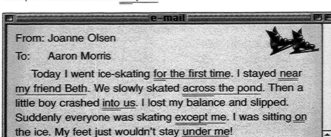

e-mail

From: Joanne Olsen

To: Aaron Morris

Today I went ice-skating for the first time. I stayed near my friend Beth. We slowly skated across the pond. Then a little boy crashed into us. I lost my balance and slipped. Suddenly everyone was skating except me. I was sitting on the ice. My feet just wouldn't stay under me!

Writing Wrap-Up

WRITING • THINKING • LISTENING • SPEAKING

CREATING

Write a Comic Strip

Draw a comic strip about your first try at a sport. Write a one-sentence caption beneath each picture. Use a prepositional phrase in each sentence. Then read your comic strip to a partner. Which picture and caption did your partner like best?

For Extra Practice see page 263.

Summing Up Help students summarize these key points about the lesson:

> A word that shows the connection between other words in a sentence is a **preposition**. A prepositional phrase begins with a preposition, and ends with a noun or a pronoun.

You may want to have students complete the parts related to this lesson on Blackline Master 7–4.

On Your Own

Remind students to check that they have found the entire prepositional phrase by making sure it ends with a noun or a pronoun.

MEETING INDIVIDUAL NEEDS

FOR STUDENTS ACQUIRING ENGLISH

Distribute SAE Practice page for Unit 7, Lesson 5. Help students describe the game. List vocabulary. Students mark the preposition twice in the underlined phrase.

1. Jason kicked the ball toward the goal.
2. The goalie jumped into the air.

Writing Wrap-Up

Writing Tip: Tell students to make a short list of steps they took to learn a sport. Then have students rephrase their lists to include prepositional phrases. See Blackline Master 7–6 for a sample comic strip.

TECHNOLOGY CONNECTION

Students may wish to use available software and hardware to publish a class comic book.

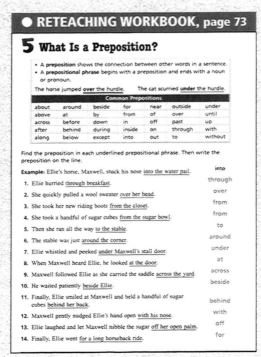

● RETEACHING WORKBOOK, page 73

5 What Is a Preposition?

- A **preposition** shows the connection between other words in a sentence.
- A **prepositional phrase** begins with a preposition and ends with a noun or pronoun.

The horse jumped **over the hurdle**. The cat scurried **under the hurdle**.

Common Prepositions						
about	around	beside	for	near	outside	under
above	at	by	from	of	over	until
across	before	down	in	off	past	up
after	behind	during	inside	on	through	with
along	below	except	into	out	to	without

Find the preposition in each underlined prepositional phrase. Then write the preposition on the line.

Example: Ellie's horse, Maxwell, stuck his nose into the water pail. **into**

1. Ellie hurried through breakfast. through
2. She quickly pulled a wool sweater over her head. over
3. She took her new riding boots from the closet. from
4. She took a handful of sugar cubes from the sugar bowl. from
5. Then she ran all the way to the stable. to
6. The stable was just around the corner. around
7. Ellie whistled and peeked under Maxwell's stall door. under
8. When Maxwell heard Ellie, he looked at the door. at
9. Maxwell followed Ellie as she carried the saddle across the yard. across
10. He waited patiently beside Ellie. beside
11. Finally, Ellie smiled at Maxwell and held a handful of sugar cubes behind her back. behind
12. Maxwell gently nudged Ellie's hand open with his nose. with
13. Ellie laughed and let Maxwell nibble the sugar off her open palm. off
14. Finally, Ellie went for a long horseback ride. for

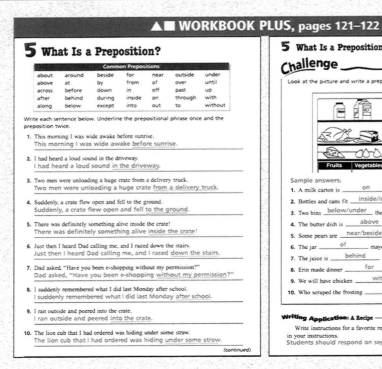

▲■ WORKBOOK PLUS, pages 121–122

5 What Is a Preposition?

Common Prepositions						
about	around	beside	for	near	outside	under
above	at	by	from	of	over	until
across	before	down	in	off	past	up
after	behind	during	inside	on	through	with
along	below	except	into	out	to	without

Write each sentence below. Underline the prepositional phrase once and the preposition twice.

1. This morning I was wide awake before sunrise.
   This morning I was wide awake before sunrise.
2. I had heard a loud sound in the driveway.
   I had heard a loud sound in the driveway.
3. Two men were unloading a huge crate from a delivery truck.
   Two men were unloading a huge crate from a delivery truck.
4. Suddenly, a crate flew open and fell to the ground.
   Suddenly, a crate flew open and fell to the ground.
5. There was definitely something alive inside the crate!
   There was definitely something alive inside the crate!
6. Just then I heard Dad calling me, and I raced down the stairs.
   Just then I heard Dad calling me, and I raced down the stairs.
7. Dad asked, "Have you been e-shopping without my permission?"
   Dad asked, "Have you been e-shopping without my permission?"
8. I suddenly remembered what I did last Monday after school.
   I suddenly remembered what I did last Monday after school.
9. I ran outside and peered into the crate.
   I ran outside and peered into the crate.
10. The lion cub that I had ordered was hiding under some straw.
    The lion cub that I had ordered was hiding under some straw.

(continued)

5 What Is a Preposition? (continued from page 121)

Challenge

Look at the picture and write a preposition to complete each sentence.

Sample answers:

1. A milk carton is ___on___ the top shelf.
2. Bottles and cans fit ___inside/into___ the refrigerator door.
3. Two bins ___below/under___ the shelves keep fruits and vegetables crisp.
4. The butter dish is ___above___ the bottles and cans.
5. Some pears are ___near/beside___ the cheese.
6. The jar ___of___ mayonnaise is new.
7. The juice is ___behind___ the milk.
8. Erin made dinner ___for___ the whole family.
9. We will have chicken ___with___ a cream sauce.
10. Who scraped the frosting ___off___ the cake?

Writing Application: A Recipe INSTRUCTING

Write instructions for a favorite recipe. Use at least five prepositional phrases in your instructions.

Students should respond on separate paper. Answers will vary.

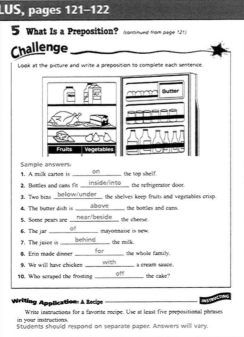

Writing with Prepositions

Lesson Objective

Students will:
- add prepositional phrases to sentences

Focus on Instruction

- Remind students that a prepositional phrase begins with a preposition, ends with a noun or pronoun, and tells *how, where, when, why,* or *which one.*
- Write these sentences on the board and discuss what each prepositional phrase tells: Cara lost her wallet at the park. (where) The dance begins at seven o'clock. (when) Todd wraps the present with care. (how)
- Explain that a prepositional phrase should be placed near the word it modifies.

Apply It

Have students complete the revising activity. Suggest that they read the poem and then read each prepositional phrase to decide what it tells and where it might fit in the poem.

Have students look in their writing in progress to find places where prepositional phrases can be added.

Sample Answers to Apply It

1. The cat looks out the window. What is swirling in the air?
2. He scratches the front door with one paw.
3. The snow in the air tickles.
4. The snow on his nose makes him sneeze.
5. He darts to the house.
6. He sleeps by the stove.

FOR STUDENTS ACQUIRING ENGLISH

- Have students choose the correct phrase (in the snow, down the hill) for each sentence below.
  1. We made a tunnel ______. (in the snow)
  2. We rode our sled ______. (down the hill)
- Show pictures of people having fun in the snow, or mention activities like *skating* or *making snowballs.* Write the example sentence below on the board. Show students how to combine the sentences. Example: I skated quickly. I skated across the pond. (I skated quickly across the pond.)

Revising Strategies

Writing with Prepositions

Elaborating Sentences You can use prepositional phrases to add helpful and interesting information to your sentences.

My friend loves snow.
My friend from Florida loves snow.
We dug a long tunnel.
We dug a long tunnel through the snow.

Apply It

1–6. Rewrite the story, elaborating each line with a prepositional phrase. Use phrases from the box, or make up your own. See TE margin for sample answers.

with one paw	on his nose
in the air	out the window
by the stove	to the house

Revising

When Snow Gets on Your Nose

Meow!
The cat looks.
What is swirling?
He scratches
the front door.
The snow tickles.
The snow makes
him sneeze.
He darts.
He sleeps.

246 Unit 7: Adverbs and Prepositions

Meeting Individual Needs

● RETEACHING WORKBOOK, page 74

Writing with Prepositions

- A preposition shows the connection between other words in a sentence.
- A prepositional phrase begins with a preposition such as *to, with, by, on, in, up, down, out, under, above, over, beside, near, around,* or *through.* It ends with a noun or pronoun.

Without a prepositional phrase	I walked my dog.
With a prepositional phrase	I walked my dog in the park.

Elaborating Sentences Write each sentence, adding the prepositional phrase in parentheses. Sample answers:

Example: People enjoy the park. **(on a sunny day)**
People enjoy the park on a sunny day.

Revising

1. The toddlers play. **(in the sandbox)**
   The toddlers play in the sandbox.
2. A rabbit chases the squirrel. **(up a tree)**
   A rabbit chases the squirrel up a tree.
3. Squawking ducks fly. **(over the pond)**
   Squawking ducks fly over the pond.
4. The grandfathers read books. **(with their grandchildren)**
   The grandfathers read books with their grandchildren.
5. The girls ride skateboards. **(down the hill)**
   The girls ride skateboards down the hill.
6. Four friends share a picnic lunch. **(beside the lake)**
   Four friends share a picnic lunch beside the lake.
7. Colorful kites drift high. **(above the branches)**
   Colorful kites drift high above the branches.
8. A tired dog rests. **(under a shady tree)**
   A tired dog rests under a shady tree.

(continued)

▲■ WORKBOOK PLUS, page 123

Writing with Prepositions

Without prepositional phrase	Rabbits nibble grass.
With prepositional phrase	Rabbits nibble grass in the meadow.

Elaborating Sentences 1–8. Rewrite the paragraph. Elaborate each sentence with a prepositional phrase from the box, or create your own. Sample answers:

into a huge pile	for the ducks	about the warm weather
under the trees	after lunch	in the morning
through the park	with the long neck	to the swan

Revising

Everyone was excited. We played outdoors. We rode our bikes. Mom brought a bag of corn and birdseed. The beautiful white swan swam toward us. I threw some of the corn. We watched the squirrels scamper. We raked our leaves and jumped in them.

Everyone was excited about the warm weather. We played outdoors in the morning. We rode our bikes through the park. Mom brought a bag of corn and birdseed for the ducks. The beautiful white swan with the long neck swam toward us. I threw some of the corn to the swan. We watched the squirrels scamper under the trees. We raked our leaves into a huge pile and jumped in them.

(continued)

Combining Sentences Sometimes you can combine two short, choppy sentences by moving a prepositional phrase from one sentence to the other. Because the two short sentences below both tell about Mia and her skiing, you can combine them by moving the phrase *across the park* from the second sentence to the first sentence.

Mia skied smoothly. She skied across the park.	Mia skied smoothly across the park.

Apply It

7–10. Rewrite this part of an essay. Combine each pair of underlined sentences by adding the highlighted phrase to the first sentence.
See TE margin for answers.

Revising

Downhill skiers race quickly. They race down steep slopes. Cross-country skiers glide more slowly. They glide along level ground. Both sports are fun and exciting.

I think, however, that cross-country skiing is better than downhill skiing. It provides better exercise. The exercise is better for the heart and the lungs. Cross-country skiing is also a safer and less complicated sport. These skiers have fewer risks. There are fewer risks of breaking an arm or a leg. Cross-country skiers can move at their own speed.

Lesson Objective

Students will:
- combine sentences by moving a prepositional phrase

Focus on Instruction

- Explain to students that if two sentences have the same subject and verb, the words and phrases describing the subject and verb can be combined into one sentence.
- Write the sentences below on the board and discuss how they've been combined.

  The players tried hard.
  They tried throughout the game.
  The players tried hard throughout the game.

Apply It

Have students complete the revising activity independently. Point out that the highlighted words are prepositional phrases that must be moved to the preceding sentence. Explain that in this exercise only, each phrase should be moved to the end of the preceding sentence. Point out that each phrase begins with a preposition and ends with a noun.

Have students find places in their own writing in progress where they can combine sentences by moving a prepositional phrase.

Answers to Apply It

7. Downhill skiers race quickly down steep slopes.
8. Cross-country skiers glide more slowly along level ground.
9. It provides better exercise for the heart and the lungs.
10. These skiers have fewer risks of breaking an arm or a leg.

● RETEACHING WORKBOOK, page 75

Writing with Prepositions *(continued from page 74)*

- Combine short, choppy sentences that tell about the same thing by moving a prepositional phrase from one sentence to the other.

Two sentences	Animals often make tracks. They make tracks to their homes.
Combined sentence	Animals often make tracks to their homes.

Combining Sentences Combine each pair of sentences. Move the underlined prepositional phrase to the first sentence.

Example: You can find animal tracks. They are near the badger's burrow.
You can find animal tracks near the badger's burrow.

Revising

9. The woodchuck burrows busily. It burrows under a rock.
The woodchuck burrows busily under a rock.
10. A woodchuck eats lots of food in the autumn. It eats before hibernation.
A woodchuck eats lots of food in the autumn before hibernation.
11. Woodchucks listen carefully. They listen for danger signals.
Woodchucks listen carefully for danger signals.
12. Badgers sleep peacefully in their burrows. They sleep during the winter.
Badgers sleep peacefully in their burrows during the winter.
13. A mother badger cares for her young. She cares for them by herself.
A mother badger cares for her young by herself.
14. A badger has white and black markings. It has markings on its head and face.
A badger has white and black markings on its head and face.
15. Moles live underground. Some moles live in nests.
Some moles live in nests underground.
16. The mole digs for insects and worms. It digs with its sharp claws.
The mole digs for insects and worms with its sharp claws.

▲■ WORKBOOK PLUS, page 124

Writing with Prepositions *(continued from page 123)*

Two sentences	The skaters glide gracefully. They glide over the ice.
Combined sentence	The skaters glide gracefully **over the ice.**

Combining Sentences 9–14. Rewrite this segment from a review of an ice skating competition. Combine each pair of related sentences by adding the underlined prepositional phrase from one sentence to the sentence before it.

Revising

Gina skated confidently. She skated onto the rink. Her colorful costume sparkled. It sparkled in the lights. Beautiful music echoed loudly. It echoed throughout the arena. She performed magnificent spins and jumps. She performed them for the audience. The audience clapped loudly. The audience clapped after her performance. Gina waved happily. She waved to the cheering fans.

Gina skated confidently onto the rink. Her colorful costume sparkled in the lights. Beautiful music echoed loudly throughout the arena. She performed magnificent spins and jumps for the audience. The audience clapped loudly after her performance. Gina waved happily to the cheering fans.

Changing Meaning with Adverbs

Lesson Objective

Students will:

- use adverbs to change the meaning of a paragraph

Focus on Instruction

- Have students read the introductory paragraph.
- Have volunteers read each example sentence and act out the action it describes. Discuss with students how changing the adverbs in the sentence changes the meaning of the sentence.

Apply It

Have students complete the activity independently. Tell them to choose their adverbs carefully. Point out that using the wrong adverb can give a sentence a meaning that is very different from what the writer intended. Have students discuss their word choices.

Suggest that students who need more support work with partners.

Have students find places in their own writing where they can change the meaning with adverbs.

Sample Answers to Apply It

The day began early. As dawn grew near, the robins chattered happily. Subway cars ran everywhere. The city woke up quickly as the sun rose in the sky. Large buses carried workers downtown. Kettles whistled loudly on kitchen stoves. People ate their breakfasts eagerly. Children slammed doors and walked noisily to school. The boys talked eagerly as they waited for class to begin. A new student walked into the classroom late.

FOR STUDENTS ACQUIRING ENGLISH

Write the following adverbs on the board: *happily, sadly, tiredly.* Have students use them in the following sentence to change its meaning: *He looked out of the window* ______. Ask them to pantomime the meaning of each adverb.

Revising Strategies — Vocabulary

Changing Meaning with Adverbs

Adverbs are powerful words for a writer. Changing one adverb can change the meaning of an entire sentence. Read the sentences below. What do you picture when you read each sentence?

The hikers are climbing slowly and carefully.

The hikers are climbing quickly and excitedly.

Apply It

1–10. Write this paragraph. Fill in the blanks with adverbs from the box. Then change the meaning of the paragraph by using other adverbs from the box. You can use any adverb more than once. Answers will vary.

happily	sadly	anywhere	carefully	easily
slowly	everywhere	late	loudly	eagerly
quietly	downtown	quickly	early	noisily

Revising

A New Day

The day began ______. As dawn grew near, the robins chattered ______. Subway cars ran ______. The city woke up ______ as the sun rose in the sky. Large buses carried workers ______. Kettles whistled ______ on kitchen stoves. People ate their breakfasts ______. Children slammed doors and walked ______ to school. The boys talked ______ as they waited for class to begin. A new student walked ______ into the classroom.

248 **Unit 7:** Adverbs and Prepositions

Meeting Individual Needs

● RETEACHING WORKBOOK, page 76

Changing Meaning with Adverbs

- Adverbs describe verbs.
- Adverbs tell how, when, or where something happens. They can change the meaning of an entire sentence.

Lisa raked **energetically.**
Lisa raked **carelessly.**

Change the meaning of each sentence by replacing the underlined adverb with another adverb from the box.

quietly	calmly	soon
loudly	sometimes	noisily

Example: Pat cheerfully took out the trash.
Pat finally took out the trash.

Revising

1. Eric and his friends always enjoy camping trips.
   Eric and his friends sometimes enjoy camping trips.
2. The campers talk excitedly as they bump along the road.
   The campers talk quietly as they bump along the road.
3. Finally they arrive at their campsite.
   Soon they arrive at their campsite.
4. Sid shouts nervously when he hears a rustling sound in the bushes.
   Sid shouts loudly when he hears a rustling sound in the bushes.
5. Then the campers bang pots and pans to scare off the enemy.
   Noisily the campers bang pots and pans to scare off the enemy.
6. Sid grins sheepishly as a chipmunk scampers away.
   Sid grins calmly as a chipmunk scampers away.

▲■ WORKBOOK PLUS, page 125

Changing Meaning with Adverbs

The crowd cheered **loudly.**
The crowd cheered **politely.**

early	nervously	finally
happily	patiently	skillfully
wildly	carefully	clumsily
late	well	noisily
sadly	anxiously	confidently

1-10. Write this paragraph. Fill in the blanks with adverbs from the box. Then compare your paragraph with one written by a classmate. Notice the difference in meaning created by using different adverbs. Sample answers:

Revising

It was a big day for the Spartans. The team had been waiting ______ for the championship game to begin. The players gathered ______ around their coach. They listened ______ to his instructions. ______, it was time for the team to take the floor. The crowd cheered ______ for the home team. ______ in the game, the score was tied. Both teams played ______. With three seconds left, Jim ______ shot the basketball. The Spartans left the court ______. They knew that they had played ______.

It was a big day for the Spartans. The team had been waiting anxiously for the championship game to begin. The players gathered nervously around their coach. They listened carefully to his instructions. Finally, it was time for the team to take the floor. The crowd cheered wildly for the home team. Early in the game, the score was tied. Both teams played confidently. With three seconds left, Jim skillfully shot the basketball. The Spartans left the court happily. They knew that they had played well.

Enrichment

Adverbs!

From Story to Script

Choose a short scene from a favorite story. Write it as a play. Before each character's words, write the name of the character. After the name, write an adverb telling how the character says the lines. Have a narrator speak the lines that describe the scene or action. Practice your play, and perform it for the class.

Example: Margarita (loudly): The diamonds are missing!
Hernando (angrily): Who could have done this?
Narrator (calmly): They began searching for clues.

Preposition Poem

Write a poem about something that moves, such as a cat, a river, or a runner. Copy the form shown below. Then draw a picture to go with your poem.

The stream flows
down the mountain,
across the field,
under the bridge,
and over my feet.

(Subject) (verb)
(prepositional phrase),
(prepositional phrase),
(prepositional phrase),
and (prepositional phrase).

Challenge Write two more verses for your poem. How many prepositional phrases can you use?

Enrichment

Objectives

Students will:
- use adverbs to describe actions
- use prepositional phrases to create a poem

Using the Activities

The Enrichment page provides fun, creative activities that reinforce students' understanding and use of adverbs and prepositions. The activities are designed to be enjoyed by all students. Here are some ideas for using the activities.

- Pair students who need extra support with more capable classmates.
- Students can work with these activities in class after they have completed other assignments.
- Activities that can be completed individually can be assigned as homework.

Focus on the Activities

FROM STORY TO SCRIPT

- Suggest that students select an emotional or action-packed story to make it easier to choose adverbs.
- As an alternative, students can write adverbs on index cards and place them in a container. As each character reads, he or she can draw a card, using it as a clue as to how to speak the lines.

PREPOSITION POEM

- Have a volunteer read the sample poem. Point out that each line includes a prepositional phrase.
- You might suggest a class theme for the poems. Then students can create a display to highlight their poems.
- Encourage students to use a thesaurus to find interesting nouns to use in their poems.

MEETING INDIVIDUAL NEEDS **CHALLENGE** Students can exchange poems with other students, each of whom writes an additional verse.

Checkup

Objectives

Students will:

- identify adverbs and the verbs they describe
- use adverbs to compare
- use *good* and *well* correctly
- use negatives in sentences correctly

Using the Checkup

Use the Checkup exercises as assessment, as review for the unit test, as extra practice, or as a diagnostic aid to help determine those students who need reteaching.

INTERNET CONNECTION The Wacky Web Tales® at www.eduplace.com/tales/ are cloze stories that students complete, using designated parts of speech. Students may choose any word to fill in a blank as long as it is the correct part of speech. As a result, the completed stories are often amusing, even "wacky," depending on the specific words chosen. Most of the stories at this Web site are student submissions.

INTERNET CONNECTION Students can take an interactive quiz for this unit at www.eduplace.com/kids/hme/ and then get immediate feedback.

Checkup: Unit 7

See TE margin for answers.

1 What Is an Adverb? *(p. 234)* Write each adverb and the verb that it describes.

1. Leo called Nick early.
2. "Let's go!" he said eagerly.
3. They both dressed quickly.
4. Then they got their fishing gear.
5. The boys met outside.
6. They found the boat quickly.
7. The boys rowed silently.
8. Finally, they found a good spot.
9. "Drop the anchor here," said Leo.
10. The boys baited their hooks carefully.
11. Nick and Leo sat patiently.
12. Suddenly Nick's line jerked.
13. A huge flounder had grabbed the worm greedily.
14. "I got one!" Nick cried excitedly.

2 Comparing with Adverbs *(p. 238)* Write each sentence. Use the correct form of the adverb in ( ).

15. This year plan your garden (carefully) than last year.
16. Order vegetable seeds (soon) than you order flowers.
17. You will work (hard) of all in the spring.
18. Plant the lettuce seeds (close) to the path.
19. Space the tomato plants (widely) apart than the rows of corn.
20. Of most spring crops, lettuce appears (soon).
21. You will find that weeds sprout (quickly) than vegetables.
22. Water the garden (long) of all in the hot weather.
23. Water the plants (heavily) in the morning than at night.

3 Using *good* and *well* *(p. 240)* Use *good* or *well* to complete each sentence.

24. The science program was ____.
25. Mr. Ray spoke ____ about animals.
26. The porcupine protects itself ____.
27. The porcupine is not ____ for other animals to eat.
28. The quills stick ____ into anything that touches them.
29. Mr. Ray also described ____ what a raccoon is like.
30. It is ____ at climbing trees.
31. Raccoons can handle objects ____ with their paws.
32. They can live ____ almost anywhere!

4 Negatives *(p. 242)* Each sentence has two negatives together. Write each sentence correctly.

33. Our school hasn't never had a band before.
34. Most students didn't know nothing about harmony.
35. Nobody never wanted to practice.
36. Now no one can't wait to learn the new songs.
37. Sam doesn't see nothing easy about this new piece.

250 Unit 7: Adverbs and Prepositions

Answers

What Is an Adverb?

1. early—called
2. eagerly—said
3. quickly—dressed
4. then—got
5. outside—met
6. quickly—found
7. silently—rowed
8. finally—found
9. here—Drop
10. carefully—baited
11. patiently—sat
12. Suddenly—jerked
13. greedily—had grabbed
14. excitedly—cried

Comparing with Adverbs

15. more carefully
16. sooner
17. hardest
18. close
19. more widely
20. soonest
21. more quickly
22. longest
23. more heavily

Using *good* and *well*

24. good
25. well
26. well
27. good
28. well
29. well
30. good
31. well
32. well

Negatives

33. Our school has never had a band before.
34. Most students didn't know anything (*or* knew nothing) about harmony.
35. Nobody ever wanted to practice.
36. Now no one can wait to learn the new songs.
37. Sam sees nothing easy about this new piece.

38. At the concert, nobody could find a seat nowhere near the stage.
39. There wasn't no sound when Ms. Conti tapped her baton to begin the performance.
40. The band didn't make no mistakes.
41. "The Stars and Stripes Forever" hadn't never sounded so good!

5 What Is a Preposition? *(p. 244)* Write each sentence. Underline the prepositional phrase once and the preposition twice.

42. The snow began before noon.
43. We ran outside the house.
44. The snow was sticking to the sidewalks.
45. It covered the tops of the cars.
46. Patti tried catching snowflakes on her tongue.
47. The snowstorm continued during the night.
48. We heard the wind howling through the trees.
49. My sister and I snuggled deeper under our blankets.
50. Everything was white in the morning!

Mixed Review 51–56. This part of a science report has four incorrect adverb forms, one mistake in using *good* and *well*, and one mistake in using negatives. Write the report correctly.

Proofreading Checklist

Did you use these words correctly?
- ✔ adverbs that compare
- ✔ *good* and *well*
- ✔ negatives

Proofreading

Venus, Lovely but Deadly

Venus is sometimes called Earth's sister. In size, it matches Earth most closely than any other planet. It's nearer to Earth than any other planet. A cloudless night is a good night to look for Venus. You'll see it more clearly than any star. It shines brighter of all the planets. The ancient Romans thought Venus was the beautifulest star in the sky. They named the planet for their goddess of love and beauty. This name doesn't fit the planet very good. Human beings couldn't never live on Venus. Its temperature rises more higher than eight hundred degrees.

(Corrections: more closely; brightest; most beautiful; well; ever; higher)

Go to www.eduplace.com/tales/ for more fun with parts of speech.

Objectives

Students will:
- identify prepositions and prepositional phrases
- proofread for correct adverb forms, correct use of *good* and *well*, and double negatives

Answers *continued*

38. At the concert, nobody could find a seat anywhere.
39. There wasn't any sound (*or* was no sound) when Ms. Conti tapped her baton to begin the performance.
40. The band didn't make any mistakes (*or* made no mistakes).
41. "The Stars and Stripes Forever" hadn't ever sounded so good *or* had never sounded so good.

What Is a Preposition?

42. The snow began before noon.
43. We ran outside the house.
44. The snow was sticking to the sidewalks.
45. It covered the tops of the cars.
46. Patti tried catching snowflakes on her tongue.
47. The snowstorm continued during the night.
48. We heard the wind howling through the trees.
49. My sister and I snuggled deeper under our blankets.
50. Everything was white in the morning!

Test Practice

Objective

Students will:

- practice completing a test format that requires them to find an error within a paragraph

Using the Test Practice

These Test Practice pages provide practice with common formats used in standardized or multiple-choice tests.

The first page works with skills taught in the basic lessons in Unit 7. The second and third pages work with skills taught in Units 1–7.

Focus on the Test Format

- Have a volunteer read the test directions aloud. Ask another volunteer to explain what the directions ask students to do.
- Remind students that the vertical line breaks the text into two columns, and that they should not read the second column until they have finished reading the first column.
- Point out that each item contains a paragraph consisting of two or three lines, and that students are required to find the mistake in the paragraph.
- Tell students to read the paragraphs carefully and look for errors. If they spot an error in a line, have them look to the left for the letter that corresponds to that line. Tell students that they should write this letter as their answer. Explain that the fourth letter is for paragraphs without mistakes.

FOR STUDENTS ACQUIRING ENGLISH

Ask for examples of adverbs. Have students use the examples in context. Review comparative and superlative adverbs with *-er, -est,* and *more, most* as well as irregulars. Distribute the SAE Test Practice pages for Unit 7. Have a volunteer read the directions aloud for each section. For the first section, students choose the line that has a mistake. If there is no mistake, they choose the last answer. Stress the importance of reading directions carefully each time. For the second section, students choose the best way to combine sentences.

Assessment Link

Test Practice

Write the numbers 1–8 on a sheet of paper. Read each paragraph. Choose the line that shows the mistake. Write the letter for that answer. If there is no mistake, write the letter for the last answer.

1 A Luis was playing catch
B with Antonio. Antonio threw
C the ball farther than Luis did.
D (No mistakes)

2 F The moon is shining
G brightlier tonight than it did
H last night. It looks like day!
J (No mistakes)

3 A Brittany was looking for
B deer tracks. She searched
C carefully in the snow.
D (No mistakes)

4 F There is a reason Keesha
G gets better grades than Mia.
H Keesha works more harder.
J (No mistakes)

5 A Nobody never puts
B anything away in this house.
C How messy it always is!
D (No mistakes)

6 F Of all the kids in the
G cabin, Sherilee snored the
H loudliest! She woke me up.
J (No mistakes)

7 A Eric makes funny
B pictures of weird creatures.
C He draws very good.
D (No mistakes)

8 F For vacation, Grandpa just
G sits on his front porch. He
H doesn't go anywhere!
J (No mistakes)

252 **Unit 7:** Adverbs and Prepositions

Now write the numbers 9–14 on your paper. Read the underlined sentences. Then find the answer that best combines them into one sentence.

9 The mayor ran in the race.
The doctor ran in the race.

A The mayor ran in the race, and the doctor ran in the race.

B The mayor ran and the doctor ran in the race.

(C) The mayor and the doctor ran in the race.

D The mayor ran in the race and the doctor also.

10 The car slid slowly.
The car slid down the hill.

(F) The car slid slowly down the hill.

G The car slid slowly and also slid down the hill.

H The car slid, and down the hill.

J The car slid down and slowly.

11 The bird gathered bits of string.
The bird made a nest.

A The bird gathered bits of string and a nest.

(B) The bird gathered bits of string and made a nest.

C The bird gathered bits of string, and the bird made a nest.

D The bird gathered and made a nest out of bits of string.

12 We will creep up the stairs.
We will creep up quietly.

F We will creep up the stairs and creep quietly up the stairs.

(G) We will creep quietly up the stairs.

H We will creep quietly up.

J We will creep up the stairs, and we will creep quietly.

13 LaToya collects buttons.
LaToya collects shells.

A LaToya collects buttons and she also collects shells.

B LaToya collects buttons and collects shells.

C LaToya collects also buttons also shells.

(D) LaToya collects buttons and shells.

14 Kevin skated fast.
His sister skated faster.

F Kevin skated faster than his sister skated fast.

G Kevin and his sister skated fast and faster.

H Kevin skated fast and his sister faster.

(J) Kevin skated fast, but his sister skated faster.

Test Practice 253

Objective

Students will:

- practice completing a test format that requires them to choose the best answer among four

Focus on the Test Format

- Have a volunteer read the test directions aloud. Ask another volunteer to explain what the directions ask students to do.
- Have students read the sentence pairs and interpret their meanings. Emphasize the importance of knowing the sentences' meanings before reading the answer choices.
- Point out that each answer choice combines the sentences differently. Students should look for grammatically correct sentences that preserve the intended meaning of the first two sentences.
- Explain that many choices may seem correct, but are not the best choice. For example, some choices may be grammatically correct, but awkwardly worded.
- After students choose their answer, have them find the letter that appears next to the sentence. Tell them that they should write this letter as their answer.

Test Practice *continued*

Objective

Students will:

- practice completing a test format that requires them to choose the best answer among four

Focus on the Test Format

The test format on this page is the same as the format on the preceding page.

Test Practice *continued*

Now write the numbers 15–20 on your paper. Read the underlined sentences. Then find the answer that best combines them into one.

15 <u>Melissa wrote the class play.</u>
<u>Melissa made the costumes.</u>

A Melissa wrote and made the class play and the costumes.
B Melissa wrote the class play, and the costumes.
C Melissa wrote it and made the costumes too.
(D) Melissa wrote the class play, and she made the costumes.

16 <u>Andrew put air in the tires.</u>
<u>Then Andrew rode his bike.</u>

(F) Andrew put air in the tires, and then he rode his bike.
G Andrew rode his bike with air in the tires.
H Andrew rode his bike, and Andrew put air in the tires.
J Andrew rode and put air in the tires of his bicycle.

17 <u>The circus came to town.</u>
<u>The circus was famous.</u>

A The circus came to town that was famous.
(B) The famous circus came to town.
C The circus came to town and was famous.
D The circus came to town, and the circus was famous.

18 <u>Jamie built the sand castle.</u>
<u>Nick built the sand castle.</u>

F Jamie built the sand castle, and Nick built the sand castle.
G Jamie built the sand castle, but Nick built the sand castle.
(H) Jamie and Nick built the sand castle.
J Jamie built the sand castle, and Nick.

19 <u>The fox ran across the field.</u>
<u>The fox ran swiftly.</u>

A The fox ran and swiftly across the field.
B The fox ran across the field and ran swiftly.
C The fox ran swiftly while it ran across the field.
(D) The fox ran swiftly across the field.

20 <u>Mom does her sit-ups.</u>
<u>Mom watches TV.</u>

F Mom does and watches her sit-ups and TV.
(G) Mom does her sit-ups while she watches TV.
H Mom does her sit-ups, and Mom watches TV.
J Mom does sit-ups and TV.

Cumulative Review

See TE margin for answers.

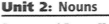

Unit 1: The Sentence

What Is a Sentence? Kinds of Sentences *(pp. 32, 36, 38)* If a group of words below is a sentence, write it correctly. If it is not, write *not a sentence*.

1. it was a rainy night
2. at the end of Nye Street
3. did you see the accident
4. please call the police
5. the driver of the car
6. went over the curb
7. how scary it was

Subjects and Predicates *(pp. 40, 42, 44)* Write each sentence. Draw a line between the complete subject and the complete predicate. Underline each simple subject once, and each simple predicate twice.

8. Nellie Bly was a famous reporter.
9. Her news stories were daring.
10. Nellie read the book *Around the World in Eighty Days*.
11. Then she went around the world.
12. Her trip around the world took fewer than eighty days.
13. She made the trip by ship, train, cart, and donkey.

Unit 2: Nouns

Common and Proper Nouns *(p. 64, 66)* Write each noun. Then write *common* or *proper* beside each one.

14. Di and her family live in the city.
15. Her father is a salesperson.
16. Mr. Hall makes trips to Mexico.
17. Her mother, Betty, is a lawyer.
18. On Saturdays Di visits parks.

Singular and Plural Nouns *(pp. 70, 72, 74)* Write the plural of each noun.

19. ox
20. shark
21. bush
22. glass
23. berry
24. deer

Possessive Nouns *(pp. 76, 78)* Write the possessive form of each noun.

25. men
26. fox
27. Cindy
28. baby
29. families
30. nurses

Unit 3: Verbs

Action Verbs, Main and Helping Verbs *(pp. 96, 98)* Write each sentence. Draw one line under the main verb and two lines under the helping verb.

31. Mr. Largo is repairing his barn.
32. Fire had damaged it.
33. The animals were roaming around the barnyard.
34. Mrs. Largo has repainted the fence.
35. The neighbors will keep some of the animals for a while.

See www.eduplace.com/kids/hme/ for a tricky usage or spelling question.

Cumulative Review 255

Cumulative Review

Objectives

Students will:

- write sentences correctly, distinguishing sentences from sentence fragments
- distinguish subjects from predicates
- identify common, proper, singular, and plural nouns
- write the possessive form of a noun correctly
- identify action verbs, helping verbs, and main verbs

Using the Cumulative Review

This Cumulative Review provides cumulative practice with basic grammar, usage, and mechanics skills taught in Units 1 through 7. You can use these pages for assessment, as a review for a test, as extra practice, or as a diagnostic aid to determine those students who may need reteaching.

INTERNET CONNECTION Send your students to www.eduplace.com/kids/hme/ for a tricky question related to usage or spelling.

Answers

Sentences, Kinds of Sentences

1. It was a rainy night.
2. not a sentence
3. Did you see the accident?
4. Please call the police.
5. not a sentence
6. not a sentence
7. How scary it was!

Subjects and Predicates

8. Nellie Bly | was
9. Her news stories | were
10. Nellie | read
11. she | went
12. Her trip around the world | took
13. She | made

Common and Proper Nouns

14. Di—p; family, city—c
15. father, salesperson—c
16. Mr. Hall, Mexico—p; trips—c
17. mother, lawyer—c; Betty—p
18. Saturdays, Di—p; parks—c

Singular and Plural Nouns

19. oxen
20. sharks
21. bushes
22. glasses
23. berries
24. deer

Possessive Nouns

25. men's
26. fox's
27. Cindy's
28. baby's
29. families'
30. nurses'

Action Verbs, Main and Helping Verbs

31. is repairing
32. had damaged
33. were roaming
34. has repainted
35. will keep

Objectives

Students will:

- identify the verb of a sentence and tell its tense
- use the correct verb form in a sentence
- write contractions with *not* correctly
- identify adjectives and the words they describe
- write the correct article for nouns
- write the correct adjective form for comparisons

Answers *continued*

Present, Past, and Future

36. will tell—future
37. built—past
38. called—past
39. will draw—future
40. live—present

Using Verbs

41. plays
42. tries
43. is
44. worn
45. have
46. hurried
47. taken

Contractions with *not*

48. hasn't
49. doesn't
50. shouldn't
51. won't

Adjectives

Adjectives are underlined.

52. two kinds, harmful snakes
53. Cobras slender
54. Long, fast cobras
55. Heads flat
56. Many vipers fat bodies

Using *a, an,* and *the*

57. an
58. a
59. the
60. an
61. a
62. the

Comparisons

63. larger
64. largest
65. most
66. better
67. worst
68. flattest

Present, Past, and Future *(p. 100)* Write the verbs in these sentences. Label each verb *present, past,* or *future.*

36. Peter will tell the class about Eskimo houses.
37. The Eskimos built snow houses in the winter.
38. They called these houses *igloos.*
39. Peter will draw a picture of an igloo for his report.
40. Most of the Eskimos live in wooden houses today.

Using Verbs *(pp. 104, 106, 108, 110, 112, 114)* Write the verb that correctly completes each sentence.

41. Grandpa (play, plays) the violin.
42. He (try, tries) to practice daily.
43. His first concert (is, are) today.
44. I have (wore, worn) my new clothes.
45. We (has, have) found our seats.
46. Grandpa (hurry, hurried) onstage.
47. He has (took, taken) a bow.

Contractions with *not* *(p. 116)* Write contractions for these words.

48. has not
49. does not
50. should not
51. will not

Unit 4: Adjectives

Adjectives *(pp. 136, 140)* Write each adjective and the word it describes.

52. Cobras and vipers are two kinds of harmful snakes.
53. Cobras are slender.
54. Long, fast cobras like to fight.
55. Heads of cobras are flat.
56. Many vipers have fat bodies.

Using *a, an,* and *the* *(p. 141)* Write each correct article.

57. (a, an) alarm
58. (a, an) book
59. (a, the) trees
60. (a, an) owl
61. (a, an) pump
62. (an, the) oxen

Comparisons *(pp. 142, 144, 146)* Write the correct word in ( ).

63. Texas is (larger, largest) than Delaware is.
64. Alaska is the (larger, largest) state of all.
65. Is Los Angeles the (more, most) exciting city in California?
66. Florida has a (better, best) climate than New England.
67. It's the (worse, worst) trip I've ever taken.
68. The Midwestern states have the (flatter, flattest) land of all.

Unit 5: Capitalization and Punctuation

Correct Sentences, Proper Nouns *(pp. 166, 170, 172)* Write these sentences correctly.

69. have you ever seen a dolphin show
70. my aunt and I went to one near redondo beach in california
71. on friday aunt megan and mrs. feld took me my uncle met us
72. how intelligent the dolphins were
73. please get me the book dolphin adventure I'd love to read it

Abbreviations *(p. 174)* Write abbreviations for these words.

74. Doctor
75. Mister
76. Road
77. April
78. Ohio
79. Utah

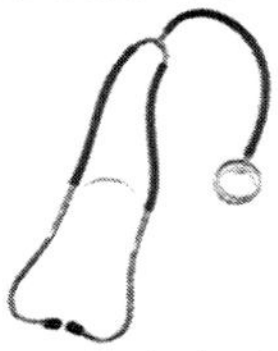

Commas *(pp. 176, 180)* Write these sentences correctly.

80. Deion tell me about storms.
81. Thunderstorms tornadoes and hurricanes are three kinds.
82. Thunderstorms Bob are common.
83. Yes most thunderstorms take place in spring and summer.
84. A thunderstorm brings lightning thunder and rain.

Quotations *(pp. 182, 184)* Write these sentences correctly.

85. Are we going to the fair asked Eva
86. Tad said I am working at a booth
87. I have entered a milking contest declared Ruben
88. How is the contest judged asked Tad
89. Ruben replied the judges will see how fast I can milk my cow

Unit 6: Pronouns

Subject and Object Pronouns *(pp. 204, 206, 208)* Write each sentence. Use a pronoun in place of the underlined word or words.

90. Mr. Hayes played a record.
91. He questioned Amy and me.
92. Amy knew the answer.
93. Johann Bach wrote the music.
94. Amy likes music by Bach.

***I* and *me*, Homophones** *(pp. 212, 218)* Write each sentence. Use the word or words that complete each sentence correctly.

95. Luis and (I, me) are learning to skate.
96. (Its, It's) lots of fun.
97. Dad drives (me and Luis, Luis and me) to the park.
98. We have our lesson (their, there).
99. Bring (you're, your) inline skates.

Objectives

Students will:

- capitalize and punctuate sentences correctly
- use periods, commas, and quotation marks properly
- use the correct pronouns to replace subjects and objects
- use the words *I* and *me* correctly
- determine the correct pronoun homophone to use in a sentence

Answers *continued*

Correct Sentences, Proper Nouns

69. Have you ever seen a dolphin show?
70. My aunt and I went to one near Redondo Beach in California.
71. On Friday, Aunt Megan and Mrs. Feld took me. My uncle met us.
72. How intelligent the dolphins were!
73. Please get me the book Dolphin Adventure. I'd love to read it!

Abbreviations

74. Dr.
75. Mr.
76. Rd.
77. Apr.
78. OH
79. UT

Commas

80. Deion, tell me about the storms.
81. Thunderstorms, tornadoes, and hurricanes are three kinds.
82. Thunderstorms, Bob, are common.
83. Yes, most thunderstorms take place in spring and summer.
84. A thunderstorm brings lightning, thunder, and rain.

Quotations

85. "Are we going to the fair?" asked Eva.
86. Tad said, "I am working at a booth."
87. "I have entered a milking contest," declared Ruben.
88. "How is the contest judged?" asked Tad.
89. Ruben replied, "The judges will see how fast I can milk my cow."

Subject and Object Pronouns

90. He
91. us
92. She
93. He
94. him

***I* and *me*, Homophones**

95. I
96. It's
97. Luis and me
98. there
99. your

Objectives

Students will:
- write possessive pronouns and pronoun contractions correctly
- identify adverbs and the verbs they describe
- make comparisons, using adverbs correctly
- use the words *good* and *well* correctly
- use negative words in a sentence correctly
- identify prepositional phrases in sentences

Answers *continued*

Possessive Pronouns

100. her
101. Their
102. His
103. Its
104. their

Contractions with Pronouns

105. you'll
106. I've
107. he's
108. he's
109. we'd
110. they're

What Is an Adverb?

111. Today—adv., made—v.
112. sewed—v., neatly—adv.
113. left—v., here—adv.
114. quickly—adv., sewed—v.
115. Later—adv., surprised—v.

Comparing with Adverbs

116. hardest
117. more quickly
118. most correctly
119. longer
120. more loudly

Using *good* and *well*, Negatives

121. anywhere
122. had
123. anyone
124. good
125. well

What Is a Preposition?

126. Ruth plays in a band.
127. She practices on Saturdays.
128. Sometimes she practices with a friend.
129. Her parents will come to her recital.
130. Ruth's younger brother will sit beside them.

Possessive Pronouns *(p. 214)* Write each sentence. Use a possessive pronoun in place of the underlined word or words.

100. Diane and Diane's brother Sam work in a pet store.
101. Diane and Sam's job is to feed the pets.
102. Sam's favorite pet is the parrot.
103. The parrot's feathers are yellow and blue.
104. The kittens snuggle with the kittens' mother.

Contractions with Pronouns *(p. 216)* Write the contractions for each of the following words.

105. you will
106. I have
107. he is
108. he has
109. we had
110. they are

Unit 7: Adverbs and Prepositions

What Is an Adverb? *(p. 234)* Write each adverb and the verb it describes.

111. Today Benita made a skirt.
112. She sewed the stitches neatly.
113. Benita left her machine here.
114. I quickly sewed a shirt.
115. Later I surprised Benita with it.

Comparing with Adverbs *(p. 238)* Write each sentence. Use the correct form of the adverb in ( ).

116. Of all the students, Beth studied (hard) for the spelling bee.
117. I lost my turn (quickly) than Steven did.
118. Beth spelled (correctly) of all.
119. She stayed in the contest (long) than any other student.
120. Our class cheered (loudly) than Mrs. Lopez's class.

Using *good* and *well*, Negatives *(pp. 240, 242)* Write the correct word to complete each sentence.

121. Pearl and Julian weren't going (nowhere, anywhere).
122. We (had, hadn't) nothing to do.
123. Can't (no one, anyone) think of something to do?
124. Pearl's idea was (good, well).
125. She studied (good, well) for her science test.

What Is a Preposition? *(p. 244)* Write each sentence. Draw one line under the prepositional phrase.

126. Ruth plays in a band.
127. She practices on Saturdays.
128. Sometimes she practices with a friend.
129. Her parents will come to her recital.
130. Ruth's younger brother will sit beside them.

Extra Practice

(pages 234–235)

1 What Is an Adverb?

- A word that describes a verb is an adverb.
- An adverb can tell *how, when,* or *where.*

Remember

● Write the adverb in each sentence.

Example: Nita always got mail. *always*

1. Erin wished that sometimes she would get letters.
2. Nita gladly told Erin about her pen pal.
3. They write letters frequently.
4. Erin then called World Pen Pals.
5. This company carefully matches pen pals.
6. They could find Erin a pen pal anywhere.

▲ Write each adverb. Then write the verb it describes.
Adverbs are underlined once; verbs, twice.

Example: Tina carefully studied the catalog. *carefully* *studied*

7. Finally, Tina spotted the perfect gift for Paco.
8. She completed the order form neatly.
9. Then she checked the name and number of the item.
10. Paco once ordered a baseball glove.
11. He carelessly wrote the wrong item number.
12. He soon received a package containing boxing gloves.

■ Use an adverb to complete each sentence. Write the sentences. The clue tells what kind of adverb to use. Sample answers are given.

Example: My uncle Jerry delivers mail ______. (where)
My uncle Jerry delivers mail downtown.

13. He rises ______ each day and puts on his uniform. (when) early
14. He greets everyone ______ as he delivers the mail. (how) pleasantly
15. ______ bad weather forces businesses to close. (when) Sometimes
16. Uncle Jerry dresses ______. (how) warmly
17. He tramps ______ through snow and sleet. (how) carefully
18. Uncle Jerry says, "I ______ deliver the mail." (when) always

Extra Practice 259

What Is an Adverb?

Objectives

Students will:

- identify whether an adverb tells *how, when,* or *where* about the verb
- identify adverbs and the verbs they describe
- use adverbs correctly in sentences

Using the Extra Practice

The Extra Practice activities provide additional practice for the basic lesson at three levels of difficulty: Easy (●), Average (▲), and Challenging (■).

The Extra Practice activities can be used in the following ways.

- Assign activities according to students' needs and abilities as homework after students have completed the basic lesson.
- Assign the Easy activities after using the lesson Reteaching instruction.
- Assign the Average activities to prepare students for the Checkup.
- Assign the Easy and/or Average activities to students who had difficulty with specific lessons on the Checkup.
- Assign the Challenging exercises as a Bonus activity.

Meeting Individual Needs — More Practice for Lesson 1

● EASY

Write *when, how,* or *where* to describe what each underlined adverb tells about the verb.

1. I quickly swept my room. (how)
2. I often drink milk for breakfast. (when)
3. A boy delivers the paper early in our neighborhood. (when)
4. He always puts it there. (where)
5. He shuts the door quietly. (how)

▲ AVERAGE

Copy each sentence. Underline the adverb twice that describes each underlined verb.

1. Today Juan used the computer.
2. He often practices his math skills on it.
3. "I love computers!" Juan said excitedly.
4. Juan and Lenny visited a computer store yesterday.
5. They stopped here on the way home from school.

■ CHALLENGING

Help create a "Neighborhood News" bulletin board. Write a news item of two or three sentences to tell about a neighborhood or school event. In each item, use adverbs that tell *how, when,* or *where* the actions happen. Underline these adverbs.

Comparing with Adverbs

Objectives

Students will:

- write the comparative and superlative forms of adverbs correctly
- use adverbs to compare two actions or three or more actions correctly

Using the Extra Practice

The Extra Practice activities provide additional practice for the basic lesson at three levels of difficulty: Easy (●), Average (▲), and Challenging (■).

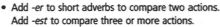

Extra Practice

(pages 238–239)

2 Comparing with Adverbs

Remember

- Add *-er* to short adverbs to compare two actions. Add *-est* to compare three or more actions.
- For adverbs that end with *-ly*, use *more* to compare two actions. Use *most* to compare three or more actions.
- Never use *-er* with *more*. Never use *-est* with *most*.

● Choose the word that correctly completes each sentence. Write the sentences.

Example: Lena runs (faster, fastest) of all the runners.
Lena runs fastest of all the runners.

1. She warms up (more carefully, most carefully) than I do.
2. Lena holds her head (higher, highest) than Lee does.
3. Sam jogs (more evenly, most evenly) than Julio does.
4. Pilar runs (more gracefully, most gracefully) of all.
5. Chan reaches the finish line (sooner, soonest) of all.

▲ Use the correct form of the adverb in ( ) to complete each sentence. Write the sentences.

Example: My brother skis _____ than I do. (skillfully)
My brother skis more skillfully than I do.

6. I like to ski _____ than he does. (slowly) more slowly
7. Kay skis _____ of everyone in the family. (fast) fastest
8. She started skiing _____ than Corliss. (soon) sooner
9. Corliss falls _____ of the three of us. (frequently) most frequently

■ For each sentence below, write two sentences. Make one compare two actions and the other compare three or more actions. Answers will vary.

Example: Connie swims expertly. *Connie swims more expertly than Alison. Connie swims most expertly of all the team members.*

10. She reaches the end of the pool soon.
11. Kiona cheers loudly for her.
12. Alex starts the race late.
13. He works hard to catch up.
14. Coach Okuda smiles proudly.

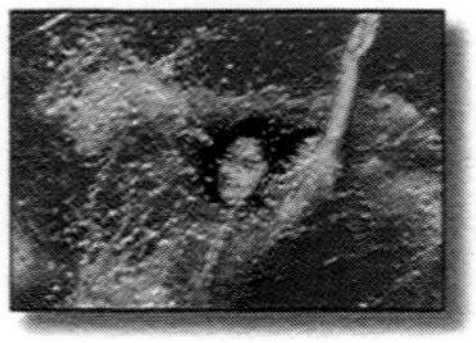

260 **Unit 7:** Adverbs and Prepositions

Meeting Individual Needs

More Practice for Lesson 2

● **EASY**

Write the missing form of each adverb.

1. loud	(louder)	loudest
2. high	higher	(highest)
3. gently	more gently	(most gently)
4. sharply	more sharply	(most sharply)

▲ **AVERAGE**

Use each adverb form in a sentence. Your sentence should show whether two, or more than two, actions are being compared. Sample answer: 1. Jo painted the most carefully of all.

1. most carefully
2. faster
3. more easily
4. hardest
5. more quickly

■ **CHALLENGING**

Write *correct* if the adverb in the sentence is correct. If it is not, write the correct form.

1. Of the three kittens, the gray one moves more quickly. (most)
2. The black one meows louder than the others do. (correct)
3. The tan one moves slowliest of all. (slowest)
4. The gray one can climb more high than the black one. (higher)
5. Do kittens or puppies act more playfully? (correct)

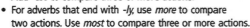

Extra Practice

3 Using *good* and *well*

(pages 240–241)

Remember

- Use the adjective *good* to describe nouns.
- Use the adverb *well* to describe verbs.

● For each sentence, write *correct* if the sentence is correct. Write *not correct* if it is not.

Example: Jade gives directions good. *not correct*

1. She gave us good directions to her house. correct
2. I listened good. not correct
3. The trip went well. correct
4. Mario's sense of direction is well. not correct
5. He and I followed Jade's directions good. not correct
6. We had a good time walking along the country roads. correct

▲ Write each sentence, using *good* or *well* correctly.

Example: Mark and his older brother Joel get along ______.
Mark and his older brother Joel get along well.

7. The trips they take together are ______. good
8. Joel is ______ at driving his car. good
9. Mark can read road maps ______. well
10. They are ______ as a team. good
11. Joel keeps his car running ______. well
12. The maps in his car are very ______. good

■ Some sentences are incorrect. Write those sentences correctly. Write *correct* if a sentence has no errors.

Example: We asked Dr. Chu to speak about eating good.
We asked Dr. Chu to speak about eating well.

13. I needed a good way to help her find our school. correct
14. Then I had an idea that was well. good
15. I knew I could make a good map. correct
16. First, I planned the map good on scrap paper. well
17. Then I made the final drawing on good paper. correct
18. I know the map worked good because Dr. Chu found us! well

Extra Practice 261

Using *good* and *well*

Objectives

Students will:

- identify the word that *good* or *well* describes in a sentence
- write sentences, using the words *good* and *well* correctly

Using the Extra Practice

The Extra Practice activities provide additional practice for the basic lesson at three levels of difficulty: Easy (●), Average (▲), and Challenging (■).

Meeting Individual Needs — More Practice for Lesson 3

● EASY

In each sentence, write the word that *good* or *well* describes.

1. It is a good day for fishing.
2. I know this stream well.
3. This new rod works well.
4. Ellen has good worms for bait.
5. I could use some good boots.

▲ AVERAGE

Underline a sentence if it is correct. If it is not, rewrite it correctly.

1. Craig plays baseball well.
2. He runs good too. (well)
3. He is a good catcher.
4. He always plays good. (well)
5. No one hits as well as Craig.

■ CHALLENGING

If a sentence is incorrect, rewrite it to correct any errors. If a sentence is correct, write *correct*.

1. Even in a good garden, some plants don't do well. (correct)
2. Sometimes good seeds don't sprout so good. (well)
3. Weeds grow good (well), but good gardeners don't let them.
4. Bugs like gardens as well as people do, but some bugs aren't good for the plants. (correct)
5. How good (well) a garden does depends a good deal on the weather.

Negatives

Objectives

Students will:

- use only one negative word in a sentence
- write sentences, using negatives correctly

Using the Extra Practice

The Extra Practice activities provide additional practice for the basic lesson at three levels of difficulty: Easy (●), Average (▲), and Challenging (■).

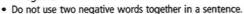

Extra Practice

(pages 242–243)

4 Negatives

Remember

- A negative is a word that means "no."
- Do not use two negative words together in a sentence.

● Write the word that makes each sentence mean *no*.

Example: Kevin hadn't met Aunt Ella until last month. *hadn't*

1. Nobody had told him she lived on a farm.
2. At first there weren't many things he could do.
3. He had never milked a cow.
4. He went to collect eggs and came back with none.
5. His aunt told him there was no need to worry.
6. A person can't do everything right the first time.

▲ Each sentence has two negatives. Write the sentences correctly. There may be more than one way to correct a sentence. Underlined portions are rewritten as sample answers.

Example: Sumi didn't know nothing about gardening.
Sumi knew nothing about gardening.

7. Nobody never told her how much work it was. Nobody ever
8. She couldn't plant nothing until the soil was ready. couldn't plant anything
9. Nothing never grows well unless the soil is loose. Nothing ever
10. Sumi didn't have no experience preparing soil. had no
11. Nothing could be no harder than digging up rocks. Nothing could be
12. She thought she wouldn't never get to plant seeds. would never

■ Answer each question with a sentence that means *no*. Use a different negative in each sentence. There may be more than one correct answer. Sample answers are g

Example: Have you ever planted a garden? *I have never planted a garden.*

13. Do you have a good place to grow vegetables? I do not have a good place.
14. Will your plants get much sun? My plants won't get much sun.
15. Have you decided which vegetables to grow? I haven't decided.
16. Can you start plants from seeds? I can't start plants from seeds.
17. Is there somewhere you can buy small plants? There is nowhere I can buy the
18. Do you know anyone who can help? I don't know anyone who can help.

262 **Unit 7:** Adverbs and Prepositions

Meeting Individual Needs — More Practice for Lesson 4

● EASY

Underline the correct word in parentheses. Then underline the one negative word that is already in the sentence.

1. She does not have (no, any) peanuts.
2. He doesn't have (no, any) money for the game tickets.
3. No one will (ever, never) understand why I was late.
4. I don't know (anything, nothing) about the new girl in class.

▲ AVERAGE

Write *correct* if the sentence is correct. If it is not, write it correctly.

1. Isn't nobody home at the Browns'? (Is nobody; Isn't anybody)
2. Ron didn't say anything about going away. (correct)
3. Aren't there no lights on in the house? (any lights; Are there no)
4. They don't never go away without telling us. (don't ever; They never)

■ CHALLENGING

Use each word pair correctly in a sentence. (Answers will vary.)

1. wasn't any
2. won't ever
3. have never
4. didn't anybody
5. has nothing

Extra Practice

(pages 244–245)

5 What Is a Preposition?

Remember

- A preposition is a word that shows the connection between two other words.
- A prepositional phrase begins with a preposition and ends with a noun or a pronoun.

● The preposition is underlined in each sentence. Write the prepositional phrase.

Example: The Sanchez family camped at a state park. *at a state park*

1. They climbed up the steep mountain. up the steep mountain
2. A beautiful view spread before them. before them
3. They looked across a green valley. across a green valley
4. A sparkling river wound through it. through it
5. Mr. Sanchez cooked over a glowing fire. over a glowing fire

▲ Copy each sentence. Underline the prepositional phrase once and the preposition twice.

Example: A trail led to the lake.
A trail led to the lake.

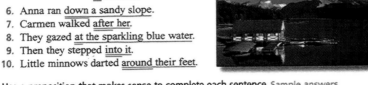

6. Anna ran down a sandy slope.
7. Carmen walked after her.
8. They gazed at the sparkling blue water.
9. Then they stepped into it.
10. Little minnows darted around their feet.

■ Use a preposition that makes sense to complete each sentence. Sample answers are given.

Example: The sun disappeared _____ the mountain.
The sun disappeared behind the mountain.

11. Their sleeping bags lay _____ the soft ground. on
12. The girls climbed _____ them. into
13. They talked _____ their wonderful day. about
14. The moon shone _____ the night. during
15. Everyone slept _____ sunrise. until
16. The sun rose _____ 4:30 A.M. at

What Is a Preposition?

Objective

Students will:

- identify the prepositions in prepositional phrases within sentences

Using the Extra Practice

The Extra Practice activities provide additional practice for the basic lesson at three levels of difficulty: Easy (●), Average (▲), and Challenging (■).

Meeting Individual Needs — More Practice for Lesson 5

● EASY

Write the preposition from each underlined prepositional phrase.

1. Yesterday, my dad took us to the carnival.
2. We got popcorn at the snack bar.
3. Then we rode on the Ferris wheel.
4. The view was lovely above the crowd.
5. Next year, we will take my friend Jack with us.

▲ AVERAGE

Copy each sentence and underline the prepositions.

1. I lost my keys during the field trip.
2. First, I searched in the school bus.
3. I started looking under my seat.
4. Then my teacher gave them to me.
5. He said he got my keys from another student.

■ CHALLENGING

Write the two prepositional phrases from each sentence. Underline the preposition from each phrase.

1. Have you ever gone to Colorado during the winter?
2. Many mountains in Colorado are capped with snow.
3. Tourists travel up chair lifts to ski down the mountains.
4. In the evening, skiers will have dinner at the ski lodge.
5. After dinner, the people will relax near the fireplace.

About Part 2

The units and lessons in Part 2 provide direct instruction in writing, listening, speaking, and viewing skills, including lessons that focus on media.

Using Part 2

The units and lessons in Part 2 may be used in any sequence or in combination or alternation with units and lessons from Part 1. Special Focus and Communication Link features are self-contained lessons that may be used independently from the rest of the unit in which they appear.

Choose among these units and lessons to address the curriculum requirements in your school and to meet the needs of your students.

Part 2

Writing, Listening, Speaking, and Viewing

264

What You Will Find in This Part:

265

Planning Part 2

The planning chart below suggests an approximate time allocation for completing the lessons in Part 2. You may want to include or skip the lessons labeled *optional* in your plans, depending on your students' needs and your district and state curricula.

Getting Started	*1 week (optional)*
Unit 8	Writing a Personal Narrative *2 weeks* Special Focus *2 days (optional)*
Unit 9	Writing a Story *2 weeks* Special Focus and Communication Links *2 weeks (optional)*
Getting Started	*1 week (optional)*
Unit 10	Writing Instructions *2 weeks* Special Focus and Communication Links *1 week (optional)*
Unit 11	Writing a Research Report *2 weeks* Special Focus and Communication Links *1 week (optional)*
Getting Started	*1 week (optional)*
Unit 12	Writing to Express an Opinion *2 weeks* Special Focus and Communication Links *1 week (optional)*
Unit 13	Writing to Persuade *2 weeks* Special Focus and Communication Links *1 week (optional)*

About Section 1

This section includes two developmental writing units for a personal narrative and a story, using the writing process.

Special Focus features provide instruction for writing a friendly letter and a play.

Communication Links lessons develop students' listening, speaking, and viewing skills.

Getting Started

- **Listening to a Narrative:** A one-page lesson with guidelines specific to listening to a narrative (A selection for reading aloud is in the Teacher's Edition.)
- **Writing a Narrative Paragraph:** A five-page segment focusing on the structure and organization of narrative paragraphs and strategies for elaboration

Unit 8 Writing a Personal Narrative

Unit features include:

Published model "A Play" from *Childtimes,* by Eloise Greenfield

Student model Personal narrative by Carolin Castillo, working draft and final copy

Mode-specific characteristics What Makes a Great Personal Narrative?

Focus Skill lessons
Prewriting: Organizing Your Narrative
Drafting: Good Beginnings
Drafting: Writing with Voice
Drafting: Good Endings

Rubric Evaluating Your Personal Narrative

Revising Strategies
Elaborating: Word Choice (similes and metaphors)
Elaborating: Details
Sentence Fluency (varying sentence structure)

Assessment Links Writing Prompts, Test Practice

Special Focus on Narrating
Friendly Letter Models and instruction for writing a friendly letter, a thank-you note, and an invitation and for addressing an envelope

Section 1

Narrating and Entertaining

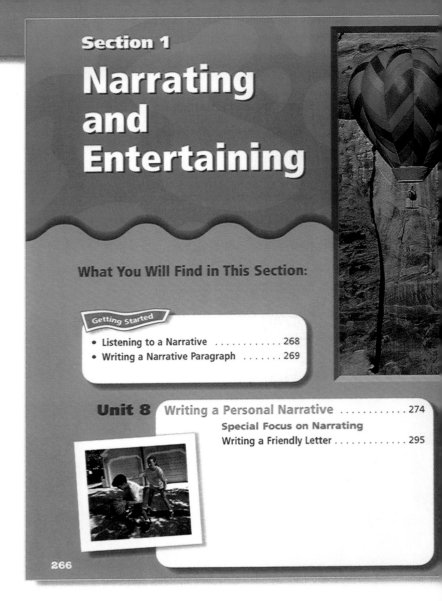

What You Will Find in This Section:

266

Independent Writing

In addition to the focused writing tasks in this section, students can benefit by having time that is set aside each day or several times a week for them to write in their journals or work on other self-selected writing activities, such as letters, poems, stories, book reviews, movie reviews, news articles, records, problem solving, announcements, written requests, or messages. Emphasize the importance of thinking about purpose and audience (noting that sometimes the students may be their own audience) and choosing an appropriate writing format that suits both.

Unit 9

267

Unit 9 Writing a Story

Unit features include:

Published model "Crows" from *Legends of the Seminoles,* by Betty Mae Jumper

Student model Story by Jessica Liu, working draft and final copy

Mode-specific characteristics What Makes a Great Story?

Focus Skill lessons

- Prewriting: Planning Characters
- Prewriting: Planning Setting and Plot
- Drafting: Developing Characters
- Drafting: Developing the Plot
- Drafting: Writing with Voice

Rubric Evaluating Your Story

Revising Strategies

- Elaborating: Word Choice (exact words)
- Elaborating: Details
- Sentence Fluency (avoiding stringy sentences)

Assessment Links Writing Prompts, Test Practice

Special Focus on Entertaining

- **Play** A model and instructions for writing a play

Communication Links

- **Speaking: Dramatizing** Guidelines and suggestions for reading aloud or performing a play
- **Viewing/Media: Comparing Stories in Books and Movies** Guidelines and practice for evaluating print and visual media versions of the same story

Listening to a Narrative

Lesson Objectives

Students will:
- use guidelines to listen to a narrative
- determine the purposes for listening, such as to enjoy and appreciate

Focus on Instruction

- Review the purposes of listening by asking these questions:

  Would you listen for enjoyment, information, or an opinion if I

  read aloud a book about volcanoes? (information)

  told you why I like banjo music? (opinion)

  told you about a funny thing that happened the first time I tried to canoe? (enjoyment)

- Discuss with students some purposes authors have for writing a story. Explain that although the general purpose is usually to entertain, an author may also want to make readers laugh or cry, scare them, share an experience, teach a lesson, or even use the story as a way to present an opinion about a topic. Have students suggest the author's purpose for some stories they know.
- Help students understand the importance of using good listening skills. Explain that important details can be learned by carefully listening to what a speaker is saying. Point out that the details can help the listeners see in their mind what the speaker is describing. Listening helps make the spoken message clearer.

Try It Out

- Ask students to use the title and the picture to predict what the selection is about. (something that involved a camel on a Sunday drive)
- Read aloud the story "Just a Sunday Drive in the Country" on the facing page. Encourage students to visualize the story as you read.

  As an alternative, students can listen to the selection on audiotape.
- Students can take notes while they are listening to a personal narrative. Refer them to page H27 for tips on taking notes while listening.

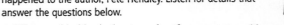

Listening to a Narrative

A **narrative** is a story about a real experience or an imagined one. Listening to a story is different from listening to a report. The general purpose for listening to a story is enjoyment. Use these guidelines to help you listen well.

Guidelines for Listening to a Story

- ▶ Listen for the one big idea. What is the story about?
- ▶ Listen for the main events. What happens? in what order?
- ▶ Listen to find out who the most important people or characters are and what they are like.
- ▶ Listen to find out where and when the story takes place.
- ▶ Listen for the author's purpose. Why is the author telling this story? Does the author want to make you laugh or cry? scare you? teach a lesson? share an experience?

Try It Out Listen as your teacher reads a true story, "Just a Sunday Drive in the Country," about an unusual experience that happened to the author, Pete Hendley. Listen for details that answer the questions below.

- What one big idea is the story about? an encounter with a camel
- When and where does the story take place? summer, in Ohio
- Who are the most important people in the story? What animal is important? the writer's daughters; camel
- Retell the story, telling the main events.

Main events: family stops at farm to buy corn; camel appears and sticks head in half-open car window to get corn; girls scream; frightened camel breaks window.

"Just a Sunday Drive in the Country"

by Pete Hendley

Read aloud the following personal narrative for the Try It Out on page 268.

You wouldn't think you'd have to worry about a camel on the loose in Ohio.

My wife and daughters and I were on vacation. We were staying at a cottage on the shore of Lake Erie and we decided to take a drive out into the countryside on our first day there. I was driving. My wife was in the front with me, and the girls were in the back.

It was a beautiful area—green rolling hills, thick with tall corn growing on both sides of the lazy country road. When we saw a sign advertising fresh sweet corn for sale, we decided to check it out.

We drove up a long dirt road and stopped in front of a large, white farmhouse. All around us were tall, old trees.

A farmer came up to the car. I talked to him through my open window, haggling over a price for the corn, our car still running. Once we came to an agreement, he opened up the back door and loaded a sack of corn onto the floor at my daughters' feet. Suddenly, on our right, a camel appeared from among the tall trees.

"Look! Look!" all three of my children screamed at once.

I couldn't believe it.

Then before we could do anything, the camel strolled up and stuck all of his huge, long head right into my wife's half-open window.

Everyone screamed at once.

"He just wants a piece of corn," the farmer said to my girls, who were in the backseat, squealing and screaming with a mixture of terror and glee.

"Give him the corn," I urged. "Give him the corn!"

The camel's head was gargantuan, as long and wide as a good-size dog, and it smelled like a wet rug. His lips moved and slopped constantly as he chewed, and his two cavernous nostrils sniffed at everything. When he turned to my wife, stuck out his tongue, and licked her smack on the face, it was more than my daughters could stand. They screamed and laughed so loud it scared the camel half to death.

He decided he would be better off somewhere else, without his head stuck in such a noisy, impolite box. He tried to pull himself out in one swift motion, but instead he got stuck in the small space created by the half-open window.

That didn't stop him, though. In terror, he yanked with all his camel strength, and amidst all the noise and confusion and panic, the window shattered, sending a shower of glass all over everyone in the car and causing complete and total pandemonium as three panicked children began to rock and bounce in their futile attempts to unbuckle their seat belts and run away.

"Go. Just drive!" my wife yelled. "Get us out of here!" A chorus of tiny voices behind me agreed.

And drive I did, backward, out the way we'd come, the perplexed and friendly farmer scratching his head and apologizing as we went. "He's just a little insistent," the man shouted. "Sorry."

We never did figure out what the camel was doing there.

Notes . . .

Writing a Narrative Paragraph

A group of sentences that tell about one main idea form a **paragraph**. The first line of a paragraph is **indented**. A paragraph has a topic and a main idea. The **topic** is the subject of the paragraph. The **main idea** is what the author wants to say about the subject.

A paragraph that tells a story is a **narrative paragraph**. What is the topic of the narrative paragraph below? What is the main idea?

Indent

Lead sentence — My first try at making pizza was like a wrestling match. First, the

Supporting sentences — dough attacked. It stuck to the rolling pin, to my fingers, and to the counter. Then the tomato sauce spilled under my feet and nearly made me slip. The cheese grater scraped my finger along with the mozzarella. Finally, I shoved the messy pizza into the oven. Twenty minutes later, I took my first bite.

Closing sentence — Mmmmmmmm. I knew I'd won the match!

The topic of this paragraph is making pizza. The main idea is that making the pizza was difficult, like a wrestling match. Which sentence tells the topic and the main idea?

The labels show the three parts of a narrative paragraph.

- The **lead sentence** introduces the topic and gives a hint about the main idea of the story.
- The **supporting sentences** follow the lead sentence. They give details about what happens in the story.
- The **closing sentence** finishes the story.

Think and Discuss Reread the pizza paragraph.

- What details are given in the supporting sentences?
Dough stuck to fingers and counter; tomato sauce spilled; cheese grater cut finger.

Writing a Narrative Paragraph

Lesson Objectives

Students will:
- identify the topic and main idea of a narrative paragraph
- discuss details that focus on paragraph structure

Focus on Instruction

- Before students read the sample narrative paragraph, explain that the blue call outs highlight the parts of a narrative paragraph and that students will learn about those parts later in the lesson.
- Have students find an indent in the first line of the paragraph. Tell students that the first line in every paragraph is indented this way. Ask why paragraphs are indented. (so readers can easily see where a new paragraph begins)
- Be sure that students understand that the topic of a paragraph is simply the subject and that the main idea is the one point that the writer has to say about the topic.
- Tell students that all three parts of a paragraph fit together like puzzle pieces to give a "complete picture" of the writer's message.

Think and Discuss

Have students explain why each detail in the supporting sentences supports the main idea.

The Lead Sentence

Lesson Objective

Students will:
- write lead sentences

Focus on Instruction

- Use the example sentence to reinforce the difference between the topic and the main idea.
- Discuss with students possible story ideas for the other two example lead sentences. (Sample answers: the difficulty the writer had choosing a pet from an animal shelter; the writer's unusual bus trip to school, caused by a flat tire) Explain that not all lead sentences break into topic and main idea as neatly as the lead sentence in the example.
- Ask students why each lead sentence might make a reader curious about the story.

Try It Out

- Ask students to identify the topic and main idea of each paragraph. (Paragraph 1: topic—keeping cool on a hot day, main idea—it's difficult to keep cool; Paragraph 2: topic—winning the soccer game, main idea—point scored in the wrong goal)
- If any students need extra support, have them list on the board what the first paragraph tells about keeping cool on a hot day. (forbidden to run through sprinkler, sat in front of fan, swam in a pool with very cold water) Ask what these details have in common with the topic. (tell the writer's difficulty in trying to keep cool) Work with students to write lead sentences that introduce the topic and the main idea.
- Follow a similar procedure with the second paragraph, or have students work with a partner and then share their ideas with the class.

The Lead Sentence

You've learned that in a narrative paragraph, the **lead sentence** introduces the topic and may give a hint about the main idea of the story. The lead sentence should also get the reader interested in the story.

Example: My first try at making pizza [Topic] was like a wrestling match. [Main idea]

What do you think stories with these lead sentences might be about?

- "It will be impossible to choose only one," I thought when we walked into the animal shelter.
- When I heard the tire go *thumpety, thumpety, thumpety,* I knew this wasn't going to be the usual bus ride to school.

Try It Out Read the paragraphs below. Each is missing the topic sentence. On your own or with a partner, write the topic and the main idea of each paragraph. Then write two possible lead sentences for each.

1. ___*Lead sentence*___. After breakfast, we tried cooling off in the sprinkler, but Dad squashed that plan. "You'll ruin the new grass!" he said. Then we tried reading in front of the fan, but we still felt sweaty. After lunch, LaToya invited us for a swim in her new pool. We swam until our lips turned blue! At least we couldn't complain about being too hot anymore.
   Topic: a hot day; main idea: staying cool not easy; lead sentence: Trying to keep cool on a hot summe can be problen

2. ___*Lead sentence*___. The score was 1–1 in the soccer game against the Rockets, and there was only one minute left. I sprinted down the field with the ball and booted it past the goalkeeper. Cheers exploded from the sidelines. "Goal!" I shouted, leaping into the air. When I saw my coach's face, I realized my mistake. I had kicked the ball into my own goal! I was the most valuable player, but for the wrong team.
   Topic: soccer game; main idea: I helped the other team win; sample lead sentence: Why was I disappointed to be the most valuable player in one of our soccer games?

Supporting Sentences

Supporting sentences follow the lead sentence. They support the main idea by telling details about it. They answer one or more of the questions *Who? What? Where? When? Why?* and *How?* In the pizza paragraph on page 269, the supporting sentences describe why making pizza was like a wrestling match.

Making Pizza = Wrestling Match

- Dough stuck to everything.
- Spilled tomato sauce nearly tripped me.
- Cheese grater scraped my finger.

Try It Out On your own or with a partner, choose one lead sentence below. List at least four details to support it. Then write at least three supporting sentences, using details from your list. Answers will vary.

1. My day at the fair gave me a prize-winning stomachache.
2. Although the rides at the fair made me dizzy, I went on every one!

GRAMMAR TIP *Use an exclamation point (!) to end a sentence that shows strong feeling.*

Keeping to the Main Idea Be sure your supporting sentences give details only about the main idea. Do not include other details.

Think and Discuss Read the paragraph below. What is the main idea? Which sentence does not keep to the main idea? Writer needs braces; sentence that does not belong is underlined.

The minute the dentist clipped up my x-ray, I suspected trouble. First, Dr. Vargas squinted at it. Then she frowned. As she examined my x-ray more closely, she mumbled something about a retainer. <u>My friend just got a retainer.</u> Finally, Dr. Vargas snapped off the light and informed me, "You need braces."

more ▶

Supporting Sentences

Lesson Objectives

Students will:

- list details to support a lead sentence
- write supporting sentences using some of their details
- identify a sentence that does not support the main idea
- identify a sentence that is out of order

Focus on Instruction

Ask students why supporting sentences are important in a paragraph. (They provide important information about the main idea.)

Try It Out

If any students need extra support, work with them to list possible details to support one of the lead sentences. Chart their ideas on the board, as in the example below, and help them write supporting sentences, using the details. Then have students share their lists of details and supporting sentences.

Topic: Fair	
Main Idea	**Supporting Details**
prize-winning stomach ache	cotton candy meatball sandwich popcorn soda caramel apple

Think and Discuss

Ask students why the sentence about the friend getting a retainer does not keep to the main idea. (The paragraph is about the writer's visit to the dentist and need for braces.)

Meeting Individual Needs

● RETEACHING WORKBOOK, page 77

Supporting Sentences

A paragraph that tells a story is a **narrative paragraph.** It often has a lead sentence, supporting sentences, and a concluding sentence. **Supporting sentences** support the main idea by giving details about it. They answer one or more of these questions: *Who? What? Where? When? Why? How?*

In the narrative paragraph below, the lead and concluding sentences are underlined. Three of the other sentences give details that support the main idea. Cross out the two sentences that do not keep to the main idea. Then write two new sentences that support the main idea. Answers will vary.

<u>I always wanted to be a lion tamer until I saw a lion lose her temper.</u> One day, I saw two cubs playing near the fence at the zoo habitat. ~~The lion habitat is a great place to visit.~~ To get the cubs' attention, I tapped on the fence. ~~Have you noticed the neat sound that tapping on a metal fence makes?~~ Suddenly, I was staring into the open jaws of a roaring mother lion. <u>Ever since then, all I can think about when I see lions is the size of their jaws!</u>

▲■ WORKBOOK PLUS, page 126

Supporting Sentences

A paragraph that tells a story is a **narrative paragraph.** It often has a lead sentence, supporting sentences, and a concluding sentence. **Supporting sentences** support the main idea by giving details about it. They answer one or more of these questions: *Who? What? Where? When? Why? How?*

Complete the narrative paragraph about this picture. Read the lead sentence below. Next, find details in the picture to support the main idea in the lead sentence. Then write three supporting sentences, using the details.

Yesterday was such a great day that I was determined to play every game.

Answers will vary.

I was worn out, but I sure had fun!

Supporting Sentences *continued*

Focus on Instruction

Have students find time clues in the dentist paragraph on the prior page. (*First, Then, Finally)*

Think and Discuss

Be sure students understand that the sentence about keeping the pumpkin should move because it tells about something that happened at the end of the visit. It should follow the reference to the pumpkin patch.

The Closing Sentence

Lesson Objective

Students will:

- write a closing sentence for a paragraph

Focus on Instruction

- Have students reread the closing sentence in the paragraph about making pizza on page 269 to see that it tells what happened at the end.
- Present these alternative closing sentences for the same paragraph. Ask students which one tells how the writer felt and which one tells what the writer thought.

  It was worth the struggle! (thought)
  I was exhausted but proud of how that pizza turned out. (felt)

Try It Out

If any students need extra support, read the lead and supporting sentences with them. Ask them to identify the topic and the main idea. (topic—family dog, Rusty; main idea—Rusty is unpredictable on a trip.) Ask students to suggest possible ways to conclude the story, and help them write concluding sentences using those ideas.

Ordering Details Events in a narrative paragraph are usually told in the order they happened. **Time-clue words and phrases**, such as *first, next,* and *in the morning,* help signal when events take place.

See page 18 for more time-clue words.

Underlined sentence is out of order; it tells the last event too soon in the paragraph. It should precede the last sentence.

Think and Discuss Which sentence is out of order in the paragraph below? Why? Tell where it should go in the paragraph.

"You're going to love Green Acres Farm!" my teacher promised. After a long bus ride, we couldn't wait to begin exploring. The best part was that everyone got to take home a pumpkin! We visited the horse stalls first. Then we learned how to milk a cow. Just before leaving, we took a hayride to a pumpkin patch. Nobody wanted to leave at the end of the day.

The Closing Sentence

The **closing sentence** in a narrative paragraph can tell the last event in the story, something learned from the story, or what the writer thought or felt about the experience. In the pizza paragraph on page 269, the concluding sentence tells how the "struggle" turned out.

Try It Out Read the paragraph below. It is missing the closing sentence. On your own or with a partner, write two different concluding sentences.
Sample answer: After that, Rusty had to sleep in the car.

We never know what's going to happen when we take our Labrador retriever, Rusty, on a trip. Last year Mom, Dad, my sister Bridget, and I were camping in a park. We set up our tent close by a stream so that we could hear the water gurgling over the rocks. In the middle of the night, I woke up and looked around for Rusty. He was gone! I woke up everybody else, and we crawled out of the tent and started calling for him. Splash, splash! Rusty was in the stream, soaking wet. ___Concluding sentence___.

Write Your Own Narrative Paragraph

Now it's time to write your own paragraph. Write about something that happened to you. First, think of a time when you felt happy, sad, scared, or embarrassed, or when something funny or unexpected happened. Then picture what happened, and make a list of details. After you have practiced telling your story to a partner, you are ready to write!

Checklist for My Paragraph

- ✓ My **lead sentence** introduces the main idea.
- ✓ Every **supporting sentence** tells details about the main idea.
- ✓ My **supporting sentences** tell what happened in order. Time-clue words and phrases make the order clear.
- ✓ My **closing sentence** sums up what happened or tells what I thought or felt.

Looking Ahead

Now that you know how to write a narrative paragraph, writing a longer narrative will be easy! The diagram below shows how the parts of a one-paragraph narrative do the same jobs as the parts of a longer narrative.

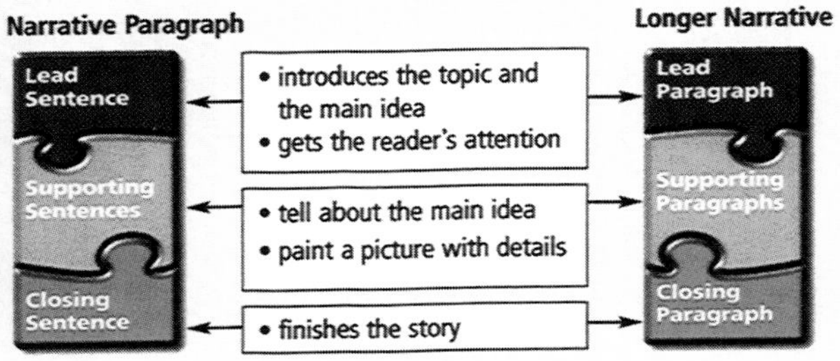

Narrative Paragraph
Longer Narrative
Lead Sentence
Supporting Sentences
Closing Sentence
• introduces the topic and the main idea
• gets the reader's attention
• tell about the main idea
• paint a picture with details
• finishes the story
Lead Paragraph
Supporting Paragraphs
Closing Paragraph

Help with Writing a Narrative Paragraph

HELP WITH CHOOSING A TOPIC
Share these ideas.

- Students can write about a funny or an unusual event at school.
- They can tell a funny story about a pet.
- They can tell about a special experience with a family member or a friend.
- They can write about something that happened on the first day of school.
- They can write about a visit to a new place.

HELP WITH PLANNING
Have students make a planning chart with these entries to help them organize their ideas. Review their charts before they write.

Topic	
Main Idea	
Lead Sentence	
Details	
Closing Sentence	

Write Your Own Narrative Paragraph

Lesson Objective

Students will:
- write a narrative paragraph

Focus on Instruction

- Remind students that the first step in writing a paragraph is to choose a topic. If students have difficulty choosing a topic, suggest ideas from the Help box on this page or brainstorm other ideas with students. List the ideas on the board or on an overhead transparency.
- Have students discuss their topic with a partner. Telling their story idea first to a partner will help students tap into their oral language skills. Explain that writing a paragraph is the same as telling it. When students write, however, they have the luxury of thinking a little more about the way they will word their sentences so that they can help their readers picture what happened more clearly.
- **Connecting to the Criteria** Review with students the Checklist for My Paragraph.
- Have volunteers read their paragraphs aloud to the class.

If students are keeping portfolios, they could include this paragraph as an example of a short writing assignment. The paragraph can be used later as a basis for comparison with longer narratives. If you want to send the paragraphs home as well, you can make copies for the portfolios.

SCHOOL-HOME CONNECTION Encourage students to share their paragraph with family members.

Looking Ahead Explain to students that in this Narrating and Entertaining section of the book, they will learn how to write a longer personal narrative and a make-believe story, using what they have learned about writing paragraphs.

Unit 8 Planning Guide

Writing a Personal Narrative

Writing a Personal Narrative: *2 weeks*
Special Focus: *2 days (optional)*

	Blackline Masters (TE)	Workbook Plus	Reteaching Workbook
PUBLISHED MODEL "A Play," by Eloise Greenfield *(275–276)*			
What Makes a Great Personal Narrative? *(277)*			
STUDENT MODEL Working Draft *(278–279)* Final Copy *(280–281)*	8–1A, 8–1B		
The Writing Process Write a Personal Narrative			
Prewriting Explore Your Personal Narrative *(283)*	8–2		
Focus Skill: Organizing Your Narrative *(284)*	8–3	127	78
Drafting Focus Skill: Good Beginnings *(285)*		128	79
Focus Skill: Writing with Voice *(286)*		129	80
Focus Skill: Good Endings *(287)*		130	81
Revising ✓ Evaluating Your Personal Narrative [rubric] *(288)*	8–4	131	82
Writing Conference *(289)*	8–5		
Revising Strategies *(290)*		132	83
Proofreading *(291)*			
Publishing and Reflecting *(292)*			
✓ **Writing Prompts and Test Practice** *(293–294)*			
SPECIAL FOCUS ON NARRATING **Writing a Friendly Letter** *(295–296)*			

Tools and Tips

- **Listening and Speaking Strategies,** *pp. H4–H10*
- **Building Vocabulary,** *pp. H11–H17*
- **Research and Study Strategies,** *pp. H18–H30*
- **Using Technology,** *pp. H35–H47*
- **Writer's Tools,** *pp. H48–H54*
- **Spelling Guide,** *pp. H65–H69*
- **Guide to Capitalization, Punctuation, and Usage,** *pp. H55–H64*
- **Thesaurus Plus,** *pp. H79–H100*

School-Home Connection

Suggestions for informing or involving family members in classroom activities and learning related to this unit are included in the Teacher's Edition throughout the unit.

Meeting Individual Needs

- **FOR SPECIAL NEEDS/INCLUSION:** *Houghton Mifflin English* Audiotape
- **FOR STUDENTS ACQUIRING ENGLISH:**
  - Notes and activities are included in this Teacher's Edition throughout the unit to help you adapt or use pupil book activities with students acquiring English.
  - Students acquiring English can listen to the published and student models on audiotape.
  - MediaWeaver™, Sunburst/Humanities software, offers bilingual features, including Spanish menus, a Spanish spelling tool, and a Spanish thesaurus.
- **ENRICHMENT:** See *Teacher's Resource Book.*

All audiotape recordings are also available on CD.

Daily Language Practice

Each sentence includes two capitalization, punctuation, usage, or spelling errors based on skills presented in the Grammar and Spelling Connections in this unit or from Grammar Unit 1. Each day write one sentence on the chalkboard. Have students find the errors and write the sentence correctly on a sheet of paper. To make the activity easier, identify the kinds of errors.

1. Yesterday we walk in a march against hunger! Yesterday we walked in a march against hunger. (past tense; end punctuation)
2. Cara help her mom with the laundry last week Cara helped her mom with the laundry last week. (past tense; end punctuation)
3. flew into our classroom window. Sample: A small bird flew into our classroom window. (complete sentences; capitalization)
4. Today at school the fourth graders Sample: Today at school the fourth graders put on a play. (complete sentences; end punctuation)
5. North Carolina beaches are wide and flait many vacationers love them. Sample: North Carolina beaches are wide and flat. Many vacationers love them. (spelling short vowel sounds; run-on sentences)
6. What a meass you've made in the kitchen. What a mess you've made in the kitchen! (spelling short vowel sounds; end punctuation)
7. What will you wish for on your birthday. What will you wish for on your birthday? (spelling short vowel sounds; end punctuation)
8. We fed bread to the ducks in the paund We fed bread to the ducks in the pond. (spelling short vowel sounds; end punctuation)
9. Ashley tripped on her laces and landed with a thaud on the gym floor? Ashley tripped on her laces and landed with a thud on the gym floor. (spelling short vowel sounds; end punctuation)
10. Wolves travel in packs, they are social animals Sample: Wolves travel in packs. They are social animals. (run-on sentences; end punctuation)

Additional Resources

Workbook Plus, Unit 8
Reteaching Workbook, Unit 8
Teacher's Resource Book
Transparencies
Posters, Unit 8
Audiotapes

Technology Tools

CD-ROM: *EasyBook Deluxe
MediaWeaver™, Sunburst/Humanities software
*Type to Learn™

*©Sunburst Technology Corporation, a Houghton Mifflin Company. All rights reserved.

INTERNET: http://www.eduplace.com/kids/hme/ *or* http://www.eduplace.com/rdg/hme/

Visit Education Place for these additional support materials and activities:

- author biographies
- student writing models
- graphic organizers
- an interactive rubric
- proofreading practice
- writing prompts
- benchmark papers

Assessment

Test Booklet, Unit 8

Keeping a Journal

Discuss with students the value of keeping a journal as a way of promoting self-expression and fluency. Encourage students to record their thoughts and ideas in a notebook. Inform students whether the journal will be private or will be reviewed periodically as a way of assessing growth. The following prompts may be useful for generating writing ideas.

Journal Prompts

- Think of a scary experience you once had. What happened?
- Think of an experience you had that taught you an important lesson. What happened?
- Think of the best holiday you ever had. Tell what happened that day.

Introducing the Unit

Using the Photograph

- Direct students' attention to the photograph, and have a volunteer read the caption aloud. Ask students why the boy in the photograph might want to outsmart his sister. (Sample responses: He feels embarrassed that his sister outplayed him. His sister is a very good player, and he wants to prove that he is equally good.)
- Ask students who the *I* in the caption refers to. (the boy) Why might this experience be fun for the boy to write about? (It could be exciting and action-packed—and funny.) Discuss with students other situations or experiences, including everyday ones, that they have had that would be interesting for others to read about.
- Explain to students that a true story about something that has happened to the writer is called a **personal narrative**. Tell students that they will learn how to write a personal narrative in this unit.

Unit 8

Writing a Personal Narrative

For weeks my sister had outplayed me on the home court. Finally, I figured out a way to outsmart her.

274

Shared Writing Activity

Work with students to write a short narrative about an experience they have had in common to share with their families, such as a class field trip or a class play.

1. Have students list words and phrases about the experience that tell *who, what, where, when, why,* and *how.* Write their suggestions on the board.
2. Ask students to group words and phrases that would go together to describe particular parts of the narrative.
3. Have them identify which group of words and phrases tells what happened first, next, and so on. Work with students to generate sentences with these word groups to describe the experience. Write the sentences on the board or on an overhead transparency.
4. Reinforce the importance of telling the events in order and keeping to the topic.
5. If students suggest fragments, remind them that a sentence has both a subject and a predicate. Reinforce the use of correct verb tenses (or other skills students need to work on) as they suggest sentences.
6. Have students copy the final story to share with family members.

A Published Model

Eloise Greenfield wrote a personal narrative about something that happened to her in school. Can you understand how she felt?

A Play

from *Childtimes*, by Eloise Greenfield

beginning — When I was in the fifth grade, I was famous for a whole day, and all because of a play. The teacher had given me a big part, and I didn't want it. I liked to be in plays where I could be part of a group, like being one of the talking trees, or dancing, or singing in the glee club. But having to talk by myself—*uh uh!*

I used to slide down in my chair and stare at my desk while the teacher was giving out the parts, so she wouldn't pay any attention to me, but this time it didn't work. She called on me anyway. I told her I didn't want to do it, but she said I had to. I guess she thought it would be good for me. — details

On the day of the play, I didn't make any mistakes. I remembered all of my lines. Only—nobody in the audience heard me. I couldn't make my voice come out loud.

For the rest of the day, I was famous. Children passing by my classroom door, children on the playground at lunchtime, kept pointing at me saying, "That's that girl! That's the one who didn't talk loud enough!" — main part of story

more ▶

Go to www.eduplace.com/kids/ for information about Eloise Greenfield.

About the Author

INTERNET CONNECTION Send your students to www.eduplace.com/kids/ for information about Eloise Greenfield.

Resources

Here are other books that model this type of writing that students might enjoy reading.

- ***The Summer My Father Was Ten*** by Pat Brisson
- ***Tallchief: America's Prima Ballerina*** by Maria Tallchief with Rosemary Wells
- ***I'm New Here*** by Bud Howlett
- ***Seven Brave Women*** by Betsy Hearne

"A Play"

Lesson Objectives

Students will:
- read a published model of a personal narrative
- identify characteristics of personal narratives
- note author's technique for tying together the beginning and the ending
- evaluate the relationship between visuals and text
- write personal and critical responses

Focus on the Model

Building Background

Ask students if they have had to take part in activities that they don't enjoy. What happened? How did they feel? Tell them that they will read a personal narrative that tells about that kind of experience.

Introducing Vocabulary

Introduce key vocabulary words by writing these sentences on the board.

Many movie actors are **famous** because many people see their films.

A bad grade on the test will **ruin** Anna's day.

Have a volunteer read each sentence aloud. Ask students to explain the meaning of the boldfaced words.

Reading the Selection

- Have students read the introduction to "A Play." The purpose-setting question focuses on a characteristic of a personal narrative, the expression of feelings about the experience.

Have students read the selection as a class, independently, or with partners, or they can listen to the selection on audiotape.

- The call outs highlight key characteristics of a personal narrative that are addressed in the Think About the Personal Narrative questions at the end of this selection.

MEETING INDIVIDUAL NEEDS — FOR STUDENTS ACQUIRING ENGLISH

Before reading, ask whether students speak as loudly or as softly in English as they do in their first language. Brainstorm with students why some may speak loudly or softly, and list the reasons on the board. Tell them this will help them think about *voice* in writing.

Answers to Reading As a Writer

Think About the Personal Narrative

- Eloise Greenfield is the *I* in the story.
- *Slide down in my chair* and *stare at my desk* help illustrate how she felt.
- The main part is when Eloise Greenfield didn't speak loud enough during the play. For the rest of the day, her classmates were talking about her.

Think About Writer's Craft

- She repeats the phrase *famous for a day* at the beginning and at the end.

Think About the Picture

- Sample answer: The photo showing Eloise as a shy-looking girl helps you understand why she disliked being in plays. A photograph shows exactly how a person looks rather than an artist's idea of how he or she looks.

After students complete the questions, work with them to generate criteria for a personal narrative, using the published model as a reference.

More About Writer's Craft

- Point out the sentences with dashes in the first and third paragraphs. Have a volunteer read the sentences aloud and then ask students why the writer used dashes. (to indicate a pause longer than one indicated by a comma) Tell students that this technique is one they can use in their own writing, but caution them to use it sparingly.
- Draw students' attention to the exclamation points in the first and fourth paragraphs. Ask why the writer made the decision to use exclamation points. (to show strong feeling) Again explain that students may want to use this technique in their own writing, but remind them to use it sparingly.

Notes on Responding

Personal Response

Ask volunteers to share their personal responses.

Critical Thinking

Encourage a discussion about the difficulty of doing something one doesn't want to do and whether or not it makes one a stronger person.

A Published Model

I felt so bad, I wanted to go home. But one good thing came out of it all. The teacher was so angry, so upset, she told me that as long as I was in that school, I'd never have another chance to ruin one of her plays. And that was such good news, I could stand being famous for a day.

Reading As a Writer See TE margin for answers.

Think About the Personal Narrative

- Who is the *I* in the story?
- What details help you understand how Eloise Greenfield felt when the teacher was handing out parts?
- What is the main part of the story?

Think About Writer's Craft

- How does Eloise Greenfield tie the beginning of her story to the ending?

Think About the Picture

- Why does the photo of Eloise Greenfield as a young girl help bring the story to life? Why might a photo be more effective than an illustration?

Responding Answers will vary.

Write responses to these questions.

- **Personal Response** Think about a time you had to do something you didn't want to do. How was your experience similar to or different from Eloise Greenfield's?
- **Critical Thinking** Why does Eloise Greenfield decide that she "could stand being famous for a day"? Give examples from her narrative to support your answer.

276 **Unit 8:** Personal Narrative

Mapping the Selection

Mapping helps students visualize the structure of a piece of writing. After students have read the personal narrative, draw the following map on the board. Have students fill in the map to identify the events and details in the story.

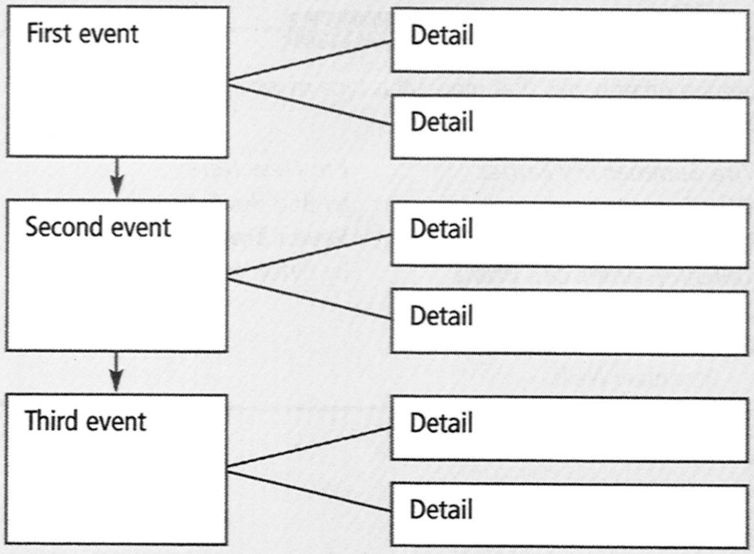

What Makes a Great Personal Narrative?

A **personal narrative** is a true story about something that happened to the person who tells it.

Remember to follow these guidelines when you write a personal narrative.

- Grab your readers' attention at the beginning.
- Use the pronoun *I*.
- Include only the important events, and tell them in order.
- Use details that tell what you saw, heard, or felt. Include dialogue if appropriate.
- Write so that it sounds like you.
- Write an ending that tells how the story worked out or how you felt.

GRAMMAR CHECK

Use complete sentences. Begin each sentence with a capital letter, and end it with the correct mark.

FOR STUDENTS ACQUIRING ENGLISH

Words such as *grab, events, details,* and *dialogue* may be unfamiliar to students. Define the words with the help of student guesses about possible definitions. Once students understand the words, they may still find the list of criteria difficult. Take time to illustrate and explain each item, turning back to "A Play" for each example.

What Makes a Great Personal Narrative?

Lesson Objective

- discuss the characteristics of a well-written personal narrative

Focus on Instruction

- Explain to students that "A Play" is an example of a well-written personal narrative. Ask volunteers to read aloud the definition and characteristics of a personal narrative. Review which ones are represented in the published model, "A Play." (uses *I,* has an interesting beginning, tells events in order, uses details, has an ending that wraps up the story)
- Have students read the Grammar Check. Tell them that the Grammar Check reminds them that great writing should also be grammatically correct. Explain that they will be asked to check their papers for correct sentences when they proofread them.

If this is students' first encounter with the cartoon dog, explain that this is Sal, the writer's pal, and that Sal will help them learn to write great personal narratives.

Connecting to the Rubric

- These criteria are tied to the rubric on page 288.
- Explain to students that they will be writing their own personal narrative and that they will learn how to include these characteristics. Students will use these characteristics as criteria to help them evaluate their papers.

This page is available as a poster.

Looking Ahead Tell students that they will next see how the characteristics listed on this page are applied in one student's working draft and final copy of a personal narrative.

Student Model: Working Draft

Lesson Objectives

Students will:

- read a working draft of a student-written personal narrative
- discuss the ways the model meets the criteria for a well-written personal narrative and ways that it could be improved

Focus on the Model

- Tell students that they will read a working draft of a personal narrative written by a real student, Carolin Castillo. Explain that a working draft is a work in progress, and that the writer was just trying to get ideas on paper, knowing that she could make revisions later.
- Have volunteers read the model aloud.

  Alternatively, students can listen to it read by a student (although not the student writer) on audiotape.

> - Reading the draft aloud gives students practice listening and responding to a writer's work in progress and provides practice for peer conferences.
> - This working draft does not include any usage, capitalization, or punctuation mistakes so that students can focus on the content of the piece.

- Tell students to think about whether or not Carolin included the important characteristics of a personal narrative. Explain that the thought balloons show Sal's thoughts about the narrative and that students will discuss his ideas after they read the model.

Student Model

WORKING DRAFT

Carolin Castillo had a shocking experience while on a family trip! She thought it would make a good topic for a personal narrative. Read Carolin's draft to find out what happened.

Carolin Castillo

This story is about my trip to Vernal Falls in Yosemite Valley with my family.

~~The drive was not the fifteen minutes my friend had told us about. It was more like an hour and a half, not including the wait for the bus.~~

I like this detail. I can really picture the squirrels.

Hiking to the waterfall was a mile UPHILL. We had lunch on the trail. Jonathan and I tossed pieces of bread to the ground squirrels, watching them nibble away.

We were glad when we finally got to a huge slab of granite where we could lie and watch the waterfall. After a little rest, we ~~walked around~~ went exploring. All we saw was granite, granite, granite! Then we found a pool of water with water skeeters all over the surface. I was still hot from the hike, so I asked

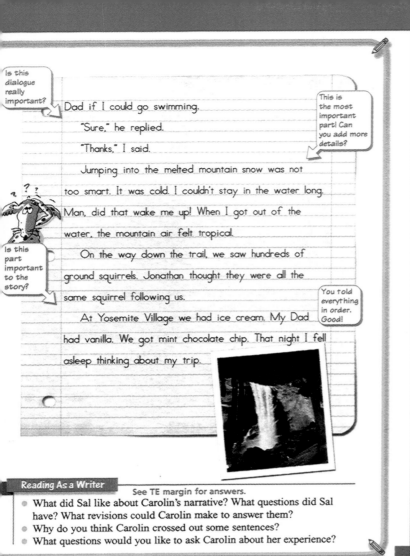

Is this dialogue really important?

Dad if I could go swimming.

"Sure," he replied.

"Thanks," I said.

This is the most important part! Can you add more details?

Jumping into the melted mountain snow was not too smart. It was cold. I couldn't stay in the water long. Man, did that wake me up! When I got out of the water, the mountain air felt tropical.

Is this part important to the story?

On the way down the trail, we saw hundreds of ground squirrels. Jonathan thought they were all the same squirrel following us.

You told everything in order. Good!

At Yosemite Village we had ice cream. My Dad had vanilla. We got mint chocolate chip. That night I fell asleep thinking about my trip.

Reading As a Writer

See TE margin for answers.

- What did Sal like about Carolin's narrative? What questions did Sal have? What revisions could Carolin make to answer them?
- Why do you think Carolin crossed out some sentences?
- What questions would you like to ask Carolin about her experience?

Answers to Reading As a Writer

- Sal liked the way Carolin described the squirrels. Sal also liked the way Carolin told everything in order. Sal asked if the dialogue between Carolin and her father was important; if Carolin could add more details to the most important part; and if the information about the ice cream flavors in the last paragraph was important. Carolin could take out the unimportant dialogue. Explain that while dialogue can help bring a story to life, unimportant dialogue should be left out. (Refer them to the dialogue between Carolin and her father.) She could tell more about swimming. She could take out the part about the ice cream.
- Carolin took out the part about the bus because it wasn't important to the main story.
- Answers will vary.

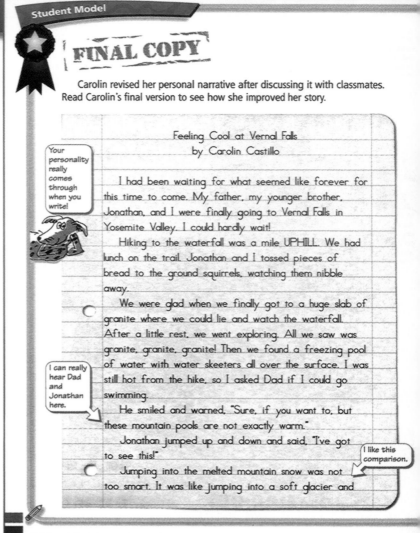

Student Model: Final Copy

Lesson Objectives

Students will:

- read a well-written final copy of a student's personal narrative
- note and compare the revisions that improved the first draft

Focus on the Model

SUMMARY OF REVISIONS In her final copy, Carolin added a title; wrote a new, interesting beginning; added details; took out sentences that didn't keep to the topic or were not important to the story; and revised her ending. Blackline Master 8–1 provides a copy of the student's working draft, showing the revisions that were made.

Have volunteers read the model aloud. Alternatively, students can listen to it read by a student (although not the student writer) on audiotape.

FINAL COPY

Carolin revised her personal narrative after discussing it with classmates. Read Carolin's final version to see how she improved her story.

Feeling Cool at Vernal Falls
by Carolin Castillo

Your personality really comes through when you write!

I had been waiting for what seemed like forever for this time to come. My father, my younger brother, Jonathan, and I were finally going to Vernal Falls in Yosemite Valley. I could hardly wait!

Hiking to the waterfall was a mile UPHILL. We had lunch on the trail. Jonathan and I tossed pieces of bread to the ground squirrels, watching them nibble away.

We were glad when we finally got to a huge slab of granite where we could lie and watch the waterfall. After a little rest, we went exploring. All we saw was granite, granite, granite! Then we found a freezing pool of water with water skeeters all over the surface. I was still hot from the hike, so I asked Dad if I could go swimming.

I can really hear Dad and Jonathan here.

He smiled and warned, "Sure, if you want to, but these mountain pools are not exactly warm."

Jonathan jumped up and down and said, "I've got to see this!"

I like this comparison.

Jumping into the melted mountain snow was not too smart. It was like jumping into a soft glacier and being able to surface again. The water was cold beyond belief, as cold as water can be without actually freezing. It was so cold that I could only stay in for about thirty seconds before my body forced me to get out. Man, did that wake me up! When I got out of the water, the mountain air felt tropical.

On the way down the trail, we saw hundreds of ground squirrels. Jonathan thought they were all the same squirrel following us.

Please take some advice from a girl who learned it the hard way. Unless you're a polar bear, DON'T go swimming at Vernal Falls!

You took out the part about the ice cream because it didn't keep to the topic. Good!

Reading As a Writer

- How did Carolin respond to Sal's questions?
- Compare the beginning and ending of Carolin's final copy with her working draft. Why are they better in the final copy?
- What details did Carolin add to tell how the water felt?

Answers to Reading As a Writer

- Carolin took out the dialogue between her father and herself that wasn't interesting, added more details to describe her swim, and took out the part about the ice cream.
- The new beginning makes the reader curious. The new ending describes how Carolin feels about her experience.
- Carolin added the following sentences: *It was like jumping into a soft glacier and being able to surface again. The water was cold beyond belief, as cold as water can be without actually freezing. It was so cold that I could only stay in for about thirty seconds before my body forced me to get out.*

More About Writer's Craft

- Direct students' attention to *UPHILL* in the second paragraph. Ask students why the writer capitalized the letters in this word. (for emphasis) Discuss how the use of capitalization emphasizes the meaning of the word. Tell students that this is a technique that they can use in their own writing. Caution them to use it sparingly.
- Have students study the model to see how it was broken into paragraphs. Point out that whenever the speaker changes, a new paragraph begins.

Connecting to the Rubric

- Have students look again at the list of characteristics on page 277 and review with them how Carolin's final copy addressed each one.
- Reinforce the Grammar Check by having students check that Carolin used complete sentences and capitalized and punctuated them correctly.

INTERNET CONNECTION Send your students to www.eduplace.com/kids/hme/ to see more models of student writing. You can also find and print these models at www.eduplace.com/rdg/hme/.

Looking Ahead Tell students that they will next write their own personal narrative, using the writing process. As they go along, they will learn how to organize their narrative, write a good beginning and ending, and write so that the reader can hear their voice.

MEETING INDIVIDUAL NEEDS

FOR STUDENTS ACQUIRING ENGLISH

Students may not be familiar with writing as a process. Reading and reviewing another student's changes is an excellent exercise to model revision and to encourage taking risks. Encourage students to notice Carolin's process (writing, talking, changing, rewriting). Tell students this is what they will do.

Write a Personal Narrative

Lesson Objectives

Students will:

- list their ideas for audience, purpose, and publishing/sharing formats
- list ideas for a personal narrative
- discuss their ideas with a partner
- choose an appropriate topic to write about

Start Thinking

Focus on Instruction

- Tell students that good writers adapt the language of their papers to their chosen audience. Ask how a personal narrative written for a classmate might differ from one for a younger child. (would use simpler language when writing for a younger child) Ask how one for a family member might differ from one for a pen pal. (might use more formal language for a pen pal)
- Ask how writing the narrative in a letter might differ from writing it as a photo essay. (Photos might provide more detail.)

Choose Your Story Idea

Focus on Instruction

- Page 293 provides writing prompts that might suggest ideas.
- Reassure students that an everyday experience is just as good a subject as an unusual one.

Have students start a writing folder titled *My Personal Narrative.* Explain that they will keep all notes, graphic organizers, and drafts for their personal narrative in this folder. Have students include their paper with their thoughts about their audience, purpose, and publishing format.

SCHOOL-HOME CONNECTION Students can discuss their topic with family members, who might be able to recall details that students can use in their writing.

MEETING INDIVIDUAL NEEDS

FOR STUDENTS ACQUIRING ENGLISH

Remember that setting individual goals for each student works best for the writing process. (Some students may do only the first steps; students who are at the intermediate and advanced stages of English development may do all.) Initially, work as a class, breaking the process into simple steps, making sure each student understands and completes a step before moving on.

The Writing Process: PREWRITING | DRAFTING | REVISING | PROOFREADING | PUBLISHING

Write a Personal Narrative

Start Thinking

Make a writing folder for your personal narrative. Copy the questions in bold print, and put the paper in your folder. Write your answers as you think about and choose your topic.

- **Who will be my audience?** Will it be my classmates? a family member? a pen pal? a younger child?
- **What will be my purpose?** Do I want to make people laugh? to share a feeling or special time?
- **How will I publish or share my personal narrative?** Will I send it in a letter or an e-mail? read it aloud for my class? add pictures and make it into a book?

Choose Your Story Idea

1. **List** five experiences you could write about.
2. **Discuss** your ideas with a partner.
   - Which ones does your partner like? Why?
   - Is any idea too big? Could you write about one part? Carolin broke one big idea, *camping in Yosemite,* into smaller parts. Each part could be a whole story.

HELP ***Stuck for an Idea?***

- What strange or funny thing happened to you?
- What experience made you say *yuck* or *wow?*
- When were you scared? proud? embarrassed?

See page 293 for more ideas.

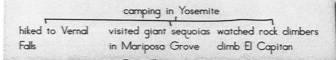

camping in Yosemite

hiked to Vernal Falls | visited giant sequoias in Mariposa Grove | watched rock climbers climb El Capitan

3. **Ask** yourself these questions about each idea. Then circle the one you will write about.
   - Can I remember enough details?
   - Would this interest my audience?
   - Would I enjoy writing about this?

Help with Choosing a Topic

TECH TIPS

- Refer students who are using a computer to page H39 to find ideas for using a computer during the writing process.
- Have students list their story ideas on the computer and then print them out to share with a partner.

EVALUATION TIP

Review students' final topic choices. If a topic is too broad, ask what one part the student would most like to tell about.

SOURCES OF TOPIC IDEAS

Suggest these activities to prompt topic ideas.

- Students can think of a favorite souvenir and how they got it.
- They can look at personal snapshots to spark memories.
- They can list special days, such as *birthday, first day of school,* or *holiday* (or specific holidays). Have them write freely about those days for five minutes. Did any topic ideas emerge?

Explore Your Story Idea

1. **Think** about your experience as a movie. Close your eyes, and watch it in your mind. You may want to draw a cartoon strip of the main events.
   - List and underline the main events. Leave a lot of space between each one.
2. **Rewind** your movie. Zoom in on the most important part. Put a star next to it.
   - A close-up shows details. Write a lot of details about this part. Use the Exploring Questions to help you.

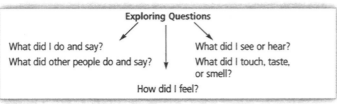

Exploring Questions

What did I do and say?
What did other people do and say?

What did I see or hear?
What did I touch, taste, or smell?

How did I feel?

3. **List** any other details that your audience might need to know.

went swimming	went exploring
cold water	granite, granite, granite
woke me up	pool of water
air felt tropical	water skeeters
hiked to Vernal Falls	got ice cream
fed ground squirrels	vanilla
one mile uphill	mint chocolate chip

▲ Part of Carolin's list

HELP ***Stuck for Details?*** If you can't think of many details, try another topic.

See page 14 for other ideas for exploring your topic.

Help with Exploring the Topic

TECH TIP

To help students loosen their thoughts, suggest they dim the computer screen and type any words or phrases that come to mind about their topics.

MORE IDEAS FOR EXPLORING

You can suggest these ideas to students as alternatives for exploring their topics.

- They can make a cluster instead of a list.
- They can pair up with a partner and interview each other about their topics.
- They can look at snapshots they have of the experience or discuss it with other people who were there.

Lesson Objectives

Students will:

- list main events and details of their experience
- identify the most important event

Explore Your Story Idea

Focus on Instruction

- See Blackline Master 8–2 for a graphic organizer that students can use to explore their topics.
- Review each student's list of details and the event chosen as most important. Make sure that the student has enough details to elaborate the experience successfully in a written personal narrative.
- Help the student elaborate by asking questions such as these:

  Who else was there? What did they say or do when this happened?

  What did you do when this happened?

  How did you feel? What did you think?

  What else did you see, hear, smell, taste, or feel?
- Discuss with students the note in the Help box. Explain that sometimes a topic that seemed like a good idea doesn't work out when a writer tries to develop it. It is better to choose another topic than to proceed with one that won't work. Support the student in choosing a new topic by reviewing the prompts on page 293 or suggesting activities in the Help with Choosing a Topic section on TE page 282.
- Students could also use the cluster graphic organizers on page H50 to explore their topic.

Organizing Your Narrative

Lesson Objectives

Students will:

- organize the main events of their narrative in sequence
- make a graphic organizer showing the sequence of events and the related details

Focus on Instruction

- Ask students why it is important for events and details to be told in order. (Otherwise, the audience might not understand what is happening.)
- Ask this question: If someone were writing about winning a soccer game, should the writer tell everything that happened before the game? (only if the details are important to winning the game)
- Help students list other clue words. (Sample words: *while, during, one month ago, today, at the end*)

Think and Discuss

If students need extra support, write Carolin's list shown on page 283 on the board. Have volunteers number the items in the order in which they happened.

Plan Your Narrative

- If students' lists are a jumbled mix of events and supporting details, have them circle each event and its related details with the same colored pencil or crayon, using a different color for each event. Then they can number the events in order.
- Explain how to create and complete the chart, if necessary. A copy of the organizer appears on Blackline Master 8–3. As an alternative, students could use a time line. Refer them to page H54 for an example.

INTERNET CONNECTION Send your students to www.eduplace.com/kids/hme/ for graphic organizers. You can also find and print these organizers at www.eduplace.com/rdg/hme/.

FOR STUDENTS ACQUIRING ENGLISH

The time clue words and phrases are very helpful once the class defines them. Use the words in sentences on the board, encouraging volunteers to help. Remind writers to use only the phrases that relate to their stories. Model each organizing tool with your own or a volunteer's story.

The Writing Process: PREWRITING | DRAFTING | REVISING | PROOFREADING | PUBLISHING

Focus Skill

Organizing Your Narrative

Tell the events in the order they happened. Be careful not to mention something in the middle that you should have told your audience at the beginning. Remember: they weren't there!

Keep to your topic. Take out any events or details that are not needed to understand the most important part.

Use time clues. Time clue words signal to your audience when events happened. What other time clue words can you add to this list?

Time Clue Words	Time Clue Phrases
first, second, third, before, after, next, later, finally, Monday, then, meanwhile, yesterday	by the time, later on, in the meantime, at last, at the same time, last summer, on Tuesday, this morning

Think and Discuss Look at Carolin's list on page 283.

- The events and details are not in the order they happened. What could she do to show the correct order without rewriting them? Sample answer: number them
- Which event and details are not important to the waterfall story? ice cream details

Plan Your Narrative

1. **Number** the events of your narrative in the order they happened. Cross out events and details that are not needed.
2. **Make a chart** that shows the events in order. Add the details that describe each event. Look at this chart as a model.

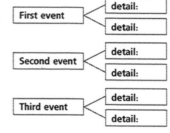

First event → detail: / detail:
Second event → detail: / detail:
Third event → detail: / detail:

284 **Unit 8:** Personal Narrative — Go to www.eduplace.com/kids/hme/ for graphic organizers.

Meeting Individual Needs

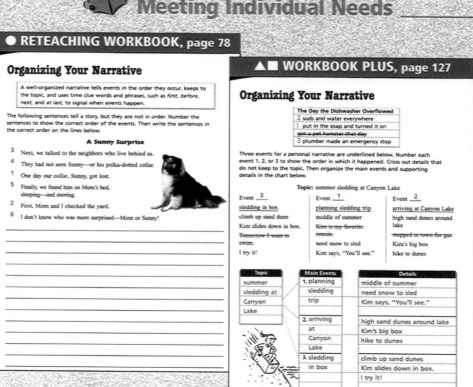

● RETEACHING WORKBOOK, page 78

Organizing Your Narrative

A well-organized narrative tells events in the order they occur, keeps to the topic, and uses time clue words and phrases, such as *first, before, next,* and *at last,* to signal when events happen.

The following sentences tell a story, but they are not in order. Number the sentences to show the correct order of the events. Then write the sentences in the correct order on the lines below.

A Sunny Surprise

3 Next, we talked to the neighbors who live behind us.
4 They had not seen Sunny—or his polka-dotted collar.
1 One day our collie, Sunny, got lost.
5 Finally, we found him on Mom's bed, sleeping—and snoring.
2 First, Mom and I checked the yard.
6 I don't know who was more surprised—Mom or Sunny!

▲■ WORKBOOK PLUS, page 127

Organizing Your Narrative

The Day the Dishwasher Overflowed
2 suds and water everywhere
1 put in the soap and turned it on
~~got a pet hamster that day~~
3 plumber made an emergency stop

Three events for a personal narrative are underlined below. Number each event 1, 2, or 3 to show the order in which it happened. Cross out details that do not keep to the topic. Then organize the main events and supporting details in the chart below.

Topic: summer sledding at Canyon Lake

Event 3	Event 1	Event 2
sledding in box	planning sledding trip	arriving at Canyon Lake
climb up sand dune	middle of summer	high sand dunes around lake
Kim slides down in box.	~~Kim is my favorite cousin.~~	~~stopped in town for gas~~
~~Tomorrow I want to swim.~~	need snow to sled	Kim's big box
I try it!	Kim says, "You'll see."	hike to dunes

Topic	Main Events	Details
summer sledding at Canyon Lake	1. planning sledding trip	middle of summer; need snow to sled; Kim says, "You'll see."
	2. arriving at Canyon Lake	high sand dunes around lake; Kim's big box; hike to dunes
	3. sledding in box	climb up sand dunes; Kim slides down in box.; I try it!

Focus Skill

Good Beginnings

Like a race, your story should begin with a BANG! A good beginning grabs your audience's attention and makes them want to keep reading. Here are three different ways to begin.

Ask a question. A question makes your readers want to know the answer.

Weak Beginning	Strong Beginning
Last Saturday we went to the grocery store and to the barber.	Have you ever gone to the barber and then wanted to hide for two months?

Make a surprising statement. Say something unexpected.

Weak Beginning	Strong Beginning
We went to Riverside Amusement Park for my birthday, and I rode on the roller coaster.	It looked as if I was going to drop into a hole as deep as the Grand Canyon, and there was nothing I could do about it.

Use dialogue. A person's exact words may be interesting.

Weak Beginning	Strong Beginning
One day my friend Ramón and I were walking home from school.	"I knew this was going to be an unlucky day," groaned my friend Ramón.

GRAMMAR TIP *Put a speaker's exact words in quotation marks.*

Try It Out

- With a partner, rewrite the first beginning as a surprising statement, the second as dialogue, and the third as a question. Answers will vary.

Draft Your Beginning

1. **Write** three beginnings for your narrative, using a question, a surprising statement, and dialogue.
2. **Choose** the beginning you like best.

Drafting 285

Good Beginnings

Lesson Objectives

Students will:

- write three beginnings for their narrative, using different techniques
- choose a beginning

Focus on Instruction

- Discuss each pair of weak and strong beginnings with students. Point out that a weak beginning makes the reader say "So what?" The strong beginnings make the reader wonder what happened at the barber shop. What huge hole was the writer dropping into? Why was Ramon's day unlucky?
- Have students read the Grammar Tip and then find the speaker's exact words in the strong beginning with dialogue.

Try It Out

- Work as a class or have students work in small groups to rewrite the weak beginnings.
- Sample answers: When I looked in the mirror that day, I knew I'd be wearing a hat for several days; "Oh, no! Oh, no!" I kept repeating as we neared the top of the first hill; Did you ever just know the day wasn't going to be a lucky one?

Draft Your Beginning

Explain that there is no one correct way to begin a narrative and that several ways might work.

MEETING INDIVIDUAL NEEDS

FOR STUDENTS ACQUIRING ENGLISH

Students may be reluctant or confused by having to write more than one beginning to the same story. With the examples and Carolin's story, highlight the great results of trying new beginnings. Students may feel more comfortable working in small groups rather than pairs.

● RETEACHING WORKBOOK, page 79

Good Beginnings

A good beginning captures your reader's interest. It makes your reader want to know what happens next. To write a good beginning, you might ask a question, make a surprising statement, or use dialogue.

Weak Beginning	Strong Beginnings: Question	Surprising Statement	Dialogue
I woke up to a loud noise very early in the morning.	What clatters and rattles when everybody else is sound asleep?	The horn on the truck sounded like a car alarm with hiccups.	"Good morning to you too!" I shouted back as the truck thundered hello.

Each short narrative below needs a stronger beginning. Read each narrative. Then write a strong beginning to replace the underlined sentence. Try using different strategies, such as asking a question, making a surprising statement, or using dialogue. Sample beginnings:

1. My dog, Sylvester, caused some trouble. I ran into the kitchen to see what was the matter. There was Sylvester in the corner chewing on a package of raw steak. All over the floor were dented cans and broken jars. On the kitchen table were scraps of paper that used to be grocery bags.

Strong Beginning: Why did I think my dog, Sylvester, was causing some trouble once again?

2. I knew I could win the race. I looked back to see where the other runners were. One was right at my heels. I burst ahead with extra speed. Suddenly the crowd cheered loudly. I had crossed the finish line first!

Strong Beginning: Something told me this would be the race of my life!

3. Guinea pigs have feelings too. I know because of Waldo, my best friend's guinea pig. I took care of Waldo for two weeks when my friend went on vacation. Now Waldo jumps and squeaks whenever he hears my voice.

Strong Beginning: "I'm sure guinea pigs have feelings just like people," I explained to Mom.

▲■ WORKBOOK PLUS, page 128

Good Beginnings

Weak Beginning	Strong Beginnings: Question	Surprising Statement	Dialogue
I walk my dog bright and early every morning.	What gets you out of bed faster than an alarm clock?	In the early morning, I often wonder whether I walk my dog or he walks me.	"Wait! Just let me tie my shoelaces!" I pleaded.

Each short narrative below needs a beginning. First, read the story. Then write a strong beginning, using the strategy suggested. Sample beginnings:

1. . . . Then I closed my eyes and concentrated really hard. I started to picture myself standing in the middle of a tropical forest surrounded by strange animals. However, it was just my dad, a would-be opera singer, singing in the shower.

Question: What in the world was I hearing?

2. . . . I planted the "wonder seeds" that I had ordered. The flowers that grew were huge, and the tomato plants filled the back porch. I grew enough tomatoes to make spaghetti sauce for the entire neighborhood!

Surprising Statement: Little did I know I was to become the gardener of the century.

3. . . . I followed her into her room. She opened a small box and took out a black pearl ring. She said, "I wore this ring when I was your age. If it fits your finger, it will bring you good luck." It fit perfectly!

Dialogue: "I have something very interesting to show you," Grandma whispered.

Writing with Voice

Lesson Objective

Students will:
- draft the body of their personal narrative, writing with voice

Focus on Instruction

Ask several students to describe the day's weather. Point out that even though each student was talking about the same topic, the words each student chose, the sentences each student used, and the sound of each student's voice made each description a little different. Explain that the same should be true of their writing—the reader should be able to hear the writer "speaking."

Think and Discuss

Have volunteers read the example of strong voice aloud to capture the expressiveness of the language. Then discuss the questions with students as a class.

Draft Your Narrative

Remind students to begin their drafts with the beginning they chose in the previous lesson.

Drafting Reminders

- Reinforce that if students change their mind while writing, they should cross out words or sentences they don't want rather than start over.
- Reassure students that they will have time to correct mistakes and check spelling later.

FOR STUDENTS ACQUIRING ENGLISH

Adding to the vocabulary log of writing terms, define *drafting* as "writing for the first time" and *voice* as "how the writer sounds." Find illustrative examples of voice throughout student and published models. As a class, label voices as *happy, sad, serious,* or *funny.*

The Writing Process: PREWRITING | DRAFTING | REVISING | PROOFREADING | PUBLISHING

Focus Skill

Writing with Voice

Your personal narrative is about you, and it should sound as if you wrote it. Writing with voice lets the audience hear the person behind the words. Writing without voice will sound flat. It won't grab the reader.

Compare the weak example below to the strong excerpt from Eloise Greenfield's narrative, "A Play."

Weak Voice	Strong Voice
I liked to be in plays if I was with other kids. I didn't like to talk by myself.	I liked to be in plays where I could be part of a group, like being one of the talking trees, or dancing, or singing in the glee club. But having to talk by myself—*uh uh!*

Think and Discuss Compare the weak and strong examples.
- Why does the weak voice sound flat? The statements have no details or interesting words.
- Why is the strong example better? uses a series of examples; uses a common expression set off by a dash for emphasis

Draft Your Narrative

1. **Write** the rest of your narrative. Skip every other line to leave room for changes. Don't worry about mistakes. Just write.
2. **Follow your chart.** Include the details. Add other details that you think of as you write. Use time clues.
3. **Let your feelings show.** Allow your audience to hear your voice.

Paragraph Tip
Look for details that tell about the same idea. Group them together in one paragraph.

286 **Unit 8:** Personal Narrative

Meeting Individual Needs

● RETEACHING WORKBOOK, page 80

Writing with Voice

You write with voice when you write the way you think and speak, using your own choice of details and words. Writing without voice sounds flat and uninteresting.

Weak Voice	Strong Voice
I like to help my mom cook. On Saturdays we make breakfast together. We cook a lot of different things.	I love cooking with my mom. You should see us on Saturday mornings! We're mixing and stirring and shaking and baking. By the time we're done, we've used every pan in the kitchen.

The personal narrative below sounds flat and dull. Put yourself in the writer's shoes, and rewrite the narrative. Picture the story in your mind, and add details and language that help the reader hear your voice.

My mom asked if I would help paint the fence in the back yard. I said yes. I spilled a whole can of white paint. I got paint all over me. My mom hosed me off, but the paint would not come out of my hair.

Stories will vary.

▲■ WORKBOOK PLUS, page 129

Writing with Voice

Weak Voice	Strong Voice
I liked school this year. Our class was putting on a play. Mr. Gee asked me if I wanted to be on the stage crew. I said I did. I moved scenery and worked the curtain.	This was my best school year ever. I had a big role in the class play, but it wasn't on-stage. When Mr. Gee asked me if I wanted to be part of the stage crew, I said, "Sign me up!" With all the cool scenery and props to get ready, I had as much fun backstage as I would have had on the stage.

The story below is dull and boring. It sounds flat. Rewrite the narrative to give it a stronger voice. Make the story your own by writing it so that it sounds like you. Let your personality shine through.

Last summer, my best friend and I decided to sell lemonade. It was easy. We went to the basketball courts near our house. That was where the boys in high school played ball. We knew that they would be thirsty. We had two pitchers of lemonade and a lot of paper cups. The basketball players bought all of the lemonade. We ran out of lemonade and made fourteen dollars.

Narratives will vary.

PREWRITING DRAFTING REVISING PROOFREADING PUBLISHING

Focus Skill

Good Endings

A good ending makes your story feel finished. Just writing THE END is not enough.

Tell how the experience worked out. Compare these endings for a narrative about a terrible haircut.

Weak Ending	Strong Ending
I went home. After I got the haircut, I didn't want to go anywhere for a long time.	My Tigers cap stayed glued to my head for the next two months. Finally, my hair grew out enough for another haircut—with a different barber!

Share your thoughts or describe your feelings about the experience. If you end this way, don't just tell how you felt. Describe it! Compare these endings for a narrative about a baseball game.

Weak Ending	Strong Ending
The ball went over the wall. I ran around the bases and scored a home run.	The ball went over the wall! I ran around the bases, my heart pounding, and tagged home plate. I leaped into the air, yelling until I was hoarse. What a great day it was!

Think and Discuss

- Why are the strong endings better? The strong endings are elaborated. They tell what the writers did or felt.
- What kind of ending does Carolin use in her final copy on page 281? She shares thoughts and feelings.

Draft Your Ending

Write two endings for your narrative. Choose the one you like better.

Tech Tip
Cut and paste different endings on your story. Which ones do you like?

Drafting 287

● RETEACHING WORKBOOK, page 81

Good Endings

A good ending makes a personal narrative feel finished. It may tell how an experience worked out or what the writer thought or felt about the experience.

Weak Ending	Strong Ending
I read the wrong story and failed the quiz. I will pay attention in English class next time.	My friends thought the quiz was easy if you read the story. I read a story, but it was the wrong one! Ms. Yu said that she doesn't give *A*'s for good daydreams. The next time I daydream, I won't do it when she's giving out homework assignments.

Each of the short narratives below needs a stronger ending. Read each story. Then write a strong ending to replace the underlined sentence. Sample endings:

1. My tenth birthday party was the best ever until Imani said six little words. Everybody on my soccer team was there. The cake looked great. The candles were purple—my favorite color. I was just thinking how easy it would be to blow out the candles, when Imani shouted the first three words, "Open your present!" I couldn't wait. I opened the present from my team. It was just what I wanted—a brand-new soccer ball. Then Imani said the other three words, "Throw it here!" The ball landed on the cake.

Without thinking, I tossed the ball, but it slipped through Imani's hands and plopped right onto the cake. I won't ever throw a ball to Imani again!

2. I went to cooking school for kids, where I learned how to separate egg yolks and whites with one hand. It was such a neat trick that I practiced it again and again at home. I used all the eggs in the refrigerator and soon had filled two big bowls, one with whites and one with yolks. I was so proud—until Dad came home. He asked what I would do with the eggs. I had not thought of that.

Dad sure has a way of spoiling my fun. Maybe in my next cooking class we'll learn how to cook eggs.

▲■ WORKBOOK PLUS, page 130

Good Endings

Weak Ending	Strong Ending
My team beat the best girl's soccer team in our league.	I couldn't believe what happened. We trounced the best girl's soccer team in our league and broke our losing streak in one afternoon! What a victory that was!

Each short narrative below needs an ending. First, read the story. Then write two endings for it. Read your story endings and decide which one is stronger. Put a check mark in front of the stronger ending. Sample endings:

1. At first I didn't want to spend Saturday afternoon with Aunt Gina. I thought I would be bored, but that changed the minute I walked in the door. First, we baked brownies and made apple crisp. Then we went to a yard sale and had a contest to see who could find the most useless thing to buy. I won when I pulled one green and purple sock out of a pile of clothes. My prize was a trip to the movies.

Ending: It was the best Saturday afternoon I had had in a long time.

Ending: I hope Aunt Gina invites me again. Next time I won't hesitate to accept.

2. The ocean was just too big and deep. I did not want to go swimming. Then I tickled my toes along the shore. The water was warm enough, so I waded in a short way. I felt something under my foot. It was a clam shell. Then I spotted something white and horn-shaped. It was a snail shell. The ocean was turning out to be a fascinating place.

Ending: I even dreamed about it that night. I guess I have a lot to learn about the ocean.

Ending: Dad said we can come again if I'd like. I can't wait!

Good Endings

Lesson Objectives

Students will:
- write two endings for their narrative, using different techniques
- choose an ending

Focus on Instruction

- For the first pair of examples, ask students what details were added to the weak ending. (wore Tigers cap for two months, got next haircut with a different barber) Point out that these details give a clearer picture of how the writer dealt with the problem until he or she had a chance to get a better haircut.
- Then ask students what feeling is described in the strong ending in the second pair of examples. (excitement, joy) Ask what details showed how the writer felt. (heart pounding, leaped into the air, yelling until hoarse)

Think and Discuss

Discuss the questions with students as a class.

Draft Your Ending

- Remind students to add details to their endings that show how they felt and not just write *I was so [feeling]!*
- As with the beginnings, remind students that there is no one correct way to end their stories. They can use either technique, or another one, as long as the ending makes the story feel finished.

MEETING INDIVIDUAL NEEDS

FOR STUDENTS ACQUIRING ENGLISH

As with each step of the writing process, students may want a clear right or wrong way of writing. Emphasize that all writers make changes as they write. Show professional writers' drafts (found in most libraries). Demonstrate different endings to your own or a volunteer's story.

Evaluating Your Personal Narrative

Lesson Objective

Students will:
- evaluate their personal narrative, using a rubric

Connecting to the Criteria

Have students reread the characteristics of a great personal narrative listed on page 277. Then explain that the rubric shown on this page refers to those characteristics. Tell them that the rubric will help them decide which parts of their narrative "ring the bell," or meet the standards of a great personal narrative, and which parts still need more work or haven't been addressed at all.

Focus on Instruction

- Review the rubric with students. Have a volunteer read the first point in each section and explain the differences among them. Follow the same procedure for the remaining points.
- After students write their criteria, have them circle the ones that indicate aspects of their personal narratives that need revision. Blackline Master 8–4 provides a copy of the rubric as a checklist.
- See the Teacher's Resource Book for scoring rubrics.

This page is also available as a poster.

INTERNET CONNECTION Have your students go to www.eduplace.com/kids/hme/ to use an interactive version of the rubric shown in the student book. Students will get feedback and support depending on how they mark the rubric items.

FOR STUDENTS ACQUIRING ENGLISH

Students may never have been asked to evaluate their own work. Encourage them to work in small groups and pretend they are teachers who use the list of criteria to grade the work. To help students focus on content, which may also be unfamiliar to them, eliminate correctness or mechanics from the list. Mechanics are important, but may distract students from the more essential tasks of reviewing and evaluating their ideas, clarity, and order. If students are too self-critical, point out the criteria they have met.

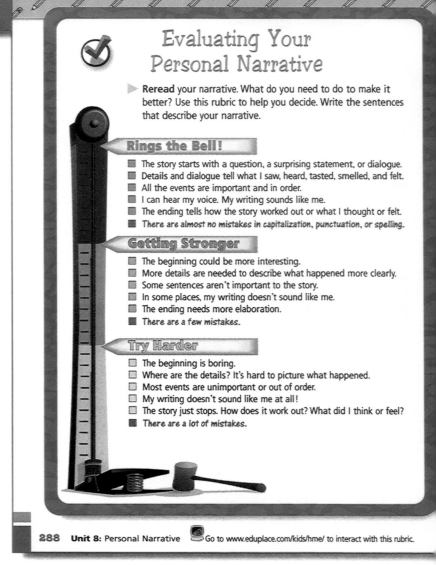

Evaluating Your Personal Narrative

▶ **Reread** your narrative. What do you need to do to make it better? Use this rubric to help you decide. Write the sentences that describe your narrative.

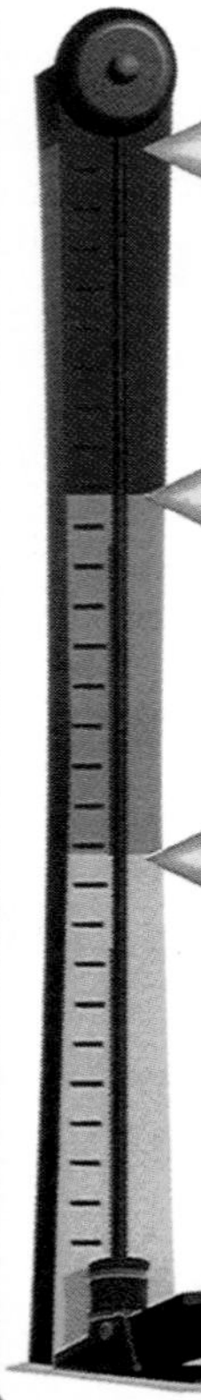

Rings the Bell!

- The story starts with a question, a surprising statement, or dialogue.
- Details and dialogue tell what I saw, heard, tasted, smelled, and felt.
- All the events are important and in order.
- I can hear my voice. My writing sounds like me.
- The ending tells how the story worked out or what I thought or felt.
- *There are almost no mistakes in capitalization, punctuation, or spelling.*

Getting Stronger

- The beginning could be more interesting.
- More details are needed to describe what happened more clearly.
- Some sentences aren't important to the story.
- In some places, my writing doesn't sound like me.
- The ending needs more elaboration.
- *There are a few mistakes.*

Try Harder

- The beginning is boring.
- Where are the details? It's hard to picture what happened.
- Most events are unimportant or out of order.
- My writing doesn't sound like me at all!
- The story just stops. How does it work out? What did I think or feel?
- *There are a lot of mistakes.*

288 **Unit 8:** Personal Narrative   Go to www.eduplace.com/kids/hme/ to interact with this rubric.

Meeting Individual Needs

● RETEACHING WORKBOOK, page 82

Revising a Personal Narrative

Have I | yes
- written a new beginning that will grab my readers' attention? ❑
- given the writing my own voice? ❑
- added details to help readers see, hear, and feel the experience? ❑
- told the events in order? ❑
- revised the ending to make the story feel finished? ❑

Revise the following narrative to make it better. Use the checklist above to help you. Check off each box when you have finished your revision. You can use the spaces above the lines, on the sides, and below the paragraph for your changes. Sample answers:

Don't Forget the Milk
~~The Day I Went to the Store and Forgot What to Buy~~
The weather can help your memory!
~~One day~~ my mother asked me to go to the store to buy
to the store.
some milk. I wanted to go ice-skating instead. I went ~~there.~~
All I could think of was skating. I could not remember what I
My mother
was supposed to buy. ~~She~~ would be angry if I came home
I looked at cereal, peanut butter, and noodles.
with the wrong thing. I went up and down every aisle. ~~I still~~
I went to the bakery and the meat case.
~~couldn't remember.~~ Then I thought about being out in the cold
"That's it! It's milk!" I cried.
air and the white snow. I quickly ran to the dairy section and
grabbed a quart of milk. At last I remembered. I bought it and
as fast as I could.
ran home.
I'm so glad it was a cold, snowy day because green grass and sunshine would not have reminded me of milk at all!

▲■ WORKBOOK PLUS, page 131

Revising a Personal Narrative

Have I | yes
- written a new beginning that will grab my readers' attention? ❑
- given the writing my own voice? ❑
- added details to help readers see, hear, and feel the experience? ❑
- told the events in order? ❑
- revised the ending to make the story feel finished? ❑

Revise the following narrative to make it better. Use the checklist above to help you. Check off each box when you have finished your revision. You can use the spaces above the lines, on the sides, and below the paragraph for your changes. Sample answers:

Strike Out or Home Run?
~~The Day I Hit the Winning Home Run~~
"Batter up!" yelled the umpire.
~~It was my turn to bat.~~ The bases were loaded. There were
put the bat on my shoulder
two outs. I walked to the plate and ~~held the bat.~~ I waited for
Then I swung as hard as I could, but "Strike!" called the umpire.
the pitch. I missed the ball. ~~The umpire called a strike.~~ The
"Strike!" yelled the umpire again.
crowd groaned. I swung again. ~~I heard the umpire say strike.~~
"Oh, no!" I thought. "If I strike out, my team will lose. It will
~~If I struck out, my team would lose. It would be my fault.~~ The
be my fault." This time I would not miss. smack
pitcher was getting ready for her next pitch. I felt the bat ~~hit~~
hard whistling and
the ball. I ran as fast as I could, and I heard the crowd cheering
as my foot touched home plate. I had hit a home run. My team
had won the game!

Revise Your Personal Narrative

1. **Revise** your narrative. Use the list of sentences you wrote from the rubric. Work on the parts that you described with sentences from "Getting Stronger" and "Try Harder."

Revising Tip
Write new paragraphs on strips of paper. Attach the strips where they belong in your narrative.

2. **Have a writing conference.**

When You're the Writer Read your narrative to a partner. Discuss any questions or problems you're having with it. Take notes to remember what your partner says.

When You're the Listener Tell at least two things you like about the narrative. Ask questions about anything that is unclear.

The Writing Conference	
If you're thinking...	**You could say...**
The beginning isn't very interesting.	**Could you start with a question? a surprising statement? dialogue?**
I don't understand when things happened.	**Can you add time clues?**
I wonder what people said.	**What did _____ say when that happened?**
What does this part have to do with the main part of this story?	**Is that part about _____ really important? Could you leave it out?**
Your story is great, but it just stops.	**I'd like to know how everything worked out.**
This doesn't sound like you.	**How did you feel when that happened?**

3. **Make more revisions** to your personal narrative. Use your conference notes and the Revising Strategies on the next page.

Help with Conferencing

ADDITIONAL CONFERENCING QUESTIONS

These questions may be useful during teacher-student conferences.

- Where and when did this happen?
- Who else was there? What did they say or do?
- What is the most important part or moment?
- What happened after [or before] _______?
- Can you tell me more about _______ so that I can picture it clearly?
- What did you learn from this experience? Can you include those ideas in your ending?
- How did you feel when this was over? Could you tell about those feelings in your ending?

EVALUATION TIP

Listen to find out if students are asking questions about their partners' papers or trying to tell the writers what to do. If the latter, have students review the conferencing questions in the student book for ideas of what to ask.

Lesson Objectives

Students will:
- revise their working draft, based on their evaluation
- discuss their working draft in a writing conference

Revise Your Personal Narrative

Focus on Instruction

Revising Reminder

Remind students that revising focuses on making their narrative clearer and more interesting. They should not worry about mistakes at this stage. If necessary, review the revising techniques on page 20.

- Direct students' attention to the Revising Tip. Have them check that their paragraphs flow easily and logically.

Conferencing Reminders

Remind students to read their paper aloud to their partner and to read slowly, clearly, and at an appropriate volume for their audience and setting.

- To reinforce giving the writer a compliment, present these examples.

  Your beginning really grabbed my attention.

  You used many vivid details.

- Tell students that it is unnecessary to make all of the changes suggested by their partner. They should keep the suggestions in mind but make their own choices.
- Students can use Blackline Master 8–5 during their writing conferences.

MEETING INDIVIDUAL NEEDS — FOR STUDENTS ACQUIRING ENGLISH

Model good conferencing skills with your own and a volunteer's work. Show how listeners look at the reader and pay attention. Model both bad and good behavior and questions. Encourage students to explain why some behavior and questions are helpful and others hurtful. Students may be more comfortable in small groups organized by similar language development levels. Students may not be accustomed to writing directly on their work. Show possible uses of arrows, question marks, cross-outs, text circling, carets, and asterisks.

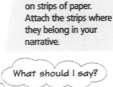

Revising Strategies

Lesson Objectives

Students will:
- add similes and metaphors to elaborate their narrative
- add details to elaborate their narrative
- vary sentence structure

Focus on Instruction

Elaborating: Word Choice

Have students identify the similes and the metaphor in the examples. (as loud as thunder and like mice in a maze; tinkling wind chimes) Discuss with students the comparisons that the similes and the metaphor suggest. Help students summarize that using similes and metaphors will help their readers to picture what is happening more clearly. Page H11 provides a vocabulary lesson about similes and metaphors.

Elaborating: Details

Ask students what details were added to the second example. (three-inch gash in leg, big lump on ankle) Help students summarize that the details help them picture what happened more clearly.

Sentence Fluency

Tell students that writers use different types of sentences for variety and to support meaning and purpose. For example, when a writer wants to highlight an additional idea, he or she can join sentences with *and*. Have students read the sample sentence joined by *and*. Ask how the two sentences are related. (The two actions happened at the same time.) Point out that the other examples express the same meaning but show alternative structure.

FOR STUDENTS ACQUIRING ENGLISH

For each revising strategy, find a point in your own or a volunteer's story where you can revise as a class using an overhead projector. Practice each strategy until all students understand how to perform it. List weak versus strong verbs (*was, were, said* versus. *stood* or *shouted*).

Revising Strategies

Elaborating: Word Choice Use similes and metaphors to create pictures in the minds of your readers. A **simile** compares two different things, using the word *like* or *as*. A **metaphor** compares without using *like* or *as*.

Simile	The crash of the cymbals was as loud as thunder. The new students wandered the halls like mice in a maze.
Metaphor	Mom's new earrings are tinkling wind chimes.

▶ Find at least one place in your narrative where you can use a simile or a metaphor. See also page H11.

Elaborating: Details Insert details within a sentence or write more sentences.

Few details	When I crashed, I hurt my leg.
Elaborated with details	When I crashed, I got a gash in my leg about three inches long. I also had a big lump on my ankle.

▶ Find at least two places in your narrative where you can add details.

Sentence Fluency Try writing sentences different ways so that not all sentences are written the same way. Don't change the meaning when you rewrite.

Two sentences	I zipped down the hill. My bike slipped.
Combined with *and*	I zipped down the hill, and my bike slipped.
Combined with *as*	My bike slipped as I zipped down the hill.
Changed order	As I zipped down the hill my bike slipped.

▶ Write at least two sentences of your narrative a different way.

GRAMMAR LINK See also page 49.

Meeting Individual Needs

● RETEACHING WORKBOOK, page 83

Elaborating: Details

Elaborate by adding interesting details that describe the people, places, and events in a narrative. You can insert details within a sentence, or write more sentences.

Few details	I got paint on my clothes.
Elaborated with details	I splattered red paint all over my new shirt.

The following narrative is boring because it does not contain enough details. Revise each sentence, adding interesting details.

I got on the airplane. It started down the runway. When we were in the air, I saw things out the window. The flight attendants served a meal. I also watched a movie.

1. I got on the airplane.
   Answers will vary.
2. It started down the runway.
3. When we were in the air, I saw things out the window.
4. The flight attendants served a meal.
5. I also watched a movie.

▲■ WORKBOOK PLUS, page 132

Elaborating: Details

Few details	Felisa cleaned off her desk.
Elaborated with details	Felisa put her pencils and her books in a drawer, lined up her toy frog collection on a shelf, and wiped her desktop clean. She even put her papers in a neat pile.

The following narrative is boring because it doesn't contain enough details. Revise the narrative, adding details to make it more interesting.

I read books to my little brother last summer. It was my job. At first it was boring. Then we both started to have fun. I liked finding good books. He laughed at the different voices I used too. It was fun to perform.

Details will vary.

PREWRITING DRAFTING REVISING PROOFREADING PUBLISHING

Proofread Your Personal Narrative

Proofread your narrative, using the Proofreading Checklist and the Grammar and Spelling Connections. Proofread for one skill at a time. Use a class dictionary to check spellings.

Proofreading Checklist

Did I

- ✓ indent all paragraphs?
- ✓ correct any run-on sentences?
- ✓ begin and end sentences correctly?
- ✓ use correct verb forms?
- ✓ correct any spelling errors?

Use the Guide to Capitalization, Punctuation, and Usage on page H55.

Proofreading Marks

- ¶ Indent
- ∧ Add
- Delete
- ≡ Capital letter
- / Small letter

Tech Tip The spelling tool on your computer cannot find words misspelled as other words.

Grammar and Spelling Connections

Past Tense Add *-ed* to most verbs to form the past tense.

Present tense	shout	holler	walk
Past tense	shouted	hollered	walked

GRAMMAR LINK *See also page 108.*

Complete Sentences A sentence has both a subject and a predicate. It begins with a capital letter and ends with a period, a question mark, or an exclamation point.

Not a sentence	Up the steep mountain trail.
Sentence	The hikers carried backpacks.

GRAMMAR LINK *See also pages 32, 36, 38, and 166.*

Spelling Short Vowels A short vowel sound before a consonant is usually spelled with just one letter: *a, e, i, o,* or *u.*

staff, slept, mist, fond, bulb

See the Spelling Guide on page H65.

Go to www.eduplace.com/kids/hme/ for proofreading practice.

Help with Proofreading

MANAGEMENT TIP

Have each student keep a personal checklist of skills that he or she needs to proofread for. Staple the list to the student's folder.

EVALUATION TIP

You may want to check students' proofread stories before they make their final copies.

Lesson Objective

Students will:

- proofread their personal narrative

Proofread Your Personal Narrative

Focus on Instruction

Proofreading Reminders

- Remind students that the proofreading stage is when they should correct capitalization, usage, punctuation, and spelling. Encourage them to use the Guide to Capitalization, Punctuation, and Usage.
- If necessary, review with students when and how to use each proofreading mark. Have students use a different colored pen or pencil to mark their proofreading corrections.
- For proofreading practice, see the usage and mechanics lessons in the grammar units and the Mixed Review practice in each grammar unit Checkup.

- Review and clarify each item in the checklist, using any related Grammar and Spelling Connections. If students need extra support, review the lessons listed in the Grammar Links.
- To review past tense verbs, write these verbs on the board: *kick, spill, clean, jump.* Then ask volunteers to show how each verb forms the past tense.
- Use the example of a sentence and a fragment from the Grammar Connection in the student book to explain that a sentence contains a subject and a predicate and expresses a complete thought. A fragment does not express a complete thought and is missing either a subject or a predicate or both.

INTERNET CONNECTION Have your students go to www.eduplace.com/kids/hme/ for online proofreading practice that is fun.

MEETING INDIVIDUAL NEEDS

FOR STUDENTS ACQUIRING ENGLISH

Expect plenty of student errors; review various samples to decide which areas need the most work. Or, encourage individual students to choose two areas of focus (verbs, spelling, or sentences). Then correct your or a volunteer's paper, using an overhead projector.

Lesson Objectives

Students will:

- make a neat final copy of their narrative
- choose a way to publish or share their narrative
- reflect on their writing experience
- evaluate their narrative in comparison to other compositions in their writing portfolio

Publish Your Personal Narrative

Focus on Instruction

- Before students make their final copy, have them decide how they will publish or share their narrative. Review their decisions with them to help them make any special plans.
- Help students make neat corrections to the final copy rather than rewrite their paper.

Keeping a Writing Portfolio

- **Selection** A paper might be selected because it is
  - ✓ generally noteworthy
  - ✓ a good example of a particular criterion
  - ✓ an example of a particular kind of writing
  - ✓ an example from a certain time in the school year
  - ✓ a typical example of the student's work
- **Labeling** For every paper, have students complete a cover sheet giving the title, date of completion, and reason for inclusion.
- **Review** Periodically have students remove papers that no longer reflect their best work or aren't needed as baselines.
- **Evaluation** Periodically review students' portfolios with them to discuss growth and areas that need improvement.

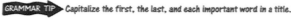

The Writing Process: PREWRITING | DRAFTING | REVISING | PROOFREADING | PUBLISHING

Publish Your Personal Narrative

1. **Make a neat final copy** of your narrative. Be sure you fixed all mistakes.
2. **Write** an interesting title for your narrative that will make your audience curious, such as "Goosebumps on the Trail" rather than "My Hiking Trip."

GRAMMAR TIP *Capitalize the first, the last, and each important word in a title.*

3. **Publish** or share your narrative in a way that suits your audience. See the Ideas for Sharing box.

Tips for Reading Aloud

- Read clearly, slowly, and loudly enough for everyone to hear.
- Read with expression. Pause at commas, and raise your voice at the end of questions. Say exclamations with feeling!
- Look at your audience from time to time.
- Let your face show your feelings.

Ideas for Sharing

Write It

- Send or e-mail your story to a magazine. See page H37 for tips.
- Send it with a greeting card.

Say It

- Read it aloud in the Author's Chair.
- Record it, adding sound effects.

Show It

- Display it with photos.

Reflect

Write about your writing experience. Use these questions to get started.

- What was easy to do? What was hard to do?
- What are your goals for the next time you write?
- How does this paper compare with other papers you have written?

Help with Publishing

TIPS FOR IDEAS FOR SHARING

E-mail Advise students to skip a line between paragraphs rather than indent for easier reading on e-mail.

Greeting Card Students may want to write their narrative on decorative stationery.

Photo Essay Have students choose the pictures they will show, and plan how much text will go on each page with one or more pictures.

TECH TIP

Students can add clip art or, if possible, scan photos into their e-mails or greeting cards.

SCHOOL-HOME CONNECTION

Suggest that students record their narrative and then play their recording to family members.

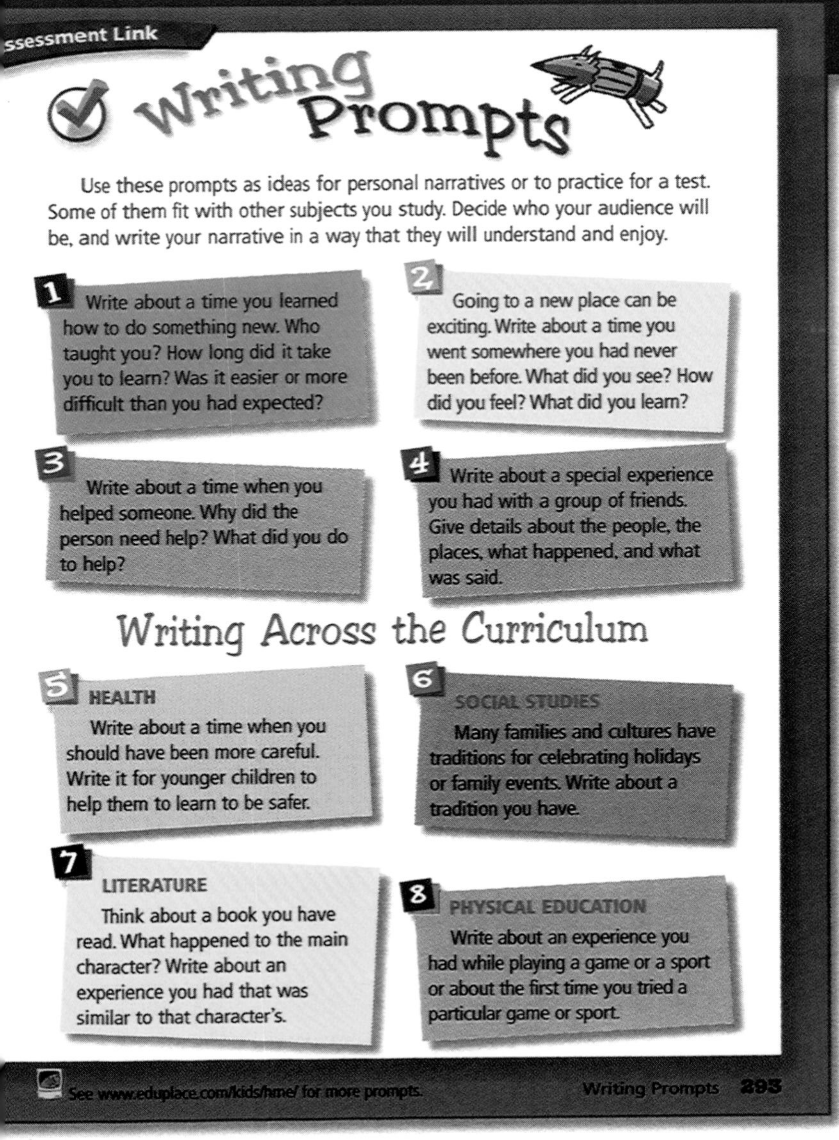

Assessment Link

Writing Prompts

Use these prompts as ideas for personal narratives or to practice for a test. Some of them fit with other subjects you study. Decide who your audience will be, and write your narrative in a way that they will understand and enjoy.

1 Write about a time you learned how to do something new. Who taught you? How long did it take you to learn? Was it easier or more difficult than you had expected?

2 Going to a new place can be exciting. Write about a time you went somewhere you had never been before. What did you see? How did you feel? What did you learn?

3 Write about a time when you helped someone. Why did the person need help? What did you do to help?

4 Write about a special experience you had with a group of friends. Give details about the people, the places, what happened, and what was said.

Writing Across the Curriculum

5 HEALTH
Write about a time when you should have been more careful. Write it for younger children to help them to learn to be safer.

6 SOCIAL STUDIES
Many families and cultures have traditions for celebrating holidays or family events. Write about a tradition you have.

7 LITERATURE
Think about a book you have read. What happened to the main character? Write about an experience you had that was similar to that character's.

8 PHYSICAL EDUCATION
Write about an experience you had while playing a game or a sport or about the first time you tried a particular game or sport.

See www.eduplace.com/kids/hme/ for more prompts. Writing Prompts 293

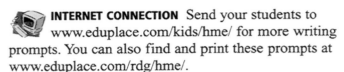

Writing Prompts

Objective

Students will:

- review prompts for choosing a topic or to practice for a writing test

Using the Prompts

You can use the prompts on this page in several ways.

- Have students review the prompts to help spark ideas when they are choosing their own topics for a personal narrative. Suggest that students choose one or two prompts and brainstorm ideas of their own.
- Choose a prompt to provide practice for a writing test. Use it with the Test Practice on the next page.
- Choose a prompt that fits with a related topic in another subject area to integrate writing a personal narrative across the curriculum.

INTERNET CONNECTION Send your students to www.eduplace.com/kids/hme/ for more writing prompts. You can also find and print these prompts at www.eduplace.com/rdg/hme/.

MEETING INDIVIDUAL NEEDS

FOR STUDENTS ACQUIRING ENGLISH

Especially useful prompts are: (1) learning English, (2) coming to America, (3) helping family members with their English, (4) remembering friends, family, and events from their native countries, and (5) celebrating holidays.

Test Practice

Objective

Students will:

- learn strategies for evaluating a writing prompt and writing a personal narrative for a test

Using the Test Practice

- Read through the page with students, discussing the strategies for evaluating and responding to a prompt to write a personal narrative.
- Review the rubric on page 288 with students before they write their practice test.
- Have students write a personal narrative in response to the prompt on this page or to one of the prompts on the previous page. Impose the time limitations or other restrictions or qualifications specific to the testing requirements used in your school.

INTERNET CONNECTION Send your students to www.eduplace.com/rdg/hme/ for examples of benchmark papers.

INTERNET CONNECTION Send your students to www.eduplace.com/kids/hme/ for graphic organizers. You can also find and print these organizers at www.eduplace.com/rdg/hme/.

MEETING INDIVIDUAL NEEDS

FOR STUDENTS ACQUIRING ENGLISH

To help students transition from the process to the product, explain that they will be working on their own, but encourage them to ask questions as they write. Allow students to use their previous stories, the text, and dictionaries. Walk about the room, stopping and conferencing with students who are having trouble.

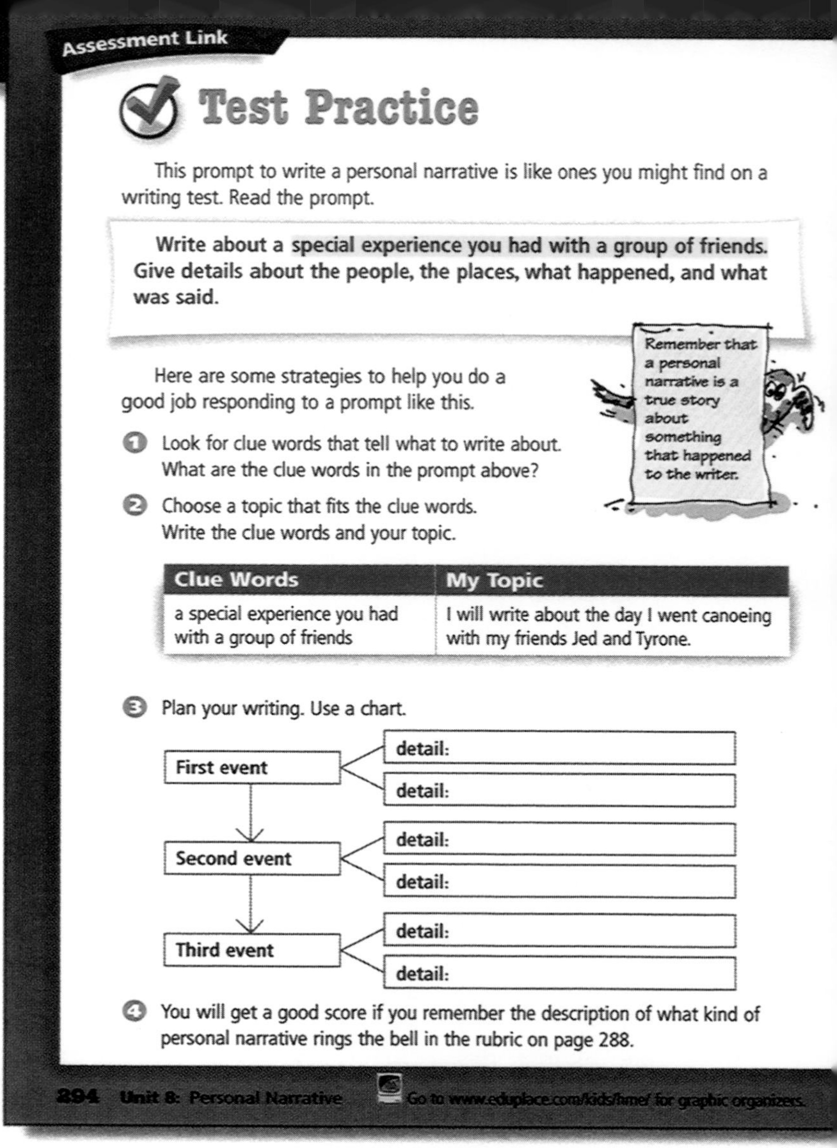
Assessment Link

Test Practice

This prompt to write a personal narrative is like ones you might find on a writing test. Read the prompt.

Write about a special experience you had with a group of friends. Give details about the people, the places, what happened, and what was said.

Here are some strategies to help you do a good job responding to a prompt like this.

1. Look for clue words that tell what to write about. What are the clue words in the prompt above?
2. Choose a topic that fits the clue words. Write the clue words and your topic.

Clue Words	My Topic
a special experience you had with a group of friends	I will write about the day I went canoeing with my friends Jed and Tyrone.

3. Plan your writing. Use a chart.

4. You will get a good score if you remember the description of what kind of personal narrative rings the bell in the rubric on page 288.

294 Unit 8: Personal Narrative — Go to www.eduplace.com/kids/hme/ for graphic organizers.

Writing a Friendly Letter

A **friendly letter** is written to a person you know well. You can write a friendly letter to share news or to find out how someone is doing. Read Callie's letter.

Heading → 2240 North Tate Street
New Orleans, LA 70113
November 29, 2001

Greeting → Dear Jerome,

Body →
How is your new school? We wish you could still be here to play tag football with us. Our team hasn't won a game since you left.

Ms. Ortega put John in our science group to take your place. He's doing a good job, but he's not as funny as you! We're still making the model of the sea urchin you started. For the spines, we are using short drinking straws instead of toothpicks. Some kids were getting hurt from the toothpicks, so Ms. Ortega asked us to use something safer.

I hope you're having fun in Baton Rouge.

Closing → Your friend,
Signature → Callie

Reading As a Writer See TE margin for answers.

- The **heading** contains the writer's address and the date. *What information is on each line?*
- The **greeting** begins with *Dear* and gives the name of the person getting the letter, followed by a comma. Capitalize each word. *To whom is Callie writing?*
- The **body** is the main part of the letter. *What did Callie write about?*
- The **closing** finishes the letter. It is followed by a comma. *What closing did Callie use?*
- The **signature** is the writer's name. *Where is the signature written?*

more ▶

Help with Writing a Friendly Letter

USING RESOURCES
Students might enjoy writing to a pen pal. Provide sources where they can obtain lists of pen pal names. Students also can research the Internet for groups that provide international pen pals for students.

Writing a Friendly Letter

Lesson Objective

Students will:
- read a model of a friendly letter and identify its parts

Focus on the Model

- Ask students what they think is the purpose of a friendly letter. (to share thoughts, news, or experiences with friends or family they don't see regularly) Point out that writing a friendly letter is like writing a personal narrative in that a letter includes interesting details about the writer's news or experiences.
- Tell students that they will read a student's letter to a friend who moved to a new city. Have students read the introduction to the letter.
- Before students read the letter, explain that the blue call outs highlight the five parts of a friendly letter and that students will learn about those five parts after they read the letter.
- Ask volunteers to read the letter aloud.

Students can also listen to the model on audiotape.

Focus on Instruction

Discuss the explanations of the call outs in the Reading As a Writer section with the class, and have volunteers answer the questions.

Answers to Reading As a Writer

- The first line contains the street address; the second line tells the city, state, and Zip Code; the third line tells the date.
- Callie is writing to Jerome.
- Callie wrote about news from school.
- Callie used *Your friend.*
- The signature is written in the closing.

FOR STUDENTS ACQUIRING ENGLISH
Discuss the parts of a friendly letter. Review the way a date is written, including the order of month, day, and year and the use of a capital letter on the month. Have students work with partners to practice writing headings using their own addresses and the current date. Then present various closings; discuss when to use each.

Lesson Objectives

Students will:
- write a friendly letter and address an envelope correctly
- recognize the characteristics of a thank-you letter and an invitation

How to Write a Friendly Letter

Focus on Instruction

- Tell students that good writers vary their word choice and style of writing to suit their audience and purpose. Ask how a letter written about an exciting vacation would differ from a letter meant to express feelings about a lost pet.
- Discuss with students the information included in the main address and the return address of an envelope. Point out that if there is an apartment number, it would follow the street address on the same line. Explain that a return address is important so that a letter can be returned to the sender if the mailing address is incorrect.

Connecting to the Criteria

Remind students to check that their letters contain all five parts described in the Reading As a Writer section of their lesson and that the information in each part is complete.

FOR STUDENTS ACQUIRING ENGLISH

Provide blank envelopes for practice. Say that a letter cannot be mailed without correct postage; show where to put the stamp(s). Say which postage is needed for letters mailed to addresses in the United States and to countries where students have family or friends. You may want to get a list of current rates from the post office.

Types of Friendly Letters

- Have a volunteer read the thank-you letter model aloud. Have students find the words that elaborate on the gift. Reinforce that a good thank-you letter shows that the recipient has enjoyed the gift or noticed special features about it. Have students write a thank-you letter to a classmate for an appreciated act.
- Explain that when an invitation says *RSVP*, a response is requested, and that *RSVP* stands for the French sentence *Répondez s'il vous plait,* which means "Please respond." Have students write an invitation to their family inviting them to visit the classroom.
- Help each student decide whether these letters should go into their portfolio.

How to Write a Friendly Letter

1. **Think** about what you want to say.
2. **Organize** your information. You may want to make notes first.
3. **Write** the letter. Include all five parts.
4. **Proofread** for mistakes. Use the Proofreading Checklist on page 291. Use a dictionary to check spellings.
5. **Write** a neat final copy of your letter.
6. **Address** the envelope correctly. Stamp and mail your letter.

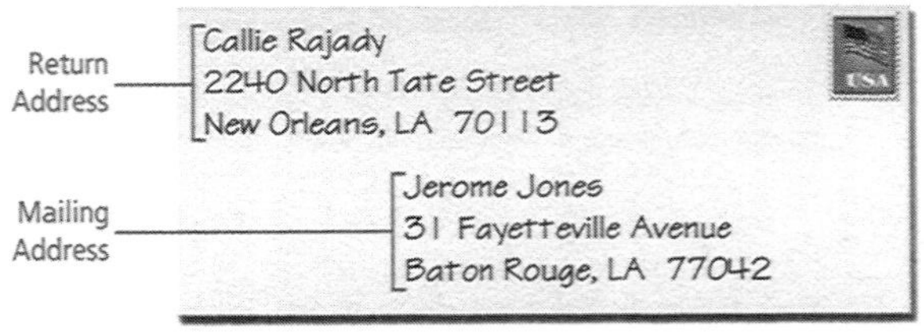

Types of Friendly Letters

Thank-you Letter Writing a thank-you letter is a way for you to express your appreciation. You can elaborate using details about the gift or favor.

> Dear Roxanne,
>
> I love the 1,000-piece jigsaw puzzle of New York City that you gave me for my birthday. I have always wanted a hard puzzle with many different pieces. My whole family wants to work on it, which is good because it will probably take a lot of time!
>
> I'm so glad you could come to my party. Thanks again for the great present!

Invitation An invitation asks someone to come to an event, usually a party. Most invitations include the name of the event, the place, the date, the time, and any special information, such as what to wear or bring. Invitations often give a phone number that you can call to respond.

Help with Writing a Friendly Letter

TOPIC IDEAS

Suggest these possibilities.
- Students can write a letter explaining favorite hobbies or after-school activities to a relative.
- They can write a letter expressing a feeling or an opinion to a friend about something that happened.
- They can write a letter describing the writer's school and activities to a student in another city or country.

TECH TIPS

- Tell students to use the tab key to indent each paragraph.
- If the necessary software and hardware are available, suggest that students add clip art or scan appropriate photos or illustrations into their letters.

Unit 9 Planning Guide

Writing a Story

Writing a Story: *2 weeks*
Special Focus and Communication Links: *2 weeks (optional)*

	Blackline Masters (TE)	Workbook Plus	Reteaching Workbook
PUBLISHED MODEL "Crows," by Betty Mae Jumper *(298–299)*			
What Makes a Great Story? *(300)*			
STUDENT MODEL Working Draft *(301–302)* Final Copy *(303–304)*	9–1A, 9–1B		
The Writing Process Write a Story			
Prewriting Focus Skill: Planning Characters *(306)* Focus Skill: Planning Setting and Plot *(307)*	9–2 9–3	133 134	84 85
Drafting Focus Skill: Developing Characters *(308)* Focus Skill: Developing the Plot *(309–310)* Focus Skill: Writing with Voice *(311)*		135 136 137	86 87 88
Revising Evaluating Your Story [rubric] *(312)* Writing Conference *(313)* **Revising Strategies** *(314)*	9–4 9–5 	138 139	89 90
Proofreading *(315)*			
Publishing and Reflecting *(316)*			
Writing Prompts and Test Practice *(317–318)*			
SPECIAL FOCUS ON ENTERTAINING **Writing a Play** *(319–323)*			
COMMUNICATION LINKS **Speaking: Dramatizing** *(324–325)* **Viewing/Media: Comparing Stories in Books and Movies** *(326–327)*			

Unit 9

Tools and Tips

- **Listening and Speaking Strategies,** *pp. H4–H10*
- **Building Vocabulary,** *pp. H11–H17*
- **Research and Study Strategies,** *pp. H18–H30*
- **Using Technology,** *pp. H35–H47*
- **Writer's Tools,** *pp. H48–H54*
- **Spelling Guide,** *pp. H65–H69*
- **Guide to Capitalization, Punctuation, and Usage,** *pp. H55–H64*
- **Thesaurus Plus,** *pp. H79–H100*

School-Home Connection

Suggestions for informing or involving family members in classroom activities and learning related to this unit are included in the Teacher's Edition throughout the unit.

Meeting Individual Needs

- **FOR SPECIAL NEEDS/INCLUSION:** *Houghton Mifflin English* Audiotape
- **FOR STUDENTS ACQUIRING ENGLISH:**
  - Notes and activities are included in this Teacher's Edition throughout the unit to help you adapt or use pupil book activities with students acquiring English.
  - Students acquiring English can listen to the published and student models on audiotape.
  - MediaWeaver™, Sunburst/Humanities software, offers bilingual features, including Spanish menus, a Spanish spelling tool, and a Spanish thesaurus.
- **ENRICHMENT:** See *Teacher's Resource Book.*

All audiotape recordings are also available on CD.

Daily Language Practice

Each sentence includes two capitalization, punctuation, usage, or spelling errors based on skills presented in the Grammar and Spelling Connections in this unit or from Grammar Units 1 and 2. Each day write one sentence on the chalkboard. Have students find the errors and write the sentence correctly on a sheet of paper. To make the activity easier, identify the kinds of errors.

1. "Look out for the turn? yelled Tyler." "Look out for the turn!" yelled Tyler. (quotations; end punctuation)
2. The captain announced, "We should be landing in orlando in ten minutes". The captain announced, "We should be landing in Orlando in ten minutes." (proper nouns; quotations)
3. Three deers grazes in our back yard each morning. Three deer graze in our back yard each morning. (plural nouns; subject-verb agreement)
4. I needs a ribbon for Marcus birthday present. I need a ribbon for Marcus's birthday present. (subject-verb agreement; possessive nouns)
5. Should wilde animales be put in cages in zoos? Should wild animals be put in cages in zoos? (spelling long *i*; plural nouns)
6. Some familys spent the hot nite camping in the park. Some families spent the hot night camping in the park. (plural nouns; spelling long *i*)
7. The dress' collar is whight. The dress's collar is white. (possessive nouns; spelling long *i*)
8. Several baseball teams have spring training camps in arizona! Several baseball teams have spring training camps in Arizona. (proper nouns; end punctuation)
9. Labrador retrievers make wonderful pets they are especially good with childrens. Sample: Labrador retrievers make wonderful pets. They are especially good with children. (run-on sentences; plural nouns)
10. Please pick only the strawberrys that are red! Please pick only the strawberries that are red. (plural nouns; end punctuation)

Additional Resources

Workbook Plus, Unit 9
Reteaching Workbook, Unit 9
Teacher's Resource Book
Transparencies
Posters, Unit 9
Audiotapes

Technology Tools

CD-ROM: *EasyBook Deluxe
MediaWeaver™, Sunburst/Humanities software
*Type to Learn™

*©Sunburst Technology Corporation, a Houghton Mifflin Company. All rights reserved.

INTERNET: http://www.eduplace.com/kids/hme/ *or* http://www.eduplace.com/rdg/hme/

Visit Education Place for these additional support materials and activities:

- author biographies
- student writing models
- graphic organizers
- an interactive rubric
- proofreading practice
- writing prompts
- benchmark papers

Assessment

Test Booklet, Unit 9

Keeping a Journal

Discuss with students the value of keeping a journal as a way of promoting self-expression and fluency. Encourage students to record their thoughts and ideas in a notebook. Inform students whether the journal will be private or will be reviewed periodically as a way of assessing growth. The following prompts may be useful for generating writing ideas.

Journal Prompts

- Think of an imaginary place you would like to visit. Describe it.
- Write about an adventure that you and your best friend could have.
- Make up a fairy tale in which you are the hero.

Unit 9

Writing a Story

Once upon a time, in their castle high on a rocky cliff, Princess Bright and her brother Prince Klever planned a surprise for the king and queen.

297

Introducing the Unit

Using the Photograph

- Direct students' attention to the photograph, and ask what it shows. (a castle on top of a mountain by the edge of the sea) Ask students who they think might live in the castle and what might happen there. Then have a volunteer read the caption aloud.
- Ask students what kind of surprise Princess Bright and her brother Prince Klever might have planned for the King and Queen. (Sample responses: a surprise birthday party, a surprise visit from their country cousins, a royal picnic by the sea) Discuss with students different plot ideas.
- Explain that plot ideas can be developed into stories. A **story** is a narrative made up by an author. Tell students that they will learn how to write a story in this unit.

Shared Writing Activity

Work with students to choose one of their plot ideas and then write a paragraph describing the main event—the surprise.

1. Have students list words and phrases describing the *who, what, where, when, why,* and *how* about the surprise event. Write their suggestions on the board.
2. Ask students to group words and phrases that would go together to describe the particular details of the surprise event.
3. Then have students identify which groups of words and phrases about the surprise event tell what happened first, next, and so on. Work with students to generate sentences with these word groups to describe the surprise event. Write the sentences on the board or on an overhead transparency.
4. Reinforce the importance of using vivid sensory words and phrases as they describe the surprise event.
5. If students suggest stringy sentences with too many *ands,* remind them that they can fix a stringy sentence by breaking it into two or more sentences. Reinforce the use of subject-verb agreement (or other skills students need to work on) as they suggest sentences.
6. Have students copy the final paragraph to share with a younger child.

"Crows"

Lesson Objectives

Students will:
- read a published model of a story
- identify characteristics of a story
- note author's technique for adding variety to her writing by varying sentence length
- evaluate the relationship between visuals and text
- write personal and critical responses

Focus on the Model

Building Background

Ask students if their curiosity has ever placed them in an unsafe situation. What happened? How did they feel about the situation? Tell students that they will read a story about two beautiful songbirds whose curiosity cost them their beauty and talent.

Introducing Vocabulary

Introduce key vocabulary words by writing these sentences on the board.

> Each year my father cleans the **soot** from our chimney and gets covered in black powder.
>
> The logs burned so long that they turned into **charcoal** and could easily be broken apart.

Ask a volunteer to read each sentence aloud. Ask students to explain the meaning of the boldfaced words.

Reading the Selection

- Have students read the introduction to "Crows." The purpose-setting question focuses on a characteristic of a story, the teaching of a lesson.

Have students read the selection as a class, independently, or with partners, or they can listen to the selection on audiotape.

- The call outs highlight key characteristics of a story that are addressed in the Think About the Story questions at the end of this selection.

FOR STUDENTS ACQUIRING ENGLISH

Before reading, ask for help describing crows. If students are unfamiliar with them, show photos. Discuss animal fables. Encourage students to share similar stories from their native countries.

A Published Model

The story "Crows" is a legend told by members of the Seminole tribe in Florida. What does this legend teach us?

Crows

from *Legends of the Seminoles*, by Betty Mae Jumper

Once, among all the flying birds in the beautiful forest, were two special birds. They had very colorful feathers that shone brightly under the sun as they flew around. All the other birds admired and envied them. And the songs they sang were out of this world. When these birds sang, the others in the forest would quiet down and just listen to them. [introd chara and settin]

One day, as these two birds were flying around, they saw a strange thing coming up in the air which was not a cloud. They looked and looked from up in the air, but they couldn't make out what it was. One said to the other, "Let us fly a little ways further and see what it is." [story probl]

"I'm scared," said the other, but he followed his friend halfway to the strange thing. Then both stopped in a tree and looked and looked.

"What is that orange color below and that strange black color going in the air?" said the one bird, begging his friend to go closer. So, they flew right to the edge of where the forest was burning— something the birds had never seen before. They sat a long time watching it. Then one bird said, "Let us fly to that black tree and see the burning from the top."

The other said, "No. Let us go back. We have seen enough." But the other kept it up, wanting to fly to the top of the tall black tree. As usual, he won the argument and they flew to the top of the tree and tried to sit on a limb. [deal with prob]

298 **Unit 9:** Story

Bibliography

Here are other books that model this type of writing that students might enjoy reading.

- ***Ashley Bryan's African Tales, Uh-huh*** by Ashley Bryan
- ***Encyclopedia Brown and the Case of the Disgusting Sneakers*** by Donald Sobol
- ***A Twist in the Tail: Animal Stories from Around the World*** by Mary Hoffman
- ***Sideways Stories from Wayside School*** by Louis Sachar

A Published Model

But the limb broke and the birds fell to the ground into the black soot, which burned their beautiful feathers into charcoal.

And their voices were gone. They couldn't get any sound out, until one day they learned to say "Caw. Caw." For this, they were ashamed and never returned to the beautiful forest they once knew.

Reading As a Writer See TE margin for answers.

Think About the Story

- What lesson does this legend teach?
- What do you find out in the beginning about the characters and setting?
- What is the problem in the story? How do the birds deal with the problem?
- What happens to the birds at the end?

Think About Writer's Craft

- The author adds variety to her writing by making her sentences different lengths. Find at least three examples of this in the story.

Think About the Picture

- What is the main color in the picture? Why do you think the artist used so much of this color?

Responding See TE margin for answers.

Write responses to these questions.

- **Personal Response** What did you like about the story? What didn't you like? Explain your answers.
- **Critical Thinking** How are the two birds alike and different?

Mapping the Selection

MAPPING THE STORY

A map helps students to visualize the story structure. After students have read the story, draw the following map on the board. Have students complete the map by answering the questions.

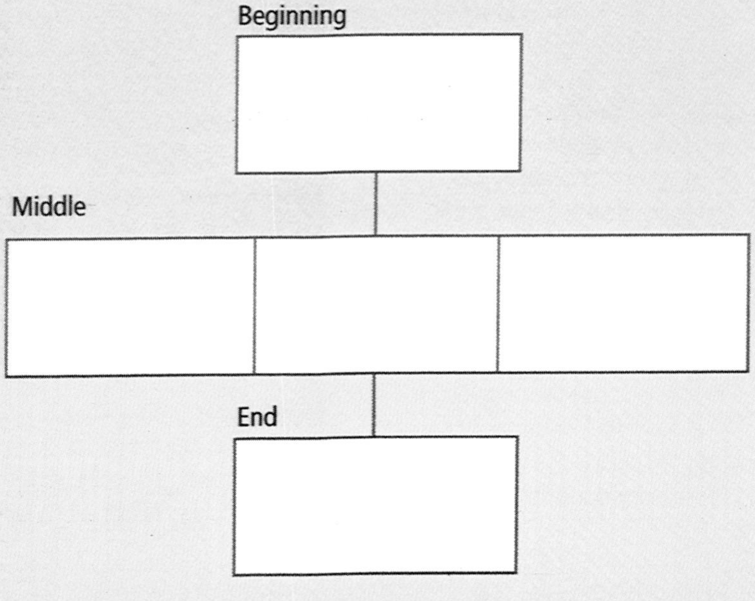

Answers to Reading As a Writer

Think About the Story

- This legend teaches the value of safety over curiosity.
- The two main characters are beautiful songbirds. The setting is an imaginary forest.
- The problem happens when both birds see something strange in the air. They can't figure out what it is. The birds fly to the top of the tree to get a better look.
- The branch breaks, and the birds fall into the black soot. They become crows after their feathers burn, and they lose their singing voices.

Think About Writer's Craft

- Sample answers: So they flew right to the edge of where the forest was burning—something the birds had never seen before. They sat a long time watching it. Then one bird said, "Let us fly to that black tree and see the burning from the top."

Think About the Picture

- The main color in the picture is orange. The artist used so much of it to show how big and hot the fire was. It also helps to contrast the colors of the crows before and after they fell into the soot.

After students answer the questions, work with them to generate criteria for a great story, using the published model as a reference.

More About Writer's Craft

Tell students that using sensory details in their writing can make it vivid and more interesting. Have students find specific words or phrases in "Crows" that give details about seeing or hearing. (Sample answers: *beautiful forest, colorful feathers, the songs they sang were out of this world, tall black tree*) Encourage students to use sensory details in their own writing to add interest and to make it more vivid. Remind students that they can also use the senses of smell, taste, and touch.

Notes on Responding

Personal Response

Ask volunteers to share their opinions with the class. Encourage students to explain their viewpoints, reminding them that each person may have a different reaction to the story.

Critical Response

Sample answer: Both birds have beautiful feathers and can sing well. One bird is curious, and the other bird is cautious.

What Makes a Great Story?

Lesson Objective

Students will:
- discuss the characteristics of a well-written story

Focus on Instruction

- Explain to students that "Crows" is an example of a well-written story. Ask volunteers to read aloud the definition and characteristics of a story. List on the board and discuss the characteristics represented in the published model. (has a plot with a beginning, middle, and end; introduces the main characters and setting in the beginning; tells only the important events in a logical order; shows how characters deal with the story problem in the middle; uses colorful detail and meaningful dialogue; explains how everything is solved in the end)
- Have students read the Grammar Check. Point out that it is a reminder that good writing must also be grammatically correct. Explain that students will be expected to use singular and plural verbs correctly.

If this is students' first encounter with the cartoon dog, explain that Sal is the writer's pal and that Sal will provide tips to help them learn to write great stories.

Connecting to the Rubric

- These criteria are tied to the rubric on page 312.
- Tell students that they will be writing their own story and they will learn how to include these characteristics. Explain that after writing their story, they will use these characteristics as criteria to help them evaluate their work.

This page is available as a poster.

Looking Ahead Tell students that they will next see how the characteristics listed on this page are applied in one student's working draft and final copy of a story.

FOR STUDENTS ACQUIRING ENGLISH

Turn back to "Crows" and the class map of the selection to find examples of each criterion. Demonstrate how the story includes each item and has left out any unimportant material. (the birds' families, eating habits) As you read Jessica's story on the next page, act out the part of the pig, so students understand and can respond with the class.

What Makes a Great Story?

A **story** is a narrative made up by the author.

Remember to follow these guidelines when you tell or write a story.

- Develop a plot with a beginning, a middle, and an end.
- Introduce the main characters, the setting, and the problem in the beginning in an interesting way.
- Show how the characters deal with the problem in the middle and how the problem works out in the end.
- Describe the events in an order that makes sense. Leave out events that are not important to the story.
- Use details and dialogue to show rather than tell about the characters, events, and setting.
- Use details to make your story scary, funny, serious, or sad.

GRAMMAR CHECK

Use singular verbs with singular subjects. Use plural verbs with plural subjects.

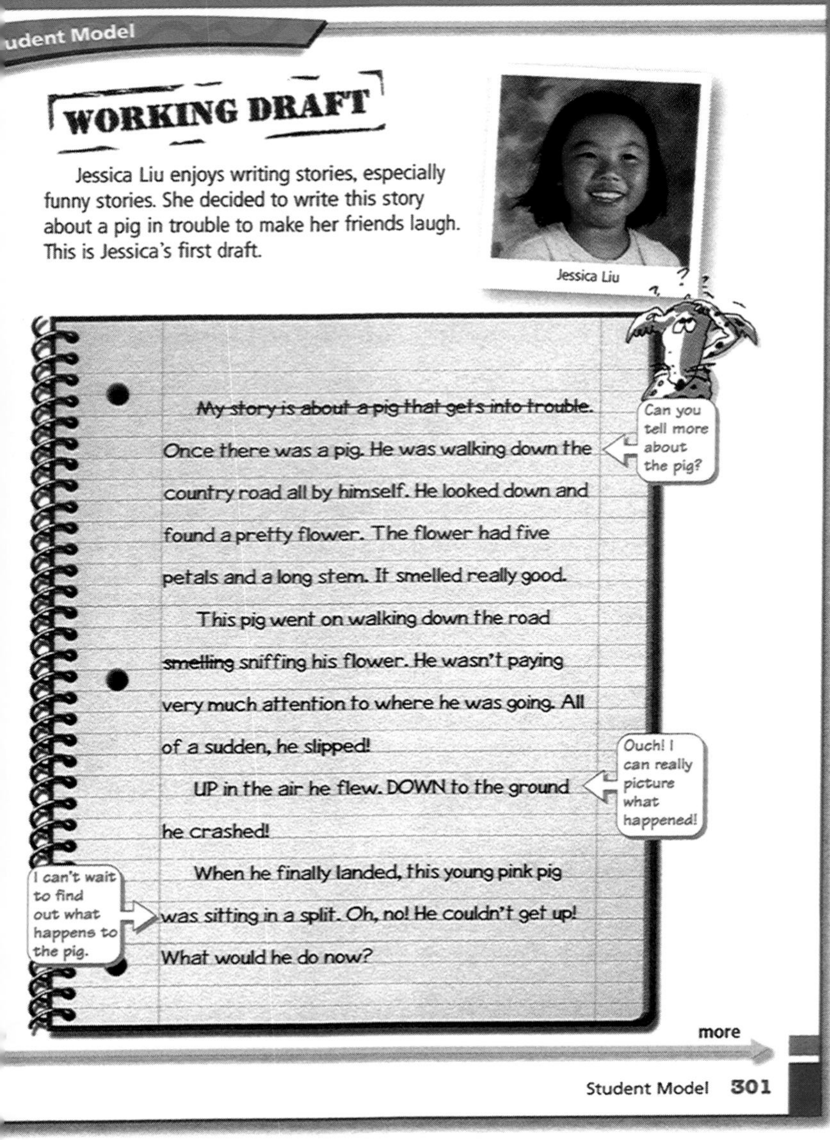

Student Model

WORKING DRAFT

Jessica Liu enjoys writing stories, especially funny stories. She decided to write this story about a pig in trouble to make her friends laugh. This is Jessica's first draft.

Jessica Liu

~~My story is about a pig that gets into trouble.~~ Once there was a pig. He was walking down the country road all by himself. He looked down and found a pretty flower. The flower had five petals and a long stem. It smelled really good.

This pig went on walking down the road ~~smelling~~ sniffing his flower. He wasn't paying very much attention to where he was going. All of a sudden, he slipped!

UP in the air he flew. DOWN to the ground he crashed!

When he finally landed, this young pink pig was sitting in a split. *Oh, no! He couldn't get up!* What would he do now?

Can you tell more about the pig?

Ouch! I can really picture what happened!

I can't wait to find out what happens to the pig.

more

Student Model 301

Student Model: Working Draft

Lesson Objectives

Students will:
- read a working draft of a student-written story
- discuss the ways the model meets the criteria for a well-written story and ways that it could be improved

Focus on the Model

- Tell students that they will read a working draft of a story written by a real student, Jessica Liu. Remind students that a working draft is the writer's attempt to get his or her ideas on paper, knowing that revisions can be made later.
- Ask volunteers to read aloud the student model.

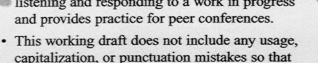

  Alternatively, students can listen to it read by a student (although not the student writer) on audiotape.

> - Reading the draft aloud gives students practice listening and responding to a work in progress and provides practice for peer conferences.
> - This working draft does not include any usage, capitalization, or punctuation mistakes so that students can focus on the content of the piece.

- Tell students to think about whether Jessica included the important characteristics of a story. Point out Sal's thoughts, enclosed in the thought balloons, about the story. Tell students that they will discuss Sal's ideas after they read the model.
- Refer students to Sal's note about the first paragraph. Discuss with students the benefits of adding details about the pig in the beginning. Help students see that the pig in the working draft is not a very interesting main character.

Answers to Reading As a Writer

- Sal liked how Jessica described the pig's fall, and he liked the humor in the story. Sal also liked that Jessica wrote her events in order. Sal asked if Jessica could tell more about the pig, and if she could say more to make the ending more interesting. Jessica could tell more about the pig in the beginning, and say more at the end to make the story feel finished.
- *The flower had five petals and a long stem. It smelled really good.* These details are not important to the story.
- Sample answer: The sentences did not add anything important to the story.

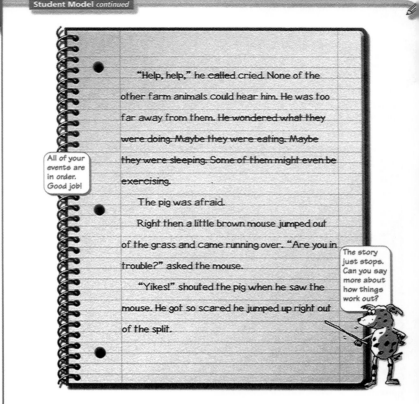

"Help, help," he ~~called~~ cried. None of the other farm animals could hear him. He was too far away from them. ~~He wondered what they were doing. Maybe they were eating. Maybe they were sleeping. Some of them might even be exercising.~~

The pig was afraid.

Right then a little brown mouse jumped out of the grass and came running over. "Are you in trouble?" asked the mouse.

"Yikes!" shouted the pig when he saw the mouse. He got so scared he jumped up right out of the split.

All of your events are in order. Good job!

The story just stops. Can you say more about how things work out?

Reading As a Writer

See TE margin for answers.

- What did Sal like about Jessica's story? What were Sal's questions? What revisions could Jessica make to answer them?
- What sentences should Jessica take out of the first paragraph on page 301? Why?
- Look at the first paragraph on this page. Why do you think Jessica crossed out some sentences?

FINAL COPY

Jessica revised her story after discussing it in a writing conference. Read her final copy to see what changes she made to improve her story.

There's More Than One Way to Scare a Pig
by Jessica Liu

These details help me picture the pig much better.

Once there lived a roly-poly young pig. He was a lovely pink fellow. He lived on a farm with other farm animals. One morning he was walking down the country road all by himself. He looked down and found a pretty flower.

This young pink pig went on walking down the road, sniffing his flower. He wasn't paying very much attention to where he was going. All of a sudden, he stepped on a wet leaf and. . . slipped!

UP in the air he flew. DOWN to the ground he crashed!

This story is really funny!

When he finally landed, this young pink pig was sitting in a split. Oh, no! He couldn't get up! What would he do now?

"Help, help," he cried. None of the other farm animals could hear him. He was too far away from them.

The pig was afraid. "Help, help," he called again. Now he was getting even more afraid because it was getting dark. "Oh, no! I can't stay here all night. It will be dark and cold."

more

Student Model: Final Copy

Lesson Objectives

Students will:

- read a well-written final copy of a student's story
- note and compare the revisions that improved the first draft

Focus on the Model

SUMMARY OF REVISIONS In her final copy, Jessica added a title; she added details to tell more about the main character; she left out unimportant information to make the story funnier; and she added more details to the ending to show how the problem was solved. Blackline Master 9–1 provides a copy of the student's working draft, showing the revisions that were made.

Have volunteers read the model aloud. Alternatively, students can listen to it read by a student (although not the student writer) on audiotape.

Answers to Reading As a Writer

- Jessica told more about the pig in the beginning. She made the story feel finished by telling what the mouse and the pig did at the end.
- Jessica added the sentences *"Help, help," he called again. Now he was getting even more afraid because it was getting dark. "Oh, no! I can't stay here all night. It will be dark and cold."*
- Jessica made these changes to the second paragraph: This *young pink* pig went on walking down the road, sniffing his flower. . . . All of a sudden he *stepped on a wet leaf and . . . slipped!*

More About Writer's Craft

- Point out the use of all capital letters in the words *UP* and *DOWN* in paragraph 3. Ask students how using this technique enhances the story. (adds a sense of drama; makes the reader say the word in a loud voice for emphasis) Suggest that students use capitalization sparingly for drama and emphasis in their own story.
- Point out the story's effective use of punctuation, especially the ellipsis. Ask students to comment on the effect this mark creates. Help them see that the ellipsis dramatizes the delay between stepping on a wet leaf and actually falling. Advise students to use punctuation effectively in their own writing.
- Help students think about criteria the writer used to break the story into paragraphs. Point out that stories often include dialogue from several speakers, and each time a new character speaks, a new paragraph begins.

Connecting to the Rubric

- Have students look again at the list of characteristics on page 300 and review with them how Jessica's final copy addressed each one.
- Reinforce the Grammar Check by having students check that Jessica correctly used singular verbs with singular subjects, and plural verbs with plural subjects.

INTERNET CONNECTION Send your students to www.eduplace.com/kids/hme/ to see more models of student writing. You can also find and print these models at www.eduplace.com/rdg/hme/.

Looking Ahead Tell students that they will next write their own story, using the writing process. As they progress, they will learn how to plan and develop convincing characters, a setting, and a plot, and also how to give a voice to each character and to the story as a whole.

Right then a little brown mouse jumped out of the grass and came running over. "Are you in trouble?" asked the mouse.

"Yikes!" shouted the pig when he saw the mouse. He got so scared he jumped up right out of the split. Then he ran back down the road right back to the farm.

The little mouse waved good-bye as the pig ran away. "I'm glad I could help you!" he said. "See you later!"

Good job! You told how everything worked out in the end. Now your story feels finished.

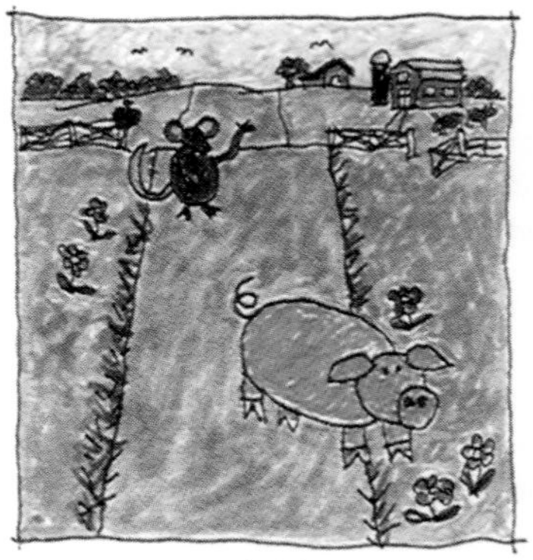

Reading As a Writer See TE margin for answers.

- How did Jessica respond to Sal's questions?
- What details and dialogue did Jessica add to tell why the pig was afraid? What other details did she add?
- What other changes did Jessica make?

 See www.eduplace.com/kids/hme/ for more examples of student writing.

FOR STUDENTS ACQUIRING ENGLISH

To answer Reading As a Writer, return to Jessica's first draft and review the questions Sal asks. Help students see Jessica's changes by placing the two drafts next to each other (using two textbooks). Also review the criteria of a story, deciding which ones Jessica satisfied and which ones she could improve.

Write a Story

Start Thinking

Make a writing folder for your story. Copy the questions in bold print, and put the paper in your folder. Write your answers as you think about and choose your topic.

- **Who will be my audience?** Will I write this story for my classmates? younger students? my family?
- **What will be my purpose?** Do I want to make people laugh? scare them? take them on an adventure?
- **How will I publish or share my story?** Will I make a book with pictures? put on a radio play? act it out?

Choose Your Story Idea

1. **List** five story ideas you could write about. Make a story chart like the one below.

Who?	Where?	What could happen?
pig	country road	an accident
boy	forest	lost in storm
cat	school	wants to win a contest

▲ Part of Jessica's chart

HELP *Stuck for Ideas?*
Share your charts with a small group. Pick items from different charts, and combine them to create new story ideas.
See page 317 for more ideas.

2. **Discuss** your ideas with a partner.
   - Which idea is the most interesting to your partner? Why?
   - Which idea has a good beginning, middle, and end?
3. **Ask** yourself these questions about each idea. Then circle the idea you will write about.
   - Do I have enough ideas for my story?
   - Will this interest my audience?
   - Will I enjoy writing about this idea?

Help with Choosing a Topic

TECH TIP

- To help students generate ideas, suggest that they key in phrases and thoughts as they come to mind. Then they can go back and add details to each idea.
- Refer students who are using a computer to page H39 to find ideas for using a computer during the writing process.

EVALUATION TIP

Review students' final topic choices. Make sure each topic can be developed into a beginning, a middle, and an end.

USING RESOURCES

Suggest that students read biographical information on various authors to find out how some professional writers come up with story ideas.

SOURCES OF TOPIC IDEAS

Suggest these activities to prompt topic ideas.

- Students can think of an extraordinary occurrence that could be the basis of a good story.
- They can think of a message to share with others.
- They can think of their favorite animal and what it might say if it could speak.

Write a Story

Lesson Objectives

Students will:

- list their ideas for audience, purpose, and publishing/sharing formats
- list ideas for a story
- discuss their ideas with a partner
- choose an appropriate topic to write about

Start Thinking

Focus on Instruction

- Explain that the language used in a story should be adapted to the audience and purpose. Ask students for examples of how appropriate story language would differ for a funny story versus an adventure story. (A funny story might use lighthearted, silly language, whereas an adventure story might use more action words.)
- Have students look at Jessica's story. Ask how she might have adapted the language if she had written the story for pre-school children. (She would have used shorter sentences and simple words.)

Choose Your Story Idea

Focus on Instruction

Page 317 provides writing prompts that might suggest ideas.

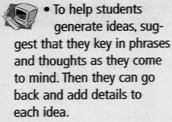

INTERNET CONNECTION Send your students to www.eduplace.com/kids/hme/ for graphic organizers. You can also find and print these organizers at www.eduplace.com/rdg/hme/.

SCHOOL-HOME CONNECTION Suggest that students discuss their story topics with family members to see if the ideas grab their interest.

Have students start a writing folder titled *My Story.* Explain that they will keep all notes, graphic organizers, and drafts for their story in this folder. Have students include their papers with their thoughts about their audience, purpose, and publishing format.

MEETING INDIVIDUAL NEEDS — FOR STUDENTS ACQUIRING ENGLISH

If students have trouble listing five possible topics, ask, "Which animals fascinate you and why? Is there an animal story from your culture that you can write about? What makes you laugh?" Then do all prewriting steps together.

Planning Characters

Lesson Objectives

Students will:
- select two main characters for their story
- describe each main character's personality in one sentence

Focus on Instruction

- Ask students why it is important to create convincing characters. (Realistic characters make the story interesting and are easy for the reader to relate to.)
- Tell students that details make characters interesting and give them life. Discuss the use of details in portraying the characters below.

  He slouched down in the overstuffed chair and buried his head in a book. (shows that the character is fatigued or that he is very interested in the book)

  She tossed her blonde ringlets away from her face, threw her shoulders back, and strutted off. (shows the character is very confident or conceited)

Try It Out

Tell students that they will need to use their imagination to address all questions about the pictured character. Point out that physical qualities alone can tell a great deal about a character.

Explore Your Story

- Use Blackline Master 9–2 to help students develop their story characters.
- Point out to students that their main characters should have personal qualities that make the plot interesting and believable. Encourage students to create lifelike characters that can step off the pages of their story.

FOR STUDENTS ACQUIRING ENGLISH

Ask students to turn to their word logs and, as a class, review the concepts of *details* and *events*. Then review the definition of *characters*. (people in a story) Students may be unfamiliar with creative writing. Encourage them to first share their ideas aloud in small groups.

The Writing Process: PREWRITING | DRAFTING | REVISING | PROOFREADING | PUBLISHING

Focus Skill

Planning Characters

You are the casting director of your story. Do you need a computer genius or a mummy that sends e-mail in Egyptian picture language? Give your story at least one **main character** and as many **minor characters** as it needs.

Use details. Help your readers get to know your main character inside and out. Here are some ideas to get you started.

What does your character look like? Describe your character's face, hair, clothes, and other features.

What is your character's personality? Is he or she smart? funny? dreamy? loud?

What does your character say? Does he or she recite poetry? make jokes?

What are your character's feelings? Is she or he curious? lonely? brave? fearful?

How does your character act? Does she or he whistle? shuffle? pout? blush?

What are your character's interests? Does he or she collect posters? love sports?

Try It Out Answers will vary.

- Work with a partner or a small group to describe the pictured character. Use the questions above. Make notes about your ideas. Then compare your ideas with those of other students.

Explore Your Story

Think of two main characters that you might like to use in your story. Draw a picture of each character, and answer the questions above about each one. Describe each character's personality in one sentence.

See page 14 for other ideas for exploring your topic.

Meeting Individual Needs

● RETEACHING WORKBOOK, page 84

Planning Characters

When you plan story characters, use details to help your readers get to know the characters inside and out. Think about what your characters look like, how they act, and what they say. Think about your characters' feelings and interests.

Think about the main character in a story you might write. Choose details from each list to describe your character, or make up some of your own. Circle each detail you choose. Then draw a picture of your character.

Details and sketches will vary.

How my character looks
tall
blue eyes
dimples

How my character feels
unhappy
scared
bored

What my character is like
friendly
funny
neat

How my character acts
wiggles nose
snaps fingers
sings

What my character says
tells funny stories
speaks Spanish
uses polite words

My character's interests
chess
gymnastics
reading

▲■ WORKBOOK PLUS, page 133

Planning Characters

When you plan your story characters, use details to help your readers get to know the characters inside and out. Think about what your characters look like, how they act, and what they say. Think about your characters' feelings and interests.

Think about the main character in a story you might write. Does the character wear a uniform? make people laugh? love computer games? Write details about the character on the lines in each category. Draw a picture of your character. Then write a sentence that describes your character's personality.

Sketches and sentences will vary. Sample details:

How my character looks
short
long hair
freckles

How my character feels
happy
nervous
excited

What my character is like
quiet
thoughtful
generous

How my character acts
winks
twists hair
blows bubbles

What my character says
talks in rhyme
reads aloud
uses good phone manners

My character's interests
loves to draw
plays the piano
enjoys animals

Focus Skill

Planning Setting and Plot

The **setting** for a story is where and when the story takes place. The setting could be in a town like yours, on the moon, in a castle, on an island, or in a make-believe place. It could be long ago, today, or in the future.

A good story has a **plot** that focuses on a problem. The plot has three main parts: a beginning, a middle, and an end. This story map shows the three parts of "Crows."

Beginning → two beautiful birds sing in the forest; see something strange; try to find out what the strange thing is
- introduces the main characters
- introduces the setting
- introduces the problem

Middle → one bird wants to fly closer; other one doesn't | fly close; sit on branch over fire | tree burns; birds fall into fire
- tells how the characters deal with the problem

End → feathers burned black; can't sing anymore
- explains how the problem works out

Try It Out

- With a partner, make a story map for Jessica's story on pages 303–304. Show the beginning, the middle, and the end. Sample answer: beginning: pig takes walk and slips, he can't get up; middle: pig cries for help, no one hears him, and he becomes afraid; end: mouse scares pig, pig jumps up and runs home

Plan Your Story

Make a story map for your story. Plan the beginning, the middle, and the end. Add notes about the characters, the setting, and the problem.

Go to www.eduplace.com/kids/hme/ for graphic organizers.

Planning Setting and Plot

Lesson Objective

Students will:
- make a story map of their story

Focus on Instruction

Read aloud the following paragraph.

> Peter looked up at the blowing wind and gazed across the vast white wilderness. As he brushed the cold powdery flakes from his wind-burned face, he wondered if he would ever feel warm again.

Ask students when this story takes place (in winter) and what clues led them to this conclusion. (blowing wind, white wilderness, cold powdery flakes, wind-burned face, need for warmth) Ask what the story might be about. (a boy who is stranded in the snowy mountains) Explain that good writers do not directly state the setting. Instead they provide clues to help readers mentally draw their own picture of the setting.

Try It Out

Remind students that their map should tell the complete story without all the details. A copy of a story map organizer appears on Blackline Master 9–3.

Plan Your Story

- If students are not yet ready to create a story map, have them discuss their story plot with a partner or in a small group.
- Remind students that their map should be brief, telling only the most important events. For a different story map design, refer students to page H54.

INTERNET CONNECTION Send your students to www.eduplace.com/kids/hme/ for graphic organizers. You can also find and print these organizers at www.eduplace.com/rdg/hme/.

MEETING INDIVIDUAL NEEDS

FOR STUDENTS ACQUIRING ENGLISH

Have students define *setting* (where and when the story happens) and *plot* (the action of the story) in their word logs. Turn back to the class map, have them identify the beginning, middle, and end of "Crows." If students are ready, encourage small groups to map Jessica's story, using the format on page 307, or map it as a class.

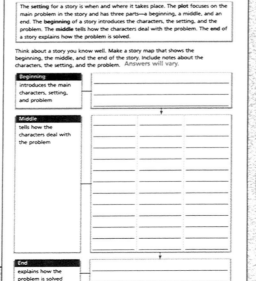

● RETEACHING WORKBOOK, page 85

Planning Setting and Plot

The **setting** for a story is when and where it takes place. The **plot** focuses on the main problem in the story and has three parts—a beginning, a middle, and an end. The **beginning** of a story introduces the characters, the setting, and the problem. The **middle** tells how the characters deal with the problem. The **end** tells how the problem is solved.

The events below show the three parts of a story. Write *Beginning*, *Middle*, or *End* to show in which part of the story each event belongs. Then write them in the story map.

End Hannah can't believe it when she wins first prize! She gives Renata the portrait as a gift.

Beginning Hannah is a shy girl with a great talent for drawing. Renata is pretty, popular, and talented. Both girls decide to enter a school drawing contest.

Middle Hannah is afraid to compete with Renata. Renata tells Hannah it's okay if they both enter the contest. Renata draws a princess on a white horse. Hannah draws a beautiful portrait of Renata.

Beginning introduces the main characters, setting, and problem — Hannah is shy, but good at drawing; Renata is pretty, popular, and talented; both enter the school drawing contest.

Middle tells how the characters deal with the problem — Hannah is afraid to compete with Renata; Renata says it's okay. | Renata draws a princess on a white horse. | Hannah draws a portrait of Renata.

End explains how the problem is solved — Hannah wins first prize; she gives Renata the portrait.

▲■ WORKBOOK PLUS, page 134

Planning Setting and Plot

The **setting** for a story is when and where it takes place. The **plot** focuses on the main problem in the story and has three parts—a beginning, a middle, and an end. The **beginning** of a story introduces the characters, the setting, and the problem. The **middle** tells how the characters deal with the problem. The **end** of a story explains how the problem is solved.

Think about a story you know well. Make a story map that shows the beginning, the middle, and the end of the story. Include notes about the characters, the setting, and the problem. Answers will vary.

Beginning introduces the main characters, setting, and problem

Middle tells how the characters deal with the problem

End explains how the problem is solved

Developing Characters

Lesson Objective

Students will:
- show characters through details, dialogue, and actions

Focus on Instruction

- Explain to students that a character's appearance and actions can reveal a great deal about his or her personality. Ask students to read the description of Will Trek and describe his personality. (He is prepared, strong, eager to get going, and a bit of a know-it-all.)
- Write this simple sentence on the board: *The puppy was afraid.* Ask students to rewrite it, using details and actions to convey the same message. Ask volunteers to write their sentences on the board and discuss.
- Ask students what the speech of the pig and mouse in the final copy of the student model show about each character. (The pig is nervous and easily frightened. The mouse is calm and easy-going.) Remind students to use dialogue to reveal the personalities of their story's main characters.

Think and Discuss

Suggest that students do this exercise with a partner so that they can discuss appropriate words to use.

Draft Some Dialogue

- Tell students to convey their character's personality or mood through word choice and tone of voice. Then have students read the dialogue aloud to see if it has the intended effect.
- Remind students of how the student writer used all capital letters for emphasis and an ellipsis for dramatic effect in the student model. Suggest that students use these techniques sparingly in their story and only where appropriate.

MEETING INDIVIDUAL NEEDS

FOR STUDENTS ACQUIRING ENGLISH

The vocabulary in the examples is challenging. Write simpler samples of telling versus showing. After looking at the text examples, ask volunteers to change some of their own descriptions from telling to showing. On the board, emphasize the use of quotations before having students use them.

The Writing Process: PREWRITING · DRAFTING · REVISING · PROOFREADING · PUBLISHING

Focus Skill

Developing Characters

Once you have planned what your characters are like, how can you help your readers imagine them?

Give details. Describe how your characters look, sound, and act.

> Will Trek slung a stuffed backpack over his shoulders, looped three cameras around his neck, grabbed two heavy suitcases, and slapped on his biggest smile before anyone could say, "Let's go!"

Show characters through their actions. Let the characters' actions reveal their personalities.

Telling	Showing
Mr. Trek told his family about the city's famous sites.	In his I-know-everything voice, Mr. Trek rattled off fifty zillion facts as he dragged his dazed family all over the city.

Show characters through dialogue. You can show your characters' thoughts, feelings, and personalities by what they say.

Telling, Without Dialogue	Showing, With Dialogue
Liane is always bragging.	"My family take trips all the time, and we see the best places. Pretty soon we'll start space traveling, I bet," Liane sighed.

Think and Discuss Answers will vary.

- Look at your notes about the character shown on page 306. What might that character say that would show what he is like?

Remember to start a new paragraph each time the speaker changes.

Draft Some Dialogue

Write some dialogue for the main characters in your story. Use it to show what your characters are like.

308 **Unit 9:** Story

Meeting Individual Needs

● RETEACHING WORKBOOK, page 86

The Writing Process: Focus Skill   Name ____________

Developing Characters

You can describe how your characters look, sound, and act, by giving details. You can show your characters' personalities through their actions. You can show their thoughts, feelings, and personalities by what they say.

Telling	Showing
My dog, Bruno, was afraid of thunder.	As soon as the sky started to rumble, Bruno's ears perked up. He stood up suddenly and scurried under the bed. Bruno stayed there, whimpering, until the storm was over.

Telling, Without Dialogue	Showing, with Dialogue
Mr. Snuffer did not like Bruno.	"How many times do I have to tell you to keep that sorry excuse for a dog out of my yard?" yelled Mr. Snuffer.

Read the following paragraphs. Then rewrite each paragraph by adding dialogue to show what the characters are like. Sample answers:

1. Niki couldn't find her dog, Bruno. Niki asked her mother if she had seen Bruno. Her mother said that she had seen an animal running quickly down the street. It was going in the direction of Mr. Snuffer's garden.
   "I've looked everywhere for Bruno," said Niki frantically. "Have you seen him, Mother?"
   Mother exclaimed, "So that was the flash of fur I saw racing down the street! It was headed toward Mr. Snuffer's flower garden."

2. Mr. Snuffer warned Niki about Bruno. Niki pleaded and offered to cut Mr. Snuffer's grass.
   "If that annoying dog sets foot in my garden one more time, I'm going to call the dog pound," growled Mr. Snuffer.
   "Bruno's just a sweet little dog," Niki said, desperately. "I'll cut

▲■ WORKBOOK PLUS, page 135

Developing Characters

Telling	Showing
Billy's brother came home from the movie and told Billy all about it.	Billy's older brother ran all the way home from the movie, rushed in the door, and immediately started acting out all the characters' parts for Billy.

Telling, Without Dialogue	Showing, with Dialogue
Abe can't stop talking about his new bike.	"Wait until you see my new bike!" exclaimed Abe. "It is so cool! I feel as though I'm flying when I ride it. I'd better be careful, though, or I'll get a speeding ticket!"

Rewrite the story below by adding dialogue to show what the characters are like. Remember that you can show your characters' thoughts, feelings, and personalities by what they say.

Rosemary gently lifted her caramel-colored kitten out of its basket. She lovingly carried it into the kitchen, where her mother was working. Rosemary had been struggling to think of a name for her adorable new pet. She hoped that her mother might have an idea. Rosemary's mom was very creative. Rosemary knew she could count on Mom for the perfect name. Stories will vary.

Focus Skill

Developing the Plot

The Beginning

The beginning may be more than one paragraph.

Catch your audience's interest in the first sentence. Beginnings such as *My story is about . . .* are boring. A good beginning makes your readers wonder, *What is going to happen?* Here are some ideas for how to begin.

Describe the setting.	Long vines looped around tree trunks and snaked along the ground in the thick rain forest.
Describe a character.	Sneaky Pete twisted the tips of his mustache and flashed a yellow-toothed grin at Clyde Clemhopper.
Describe an action.	The white horse pushed its hind legs against the ground and flew majestically into the clouds.

Think and Discuss Answers will vary.

- What clues do the beginnings above give you about the stories?
- What catches your attention in each one?

The Middle

Include only the events that are important to the main idea. If your story is about a baseball game, include only important events related to the game. Don't include everything the characters did before, during, and after the game. Remember to begin a new paragraph for each new event.

Write the events in an order that makes sense. Use time clues, such as *before, after, later,* and *the next day,* to make the order clear.

Think and Discuss Answers will vary.

- Choose one of the story beginnings above. What are some possible events for this beginning?

more ▶

Developing the Plot

Lesson Objectives

Students will:
- write three different beginnings for their story
- select their favorite story beginning

The Beginning

Focus on Instruction

Tell students that the beginning of a story introduces the reader to the problem that will be solved. A good beginning sets the stage by telling *who, where,* and *when.*

Think and Discuss

- Sample answers: The clues in the first beginning tell that the story might involve an adventure. The second beginning tells that it might be a funny story. The clues in the third beginning tell that it will probably involve fantasy.
- Have volunteers share their answers with the class.

The Middle

Focus on Instruction

- Explain to students that time clues are like directions on a map that help readers follow the story events. Have students find time clue words and phrases in the published and student models. Remind them that dependent clauses such as *After the game ended,* can also signal time. Tell students to signal readers with a time clue word or phrase each time an event in their story changes.
- Students can use a time line like the one on page H54 to order the events of their story.

Think and Discuss

Students can use a flow chart like the one below to organize the series of events that might follow each story beginning. Have students share their ideas.

Beginning → Event → Event → Event → Event

The Ending

Focus on Instruction

Point out that the last paragraph of the published model explains why it is called "Crows," and it concludes the legend's lesson. The story's problem is solved. Remind students to write endings for their stories that make the writing feel finished.

Try It Out

Tell students to keep the theme of "Crows" in mind as they create a new ending. Remind them that their ending still needs to explain the transformation of the beautiful songbirds into crows.

Draft Your Beginning

Tell students to keep the mood of their story in mind as they compose their different beginnings. Advise them to select the beginning that best conveys the intended mood and the one that motivates them to continue writing.

MEETING INDIVIDUAL NEEDS — FOR STUDENTS ACQUIRING ENGLISH

Before considering the samples in the text, turn back to "Crows" and Jessica's story to identify what kind of beginnings they have. Then consider the examples in the text. Briefly act out or draw the scenes to enhance student comprehension. Before moving on to writing with voice, ask students to draft their stories.

Focus Skill continued

The Ending

A good ending makes sense of how the problem works out. Look again at this paragraph near the end of "Crows."

> But the limb broke and the birds fell to the ground into the black soot, which burned their beautiful feathers into charcoal.

If the story had ended there, you might have wondered, *Then what happened to the birds?* The last paragraph tells you. It finishes the story.

> And their voices were gone. They couldn't get any sound out, until one day they learned to say "Caw. Caw." For this, they were ashamed and never returned to the beautiful forest they once knew.

Try It Out Answers will vary.

- Work with a small group of classmates to write another last paragraph for "Crows." Compare your ending with ones written by other groups.

Draft Your Beginning

1. **Write** three beginnings for your story.
2. **Choose** the beginning you like best.

Tech Tip
You may want to write your draft on a computer.

Meeting Individual Needs

● RETEACHING WORKBOOK, page 87

Developing the Plot

A good **beginning** catches the reader's interest right away. A good **middle** includes events that are important to the plot of the story. A good **ending** tells how the problem in the story is worked out.

You might begin a story in one of these ways.

Describe the setting	The smell of hot dogs and peanuts filled the air, as fans wearing baseball caps impatiently waited for the game to begin.
Describe a character	The detective tucked her shiny blonde hair under a stocking cap and put on a pair of wire-rimmed glasses.
Describe an action	The turtle plodded along the side of the road, slowly picking up one foot, putting it down, and then picking up another.

The underlined story beginning below does not grab the reader's attention. Think of two good beginnings for the story and write them on the lines. Try describing the setting, describing a character, or describing an action. Put a checkmark by the beginning that you like best. Sample answers:

This story tells how brave Erica was.

Rose was an old, gray-pink sow who was too old to be sold at market. Farmer Jones let her do as she pleased.

One foggy day Rose wandered into the forest, scouting the way with her wrinkled old snout. Suddenly, something fell on her leg with a loud thump. Rose's wails led Erica right to her. Erica pulled the log from the screaming sow.

Erica had always wanted to be a hero. Maybe she would never save nations or slay dragons, but she knew that her courage had set Rose free.

My beginning: Erica edged toward the terrible sound step by step, even though she couldn't see a thing. It sounded like Rose, but she couldn't be sure.

My beginning: Erica was so scrawny that she didn't look like she could defend herself against a fly. One day something happened to change all that.

▲■ WORKBOOK PLUS, page 136

Developing the Plot

Good Beginnings	
Describe the setting	The waves crashed against the rugged rocks on the shore as the spindly trees twisted in the wind.
Describe a character	The crowd gasped as Trina glided onto the ice in her glittering sequined costume and her sparkling silver tiara.
Describe an action	The boys carefully positioned themselves on the toboggan, pushed off, and whizzed down the hill at breakneck speed!

The story below needs a good beginning. Write two good beginnings. The strategies above will help you. Put a check by the beginning that you like better.
Sample answers:

Elizabeth thought she would never be able to stay calm under such pressure. As she walked up the steps to the high dive, she thought, "I know I can do this. I know I can do this."

When she reached the end of the diving board, Elizabeth raised her hands over her head to get into position. She whispered to herself, "You've done a back dive hundreds of times. Just pretend you're doing it for the coach."

After the dive was completed and she hit the water, Elizabeth knew she had done a good job. She swam to the edge of the pool and looked up at her coach. "Way to go, Champ," he said. "That dive clinched first place."

My Beginning: The crowd was chanting her name, "Elizabeth! Elizabeth!" Then, suddenly, a hush spread through the stands. This was the moment everyone had been waiting for.

My Beginning: Elizabeth looked confident as her name was called. She held her head high and her body straight. However, looks can be deceiving. What was really going through her mind?

PREWRITING DRAFTING REVISING PROOFREADING PUBLISHING

Focus Skill

Writing with Voice

As the writer, you can give your characters a voice by letting your audience know your characters' thoughts, feelings, and personalities. You use another voice to tell the story. The details you write help to make the story sound sad, or funny, or scary. It's up to you!

Compare the weak examples below to the strong examples from Jessica's story.

HELP **Adding Voice**

Does your story have more than one character? Use a different voice for each character.

Weak Voice	Strong Voice
Once there was a big pig. He was pink. He went up in the air. He fell down.	Once there lived a roly-poly young pig. He was a lovely pink fellow. UP in the air he flew. DOWN to the ground he crashed!

Think and Discuss Compare the weak and strong voices in each example.

- How does the voice sound in each weak example? each strong example? *dull, flat; lively, humorous*
- What details make each strong example sound the way it does? *roly-poly young pig; a lovely pink fellow; DOWN to the ground he crashed*

Draft Your Story

1. **Decide** how you want your story to sound.
2. **Write** the rest of your story. Use your story map and any dialogue and beginnings you have written.
3. **Write** a good ending that wraps up your story. Skip every other line. Don't worry about mistakes until later.

Describe your characters and their actions in a lively, interesting way, so your audience will want to keep reading.

Drafting 311

Writing With Voice

Lesson Objectives

Students will:

- give voice to their characters and their story
- write their complete story

Focus on Instruction

Tell students to close their eyes as you read this sentence:

She waited impatiently.

Ask volunteers to describe the picture that forms in their mind. Next, read the following sentence and have students tell how their visualization of it is clearer than that of the first sentence.

She drummed the fingers of her right hand against the table and, with her left hand, twisted a strand of hair into a knot.

Think and Discuss

Have volunteers read aloud the examples of strong voice to capture the expressiveness of the language.

Draft Your Story

- Encourage students to keep the voice of their story in mind as they write. Explain that they can enhance the voice by adding details to nearly every sentence.
- Remind students to use dialogue whenever appropriate.
- Remind students of the way Jessica used exclamation points and an ellipsis to enhance her story. Tell students to use similar techniques in their own story.

Drafting Reminders

- Reinforce that if students change their mind while writing, they should cross out words or sentences they don't want rather than start over.
- Reassure students that they will have time to correct mistakes and check spelling later.

● RETEACHING WORKBOOK, page 88

Writing with Voice

Give a character **voice** by letting the reader know what your character thinks and feels. Use details that help make your story sound sad, funny, scary, or however you wish.

Weak Voice	Strong Voice
There was once a mom who didn't like doing laundry. She always put it off.	Supermom loved to cook and clean and work in the garden, but she hated doing laundry. Just thinking about the washing machine gave her a nervous twitch. She would use any excuse to avoid it.

Rewrite the story below to give it a strong voice. Let your audience know what the character is like. Add details to make the story sound special. Then write an ending that wraps up your story.

Once there was a mom who hated doing laundry. She daydreamed through each and every laundry day. One day, she dreamed up a sock-sorting machine. The next day she invented an automatic ironing machine. Her best invention ever was a laundry robot. This mom became rich and famous.

Stories will vary.

▲■ WORKBOOK PLUS, page 137

Writing with Voice

Weak Voice	Strong Voice
Billy opened his birthday present and smiled. It was what he wanted.	Billy tore open the wrapping on his birthday gift. When he saw what was inside, he could barely speak. The words came out garbled. He had thought no one knew his secret birthday wish.

The story below is dull and boring. It does not have a voice. Rewrite the story, using voice to let the audience know the characters' personalities. Use details to make the story sound the way you want it to. Then give the story a good ending.

Stories will vary.

The king called his three daughters together. He told them it was time to choose the one who would wear the crown. He explained that he would give the girls a test. Each daughter had to solve a puzzle. This would be a challenge.

The girls thought and thought. Each knew she would have to use her wits to win the crown.

Evaluating Your Story

Lesson Objective

Students will:

- evaluate their story, using a rubric

Connecting to the Criteria

Have students reread the characteristics of a great story listed on page 300. Then explain that the rubric shown on this page refers to those characteristics. Tell students that the rubric will help them decide which parts of their stories "ring the bell," or meet the requirements of a great story, and which parts need more work or haven't been addressed at all.

Focus on Instruction

- Review the rubric with students. Have a volunteer read the first point in each section and explain the differences among them. Follow the same procedure for the remaining points.
- After students write their criteria, have them circle the ones that indicate aspects of their own story that need revision. Blackline Master 9–4 provides a copy of the rubric as a checklist.
- See the Teacher's Resource Book for scoring rubrics.

This page is also available as a poster.

INTERNET CONNECTION Have your students go to www.eduplace.com/kids/hme/ to use an interactive version of the rubric shown in the student book. Students will get feedback and support depending on how they mark the rubric items.

FOR STUDENTS ACQUIRING ENGLISH

Before using the rubric, review vocabulary from the word logs. Add definitions for *audience* and *dialogue*. Encourage students to write on their drafts, labeling each paragraph according to the rubric. Students often benefit from reading their drafts aloud. Make time and space for students to feel comfortable. Designating corners of the room and providing chairs and privacy will facilitate reading aloud. Also try making a template of the rubric so students can easily check the areas on which they need work. Remind students to consider each part of the rubric because their writing will have both strengths and weaknesses.

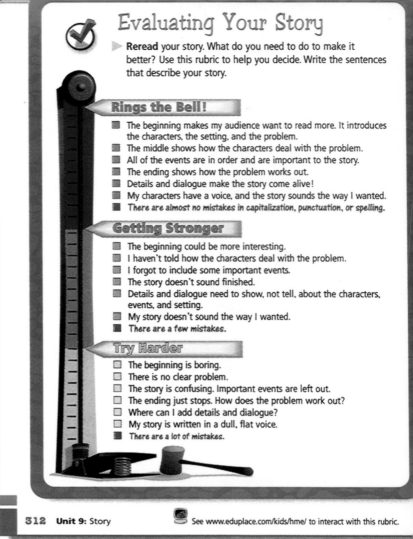

Evaluating Your Story

Reread your story. What do you need to do to make it better? Use this rubric to help you decide. Write the sentences that describe your story.

Rings the Bell!

- The beginning makes my audience want to read more. It introduces the characters, the setting, and the problem.
- The middle shows how the characters deal with the problem.
- All of the events are in order and are important to the story.
- The ending shows how the problem works out.
- Details and dialogue make the story come alive!
- My characters have a voice, and the story sounds the way I wanted.
- *There are almost no mistakes in capitalization, punctuation, or spelling.*

Getting Stronger

- The beginning could be more interesting.
- I haven't told how the characters deal with the problem.
- I forgot to include some important events.
- The story doesn't sound finished.
- Details and dialogue need to show, not tell, about the characters, events, and setting.
- My story doesn't sound the way I wanted.
- *There are a few mistakes.*

Try Harder

- The beginning is boring.
- There is no clear problem.
- The story is confusing. Important events are left out.
- The ending just stops. How does the problem work out?
- Where can I add details and dialogue?
- My story is written in a dull, flat voice.
- *There are a lot of mistakes.*

312 **Unit 9:** Story

See www.eduplace.com/kids/hme/ to interact with this rubric.

Meeting Individual Needs

RETEACHING WORKBOOK, page 89

Revising a Story

Have I — yes

- written a new beginning that grabs readers' attention and introduces the characters, the setting, and the problem? ❑
- added details and dialogue that make the story come alive? ❑
- given the characters a voice and made the story sound the way I want? ❑
- ended the story by telling how the problem worked out? ❑

Revise the following story to make it better. Use the checklist above to help you. Check each box when you have finished your revision. You can use the spaces above the lines, on the sides, and below the paragraph for your changes. Sample answers:

A Job for Dina
~~The Lost Video~~

~~Dina was in trouble.~~ Dina was happy when she had found
in Wrigley's doghouse
the lost videotape. However, she did not stop to think about
paying for the damage.
"The cost to replace this video is $33," said Mr. Wilson.
~~Mr. Wilson told Dina it would cost $33 to replace the videotape.~~
"Do you have the money to pay for it?"
~~He asked her if she had the money to pay for it.~~ He knew what
Dina's answer would be before she began to shake her head.

Dina spent all day Saturday sorting videos and putting
She was proud of her work, and so was Mr. Wilson.
them on their shelves. ~~She did such a good job that Mr.~~
In fact, now Dina is the "Special Saturday Assistant" at
~~Wilson hired her to be his assistant.~~ Hometown Video.

"How can one kid get into so much trouble in so little time?" asked Mr. Wilson. He looked at the crushed videotape on the counter.

WORKBOOK PLUS, page 138

Revising a Story

Have I — yes

- written a new beginning that grabs readers' attention and introduces the characters, the setting, and the problem? ❑
- added details and dialogue that make the story come alive? ❑
- given the characters a voice and made the story sound the way I want? ❑
- ended the story by telling how the problem works out? ❑

Revise the following story to make it better. Use the checklist above to help you. Check each box when you have finished your revision. You can use the spaces above the lines, on the sides, and below the paragraph for your changes. Sample answers:

Travel Adventure
"There isn't a thing in the world that I haven't seen at
~~Jason told his brother Ben that there was nothing left to discover~~
least in a book or on television," said Jason.
~~in the world. He was sure that he had seen everything, at least in a~~
~~book or on television. Ben said no way. So~~ the two brothers set off
on an adventure trip.

They saw a chameleon in Saudi Arabia and a cheetah in Sri Lanka. "I've seen those," said Jason, yawning.

The trip was almost over, and nothing had surprised Jason. The boys were sitting on a hillside in Ethiopia when Jason shouted,
"What's that?" He was staring at a big, wild goat with huge, jagged
"Aha," said Ben. "It's a Walia ibex." He smiled as he thought
horns. ~~Ben told him that it was a Walia ibex.~~
about all the free time he would have when they got home.

"If you're wrong," said his brother Ben, "you'll have to clean my room for a year."
"No problem," said Jason, and

PREWRITING DRAFTING REVISING PROOFREADING PUBLISHING

Revise Your Story

1 **Revise** your story. Use the list of sentences you wrote from the rubric. Work on the parts that you described with sentences from "Getting Stronger" and "Try Harder."

Tech Tip
Always make a backup copy of your story when using a computer. Use the backup copy for revisions. Save the original version for reference.

2 **Have a writing conference.**

When You're the Writer Read your story to a partner. Discuss any questions or problems you are having with it. Take notes to remember what your partner says.

When You're the Listener Tell at least two things you like about the story. Ask questions about anything that is unclear.

The Writing Conference

If you're thinking . . .	**You could say . . .**
I can't follow this story.	What is the main idea of this story?
The story is great, but the beginning doesn't catch my interest.	Can you begin by describing an action, a character, or the setting?
I can't picture these characters. The characters all have the same personality.	What do the characters look like? How do they act? Can you give each character his or her own voice?
I don't understand what the part about _______ has to do with the story.	Why is the part about _______ in the story? Do you need it?
The story just stops.	Can you tell how the problem works out?

3 **Make more revisions** to your story. Use your conference notes and the Revising Strategies on the next page.

Help with Conferencing

ADDITIONAL CONFERENCING QUESTIONS

These questions may be useful during teacher-student conferences.

- Can you add more dialogue to your story?
- Can you add time clues to make the order of events clearer?
- Can you give more details about _________ so that I can picture it clearly?
- Can you add more details to strengthen voice of the story and characters?

EVALUATION TIP

Be alert for students who respond defensively to listeners' questions, and try to determine the reason for it. Point out to writers that it is easier for listeners to find a story's weak points than strong ones. That is because listeners are not as intimately involved with the plot and characters as the writer is.

Lesson Objectives

Students will:

- revise their working draft, based on their evaluations
- discuss their working draft in a writing conference
- make additional revisions to their story, based on their conference notes

Revise Your Story

Focus on Instruction

Revising Reminder

Remind students that revising focuses on making their story clearer and more interesting. They should not worry about mistakes at this stage. If necessary, review the revising techniques on page 20.

- Tell students to look for places where they can add dialogue to their story to make it more interesting.

Conferencing Reminder

Remind students to read their story aloud to their partners and to read slowly, clearly, and at an appropriate volume for their audience and setting.

- Ask listeners to retell the story they hear before beginning the writing conference. This technique will tell writers if any sections of their story are unclear.
- To encourage students to give the writer positive feedback, present these examples: I can easily follow your story events. Your characters are so realistic!
- Students may need help deciding which peer suggestions to implement. Tell them to make those changes that would make the story clearer and more interesting. Then they can make other changes they want.
- Students can use Blackline Master 9–5 during their writing conferences.

MEETING INDIVIDUAL NEEDS — FOR STUDENTS ACQUIRING ENGLISH

Initially, students may not consider peers capable of helping in conferences. Model with a volunteer's story. Ask him or her to read while you model both behavior and questions. Then, on an overhead, demonstrate using the conference notes and the student's own evaluation to make changes to the story. Ask the class if they prefer the original or the changes and why. Finally, provide pens in different colors for revision and then proofreading.

Revising Strategies

Lesson Objectives

Students will:

- add exact nouns, verbs, adjectives, and adverbs to their story
- add prepositional phrases to their story
- rewrite stringy sentences

Focus on Instruction

Elaborating: Word Choice

Ask students what questions they have after reading the sentence in the left column. (Which uncle? How quickly? What contest? What people?) Point out the exact words in the right column that answer their questions.

Elaborating: Details

Have students rewrite the sentence without details by adding prepositional phrases that tell *which one, when,* and *how.* Then have volunteers write their sentences on the board. Discuss how the meaning of the sentence varies as the prepositional phrases change.

Sentence Fluency

- Tell students that stringy sentences are hard to read because too many ideas run together. Ask students to identify the ideas in the stringy sentence. (Jessica had a lot of trading cards; one was old; a collector offered her fifty dollars for it)
- Point out how two sentences are joined with *and* in the smoother sentences. Explain that joining these sentences with *and* shows that they are closely related.

FOR STUDENTS ACQUIRING ENGLISH

Offer more examples of exact nouns, verbs, adjectives, and adverbs. (*puppy* versus *little dog*; *skated* versus *went*; *coffee-colored* versus *brown*; *lazily* versus *slowly*) Instead of explaining these parts of speech at this point, you can give a mini-lesson on prepositions and their uses.

Revising Strategies

Elaborating: Word Choice Exact words help your audience picture the characters, setting, and action in your story.

Without Exact Words	With Exact Words
Lindy's uncle completed the contest quickly while people watched.	Lindy's favorite uncle completed the skateboarding contest in record time while her friends watched.

▶ Find two places in your story where you can add exact nouns, verbs, adjectives, and adverbs.

Use the Thesaurus Plus on page H79.

Elaborating: Details Insert prepositional phrases to add more information to a sentence.

Without Details	Elaborated with Details
Carlos wrote a story.	Carlos wrote a story with his friends for a class assignment.

▶ Add at least two prepositional phrases to your story.

GRAMMAR LINK *See also page 246.*

Sentence Fluency Avoid stringy sentences. Your audience may get lost if your sentence has too many *ands*. Rewrite your sentence to make it clearer.

Stringy Sentence	Smoother Sentences
Jessica had a lot of trading cards **and** one was old **and** a collector offered her fifty dollars for it.	Jessica had a lot of trading cards. One was old. A collector offered her fifty dollars for it. Jessica had a lot of trading cards. One was old, and a collector offered her fifty dollars for it.

▶ Look for stringy sentences in your story, and rewrite them to make them clearer.

314 **Unit 9:** Story

Meeting Individual Needs

● RETEACHING WORKBOOK, page 90

Elaborating: Details

Elaborate by adding details to a story. You can insert prepositional phrases to add more information to a sentence.	
Without details	Monica packed everything she needed.
Elaborated with details	Monica packed everything she needed for her stay with Grandma.

The following story is boring because it does not contain enough details. Revise each sentence of the story. Use prepositional phrases to add information.

The Dove family stayed at the Red Rooster Resort. The family watched birds. The flamingos reminded Susan Dove of people on stilts. Darryl Dove watched a hawk gliding. Edie Dove won a hummingbird feeder.

1. The Dove family stayed at the Red Rooster Resort.
   The Dove family stayed at the Red Rooster Resort in Florida.
2. The family watched birds.
   The family watched birds by the lake.
3. The flamingos reminded Susan Dove of people on stilts.
   The flamingos in the water reminded Susan Dove of people on stilts.
4. Darryl Dove watched a hawk gliding.
   Darryl Dove watched a hawk gliding across the sky above the trees.
5. Edie Dove won a hummingbird feeder.
   Edie Dove won a hummingbird feeder in a contest.

▲■ WORKBOOK PLUS, page 139

Elaborating: Details

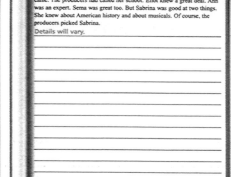

Without details	Sandra ate an apple.
Elaborated with details	Sandra ate an apple in the kitchen with her sister.

The following story would be more interesting if it had more details. Revise the story by adding prepositional phrases to some of the sentences.

Sabrina never dreamed that she might be on a quiz show. Then the call came. The producers had called her school. Eliot knew a great deal. Ann was an expert. Sema was great too. But Sabrina was good at two things. She knew about American history and about musicals. Of course, the producers picked Sabrina.

Details will vary.

PREWRITING DRAFTING REVISING PROOFREADING PUBLISHING

Proofread Your Story

Proofread your story, using the Proofreading Checklist and the Grammar and Spelling Connections. Proofread for one skill at a time. Use a class dictionary to check spellings.

Proofreading Checklist

Did I
- ✓ indent each paragraph?
- ✓ begin and end sentences correctly?
- ✓ write dialogue correctly?
- ✓ make subjects and verbs agree?
- ✓ spell all words correctly?

Use the Guide to Capitalization, Punctuation, and Usage on page H55.

Proofreading Marks
- ¶ Indent
- ∧ Add
- Delete
- ≡ Capital letter
- / Small letter

Proofreading Tip

Read your story aloud to a friend. You may notice mistakes when you hear them.

Grammar and Spelling Connections

Writing Dialogue Put quotation marks around a speaker's exact words. Put the end punctuation inside the quotation marks.

"Watch out for the runaway horses!" warned Jake Johnson.
Theresa said slyly, "I know who can solve the mystery."

GRAMMAR LINK *See also pages 182 and 184.*

Subject-Verb Agreement Use singular verbs with singular subjects. Use plural verbs with plural subjects.

Singular Subjects	Plural Subjects
The eagle scoops me up.	The eagles scoop me up.
It circles the sky.	They circle the sky.

GRAMMAR LINK *See also page 104.*

Spelling Long *i* The |ī| sound is often spelled *i, igh,* or *i*-consonant-*e*.

mild, slight, strike

See the Spelling Guide on page H65.

Go to www.eduplace.com/kids/hme/ for proofreading practice.

Help with Proofreading

MANAGEMENT TIP

Have each student keep a personal checklist of skills that he or she needs to proofread for. Staple the list to the student's folder.

TECH TIP

Have students boldface or highlight any words that might be misspelled to remember to check them in a dictionary.

EVALUATION TIP

Check proofread stories with students to make sure all proper nouns, such as character names, begin with a capital letter.

Lesson Objective

Students will:
- proofread their story

Proofread Your Story

Focus on Instruction

Proofreading Reminders

- Remind students that the proofreading stage is when they should correct capitalization, usage, punctuation, and spelling. Encourage them to use the Guide to Capitalization, Punctuation, and Usage.
- If necessary, review with students when and how to use each proofreading mark. Have students use a different colored pen or pencil to mark their proofreading corrections.
- For proofreading practice, see the usage and mechanics lessons in the grammar units and the Mixed Review practice in each grammar unit Checkup.

- Review each item in the checklist, using any related Grammar and Spelling Connections. For additional support, review the lessons listed in the Grammar Links.
- Use the dialogue examples in the student book to point out that when the speaker is mentioned after the dialogue, a period ends the sentence. When the speaker is mentioned before the dialogue, a comma precedes the dialogue.
- Point out that only present tense verbs require different endings for singular and plural.
- Write on the board the three different ways to spell |ī|. Then have volunteers suggest words for each spelling. Students should use a dictionary to help with spelling.

INTERNET CONNECTION Have your students go to www.eduplace.com/kids/hme/ for online proofreading practice that is fun.

MEETING INDIVIDUAL NEEDS

FOR STUDENTS ACQUIRING ENGLISH

Make sure students have a different colored pen and understand that they will be correcting their work as if they were the teacher or editor. Begin proofing as a class. Go through each item together. Encourage students to work on their stories as you edit yours or a volunteer's on an overhead projector.

Lesson Objectives

Students will:

- make a neat final copy of their story
- choose a way to publish or share their story
- reflect on the writing experience
- evaluate their story in comparison to other compositions in their writing portfolio

Publish Your Story

Focus on Instruction

- Before students make their final copy, have them decide how they will publish or share their story. Review their decision with them to help them make any special plans.
- Help students make neat corrections to the final copy rather than rewrite their paper.

Keeping a Writing Portfolio

- **Selection** A paper might be selected because it is
  - ✓ generally noteworthy
  - ✓ a good example of a particular criterion
  - ✓ an example of a particular kind of writing
  - ✓ an example from a certain time in the school year
  - ✓ a typical example of the student's work
- **Labeling** For every paper, have students complete a cover sheet giving the title, date of completion, and reason for inclusion.
- **Review** Periodically have students remove papers that no longer reflect their best work or aren't needed as baselines.
- **Evaluation** Periodically review students' portfolios with them to discuss growth and areas that need improvement.

The Writing Process: PREWRITING · DRAFTING · REVISING · PROOFREADING · PUBLISHING

Publish Your Story

1. **Make a neat final copy** of your story. Be sure you have fixed all mistakes.
2. **Title** your story. Make your audience curious with a title that attracts their attention, such as "There's More Than One Way to Scare a Pig," rather than "A Scared Pig."

GRAMMAR TIP *Capitalize the first, last, and all important words in the title.*

3. **Publish** or share your story. Think about your audience to help you decide how to share. See the Ideas for Sharing box.

Tips for Making a Picture Book

- Plan what part of the story you will put on each page.
- Include interesting pictures to illustrate the story.
- Make an eye-catching cover with a title.

Ideas for Sharing

Write It

- Make your story into a picture book for a young child.
- Write your story in the form of a comic strip.

Say It

- With a partner or small group, read your story aloud as though it is on the radio.

Show It

- Make puppets of the main characters.
- Act out your story with props. See page 324 for tips.

Reflect

Write about your writing experience. Use these questions to get started.

- What did you enjoy most about writing your story? What was hard to do?
- How does this story compare with other papers you have written?

316 **Unit 9:** Story

Help with Publishing

TIPS FOR IDEAS FOR SHARING

Comic Strip Tell students that some comic strip frames might contain only a picture; others will contain a picture and dialogue in speech balloons.

Reading Aloud Remind students who choose to read their story to use appropriate rate, volume, pitch, and tone.

Puppets Provide students with cloth, markers, glue, and string to shape the puppets and create their physical characteristics.

TECH TIP

Show children how to increase the top or bottom margins on the computer to allow room for illustrations.

SCHOOL-HOME CONNECTION

Have students act out their story for family members.

Assessment Link

Writing Prompts

Use these prompts as story ideas or to practice for a test. Decide who your audience will be, and write your story in a way that they will understand and enjoy.

1 Write a fantasy story about an animal that becomes a hero. Where will the story take place? What problem does the animal solve? Will your story be silly? scary?

2 A character is walking through the woods and discovers a footprint that is eight feet long. Write a story that tells what happens next.

3 Write a story about a character who finds a jeweled box that has a secret message inside. Who finds the box? What does the secret message say? What does the character do next?

4 What would it be like to live on the moon? What would everyday life be like? What problems could happen? Write a story about a character living in a moon colony one hundred years from now.

Writing Across the Curriculum

5 **FINE ART**
Who is the girl in this picture? Where is she going, or where has she been on her bicycle? Does the dog belong to her? Write a story about the girl and the dog.

Oklahoma City Art Museum

Carri and Cocoa, by Robert Vickrey

About the Artist

About Robert Vickrey

Robert Vickrey is a modern artist known for his detailed, realistic paintings of such scenes as children playing on pavement; finely textured old stone walls and trees; and bicycles casting intricate shadows.

He was born in 1926 in New York but grew up on a ranch in Nevada. Vickrey recalls that the first picture he ever drew was of the brand on the cattle at the ranch. His choice of subject matter as a boy reflected an interest that continues in his adult paintings: finding abstract shapes in realistic settings.

Vickrey gets ideas for his paintings from scenes glimpsed on the street, in theaters, on boats, or in nature around him. He often uses his children as subjects. For instance, his daughter Carri posed for the painting *Carri and Cocoa*. Vickrey has also done magazine illustrating, including more than seventy-five cover portraits for *Time*.

Writing Prompts

Objectives

Students will:
- review prompts for choosing a topic or to practice for a writing test
- view critically a work of fine art and use it to write a story

Using the Prompts

You can use the prompts on this page in several ways.

- Have students review the prompts to help spark ideas when they are choosing their own topics for a story. Suggest that students choose one or two prompts that interest them and brainstorm ideas of their own.
- Choose a prompt to provide practice for a writing test. Use it with the Test Practice on the next page.
- Choose a prompt that fits with a related topic in another subject area to integrate writing a story across the curriculum.
- Direct students' attention to *Carrie and Cocoa* by Robert Vickrey. Explain that the artist doesn't give specific details about the girl and the dog in the painting. Instead, he uses lines, patterns, and shadows to create a mood. Ask students what emotions they feel when they look at this scene.

INTERNET CONNECTION Send your students to www.eduplace.com/kids/hme/ for more writing ideas. You can also find and print these prompts at www.eduplace.com/rdg/hme/.

MEETING INDIVIDUAL NEEDS

FOR STUDENTS ACQUIRING ENGLISH

Read through each prompt, acting out and making sure students understand the ideas presented. Note that the writing prompts lend themselves to long stories. Help students narrow the topics to a manageable size for the time allowed and their abilities. (For example: Prompt 4–Write one moon dweller's adventure; Prompt 5–make up a specific event from the details in the picture.)

Test Practice

Objective

Students will:

- learn strategies for evaluating a writing prompt and writing a story for a test

Using the Test Practice

- Guide students through the page and discuss the strategies for evaluating and responding to a prompt to write a story.
- Review the rubric on page 312 with students before they write their practice test.
- Have students use the prompt on this page or one on the previous page to write a story. Apply the same time constraints or other restrictions or qualifications specific to the testing requirements used in your school.

INTERNET CONNECTION Go to www.eduplace.com/rdg/hme/ for examples of benchmark papers.

INTERNET CONNECTION Send your students to www.eduplace.com/kids/hme/ for graphic organizers. You can also find and print these organizers at www.eduplace.com/rdg/hme/.

MEETING INDIVIDUAL NEEDS

FOR STUDENTS ACQUIRING ENGLISH

Prewriting may be the biggest challenge for students acquiring English. Encourage students to draw or map their ideas before writing. Also give them an opportunity to talk in small groups about what they might write. As a class, generate a list of possible words to be used in the story: *beware, treasure, fairy,* and so on.

Assessment Link

Test Practice

This prompt to write a story is like ones you might find on a writing test. Read the prompt.

> **Write a story about a character who finds a jeweled box that has a secret message inside. Who finds the box? What does the secret message say? What does the character do next?**

Here are some strategies to help you do a good job responding to a prompt like this.

Remember that a story is a narrative made up by the author.

1. Look for clue words that tell what to write about. What are the clue words in the prompt above?
2. Choose a topic that fits the clue words. Write the clue words and your topic.

Clue Words	My Topic
a character who finds a jeweled box that has a secret message inside	I will write about a detective who discovers a treasure map inside a jeweled box.

3. Plan your writing. Use a story map.

Characters	Setting	Plot
		Beginning: **Middle:** **End:**

4. You will get a good score if you remember the description of what kind of story rings the bell in the rubric on page 312.

 Go to www.eduplace.com/kids/hme/ for graphic organizers.

Writing a Play

A **play** is a story written to be performed on a stage by actors. The author tells the story through the characters' words and actions. Read Jillian's play.

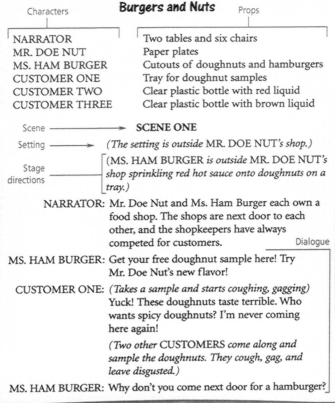

Burgers and Nuts

Characters	Props
NARRATOR	Two tables and six chairs
MR. DOE NUT	Paper plates
MS. HAM BURGER	Cutouts of doughnuts and hamburgers
CUSTOMER ONE	Tray for doughnut samples
CUSTOMER TWO	Clear plastic bottle with red liquid
CUSTOMER THREE	Clear plastic bottle with brown liquid

Scene → **SCENE ONE**

Setting → *(The setting is outside* MR. DOE NUT*'s shop.)*

Stage directions: *(*MS. HAM BURGER *is outside* MR. DOE NUT*'s shop sprinkling red hot sauce onto doughnuts on a tray.)*

NARRATOR: Mr. Doe Nut and Ms. Ham Burger each own a food shop. The shops are next door to each other, and the shopkeepers have always competed for customers.

Dialogue

MS. HAM BURGER: Get your free doughnut sample here! Try Mr. Doe Nut's new flavor!

CUSTOMER ONE: *(Takes a sample and starts coughing, gagging)* Yuck! These doughnuts taste terrible. Who wants spicy doughnuts? I'm never coming here again!

(Two other CUSTOMERS *come along and sample the doughnuts. They cough, gag, and leave disgusted.)*

MS. HAM BURGER: Why don't you come next door for a hamburger?

more ▶

Writing a Play

Lesson Objective

Students will:

- read a model of a play and identify its parts

Focus on the Model

- Ask students what they think is the purpose of a play. (for actors to use words and actions to tell a story that entertains an audience) Point out that a play is like a story that is told through the characters' dialogue and action.
- Tell students they will read Jillian's play about two shop owners. Have students read the introduction to the play.
- Before students read the play, explain that the blue call outs highlight the parts of a play and that students will learn about those parts after they read the play.
- Ask volunteers to choose a character and act out the play. Props are not necessary for this read-through.

Students can also listen to the model on audiotape.

FOR STUDENTS ACQUIRING ENGLISH

Make sure students understand the humor of the two main characters' names. Have students say the names aloud. After students read the model, have volunteers explain *doughnut, hamburger, hot sauce,* and *syrup.* Ask: "Would you put hot sauce on a doughnut? Would you put syrup on a hamburger? Why or why not?"

MR. DOE NUT: *(*MR. DOE NUT *sees* MS. HAM BURGER *taking his customers.)* Where's everyone going? What have you done to my doughnuts, Ms. Ham Burger?

SCENE TWO

(The setting is MS. HAM BURGER*'s shop.)*

MR. DOE NUT: *(Walking into the shop and speaking in a sly voice)* Why, hello, Ms. Burger. I have something for you. *(He pulls a bottle of brown liquid out of his apron pocket.)* It's a new cooking oil. It will make your burgers taste terrific. It smells like syrup, but it works like cooking oil, and customers love it!

MS. HAM BURGER: Gee, that's great! Thanks!

*(*MS. HAM BURGER *takes the bottle, although she's a bit suspicious.)*

MR. DOE NUT: Have a nice day! *(He walks out giggling.)*

*(*MS. HAM BURGER *cooks a fresh batch of hamburgers with* MR. DOE NUT*'s sauce and serves them to two customers who come in.)*

CUSTOMER TWO: *(Taking a bite)* Oh, gross! This tastes awful!

CUSTOMER THREE: Yuck! What is that terrible taste? I'm never coming here again!

*(*MS. HAM BURGER *looks at the bottle from* MR. DOE NUT *and storms out of her shop.)*

SCENE THREE

(The setting is MR. DOE NUT*'s shop.)*

MS. HAM BURGER: *(Racing into* MR. DOE NUT*'s shop)* You . . . you knew that wasn't cooking oil!

MR. DOE NUT: That's right. Just like you knew that awful hot sauce would ruin my doughnuts!

MS. HAM BURGER: *(Sighs)* This is crazy.

MR. DOE NUT: We should work this out. *(Holds out his hand)*

MS. HAM BURGER: *(Looking at the floor)* I guess so. *(Shaking hands with* MR. DOE NUT*)* You know, instead of fighting, maybe if we put our heads together, we could come up with some new ideas for a business together.

MR. DOE NUT: As a matter of fact, I have a great idea! I can use the syrup to make a new doughnut flavor and you can use the hot sauce on your hamburgers. *(The shopkeepers sit down and pretend to keep talking.)*

NARRATOR: Mr. Doe Nut and Ms. Ham Burger became best of friends. Two months later they opened a new shop called Burgers and Nuts. Business has never been better.

CURTAIN

Reading As a Writer See TE margin for answers.

- The list of **characters** tells who is in the play. *Who are the characters in Jillian's play?*
- The **props** are the items the characters will use in the play. *What props are used in Jillian's play?*
- A **scene** presents the action that happens in one place at a certain time. *What happens in Scene One?*
- The **setting** tells where and when the action takes place. *What is the setting for Scene One?*
- The **stage directions** tell what the characters do, how they do it, and how they speak. *Which stage directions in Scene Two tell what the customers do?*
- The **dialogue** is what the characters say. It can reveal what they are thinking, seeing, and feeling. *What does Ms. Ham Burger say when she races into Mr. Doe Nut's shop at the beginning of Scene Three?*

more ▶

Writing a Play *continued*

Focus on Instruction

- Discuss with the class the explanations of the call outs given in the Reading As a Writer section.
- Point out that a character's dialogue follows the colon after the character's name.
- Have students find the stage directions before the dialogue of Customer One. Point out that stage directions are in parentheses and italics.
- Have volunteers answer the questions.

Answers for Reading As a Writer

- The characters are the Narrator, Mr. Doe Nut, Ms. Ham Burger, Customer One, Customer Two, and Customer Three.
- The props include two tables, six chairs, paper plates, cutouts of doughnuts and hamburgers, clear plastic bottle with brown liquid, clear plastic bottle with red liquid, and a tray for doughnut samples.
- Ms. Ham Burger tries to ruin Mr. Doe Nut's business.
- The setting for Scene One is outside Mr. Doe Nut's shop.
- *Taking a bite* tells what the customers do.
- Ms. Ham Burger says *You . . . you knew that wasn't cooking oil!*

MEETING INDIVIDUAL NEEDS

FOR STUDENTS ACQUIRING ENGLISH

Point out each of the highlighted words in the description. Ask students to find an example of stage directions. Ask how these are different from the lines the actors say. Name and explain the parentheses and italics. Have volunteers act out stage directions such as *storms out*. Also explain the word *curtain*.

Lesson Objective

Students will:
- choose a story idea and plan to write a short play

How to Write a Play

Focus on Instruction

- Remind students that the purpose of a play is to entertain the audience. Tell students to keep the action and dialogue in their play simple so the audience can follow what is happening.
- Tell students that a character's dialogue should not only help tell the story but it should also give the audience a picture of the speaker's personality. Point out that word choice can be used to develop characters.
- Review how to use a story map. You may also wish to put a sample story map on the board.
- Have students discuss their story idea in small groups before they write. Have them ask questions of each other to help focus their ideas.

Connecting to the Criteria

Have students review the characteristics of a good play described in the Reading As a Writer section of this lesson. Tell students to evaluate their play by using these characteristics.

How to Write a Play

1. **Think** about your audience. Choose a story idea for a short play that will interest or entertain them. You will need characters who do a lot of talking. Include only a few characters and one or two settings.

   You can use a T-chart to help you list details about your characters. Look at the sample T-chart below for Mr. Doe Nut and Ms. Ham Burger. Notice that the characters' names are across the top and details about each character are listed below his or her name.

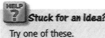

> HELP
> ***Stuck for an Idea?***
> Try one of these.
> - a favorite story or scene from a book
> - a story of your own
> - an exciting, funny, or surprising experience that you or someone else had

Mr. Doe Nut	Ms. Ham Burger
• owns a food shop	• owns a food shop
• competes with Ms. Ham Burger for business	• competes with Mr. Doe Nut for business
• forgiving	• prankster

2. **Plan** your play. Just like a story, a play has a beginning, a middle, and an end. Look at the story map below to help you plan your play. Add more details about your characters, setting, and plot as you plan.

Character	Setting	Plot
		Beginning
		Middle
		End

Help with Writing a Play

MORE TOPIC IDEAS

Suggest these possibilities.
- Students can describe a make-believe adventure they might have on a school day.
- They can write a play with characters that are inanimate objects, such as food in a cafeteria.

TECH TIP

Show students how to set up their document with tabs and hanging indents to achieve a play format.

USING RESOURCES
- Invite a local theater director to speak to students about the qualities of a good play.
- Have students attend a performance of a play or have them watch one on video.
- Students can e-mail their questions about plays to a member of a local theater group.

EVALUATION TIP

Tape-record each student reading the first draft of his or her play. Later, play the tape back and have each writer answer the questions for revision.

3. **Write** your play.
   - List your characters.
   - Write stage directions telling what actions the characters will be taking at the beginning of the play.
   - Write the dialogue. Write it the way you think the characters would talk. The dialogue should help tell the story.
   - Write more stage directions throughout the play to tell how the characters talk and act.
   - If the action moves from one place to another, divide your play into scenes. Describe each setting in stage directions.
   - End your play in a way that wraps up the action. When you have finished, write BLACKOUT or CURTAIN.
4. **Revise** your play. Ask yourself these questions.
   - Is the plot clear?
   - Does the characters' dialogue sound natural?
   - Should any characters be taken out or added?
   - Do the final events make the play feel finished?
5. **Proofread** your play. Use a dictionary to check your spelling. Check that you have included punctuation such as exclamation points and question marks. These will help the actors read their lines with feeling.
6. **Make** a neat final copy.
7. **Perform** your play for an audience, such as your classmates or another class.

See pages 324–325 for tips on dramatizing.

Ask some classmates to read the draft of your play aloud with you. Do they have any suggestions?

Lesson Objective

Students will:
- write, revise, proofread, and perform their play for an audience

Focus on Instruction

- Suggest that students refer to their story map as they list their characters. Students can list the characters in the order in which they will appear.
- Point out that stage directions do not have to indicate every little action or tell how every bit of dialogue should be spoken. Remind students that they will tell their story mostly through dialogue, using stage directions only as necessary.
- Ask a few volunteers to tell characteristics of one of their characters. Then ask students if they think all the characters mentioned would talk the same way. Discuss with students how the different characters' dialogue might vary.
- Before students revise their play, they might work with a partner, reading aloud all or part of the play, using a different voice for each character and reading the stage directions to help the partner visualize the action. Encourage partners to discuss what they liked about the play and what might have been confusing.
- Review with students the Proofreading Checklist on page 315 and the use of proofreading marks.

SCHOOL-HOME CONNECTION Invite families to visit the school and watch students perform their play.

Discuss with each student whether his or her play should go into the portfolio. Consider these possible reasons: (1) it is an especially good piece of writing; (2) it reflects a particular aspect of writing that the student did well; (3) it shows an aspect of writing that needs more work and could be used as a baseline for measuring growth.

Dramatizing

Lesson Objectives

Students will:

- prepare and present a dramatic interpretation of a poem, experience, story, or play
- communicate with a rate, volume, pitch, and tone appropriate for the audience and setting

Focus on Instruction

- Tell students that the root word for *dramatize* is *drama*. A drama is a story told through action and dialogue before an audience.
- To generate discussion about the interpretive nature of drama, ask students if they have ever acted in plays or other performances. Which characters did they play? How did they decide how to move and speak in the role they performed?
- Have volunteers read the example aloud, using variations in the way they speak and act to show how they think Annika feels.
- Have students identify the feelings expressed in each photograph. Ask volunteers to stand and demonstrate similar emotions, without speaking. Then have volunteers demonstrate those emotions with words alone. Finally, have volunteers express the emotions through words, facial expressions, and gestures.
- Then ask students to describe a character from a television show, movie, or play. Have students speculate about how the actor knew which voice and tone to use. Explain that actors try to speak and behave as they think their characters might. Often, professional actors do research to prepare for a new role. They may study history if the story took place in the past, or they may observe real people who hold jobs similar to ones held by the characters they will play. This helps actors behave in more believable ways.

Dramatizing

Have you ever thought about being an actor? Actors dramatize, or act out, characters from stories, poems, or plays. They do this by speaking and moving the way they think the characters would.

Start Thinking

Read the example below. How do you think Annika feels? How might the sound of her voice change as she talks?

> "We played our hearts out, but we still lost the game. The most frustrating part is that we only lost by two points. I know we can play better next week if everyone keeps practicing. If we all put in some extra practice time this weekend, we could be great!"

Look at the photographs below. Can you figure out which face goes with which words or phrases from the example? If you were to act out the example, how and when would you change the look on your face? Would your expressions look like Annika's?

Note on Oral Traditions

- Explain to students that before books were widespread and people could read, stories were shared and passed on orally through storytelling or dramatizing. Different regions of the country and the world had their own stories. Those stories incorporated the climate, geography, plants, and animals of the region as well as the way of life of the people who lived there. Different cultures also created stories that expressed their beliefs and traditions.
- Discuss with students some of the stories that reflect their own region and cultures. Have them read the stories in the books listed with this lesson or in others available in your school or local library to compare oral traditions from other regions and cultures with their own.

Here are some guides to help you dramatize a story, a poem, or a play.

Guides for Dramatizing

1. Put yourself in your character's shoes. What is the character like? How does the character feel?
2. Use your speaking voice. Change the volume, rate, pitch, and tone of your voice to show your character's feelings and mood. A shaky, high voice could show fear. A low, loud voice might show courage.
3. Use facial expressions. A wink might tell your audience that your character is up to something.
4. Use movements instead of words to show what you mean. A character might shrug his shoulders when he doesn't know how to answer a question.
5. Speak clearly but naturally. Think about your audience and the place in which you will be performing. Be sure everyone can hear you.
6. Practice reading your lines. Write key words or entire lines on note cards. Use these if you need a hint to remember your lines.

Using Your Voice	
volume	means loudness
rate	means speed
pitch	means how high or how low it sounds
tone	means mood

Apply It

Answers will vary.

Choose a poem or part of a story or play to dramatize. Follow the Guides for Dramatizing as you practice. Perform for another group or for the class.

- What was your character's mood? Did it change?
- In what ways did you show different feelings?
- What worked well? What would you do differently if you were to dramatize this character again?

Bibliography

Regional

- ***The Bunyans*** by Audrey Wood
- ***Cendrillon*** by Robert D. San Souci
- ***Pecos Bill*** by Steven Kellogg
- ***The Lizard and the Sun*** by Alma Flor Ada

Cultural

- ***Senor Cat's Romance*** by Lucía M. González
- ***The Ox of the Wonderful Horns*** by Ashley Bryan
- ***How the Stars Fell into the Sky*** by Jerrie Oughton
- ***Brother Rabbit*** by Minfong Ho

Focus on Instruction

- Have volunteers read aloud the Guides for Dramatizing. Discuss each guide as necessary to clarify meaning. Ask students to think of other ways they could change the volume, rate, pitch, and tone of their voice to show feelings and mood. For instance, how could they use voice to show excitement? (Sample answer: speak very quickly and loudly) How could they use voice to show fatigue? (Sample answer: speak very slowly, quietly, or in a monotone)
- Remind students that if speaking to a large group or in a large room, they should project their voices so that they can be heard throughout the room. This requires that they speak loudly without shouting.
- Tell students that there is no single way to dramatize a scene. There can be many different interpretations.
- To provide practice applying the guides, have students imagine that they are a ten-year-old who gets locked in a toy store overnight. Have volunteers take turns using dialogues, facial expressions, and gestures to respond to the following prompts.

  How does the character feel when he or she first realizes the situation?

  How does the character feel in the middle of the night?

  How does the character feel when the store manager unlocks the door in the morning?

Apply It

- Tell students to keep their dramatizations short (one or two minutes) and to take that amount of time into consideration when choosing what to dramatize. Remind students that if they are presenting part of a play or story, they should choose lines that still will make sense out of context.
- Before answering the questions in the book, have students work with partners to provide feedback about what in the performance worked well and what could have been improved.

FOR STUDENTS ACQUIRING ENGLISH

As students read the example and guides, pause to discuss *played our hearts out, put yourself in your character's shoes, shrug his shoulders* and the word *wink*. Use examples to help students understand volume, rate, pitch, and tone. Discuss how gestures can have different meanings in different cultures.

Comparing Stories in Books and Movies

Lesson Objectives

Students will:

- compare and contrast print media with film
- evaluate a filmed version of a book

Focus on Instruction

- Ask students which books they have read and also seen as films. Have volunteers tell how the movie was similar to and different from the book. Ask students what they liked best about the movie and about the book. Discuss which version they preferred and why.
- Ask students why a movie might be better than a book and a book better than a movie. (Sample answers: A movie can show vivid scenes, and it can show feelings through the characters' actions. A book lets the reader use his or her imagination.)
- Emphasize that a movie does not have to be the same as the original story in order to be good.
- Ask students which they prefer and why: seeing a movie and then reading the book, or reading the book and then seeing the movie.
- Tell students that many people influence how a movie tells a story. The movie studio determines how much money to spend on the movie, which in turn affects who and how many people will act in the film, and how elaborate the costumes, set, and special effects can be. Others who affect a movie include the producer, who is responsible for the overall management of the movie; the director, who directs the actors; a screenwriter, who writes the script; and actors, who interpret the story. In contrast, usually the author, the editor, and perhaps an illustrator influence how a book tells a story.

Comparing Stories in Books and Movies

Movies are often made from stories that were first written in books. Often moviemakers change the stories. That's because books and movies tell stories in different ways. The chart below shows some of the reasons why telling a story in a book is different from telling it in a movie.

Reading the Story	Watching the Story
Books use words to tell the story. The words describe the characters and the setting. Readers use the words to create pictures in their minds.	Movies use images and sounds to tell the story. The audience sees and hears the characters. Often, the action takes place in settings built by the moviemakers.
Readers can tell what a character is thinking or feeling from what the writer says about the character.	Actors show what the characters are thinking and feeling. They look, speak, and behave the way they think the characters would.
Readers can flip back and forth in a book to reread or to look ahead in the story. They can read the book as quickly or as slowly as they like.	People watching a movie in a theater cannot go back to watch something they have already seen. They also must wait to see what happens next and how the story ends.

Thinking Further

Written stories can be long or short, but most movies are about two hours long. When a story is too long for a movie, moviemakers may choose to leave out parts of it. They may add scenes when a story is too short.

Was a story you like changed when it became a movie? Use these guides to see how the movie version is different from the written story.

Guides for Comparing Stories in Books and Movies

1 Plot
- Are there events in the book that weren't in the movie? If so, why do you think they were left out?
- Are there events in the movie that weren't in the book? If so, why do you think they were added?
- Does the movie end the same way as the book?

2 Characters
- Are there any characters in the book who don't appear in the movie? Are there any characters in the movie who aren't in the book?
- Are the main characters the same in both versions? Are they different? In what ways?

3 Setting
- Is the setting in the book the same as in the movie?
- If the setting is different, how does it change the story?

Apply It

Choose a book you have read that has been made into a movie. After watching the movie, make a list of things that are the same and that are different between the two stories. Use the guides above and these questions to help you. Answers will vary.

- Which did you like better, the book or the movie? Why?
- What were the biggest differences between the book and the movie? Why do you think these changes were made?

Books with Movie Versions
- *Jumanji*
- *Harriet the Spy*
- *The Secret Garden*
- *Sarah, Plain and Tall*
- *James and the Giant Peach*

Focus on Instruction

- Have volunteers read aloud the Guides for Comparing Stories in Books and Movies. Discuss each guide as necessary to clarify meaning.
- To provide practice comparing books and movies, examine with students how mood is created in a book and in a movie and how it is translated from the page to the screen. Start by reading aloud a chapter from a book. Discuss with students how the author uses specific words to create the mood in the reader's mind. Then show the corresponding scene in the movie version. Discuss the effect of lighting, music, actors' actions, and the tone of voice used to speak the dialogue. Sample questions:

  How do the actors' facial expressions, body language, and tone of voice affect the viewers' understanding of the characters?

  How does the visualization of the setting affect the viewers' understanding or feelings about the story?

  What technical effects were used? How do they affect the viewers' understanding or enjoyment of the story?

Apply It

- Suggest that students make a chart to record information about the plot, characters, and setting in the movie and the book. Before students watch the movie, have them fill in information about the book. Have them complete the chart after viewing the movie.
- Remind students to include a topic sentence and concluding sentence and to give strong reasons for the opinions they express. Tell them to include examples from the movie or book to clarify information.

MEETING INDIVIDUAL NEEDS

FOR STUDENTS ACQUIRING ENGLISH

Write *plot, characters, setting*. Have students say the terms after you; review the meaning. Ask for examples from stories students have read in class. List the students' examples under the three terms; use words or brief phrases. Later, help students compare a specific book and movie and respond to the "Guides" questions.

About Section 2

This section includes two developmental writing units for instructions and a research report, using the writing process.

Special Focus features provide instruction for writing to compare and contrast, writing to solve a problem, writing a news article, and completing a form.

Communication Links lessons develop students' listening, speaking, and viewing skills.

Getting Started

- **Listening for Information:** A one-page lesson with guidelines specific to listening for information (A selection for reading aloud is in the Teacher's Edition.)
- **Writing Informational Paragraphs:** A seven-page segment focusing on the structure and organization of expository paragraphs and strategies for elaboration

Unit 10 Writing Instructions

Unit features include:

Published model "Knuckle Down That Taw" by Beth Kennedy, from *Highlights for Children*

Student model Instructions by Colin McMillan, working draft and final copy

Mode-specific characteristics What Makes Great Instructions?

Focus Skill lessons
Prewriting: Organizing Your Instructions
Drafting: Using Details
Drafting: Good Beginnings and Endings

Rubric Evaluating Your Instructions

Revising Strategies
Elaborating: Word Choice (exact verbs)
Elaborating: Details (adverbs)
Sentence Fluency (varying sentence length)

Assessment Links Writing Prompts, Test Practice

Special Focus on Explaining
Compare and Contrast Model and instructions for writing about the similarities and differences between two subjects

Communication Links
Listening/Speaking: Giving and Following Instructions Guidelines and practice for giving and following verbal instructions

Viewing/Media: Comparing Visual Information Guidelines and practice for evaluating different forms of visual presentation

Section 2

Explaining and Informing

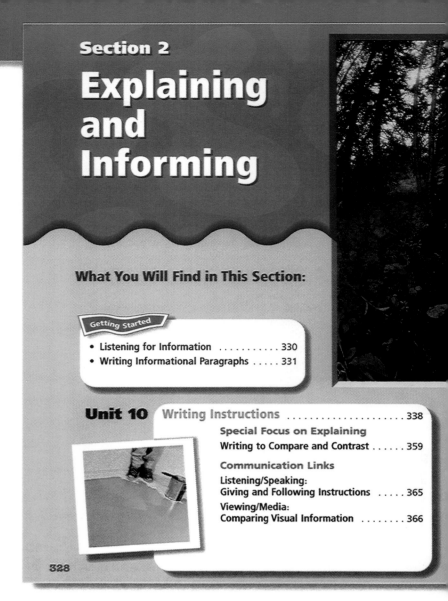

What You Will Find in This Section:

Getting Started

328

Independent Writing

In addition to the focused writing tasks in this section, students can benefit by having time that is set aside each day or several times a week for them to write in their journals or work on other self-selected writing activities, such as letters, poems, stories, book reviews, movie reviews, news articles, records, problem solving, announcements, written requests, or messages. Emphasize the importance of thinking about purpose and audience (noting that sometimes the students may be their own audience) and choosing an appropriate writing format that suits both.

Supporting Sentences

Supporting sentences usually follow the topic sentence. They contain details that explain the main idea. In informational writing, some details are facts, such as numbers. **Facts** can be proved true. Other details are **sensory words** that describe how things look, smell, feel, taste, and sound.

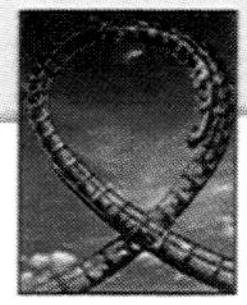

Roller coasters are built to scare you. Some are 400 feet high and 5,000 feet long. A coaster's hair-raising speed can strike fear into a rider's heart. A California coaster, for example, zips around at 100 miles per hour. Scariest of all are the steep drops. On some coasters, the fall can be 200 feet. That's like dropping from a 10-story building! No wonder people scream!

Think and Discuss What facts do you find about roller coasters? What sensory words? Sample answers: facts—400 feet high, 5,000 feet long, fall 200 feet; sensory words—steep, hair-raising, fear, scream

Ordering Details Supporting sentences are arranged in an order that makes sense. In the capybara paragraph on page 331, the details start at the animal's head and work backward. Details in the roller coaster paragraph above are arranged from least scary to scariest. **Transitional words**, such as *also, however, for example, more important,* and *finally,* help the reader see connections between sentences. How are details ordered in the paragraph below? What transitional words can you find?

Visitors to a railroad museum discover just how different train travel was long ago. For example, the 1890 locomotive engine ran on steam. It was like a giant furnace fed by workers who shoveled chunks of dusty black coal into its firebox. Passenger cars, however, were dressed up in bright red paint, gold trim, and lacy curtains. The dining car seats were covered in soft velvet. Visitors can see how train travel was both dirtier and fancier than it is today.

See page 16 for tips on ordering details. See page 18 for more transitional words.

more ▶

Supporting Sentences

Lesson Objectives

Students will:

- list facts and sensory words that support a main idea
- write supporting sentences, using facts from a diagram
- use transitional words or phrases to link supporting sentences

Focus on Instruction

- Have students give examples of different kinds of facts they might use when writing to inform. (Sample answers: numbers, dates, descriptions, names) Ask what resources they could use to make certain their facts were correct. (Sample answers: reference books, maps and globes, the Internet, experts)
- Discuss with students why including facts is necessary in an informational paragraph. (Informational paragraphs are meant to inform, so they need to include facts to back up and elaborate on the main idea.)

Think and Discuss

Ask students how the facts and sensory words in the roller-coaster paragraph enhance the writing. (Sample answers: The facts help the reader to visualize the size and speed of the roller coaster; the sensory words help the reader feel as if he or she is actually on a roller coaster.)

Focus on Instruction

- Explain that the details in the paragraph on the railroad museum are ordered spatially, from the front of the train to the back. Ask students how each transitional word helps connect sentences.
- Transitional words and phrases include *For example* and *however*. Ask students how each transitional word helps connect sentences.

Meeting Individual Needs

● RETEACHING WORKBOOK, page 91

Supporting Sentences

A paragraph that gives factual information is called an **informational paragraph**. It often has a topic sentence, supporting sentences, and a closing sentence. **Supporting sentences** give details that tell about the main idea of the paragraph. These details often include facts. They may also include sensory words that describe how things look, smell, feel, taste, and sound.

Read the informational paragraph below. The topic sentence and the closing sentence are underlined. Two of the other sentences do not help explain the main idea. Cross out the two sentences that do not keep to the main idea. Then write two new sentences that support the main idea. Use the picture to help you. Answers will vary.

Before engine-powered vehicles were invented, travel was a slow process. One of the first kinds of wheeled vehicles were simple carts pulled by one horse or another animal. Not only were these carts slow, but poor roads made it impossible to travel more than about twenty miles a day. Some improvements made travel faster and easier, but still it could take ten hours to travel by wagon to a town one hundred miles away. ~~Do you like the hat the man in the stagecoach is wearing?~~ Travel was not always pleasant, either. ~~They should have taken an airplane.~~ As improvements were made to roads and vehicles, more people traveled. Now we can travel all the way across the United States in just a few hours.

▲■ WORKBOOK PLUS, page 140

Supporting Sentences

A paragraph that gives factual information is called an **informational paragraph**. It often has a topic sentence, supporting sentences, and a closing sentence. **Supporting sentences** give details that tell about the main idea of the paragraph. These details often include facts. They may also include sensory words that describe how things look, smell, feel, taste, and sound.

Complete the informational paragraph. Look at the diagram, and read the topic sentence and the closing sentence below. Then write at least three supporting sentences, using information from the diagram.

College Basketball Scoring

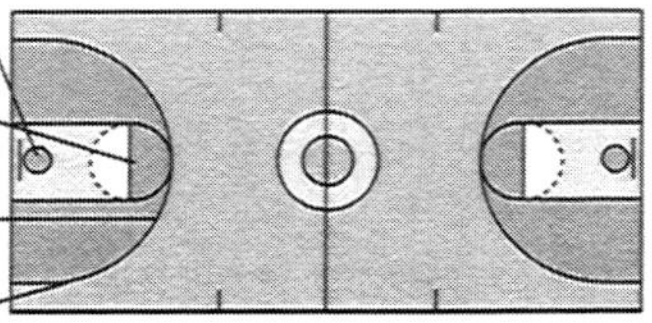
basket
Score one point from here if awarded free throw after a foul.
Score two points from inside this line during play.
Score three points from outside this line during play.

The only way to make points in basketball is to throw the ball into the basket.
Answers will vary.

Where you are when you shoot makes an important difference to your score.

Supporting Sentences *continued*

Try It Out

- Discuss with students how they would arrange the supporting sentences in a paragraph about the bald eagle. (Sample answer: The sentences could start at the eagle's head and work down to the talons, or they might be arranged from most important to least important.)
- If students need extra support, write the facts and transitional words on slips of paper, putting the facts on paper of one color and the transitional words on another. Put the facts facedown on a desktop. Have two volunteers each choose a fact and write on the board a sentence based on their fact. Display the transitional words faceup. Discuss each transitional word and whether it could be used to connect the two factual sentences.

The Closing Sentence

Lesson Objective

Students will:
- write a closing sentence for a paragraph

Focus on Instruction

- Have students reread the closing sentence in the paragraph about the capybara on page 331 to see how it makes a final comment.
- Present these alternative closing sentences for the same paragraph. Ask students which one repeats the topic sentence in different words and which one makes a final comment.

  Can you imagine such a sight?
  (makes a final comment)

  No other animal looks quite like the capybara!
  (repeats the topic sentence)

- If necessary, ask students to identify types of closing sentences in other paragraphs.

Try It Out

If any students need extra support, help them identify the topic and the main idea. (topic—exercise; main idea—exercise is good for you) Then have them identify the details. Finally, have students suggest ideas for possible endings for the paragraph, and help them write closing sentences using those ideas.

Try It Out Work on your own or with a partner. Use the diagram and the facts below to write some supporting sentences for the topic sentence. Link two of your sentences with a transitional word or phrase. Answers will vary.

Topic sentence: The bald eagle has every tool it needs to be a fierce hunter.

Sharp eyesight for spotting prey from the air; better eyesight than most other birds or people have
Curved, pointed beak, more than two inches long; extremely powerful
Featherless legs and talons for ease in grabbing fish out of water
Strong talons for catching and holding onto prey

GRAMMAR TIP *Use a comma after most order words at the beginning of a sentence.*

The Closing Sentence

The **closing sentence** wraps up the paragraph by repeating the main idea in different words or by adding one last comment. For example, the closing sentence makes a final comment in both the capybara paragraph and the roller coaster paragraph. In the railroad paragraph, the main idea is repeated, and more information is given.

Try It Out Read the paragraph below. It is missing the closing sentence. On your own or with a partner, write two possible closing sentences.

> Exercise is a healthful activity. For one thing, it helps your circulatory system. As you exercise, your heart beats faster, and your heart muscle becomes stronger. Exercise also helps prevent your arteries from becoming clogged with fat. Finally, exercise helps you sleep better, so you wake up feeling ready to go. _Closing sentence_.

Sample answer: The more you exercise, the better you will feel.

Paragraphs That Compare and Contrast

One kind of informational paragraph compares and contrasts two subjects. When you tell how two subjects are alike, you **compare** them. When you show how two subjects are different, you **contrast** them.

A **paragraph that compares and contrasts** has a topic sentence, supporting sentences with details that show how the subjects are alike and different, and a closing sentence. Transitional words, such as *on the other hand* or *in contrast*, connect the supporting sentences and help the reader follow the details.

Notice which sentences compare and which contrast in the paragraph below. What transitional words and phrases do you find?

Topic sentence — Transitional word — Supporting sentences — Closing sentence

> Although radio commercials and TV commercials have many things in common, they are not exactly alike. Both have the goal of selling products. In addition, they send their messages in just a few seconds. Radio is heard, however, while television is heard *and* seen. That means radio must use powerful words and sound effects to make the audience listen. Television, on the other hand, can use attractive pictures to carry part of its message. Another difference is that television and radio don't have the same audience. Because more children watch TV than listen to radio, there are more ads for toys and certain foods on television. TV and radio commercials are not exactly alike, but they are both important in the advertising world.

Try It Out Compare and contrast softball and soccer or two other sports. With a partner, list details that tell how the two subjects are alike and how they are different. Then use these details to write at least three supporting sentences. Use transitional words. Answers will vary.

Paragraphs That Compare and Contrast

Lesson Objective

Students will:
- write sentences that compare and contrast two topics

Focus on Instruction

- Before students read the paragraph, explain that the call outs highlight the main parts of a paragraph that compares and contrasts and that students will learn about those parts as they read the paragraph.
- Ask students how the information in the paragraph is organized. (Similarities are discussed first; then the differences are noted.)

Try It Out

If any students need extra support, work with them to organize the similarities and differences between the two sports in a Venn diagram like the one below. Have students use the information to write supporting sentences that compare and contrast the sports. Then help students organize the sentences into a paragraph, using transitional words to connect ideas.

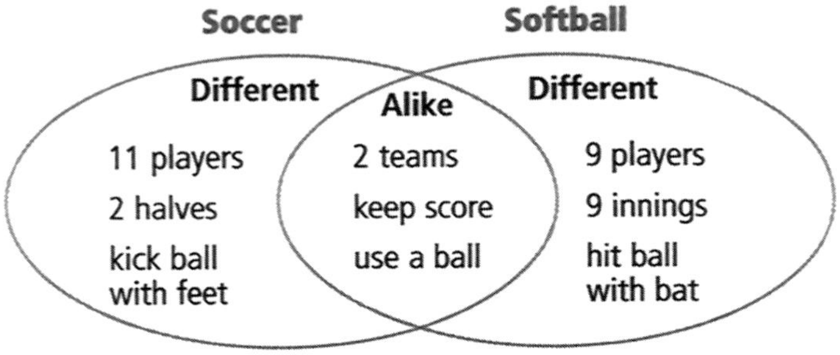

Paragraphs That Show Cause and Effect

Lesson Objective

Students will:
- write sentences that show cause and effect

Focus on Instruction

- Before students read the paragraph, explain that the call outs highlight the main parts of a cause-and-effect paragraph and that students will learn about those parts as they read the paragraph.
- Explain that sometimes a cause can result in more than one effect. Draw the organizer below on the board to help students identify the relationship between the causes and effects in the paragraph. Help them see how effects can become causes. For example, new families moving to town was the effect of the new store and factory being built, but the action was also the cause of more homes and apartments being built.

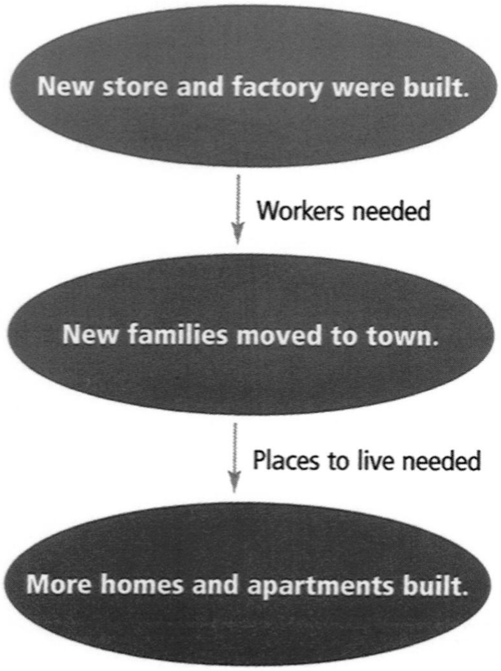
New store and factory were built.
Workers needed
New families moved to town.
Places to live needed
More homes and apartments built.

Try It Out

Students can use a graphic organizer like the one above when planning cause-and-effect paragraphs.

Paragraphs That Show Cause and Effect

An **informational paragraph that shows cause and effect** explains why or how one thing (cause) makes another thing (effect) happen. In this kind of paragraph, the topic sentence tells the cause, an effect, or both. The supporting sentences give more details about causes and effects. Transitional words, such as *first, then, later that day,* and *as a result,* help readers follow what happened. A closing sentence wraps up the paragraph.

Read the paragraph below. What is the cause? What are the effects?

Topic sentence — Our town has really grown! Three years ago a new store and a new factory were built.
Supporting sentences — Then, because the store and the factory needed workers, new families moved into town. These families needed places to live, so builders constructed more homes and apartments. Soon we needed more schools and shops. Our town used to be small, but
Closing sentence — now it is big. It is finally catching up to its neighbors.

Try It Out On your own or with a partner, look at the picture below and read the topic sentence. Identify the cause stated in the topic sentence. Then write at least three supporting sentences that explain its effects. Answers will vary.

Topic sentence: A power failure can cause lots of problems for a family.

Write Your Own Informational Paragraph

Now you're ready to write your own informational paragraph. You may choose to write a paragraph that compares and contrasts, one that shows cause and effect, or one that explains what something is or does.

First, think of a topic that interests you. Then make a list of details to include. After discussing your ideas with a partner, begin to write!

Checklist for My Paragraph

- ✓ My **topic sentence** introduces the subject and the main idea.
- ✓ Every **supporting sentence** gives facts and sensory details about the main idea.
- ✓ My **supporting sentences** are in a clear order. Transitional words make the meaning clear.
- ✓ My **closing sentence** repeats the main idea in different words or makes a final comment.

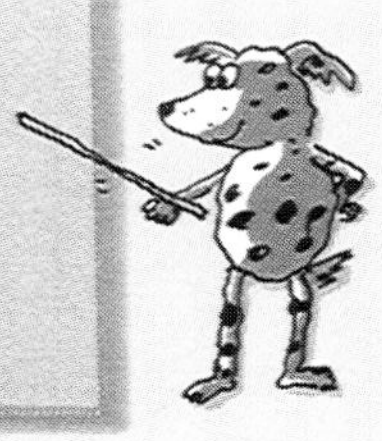

Looking Ahead

Once you know how to write an informational paragraph, writing a longer composition will be easy. The diagram below shows how the parts of an informational paragraph match the parts of a longer piece.

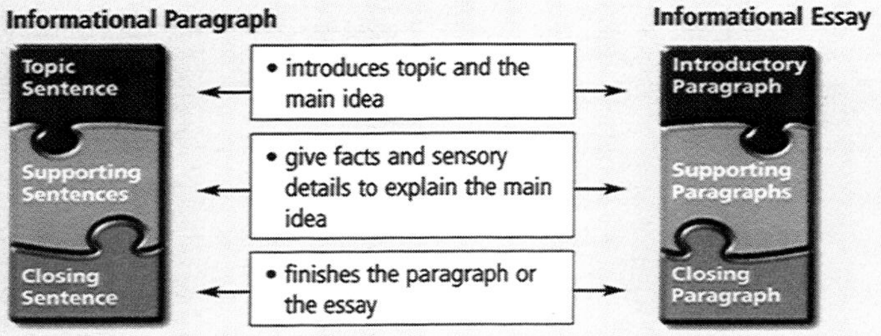

Help with Writing

HELP WITH CHOOSING A TOPIC

Share these ideas.

- Students can explain the facts about an activity they are involved in.
- They can write about a favorite kind of animal.
- They can give information about a club or organization.

HELP WITH PLANNING

Have students make a planning map with these entries to help them organize their ideas. Review their maps before they write.

Topic	Main Idea
Topic Sentence	
Details	
Closing Sentence	

Write Your Own Informational Paragraph

Lesson Objective

Students will:

- write an informational paragraph

Focus on Instruction

- Remind students that the first step in writing a paragraph is to choose a topic. If students have difficulty choosing a topic, suggest ideas from the Help box on this page or brainstorm other ideas with students. List the ideas on the board or on an overhead transparency.
- Tell students that it is important to discuss their topic with a partner before they begin to write. Discussing their topic will help students tap into their oral language skills. Encourage partners to give feedback about what information he or she feels is interesting and relevant.

Connecting to the Criteria Review with students the Checklist for My Paragraph.

- Have volunteers read their paragraph aloud to the class.

> If students are keeping portfolios, they could include this paragraph as an example of a short writing assignment. The paragraph can be used later as a basis for comparison with longer informational paragraphs. If you want to send the paragraphs home as well, you can make copies for the portfolios.

SCHOOL-HOME CONNECTION Encourage students to share their paragraph with family members.

Looking Ahead Explain to students that in this Explaining and Informing section of the book they will learn how to write instructions and a research report, using what they have learned about writing paragraphs.

Unit 10 Planning Guide

Writing Instructions

Writing Instructions: *2 weeks*
Special Focus and Communication Links: *1 week (optional)*

	Blackline Masters (TE)	Workbook Plus	Reteaching Workbook
PUBLISHED MODEL "Knuckle Down That Taw!," by Beth Kennedy *(339–341)*			
What Makes Great Instructions? *(342)*			
STUDENT MODEL Working Draft *(343–344)* Final Copy *(345–346)*	10-1A, 10-1B		
The Writing Process Write Instructions			
Prewriting Explore the Topic *(348)*	10–2		
Focus Skill: Organizing Your Instructions *(349)*	10–3	141	92
Drafting Focus Skill: Using Details *(350)*		142	93
Good Beginnings and Endings *(351)*		143	94
Revising Evaluating Your Instructions [rubric] *(352)*	10–4	144	95
Writing Conference *(353)*	10–5		
Revising Strategies *(354)*		145	96
Proofreading *(355)*			
Publishing and Reflecting *(356)*			
Writing Prompts and Test Practice *(357–358)*			
SPECIAL FOCUS ON EXPLAINING **Writing to Compare and Contrast** *(359–364)*			
COMMUNICATION LINKS **Listening/Speaking: Giving and Following Instructions** *(365)* **Viewing/Media: Comparing Visual Information** *(366–367)*			

Unit 10

Tools and Tips

- **Listening and Speaking Strategies,** *pp. H4–H10*
- **Building Vocabulary,** *pp. H11–H17*
- **Research and Study Strategies,** *pp. H18–H30*
- **Using Technology,** *pp. H35–H47*
- **Writer's Tools,** *pp. H48–H54*
- **Spelling Guide,** *pp. H65–H69*
- **Guide to Capitalization, Punctuation, and Usage,** *pp. H55–H64*
- **Thesaurus Plus,** *pp. H79–H100*

School-Home Connection

Suggestions for informing or involving family members in classroom activities and learning related to this unit are included in the Teacher's Edition throughout the unit.

Meeting Individual Needs

- **FOR SPECIAL NEEDS/INCLUSION:** *Houghton Mifflin English* Audiotape
- **FOR STUDENTS ACQUIRING ENGLISH:**
  - Notes and activities are included in this Teacher's Edition throughout the unit to help you adapt or use pupil book activities with students acquiring English.
  - Students acquiring English can listen to the published and student models on audiotape.
  - MediaWeaver™, Sunburst/Humanities software, offers bilingual features, including Spanish menus, a Spanish spelling tool, and a Spanish thesaurus.
- **ENRICHMENT:** See *Teacher's Resource Book.*

All audiotape recordings are also available on CD.

Daily Language Practice

Each sentence includes two capitalization, punctuation, usage, or spelling errors based on skills presented in the Grammar and Spelling Connections in this unit or from Grammar Units 1–3. Each day write one sentence on the chalkboard. Have students find the errors and write the sentence correctly on a sheet of paper. To make the activity easier, identify the kinds of errors.

1. I cann't do nothing with my hair today. Sample: I can't do anything with my hair today. (contractions; negatives)
2. The three fisherman hadn't no time to prepare for the storm. Sample: The three fishermen hadn't any time to prepare for the storm. (plural nouns; negatives)
3. They gives away old clothing, household items and canned goods each year. They give away old clothing, household items, and canned goods each year. (subject-verb agreement; commas)
4. You need bananas ice cream, and cherrys to make that dessert. You need bananas, ice cream, and cherries to make that dessert. (commas; plural nouns)
5. Gloria's sunflowers have grew sow tall. Gloria's sunflowers have grown so tall. (irregular verbs; spelling long *o*)
6. Frost or snoe can destroy Floridas orange crop. Frost or snow can destroy Florida's orange crop. (spelling long *o*; possessive nouns)
7. Max eat tost and juice for breakfast. Sample: Max eats toast and juice for breakfast. (subject-verb agreement; spelling long *o*)
8. Several mouses make their hoam in our basement. Several mice make their home in our basement. (plural nouns; spelling long *o*)
9. Tina goes home after school each day, she is eager to play her guitar Sample: Tina goes home after school each day. She is eager to play her guitar. (run-on sentences; end punctuation)
10. Justin joged to the corner to mail Mrs. Prices' letter. Justin jogged to the corner to mail Mrs. Price's letter. (past tense; possessive nouns)

Additional Resources

Workbook Plus, Unit 10
Reteaching Workbook, Unit 10
Teacher's Resource Book
Transparencies
Posters, Unit 10
Audiotapes

Technology Tools

CD-ROM: *EasyBook Deluxe
MediaWeaver™, Sunburst/Humanities software
*Type to Learn™

*©Sunburst Technology Corporation, a Houghton Mifflin Company. All rights reserved.

INTERNET: http://www.eduplace.com/kids/hme/ *or* http://www.eduplace.com/rdg/hme/

Visit Education Place for these additional support materials and activities:

- author biographies
- student writing models
- graphic organizers
- an interactive rubric
- proofreading practice
- writing prompts
- benchmark papers

Assessment

Test Booklet, Unit 10

Keeping a Journal

Discuss with students the value of keeping a journal as a way of promoting self-expression and fluency. Encourage students to record their thoughts and ideas in a notebook. Inform students whether the journal will be private or will be reviewed periodically as a way of assessing growth. The following prompts may be useful for generating writing ideas.

Journal Prompts

- What is the hardest thing you ever learned to do? How did you learn it?
- Think of something you made once. Explain the steps you took to make it.
- Think of something unusual that you know how to do. How would you teach it to others?

Introducing the Unit

Using the Photograph

Have students look at the photograph. What has happened? (A person has painted himself or herself into a corner.) Ask students why this may have happened. (Sample response: The person either did not follow instructions or received poor instructions.)

Have a volunteer read the caption aloud. Have students supply answers to the painter's question. (Sample responses: jump across the floor, wait until the paint dries) Have students suggest instructions they might give a painter to avoid this problem. (Sample response: Start at the back corners and work outward.) Ask students to share problems they have had when they failed to follow instructions or when they received poor instructions.

Explain to students that **instructions** explain how to do something. Tell students that in this unit they will learn how to write instructions.

Shared Writing Activity

Work with students to write a short paragraph of instructions explaining how to do a simple activity, such as brush their teeth or make a craft.

1. Make a two-column chart on the board or on an overhead transparency. Write *Materials* as the head of one column and *Steps* as the head of the other.
2. Have students list the materials needed for the activity or craft in the column headed *Materials*. Then have students list the steps in any order in the *Steps* column. Discuss the order of the steps, and have volunteers number the steps correctly.
3. Work with students to use the information in the chart to write their instructions as a paragraph, beginning with a topic sentence. Help them substitute order words, such as *first, next,* and *then,* for the numbers. As students suggest sentences, write them on the board or on an overhead transparency.
4. Reinforce the importance of including all the steps and putting them in the correct order.
5. If students suggest run-on sentences, remind them that they can fix a run-on by making it into a compound sentence. Reinforce the use of commas to separate items in a series (or other skills students need to work on) as they suggest sentences.
6. Have students copy the final paragraph to share with a friend or a younger child.

A Published Model

In "Knuckle Down That Taw!" Beth Kennedy gives instructions for a marble game called *ringer.* What steps does she describe for playing this game?

Knuckle Down That Taw!

by Beth Kennedy

The game of marbles dates back to ancient times. Historians think that children in Egypt, Rome, and North America may have played marbles thousands of years ago. In fact, signs of marble playing have been found in countries all over the world.

Marbles from long ago were not like those of today. People used stones, clay balls, nuts, and fruit pits as the first marbles. Later, people made marbles from materials such as glass, china, and real chips of marble. This gave the game its present name.

Adults as well as children enjoy marbles. Some people say that Presidents George Washington and Thomas Jefferson liked to play. Abraham Lincoln is thought to have been an expert at a marble game called *old bowler.*

more ▶

Bibliography

Here are other books that model this type of writing that students might enjoy reading.

- ***The Kids Campfire Book*** by Jane Drake and Ann Love
- ***Gardening Wizardry for Kids*** by Patricia Kite
- ***Cody Coyote Cooks! A Southwest Cookbook for Kids*** by Denise Skrepcinski, Melissa T. Stock, and Lois Bergthold

"Knuckle Down That Taw!"

Lesson Objectives

Students will:

- read a published model of instructions
- identify characteristics of instructions
- identify examples of headings
- evaluate the relationship between visuals and text
- write personal and critical responses

Focus on the Model

Building Background

Ask students if they know any marble games. If possible, provide marbles and have a volunteer demonstrate. What are the rules? Tell students that they will read instructions that tell how to play a marble game called *ringer.*

Introducing Vocabulary

Introduce key vocabulary word by writing this sentence on the board.

> **Historians** often learn surprising things about people who lived in the past.

Ask a volunteer to read the sentence aloud. Ask students to explain the meaning of the boldfaced word.

Reading the Selection

Have students read the introduction to "Knuckle Down That Taw!" The purpose-setting question focuses on a characteristic of instructions, telling steps in a process.

Have students read the selection as a class, independently, or with partners, or they can listen to the selection on audiotape.

MEETING INDIVIDUAL NEEDS — FOR STUDENTS ACQUIRING ENGLISH

Before reading, show some marbles to the class. Then ask about marble games students play. Encourage them to explain their games. As students share, list the rules and draw diagrams to illustrate.

A Published Model

How do you play marbles? Here are directions for *ringer,* a game that is popular today.

details

Getting Ready

Find a large flat surface where it's safe to play. It can be outside or inside. Use chalk or string to make a circle that is ten feet from one side to the other. Inside the circle, place thirteen marbles in the shape of a cross. Each marble should be three inches from the next one. These target marbles are sometimes called *mibs.*

steps

How to Shoot

Turn your hand so that at least one knuckle rests on the ground. This is called "knuckling down." Hold your shooting marble between your curled index and middle fingers. Aim, then flick the shooter with your thumb. Shooters are also called *taws,* and they may be larger than the target marbles.

Let's Play!

From outside the circle, shoot at the marbles in the cross shape. Try to knock them out of the circle without having your shooter roll out. Shoot again from the spot where your shooter stopped. Your turn ends when you fail to knock a marble out of the circle or when your shooter rolls out.

Players take turns. The winner is the player who has knocked out the most marbles by the end of the game.

340 **Unit 10:** Instructions

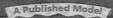

Ringer is just one kind of marble game. There are dozens of other marble games you can learn to play. So polish up those mibs and taws, call your friends, and knuckle down to an exciting and historic game.

ending

Reading As a Writer
See TE margin for answers.

Think About the Instructions

- What are the steps for playing marbles? What would happen if the steps were out of order?
- In "Getting Ready," what details does the author give about the kind of surface to play on? What problem might a player have if the author left out these details?
- What information does the author put in the last paragraph? Why is this better than stopping with the last step?

Think About Writer's Craft

- Why are the headings in bold print helpful?

Think About the Picture

- What additional information about playing marbles is shown in the picture on page 340?

Responding
Answers will vary.

Write responses to these questions.

- **Personal Response** Explain why *ringer* does or does not seem like an interesting game to play.
- **Critical Thinking** Think of a game you know. How is the game like *ringer*? How is it different?

Mapping the Selection

Mapping helps students identify and visualize the elements in a set of instructions. After students read the model, draw this chart on the board. Have students complete the chart, adding rows as needed, to show the materials, steps, and details in the model set of instructions.

Steps	Materials Needed	Details
1.		
2.		
3.		
4.		

Answers to Reading As a Writer

Think About the Instructions

- Make a circle, place thirteen marbles in the shape of a cross inside the circle, and then shoot the taw so it knocks marbles out of the circle. Sample answer: People wouldn't understand how to shoot the marbles.
- She says it should be large and flat. Sample answers: A player might use a slanting or bumpy surface, and the marbles wouldn't roll properly. A player might choose too small a space and not have room to draw the circle.
- She says that besides *ringer,* there are many other marble games to play. Sample answer: This ending leaves the reader excited about playing marbles.

Think About Writer's Craft

- By telling what each section teaches, the headings make the instructions easier to follow.

Think About the Picture

- Sample answer: The picture shows the correct body position and the proper distance from player to marbles.

After students complete the questions, work with them to generate criteria for writing instructions, using the published model as a reference.

More About Writer's Craft

Point out that italics were used for games and marble names. (*old bowler* and *ringer; mibs* and *taws*) Explain to students that italics are often used in printed materials to call attention to the name of things. Advise students that when they write by hand they will need to underline the name of things rather than use italics.

Notes on Responding

Personal Response
Encourage students to share opposing opinions but to do so respectfully.

Critical Thinking
Suggest that students draw a Venn diagram to compare and contrast the two games.

What Makes Great Instructions?

Lesson Objective

Students will:
- discuss the characteristics of well-written instructions

Focus on Instruction

- Tell students that "Knuckle Down That Taw!" is an example of well-written instructions. Ask students to read aloud the definition and characteristics of instructions. Discuss why each element is important, referring to the published model and to students' own experiences in learning new things. Note that in the published model, only two materials are needed, so the author mentions but does not list them.
- Point out that the topic sentence does not have to be the first sentence. The published model begins with a history of marbles, but the topic sentence about *ringer* comes just before the instructions.
- Have a student read the Grammar Check. Explain that it reminds them that great instructions are mistake free. On the board, write sentences that list a series of items. Have students insert commas to correct the sentences.

If this is students' first encounter with the cartoon dog Sal, the writer's pal, explain that he will provide tips to help them learn how to write great instructions.

Connecting to the Rubric

- These criteria are tied to the rubric on page 352.
- Explain to students that they will be writing their own instructions and that they will learn how to include these characteristics. Students will use these characteristics as criteria to help them evaluate their papers.

This page is available as a poster.

Looking Ahead Tell students that they will next see how the characteristics listed on this page are applied in one student's working draft and final copy of instructions.

FOR STUDENTS ACQUIRING ENGLISH

The words *instructions, topic* and *closing sentence, material,* and *order* are essential to this unit. Define them by listing them on the board and encouraging student suggestions of definitions based on the context of the unit. Then ask volunteers to point out examples of each word in the text.

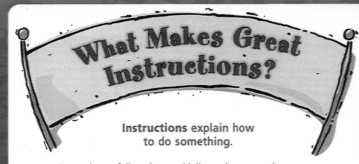

What Makes Great Instructions?

Instructions explain how to do something.

Remember to follow these guidelines when you write instructions.

- Begin with an interesting topic sentence that states the main idea.
- List all the materials that will be needed.
- Include all the steps. Leave out anything that doesn't belong.
- Put the steps in the correct order. Use order words.
- Include exact details that make each step clear.
- End with a closing sentence that wraps up the instructions.

GRAMMAR CHECK

Use commas to separate three or more items in a series. Put a comma after each item except the last one.

WORKING DRAFT

Colin McMillan enjoys building models. He made a papier-mâché model of a hot-air balloon and wrote down the instructions so his classmates could make one. Here is a working draft of his instructions.

Colin McMillan

This is a great beginning!

Do you like high-flying adventure? Well, ~~get ready~~ strap on your safety belts. I'll show you how to make a model hot-air balloon.

First, make a papier-mâché balloon. Blow up the balloon and knot it. ~~I used a balloon left over from my last birthday party.~~ Take the newspaper and tear it up into strips. Put some papier-mâché paste into a bowl. You can also make papier-mâché masks this way. Take a piece of paper and ~~put~~ dip it into the paste. Take the strip of paper and lay it on the balloon. Do that with lots of strips of newspaper until the whole balloon is covered. Leave a space at the bottom. Give it another four layers of newspaper dipped in the paste. Once the balloon is dry, it's time to pop the balloon and pull it out.

Does this part belong in your instructions?

more

Student Model: Working Draft

Lesson Objectives

Students will:

- read a working draft of student-written instructions
- discuss the ways the model meets the criteria for well-written instructions and ways that it could be improved

Focus on the Model

- Tell students that they will read a working draft of instructions written by Colin McMillan, a real student. Remind students that a working draft is a work in progress, and that Colin was just trying to get his ideas on paper, knowing that he could make revisions later.
- Have volunteers read the model aloud.

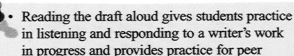

  Alternatively, students can listen to it read by a student (although not the student writer) on audiotape.

> - Reading the draft aloud gives students practice in listening and responding to a writer's work in progress and provides practice for peer conferences.
> - This working draft does not include any usage, capitalization, or punctuation mistakes so that students can focus on the content of the piece.

- Tell students to think about whether Colin included the important characteristics of instructions. Explain that Sal's thoughts about the essay appear in thought balloons and that students will discuss his ideas after they read the model.

Answers to Reading As a Writer

- Sal liked the beginning Colin used for his instructions. Sal asked if a certain part really belonged in the instructions; if one step was in the right order; what the thread was for; if Colin could list his materials closer to the beginning of his instructions. In the second paragraph, Colin could cross out the sentence about masks, and he could move up the sentence *Let the papier-mâché dry out for a day or two* to follow *Give it another four layers of newspaper dipped in the paste.* After the first paragraph, he could add a paragraph listing all the materials needed. In the fourth paragraph, he could explain what the thread is for.
- The sentence wasn't important to the instructions.
- Answers will vary.

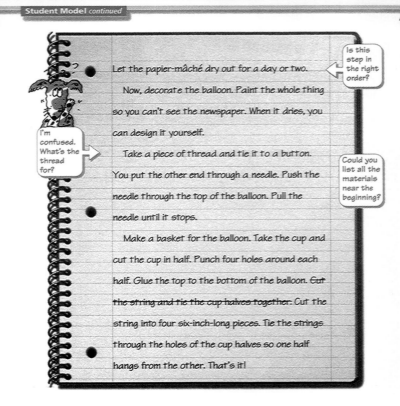

Let the papier-mâché dry out for a day or two.

Now, decorate the balloon. Paint the whole thing so you can't see the newspaper. When it dries, you can design it yourself.

Take a piece of thread and tie it to a button. You put the other end through a needle. Push the needle through the top of the balloon. Pull the needle until it stops.

Make a basket for the balloon. Take the cup and cut the cup in half. Punch four holes around each half. Glue the top to the bottom of the balloon. ~~Cut the string and tie the cup halves together.~~ Cut the string into four six-inch-long pieces. Tie the strings through the holes of the cup halves so one half hangs from the other. That's it!

Is this step in the right order?

I'm confused. What's the thread for?

Could you list all the materials near the beginning?

Reading As a Writer

See TE margin for answers.

- What did Sal like about Colin's instructions? What questions did he have? What changes could Colin make to answer Sal's questions?
- Look at the second paragraph on page 343. Why did Colin cross out a sentence?
- What questions would you like to ask Colin about his instructions?

Student Model

FINAL COPY

Colin revised his instructions after discussing them with his classmates. Read his final version to see what changes he made.

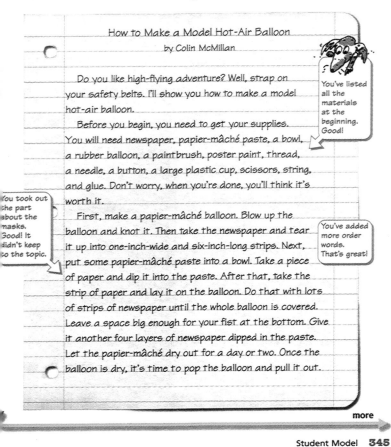

How to Make a Model Hot-Air Balloon

by Colin McMillan

Do you like high-flying adventure? Well, strap on your safety belts. I'll show you how to make a model hot-air balloon.

Before you begin, you need to get your supplies. You will need newspaper, papier-mâché paste, a bowl, a rubber balloon, a paintbrush, poster paint, thread, a needle, a button, a large plastic cup, scissors, string, and glue. Don't worry, when you're done, you'll think it's worth it.

> You've listed all the materials at the beginning. Good!

First, make a papier-mâché balloon. Blow up the balloon and knot it. Then take the newspaper and tear it up into one-inch-wide and six-inch-long strips. Next, put some papier-mâché paste into a bowl. Take a piece of paper and dip it into the paste. After that, take the strip of paper and lay it on the balloon. Do that with lots of strips of newspaper until the whole balloon is covered. Leave a space big enough for your fist at the bottom. Give it another four layers of newspaper dipped in the paste. Let the papier-mâché dry out for a day or two. Once the balloon is dry, it's time to pop the balloon and pull it out.

> You took out the part about the masks. Good! It didn't keep to the topic.

> You've added more order words. That's great!

more

Student Model: Final Copy

Lesson Objectives

Students will:

- read a well-written final copy of a student's instructions
- note and compare the revisions that improved the first draft

Focus on the Model

SUMMARY OF REVISIONS In his final copy, Colin added a title; listed his materials in a paragraph near the beginning, added more order words, took out the sentence about papier-mâché masks, put the steps in the correct order, and improved his description of the process for attaching the thread and button to the balloon. Blackline Master 10–1 provides a copy of the student's working draft, showing the revisions that were made.

Have volunteers read the model aloud. Alternatively, students can listen to it read by a student (although not the student writer) on audiotape.

Answers to Reading As a Writer

- Colin added a paragraph after the opening paragraph listing all the materials. In the third paragraph, he took out the sentence about masks, and he corrected the order of the steps by moving up the sentence *Let the papier-mâché dry out for a day or two* to follow *Give it another four layers of newspaper dipped in the paste.* He made the fifth paragraph clearer by adding details about how long the thread should be, how to push the needle through the top, what the button is for, where to knot the thread, and what the thread is for. Sal liked the way Colin added more order words.
- In the third paragraph, Colin added a detail about the size of the strips. This detail is important because without it someone might make the strips the wrong size.
- Sample answer: The new ending is better because it gets you excited about making a hot-air balloon.

More About Writer's Craft

- Draw students' attention to the paragraph structure of the student model. The first paragraph establishes the purpose and builds enthusiasm. The second paragraph lists materials. Subsequent paragraphs each develop one main step in the instruction set. Tell students that they may want to apply these same considerations for paragraphing in their writing.
- Direct students' attention to the prepositional phrases *into the paste, on the balloon,* and *at the bottom.* Ask students why the writer included these phrases. Discuss how prepositional phrases clarify the instructions. Tell students that they can use this technique in their own writing.

Connecting to the Rubric

- Have students look again at the list of characteristics on page 342. Review with them how Colin's final copy addressed each characteristic.
- Reinforce the Grammar Check by having students verify that Colin used commas after all but the last item in a series.

INTERNET CONNECTION Send your students to www.eduplace.com/kids/hme/ to see more models of student writing. You can also find and print these models at www.eduplace.com/rdg/hme/.

Looking Ahead Tell students that they will next write their own set of instructions, using the writing process. As they go along, they will learn how to organize their instructions, use details, and write a good beginning and ending.

Student Model *continued*

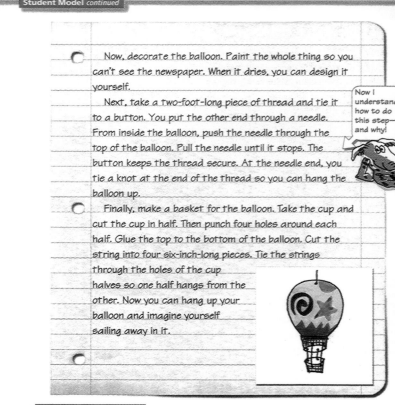

Now, decorate the balloon. Paint the whole thing so you can't see the newspaper. When it dries, you can design it yourself.

Next, take a two-foot-long piece of thread and tie it to a button. You put the other end through a needle. From inside the balloon, push the needle through the top of the balloon. Pull the needle until it stops. The button keeps the thread secure. At the needle end, you tie a knot at the end of the thread so you can hang the balloon up.

Now I understand how to do this step—and why!

Finally, make a basket for the balloon. Take the cup and cut the cup in half. Then punch four holes around each half. Glue the top to the bottom of the balloon. Cut the string into four six-inch-long pieces. Tie the strings through the holes of the cup halves so one half hangs from the other. Now you can hang up your balloon and imagine yourself sailing away in it.

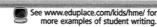

Reading As a Writer See TE margin for answers.

- What changes did Colin make after thinking about Sal's questions? What else did Colin do that Sal liked?
- Look at the third paragraph on page 345. What detail did Colin add about the strips of newspapers? Why is this detail important?
- Compare the endings in Colin's working draft and final copy. Why is the ending in the final draft better?

346 **Unit 10:** Instructions

See www.eduplace.com/kids/hme/ for more examples of student writing.

FOR STUDENTS ACQUIRING ENGLISH

In order to help students understand Colin's essay, bring in or draw the materials. You may even want to partially construct a balloon to illustrate the steps. Whether you construct or not, encourage students to reread the passage and draw diagrams of each step. Then together answer the questions after draft two.

Write Instructions

Start Thinking

Make a writing folder for your instructions. Copy the questions in bold print, and put the paper in your folder. Write your answers as you think about and choose your topic.

- **Who will be my audience?** Will it be my classmates? a family member? a younger child?
- **What will be my purpose?** Do I want to explain how to do something? how to make something?
- **How will I publish or share my instructions?** Will I write a "How To" book? give a demonstration? make a poster?

HELP *Stuck for a Topic?*

Use these questions.
- What do I like to do in my free time?
- What could I make for someone?
- What am I good at doing?

See page 357 for more ideas.

Choose Your Topic

1. **List** five topics you could write instructions for. Colin made a list to help him think of topics.

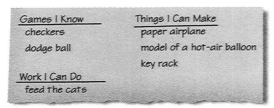

Games I Know	Things I Can Make
checkers	paper airplane
dodge ball	model of a hot-air balloon
	key rack
Work I Can Do	
feed the cats	

2. **Discuss** each topic idea with a partner. Would your audience like to learn how to do this? Can you explain the topic in a few paragraphs?
3. **Ask** yourself these questions about each topic. Circle the topic you will write about.
   - Have I done this myself? Do I know all the steps?
   - Would I enjoy explaining how to do this?

Help with Choosing a Topic

TECH TIP

Refer students who are using a computer to page H39 to find ideas for using a computer during the writing process.

EVALUATION TIP

Review students' final choices. Make sure that topics can be explained in about five to eight steps.

USING RESOURCES

Suggest that students look through "How To" books for help with identifying topics. Or ask students if they have a friend or relative who might be a good resource for expert advice on a topic. If so, suggest that students interview that person.

SOURCES OF TOPIC IDEAS

Suggest these activities to prompt topic ideas.
- Students can think of something they made for a celebration.
- They can think of a time they fixed something that was broken.
- They can think of a request someone made of them. Is it something they could teach other people to do for themselves?

Write Instructions

Lesson Objectives

Students will:
- list their ideas for audience, purpose, and publishing/sharing formats
- list ideas for instructions
- discuss their ideas with a partner
- choose an appropriate topic to write about

Start Thinking

Focus on Instruction

- Tell students that good writers adapt their language to their chosen audience. Ask students how instructions written for beginners might differ from instructions written for those with more experience. (might include more details for beginners; might skip steps and use informal language for those with more experience)
- Ask how instructions for a skill, such as kicking a soccer ball, might differ from instructions for the game of soccer. (Skill instructions may include suggestions and list more than one technique; game instructions may have formal rules and be very specific.)

Choose Your Topic

Focus on Instruction

- Page 357 provides writing prompts that might suggest ideas.
- Have students list their activities in the past twenty-four hours. Have them review the list to identify which things they like and know well enough to teach someone else.
- If a student can't decide between two good topics, have him or her pick both so that if the first topic doesn't work out, the second one can take its place.

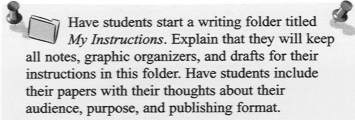

Have students start a writing folder titled *My Instructions*. Explain that they will keep all notes, graphic organizers, and drafts for their instructions in this folder. Have students include their papers with their thoughts about their audience, purpose, and publishing format.

SCHOOL-HOME CONNECTION Have students ask a family member to name something the student knows or does well. Suggest that students consider that as a possible topic for instructions.

Lesson Objectives

Students will:

- visualize the steps in the process they are describing
- illustrate the steps in the process
- describe the steps in a set of instructions, based on the illustrations

Explore Your Topic

Focus on Instruction

- See Blackline Master 10–2 for a graphic organizer students can use as they draw pictures of the steps in their "how-to" topic.
- Tell students to picture the order of steps in the process they are describing. Have students pantomime the activity to a partner while explaining the steps. This action will help them to remember details.
- Ask students to decide which steps are important or difficult to describe. Have students make rough sketches of those steps on index cards and then add a caption to describe each sketch.
- Have students put the index cards in the proper order. As students discuss their steps, have them jot words they used to describe the steps on the reverse side of the index cards. Students may use these words when they write their instructions.

FOR STUDENTS ACQUIRING ENGLISH

Writing explanations may be difficult for students. Students may need bilingual dictionaries to find words for their rules. Ask them to form small groups and then orally explain their games. Have them write down the instructions, making sure the explanation is clear, and read them to their group.

Explore Your Topic

1. **Think** about your "how-to" topic. Picture yourself doing it.
2. **Draw** pictures or diagrams of the steps. Write notes about what is happening. Colin drew these pictures.

3. **Use your pictures or diagrams** to explain the steps to a partner. Have your partner ask about anything that is not clear.

See page 14 for other ideas for exploring your topic.

Help with Exploring the Topic

TECH TIP

To help students put their ideas in order, have them assemble the steps in a table and then cut and paste them until all of the steps are in the proper order.

IDEAS FOR EXPLORING

You can suggest these ideas to students as alternative ways to explore their topics.

- Students can make a time line instead of a flow chart to show the steps in order.
- They can try doing the activity first to find out whether the topic is too easy or too broad.
- Students can list and count all the steps in the process they wish to describe to see whether there are too many or too few steps to write about.

Focus Skill

Organizing Your Instructions

Think of your instructions as stepping-stones across a brook. Your audience must follow the steps in order. Otherwise, they might fall in!

Put your steps in the right order. If the order doesn't make sense, your audience might be confused and make a mistake.

Use order words. Order words signal the sequence of steps. Use order words such as *first, second, next, finally, at the end, when, before, later, during, while.*

Colin numbered his pictures in order. Then he made a Step-by-Step Chart. Here is part of Colin's chart.

Steps	Materials Needed	Details
1. First, make a papier-mâché balloon. 2. Now, decorate the balloon.	rubber balloon newspaper bowl paste poster paint paintbrush	

Think and Discuss Look back at Colin's pictures on page 348.

- What should steps 3 and 4 be on Colin's chart? Step 3: attach thread; Step 4: make basket
- What order words could he add to steps 3 and 4? Answers will vary.

Plan Your Instructions

1. **Number** your pictures in the right order.
2. **Use** the pictures to help you make a Step-by-Step Chart. List your steps with order words. Write the materials for each step.

Go to www.eduplace.com/kids/hme/ for graphic organizers.

Organizing Your Instructions

Lesson Objectives

Students will:

- organize the main steps of the process in sequence
- make a graphic organizer showing the steps, materials, and details of the process

Focus on Instruction

- Ask students why it is important to put the steps in order. (so the instructions aren't confusing)
- Ask students what would happen if the last step in the instructions started with the order word *Next.* (The reader might think some instructions were left out.) Point out that order words, just like steps, must appear in the correct sequence.
- Help students list other order words. (Sample answers: *then, now, after*)

Think and Discuss

- If students need extra support, have them list Colin's steps on a flow chart.
- Sample answers: *next, finally*

Plan Your Instructions

- Students may have difficulty distinguishing steps from details. Tell students to write only about the big steps. They will supply details later.
- Be sure that students make their charts big enough to show the details they will add later. A copy of the Step-by-Step Chart appears on Blackline Master 10–3.

INTERNET CONNECTION Send your students to www.eduplace.com/kids/hme/ for graphic organizers. You can also find and print these organizers at www.eduplace.com/rdg/hme/.

FOR STUDENTS ACQUIRING ENGLISH

After you lead the class through the prewriting exercises, model the order words to show the steps of your own instructions. Write the phrases you use on the board. Then turn back to the other models; ask students to read aloud the phrases that include order words. Make a game of finding the words.

Meeting Individual Needs

● RETEACHING WORKBOOK, page 92

Organizing Your Instructions

To organize your instructions, put the steps in order, and list the materials needed. Use order words such as *first, second, next, then, now, finally, last, before, while, when, later,* and *during.*

The pictures and steps below describe how to make balloon invitations for a party, but they are out of order. Number the steps in the correct order. Then write the sentences in order on the lines below.

3 After that, let the air out of the balloon.

2 While you hold the end closed with a paperclip, write your message.

5 Finally, address it, add a stamp, and mail it.

1 To begin with, blow up a balloon.

4 Then put the balloon into an envelope.

▲■ WORKBOOK PLUS, page 141

Organizing Your Instructions

Steps	Materials Needed	Details
1 First, arrange the chairs.	chairs (one per player, minus one)	
2 Now start the music.	music CD, CD player with remote control	

The pictures and steps below describe how to make sock puppets, but they are out of order. Number the steps to show the correct order. Then fill in the chart by writing the steps in order and listing materials that are needed.

3 Then glue on yarn for hair.

2 Next, glue on felt lips.

4 Finally, when the glue has dried, put on a show!

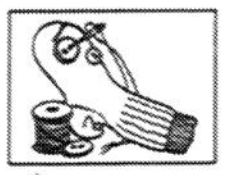

1 First, sew buttons on for eyes and nose.

Steps	Materials Needed
1 First, sew buttons on for eyes and nose.	Sample answers: sock, needle and thread, buttons
2 Next, glue on felt lips.	white glue, lips cut from red felt
3 Then glue on yarn for hair.	white glue, pieces of yarn
4 Finally, when the glue has dried, put on a show!	finished puppet

Using Details

Lesson Objectives

Students will:

- add details to their Step-by-Step Charts
- use their charts to help them draft a set of instructions

Focus on Instruction

- Point out that in the example with exact details, Colin added the following prepositional phrases: *into four six-inch-long pieces, through the holes, of the cup halves,* and *from the other.* Tell students that they can use this technique to elaborate steps in their own writing.
- Remind students to clarify the meaning of nonstandard words by using quotation marks.

Think and Discuss

Have students list the details that made the instructions with exact details easier to follow.

Draft Your Instructions

- Tell students that they do not need to use complete sentences when they add details to their chart.
- Draw attention to the Paragraph Tip. Point out that details can often make a single step of instructions take up an entire paragraph. Tell students to start a new paragraph for each major step.

Drafting Reminders

- Reinforce that if students change their mind while writing, they should cross out words or sentences they don't want rather than start over.
- Reassure students that they will have time to correct mistakes and check spelling later.

FOR STUDENTS ACQUIRING ENGLISH

Model pantomiming with a volunteer who reads his/her instructions while you act. Encourage students to practice their instructions in pairs and at home with materials. Students may have trouble with sequencing their instructions. Make an overhead transparency of the detail chart to help students organize their steps.

The Writing Process: PREWRITING · DRAFTING · REVISING · PROOFREADING · PUBLISHING

Focus Skill

Using Details

Include exact details for each step so that your audience won't make a mistake. Be sure to include all the important details. Remember that your audience has never followed your instructions before.

Without Exact Details	With Exact Details
Cut the string and tie the cup halves together.	Cut the string into four six-inch-long pieces. Tie the strings through the holes of the cup halves so one half hangs from the other.

Think and Discuss Compare the examples above.

- Which example is clearer? Why? *the second example, because it gives exact details about how to cut the string and how to tie up the cup halves*
- What might happen if the exact details were left out of the instructions? *Answers will vary.*

Draft Your Instructions

1. **Add** details to your Step-by-Step Chart. Here is an example from Colin's chart.

Steps	Materials Needed	Details
1. First, make a papier-mâché balloon.	rubber balloon newspaper bowl paste	blow up balloon tear newspaper put strips in paste

2. **Use your chart** to help you write your instructions. It's never too late to add more details if you need them.
3. **Skip** every other line. You can make corrections and changes later.
4. **Read** your instructions to a partner. Have your partner pantomime the steps.

Paragraph Tip
Start a new paragraph when you begin a step that has many details.

350 Unit 10: Instructions

Meeting Individual Needs

● RETEACHING WORKBOOK, page 93

Using Details

Exact details help make instructional steps easier to follow. They describe the materials needed and tell how to do each step.

Without Exact Details	With Exact Details
Tape plastic cups together. Number them. Throw buttons in, and count your score.	Tape six plastic cups together in the shape of a triangle. Write a number, from 1 to 6, inside each cup. Stand back and throw six buttons into the cups. The player with the highest total wins.

The Step-by-Step Chart below lists the steps and materials for making an indoor super-mini golf course. Look at the picture, and add exact details in the third column of the chart. Sample details:

Steps	Materials Needed	Details
1. First, put clay in bottle cap.	plastic bottle cap modeling clay	Roll clay into a small ball. Press it into the bottle cap.
2. Then make nine holes.	nine paper cups marker, masking tape	Use the marker to number paper cups 1 through 9. Tape the cups to the floor in order, with room between them.
3. Now play golf.	ruler, bottle cap weighted with clay	Use the ruler as a golf club to hit the cap toward a cup. Count the number of shots it takes to get the cap into each "hole."

▲■ WORKBOOK PLUS, page 142

Using Details

Without Exact Details	With Exact Details
Fold a piece of paper. Attach the pieces with string.	Fold a piece of paper in half, and then fold it again. Cut the squares apart, and punch a hole in the top of each. Next, string the squares together.

The Step-by-Step Chart below lists the steps and materials for making a mobile. Look at the picture, and add details to the chart. Then use the chart to help you write a set of instructions. Remember to include exact details. Sample details:

Steps	Materials Needed	Details
1 First, make interesting paper shapes.	old newspaper and magazines, scissors, glue	Cut the paper into small pieces. Glue pieces together to make designs.
2 Next, attach bottles to hanger.	plastic bottles, shoelaces or used string, wire coat hanger	Tie the string around the tops of the bottles. Tie them to the hanger.
3 When glue dries, attach shapes to hanger.	shapes from Step 1, more string, mobile	Attach the paper designs with string. Make them all different lengths.

Instructions will vary.

Focus Skill

Good Beginnings and Endings

When you write instructions, think of yourself as a coach. Your beginning should get your team interested in the game, and your ending should leave them eager to play.

A good beginning includes a topic sentence that states the main idea. The beginning should also catch the interest of your audience.

Weak Beginning	Strong Beginning
This is how to grow carrots.	Here's how to have fun outdoors and grow the best carrots you've ever eaten.

A good ending wraps up your instructions. End with a closing sentence that makes your audience want to try out your instructions.

Weak Ending	Strong Ending
Now you can pick and eat your carrots.	After tasting your fresh, homegrown carrots, you'll never want to eat canned or frozen carrots again.

Try It Out With a partner compare the examples above. Answers will vary.

- Write a different strong beginning.
- Write a different strong ending.

Don't just end with the last step.

Draft Your Beginning and Ending

1. **Write** two beginnings and two endings for your instructions.
2. **Choose** the beginning and ending you like better.

Good Beginnings and Endings

Lesson Objectives

Students will:
- write two beginnings and endings for their instructions
- select the beginning and the ending that fit the instructions best

Focus on Instruction

- Point out the use of the superlative adjective *best* in the strong beginning. Discuss how this word builds enthusiasm. Suggest that students use this form in their own writing to achieve the same effect.
- Ask students which ending gets the reader excited about the topic. (strong ending) Discuss how the adjectives *fresh* and *homegrown* contrast with *canned* and *frozen* and motivate readers to carry out the instructions.
- Remind students that they can build enthusiasm with judicious use of exclamation points.

Try It Out

Have students share their beginnings and endings. Discuss different ways to draw in readers at the beginning: ask a question; use humor; make a surprising statement; or stir up feelings of curiosity, concern, or pleasure.

Draft Your Beginning and Ending

Have students consider their audience as they write. What tone should they use? Should it appeal to someone younger? older? their own age?

● RETEACHING WORKBOOK, page 94

Good Beginnings and Endings

A good beginning gets your audience's attention. It includes a strong topic sentence that clearly states the main idea. A good ending wraps up your instructions and makes your audience want to try them out.

Weak Beginning	Strong Beginning
Making dinner takes time.	A scrumptious home-cooked dinner is worth the time and effort it takes.

Weak Ending	Strong Ending
You'll enjoy the dinner you made.	A good plan, fresh ingredients, and just a little extra work will result in a meal worth waiting for!

Each set of instructions below needs a stronger beginning and ending. Write a better beginning and ending to replace the underlined sentences.
Sample answers:

1. Oatmeal is a good breakfast. First, boil a cup of water. While you wait for the water to boil, pour the instant oatmeal into a bowl. Carefully pour the boiling water over the oatmeal. Stir until the oatmeal flakes have absorbed all the water. Finally, add some milk, raisins, fresh fruit, or any combination of these ingredients. Now your oatmeal is ready to eat.

Beginning: Make oatmeal special by adding your own ingredients.

Ending: My favorite way to start the day is with my own special oatmeal breakfast.

2. Try a new and different juice drink. Make a smooth tutti-frutti shake. Use two cups of prepared lemonade, one cup of partially melted orange or strawberry sherbet, and 1/4 cup of cherry or grape juice. Put all the ingredients in a blender or shaker. Blend for three minutes and pour into two glasses. Drink up.

Beginning: Are you tired of the same old juice drinks?

Ending: Your mouth and stomach will thank you!

▲■ WORKBOOK PLUS, page 143

Good Beginnings and Endings

Weak Beginning	Strong Beginning
You can make a box with art sticks.	Do you need a place to keep small personal objects?

Weak Ending	Strong Ending
Now your little box is ready to use.	It's small, it's private, and it's ready to use!

The instructional paragraph below needs a better beginning and a better ending. First, read the paragraph. Then replace the underlined sentences. Write two interesting beginnings and circle the one that you think is stronger. Then write two strong endings and circle the one that you like better.
Sample answers:

Planting a flower garden is a good idea. You will need some seeds, a small shovel, and a plot with rich soil. First, read the instructions on the seed packet to find out how deeply you should dig. Then find a small area that gets enough sunlight. Now dig the holes and place the seeds in the ground. Next, cover them with dirt. Finally, drench the area with water. Be sure to water your plants regularly while they are growing. That's how you grow flowers.

Beginning: Even the smallest bit of earth can produce beautiful flowers.

Beginning: How would you like to grow smiles along with flowers?

Ending: When you have grown enough flowers, make a bouquet for someone special.

Ending: When colorful blossoms burst open like fireworks in the evening sky, you will know your hard work was worthwhile.

MEETING INDIVIDUAL NEEDS — FOR STUDENTS ACQUIRING ENGLISH

Students have had much practice with beginnings thus far. Remind them of the work they have done writing different versions of their beginnings. Ask them if they think this exercise has helped them write good beginnings. As a class, draft versions of volunteers' beginnings on the board. Encourage students to be innovative with both the openings and closings of their instructions. If they have trouble, suggest turning back to the models, or ask if they can use a quotation or a person or place they can describe.

Evaluating Your Instructions

Lesson Objective

Students will:
- evaluate their instructions, using a rubric

Connecting to the Criteria

Have students reread the characteristics of great instructions listed on page 342. Then explain that the rubric shown on this page refers to those characteristics. Tell students that the rubric will help them decide which parts of their instructions "ring the bell," or meet the standards of great instructions, and which parts need more work or haven't been addressed at all.

Focus on Instruction

- Review the rubric with students. Have a volunteer read the first point in each section and explain the differences among them. Follow the same procedure for the remaining points.
- Suggest that students read their instructions three times, each time thinking about only one or two of the rubric items. Blackline Master 10–4 provides a copy of the rubric as a checklist.
- See the Teacher's Resource Book for scoring rubrics.

This page is also available as a poster.

INTERNET CONNECTION Have your students go to www.eduplace.com/kids/hme/ to use an interactive version of the rubric shown in the student book. Students will get feedback and support depending on how they mark the rubric items.

FOR STUDENTS ACQUIRING ENGLISH

A reproduction of this page on a transparency would be helpful for students to use as a checklist. However, remind students to write the sentences that describe their instructions on their draft. When students are ready, they should write some questions about improving their drafts. Model questions such as: *My ending is boring, but I'm having trouble. What can I do? I can't explain how to tie the basket on. Can you help?* Questions like these can help when students are conferencing with you or their peers. Because this is a new skill, require students to write a minimum of two questions about their draft.

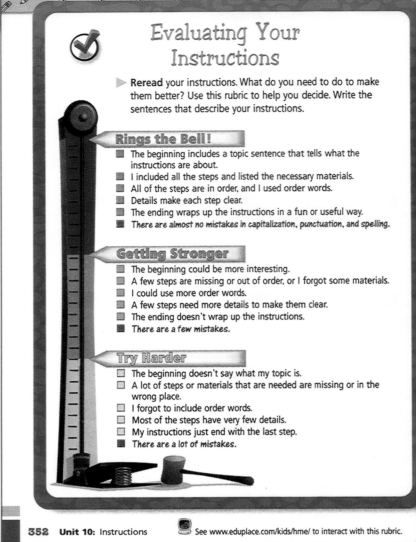

Evaluating Your Instructions

Reread your instructions. What do you need to do to make them better? Use this rubric to help you decide. Write the sentences that describe your instructions.

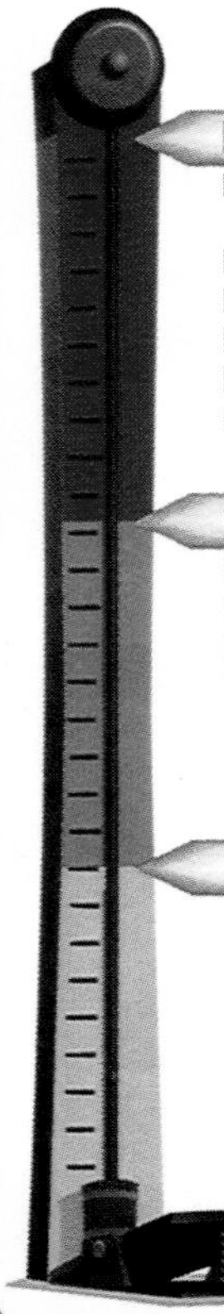

Rings the Bell!
- The beginning includes a topic sentence that tells what the instructions are about.
- I included all the steps and listed the necessary materials.
- All of the steps are in order, and I used order words.
- Details make each step clear.
- The ending wraps up the instructions in a fun or useful way.
- *There are almost no mistakes in capitalization, punctuation, and spelling.*

Getting Stronger
- The beginning could be more interesting.
- A few steps are missing or out of order, or I forgot some materials.
- I could use more order words.
- A few steps need more details to make them clear.
- The ending doesn't wrap up the instructions.
- *There are a few mistakes.*

Try Harder
- The beginning doesn't say what my topic is.
- A lot of steps or materials that are needed are missing or in the wrong place.
- I forgot to include order words.
- Most of the steps have very few details.
- My instructions just end with the last step.
- *There are a lot of mistakes.*

352 **Unit 10:** Instructions

See www.eduplace.com/kids/hme/ to interact with this rubric.

Meeting Individual Needs

● RETEACHING WORKBOOK, page 95

Revising Instructions

Have I | yes
- written a new beginning that states the topic in an interesting way? ❑
- included all the steps in the correct order? ❑
- listed all the materials needed for each step? ❑
- added clear, exact details for the steps? ❑
- revised the ending to wrap up the instructions? ❑

Revise the following instructional paragraph to make it better. Use the checklist above to help you. Check off each box when you have finished your revision. You can use the spaces above the lines, along the sides, and below the paragraph for your changes. Sample answers:

Always Ready for
S'Mores

~~S'Mores are delicious.~~ First, find an adult to build a campfire. Second, get a plain flat graham cracker, a chocolate bar, and a marshmallow for each S'More. Break the graham cracker and the chocolate bar in two, and put one piece of the chocolate on each cracker half. Next, use a long-handled fork to hold the marshmallow over the campfire. Put the toasted marshmallow between the chocolate layers. Squish the sandwich together. When your S'More is cool enough, eat it up. You know what to do next. Make s'more!

It's amazingly easy to make the cookie-candy-marshmallow sandwiches that deserve their special name—S'Mores.

▲■ WORKBOOK PLUS, page 144

Revising Instructions

Have I | yes
- written a new beginning that states the topic in an interesting way? ❑
- included all the steps in the correct order? ❑
- listed all the materials needed for each step? ❑
- added clear, exact details for the steps? ❑
- revised the ending to wrap up the instructions? ❑

Revise the following instructional paragraph to make it better. Use the checklist above to help you. Check off each box when you have finished your revision. You can use the spaces above the lines, along the sides, and below the paragraph for your changes. Sample answers:

Make Them Wonder!
~~Puzzle Party Invitations~~

Puzzle party invitations are fun to make and fun to receive. ~~Here's how to make puzzle party invitations.~~ Write each invitation on a card or thick construction paper. Use colorful felt pens. Then cut each invitation into eight or ten puzzle pieces. Put all the pieces for each invitation into an envelope. Address the envelopes, seal them, and put a stamp on each one. Finally, mail the invitations.

Your friends will begin having fun as soon as they open the invitations.

You can decorate the invitations creatively with stickers and glitter.

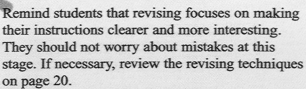

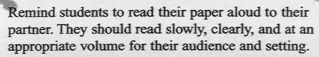

PREWRITING DRAFTING REVISING PROOFREADING PUBLISHING

Revise Your Instructions

Revising Tip

To add a step, write it on another piece of paper. Label it with a letter, such as *A*. Put a caret where the new step goes and write "Insert A."

1. **Revise** your instructions. Use the list of sentences you wrote from the rubric. Work on the parts that you described with sentences from "Getting Stronger" and "Try Harder."
2. **Discuss** your instructions in a writing conference.

   When You're the Writer Read your instructions to a partner. Discuss any problems you're having. Take notes to remember what your partner says.

   When You're the Listener Tell at least two things you like about the instructions. Ask questions about anything that is unclear. Use the chart below as a guide.

The Writing Conference

If you're thinking . . .	**You could say . . .**
The beginning doesn't get me interested.	**Could you begin with an interesting point about the topic?**
I can't picture how to do this step.	**What other details could you add to make this step clearer for your audience?**
What does this part have to do with the topic?	**You have a lot of good details, but does this really belong in the instructions?**
I'm confused.	**Are the steps in the right order?**
The instructions just end with the last step.	**Can you add something to wrap up the instructions?**

3. **Make more revisions** to your instructions. Use your conference notes and the Revising Strategies on the next page.

Revising 353

Help with Conferencing

ADDITIONAL CONFERENCING QUESTIONS

These questions may be useful during teacher-student conferences.

- Can you tell the reader how he or she will benefit from following these instructions?
- How can you direct the reader to the most important part of the instructions?
- Can you explain ______ better so I can picture it?
- Can you add more order words to guide the reader in the proper sequence of steps?
- Can you omit ______ so that it doesn't distract the reader away from the instructions?

EVALUATION TIP

Hold a model writing conference. Play the part of a student. Use Colin's working draft as the paper to be evaluated, or have a student volunteer his or her paper. Evaluate the success of students' writing conferences in relation to the model.

Lesson Objectives

Students will:

- revise their working draft, based on their evaluation
- discuss their working draft in a writing conference

Revise Your Instructions

Focus on Instruction

Revising Reminder

Remind students that revising focuses on making their instructions clearer and more interesting. They should not worry about mistakes at this stage. If necessary, review the revising techniques on page 20.

- Before the writing conference, have students highlight order words in their paper. The order words and the steps they refer to should be in the correct sequence.

Conferencing Reminders

Remind students to read their paper aloud to their partner. They should read slowly, clearly, and at an appropriate volume for their audience and setting.

- Remind students to give their partners a compliment about the work, such as *I can picture all the steps!,* before they ask questions and suggest changes.
- Tell students that they don't need to make every change their partners suggest. They should keep the comments in mind but make their own choices.
- Students can use Blackline Master 10–5 during their writing conferences.

MEETING INDIVIDUAL NEEDS

FOR STUDENTS ACQUIRING ENGLISH

Based on the self-evaluations and questions they have formulated, students should be well aware of the areas they wish to change. Still, students will need help with the actual revising. Sometimes, as students learn so many new skills, drafts actually appear to worsen with revision, but students improve over the long term. Continue to act out a sample conference for students, modeling helpful and hurtful behavior (looking at the reader vs. turning away, or asking leading questions vs. making harsh statements). Also model taking notes on the actual draft or in a notebook.

Revising Strategies

Lesson Objectives

Students will:
- replace vague verbs with exact ones
- use adverbs to add details to their instructions
- vary sentence length in their instructions

Focus on Instruction

Elaborating: Word Choice

Discuss the example with students. Point out how vague verbs might lead to mistakes or confusion. On the board, list some vague verbs, such as *put, have, make, do, go,* and *take*. Have students search for these verbs in their instructions and replace them with more exact ones.

Elaborating: Details

Remind students that adverbs can describe verbs and tell *how, where*, or *when*. Mention that many, but not all, adverbs end in *-ly*. Discuss how the adverbs in the example add details to the instructions.

Sentence Fluency

- Read the two examples aloud. Tell students to listen and then decide why the example using sentences of different lengths sounds better. (It sounds more natural and conversational.)
- Continue the discussion of sentence fluency by telling students that writers often vary sentence types to serve specific purposes. Write the following sentence on the board.

  After the paint is dry, paste the feather to the box.

  Point out that this complex sentence construction provides a time clue that makes the instructions more exact. Tell students to check for places in their writing where they could use introductory phrases to add time clues.

FOR STUDENTS ACQUIRING ENGLISH

Allow student use of dictionaries in their first language for specific verbs and nouns. Also brainstorm and list possibly useful words such as *punch, dip, spin, lightly, evenly,* and *quickly.* Then reinforce sentence combining with the use of *and.* If they wish, students can use other connectors *(or, but, nor).*

Revising Strategies

Elaborating: Word Choice Use exact verbs to tell your audience exactly what to do.

Without Exact Verbs	With Exact Verbs
Make a row of holes in the paper. Then **put** the yarn through them.	Punch a row of holes in the paper. Then weave the yarn through them.

▶ Change at least two verbs in your instructions to be more exact.

Use the Thesaurus Plus on page H79. See also page 118.

Elaborating: Details Insert adverbs to add details to help your audience picture the steps of your instructions more clearly.

Without Adverbs	With Adverbs
Open the lid. Hold the oars and pull.	Open the lid slightly. Hold the oars firmly and pull hard.

▶ Add adverbs in at least two places in your instructions.

Sentence Fluency Make your writing interesting to your readers by varying the lengths of your sentences.

All the Same Length	Different Lengths
The double checkers are called kings. Kings are the most useful checkers. They can move in both directions.	The double checkers are called kings. Kings are the most useful checkers because they can move in both directions.

▶ Find a group of at least three sentences in your instructions that are all short or all long. Rewrite them to vary their lengths.

GRAMMAR LINK See also pages 49 and 211.

Meeting Individual Needs

● RETEACHING WORKBOOK, page 96

Sentence Fluency

Make your writing more interesting by varying the length of your sentences.	
Sentences all the same length	Find two empty milk containers. Find a spongy rubber ball. Rinse the containers. Dry the containers. Cut off the bottoms of the containers. Play pitch with a friend.
Sentences different lengths	Find two empty milk containers and a spongy rubber ball. Rinse and dry the containers, and cut off the bottoms of the containers. Use the containers and the ball to play pitch with a friend.

The instructions below are boring because the sentences are all the same length. Revise the instructions, using sentences of different lengths to make them more interesting. Sentences will vary.

1. How talented are your toes? You will need a paper cup. You will need five peanuts. Take off one of your socks. Pick up one of the peanuts. Put it in the cup. Use just your toes.

2. Here's a game for two. Take off your shoes. Keep on your socks. Sit on the floor. Pick up a ball. Use just your feet. Pass the ball. Use just your feet.

▲■ WORKBOOK PLUS, page 145

Sentence Fluency

Sentences all the same length	Find some clear plastic wrap. Cut off a large piece. Tape it to a mirror. Stand in front of it. Use a marking pen. Trace your face.
Sentences different lengths	Cut off a large piece of clear plastic wrap, and tape it to a mirror. Then stand in front of it. Use a marking pen to trace your face.

These two sets of instructions sound boring because the sentences are all the same length. Revise the instructions, using sentences of different lengths to make them more interesting.

1. Take two empty cans. Wash them out. Punch a hole in the bottom of each can. Connect the cans with string. Ask a friend to put one can up to an ear. Tell your friend to listen. Pull the string taut. Talk into the other can. Can your friend hear you?
   Sentences will vary.

2. Find an empty cardboard tube. Hold it up to one eye. Keep both eyes open. Put one hand next to the tube. Hold the hand a few inches from your face. You will see a hole in your hand.

PREWRITING DRAFTING REVISING PROOFREADING PUBLISHING

Proofread Your Instructions

Proofread your instructions, using the Proofreading Checklist and the Grammar and Spelling Connections. Proofread for one skill at a time. Use a class dictionary to check spellings.

Proofreading Checklist

Did I
- ✓ indent all paragraphs?
- ✓ correct run-on sentences?
- ✓ use commas correctly?
- ✓ use negatives correctly?
- ✓ correct any spelling errors?

Use the Guide to Capitalization, Punctuation, and Usage on page H55.

Proofreading Marks
- ¶ Indent
- ∧ Add
- Delete
- ≡ Capital letter
- / Small letter

Tech Tip
Scroll down your instructions until just the top line shows. Then proofread your instructions one line at a time.

Grammar and Spelling Connections

Negatives Words that contain the meaning "no" or "not" are called negatives. Never use two negatives together in a sentence.

Incorrect: Play until there aren't no letters left.
Correct: Play until there aren't any letters left.
Correct: Play until there are no letters left.

GRAMMAR LINK See also page 242.

Commas in a Series Use commas to separate three or more items in a series. Put a comma after each item except the last one.

You need sand, food coloring, paper, a pencil, and glue.

GRAMMAR LINK See also page 176.

Spelling Long *o* The |ō| sound is often spelled *o*, *o*-consonant-*e*, *oa*, or *ow*.

no, note, float, grow

See the Spelling Guide on page H65.

Go to www.eduplace.com/kids/hme/ for proofreading practice.

Help with Proofreading

MANAGEMENT TIP
Have each student keep a personal checklist of skills that he or she needs to proofread for. Staple the list to the student's folder.

TECH TIP
Remind students that spelling tools on a computer will not find errors in punctuation. For example, a spelling tool will not flag a missing comma.

EVALUATION TIP
Check to see that students are using available resources for proofreading, such as the class dictionary and the Guide to Capitalization, Punctuation, and Usage, rather than relying heavily on you or other students for assistance.

Lesson Objective

Students will:
- proofread their instructions

Proofread Your Instructions

Focus on Instruction

Proofreading Reminders
- Encourage students to use the Guide to Capitalization, Punctuation, and Usage.
- If necessary, review with students when and how to use each proofreading mark. Have students use a different colored pen or pencil to mark their proofreading corrections.
- For proofreading practice, see the usage and mechanics lessons in the grammar units and the Mixed Review practice in each grammar unit Checkup.

- Review and clarify each item in the checklist, using any related Grammar and Spelling Connections. If students need extra support, review the lessons listed in the Grammar Links.
- On the board, write the following sentence, and have students restate it to correct the double negative.

  Can't nobody fix this for me? (Can't anybody fix this for me? Can nobody fix this for me?)
- Direct students' attention to the sentence with items in a series. Point out that the commas make the list of items much easier to read and can prevent misunderstandings.
- Present other words that fit the long *o* spelling principle, such as *go, row, coat,* and *tone*. Ask volunteers to name other words with the long *o* sound. Write the words on the board to see which spelling pattern they follow.

INTERNET CONNECTION Have your students go to www.eduplace.com/kids/hme/ for online proofreading practice that is fun.

MEETING INDIVIDUAL NEEDS

FOR STUDENTS ACQUIRING ENGLISH
Commands may be unfamiliar for students, especially those who speak first languages with different command verb forms. Give a mini-lesson on command forms in English. Demonstrate that students needn't use the pronoun *you* but merely the verb in the second person form, for example, *Put it down* vs. *You put it down.*

Lesson Objectives

Students will:

- make a neat final copy of their instructions
- choose a way to publish or share their instructions
- reflect on their writing experience
- evaluate their instructions in comparison to other compositions in their portfolio

Publish Your Instructions

Focus on Instruction

- Before students make their final copy, have them decide how they will publish or share their instructions. Review their decisions with them to help them make any special plans.
- Help students make neat corrections to their final copy rather than rewrite their paper.

Keeping a Writing Portfolio

- **Selection** A paper might be selected because it is
  ✓ generally noteworthy
  ✓ a good example of a particular criterion
  ✓ an example of a particular kind of writing
  ✓ an example from a certain time in the school year
  ✓ a typical example of the student's work
- **Labeling** For every paper, have students complete a cover sheet giving the title, date of completion, and reason for inclusion.
- **Review** Periodically have students remove papers that no longer reflect their best work or aren't needed as baselines.
- **Evaluation** Periodically review students' portfolios with them to discuss growth and areas that need improvement.

SCHOOL-HOME CONNECTION Have students recruit family members to conduct a "usability test" of their instructions. First, have the student present his or her instructions in their published form. Then have the family member follow the instructions. Have students critique the effectiveness of their instructions.

The Writing Process: PREWRITING · DRAFTING · REVISING · PROOFREADING · PUBLISHING

Publish Your Instructions

1. **Make a neat final copy** of your instructions. Check to make sure you corrected all mistakes.
2. **Write** a title for your instructions. The title should make the topic clear and stir up interest in it. For example, "The Smart, Safe Way to Bike" is better than "How to Ride a Bike."

GRAMMAR TIP *Capitalize the first, the last, and each important word in a title.*

3. **Publish** or share your instructions in a way that suits your audience. See the Ideas for Sharing box.

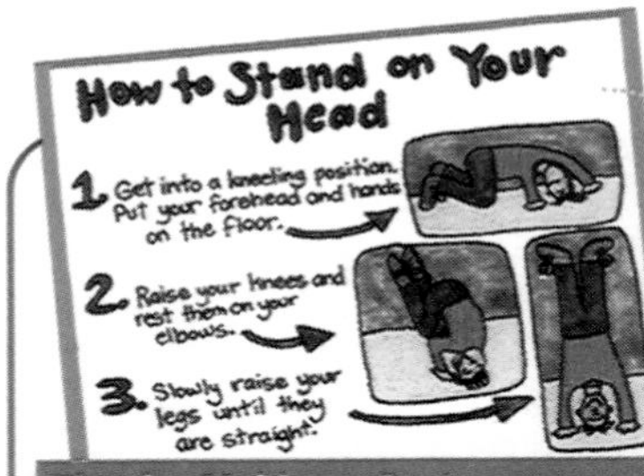
How to Stand on Your Head
1. Get into a kneeling position. Put your forehead and hands on the floor.
2. Raise your knees and rest them on your elbows.
3. Slowly raise your legs until they are straight.

Tips for Making a Poster

- Use color to make the main ideas stand out.
- Make separate sections for the materials and each main step.
- Number the steps.
- Include helpful photos or drawings.

Ideas for Sharing

Write It

- Make a class "How To" activity book.
- Make an instructions sheet. Use a computer to create a layout.

Say It

- Present the instructions to a group as you demonstrate.

Show It

★ Make a poster.

Reflect

Write about your writing experience. Use these questions to get started.

- What was challenging about writing instructions? What was easy?
- What will you do differently the next time you write instructions?
- How do your instructions compare with other papers you have written?

Help with Publishing

TIPS FOR IDEAS FOR SHARING

Activity Book Have students put each step of their instructions on an index card. Place illustrations or diagrams on the front. Write details on the back. Punch a hole in the top left corner of each card, and thread a metal ring, twist tie, or string through the holes to join the cards.

Reading Aloud Remind students who plan to present their instructions aloud to speak with a rate, volume, pitch, and tone that is appropriate for their audience.

TECH TIP

Students can scan photos or use a paint or draw computer program to illustrate their instruction sheets or posters.

Assessment Link

Writing Prompts

Use these prompts as ideas for writing instructions or to practice for a test. Some of them fit with other subjects you study. Decide who your audience will be, and write your instructions in a way that they will understand and enjoy.

1 Do you collect something, such as stamps, cards, or shells? Write instructions for how to start, build, or take care of a collection.

2 What do you do to help out at home? Write instructions for a chore you know how to do, such as setting the table or washing clothes.

3 Do you have your own special way of doing something? Have you discovered the perfect way to entertain a cat? get to sleep? eat a slice of pizza? Share your secret by writing instructions for it.

4 Imagine that you are entertaining a young child on a rainy day. What indoor game or activity do you know that the child could learn? Write the instructions for the game or activity.

Writing Across the Curriculum

5 SCIENCE
Write instructions for doing a science experiment. Include materials and safety information.

6 ART
Write instructions explaining how to do an art or crafts project. Can you make a necklace? paint a picture? Include a materials list.

7 MATH
Suppose you had a huge bank loaded with pennies, nickels, dimes, quarters, and half dollars. Write instructions for an easy way to count the money.

8 PHYSICAL EDUCATION
What athletic skill could you teach to a beginner? Can you hit a baseball? do a simple dive? skate without falling? Write instructions to help a beginner get started.

See www.eduplace.com/kids/hme/ for more prompts. Writing Prompts 357

Writing Prompts

Objective

Students will:

- review prompts for choosing a topic or to practice for a writing test

Using the Prompts

You can use the prompts on this page in several ways.

- Have students review the prompts to help spark ideas as they choose their own topics for instructions. Suggest that students choose one or two prompts that interest them and brainstorm ideas of their own.
- Choose a prompt to provide practice for a writing test. Use it with the Test Practice on the next page.
- Choose a prompt that fits with a related topic in another subject area to integrate the skill of writing instructions across the curriculum.

INTERNET CONNECTION Send your students to www.eduplace.com/kids/hme/ for more writing prompts. You can also find and print these prompts at www.eduplace.com/rdg/hme/.

MEETING INDIVIDUAL NEEDS

FOR STUDENTS ACQUIRING ENGLISH

Define vocabulary to help students understand each prompt. Essential words include *collect, chore,* and *entertain*. First read the prompts, and then encourage students to guess the meaning of the vocabulary based on context. Prompts that are especially suitable for ESL learners are *making a special dish,* and *playing a special game.*

Test Practice

Objective

Students will:

- learn strategies for evaluating a writing prompt and writing instructions for a test

Using the Test Practice

- Read through the page with students. Discuss strategies for identifying clue words, using the pictures, and planning the writing. Suggest to students that they look at the last picture first to see what the instructions are about and then look at all of the pictures in order before planning their writing.
- Review the rubric on page 352 and the items in What Makes Great Instructions? with students before they write their practice test. Summarize the main points about organizing, using details, and writing good beginnings and endings.
- Have students write instructions in response to the prompt on this page or to one of the prompts on the previous page. Apply the same time constraints or other restrictions or qualifications specific to the testing requirements used in your school.

INTERNET CONNECTION Go to www.eduplace.com/rdg/hme/ for examples of benchmark papers.

MEETING INDIVIDUAL NEEDS — FOR STUDENTS ACQUIRING ENGLISH

Be sure students understand what a bookmark is. Bring in examples to pass around before asking students to write the instructions. As a class, briefly describe the steps in making the bookmark. Then brainstorm possibly useful words such as *measure, cut, felt, strip, fringe, ribbon, glue,* and so on.

Assessment Link

Test Practice

Sometimes on a test you will be asked to write a paper in response to a picture prompt like this one.

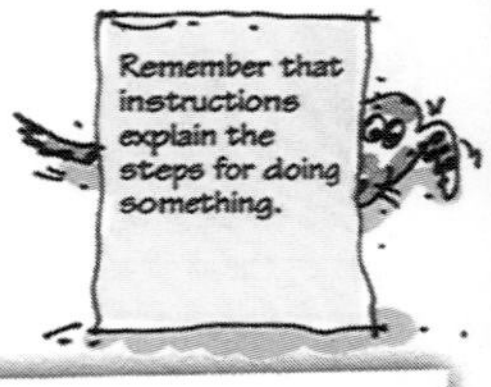

Remember that instructions explain the steps for doing something.

These pictures show how to make a bookmark. Look carefully at each picture. Then write instructions to go with the pictures that explain how to make the bookmark.

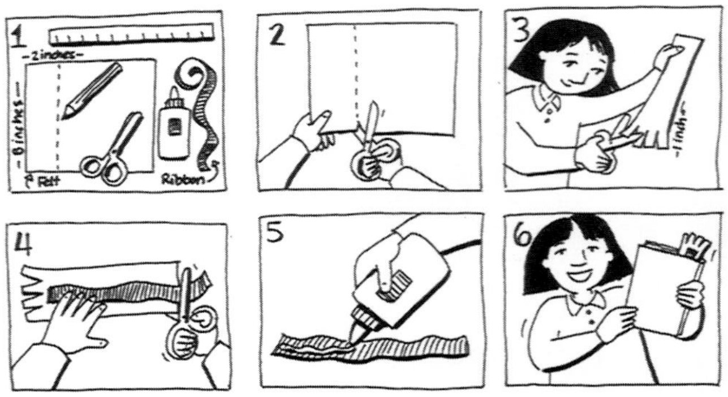

Here are some strategies to help you do a good job responding to a prompt like this one.

1. Look at each picture and answer these questions.
   - What materials are shown?
   - What has been done with the materials in each picture?
2. Plan your writing. Use the graphic organizer on page 349.
3. You will get a good score if you remember the description of what kind of instructions ring the bell in the rubric on page 352.

Writing to Compare and Contrast

When you write to **compare**, you explain how two things are alike. When you write to **contrast**, you explain how two things are different. Read Jane's essay that explains ways in which ballet and football are different and alike.

Pointe Shoes and Cleats

Introduction — Some people say ballet is just for girls, but it's not. Some say football is just for boys, but it's not. In fact, ballet and football have many things in common even though they seem very different. (Connecting words)

Topic sentence / Paragraph of contrast — It's easy to think of ways that ballet dancers and football players are different. In ballet, dancers can be short, tall, big, or small. It's not size that counts. It's flexibility. In football, though, the bigger the better, and speed helps, too. Some players need to be big to stop the other team. Some players need to run fast to carry the ball. Football players catch and throw footballs. In ballet, though, dancers catch and throw people—carefully! Finally, another difference is that ballet is danced on a stage, but football is played on a field.

Topic sentence / Paragraph of comparison — Ballet and football are also similar in some ways. They both take strength because practice sessions are long and hard. Both take concentration. Ballet dancers have to concentrate on all the dance steps, just as football players have to concentrate on all the plays. Also, the pointe shoes that dancers wear are as uncomfortable as football cleats. In fact, my sister who wears them says, "Pointe shoes hurt so badly I can't even say!" It takes guts to keep dancing or playing when your feet hurt.

Conclusion — The next time you see ballet dancers or football players, remember that they are more alike than you might think. They are all athletes who enjoy their sports, and we can too.

more ▶

Writing to Compare and Contrast

Lesson Objective

Students will:

- read a student model of an essay that compares and contrasts

Focus on the Model

- Ask students what they think is the purpose of a compare-contrast essay. (to show how two or more subjects are alike and different) Explain that to compare and contrast is one kind of explanation.
- Tell students that they will read an essay written by a student named Jane. Have students read the introduction to the model.
- Before students read the model, explain that the blue call outs highlight important elements of a comparison and contrast essay and that they will learn more about those elements after they read Jane's paper.
- Ask volunteers to read the model aloud. Have students look for details about how ballet and football are alike and different.

Students can also listen to the model on audiotape.

Writing to Compare and Contrast *continued*

Lesson Objective

Students will:
- identify the characteristics of a compare-contrast essay

Focus on Instruction

Discuss with the class the explanations of the call outs given in the Reading As a Writer section. Have volunteers answer the questions.

Answers to Reading As a Writer

- Jane says that ballet isn't just for girls, that football isn't just for boys, and that both activities have things in common.
- In Jane's first topic sentence, the main idea is that ballet dancers and football players are different in some ways. In her second topic sentence, the main idea is that ballet and football are also similar in some ways.
- Dancers can be any size as long as they're flexible, but it helps if football players are big and fast; players catch and throw footballs, but dancers catch and throw people; dancers dance on a stage, but players play on a field.
- Jane uses these transition words: *in fact, though, but, too, finally, just as,* and *also.*
- Jane thinks that people in ballet and football share strength, concentration, and guts.
- Both ballet dancers and players are athletes and more alike than people might think.

FOR STUDENTS ACQUIRING ENGLISH

Students may find the specialized words in this essay challenging. Assist with vocabulary such as *ballet* and *cleats* as needed. Most of the world calls soccer "football," so make sure students understand that the essay refers to American football. Ask students to find examples of connecting words and phrases in the essay. Explain the phrase *sums up*.

Reading As a Writer

See TE margin for answers.

- The **introduction** presents the subjects being compared and contrasted. It also says something interesting about them to catch the attention of the reader.
  What does Jane say about ballet and football in her introduction that might surprise you?
- **Topic sentences** tell the main idea of each paragraph.
  What is the main idea of each topic sentence in Jane's essay?
- The **paragraph of contrast** gives details that tell how the two subjects are different.
  What differences does Jane describe?
- **Connecting words**, such as *of course, too,* and *also,* help readers move smoothly from one idea to the next.
  What connecting words does Jane use?
- The **paragraph of comparison** gives details about how the two subjects are alike.
  In what ways does Jane think that ballet and football are alike?
- The **conclusion** sums up the likenesses and differences.
  What does Jane want the reader to remember?

How to Write to Compare and Contrast

1. **Choose** two subjects that are alike in some ways and different in other ways. You can pick people, places, animals, or objects. As you think about your subjects, ask yourself these questions.
   - Are there at least two ways they are alike and two ways they are different?
   - Will I be able to explain these likenesses and differences in writing?
   - Are my choices too broad? Is there just too much to say about each subject?

HELP ***Stuck for an Idea?***

Here are some suggestions.
- penguins and eagles
- two places I have visited
- rock 'n' roll and hip-hop music
- my hand and my foot
- a cactus and a tree

2. **List** details about each subject in a T-chart.
   - Write details about one subject on the left. Write details about the other subject on the other side.
   - Then find the likenesses and differences between your subjects. Draw lines to match the items in each column that are alike. See the T-chart on page 362.

Tech Tip

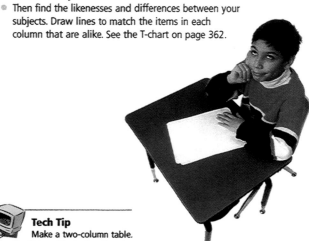

Make a two-column table. Use the Cut and Paste functions to line up likenesses and differences.

more ▶

Help with Writing to Compare and Contrast

MORE TOPIC IDEAS

Provide these suggestions:
- fourth grade and third grade
- a pencil and a pen
- rain and snow
- two kinds of pets
- two kinds of fruit
- two places where the student has lived
- two cars
- a book and its movie version

EVALUATION TIP

Review students' final topic choices. If the chosen subjects seem too similar, ask what differences the student can identify. If the subjects are very different, ask the student to identify the similarities. If the student doesn't have at least two or three details for each point of view, encourage him or her to choose another topic.

Lesson Objective

Students will:
- choose two subjects that they can compare and contrast

How to Write a Compare-Contrast Essay

Focus on Instruction

- Have students create a writing folder titled *My Compare-Contrast Essay*. Tell students to keep all their notes, graphic organizers, and drafts in this folder.
- Discuss with students different characteristics that can be used to compare and contrast two subjects, such as appearance, quality, performance or behavior, and appeal. Ask which characteristics might be used to compare and contrast two dogs (size, personality, appearance, behavior) and two movies about the same subject (actors' performances, audience appeal).
- The suggestion in Stuck for an Idea? that students compare "My hand and my foot" isn't meant to make students think self-consciously about body parts; however, with teacher help it could lead to great fun—students comparing their left and right hands—and lead students to become more fluent in the techniques of compare-contrast writing.
- Ask how a compare-contrast essay written for someone unfamiliar with the subjects might differ from one written for a person familiar with the subjects. (The knowledgeable person would need fewer details.)
- Ask how a compare-contrast essay written to clear up confusion about two similar subjects would differ from one that shows one subject is better than another. (Clearing up confusion requires many details and distinctions. Showing the superiority of one thing over another requires persuasion and convincing.)
- Remind students that formal language is required for some audiences and occasions.
- Explain that a T-chart is a good way to separate two sets of details. Ask students to find the details that are similar on Jane's T-chart, which is shown on the next page; (Possible answer: takes strength, takes concentration) and two that are different. (Possible answer: In football players are big; in ballet they are small.)

MEETING INDIVIDUAL NEEDS **FOR STUDENTS ACQUIRING ENGLISH**

With students, brainstorm words used for comparison and contrast. Set up two categories on the board. Include related word forms such as *differ, different, difference*. Students may have difficulty with words such as *likeness* and similar words such as *like* and *alike*. Call on students to write sentences presenting words in context.

Writing to Compare and Contrast *continued*

Lesson Objectives

Students will:

- list and organize details about their subject
- write an introduction that makes readers curious

Focus on Instruction

- If students have not previously worked with a Venn diagram, explain that it shows the characteristics two subjects have in common and the characteristics that are different. Shared characteristics appear where the circles overlap. Ask students what characteristics Jane listed in the overlapping circles. (take strength, take concentration, take guts, uncomfortable shoes, for athletes)
- Have students look at the details in the other areas of the circles. Have them read the top detail on each side, noting that the two details focus on the same characteristic (size of participants) and how it is different in ballet and football. Repeat line by line to reinforce the parallel listing of differences.
- Have students work in small groups and discuss the two subjects they plan to compare.

SCHOOL-HOME CONNECTION Have students share their Venn diagram with family, asking for any additional similarities or differences family members might suggest.

Ballet	Football
Dancers can be short. They can also be tall, big, or small.	played on a field
takes strength	helps if players are big or fast
takes concentration	players catch and throw footballs
takes guts	uncomfortable shoes
for athletes	for athletes
uncomfortable shoes	takes strength
danced on a stage	takes concentration
	takes guts

▲ Part of Jane's chart

Are you having trouble finding enough details? Choose new subjects to compare and contrast.

3 **Organize** your details by putting them in a Venn diagram.

- Label your diagram with the names of your subjects, as shown below.
- Write what is different about each subject in the outside sections.
- Write how the subjects are alike in the inside section.

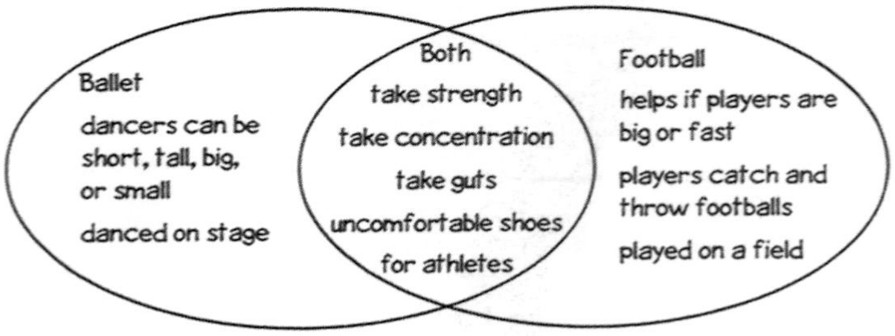

4 **Introduce** your two subjects by telling something that will make your readers curious about them.

Help with Writing to Compare and Contrast

TECH TIP

Using the draw feature of available software, students can create both a T-chart and a Venn diagram in the same document. Then they can use the Cut and Paste functions to move text from the T-chart to the appropriate part of the Venn diagram.

5 **Write** two paragraphs, one comparing and one contrasting your subjects.

- Write the paragraph that compares your subjects, using the details listed in the inside section of your Venn diagram.
- Write the paragraph that contrasts your subjects, using the differences listed in the outside sections.
- For each paragraph, write a clear topic sentence that gives the paragraph's main idea. Make sure all of the sentences that follow each topic sentence explain or tell more about the main idea.
- Use connecting words to help your readers pass easily from one idea to the next.

Connecting Words
To Show Likenesses and Differences in contrast however though although in fact but
To Tell More another also in addition too finally

6 **Sum up** the likenesses and differences between your subjects in your conclusion. You could tell how you think or feel about these likenesses and differences.

7 **Revise** your essay, using the Revising Checklist.

Revising Checklist

- ✓ What information did I include in my introduction to get my readers' attention?
- ✓ Have I included at least two likenesses and two differences?
- ✓ Did I write all the likenesses in one paragraph and all the differences in another paragraph?
- ✓ Do my topic sentences clearly tell the main idea of each paragraph?
- ✓ Where can I add connecting words?
- ✓ Does my conclusion sum up the main points?

more ▶

Help with Writing to Compare and Contrast

REVISING TIP
Tell students to use at least two connecting words in their essays.

EVALUATION TIP
Have students highlight the topic sentence in each paragraph to be sure that they have one. Help them check each topic sentence to see if it states the main idea of the paragraph.

TECH TIP
Students can highlight their topic sentences in bold and then check to see if all of the other sentences in the paragraph support the topic sentence.

Lesson Objectives

Students will:

- write a first draft of their essay
- revise their essay, using the Revising Checklist

Focus on Instruction

- Have a volunteer read the directions for drafting the essay. Be sure that students understand which part(s) of the Venn diagram relate to each paragraph.
- To reinforce student learning, model possible topic sentences for compare and contrast essays on the board. For example, if students were writing to compare and contrast wolves and coyotes, their two paragraphs might have topic sentences something like these. Comparison paragraph: *Wolves and coyotes are alike in many ways.* Contrast paragraph: *Although wolves and coyotes are similar in some ways, they are very different in other ways.*
- Suggest that students first write their paragraphs and then go back to add connecting words.
- Before students write their conclusions, have a volunteer reread Jane's conclusion.

Revising Reminder

Remind students that the purpose of revising is to make their writing clearer and more interesting. They should not worry about correcting mistakes at this stage.

Connecting to the Criteria

Have students review the characteristics of a good compare-contrast essay listed on the Reading As a Writer section on page 360. Explain that the Revising Checklist on this page will help them evaluate their essay in relation to those characteristics.

Lesson Objectives

Students will:
- discuss their essay in a writing conference
- proofread their essay
- publish and share their final copy

Focus on Instruction

Conferencing Reminders

Remind students
- to read their papers aloud to their partners during the writing conference;
- to summarize the main points of the essay first when they are the listeners so that the writer knows whether the essay was clear and which parts, if any, were not; and
- that questions or comments from their partners are only suggestions and that the writers should decide what changes they want to make.

Proofreading Reminders

- Tell students to circle any words they think are misspelled and to check them in a dictionary.
- Remind student to refer to the Guide to Capitalization, Punctuation, and Usage and to the Spelling Guide at the back of their book.
- Check students' proofread papers before they make their final copies.

- Review the Proofreading Checklist on page 355 and the use of proofreading marks with students.
- To support proofreading skills, have students proofread a partner's essay as well as their own.

Help each student decide whether this paper should go in the portfolio.

- Review students' publishing plans with them to help them address any special requirements.
- After students publish their work, ask them to evaluate how well their writing achieved its purpose.

FOR STUDENTS ACQUIRING ENGLISH

Students may need guidance and practice in providing feedback in English. You may find it useful to have students practice asking polite questions such as those in the book and providing polite criticism. Model and discuss correct intonation in information and yes-no questions as well as appropriate body language.

8 **Hold a writing conference.** Take notes to remember your partner's ideas, and then decide whether you want to make further changes to your essay. These questions may help during your conference.

The Writing Conference

If you're thinking...	**You could say...**
This needs an introduction.	**Could you start with a question or a statement that will make your readers curious about your subjects?**
I can't tell how these subjects are different.	**Tell me more about how ______ is different from ______ .**
I can't tell how these subjects are alike.	**Tell me more about how ______ is like ______ .**
The likenesses are mixed up with the differences.	**Are you comparing or contrasting in this paragraph? Could you add a topic sentence that tells me that?**
That sentence seems out of place.	**What is this sentence telling more about? Does it tell more about the main idea of this paragraph?**
There's no conclusion.	**Can you sum up your main idea in a final paragraph?**

9 **Proofread** your essay, using the Proofreading Checklist on page 355. Use a dictionary to check spellings.

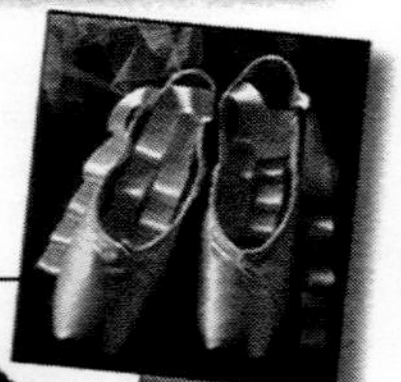

10 **Publish** or share a final copy of your essay with your audience. For example, on a long piece of yarn you might string some pictures showing how your subjects are different and alike.

Help with Writing to Compare and Contrast

MORE CONFERENCING QUESTIONS

These questions may be useful during teacher-student conferences.
- In addition to naming your subjects in the introduction, can you also tell something interesting about them or why you are writing about them?
- What connecting word could you use to begin [a specific sentence, a new paragraph]?
- Can you give more details to explain why these two subjects are alike (or different) in [a certain way]?
- Can you add a conclusion that tells what you think or feel about these subjects?

Giving and Following Instructions

When instructions are clear, the task or game is easier to figure out. Use these guides to give instructions.

Guides for Giving Instructions

1. Explain the purpose of the instructions.
2. Tell one step at a time. Use words such as *first, next,* and *finally* to show the order of the steps.
3. Include enough details to make each step clear. If you can, show how to do each step as you explain it.
4. Speak clearly. Adjust the volume of your voice to fit your audience and setting.

Before you give your instructions, plan what you are going to say. Write down the steps first. Then try to follow them to see if they work.

If you follow instructions carefully, you will make fewer mistakes. These guides will help.

Guides for Following Instructions

1. Listen carefully to each step.
2. Listen to the order of the steps. Words like *first, then,* and *next* will help you.
3. Try to picture each step in your mind. If the person is showing you what to do, watch carefully.
4. Ask questions if you do not understand.

Apply It

Find or sketch a simple picture made up of different geometric shapes, including circles, triangles, and rectangles. Give instructions to your partner on how to draw the picture. Use words and phrases such as *above, on top of, to the right side,* and *below.* Switch roles and follow your partner's instructions.

- Does your partner's drawing look like the picture you described?
- How can you improve your instructions? Answers will vary.

FOR STUDENTS ACQUIRING ENGLISH

Ask students to comment on the way they used the drawing to help them understand the instructions. In particular, ask students to talk about vocabulary that was clarified by the drawings. Also ask students to mention words in the written directions that remain unclear and to talk about what they could do to figure out the meaning.

Giving and Following Instructions

Lesson Objectives

Students will:

- prepare and present precise instructions for tasks, speaking clearly and appropriately for the audience
- determine the purpose for listening
- listen actively and purposefully to gain information
- follow a set of oral instructions

Focus on Instruction

- Have volunteers read aloud the Guides for Giving Instructions. Discuss each guide.
- Remind students that the *volume* refers to how loudly or softly a person is speaking. Ask students how they would adjust the volume of their voice if they were presenting instructions to the whole class. (speak more loudly than normal) if presenting in a very large room, such as an auditorium full of people? (speak even louder, but without shouting) Explain that effective public speaking involves adjusting the volume, rate, pitch, and tone of the voice, as well as choosing appropriate vocabulary and sentence structure for the audience.
- Have volunteers read aloud the Guides for Following Instructions. Discuss each guide as necessary to clarify meaning.
- Tell students that as they listen to instructions, they should establish a purpose for listening. Are they listening to gain information about how to fix something, accomplish a task, or solve a problem?
- On the board, write a list of possible tasks or games, such as tying a shoe, wrapping a package, drawing a star, or playing tag. Have students work in pairs, taking turns giving and following instructions. Remind students to refer back to the Guides for Giving and Following Instructions.

Apply It

- Emphasize that speakers should use cues from the audience to gauge their understanding. For instance, a wrinkled eyebrow or frown may show confusion. In that situation, a speaker should speak more slowly and perhaps pause to answer questions or add detail.
- To help students focus on the voice of the person giving instructions, tell them to try to block out background noise.
- Tell students they can evaluate how well they give instructions by looking at how well their partner can follow their instructions.

Comparing Visual Information

Lesson Objectives

Students will:

- analyze and interpret the significance, message, and meaning of visual images
- compare and contrast the information received from a technical illustration and a photograph

Focus on Instruction

- Ask students when visual information might be more useful than text. (Possible answers: when an object being discussed has many parts, when a process has many steps) Explain that often visual information is accomplished by text, but at times, visuals can stand alone.
- Discuss with students the saying "A picture is worth a thousand words." Ask if students agree with the statement.
- Tell students that there are camera techniques, such as close-ups, aerial views, and wide-angle shots, that influence how people view or feel about an image. Photographers can create feelings of excitement, fear, joy, and sorrow by manipulating how a photograph is taken.
- Tell students to examine the photograph of the volcano. Then have them describe what they feel when they look at the picture. Present additional questions, such as the following:

  What message did the photographer try to deliver?

  Are you worried about the people inside the helicopter?

  What do you imagine the area looks like beyond the edge of the photo?

  If a group of tourists were standing on the hillside, how would that change your view of the danger?

Comparing Visual Information

Information comes to you in many ways. Visual information is information that you see in pictures. A photograph, a diagram, a graph, a map, or a drawing can show ideas that may not be given in words.

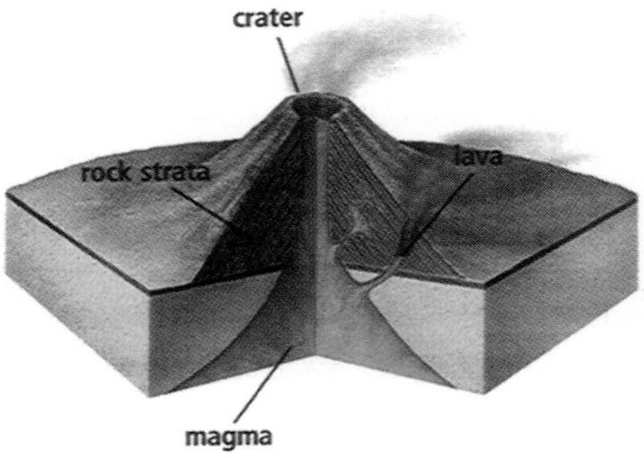

Photographs

Do photographs show things just the way they are? Not really. A photograph captures a single instant in time. Most things won't appear that way again.

Also, a camera shoots only what is in front of it. Photographers choose what to include and what to leave out in a photo. They decide on a center of interest. Their choices can make a difference in what you feel and think about when you look at a photograph.

Look at the photo of the volcano. What is the center of interest? How does the photographer bring out the idea of danger? Think about the information the photo gives about volcanoes.

Cut-away Diagrams

A cut-away diagram lets you see inside something. The artists who draw diagrams choose a center of interest for the picture. They may label different parts. Diagrams, though, often don't include as many details as a photograph.

Look at the cut-away diagram on page 366. Compare it to the photograph. What can you learn from each one? What information does the diagram give that the photograph doesn't?

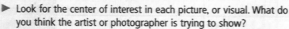

Guides for Comparing Visuals

- ▶ Look for the center of interest in each picture, or visual. What do you think the artist or photographer is trying to show?
- ▶ Think about the kind of information the visuals show. Do the pictures include details? Which picture gives more information?
- ▶ Remember that photographers and artists leave out information in their work. Think about the kinds of information they left out of the visuals and why.
- ▶ Suppose that you have been given only one of the visuals to view. What information would you miss if one of them were gone?

Apply It

Use the guides above to compare the information in two different kinds of visuals. Then answer these questions. Answers will vary.

- Did you learn more from one of the visuals than the other? Explain.
- Did either visual create a special feeling, such as enjoyment or tiredness? Why do you think this is so?
- What were the main differences between the two visuals?

Need ideas?

You can compare

- a photo and a cartoon of a famous person;
- a photo and a painting of a person, a place, or an event;
- a photo of a mountain and a relief map;
- a photo and a diagram from a news story.

Focus on Instruction

- After students have a chance to examine the cut-away diagram, ask them how their understanding of volcanoes would change if there was no photo. (They would understand the details, but not the whole picture.)
- Have volunteers read aloud the Guides for Comparing Visuals. Discuss each guideline as necessary to clarify meaning. If possible, show a photograph and a map or illustration of the same location, such as a national park. Have students evaluate the images according to the guides. Then ask additional questions, such as the following.

  How do the artists' purposes differ? How are they the same?

  Is one of the images more "factual" than another? In what ways?

  Which image do you think does the better job of communicating? Why?

Apply It

- Assemble pairs of different kinds of visuals ahead of time. You might find appropriate photos, maps, and diagrams of the same subjects in social studies or science textbooks. History textbooks may have photos and paintings of the same subject. News magazines often group together many kinds of visuals on the same subject.
- Remind students to give strong reasons for opinions they express in their evaluations. Emphasize that they should support their opinions with specific examples from the visuals.

FOR STUDENTS ACQUIRING ENGLISH

First ask a volunteer to explain the meaning of *visual.* Then ask if anyone knows a word that is related to *visual. (vision)* Ask for examples of types of visuals; list ideas on the board. Write *cut-away diagram* on the board; discuss what this type of diagram helps one see. How is a diagram different from a photo?

Unit 11 Planning Guide

Writing a Research Report

Writing a Research Report: *2 weeks*
Special Focus and Communication Links: *1 week (optional)*

	Blackline Masters (TE)	Workbook Plus	Reteaching Workbook
Published Model "What Do Sea Otters Look Like?" by Alvin, Virginia, and Robert Silverstein *(369–370)*			
What Makes a Great Research Report? *(371)*			
Student Model Working Draft *(372–373)* Final Copy *(374–376)*	11-1A, 11-1B		
The Writing Process Write a Research Report			
Prewriting Explore the Topic *(378)*	11–2		
Focus Skill: Finding the Best Information *(379–380)*		146	97
Plan Your Report *(383)*	11–3		
Drafting Focus Skill: Writing from an Outline *(384)*		147	98
Focus Skill: Good Openings and Closings *(385)*		148	99
Revising Evaluating Your Research Report [rubric] *(386)*	11–4	149	100
Writing Conference *(387)*	11–5		
Revising Strategies *(388)*		150	101
Adding Graphics and Visuals *(389–390)*			
Proofreading *(391)*			
Publishing and Reflecting *(392)*			
Writing Prompts and Test Practice *(393)*			
SPECIAL FOCUS ON INFORMING Writing to Solve a Problem *(394–395)* Writing a News Article *(396–397)* Completing a Form *(398–399)*	11–6		
COMMUNICATION LINKS Speaking/Viewing/Media: Giving an Oral Report *(400–401)* Viewing/Media: Looking at the News *(402–403)*			

Unit 11

Tools and Tips

- **Listening and Speaking Strategies,** *pp. H4–H10*
- **Building Vocabulary,** *pp. H11–H17*
- **Research and Study Strategies,** *pp. H18–H30*
- **Using Technology,** *pp. H35–H47*
- **Writer's Tools,** *pp. H48–H54*
- **Spelling Guide,** *pp. H65–H69*
- **Guide to Capitalization, Punctuation, and Usage,** *pp. H55–H64*
- **Thesaurus Plus,** *pp. H79–H100*

School-Home Connection

Suggestions for informing or involving family members in classroom activities and learning related to this unit are included in the Teacher's Edition throughout the unit.

Meeting Individual Needs

- **FOR SPECIAL NEEDS/INCLUSION:** *Houghton Mifflin English* Audiotape
- **FOR STUDENTS ACQUIRING ENGLISH:**
  - Notes and activities are included in this Teacher's Edition throughout the unit to help you adapt or use pupil book activities with students acquiring English.
  - Students acquiring English can listen to the the published and student models on audiotape.
  - MediaWeaver™, Sunburst/Humanities software, offers bilingual features, including Spanish menus, a Spanish spelling tool, and a Spanish thesaurus.
- **ENRICHMENT:** See *Teacher's Resource Book.*

All audiotape recordings are also available on CD.

Daily Language Practice

Each sentence includes two capitalization, punctuation, usage, or spelling errors based on skills presented in the Grammar and Spelling Connections in this unit or from Grammar Units 1–4. Each day write one sentence on the chalkboard. Have students find the errors and write the sentence correctly on a sheet of paper. To make the activity easier, identify the kinds of errors.

1. We dives only into the most deepest part of the pool. We dive only into the deepest part of the pool. (subject-verb agreement; comparing with adjectives)
2. A elevatar will take us to the top floor. An elevator will take us to the top floor. (articles; spelling final |ər|)
3. The Empire State building has drew visitors from around the world. The Empire State Building has drawn visitors from around the world. (proper nouns; irregular verbs)
4. My brother tryed to win the pie-eating contest at the picnic on Labor day. My brother tried to win the pie-eating contest at the picnic on Labor Day. (past tense; proper nouns)
5. My coat musst up my shirt coller. My coat mussed up my shirt collar. (past tense; spelling final |ər|)
6. Dont you know the name of your town's mayer? Don't you know the name of your town's mayor? (contractions; spelling final |ər|)
7. That bakor makes the goodest blueberry muffins. That baker makes the best blueberry muffins. (spelling final |ər|; comparing with adjectives)
8. Chess is hardest to play than checkers you must learn many different moves. Sample: Chess is harder to play than checkers. You must learn many different moves. (comparing with adjectives; run-on sentences)
9. The police officer tapt on the front window of the mans' car. The police officer tapped on the front window of the man's car. (past tense; possessive nouns)
10. My mother worrys about everyone and everything? My mother worries about everyone and everything. (present tense; end punctuation)

Additional Resources

Workbook Plus, Unit 11
Reteaching Workbook, Unit 11
Teacher's Resource Book
Transparencies
Posters, Unit 11
Audiotapes

Technology Tools

CD-ROM: *EasyBook Deluxe
MediaWeaver™, Sunburst/Humanities software
*The Writer's Resource Library
*Type to Learn™

*©Sunburst Technology Corporation, a Houghton Mifflin Company. All rights reserved.

INTERNET: http://www.eduplace.com/kids/hme/ *or* http://www.eduplace.com/rdg/hme/

Visit Education Place for these additional support materials and activities:

- author biographies
- student writing models
- graphic organizers
- an interactive rubric
- proofreading practice
- writing prompts
- help with research papers
- benchmark papers

Assessment

Test Booklet, Unit 11

Keeping a Journal

Discuss with students the value of keeping a journal as a way of promoting self-expression and fluency. Encourage students to record their thoughts and ideas in a notebook. Inform students whether the journal will be private or will be reviewed periodically as a way of assessing growth. The following prompts may be useful for generating writing ideas.

Journal Prompts

- What hobbies do you have? What do you know about the history of your favorite hobby?
- Scientific discoveries are often in the news. What new discovery would you like to know more about?
- Who is your favorite movie star? How did he or she get started? What films has he or she been in?

Introducing the Unit

Using the Photograph

Note on the Photograph This color-enhanced NASA photograph shows the planet Saturn, the second largest planet in our solar system.

- Have students look at the photograph and describe what they see. (Sample responses: a spherical object with rings; a planet) Then have a volunteer read the caption aloud, and share the information about Saturn provided in the Note on the Photograph.
- Ask students what else they would like to know about the planet Saturn. Have them give their responses in the form of questions. (Sample responses: Why does Saturn have rings? How far is Saturn from Earth? What other information did the Voyager explorations reveal?)
- Tell students that to answer questions like these, they would need to gather information from a variety of sources. Explain that the process of gathering information about a topic, such as Saturn, from different sources is called research.
- Explain that a **research report** gives factual information found through research. Tell students that in this unit they will learn how to write a research report.

Unit 11

Writing a Research Report

NASA's *Voyager* explorations revealed more of Saturn's rings.

Shared Writing Activity

Work with students to write a paragraph about Saturn that might be part of a research report about this planet.

1. Write the following facts about Saturn on the board or on an overhead transparency:
   - second largest planet
   - sixth closest planet to sun
   - made up mostly of gases
   - temperature: –285°F (–176°C)
   - has seven flat thin rings
   - has 18 satellites
2. Help students use the facts to make up a topic sentence for a paragraph about Saturn. Write their topic sentence on the board or on an overhead transparency.
3. Work with students to use the facts to generate sentences that support their topic sentence. Write students' sentences as they suggest them.
   - Reinforce the importance of including only supporting facts and details and of sticking to the topic.
4. If students suggest sentences that all begin the same way, remind them that they can move certain words and phrases around to vary sentence beginnings.
   - Reinforce the correct use of capitalization for a proper noun or proper adjective (or other skills students need to work on) as they suggest sentences.
5. Have students copy the final paragraph about Saturn to share with family members.

A Published Model

This report gives well-organized, detailed information about sea otters. What is the main idea of each paragraph?

What Do Sea Otters Look Like?

from *The Sea Otter*, by Alvin, Virginia, and Robert Silverstein

topic sentence/main idea

Sea otters have a streamlined appearance. They have a small round head, a long heavy body, and a thick, tapering tail that is flat on the bottom. Their eyes are dark, and their noses flat and diamond-shaped. Little pointed ears close when a sea otter dives underwater. The sea otter's whiskers, 4 inches long, point downward to act like feelers, helping the animal to find food as it swims along the bottom of the sea.

supporting details

A sea otter's front paws look like mittens, but they are actually very useful hands. The backs of its front paws are covered with fur, but the palms have tough pads that help the otter to grip prey better. Its claws are retractable like those of a cat. The otter uses them to comb its fur and to snatch up clams from the sea bottom or mussels from a reef.

more ▶

See www.eduplace.com/kids/ for information about Robert and Virgina Silverstein.

About the Author

INTERNET CONNECTION Send your students to www.eduplace.com/kids/ for information about Alvin, Virginia, and Robert Silverstein.

Bibliography

Here are other books that model this type of writing that students might enjoy reading.

- ***Eagles of America*** by Dorothy Hinshaw Patent
- ***Manatee: On Location*** by Kathy Darling
- ***Fox*** by Caroline Arnold
- ***Earthquakes*** by Seymour Simon

"What Do Sea Otters Look Like?"

Lesson Objectives

Students will:

- read a published model of a research report
- identify characteristics of research reports
- identify examples of comparisons
- evaluate the relationship between visuals and text
- write personal and critical responses

Focus on the Model

Building Background

Ask students what they know about sea otters. Then ask them what they would like to know. Tell students that they will read a research report that tells about what sea otters look like.

Introducing Vocabulary

Introduce key vocabulary words by writing these sentences on the board.

The **streamlined** shape of the aircraft helps it to move more efficiently.

The antenna on our car is **retractable** so we pull it up when we use the radio.

Mussels are water animals that have soft bodies protected by hard shells.

Have a volunteer read each sentence aloud. Ask students to explain the meaning of the boldfaced words.

Reading the Selection

- Have students read the introduction to "What Do Sea Otters Look Like?" The purpose-setting question focuses on a characteristic of a research report, a main idea in each paragraph.

Have students read the selection as a class, independently, or with partners, or they can listen to the selection on audiotape.

- The call outs highlight key characteristics of a research report that are addressed in the Think About the Report questions at the end of this selection.

FOR STUDENTS ACQUIRING ENGLISH

Before reading the model, look at the pictures and any photos you can bring in of sea otters. With students, label the parts of the animal from the student book. (head, body, tail, ears, whiskers, and so on)

Answers to Reading As a Writer

Think About the Report

- The main idea of paragraph one is the overall appearance of sea otters. The first sentence tells the main idea.
- Sample answer: The details are *small round head; long heavy body; thick, tapering tail; eyes are dark, and their noses flat and diamond-shaped; little pointed ears; whiskers, 4 inches long.*
- Sample answer: The average male is a little more than four feet long, and the average female is a little shorter.

Think About Writer's Craft

- The comparisons are *like feelers, like mittens,* and (claws) *like those of a cat.*

Think About the Picture

- Report details shown in the photo include small round head; eyes are dark, and their noses flat and diamond shaped; little pointed ears; whiskers four inches long.

After students answer the questions, work with them to generate criteria for a research report, using the published model as a reference.

More About Writer's Craft

Draw students' attention to the word *shorter* in the last paragraph of the model. Tell students that this is a form of the adjective *short* and it is used to compare two things. Ask what is being compared. (the female and male sea otters) Have students find another comparative adjective in the paragraph. *(larger)* Explain that this comparison helps the reader visualize relative size. Tell students that they can use comparative and superlative adjectives in their writing to achieve the same purpose.

Notes on Responding

Personal Response

Encourage students to share their personal responses. Emphasize that there are no right or wrong answers to the questions. Point out that something that is surprising to one person may not be to another.

Critical Thinking

Answers should include details from the model.

A Published Model

The sea otter's hind feet are very different from its front paws. They are wide with long webbed toes, forming large flippers for swimming.

The average male southern sea otter is a little more than 4 feet long, including a tail about 12 inches long. He weighs about 65 pounds. The average female is a little shorter and weighs about 45 pounds. Northern sea otters are generally somewhat larger. facts

Reading As a Writer See TE margin for answers.

Think About the Report

- What is the main idea of the first paragraph on page 369? Which sentence in this paragraph tells the main idea?
- What are the supporting details in the first paragraph?
- What facts did you learn about the size of the sea otter?

Think About Writer's Craft

- Look at the first two paragraphs. What comparisons help you picture the sea otter's whiskers and front paws?

Think About the Picture

- Look at the photo on page 369. Which details from the report are shown in the photo?

Responding Answers will vary.

Write responses to these questions.

- **Personal Response** Which facts about the sea otter did you find surprising? Why?
- **Critical Thinking** What other animal does the sea otter make you think of? How is it the same? How is it different?

370 **Unit 11:** Research Report

Mapping the Selection

Mapping can help students review what they have learned in a report and help them understand how the information is organized. After students have read the report about sea otters, draw the following map on the board. Have students fill in the map with facts that tell how the sea otter looks.

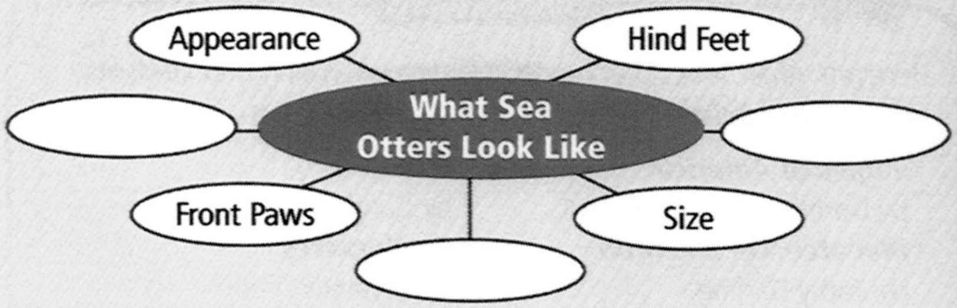

What Makes a Great Research Report?

A **research report** gives factual information found through research.

Remember to follow these guidelines when you write a research report.

- Research your topic. Organize your information carefully.
- Include facts, not opinions.
- Write an interesting opening that states the main idea.
- Write a paragraph for each main topic. Give supporting details.
- Use your own words. Don't copy!
- Write a closing that sums up your report.
- Include an accurate list of sources.

GRAMMAR CHECK
A proper noun names a particular person, place, or thing. Capitalize proper nouns.

What Makes a Great Research Report?

Lesson Objective

Students will:
- discuss the characteristics of a well-written research report

Focus on Instruction

- Tell students that "What Do Sea Otters Look Like?" is an example of a well-written research report. Have a volunteer read aloud the definition and characteristics of a research report. Then review which ones are represented in "What Do Sea Otters Look Like?" (The information is well organized; each paragraph tells about a different topic.)
- Explain that since the model is an excerpt from a report, it does not have an attention-grabbing opening paragraph or a formal closing.
- Tell students that the Grammar Check reminds them to check their papers for correct capitalization of proper nouns as they proofread.

If this is students' first encounter with the cartoon dog, explain that this is Sal, the writer's pal, and that Sal will help them learn to write great research reports.

Connecting to the Rubric

- These criteria are tied to the rubric on page 386.
- Tell students that they will be writing their own research report and that they will learn how to include these characteristics. Students will use these characteristics as criteria to help them evaluate their paper.

This page is available as a poster.

Looking Ahead Tell students that they will next see how the characteristics listed on this page are applied in one student's working draft and final copy of a research report.

FOR STUDENTS ACQUIRING ENGLISH

As you read the rubric for a research report, define the words *topic, sources,* and *sums up.* Simply restating the words may be sufficient; ask students to enter the words in their word logs. When all students understand the rubric, turn back to the published model and find the points cited in it.

Student Model: Working Draft

Lesson Objectives

Students will:
- read a working draft of a student-written research report
- discuss the ways the model meets the criteria for a well-written research report and ways that it could be improved

Focus on the Model

- Tell students that they will read a working draft of a research report written by a real student, James Lee. Remind students that a working draft is just a beginning and that there will always be later changes and revisions to the writing.
- Have volunteers read the model aloud.

  Alternatively, students can listen to it read by a student (although not the student writer) on audiotape.

> - Reading the draft aloud gives students practice in listening and responding to a writer's work in progress and provides practice for peer conferences.
> - This working draft does not include any usage, capitalization, or punctuation mistakes so that students can focus on the content of the piece.

- Tell students to think about whether or not James included the important characteristics of a research report. Explain that the thought balloons show Sal's thoughts about the report and that students will discuss his ideas after they read the model.

Student Model

WORKING DRAFT

When James Lee read a story that took place in the Tropics, he decided that tropical rain forests would make a good topic for a research report. Here is his working draft.

James Lee

Working Draft

Rain Forests

Tropical rain forests are a wonderful part of our environment. Many different species of plants and animals live there. Some are really strange-looking! Rain forests give us good things like food and medicine.

Tropical rain forests grow near the equator in an area called the Tropics. Brazil, Nigeria, and Thailand have rain forests. Most rain forests get at least 80 inches of rain every year. Usually they get rain all year round. It is always warm and humid, even in winter. Temperatures are between 68°F and 82°F all year.

Many different kinds of plants and animals live in these forests. The rafflesia grows on the roots of vines. The smallest mammal in the world is a bat. It lives in the rain forests of Thailand. This bat is only about one inch long. Many of these plants and animals live only in the rain forest.

Your opening is great!
You've done good research!
Can you tell more about the rafflesia? about this bat?

Working Draft

Things that we use every day come from the rain forest. We get rubber from the rubber tree to make tires for cars. Some medicines come from there too.

Some scientists estimate that 35 million acres of rain forest were destroyed each year in the 1990s. I think this is very bad. Well, that's everything I learned about rain forests.

Can you give more facts about rain forests being destroyed, without stating your opinion?

Rafflesia Flower

Reading As a Writer

See TE margin for answers.

- What did Sal like about James's report? What suggestions does he make? What changes can James make to answer Sal's questions?
- Which sentence in the last paragraph states an opinion? What words tell you that it's an opinion?
- What else would you like to know about this topic?

Answers to Reading As a Writer

- Sal liked the opening and the thoroughness of the research. Sal asked if James could tell more about the rafflesia and more about the bat in the third paragraph. Sal also asked James to give more facts about the destruction of rain forests. James can include more details about the rafflesia plant and the bat. James can also replace his opinion in the final paragraph with facts.
- *I think this is very bad.* He uses *I* and tells what he thinks about the problem—he doesn't give a proven fact.
- Answers will vary.

Student Model: Final Copy

Lesson Objectives

Students will:
- read a well-written final copy of a student's research report
- note and compare the revisions that improved the first draft

Focus on the Model

SUMMARY OF REVISIONS In his final copy, James made his title more interesting, added facts and examples, added supporting details, took out an opinion, revised his conclusion, and added a list of sources. Blackline Master 11–1 provides a copy of the student's working draft, showing the revisions that were made.

Have volunteers read the model aloud. Alternatively, students can listen to it read by a student (although not the student writer) on audiotape.

Student Model

FINAL COPY

James revised his report after discussing it with his classmates. Read his final copy to see what he changed.

The Wonders of the Rain Forest

by James Lee

Tropical rain forests are a wonderful part of our environment. Many different species of plants and animals live there. Some are really strange-looking! Rain forests give us good things like food and medicine.

Tropical rain forests grow near the equator in an area called the Tropics. Brazil, Nigeria, and Thailand have rain forests. Most rain forests get at least 80 inches of rain every year. Usually they get rain all year round. It is always warm and humid, even in winter. Temperatures are between 68°F and 82°F all year.

Many different kinds of plants and animals live in these forests. The rafflesia plant has the biggest flowers in the world. It grows on the roots of vines. One flower can be 3 feet wide and weigh 24 pounds. This flower actually smells like a rotting cheeseburger! The smallest mammal in the world is a bat. It is called the hog-nosed bat and lives in the rain forests of

Your information is well-organized.

Thailand. This bat is only about one inch long. Many of these plants and animals live only in the rain forest.

More Creatures of the Rain Forest

Animals	*Plants*
Leaf-cutter ants grow their own food. They raise funguses to eat.	**Pitcher plants** eat insects that fall into their tube-shaped leaves.
Three-toed sloths like to hang upside down from trees. They don't move much.	**Kapok trees** have huge trunks. The fruit fiber from the tree is used to fill mattresses.
Many kinds of **beetles** live in rain forests. Some can be 5 inches long.	**Lianas** are vines that climb up tall trees to reach the sunlight.
Monkeys use their tails to hold branches as they swing from tree to tree.	**Orchids** are beautiful flowers that grow on tree trunks in the forest.

Using a chart is a great idea!

Things that we use every day come from the rain forest, such as cinnamon, pineapples, bananas, sugar, and vanilla. We get rubber from the rubber tree to make tires for cars. Medicines are made from plants of the rain forest. Some medicines are used in heart and lung surgery.

These are strong supporting details.

A lot of the rain forest is being destroyed. This happens when people clear land. Some scientists estimate that 35 million acres of rain forest were destroyed each year in the 1990s. This destruction is still going on. Some people are trying to change this. Many children belong to groups that work to protect these lands.

more

Focus on Instruction

Point out to students that James's list of sources cites titles using both *Rain forest* and *Rainforest.* Explain that the spellings vary as one word or two according to the source, but most dictionaries cite it as two words. Tell students that book titles should always be written as they appear in the book.

Answers to Reading As a Writer

- James wrote more details about the rafflesia. He explained how the rain forest is being destroyed.
- He compared the smell of the rafflesia with that of a rotting cheeseburger.
- James added *Some scientists have estimated that 35 million acres of rain forest were destroyed each year in the 1990s.* He also added *Many children belong to groups that work to protect these lands.*
- The revised closing doesn't give an opinion, as the draft did. It sums up the main points of the paper.

More About Writer's Craft

- Draw attention to the exclamation point in the opening paragraph. Explain that the student writer used it for emphasis. Suggest that students use an exclamation point in their own writing if they think it will help emphasize an idea, but remind them to use it sparingly.
- Explain that in reports with many numerical facts, it is sometimes preferable to use all numerals rather than spelled-out numbers.
- Draw students' attention to the paragraphs in the working draft. Point out that each paragraph has a different topic.

Connecting to the Rubric

- Have students look again at the list of characteristics on page 371 and review with them how James's final copy addressed each one.
- Reinforce the Grammar Check by having students check that James has capitalized all proper nouns.

INTERNET CONNECTION Send your students to www.eduplace.com/kids/hme/ to see more models of student writing. You can also find and print these models at www.eduplace.com/rdg/hme/.

Looking Ahead Tell students that they will next write their own research report, using the writing process. As they go along, they will learn how to find the best information, how to write from an outline, and how to write good openings and closings.

Student Model *continued*

Scientists keep studying rain forests. They want to find cures for disease. They would like to learn more about the creatures that live there. Many people are working to preserve this part of nature.

You've summarized like an expert!

Sources

Burton, John A. *Jungles and Rainforests.* San Diego, CA: Thunder Bay Press, 1996.

Losos, Elizabeth. "Rain Forest." *Microsoft Encarta Online Deluxe Encyclopedia.* 1997–99. 24 Nov. 2001.

Ricciuti, Edward R. *Rainforest.* Biomes of the World Series. Tarrytown, NY: Benchmark Books, 1996.

Silver, Donald, and Patricia J. Wynne (illus.). *Tropical Rain Forest.* New York: McGraw-Hill, 1998.

This shows exactly where you found your information. That's great!

Reading As a Writer See TE margin for answers.

- What did James do in response to Sal's suggestions?
- What comparison did James add to the third paragraph on page 374?
- What facts did James add about rain forests being destroyed?
- What did James do to improve his closing?

See www.eduplace.com/kids/hme/ for more examples of student writing.

FOR STUDENTS ACQUIRING ENGLISH

Before reading the first draft of the student model, have students form groups of three to brainstorm the topic of *rain forest.* As you or a volunteer reads the models aloud, pause often to restate challenging passages. Highlight James's voice, noting how he wrote in his own words.

Write a Research Report

Start Thinking

Make a writing folder for your research report. Copy the questions in bold print, and put the paper in your folder. Write your answers as you think about and choose your topic.

- **Who will be my audience?** Will it be my classmates? a family member? a younger child?
- **What will be my purpose?** What do I want to learn? What do I want my readers to learn?
- **How will I publish or share my report?** Will I publish it as a magazine article? read it aloud as a news report? display it with visuals?

Choose Your Topic

1. **List** five possible topics by making an "I Wonder" list. Here is part of James's list.

   I Wonder
   Australia
   Wild West
   The Tropics
   Pandas

> **I Need Ideas!**
> Use these questions.
> - What TV shows or movies on real-life topics do you like? Which ones do you want to learn more about?
> - What do you like to read about?
> - Does something about the past interest you?
>
> See page 393 for more ideas.

2. **Discuss** your ideas with a partner. Which ones does your partner like? Why? Which ones do you like best?
3. **Narrow** your list. Choose the top three topics you might write about. Ask yourself these questions about each one.
   - Will it be interesting to research?
   - Can I find information about it?
   - Is it too large for a short report?
4. **Choose** one topic and circle it. Keep your list of three topics in case you need them later.

Help with Choosing a Topic

TECH TIP
Refer students who are using a computer to page H39 to find ideas for using a computer during the writing process.

EVALUATION TIP
Review students' final choices. If a topic is too broad, ask how it might be narrowed down.

MANAGEMENT TIP
As a class, create a list of topics related to a theme of study. Display the list, and add to it over the next few days. Allow "incubation time" for research ideas to take hold. Discuss what information students might research about each topic.

SOURCES OF TOPIC IDEAS
Suggest these activities to prompt topic ideas:
- Students can browse through magazines, newspapers, and books.
- They can choose a letter of the alphabet and find in an encyclopedia five possible report topics that begin with that letter.
- They can make clusters to narrow their topic.

USING RESOURCES
Keep a class file of experts on various topics whom students might interview. Remind students that people can be good sources of information.

Write a Research Report

Lesson Objectives

Students will:
- list their ideas for audience, purpose, and publishing/sharing formats
- list ideas for a research report
- discuss their ideas with a partner
- choose an appropriate topic to write about

Start Thinking

Focus on Instruction

- Discuss with students how the language of a report might be adapted to the chosen audience, purpose, and occasion. Point out that more formal language will be expected for some occasions and audiences than for others. Ask students to give examples of occasions and audiences that might require less formal language. (A writer might be less formal with a family member or a classmate than with a teacher.)
- Ask how writing the report as a magazine article might be different from displaying it with visuals. (Visuals might provide details that a written report would lack.)

Choose Your Topic

Focus on Instruction

- Page 393 provides writing prompts that might suggest ideas.
- Have students ask themselves these questions: *Can I find enough information about this topic? Are sources readily available?*
- Reassure students that they can always change their mind about a topic if they decide they don't want to write about it.

Have students start a writing folder titled *My Research Report*. Explain that they will keep all notes, graphic organizers, and drafts for their research report in this folder. Have students include their paper with their thoughts about their audience, purpose, and publishing format.

MEETING INDIVIDUAL NEEDS — FOR STUDENTS ACQUIRING ENGLISH
Help students determine which topics they will truly be able to research easily and well. If they are having trouble listing topics, ask "What American holiday or event would you like to know more about? What tradition from your culture (food, dance, music, etc.) would you like people in the United States to know about?"

Lesson Objectives

Students will:
- narrow their topic
- make a K-W-S chart to explore their topic

Explore Your Topic

Focus on Instruction

- See Blackline Master 11–2 for a K-W-S chart students can use to explore their topics. As an alternative, students could use an inverted triangle to narrow their topic. Refer students to page H50 for an example.
- Encourage students to break their topic into smaller parts.
- The K-W-S chart serves as a rough outline for the student to use while doing research. Good questions on the chart will result in good research. Make sure the questions are specific enough and don't go in too many different directions.
- When researching, students should also confirm facts in the What I Know column. Point out that what we think we know isn't always correct!
- Discuss with students the note in the Help box. Explain that a topic that seems interesting can turn out to be dull once a writer starts gathering information about it.
- If students find they do not have enough information about a topic, help them choose a new topic by reviewing the prompts on page 393 or suggesting activities in the Help with Choosing a Topic section on TE page 377.

INTERNET CONNECTION Send your students to www.eduplace.com/kids/hme/ for graphic organizers. You can also find and print these organizers at www.eduplace.com/rdg/hme/.

FOR STUDENTS ACQUIRING ENGLISH

Help students brainstorm their topics by reviewing word webs. On the board write and circle *who, what, where, when, why,* and *how.* Then draw lines with smaller circles off each large one, writing one idea, question, or detail in each small circle. Help students organize their own ideas in a web.

The Writing Process: PREWRITING | DRAFTING | REVISING | PROOFREADING | PUBLISHING

Explore Your Topic

1. **Narrow** your topic. If it is too big, you can write about a part of it. Here is how James narrowed his topic to *tropical rain forests.*

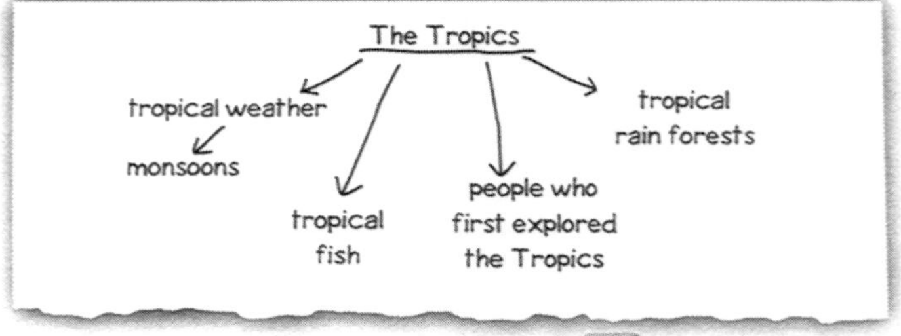

2. **Explore** your topic by making a K-W-S chart. Write what you already know in the first column. Write your questions in the second column. Ask *Who? What? When? Where? Why? How?* Here is part of the chart that James made.

HELP Read All About It!
To make sure that you're interested in your topic, read a short encyclopedia article about it.

What I Know	What I Want to Know	Possible Sources
Rain forests are wet.	What is the climate?	
They have many different plants and animals.	What are some of the interesting plants and animals?	
Rubber comes from there.	What other products come from rain forests?	
They are being destroyed.	Why are they being destroyed?	

Go to www.eduplace.com/kids/hme/ for graphic organizers.

Help with Exploring the Topic

MORE IDEAS FOR EXPLORING

You can suggest these ideas to students as alternatives for exploring their topics.
- They can brainstorm topic ideas with students who share their interests.
- They can have a partner ask them three questions about their topic ideas. Would any of the questions make a better topic?
- They can find photographs in resource books or magazines that go with their topic. Do these sources give ideas for things to write about?

MANAGEMENT TIP

Create a class chart of report topics. Determine four or five categories, such as people, animals, places, events, and things. Have groups of students brainstorm topics for individual categories and list their ideas on the chart.

PREWRITING DRAFTING REVISING PROOFREADING PUBLISHING

Focus Skill

Finding the Best Information

Locating Sources

Now it's time to dig into your topic. To find information, you can talk to experts, use technology, and look in print sources.

Talk to people. Interview an expert to get inside information. You might speak to a high school biology teacher, a reporter at your local newspaper, an artist, or a person who was born in China. It all depends on your topic!

See page H9 for information on interviewing.

Use technology. Surf the Internet to find online encyclopedias and Web sites related to your topic. Find out if your library has information on CD-ROM.

See page H43 for more about using the Internet.

Look at print sources. Find sources in your library. Ask the librarian for help when you need it.

Your library is a gold mine of information!

Source	Examples	Tips
Encyclopedias have short entries about many topics.	*The World Book Encyclopedia*	• Get basic facts about your topic.
Nonfiction books give facts about real people, places, events, and things.	*The Wright Brothers* by Russell Freedman *Oceans* by Seymour Simon	• Find a book that tells all about your topic. • Find a book with one chapter on your topic.
Reference books are special nonfiction books. They are packed with different kinds of facts.	*Information Please Kids' Almanac* *Macmillan Color Atlas of the States*	• Find all kinds of facts in an almanac. Use a recent one. • Check maps in an atlas.
Magazines and **newspapers** give up-to-date information.	*National Geographic World* *Weekly Reader*	• Use these sources when you need the latest facts.

See page H21 for more about using the library.

more ▶

Go to www.eduplace.com/kids/hme/ for topic links.

Finding the Best Information

Lesson Objectives

Students will:

- find information by talking to people, using technology, and looking at print sources
- write their sources on their K-W-S chart

Locating Sources

Focus on Instruction

- Ask students to think of people who are knowledgeable in certain fields. Then discuss how to plan and conduct a successful interview with one of these experts. Refer students to page H9 for help with interviewing.
- Ask a student volunteer to demonstrate how to find specific information on the Internet. Pages H43 and H44 can help with this task. Make a chart showing the steps to follow so that students can refer to it when they do it on their own. Display the chart until students are comfortable using the Internet.
- Make sure students know where to find the sources they will need to write their paper. If students need help using the library, refer them to pages H21–H23.

INTERNET CONNECTION Send your students to www.eduplace.com/kids/hme/ for Internet links to help students find information about different topics for their research reports.

MEETING INDIVIDUAL NEEDS

FOR STUDENTS ACQUIRING ENGLISH

Take students on a field trip to the library to show students how to use all its resources, especially the computer. Arrange for your librarian and computer teacher to give mini-lessons to teach students how to use the card catalogues and computers. This may be new, but students will learn fast.

Meeting Individual Needs

● RETEACHING WORKBOOK, page 97

Finding the Best Information

Encyclopedias have short entries about many topics.
Nonfiction books give facts about real people, places, events, and things.
Reference books are special nonfiction books. They are packed with different kinds of facts. **Dictionaries, almanacs,** and **atlases** are reference books.
Magazines and **newspapers** give up-to-date information.
Web sites link information related to a topic.
Interviews with family members and experts can provide inside information on a topic.

Write *encyclopedia, nonfiction book, dictionary, almanac, atlas, magazine, newspaper, Web site,* or *interview* to tell where you would look for the answer to each of the following questions. Sample answers:

1. What are some facts about John Adams? encyclopedia
2. How large is the city of Tokyo, Japan? almanac
3. What are some different kinds of airplanes? encyclopedia
4. How many people live in Canada? almanac
5. What lake borders Cleveland, Ohio? atlas
6. How deep is the Grand Canyon? encyclopedia
7. What camping sites are near the Grand Canyon? Web site
8. What was the temperature at the Grand Canyon National Park yesterday? newspaper
9. Who was Grandma Moses? encyclopedia
10. Have there been any space explorations in the past year? magazine
11. What does your coach think of Babe Ruth? interview
12. How does a filmmaker go about making a movie? nonfiction book
13. What shape is the state of Wyoming? atlas
14. What does the word *tinder* mean? dictionary
15. When was the first car built and who built it? encyclopedia

▲■ WORKBOOK PLUS, page 146

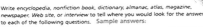

Finding the Best Information

What I Know	What I Want to Know	Possible Sources
Jesse Owens was a famous Olympic athlete.	When did he participate in the Olympics? What sport did he participate in?	*The Grolier Student Encyclopedia of the Olympic Games,* by Ron Thomas and Joe Herran
He worked with and helped young people.	What did he do, and how did he help?	*Jesse Owens,* by Tony Gentry

Read the following K-W-S chart for a research report on the Olympic Games. Then look at the sources listed in the box. Write the names of the sources that you think would provide the best information to answer the questions. When you write, underline the names in italics. Sample answers:

Weekly Reader	Olympics Web site
The Olympic Games, by Theodore Knight	*The Story of the Olympics,* by Dave Anderson
Microsoft Encarta Online Deluxe Encyclopedia	*Scholastic Kid's Almanac for the 21st Century*

K-W-S Chart

What I Know	What I Want to Know	Possible Sources
The Olympic Games began a long time ago.	When and how did the Olympic Games begin?	The Olympic Games, by Theodore Knight
Swimming and skiing are sports in the modern games.	What are some other sports that make up the games?	The Story of the Olympics, by Dave Anderson
The United States, China, and Russia participate in the games.	What are some other countries that send athletes to the games?	Microsoft Encarta Online Deluxe Encyclopedia
The Summer Games were held in Sydney, Australia, in 2000.	When and where will the next Olympic Games be held?	Olympics Web site

Lesson Objectives

Students will:

- test their sources
- choose their strongest sources

Choosing the Best Sources

Focus on Instruction

- Read aloud the following statements. Ask students which are opinions and which are facts.

  September is the most beautiful month. (opinion)

  There are thirty days in April. (fact)

  Austin is the capital of Texas. (fact)

  Apples are the best fruit in the world. (opinion)
- Ask volunteers to explain why it is important to use facts rather than opinions in a research report. (The goal of a research report is to inform.)
- Show students where to find information about an author or expert in a resource book. Discuss why it is important that the author have expertise in the subject. (so the source is dependable)

Think and Discuss

Have students work in small groups to answer the questions. Tell students that a report on George Washington can probably be researched from older sources without causing problems because a source such as Washington's writings will not be updated as other sources might be. A new invention would require up-to-date sources. Talking with a scientist or technician who understands the invention would be ideal.

Explore Your Topic

Advise students that they may find an overabundance of information about some topics, while information about other topics may be scarce. Explain that information about the topic *frogs* might be plentiful; however, information about a specific type of frog from a specific place might be harder to find. If students have trouble locating enough information, advise that they choose a different topic.

Focus Skill continued

Choosing the Best Sources

Sift through your sources. Which ones are the most valuable?

Test your sources. Use this checklist.

Is the Source...	How to Tell
____ related to your topic?	Check the title and the headings. Read a few sentences.
____ factual?	Look for facts, not opinions. Facts can be proved. Your report should give facts.
____ dependable?	The writer should have experience or education in the topic you are researching.
____ up-to-date?	Find out when the source was published. Use the most recent sources you can find.

WARNING: Web sites often have errors. You might want to check with your teacher before you use an Internet source.

Think and Discuss Sample answers: encyclopedia, nonfiction books, online referen works, collections of Washington's writings; facts long establish well-know topic cove man sour

- If you were doing research on George Washington, what sources would you explore first? Why?
- If you were doing research on a recent invention, what sources would you explore first? Why? Sample answers: newspapers, magazines, Web sites, interviews; give the latest facts

Explore Your Topic

If you can't find good sources, choose a different topic from your top three.

1. **Find** information. Look in your library for a variety of sources. Which ones answer the questions on your K-W-S chart? Write these sources in the third column of your chart.
2. **Test** your sources. Choose the strongest ones. You should have at least three sources for your report. Only one should be an encyclopedia article.

Research Your Topic

1 Take notes to help you remember what you have heard or read. The questions on your K-W-S chart will guide you.

- Write the question you are answering at the top of the card. You may end up with more than one card for each question.
- Write facts that answer the question. Write just enough to help you remember the important ideas.
- Take notes in your own words.
- As you take notes, write the source on the bottom of each card.

Here is a source that James used, along with one of his note cards.

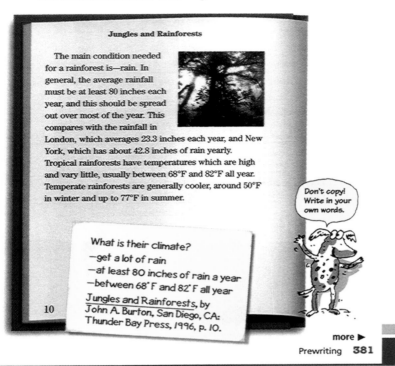

Jungles and Rainforests

The main condition needed for a rainforest is—rain. In general, the average rainfall must be at least 80 inches each year, and this should be spread out over most of the year. This compares with the rainfall in London, which averages 23.3 inches each year, and New York, which has about 42.8 inches of rain yearly. Tropical rainforests have temperatures which are high and vary little, usually between 68°F and 82°F all year. Temperate rainforests are generally cooler, around 50°F in winter and up to 77°F in summer.

10

What is their climate?
—get a lot of rain
—at least 80 inches of rain a year
—between 68° F and 82° F all year
Jungles and Rainforests, by John A. Burton, San Diego, CA: Thunder Bay Press, 1996, p. 10.

Don't copy! Write in your own words.

more ▶

Help with Exploring the Topic

IDEAS FOR RESEARCHING

Suggest these ideas to students for researching their topics.

- They can keep a research log. They can write their questions on separate pages of a booklet and then write notes that answer the questions. Then students can record their sources.
- They can use a data chart to keep all notes for one question together.
- They can ask a partner to suggest other resources they might use for their topic.

Lesson Objectives

Students will:

- take notes for their report
- write down their sources
- focus on their topic
- review and revise their K-W-S chart

Research Your Topic

Focus on Instruction

- Suggest that students take notes on different colored note cards (one color per question) or use markers to color-code cards.
- Tell students to write only one question on each card.
- Remind students not to write down too much information when taking notes. They should write just enough to answer the question.
- Emphasize that students should not copy word for word from a source. For an interview, they should put quotation marks around the speaker's exact words.
- Tell students that each fact should be confirmed in at least one reliable source. Students should confirm the items in the What I Know column of their charts if they plan to use these facts in their report.
- Have students read the source information and James's notes. Then ask questions such as "Did James write the whole sentence or just key words?" and "Did James write only facts that answer the question?"
- If students aren't sure whether they should include some of the facts they have found, suggest that they work with a partner to help them decide.

Focus on Instruction

- Explain that just as some topics might not have enough information, others might have too much. Help students determine how to prioritize their facts. Use the ideas in Help with Researching on this page.
- The information on summarizing on page H29 might be helpful to students as they research their topic.

INTERNET CONNECTION Send your students to www.eduplace.com/kids/hme/ for graphic organizers. You can also find and print these organizers at www.eduplace.com/rdg/hme/.

2 **Focus** on your topic. Don't write every fact you find. Ask yourself these questions.

- Does this fact answer one of my questions?
- Will it help my audience understand my topic?
- Is the fact interesting?

See page H26 to find out more about taking notes.

3 **Review** your K-W-S chart as you do research. Cross out questions that don't seem important anymore, and add questions about interesting information you want to use.

As he took notes from different sources, James added the question *What medicines come from the rain forest?* to his chart. Before working on his report, he didn't know that medicine was made from rain-forest plants. Here is part of his updated chart.

What I **K**now	What I **W**ant to Know	Possible **S**ources
Rain forests are wet.	What is the climate?	Burton, Jungles and Rainforests
They have many different plants and animals.	What are some of the interesting plants and animals?	Ricciuti, Rainforest
Rubber comes from there.	What other products come from rain forests?	
They are being destroyed.	Why are they being destroyed?	
	What medicines come from the rain forest?	

Help with Researching

MANAGEMENT TIP

Students can use one of these ideas if they have too much information.

- They can cross some questions off their K-W-S chart and then take notes on the most important ones.
- They can collect a few facts and examples for each question.

Plan Your Report

1. **Sort** your note cards.
   - Make a stack for each question you answered. Put the cards in each stack in an order that makes sense.
   - Remove cards that have repeated or unimportant information.
   - Put the stacks in an order that makes sense.
2. **Make an outline** from your notes. Each question you answered will become a **main topic**. Each supporting detail will become a **subtopic**.
   - List each main topic with a Roman numeral.
   - List each subtopic with a capital letter.
   - Give your outline a title.

Here are two of the note cards James wrote and part of his outline.

What is their climate?
—get a lot of rain
—at least 80 inches of rain a year
—between 68° F and 82° F all year
Jungles and Rainforests, by John A. Burton, San Diego, CA: Thunder Bay Press, 1996, p. 10.

What is their climate?
—very few dry periods or none at all
—always warm and humid
"Rain Forest" by Elizabeth Losos, Microsoft Encarta Online Deluxe Encyclopedia: 1997–99. 24 Nov. 2001

II. Climate in the rain forest
   A. Get a lot of rain
   B. At least 80 inches of rain a year
   C. Few dry periods
   D. Always warm and humid
   E. Between 68°F and 82°F all year

Your outline is a map that will guide you as you write your report.

See page H28 for more about outlining.

Lesson Objectives

Students will:
- sort and organize their note cards
- use their note cards to make an outline

Plan Your Report

Focus on Instruction

- Suggest that students spread out their note cards faceup in front of them. Remind students to think carefully about how they will order their ideas. Explain that in order for their reports to be effective, students must put their ideas in a logical order. Suggest that students sort their cards in time order, from most familiar to least familiar, from most important to least important, or by cause and effect.
- Ask students how an outline might be useful in writing. (An outline shows how facts can be arranged in an order that makes sense.) Reinforce the conventions of outlining. Students can use Blackline Master 11–3 as they make their outline.
- Tell students that some researchers include a focus, or thesis, statement on the outline. In this book, the focus statement is included later in the lesson on Good Openings and Closings, since the focus of the paper may still be evolving throughout the drafting process.
- Have students compare the information on the note cards with the information on James's outline. Ask if James ordered his facts in a logical manner.

Help with Planning

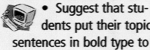

IDEAS FOR PLANNING

You can suggest this plan for turning notes into outlines: Research questions can become main topics. Facts that answer the questions can become subtopics.

TECH TIPS

- Suggest that students put their topic sentences in bold type to help stay focused on their main ideas.
- Some word-processing programs automatically format outlines after the first Roman numeral and topic are typed. Demonstrate for students how this works.

Writing from an Outline

Lesson Objectives

Students will:
- write a topic sentence for each main topic
- write a paragraph for each topic sentence

Focus on Instruction

- Remind students that a topic sentence can come at the beginning, the middle, or the end of a paragraph.
- Explain that two subtopics were combined to form the fourth sentence of the paragraph about Ben Franklin. Tell students that it is not necessary to begin a new sentence for each subtopic. Similarly, one subtopic can be used to write more than one sentence.
- Remind students to write quotations correctly and to check them for accuracy.

Think and Discuss

Have partners discuss how the writer changed each subtopic into a sentence that supports the main idea.

Draft Your Report

- Students should write in the third person. However, in a less formal research report, sometimes a catchy beginning or ending, or one sentence, may address the audience as "you." Decide whether this is appropriate for the writing assignment.
- Tell students to write on every other line so there will be room for changes.

Drafting Reminders

- Reinforce that if students change their mind while writing, they should cross out words or sentences they don't want rather than start over.
- Reassure students that they will have time to correct mistakes and check spelling later.

FOR STUDENTS ACQUIRING ENGLISH

Students will need much practice in writing note cards with facts in their own words. Help students by modeling. Model this activity, as well as outlining. Explain each step; show how an outline helps organize facts or ideas.

The Writing Process: PREWRITING | DRAFTING | REVISING | PROOFREADING | PUBLISHING

Focus Skill

Writing from an Outline

Write topic sentences. For each main topic on your outline, write a topic sentence. It should tell what the paragraph is about.

Write paragraphs. Using the subtopics on your outline, write a paragraph for each topic sentence.

Here is part of an outline for a report on the career of Benjamin Franklin, along with the paragraph written from it.

II. Franklin's government jobs
   A. Ran the post office
   B. Provided army with gunpowder
   C. Directed printing of money
   D. Was ambassador to France

Ben Franklin did many jobs for the government of the United States. He ran the post office. He provided the army with gunpowder. In addition, he directed the printing of money and was ambassador to France.

Connect your ideas. Help your reader move smoothly through your report. Connect your thoughts with words such as *also, in addition, for example,* and *in conclusion.*

Think and Discuss Use the outline and paragraph to answer these questions.

- What is the topic sentence in the paragraph? *Ben Franklin did many jobs for the government of the United States*
- What words did the writer use to connect ideas smoothly? *In addition*
- Which sentence includes subtopic A? B? C? D?
  subtopic A: sentence 2; subtopic B: sentence 3; subtopics C and D: sentence 4

Draft Your Report

1. **Write a topic sentence** for each main topic on your outline.
2. **Write a paragraph** for each topic sentence. Include interesting details.

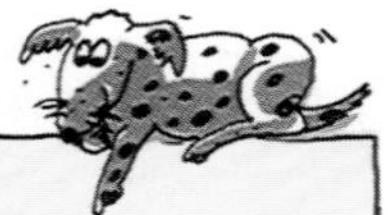

Write with voice! Show how interesting your topic is.

Meeting Individual Needs

● RETEACHING WORKBOOK, page 98

Writing from an Outline

Each section of an **outline** is about one main topic. When you write a **paragraph** from an outline, use the main topic to help you write a **topic sentence**. Use the subtopics to write complete sentences that support the main idea.

The parts of an outline below are for a report on maple trees. In each outline, the main topic has been used to write a topic sentence. Write the subtopics as complete sentences that support the main idea.
Sample answers:

I. Appearance
   A. Tall with full branches
   B. Trunks can measure five to six feet around.
   C. Gray or dark brown bark
   D. Yellowish or reddish leaves in fall

Topic sentence: Maple trees are large, colorful trees.

Maple trees are tall with full branches. Their trunks can measure five to six feet around. Maple trees have gray or dark brown bark. In the fall, the leaves on maple trees turn a yellowish or reddish color.

II. Uses
   A. Excellent shade trees
   B. Syrup made from sap of sugar maples
   C. Furniture, such as desks and chairs
   D. Firewood

Topic sentence: Maple trees have many different uses.

Maple trees make excellent shade trees. Sap from sugar maple trees is used to make maple syrup. The wood from maple trees is used to make fine furniture, such as desks and chairs. Finally, the wood from maple trees is used as firewood for heating.

▲■ WORKBOOK PLUS, page 147

Writing from an Outline

Each section of an **outline** is about one main topic. When you write a **paragraph** from an outline, use the main topic to write a **topic sentence** for the paragraph. Write the subtopics as complete sentences that support the main idea.

The outline below is for a report on Earth's solar system. Write a paragraph from each outline section. Start by writing the topic sentence. Remember to indent each paragraph. Sample answers:

I. The moon, Earth's closest neighbor
   A. About one-quarter the size of Earth
   B. About two hundred thirty-nine thousand miles away
   C. Takes twenty-seven and one-third days to circle Earth
   D. Same side always faces Earth

The moon is Earth's closest neighbor. It is about one-quarter the size of Earth. The moon is about two hundred thirty-nine thousand miles away from Earth. It takes twenty-seven and one-third days for the moon to circle Earth. The same side of the moon always faces Earth.

II. The sun, closest star to Earth
   A. Ninety-three million miles from Earth
   B. Sun's light reaches Earth in eight minutes
   C. Provides heat and light for life
   D. More than one hundred times the size of Earth

The sun is the closest star to Earth. It is ninety-three million miles from Earth. The sun's light reaches Earth in eight minutes. The sun provides heat and light for life. The sun is more than one hundred times the size of Earth.

PREWRITING DRAFTING REVISING PROOFREADING PUBLISHING

Focus Skill

Good Openings and Closings

Write an opening paragraph. Tell the main idea of your report in one sentence. Ask a question or state a surprising fact to catch the reader's interest.

Weak Opening	Strong Opening
The transcontinental railroad linked the East and the West in the United States. It took a lot of hard work.	What took seven years to build and linked the East to the West in the United States? The transcontinental railroad, begun in 1862, is the answer. With picks, shovels, and sledgehammers, workers built this historic railway.

Write a closing. A strong closing sums up the report and connects with the main idea in the opening.

Weak Closing	Strong Closing
The hard work was done. Now people could cross the United States by train. Most people would think this was important.	After the dangers of blasting through mountains and building bridges over deep gorges, the transcontinental railroad was complete. Passengers could now travel from New York to San Francisco by rail.

GRAMMAR TIP *If you give an exact date, put a comma between the day and the year.*

Think and Discuss Compare the weak and strong examples above.

- Why doesn't the weak opening above seem interesting? It lacks interesting facts and shows no excitement about the topic.
- Why is the weak closing less interesting than the strong one? The weak one makes this great feat sound boring and doesn't sum up the most interesting content in the report.

Draft Your Opening and Closing

1. **Draft** two openings for your report. Choose the one that fits better.
2. **Write** a closing that connects to your opening.
3. **Make** a list of sources as shown on page 376.

Good Openings and Closings

Lesson Objectives

Students will:

- draft two openings for their report, using different techniques
- choose an opening
- write a strong closing

Focus on Instruction

- Discuss the weak and strong openings. Explain that opening with a question makes the reader want to continue reading to find the answer.
- Compare the weak and strong closings. Ask how the strong closing connects with the main idea in the strong opening. (It talks about blasting through mountains and building bridges.) Ask what the last sentence does. (It sums up the report.)

Think and Discuss

Discuss the questions with students. As a class, brainstorm ideas for more examples of strong openings and closings.

Draft Your Opening and Closing

- Tell students to vary the approach of the two openings they write. For example, students can write one opening that asks a question and one that states a surprising fact. Students can then choose the one that works best with their topic.
- Have students read their opening and closing to a partner for feedback.

MEETING INDIVIDUAL NEEDS

FOR STUDENTS ACQUIRING ENGLISH

The step of rewriting openings and closings will be familiar. For openings, focus students' attention on writing interesting questions or on the use of quotes found in sources. For closings, provide these words: *finally, as a result, lastly, to sum up, in short,* and *in conclusion.*

● RETEACHING WORKBOOK, page 99

Good Openings and Closings

A good, strong **opening** captures your reader's interest and tells what your report is about. A strong **closing** sums up the report and connects to the main idea in the opening.

1. Read the following paragraph from a report on the yellow ice plant, a California wildflower. Write a strong opening for the report. Try asking a question or stating a surprising fact. Sample opening:

The yellow ice plant is a colorful wildflower. The flower of the yellow ice plant has many petals. The fat leaves have three sides. This pretty wildflower blooms from April to October. It grows on sand dunes and banks. The yellow ice plant can be found along the California coast.

Opening: Does the color yellow make you think of buttercups? It is also the color of another wildflower, the yellow ice plant.

2. Read the following paragraph from a report on the Gateway Arch in St. Louis, Missouri. Write a strong closing for the report. Sample closing:

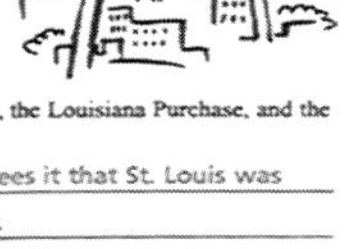

The first thing visitors notice when they come to St. Louis, Missouri, is the beautiful Gateway Arch. Designed by the famous architect Eero Saarinen, the Gateway Arch stands 630 feet tall along the Mississippi River. It is the tallest monument in the United States. Inside the arch, small trains carry visitors to the top. From there visitors have a magnificent view of the city. The arch is part of the Jefferson National Expansion Memorial. It was built to honor Thomas Jefferson, the Louisiana Purchase, and the pioneers who settled the West.

Closing: The arch reminds everyone who sees it that St. Louis was once the gateway to the western frontier.

▲■ WORKBOOK PLUS, page 148

Good Openings and Closings

A strong **opening** captures your reader's interest and tells what your report is about. A strong **closing** sums up the report and connects to the main idea.

1. Below are two possible openings and closings for a research report about the Loch Ness monster. Put a check beside the stronger opening and closing.

Openings	Closings
___ I don't think there is a Loch Ness monster.	___ Maybe I will try to catch Nessie someday!
✓ Is some huge, mysterious creature lurking near the calm surface of a lovely Scottish lake?	✓ Thus, the mystery of the Loch Ness monster still remains to be solved.

2. Write two good openings and two good closings for a report on icebergs using the outline. Ask a question and state a surprising fact. For the closing, try connecting to the main idea in the opening. Then put a check beside the opening and closing you think are stronger. Sample answers:

I. Description of iceberg
   A. Mountain of ice floating in ocean
   B. Piece broken off glacier (huge field of ice)
   C. In summer, floats south from Arctic to Canada
II. Size of iceberg
   A. Most of iceberg under water
   B. May be 400 feet above water
   C. Can be many miles long

Opening: What kind of mountain is not made of rock? An iceberg. An iceberg is a towering mountain made, not of rock, but of ice.

Opening: Picture in your mind a huge mountain made entirely of ice and floating in the ocean. That is an iceberg.

Closing: As you can see, icebergs, like mountains, are extremely large.

Closing: When you hear the expression "It was only the tip of the iceberg," you'll appreciate what it means.

Evaluating Your Research Report

Lesson Objective

Students will:

- evaluate their research report, using a rubric

Connecting to the Criteria

Have students reread the characteristics of a great research report listed on page 371. Then explain that the rubric shown on this page refers to those characteristics. Tell students that the rubric will help them decide which parts of their report "ring the bell," or meet the standards of a great research report, and which parts need more work or haven't been addressed at all.

Focus on Instruction

- Review the rubric with students. Have a volunteer read the first point in each section and explain the differences among them. Follow the same procedure for the remaining points.
- After students write their criteria, have them circle the ones that indicate aspects of their research report that need revision. Blackline Master 11–4 provides a copy of the rubric as a checklist.
- See the Teacher's Resource Book for scoring rubrics.

This page is also available as a poster.

INTERNET CONNECTION Have your students go to www.eduplace.com/kids/hme/ to use an interactive version of the rubric shown in the student book. Students will get feedback and support depending on how they mark the rubric items.

FOR STUDENTS ACQUIRING ENGLISH

To discourage students from copying directly from sources (and to encourage independent writing), have students rewrite all or part of their report from memory. However, expect opinion statements in students' writing during this exercise. Using the rubric as a checklist is helpful, but stress that students must use all the rubric categories; strengths and areas for improvement must be considered. If students have trouble evaluating their own work, give them a few days away from their report. In the writing process, time spent away from writing can be as valuable as time spent on writing.

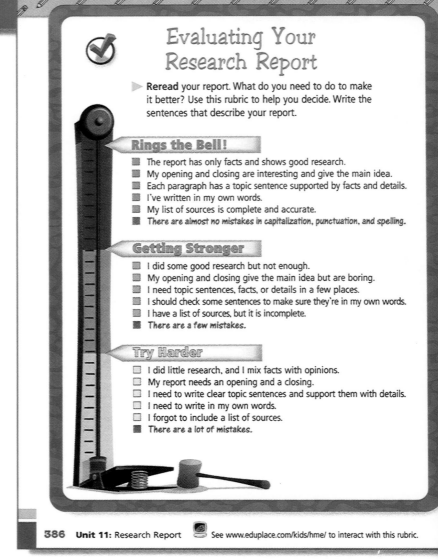

Evaluating Your Research Report

Reread your report. What do you need to do to make it better? Use this rubric to help you decide. Write the sentences that describe your report.

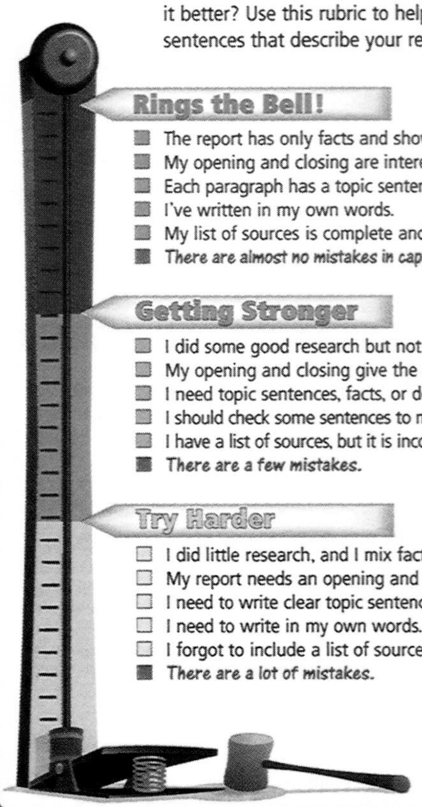

Rings the Bell!

- The report has only facts and shows good research.
- My opening and closing are interesting and give the main idea.
- Each paragraph has a topic sentence supported by facts and details.
- I've written in my own words.
- My list of sources is complete and accurate.
- *There are almost no mistakes in capitalization, punctuation, and spelling.*

Getting Stronger

- I did some good research but not enough.
- My opening and closing give the main idea but are boring.
- I need topic sentences, facts, or details in a few places.
- I should check some sentences to make sure they're in my own words.
- I have a list of sources, but it is incomplete.
- *There are a few mistakes.*

Try Harder

- I did little research, and I mix facts with opinions.
- My report needs an opening and a closing.
- I need to write clear topic sentences and support them with details.
- I need to write in my own words.
- I forgot to include a list of sources.
- *There are a lot of mistakes.*

386 **Unit 11:** Research Report

See www.eduplace.com/kids/hme/ to interact with this rubric.

Meeting Individual Needs

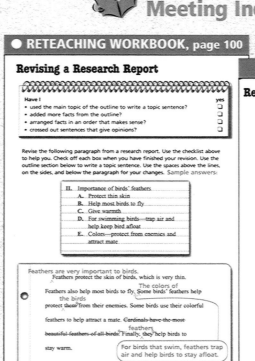

● RETEACHING WORKBOOK, page 100

Revising a Research Report

Have I | yes
- used the main topic of the outline to write a topic sentence? ❑
- added more facts from the outline? ❑
- arranged facts in an order that makes sense? ❑
- crossed out sentences that give opinions? ❑

Revise the following paragraph from a research report. Use the checklist above to help you. Check off each box when you have finished your revision. Use the outline section below to write a topic sentence. Use the spaces above the lines, on the sides, and below the paragraph for your changes. Sample answers:

II. Importance of birds' feathers
  A. Protect thin skin
  B. Help most birds to fly
  C. Give warmth
  D. For swimming birds—trap air and help keep bird afloat
  E. Colors—protect from enemies and attract mate

Feathers are very important to birds.
Feathers protect the skin of birds, which is very thin.
The colors of
Feathers also help most birds to fly. Some birds' feathers help
the birds
protect them from their enemies. Some birds use their colorful
feathers to help attract a mate. ~~Cardinals have the most~~
feathers
~~beautiful feathers of all birds.~~ Finally, they help birds to
stay warm.
For birds that swim, feathers trap air and help birds to stay afloat.

▲■ WORKBOOK PLUS, page 149

Revising a Research Report

Have I | yes
- written a topic sentence using the main topic of the outline? ❑
- arranged facts in an order that makes sense? ❑
- added more facts from the outline? ❑
- added details from the outline? ❑
- crossed out sentences that give opinions? ❑

Revise the following paragraph from a research report. Use the checklist above to help you. Check off each box when you have finished your revision. Use the outline section below to write a topic sentence. Use the spaces above the lines, on the sides, and below the paragraph for your changes. Sample answers:

II. Electric eels' use of electricity
  A. To hunt for food—fish and frogs
  B. Can stun an animal as big as a horse
  C. In place of eyesight, to find way around in muddy water
  D. To communicate with other electric eels, so some scientists think
  E. To protect self from enemies

Electric eels use their electricity in several ways.
An eel uses its electricity to hunt for food. The electricity
fish and frogs | as big as a horse
can easily kill ~~its food.~~ It can even stun an animal. An eel also
Some scientists think that electric
uses electricity to protect itself from enemies. ~~I certainly~~
eels may use electricity to communicate with each other.
~~wouldn't want to meet an electric eel in the water!~~ After a
while, electricity damages the eel's eyes, but the eel can use
in the muddy water where it lives.
electricity to find its way around.

PREWRITING DRAFTING REVISING PROOFREADING PUBLISHING

Revise Your Research Report

1. **Revise** your report. Use the list of sentences you wrote from the rubric. Work on the parts that you described with sentences from "Getting Stronger" and "Try Harder."

Revising Tip
To add sentences, write them at the bottom of your paper, circle them, and draw an arrow to show where to add them.

2. **Have a writing conference.**

When You're the Writer Read your report aloud to a partner. Discuss any questions or problems you have. Take notes to remember what your partner says. Then make the changes you want to make.

When You're the Listener Tell at least two things you like about the report. Ask questions about anything that seems unclear or boring. Use this chart to help you.

The Writing Conference

If you're thinking . . .	You could say . . .
Did you just make this up?	Where did you find this information?
The opening isn't very interesting.	Can you start with a question or a surprising fact?
Some facts aren't important.	Does your reader really need to know this?
The report is choppy. It's just one fact after another.	Can you add words to connect your ideas?
This part is hard to understand.	It would help your readers if you could give details to make this part clearer.
The report ends suddenly.	Can you write a closing to sum up the report?

3. **Make more revisions** to your research report. Use your conference notes and the Revising Strategies on the next page.

Help with Conferencing

ADDITIONAL CONFERENCING QUESTIONS

These questions may be useful during teacher-student conferences.

- What were you trying to learn from your report? Does your report give the answers?
- _____ does not seem quite right. Where did you find this fact? Could you double-check it?
- What does _____ mean? Could you define it?
- Were you careful to paraphrase your sources? Show me an example.
- Facts about _____ appear in several places. Can you place them all in one part of your paper?

EVALUATION TIP

Listen to find out whether students are really dialoguing and to make sure that one student isn't monopolizing the conversation. Glance at each writer's notes to make sure they are appropriate and will be useful.

Lesson Objectives

Students will:

- revise their working draft, based on their evaluations
- discuss their working draft in a writing conference

Revise Your Research Report

Focus on Instruction

Revising Reminder

Remind students that revising focuses on making their research report clear and interesting. They should not worry about mistakes at this stage. If necessary, review the revising techniques on page 20.

- Direct students' attention to the Revising Tip. Have them check that any new sentences fit easily and logically into the paragraph.
- Have students highlight each topic sentence, underline each sentence in the paragraph that supports the topic sentence, and cross out each sentence that doesn't support the topic sentence.
- Explain that students may need to do more research if they are missing some necessary information.

Conferencing Reminders

Remind students to read their paper aloud to their partner. Remind them to read slowly, clearly, and at an appropriate volume for their audience and setting.

- Reinforce the importance of the listener's compliments to the writer before asking questions. Provide examples, such as "What an interesting topic!" or "I can tell you researched your paper thoroughly."
- Students can use Blackline Master 11–5 during their writing conference.

MEETING INDIVIDUAL NEEDS

FOR STUDENTS ACQUIRING ENGLISH

Set aside quiet spaces for students to read their work aloud to themselves or a partner. Students may be more comfortable working alone or with you but should increasingly work in small groups. Give a mini-lesson on different types of sentences. Using a volunteer's report, list some sentences on the board and rewrite them as combined sentences or ones that begin with verb phrases (for example, *The hard work was done* instead of *Finishing the hard work, the engineers rested.*) Encourage risk-taking; students can always choose the original sentence after trying variations.

Revising Strategies

Lesson Objectives

Students will:

- add definitions of special words
- add details to elaborate their report
- vary sentence structure

Focus on Instruction

Elaborating: Word Choice

Have students identify the words that describe *lava* and *irrigate.* Point out that the definition for *lava* is separated by commas and that *irrigate* is defined in a separate sentence. Explain to students that the definitions help them understand the meanings of the words.

Elaborating: Details

Ask students which details were added to the second example. (in Alaska; It towers 20,320 feet above sea level.) Ask what type of detail each one is. (location; measurement) Tell students that details help them picture something more clearly.

Sentence Fluency

- Explain that sometimes sentences are written in different ways to support meaning or purpose. Refer students to the published model on page 369. Point out the compound sentences that contain related ideas. *(The otter uses them to comb its fur and to snatch up clams from the sea bottom or mussels from a reef; The average female is a little shorter and weighs about 45 pounds.)* Ask students to think of more compound sentences that contain related ideas.
- If students need extra support, review the lessons listed in the Grammar Link.

FOR STUDENTS ACQUIRING ENGLISH

To help students decide on which words to elaborate, ask them to list all the vocabulary they learned from their own report. Ask them to determine whether the words are special terms important to the report. Once the students have a list, practice defining the words as a class, using sentences on the board.

Revising Strategies

Elaborating: Word Choice Definitions of special words will help your audience understand your report.

Without a Definition	With a Definition
Lava pours out of a volcano.	Lava, a flow of hot, melted rock, pours out of a volcano.
Some farmers **irrigate** their crops.	Some farmers irrigate their crops. This means they supply water to plants by using ditches, pipes, or canals.

▶ Find at least two places in your report where you can define special words.

Elaborating: Details Exact details such as dates, amounts, measurements, and locations help make the information clear.

Few Details	Elaborated with Details
Mount McKinley is the tallest peak in the United States.	Mount McKinley in Alaska is the tallest peak in the United States. It towers 20,320 feet above sea level.

▶ Find at least two places in your report where you can add exact details.

Sentence Fluency To keep your writing interesting for your readers, begin sentences in different ways.

Death Valley in California has very high temperatures.
In Death Valley, temperatures are very high.
When summer arrives, temperatures climb high in Death Valley.

▶ Find at least two places in your report where you can vary the sentence beginnings.

GRAMMAR LINK *See also page 246.*

388 Unit 11: Research Report

Meeting Individual Needs

● RETEACHING WORKBOOK, page 101

Elaborating: Details

Elaborate by adding exact details, such as dates, amounts, measurements, and locations, to help make information clear.

Few details	The tarantula is the largest spider in the world.
Elaborated with details	The hairy, long-legged tarantula of South America is the largest spider in the world. With its legs extended, it measures up to 10 inches—about the size of a dinner plate!

Revise the following paragraph from a report on the armadillo. Elaborate each sentence by adding exact details from the diagram. The topic sentence is in dark print. Sample answers:

The armadillo is an unusual animal. It has a hard shell. It has bony plates on its body. The armadillo has bands on its back. It has claws on its legs. The armadillo uses its claws a lot.

Topic sentence: The armadillo is an unusual animal.

1. It has a hard shell.
   It has a hard shell that looks like armor.
2. It has bony plates on its body.
   It has bony plates on its head, neck, and shoulders.
3. The armadillo has separate bands on its back.
   The armadillo has separate bands on its back that move as it moves.
4. It has claws on its legs.
   It has large claws on its front legs.
5. The armadillo uses its claws a lot.
   The armadillo uses its large claws to dig tunnels, burrows, and holes to hide in.

▲■ WORKBOOK PLUS, page 150

Elaborating: Details

Few details	The hummingbird beats its wings fast.
Elaborated with details	When gathering nectar, the hummingbird beats its wings more than 70 times a second, making a sort of humming sound.

Revise the supporting sentences in the paragraph below from a report on the ostrich, adding exact details from the picture and captions. The topic sentence is in dark print.

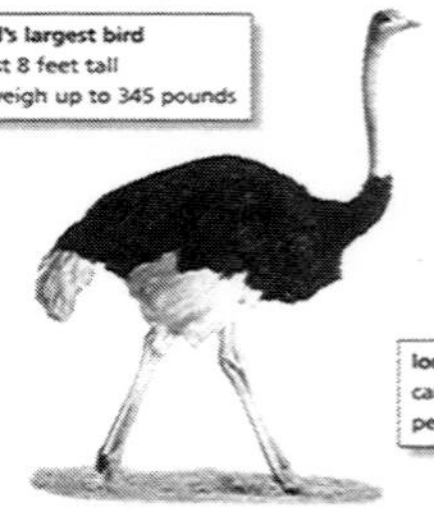

The ostrich is an unusual bird. It is very tall and weighs a lot. The ostrich cannot fly, but it can run fast. An ostrich hen lays big eggs. The ostrich lives a long time too.

The ostrich is an unusual bird. The world's largest bird, it is almost eight feet tall and can weigh up to 345 pounds. The ostrich cannot fly, but it has long legs and can run 40 miles per hour. An ostrich hen lays eggs that weigh three pounds. The ostrich lives up to 70 years. Few birds live as long.

Adding Graphics and Visuals

Sometimes a visual can add interesting information to a report. Here are some ideas.

Pictures and Maps Draw or copy a picture to show something about your topic. Including a map can be helpful if you've written about a place or described a journey.

▶ Add a picture or a map if it fits your report.

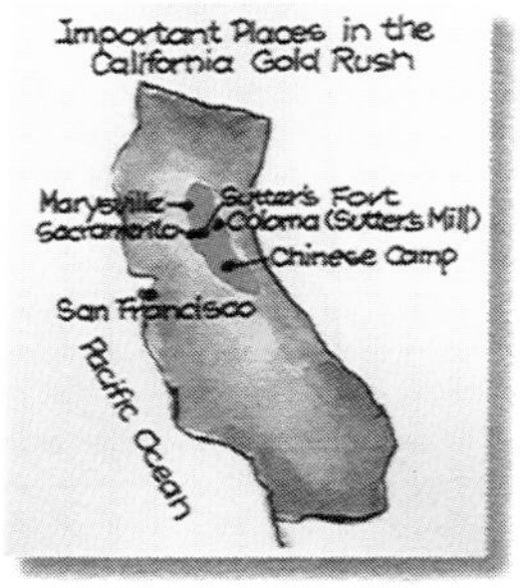

Charts and Graphs Using a chart or a graph is a good way to organize extra information.

Speedy Animals	
Animal	Speed
Cheetah	70 miles per hour
Pronghorn antelope	61 miles per hour
Wildebeest, lion, Thomson's gazelle	50 miles per hour
Quarter horse	47.5 miles per hour

▶ Add a chart or a graph to your report if you need to organize detailed information.

You can put visuals on your report cover or in the report.

Adding Graphics and Visuals

Lesson Objectives

Students will:

- add visuals to their report, if appropriate
- add a chart or a graph, if appropriate

Focus on Instruction

- Ask what the proverb "A picture is worth a thousand words" means. Discuss how pictures might enhance a report.
- Point out the map of California. Have volunteers tell how this map would be helpful in a research report about the California Gold Rush. (It would help the reader visualize where events took place.)
- Help students understand that a map can be used to emphasize a certain feature, such as rainfall, crops, or population distribution. Explain that maps can also give information about geographical features, such as countries, rivers, cities, and so on.
- Point out that the chart on page 389 gives the information about speedy animals in an organized manner. Tell students that they may use a chart from a book that fits with their report or they may create their own chart in a drawing or on a computer.
- Explain that a graph helps the reader understand numerical information by presenting the information in picture form.
- Refer students to pages H24 and H25 for additional information about visuals.

MEETING INDIVIDUAL NEEDS

FOR STUDENTS ACQUIRING ENGLISH

Refer students back to their visuals for the instructional essays. Ask them how research visuals differ from instructional ones. (They have more labels, facts, and charts.) Define each type of visual in the word logs. If students have trouble deciding which visual to use, team them with partners who will help decide.

Lesson Objectives

Students will:

- create a time line, if appropriate
- draw a diagram, if appropriate

Focus on Instruction

- Brainstorm with students different topics that might use a time line to enhance a report. (Sample answer: history of a specific invention and how it has changed over time)
- Point out the labels for the diagram. Discuss how diagrams can give the reader a better understanding of how something looks or works.
- Make sure students understand that it is not mandatory to use graphics and visuals. Students should not force them into the report if they don't fit.

Time Line If your report tells about a person's life or a series of events, you might show important dates on a time line.

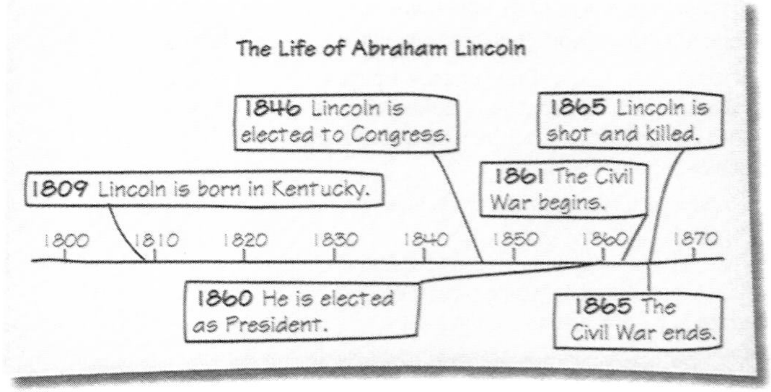

Create a time line if it fits your report.

Diagrams Draw a diagram to show the parts of something in your report.

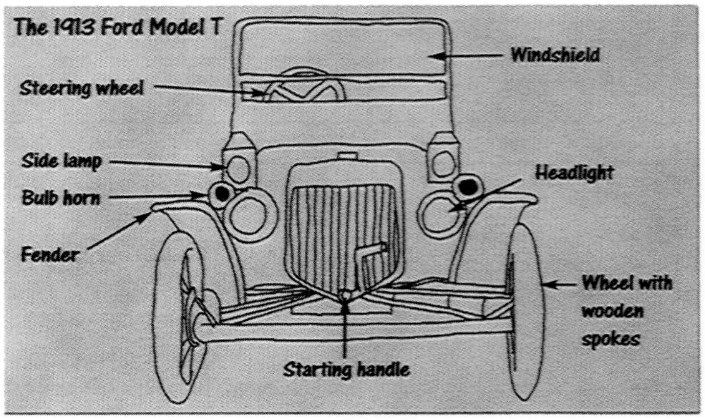

Add a diagram to your report if it will help your readers.

PREWRITING DRAFTING REVISING PROOFREADING PUBLISHING

Proofread Your Research Report

Proofread your report, using the Proofreading Checklist and the Grammar and Spelling Connections. Proofread for one skill at a time. Use a class dictionary to check spellings.

Proofreading Checklist

Did I
- ✓ indent all paragraphs?
- ✓ correct any run-on sentences?
- ✓ begin proper nouns with capital letters?
- ✓ use comparisons with *-er* and *-est* correctly?
- ✓ correct all spelling errors?

Use the Guide to Capitalization, Punctuation, and Usage on page H55.

Proofreading Marks
- ¶ Indent
- ∧ Add
- Delete
- ≡ Capital letter
- / Small letter

Tech Tip The spelling tool will not catch every capitalization mistake.

Grammar and Spelling Connections

Proper Nouns The names of particular people, places, and things are called **proper nouns.** Capitalize every important word in a proper noun.

Common Nouns	Proper Nouns
scientist	Marie Curie
park	Yellowstone National Park
city, state	Tampa, Florida
holiday	Fourth of July

GRAMMAR LINK See also pages 66, 170, and 172.

Spelling final |ər| The final |ər| sounds in two-syllable words are often spelled *ar, or,* or *er.*

cellar	sailor	ladder
sugar	harbor	proper

See the Spelling Guide on page H65.

Go to www.eduplace.com/kids/hme/ for proofreading practice.

Help with Proofreading

EVALUATION TIP
You may want to check your students' proofread reports before they make their final copy.

TECH TIP
Students may highlight or put in bold type any words that might be misspelled and then check those words in a dictionary.

MANAGEMENT TIP
Have each student keep a personal checklist of skills that he or she needs for proofreading. Staple the list to the student's folder.

Lesson Objective

Students will:
- proofread their research report

Proofread Your Research Report

Focus on Instruction

Proofreading Reminders

- Remind students that the proofreading stage is the time to correct capitalization, usage, punctuation, and spelling. Encourage students to use the Guide to Capitalization, Punctuation, and Usage.
- If necessary, review with students when and how to use each proofreading mark. Have students use a different colored pen or pencil to mark their proofreading corrections.
- For proofreading practice, see the usage and mechanics lessons in the grammar units and the Mixed Review practice in each grammar unit Checkup.

- Have students use the Proofreading Checklist in the student book or a checklist of personal skills. Make sure students understand each item in the checklist and the related Grammar and Spelling Connections.
- Tell students to double-check that they have capitalized every important word in a proper noun and have spelled words that end with *ar, or,* or *er* correctly.

INTERNET CONNECTION Have your students go to www.eduplace.com/kids/hme/ for online proofreading practice that is fun.

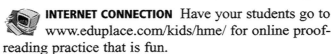

MEETING INDIVIDUAL NEEDS **FOR STUDENTS ACQUIRING ENGLISH**
Students often need help with run-ons and subject-verb agreement. In addition to worksheet practice, play a game. Give pairs of students 5–10 minutes to find and correct all the run-ons and subject-verb agreement errors in their reports. Offer prizes for the teams that correct the most, best, and fastest.

Lesson Objectives

Students will:
- make a neat final copy of their report
- choose a way to publish or share their report
- reflect on the writing experience
- evaluate their report in comparison to other compositions in their writing portfolio.

Publish Your Research Report

Focus on Instruction

- Before students make their final copy, have them decide how they will publish or share their report. Review their decisions with them to help them make any special plans.
- Help them make neat corrections to their final copy rather than rewrite their paper.

Keeping a Writing Portfolio

- **Selection** A paper might be selected because it is
  - ✓ generally noteworthy
  - ✓ a good example of a particular criterion
  - ✓ an example of a particular kind of writing
  - ✓ an example from a certain time in the school year
  - ✓ a typical example of the student's work
- **Labeling** For every paper, have students complete a cover sheet giving the title, date of completion, and reason for inclusion.
- **Review** Periodically have students remove papers that no longer reflect their best work or aren't needed as baselines.
- **Evaluation** Periodically review students' portfolios with them to discuss growth and areas that need improvement.

Publish Your Research Report

1. **Make a neat final copy** of your report. Be sure you fixed all mistakes.
2. **Write** an interesting title for your report that will make your audience curious, such as "Ford's Tin Lizzie" rather than "An Old Car."
3. **Publish** or share your report in a way that suits your audience. See the Ideas for Sharing box.

Tips for Creating a Visual Display

- Make large visuals to go with your report. Use nice lettering.
- Find objects related to your report, make a cardboard or clay model, or create a mural or a collage. Add helpful labels.
- Put your visuals on poster board, or arrange them on a table. Display your report with them.

See page H24 for more tips.

Ideas for Sharing

Write It
- Put your report in a homemade booklet.

Say It
- Present your report orally. See page 400 for tips.
- With other classmates, form a panel of experts. Record your reports on videotape.

Show It
- Make a multimedia presentation. See page H45 for tips.
- Create a visual display for your report.

Reflect

Write about your writing experience. Use these questions to get started.
- What was hard about writing a research report? What was easy?
- What else would you like to learn about your topic?
- How does this paper compare with other papers that you have written?

Help with Publishing

TIPS FOR IDEAS FOR SHARING

Booklet Suggest that students make decorative covers for their booklets. Have them think of ways to share their booklets with readers outside the classroom.

Oral Report Remind students who choose to read their report to use appropriate rate, volume, pitch, and tone.

Panel of Experts Encourage students to practice presenting their report with one another. Use the videotape as a teaching tool the next time students prepare for an oral presentation.

TECH TIP

Students can choose different fonts and type sizes to use as headings for their visual display. They can print and cut out the words and glue them to their visuals.

SCHOOL-HOME CONNECTION

Students can share their booklet with family members. Family members can ask questions and give feedback.

Assessment Link

Writing Prompts

Use these prompts as ideas for writing research reports. Think about who your audience will be, and write your report in a way that they will enjoy and understand.

Writing Across the Curriculum

1 CAREER EDUCATION
What career interests you most? Would you like to be a computer programmer? a cook at a fancy restaurant? a singer? a doctor? Write a report on the career. Try to interview someone who works in that area.

2 MATH
People have invented many things to help them keep track of numbers and amounts. Research the history of the calendar, the abacus, early units of measure, or an instrument such as the barometer. Include diagrams or pictures if you'd like.

3 HEALTH
What does exercise do for health? Would you like to know more about vitamins or nutrition? Write a report on a health topic that interests you. Report facts without giving your opinion. Use up-to-date sources.

4 PHYSICAL EDUCATION
Who first played soccer? Who made up the rules for tennis? Who designed golf clubs? Report on the history of your favorite sport or pastime. You might include diagrams of special equipment.

5 FINE ART
The Mexican artist Rufino Tamayo was important in modern art. Research the man and his career, and write a report. Which artists did he learn from? What is his style of painting? Tell about some of his major works of art.

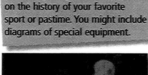

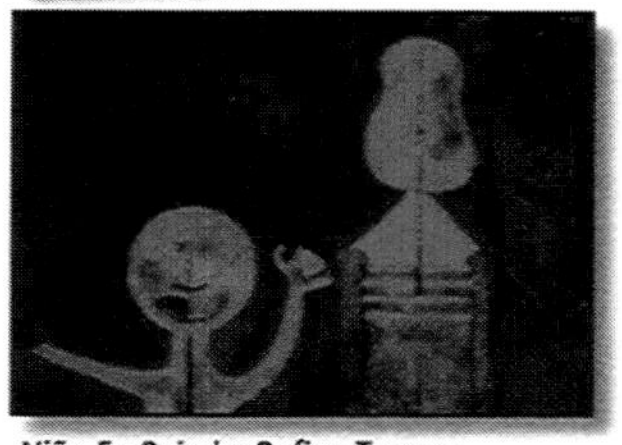
Niño En Rojo, by Rufino Tamayo

See www.eduplace.com/kids/hme/ for more prompts.

About the Artist

About Rufino Tamayo

Rufino Tamayo (1899–1991) was an important Mexican painter who was known for his use of bright colors. Born in Oaxaca, Mexico, Tamayo found inspiration in the landscape, history, and folklore of his native country. His painting style was semiabstract, which means he distorted his forms to make them appear more expressive.

Tamayo enrolled in the San Carlos Academy of Fine Arts in 1917 but soon left to venture out on his own. He became the head designer of the department of ethnographic drawings at the National Museum of Archaeology in Mexico City.

Over the following decades, Tamayo's work was exhibited in many galleries and art museums around the world. Tamayo painted murals for various libraries, museums, and universities. Tamayo's Indian origins influenced his work, as did the artistic movements of Surrealism, Cubism, and Expressionism.

The Rufino Tamayo Museum of International Contemporary Art opened in Mexico in 1981. One can view the artist's works as well as many items from his private collection, which includes paintings, sculpture, and drawings by Miró, Dali, and Picasso.

Writing Prompts

Objective

Students will:
- review prompts for choosing a topic
- view critically a work of fine art and use it to write a research report

Using the Prompts

You can use the prompts on this page in several ways.

- Have students review the prompts to help spark ideas when they are choosing their own topics for a research report. Suggest that students choose one or two prompts that interest them and brainstorm ideas of their own.
- Choose a prompt that fits with a related topic in another subject area to integrate writing a research report across the curriculum.
- Share information about Mexican artist Rufino Tamayo. Brainstorm ideas about sources students could use to find information about this artist. (Sample ideas: They could use the Internet, read books on art, or visit an art museum that contains his works in its collections.)

INTERNET CONNECTION Send your students to www.eduplace.com/kids/hme/ for more writing prompts. You can also find and print these prompts at www.eduplace.com/rdg/hme/.

MEETING INDIVIDUAL NEEDS

FOR STUDENTS ACQUIRING ENGLISH

If you would like students to gain more practice in reports but know they can't produce another long work, assign them a paper to write with a partner. Students should write the report just as they did for their own reports (decide on a topic, research, outline, and so on). However, this time they can work together or split each step.

Writing to Solve a Problem

Lesson Objective

Students will:

- read a student model of how to write to solve a problem

Focus on the Model

- Ask students what they think is the purpose of writing to solve a problem. (to find and organize information that will help solve a problem) Point out that writing to solve a problem is similar to writing a research report because the writer must do research to find facts.
- Tell students they will read about how a girl solved the problem of how to start a stamp collection. Have students read the introduction to the lesson.
- Before students read about how the girl solved her problem, explain that the blue callouts highlight the four parts of writing to solve a problem and that students will learn about those four parts after they read the completed report.
- Ask volunteers to read the report aloud.

Students can also listen to the model on audiotape.

Focus on Instruction

- Discuss with the class the explanations of the callouts given in the Reading As a Writer section on page 395. Have volunteers answer the questions.
- Ask students to name some other types of problems that could be researched and solved.

Answers for Reading As a Writer

- The student wants to learn how to start a stamp collection.
- Sources of information are the U.S. Postal Service Web site, a postal clerk, and library books.
- *My problem was finding out how to start a stamp collection* retells the problem. The student visited the Postal Service Web site, the post office, and the library to gather information.
- She decides to start her collection with stamps from mail received by friends and family members.

FOR STUDENTS ACQUIRING ENGLISH

Have students work with partners to practice writing a problem in a single clear statement or question. Most students will find questions easier, so you may want to provide a model for statements. For example: *I need to find out how to start a stamp collection.* Provide basic topic ideas such as getting a pet or using the Internet. Ask students for examples of resources they might use to solve a problem. Remind students that people can be resources.

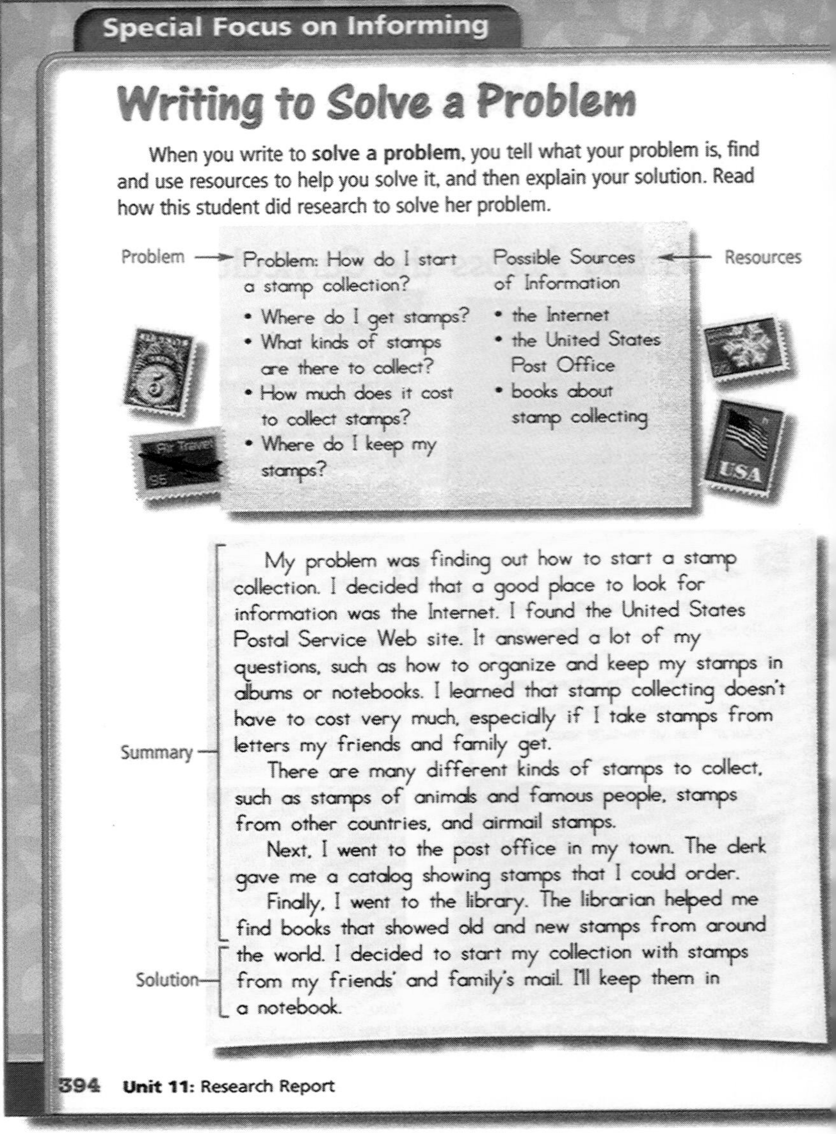
Special Focus on Informing

Writing to Solve a Problem

When you write to **solve a problem**, you tell what your problem is, find and use resources to help you solve it, and then explain your solution. Read how this student did research to solve her problem.

Problem → Problem: How do I start a stamp collection?

- Where do I get stamps?
- What kinds of stamps are there to collect?
- How much does it cost to collect stamps?
- Where do I keep my stamps?

Possible Sources of Information ← Resources

- the Internet
- the United States Post Office
- books about stamp collecting

Summary

My problem was finding out how to start a stamp collection. I decided that a good place to look for information was the Internet. I found the United States Postal Service Web site. It answered a lot of my questions, such as how to organize and keep my stamps in albums or notebooks. I learned that stamp collecting doesn't have to cost very much, especially if I take stamps from letters my friends and family get.

There are many different kinds of stamps to collect, such as stamps of animals and famous people, stamps from other countries, and airmail stamps.

Next, I went to the post office in my town. The clerk gave me a catalog showing stamps that I could order.

Finally, I went to the library. The librarian helped me find books that showed old and new stamps from around the world.

Solution

I decided to start my collection with stamps from my friends' and family's mail. I'll keep them in a notebook.

394 **Unit 11:** Research Report

Reading As a Writer

See TE margin for answers.

- The **problem** is a question or a situation that needs to be solved. *What is this student's problem?*
- **Resources** are people, places, and materials that might give you information to solve the problem. *What possible sources are listed?*
- The **summary** retells the problem and explains the actions taken to solve the problem. *Which paragraph retells the problem?*
- The **solution** is the decision you make. *What decision does this student make?*

How to Write to Solve a Problem

1. **State** your problem in one clear sentence.
2. **Write** a list of questions you want to answer, or make notes about parts of the problem.
3. **Find** sources of information to help you. Then do the research you need to do. Organize your questions, information, and sources in a chart.

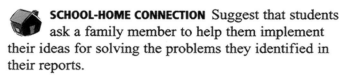

Question	Information	Source
Where do I get stamps?	from mailed envelopes or from a catalog	the U.S. Postal Service Web site and a postal clerk
What kinds of stamps are there to collect?	many different kinds, like stamps from other countries or that show famous people	the U.S. Postal Service Web site, a postal clerk, and library books
How much does it cost to collect stamps?	not much if I start with used ones	the U.S. Postal Service Web site
Where do I keep my stamps?	in albums or notebooks	the U.S. Postal Service Web site

4. **Solve** the problem using the information you collected. Write a summary paragraph explaining what you learned and what you decided.

Help with Writing to Solve a Problem

TOPIC IDEAS

Suggest these ideas to prompt topics.

- Students can find out how to improve performance in a particular sport.
- They can find out how to train a pet.
- They can solve the problem of how to earn extra money.

TECH TIPS

Show students how to use the table function to set up their chart.

EVALUATION TIP

Review students' chosen problems to be sure that they can be solved.

Lesson Objectives

Students will:

- research and solve a problem and write a summary paragraph explaining what they learned
- revise and proofread the paragraph

How to Write to Solve a Problem

Focus on Instruction

- Remind students that people write for a variety of purposes. In this case, they are writing to help themselves solve a problem.
- Point out that problem-solving is easier when students establish a clear, central focus with little or no irrelevant or repetitious information.
- Have students work in small groups to discuss the problems they wish to solve. Groups can help individuals formulate a clear sentence to state their problem.
- Before students begin writing, review their charts to make sure that they have asked relevant questions and used appropriate sources of information.

Connecting to the Criteria

Remind students to check that their completed summary contains the four main parts described in the Reading As a Writer section of this lesson.

SCHOOL-HOME CONNECTION Suggest that students ask a family member to help them implement their ideas for solving the problems they identified in their reports.

Discuss with each student whether this paper should go into the portfolio. Consider these possible reasons: (1) it is an especially good piece of writing; (2) it reflects a particular aspect of writing that the student did well; (3) it shows an aspect of writing that needs more work and could be used as a baseline for measuring growth.

Writing a News Article

Lesson Objective

Students will:

- read a model of a news article and identify its parts

Focus on the Model

- Ask students what they think is the purpose of a news article. (to inform readers about the facts of current events) Point out that writing a news article is like writing a research report in that a good news article is factual and shows good research.
- Tell students that they will read Jeremy's news article about a basketball playoff game. Have students read the introduction.
- Before students read the news article, explain that the blue callouts highlight the four parts of a news article and that they will learn more about those parts after they read the article.
- Have volunteers read the article aloud.

Students can also listen to the model on audiotape.

Focus on Instruction

- Discuss with the class the explanations of the characteristics highlighted in the Reading As a Writer section on page 397. Have volunteers answer the questions.
- Point out that the news article uses short sentences and paragraphs for easier reading.

Answers to Reading As a Writer

- The main idea of Jeremy's news article is that the Bulldogs beat the Cougars in the basketball game.
- The basketball game took place Friday night at the Beechmont Civic Arena.
- Jeremy noted that the crowd was cheering wildly and that Michael Hernandez ran for the ball and made a slam dunk. He added that Tim Jackson bounced the ball under his leg and then made a basket. After that, Joey Wong made a three-pointer for the win.
- Jeremy ends his article by quoting a player.

FOR STUDENTS ACQUIRING ENGLISH

First, ask for suggestions for other possible headlines for this article. Then have students find the answers to *who, what, where, when, why,* and *how* questions in the lead paragraph of the article. Partners can alternate asking each other a question. Explain the compound word *playoffs*.

Writing a News Article

A **news article** tells about a recent event. It reports facts about what happened. Read Jeremy's news article below about a sporting event.

Headline → **Bulldogs Beat Cougars**

Lead paragraph: At the Beechmont Civic Arena Friday night, the Beechmont Bulldogs beat the Cannonstown Cougars in the Junior Varsity basketball playoffs.

Supporting details: The scores were close up to the very end. With four minutes left on the clock, one of the Beechmont players raced with the ball to the basket. A Cougar caught up with him and stole the ball to make a two-point lay-up. Then the Cougars fouled the Beechmont Bulldogs. Joey Wong, Beechmont's best free thrower, went to the line and made the two baskets.

With two minutes to go, the crowd cheered wildly for each team. Bulldog Michael Hernandez made a slam dunk. The score was tied. Cougar Tim Jackson bounced the ball under his leg and shot a terrific basket. The score then was 42 to 40. Then, Wong shot a dramatic three-pointer on the buzzer and won the game for the Bulldogs!

Conclusion: Asked about the game, Wong said, "This was really a team effort. Everyone deserves credit."

Reading As a Writer

See TE margin for answers.

- The **headline** gets the reader's attention and tells the main idea of the news article. *What is the main idea of Jeremy's article?*
- The **lead paragraph** tells the most important facts about the event. It answers the questions *Who? What? Where? When? Why?* and *How? Where and when did the event in Jeremy's article take place?*
- The **supporting details** give more information about the facts. *How did Joey Wong win the game for the Bulldogs?*
- The **conclusion** ends the article. The writer may quote someone or give some final details about the event. *How does Jeremy end his article?*

How to Write a News Article

1. **Choose** a recent event to write about. Think about what your audience would want to know.
2. **Outline** your news article, using a pyramid like the one shown.
3. **Research** your subject. Take careful notes to answer each of the six questions. If possible, interview people who were at the event, or know about it, for quotations.
4. **Write** your article. Remember to write only the facts, not your opinions. Start with a lead paragraph that tells about the event. Quote people who were there. End with a conclusion that wraps up the story.
5. **Think** of a short, attention-getting headline for your news article.
6. **Revise and proofread** your article. Check to be sure that the names you've used are spelled correctly.
7. **Make a final copy.** Work with classmates and make a class newspaper.

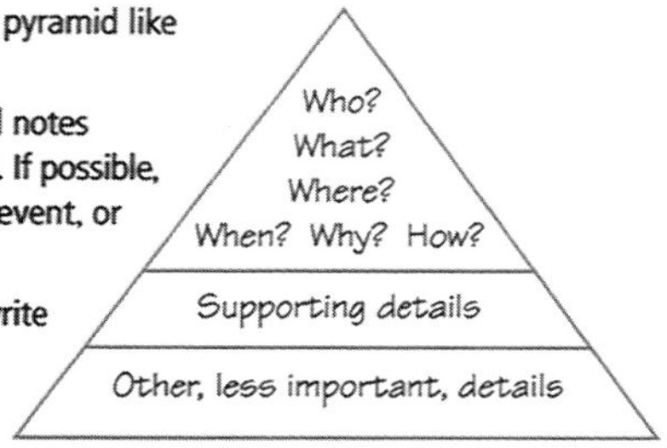

Help with Writing a News Article

MORE TOPIC IDEAS
Suggest these possibilities.
- a news article describing a student election
- an article about an award or honor received by a student, teacher, or principal

TECH TIPS
Have students use available software that provides newspaper templates to create a class newspaper. Students can scan photos or artwork into their articles.

SCHOOL-HOME CONNECTION
Suggest that students share their class newspaper with family members.

EVALUATION TIP
Review students' topic choices to make sure they are appropriate and that students have gathered enough facts to write a solid news article that answers the questions *Who? What? Where? When? Why?* and *How?*

COLLABORATIVE WRITING
Have students review different newspapers to analyze headline structure and newspaper layouts. Then have groups of students work together to gather and organize information for news articles, revise the articles, and compile them into a class newspaper.

Lesson Objectives

Students will:
- choose a topic
- outline, research, organize, and write a news article
- revise and proofread their article and then make a final copy for publication

How to Write a News Article

Focus on Instruction

- Emphasize that the purpose of a news article is to inform the audience about the facts of an event. Tell students that facts give information that can be proved.
- Emphasize that reporters write news articles in the third person and do not give the writer's opinion.
- Review the use of the pyramid graphic organizer. Remind students that supporting details should give facts that strengthen the main idea of the article.
- Ask students how the purpose of various news articles might differ. (Sample answer: One article might report on a funny happening whereas another might tell about a serious accident.) Ask how students would alter their word choice and style of writing for each purpose.
- Suggest that students talk about their topic with a partner or in a small group before they write.
- Tell students to write the most important facts at the beginning of their article.
- Review with students the Proofreading Checklist on page 391 and the use of proofreading marks.
- Encourage students to incorporate visuals, such as photos or drawings, into their article to enhance the meaning of the written message.

Help each student decide whether this paper should go into the portfolio.

Connecting to the Criteria

Remind students to check that their article contains the four main parts of a good news article described in the Reading As a Writer section of this lesson.

MEETING INDIVIDUAL NEEDS
FOR STUDENTS ACQUIRING ENGLISH
Have students work in small groups to think of possible topics for a news article. Remind students to think about recent events. Discuss the pyramid outline in the graphic organizer. Ask students why the pyramid is divided into three sections. Which part is most important? Which is least important?

Completing a Form

Lesson Objective

Students will:
- read a student model of a properly completed public library card application and identify its parts

Focus on the Model

- Ask students what they think is the purpose of filling out a form. (to provide information) Point out that a completed form is similar to a research report in that it contains factual information. Explain that a form organizes information so it can be found quickly. Ask students who might use forms. (any person or group that needs quick access to organized information)
- Tell students they will read a library card application form that a boy named Michael completed. Have students read the introductory paragraph.
- Before students read Michael's application, explain that they will learn about the parts of the application after they read the completed application.
- Ask volunteers to read the application aloud.

Focus on Instruction

- Discuss with students the parts of a form given in the Reading As a Writer section on page 399. Have volunteers answer the questions.
- Point out to students that providing a middle initial on a form can be helpful because it differentiates people with common first and last names.
- Explain that the # symbol after *Apt.* is an abbreviation for the word *number.*

Answers to Reading as a Writer

- He should leave those boxes blank.
- He wrote one letter or number in each box.
- He lives at 325 W. Palm Drive, Anytown, Florida.
- He agreed to return anything he borrows from the library in good condition and on time. He also agreed to pay any fines.
- He filled out the form on January 16, 2001.

FOR STUDENTS ACQUIRING ENGLISH

Ask a volunteer to explain what an application is. Discuss what a library card is used for; if possible, show one from your local library. Make sure students understand that their last name is the same as their family name. Explain that they should always print on an application. Talk about the Zip Code and Area Code.

Completing a Form

One way to supply information to another person, to an organization, or to a business is to **complete a form**. Forms are sometimes needed to register a bicycle, to order from a catalog, to get a dog license, or to join a book club. Read this form.

APPLICATION **Public Library Card**

Directions — *Fill in the information. Print one letter or number in each box. If something does not apply to you, leave those boxes blank.*

First Name: Michael   Middle Initial: S

Last Name: Baker

Boxes for letters and numbers

Date of Birth (month/day/year) (sample: 03/16/1991): 07 23 1992

Information about you

Street Address: 325 W. Palm Drive   Apt. #:

City: Anytown

County: Manatee   State: FL   Zip Code: 34205

Area Code: 941   Home Phone: 555 9876

I agree to be responsible for the materials I check out with this card. I will return all materials, including books, tapes, and videos, in good condition and on time. I agree to pay any fines charged to me.

Signature — Michael S. Baker   January 16, 2001 — Date

Signature of Applicant   Date

Reading As a Writer

See TE margin for answers.

- The **directions** tell you how to fill out the form. *What should Michael do if something does not apply to him?*
- Some forms have **boxes for letters and numbers**. Only one letter or number is written in each box. *How many letters or numbers did Michael write in each box?*
- The **information about you** is often your name, address, and phone number. *Where does Michael live?*
- Some forms ask for your **signature**, which is your name written in cursive. Your signature means that you understand and agree with everything on the form. *What did Michael agree to do?*
- The **date** gives the month, day, and year on which you fill out the form. Sometimes a zero is needed before the digit, as in 01, 02, 03, and so on. *When did Michael fill out this form?*

How to Complete a Form

1. **Read** the directions carefully.
2. **Complete** the form by filling in the boxes. Put only one letter or number in each box. For any information you don't know, ask a family member to help you.
3. **Sign** the form.
4. **Date** the form.
5. **Proofread** your form for mistakes. Check to see that the information is correct and that you have filled in all of the information.

Help with Completing a Form

USING RESOURCES
Provide students with a variety of forms so that they can see the kinds of information that are requested on each.

TECH TIP
Students can use available software to create their forms. Show them how to provide write-on lines and check boxes.

COLLABORATIVE WRITING
Have small groups of students review different forms in order to analyze the kinds of information requested by each. Then have groups work together to compose, organize, and revise forms for classroom use. For example, they might create a form for a library card that students can use to borrow books from the classroom.

Lesson Objectives

Students will:

- complete and proofread a sample library application form
- recognize the characteristics of an application form

How to Complete a Form

Focus on Instruction

- Students can use Blackline Master 11–6 to practice completing a form.
- Remind students that if something on the form does not apply to them, they should leave the boxes blank. In this case, some students may not have an Apt. #.
- Remind students that it is important to check with a parent or guardian before giving out detailed information about themselves or their families.
- Remind students to check that only one number or letter appears in each box.
- Explain to students that by putting their signature on a document they are giving a solemn promise to meet the requirements discussed on the form.

Connecting to the Criteria

Remind students to check that they have followed all the guidelines stated in the Reading As a Writer section and that their completed form follows the format shown in the model.

SCHOOL HOME CONNECTION Suggest that students go with their parents or guardians to their local library and apply for a library card.

FOR STUDENTS ACQUIRING ENGLISH

Ask how directions on a form are the same as or different from directions to a place. Review ways to write dates. Remind students that the month always precedes the day in English; give several examples, such as 10/12/01 and 5/7/95, and ask students to read the dates out loud.

Giving an Oral Report

Lesson Objectives

Students will:

- demonstrate effective communication skills by presenting a multimedia report
- present information in an organized speech
- present information in various forms, using available technology
- select, organize, or produce media to complement and extend an oral report
- adapt spoken language, such as word choice, diction, and usage, to the audience, purpose, and occasion

Focus on Instruction

- As students think about their oral report topic choices, they should consider the media they want to use to make their presentation. Their selection of media should support and enhance the subject matter.
- Tell students to consider the size of their audience and the presentation site before selecting which media to use. Small illustrations or complicated diagrams or tables will not be easy for a large group to see, unless the images are projected on an overhead or computer projection device.
- Have volunteers read aloud the Which Media? table. Define and discuss the usefulness of each of the media listed. Explain that the table is not a complete list, and that students might have other good ideas for media support. For instance, students could create a computer-generated multimedia presentation by incorporating into slide-presentation software audio and video clips, scanned photography, computer-generated charts or diagrams, and text.
- Name topics such as those that follow and have students tell what media they might use to support an oral presentation on that topic.

  Earth and moon (Sample answers: papier-mâché or a solid foam model; diagrams; satellite photography from the Internet)

  Life in the early 1800s (Sample answers: diorama; diagram; music CD or audiotape cassette; computer or hand-drawn chart)

  Earthquakes (Sample answers: clay model; videotape; diagrams or photography from the Internet)

  Roller coasters (Sample answers: toothpick-and-clay model; diagram; videotape; tape-recorded interviews; computer simulation)

Giving an Oral Report

The research you do for an oral report can include finding different kinds of media to present, such as photographs or videos. These help make your topic more interesting for your audience. You might make visual aids of your own, such as models, charts, or slides, to support your spoken ideas.

Which Media?

Models Models give a sense of size. They show subjects in three dimensions. Would your listeners better understand your topic if you made a model?	Dioramas, clay models, and papier-mâché objects
Photographs Photographs can show hard-to-explain events or details. Would your report be clearer if you used pictures to explain what you mean?	Posters, slides, and pictures from newspapers, magazines, or books
Illustrations Can you present data from your report? Information presented in charts and drawings can help explain your ideas.	Charts, graphs, diagrams, and tables 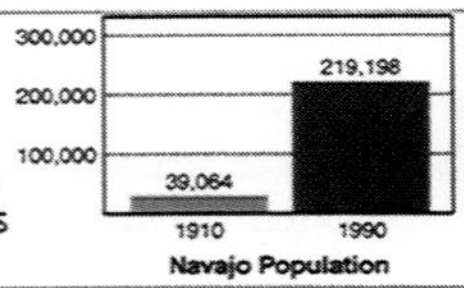
Technology Can you present your ideas through music? Could you show part of a video on your topic to interest your audience?	Videotapes, CDs, cassette tapes, the Internet, CD-ROMs, and digital photography 

See also pages H45–H47 in the Tools and Tips Handbook.

Getting Ready

Prepare your materials ahead of time. If you plan to show photographs from books, use bookmarks so that you can easily turn to the right pages. If you are using cassettes or videos, be sure the equipment is set up and that it works. Here are some guides to help you give your report.

Before the Talk

- Write notes, or key words and phrases, on cards.
- Practice your talk using the cards.
- Add more notes if you need to.
- Practice saying words that are hard to pronounce.

Guides for Giving an Oral Report

- Stand up straight.
- Speak clearly and loudly enough to be heard by everyone in the room.
- Don't fidget or rock back and forth. Keep your hands out of your pockets.
- Be sure not to say *ah, well,* and *um.*
- Make eye contact with your audience.
- Be sure everyone in the audience can see or hear the media you are using.
- Sound interested in what you are saying. Vary the tone of your voice to keep your listeners interested.

Apply It

Answers will vary.

Choose a report you have already written and prepare media to use in presenting it orally. Make sure the topic would interest your audience. Use the guides above as you give your report. Then answer the following questions.

- Which media did you choose for your report? Why?
- Did your presentation hold the attention and interest of your audience? How do you know?
- If you could present your report again, what would you do differently?

Focus on Instruction

- Stress that students should not read their oral reports as they present them, so students need only write notes, not complete sentences and paragraphs, on cards.
- Suggest that students time themselves as they practice their oral reports. Because many people present oral information too quickly, students can use their timings to compare one practice session with another until they are satisfied with their rate of speaking.
- Have volunteers read aloud the guidelines. Discuss each one. Remind students that they need to consider the size of the room and the number of people in the room when choosing how loudly to speak.
- Tell students that they should stop and take a deep breath, rather than say *ah*, *well*, or *um*.
- Emphasize that in any oral presentation, word choice, diction, and usage should be appropriate for the needs of the audience, as well as for the subject matter. For instance, a light-hearted subject might lend itself to a less-formal presentation style than a serious subject.

Apply It

- Discuss how to use a video camera to document pertinent information.
- Students may choose to videotape and show their own footage or present commercially prepared videos. In either case, encourage students to provide accompanying explanation either in tandem with, preceding, or following the presentation.
- If students are using videotape, preview the videotape before showing it to the class.
- Assist students with the use of certain media, especially those requiring batteries or an electrical outlet. Some media may require advance time for set-up. Students should have the tape set to the sounds or images they want to present.
- Encourage students to use at least two different media in their oral reports. Have students make one visual and one non-visual, if possible.

MEETING INDIVIDUAL NEEDS — FOR STUDENTS ACQUIRING ENGLISH

Write *media* on the board. Say that this word is an irregular plural; explain that it includes all the things that we can use to help us present or explain our ideas in an oral report. Name a map as an example; ask students for other examples of media. Compare their ideas to those in the book; assist with vocabulary and pronunciation.

Looking at the News

Lesson Objectives

Students will:
- interpret messages conveyed through mass media
- use media to compare ideas and points of view
- distinguish between a speaker's opinion and fact
- compare and contrast print, visual, and electronic media

Focus on Instruction

- Draw attention to the web. Have students describe what they might hear or see in each of the listed news features. Explain that local news is about the community, city, or state; national news is about the entire United States; and international news is about events from other countries.
- Tell students that visuals, including text, video, and computer images, may run in the background of news stories. Other elements of the evening news not shown on the Internet include promotions within the newscast that attempt to keep viewers watching for a particular feature, and theater, book, or movie reviews.
- To extend student thinking about how news features are chosen, have students name what most interests them on the news. Ask students to consider whether the news provides information or entertainment. Use their answers as a springboard for discussion about why newscasts devote significant amounts of time to "softer" news items, such as human-interest stories.

Looking at the News

What is news? It is information about current events. To get the day's news, your family may watch a television news program. News is also found on the radio, in newspapers, and on the Internet.

You probably expect the news to be true and fair. Is it? When you watch the evening news on TV, what are you actually seeing and hearing?

Behind the News

Television is a business. That means that most TV networks must make money. They do this by selling time during their programs for companies to play commercials. Even news programs have commercials.

Look at the word web above. Many topics are part of an evening news program. Stories about weather and sports are included along with the national news. Think of a reason to explain why so many topics are included.

Thinking Further

News people make decisions about what you see on TV. They select stories for a purpose. Some news people cover issues they believe are important. Others choose stories that will entertain their audience. Use the guides below to think about the news.

Guides for Looking at the News

- ▶ Notice the first story. Why do you think that story was chosen to lead or begin the news? Count how many are meant to inform. Count how many are meant to catch the interest of the audience.
- ▶ Notice which stories take more time than the others. What information do you think is left out of the shorter stories? Do you think information has been left out of the longer stories too? Why or why not?
- ▶ Notice how much time is given to sports and weather. Why do you think these subjects receive this much coverage?
- ▶ Pay attention to the commercials. Can you tell who the audience of the news program is? Are the commercials aimed at voters? teenagers? workers? or retired people?
- ▶ Listen to the chitchat among the news people. Why do you think they talk like that?

Apply It Answers will vary.

Watch an evening news program on television. Use the guides above and take notes. Answer these questions.

- What businesses paid to have their commercials played during the news?
- Do you think the news stories you watched gave the whole picture about what happened that day? Explain why or why not.
- Why do you think the news people picked the stories they ran?
- What part of the news did you like to watch?

Focus on Instruction

- Explain that "news people" have a wide variety of talents and skills. This group of people may include newscasters who deliver the news, reporters who gather the news, editors who write or edit the scripts, video photographers who shoot film clips, graphic designers who create diagrams and illustrations, and researchers who locate and summarize background information.
- Have volunteers read aloud the Guides for Looking At the News. Discuss each guideline. Make sure students understand that television stations choose which news and features appear, how much time is devoted to each story, and the order in which the stories are aired.
- Ask students which news features are most likely to contain more opinion than fact. (commercials, chitchat, public service announcements) Tell them that as they watch the news, they should listen to distinguish between a speaker's opinion and fact. Remind students that facts can be proved true or false.
- Have students compare news on TV to news found in a newspaper. How might it be more difficult to tell fact from opinion in a newspaper? (Sample answer: can't see facial expressions) How might it be easier to tell fact from opinion in a newspaper? (A newspaper has all of its news in sections, so you know exactly what you're reading.)

Apply It

- Videotape an evening news program to show the entire class. Tell students to take notes while viewing the news, and to list specific examples as they watch.
- Ask students to give examples of factual news statements. Have them identify examples of opinion. Ask students whether they noticed instances when a speaker's tone of voice, facial expression, or gestures revealed opinion, even if the words did not.
- If possible, share a newspaper written the same day or the day after the television news show. Read the newspaper headlines. How do they compare with the television news? What other newspaper features and stories relate to those on the television news? Compare and contrast the amount of detail, fact, and opinion in each medium.
- The Guides for Looking at the News can be applied to listening to radio news broadcasts and to other types of television news programs. Extend the activity by having students use the guidelines to evaluate an alternate news broadcast.

About Section 3

This section includes two developmental writing units for an opinion essay and a persuasive essay, using the writing process.

Special Focus features provide instruction for writing a book report, a poem, and a business letter.

Communication Links lessons develop students' listening, speaking, and viewing skills.

Getting Started

- **Listening to an Opinion:** A one-page lesson with guidelines specific to listening to an opinion (A selection for reading aloud is in the Teacher's Edition.)
- **Writing an Opinion Paragraph:** A five-page segment focusing on the structure and organization of opinion paragraphs and strategies for elaboration

Unit 12 Writing to Express an Opinion

Unit features include:

Published model "Why I Like to Take Pictures" by George Ancona

Student model Opinion essay by Asa Horvitz, working draft and final copy

Mode-specific characteristics What Makes a Great Opinion Essay?

Focus Skill lessons
Prewriting: Choosing Strong Reasons
Prewriting: Elaborating Your Reasons
Drafting: Writing with Voice
Drafting: Openings and Closings

Rubric Evaluating Your Opinion Essay

Revising Strategies
Elaborating: Word Choice (synonyms)
Elaborating: Details
Sentence Fluency (varying sentence length)

Assessment Links Writing Prompts, Test Practice

Special Focus on Expressing
Book Report A model and instructions for summarizing a book
Poem Published models and instructions for writing poetry

Communication Links
Listening/Speaking: Having a Panel Discussion
Guidelines and practice for having an organized group discussion
Viewing/Media: Finding Points of View in Visuals
Guidelines and practice for finding the messages in visual images

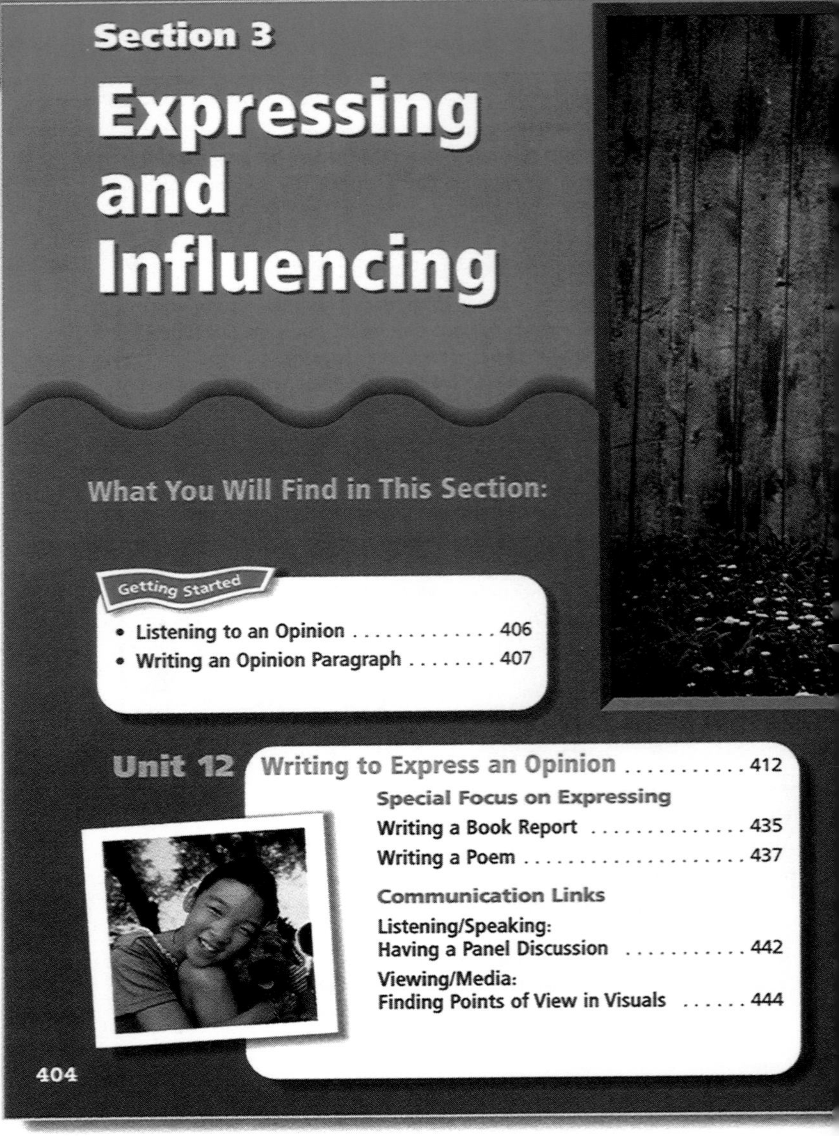
Section 3

Expressing and Influencing

What You Will Find in This Section:

Getting Started

404

Independent Writing

In addition to the focused writing tasks in this section, students can benefit by having time that is set aside each day or several times a week for them to write in their journals or work on other self-selected writing activities, such as letters, poems, stories, book reviews, movie reviews, news articles, records, problem solving, announcements, written requests, or messages. Emphasize the importance of thinking about purpose and audience (noting that sometimes the students may be their own audience) and choosing an appropriate writing format that suits both.

Supporting Sentences

Supporting sentences usually follow the opinion statement. They give reasons that answer the question *Why?* about the opinion. Details, such as facts and examples, explain the reasons. In the neighborhood paragraph on page 407, the supporting sentences explain why the writer thinks the neighborhood is great for kids.

Reason: lots of people my age
Detail: always have someone to play with

Read the paragraph below. Look for reasons and details that support the writer's opinion.

Our town has an excellent summer recreation program. First, it teaches kids new skills. It offers classes in arts and crafts, math puzzles, and golf. It also helps kids discover new interests. Every summer many children try hiking, bird watching, or drama for the first time. Most important, the program gives children a place to make new friends. Four hundred excited kids take part in the program every summer. This program helps make summer fun here!

Reasons: learn new skills, discover new interests, meet new people and make friends; details: classes in arts and crafts, math puzzles, and golf; hiking, bird watching, drama activities; four hundred kids every summer

Think and Discuss What reasons and details are in the paragraph above?

Ordering Reasons and Details The supporting sentences in an opinion paragraph are often arranged from most important to least important or from least important to most important. **Transitional words**, such as *first, also, another reason, the best, for example,* and *finally,* help the reader see the connections between reasons and details. Which reason is most important to the writer of the paragraph above? What transitional words can you find?

See page 18 for more transitional words.

more ▶

Supporting Sentences

Lesson Objectives

Students will:
- list reasons and details that support an opinion statement
- write supporting sentences, using an opinion statement and a picture
- use transitional words or phrases to link supporting sentences

Focus on Instruction

- Be sure students understand that in order for an opinion paragraph to be effective, it must have strong reasons that support the opinion statement. Explain that if the reasons are weak, the reader may say, "This person doesn't really care about the topic."
- Discuss with students how the details relate to the reasons in the neighborhood paragraph on page 407. Have students suggest reasons and details they would include if they were writing about their own neighborhood.

Think and Discuss

Discuss with students how each detail explains each reason.

Focus on Instruction

- Ask students to name the most important reason in the paragraph about the summer recreation program. (Children meet new people.) Ask what transitional words the writer used to give this message. *(Most important)*
- Students should find these transitional words and phrases in the paragraph: *First, also,* and *Most important.*

Meeting Individual Needs

● RETEACHING WORKBOOK, page 102

Supporting Sentences

An **opinion paragraph** tells what someone thinks or believes. It usually has a focus statement, which tells the writer's opinion. The **supporting sentences** give strong reasons to support this opinion. They also give details that help the reader understand the reasons. The concluding sentence finishes the paragraph.

In the opinion paragraph below, the focus statement and concluding sentence are underlined. Four of the other sentences give reasons and details that support the writer's opinion. Cross out the two sentences that do not keep to the main idea. Rewrite the corrected paragraph, adding one new sentence to support the opinion that a zoo is a great place to go for a field trip. Use the picture to help you.

When my class plans its field trips for fall and spring, visiting the zoo gets my vote every time. ~~The zoo is often very crowded.~~ Land and sea animals from all over the world live there. ~~Last week I saw a squirrel munching on an acorn in my back yard.~~ Signs posted near the exhibits give lots of information about the animals. We can learn about their natural habitats and the types of food they thrive on. Some zoos have nurseries to care for baby animals. The zoo is a great place to get close to animals and learn about them.

Answers will vary.

▲■ WORKBOOK PLUS, page 151

Supporting Sentences

An **opinion paragraph** tells what someone thinks or believes. It often has a focus statement, supporting sentences, and a concluding sentence. **Supporting sentences** give strong reasons for an opinion. They usually include facts and examples that make the reasons clear and convincing.

Complete the opinion paragraph about this picture. Write three supporting sentences that give reasons for the opinion presented in the focus statement below. Use details in the beach scene to elaborate each reason with facts and examples.

When you're ready for fun in the sun, a beach is the place to be!

Answers will vary.

A beach is definitely the best place to spend a warm summer afternoon.

Supporting Sentences *continued*

Try It Out

- Have students first list reasons with supporting details that tell *why* about the opinion statement. Then have them write their supporting sentences.
- Sample answer: Summer is the best season of all for many reasons. First, there is no school, which means there is no homework. Second, summer brings warm weather and people can go outside without bundling up. A third reason summer is the best season is that many families are able to go on vacations without worrying about students missing school.

The Closing Sentence

Lesson Objective

Students will:

- write a closing sentence for a paragraph

Focus on Instruction

- Have students reread the closing sentence in the paragraph about the neighborhood on page 407 to see how it repeats the opinion statement in an interesting way.
- Present these alternative closing sentences for the same paragraph. Ask students which one sums up the writer's reasons and which one makes a final comment.

  I'm so lucky to live in my neighborhood. (final comment)

  Kids my age, the park, and our neighbors all make it a super place to live! (sums up reasons)
- Have students identify other types of closing sentences in the sample paragraphs.

Try It Out

If any students need extra support, read the opinion statement and the supporting sentences with them. Have them identify the opinion and the reasons. Review what a closing sentence might do. (sum up reasons, repeat the opinion statement another way, make a final comment) Have volunteers suggest ways to conclude the paragraph, and help them write closing sentences using these ideas.

Try It Out Look at the picture of the summer outdoor scene. On your own or with a partner, use the opinion statement and the picture to write at least three sentences that support the opinion. Include reasons and details such as facts and examples. Link at least two of your sentences with a transitional word or phrase. Answers will vary.

Opinion statement: Summer is the best season of all.

GRAMMAR TIP *Watch out for run-on sentences!*

The Closing Sentence

The **closing sentence** finishes the opinion paragraph. It can repeat the writer's opinion in an interesting way or make a final comment. In the summer-program paragraph on page 409, the closing sentence makes a final comment.

Try It Out The paragraph below is missing its closing sentence. On your own or with a partner, write two different closing sentences for it.

> I'm lucky because I know how to read. Reading helps me many times each day. Because I can read, I know whether a store is open or closed or whether to wait or walk at a crosswalk. Reading also helps me find out how to build and fix things. For example, reading the directions helped me build a birdhouse last summer. Best of all, reading introduces me to new people and carries me to faraway lands. I have met Abraham Lincoln and traveled to Antarctica through books. ___*Closing sentence*___.
> Sample answer: My life would be harder and less interesting if I didn't know how to read.

Write Your Own Opinion Paragraph

Now it's your turn to write a paragraph. What do you have an opinion about? It might be something that is happening at school. It might be something you like or do not like. Write reasons for your opinion. Include details, such as facts and examples, to support your reasons. Share your opinion and reasons with a partner. Then go ahead and write!

Checklist for My Paragraph

✓ I wrote an **opinion statement** that introduces the topic and main idea.
✓ My **supporting sentences** give reasons for my opinion and details that elaborate the reasons.
✓ I wrote a **closing sentence** that restates the main idea or makes a final comment.

Looking Ahead

Now that you know how to write an opinion paragraph, writing a longer composition will be a snap! The diagram below shows how the parts of an opinion paragraph do the same jobs as the parts of an opinion essay.

Opinion Paragraph

- introduces the topic and the main idea—the writer's opinion
- give reasons for the opinion
- give details to support the reasons
- finishes the paragraph or the essay

Opinion Essay

Help with Writing

HELP WITH CHOOSING A TOPIC

Share these ideas.

- Students can write about something everyone should learn to do.
- They can write about a place they think the class should visit.
- They can tell about a game they like or don't like.
- They can give their opinion about a favorite song or type of music.
- They can write about a book they read recently.

HELP WITH PLANNING

Have students make a planning chart with these entries to help them organize their ideas. Review their charts before they write.

Topic	Main Idea
Opinion Statement	
Details	
Closing Sentence	

Write Your Own Opinion Paragraph

Lesson Objective

Students will:

- write an opinion paragraph

Focus on Instruction

- Remind students that the first step in writing a paragraph is to choose a topic. If students have difficulty choosing a topic, suggest ideas from the Help box on this page or brainstorm other ideas with students. List the ideas on the board or an overhead transparency.
- Build on students' oral language skills by having them tell their opinion to a partner before they write it down. Encourage partners to give feedback about what information they feel is relevant and interesting. It is important to get students in the habit of sharing their ideas orally before putting them down on paper.
- **Connecting to the Criteria** Review with students the Checklist for My Paragraph.
- Have volunteers read their paragraph aloud to the class.

If students are keeping portfolios, they could include this paragraph as an example of a short writing assignment. The paragraph can be used later as a basis for comparison with longer opinion pieces. If you want to send the paragraphs home as well, you can make copies for the portfolios.

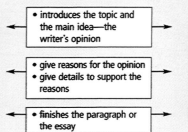

SCHOOL-HOME CONNECTION Encourage students to share their paragraph with family members. Have students discuss with family members whether they agree with the student's opinion.

Looking Ahead Explain to students that in this Expressing and Influencing section of the book they will learn how to write an opinion essay and a persuasive essay, using what they have learned about writing paragraphs.

Unit 12 Planning Guide

Writing to Express an Opinion

Writing to Express an Opinion: *2 weeks*
Special Focus and Communication Links: *1 week (optional)*

	Blackline Masters (TE)	Workbook Plus	Reteaching Workbook
PUBLISHED MODEL "Why I Like to Take Pictures," by George Ancona *(413–416)*			
What Makes a Great Opinion Essay? *(417)*			
STUDENT MODEL Working Draft *(418–419)* Final Copy *(420–421)*	12-1A, 12-1B		
The Writing Process Write an Opinion Essay			
Prewriting Focus Skill: Choosing Strong Reasons *(423)* Focus Skill: Elaborating Your Reasons *(424)*	12–2 12–3	152 153	103 104
Drafting Focus Skill: Writing with Voice *(425)* Openings and Closings *(427)*		154 155	105 106
Revising Evaluating Your Opinion Essay [rubric] *(428)* Writing Conference *(429)* **Revising Strategies** *(430)*	12–4 12–5 	156 157	107 108
Proofreading *(431)*			
Publishing and Reflecting *(432)*			
Writing Prompts and Test Practice *(433–434)*			
SPECIAL FOCUS ON EXPRESSING **Writing a Book Report** *(435–436)* **Writing a Poem** *(437–441)*			
COMMUNICATION LINKS **Listening/Speaking: Having a Panel Discussion** *(442–443)* **Viewing/Media: Finding Points of View in Visuals** *(444–445)*			

Tools and Tips

- **Listening and Speaking Strategies,** *pp. H4–H10*
- **Building Vocabulary,** *pp. H11–H17*
- **Research and Study Strategies,** *pp. H18–H30*
- **Using Technology,** *pp. H35–H47*
- **Writer's Tools,** *pp. H48–H54*
- **Spelling Guide,** *pp. H65–H69*
- **Guide to Capitalization, Punctuation, and Usage,** *pp. H55–H64*
- **Thesaurus Plus,** *pp. H79–H100*

School-Home Connection

Suggestions for informing or involving family members in classroom activities and learning related to this unit are included in the Teacher's Edition throughout the unit.

Meeting Individual Needs

- **FOR SPECIAL NEEDS/INCLUSION:** *Houghton Mifflin English* Audiotape
- **FOR STUDENTS ACQUIRING ENGLISH:**
  - Notes and activities are included in this Teacher's Edition throughout the unit to help you adapt or use pupil book activities with students acquiring English.
  - Students acquiring English can listen to the published and student models on audiotape.
  - MediaWeaver™, Sunburst/Humanities software, offers bilingual features, including Spanish menus, a Spanish spelling tool, and a Spanish thesaurus.
- **ENRICHMENT:** See *Teacher's Resource Book.*

All audiotape recordings are also available on CD.

Daily Language Practice

Each sentence includes two capitalization, punctuation, usage, or spelling errors based on skills presented in the Grammar and Spelling Connections in this unit or from Grammar Units 1–5. Each day write one sentence on the chalkboard. Have students find the errors and write the sentence correctly on a sheet of paper. To make the activity easier, identify the kinds of errors.

1. The children race down the beach the children love to play by the water's edge. Sample: The children race down the beach. They love to play by the water's edge. (run-on sentences; pronouns)
2. Mike's mother am a pilot. Mike's mother flies planes for an airline. Mike's mother is a pilot. She flies planes for an airline. (verb *be*; pronouns)
3. The libraries in our city are'nt open on holidaies. The libraries in our city aren't open on holidays. (contractions; plural nouns)
4. Didnt you read the book An Island Adventure once before? Didn't you read the book An Island Adventure once before? (contractions; book titles)
5. "Handle the dishes carefuly", Mother warned us. "Handle the dishes carefully," Mother warned us. (spelling suffixes; quotations)
6. Grace grabed a handfull of nuts from the bowl. Grace grabbed a handful of nuts from the bowl. (past tense; spelling suffixes)
7. Janeen were speechles at her surprise party. Janeen was speechless at her surprise party. (subject-verb agreement; spelling suffixes)
8. "Well what do we have here? Grandfather asked." "Well, what do we have here?" Grandfather asked. (commas; quotations)
9. The waiter brung us drinks, plates and pizza. The waiter brought us drinks, plates, and pizza . (past tense; commas)
10. Mrs Lee and her husband gave us a tour of the museum Mrs. Lee and her husband gave us a tour of the museum. (abbreviations; end punctuation)

Additional Resources

Workbook Plus, Unit 12
Reteaching Workbook, Unit 12
Teacher's Resource Book
Transparencies
Posters, Unit 12
Audiotapes

Technology Tools

CD-ROM: *EasyBook Deluxe
MediaWeaver™, Sunburst/Humanities software
*Type to Learn™

*©Sunburst Technology Corporation, a Houghton Mifflin Company. All rights reserved.

INTERNET: http://www.eduplace.com/kids/hme/ *or* http://www.eduplace.com/rdg/hme/

Visit Education Place for these additional support materials and activities:

- author biographies
- student writing models
- graphic organizers
- an interactive rubric
- proofreading practice
- writing prompts
- benchmark papers

Assessment

Test Booklet, Unit 12

Keeping a Journal

Discuss with students the value of keeping a journal as a way of promoting self-expression and fluency. Encourage students to record their thoughts and ideas in a notebook. Inform students whether the journal will be private or will be reviewed periodically as a way of assessing growth. The following prompts may be useful for generating writing ideas.

Journal Prompts

- What movie have you seen recently? Would you recommend it or not? Why?
- What is your favorite sports team? Tell how you think it will do this year and why.
- Think of a popular fad in your school. Would you recommend it to someone in another school? Why or why not?

Introducing the Unit

Using the Photograph

- Have students look at the photograph. Ask students what feeling, or emotion, it expresses and how they can tell. (Sample response: love, because the girl is smiling and hugging the dog, and the dog is willingly cuddling up to the girl)
- Then have a volunteer read the caption aloud. Point out that the caption expresses an opinion because it expresses what the girl believes is true. Ask what the girl's opinion is. (Everyone needs someone or something special to love.) Ask whether students agree or disagree. (Most will undoubtedly agree.)
- Explain that in an **opinion essay**, the writer expresses an opinion and then supports his or her opinion with strong reasons and lots of good details. Tell students that they will learn to write an opinion essay in this unit.

Unit 12

Writing to Express an Opinion

Everyone needs someone or something special to love. For me it's Jamie, my pet dog.

412

Shared Writing Activity

Work with students to write a short paragraph about an opinion they share, such as *Pets make good friends* or *Our school is a great place to learn.*

1. Write the students' shared opinion on the board or on an overhead transparency. Have students suggest reasons why they think or feel as they do. List each reason under the opinion statement.
2. Ask students to review the reasons and choose the three they think are most important. Then have students decide the reasons' order of importance, and have a volunteer number them *1, 2, 3.*
   - Reinforce the importance of choosing reasons that are exact and that directly relate to the topic in the opinion statement.
3. Write the opinion statement as the first sentence in the paragraph. Then help students use their numbered reasons to generate sentences that support their opinion. Encourage students to add details and examples that help elaborate, or explain, their reasons.
4. If students suggest a series of short, choppy sentences, suggest that they combine two or more of them to make a compound sentence. Reinforce the correct use of singular and plural pronouns to replace nouns (or other skills students need to work on) as they suggest sentences.
5. Have students copy their opinion paragraph to share with family members.

A Published Model

George Ancona is a freelance photographer, and he wrote this essay to explain why he enjoys taking pictures. What reasons does he give to support his opinion?

Why I Like to Take Pictures

by George Ancona

A long time ago, I began to take pictures with my father's camera. We lived on Coney Island, and I would wander the empty streets in winter taking pictures of the snow-covered clowns. I found that I really enjoyed taking pictures. opening

What I liked most was to take pictures of my family. After high school I went to Mexico to meet my grandparents, aunts, uncles, and cousins. I took pictures of them, and with these pictures I began my family album.

more ▶

See www.eduplace.com/kids/ for information about George Ancona. A Published Model 413

About the Author

INTERNET CONNECTION Send your students to www.eduplace.com/kids/ for information about George Ancona.

Resources

Encourage students to look for opinions as they read nonfiction and fiction books, such as an author's expression of opinion about the subject of his or her book. Provide opportunities to share some of their finds with the class.

"Why I Like to Take Pictures"

Lesson Objectives

Students will:

- read a published model of an opinion essay
- identify characteristics of an opinion essay
- note how the author elaborated on reasons
- evaluate the relationship between visuals and text
- write personal and critical responses

Focus on the Model

Building Background

Ask students if they like taking pictures. Then ask students to explain why or why not. Tell students they will read an opinion essay by a professional photographer that explains why he enjoys taking pictures.

Introducing Vocabulary

Introduce the key vocabulary word by writing this sentence on the board.

> Because my mother is a **freelance** writer, she works for different companies instead of just one.

Ask a volunteer to read the sentence aloud. Ask students to explain the meaning of the boldfaced word.

Reading the Selection

- Have students read the introduction to "Why I Like to Take Pictures." The purpose-setting question focuses on a characteristic of an opinion essay, reasons that support the opinion.

Have students read the selection as a class, independently, or with partners, or they can listen to the selection on audiotape.

- The call outs highlight key characteristics of an opinion essay that are addressed in the Think About the Opinion Essay questions at the end of this selection.

FOR STUDENTS ACQUIRING ENGLISH

Students' previous schooling may not have taught them to value or practice giving their own opinion. Emphasize that this is important in schools in the United States. Discuss why. (Build background around the terms *democracy, voting, rights,* and so on.)

A Published Model

reason

I also like to take pictures because it gives me a chance to travel. When I returned from Mexico, I became a freelance professional photographer. This has allowed me to go to many wonderful places around the world, including Iceland, Tunisia, France, Brazil, Japan, Cuba, and many other countries.

details

One of my favorite reasons for taking pictures is to meet people. In countries where I do not speak the language, I will meet a person who sees me as a stranger. I look him or her in the eyes and smile. Usually the response is a twinkle in the eyes, and then I take a picture. If it's a frown, I move on.

Once, in a small village in Mexico, I saw a man loading his ox cart with corn stalks. I asked if I could take a picture of his ox. He said no. As I moved on down the street I wondered why, so I turned

414 **Unit 12:** Opinion

back and asked him. He had no answer, but he said I could take the picture. Then I asked him to stand next to the ox, and he did. Soon his whole family came to have their picture taken.

Once I took my granddaughter with me, and she would complain, "Poppi, you are always talking to people. You don't even know that man." "Yes, Sweetie," was my answer, "but now I do!"

Today, when I look through my photographs, my thoughts go beyond them to the fond memories of the people I have met, of meals shared with strangers that became friends, of long walks and long talks, of music and dances and festivals, and of how alike we all are—the peoples of the world. closing

Answers to Reading As a Writer

Think About the Opinion Essay

- He enjoys taking pictures because it gives him a chance to travel and to meet people.
- The author states his opinion in the final paragraph of the essay.
- He includes the details *many wonderful places around the world, including Iceland, Tunisia, France, Brazil, Japan,* and *Cuba.*
- The important points are summed up in the last paragraph so that the reader will remember them.

Think About Writer's Craft

- The writer includes a personal experience about a time he wanted to take a picture of a man and his ox. This story helps explain the writer's pleasure in meeting people as a reason for taking pictures.

Think About the Pictures

- The photos show some of the different places the author has visited and some of the people he has met. After students complete the questions, work with them to generate criteria for an opinion essay, using the published model as a reference.

More About Writer's Craft

Call students' attention to the exclamation point in the sixth paragraph. Point out that the writer uses this type of punctuation to show that the speaker is excited. Encourage students to occasionally use exclamation points to show emphasis or to enhance meaning in their own writing.

Notes on Responding

Personal Response

Encourage students to share their opinions. Emphasize that an opinion is the way a person feels about something and is very personal, and explain that opinions are not right or wrong.

Critical Thinking

Discuss what the author has done, where he has been, and how he relates to people. Then help students conclude that the author is outgoing, adventurous, and fun loving.

A Published Model

Reading As a Writer See TE margin for answers.

Think About the Opinion Essay

- What reasons does the author give to support his opinion?
- In which paragraph does the author state his opinion?
- In the first paragraph on page 414, what details does the author give to support his reason?
- In which paragraph does the author sum up why he likes photography?

Think About Writer's Craft

- Reread the third paragraph on page 414. What story does the author tell? Which reason does this story help explain?

Think About the Pictures

- What do the photos show that helps you understand why the author enjoys taking pictures?

Responding Answers will vary.

Write responses to these questions.

- **Personal Response** Think of something you like to do. Are your reasons for liking it similar to the author's reasons for liking photography? In what ways are they different?
- **Critical Thinking** After reading this essay, how would you describe the kind of person George Ancona is?

416 **Unit 12:** Opinion

Mapping the Selection

Mapping can help students review what they have learned in an essay and help them understand how the information is organized. After students have read the essay about why the author likes to take pictures, draw the following cluster on the board. Have students fill in the cluster with reasons and details.

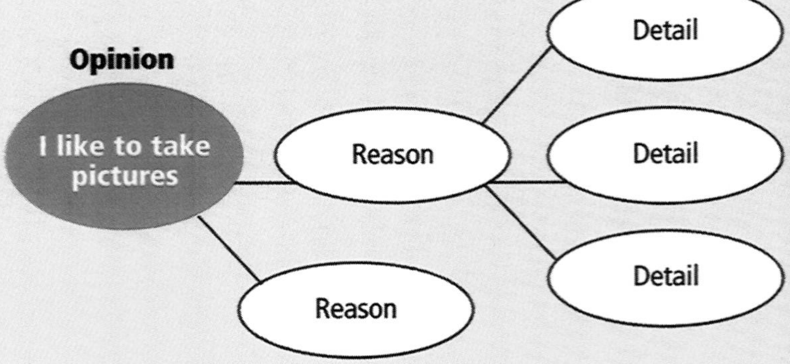

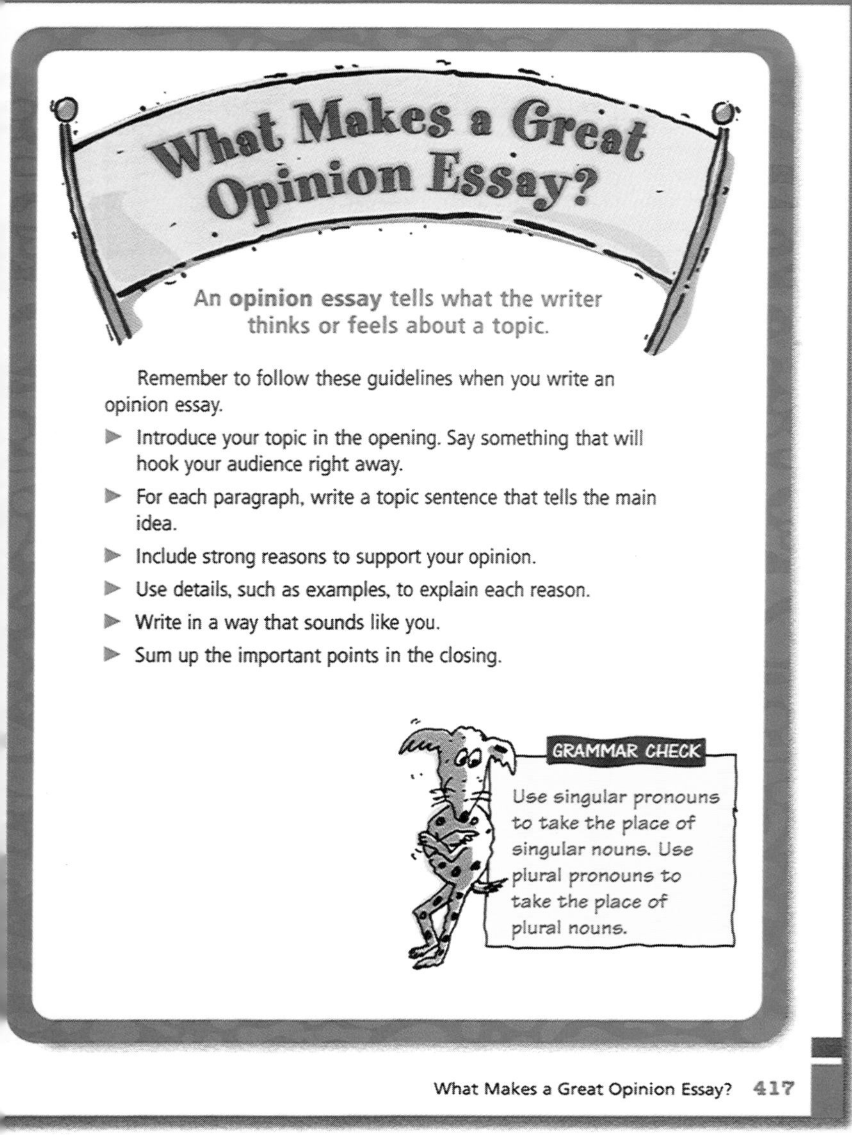

What Makes a Great Opinion Essay?

An **opinion essay** tells what the writer thinks or feels about a topic.

Remember to follow these guidelines when you write an opinion essay.

- Introduce your topic in the opening. Say something that will hook your audience right away.
- For each paragraph, write a topic sentence that tells the main idea.
- Include strong reasons to support your opinion.
- Use details, such as examples, to explain each reason.
- Write in a way that sounds like you.
- Sum up the important points in the closing.

GRAMMAR CHECK

Use singular pronouns to take the place of singular nouns. Use plural pronouns to take the place of plural nouns.

What Makes a Great Opinion Essay? 417

What Makes a Great Opinion Essay?

Lesson Objective

Students will:
- discuss the characteristics of a well-written opinion essay

Focus on Instruction

- Explain to students that "Why I Like to Take Pictures" is an example of a well-written opinion essay. Ask volunteers to read aloud the definition and characteristics of an opinion essay. Review the ones that were represented in the published model, "Why I Like to Take Pictures." (an opening that introduced the topic, strong reasons and details, an ending that summed up the important points)
- Have students read the Grammar Check. Tell students to keep the tip in mind as they write their papers. Remind students that they will check their papers for correct correct use of singular and plural pronouns.

If this is students' first encounter with the cartoon dog, explain that this is Sal, the writer's pal, and that Sal will help them learn to write a great opinion essay.

Connecting to the Rubric

- These criteria are tied to the rubric on page 428.
- Explain to students that they will be writing their own opinion essay and that they will learn how to include these characteristics. Students will use these criteria to help them evaluate their papers.

This page is available as a poster.

Looking Ahead Tell students that they will next see how the characteristics listed on this page are applied in one student's working draft and final copy of an opinion essay.

FOR STUDENTS ACQUIRING ENGLISH

To illustrate the use of *I, me, to, with, for,* and *at,* turn back to the published model and highlight each use of these words. Once you have done a few examples, encourage students to make a game of finding the words in the essay. Next, compare the other aspects of the rubric to the model. Ask students to give opinions on how the writer did.

Student Model: Working Draft

Lesson Objectives

Students will:

- read a working draft of a student-written opinion essay
- discuss the ways the model meets the criteria for a well-written opinion essay and ways that it could be improved

Focus on the Model

- Tell students that they will read a working draft of an opinion essay written by a real student, Asa Horvitz. Remind students that the purpose of the working draft is to get ideas on paper. The writer can make corrections and revisions later.
- Have volunteers read the model aloud.

Alternatively, students can listen to it read by a student (although not the student writer) on audiotape.

> - Reading the draft aloud gives students practice in listening and responding to a writer's work in progress and provides practice for peer conferences.
> - This working draft does not include any usage, capitalization, or punctuation mistakes so that students can focus on the content of the piece.

- Tell students to think about whether Asa included the important characteristics of an opinion essay. Remind students that the thought balloons show Sal's thoughts about the essay and that they will discuss his ideas after they read the model.

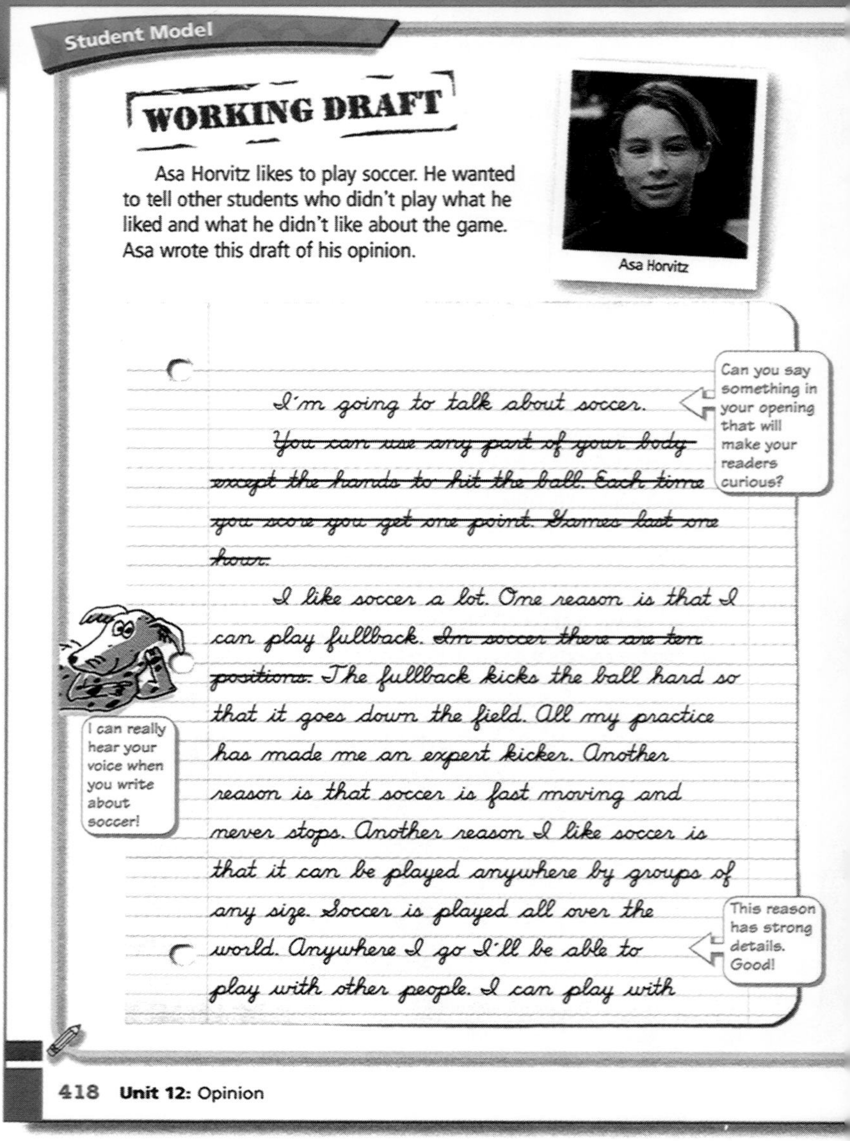
Student Model

WORKING DRAFT

Asa Horvitz likes to play soccer. He wanted to tell other students who didn't play what he liked and what he didn't like about the game. Asa wrote this draft of his opinion.

Asa Horvitz

I'm going to talk about soccer. ~~You can use any part of your body except the hands to hit the ball. Each time you score you get one point. Games last one hour.~~

I like soccer a lot. One reason is that I can play fullback. ~~In soccer there are ten positions.~~ The fullback kicks the ball hard so that it goes down the field. All my practice has made me an expert kicker. Another reason is that soccer is fast moving and never stops. Another reason I like soccer is that it can be played anywhere by groups of any size. Soccer is played all over the world. Anywhere I go I'll be able to play with other people. I can play with

Can you say something in your opening that will make your readers curious?
I can really hear your voice when you write about soccer!
This reason has strong details. Good!

418 Unit 12: Opinion

two people or as many as twenty. Sometimes I just kick the ball around the yard with my family or with my friends at the park. Another reason is that the coach gives me a ride to all of the games.

Is this reason really important?

There are some things I don't like. I don't like soccer because goalie is a dumb position. When I play goalie, I don't ~~play much~~ see much action. I usually just stand around and watch the other players having fun. Another reason I don't always like soccer is that you have to work with the team, and sometimes that can be hard. I might have to sit out for a long time. This can happen if there are twelve people on a team because only eleven play at a time.

This isn't a good reason. Can you be more exact?

Reading As a Writer

See TE margin for answers.

- What did Sal like about Asa's essay? What were Sal's questions? What revisions could Asa make to answer them?
- Why did Asa cross out the second paragraph?
- Look at the paragraph that tells why Asa likes soccer. Which reason needs details?
- What questions would you like to ask Asa about his opinion?

Answers to Reading As a Writer

- Sal liked Asa's clear voice and the strong details that supported the second reason. Sal asked Asa to use an opening that makes the reader curious, he asked if getting a ride to the game was important, and he asked Asa to give a more exact reason. Asa could change his opening to make it grab the reader's attention; he could give a more important reason than getting a ride from the coach; and he could give a more exact reason than goalie being a dumb position.
- He crossed out the sentence because it is not related to his opinion.
- *It is fast moving and never stops* is the reason that needs details.
- Answers will vary.

Student Model: Final Copy

Lesson Objectives

Students will:

- read a well-written final copy of a student's opinion essay
- note and compare the revisions that improved the first draft

Focus on the Model

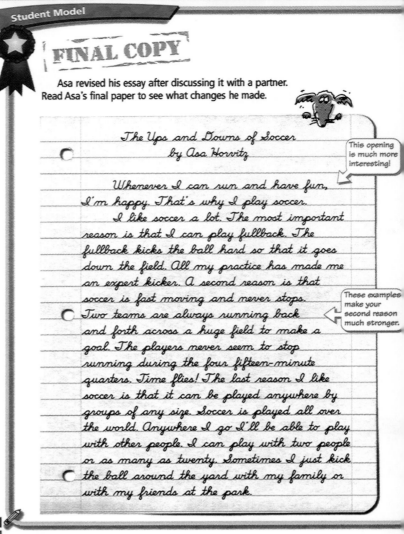

SUMMARY OF REVISIONS In his final copy, Asa added a catchy title, made the opening more interesting, took out an unimportant reason, clarified reasons with details, and summed up his ideas in the closing.

- Blackline Master 12–1 provides a copy of the student's working draft, showing the revisions that were made.
- Point out that Asa has three reasons for liking soccer and three reasons for disliking it. All reasons are supported by at least two details. Asa uses transitional words to connect reasons and details.

Have volunteers read the model aloud. Alternatively, students can listen to it read by a student (although not the student writer) on audiotape.

Student Model

FINAL COPY

Asa revised his essay after discussing it with a partner. Read Asa's final paper to see what changes he made.

The Ups and Downs of Soccer
by Asa Horwitz

Whenever I can run and have fun, I'm happy. That's why I play soccer.

I like soccer a lot. The most important reason is that I can play fullback. The fullback kicks the ball hard so that it goes down the field. All my practice has made me an expert kicker. A second reason is that soccer is fast moving and never stops. Two teams are always running back and forth across a huge field to make a goal. The players never seem to stop running during the four fifteen-minute quarters. Time flies! The last reason I like soccer is that it can be played anywhere by groups of any size. Soccer is played all over the world. Anywhere I go I'll be able to play with other people. I can play with two people or as many as twenty. Sometimes I just kick the ball around the yard with my family or with my friends at the park.

This opening is much more interesting!

These examples make your second reason much stronger.

Soccer isn't always a dream sport, and there are some things I don't like. The worst part about soccer is that the goalie position can be lonely. When I play goalie, I don't see much action. I usually just stand around and watch the other players having fun. Another reason I don't always like soccer is that you have to work with the team, and sometimes that can be hard. I might have to sit out for a long time. This can happen if there are twelve people on a team because only eleven play at a time. Then there is the weather. We play under the hottest sun, the wettest rain, and the coldest snow. The cold weather is the hardest to play in because the ball hurts if it hits me.

The cheers from the crowd make me feel good. I forget about being cold or sitting out. I know I'll get to run and play fullback again in the next game.

This reason is more exact now. Good!

These details help me understand how you feel about the weather. I feel the same way!

Reading As a Writer

See TE margin for answers.

- How did Asa respond to Sal's questions?
- Asa added a closing to his final copy. Why does this make his essay better?
- What words did Asa add to the beginning of each reason? Why does adding these words make his paper easier to read?

See www.eduplace.com/kids/hme/ for more examples of student writing.

Answers to Reading As a Writer

- He responded by making the opening more interesting, by taking out an unimportant reason, and by making one reason more exact.
- He added information to sum up main points. His essay now has more detail, and Asa's voice is very clear.
- Asa added the transitional phrases *most important, second reason, last reason, worst part, another reason,* and *then.* Transitional words help the reader move smoothly from one idea to the next.

More About Writer's Craft

- Call students' attention to details that were added that contain prepositional phrases, such as *Two teams are always running back and forth across a huge field to make a goal.* Explain that the phrase *across a huge field* elaborates on where the teams are running. Encourage students to use this technique in their own writing.
- Point out how the writer uses the superlative adjectives *hottest, wettest, coldest,* and *hardest* to make his writing more precise. Encourage students to use comparatives and superlatives in their writing.
- Draw students' attention to the structure of the paragraphs in the student model. Point out that each paragraph includes a topic sentence and details that support it.

Connecting to the Rubric

- Have students look again at the list of characteristics on page 417 and review with them how Asa's final copy addressed each one.
- Reinforce the Grammar Check by having students check that Asa used *I, me,* and *it* correctly.

INTERNET CONNECTION Send your students to www.eduplace.com/kids/hme/ to see more models of student writing. You can also find and print these models at www.eduplace.com/rdg/hme/.

Looking Ahead Tell students that next they will write their own opinion essay, using the writing process. As they go along, they will learn how to choose strong reasons, elaborate their reasons with details, express their voice clearly, and write a good opening and closing.

MEETING INDIVIDUAL NEEDS

FOR STUDENTS ACQUIRING ENGLISH

Most students will be familiar with soccer and may be fans of it. Encourage them to state their opinions about how Asa has presented soccer. If they disagree, ask them to provide details supporting their opinion. After reading Asa's final copy, have students list his changes. Then ask students if Asa made the right changes and why.

Write an Opinion Essay

Lesson Objectives

Students will:

- list their ideas for audience, purpose, and publishing/sharing formats
- list ideas for an opinion essay
- discuss their ideas with a partner
- choose an appropriate topic to write about

Start Thinking

Focus on Instruction

- Ask how an essay written for a classmate might differ from one written for the school principal. (An essay for the principal might use more formal language.)
- Discuss with students how the purpose for writing can affect the essay. Explain that writing to express an opinion often includes expressions of strong feelings supported by strong reasons.
- Ask how writing the essay for the school newspaper might differ from making it into a poster. (A poster might rely more on visuals to support the goal.)
- Discuss with students how they might adapt the language of their paper to their chosen audience, purpose, and the occasion. Ask students to think of occasions and audiences that might call for formal language.

Choose Your Topic

Focus on Instruction

- The writing prompts on page 433 might suggest ideas.
- Have students support one viewpoint or two, depending on your school district or state requirements.

Have students start a writing folder titled *My Opinion Essay.* Explain that they will keep all notes, graphic organizers, and drafts for their essays in this folder. Have students include their paper with their thoughts about their audience, purpose, and publishing format.

FOR STUDENTS ACQUIRING ENGLISH

Some students may feel uncomfortable writing their opinions about the United States. To help them structure their answers, ask: "What do you like best/least about the United States and why? What do/don't you miss from your native country and why? If you could change one thing about the U.S., what would it be?"

The Writing Process: PREWRITING · DRAFTING · REVISING · PROOFREADING · PUBLISHING

Write an Opinion Essay

Start Thinking

Make a writing folder for your opinion essay. Copy the questions in bold print, and put your paper in your folder. Write your answers as you think about and choose your topic.

- **Who will be my audience?** Will it be my classmates? a family member? the school principal?
- **What will be my purpose?** Do I want to tell my audience about a place I like to visit? Do I want to help myself make a decision?
- **How will I publish or share my opinion essay?** Will I send it as a letter to a newspaper? make a tape recording? make a collage?

Choose Your Topic

1. **List** five topics that you have a strong opinion about. There should be things you like and dislike about each one. (Don't list people.) Look at part of Asa's list.

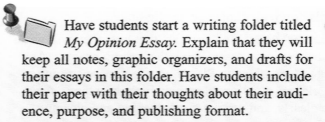

   chores–earn money, but less time for fun
   soccer–can play fullback, but goalie position dumb
   television–can learn a lot, but watch too much

2. **Discuss** your topics with a partner. What are your reasons for liking and not liking each one?
3. **Ask** yourself these questions about each topic. Circle the topic you will write about.
   - Do I feel strongly about this topic?
   - Do I have several good reasons for why I like it? why I dislike it?

Stuck for a Topic?

Here are some ideas.
I like/I don't like . . .

- playing computer games
- studying math
- owning a pet
- playing an instrument

See page 433 for more ideas.

An opinion essay can also be about what you like about a topic *or* about what you dislike.

Help with Choosing a Topic

TECH TIPS

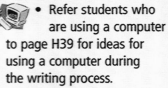

- Refer students who are using a computer to page H39 for ideas for using a computer during the writing process.
- Students may also create a two-column table on the computer in which they can list their likes and dislikes.

SCHOOL-HOME CONNECTION

Have students share their topic and reasons with their family and ask family members to help think of more reasons.

SOURCES OF TOPIC IDEAS

Suggest these activities to prompt topic ideas.

- Students can create a personal inventory chart about what they like and don't like about topics such as a specific season or sport.
- They can look in magazines for words or pictures to spark ideas.
- They might list ways they have spent time during the past week. Have them think of what they liked and didn't like about each activity.

EVALUATION TIP

Review each student's final topic choice. Make sure he or she has enough strong reasons to support the topic.

PREWRITING | DRAFTING | REVISING | PROOFREADING | PUBLISHING

Focus Skill

Choosing Strong Reasons

Reasons tell why you feel or think a certain way. To help you think of reasons, ask *Why?* about your opinion. Compare the weak and strong reasons below.

I like ___ because ___
I don't like ___ because ___

Opinion: I like walking the dog.

Weak Reasons	Strong Reasons
general reason: have fun	**exact reason:** playing outside together
unimportant reason: get to wear new sneakers	**important reason:** make friends with other dog walkers

Think and Discuss Compare the examples above.

- Why is the exact reason better? Why is the important reason better?
  gives specific information; more meaningful to support opinion

Explore Your Reasons

Make a T-Chart. Write three or four reasons why you like the topic and three or four reasons why you don't like it. Cross out any reasons that are not important.

If you can't think of three strong reasons, try another topic.

I like soccer.	I don't like soccer.
fast-moving game	goalie a dumb position
play anywhere	~~early games on weekends~~
~~great snacks~~	work with the team
fullback position	

▲ Part of Asa's chart

See page 14 for other ideas for exploring your topic.

Go to www.eduplace.com/kids/hme/ for graphic organizers.

Choosing Strong Reasons

Lesson Objectives

Students will:
- write reasons why they like or don't like their topic
- eliminate unimportant reasons

Focus on Instruction

- Have students think of reasons why they like or don't like summer. List responses on the board. Then help students determine whether the reasons are weak or strong. Point out that strong reasons need to be exact and important enough to support the opinion.
- Read the following reasons aloud. Discuss with students whether each reason is weak or strong, and why.

  I don't like to swim because I always get water in my nose.

  I don't like to swim because my best friend says it's boring.

Think and Discuss

If students need extra support, have them turn back to Asa's working and final drafts. Help students find weak reasons in the working draft. (the coach gives me a ride; goalie is a dumb position) Discuss what Asa did in the final copy to make each reason stronger.

Explore Your Reasons

- See Blackline Master 12–2 for a graphic organizer students can use to explore their reasons. As an alternative, students could use a cluster graphic organizer on page H50.
- Tell students that Asa's chart has weak and strong reasons. Asa did not include *great snacks* and *early games on weekends* in his working draft.

INTERNET CONNECTION Send your students to www.eduplace.com/kids/hme/ for graphic organizers. You can also find and print these organizers at www.eduplace.com/rdg/hme/.

FOR STUDENTS ACQUIRING ENGLISH

Students will need help seeing the subtle difference between the weak and strong reasons. First, offer clearer examples: *I like bikes. They're cool.* versus *They're easy to ride, but challenging for tricks.* Explain that the weak reason does not tell enough, and that the strong one gives details and is specific.

Meeting Individual Needs

● RETEACHING WORKBOOK, page 103

Choosing Strong Reasons

- Strong reasons tell why you feel and think a certain way.
- To help you think of reasons, ask yourself *Why?*

Opinion: I like wearing a uniform to school.

Weak Reasons	Strong Reasons
general reason: look the same	**exact reason:** no competition about who has the best outfits
unimportant reason: can buy them at the mall	**important reason:** don't have to decide what to wear every day

The following ideas were listed when a group of fourth graders brainstormed reasons why they like and dislike summer.

summer—

hot weather	picnics
camping	family vacations
fun	boring hours
no school	nice days

List the reasons on the T-Chart below. Cross out reasons that seem unimportant or too general. Answers will vary.

I like summer.	I do not like summer.

▲■ WORKBOOK PLUS, page 152

Choosing Strong Reasons

Opinion: I don't like windy days.

Weak Reasons	Strong Reasons
general reason: feels cold	**exact reason:** icy chill makes me shiver
unimportant reason: makes flags flutter	**important reason:** makes it difficult to pedal my bike

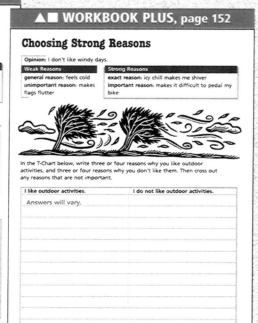

In the T-Chart below, write three or four reasons why you like outdoor activities, and three or four reasons why you don't like them. Then cross out any reasons that are not important.

I like outdoor activities.	I do not like outdoor activities.
Answers will vary.	

Elaborating Your Reasons

Lesson Objectives

Students will:
- organize their reasons in clusters
- put their reasons in order

Focus on Instruction

- Ask students why it is important to include details to support their reasons. (Details make the reasons stronger.)
- Ask students what they should do if they can't think of any details for a reason. (They should choose another reason.)

Think and Discuss

Work as a class or have students work in small groups to rewrite the weak details. (Sample answers: Change *do fun things* to *get to go to a movie*; change *have a good time* to *have a good time fishing in the pond.*)

Explore and Plan Your Essay

- Remind students that reasons support the opinion and that details elaborate on the reasons.
- The graphic organizer will help students determine if they have enough details to support their reasons. A copy of the organizer appears on Blackline Master 12–3.

INTERNET CONNECTION Send your students to www.eduplace.com/kids/hme/ for graphic organizers. You can also find and print these organizers at www.eduplace.com/rdg/hme/.

FOR STUDENTS ACQUIRING ENGLISH

Help students see that details answer the question "Why?" As a class, brainstorm details for a volunteer's reasons, modeling the cluster activity. If students have trouble thinking of details, encourage them to look at photos or draw pictures of their topic. Ask them to explain the images to a peer.

The Writing Process: PREWRITING | DRAFTING | REVISING | PROOFREADING | PUBLISHING

Focus Skill

Elaborating Your Reasons

Reasons are like the wheels on a bike. Wheels support a bike, and reasons support your opinion. Details are like the spokes that make the wheels strong.

Use details to elaborate, or explain, your reasons. Give examples. Include enough details to make your reasons exact and clear. Suppose your opinion is *I like Saturdays*. Compare the weak and strong details below.

Reason: I see my best friends.

Weak Details	Strong Details
do fun things	get to play outdoors
have a good time	have a good time riding our bikes down the dirt path

Think and Discuss Compare the examples above.
- Why are the strong details better? more exact; elaborate the reason
- Suggest other ways to make the weak details stronger. Answers will vary.

Explore and Plan Your Essay

1. **Make two clusters.** Label one main circle *I like* ______. Label the second main circle *I don't like* ______. Write your reasons from your T-Chart, circle them, and connect them to the main circles. Add details in circles for each reason. Here's an example from one of Asa's clusters.

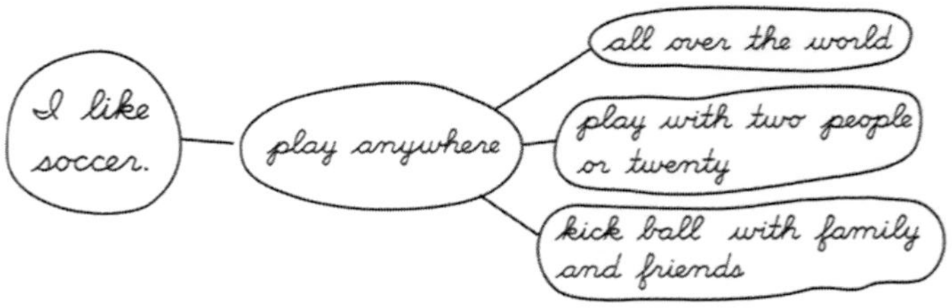

2. **Number** the reasons in the order you will write about them.

424 **Unit 12:** Opinion

Go to www.eduplace.com/kids/hme/ for graphic organizers.

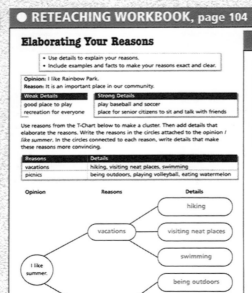

Meeting Individual Needs

● RETEACHING WORKBOOK, page 104

Elaborating Your Reasons

- Use details to explain your reasons.
- Include examples and facts to make your reasons exact and clear.

Opinion: I like Rainbow Park.
Reason: It is an important place in our community.

Weak Details	Strong Details
good place to play	play baseball and soccer
recreation for everyone	place for senior citizens to sit and talk with friends

Use reasons from the T-Chart below to make a cluster. Then add details that elaborate the reasons. Write the reasons in the circles attached to the opinion *I like summer*. In the circles connected to each reason, write details that make these reasons more convincing.

Reasons	Details
vacations	hiking, visiting neat places, swimming
picnics	being outdoors, playing volleyball, eating watermelon

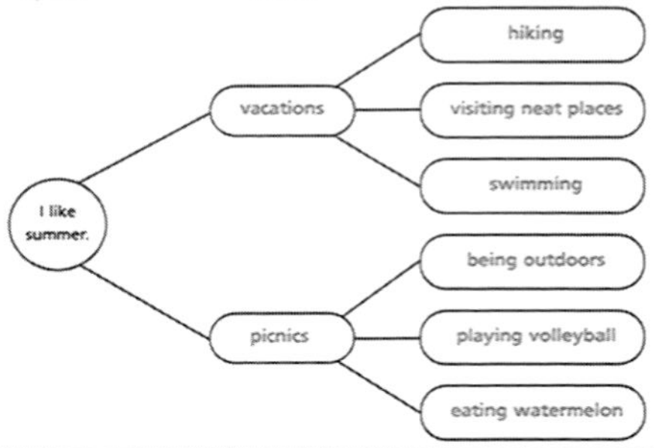

▲■ WORKBOOK PLUS, page 153

Elaborating Your Reasons

Opinion: I like mystery stories.
Reason: Mystery stories challenge readers to think.

Weak Details	Strong Details
good plot	complex plot with twists and turns
interesting story	clues that help solve the mystery

Choose two reasons from the T-Chart about outdoor activities on the previous page and write them in the cluster below *Reasons*. Under *Details*, write details that make each reason more convincing. Sample answers:

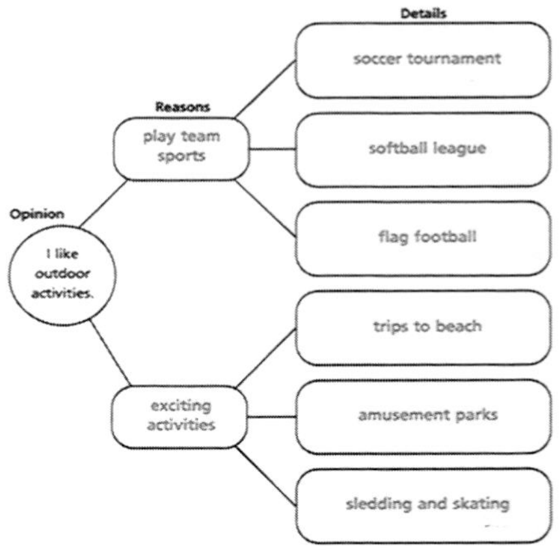

PREWRITING DRAFTING REVISING PROOFREADING PUBLISHING

Focus Skill

Writing with Voice

When you write something as personal as an opinion, you should tell your audience how you really feel. Let your audience hear your voice.

Look at one student's working draft and final copy.

Working Draft

Dogs can be annoying. They can wake you up. If you're not looking, they chew things. They bark at everything. Sometimes they bark really loudly for a long time.

Final Copy

Dogs don't always have the best habits. Before the sun is up, they dive into your bed. Oh, no! If you're not looking, they'll chew your shoes to a pulp. When the phone rings or someone comes over—yap, yap, yap—they bark forever.

Think and Discuss Compare the examples above.

- What is the weak example about? the strong example? Dogs can be pests.
- What words and details make the strong example better than the weak example? details such as *dive into your bed* or *chew your shoes*; words such as *pulp* or *yap, yap, yap*.

more ▶

Drafting 425

Writing With Voice

Lesson Objectives

Students will:

- compare weak and strong examples of writing with voice
- write two paragraphs about their topic for the body of their opinion essay

Focus on Instruction

Send two volunteers out of the classroom. Then have the class choose a topic, such as an object or an event, for the volunteers to describe. Have one volunteer return to the classroom and tell about the chosen topic. Repeat the procedure with the other volunteer and compare the descriptions. Point out that each volunteer used different words and ways of saying things. Tell students that when people speak and write they all have their own style, or voice. Remind students that they need to let their voice come through as they write their opinion essay.

Think and Discuss

Ask a volunteer to read both models aloud. Ask students to identify the words and phrases that make the strong model strong. *(dive in to your bed; chew your shoes to a pulp; yap, yap, yap)* Have students compare these words and phrases with the weaker words and phrases in the weak model. *(annoying; wake you up; chew things; bark really loudly)*

MEETING INDIVIDUAL NEEDS

FOR STUDENTS ACQUIRING ENGLISH

Ask a volunteer to read the definition of *voice* from the word log. Using the text example, show how voice is often conveyed through slang or exclamations. Encourage students to speak their ideas to a partner and then write them as if they were speaking. Some student voices will remain formal; this is normal for students acquiring English. In time, students will grow more comfortable with English, and their speech will reflect an informal voice.

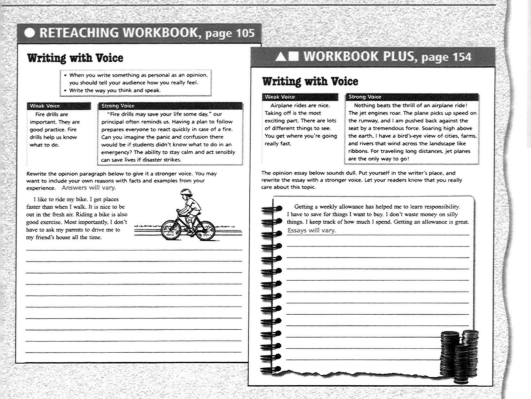

● **RETEACHING WORKBOOK, page 105**

Writing with Voice

- When you write something as personal as an opinion, you should tell your audience how you really feel.
- Write the way you think and speak.

Weak Voice

Fire drills are important. They are good practice. Fire drills help us know what to do.

Strong Voice

"Fire drills may save your life some day," our principal often reminds us. Having a plan to follow prepares everyone to react quickly in case of a fire. Can you imagine the panic and confusion there would be if students didn't know what to do in an emergency? The ability to stay calm and act sensibly can save lives if disaster strikes.

Rewrite the opinion paragraph below to give it a stronger voice. You may want to include your own reasons with facts and examples from your experience. Answers will vary.

I like to ride my bike. I get places faster than when I walk. It is nice to be out in the fresh air. Riding a bike is also good exercise. Most importantly, I don't have to ask my parents to drive me to my friend's house all the time.

▲■ **WORKBOOK PLUS, page 154**

Writing with Voice

Weak Voice

Airplane rides are nice. Taking off is the most exciting part. There are lots of different things to see. You get where you're going really fast.

Strong Voice

Nothing beats the thrill of an airplane ride! The jet engines roar. The plane picks up speed on the runway, and I am pushed back against the seat by a tremendous force. Soaring high above the earth, I have a bird's-eye view of cities, farms, and rivers that wind across the landscape like ribbons. For traveling long distances, jet planes are the only way to go!

The opinion essay below sounds dull. Put yourself in the writer's place, and rewrite the essay with a stronger voice. Let your readers know that you really care about this topic.

Getting a weekly allowance has helped me to learn responsibility. I have to save for things I want to buy. I don't waste money on silly things. I keep track of how much I spend. Getting an allowance is great.

Essays will vary.

Lesson Objectives

Students will:

- draft the body of their opinion essay
- use transitional words or phrases in their personal essay

Draft your Essay

Focus on Instruction

- Encourage students to refer to their cluster as they write their paragraphs.
- Have students underline the topic sentence in each paragraph. They can write a number above each detail that supports the reasons in the topic sentence. The numbers will help students check that they have adequately supported their reasons and that they have a balance of details for each reason in the opinion essay. Alternatively, students could write one paragraph for each reason.

Drafting Reminders

- Reinforce the idea that if students change their mind while writing, they should cross out the words or sentences they don't want rather than start over.
- Reassure students that they will have time to correct mistakes and check spelling later.

- Demonstrate how to use transitional words and phrases as a way to organize an opinion essay.

  The most important reason is . . .

  My second reason is . . .

  Students can circle the transitional words and phrases they use in their essays.
- Remind students that neatness does not count in a draft but that ideas do. Encourage students to cross out sentences that don't work, to replace examples, and to let their thoughts flow.

The Writing Process: PREWRITING | DRAFTING | REVISING | PROOFREADING | PUBLISHING

Draft Your Essay

1. **Write** your draft. Leave some space so that you can write an opening later. Make your writing sound like you.

   Skip every other line, and don't worry about mistakes. You can fix them later.

2. **Write** two paragraphs. In the first paragraph, tell what you like about your topic. In the second paragraph, tell what you don't like. Use the reasons and details from your clusters.
   - Write a topic sentence for each paragraph that states the main idea.
   - Write the reasons that tell more about the main idea.
   - Use the details to write supporting sentences for each reason.
3. **Use transitional words or phrases.** Help your reader move smoothly from reason to reason.

Transitional Words	Transitional Phrases
also	the first reason
then	the most important reason
next	
besides	for example
finally	worst of all
	another reason

Tech Tip You might want to use a computer to draft your essay.

Help with Drafting

MORE IDEAS FOR DRAFTING

Suggest these ideas to students as they draft their essay.

- Students can picture themselves talking to their audience as they write.
- Students can underline words or phrases to replace later and circle words that need a spell check.

MANAGEMENT TIP

Suggest that students keep a list of transitional words and phrases in their writing folder for future reference.

Focus Skill

Openings and Closings

Good Openings

A good opening gives a clue, or preview, of what the topic is about and hooks the reader right away. Avoid dull openings. Compare these examples.

Weak Opening	Strong Opening
Here are some reasons why I like Saturdays.	One day a week I hop out of bed as soon as my eyes pop open. It's Saturday!

Good Closings

A good closing sums up the important points. Don't just stop after your last reason. End in a way that your reader will remember.

Weak Closing	Strong Closing
So that's why I like Saturdays.	Saturdays just aren't long enough. My friends, family, sports, and games keep me extra busy. Next week I'm getting up even earlier and doing more!

Think and Discuss Compare the examples above.

- What makes the strong opening better than the weak one?
- What makes the strong closing better than the weak one?

Draft Your Opening and Closing

1. **Write** two openings and two closings for your opinion essay.
2. **Choose** the opening and the closing you like better.

Openings and Closings

Lesson Objectives

Students will:
- write two openings and two closings
- choose an opening and a closing for their essay

Focus on Instruction

- Read these openings aloud.

  Camping is fun for many reasons.

  There's never a dull moment when my family goes camping!

  Ask students which opening makes them want to read more and why. (The second reason makes the reader curious about why camping is so exciting.)

- Write these closings on the board. Call on volunteers to make each closing stronger.

  That's why I don't like winter.

  These are reasons I think amusement parks are fun.

  Discuss volunteers' suggestions. Make sure that students understand that they should sum up their ideas in their closing.

Think and Discuss

Have students work in pairs to write a strong opening or closing about a different day of the week.

Draft Your Opening and Closing

Remind students to use the guidelines for strong openings and closings as they write these sections.

MEETING INDIVIDUAL NEEDS — FOR STUDENTS ACQUIRING ENGLISH

Before looking at the text, ask students to give you a weak and a strong opening or closing. Then, as a class, rewrite these sections. Remind students to use dialogue, actions, or thoughts to hook a reader in the beginning and to summarize by giving opinions at the end. Then rewrite the text's examples.

Meeting Individual Needs

● RETEACHING WORKBOOK, page 106

Openings and Closings

- A good opening captures your reader's interest. It gives a clue about the topic.
- A good closing sums up your main points in an interesting way.

Weak Opening	Strong Opening
I like hamsters.	Who eats fruit and nuts, has a furry coat, and likes to play at night? My pet hamster, of course!

Weak Closing	Strong Closing
That's why hamsters are great.	When my hamster nuzzles in the palm of my hand, I know it's the only pet for me.

Replace the underlined sentence of the paragraph below with a stronger opening. Be sure that your opening will grab your reader's attention.
Sample answers:

I like to look around in the attic. Each time I explore there I find new treasures. Once I discovered a pocket watch with my great-grandfather's name engraved on the back. I always love to look through dusty albums filled with old family photos. There is even a box of antique dolls that my grandmother played with when she was my age. I could easily spend hours investigating this storehouse of family memories.

Strong Opening: When a rainstorm keeps me inside on a summer afternoon, I head for the attic.

Replace the underlined sentence in the paragraph below with a stronger closing. Your closing should sum up the reasons that support your opinion.

When I watch a play, I am transported to a different time and place. I become one of the characters, experiencing joy or sadness or fear. Suddenly I am part of the action as the story unfolds. Sometimes I hold my breath as the hero deals with a tense situation. At other times the scenes are funny, and I laugh until my sides hurt. That's why I like watching plays.

Strong Closing: Being in the audience when the curtain rises on-stage is definitely the most exciting way to enjoy a story.

▲■ WORKBOOK PLUS, page 155

Openings and Closings

Weak Opening	Strong Opening
Here is why I like computers.	Have you ever considered the many ways that we use computers?

Weak Closing	Strong Closing
That's why I think computers are great.	Whether I'm searching for information, practicing my math, or playing games with a friend, computers are an important part of everyday life.

The short opinion essay below needs an opening. First, read the essay. Then write two strong openings. Read both your openings and decide which one you like best. Put a check mark in front of the stronger opening. Sample openings:

Every hockey game is packed with fast action. Players skate around the rink at a furious pace, passing the puck back and forth like a hot potato. A member of the home team fakes left, almost colliding with his opponent. Suddenly, the puck flies past the goalie, a light flashes behind the net, and the fans go wild. Only at a hockey rink will you experience action like this!

Strong Opening: Many skaters practice their spins and jumps, but for members of a hockey team, speed and stickhandling make the difference.

Strong Opening: "A shot! A goal!" yells the announcer, as the crowd cheers enthusiastically.

The opinion essay below needs a closing. First, read the paragraph. Then write two closings for it. Read both closings and decide which one you like better. Put a check mark in front of the stronger closing. Sample closings:

Whether I'm feeling a little bit blue or floating on top of the world, painting is my favorite way to share what I'm thinking and feeling. Creating pictures is my special way of showing others how I see the world. I love to play with different forms and shapes.

Strong Closing: With a few brush strokes, I can bring sunshine to a gloomy day.

Strong Closing: As shapes and colors dance across the page, I feel like dancing with them.

Evaluating Your Opinion Essay

Lesson Objective

Students will:

- evaluate their opinion essay, using a rubric

Connecting to the Criteria

Have students reread the characteristics of a great opinion essay listed on page 417. Explain that the rubric shown on this page refers to those characteristics. Tell students that the rubric will help them decide which parts of their essay "ring the bell," or meet the standards of a great opinion essay, and which parts still need more work or haven't been addressed at all.

Focus on Instruction

- Review the rubric with students. Have a volunteer read the first point in each section and explain the differences among them. Follow the same procedure for the remaining points.
- After students write their criteria, have them circle the ones that indicate aspects of their opinion essays that need revisions. Blackline Master 12–4 provides a copy of the rubric as a checklist.
- See the Teacher's Resource Book for scoring rubrics.

This page is also available as a poster.

INTERNET CONNECTION Have your students go to www.eduplace.com/kids/hme/ to use an interactive version of the rubric shown in the student book. Students will get feedback and support depending on how they mark the rubric items.

FOR STUDENTS ACQUIRING ENGLISH

Before looking at the rubric in the text, ask the class to generate lists of criteria for Rings the Bell, Getting Stronger, and Try Harder. Then compare the class lists to the text, adding any omissions. Ask students to decide, based on the criteria, what the best part of their essay is and which part needs the most work. Then encourage them to exchange their essays with a partner, who will also determine the essay's strengths and weaknesses. Ask students to return to the checklist and decide how best to fix the weak areas.

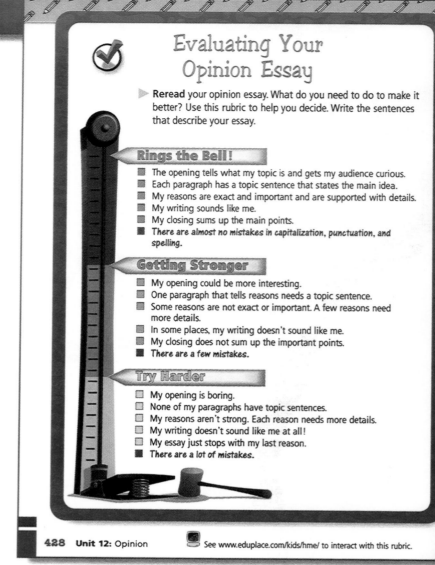

Evaluating Your Opinion Essay

Reread your opinion essay. What do you need to do to make it better? Use this rubric to help you decide. Write the sentences that describe your essay.

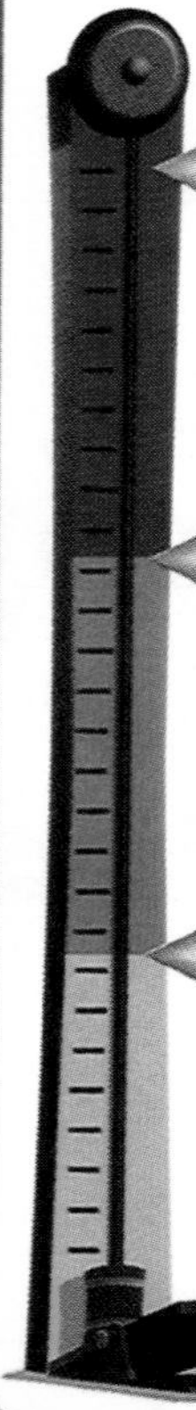

Rings the Bell!

- The opening tells what my topic is and gets my audience curious.
- Each paragraph has a topic sentence that states the main idea.
- My reasons are exact and important and are supported with details.
- My writing sounds like me.
- My closing sums up the main points.
- ***There are almost no mistakes in capitalization, punctuation, and spelling.***

Getting Stronger

- My opening could be more interesting.
- One paragraph that tells reasons needs a topic sentence.
- Some reasons are not exact or important. A few reasons need more details.
- In some places, my writing doesn't sound like me.
- My closing does not sum up the important points.
- ***There are a few mistakes.***

Try Harder

- My opening is boring.
- None of my paragraphs have topic sentences.
- My reasons aren't strong. Each reason needs more details.
- My writing doesn't sound like me at all!
- My essay just stops with my last reason.
- ***There are a lot of mistakes.***

428 **Unit 12:** Opinion

See www.eduplace.com/kids/hme/ to interact with this rubric.

Meeting Individual Needs

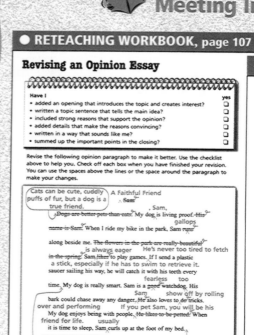

● RETEACHING WORKBOOK, page 107

Revising an Opinion Essay

Have I	yes
• added an opening that introduces the topic and creates interest?	❑
• written a topic sentence that tells the main idea?	❑
• included strong reasons that support the opinion?	❑
• added details that make the reasons convincing?	❑
• written in a way that sounds like me?	❑
• summed up the important points in the closing?	❑

Revise the following opinion paragraph to make it better. Use the checklist above to help you. Check off each box when you have finished your revision. You can use the spaces above the lines or the space around the paragraph to make your changes.

Cats can be cute, cuddly puffs of fur, but a dog is a true friend.
A Faithful Friend
~~Sam~~
, Sam,
~~Dogs are better pets than cats.~~ My dog is living proof. ~~His~~
gallops
~~name is Sam.~~ When I ride my bike in the park, Sam ~~runs~~
along beside me. ~~The flowers in the park are really beautiful~~
is always eager He's never too tired to fetch
~~in the spring.~~ Sam ~~likes~~ to play games. If I send a plastic
a stick, especially if he has to swim to retrieve it.
saucer sailing his way, he will catch it with his teeth every
fearless too
time. My dog is really smart. Sam is a ~~good~~ watchdog. His
Sam show off by rolling
bark could chase away any danger. ~~He~~ also loves to ~~do~~ tricks.
over and performing If you pet Sam, you will be his
My dog enjoys being with people. ~~He likes to be petted.~~ When
friend for life. usually
it is time to sleep, Sam curls up at the foot of my bed.
In addition to having a gentle disposition,
Cat lovers may disagree, but I think the friendship of a loyal dog is the best thing in the world.

▲■ WORKBOOK PLUS, page 156

Revising an Opinion Essay

Have I	yes
• added an opening that introduces the topic and creates interest?	❑
• written a topic sentence that tells the main idea?	❑
• included strong reasons and details that support the opinion?	❑
• written in a way that sounds like me?	❑
• summed up the important points in the closing?	❑

Revise the following opinion essay to make it better. Use the checklist above to help you. Check off each box when you have finished your revision. You can use the spaces above the lines or the space around the paragraph to make your changes.

¶If you think baby-sitting is easy, you may be in for a big surprise.
Energy in Motion
~~Baby-sitting~~
She likes to be a flying bird or a leaping frog.
The job ~~Baby-sitting~~ is harder than it looks. When I baby-sit for five-
year-old Carolyn, I am always on the go. When we play, she wants
to do a dozen things at once. ~~It was a beautiful sunny day.~~ After
another exciting activity. nervously
ten minutes, I have to come up with ~~something else to do.~~ I watch
Carolyn
her every move so that she doesn't fall and get hurt. ~~She~~ always
First, and she wants some crackers
needs something. She is hungry. Then she ~~wants a drink.~~ I read her
, and only when she falls asleep
a story. She begs for another. Carolyn ~~never~~ stops. I am always
exhausted. ~~Baby-sitting is a tough job.~~
My advice for any would-be baby-sitters is simple—be prepared for action.
is thirsty, so I give her apple juice.

PREWRITING DRAFTING REVISING PROOFREADING PUBLISHING

Revise Your Opinion Essay

1. **Revise** your essay. Use the list of sentences you wrote from the rubric. Work on the parts that you described with sentences from "Getting Stronger" and "Try Harder."

Tech Tip
Insert your partner's comments in bold print so that you can think about which changes you want to make.

2. **Have a writing conference.**

When You're the Writer Read your essay to a partner. Discuss the parts that are giving you trouble. Take notes to remember what your partner says. Make any other changes you want.

When You're the Listener Tell at least two things you like about the essay. Ask questions about anything you don't understand. Use this chart to help you.

The Writing Conference

If you're thinking . . .	**You could say . . .**
The opening doesn't tell what the essay is about.	**Could you give your audience a clue about your topic?**
This reason isn't important.	**Are you sure you want to include this reason?**
I don't understand some reasons.	**Can you include more details to explain your reasons?**
I can't tell when one reason stops and the next one starts.	**Can you add transitional words to connect your reasons?**
The paper just stops after the last reason.	**Can you sum up the important points?**

3. **Make more revisions** to your essay. Use your conference notes and the Revising Strategies on the next page.

Help with Conferencing

ADDITIONAL CONFERENCING QUESTIONS

These questions may be useful during teacher-student conferences.

- I'm having trouble following your essay. Could you add transitional phrases, such as *My first reason is . . .* ?
- This reason does not support your opinion. What did you have in mind?
- Is this reason (or example) a fact or simply your opinion? What examples can you give to support this reason?
- Would changing the order of the reasons make your writing easier to read or more convincing?
- This part of your writing has a strong voice. How can you let your voice show in the rest of your writing?

EVALUATION TIP

Have pairs of students role-play a writing conference. Encourage them to include the tips provided on the page. Have students make suggestions for improving the conference.

Lesson Objectives

Students will:

- revise their working draft, based on their evaluations
- discuss their working draft in a writing conference

Revise Your Opinion Essay

Focus on Instruction

Revising Reminder

Remind students that revising focuses on making their essay clearer and more interesting. They should not worry about mistakes at this stage. If necessary, review the revising techniques on page 20.

Conferencing Reminders

Remind students to read their paper aloud to their partner. Remind them to read slowly, clearly, and at an appropriate volume for their audience and setting.

- Remind the listener that is important to give the writer a compliment before asking questions. Give students examples of compliments, such as *Your strong reasons made your essay convincing* or *I liked the way you summed up your ideas in your closing.*
- Explain that it is not necessary for students to address all of their listener's comments or questions in their revision. Students should make their own choices as to how to revise their paper.
- Students can use Blackline Master 12–5 during their writing conferences.

MEETING INDIVIDUAL NEEDS

FOR STUDENTS ACQUIRING ENGLISH

Before looking at the text, the class should list the guidelines for conferencing. (look at the reader, ask helpful questions, take notes as a writer, and so on) Then have the class generate questions based on the possible conferencing thoughts. Write on the board *This opening is boring* and have students provide the helpful question that listeners would ask. Continue until the class has generated all the conferencing questions, and then have students compare them with those in the student book. Note: Students should conference with someone other than their evaluating partner.

Revising Strategies

Lesson Objectives

Students will:
- replace overused words with synonyms
- add details to elaborate their essays
- vary sentence length

Focus on Instruction

Elaborating: Word Choice

Have students identify the synonyms and the words that the synonyms replaced in the examples. *(icy/cold; delicious/good; scorching/hot)* Discuss how the sentence with the synonyms helps the reader more easily form a picture in his or her mind. Ask students to think of additional synonyms that would fit in the sentence. (Sample answers: *frosty, refreshing,* and *blistering*) Page H13 provides a lesson about synonyms.

Elaborating: Details

Ask students what details were added to the second example. (*splashing, throwing a ball,* and *The best part is wearing my new goggles.*) What do the details tell? (what the writer enjoys doing in the water) Give students a simple sentence, such as *I read an exciting book* and have them add details to make the sentence more interesting.

Sentence Fluency

Discuss with students how the choppy sentences were changed to make smoother sentences. Have students read the first set of smoother sentences. Explain that two simple sentences were joined by the word *and* to make a compound sentence that links related ideas. Point out that the other example uses the conjunction *when* and makes the sentences smoother by giving a time clue.

FOR STUDENTS ACQUIRING ENGLISH

Synonyms: Provide focus to students' revision by asking them to circle words they use too often. (*fun, good, great,* and so on) Then, as a class, brainstorm synonyms or learn to use a thesaurus. Next, ask the class to look for choppy areas in their essays where sentences are all one length. Remind students about the use of *and* to join sentences when appropriate.

Revising Strategies

Elaborating: Word Choice **Synonyms** are words that have the same or almost the same meaning. Choosing the best synonym will help make your writing more interesting and exact.

Without Synonyms	With Synonyms
The **cold** lemonade tastes **good** on **hot** summer days.	The icy lemonade tastes delicious on scorching summer days.

▶ Replace at least three words in your essay with synonyms.

Use the Thesaurus Plus on page H79. See also page H13.

Elaborating: Details Insert details within a sentence, or write more sentences.

Without Details	Elaborated with Details
I enjoy playing in the water.	I enjoy splashing and throwing a ball in the water. The best part is wearing my new goggles.

▶ Add details in at least two places in your essay.

Sentence Fluency Your sentences won't be choppy if you make them different lengths.

Choppy Sentences	Smoother Sentences
I like summer vacation. My friends stop over. I get to stay up late.	I like summer vacation. My friends stop over, and I get to stay up late. I like summer vacation. When my friends stop over, I get to stay up late.

▶ Change at least two sentences in your essay to make them different lengths.

GRAMMAR LINK See also pages 49 and 169.

Meeting Individual Needs

● RETEACHING WORKBOOK, page 108

Elaborating: Word Choice

- Synonyms are words that have the same or almost the same meaning.
- Use synonyms to help make your writing more interesting and exact.

Without synonyms	The **shiny car** was **loud**.
With synonyms	The **sparkling automobile** was **noisy**.

Revise the following opinion essay to make it more interesting. Rewrite each sentence, replacing the underlined words with more colorful synonyms.

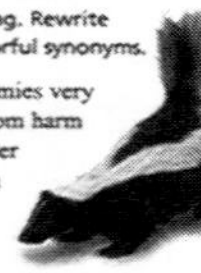

Skunks are neat animals. They cannot move away from enemies very fast because their legs are short. Skunks protect themselves from harm by spraying. The spray has a bad smell. It also can blind another animal for a time, so the skunk can get away. Nature has given skunks a good way to defend themselves.

1. Skunks are neat animals.
   Answers will vary.
2. They cannot move away from enemies very fast because their legs are short.
3. Skunks protect themselves from harm by spraying.
4. The spray has a bad smell.
5. It can also blind another animal for a time, so the skunk can get away.
6. Nature has given skunks a good way to defend themselves.

▲■ WORKBOOK PLUS, page 157

Elaborating: Word Choice

Without synonyms	The **big, pretty** snowflakes fell **fast**.
With synonyms	The **giant, lacy** snowflakes fell **swiftly**.

Revise the following opinion essay to make it more interesting. Underline words that seem too general or dull. Then rewrite the essay, replacing the underlined words with colorful synonyms that have a more exact meaning.

Volunteering to visit senior citizens is a good thing to do. A lot of elderly people feel bad because no one comes to see them. When someone takes time to talk to them, they are better. Listening to them tell about their experiences can be great. We can learn a lot from their stories. Most volunteers will tell you that they get back much more than they give when they help others.

Essays will vary.

PREWRITING DRAFTING REVISING PROOFREADING PUBLISHING

Proofread Your Opinion Essay

Proofread your opinion essay, using the Proofreading Checklist and the Grammar and Spelling Connections. Proofread for one skill at a time. Use a class dictionary to check spellings.

Proofreading Checklist

Did I
- ✓ indent all paragraphs?
- ✓ correct any run-on sentences?
- ✓ use pronouns correctly?
- ✓ write contractions correctly?
- ✓ correct any spelling errors?

Use the Guide to Capitalization, Punctuation, and Usage on page H55.

Proofreading Marks
- ¶ Indent
- ∧ Add
- Delete
- ≡ Capital letter
- / Small letter

Proofreading Tip

Read one line at a time. Hold a ruler or a piece of paper under each line to help you focus on each word.

Grammar and Spelling Connections

Pronouns Use singular pronouns to take the place of singular nouns. Use plural pronouns to take the place of plural nouns.

Singular noun	Fishing is important to me.
Singular pronoun	It is important to me.
Plural noun	The waves splash over the boat.
Plural pronoun	They splash over the boat.

GRAMMAR LINK See also pages 204 and 206.

Contractions Use an apostrophe to take the place of letters left out.

Two Words	Contraction
is not	isn't
I am	I'm

GRAMMAR LINK See also pages 116 and 216.

Spelling Suffixes A **suffix** is a word part added to the end of a base word.
kind**ly**, peace**ful**, hope**less**

See the Spelling Guide on page H65.

Go to www.eduplace.com/kids/hme/ for proofreading practice.

Help with Proofreading

MANAGEMENT TIP
Have each student keep a personal checklist of skills that he or she needs to proofread for. Staple the list to the student's folder.

EVALUATION TIP
Keep a record of errors students consistently miss when they proofread. Encourage students to review their writing for these specific mistakes.

TECH TIP
Students using a word-processing program can rearrange their paragraphs, using the Cut and Paste functions.

Lesson Objective

Students will:
- proofread their opinion essay

Proofread Your Opinion Essay

Focus on Instruction

Proofreading Reminders

- Encourage students to use the Guide to Capitalization, Punctuation, and Usage.
- If necessary, review with students when and how to use each proofreading mark. Have students use a different colored pen or pencil to mark their proofreading corrections.
- For proofreading practice, see the usage and mechanics lessons in the grammar units and the Mixed Review practice in each grammar unit Checkup.

- Review and clarify each item in the Proofreading Checklist, using any related Grammar and Spelling Connections. If students need extra support, review the lessons listed in the Grammar Links.
- Make a comment such as *The books are on the table.* Ask a student to repeat the sentence, substituting a pronoun for the object or objects. *(They are on the table.)* Have the student explain his or her choice of pronouns. If necessary, repeat the procedure with different objects or an individual object or a person.
- Write the following words in a column on the board: *will, are, did, has, were,* and *could.* Tell students that you want them to make a contraction with each word and the word *not.* Call on students to choose a word on the list, to write the contraction next to the chosen word, and to identify the letters replaced by the apostrophe.
- Write the base words *paint, use, care,* and *report* on the board. Ask volunteers to add the suffix *-er, -ful,* or *-less* to make new words.

INTERNET CONNECTION Have your students go to www.eduplace.com/kids/hme/ for online proofreading practice that is fun.

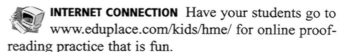

MEETING INDIVIDUAL NEEDS **FOR STUDENTS ACQUIRING ENGLISH**

Have students brainstorm a proofreading checklist. When they are done, ask them to compare the class list with the text. If students have trouble with conjugating *I,* make a worksheet of incorrect student sentences and ask students to correct them. Then share answers as a class.

Lesson Objectives

Students will:
- make a neat final copy of their essay
- choose a way to publish or share their essay
- reflect on their writing experience
- evaluate their opinion essay in comparison to other compositions

Publish Your Opinion Essay

Focus on Instruction

- Before students make their final copy, have them decide how they will publish or share their essay. Review their decisions with them to help them make any special plans.
- Help students make neat corrections rather than rewrite their papers.

Keeping a Writing Portfolio

- **Selection** A paper might be selected because it is
  - ✓ generally noteworthy
  - ✓ a good example of a particular criterion
  - ✓ an example of a particular kind of writing
  - ✓ an example from a certain time in the school year
  - ✓ a typical example of the student's work
- **Labeling** For every paper, have students complete a cover sheet giving the title, date of completion, and reason for inclusion.
- **Review** Periodically have students remove papers that no longer reflect their best work or aren't needed as baselines.
- **Evaluation** Periodically review students' portfolios with them to discuss growth and areas that need improvement.

The Writing Process: PREWRITING · DRAFTING · REVISING · PROOFREADING · PUBLISHING

Publish Your Opinion Essay

1. **Make a neat final copy** of your essay. Be sure you fixed all mistakes.
2. **Write a title** to make your reader curious, such as "The Ups and Downs of Soccer" rather than "Playing Soccer."

GRAMMAR TIP *Capitalize the first, the last, and each important word in the title.*

3. **Publish** or share your essay in a way that suits your audience. See the Ideas for Sharing box.

Tips for Sending a Letter to the Editor
- If you are sending the letter to your town newspaper, include the name and address of the newspaper in the inside address.
- Include your name and phone number so that the paper can verify who wrote the essay.
- Address the envelope *Letter to the Editor.* Most newspapers also accept letters by e-mail and by fax.

Ideas for Sharing

Write It
- Write a letter to the editor of your school or town newspaper.

Say It
- Make a tape recording of your opinion essay.

Show It
- Make a collage with pictures or drawings. Show what you like on one side and what you don't like on the other side.

Reflect

Write about your writing experience. Use these questions to get started.
- What did you learn about writing an opinion essay?
- What was the easiest part? What was most difficult?
- How does this paper compare with other papers you have written?

432 **Unit 12:** Opinion

Help with Publishing

TIPS FOR IDEAS FOR SHARING

Tape Recording Suggest that students practice speaking into a tape recorder before they actually read their essay. Remind them to speak at a volume appropriate to the setting and to use their voice to emphasize important points and add interest. See page H5 for tips on giving a talk.

Collage Students may also wish to include cut out words of magazines or newspapers that represent their feelings.

TECH TIP

If students wish to send their letter to more than one person, they can copy the letter and change the heading and greeting for new addresses.

SCHOOL-HOME CONNECTION

Students can share their collage with a family member. They can explain how their pictures or drawings tell a story about what they like and don't like about their topic.

Assessment Link

Writing Prompts

Use these prompts as ideas for opinion essays or to practice for a test. Decide who your audience will be. Write your essay in a way that they will enjoy.

1. Your teacher asks your opinion about places your class might go for a field trip. Write your opinion about a special place you have visited. Tell what you liked about it.

2. Write about a ride at an amusement park. What did you like about the ride? What didn't you like? Would you recommend it to a friend?

3. Write about an animal that interests you. Tell why you would like to have it for a pet, and why you would not.

4. Think about a book or story you have read recently. Write a review of it. Tell what you liked about the book or what you didn't like. Support your opinions with strong reasons.

Writing Across the Curriculum

5. **FINE ART** Have you ever seen a camel like this one? Did the artist want to show what a real camel looks like, or was he trying to be funny? Write your opinion about this sculpture.

National Gallery of Art, Washington, D.C.

Black Camel with Blue Head and Red Tongue, by Alexander Calder (1898–1976)

See www.eduplace.com/kids/hme/ for more prompts. Writing Prompts 433

About the Artist

About Alexander Calder

Twentieth-century sculptor Alexander Calder used his training as a mechanical engineer to create abstract constructions known as "stabiles" (static sculptures) and "mobiles" (abstract sculptures capable of moving).

Born in 1898, Calder gained widespread recognition in the late 1920s with "Calder's Circus," a miniature troupe of circus animals and performers made of wires, wheels, string, cloth, wood, and cork. These figures showed his fascination for how things move.

Calder's focus changed from representation to abstraction with a visit to Dutch artist Piet Mondrian. Mondrian's brightly colored geometric compositions inspired Calder's first stabiles, and his mobiles were exhibited the following year. Calder's early mobiles, like his toys, were driven by motor or hand crank. His later mobiles were set in motion by slight air drafts.

As Calder grew older, he made larger works, some having enormous proportions. His outdoor sculpture in Spoleto, Italy, is so large that cars and buses can fit beneath it. Besides making sculptures, Calder painted, designed stage sets, made jewelry, and illustrated books.

Writing Prompts

Objective

Students will:
- review prompts for choosing a topic or to practice for a writing test
- view critically a work of fine art and use it to write an opinion essay

Using the Prompts

You can use the prompts on this page in several ways.

- Have students review the prompts to help spark ideas when they are choosing their own topics for an opinion essay. Suggest that students choose one or two prompts that interest them and brainstorm ideas of their own.
- Choose a prompt to provide practice for a writing test. Use it with Test Practice on the next page.
- Choose a prompt that fits with a related topic in another subject area to integrate writing an opinion essay across the curriculum.

INTERNET CONNECTION Send your students to www.eduplace.com/kids/hme/ for more writing prompts. You can also find and print these prompts at www.eduplace.com/rdg/hme/.

FOR STUDENTS ACQUIRING ENGLISH

Students who are new to this country may have trouble responding to prompts 1, 2, and 4. Suggest alternatives: What is your opinion of television in the United States? Explain your answer. What do you think about schools here? What is good, and what needs improvement? Describe your favorite music and why you like it.

Test Practice

Objective

Students will:

- learn strategies for evaluating a writing prompt and writing an opinion essay for a test

Using the Test Practice

- Discuss the strategies for evaluating and responding to a prompt to write an opinion essay as you read through the page with students.
- Review the rubric on page 428 with students before they write their practice test.
- Have students write an opinion essay in response to the prompt on this page or to one of the prompts on the previous page. Impose the time limitations or other restrictions or qualifications specific to the testing requirements used in your school.

INTERNET CONNECTION Send your students to www.eduplace.com/kids/hme/ for graphic organizers. You can also find and print these organizers at www.eduplace.com/rdg/hme/.

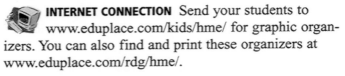

FOR STUDENTS ACQUIRING ENGLISH

After reading the prompt, encourage students to make a list of suggestions for writing this opinion essay. To support brainstorming, ask "What vocabulary will you need? What criteria should you use? What are some difficult spots to watch out for?"

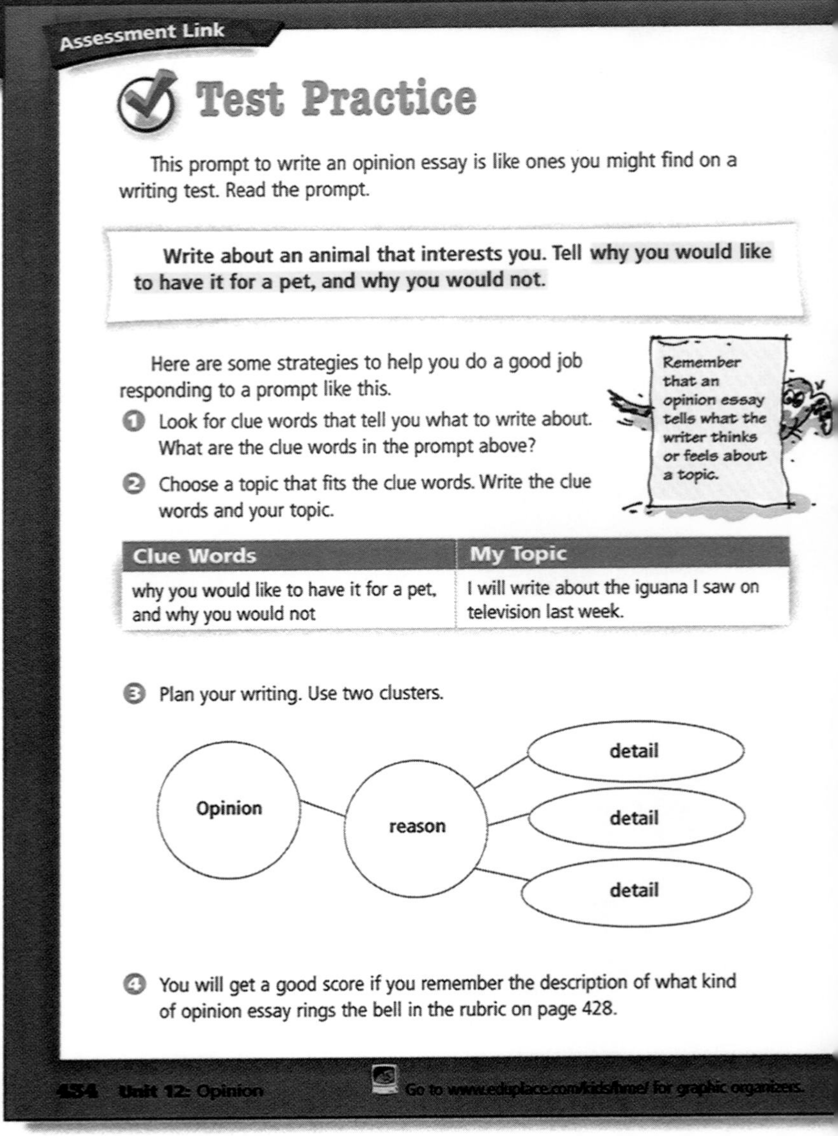

Assessment Link

Test Practice

This prompt to write an opinion essay is like ones you might find on a writing test. Read the prompt.

Write about an animal that interests you. Tell why you would like to have it for a pet, and why you would not.

Here are some strategies to help you do a good job responding to a prompt like this.

1. Look for clue words that tell you what to write about. What are the clue words in the prompt above?
2. Choose a topic that fits the clue words. Write the clue words and your topic.

Remember that an opinion essay tells what the writer thinks or feels about a topic.

Clue Words	My Topic
why you would like to have it for a pet, and why you would not	I will write about the iguana I saw on television last week.

3. Plan your writing. Use two clusters.

Opinion — reason — detail, detail, detail

4. You will get a good score if you remember the description of what kind of opinion essay rings the bell in the rubric on page 428.

434 Unit 12: Opinion — Go to www.eduplace.com/kids/hme/ for graphic organizers.

Writing a Book Report

Writing a **book report** is a way to share information and opinions about a book you have read. Read Aimee's report on *Little House on the Prairie*, which is a story of fiction that is set in the past.

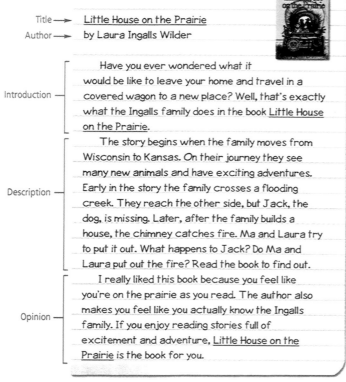

Title → Little House on the Prairie
Author → by Laura Ingalls Wilder

Introduction — Have you ever wondered what it would be like to leave your home and travel in a covered wagon to a new place? Well, that's exactly what the Ingalls family does in the book Little House on the Prairie.

Description — The story begins when the family moves from Wisconsin to Kansas. On their journey they see many new animals and have exciting adventures. Early in the story the family crosses a flooding creek. They reach the other side, but Jack, the dog, is missing. Later, after the family builds a house, the chimney catches fire. Ma and Laura try to put it out. What happens to Jack? Do Ma and Laura put out the fire? Read the book to find out.

Opinion — I really liked this book because you feel like you're on the prairie as you read. The author also makes you feel like you actually know the Ingalls family. If you enjoy reading stories full of excitement and adventure, Little House on the Prairie is the book for you.

See www.eduplace.com/kids/hme/ for more examples of book reports.

more ▶

Writing a Book Report

Lesson Objective

Students will:

- read a model of a book report and identify its parts

Focus on the Model

- Ask students what they think is the purpose of a book report. (to inform others about the book and to share the reviewer's opinion of the book) Point out that writing a book report is similar to writing an opinion essay, in that a book report tells the writer's opinion of the book and gives reasons for the opinion.
- Tell students they will read Aimee's book report on *Little House on the Prairie* by Laura Ingalls Wilder. Survey the class to see how many students have read Wilder's book. Tell students to see if their opinion of the book is the same as Aimee's.
- Before students read Aimee's book report, explain that the blue call outs highlight the five parts of a book report and that students will learn about those five parts after they read the report.
- Ask volunteers to read the model aloud. Have students look for ways the writer makes her audience curious about the book.

Students can also listen to the model on audiotape.

Focus on Instruction

Discuss with the class the explanations of the call outs given in the Reading As a Writer section on page 436.

Answers to Reading As a Writer

- The title of this book is *Little House on the Prairie.*
- The author is Laura Ingalls Wilder.
- Aimee began her report with a question.
- This book is about a family that travels from Wisconsin to Kansas in a covered wagon. Aimee writes about an incident at the beginning of the book.
- Aimee liked the book because the author made her feel as if she were on the prairie with the Ingalls family.

MEETING INDIVIDUAL NEEDS

FOR STUDENTS ACQUIRING ENGLISH

Ask if anyone knows what a prairie is. Show photos of the prairies and of a covered wagon. Find out what students know about life in the United States in the 1800s. Help students locate Wisconsin and Kansas on a map; talk about what a journey from Wisconsin to Kansas might have been like during the 1800s.

Lesson Objectives

Students will:

- write a book report
- revise and proofread their book report and make a final copy for display

How to Write a Book Report

Focus on Instruction

- Remind students that one purpose of a book report is to inform the reader by providing a summary of the book and telling the writer's opinion of it. Emphasize that in their summary students should state only the most important events in the book, not everything that happens.
- Tell students that they should write in the first person when sharing their opinions about a book.
- Remind students to keep their intended audience and purpose in mind as they write. Ask how a book report written for a class newsletter might differ from one written to encourage a friend to read the book.
- Before students begin writing, have them summarize their book to a partner and discuss what they liked and didn't like about it.
- Tell students that they should introduce the main characters in their book report.
- Review with students the Proofreading Checklist on page 431 and the use of proofreading marks.
- Review students' publishing plans with them to help them address any special requirements.

Connecting to the Criteria

Have students review the characteristics of a book report described in the Reading As a Writer section of this lesson. Remind them to check that the information in each part is complete and written accurately.

SCHOOL-HOME CONNECTION Suggest that students share the final draft of their book report with their families.

Discuss with each student whether this paper should go into the portfolio. Consider these possible reasons: (1) it is an especially good piece of writing; (2) it reflects a particular aspect of writing that the student did well; (3) it shows an aspect of writing that needs more work and could be used as a baseline for measuring growth.

Reading As a Writer See TE margin for answers.

- The **title** gives the name of the book.
  What is the title of this book?
- The **author** is the person who wrote the book.
  Who is the author?
- The **introduction** presents the subject of the report and captures the interest of the reader.
  How did Aimee begin her report?
- The **description** tells what the book is about.
  What is this book about? What did Aimee tell about the book she read?
- The **opinion** explains what the writer thought about the book.
  Why did Aimee like this book?

How to Write a Book Report

1. **List** the title of the book and the author's name.
2. **Introduce** your book by making your reader curious about it. You might ask a question, give a startling piece of information, or use a quotation from the book.
3. **Describe** the book. Include at least one event from the story in your summary.
4. **Give** your opinion. Tell what you thought about this book and why. Did the picture on the book's cover or the illustrations in the book help bring the story to life?
5. **Revise and proofread** your book report. Use the Proofreading Checklist on page 431. Use a dictionary to check your spelling.
6. **Display** a neat final copy of your book report in your classroom's reading center, or place it in the school library for others to read.

Need help?

Ask yourself these questions to help you decide what to write.

- Is the book nonfiction (a real story) or fiction (a made-up story)?
- Is the story funny, exciting, scary, or sad?
- What is the setting?
- Who are the main characters?
- How do the photos or illustrations help tell the story?

Help with Writing a Book Report

USING RESOURCES

- Provide examples of book reviews from magazines and newspapers. Have students identify the strategies that are used to make readers want to read the book.
- Invite a book reviewer from a local newspaper to speak or have students e-mail questions to the reviewer if a visit is not possible.

TECH TIPS

If the necessary software and hardware are available, suggest that students scan their book cover to post beside their report in the classroom reading center or school library.

EVALUATION TIP

Review students' drafts to be sure their opinions about the book are clear and supported with reasons.

Writing a Poem

Poets put words into interesting patterns. One kind is **rhythm**, a pattern of beats that you can tap out with your finger as you read the words. Some poems have the same number of beats in every line.

Another kind of pattern is **rhyme**. Words rhyme when they have the same ending sound, such as *moose*, *goose*, and *caboose*. In lots of poems, the rhyme comes at the ends of lines.

Read these poems to see how the writers used rhythm and rhyme.

Keziah

I have a secret place to go.
Not anyone may know.

And sometimes when the wind is rough
I cannot get there fast enough.

And sometimes when my mother
Is scolding my big brother,

My secret place, it seems to me,
Is quite the only place to be.

Gwendolyn Brooks

A Matter of Taste

What does your tongue like the most?
Chewy meat or crunchy toast?

A lumpy bumpy pickle or tickly pop?
A soft marshmallow or a hard lime drop?

Hot pancakes or a sherbet freeze?
Celery noise or quiet cheese?

Or do you like pizza
More than any of these?

Eve Merriam

more ▶

Writing a Poem

Lesson Objective

Students will:

- read published and student models of poems that have rhyme and rhythm

Focus on the Models

- Ask students what they think is the purpose of a poem. (Answers will vary.) Point out that in writing a poem, the poet uses words in interesting patterns to express thoughts and feelings in new ways.
- Tell students they will read four poems that have different patterns of rhyme and rhythm. The first three are by adult poets and one is by a student writer. You may want to mention that "Keziah" is from a book of poems by Gwendolyn Brooks in which each poem is written from the viewpoint of a different child.
- Ask volunteers to read the models aloud. Tell students to listen for the patterns of rhythm and rhyme in each poem.

Students can also listen to the models on audiotape.

Focus on Instruction

- To help students discern the beats, have them tap their finger on the desk for each "beat" they hear in the poem. If they are having difficulty, read the first two or four lines of the poem aloud, emphasizing the accented syllables, having students clap for each beat. Then continue reading that poem in a rhythmic, but more natural, tone as they continue clapping.
- Have volunteers answer the Reading As a Writer questions.

FOR STUDENTS ACQUIRING ENGLISH

Read the poems aloud or call on volunteers to do so. Discuss each of the poems after it is read. Point out invented words such as *Keziah,* the title of the Brooks poem. Help students find the rhyming words at the end of the lines. Have partners practice reading the poems to each other.

Lesson Objective

Students will:

- identify patterns of rhythm and rhyme in poems

Answers to Reading As a Writer

- There are three beats.
- In lines 1–6, each two lines rhyme. The word *pizza* at the end of line 7 breaks the pattern, and the word *these* at the end of line 8 rhymes with lines 5 and 6.
- There are four beats in each line. The rhyming words are *try/fly, birth/earth, wings/kings, why/sky.*

FOR STUDENTS ACQUIRING ENGLISH

Present examples of rhyming words such as *red* and *head.* Practice by calling out various words and having students take turns thinking of words that rhyme. Let them continue until they can think of no more possibilities. Show students how to count out beats for the poems on this page.

Penguin

O Penguin, do you ever try
To flap your flipper wings and fly?
How do you feel, a bird by birth
And yet for life tied down to earth?
A feathered creature, born with wings
Yet never wingborne. All your kings
And emperors must wonder why
Their realm is sea instead of sky.

Mary Ann Hoberman

I'm Hungry

My dish is empty. They're all in bed.
Don't they know I need to be fed?

I start to meow to get them awake.
I am so hungry, I could eat a steak!

I jump on their bed and lick their ears.
My stomach is growling. I am close to tears!

Finally Jack gets up and gets my dish.
He feeds me my favorite, tunafish.

My tummy is full, my eyes start to close,
and I start to dream as off I doze.

Elizabeth Allen,
Student Writer

Reading As a Writer See TE margin for answers.

- Most of the lines in the poem "Keziah" have four beats. How many beats are in lines 2, 5, and 6?
- In "A Matter of Taste," how do lines 7 and 8 change the way the poem rhymes?
- How many beats are in each line of "Penguin"? What words rhyme?

How to Write a Poem in Couplets

1. **Choose** a topic. You can write a poem about almost anything—an experience you had, or a favorite place, person, or activity.
2. **Make** an idea tree to explore your topic.
   - Write your topic under the trunk.
   - On each branch, write an idea you'd like to include in the poem. It may be a thought, a feeling, or something that happens.
   - Add some twigs to each branch. Put exact words, details, and rhyming words on the twigs.

Here is Elizabeth Allen's idea tree ▶

Here are more ideas.

- Write as if you were speaking as a different girl or boy, as Gwendolyn Brooks did in "Keziah."
- Write to an animal, as in the poem "Penguin." What would you like to ask your dog? a porcupine in the woods? a lion at the zoo?
- Write as if you were an animal, as in "I'm Hungry." What might your parakeet say about the room it lives in?

3. **Write** your poem in **couplets**. A couplet is made of two lines (a *couple* of lines). Both lines should have the same or almost the same number of beats. The words at the end of each line should rhyme.

   Don't worry if your poem doesn't come out perfectly the first time!

more ▶

Help with Writing a Poem in Couplets

MORE TOPIC IDEAS

Suggest these ideas.

- Students can write about their lunch, using descriptive words.
- They can write about a bicycle ride to a favorite place.
- They can tell about their pet animal.

How to Write a Poem in Couplets

Lesson Objectives

Students will:

- choose a topic and make an idea tree to explore the topic
- write a poem in couplets, considering rhyme and rhythm

Focus on Instruction

- Suggest that students consider two opposite possibilities for their poem topic: they can write about either a very unusual idea or something that will be very familiar to their audience.
- Have small groups of students brainstorm topics for their poem before they begin writing.
- Discuss with the class the meaning of the word *beat* in poetry. ("accent or stress in the rhythm of a verse")
- Remind students that they should keep their purpose in mind as they choose words to write their poem. Have students tell how word choice might differ in a poem meant to describe an object and a poem meant to describe an adventure. (Sample answer: A poem meant to describe an object would have many sensory words; an adventure poem would have many action words.)
- Ask students how they might vary their writing if they wrote as if they were animals; how would their writing differ for different kinds of animals? (Sample answers: A poem "written" by a bird might use short words and sentences to give the feeling of a bird's chirping. A poem written about a lion might use longer words with a lot of consonants to mimic the roaring sounds of the lion's voice.)
- Tell students that poetry allows writers to find new and interesting ways to express their thoughts. Explain that sometimes poets "bend the rules" for capitalization and punctuation, but that writers should take care that this does not make their poem hard for readers to understand.
- Encourage students to write at least three couplets. If they don't have enough details or rhyming words for three couplets, have them look back at their idea tree and think of other ideas to add to it.

MEETING INDIVIDUAL NEEDS — FOR STUDENTS ACQUIRING ENGLISH

Explain the meaning of *couplets;* ask if anyone knows what *couple* means. Have partners make lists of rhyming words that they can use in couplets; remind students that it is the way a word sounds that matters, not the way it is spelled. Have partners use words from their lists to write couplets. Remind students to tap out the beats.

Lesson Objectives

Students will:
- reread their poem to evaluate rhythm and rhyme
- proofread their poem
- publish the poems in a class booklet

Focus on Instruction

- As students revise their poem, remind them to use precise words and vivid images whenever possible to give the reader the best picture.
- If students read their poem aloud, they can have a partner supply sound effects, such as the barking of a dog or whooshing noises for wind. Partners should practice before reading to an audience in order to make sure the sound effects do not drown out the poem.
- Review with students the Proofreading Checklist on page 431 and the use of proofreading marks.
- Review students' publishing plans with them to help them address any special requirements.

Connecting to the Criteria

Remind students to check that each of the couplets in their poem has the same number of beats and that the end words of each couplet rhyme.

Discuss with each student whether this paper should go into the portfolio. Consider these possible reasons: (1) it is an especially good piece of writing; (2) it reflects a particular aspect of writing that the student did well; (3) it shows an aspect of writing that needs more work and could be used as a baseline for measuring growth.

4 **Reread** your poem.
- Have you said everything you want to say?
- Check the rhythm of your poem. Does each line have the right number of beats? Most lines should follow the pattern you have chosen.
- Check your rhymes. Does each pair of lines end with rhyming words?

Reread your favorite poem in this lesson. Feel the rhythm of the lines. Then put that rhythm in your poem.

I Can't Make It Rhyme!

It can be hard to make the second line of a couplet rhyme. Here are two things to try.
- If one line ends with a word that's hard to rhyme, rewrite that line to end with a better word.
- Brainstorm a list of possible rhyming words. Have a partner help you. Then choose the best one.

Ask a partner to read your poem aloud. Does it sound the way you want it to? Make any changes.

5 **Proofread** your poem. Use a dictionary to check spellings. Remember that the ends of rhyming words may be spelled differently, even though they sound the same, as in *crews, choose,* and *use.*

6 **Publish** your poem. Make a neat final copy of your poem to include in a class booklet. You can also display your poems on a bulletin board.

Draw a picture for your poem, if you wish. Here are more ideas.
- Have a class poetry fair. Take turns reading your poems. Select one or two poems for a group to dramatize for your class.
- Make a tape recording of class poems. Share it with a younger class.

Help with Writing Couplets

USING RESOURCES

Refer students to the Thesaurus Plus on page H79, or provide them with other thesauruses so they can find more precise words for their poem.

TECH TIP

Students can experiment with the font, type size, tab, and centering features of available software to create a professional-looking layout for their poem.

EVALUATION TIP

To make sure students are using rhythm in their poem, read each student's poem aloud as he or she gently taps out the beat. Students are often sensitive about revising their creative efforts; this technique allows them to hear for themselves what needs work, rather than reacting to what they perceive to be the teacher's criticism.

Writing a Nonsense Poem

Writing a nonsense poem about yourself is like dressing in a silly costume or drawing a cartoon portrait of yourself. It's also a way to play with words. Read these two examples.

As I Was Going Out One Day

As I was going out one day
My head fell off and rolled away.
But when I saw that it was gone,
I picked it up and put it on.

And when I got into the street
A fellow cried: "Look at your feet!"
I looked at them and sadly said:
"I've left them both asleep in bed!"

Anonymous

My Name Is . . .

My name is Sluggery-wuggery
My name is Worms-for-tea
My name is Swallow-the-table-leg
My name is Drink-the-Sea.

My name is I-eat-saucepans
My name is I-like-snails
My name is Grand-piano-George
My name is I-ride-whales.

My name is Jump-the-chimney
My name is Bite-my-knee
My name is Jiggery-pokery
And Riddle-me-ree, and ME.

Pauline Clarke

Reading As a Writer

See TE margin for answers.

- What makes each of these poems funny?
- What patterns of rhymes and beats can you find in the poems?

How to Write a Nonsense Poem

1. **Choose** an idea for a nonsense poem about yourself. It could be about funny names for yourself, odd things you collect, or silly things you'd like to do. List the things you'll put in your poem.
2. **Write** your poem. You might try using a pattern of rhymes and beats.
3. **Revise** your poem to make it as humorous as you can. Use exact words to paint clear pictures in your reader's mind, and try to find words with interesting sounds. If you wish, make up some words!

Use the Thesaurus Plus on page H79 to find words with pizzazz.

Writing a Nonsense Poem

Lesson Objectives

Students will:

- read two examples of nonsense poems
- write a nonsense poem

Focus on the Models

- After students read the two poems aloud, ask them why they think these are called nonsense poems. (The poems don't make sense.)
- Have students experiment with reading each poem in two or three different ways (for example, very fast, in a very serious voice, with silly gestures). Discuss with students which reading made each poem sound silliest.

Students can also listen to the models on audiotape.

Answers to Reading As a Writer

- "As I Was Going Out One Day" describes things that could not possibly happen, but describes them as though they were perfectly normal. In "My Name Is . . . ," the names are all nonsense names.
- In "As I Was Going Out One Day," each stanza has two rhyming couplets, and each line has the same beat. In "My Name Is . . . ," the second and fourth lines in each stanza rhyme, and every line has three beats; even-numbered lines, however, are one syllable shorter than odd-numbered lines.

How to Write a Nonsense Poem

Focus on Instruction

Tell students that they might make an idea tree again but try making it backwards. They can write silly words on the twigs and work back from those words to the ideas on the branches and the trunk.

Help each student decide whether this paper should go into the portfolio.

Connecting to the Criteria

Explain to students that although the content of nonsense poems is silly, the structure still should have rhythm or rhyme.

MEETING INDIVIDUAL NEEDS — FOR STUDENTS ACQUIRING ENGLISH

Explain what *nonsense* means. Read the nonsense poems aloud or call on volunteers to do so. Discuss each after it is read. Ask students what the nonsense is; point out invented words. Help students find the rhyming words at the end of the lines. Have partners practice reading the poems to each other.

Help with Writing a Nonsense Poem

TOPIC IDEAS

Suggest these ideas.

- Students can start by jotting down something that actually happened to them and then change every other noun or verb to a sillier noun or verb.
- They can follow the structure of "My Name Is . . ." to write a poem called "My Pet Is . . ." or "My Shoes Are . . ."
- They can list words that are opposites and try to combine at least two opposites in a silly way in each stanza.

USING RESOURCES

Students can read the poetry of Edward Lear or Ogden Nash as models of nonsense poems.

TECH TIP

If illustration software is available, suggest that students create computer-generated illustrations for their poems.

SCHOOL-HOME CONNECTION

Suggest that students plan a poetry reading and invite family members to be the audience.

Having a Panel Discussion

Lesson Objectives

Students will:

- plan and present a panel discussion, adapting voice, diction, and word choice to the audience and setting
- use nonverbal cues to convey a message to an audience
- interpret speakers' verbal and nonverbal messages, purposes, and perspectives
- clarify and support spoken ideas with evidence, elaboration, and examples
- understand the major ideas and supporting evidence in spoken messages

Focus on Instruction

- Explain to students that a panel discussion can be a good way to create a forum for presenting diverse viewpoints. Ask in what kinds of situations a panel discussion might be used. (Sample answers: television news program, community meeting)
- Have volunteers share possible topics for a panel discussion. Remind students that the topic should be something people would have strong opinions about, such as commercial advertising in public schools.
- Ask students why it is important to have a moderator in a panel discussion. (Sample answers: to introduce the panelists; to make sure the panelists speak only for the allotted time; to ensure that the audience has time to ask questions; and to keep the discussion running smoothly)
- Ask students why they think it makes more sense to have three panelists versus ten or more. (Sample answers: Three panelists would be enough to cover most possible viewpoints about a topic, and more panelists would just repeat these views. The discussion would take too much time with more panelists, and the audience would lose interest.)

Having a Panel Discussion

In a panel discussion, a group of people talk about a topic in front of an audience. Each member of the group is called a panelist. Panelists take turns sharing their information and ideas. Look at the chart below to see one way a classroom panel discussion can work.

The moderator	• tells the audience the topic • introduces the panelists
Panelist 1	• speaks on the topic for three minutes
Panelist 2	• speaks on the topic for three minutes
Panelist 3	• speaks on the topic for three minutes
The moderator	• announces that the panelists can now discuss the topic together for ten minutes
The panelists	• talk and disagree politely
The audience	• asks questions of any or all of the panelists for ten minutes; panelists respond

When you take part in a panel discussion, you are both a speaker and a listener. Be sure that you understand the other speakers' opinions and reasons before you agree or disagree.

The guides below can help you be a good panelist.

Guides for Being a Panelist

Organize your ideas before you speak. Write key ideas on note cards.

When You Are Speaking

- Clearly state your opinion about the topic.
- Give reasons for your opinions. Support your reasons with facts.
- Speak loudly enough so that everyone can hear you.
- Be polite when you disagree with others.

When You Are Listening

- Pay close attention to the person who is speaking. Try to block out sounds that make your mind wander away from the discussion.
- Try to understand each speaker's point of view. Listen to the reasons the speaker gives for his or her views. Are the reasons based on facts or opinions? Do they make sense?
- Don't interrupt another panelist. Ask questions after the speaker has finished.
- Be sure that you understand a speaker's opinions and reasons before you agree or disagree.

Apply It Answers will vary.

Plan a panel discussion. Choose a topic and decide on time limits for the panelists. Research the topic. Write your opinion about it. Follow the guides above during the discussion. After the discussion, answer these questions.

- Which guides were difficult to follow? Why do you think so?
- What kinds of topics do you think would work well for a panel discussion? Explain why.

Need a Topic?

Try one of these.

- favorite kinds of music
- the best way to spend free time
- peer tutors

Having a Panel Discussion 443

Focus on Instruction

- Have volunteers read aloud the Guides for Being a Panelist. Clarify and discuss each guideline.
- Ask students to explain how they can decide whether a speaker's reasons are based on fact or opinion. (Sample answer: Facts can be proved true or false.)
- Have students demonstrate appropriate nonverbal cues to use when presenting, such as raised eyebrows to suggest doubt, head-nodding to suggest agreement, hand gestures to emphasize an important point, and so on.
- Tell students that listening during a panel discussion is just as important as speaking. Emphasize that little is accomplished when speakers argue their point of view without listening to those of others.

Apply It

- Have students take turns listening and presenting. Ask listeners to provide feedback and cite examples about what panel members did well.
- Remind students to speak loudly enough for their audience, not just other panel members, to hear.
- Emphasize that students can show disagreement without using an angry tone or a loud voice.
- Tell students that sometimes when people get excited, the pitch of their voice becomes too high. Remind students to guard against this.
- Emphasize to students that they must use proper word choice for their audience. Tell students they should explain any words their audience might not know.
- Have students take notes as they listen to panel discussions. Suggest that if students have questions, they should begin by restating what they thought they heard the panelist say. In this way listeners can verify that they correctly understood and interpreted a presenter's ideas and evidence.

MEETING INDIVIDUAL NEEDS — FOR STUDENTS ACQUIRING ENGLISH

Ask students to read the introduction to learn what a panel discussion is. Call attention to the *-ist* suffix on *panelist.* Ask for other examples of nouns for people that end in this suffix. Other examples include *artist, specialist, dentist.* Have English speakers act out the behaviors in the guides for speaking and listening.

Finding Point of View in Visuals

Lesson Objectives

Students will:
- evaluate, compare, and contrast point of view, main idea, and supporting details in visual media messages
- convey point of view with media

Focus on Instruction

- Tell students that a *medium* is a means for communicating information to large numbers of people. Newspapers, magazines, radio, television, billboards, paintings, sculpture, and the Internet, are examples of media. Explain that the plural of *medium* is *media*.
- Tell students to cover the photograph on the right and focus on the photo on the left. Ask volunteers to share their viewpoints about the picture of the child with the hat. (Sample answer: The child might be afraid of something and could be feeling cold and tired.) Then have students uncover the right-hand photo and share how their viewpoint changes after viewing the larger picture. (Sample answers: The larger photo shows that most of the people are smiling; therefore, it makes one wonder why this child is so serious. The larger photograph also tells more about where the child is—a parade or other spectator event.)

Think and Discuss

Encourage students to explain their viewpoints. Remind students that there are no right or wrong answers to these questions. Sample answers:

The photo on the left shows a child looking at something and appearing a bit afraid.

The focus is on the child and the expression on the child's face.

The focus in the photo on the right is on an entire crowd of happy-looking people, rather than just one person in that crowd

Answers will vary.

Finding Points of View in Visuals

The visuals that you see in the media have many different purposes. The people who make the visuals give them a certain message about a subject. The message can tell you what those people think about the subject.

A way of thinking about a subject is called a point of view, or viewpoint. The photographs below show two different viewpoints.

Visuals do not always tell the whole story. They may leave out information that could greatly change the message. Further, when you change the focus of a visual, you can also change the viewpoint.

Think and Discuss See TE margin for answers.

- What is shown in the photo on the left?
- What is its focus, or center of attention?
- How is that focus different from the focus in the photograph on the right?
- Did you notice that the photo on the left is a part of the photo on the right?

Use the guides below to help you look at visuals.

Guides for Finding Points of View in Visuals

1. **Focus** • Look for the main subject of the visual. What captures your attention?
2. **Purpose** • Look at the details. What do you think is the purpose of the visual?
3. **Audience** • If you know who the audience is, you can tell a great deal about the purpose of a visual. Who does the visual appeal to?
4. **Message** • Look for the message. What is the visual telling you? Ask yourself whether you are seeing all of the information. Could important details be missing?
5. **Viewpoint** • The person or persons who made the visual have a way of thinking about the subject. What do you think it is?

Visuals have many purposes! These include:

- *to persuade*
- *to sell*
- *to express an opinion*
- *to inform*
- *to mislead*
- *to entertain*
- *to influence*

Apply It Answers will vary.

Use the guides above to help you show different points of view with visuals.

- Find a newspaper photograph, magazine advertisement, or other visual. Think about the point of view of the image. Then change the image to give a different point of view. You might cut the image apart, cover up parts, or add details.
- Draw, photograph, or videotape the same subject to create two visuals. Design each visual for a different audience. Each visual should show a different point of view or send a different message.

Focus on Instruction

- Have volunteers read aloud the guidelines. Discuss each one. Have students use the guidelines to evaluate the point of view, main idea, and supporting details of each of the images on page 444.
- To provide further practice evaluating point of view in media messages, show another pair of images. For instance, show a newspaper or news magazine photo of a soldier and a picture of a soldier from a military recruitment ad. Ask students how the images differ. What is the purpose of each visual? What message or point of view does each convey?
- You may want to have students review pages 402–403 for additional guidelines on evaluating the media.

Apply It

- Students with cameras might use a zoom lens to create and manipulate images showing different points of view.
- Students with access to a computer scanner could scan photographs into a computer program, and then manipulate the visuals by cropping, enlarging, or distorting the images to convey different messages.
- Students may need additional support identifying visuals. Tell students to look through magazines or other resources to find one strong visual and then to narrow their search to find another image that presents a different message about the same general topic. If students cannot find a second visual, have them draw one or make a copy of the first visual, which they then can change to show another point of view.

MEETING INDIVIDUAL NEEDS

FOR STUDENTS ACQUIRING ENGLISH

Students from different cultures may interpret visuals in different ways. As students look at visuals, use the guides as a basis for discussion and comparison. Does the same thing capture everyone's attention? Do some details carry special meaning for some viewers? Is the message always the same? What about viewpoint?

Unit 13 Planning Guide

Writing to Persuade

Writing to Persuade: *2 weeks*
Special Focus and Communication Links: *1 week (optional)*

	Blackline Masters (TE)	Workbook Plus	Reteaching Workbook
PUBLISHED MODEL "Bats," by Betsy Maestro *(447–449)*			
What Makes a Great Persuasive Essay? *(450)*			
STUDENT MODEL Working Draft *(451–452)*	13-1A, 13-1B		
Final Copy *(453–454)*			
The Writing Process Write a Persuasive Essay			
Prewriting Explore Your Goal *(456)*	13–2		
Focus Skill: Supporting Your Reasons *(457)*		158	109
Focus Skill: Evaluating Your Reasons *(458)*		159	110
Focus Skill: Organizing Your Essay *(459)*	13–3	160	111
Drafting Focus Skill: Openings and Closings *(460)*		161	112
Focus Skill: Writing with Voice *(461)*		162	113
Revising ✓ Evaluating Your Persuasive Essay [rubric] *(462)*	13–4	163	114
Writing Conference *(463)*	13–5		
Revising Strategies *(464)*		164	115
Proofreading *(465)*			
Publishing and Reflecting *(466)*			
✓ **Writing Prompts and Test Practice** *(467–468)*			
SPECIAL FOCUS ON INFLUENCING Writing a Business Letter *(469–470)*			
COMMUNICATION LINKS **Listening:** Listening for Persuasive Tactics *(471–472)*			
Viewing/Media: Watching for Persuasive Tactics *(473–475)*			

Tools and Tips

- **Listening and Speaking Strategies,** *pp. H4–H10*
- **Building Vocabulary,** *pp. H11–H17*
- **Research and Study Strategies,** *pp. H18–H30*
- **Using Technology,** *pp. H35–H47*
- **Writer's Tools,** *pp. H48–H54*
- **Spelling Guide,** *pp. H65–H69*
- **Guide to Capitalization, Punctuation, and Usage,** *pp. H55–H64*
- **Thesaurus Plus,** *pp. H79–H100*

School-Home Connection

Suggestions for informing or involving family members in classroom activities and learning related to this unit are included in the Teacher's Edition throughout the unit.

Meeting Individual Needs

- **FOR SPECIAL NEEDS/INCLUSION:** *Houghton Mifflin English* Audiotape
- **FOR STUDENTS ACQUIRING ENGLISH:**
  - Notes and activities are included in this Teacher's Edition throughout the unit to help you adapt or use pupil book activities with students acquiring English.
  - Students acquiring English can listen to the published and student models on audiotape.
  - MediaWeaver™, Sunburst/Humanities software, offers bilingual features, including Spanish menus, a Spanish spelling tool, and a Spanish thesaurus.
- **ENRICHMENT:** See *Teacher's Resource Book.*

All audiotape recordings are also available on CD.

Daily Language Practice

Each sentence includes two capitalization, punctuation, usage, or spelling errors based on skills presented in the Grammar and Spelling Connections in this unit or from Grammar Units 1–7. Each day write one sentence on the chalkboard. Have students find the errors and write the sentence correctly on a sheet of paper. To make the activity easier, identify the kinds of errors.

1. Chin and me worked hardest than anyone else. Chin and I worked harder than anyone else. (subject pronouns; comparing with adverbs)
2. Jamal always runs faster and finishes ahead of the other racers. Jamal always runs fastest and finishes ahead of the other racers. (comparing with adverbs; present tense)
3. Our bird sings more happilier in it's big new cage. Our bird sings more happily in its big new cage. (comparing with adverbs; homophones)
4. Of all the stars, the North star shines brightlye Of all the stars, the North Star shines most brightly. (proper nouns; comparing with adverbs)
5. You should'nt fource anyone to eat. You shouldn't force anyone to eat. (contractions; spelling |ôr|)
6. I don't have no more chors to do. Sample: I don't have any more chores to do. (negatives; spelling |ôr|)
7. The lions rored from inside there cages. The lions roared from inside their cages. (spelling |ôr|; homophones)
8. A guinea pigs fur are soft and silky. A guinea pig's fur is soft and silky. (possessive nouns; subject-verb agreement)
9. The kittens bellys are round and full. The kittens' bellies are round and full. (possessive nouns; plural nouns)
10. I wanted to sing especially good for she. I wanted to sing especially well for her. (*good/well*; object pronouns)

Additional Resources

Workbook Plus, Unit 13
Reteaching Workbook, Unit 13
Teacher's Resource Book
Transparencies
Posters, Unit 13
Audiotapes

Technology Tools

CD-ROM: *EasyBook Deluxe
MediaWeaver™, Sunburst/Humanities software
*Type to Learn™

*©Sunburst Technology Corporation, a Houghton Mifflin Company. All rights reserved.

INTERNET: http://www.eduplace.com/kids/hme/ *or* http://www.eduplace.com/rdg/hme/

Visit Education Place for these additional support materials and activities:

- author biographies
- student writing models
- graphic organizers
- an interactive rubric
- proofreading practice
- writing prompts
- benchmark papers

Assessment

Test Booklet, Unit 13

Keeping a Journal

Discuss with students the value of keeping a journal as a way of promoting self-expression and fluency. Encourage students to record their thoughts and ideas in a notebook. Inform students whether the journal will be private or will be reviewed periodically as a way of assessing growth. The following prompts may be useful for generating writing ideas.

Journal Prompts

- Is there anything you wish your best friend did differently? What could you say to persuade him or her to change?
- Is there an important skill you think everyone should learn? What could you say to persuade people to learn it?
- Think of a book you really enjoyed. What points could you make to persuade your friends to read it?

Introducing the Unit

Using the Photograph

- Have students look at the photograph and ask what is happening. (Sample responses: The woman is teaching the girl how to play chess. A mother is watching proudly while her daughter plays.)
- Have a volunteer read the caption aloud. Ask what the writer is trying to persuade readers to do. (learn a new game, such as chess, that will challenge them)
- Ask students whether they think the writer has stated his or her goal convincingly and to tell why or why not. (Sample response: yes, because the writer challenges the reader not to play the same old games but to learn a new, challenging game that makes you think)
- Explain to students that the caption would make a good opening for a **persuasive essay**, in which a writer tries to persuade an audience to do something. Tell students that they will learn to write a persuasive essay in this unit.

Unit 13

Writing to Persuade

Why spend time on games you played last year? Move up to a game that will really test your strategy skills.

446

Shared Writing Activity

Work with students to write a short persuasive paragraph about a common goal, such as *Everyone should learn to play chess* or *Our teacher should play music during free-reading time.*

1. Help students select a common goal based on who their audience will be. If you are the audience, discuss with students your interests and concerns. Then help them select a reasonable goal—one you would be willing to agree to if they persuade you.
2. Write the goal in the main circle of a web on the board or on an overhead transparency. Then have students suggest reasons explaining why you (or whoever the audience is) should do whatever their goal states. List each reason in a circle radiating from the goal.
3. Have students review the reasons and choose the three they think are the strongest. Then have them decide the reasons' order of importance, and have a volunteer number them *1, 2, 3.*
   - Reinforce that strong reasons are those that best address the audience's interests and concerns.
4. Write the goal as the first sentence in the paragraph on the board or on an overhead transparency. Then help students use their numbered reasons to generate sentences that explain their goal. Encourage them to add a simple fact or two—or an example—to help support one or more of their reasons.
5. If students suggest fragments and phrases that begin with *because* or *since,* remind them that every sentence should express a complete thought. They can usually combine a phrase or groups of words beginning with *because* or *since* with another sentence.
6. Have students copy their persuasive paragraph and present it to their audience. If the audience agrees to do what the students want, then they know their argument was convincing.

A Published Model

Betsy Maestro believes that bats can help people. What does she want her readers to do?

Bats

from *Bats: Night Fliers*, by Betsy Maestro

goal

No one knows exactly how many bats there are on Earth. But we do know that Earth would not be the same without bats. A large colony of bats can consume 6,000 tons of insects in a year. A single bat can eat as many as 600 mosquitoes in an hour. Without bats, night-flying insects would rapidly multiply. reason

Tropical bats are like the bees of the night. They are the only pollinators of some night-opening flowers. And in the rain forests, where too much timber is being cut, seed dispersal aids in new tree growth. In these areas, over 300 kinds of trees and plants depend on fruit-eating bats for their survival.

more ▶

See www.eduplace.com/kids/ for information about Betsy Maestro.

A Published Model 447

"Bats"

Lesson Objectives

Students will:

- read a published model of a persuas
- identify characteristics of persuasive
- identify examples of comparison
- evaluate the relationship between visuals and text
- write personal and critical responses

Focus on the Model

Building Background

Ask volunteers to tell something they know about bats. Help students identify each statement as fact or opinion. Tell students that many people fear bats and don't realize their valuable role. Tell students that they will read a persuasive essay that explains why people should protect bats.

Introducing Vocabulary

Introduce key vocabulary words by writing these sentences on the board.

My dog can quickly **consume** a big bowl of food.

Pollinators, such as bees, pick up pollen and carry it from flower to flower as they feed on nectar.

A raccoon aids **seed dispersal** by carrying seeds stuck to its fur from place to place.

Ask a volunteer to read each sentence aloud. Ask students to explain the meaning of the boldfaced words.

Reading the Selection

- Have students read the introduction to "Bats." The purpose-setting question focuses on a characteristic of a persuasive essay, stating a goal.

Have students read the selection as a class, independently, or with partners, or they can listen to the selection on audiotape.

- The call outs highlight key characteristics of a persuasive essay that are addressed in the Think About the Persuasive Essay questions at the end of this selection.

MEETING INDIVIDUAL NEEDS — FOR STUDENTS ACQUIRING ENGLISH

Before reading the model, ask students to use a dictionary to define *persuasive* in their word logs. Then have them look at bats in photos. As a class, brainstorm phrases about bat behavior. List ideas on the board.

About the Author

INTERNET CONNECTION Send your students to www.eduplace.com/kids/ for information about Betsy Maestro.

Resources

Encourage students to look for examples of persuasion in their reading, such as one character trying to persuade another to do something. Provide opportunities for students to share some of their finds with the class.

A Published Model

Bats can live for 25 to 30 years. But many are eaten by natural enemies like owls, snakes, raccoons, and hawks. Spring floods can wash out caves and destroy whole colonies of bats. But the most harmful enemies of bats are human beings. Sadly, many bats are killed by humans, accidentally or on purpose.

The use of insecticides and poisons in the environment can also cause the death of many bats. Farmers kill bats for eating their fruit. However, bats only eat fruit that is too ripe to be sold. Cave explorers and vandals often disturb or destroy hibernating bats, resulting in the death of thousands of bats.

facts

Some people believe bats attack and bite humans. They also mistakenly think all bats carry the disease *rabies*. But bats are very gentle creatures that rarely bite except when caught and frightened. They don't carry rabies any more often than other mammals. Bats are helpful, not harmful.

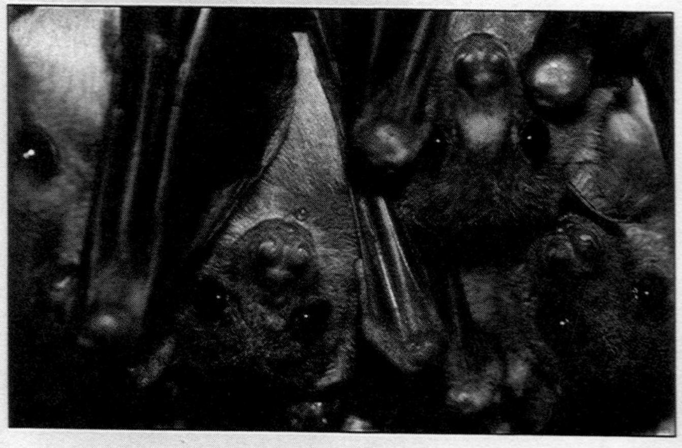

A Published Model

By protecting bats, people also help themselves. The Chinese have always believed that bats bring good luck. And they probably do. Places where bats live are usually healthy places where all life exists together in the right balance. Humans must learn to be kind to bats. They are nature's helpers and true friends of the earth.

Reading As a Writer See TE margin for answers.

Think About the Persuasive Essay

- What does the author want her audience to do?
- Look at the second paragraph on page 447. What reason does the author give to support her goal?
- Some people believe that bats harm humans. What facts does the author use to show that this isn't true?

Think About Writer's Craft

- In the second paragraph on page 447, the author compares bats to bees. In what ways does she think bats and bees are alike?

Think About the Pictures

- Look at the photos of bats on pages 447 and 448. Which photo gives you a closer view? What does the photo with the more distant view let you see that the close-up photo does not?

Responding Answers will vary.

Write responses to these questions.

- **Personal Response** What was your opinion of bats before you read this excerpt? after you read this excerpt?
- **Critical Thinking** Why might it be difficult to persuade people not to be afraid of bats?

A Published Model 449

Mapping the Selection

Mapping helps students isolate and analyze the elements of a persuasive essay. After students read "Bats," draw the map below on the board. Have students complete the map, adding circles as needed, to show the goal, reasons, and facts presented in the persuasive essay.

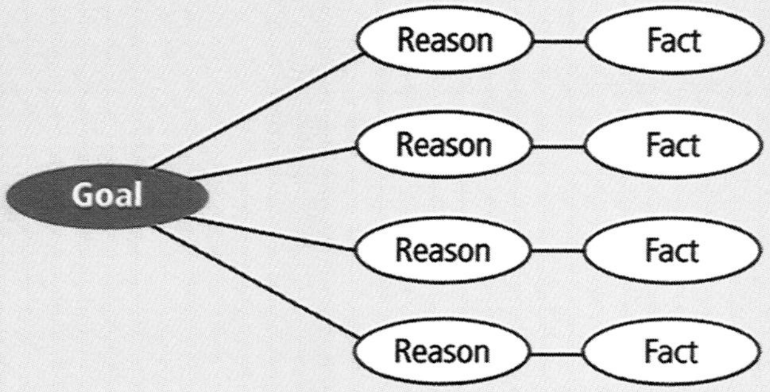

Answers to Reading As a Writer

Think About the Persuasive Essay

- The author wants the audience to protect bats.
- Bats pollinate flowers and spread seeds.
- Bats rarely bite except when caught and frightened. Bats carry rabies no more often than other mammals.

Think About Writer's Craft

- They pollinate flowers.

Think About the Pictures

- The photo on page 448 gives a closer view. The photo with the more distant view (page 447) lets you see the bat's wings. It allows you to see how large a bat's wingspan is in comparison to its body.

After students complete the questions, work with them to generate criteria for a persuasive essay, using the published model as a reference.

More About Writer's Craft

Draw students' attention to the use of *most harmful* in the third paragraph. If necessary, review Unit 4, Lesson 5, Comparing with *more* and *most.* Then ask what is being compared in the sentence. (humans and other enemies of bats) Discuss how the use of *most* clarifies that humans are bats' worst enemies. Tell students to use similar comparisons in their own writing to make it more precise.

Notes on Responding

Personal Response

Ask volunteers to share how the reading changed their opinion of bats and which reasons or facts persuaded them. Acknowledge that some students might still fear bats.

Critical Thinking

Have students tell which fears the author mentions in her essay. (that bats attack, bite, and carry rabies) Share a childhood fear, such as sleeping in the dark, or ask students to share one. Discuss the difficulty of dislodging long-held notions even when they have no basis in fact.

What Makes a Great Persuasive Essay?

Lesson Objective

Students will:
- discuss the characteristics of a well-written persuasive essay

Focus on Instruction

- Ask students to read aloud the definition and characteristics of a persuasive essay. Revisit "Bats," an example of a well-written persuasive essay, to see which characteristics it meets. (tells a goal, supports the goal with reasons and the reasons with facts, uses a strong voice, sums up goal and reasons)
- Have students read the Grammar Check. Explain that the Grammar Check reminds them that a great persuasive essay should also be grammatically correct. Tell students that when they proofread, they will be asked to check for correct use of possessives.

If this is students' first encounter with the cartoon dog, explain that this is Sal, the writer's pal, and that Sal will help them learn to write great persuasive essays.

Connecting to the Rubric

- These criteria are tied to the rubric on page 462.
- Explain to students that they will be writing their own persuasive essay and that they will learn how to include these characteristics. Students will use these characteristics as criteria to help them evaluate their papers.

This page is available as a poster.

Looking Ahead Tell students that they will next see how the characteristics listed on this page are applied in one student's working draft and final copy of a persuasive essay.

FOR STUDENTS ACQUIRING ENGLISH

Ask students what a persuasive essay might include. Students should be familiar enough with the writing process to list some characteristics of an essay. Have students compare their list with the one in the student book. Have students form pairs and turn back to "Bats" to illustrate each item from the rubric.

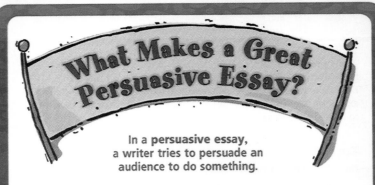

What Makes a Great Persuasive Essay?

In a **persuasive essay,** a writer tries to persuade an audience to do something.

Remember to follow these guidelines when you write a persuasive essay.

- Start by telling your goal. Your goal is what you want your audience to do.
- Write a paragraph for each reason. State the reason in a topic sentence.
- Give strong reasons that support your goal. Back up your reasons with facts and examples.
- Tell your reasons from most important to least important.
- Use a confident voice.
- Write an ending that sums up your goal and your reasons.

GRAMMAR CHECK

Add an apostrophe and s ('s) to a singular noun to make it possessive. When a plural noun ends in s, add an apostrophe (') to make it possessive.

WORKING DRAFT

Andrea Zawoyski wants a dog, and she has many good reasons why. She wrote this draft to persuade her parents to get her one.

Andrea Zawoyski

Working Draft

A Dog for a Pet

What is your goal?

A friendly puppy can make you as happy as a clam!

I could teach our dog to be a loyal watchdog. We worry so much about James wandering off. "Where's James?" someone asks a dozen times a day. Well, if we got a dog, that wouldn't be a worry for us any longer. A faithful dog would bark as loudly as an alarm if James walked out of our cozy, warm house. It would also bark if any strangers came to the door.

This reason supports your goal. Well done!

What facts and examples support this reason?

A dog would teach responsibility. That is one of the most important skills to learn.

A dog would be a fantastic furry friend. If you play with it as much as you can, it'll grow up to be a great loving dog. A puppy is like a pal. It would be fun to teach it new tricks too.

more

Student Model: Working Draft

Lesson Objectives

Students will:

- read a working draft of a student-written persuasive essay
- discuss the ways the model meets the criteria for a well-written persuasive essay and ways that it could be improved

Focus on the Model

- Tell students that they will read a working draft of a persuasive essay written by Andrea Zawoyski, a real student. Remind them that a working draft is a work in progress in which a writer puts ideas on paper, knowing that he or she will revise it later.
- Have volunteers read the model aloud.

  Alternatively, students can listen to it read by a student (although not the student writer) on audiotape.

- Reading the draft aloud gives students practice in listening and responding to a writer's work in progress and provides practice for peer conferences.
- This working draft does not include any usage, capitalization, or punctuation mistakes so that students can focus on the content of the piece.

- Tell students to think about whether or not Andrea included the important characteristics of a persuasive essay. Explain that the thought balloons show Sal's thoughts about the essay and that students will discuss his ideas after they read the model.

Answers to Reading As a Writer

- Sal asked what Andrea's goal is; if she has facts and examples to support one reason; whether a certain reason will convince her parents; and if Andrea could restate why she wants a dog so much. Andrea might state her goal clearly in the introduction; add support to the reason about learning responsibility; delete the reason about buying things; and sum up her reasons in the conclusion.
- This reason, buying things for the dog, might not be convincing; all the money Andrea's parents will have to spend is more of a reason *not* to get a dog.
- Answers will vary.

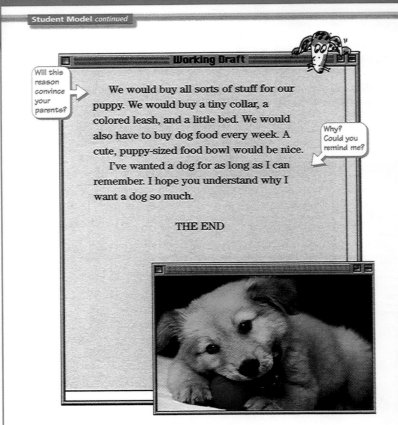

Working Draft

Will this reason convince your parents?

We would buy all sorts of stuff for our puppy. We would buy a tiny collar, a colored leash, and a little bed. We would also have to buy dog food every week. A cute, puppy-sized food bowl would be nice.

Why? Could you remind me?

I've wanted a dog for as long as I can remember. I hope you understand why I want a dog so much.

THE END

Reading As a Writer

See TE margin for answers.

- What questions did Sal ask? What revisions might Andrea make?
- Find the reason about buying things for the puppy. Why might this reason not be convincing to Andrea's parents?
- Think of some reasons for buying a dog that Andrea didn't use. Which of these reasons might help convince her parents?

FINAL COPY

Andrea revised her persuasive essay after discussing it with a classmate. Read her final version to see how she improved it.

My Furry Wish

by Andrea Zawoyski

Your opening states your goal clearly.

What do you think I've wanted for the longest time? I want a furry, friendly dog for a pet! Yes, I would love to get a small puppy.

Your reasons are clearly ordered.

My first reason for getting a dog is that I could teach it to be a loyal watchdog. We worry so much about James wandering off. "Where's James?" someone asks a dozen times a day. Well, if we got a dog, that wouldn't be a worry for us any longer. A faithful dog would bark as loudly as an alarm if James walked out of our cozy, warm house. It would also bark if any strangers came to the door.

You sound so confident!

My second reason is that a dog would teach responsibility. That is one of the most important skills to learn. James and I would be the ones feeding, bathing, and playing with it. We would brush it so its fur would be as soft as silky cotton. I wouldn't be able to walk it because I am not old enough, and it would probably pull me to Poland. However, I would be responsible for many other things.

You support this reason well now.

My final reason is that a puppy would be a fantastic furry friend. A friendly puppy can make you as happy as a clam! If you play with it as much as you can, it'll grow up to be a great loving dog.

more

Student Model: Final Copy

Lesson Objectives

Students will:

- read a well-written final copy of a student's persuasive essay
- note and compare the revisions that improved the first draft

Focus on the Model

SUMMARY OF REVISIONS In her final copy, Andrea changed her title; strengthened her opening goal statement; added facts and examples to support her reason about responsibility; deleted the original reason about buying things for the dog; and summarized her goal and reasons at the end. Blackline Master 13–1 provides a copy of the student's working draft, showing the revisions that were made.

Have volunteers read the model aloud. Alternatively, students can listen to it read by a student (although not the student writer) on audiotape.

Answers to Reading As a Writer

- She stated her goal clearly; she added facts and examples to support her reason about responsibility; she deleted her reason about buying things; she summed up her goal and her reasons at the end.
- Andrea and James would be the ones taking care of the dog: feeding, bathing, brushing, and playing with it.
- Because parents care a great deal about safety, the most convincing reason to Andrea's parents will be that a dog can be a good watchdog and protect the family.

More About Writer's Craft

- Point out the use of commas to set off items in a series in the third paragraph. Have a volunteer read the sentence aloud. Discuss how the commas tell the reader where to pause, making the meaning of the sentence clearer. Remind students to use commas to separate items in a series in their own writing.
- Direct students to look through the model to see how the student writer broke it into paragraphs. Point out that whenever a new reason is presented, a new paragraph begins. Discuss how this organization of paragraphs adds to the persuasiveness of the essay.

Connecting to the Rubric

- Have students look again at the list of characteristics on page 450 and review with them how Andrea's final copy addressed each one.
- Reinforce the Grammar Check by having students make sure that Andrea used possessives correctly.

INTERNET CONNECTION Send your students to www.eduplace.com/kids/hme/ to see more models of student writing. You can also find and print these models at www.eduplace.com/rdg/hme/.

Looking Ahead Tell students that they will next write their own persuasive essay, using the writing process. As they go along, they will learn how to support and evaluate their reasons, organize their essay, write a strong opening and closing, and write with a positive, confident voice.

MEETING INDIVIDUAL NEEDS

FOR STUDENTS ACQUIRING ENGLISH

Encourage students who are at the intermediate and advanced levels of English fluency to read the student models alone. As a class, summarize Andrea's ideas by outlining or clustering them. Then have students continue working alone or in pairs, identifying the parts of the second draft that illustrate the Persuasive Essay rubric. Finally, answer the questions together.

Student Model *continued*

You sum up your goal and reasons nicely.

A puppy is like a pal. It would be fun to teach it new tricks too.

I've wanted a dog for as long as I can remember. I hope you understand why I want a dog so much. Dogs are very lovable animals. They teach responsibility. They can become good watchdogs. I know as soon as we get one, you'll feel the same way I do!

Reading As a Writer

See TE margin for answers.

- How did Andrea respond to Sal's questions?
- What facts and examples did Andrea give to support her reason that a dog teaches responsibility?
- Which reason do you think will be most convincing to Andrea's parents? Why?

454 **Unit 13:** Persuasion

See www.eduplace.com/kids/hme/ for more examples of student writing.

Write a Persuasive Essay

Start Thinking

Make a writing folder for your persuasive essay. Copy the questions in bold print, and put the paper in your folder. Write your answers as you think about and choose your topic.

- **What is my purpose or goal?** What do I want to persuade someone to do? Why do I care about this?
- **Who is my audience?** Do I want to persuade my parents? my friends? the principal of my school?
- **How will I publish or share my essay?** Will I reach my audience through a newspaper editorial? in a flier? in a speech?

Stuck for an Idea?

Try these goal-starters.
- My school should have a ______.
- Our class should take a trip to ______.
- Everyone should learn to ______.

See page 467 for more ideas.

Choose a Goal

1. **List** five goals on a chart. Write what should be done (your goal) and who should do it (your audience). Part of Andrea's chart is shown below.

What Should Be Done?	Who Should Do It?
join the games club at school	my friends
get a dog	my parents

2. **Discuss** each goal with a partner. Is any goal too large? Can you write about only one part? What reasons will you use? Will these reasons convince your audience?
3. **Ask** yourself these questions about each goal. Then circle the goal you will write about.
   - Do I really care about this goal? Will it interest my audience?
   - Can I think of enough facts and examples to support my reasons?

Help with Choosing a Topic

TECH TIP
Refer students who are using a computer to page H39 to find ideas for using a computer during the writing process.

SCHOOL–HOME CONNECTION
Students can discuss their goal with family members who can help with reasons and facts to support the goal.

USING RESOURCES
Suggest that students look up letters to the editor in magazines or newspapers for ideas on how writers use persuasion based on the audience, purpose, or occasion.

SOURCES OF TOPIC IDEAS
Suggest these activities to prompt topic ideas.
- Students can think of a privilege they want and why they deserve it.
- They can think of a movie they like and why a friend should see it.
- They can think of a rule that they'd like to change and tell why that's fair.

EVALUATION TIP
Review students' final topic choices. If a topic is too broad, ask students to focus on a specific action they want the audience to take.

Write a Persuasive Essay

Lesson Objectives

Students will:
- list their ideas for audience, purpose, and publishing/sharing formats
- list ideas for a persuasive essay
- discuss their ideas with a partner
- choose an appropriate topic to write about

Start Thinking

Focus on Instruction

- Direct students' attention to the bulleted list. Tell them that good writers adapt the language in their writing to their purpose and audience. Ask students how a persuasive essay with a goal of staying up late would differ from one with a goal of buying a computer game. (An essay on buying a computer game might address financial considerations such as who would pay and how.)
- Ask students how writing the persuasive essay as a flier might differ from writing it as a letter to the editor. (The persuasive essay for the flier could include graphics. The persuasive essay for the newspaper editorial should be in a business letter format.)

Choose a Goal

Focus on Instruction

- Page 467 provides writing prompts that might suggest ideas.
- Explain that a persuasive essay need not be about a serious issue or a world problem. Tell students that people use persuasion everyday as they seek permission and try to convince others to do things.

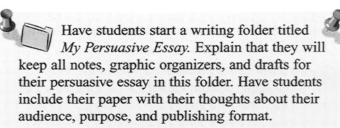

Have students start a writing folder titled *My Persuasive Essay.* Explain that they will keep all notes, graphic organizers, and drafts for their persuasive essay in this folder. Have students include their paper with their thoughts about their audience, purpose, and publishing format.

MEETING INDIVIDUAL NEEDS

FOR STUDENTS ACQUIRING ENGLISH

To help students generate ideas, ask them to list responses to these questions: *What's wrong in this school? What's wrong in this town? What's wrong in this country? What's wrong in this world?* Share ideas as a class, and then decide together which topics are too broad for this essay.

Lesson Objectives

Students will:

- identify the audience and the goal for a selected topic
- develop a persuasive strategy appropriate for the selected audience
- list reasons to support the goal

Explore Your Goal

Focus on Instruction

- See Blackline Master 13–2 for a graphic organizer that students can use to explore their topic.
- Review each student's goal statement. If students need help clarifying their goal, have them work with a partner to act out talking to their audience. As an alternative, students can use a planning chart similar to the one on page H51.
- Blackline Master 13–3 will help students as they imagine themselves talking to an audience in Step 2.
- Help students support their goal with strong reasons by asking questions such as these:

  Who will benefit from this request?

  What might your audience get if they do as you ask?

  How difficult or costly is it to grant your request?

  What are the consequences if your audience does not do as you ask?
- Discuss with students the note in the Help box. Explain that strong reasons make convincing essays. Tell students a goal may sound good at first but if they are unable to identify strong reasons that support it, they are better off choosing another goal rather than proceeding with one that isn't working. Support the student in choosing a new goal by reviewing the writing prompts on page 467 or suggesting activities in the Help with Choosing a Topic section on TE page 455.

INTERNET CONNECTION Send your students to www.eduplace.com/kids/hme/ for graphic organizers. You can also find and print these organizers at www.eduplace.com/rdg/hme/.

FOR STUDENTS ACQUIRING ENGLISH

Have students review their ideas orally before writing. They can share ideas in pairs; give them time to take notes in their conferences. Finally, model the webbing activity with a volunteer's notes. Remind students to think of their audience as they generate reasons.

Explore Your Goal

1. **Start** a web. Complete the sentence shown to tell your goal.

Goal: I want (name your audience) to (name your goal).

2. **Imagine** yourself talking to your audience.

3. **Add reasons** to your web. Each reason should explain why your audience should do what you want.

Stuck for a Reason?
If you can't think of at least three reasons, try another goal.

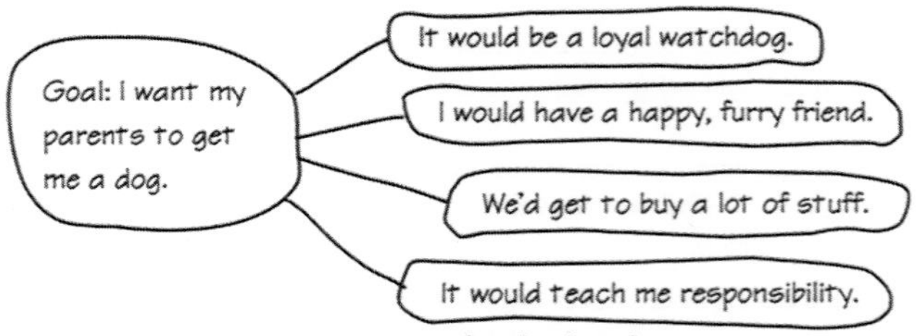

▲ Part of Andrea's web

See page 14 for other ideas about exploring your topic.

Go to www.eduplace.com/kids/hme/ for graphic organizers.

Help with Exploring Your Goal

TECH TIP
Have students use the numbering function when they compose their list of reasons at the computer. As they edit the list, the computer will automatically renumber the reasons.

MORE IDEAS FOR EXPLORING
Suggest these ideas to students as alternatives for exploring their goal.

- They can role-play the parts of the audience and the presenter. Have them take turns.
- They can make a chart. In one column have students write reasons. In a second column have them write responses from someone opposed to the goal. Students can strengthen their reasons or pick new ones to answer the responses.

Focus Skill

Supporting Your Reasons

Pillars are strong posts that hold up a building. Facts and examples are the pillars that support your reasons and your goal.

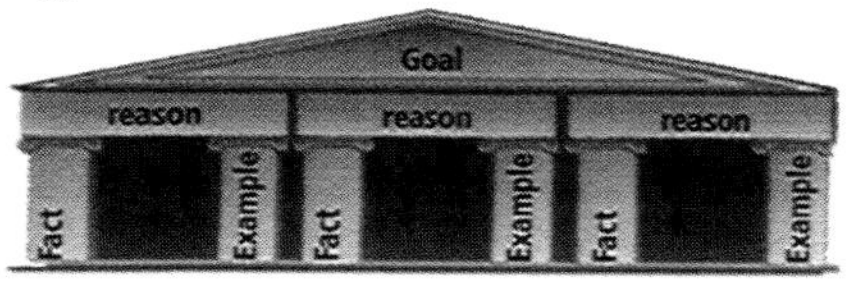

Elaborate reasons with facts and examples. Don't use opinions to support your reasons. An opinion tells feelings or thoughts. A fact can be proved. An example tells what has happened to you or someone you know.

Reason: *You should join the swim team because we have a good coach.*

Weak Support	Strong Support
Opinion: I think Coach Roth is the nicest guy!	**Fact:** For the last three years, Coach Roth's teams have all won the championships.
Opinion: I think Coach Roth is a good teacher.	**Example:** Coach Roth helped improve my backstroke by taking time to teach me after practice.

Think and Discuss Look at the published model on pages 447–449.

- Find three facts or examples that the writer uses to support her reasons.
  Sample answer: A single bat can eat 600 mosquitoes in an hour.

Explore Your Reasons

Add facts and examples to support each reason on your web.

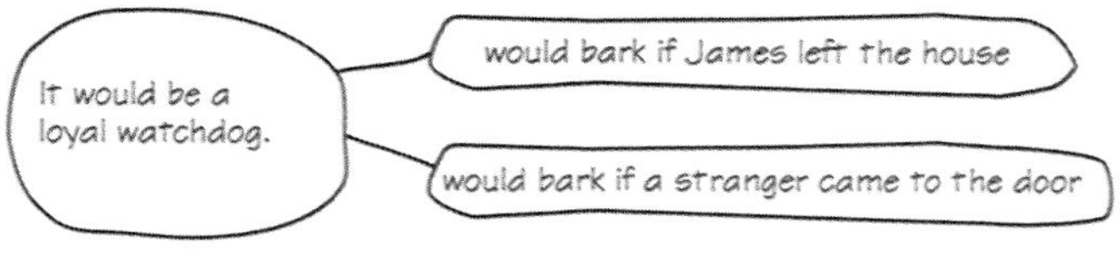

▲ Part of Andrea's web

Go to www.eduplace.com/kids/hme/ for graphic organizers.

Supporting Your Reasons

Lesson Objective

Students will:
- elaborate reasons and goals with facts and examples

Focus on Instruction

- Have students read the first paragraph and look at the illustration. Ask what might happen if the pillars were weak. (The building might collapse.) Explain that, likewise, without strong facts and examples, a persuasive essay falls apart.
- Write the following sentences on the board.

  My bike is too old.

  My bike is a hand-me-down from my older brother.

  Ask students to tell which statement is a fact. (the second) How can they tell it is a fact? (They could prove it right or wrong by asking a family member.)

Think and Discuss

- Tell students to locate facts and examples by finding the answers to questions such as *Where? How?* and *Why?*
- Sample answer: In these areas, over 300 kinds of trees and plants depend on fruit-eating bats for their survival.

Explore Your Reasons

Have students think of at least two facts and examples for each of the reasons on their web.

Meeting Individual Needs

FOR STUDENTS ACQUIRING ENGLISH

Turn back to the word log and review the definition of *fact.* Ask students to restate the definition of *opinion.* Then play a game in which you state a fact or opinion and students call out which it is. Then ask students to look at their webs and offer either a fact or an opinion that the class can identify.

Meeting Individual Needs

● RETEACHING WORKBOOK, page 109

Supporting Your Reasons

- Use facts and examples to support your goal and reasons. A **fact** can be proved. An **example** tells something that has happened to you or to someone else.
- Don't use opinions. They tell feelings and thoughts.

Reason: You should go to the circus because it has entertaining acts.

Weak Support	Strong Support
Opinion: I think the trapeze artists are very talented.	**Fact:** The trapeze artists flew through the air thirty feet overhead.
Opinion: I think the clowns are hilarious.	**Example:** I laughed hysterically when ten clowns piled into a tiny car.

Read the goal and reasons in the web below. Choose details from the box to complete the web.

Facts and Examples	
food wrappers against fence	would give school a pleasant appearance
lesson in planning	chance to work together
rusty cans in play area	would make playground a safe place

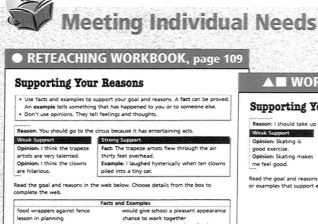

▲■ WORKBOOK PLUS, page 158

Supporting Your Reasons

Reason: I should take up ice skating because skating is good for my body.

Weak Support	Strong Support
Opinion: Skating is good exercise.	**Fact:** My doctor says the exercise I get while skating helps build strong muscles.
Opinion: Skating makes me feel good.	**Example:** I can feel my heart beating faster when I skate.

Read the goal and reasons in the web below. Write two facts or examples that support each reason.

Goal: You should hire me to feed your cat while you're away.
Reason: It would be convenient for you.
I live nearby.
I already know what your cat eats.
Reason: I am responsible.
I have several regular chores at home.
I run errands for my neighbor.
Reason: I am good with animals.
I'm teaching my dog to do tricks.
I play with my grandma's cat.

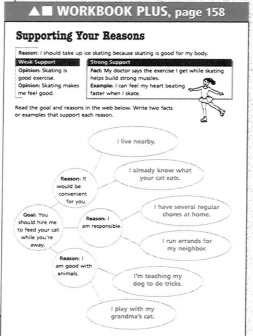

Evaluating Your Reasons

Lesson Objective

Students will:

- evaluate the audience appeal and credibility of the reasons in their persuasive essay

Focus on Instruction

- Tell students that an audience profile is a helpful tool that shows what is important to an audience. As a class, create an audience profile for teachers by listing and ranking things teachers care about. Then point out that the Reason for Teacher shown in the book addresses something teachers value most—helping students learn. Compare that reason to the one for classmates.
- Have students read the weak reason. Ask why it is unconvincing. (It is exaggerated. Learning everything about computers is impossible on one trip to a museum.) Then point out how the strong reason tells exactly what students will learn.

Try it Out

- Tell students to address the specific values and concerns of their own friends.
- Possible answers: You will have time for other activities including schoolwork, reading, or spending time with family and friends. You will have time to learn a new hobby or develop an interest you already have.

Explore Your Reasons

- Students may need additional help determining which reasons matter most to their audience. Have students create an audience profile for a partner's persuasive essay. Then have both partners evaluate audience appeal and support.
- For more ideas see Help with Exploring Your Goal on TE page 456.

FOR STUDENTS ACQUIRING ENGLISH

Before deciding which reasons are most convincing, students may have to get a clearer idea of their audience. Ask students to imagine their audience. Are the people patient and polite? Are they in a hurry? Using Andrea's essay or a volunteer's web, model a drawing of the audience described by students. (Use labels to describe some people.) Point out that details often turn weak reasons into strong ones.

The Writing Process: PREWRITING · DRAFTING · REVISING · PROOFREADING · PUBLISHING

Focus Skill

Evaluating Your Reasons

Be sure each reason is right for your audience. Different reasons work for different people. Think about what matters to your audience.

Goal: *Our class should take a trip to the computer museum.*

Reason for Teacher	Reason for Classmates
We will learn how new inventions can change our lives.	We will get to try new computer games.

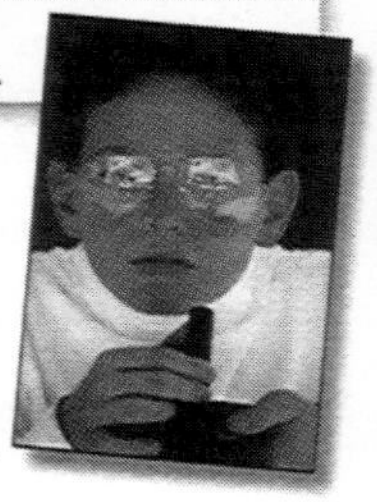

Check your support for each reason. Do not exaggerate. Choose reasons that you can explain simply and honestly.

Goal: *Our class should take a trip to the computer museum.*

Weak: Unconvincing Reason	Strong: Convincing Reason
We will learn everything about computers.	We will get an introduction to how computers work. We will learn how software programs are written.

Try It Out

- With a partner, think of two strong reasons to persuade your friends not to watch any television for a week. Answers will vary.

Explore Your Reasons

1. **Reread** your web. Which reasons will matter most to your audience? Which reasons are supported by the most facts and examples?
2. **Choose** your most convincing reasons. You need at least three. Star them.

458 **Unit 13:** Persuasion

Meeting Individual Needs

● RETEACHING WORKBOOK, page 110

Evaluating Your Reasons

- Check your reasons. Are they right for your audience? Different reasons work for different people.
- Check your support. Back up your reasons with facts and examples.

Goal: Our class should take a trip to the forest preserve.

Reason for Teacher	Reason for Classmates
We will learn about plant life in our area.	We will learn about nature and be outdoors at the same time.

Goal: My friend and I should study together.

Unconvincing Reason	Convincing Reason
We could help each other.	I'm good at math, and my friend is good at geography. We could coach each other.

Read each goal below and the reasons to support it. Cross out the reason that does not support the goal well or will not appeal to the audience. Then add one reason of your own that would appeal to the audience. Sample answers:

Goal: My father should redecorate my room.
Reason: The wallpaper is too childish.
Reason: ~~My room is smaller than my brother's.~~
Reason: My room is the only one that hasn't been redecorated.

Goal: My mother should order pizza on Fridays.
Reason: ~~I really like pizza.~~
Reason: No one would have to cook that night.
Reason: Friday night is "family night," and ordering pizza would make it extra special.

Goal: My teacher should change my seating assignment.
Reason: I can't see the board from where I sit.
Reason: ~~I would like to be able to look out the window.~~
Reason: The kids who sit near me are always talking.

▲■ WORKBOOK PLUS, page 159

Evaluating Your Reasons

Goal: My principal should have a career day at school.

Reason for Principal	Reason for Students
Inviting adults to tell about their jobs will get the community involved with the school.	We would learn about a variety of jobs and careers.

Goal: My sister should let me borrow her bike.

Unconvincing Reason	Convincing Reason
I can't ride my bike.	My bike has a flat tire. The bike shop is closed.

Cross out the reasons below that do not show strong support or would not matter to the audience. Then fill in the web.

Reasons	Facts or Examples
My skills have improved.	running; ball handling
I am a team player.	willing to pass; don't need to be the star
~~I enjoy sporting events.~~	soccer; baseball
The team needs another member.	Mia quit the team; Zoe hurt her leg.
~~My parents go to all the games.~~	bring snacks; cheer loudly

Goal: The coach should let me be on the team.
- Reason: My skills have improved.
  - running
  - ball handling
- Reason: I am a team player.
  - willing to pass
  - don't need to be the star
- Reason: The team needs another member.
  - Mia quit the team.
  - Zoe hurt her leg.

Focus Skill

Organizing Your Essay

Order your reasons from most important to least important. Tell your most convincing reason first. Tell your least convincing reason last.

Make each of your reasons a paragraph. The reason itself will be your topic sentence. The facts and examples will be the supporting details.

Keep to your topic. Leave out reasons that do not support your goal. Leave out facts and examples that do not support your reasons.

Use transitional words. Transitional words help your readers move smoothly from paragraph to paragraph. What other words can you add to this list?

First Reason	Second Reason	Third Reason
first, in the first place, my first reason	also, too, another, next, my second reason	in the third place, lastly, last of all, finally

Think and Discuss Look at Andrea's web below and her final copy on pages 453-454.

- Which reason does she tell first? Why? that they would have a watchdog; because this reason will be most convincing to her parents
- Which reason does she leave out of her final copy? Why? the one about all the things they would have to buy; because it will not help convince her parents

Plan Your Essay

Reread your web. Cross out reasons, facts, or examples that don't keep to your topic. Number your reasons from most to least convincing.

▲ Part of Andrea's web

Go to www.eduplace.com/kids/hme/ for graphic organizers.

Organizing Your Essay

Lesson Objectives

Students will:

- organize their persuasive essay reasons in order of importance
- evaluate the relevance of their persuasive essay reasons, facts, and examples

Focus on Instruction

- Ask students why the most important reason should be listed first when organizing information for a persuasive essay. (to immediately convince the audience)
- Refer students to their web. Tell students that it represents the structure for their paragraphs. Each box circling the center circle should be a new paragraph.
- Ask the question, "If the goal is to have a friend sleep at your house overnight, should you include facts about your friend's house?" (not unless this helps persuade your parents)
- Discuss the transitional words in the chart. Help students list other transitional words. (Sample answers: *for this reason, likewise, more importantly*)

Think and Discuss

If students need extra support, write on the board Andrea's reasons as shown on the web. Have volunteers number the reasons from most important to least important.

Plan Your Essay

If students are having difficulty ranking their reasons, tell them to identify the most convincing reason by finding the one that has the most support and will matter the most to the audience. Then they can give this reason first and give the other two in an order that makes sense.

INTERNET CONNECTION Send your students to www.eduplace.com/kids/hme/ for graphic organizers. You can also find and print these organizers at www.eduplace.com/rdg/hme/.

MEETING INDIVIDUAL NEEDS

FOR STUDENTS ACQUIRING ENGLISH

Write the words *Transitional Words and Phrases* on index cards and distribute them to students. Students write words for each category and then find or write sentences for the words they wrote. Before referring them to the student book, encourage students to write examples of weak and strong openings.

● RETEACHING WORKBOOK, page 111

Organizing Your Essay

- A well-organized essay tells your reasons from most important to least important.
- It keeps to the topic and uses transitional words and phrases, such as *my first reason, my second reason, next,* and *finally,* to help readers move smoothly from paragraph to paragraph.

The sentences below form a persuasive essay, but they are not in order. Cross out the two sentence groups that do not support the goal. Number the other sentences to show the order in which they would be written. The goal of the essay is numbered for you. Rewrite the essay in order on the lines below.

2 First, we could learn about our country's past. Books such as *Ben and Me* and *Johnny Tremain* would introduce us to life in early America.

___ ~~There are also interesting history shows on TV. You should watch them.~~

4 Finally, we could learn about everyday life of long ago. *All-of-a-Kind Family* tells about family life in New York during the same time period as *Dragonwings*.

5 Our school should order some of these books. We would enjoy going back in time.

___ ~~The public library has many history books. I like going there.~~

1 Our school library should have more books about history.

3 Also, we could learn how people in the past faced challenges. *Dragonwings* tells about the life of Chinese immigrants in San Francisco in the early 1900s.

▲■ WORKBOOK PLUS, page 160

Organizing Your Essay

Goal: Mom should let my friend Zach stay for dinner.
2 Also, you made a big pot of spaghetti, so there's plenty of food.
~~The spaghetti smells delicious.~~
1 In the first place, we all like Zach and enjoy his funny stories.
3 Finally, you know how much Zach loves your spaghetti.

Three reasons for a persuasive essay are underlined below. Cross out the facts or examples that do not support the reasons. Number each reason 1, 2, or 3 to show the order in which you would write about them. Then organize the reasons and the facts and examples in the web below. Numbering will vary.

Goal: I want to persuade my friends that school is a good place to be.		
Reason ____	Reason ____	Reason ____
School is a caring place.	We learn and do interesting things.	Our friends are there too.
Classmates made me get-well cards.	~~winter and spring vacations~~	play together during recess
Teacher gives me extra help	fascinating field trips	~~Martin is my friend.~~
~~I sit in the front of the room.~~	scientific experiments	eat lunch together

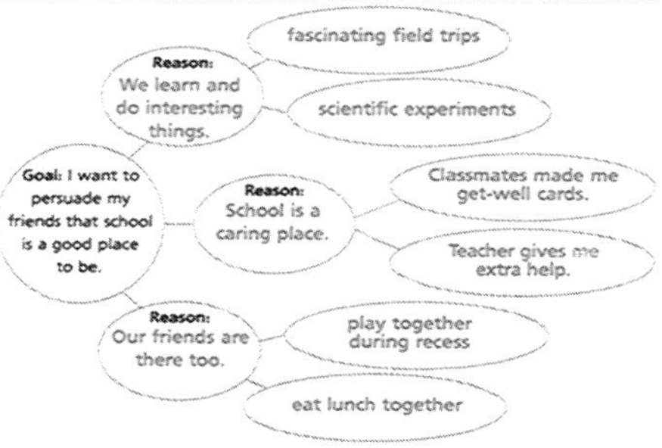

Openings and Closings

Lesson Objective

Students will:

- write a strong opening for their persuasive essay

Focus on Instruction

- Read the pair of weak and strong openings with students. Point out that the weak opening makes the reader ask, "What do you want me to do about it?" The strong opening states what the writer wants, making it easy for the reader to see the essay's direction.
- Read the pair of weak and strong closings with students. Point out that the weak closing introduces a new example—one that might have been useful earlier in the essay. However, the closing should have summarized and defined the next steps for the audience.

Try It Out

- Work as a class or have students work with partners to write a strong opening for the goal.
- Sample answers: What do you know about bicycle safety? How do you protect your bike from being stolen? We should have a bicycle safety class at school. All students would benefit from this type of class.

Draft Your Opening

- Explain that there are many effective ways to write a strong opening. Have students look at the example of a strong opening on this page. How does the writer grab our attention? (asks a question)
- Suggest that students write three different openings for their persuasive essay. Then have them choose the most effective one.

The Writing Process: PREWRITING | DRAFTING | REVISING | PROOFREADING | PUBLISHING

Focus Skill

Openings and Closings

Reasons, supported by facts and examples, are the meat of a good persuasive essay. The opening and closing are like the slices of bread that hold the whole sandwich together.

An opening clearly states your goal. Start by telling your audience exactly what you want them to do. You should also try to grab their attention.

Weak Opening	Strong Opening
Different flowers bloom at different times. This means you can plant a garden that will bloom and bloom. Wouldn't that be nice?	How often have you smiled at a flower? We should plant a flower garden at the senior center. All the blooms will make everyone smile.

A closing makes a call to action. Remind your audience of what you want. Sum up your reasons. Then get them excited about doing what you ask!

Weak Closing	Strong Closing
Once my friend was on his bike, and he didn't stop at a corner. He got hit by a car. Now do you see that we need a bicycle-safety class?	A bicycle-safety class will make biking safer, cut down on stolen bikes, and help us have more fun. This class is one more way school can make our lives better.

Try It Out See TE margin for sample answer.

- With a partner, reread the strong closing above. Then write a strong opening for an essay about having a bicycle class at school.

Draft Your Opening

Write an opening that states your goal. Use the goal statement from your web. Try to think of ways to make your audience interested in reading your essay.

Meeting Individual Needs

● RETEACHING WORKBOOK, page 112

Openings and Closings

- A strong opening clearly states your goal and grabs your audience's attention.
- A strong closing sums up your reasons and calls your audience to action.

Weak Opening	Strong Opening
People should not litter. It costs taxpayers lots of money to clean up litter.	Do you want to spend thousands of dollars a week to keep our city streets clean? We must put a stop to littering.

Weak Closing	Strong Closing
Pizza is good for you, and it also tastes great!	Eating pizza is a mouthwatering experience. Many of the ingredients are good for you too. I'd like to eat a piece right now! How about you?

Read each goal and the opening below it. Rewrite the opening so that it states the goal and makes your audience interested in your essay. Sample answers:

1. **Goal:** My father should let me take karate lessons.
   Opening: I think karate lessons would be fun.
   My Opening: Karate lessons would be an exciting adventure. I would have fun and learn new skills.
2. **Goal:** My friend should eat healthful foods.
   Opening: Eating healthful foods is good for you.
   My Opening: What are your favorite foods? Are they good for your body? It's important to eat the right foods if you want to stay healthy.
3. **Goal:** City officials should extend the hours for the swimming pool.
   Opening: The swimming pool should stay open later at night.
   My Opening: The swimming pool is my favorite spot in the summer, but it closes too early. Please keep it open longer and give families something to do together on warm summer nights.

▲■ WORKBOOK PLUS, page 161

Openings and Closings

Weak Opening	Strong Opening
The school band needs new uniforms. The present uniforms are old and shabby looking. We should raise money to buy new ones.	The school band sounds great. There's no reason why we can't look great too. We need new uniforms. Let's all pitch in and start that fundraising.

Weak Closing	Strong Closing
The band uniforms in this school need to be changed. It's embarrassing to wear them. We need to buy new ones.	Our band uniforms are old, faded, and in need of repair. Together we can do something about it. Let's organize and raise money to buy new uniforms!

Write two strong openings for persuasive essays about each goal below.
Sample openings:

Goal: My mother should let me have a birthday party next month.
Opening: Birthdays come but once a year. I would like to share my birthday with my friends. You should let me have a party.
Opening: ______

Goal: My friend should let me borrow her new T-shirt.
Opening: Wouldn't you like to be seen with a smartly dressed friend? I need something unique to wear to the play.
Opening: ______

Goal: My grandmother should let me visit her this summer.
Opening: Please let me visit you this summer. Remember the great time we had when I stayed with you last August? Let's do it again.
Opening: ______

Focus Skill

Writing with Voice

Writing with voice means writing so that your thoughts and feelings come through clearly. Your own voice can make your essay more persuasive.

Show that you care. Choose words and phrases that show your goal is important to you. Try to sound positive, however. Don't sound angry.

Weak: Negative Voice	Strong: Positive Voice
Some people are too careless to recycle. Haven't these lazy people heard that we're running out of places to put all our trash?	What if all our fields and forests became garbage dumps? Recycling can prevent such a sorrowful disaster.

Write with a confident tone. Say "Follow me!" to your audience. Use persuasive words such as *certainly, clearly, definitely, obviously,* and *really.*

Weak: Not Confident Voice	Strong: Confident Voice
Let's get a second computer, okay? Maybe that will mean fewer arguments about whose turn it is.	Obviously, a second computer means less time waiting. This will really help our whole family, and clearly it will mean fewer arguments.

Think and Discuss Compare the examples of weak and strong voices.

- What words and phrases make the writer sound angry in the example of negative voice? Sample answers: *too careless, lazy people*
- Find the persuasive words in the example of confident voice. *Obviously, really, clearly*

Draft Your Essay

1. **Write** the rest of your essay. Follow your web. Skip every other line.
2. **Write** a closing that sums up your goal and your reasons.
3. **Use** a confident voice.

Writing with Voice

Lesson Objective

Students will:

- draft the body and closing of their persuasive essay, writing with a confident voice

Focus on Instruction

- Ask a volunteer to complete this sentence: *Everyone should learn to ______.* Have volunteers speak in support of the goal. Point out that although each student supported the same goal, each student's words and tone made the speeches different. Explain that the same should be true of students' writing.
- Have students tell how they feel when they are accused of doing something wrong. Discuss the tendency for people to get defensive. Then read aloud the examples of negative and positive voice.
- Read aloud the examples of writing with strong and weak confidence. Point out that it is unlikely the audience could believe in a goal when it sounds as if the writer doesn't believe in it.

Think and Discuss

Have volunteers read the examples of strong and weak voice aloud to capture the expressiveness of the language. Then discuss the questions together as a class.

Draft Your Essay

- Share the following list of additional persuasive words with students: *absolutely, surely, greatly, highly, plainly, strongly.*
- Tell students that reading their own work aloud may help them hear how their writing will sound to others.

Drafting Reminders

- Reinforce the idea that if students change their mind while writing, they should cross out words or sentences they don't want rather than start over.
- Reassure students that they will have time to correct mistakes and check spelling later.

● RETEACHING WORKBOOK, page 113

Writing with Voice

Let your thoughts and feelings show to make your essay more persuasive.
- Use voice to show that you care about something.
- Be positive and confident.

Weak: Negative Voice	Strong: Positive Voice
Kids at our school have no manners. They push and shove. They yell in the lunchroom. It's embarrassing.	Our school has great kids. We just need to learn manners. Let's walk in the halls and be quiet in the lunchroom.

Weak: Not Confident Voice	Strong: Confident Voice
I think I should have a phone in my room. Then maybe I could talk to my friends without disturbing the family.	A phone in my room would certainly benefit the entire family. The house would definitely be quieter without me talking and disturbing everyone else.

The persuasive paragraph below sounds flat and dull. Put yourself in the writer's shoes and rewrite it so that your thoughts and feelings come through. Be positive and confident. Give reasons that show your goal is important to you. Be sure to write a closing that sums up your goal and your reasons.

I think we should have cake for dessert tonight, Mom. First, maybe I could do some of the work. Also, it's been kind of a long time since we had cake. Finally, you make pretty good cake. May we have cake for dessert tonight?

Essays will vary.

▲■ WORKBOOK PLUS, page 162

Writing with Voice

Weak: Negative Voice	Strong: Positive Voice
Our team is terrible! We haven't won a game this year. Without more practice sessions, I doubt if we ever will.	If we practice more and change our attitude, we'll get out of this slump. Our team is better than our record shows.

Weak: Not Confident Voice	Strong: Confident Voice
I think you should study more. Doing well in school is sort of important.	Success in school is a definite sign of how well you will do in the future. Clearly, studying prepares you for success.

The paragraph below isn't very persuasive. Rewrite the paragraph to give it a stronger voice. Show that your goal is important to you by adding words and phrases that persuade your reader. Then make sure you write a closing that sums up your goal and your reasons.

I think we should get a pet bird. First, a bird probably isn't hard to take care of. Second, a bird is quiet and would never bark at night. Finally, I think I'm old enough to take care of a pet. Most likely a bird would be the perfect pet.

Answers will vary.

Evaluating Your Persuasive Essay

Lesson Objective

Students will:
- evaluate their persuasive essay, using a rubric

Connecting to the Criteria

Have students reread the characteristics of a great persuasive essay listed on page 450. Then explain that the rubric shown on this page refers to those characteristics. Tell them that the rubric will help them decide which parts of their essay "ring the bell," or meet the standards of a great persuasive essay, and which parts still need more work or haven't been addressed at all.

Focus on Instruction

- Review the rubric with students. Have a volunteer read the first point in each section and explain the differences among them. Follow the same procedure for the remaining points.
- After students write their criteria, have them circle the ones that indicate aspects of their persuasive essays that need revision. Blackline Master 13–4 provides a copy of the rubric as a checklist.
- See the Teacher's Resource Book for scoring rubrics.

This page is also available as a poster.

INTERNET CONNECTION Have your students go to www.eduplace.com/kids/hme/ to use an interactive version of the rubric shown in the student book. Students will get feedback and support depending on how they mark the rubric items.

FOR STUDENTS ACQUIRING ENGLISH

Before students look at the rubric in the book, ask the class to generate lists of criteria for *Rings the Bell, Getting Stronger,* and *Try Harder.* Then compare the class lists to the student book rubric, adding items students may have omitted.

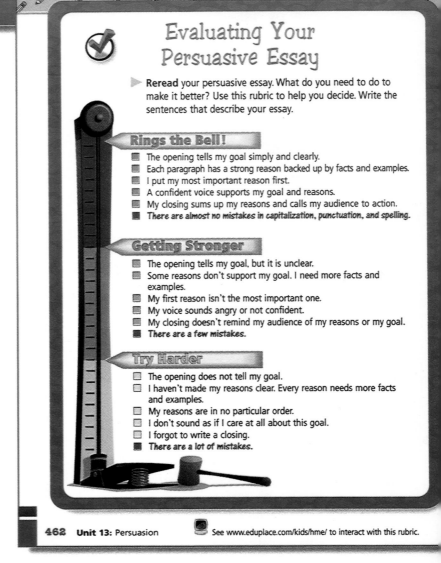

Evaluating Your Persuasive Essay

Reread your persuasive essay. What do you need to do to make it better? Use this rubric to help you decide. Write the sentences that describe your essay.

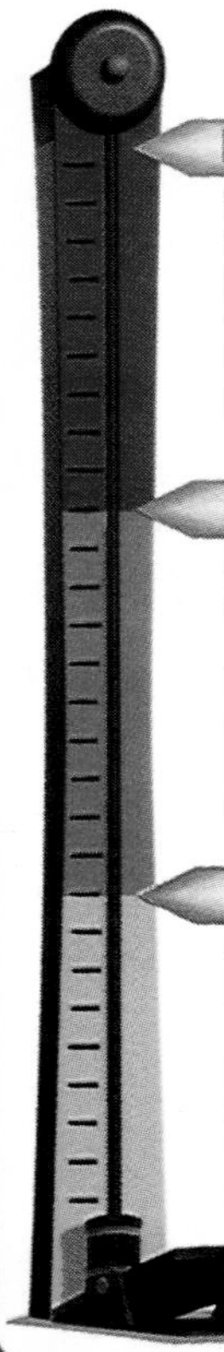

Rings the Bell!

- ☐ The opening tells my goal simply and clearly.
- ☐ Each paragraph has a strong reason backed up by facts and examples.
- ☐ I put my most important reason first.
- ☐ A confident voice supports my goal and reasons.
- ☐ My closing sums up my reasons and calls my audience to action.
- ☐ *There are almost no mistakes in capitalization, punctuation, and spelling.*

Getting Stronger

- ☐ The opening tells my goal, but it is unclear.
- ☐ Some reasons don't support my goal. I need more facts and examples.
- ☐ My first reason isn't the most important one.
- ☐ My voice sounds angry or not confident.
- ☐ My closing doesn't remind my audience of my reasons or my goal.
- ☐ *There are a few mistakes.*

Try Harder

- ☐ The opening does not tell my goal.
- ☐ I haven't made my reasons clear. Every reason needs more facts and examples.
- ☐ My reasons are in no particular order.
- ☐ I don't sound as if I care at all about this goal.
- ☐ I forgot to write a closing.
- ☐ *There are a lot of mistakes.*

462 **Unit 13:** Persuasion

See www.eduplace.com/kids/hme/ to interact with this rubric.

Meeting Individual Needs

● RETEACHING WORKBOOK, page 114

Revising a Persuasive Essay

Have I — yes
- made sure the goal is stated clearly? ☐
- given strong reasons to support the goal? ☐
- backed up the reasons with facts and examples? ☐
- made sure the reasons stick to the topic? ☐
- added a strong, positive voice? ☐
- summed up the goals and reasons? ☐

Make the following persuasive essay better. Use the checklist above to help you. Check off each box when you have finished your revision. Use the spaces above the lines, on the sides, and below the paragraph for your changes. Sample answers:

I Need Cash
~~A Bigger Allowance~~

[It's time for] ~~I think~~ my parents [to] ~~should~~ increase my allowance. In the first place, I have more responsibilities around the house[, like cleaning my room and clearing the table]. I think I should be compensated for them. I also buy more of my own personal things now that I'm older. ~~I don't waste money on unnecessary things.~~ [I buy notebooks at the school supply store and snacks after school.] Finally, with a bigger allowance, I could be required to pay for my ~~entertainment~~ [movies and videos], too. That would help me learn to budget my money. ~~For all these reasons, I should get~~ [I'm a responsible person. I know I could handle] a bigger allowance.

▲■ WORKBOOK PLUS, page 163

Revising a Persuasive Essay

Have I — yes
- made sure the goal is stated clearly? ☐
- given strong reasons to support the goal? ☐
- backed up the reasons with facts and examples? ☐
- made sure the reasons stick to the topic? ☐
- added a strong, positive voice? ☐
- summed up the goals and reasons? ☐

Revise the following persuasive essay to make it better. Use the checklist above to help you. Check off each box when you have finished your revision. You can use the spaces above the lines, on the sides, and below the paragraph for your changes. Sample answers:

Let's Recycle
~~Recycling Is Important~~

[Attention, classmates!] ~~I think~~ our school should begin a recycling program. First of all, recycling would reduce the amount of trash. Lots of [cans, paper, and plastic are] ~~trash is~~ thrown away every day. Landfills are getting full[. Where will all the trash go?] ~~We have garbage pick-up twice a week.~~ In addition, recycling at school would foster good habits. We would think twice before throwing things away. Finally, our school could earn some money. Some companies pay for things [like newspapers and aluminum cans.] ~~that can be recycled. A recycling program would~~ [Let's] help the environment [by recycling] and our school. [We could use the money for new playground equipment or a new computer for the library.]

Revise Your Persuasive Essay

Revising Tip
If you reorder your reasons, don't forget to change the transition words also.

1. **Revise** your essay. Use the list of sentences you wrote from the rubric. Work on the parts that you described with sentences from "Getting Stronger" and "Try Harder."

2. **Have a writing conference.**

When You're the Writer Read your essay aloud to a partner. Ask questions about any problems you are having. Take notes to remember what your partner says.

When You're the Listener Say at least two things you like about the essay. Ask questions about parts that are unclear. Use the chart for help.

The Writing Conference

If you're thinking . . .	**You could say. . .**
The opening could be more interesting.	**Could you start with a personal experience or a question to get your audience's attention?**
I don't understand the goal.	**What do you want your audience to do?**
Why should I do that?	**Can you give me some more reasons to support your goal?**
This reason is not very convincing.	**You explained most of your reasons clearly. Can you elaborate this one with facts and examples?**
I'm confused. The reasons flow together.	**Is each reason a separate paragraph? Can you add transition words?**
The writer sounds uncertain.	**Where can you use persuasive words?**

3. **Make more revisions** to your persuasive essay. Use your conference notes and the Revising Strategies on the next page.

Lesson Objectives

Students will:
- revise their working draft, based on their evaluation
- discuss their working draft in a writing conference

Revise Your Persuasive Essay

Focus on Instruction

Revising Reminder

Remind students that revising focuses on making their essay clearer and more interesting. Students should not worry about mistakes at this stage. If necessary, review the revising techniques on page 20.

- Direct students' attention to the Revising Tip. Remind students to also check that their transitional words help the paragraphs flow easily and logically.
- Tell students to underline once the reason in each paragraph. They should underline twice any facts or examples that support their reasons.
- Remind students to use the comparative and superlative forms of adjectives, when appropriate, to enhance their writing.

Conferencing Reminder

Remind students to read their paper aloud to their partner. Remind them to read slowly, clearly, and at an appropriate volume for their audience and setting.

- To reinforce giving the writer a compliment, present these examples.

  Your reasons make a lot of sense.
  I like the way you back up your reason.

- Tell students to listen carefully when they are the listeners to distinguish fact from opinion.
- Students can use Blackline Master 13–5 during their writing conference.

MEETING INDIVIDUAL NEEDS

FOR STUDENTS ACQUIRING ENGLISH

As a class, review conference behavior. (eyes on the reader, ask helpful questions, listen) Before looking at the text, students should generate a list of possible problem areas and helpful questions. Then ask them to compare their list to the one in the book and to add anything they omitted. Encourage students to read their essays to a partner.

Help with Conferencing

ADDITIONAL CONFERENCING QUESTIONS

These questions may be useful during teacher-student conferences.
- How many _______ does this affect?
- Where is this a problem?
- How long has this been going on?
- What caused _______ to happen?
- What will happen if we _______?
- What will happen if we don't _______?

EVALUATION TIP

Listen as students conference to see if they ask appropriate questions. If not, have them stop the conference and reread Sal's comments about Andrea's essay on page 451. Tell them to write down compliments and questions, using Sal's comments as a model. Then have them continue the conference.

Revising Strategies

Lesson Objectives

Students will:

- replace inaccurate words with correct ones
- add details to elaborate their essay
- correct incomplete sentences in their essay

Focus on Instruction

Elaborating: Word Choice

Have students identify the word that was replaced in the example. *(smashed)* Discuss how the replacement changed the meaning of the sentence. Tell students that although both *smashed* and *bumped* are used to mean "hit," the implied force of the hit differs, so the words are not necessarily interchangeable.

Elaborating: Details

Have volunteers read aloud both examples. Then discuss how they differ. (The first example doesn't create a strong picture or feeling for the reader. The second example provides a picture of the bike owner's behavior and insight into his or her feelings.)

Sentence Fluency

- Look at the first example. Ask a volunteer to tell why the first statement is a sentence. (It expresses a complete thought.) Point out that the second statement answers the question *Why?* but is not a complete thought.
- Look at the second example. Discuss how the phrase beginning with *because* has been combined with another complete sentence so that the entire statement expresses a complete thought. Discuss with students the use of complex sentences, such as the one used in the complete sentence example, to support a writer's purpose by showing a cause-effect relationship.
- Remind students to break their essay into paragraphs for each new reason.

FOR STUDENTS ACQUIRING ENGLISH

In addition to elaborating word choice, focus on overused phrases such as *I like* or *I love*. Give a mini-lesson on using a thesaurus by asking the students to find alternatives for the words *like* and *love*. Encourage students to identify their own overused words and replace them with stronger ones.

Revising Strategies

Elaborating: Word Choice Choose words that support your goal and reasons. A word that is right for one goal can be wrong for another.

Wrong Word	Right Word
Your store should replace my computer monitor. It cracked when I **smashed** it against a table.	Your store should replace my computer monitor. It cracked when I bumped it against a table.

▶ Find at least two places in your essay where you can use a better word to support your goal and reasons.

Use the Thesaurus Plus on page H79. See also page H13.

Elaborating: Details Make your facts and examples come alive for your audience. Use vivid, descriptive details.

Few Details	Elaborated with Details
We can prevent kids from getting their bikes stolen.	We can prevent the awful experience of finding only an empty hole in the bicycle rack.

▶ Find at least two places in your essay where you can add vivid details.

Sentence Fluency Be sure every sentence tells a complete thought. Watch out for phrases, or groups of words, beginning with *because* or *since*.

Not a Complete Sentence	Complete Sentence
We should plant a garden at the senior center. Because this would help us get to know senior citizens.	We should plant a garden at the senior center because this would help us get to know senior citizens.

Find and fix any incomplete sentences in your essay.

GRAMMAR LINK *See page 34.*

Meeting Individual Needs

● RETEACHING WORKBOOK, page 115

Elaborating: Details

Use vivid details to describe your facts and examples.	
Few details	Our class should visit the county fair.
Elaborated with details	The amusement rides, the farm animals, and the delicious food would make a visit to the fair a fun-filled learning experience!

The persuasive paragraph below is boring because it doesn't contain enough details. Revise each reason by adding facts and examples. Use the picture to help you. Answers will vary.

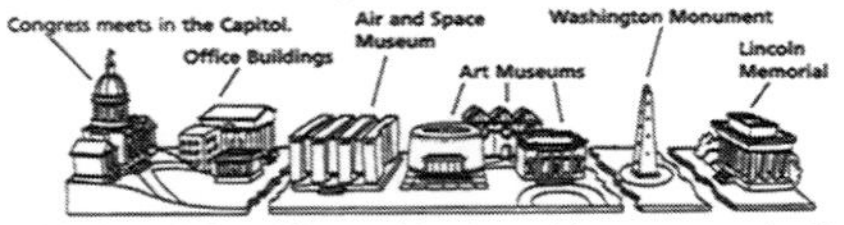

Washington, D.C., would be an exciting place to visit on our next vacation. First, there are government buildings to see. In addition, it is the site of many historic monuments. There are also interesting things to see in the city's museums. Finally, we might see some important people.

1. First, there are government buildings to see.
2. In addition, it is the site of many historic monuments.
3. There are also interesting things to see in the city's museums.
4. Finally, we might see some important people.

▲■ WORKBOOK PLUS, page 164

Elaborating: Details

Few details	We can prevent injuries from skateboard accidents.
Elaborated with details	We can prevent ninety percent of the injuries from skateboard accidents by wearing safety helmets and knee and elbow pads.

Revise the persuasive writing below by adding vivid, descriptive details to make it more interesting.

My mom should let me do odd jobs for the neighbors. Most important, I could use the money to buy some things that I want. It would also save my mom money. Finally, it would keep me from being bored. Extra cash, savings for Mom, and something interesting for me to do are all good reasons for me to do odd jobs. Let the job hunt begin!

Answers will vary.

Proofread Your Persuasive Essay

Proofread your essay, using the Proofreading Checklist and the Grammar and Spelling Connections. Proofread for one skill at a time. Use a class dictionary to check spellings.

Proofreading Checklist

Did I
- ✓ indent all paragraphs?
- ✓ use complete sentences?
- ✓ use correct adverb forms?
- ✓ use apostrophes correctly?
- ✓ correct any spelling errors?

Use the Guide to Capitalization, Punctuation, and Usage on page H55.

Proofreading Marks

¶	Indent
∧	Add
⌐	Delete
≡	Capital letter
/	Small letter

Tech Tip Use the Find function to locate words you may have overused, such as *really* or *very*.

Grammar and Spelling Connections

Adverbs Add *-er* to short adverbs to compare two actions. Add *-est* to short adverbs to compare three or more actions.

Juan ran faster than Charles. Of all the runners, Juan ran fastest.

GRAMMAR LINK *See also page 238.*

Possessive Nouns Add an apostrophe and *s* ('s) to a singular noun to make it possessive. When a plural noun ends with *s*, add an apostrophe (') to make it possessive.

the student's speech   the students' speeches

GRAMMAR LINK *See also pages 76 and 78.*

Spelling |ôr| The |ôr| sounds are often spelled *or, ore,* or *oar.*

horse, more, soar

See the Spelling Guide on page H65.

Go to www.eduplace.com/kids/hme for proofreading practice.

Help with Proofreading

EVALUATION TIP

Observe students' use of proofreading marks. If students are spending too much time determining which marks to use, have them write the marks on a note card for reference as they work.

TECH TIP

Encourage students to determine if they find a printout easier to proofread than text on a computer screen.

MANAGEMENT TIP

Have each student keep a personal checklist of skills that he or she needs to proofread for. Staple that list to the student's folder.

Lesson Objective

Students will:
- proofread their persuasive essay

Proofread Your Persuasive Essay

Focus on Instruction

Proofreading Reminders

- Remind students that the proofreading stage is the time to correct capitalization, usage, punctuation, and spelling. Encourage students to use the Guide to Capitalization, Punctuation, and Usage.
- If necessary, review with students when and how to use each proofreading mark. Have students use a different colored pen or pencil to mark their proofreading corrections.
- For proofreading practice, see the usage and mechanics lessons in the grammar units and the Mixed Review practice in each grammar unit Checkup.

- Review and clarify each item in the checklist, using any related Grammar and Spelling Connections. If students need extra support, review the lessons listed in the Grammar Links.
- Write the following sentences on the board. Then have students select the correct adverb and tell the rule.

  Mandy jumped higher/highest *(higher)* than Luis.

  Of all the runners, Daryl ran more swiftly/most swiftly. *(most swiftly)*
- After reviewing the rule for possessive nouns, write the following words on the board: *dog, baby,* and *girl.* Then have volunteers write the singular possessive and plural possessive for each noun.

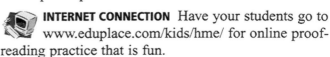

INTERNET CONNECTION Have your students go to www.eduplace.com/kids/hme/ for online proofreading practice that is fun.

FOR STUDENTS ACQUIRING ENGLISH

Run-ons and fragments are often a challenge for students. Review the use of contractions by taking run-ons from student drafts and correcting them on the board. Also, find fragments in their drafts and correct them in the same way, asking "Who?" or "What?" for phrases that are missing subjects and "Did what?" for phrases that lack verbs.

Lesson Objectives

Students will:

- make a neat final copy of their persuasive essay
- choose a way to publish or share their essay
- reflect on their writing experience
- evaluate their essay in comparison to other compositions in their writing portfolio

Publish Your Persuasive Essay

Focus on Instruction

- Before students make their final copy, have them decide how they will publish or share their essay. Review their decisions with them to help them make any special plans.
- Help students make neat corrections to their final copy rather than rewrite their paper.

Keeping a Writing Portfolio

- **Selection** A paper might be selected because it is
  - ✓ generally noteworthy
  - ✓ a good example of a particular criterion
  - ✓ an example of a particular kind of writing
  - ✓ an example from a certain time in the school year
  - ✓ a typical example of the student's work
- **Labeling** For every paper, have students complete a cover sheet giving the title, date of completion, and reason for inclusion.
- **Review** Periodically have students remove papers that no longer reflect their best work or aren't needed as baselines.
- **Evaluation** Periodically review students' portfolios with them to discuss growth and areas that need improvement.

Publish Your Persuasive Essay

1. **Make a neat final copy** of your essay. Be sure you fixed all mistakes.
2. **Title** your essay. Choose an attention-grabbing title, such as "Send Your Dog to College" rather than "Obedience School."

GRAMMAR TIP *Capitalize the first, the last, and each important word in a title.*

3. **Publish** or share your essay in a way that fits both your goal and your audience. See the Ideas for Sharing box.

Tips for Giving a Speech

- Practice your speech beforehand.
- Speak with expression. Use a persuasive tone.
- Use your face and hands to express your feelings.
- Speak loudly and slowly enough for your audience to hear and understand you.

See page H5 for more tips.

Ideas for Sharing

Write It
- Post your essay on your school's Internet site.

Say It
- Present your essay as a speech.

Show It
- Make a flier and pass out copies. Include pictures that illustrate your reasons.

Reflect

Write about your writing experience. Use these questions to get started.

- What have you learned about writing persuasively?
- What was most difficult about writing a persuasive essay? What was easiest?
- How does this paper compare with other papers you have written?

Help with Publishing

TIPS FOR IDEAS FOR SHARING

Internet Site Have students include links to Internet sites that support their opinion.

Flier Have students pick a flier style, such as trifold or bifold. Tell them to adjust the margins of their final copy to match the flier layout.

TECH TIP

Have students use an available flier template from their word processing or publication software. If possible, have students insert clip art or scan photos into their fliers.

SCHOOL-HOME CONNECTION

Students who publish their final composition in the form of a flier can share it with family members by taping it to the refrigerator for everyone to read, or students can mail a flier to each family member.

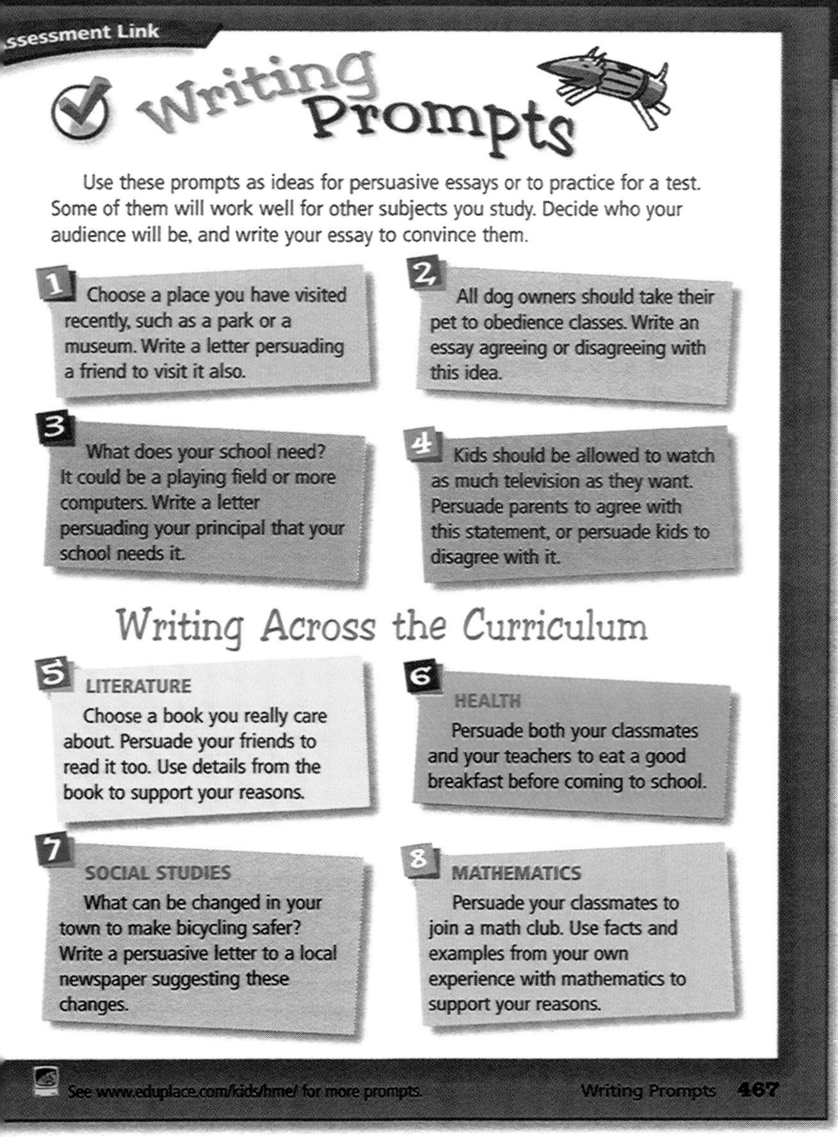
Assessment Link

Writing Prompts

Use these prompts as ideas for persuasive essays or to practice for a test. Some of them will work well for other subjects you study. Decide who your audience will be, and write your essay to convince them.

1 Choose a place you have visited recently, such as a park or a museum. Write a letter persuading a friend to visit it also.

2 All dog owners should take their pet to obedience classes. Write an essay agreeing or disagreeing with this idea.

3 What does your school need? It could be a playing field or more computers. Write a letter persuading your principal that your school needs it.

4 Kids should be allowed to watch as much television as they want. Persuade parents to agree with this statement, or persuade kids to disagree with it.

Writing Across the Curriculum

5 LITERATURE
Choose a book you really care about. Persuade your friends to read it too. Use details from the book to support your reasons.

6 HEALTH
Persuade both your classmates and your teachers to eat a good breakfast before coming to school.

7 SOCIAL STUDIES
What can be changed in your town to make bicycling safer? Write a persuasive letter to a local newspaper suggesting these changes.

8 MATHEMATICS
Persuade your classmates to join a math club. Use facts and examples from your own experience with mathematics to support your reasons.

See www.eduplace.com/kids/hme/ for more prompts. Writing Prompts 467

Writing Prompts

Objective

Students will:

- review prompts for choosing a topic or to practice for a writing test

Using the Prompts

You can use the prompts on this page in several ways.

- Have students review the prompts to help spark ideas when they are choosing their own topics for a persuasive essay. Suggest that students choose one or two prompts and brainstorm ideas of their own.
- Choose a prompt to provide practice for a writing test. Use it with the Test Practice on the next page.
- Choose a prompt that fits with a related topic in another subject area to integrate persuasive writing across the curriculum.

INTERNET CONNECTION Send your students to www.eduplace.com/kids/hme/ for more writing prompts. You can also find and print these prompts at www.eduplace.com/rdg/hme/.

FOR STUDENTS ACQUIRING ENGLISH

Useful topics with students acquiring English are: What does the United States need in order to be a better place for immigrants? What should the city or town do to help new families? What should the school do to help new students? What is the best sport to play?

Test Practice

Objective

Students will:

- learn strategies for evaluating a writing prompt and writing a persuasive essay for a test

Using the Test Practice

- Read through the page with students, discussing the strategies for identifying clue words, choosing a relevant topic, and planning the essay.
- Review the rubric on page 462 with students before they write their practice test.
- Have students write a persuasive essay in response to the prompt on this page or to one of the prompts on the previous page. Impose the time limitations or other restrictions or qualifications specific to the testing requirements used in your school.

INTERNET CONNECTION Send your students to www.eduplace.com/kids/hme/ for graphic organizers. You can also find and print these organizers at www.eduplace.com/rdg/hme/.

INTERNET CONNECTION Send your students to www.eduplace.com/rdg/hme/ for examples of benchmark papers.

FOR STUDENTS ACQUIRING ENGLISH

After reading the prompt, ask the class to list the steps and rubric that they will use for this essay. Also, requiring that these letters actually be given to the principal may promote better writing and make for a fulfilling publishing experience. Write a cover letter to the principal explaining the exercise.

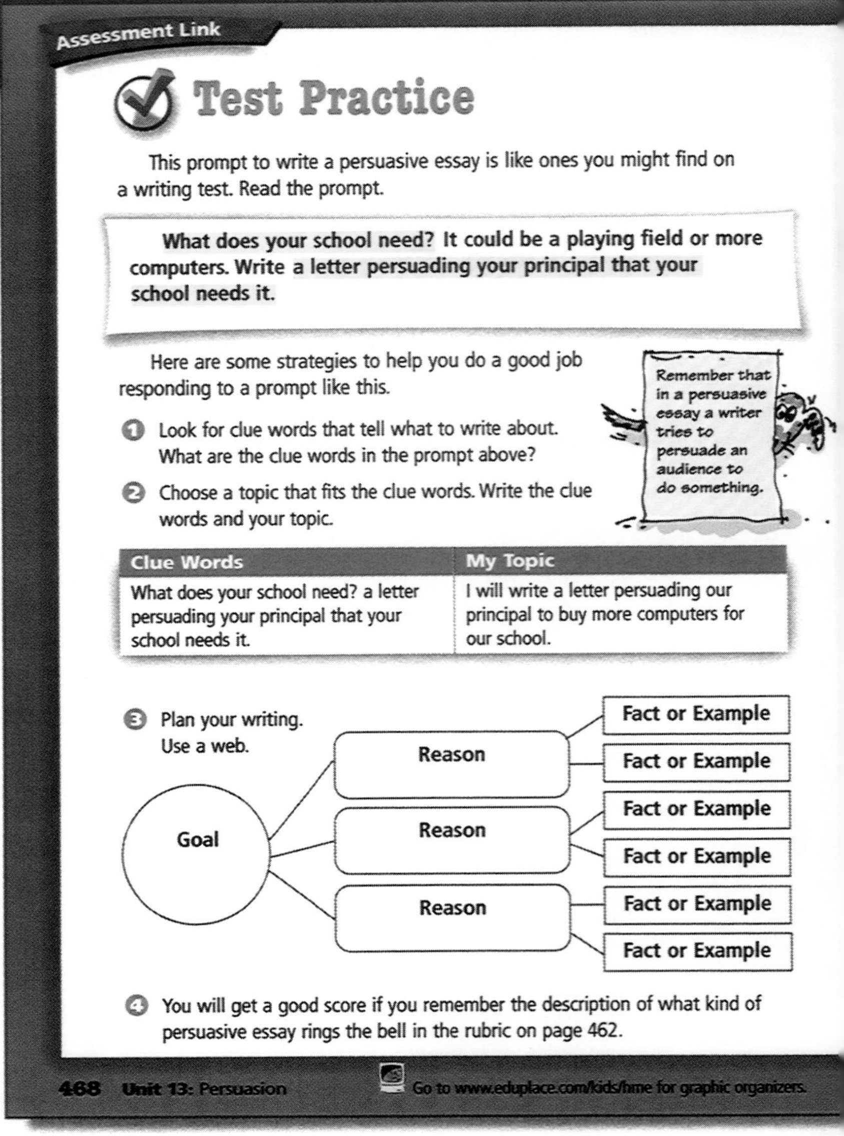
Assessment Link

Test Practice

This prompt to write a persuasive essay is like ones you might find on a writing test. Read the prompt.

What does your school need? It could be a playing field or more computers. Write a letter persuading your principal that your school needs it.

Here are some strategies to help you do a good job responding to a prompt like this.

Remember that in a persuasive essay a writer tries to persuade an audience to do something.

1. Look for clue words that tell what to write about. What are the clue words in the prompt above?
2. Choose a topic that fits the clue words. Write the clue words and your topic.

Clue Words	My Topic
What does your school need? a letter persuading your principal that your school needs it.	I will write a letter persuading our principal to buy more computers for our school.

3. Plan your writing. Use a web.

4. You will get a good score if you remember the description of what kind of persuasive essay rings the bell in the rubric on page 462.

468 Unit 13: Persuasion — Go to www.eduplace.com/kids/hme for graphic organizers.

Writing a Business Letter

A **business letter** is usually written to someone you do not know. It may ask for information, order a product, give an opinion, or persuade someone to do something. Read Wesley's business letter.

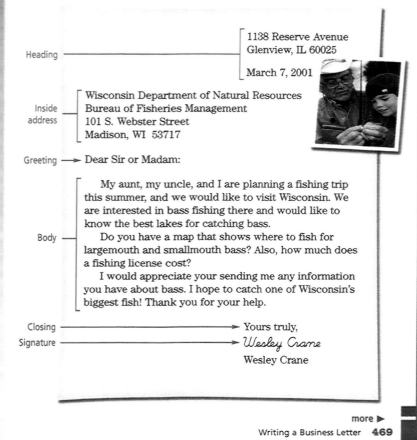

Heading — 1138 Reserve Avenue
Glenview, IL 60025

March 7, 2001

Inside address — Wisconsin Department of Natural Resources
Bureau of Fisheries Management
101 S. Webster Street
Madison, WI 53717

Greeting → Dear Sir or Madam:

Body —
My aunt, my uncle, and I are planning a fishing trip this summer, and we would like to visit Wisconsin. We are interested in bass fishing there and would like to know the best lakes for catching bass.

Do you have a map that shows where to fish for largemouth and smallmouth bass? Also, how much does a fishing license cost?

I would appreciate your sending me any information you have about bass. I hope to catch one of Wisconsin's biggest fish! Thank you for your help.

Closing → Yours truly,

Signature → *Wesley Crane*

Wesley Crane

more ▶

Help with Writing a Business Letter

USING RESOURCES

Show students examples of business letters, such as a letter to the editor or a job application letter, that they can use as models as they write, revise, and edit their own writing.

COLLABORATIVE WRITING

Have groups of students select a change that they would like to see in school policy. Then have them gather and organize information to help them compose a business letter to the appropriate school officials that persuades them to make the change. Have groups discuss their letter with other groups, revise the letter, and then send it.

Writing a Business Letter

Lesson Objective

Students will:

- read a model of a business letter and identify its parts

Focus on the Model

- Ask students why people write business letters. (to request information, order a product, share an opinion, or persuade someone to do something) Point out that business letters attempt to influence someone to take some form of action by providing strong reasons that are backed up by facts.
- Tell students they will read a business letter written by a student named Wesley to request information about fishing. Have students read the introduction to the letter.
- Before students read the letter, explain that the blue call outs highlight the six parts of a business letter and that students will learn about those six parts after they read the letter.
- Ask volunteers to read the letter aloud. Have students listen for the specific information the writer requests.

Students can also listen to the model on audiotape.

Focus on Instruction

- Discuss with the class the explanations of the call outs given in the Reading As a Writer section on page 470.
- Point out that *Dear Sir or Madam* is a common formal greeting for a business letter when the sender does not know the name of the recipient.
- Explain that the body of a letter should be brief and give all the necessary details in polite but formal language.
- Point out the typed name under the signature. Explain to students that a business letter always contains both.
- Have volunteers answer the questions on the next page.

Answers to Reading As a Writer

- The date follows the sender's address.
- The Wisconsin Department of Natural Resources is in Madison.
- Wesley probably didn't know the name of the person to whom he was writing.
- Wesley requested information on where to go bass fishing.
- Wesley used the closing *Yours truly*.
- His full name is Wesley Crane.

Lesson Objective

Students will:

- write a business letter and address an envelope correctly

How to Write a Business Letter

Focus on Instruction

- Ask students to name some reasons for writing a business letter and to whom they might write. Tell students that regardless of the purpose or audience, they should always be brief and give all the necessary details in polite but formal language.
- Have students discuss the purpose of their letter with a partner or small group before they write. Groups can help individuals identify the information that should be included in their letter.
- Emphasize the importance of proofreading a letter before it is sent because the letter may affect the recipient's opinion of the writer. Mistakes may indicate a lack of consideration for the reader. Students should check their final copy before sending it.
- Review with students the Proofreading Checklist on page 465 and the use of proofreading marks.

Connecting to the Criteria

Have students refer to the characteristics of a business letter described in the Reading As a Writer section of this lesson. Explain that using these characteristics will help students evaluate their own writing.

Discuss with each student whether this paper should go into the portfolio. Consider these possible reasons: (1) it is an especially good piece of writing; (2) it reflects a particular aspect of writing that the student did well; (3) it shows an aspect of writing that needs more work and could be used as a baseline for measuring growth.

MEETING INDIVIDUAL NEEDS — FOR STUDENTS ACQUIRING ENGLISH

Call on students to read aloud the various sections of the business letter. Remind students how to read an address. Help with pronunciation and two-letter abbreviations for the states as needed. Point out that, except for the abbreviations for the states, students should write out the full forms of words.

Reading As a Writer

See TE margin for answers.

- The **heading** contains the writer's address and the date. *Where is the date?*
- The **inside address** is the name and address of the person, business, or agency to whom you are writing. *In what city is the Wisconsin Department of Natural Resources?*
- The **greeting** usually begins with *Dear* and includes the title and the last name of the person receiving the letter. A colon follows the name. *Why didn't Wesley use a person's name?*
- The **body** is the main part of the letter. It has one or more paragraphs. *What did Wesley request?*
- The **closing** finishes the letter, and it is followed by a comma. Common closings are *Sincerely* and *Yours truly*. *What closing did Wesley use?*
- The **signature** is the writer's name written in cursive. *What is Wesley's full name?*

How to Write a Business Letter

1. **Think** about the purpose of your letter and your reader. What do you want your reader to know or do?
2. **Organize** your thoughts. Jot down notes about what you want to say.
3. **Write** the letter. Include all six parts of a business letter.
4. **Use** polite, formal language. Make your point and include all necessary details. You can be friendly without being chatty.
5. **Revise** your business letter. Reorder sentences or change wording.
6. **Proofread** for mistakes. Use the Proofreading Checklist on page 465. Use a dictionary to check spellings.
7. **Write or type** a neat, correct final copy of your letter.
8. **Address** the envelope correctly and put a stamp on it. Make sure the addresses in the letter match those on the envelope. Mail the letter.

Help with Writing a Business Letter

TOPIC IDEAS

Suggest these possibilities.

- Students can write a letter to the editor responding to an article in the local newspaper.
- They can write a letter to a store or a company expressing an opinion about a product or service.
- They can write a letter to a government agency requesting information for a school project.

TECH TIPS

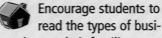

- Students can go to company Web pages to check the spellings of company names and addresses.
- Suggest that students use computers to design a letterhead for their stationery.

SCHOOL-HOME CONNECTION

Encourage students to read the types of business letters their families receive at home. These may include letters from companies soliciting business.

Listening for Persuasive Tactics

When a speaker is trying to persuade you, he or she wants you to do something. Listen for the reasons the speaker gives. Then ask yourself why you should take the action the speaker wants. Watch out for persuasive tactics that can tug on your feelings and keep you from thinking clearly.

Look at the tactics shown below.

Promise

Flattery

Other Tactics

Sometimes a speaker may use the fact that he or she is older than you to convince you to do something. Other times, a speaker may use taunts or dares, claiming that you can't do something, just so you will try to prove that you can. What other tactics are familiar to you?

more ▶

Listening for Persuasive Tactics

Lesson Objectives

Students will:

- understand and interpret speakers' verbal and nonverbal messages, purposes, and perspectives
- identify and analyze a speaker's persuasive techniques
- distinguish between a speaker's opinion and facts

Focus on Instruction

- Have volunteers role-play the situations shown in their book. Tell them to continue the dialogue, using different tactics to persuade the listener. After each dramatization, discuss with students how the speaker used body language and tone of voice to persuade.
- Ask students to share times when people have used persuasive tactics to get them to do something. Have students analyze their experiences by responding to questions such as these:

  What was the speaker's goal or request?

  What reasons did the speaker provide? How did the speaker support the reasons?

  Did you feel pressure to respond in a certain way?

  How did you react?

  Did you realize at the time that persuasive tactics were being used?

  How might an understanding of persuasive tactics have influenced your reaction? Would it have helped you respond objectively to the request?

- Explain that speakers use persuasive tactics for both noble and inappropriate causes. The important point is for listeners to be aware that persuasive tactics are being used, and not let the tactics muddy their decision-making abilities.

Focus on Instruction

- Make sure students understand what makes a strong reason: (1) It supports the speaker's goal by telling why you should take a particular action, (2) It is supported by facts and examples.
- Emphasize the importance of distinguishing persuasive tactics from strong reasons. Encourage students to analyze what they hear by asking these questions: Is this statement a strong reason for doing what the speaker wants? Is this statement true? Is it supported by facts and examples?
- Discuss with students the definition of *opinion, fact,* and *example*. An opinion tells feelings or thoughts. A fact can be proved. An example is something that has happened or that might happen to you or someone you know. Tell students that when they listen to a speaker's reasons, they should distinguish between the speaker's opinion and verifiable facts.
- Have volunteers read aloud the Guides for Listening for Persuasive Tactics. Point out that these techniques are only some of the persuasive techniques they may hear.

Apply It

As an alternative or extension activity, videotape an appropriate television segment from a talk show interview, a paid commercial advertisement, or a public service announcement. Show the video to the class, having students take notes as they watch. Discuss the speakers' key points and examine specific examples of persuasive tactics. Have students classify some of the speakers' statements as opinion or fact.

MEETING INDIVIDUAL NEEDS

FOR STUDENTS ACQUIRING ENGLISH

Review the meaning of *tactics*. Then before students read, ask volunteers to explain *promises, flattery, taunts,* and *dares,* using definitions and examples. As students read, suggest that they keep in mind the definitions and examples their classmates gave. Remind students to ask themselves the questions in the guides.

Decide for Yourself

Think about what you hear. Then decide for yourself what to do.

- **Think about the goal.** What does the speaker want you to do? Why is this goal important to him or her?
- **Think about the reasons.** Why does the speaker think you should do this? Does each reason make sense to you?
- **Think about the support.** How does the speaker explain each reason? Does the speaker just repeat an opinion or does he or she give facts and examples?

Guides for Listening for Persuasive Tactics

1. Listen for promises. Is the speaker saying that you'll get something good if you do this? Will this promise really be kept? How?
2. Listen for flattery. Is the speaker saying good things about you? Does this person really mean it? Has the speaker given you a good reason for doing what he or she asks?
3. Listen for taunts or dares. Is the speaker telling you that you're afraid to do something or that you don't really know how? Is the speaker asking you to prove something about yourself that you already know? Is the speaker trying to scare you into doing this? Is what the speaker saying true? Is it fair?

Apply It

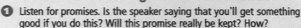

For the next week, listen carefully every time someone asks you to do something. Take notes on what you hear. Answers will vary.

- What did each speaker want you to do?
- What reasons did each speaker give? What facts and examples did each speaker give?
- Were persuasive tactics used? Did you notice them at the time?

COMMUNICATION LINK Viewing

Media

Watching for Persuasive Tactics

Mass media are used to get information to large numbers of people. Television, billboards, and magazines are types of mass media.

Advertising is a big part of many forms of mass media. Companies pay to place ads so that they can be seen by large audiences. These ads are meant to persuade you that you need the products or services that they show.

Tactics You've Seen

The people who make ads use tactics, or ways, to get people to buy products. Some tactics are meant to play on your feelings. Look at the examples below. You've probably seen these used on television or in magazines.

Persuasive Tactics	
Bandwagon Everyone else has one, so you should too. You'll feel left out if you don't.	
Superstars A sports star or a movie star says the product is good.	
Friendly Face Someone who seems trustworthy says you should use the product.	
Flattery You are wonderful. You deserve this product.	
Before and After The plant looks bad. Use the product and—wow! The plant looks great.	

more ▶

Watching for Persuasive Tactics

Lesson Objectives

Students will:

- understand and interpret mass media messages, purposes, and perspectives
- identify and analyze mass media persuasive techniques
- distinguish between opinion and facts in mass media

Focus on Instruction

- Have volunteers read aloud the examples of persuasive tactics. Point out that these techniques are only some of the persuasive techniques that students may see in mass media.
- Promote discussion by asking students to identify media ads that they are familiar with. Ask which ads use the tactics in the examples. Have students analyze their responses to the ads by responding to questions such as these:

  What feeling did the ad prompt?

  Did you realize at the time that persuasive tactics were being used?

  How might an understanding of persuasive tactics have influenced your reaction? Would you have reacted differently?
- Ask how viewers can avoid letting the tactics influence their decision-making abilities. (by recognizing persuasive tactics)

Focus on Instruction

- Have students look at the ads on this page. Ask students what persuasive tactics are being used. (bandwagon, superstar) Ask students if they think another tactic might also work to advertise the product. (Sample answers: The roller coaster ad might use flattery and say *Come on! You're tough enough for it!* The sports drink ad might show an athlete looking weak before drinking it and strong after drinking it.)
- Explain that a bandwagon is an ornate wagon that carries a musical band in a parade. Tell students that the wagon attracts attention and, especially in the past, followers.

Stop and Think

When you look at an advertisement, remember that you are seeing only what the people who made it want you to see. Because an advertiser's goal is to sell the product, important information about the product may be left out of the ad.

Most advertisers want you to feel before you think. If you act on your feelings, you might buy the product. If you think about it first, you might find reasons not to buy the product.

The billboard above uses the bandwagon tactic. It makes it seem as if "everyone else" is riding the roller coaster. It wants you to believe that if you don't go to the amusement park, you won't get to take part in something special.

Sometimes a star athlete sells a product. The people who make this kind of ad hope that you will buy the product because you admire famous sports figures. Ads like this often suggest that if you use the product, you will become strong or famous too.

When you look at an ad or a commercial, notice how it tries to persuade you. Here are some guides to follow.

Guides for Looking at Media Advertising

- Look carefully at the advertisement. Who made it? What does it want you to do?
- Think about how the ad is trying to make you feel.
- Check the ad to see whether it uses facts or opinions. Does it tell you all there is to know about the product or service? Does it make something seem too easy?
- Study the ad to see if any persuasive tactics were used. If so, which?
- Ask yourself if the ad is fair. Do you think it is truthful?
- Ask yourself what the ad is trying to make you believe. Make up your own mind about what you see.

Apply It

Watch the commercials that air during a television show you like. Videotape them if you can. Following the guides above, take notes on one. Then answer these questions. Answers will vary.

- What product or service is being advertised?
- Is the commercial fun and entertaining? What do you like about it?
- If you could talk to the people who made it, what questions would you ask?

Look through several children's magazines. Find an ad that uses one of the persuasive tactics described in this lesson. Share the ad with your classmates and talk about the messages it uses. Then create an ad of your own, using the same tactic.

Focus on Instruction

- Review with students the definition of *opinion, fact,* and *example.* Explain that an opinion tells feelings or thoughts. A fact can be proved. An example is something that has happened or that might happen to you or someone you know.
- Have volunteers read aloud the Guides for Listening for Looking at Media Advertising.

Apply It

Extend the activity by having students view commercials during different kinds of programs, such as a sports event, a news program, and a children's show. Have students compare the kinds of messages and persuasive tactics used during each kind of program. Ask how the commercials target the intended program audience.

MEETING INDIVIDUAL NEEDS

FOR STUDENTS ACQUIRING ENGLISH

Direct students' attention to *media* and *mass media.* Explain that in this case *media* refers to television, radio, newspapers, magazines, and the Internet—all the ways we get information through mass communication. Ask small groups to think of ways that the media get our attention in advertisements. Explain *tactics*.

About Part 3

This part of the book includes valuable resources for instruction or reference.

Using Part 3

The resources in Part 3 can be used at any time, either independently or in combination with lessons and features in Parts 1 and 2. The Listening and Speaking Strategies, Building Vocabulary, Research and Study Strategies, Using Technology, and Test-Taking Strategies sections provide instruction in these areas.

Draw students' attention to the Thesaurus Plus, the Writer's Tools, the Spelling Guide, and the Guide to Capitalization, Punctuation, and Usage at the beginning of the year so that they can refer to them throughout the year as they work on their assignments.

The Diagramming Guide may be used as you introduce sentence elements, sentence parts, and parts of speech. Practice exercises are included.

Cross-references to lessons and sections in Part 3 are included in the body of the pupil book at particularly appropriate points of use.

Part 3

Tools and Tips

H2

What You Will Find in This Part:

H3

Taking and Leaving Messages

Lesson Objectives

Students will:

- listen to a caller and write a complete telephone message
- leave a telephone message including important details
- use effective rate, volume, pitch, and tone for the telephone

Focus on Instruction

- Have students take the parts of Keisha and Mr. Bay and read aloud their telephone conversation. Draw attention to the way that Keisha explained that her father couldn't take the call. Ask students why her response is a good safety precaution. (She told the caller only that her father could not take the call. You should not tell callers that you are home alone.)
- Tell students that when they take a message, they should ask the caller to spell his or her name if they are not sure of the spelling. Students should also verify the caller's message and phone number. Stress the importance of correctly recording the phone number.
- Have volunteers read aloud the Guidelines for Taking and Leaving Messages. Discuss each point with students.
- Emphasize the importance of speaking slowly and at an appropriate volume for the telephone, especially when leaving a message on an answering machine. Suggest to students that they say their phone number more than once when leaving a message on an answering machine.

Apply It

A. Read the following message for students.

> Danielle, please have your mother call the nurse at Dr. Preston's office to schedule a dental visit. Our number is 555-2357. Thank you.

B. If students need ideas for telephone conversations, suggest these possibilities:

> a request for a contribution to the school bake sale
>
> a call from a car repair shop
>
> a coworker from a parent's office

Taking and Leaving Messages

Listening and Speaking Strategies

People keep in touch by using the telephone. If you answer a call for someone else, take a message. If you make a call and no one answers, you can leave a message on an answering machine. Read this conversation and Keisha's message. What information did she write?

MR. BAY: Hello, Keisha. This is Mr. Bay. May I speak to your father?
KEISHA: I'm sorry, he can't come to the phone right now. May I take a message?
MR. BAY: Yes, please ask him to call me at 555-2197.
KEISHA: I'll tell him to call Mr. Bay at 555-2197.

> Saturday, 10:15 a.m.
> Dad, please call Mr. Bay at 555-2197.
> Keisha

Keisha included all of the information that her father would need in her message. When you take or leave messages, follow these guidelines.

Guidelines for Taking and Leaving Messages

1. When you take a message, write the caller's name, the telephone number, and the message. Ask questions if any part of the message is not clear, and retell the message to be sure you have taken it correctly. Include the day and time that you take the call.
2. When you leave a message, give your name, your telephone number, and a brief message, including the day and time you called.
3. Be polite. Speak slowly and clearly.

Apply It

A. Follow the guidelines and practice taking notes as your teacher reads a telephone message.
B. Role-play giving and taking telephone messages with a classmate.

MEETING INDIVIDUAL NEEDS

FOR STUDENTS ACQUIRING ENGLISH

Explain *keep in touch*. Using the telephone can be especially difficult in another language. Many students are reluctant to use the phone out of fear they will not understand, so students benefit greatly from additional practice. Students who can become comfortable using the phone can assist family members who speak little English. Have pairs of students role-play the dialogue; telephones and an answering machine make the practice more realistic. Have students suggest variations. Read through the guidelines with students. Stress the importance of reading the phone number back to make sure they heard it correctly. Also suggest that students ask the caller to spell his or her name. You may want to list two sets of guidelines on the board, one set for personally taking a message and the other for leaving a message on an answering machine. Make sure students understand how area codes work.

Giving a Talk

When you give a talk, you speak about a certain topic. You need to plan, prepare, and practice your talk before you present it. Follow these guidelines when you give a talk.

Guidelines for Giving a Talk

1 Plan your talk.

- Decide if the purpose of your talk will be to inform, to persuade, or to entertain. The tone of your talk, such as humorous or serious, should match your purpose.
- Think about your audience. Should you use formal or informal language? How much do the listeners know about your topic?

2 Prepare your talk.

- Find the information you need. Gather any graphics or visuals, such as maps, pictures, or objects, that you want to show.
- Jot down notes or key words on note cards. Be sure to use words that are appropriate for your audience.

Kennedy Space Center
- full name: John F. Kennedy Space Center of the National Aeronautics and Space Administration (NASA)
- location: Merritt Island, Florida, near Cape Canaveral (show map)
- what they do: test, repair, and launch all manned U.S. space missions

- Be sure your talk has a beginning, a middle, and an end. Put notes in the order you will talk about them. You might want to highlight key words.

more ▶

Giving a Talk

Lesson Objectives

Students will:
- plan, prepare, practice, and present a talk
- adapt spoken language such as word choice, diction, and usage to the audience, purpose, and occasion
- use effective rate, volume, pitch, and tone for the audience and setting
- clarify and support spoken ideas with evidence, elaborations, and examples

Focus on Instruction

- Ask students to tell about talks that they have given or have heard. (Sample answers: book reports, school projects, school assemblies, speeches on television or in the community)
- Have volunteers read the guidelines. Discuss each point. Ask students to explain why it is important to practice a talk before giving it to an audience. (Sample answers: so that the talk can be delivered from notes alone; to time the length; to practice speaking aloud with appropriate rate, volume, pitch, and tone)
- Describe different purposes and types of audiences, such as the following.

  to persuade a family member to buy a new bicycle

  to explain to kindergartners how to play a game

  to tell classmates about a trip to Alaska

  Ask students to tell what tone and language they might use for each situation. Have students explain their answers.
- Remind students that all talks, including those that have a serious purpose or topic, should start out with something interesting to grab the audience's attention.
- Suggest that students first list the points they want to make, and then choose a logical order in which to make them. Remind students to start by introducing the topic, then to move to the body of the talk, and finally, to wrap up with a conclusion.

MEETING INDIVIDUAL NEEDS

FOR STUDENTS ACQUIRING ENGLISH

Ask students to comment on giving a talk in English. How easy or difficult is it, for example, to express humor? What would they like their English-speaking classmates to know about how it feels to give a talk in another language? What do students find most difficult about speaking in English in front of the class? What would they like to be able to do better?

Giving a Talk *continued*

Focus on Instruction

- Explain that speakers should always allow extra time before presentations in order to set up electronic equipment, such as overhead projectors, slide projectors, or computer projection devices.
- Suggest that students tape-record their talk as they practice. Tell them to use their tapes to help them evaluate the rate, volume, pitch, and tone of their voice. Have students repeat the process until they are confident they are ready to give their talk before an audience.

MEETING INDIVIDUAL NEEDS — FOR STUDENTS ACQUIRING ENGLISH

Discuss the Tips for Using Visual Aids. Say that an advantage of visual aids is that they can be prepared ahead of time. Remind students to check the spelling and grammar of any text on their visuals. Discuss the Speaking Tips. Often students acquiring English speak softly to avoid calling attention to mistakes. Demonstrate appropriate rate, volume, pitch, and body language. Remind students that the tone and formality or informality of the language they use should fit their purpose.

Apply It

- If students need ideas for talks, suggest these possibilities:

  Students can teach a skill or a game.

  They might persuade others to support a cause.

  Students can describe a different neighborhood, city, or other location.

  They can explain a lesson that they learned and its significance.

- Provide students with note cards for writing key words and notes.
- Have students work in groups, taking turns listening to and presenting talks. Tell each group to listen attentively and offer suggestions for improvement.

MEETING INDIVIDUAL NEEDS — FOR STUDENTS ACQUIRING ENGLISH

Provide ample opportunities for students to practice their talks before presenting to the class. Help students decide what to say and in what order to present information. Help them decide on visuals; have them do a draft of text so that you can review spelling and grammar. If possible, videotape each student. Review the tape, providing feedback on body language and eye contact, volume, and word choice and grammar. You may also want to show students tapes of effective talks.

Listening and Speaking Strategies

Giving a Talk *continued*

3. **Practice** your talk.
   - Give your talk to a friend or family member, using your notes and your visual aids. Revise your talk after listening to their comments.

Tips for Using Visual Aids

- Make sure any lettering is large enough for your audience to read.
- Practice using any machines, such as an overhead projector or a slide projector, before you give your talk.
- Don't block the visuals from the view of the audience.

   - Practice how you say your words. Think about the rate, volume, pitch, and tone of your voice.

Speaking Tips

- Don't talk too fast or too slowly.
- Talk loudly enough to be heard, and remember to talk more loudly in a big room than in a small space.
- Speak with expression.

HELP — Talk About Talk

Rate: how fast or slowly you talk
Volume: how loud or soft your voice is
Pitch: how high or low your voice is
Tone: how happy, sad, funny, or angry you sound

   - Practice until you have almost memorized your talk.

4. **Present** your talk.
   - Remember to use your voice and visual aids in the same way you practiced.
   - Project your voice. Avoid saying *um, ah,* and *well.*
   - Make eye contact with people in your audience.

Apply It

Give a talk about a funny experience, an opinion you have, or another topic that interests you. Then follow the guidelines as you **plan, prepare, practice,** and then **present** your talk.

H6 **Tools and Tips: Listening and Speaking Strategies**

Understanding Nonverbal Cues

Look at the students pictured below. Imagine they are talking about having to take part in a new school sport—tennis. How do you think each one feels about it?

Just like words, your face and body movements or positions can let others know what you think or how you feel. This "body language" is known as **nonverbal cues**.

Using Nonverbal Cues

You can use nonverbal cues to support what you are saying. Here are some examples.

- Use facial expressions to match your message.
- Use hand motions to stress a point when persuading.
- Use your hands to show sizes and shapes.
- Point to show a direction or an object. (Don't point to people!)
- Make eye contact to show you're aware of your listeners.

more ▶

Understanding Nonverbal Cues

Lesson Objectives

Students will:
- demonstrate and interpret nonverbal cues
- use nonverbal communication effectively

Focus on Instruction

- Explain that people express both positive and negative feelings with nonverbal cues, often without being aware of them. Ask volunteers to share some of their own nonverbal cues or mannerisms, such as rolling their eyes to show disapproval, clenching their teeth when tense or determined, clapping their hands to show enthusiasm, drumming their fingers when nervous, and so forth.
- Discuss family and cultural differences in the use of nonverbal cues. For example, a common Japanese mannerism is to touch the tip of the finger to the tip of the nose when referring to oneself. Explain that nonverbal cues that are acceptable in one culture may not be acceptable in another. For instance, the American gestures of pointing with the index finger and of touching index finger to thumb in the OK sign are both considered rude gestures in some other countries.

MEETING INDIVIDUAL NEEDS

FOR STUDENTS ACQUIRING ENGLISH

Nonverbal cues vary among cultures. Though some of the differences are obvious, many are subtle, and cross-cultural misinterpretation of nonverbal cues can lead to misunderstandings and hurt feelings. Ask students to decide on their own what the faces in the book represent. As a class, compare waving hello or goodbye; motioning for a person to come; measuring the height of a person, an animal, or a thing; handing something such as money to someone—all of which vary among cultures.

Understanding Nonverbal Cues *continued*

Focus on Instruction

- Ask volunteers to demonstrate other nonverbal cues that express interest, understanding, support, friendship, friendliness, success, and so forth.
- Discuss ways that observers can verify the meaning of someone else's nonverbal cues. For example, observers could say, "It looks as if you might be feeling ______," or "I'm wondering what you're thinking."
- Remind students that nonverbal cues are best used to strengthen their communication with others, and that they should not use nonverbal cues to deliver messages that they would not say aloud.
- Have students read aloud the guidelines. Discuss each guideline to clarify its meaning.

MEETING INDIVIDUAL NEEDS — FOR STUDENTS ACQUIRING ENGLISH

Explore similarities and differences in nonverbal cues across cultures. Have students show how they would look at an adult in their culture when talking. Follow up by saying that in the United States making eye contact is considered good manners. What does it mean to nod? Make sure students understand that here we nod only when we truly agree or truly have understood. Would students ever toss something, such as car keys, to a family member? How does a clerk hand change to person?

Apply It

Provide scenarios like the ones below, or have student groups create others.

Your friend just scored the winning goal.

Your little sister is crying because she broke her toy.

You are listening to a student give a talk about your favorite book.

Then have students take turns using nonverbal cues to demonstrate their reactions.

MEETING INDIVIDUAL NEEDS — FOR STUDENTS ACQUIRING ENGLISH

To promote cross-cultural understanding, do the following as a whole class activity. First, ask the English-speaking students to use facial expression and body movements to demonstrate anger, happiness, excitement, fear, surprise, agreement, or love. Have the students acquiring English write down what they think their classmate is showing. You may want to provide a list of emotions for students to choose from. Then reverse the roles. Does everyone agree? Where are the differences?

Listening and Speaking Strategies

Understanding Nonverbal Cues *continued*

You can use nonverbal cues to send a message without words. Here are some examples.

- Smile and nod your head to show interest and understanding. Look puzzled when something is not clear.
- Put your arm around a family member to show affection or around a friend to show comfort.
- Give a thumbs up to show support.
- Give a high-five to show friendship.
- Smile to show friendliness. Frown to show unhappiness.
- Sit back to show you're relaxed. Lean forward to show special interest.

Warning! Nonverbal cues can give away your true feelings or send the wrong message!

Observing Nonverbal Cues

Watch others' nonverbal cues. A pained look on someone's face may show that you said something that hurt. Someone looking at the ground while talking may be shy or embarrassed. Someone slouching or staring into space may be bored. If you are aware of a person's nonverbal cues, you will know better how to react appropriately.

Guidelines for Nonverbal Cues

1. Always have good eye contact when speaking.
2. Use nonverbal cues to support your words.
3. Use nonverbal cues to show what you think or feel without words.
4. Watch others' nonverbal cues as clues to their thoughts and feelings, and respond appropriately.

Apply It

With your class or in a small group, take turns demonstrating different nonverbal cues. Discuss what message each nonverbal cue sends.

H8 Tools and Tips: Listening and Speaking Strategies

Interviewing

One way to get facts for a report or a news article is to **interview** someone who knows that information. An interview is a kind of conversation. One person asks questions and the other person answers them. The **interviewer** is the person who asks the questions.

To get all the facts you want during an interview takes careful planning. The guidelines below will help you.

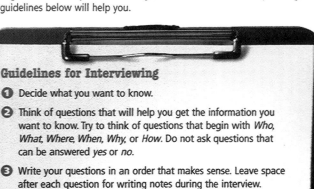

Guidelines for Interviewing

1. Decide what you want to know.
2. Think of questions that will help you get the information you want to know. Try to think of questions that begin with *Who, What, Where, When, Why,* or *How.* Do not ask questions that can be answered *yes* or *no.*
3. Write your questions in an order that makes sense. Leave space after each question for writing notes during the interview.
4. Before you ask your first question, tell the person the reason for your interview.
5. Ask your questions clearly and politely. Pay close attention to the answers.
6. Take notes to help you remember the answers. You may want to write the person's exact words if it is an important piece of information. Write these words as a quotation and use quotation marks.
7. If you don't understand something, ask more questions about it.

more ▶

Interviewing

Lesson Objective

Students will:

- conduct an interview to gather facts

Focus on Instruction

- Ask students to identify and describe interviews they have seen on TV. (Sample answers: interviews with sports figures, actors, government leaders, witnesses to an event)
- Review with students the Guidelines for Interviewing. Ask them why it is important not to ask questions that can be answered simply with *yes* or *no*. (They won't get detailed information.)
- Explain that an interview should be arranged in advance by telephone, letter, or e-mail. A start time and an approximate end time should be established prior to the interview.
- Discuss with students the importance of planning questions in advance to draw out the information they need, as the interviewee's time is valuable.
- Stress the importance of taking notes during an interview. Point out that note-taking will result in more accurate information than will relying on memory alone.

MEETING INDIVIDUAL NEEDS — FOR STUDENTS ACQUIRING ENGLISH

Emphasize the importance of planning and writing interview questions in advance and of taking good notes. Discuss why information questions are more helpful than yes-no questions. Demonstrate the difference by asking students several of each type of question, perhaps about what they did that morning. Have students copy the questions you ask and take notes on the answers given. Then have students compare the completeness and usefulness of the responses.

Interviewing *continued*

Think and Discuss

- The interviewer asked questions that began with *Who*, *What*, *Why*, *Where*, *When*, and *How*.
- None of the questions could be answered with *yes* or *no* because answers to such questions do not provide enough detail.
- Sample questions: What do you like best about playing the steel drums? How long does it take to learn to play steel drums? When and where will your next performance be held?

FOR STUDENTS ACQUIRING ENGLISH

Ask students if any of them have ever seen or heard a steel drum band play. If possible, play an audiotape. Make sure students understand that the book shows the interviewer's questions and notes, not the actual responses of the person interviewed. Have students work with partners to write three additional questions for the steel drum player interview. Then have partners role-play the complete interview, including their new questions and some possible responses.

Apply It

A. If students need topic ideas, suggest ideas such as playing soccer, joining a club, or owning a pet.

B. Depending on the topic, have students work with one or two partners to conduct the interview.

Remind students to follow all guidelines to conduct their interview.

Suggest that students keep the interviews to no longer than ten minutes.

Review students' questions with them prior to the interview.

Provide an opportunity for students to share the results of their interview with a small group of students or with classmates.

Have students write thank-you notes to the interviewee. Point out that a written summary of the interview would be a thoughtful enclosure.

Interviewing *continued*

The following notes were taken during an interview with a person who plays the steel drums.

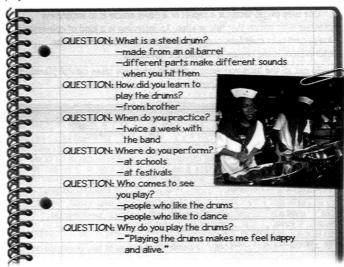

QUESTION: What is a steel drum?
—made from an oil barrel
—different parts make different sounds when you hit them
QUESTION: How did you learn to play the drums?
—from brother
QUESTION: When do you practice?
—twice a week with the band
QUESTION: Where do you perform?
—at schools
—at festivals
QUESTION: Who comes to see you play?
—people who like the drums
—people who like to dance
QUESTION: Why do you play the drums?
—"Playing the drums makes me feel happy and alive."

Think and Discuss See TE margin for sample answers.

- What kinds of questions did the interviewer ask?
- Do any of the questions call for *yes* or *no* answers? Why not?
- Work with a partner. Make up three more questions you could ask during the interview with the person who plays the steel drums.

Apply It

A. Pair up with a classmate. Tell each other a topic that you know about. Then interview each other, using questions each of you has written about the other person's topic. Follow the guidelines.

B. Interview a parent, a relative, or a neighbor about that person's job, hobby, or other interest. Use the guidelines. Share your questions and what you learned with your class.

FOR STUDENTS ACQUIRING ENGLISH

Tell students that the interview of a parent, relative, or neighbor can be conducted in English, or in another language if the student and person being interviewed would be more comfortable that way. Remind students that regardless of the language, they should plan to ask information questions. The students can take notes in whichever language they prefer, or a mix, as long as the notes will make sense to them later.

Similes and Metaphors

Writers often try to describe something by using a comparison to create a picture in your mind. One way they do this is by using similes. **A simile compares two different things using the word *like* or *as*.** What two things are being compared in each sentence below?

The circling helicopter was as annoying as a giant mosquito.

The hose looked like a coiled green snake ready to strike.

The night sky was like black velvet sprinkled with glitter.

Sometimes writers use a different kind of comparison. **A metaphor is a comparison of two things without using *like* or *as*.** What two things are being compared in each of these sentences?

The broken window was a ragged web of cracks and holes.

The shirts on the clothesline were colorful banners flapping in the wind.

The dog was a detective investigating every corner of the yard.

Why do the similes and metaphors above help you better picture what the writer is describing?

Building Vocabulary

Apply It

Complete each sentence with a simile or a metaphor. Use the kind of comparison shown in ( ). Sample answers are shown.

1. The bike seat felt like ______. (simile) hot tar
2. The clouds were ______. (metaphor) floating white marshmallows
3. The thunder sounded like ______. (simile) a giant's yawn
4. The cat was ______. (metaphor) a statue
5. The dog's eyes were as ______. (simile) brown as chocolate candies

Similes and Metaphors

Lesson Objective

Students will:

- write similes and metaphors

Focus on Instruction

- To introduce the lesson, have students close their eyes and try to envision the scene as you read aloud the following sentence.

  The train was long and silver, and it wound around the mountain.

  Then read aloud this sentence.

  The train was a silver snake, curled around the mountainside.

  Discuss the two sentences. Point out that both sentences offer descriptions of the train and the setting but that the second sentence creates an especially vivid and interesting image.
- Explain that similes and metaphors are two kinds of figurative language. Figurative language creates pictures through comparisons rather than through direct description of how things look, feel, or sound.

Apply It

Explain that each item can be completed in many different ways. Tell students to try to think of images that will help readers picture the subjects of the sentences. Encourage students to look for comparisons between two things that people would not ordinarily compare. Have students share their similes and metaphors to appreciate the variety.

Students who need extra support should complete the exercises with a partner.

Have students look for places in their writing in progress where they can add similes and metaphors. Explain that using similes and metaphors is a good way to liven up their writing and to make it clearer and more interesting. Caution students not to overuse these techniques, however, or the similes and metaphors will lose their impact.

FOR STUDENTS ACQUIRING ENGLISH

Say and write *simile* and *metaphor*. Have students repeat the words. Direct students' attention to the definition of a simile, pointing out *like* and *as*. Make sure students understand that this *like* means "similar"; it is not the verb that they use when they say, for example, "I like movies." Explain that a metaphor is a comparison but without the words *like* or *as*. Students may need help understanding some of the examples. Use explanations, actual objects such as glitter or velvet, the dictionary, and sketches as needed. Have students work with partners to do these activities. Remind students that similes have *like* or *as*; metaphors do not.

Idioms

Lesson Objective

Students will:
- interpret the meaning of idioms

Focus on Instruction

- Have volunteers read the example sentences. Ask students to name other idioms they have used or heard, and write them on the board. Then write the examples listed below.

  Ira and Ann didn't hit it off. (like each other)

  Let's knock off and go for a swim. (stop)

  That idea is for the birds. (weak, insufficient)

  Keep your nose to the grindstone until you finish. (stay on task)

  Point out that the meaning of the individual words added together differs from the meaning of the phrase.
- Explain that because the meaning of the idiom differs from the meaning of its individual words, it is especially difficult for people to use and understand idioms in a language they don't know well. Ask volunteers to share experiences with idioms in a new or unfamiliar language.
- Tell students that idioms are usually considered informal language. They are more appropriate in spoken, rather than written communication.

Apply It

Tell students to skip items they cannot readily answer and return to them last. Then students can use the process of elimination to choose the word or phrase in the word box that best fits the context of the sentence.

If students experience difficulty, have them work with partners to complete the exercises.

FOR STUDENTS ACQUIRING ENGLISH

Because of the difficulty idioms present, students acquiring English may be more aware of idioms than English speakers are. Informal language tends to be highly idiomatic, and many idioms in English are actually much less obvious than those in the book. A look at a good idioms dictionary will help you imagine the sheer number of phrases English speakers routinely use. Read the definition and description in the book aloud. Then ask students for their own examples of idioms that have caused them difficulties. You may want to show students how to use an idioms dictionary. Have students work with English speakers for this activity.

Building Vocabulary

Idioms

An idiom is a phrase with a special meaning. The meaning of an idiom is completely different from the meaning of its separate words added together. Did anyone ever offer to sell you something for a song? The salesperson probably wasn't really asking you to sing. He or she was just telling you that the item cost very little. The expression *for a song* is an idiom. Here are some more examples.

Idiom: The lesson was over my head.
Meaning: The lesson was too hard for me to understand.

Idiom: What are you driving at?
Meaning: What are you trying to say?

Apply It

Write each sentence. Replace the underlined idiom with a meaning from the word box. Be sure that the answer makes sense in the sentence.

agree	became afraid
better than	exactly
hurry	immediately
listening carefully	teasing you
told me about	trouble

1. We'll have to step on it to get home in time. hurry
2. I was just pulling your leg about going to school on Saturday. teasing you
3. Max was all ears when the teacher talked about space travel. listening carefully
4. Karen filled me in on the swim meet. told me about
5. Dan was going to dive, but he got cold feet. became afraid
6. Please wash the dishes right away. immediately
7. This book is a cut above other books by that author. better than
8. My teacher and I don't see eye to eye about homework. agree
9. Tia was in hot water for being late again. trouble
10. Theodore guessed the price on the nose. exactly

Synonyms

Words that have nearly the same meaning are called synonyms. Notice how this writer uses two different words for *happy.*

The family was **glad** to have a picnic.
The family was **pleased** to have a picnic.

glad **pleased**

Here are some more synonyms for *happy.*

delighted thrilled overjoyed

Your writing will be more interesting if you do not use the same words over and over again. You can vary your writing by using synonyms. Use a thesaurus to find synonyms.

Building Vocabulary

Apply It

Rewrite these sentences. Replace each underlined word with a synonym from the word box.

drowsy	blazed	hurried
frosty	sack	tasks
scraps	tossed	

1. Madeline awoke on a <u>cold</u> winter morning. frosty
2. She <u>threw</u> off her warm covers. tossed
3. Then she <u>rushed</u> over to the wood-burning stove. hurried
4. Madeline grabbed the <u>bag</u> filled with kindling. sack
5. She stacked a few <u>pieces</u> of wood in the stove. scraps
6. Soon the fire <u>burned</u> cheerfully. blazed
7. The warmth made her <u>sleepy</u>. drowsy
8. However, she had many more <u>jobs</u> to do. tasks

Synonyms

Lesson Objective

Students will:

- use synonyms to vary sentences

Focus on Instruction

- To introduce the lesson, have students listen to the following sentences as you read them aloud.

  The <u>small</u> rabbit <u>ran</u> through the forest.

  The <u>tiny</u> rabbit <u>dashed</u> through the forest.

  Have students name other synonyms for *small (little, teeny, wee, baby, petite, puny, dainty)* and for *ran (raced, sprinted, zoomed, zipped, rushed)*. Explain that synonyms can be used to make writing more precise and interesting. By using synonyms, writers can avoid using the same words over and over again.
- Explain that when students check verbs in a thesaurus, they may need to search under a different tense. For instance, the verb *ran* is most likely not a thesaurus entry. Students should check the present tense, *run*, and then change the tense as appropriate to their writing.
- Explain that students should not use an unfamiliar synonym in their writing without first checking the word in a dictionary. Point out that even small variations in word meaning can change the overall meaning of a sentence.

Apply It

Tell students to read each word box entry, then select the most appropriate word for each sentence.

Have students who need extra support work in pairs to complete the exercises.

Tell students to use synonyms in their own writing to add interest, variety, and precision. Remind students to use a thesaurus to find synonyms.

FOR STUDENTS ACQUIRING ENGLISH

List several examples of synonyms such as *big/large, small/tiny, smart/intelligent, car/auto, buy/purchase, help/assist*. Call on students to use each one in a sentence. Write the sentences on the board, and discuss small differences in meaning. Make sure students understand that synonyms mean more or less the same thing, and they are always the same part of speech. Point out the parts of speech for the words you have listed, or have students do so. Have students work individually or with partners to complete the items in the book. Remind students that the synonym will be the same part of speech. Suggest that students use dictionaries.

Antonyms

Lesson Objective

Students will:

- use antonyms to express opposite meanings

Focus on Instruction

- Ask volunteers to read the list of antonyms. Have students give examples of other antonyms. Then present words, such as those shown below, and ask students to name an antonym for each word.

hot (cold)	yes (no)	up (down)
raise (lower)	day (night)	tall (short)

- Explain that a single word can have many antonyms, just as it can have many synonyms. Have students identify a variety of antonyms for *happy*. (Sample answers: *sad, upset, unhappy, depressed, somber*)
- If students have trouble remembering the difference between synonyms and antonyms, tell them to use prefixes to help them. The word *antonym* is formed from the prefix *ant(i)*-, which means "opposite," while the word *synonym* is formed from the prefix *syn*-, which means "along with or together."

Apply It

Before beginning the exercises, have students look at the Thesaurus Plus on page H79. Draw attention to the antonyms. Encourage students to use the Thesaurus Plus, another thesaurus, or a dictionary as needed to complete the exercises.

Encourage students who need extra support to work together to complete the exercises.

Have students look for places in their writing in progress where they can add antonyms to show how people, places, or things differ.

FOR STUDENTS ACQUIRING ENGLISH

Ask students what two words that mean the same thing are called. Write *synonym* on the board. Then write *antonym*. Point out the prefixes on each, explaining that the first means "same," the second means "opposite." Call out common words and ask for the opposite: *hot/cold, dirty/clean, old/new, buy/sell, in/out, above/below, salt/pepper*. Say that antonyms are always the same part of speech. Discuss parts of speech for some of the words listed and in the book. Have students work individually or with partners to complete the items in the book. Remind students that the antonym will be the same part of speech.

Antonyms

Antonyms are words that have opposite meanings. You can use antonyms to show how people, places, or things are different. Here are some antonyms for common words.

Antonyms			
stop—start	left—right	shiny—dull	sharp—dull
lost—found	good—bad	love—hate	hard—easy
dark—light	heavy—light	top—bottom	under—over

Apply It

Complete each sentence with the word from the word box that is an antonym for the underlined word. Write the sentences. You may use a dictionary for help.

long	enjoyed
important	eagerly
interesting	ancient
frequently	strange
rural	bought

1. Karen never reads dull books because she can always find ______ ones. interesting
2. Sometimes she reads about familiar places, but more often she reads about ______ places. strange
3. She read one book about modern Greece, but she preferred a book about ______ Greece. ancient
4. She disliked one book about Iceland, but she ______ another book about that country. enjoyed
5. Karen rarely travels, but she ______ visits other lands in her imagination. frequently

Maps

A map is a drawing or chart of all or part of the earth's surface, including features such as mountains, rivers, boundaries, and cities.

Legend Every map has a legend, which usually appears in a box near the map. The legend explains the map's **symbols,** the marks that stand for various things. For example, a star is a symbol for a state capital.

Distance Scale A distance scale is usually shown below the legend. It shows how a particular distance on the map relates to real distance in miles or kilometers.

Compass Rose Another important part of a map is the compass rose. Arrows show the directions *north, south, east,* and *west.*

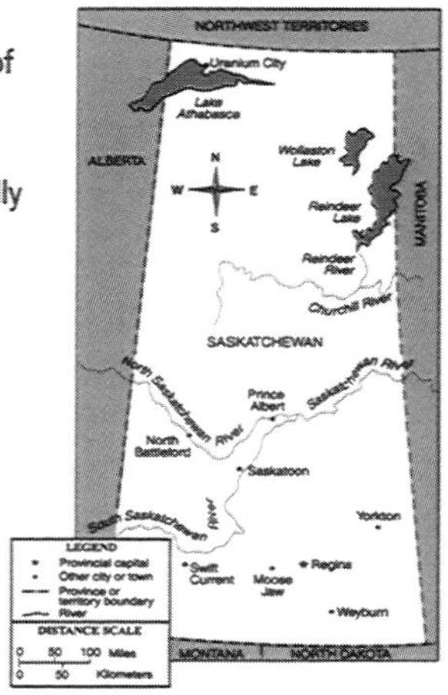

Diagrams

A diagram shows how something is put together or how it works. To understand a diagram, read the captions and all the labels.

GREAT HORNED OWL

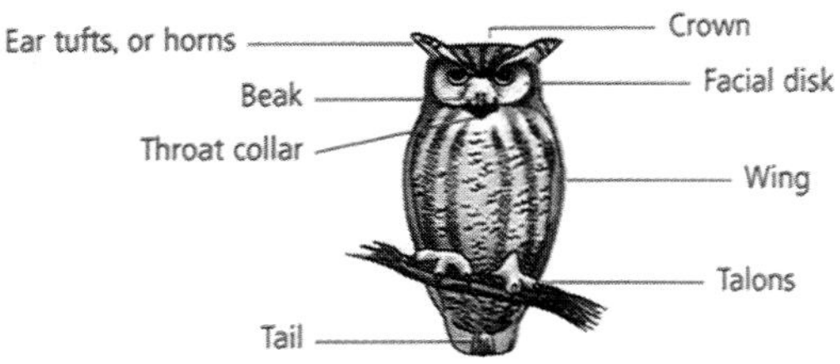

If a diagram uses unfamiliar words, check the text near it for definitions. If you found this owl diagram in a book and did not understand the term *facial disk,* you would read the paragraphs near the diagram. You might discover that a facial disk is the ring of short feathers surrounding the owl's eyes.

Practice

A. Have students use the map in their books to answer the following questions.

1. What is the capital of Saskatchewan? (Regina)
2. Approximately how many miles is it from Moose Jaw to Weyburn? (100 miles)
3. What direction is the Churchill River from the Saskatchewan River? (north)
4. What province borders Saskatchewan to the West? (Alberta)
5. What lake is farthest north? (Lake Athabasca)
6. What cities are on the North Saskatchewan River? (North Battleford, Prince Albert)
7. Which river flows out of Reindeer Lake? (Reindeer River)
8. Which part of the province has the largest number of cities and towns? (southern)
9. Which city is farthest north? (Uranium City)
10. What two states border Saskatchewan? (Montana, North Dakota)
11. What three rivers meet near the city Prince Albert? (North Saskatchewan River, South Saskatchewan River, Saskatchewan River)
12. What lake is north and a little west from Reindeer Lake? (Wollaston Lake)

B. Have students use the diagram of the owl in their books to answer these questions.

1. What are the feathers around the eyes called? (facial disk)
2. Why is this creature called a horned owl? (Ear tufts are called horns.)
3. What does an owl use to grasp a tree branch? (talons)
4. What is the top of the owl's head called? (crown)
5. How would you describe the owl's beak? (Possible answer: long and narrow)

Research Skills

Using This Section

This section provides guidelines for taking notes while reading, listening, or viewing. It includes instruction for outlining as well as explanations and models for summarizing fiction and nonfiction selections.

Research and Study Skills

Taking Notes

Whether you are reading, listening to a speaker, or watching a movie, taking notes will help you remember what you read, hear, or see. Good notes will help you remember much more than what you actually write down. The following guidelines tell you important things to remember when taking notes.

Guidelines for Taking Notes

1. Don't copy what you read. Summarize main ideas in your mind, and restate them in your own words.
2. Use quotation marks to give credit for someone's exact words.
3. Write only key words and phrases, not entire sentences.
4. Below each main idea, list the details that support it.
5. Keep careful records of the sources you are using.

Here is text from an encyclopedia entry about Robert E. Lee. A card with notes is also shown. Notice that the card lists the source of the information.

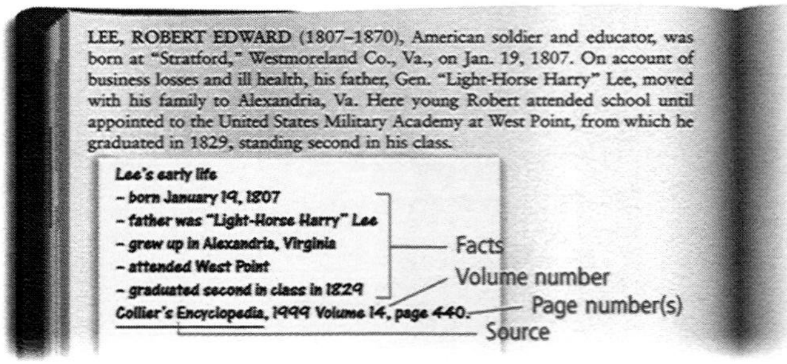
LEE, ROBERT EDWARD (1807–1870), American soldier and educator, was born at "Stratford," Westmoreland Co., Va., on Jan. 19, 1807. On account of business losses and ill health, his father, Gen. "Light-Horse Harry" Lee, moved with his family to Alexandria, Va. Here young Robert attended school until appointed to the United States Military Academy at West Point, from which he graduated in 1829, standing second in his class.

Lee's early life
- born January 19, 1807
- father was "Light-Horse Harry" Lee
- grew up in Alexandria, Virginia
- attended West Point
- graduated second in class in 1829

Collier's Encyclopedia, 1999 Volume 14, page 440.

Taking Notes While Listening When you take notes while reading, you can always look back and check facts to see if you missed anything. When listening to a speaker, you have just one chance to hear what is being said. Use the following guidelines to help you take good notes while listening.

Practice

A. Have students write *True* or *False* for each statement about taking notes while reading. Then have students rewrite false statements so they are true.
   1. Copy nearly everything you read. (F; Sample answer: Restate what you read in your own words.)
   2. Write only key words and phrases. (T)
   3. Don't worry about keeping records of the sources you use. (F; Sample answer: Keep careful records of the sources you use.)
   4. Write as many details as possible on a line. (F; Sample answer: List details below the main idea they support.)
   5. Use quotation marks around the exact words of someone you want to quote and give him or her credit. (T)

Guidelines for Taking Notes While Listening

1. Keep your mind on what the speaker is saying.
2. Pay careful attention to the speaker's introduction and conclusion. A good speaker will outline the speech in an introduction and sum up the main points in the conclusion.
3. Listen for cue words, such as *first, the main point,* and *most important,* that signal important information.
4. Don't write everything. Write only key words or phrases.
5. Go over your notes after the speech to make sure you have included all of the main points.
6. Note the speaker's name, the location, and the date of the speech.

Taking Notes While Viewing It takes practice to view something, think about it, and take notes all at the same time. Unless you are watching a video, you can't stop the action and watch the film again. In addition to the general guidelines for taking notes, the following guidelines will help improve your note-taking skills.

Guidelines for Taking Notes While Viewing

1. Prepare for the film or event by reading related material ahead of time.
2. Look and listen carefully during the introduction.
3. Be selective. Don't write everything. Listen for important ideas and write only the key words.
4. Use symbols and abbreviations, such as *w/* for *with* and *#* for *number.*
5. Even though you can't watch while taking notes, listen to the dialogue and learn new information.
6. As soon as the film is over, go over your notes and fill in missing details while they are still fresh in your mind.
7. Be sure to record the title of the film.

more ▶

Practice

A. Have students write *True* or *False* for each statement about taking notes while listening. Then have students rewrite false statements so they are true.

1. Don't allow your mind to wander. (T)
2. Write down as much as you can. (F; Sample answer: Write only key words and phrases.)
3. Put your notes aside for a few days before reviewing them. (F; Sample answer: Review your notes immediately to make sure you have included all the main points.)
4. Listen for cue words that signal important information. (T)
5. Don't worry if you miss the speaker's introduction or conclusion. (F; Sample answer: Pay careful attention to the speaker's introduction and conclusion.)

B. Have students write *True* or *False* for each statement about taking notes while viewing. Then have students rewrite false statements so they are true.

1. Write down only complete words. (F; Sample answer: Use symbols and abbreviations when possible.)
2. Be sure to record the title of the film. (T)
3. Go over your notes as soon as the film is over. (T)
4. Do not worry about preparing for the film or performance. (F; Sample answer: Read related material ahead of time to prepare for the film or performance.)
5. Look and listen carefully during the introduction. (T)

Research Skills *continued*

Outlining

An **outline** is a useful tool for sorting out main ideas and supporting details when you are reading or writing. When you use an outline to organize a piece of writing, it helps you plan the best order for your ideas.

An outline has a title and is made up of main topics, subtopics, and details. A **main topic** tells a main idea. **Subtopics** give supporting facts or details for the main topics. **Details** give more information about a subtopic. Use the following guidelines to write an outline.

Guidelines for Writing an Outline

1. Use a Roman numeral followed by a period to show each main topic.
2. Use a capital letter followed by a period to show each subtopic.
3. Use a number followed by a period to show each detail.

Here is an example of a topic outline. Note that the outline has a title. Usually the topics, marked with Roman numerals, are answers to questions about the subject.

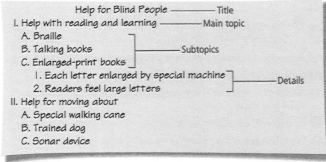

Help for Blind People —— Title
I. Help with reading and learning —— Main topic
  A. Braille
  B. Talking books —— Subtopics
  C. Enlarged-print books
    1. Each letter enlarged by special machine —— Details
    2. Readers feel large letters
II. Help for moving about
  A. Special walking cane
  B. Trained dog
  C. Sonar device

Topics, subtopics, and details can be words, phrases, or sentences. The first word in each entry begins with a capital letter. There should always be at least two main topics, two subtopics under a main topic, or two details under a subtopic.

Practice

A. Have students refer to the outline in their book to answer the questions below.

1. What general kinds of help can blind people receive? (help with reading, learning, and moving about)
2. How are the general kinds of help labeled in the outline? (with Roman numerals)
3. What reading and learning help is available? (Braille, talking books, enlarged-print books)
4. What help for moving about is available? (special walking canes, trained dogs, sonar devices)
5. How are the more specific kinds of help labeled? (with capital letters)
6. How are the details about the enlarged-print books labeled? (with numerals)

B. Have students write an outline from the notes below. Have them put the notes in an order that makes sense and give their outline a title.

What is the earliest known form of the horse?
- found in N. America, Europe
- called *Eohippus*
- lived about 55 million years ago

What did this animal look like?
- very small, 10 to 20 in. high
- several toes each foot
- short neck, arched back
- very different from horse today

Answers will vary. Sample outline:

The Earliest Horse

I. Kind of horse
  A. Called *Eohippus*
  B. Found in North America, Europe
  C. Lived about 55 million years ago
II. Appearance of animal
  A. Very different from horse of today
  B. Very small, 10–20 inches high
  C. Several toes on each foot
  D. Short neck, arched back

Summarizing

Summarizing helps you remember key points when you are reading or studying. A summary includes only the most important information.

Summarizing an Article Suppose that you read a lengthy article. Writing a summary can help you understand and remember details in the article. Read this summary of an article about sea otters, found on pages 369–370.

> Sea otters make great swimmers. Their bodies are shaped to move easily in water. Using front paws that are like hands, sea otters can pick up clams and other food. They have back feet that they use to push through the water. Sea otters can grow to be several feet long.

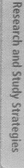

Notice that this summary begins with a clear statement of the main idea. The other sentences give details that support this main idea. The following guidelines should help you to write your own summary of an article.

Guidelines for Summarizing an Article

1. State the main idea of the article clearly and briefly.
2. Look for key words and important names, dates, and places from the article.
3. Use these facts to write sentences that support the main idea.
4. Be sure to explain events or steps in the correct order.
5. Use as few words as possible. Put the facts into your own words without changing the meaning of what you have read.

more ▶

Practice

A. Have students write *True* or *False* for each statement about summarizing an article. Then have students rewrite false statements so they are true.

1. State the main idea clearly and briefly. (T)
2. Record only the general ideas, not any names, dates, or places. (F; Sample answer: Look for key words and important names, dates, and places.)
3. The order of events does not matter. (F; Sample answer: Explain events or steps in the correct order.)
4. Use the same words that the article uses. (F; Sample answer: Put the facts into your own words without changing the meaning.)
5. Use as many words as you need to. (F; Sample answer: Use as few words as possible.)

B. Have students reread "Bats" on pages 447–449 and write a summary. They should try to use no more than ten sentences.

Sample summary:

Bats are very helpful creatures. They control the population of night-flying insects, eating thousands of tons a year. Also, they help preserve the rain forests by spreading the seeds of more than 300 kinds of trees and plants.

Bats can live up to thirty years, but there are many threats to their survival. Owls, snakes, raccoons, and hawks are natural enemies. Spring floods and the use of pesticides and other poisons kill many bats. Cave explorers, vandals, and even farmers destroy bats.

Bats are not the harmful creatures some people think. They rarely bite and don't carry rabies any more often than other mammals. People should be kind to these friends of nature.

Research Skills *continued*

Summarizing a Story When summarizing a story, briefly retell what happens. Be sure to include all the important characters and events. Read the following summary of "Crows," the story found on pages 298–299.

> Two crows with beautiful feathers and wonderful voices used to live in a forest. One crow was curious and one crow was careful. The curious crow talked the careful crow into flying near a forest fire. They were burned by the hot fire. Their feathers turned black, and they lost their beautiful call. They never went back home.

Notice that this summary includes the main events of the story. It also describes the characters' actions and their results. Use the following guidelines when you summarize a story.

Guidelines for Summarizing a Story

1. Decide what is the most important feature of the story. If it is a mystery, you might write about the plot. If the story is about friendship, you might write about the characters.
2. Write clear, brief sentences stating the most important ideas. Include important names, dates, and places from the story but don't include other details.
3. Be sure to give enough information so that the summary makes sense. The order of events in a summary should be the same as the order in the story.
4. To catch the tone or mood of the story, describe a specific character's actions or give a direct quotation.

Practice

A. Have students write *True* or *False* for each statement about summarizing a story. Then have students rewrite false statements so they are true.
1. Record all the details from the story. (F; Sample answer: Record only important details from the story, such as names, dates, and places.)
2. Don't worry about the order of events. (F; Sample answer: The order of events in a summary should be the same as in the story.)
3. A summary should be about the most important feature of the story. (T)
4. A direct quotation can capture the tone or mood of the story. (T)

B. Have students summarize a fictional story they've read recently. They should use no more than ten sentences. (Answers will vary.)

Word Analogies

Many tests ask you to complete **word analogies** that show how two pairs of words are alike.

Wet is to *dry* as *hot* is to cold.

In this example, *wet* and *dry* are opposites. *Cold* completes the word analogy correctly because it means the opposite of *hot*. Now both pairs of words show opposites.

Often a word analogy is set up with colons. To help you answer it, think of it as a sentence.

Wet : dry :: hot : ______

Wet is to dry as hot is to ______.

This chart shows some ways words can be related.

Word Relationship	Example
antonyms (opposites)	*Fast* is to *slow* as *narrow* is to *wide*.
synonyms (same meanings)	*Surprising* is to *amazing* as *unhappy* is to *sad*.
a part to the whole thing	*Toe* is to *foot* as *finger* is to *hand*.
a whole thing to one of its parts	*Car* is to *wheel* as *airplane* is to *wing*.
a thing to a category that it belongs to	*Banana* is to *fruit* as *carrot* is to *vegetable*.
a person to something he or she does	*Farmer* is to *planting* as *doctor* is to *healing*.
a thing to one of its characteristics	*Ball* is to *round* as *knife* is to *sharp*.

Test-Taking Strategies

more ▶

Word Analogies

Lesson Objective

Students will:

- follow test-taking guidelines to complete word analogies

Focus on Instruction

Discuss with students the word relationships presented in the chart. Provide these additional examples, and ask students to identify the relationships.

tree is to *leaf* (whole to part)

water is to *wet* (thing to a characteristic)

calf is to *animal* (thing to category)

melt is to *thaw* (synonyms)

handle is to *cup* (part to whole)

sure is to *uncertain* (antonyms)

wheel is to *bicycle* (part to whole)

actor is to *perform* (person to job)

easy is to *difficult* (antonyms)

bus is to *engine* (whole to part)

ice is to *slippery* (thing to characteristic)

airplane is to *transportation* (thing to category)

teacher is to *instruct* (person to job)

safe is to *secure* (synonyms)

Word Analogies *continued*

Practice

Point out that in Section B, the analogies are set up with colons. Remind students to think of analogies with colons as sentences.

Guidelines for Completing Word Analogies

1. Figure out how the first two words are alike.
2. If the analogy uses colons, say it as a sentence.
3. If you are asked to choose the second pair of words from a list, choose the pair that has the same relationship as the first pair.
4. If you are asked to fill in the last word, write a word that will make the second pair of words have the same relationship as the first pair.

Practice

A. Choose the pair of words that best completes each word analogy.

1. *Bark* is to *dog* as
   a. *scratch* is to *cat*.
   b. *tail* is to *pig*.
   (c.) *hoot* is to *owl*.
   d. *bark* is to *tree*.
2. *Chair* is to *furniture* as
   a. *car* is to *automobile*.
   (b.) *shirt* is to *clothing*.
   c. *paper* is to *book*.
   d. *dog* is to *poodle*.
3. *Day* is to *night* as
   (a.) *tall* is to *short*.
   b. *happy* is to *glad*.
   c. *car* is to *engine*.
   d. *horse* is to *pony*.
4. *Quiet* is to *silent* as
   a. *unhappy* is to *joyful*.
   b. *eager* is to *bored*.
   (c.) *sloppy* is to *messy*.
   d. *hour* is to *minute*.

B. Write the word that best completes each analogy.

5. Chef : cook :: pilot : ______.
   a. eat b. write
   c. build (d.) fly
6. Month : year :: classroom : ______.
   a. teacher (b.) school
   c. chalk d. study
7. Pie : slice :: door : ______.
   (a.) doorknob b. house
   c. tall d. window
8. Hurry : rush :: jump : ______.
   a. fall b. swim
   (c.) leap d. high

Open-Response Questions

Sometimes on a test you must read a passage and then write answers to questions about it. Remember these guidelines to help you write a good answer.

Guidelines for Answering an Essay Question

1. Read the question carefully. Find clue words that tell what kind of answer to write, such as *explain, compare, contrast,* and *summarize.*
2. Look for other clue words that tell what the answer should be about.
3. Write a topic sentence that uses clue words from the question. Write other sentences that give details to support the topic sentence.
4. Answer only the question that is asked.

Test-Taking Strategies

Read the following passage and follow the instructions at the end.

Animals in the Arctic

The Arctic is the region at the top of the world. Because it lies so far north, it has very cold, long winters. The temperature can drop to sixty degrees below zero!

Even though the Arctic has bitter winters, many kinds of animals make their home there year round. If you went for a walk on the tundra, you might see caribou, a polar bear, or an arctic fox. These animals have thick fur coats that keep them warm. Some animals that live part-time in the water, such as seals and walrus, also have fur. They also have a thick layer of blubber under their skin to help warm them in the icy water.

The arctic hare, which looks like a rabbit, and the lemming, a mouselike rodent, are small furry animals that protect themselves from the cold by living in tunnels under the snow.

more ▶

Open-Response Questions

Lesson Objective

Students will:

- analyze answers to a test prompt based on guidelines

Focus on Instruction

- Discuss the guidelines and examples with students.
- To provide practice answering open-response questions, remind students to follow the guidelines as they answer the Critical Thinking questions that accompany the Published Models in each writing unit in this book or as they answer other questions in their reading and content area textbooks. Help them study each question to identify the kind of answer expected and any clue words. When they share their answers, discuss with them and model the content of an appropriate response.

Open-Response Questions *continued*

- To help students understand why the first answer is not a good one, ask them to explain why the various animals in the Arctic are able to survive. Then have them reread the first answer to see that those facts are not included.
- Then ask students to find the facts in the first answer that are not needed to answer the question. (Arctic is at the top of the world; really cold; sometimes 60 degrees below zero; no snakes there; definition of lemming) Point out that since these facts don't explain how the animals survive, they should not be included.

Open-Response Questions *continued*

Birds have their own warm coats made of feathers. However, they have a special problem because they have no "leggings" to warm their feet and legs. Only a few birds whose feet and legs can stand very low temperatures, such as the ptarmigan, live in the Arctic.

There's one kind of animal you will rarely find, though—snakes and other reptiles. Very few of these cold-blooded animals could survive an Arctic winter!

Summarize why arctic animals are able to survive the cold winters.

Test-Taking Strategies

Read these two answers to the instruction. Which one is a better answer?

The Arctic is at the top of the world. It's really, really cold there. Sometimes it gets as cold as 60 degrees below zero. A lot of furry animals live there but few snakes! There are the polar bear, the arctic fox, seals, walrus, and the lemming. If you don't know what a lemming is, it's a rodent that looks like a mouse. Birds and insects live there too because they don't freeze.

Animals in the Arctic have different ways that help them survive the cold winters. Some animals, such as the polar bear, have thick coats of fur. Water animals like seals have fur and blubber. Some small animals live in tunnels in the snow. The birds have feathers and special feet and legs that don't get too cold. These are the ways the animals stay alive in winter.

The first answer names the kinds of animals in the Arctic, but it doesn't tell about why they are able to survive. It also gives facts about the Arctic that the question doesn't ask for.

The second answer uses clue words from the instruction in the topic sentence, such as *survive* and *cold winters.* The other sentences summarize the main points about how the animals survive the cold. This answer gives only the information asked for.

H34 **Tools and Tips: Test-Taking Strategies**

Technology Terms

Computer Terms

Your school may be equipped with computers, or you may have your own. Try to become familiar with the following terms to understand how the computer works.

CD-ROM A flat, round, plastic disc where computer data or music can be stored and read with a laser; many computers have built-in CD-ROM drives.

cursor The blinking square, dot, or bar on a computer screen that shows where the next typed character will appear.

disk drive A device that can read information from a disk or write information onto a disk; you insert a disk into a disk drive through a thin slot.

document A written or printed piece of writing.

floppy disk A somewhat flexible plastic disk coated with magnetic material and used to store computer data.

font Any one of various styles of letters in which computer type can appear.

hard copy A computer document that is printed on paper.

hard drive A computer disk that cannot be easily removed from the computer; hard disks hold more data and run faster than floppy disks.

hardware The parts of a computer system, including the keyboard, monitor, memory storage devices, and printer.

keyboard A part of the computer containing a set of keys.

menu A list of computer commands shown on a monitor.

more ▶

Using Technology

Technology Terms

Using This Page

This page presents common technology terms. If students are just learning about using computers, draw their attention to this page as a helpful resource.

Technology Terms *continued*

modem A part of a computer that allows it to communicate with other computers over telephone lines. It can be a separate device or inside the computer.

monitor A part of a computer system that shows information on a screen.

printer A part of a computer system that produces printed documents.

software Programs that are used in operating computers.

Using Technology

Word-Processing Commands

These commands are often used in word processing. You can give each command by typing a series of keys or by selecting it from a menu.

Close Closes the displayed document.

Copy Copies selected, or highlighted, text.

Cut Removes selected, or highlighted, text.

delete Removes selected, or highlighted, text.

Find Locates specific words or phrases in a document.

New Opens a new document.

Open Displays a selected document.

Paste Inserts copied or cut text in a new location in the same document or in another document.

Print Prints the displayed document.

Quit Leaves the program.

return Moves the cursor to the beginning of the next line.

Save Stores a document for later use.

shift Allows you to type a capital letter.

Spelling Activates the spelling tool.

tab Indents the cursor to the right.

Using E-mail

Writing an e-mail is different from writing a letter or talking on the phone. Follow these guidelines to write good e-mail messages.

Guidelines for Using E-mail Effectively

1. Give your message a specific title in the subject line. The person receiving your message should know the subject before opening it.
2. Use short paragraphs. Long paragraphs are difficult to read onscreen.
3. Skip a line instead of indenting when you begin a new paragraph. Your message will be easier to read onscreen.
4. Remember that special type, such as italics or underlining, may not show up on the other person's screen.
5. Be careful how you use humor. The other person can't hear your tone of voice and may not be able to tell when you're joking.
6. Even though an e-mail may seem more casual than a letter, you should still follow the rules of good writing.
7. Proofread your messages, and fix all capitalization, punctuation, usage, and spelling mistakes.

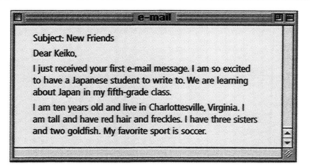

> **e-mail**
>
> Subject: New Friends
>
> Dear Keiko,
>
> I just received your first e-mail message. I am so excited to have a Japanese student to write to. We are learning about Japan in my fifth-grade class.
>
> I am ten years old and live in Charlottesville, Virginia. I am tall and have red hair and freckles. I have three sisters and two goldfish. My favorite sport is soccer.

Using E-mail

Using This Page

This page provides helpful information about constructing e-mail messages to promote easy readability and access to the content. It also addresses the formal and informal e-mails and the issue of correctness. If students are using e-mail in the classroom, draw their attention to this page when you introduce the e-mail activities. Otherwise, a good time to discuss this page would be in combination with the Special Focus features on writing friendly and business letters.

Using A Spelling Tool

Using This Page

This page describes the merits of a spelling tool and also cautions students about its limitations. Examples of different kinds of misspellings are highlighted and described. Discuss the examples with students and emphasize the need to proofread their papers themselves to check for spelling. A good time to discuss this page is during the proofreading stage of the first writing assignment.

Using a Spelling Tool

Your word-processing program's spelling tool can help you proofread your writing. Having a spelling tool on your computer doesn't mean you don't have to know how to spell, though.

Look at this paragraph. Do you see any misspelled words? If you do, you're smarter than a spelling tool because it didn't find any of the mistakes.

Document

Summer Vacation

This summer my family and I went on a vacation to the beech. I can still remember the scent of the ocean and the feel of the sand under my bare feet. I spent ours helping my little sister build a sandcastle with a pail and a shovel. One day we saw a pair of star fish. There is no place like the beach!

A spelling tool can't tell the difference between homophones.

A spelling tool can't find a misspelled word that is the correct spelling of another word.

A spelling tool doesn't know whether two words are supposed to be one word.

Think of a spelling tool as a proofreading partner. The spelling tool can help you find mistakes in your writing, but you still need to proofread to make sure the spelling tool didn't miss anything.

Computers and the Writing Process

Computers can help you plan, draft, revise, proofread, and publish your writing more efficiently. Here are some ideas for using a computer in the writing process.

PREWRITING

Type your thoughts as you think of them. Don't worry about finishing your sentences or grouping ideas. You can use the Cut and Paste features to make changes later.

Dim the screen to help you concentrate on your thoughts rather than on correctness.

Create outlines, charts, or graphic organizers to help you plan your writing.
Tip: Some word-processing programs have ready-to-use graphic organizers that you just fill in.

Benjamin Franklin's Career

I. What Ben Franklin printed
  A. City laws
  B. Notices of meetings and events
  C. Pennsylvania Gazette

II. Other jobs Ben Franklin had
  A. Statesman
  B. Scientist
  C. Inventor
  D. Writer

DRAFTING

Save your prewriting notes and ideas under a new file name, and then expand a list or outline into a draft.

Double-space your draft so that you can write revisions on your printout.

Boldface or underline words you may want to change later.

more ▶

Using Technology

Computers and the Writing Process

Using This Section

This section provides tips for taking advantage of the features of a computer and the available software to help with the writing process stages of prewriting, drafting, revising, proofreading, and publishing. If students have access to a computer for writing, draw their attention to these pages at the beginning of the first writing assignment, and remind students to try different ideas over the course of the year to find ones that are helpful to them.

Another possibility is to review the suggestions for each stage as students work through that stage of the process. Encourage students to try one of the ideas and to discuss which suggestions they found most helpful.

Computers and the Writing Process *continued*

Using Technology

REVISING

Save a copy of your file under a new name before you begin making changes.

Have a conference with a partner right at the computer. Read your draft aloud and discuss any questions or problems you have. Then insert your partner's comments in capital letters. Later you can decide which comments you agree with.

Use the Find and Replace functions to check for overused words. Enter words such as *and, then, pretty,* or *nice* in the Find function. When the word is found, highlight it and click Replace. You can also simply boldface the word and revise it later.

Use the Cut and Paste functions to make changes. Move or delete words, sentences, or paragraphs with just a few clicks. **Tip:** If you're unsure about cutting something, just move the text to the end of your document. You can always cut those "throwaways" later.

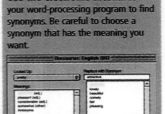

Rewrite problem sentences or paragraphs under your original text. Boldface your new text and compare the different versions. Delete the version you don't want.

Use the electronic thesaurus in your word-processing program to find synonyms. Be careful to choose a synonym that has the meaning you want.

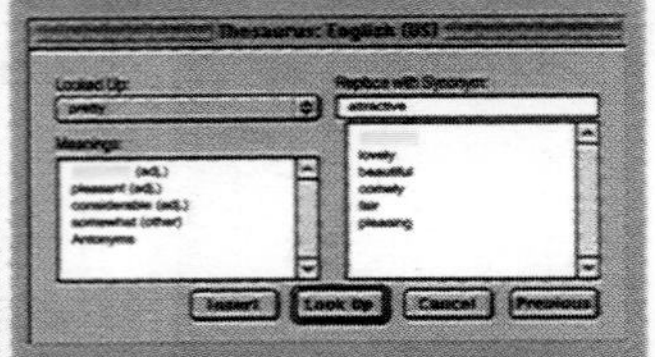

PROOFREADING

Check your spelling with your word processor's spelling tool. Then check for errors a spelling tool won't catch! See "Using a Spelling Tool" on page H38.

Turn your sentences into a list. Place the cursor after each end punctuation mark and press Return. Now you can easily spot sentences that are too long or too short, run-on sentences, and fragments. You can also make sure that each sentence begins with a capital letter. When you're finished proofreading, simply delete the extra returns.

PUBLISHING

Computers make publishing your writing a snap. Here's how you can create professional-looking final products.

Choose your fonts carefully. Designers suggest using no more than three fonts per page.

Helvetica Century
Times Roman

Choose a type size that can be read easily, but remember, type that is too big can look silly. Twelve-point type is usually a good choice.

8 pt
12 pt
16 pt

Use bullets to separate the items on a list or to highlight a passage. Typing Option + 8 usually produces a bullet.

Design your title by changing the type size or font. Make a separate title page, if you like, and use your word processor's Borders and Shading functions to make the page fancy.

Add art to your paper or report.

- **Use the computer's Paint or Draw features** to create your own picture.
- **Cut and paste** clip art, which comes with some software.
- **Use a scanner** to copy images such as photographs onto your computer. You can then insert them electronically into your document.

If you don't have the equipment to create electronic art, simply leave a space in your document, print out a hard copy, and draw or paste in a picture.

Other key combinations will make special pictures and symbols called dingbats. See how many you recognize.

Using Technology

more ▶

Computers and the Writing Process *continued*

PUBLISHING

Create tables, charts, or graphs to accompany your writing. For example, you can chart or graph the results of a class survey on birthdays.

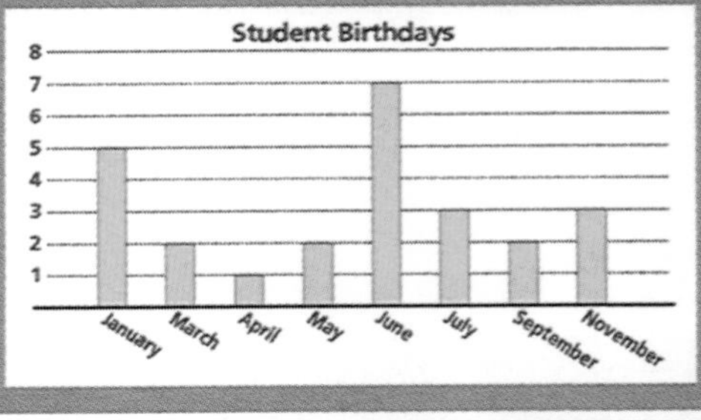

Choose your paper. White paper is always fine, but sometimes you may want to try colored paper or stationery with borders or pictures. **Tip:** Check with an adult before changing the printer paper. Paper that is too thick or heavy can jam your printer.

Create newsletters, magazines, or brochures using word-processing templates. Look at examples of real newspapers and magazines to see what kind of type to use, how big to make titles, and where to put pictures. Try combining electronic files to create a class newsletter that contains articles written by each of your classmates.

Organize your writing in electronic folders. Create separate folders to store poems, stories, research reports, and letters. You can also make a folder for unfinished pieces. Think of your computer as a giant storage cabinet!

Start an electronic portfolio for special pieces of your writing. You can create a portfolio folder on your hard drive or copy your files onto a floppy disk. Add pieces you choose throughout the year.

Using Technology

The Internet

What Is the Internet?

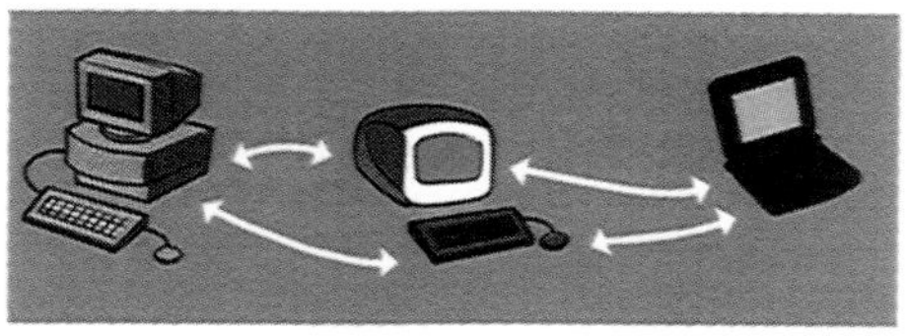

The **Internet** is a network of computers that connects people, businesses, and institutions all over the world. It lets computer users communicate with other computer users quickly and easily. Here are some of the many things you can do on the Internet.

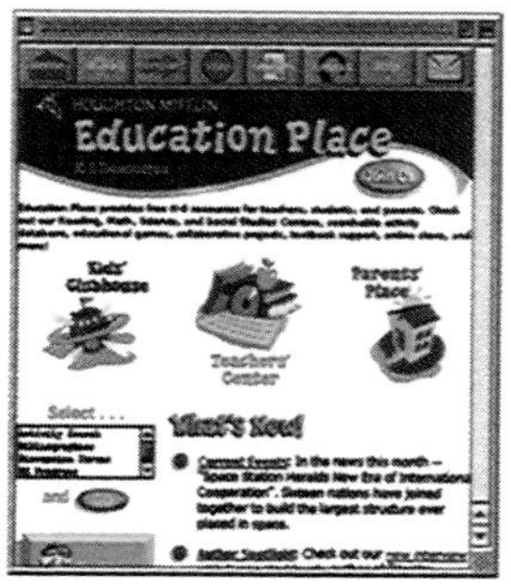

- Do research. You can watch a volcano erupt, take a tour of the Smithsonian, or hear music from the Revolutionary War. You can search for current articles or historical documents.
- Visit an electronic bulletin board or a chat room, where users "meet" to discuss specific topics. Here you can join an online book club, chat with other students who enjoy playing basketball, or debate current events.
- Send e-mail to your friends and family. Anyone who is online is reachable. See "Using E-mail" on page H37.

Tech Tip
Visit Education Place at www.eduplace.com/kids/hme/ for fun activities and interesting information.

more ▶

The Internet

Using This Page

This page provides an overview of ideas for using the Internet to learn information, to support school assignments, and to communicate with others. It also includes tips for using the Internet effectively. If students have access to the Internet in your class or school, discuss this page early in the school year. Another good time to review this page with students is while they are doing research for a research report.

INTERNET CONNECTION Send your students to www.eduplace.com/kids/hme/ for language arts activities and models. They will also find Internet links to sites with information about different topics to help with research reports.

The Internet *continued*

The Internet *continued*

- Use special software to create your own Web site. You design the page, write the text, and choose links to other sites. Your school may also have its own Web site where you can publish your work.

Tips for Using the Internet

Although the Internet can be a great way to get information, it can be confusing. Use these tips to make the most of it!

- Search smart! Use a search engine to help you find Web sites on your topic or area of interest. Type in a key word or search by topics. Most search engines give tips on searching. Some search engines are designed just for kids.

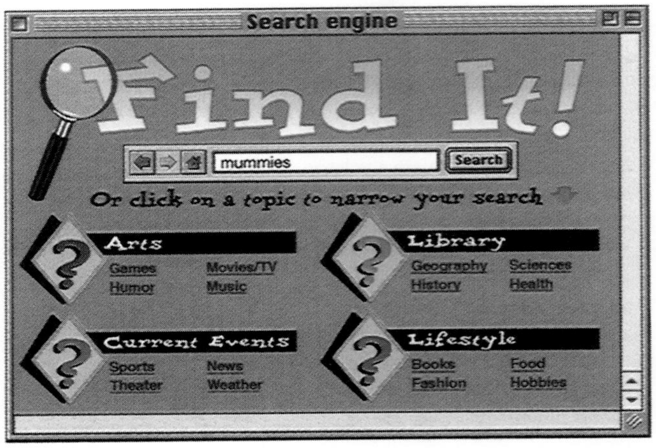

- Write down the source of any information you find on the Internet just as you would for a book. Along with the author, title, date of the material, and online address (URL), make sure you include the date you found the information. Information on the Internet can change daily.
- Check your sources carefully. The Internet is full of information, but not all of it is reliable. Web sites published by well-known organizations may be more trustworthy than those published by individuals.
- Protect your privacy. Never give your full name or address in a chat room.

Creating an Electronic Multimedia Presentation

An electronic multimedia presentation is a combination of words, pictures, and sound. It lets you express much more than you could with just words. For example, an electronic multimedia presentation on rain forests could contain descriptions of the plants found in a rain forest, recordings of animal sounds, photographs of the Amazon rain forest, and a video of flying squirrels.

Equipment

Here is what you need:

- a personal computer with a large memory
- high-quality video and audio systems
- a CD-ROM drive
- a multimedia software program

Check with your school librarian or media specialist to find out what equipment is available.

Parts of an Electronic Multimedia Presentation

An electronic multimedia presentation may include text, photos and video, sound, and animation.

Text The text of your presentation may include informative summaries, descriptions, directions, or photo captions. How the text appears onscreen is also important. You can adjust the font, size, and color of your text. **Tip:** Don't make your letters too small or put too many words on a single screen. Text should be easy to see and to read.

more ▶

Creating an Electronic Multimedia Presentation

Using This Section

This section provides suggestions for using various electronic media to create a presentation that combines text, visuals, and perhaps sound. If students have access to various electronic media, draw their attention to these ideas at the beginning of a writing assignment as well as at the publishing stage. Having students think about the possibility of creating a multimedia presentation as they begin their writing would affect how they compose, organize, and write their text.

In addition to using the ideas on these pages to create an electronic multimedia presentation, have students use the following guidelines to assess their own presentations as well as help them interpret information when viewing others' presentations.

Guidelines for Planning/Viewing an Electronic Multimedia Presentation

- Look for characteristics of the text fonts, such as color, size, or style, that alert you to key words or main ideas. Bright colors, larger type, or italics or underlines often signal important points.
- Look for design elements, such as bullets, icons, or arrows, that show key points or signal meanings. For example, an icon of a light bulb might indicate an idea to remember. An arrow might signal to go to the next step.
- Think about the visuals in combination with printed or voiced text. Are the visuals more dominant than the text, or is it the other way around?
- Listen to the sounds. Are they used just for background, or do they provide more information? If music is used, does it relate to something that is described or pictured, or is it used to create a feeling?

Creating an Electronic Multimedia Presentation *continued*

Photos and Videos Pictures can be powerful, so choose them carefully. Here are some ways you can include pictures.

- Include video you film yourself.
- Scan in photos or artwork.
- Generate your own computer artwork.

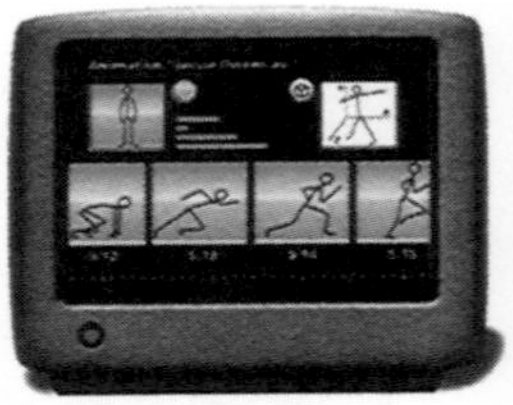

Animation Computer animation lets you create objects and then bring them to life. Here are some things you can do with animation.

- Tell a story with animated figures.
- Show an experiment being performed.
- Track changes in a chart or graph.
- Show how something is put together.
- Show how something grows.
- Display an object from all sides.

Sound Sound can help make an image or text come alive. Imagine viewing a video of the track star Jesse Owens. Then imagine viewing the same image while listening to the cheers of the crowd and the crackle of the announcer's voice. Here are some suggestions for using sound in your multimedia presentation.

- Add appropriate background sounds—birds calling, water dripping, bells ringing.
- Use music to set a mood.
- Include songs that represent a time in history or emphasize a theme.
- Include a button to let users hear the text read aloud.
- Include audio to accompany video clips.

Designing an Electronic Multimedia Presentation

The process of designing an electronic multimedia presentation is similar to that of creating a piece of writing, but here are some additional things to consider.

Types of Media If you are planning a presentation on the moon, you might come up with the following list:

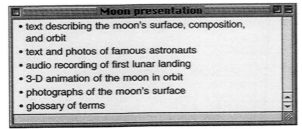

Moon presentation

- text describing the moon's surface, composition, and orbit
- text and photos of famous astronauts
- audio recording of first lunar landing
- 3-D animation of the moon in orbit
- photographs of the moon's surface
- glossary of terms

Order of Presentation Will the presentation have a specific order, or will you allow the user to choose his or her own path? A diagram, such as the one below, will help you plan.

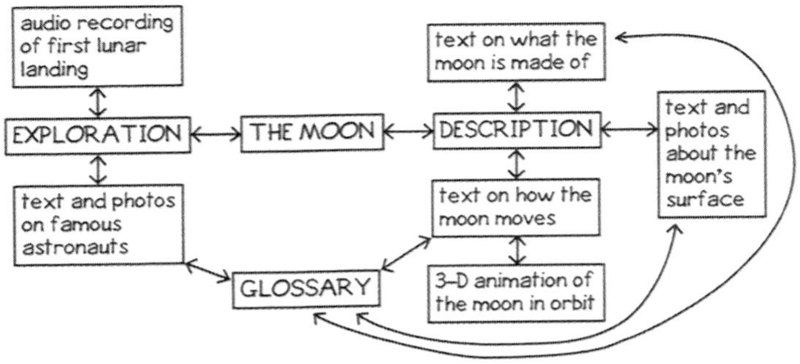

Designing and creating a multimedia presentation can be challenging and fun! **Tip:** As always, cite your sources and write text in your own words.

Using Technology

Keeping a Learning Log

Lesson Objective

Students will:

- learn about and use a learning log independently and collaboratively

Focus on Instruction

Discuss with students the example of a learning log and how you would like them to use a learning log in your classroom.

Ideas for Organizing a Learning Log

Students can keep their learning log in a three-ring binder or a spiral notebook. Here are some ideas for organizing a learning log.

- Have students write in their logs on a day-by-day basis, dating each entry.
- Have students divide their logs by subject, using tabbed pages (for three-ring binders) or by starting a page for one subject and then leaving a few blank pages before starting a page for a different subject (for spiral notebooks).

Try It Out

When students collaborate with other writers to make entries in a learning log, encourage them to do the following as they compose, organize, and revise their information.

- Discuss how to record the information. Will they write? draw pictures? make charts or graphs?
- Decide how to label and organize the information they are recording.
- Divide the tasks among themselves. One student might write the information; another might draw charts, graphs, or pictures; and a third might check the entry for errors.
- Discuss how to evaluate and revise their entry before completing it. Have they included all the important information? Have they explained their thoughts or feelings clearly? Did they record any predictions or conclusions?

Keeping a Learning Log

A **learning log** is a notebook for keeping track of what you learn in different subjects. It is a place to write facts as well as your thoughts about each subject.

Getting Started Write the date at the top of the page. Then use words, charts, or pictures to help you remember what you have learned. An example from one student's learning log is shown below.

November 17
Subject: Math

1. Our class put ten colored cubes in a bag: one yellow, two blue, two green, and five red cubes
2. Question: If we pick cubes from the bag, which color will we pick most often?
3. Our Predictions: We will pick yellow least often and red most often.
4. We picked cubes to test our predictions.

Our Results

	Tally	Total
Blue	7 tally marks	7
Red	16 tally marks	16
Green	5 tally marks	5
Yellow	2 tally marks	2

← We were right!

Try It Out Here are some suggestions for using a learning log.

- Make a vocabulary list for one subject. Include definitions.
- With a small group, record coin flips. Show the results in a bar graph.
- Work with classmates to record and graph weather data for a week.
- Explain how multiplication is similar to addition. How is it different?
- Describe your observations during a nature walk.
- Record what you know about your state. What do you want to know?
- Summarize what you have learned in a lesson in school.

ISP charts show **information (I), sources (S),** and, if appropriate, the **page references (P)** where you found the information.

I	S	P
Adult grizzlies can weigh about 850 pounds!	Know-It-All Encyclopedia	246
Mother grizzlies will adopt strays or orphaned grizzlies.	Mr. Ed Ucation, tour guide at the Natural History Museum	139

Step-by-step charts help you to plan your instructions. List the materials that are needed to follow your instructions. Then write each step in order. Include details your audience needs to know to complete each step.

Materials	
Steps	**Details**
Step 1	
Step 2	
Step 3	
Step 4	
Step 5	

Writer's Tools

more ▶

Graphic Organizers *continued*

Graphic Organizers *continued*

Story maps help you to gather details for your stories. Write notes about your character, setting, and plot.

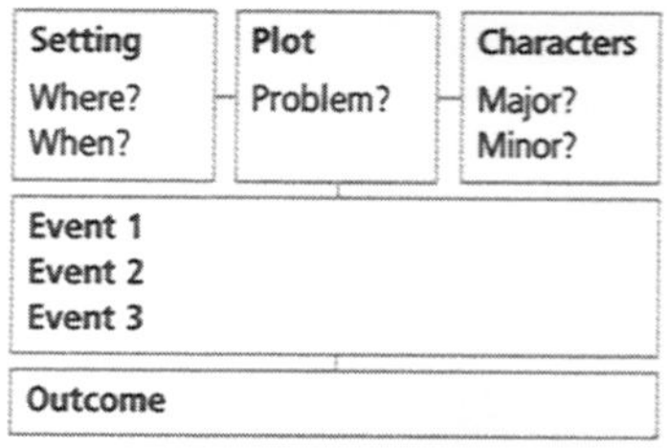

Time lines show events in order and tell when they happened. Draw an arrow, and write events along it in order from left to right. Add dates for each event.

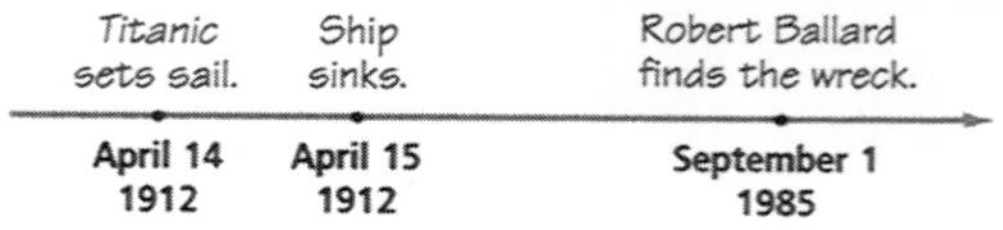

Venn diagrams are used to compare and contrast two subjects. Write details that tell how the subjects are different in the outer circles. Write details that tell how the subjects are alike where the circles overlap.

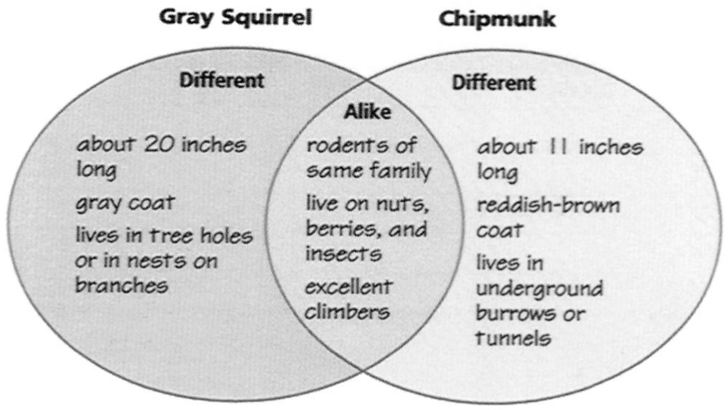

Writer's Tools

Guide to Capitalization, Punctuation, and Usage

Abbreviations

Abbreviations are shortened forms of words. Most abbreviations begin with a capital letter and end with a period. Use abbreviations only in special kinds of writing, such as addresses and lists.

Titles	Mr. *(Mister)* Mr. Juan Albino	Sr. *(Senior)* John Helt Sr.	
	Mrs. *(Mistress)* Mrs. Frances Wong	Jr. *(Junior)* John Helt Jr.	
	Ms. *(Any Woman)* Leslie Clark	Dr. *(Doctor)* Dr. Janice Dodds	
	Note: *Miss* is not an abbreviation and does not end with a period.		
Words used in addresses	St. *(Street)*	Blvd. *(Boulevard)*	Mt. *(Mount or Mountain)*
	Rd. *(Road)*	Rte. *(Route)*	Expy. *(Expressway)*
	Ave. *(Avenue)*	Apt. *(Apartment)*	
	Dr. *(Drive)*	Pkwy. *(Parkway)*	
Words used in business	Co. *(Company)*	Inc. *(Incorporated)*	
	Corp. *(Corporation)*	Ltd. *(Limited)*	
Other abbreviations	**Some abbreviations are written in all capital letters, with a letter standing for each important word.**		
	P.D. *(Police Department)*	P.O. *(Post Office)*	
	J.P. *(Justice of the Peace)*	R.N. *(Registered Nurse)*	
	The United States Postal Service uses two capital letters and no period in each of its state abbreviations.		
	AL *(Alabama)*	IL *(Illinois)*	MO *(Missouri)*
	AK *(Alaska)*	IN *(Indiana)*	MT *(Montana)*
	AZ *(Arizona)*	IA *(Iowa)*	NE *(Nebraska)*
	AR *(Arkansas)*	KS *(Kansas)*	NV *(Nevada)*
	CA *(California)*	KY *(Kentucky)*	NH *(New Hampshire)*
	CO *(Colorado)*	LA *(Louisiana)*	NJ *(New Jersey)*
	CT *(Connecticut)*	ME *(Maine)*	NM *(New Mexico)*
	DE *(Delaware)*	MD *(Maryland)*	NY *(New York)*
	FL *(Florida)*	MA *(Massachusetts)*	NC *(North Carolina)*
	GA *(Georgia)*	MI *(Michigan)*	ND *(North Dakota)*
	HI *(Hawaii)*	MN *(Minnesota)*	OH *(Ohio)*
	ID *(Idaho)*	MS *(Mississippi)*	OK *(Oklahoma)*

Capitalization / Punctuation / Usage

more ▶

Guide to Capitalization, Punctuation, and Usage

Using This Guide

The Guide to Capitalization, Punctuation, and Usage provides a useful reference resource for grammar and mechanics rules about capitalization, punctuation, and the correct usage of adjectives, adverbs, pronouns, verbs, and specific problem words, such as *can* and *may*. Encourage students to refer to this section while proofreading. The following sections are included.

- Abbreviations
- Titles
- Quotations
- Capitalization
- Punctuation
- Problem Words
- Adjective and Adverb Usage
- Negatives
- Pronoun Usage
- Verb Usage

Guide to Capitalization, Punctuation, and Usage *continued*

Abbreviations *continued*

Other abbreviations *(continued)*	OR *(Oregon)* PA *(Pennsylvania)* RI *(Rhode Island)* SC *(South Carolina)* SD *(South Dakota)* TN *(Tennessee)* TX *(Texas)* UT *(Utah)* VT *(Vermont)* VA *(Virginia)* WA *(Washington)* WV *(West Virginia)* WI *(Wisconsin)* WY *(Wyoming)*
	Initials are abbreviations that stand for a person's first or middle name. Some names have both a first and a middle initial. E.B. White *(Elwyn Brooks White)* T. James Carey *(Thomas James Carey)*

Titles

Italicizing/ Underlining	**The important words and the first and last words in a title are capitalized. Titles of books, magazines, TV shows, movies, and newspapers are italicized or underlined.** *Oliver Twist (book)* *Cricket (magazine)* *Nova (TV show)* *Star Wars (movie)* *The Phoenix Express (newspaper)*
Quotation marks with titles	**Titles of short stories, songs, articles, book chapters, and most poems are set off by quotation marks.** "The Necklace" *(short story)* "Home on the Range" *(song)* "Three Days in the Sahara" *(article)* "The Human Brain" *(chapter)* "Deer at Dusk" *(poem)*

Quotations

Quotation marks with commas and periods	**Quotation marks are used to set off a speaker's exact words. The first word of a quotation begins with a capital letter. Punctuation belongs *inside* the closing quotation marks. Commas separate a quotation from the rest of the sentence.** "Where," asked the stranger, "is the post office?" "Please put away your books now," said Mr. Emory. Linda whispered, "What time is it?" "It's late," replied Bill. "Let's go!"

Capitalization

Rules for capitalization	
	Capitalize the first word of every sentence. What an unusual color the roses are!
	Capitalize the pronoun *I*. What should I do next?
	Capitalize proper nouns. If a proper noun is made up of more than one word, capitalize each important word. Emily G. Messe District of Columbia Lincoln Memorial
	Capitalize titles or their abbreviations when used with a person's name. Governor Bradford Senator Smith Dr. Ling
	Capitalize proper adjectives. We ate at a French restaurant. She is French. That is a North American custom.
	Capitalize the names of days, months, and holidays. My birthday is on the last Monday in March. We watched the parade on the Fourth of July.
	Capitalize the names of nationalities, races, religions, languages, organizations, buildings, and companies. Able Supply Company Chinese Central School American Kennel Club Protestant African American
	Capitalize the first, last, and all important words in a title. Do not capitalize words such as *a, in, and, of,* and *the* unless they begin or end a title. *From the Earth to the Moon* *The New York Times* "The Rainbow Connection" "Growing Up"
	Capitalize the first word of each main topic and subtopic in an outline. 1. Types of libraries A. Large public library B. Bookmobile
	Capitalize the first word in the greeting and the closing of a letter. Dear Marcia, Yours truly,

Capitalization / Punctuation / Usage

more ▶

Guide to Capitalization, Punctuation, and Usage *continued*

Punctuation

End marks	**There are three end marks. A period (.) ends a declarative or imperative sentence. A question mark (?) follows an interrogative sentence. An exclamation point (!) follows an exclamatory sentence.** The scissors are on my desk. *(declarative)* Look up the spelling of that word. *(imperative)* How is the word spelled? *(interrogative)* This is your best poem so far! *(exclamatory)*
Apostrophe	**To form the possessive of a singular noun, add an apostrophe and *-s*.** doctor's boss's grandmother's family's
	For a plural noun that ends in *s*, add only an apostrophe. sisters' families' hound dogs' Smiths'
	For a plural noun that does not end in *s*, add an apostrophe and *-s* to form the plural possessive. women's mice's children's geese's
	Use an apostrophe in contractions in place of dropped letters. Do not use contractions in formal writing. isn't *(is not)* can't *(cannot)* won't *(will not)* wasn't *(was not)* we're *(we are)* it's *(it is)* I'm *(I am)* they've *(they have)* they'll *(they will)* could've *(could have)* would've *(would have)* should've *(should have)*
Colon	**Use a colon after the greeting in a business letter.** Dear Mrs. Trimby: Dear Realty Homes:
Comma	**A comma tells your reader where to pause. For words in a series, put a comma after each item except the last. Do not use a comma if only two items are listed.** Clyde asked if we had any apples, peaches, or grapes.
	Use commas to separate two or more adjectives that are listed together unless one adjective tells how many. The fresh, ripe fruit was placed in a bowl. One red apple was especially shiny.

Punctuation *continued*

Comma *(continued)*	**Use a comma before the conjunction in a compound sentence.** Some students were at lunch, but others were studying.
	Use commas after introductory words such as *yes, no, oh,* and *well* when they begin a sentence. Well, it's just too cold out. No, it isn't six yet.
	Use a comma to separate a noun in direct address. Jean, help me fix this tire. How was your trip, Grandpa? Can you see, Joe, where I left my glasses?
	Use a comma between the names of a city and a state and between a city and a country. Chicago, Illinois Sydney, Australia
	Use a comma after the greeting in a friendly letter. Dear Deena, Dear Uncle Rudolph,
	Use a comma after the closing in a letter. Your nephew, Sincerely yours,

Capitalization / Punctuation / Usage

Problem Words

Words	Rules	Examples
a, an, the	These words are articles.	
a, an	Use *a* and *an* before singular nouns. Use *a* before a word that begins with a consonant sound. Use *an* before a word that begins with a vowel sound.	a banana an apple
the	Use *the* with both singular and plural nouns. Use *the* to point out particular persons, places, or things.	the apple the apples The books that I like are long.
can	*Can* means "to be able to do something."	Nellie can read quickly.
may	*May* means "to be allowed or permitted."	May I borrow your book?
good	*Good* is an adjective.	The weather looks good.

more ▶

Guide to Capitalization, Punctuation, and Usage *continued*

Problem Words *continued*

Words	Rules	Examples
well	*Well* is usually an adverb. It is an adjective only when it refers to health.	She swims well. Do you feel well?
its	*Its* is a possessive pronoun.	The dog wagged its tail.
it's	*It's* is a contraction of *it is.*	It's cold today.
let	*Let* means "to permit or allow."	Please let me go swimming.
leave	*Leave* means "to go away from" or "to let remain in a place."	I will leave soon. Leave it on my desk.
raise	*Raise* means "to move something up," "grow something," or "increase something."	Our principal raises the flag. Julio and Myra raise rabbits. The bus line raised its prices.
rise	*Rise* means "to get up or go up."	This ski lift rises quickly.
sit	*Sit* means "to rest in one place."	Please sit in this chair.
set	*Set* means "to place or put."	Set the vase on the table.
teach	*Teach* means "to give instruction."	He teaches us how to dance.
learn	*Learn* means "to receive instruction."	I learned about history.
their	*Their* is a possessive pronoun.	Their coats are on the bed.
there	*There* is an adverb. It may also begin a sentence.	Is Carlos there? There is my book.
they're	*They're* is a contraction of *they are.*	They're going to the store.
two	*Two* is a number.	I bought two shirts.
to	*To* means "in the direction of."	A squirrel ran to the tree.
too	*Too* means "more than enough" and "also."	I ate too many cherries. Can we go too?
who	Use the pronoun *who* as a subject.	Who can solve the math problem?
whom	Use the pronoun *whom* as a direct object.	Whom did she ask for an autograph?
your	*Your* is a possessive pronoun.	Are these your glasses?
you're	*You're* is a contraction for *you are.*	You're late again!

Capitalization / Punctuation / Usage

Adjective and Adverb Usage

Adjective or adverb?	**Adjectives describe nouns or pronouns. Adverbs describe verbs.** Lena is a quick runner. *(adjective)* Lena runs quickly. *(adverb)*
Comparing	**To compare two things or actions, add *-er* to adjectives and adverbs or use the word *more*.** This plant is taller than the other one. It grew more quickly.
	To compare three or more things or actions, add *-est* or use the word *most*. This plant is the tallest of the three. It grew most quickly.
	Use *more* or *most* with an adjective or adverb that has two or more syllables, such as *careful* or *politely*. Do not add *-er* or *-est* to long adjectives or adverbs. agreeable–more agreeable–most agreeable slowly–more slowly–most slowly
good, bad	**The adjectives *good* and *bad* have special forms for making comparisons.** good–better–best bad–worse–worst

Negatives

	Do not use double negatives in a sentence. INCORRECT: We didn't go nowhere. CORRECT: We didn't go anywhere.

Pronoun Usage

Agreement	**A pronoun must agree with the noun to which it refers.** Kee bought a newspaper. Mary read it. Jeff and Cindy came to dinner. They enjoyed the meal.
Double subjects	**Do not use a double subject—a noun and a pronoun—to name the same person, place, or thing.** INCORRECT: The food it was delicious. CORRECT: The food was delicious.

more ▶

Capitalization / Punctuation / Usage

Guide to Capitalization, Punctuation, and Usage *continued*

Pronoun Usage *continued*

I, me	**Use *I* as the subject of a sentence and after forms of *be*. Use *me* after action verbs or prepositions such as *to, in,* and *for*. (See subject and object pronouns below.)** Jan and I are going to the show. She is taking me. Will you hold my ticket for me?
	When using *I* or *me* with nouns or other pronouns, always name yourself last. Beth and I will leave. Give the papers to Ron and me.
Possessive pronouns	**A possessive pronoun shows ownership. Use *my, your, his, her, its, our,* and *their* before nouns.** My report was about our trip to the zoo.
	Use *mine, yours, his, hers, its, ours,* and *theirs* to replace nouns in a sentence. Hers was about a visit to the museum.
Subject and object pronouns	**Use subject pronouns as subjects and after forms of the verb *be*.** He composed many works for the piano. I am she. The most talented singers are we.
	Use object pronouns after action verbs and prepositions like *to* and *for*. Clyde collected old coins and sold them. *(direct object)* Let's share these bananas with her. *(object of preposition)*
	Use the pronoun *who* as a subject. Use the pronoun *whom* as an object. Who traveled around the world? Whom did they see? To whom did they speak?
Demonstrative pronouns	**A pronoun that points out something is called a demonstrative pronoun. It must agree in number with the noun it points out or with its antecedent. Use *this* and *these* to point to things nearby. Use *that* and *those* to point to things farther away.** This is a jellyfish. These are sand dollars. That is a shark. Those are striped bass.

Pronoun Usage *continued*

Compound subjects and compound objects

To decide which pronoun to use in a compound subject or a compound object, leave out the other part of the compound. Say the sentence with the pronoun alone.

Lu and _______ ride the bus. *(we, us)*	
We ride the bus.	Lu and we ride the bus.
I saw Dad and _______. *(he, him)*	
I saw him.	I saw Dad and him.

***We* and *us* with nouns**

Use *we* with a noun that is a subject or a noun that follows a linking verb.

INCORRECT: Us girls are the stagehands.
CORRECT: We girls are the stagehands.
INCORRECT: The ushers are us boys.
CORRECT: The ushers are we boys.

Use *us* with a noun that follows an action verb or that follows a preposition such as *to, for, with,* or *at*.

INCORRECT: Dr. Lin helped we players.
CORRECT: Dr. Lin helped us players.
INCORRECT: She talked to we beginners.
CORRECT: She talked to us beginners.

Verb Usage

Agreement: subject-verb

A present tense verb and its subject must agree in number. Add *-s* or *-es* to a verb if the subject is singular. Do not add *-s* or *-es* to a verb if the subject is plural or if the subject is *I*.

The road bends to the right.	Mr. Langelier teaches fifth graders.
These books seem heavy.	I like camping.

Change the forms of *be* and *have* to make them agree with their subjects.

He is taking the bus today.	Have you seen Jimmy?
They are going swimming.	Mary has a large garden.

Agreement: compound subjects

A compound subject with *and* takes a plural verb.

Jason, Kelly, and Wanda have new dictionaries.

more ▶

Guide to Capitalization, Punctuation, and Usage *continued*

Verb Usage *continued*

could have, should have

Use *could have, would have, should have, might have, must have*. Avoid using *of* with *could, would, should, might*, or *must*.

She could have (*not* could of) spoken louder.
Juan would have (*not* would of) liked this movie.
We should have (*not* should of) turned left.
I might have (*not* might of) left my wallet on my desk.
It must have (*not* must of) rained last night.

Irregular verbs

Irregular verbs do not add *-ed* or *-d* to form the past tense. Because irregular verbs do not follow a regular pattern, you must memorize their spellings. Use *has, have*, or *had* as a helping verb with the past tense.

Verb	Past	Past with helping verb
be	was	been
begin	began	begun
blow	blew	blown
bring	brought	brought
choose	chose	chosen
come	came	come
fly	flew	flown
freeze	froze	frozen
go	went	gone
have	had	had
know	knew	known
make	made	made
ring	rang	rung
run	ran	run
say	said	said
sing	sang	sung
speak	spoke	spoken
steal	stole	stolen
swim	swam	swum
take	took	taken
tear	tore	torn
think	thought	thought
wear	wore	worn
write	wrote	written

Words Often Misspelled

You probably use many of the words on this list when you write. If you cannot think of the spelling of a word, you can always use this list. The words are in alphabetical order.

A
again
all right
a lot
also
always
another
anyone
anything
anyway
around

B
beautiful
because
before
believe
brought
buy

C
cannot
can't
caught
clothes
coming
could
cousin

D
didn't
different
don't

E
enough
every
everybody
everyone
everything

F
family
field
finally
friend

G
getting
girl
goes
going
guess

H
happened
happily
haven't
heard
here

I
I'd
I'll
I'm
instead
into
its
it's

K
knew
know

L
letter

M
might
millimeter
morning
mother's
myself

O
o'clock
off
once
other

P
people
pretty
probably

R
really
right

S
Saturday
school
someone
sometimes
stopped
suppose
sure
swimming

T
than
that's
their
then
there
there's
they
they're
thought
through
to
tonight
too
tried
two

U
until
usually

W
weird
we're
where
whole
would
wouldn't
write
writing

Y
your
you're

Spelling Guide

Words Often Misspelled

About the List

This list includes 104 words commonly misspelled by students in the intermediate grades. The words have been organized alphabetically for easy reference. Encourage students to refer to this list when proofreading their writing.

Spelling Guidelines

Using the Guidelines

This section of the Spelling Guide includes spelling generalizations that are developmentally appropriate for students in the intermediate grades. Examples are included for each generalization that show the most common spelling patterns for that generalization. Encourage students to refer to these guidelines and examples as they proofread.

If you find that a student is having trouble with a particular word or a certain spelling principle, find the appropriate spelling generalization and discuss it with the student. The student could then copy the generalization and the examples into a personal proofreading list or a writing notebook or staple it to his or her writing folder for easy reference when proofreading.

Spelling Guide

Spelling Guidelines

1. A short vowel sound before a consonant is usually spelled with just one letter: **a, e, i, o,** or **u.**

staff	grasp	slept	dwell	mist
split	fond	crush	bulb	

2. The |ā| sound is often spelled **ai, ay,** or **a-consonant-e.** The |ē| sound is often spelled **ee** or **ea.**

claim	sway	stake	fleet	greet	lease
brain	stray	male	speech	seal	beast

3. The |ī| sound is often spelled **i, igh,** or **i-consonant-e.** The |ō| sound is often spelled **o, o-consonant-e, oa,** or **ow.**

mild	thigh	strike	stole	loaf	sow
slight	stride	stroll	hose	boast	flow

4. The |o͞o| or the |yo͞o| sound is often spelled **ue, ew,** or **u-consonant-e.** The |o͞o| sound may also be spelled **oo** or **ui.** The |o͝o| sound is often spelled **oo** or **u.**

hue	brew	flute	boom	wood	put
clue	fume	troop	cruise	brook	bush
dew	duke	mood	bruise	poor	pull

5. The |ou| sound is often spelled **ou** or **ow.** The |ô| sound is often spelled **aw, au,** or **a** before **l.** The |oi| sound is spelled **oi** or **oy.**

ounce	coward	claw	fawn	fault	bald	joint	loyal
sour	scowl	hawk	haunt	stalk	moist	royal	

6. The |ûr| sounds are often spelled **ir, ur, er, ear,** or **or.** The |îr| sounds are often spelled **eer** or **ear.**

squirm	blur	stern	pearl	worm	smear
chirp	hurl	germ	earl	steer	rear

7. The |ôr| sounds are often spelled **or, ore,** or **oar.** The |âr| sounds are often spelled **are** or **air.** The |är| sound is usually spelled **ar.**

lord	tore	bore	hare	snare	flair	scar	barge
torch	sore	soar	fare	lair	harsh	carve	

H66 **Tools and Tips: Spelling Guide**

8. Homophones sound alike but have different spellings and meanings.

loan lone	flea flee	berry bury

9. The final |ər| sounds in two-syllable words are often spelled **ar, or,** or **er.**

lunar	burglar	major	clover	thunder
pillar	humor	tractor	banner	

10. The final |l| or |əl| sounds in two-syllable words are often spelled **le, el,** or **al.**

single	whistle	bushel	normal	local
angle	jewel	angel	legal	

11. Compound words may be spelled as one word, as a hyphenated word, or as separate words.

railroad	afternoon	ninety-nine	seat belt
watermelon	classmate	baby-sit	post office

12. A word with the VCCV syllable pattern is divided between the consonants.

at | tend	of | fer	traf | fic	tun | nel
sur | vive	es | cape	em | pire	wit | ness

13. If the consonants in a VCCV word are different and form a cluster or spell one word, divide the word before or after the two consonants.

a | fraid	de | gree	se | cret	ma | chine
rock | et	chick | en	oth | er	pack | age

14. If the first vowel sound in a VCV word is long, divide the word into syllables before the consonant.

pi | lot	fe | ver	sto | len	ba | sic
be | have	na | tion	de | tail	pre | fer

15. If the first vowel sound in a VCV word is short, divide the word into syllables after the consonant.

cab | in	hab | it	tal | ent	mod | ern
van | ish	rap | id	rec | ord	shad | ow

more ▶

Spelling Guidelines *continued*

Spelling Guidelines *continued*

16. When two different consonants in a VCCCV word spell one sound or form a cluster, divide the word into syllables before or after those two consonants.

dis | trict	al | though	com | plain	or | phan
mon | ster	or | chard	dol | phin	com | plex

17. When two vowels in a VV pattern spell two vowel sounds, divide the word into syllables between the vowels.

po | em	gi | ant	li | on	sci | ence
cru | el	di | al	cre | ate	qui | et

18. The **-ed** or **-ing** ending may simply be added to some words. A final **e** is usually dropped before adding **-ed** or **-ing**.

arrested	attending	seeking	borrowed	rising	freezing
offered	directing	awaiting	squeezing	amusing	providing

19. In one-syllable words ending with a single vowel and consonant, the consonant is usually doubled when **-ed** or **-ing** is added. In two-syllable words ending with an unstressed syllable, the final consonant is usually not doubled.

winning	bragging	shipped	stunned	suffering	covered
hitting	wrapped	whipped	chopped	gathering	wandered
swimming	dropped	begged	spotted	visiting	ordered

20. A suffix is a word part added to the end of a base word.

dreadful	breathless	countless	actively	settlement	softness

21. The final |ē| sound in a two-syllable word is often spelled **y** or **ey**.

ready	sorry	beauty	monkey	hockey
lonely	hobby	turkey	valley	

22. Final |ĭj| sounds are often spelled **age**. Final |tĭv| sounds are often spelled **tive**. Final |tĭs| sounds are often spelled **tice**.

baggage	postage	language	creative	practice
luggage	voyage	captive	defective	justice
savage	yardage	native	detective	notice

Spelling Guide

23. The |k| sound in a one-syllable word is often spelled **k** or **ck**. In a two-syllable word, it is often spelled **k, ck,** or **c**. The |ng| sound before **k** is spelled **n**.

shark	track	jacket	music	junk	blank
risk	lack	attack	active	drink	sink
struck	mistake	public	topic	rank	blanket

24. The final |j| sound is usually spelled **dge** or **ge**. The final |s| sound is often spelled **ce**.

lodge	bridge	dodge	change	chance	glance	fence
edge	ridge	strange	cage	twice	since	

25. Final |n| or |ən| sounds may be spelled **ain**. Final |chər| sounds may be spelled **ture**. Final |zhər| sounds may be spelled **sure**.

captain	mountain	fixture	exposure
fountain	creature	lecture	treasure
curtain	adventure	measure	pleasure

26. Prefixes are added to beginnings of words or word roots. Suffixes are added to ends of words.

decide	unknown	excuse	painful	careless
improve	comfort	prefix	movement	

27. The suffix **-ion** changes verbs to nouns. Sometimes the spelling changes.

correct	reduce	explode
correction	reduction	explosion

28. If a word ends with a consonant + **y**, change the **y** to **i** when adding **-es, -ed, -er,** or **-est.**

hobbies	spied	noisier	tiniest	loneliest
abilities	copied	earlier	happiest	

29. The suffixes **-able, -ible, -ant,** and **-ent** are added to words or word roots.

suitable	valuable	horrible	vacant	different
comfortable	possible	servant	student	

30. Some words have unexpected spellings.

acre	special	lamb	says	guide	knight

Spelling Guide

Diagramming Guide

Using the Guide

The Diagramming Guide is divided into the following segments that provide instruction and practice in diagramming sentences.

- Simple Subjects and Simple Predicates
- Compound Subjects
- Compound Predicates
- Direct Objects
- Linking Verbs
- Adjectives
- Adverbs
- Prepositional Phrases
- Nouns in Direct Address

Diagramming Guide

A diagram of a sentence is a set of lines that show how the words of that sentence are related. You will begin by diagramming the most important words in the sentence. In beginning lessons, sentences contain words that you do not yet know how to diagram. Work only with the words that you are asked to diagram. You will learn about the others as you work through the lessons.

Simple Subjects and Simple Predicates

The simple subject and the simple predicate are written on a horizontal line called the **base line**. The simple subject is separated from the simple predicate by a vertical line that cuts through the horizontal line.

Find the simple subject and the simple predicate in the sentence below.

Wheat has lost its Number 1 place.

Study this diagram of the simple subject and the simple predicate from the sentence above.

Wheat | has lost

Find the simple subject and the simple predicate in this sentence. Note that the subject, *you*, is understood.

Guess the largest crop.

Study the diagram of this sentence.

(you) | Guess

Practice

Diagram only the simple subjects and the simple predicates in these sentences.

See TE margin for answers.

1. Rice has gained first place.
2. It must have a hot, wet climate.
3. Name some rice exporters.
4. The biggest growers are in the Rice Bowl.
5. This area stretches from Japan to Indonesia.

Answers to Practice

Simple Subjects and Simple Predicates

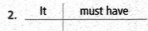

1. Rice | has gained
2. It | must have
3. (you) | Name
4. growers | are
5. area | stretches

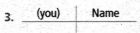

Compound Subjects

Each part of a compound subject is written on a separate horizontal line. The word *and* is written on a vertical dotted line that joins the horizontal lines.

Find the compound subject in this sentence.

India and China grow the most rice.

Study this diagram of the compound subject.

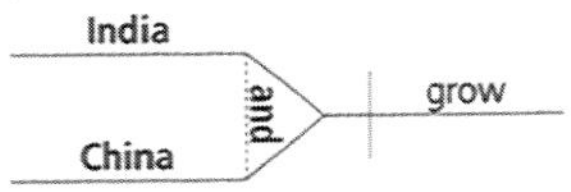

A compound subject can have more than two parts. Find the compound subject in this sentence.

Japan, Myanmar, and South Korea export more.

Study the diagram of this sentence. Note that the conjunction *and* is placed on the dotted line that connects the parts of the compound subject.

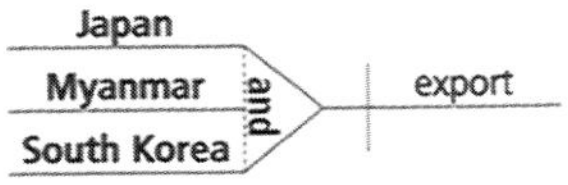

The word *or* can also join the parts of a compound subject.

Does Brazil or the United States grow more rice?

Although the sentence above is a question, it is diagrammed just like a statement. Study the diagram.

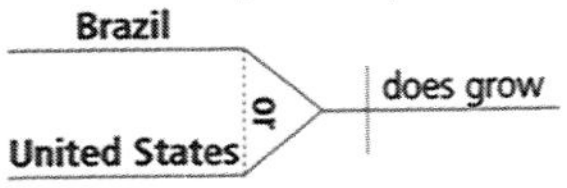

Practice

Diagram the subjects and the predicate in each of these sentences.

See TE margin for answers.

1. Rice and corn supplied Native Americans.
2. Quebec, the Midwest, and Louisiana had wild rice.
3. Europe and colonial America liked white rice better.
4. Is rice, potatoes, noodles, or tortillas your favorite food?

more ▶

Answers to Practice

Compound Subjects

1.

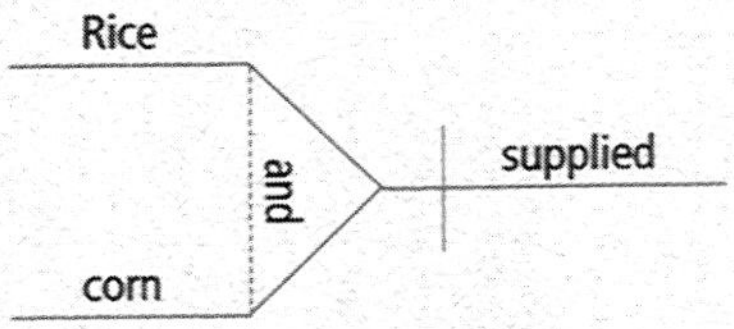

3.

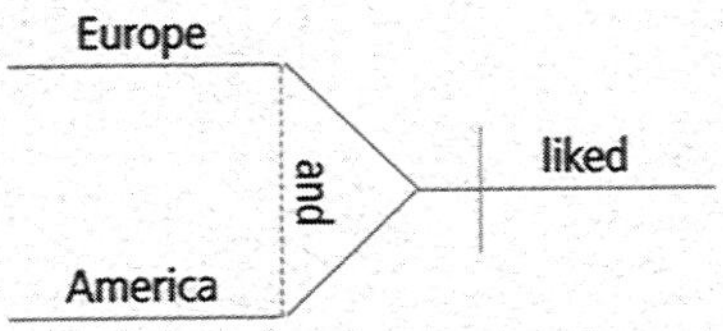

2.

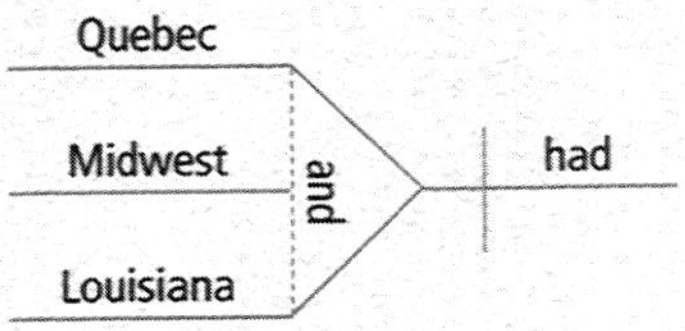

4.

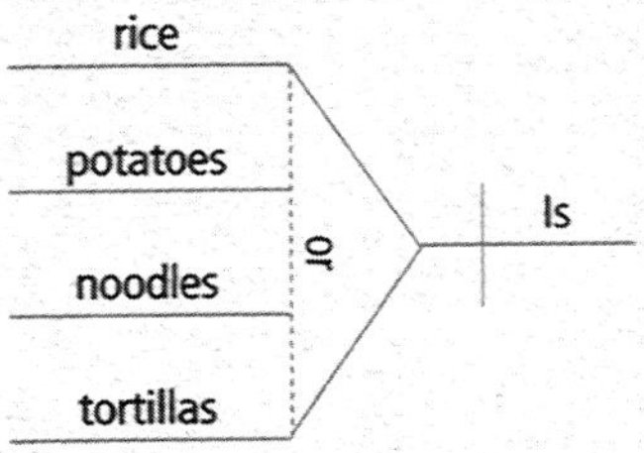

Diagramming Guide *continued*

Compound Predicates

Each part of a compound predicate is written on a separate horizontal line. The words *and, or,* and *but* are written on a vertical dotted line that joins the horizontal lines.

Find the compound predicate in this sentence.

We dressed and raced outside.

Study this diagram of the compound predicate.

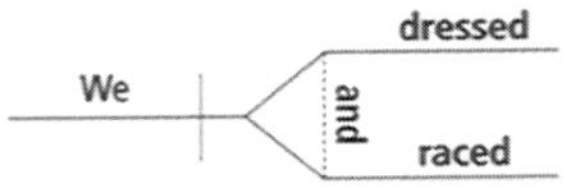

A sentence may have both a compound subject and a compound predicate.

My twin and I stumbled, slipped, and skidded along.

Study this diagram. Note where each *and* is placed.

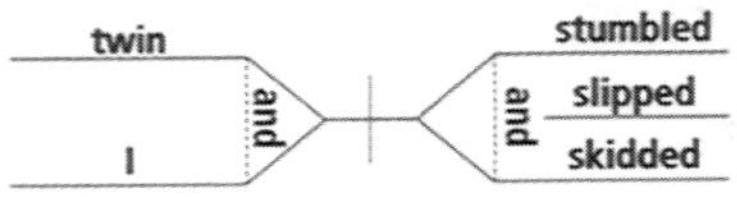

Practice

Diagram only the subjects and the predicates in each sentence. Either or both may be compound. See TE margin for answers.

1. Our yard sparkled and shone after the winter storm.
2. Each branch and twig had grown and had changed.
3. Pine needles looked and felt like diamond spikes.
4. Trees groaned and complained to the wind.
5. The heavy ice bent, broke, or cracked many branches.

Answers to Practice

Compound Predicates

1.

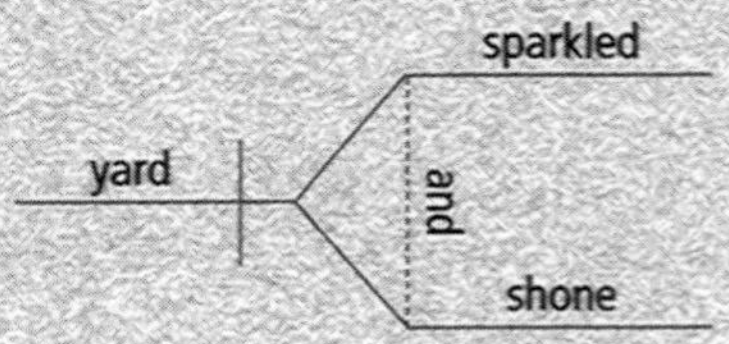

3.

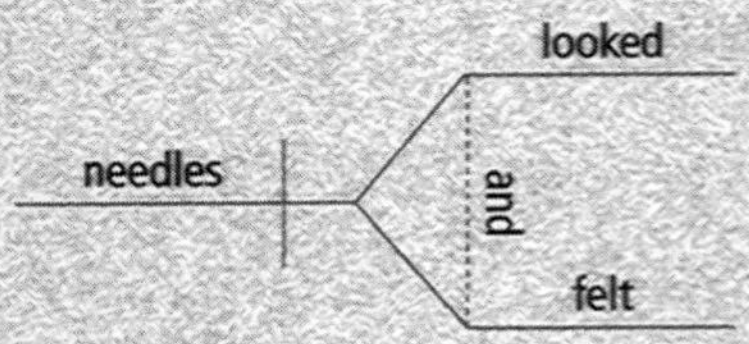

4.

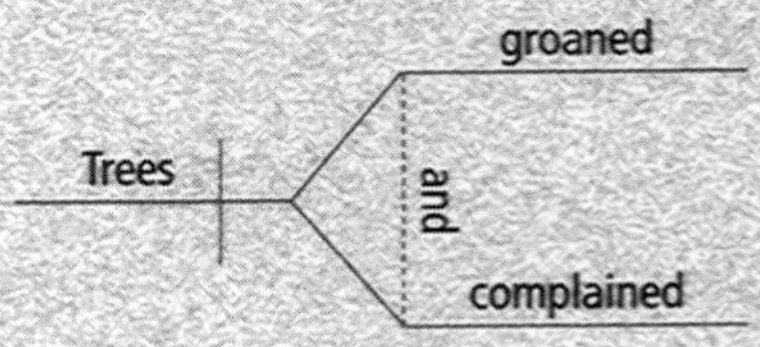

2.

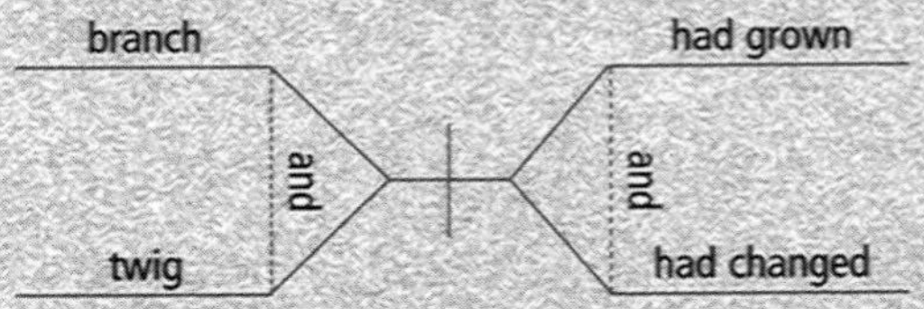

5.

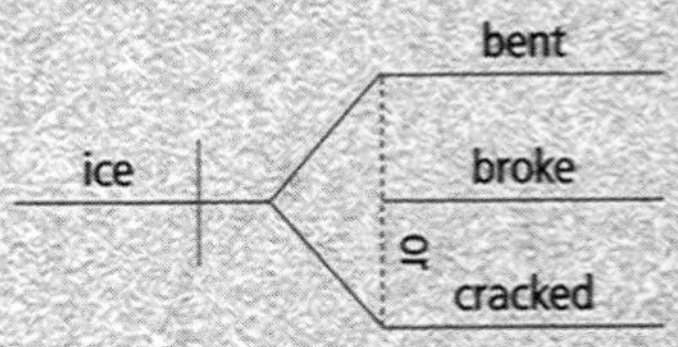

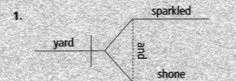

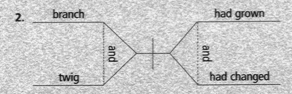

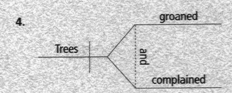

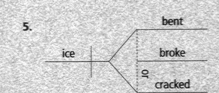

Direct Objects

A direct object is diagrammed on the base line after the verb. A vertical line is placed between the verb and the direct object. Notice that it does not cut through the base line.

Find the direct object in this sentence.

Paul needed some new clothes.

A verb can have more than one direct object. Find the compound direct object in this sentence.

Yesterday he bought boots and a jacket.

Study this diagram of the compound direct object.

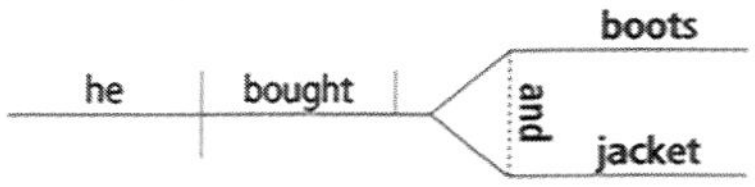

Each verb in a compound predicate can have its own direct object. Read this sentence. Find each verb and its direct object.

He liked the boots but disliked the jacket.

Study the diagram of the compound predicate and its separate direct objects.

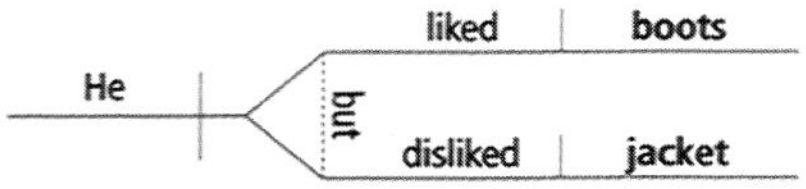

Practice

Diagram only the subjects, the verbs, and the direct objects in these sentences.

See TE margin for answers.

1. First, Paul found boots.
2. Then he saw a red wool jacket.
3. It had a hood and yarn cuffs.
4. Paul paid half and charged the rest.
5. Later he changed his mind and returned the jacket.

more ▶

Answers to Practice

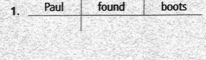

Direct Objects

1.

2.

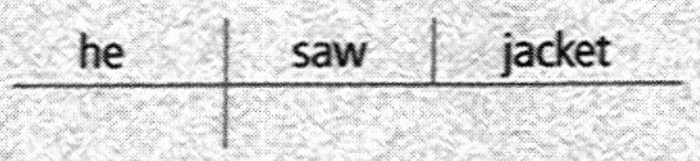

3.

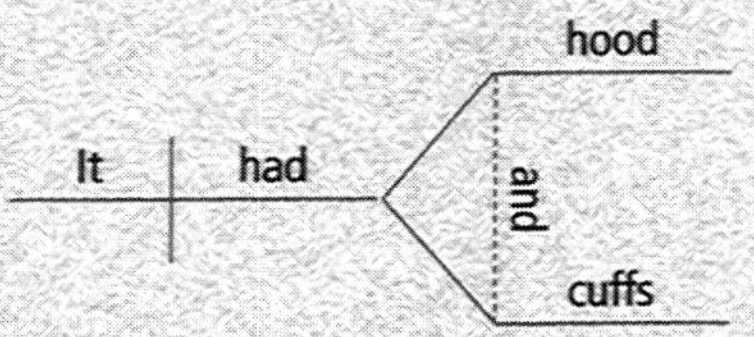

4.

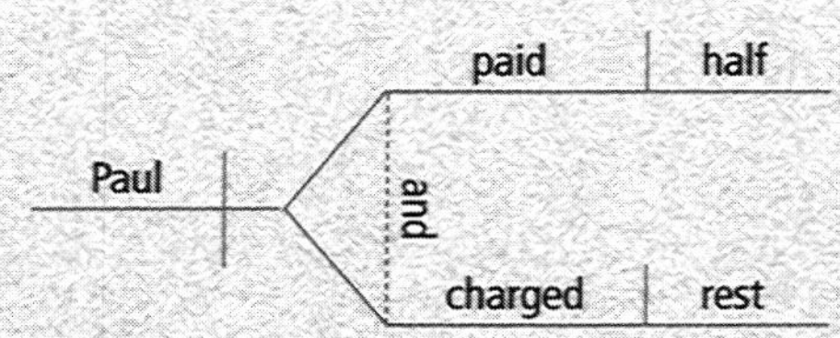

5.

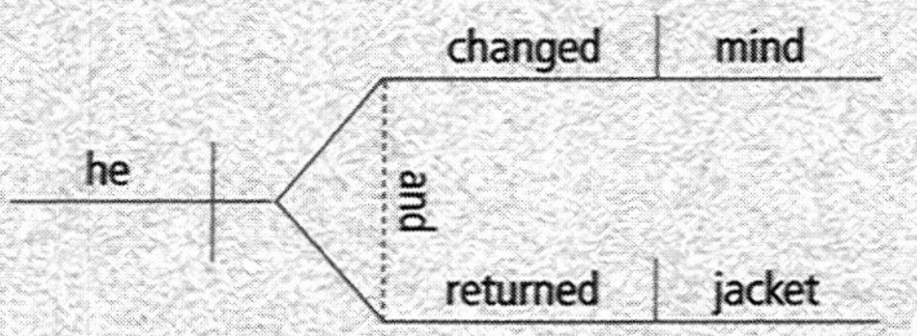

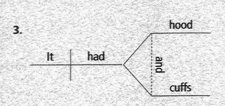

Diagramming Guide

Linking Verbs

A linking verb is diagrammed differently from an action verb. A slanting line, not a vertical one, follows a linking verb.

Remember, a linking verb joins the subject of a sentence with a word in the predicate. The word after the slanting line may name the subject or describe what it is like.

Find the linking verb in this sentence.

A cold feels horrible.

Now study this diagram. Notice that the slanting line points back toward the subject but does not cut through the base line.

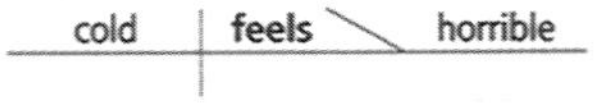

More than one word can follow a linking verb to describe the subject. Find the two words that describe the subject of this sentence.

Sally is miserable and cranky.

Study how these compound parts are diagrammed.

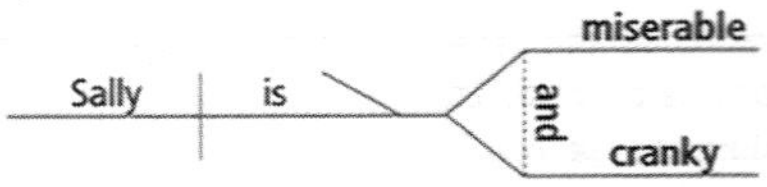

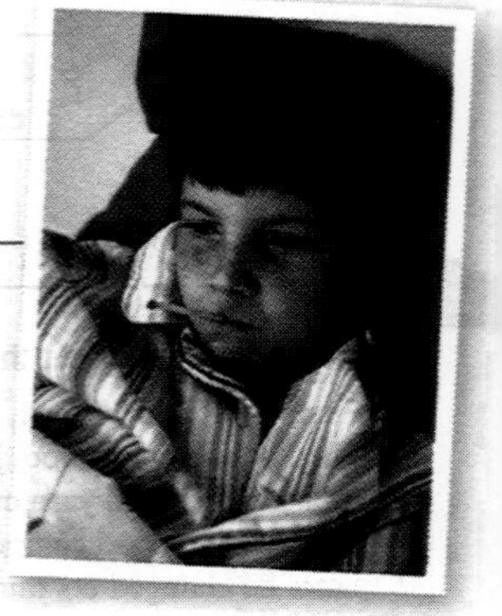

Practice

See TE margin for answers.

Diagram each linking verb and the two parts of the sentence that it joins.

1. Meals are not fun for a cold sufferer.
2. Food was tasteless yesterday.
3. Today my nose is red.
4. I am feverish and dizzy.
5. This head cold is a real pain.

Answers to Practice

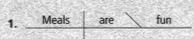

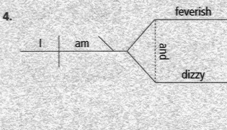

Linking Verbs

1.
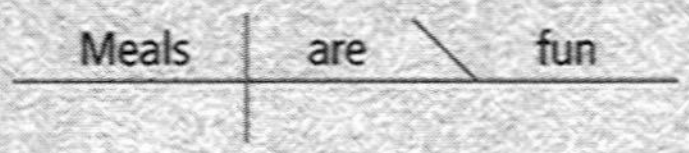

2.
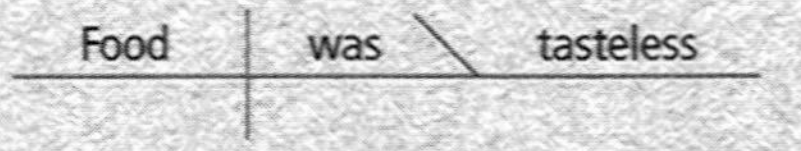

3.
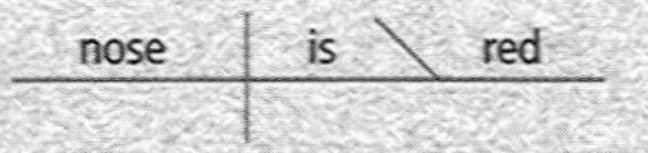

4.
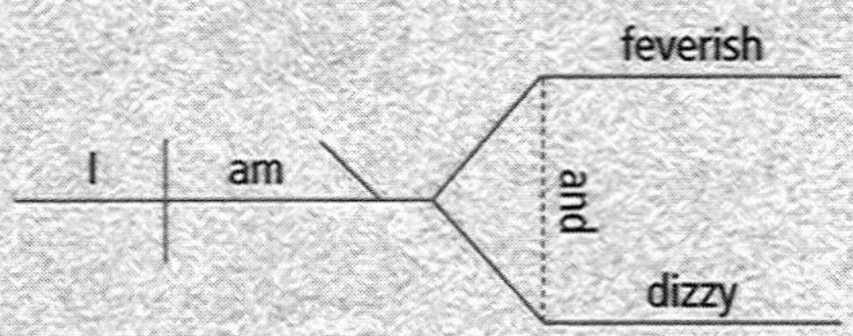

5.
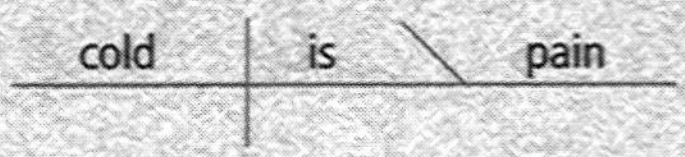

Adjectives

Adjectives are diagrammed on a slanting line right below the word that they describe.

Find the adjectives in this sentence.

I have brown, curly hair.

Study this diagram of the sentence.

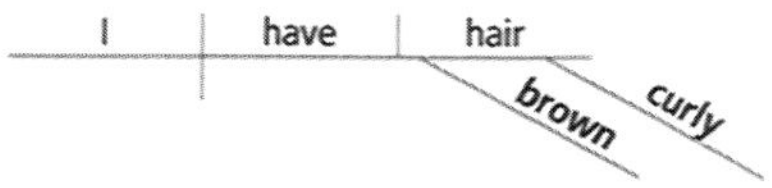

The words *a, an,* and *the* are diagrammed like adjectives.

My older sister has a long ponytail.

Study this diagram of the sentence.

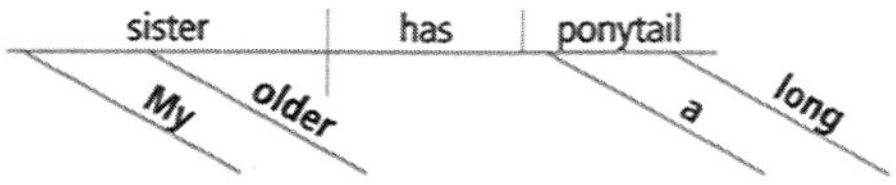

More than one adjective can describe the same word. Sometimes the word *and, or,* or *but* joins adjectives.

A long, braided, or straight hairstyle is not for me!

Note the position of the word *or* in this diagram.

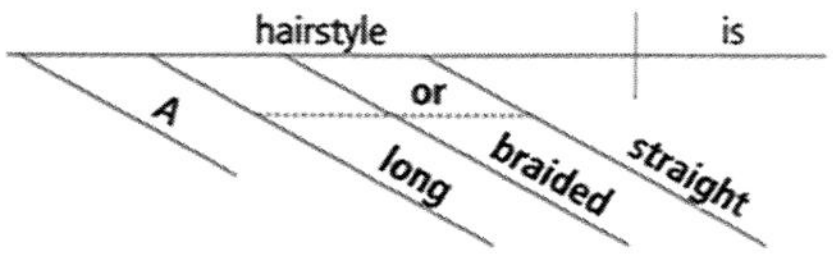

Practice

Diagram all the words in these sentences. See TE margin for answers.

1. This magazine has funny costumes.
2. See the blue, pink, and green wig!
3. That outfit wins the ugly prize.
4. I like that red satin cape.
5. You have unusual taste.

more ▶

Answers to Practice

Adjectives

1. 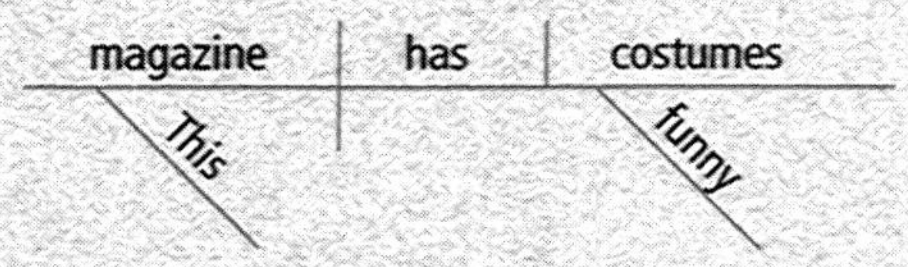

2. 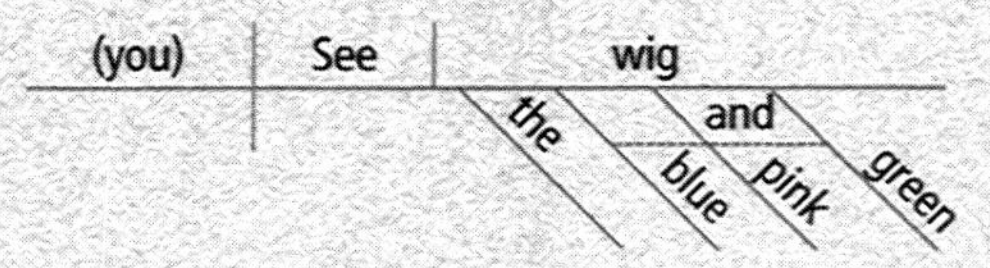

3. 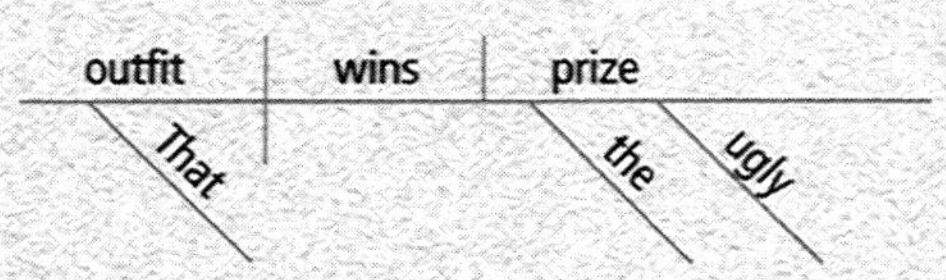

4. 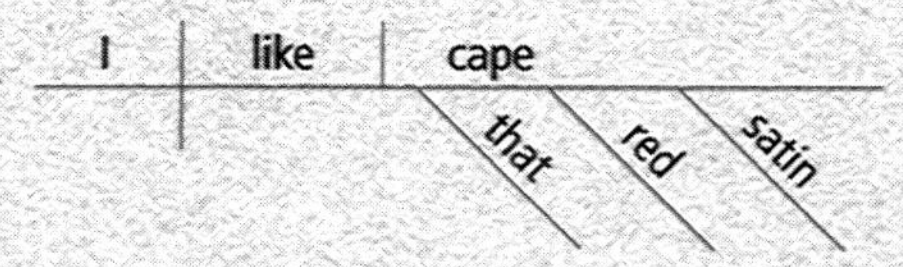

5. 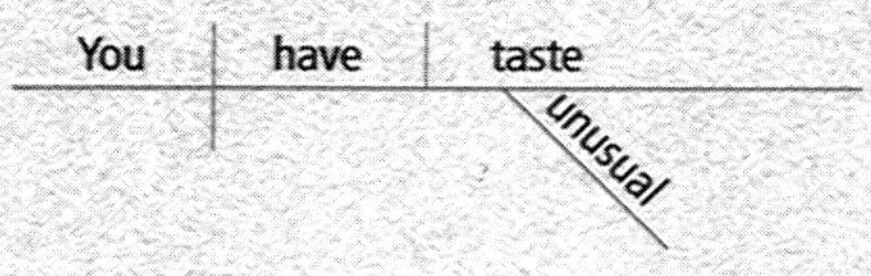

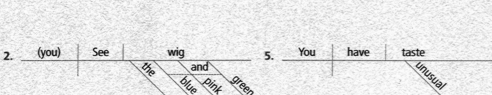

Diagramming Guide *continued*

Adverbs

Adverbs are diagrammed in the same way that adjectives are. An adverb is placed on a slanting line below the word that it describes. Find the adverb and the verb that it describes in the following sentence.

We patiently watched the tadpoles.

Study this diagram of the sentence.

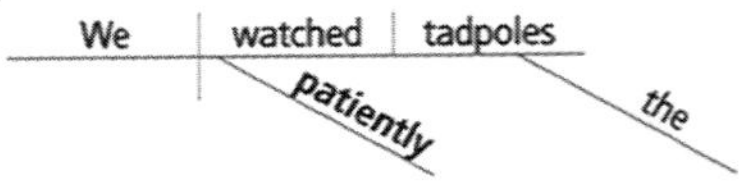

An adverb can appear anywhere in a sentence. It is not always right next to the word that it describes. Find the adverb in this sentence.

Soon the tadpoles became frogs.

Study this diagram of the sentence.

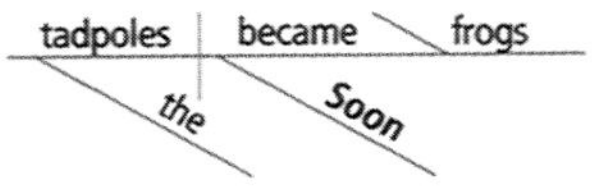

Several adverbs can describe the same word. In this sentence, find the adverbs and the words that they describe.

Then they changed swiftly and completely.

Notice the position of the word *and* in this diagram.

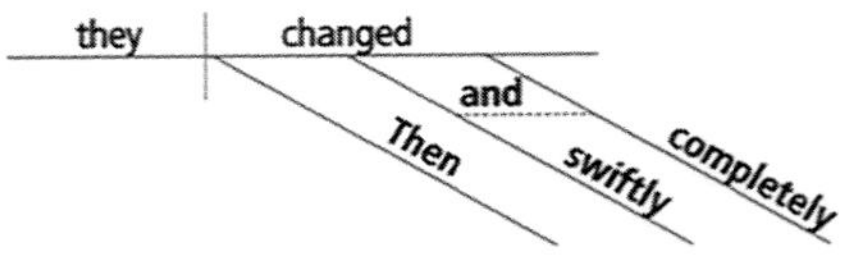

Practice

Diagram all of the words in these sentences. See TE margin for answers.

1. Recently a box arrived.
2. We put a heater nearby.
3. It had twelve eggs inside.
4. Monday we heard one faint peep.
5. Now all the chicks peep constantly and happily.

Answers to Practice

Adverbs

1.
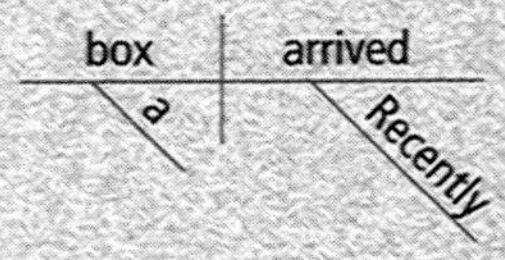

4.
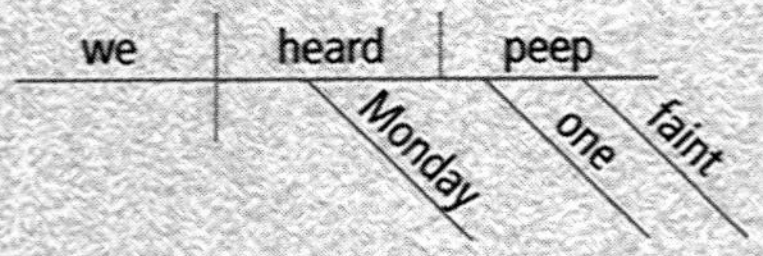

2.
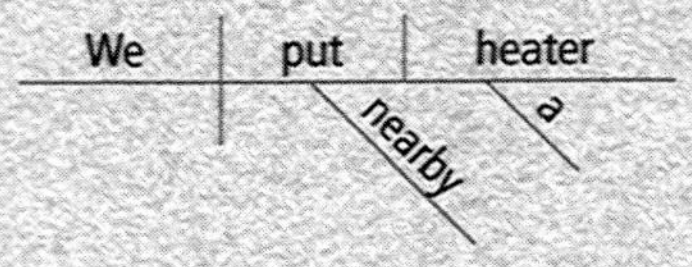

5.
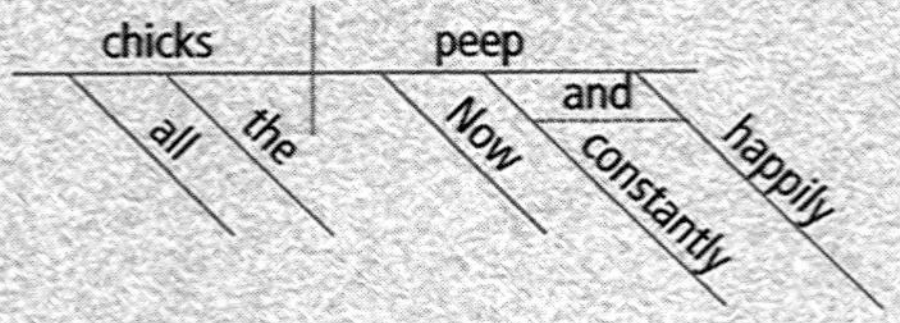

3.
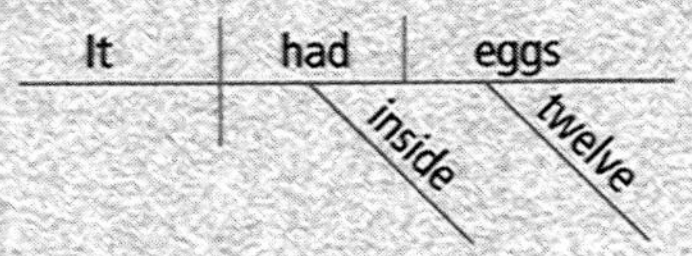

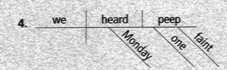

Prepositional Phrases

A prepositional phrase is diagrammed below the word that it describes. Prepositional phrases that tell where, when, or how often describe verbs. On the other hand, a prepositional phrase that tells what kind, how many, or which one describes a noun.

Find the prepositional phrase in this sentence. What word does it describe?

I like stories about twins.

Study this diagram of the sentence. Notice that the preposition is written on a slanting line below the word that it describes.

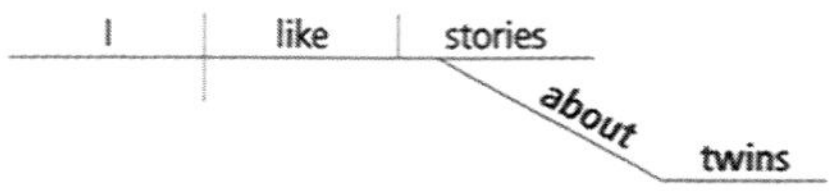

Find the prepositional phrase in this sentence. What word does it describe?

We have two sets in our family.

Study the diagram of this prepositional phrase.

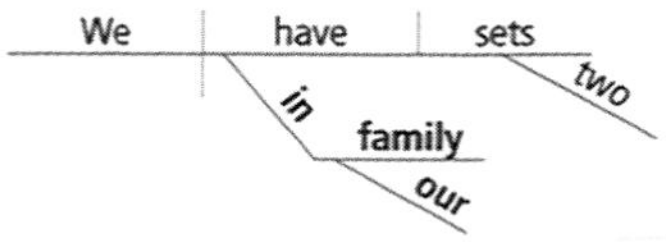

Practice

Diagram all of the words in the following sentences. See TE margin for answers.

1. Jamie lives near me.
2. He plays with some twins.
3. Once we wrote invitations for his party.
4. Jamie drew a funny picture on one invitation.
5. The two girls laughed about it.

more ▶

Answers to Practice

Prepositional Phrases

1.
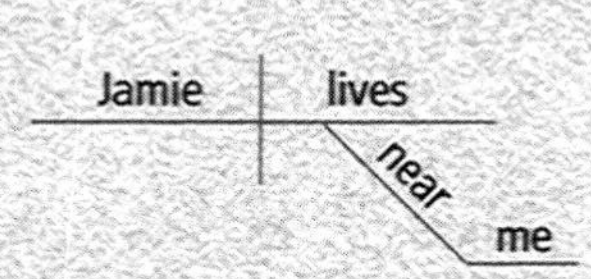

2.
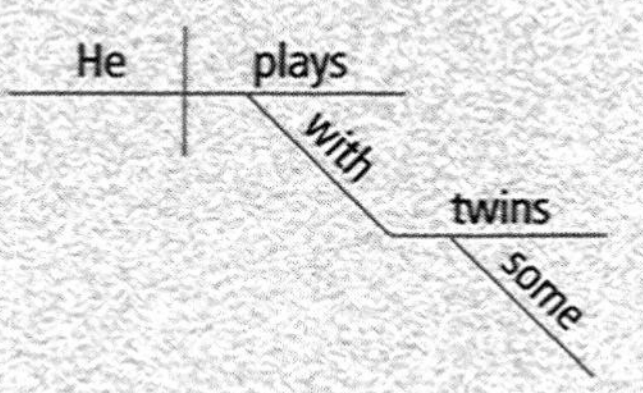

3.
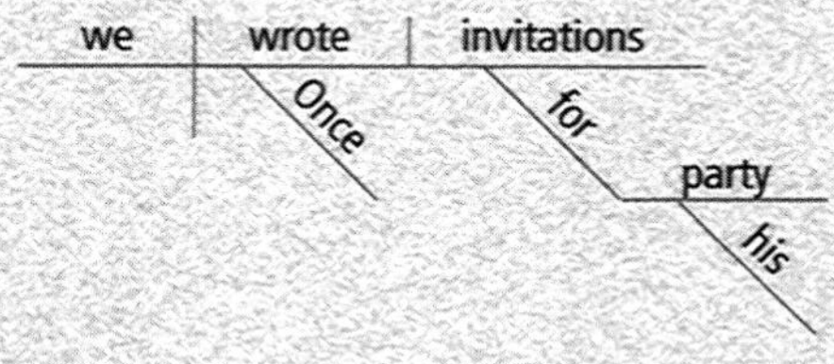

4.
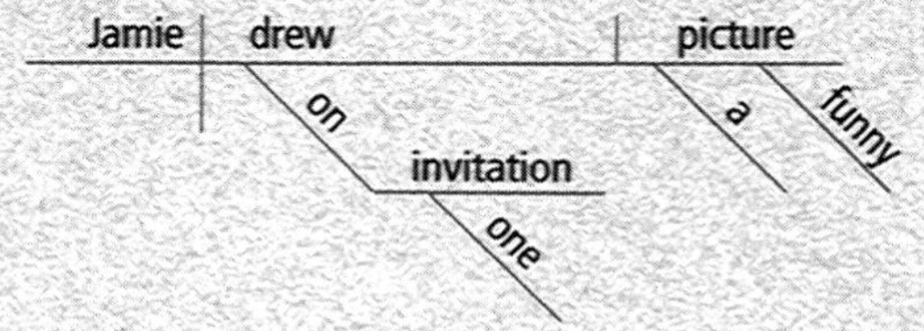

5.
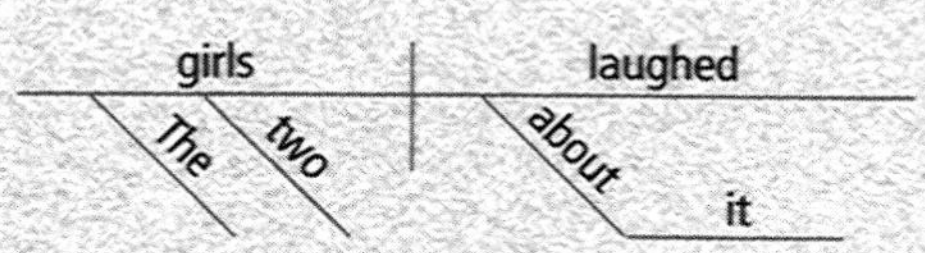

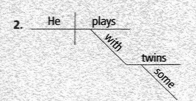

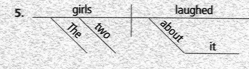

Nouns in Direct Address

Diagram a noun in direct address on a short line above and just to the left of the base line.

Find the noun in direct address in this sentence.

Students, today we are having a quiz.

Study this diagram of the sentence.

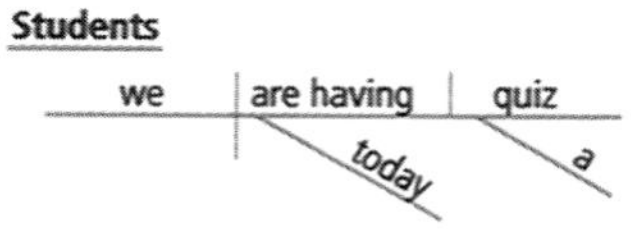

A noun in direct address is diagrammed in the same way no matter where the word appears in the sentence. Find the noun in direct address in this sentence.

Share that book with Aaron, Suzie.

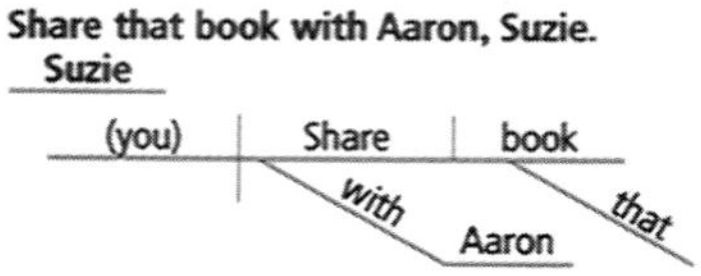

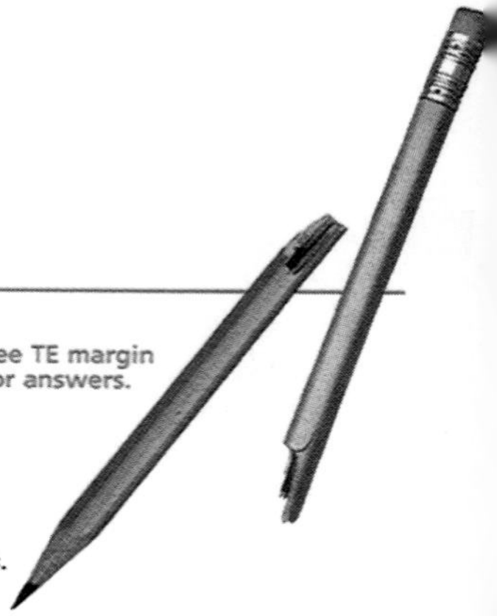

Practice

Diagram all of the words in these sentences. See TE margin for answers.

1. Mr. Savchick, I have a problem.
2. My only pencil, sir, just broke.
3. You may use this pen, Liz.
4. Listen carefully, class.
5. Everyone, I will read each question twice.

Answers to Practice

Nouns in Direct Address

1.
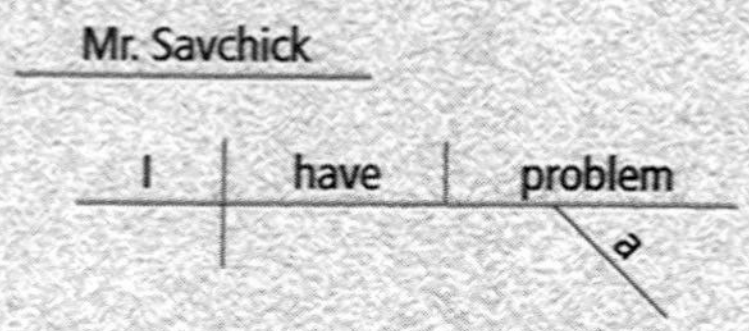

2.
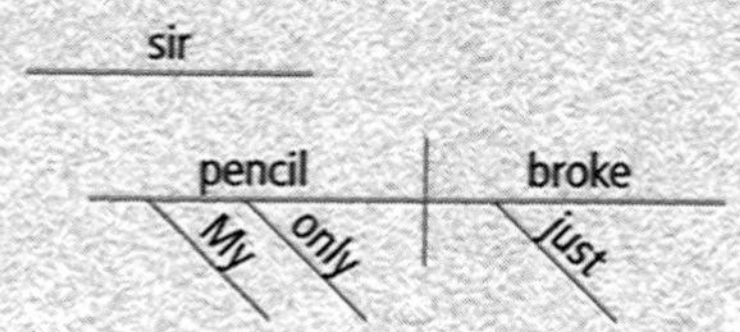

3.
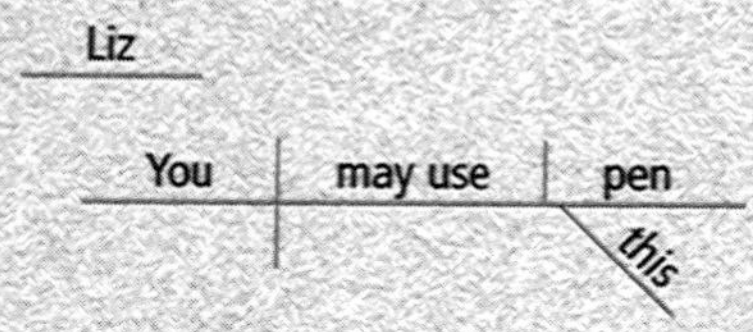

4.
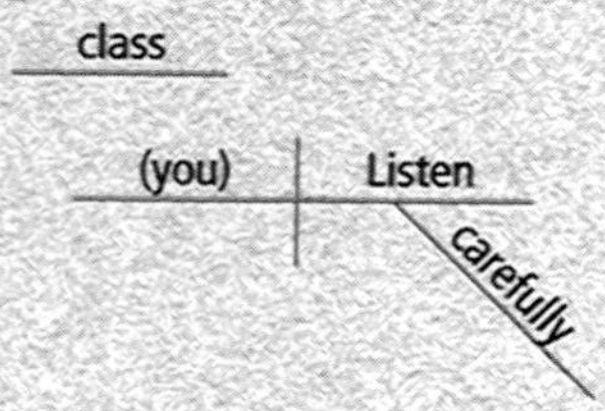

5.
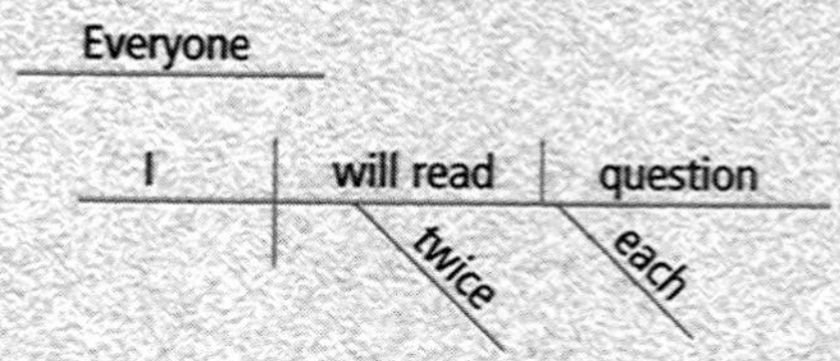

How to Use This Thesaurus

Why do you use a thesaurus? One reason is to make your writing more exact. Suppose you wrote the following sentence:

The thin ballerina twirled gracefully.

Is *thin* the most exact word you can use? To find out, use your Thesaurus Plus.

Look up Your Word Turn to the Thesaurus Plus Index on page H86. You will find

thin, *adj.*

Entry words are printed in blue type. Because *thin* is blue, you can look up *thin* in the Thesaurus Plus.

Use Your Thesaurus The main entries in the Thesaurus Plus are listed in alphabetical order. Turn to *thin*. You will find

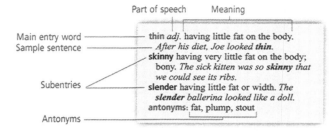

Part of speech — Meaning

Main entry word — **thin** *adj.* having little fat on the body.
Sample sentence — *After his diet, Joe looked* ***thin.***
Subentries — **skinny** having very little fat on the body; bony. *The sick kitten was so* ***skinny*** *that we could see its ribs.*
slender having little fat or width. *The* ***slender*** *ballerina looked like a doll.*
Antonyms — **antonyms:** fat, plump, stout

Which word might better describe the ballerina in the sentence at the top of the page? Perhaps you chose *slender*.

more ▶

How to Use This Thesaurus

Lesson Objectives

Students will:

- use an index for a thesaurus
- use a thesaurus to find synonyms or replacement words

Introducing the Thesaurus Plus

This introduction explains how to use the Thesaurus Plus Index and how the entries in the Thesaurus Plus are organized. Review this introduction with students prior to their using the Thesaurus Plus. Use the Practice exercises with students as guided practice prior to their using the Thesaurus Plus independently.

Focus on Instruction

- Explain that the Thesaurus Plus has features that most thesauruses do not have. Point out the information provided in the listing for the word *thin.*
- Write the following sentence on the chalkboard, and ask students to use Thesaurus Plus to find a more exact word for *easy*.

  Frozen meals make food preparation easy.

  Guide students in finding the word *easy* in the index and in the Thesaurus Plus. Point out that words listed in blue are alphabetized, main entry words. Ask students what words are listed as synonyms of *easy. (simple, uncomplicated, effortless)* Discuss the word choices with students to decide which has the most appropriate meaning for the sentence. Tell students to use the Thesaurus Plus to determine the best words to use in their writing. Point out to students that they can also use a thesaurus to avoid repeating the same word too often.
- Point out that only the index entries in blue have direct alphabetical listings in the Thesaurus Plus. Explain to students that they can find synonyms for italicized and regular-type index words only by looking up the words listed in bold type beside these words.

How to Use This Thesaurus *continued*

Focus on Instruction

- Have students look up the word *spring* under the word *jump* in the Thesaurus Plus. Ask them what other synonyms are listed. *(hurdle, leap)*
- Have students look up the word *start* in the index. Point out that it is listed in both blue and regular type. Explain to students that they can find synonyms for the word *start* either by looking it up as a direct entry in the Thesaurus Plus or by looking up its antonym *finish* and seeing what other antonyms are listed under this word. Point out to students that when a word is listed only in regular type, they can find its synonym only by looking up the antonym first and seeing what other antonyms of that word are listed.

Practice

- Before beginning the Practice exercises, review with students what each kind of type indicates about a word's listing.
- Do several of the exercises in both parts of the Practice as a class. Then have students work in pairs to complete the remaining exercises. Have students share their answers with the class.

How to Use This Thesaurus *continued*

Other Index Entries There are two other types of entries in your Thesaurus Plus Index.

1. The slanted type means you can find other words for *splendid* if you look under *nice*.
2. The regular type tells you that *start* is the opposite of *finish*.

splendid **nice**, *adj.*
spotless **clean**, *adj.*
spring **jump**, *v.*
sputter **say**, *v.*
spy **look**, *v.*

start **finish**, *v.*

Thesaurus Plus

Practice

A. Write each word. Look it up in the Thesaurus Plus Index. Then write *main entry*, *subentry*, or *antonym* to show how it is listed.

1. required subentry
2. calm main entry, antonym
3. get main entry
4. instant subentry
5. ask main entry
6. gloomy antonym
7. shout main entry, subentry
8. smash subentry

B. Use the Thesaurus Plus Index and the Thesaurus Plus. Replace each underlined word with a more exact or interesting word. Write the new sentence. Sample answers are shown.

9. As long as it kept raining, we stayed inside. While
10. It was really too cold to go out anyway. chilly
11. Later we looked at a great rainbow. stared, fantastic
12. We were nervous about the weather. anxious
13. We had to start planning our museum trip. begin
14. Clara was worried that there was little time. upset
15. Jim thought she was being comical. funny
16. Jim's thoughts angered Clara. annoyed
17. Mrs. Lee helped us to create a plan. establish
18. We decided to stick to her plan. resolved
19. We were grateful for Mrs. Lee's help. thankful
20. Everyone was now happy. glad

Thesaurus Plus Index

more ▶

Thesaurus Plus

How to Use This Thesaurus *continued*

Thesaurus Plus

Thesaurus Plus

more ▶

Thesaurus Plus H83

How to Use This Thesaurus *continued*

Thesaurus Plus

more ▶

How to Use This Thesaurus *continued*

Thesaurus Plus

How to Use This Thesaurus *continued*

Thesaurus Plus

A

active *adj.* full of movement. *Tennis is an **active** sport.*
energetic full of strength and energy. *My **energetic** friend Janet is always busy.*
lively full of life, alert. *The **lively** puppy kept tugging at his leash.*
antonyms: lazy, sluggish

agree *v.* to express willingness. *My parents **agreed** to get a dog.*
consent to say yes. *Did Judy **consent** to your plan?*
approve to say officially that something is correct or should be done. *The principal **approved** of the field trip.*
comply with to follow a request or a rule. *Please **comply with** the rules when you visit the museum.*
antonyms: deny, refuse

also *adv.* too. *Peter likes that album, but he likes this one **also**.*
in addition plus, as well. *We went to the park and to the zoo **in addition**.*
besides together with, over and above. *Tom plays two instruments **besides** the guitar.*

How Angry Were You?

angry *adj.* feeling or showing displeasure.

1. slightly angry: *displeased, annoyed, irritated, peeved*
2. very angry: *upset, cross, mad*
3. extremely angry: *furious, enraged, irate, fuming, outraged*

antonyms: calm, peaceful, delighted, happy, pleased

argue *v.* to give reasons for or against something, especially to someone with a different opinion. *Jo favored a town pool, but Jean **argued** against it.*
quarrel to have a fight with words. *We **quarreled** about who was smarter.*
clash to be against one another on an issue. *Employers and employees **clashed** during a recent strike.*
disagree to have a different opinion. *The senators **disagreed** with each other.*
antonyms: accept, agree, consent

ask *v.* to put a question to. *I will **ask** Donna to come with me.*
question to try to get information from. *Please **question** him about his plans.*
inquire to try to find out information. *We **inquired** about her address.*
antonyms: reply, answer

B

before *adv.* in the past. *He was excited since he hadn't been to Texas **before**.*
earlier sooner or at a past time. *The game ended **earlier** than usual.*
previously taking place in the past. ***Previously** she wore her hair long.*
antonyms: after, later

Word Bank

big *adj.* of great size or importance.

huge, immense, large, mighty, jumbo, bulky, massive, giant, colossal, mammoth, enormous, gigantic, sizeable, great

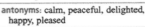

antonyms: little, tiny, miniature, small, wee, petite, microscopic

boast *v.* to praise oneself, one's belongings, or one's actions. *Sara always **boasts** about how fast she runs.*
brag to use words about oneself to show off. *Leroy **bragged** about everything.*
crow to utter a cry of delight or victory. *Pat grinned and **crowed**, "I won!"*

bold *adj.* not timid or fearful. *Mary Read was a **bold** woman.*
daring brave enough to take on a big challenge; adventurous. *Two **daring** climbers reached the top at last.*
audacious not afraid of any risk. *One **audacious** bear came up to our tent.*
antonym: cautious

boring *adj.* not interesting. *The TV show was **boring** so I fell asleep.*
dull lacking excitement. *Not one player scored during the **dull** soccer match.*
dry tiresome. *It was hard to finish reading the lengthy, **dry** report.*
monotonous not interesting because always the same. ***Monotonous** songs repeat the same words over and over.*
antonyms: exciting, lively, interesting, varied

brave *adj.* able to face danger or pain without fear. *You seemed **brave** when the doctor set your broken leg.*
courageous able to face difficult situations. *That pilot is **courageous**.*
valiant acting with great courage. *The **valiant** soldiers risked their lives.*
fearless without fright. *The **fearless** cat stood still as a dog ran toward it.*
antonyms: cowardly, frightened

break *v.* to separate into pieces as the result of force or strain. *A beam **broke** under the weight of the snow.*
shatter to come apart suddenly into many pieces. *The delicate cup **shattered** against the floor.*
smash to crush into pieces. *The car **smashed** into the orange crates.*
crack to come apart with a sharp sound. *Dale **cracked** the bat when he hit the ball.*
antonyms: mend, patch, repair

C

calm *adj.* without excitement or motion. *The **calm** water looked like a mirror.*
peaceful without worry or trouble. *Their argument spoiled our **peaceful** day.*
tranquil quiet and undisturbed. *We found a **tranquil** picnic spot.*
sedate composed; dignified. *He remained **sedate** during the trial.*
antonyms: excited, frantic, raging, wild

Shades of Meaning

careful *adj.* giving serious thought and attention to what one is doing.

1. alert for danger or trouble: *cautious, vigilant, watchful*

2. wise and thoughtful: *prudent, studious, mindful*
3. paying attention to details: *meticulous, conscientious, particular, thorough, strict*
4. showing lack of trust: *wary, guarded, protective*

antonyms: heedless, careless, thoughtless, slack, lax

change *v.* to make or become different. *I like how you **changed** your hair.*
convert to put something to a new use. *They **converted** the barn into a house.*
transform to alter completely the form of something. *We know how to **transform** fuel into energy.*
antonyms: continue, remain

chief *adj.* highest in rank or importance. *The **chief** product of the state is wheat.*
main most important. *The **main** library is bigger than its branches.*

more ▶

Thesaurus Plus

How to Use This Thesaurus *continued*

principal leading all others. *The panda's **principal** food is a kind of bamboo.*
antonyms: minor, unimportant

choice *n.* the act of choosing or deciding. *Please make your **choice** now.*
selection the act of picking one or a few out of several. *I tried on eight pairs of shoes before I made my **selection**.*
preference a liking for one thing over another. *My color **preference** is red.*
alternative decision between two or more possibilities. *The **alternative** is between walking or riding to school.*

clean *adj.* free from dirt, stains, and clutter. *Dad needs a **clean** shirt.*
spotless completely free of dirt. *The hospital operating room is **spotless**.*
antonyms: dirty, filthy, soiled

clear *adj.* free from clouds, dust, or anything that would make it hard to see through. *The sky was so **clear** that we could see the Milky Way.*
transparent able to be seen through easily. *We watched the sharks through a **transparent** tank.*
antonyms: cloudy, foggy, misty

cold *adj.* at a low temperature. ***Cold** water is the most refreshing drink of all.*
chilly not warm enough for comfort. *If you feel **chilly**, you can sit in the sun.*
cool at a somewhat low temperature. *The **cool** wind felt good in the sun.*
icy feeling like ice. *How do birds stay alive in such **icy** winds?*
freezing producing icy conditions. *The **freezing** rain made driving difficult.*
antonyms: hot, warm

common *adj.* often found or occurring; familiar. *A **common** response to a kind host is a thank-you note.*
familiar well known because it is often seen or heard. *The bus route home is very **familiar**.*
ordinary not unusual in any way. *On an **ordinary** day, I eat cereal.*
normal of the usual kind; natural. *It was not our **normal** school schedule.*
general widespread; prevalent. *The students had a **general** feeling of excitement before the big game.*
regular usual or standard. *They said our **regular** teacher was ill.*
antonyms: abnormal, extraordinary, rare, strange, unusual

create *v.* to bring into being. ***Spiders create** webs to trap insects.*
establish to begin or set up. *The settlers soon **established** a small town.*
invent to make something that did not exist before. *No one is sure who really **invented** the camera.*
produce to bring forth, manufacture. *How many cars do they **produce**?*
design to make a plan or a drawing for something. *An art student **designed** the school's new sign.*
antonym: destroy

D

danger *n.* the chance of great harm or loss. *There was no **danger** of getting lost if we stayed on the path.*
hazard something that could cause harm. *A blocked door can be a fire **hazard**.*
risk the possibility of harm in an activity. *The **risk** of an accident increases on icy roads.*
peril a condition that can threaten lives. *Anyone out in this storm will be in great **peril**.*
antonyms: safety, security, protection

dark *adj.* without light or sun. *It was so **dark** that we turned on the lights.*
dim not well lit. *Do not read in such **dim** light.*
murky very gloomy. *Evans was afraid to step into the **murky** cell.*
antonyms: bright, light

decide *v.* to make up one's mind. *I **decided** to buy the red bike.*
determine to make a firm decision. *Dr. Tsao **determined** to do all that he could to save the cat.*
resolve to make a firm plan. *I **resolve** to eat a good breakfast every day.*

deserve *v.* ought to have or receive. *An animal lover like Paul **deserves** a pet.*
merit earn the right to something. *June's courage **merits** high praise.*
be worthy of be good or valuable enough to receive. *The animal shelter **is worthy of** your support.*

Shades of Meaning

do *v.*

1. to carry out an action: *perform, execute, produce, make, work, act*
2. to solve something: *unscramble, solve, work out, decode, resolve*

3. to complete an action: *fulfill, finish, complete, achieve, attain, accomplish*

antonyms: omit, undo, fail, quit

E

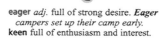

eager *adj.* full of strong desire. ***Eager** campers set up their camp early.*
keen full of enthusiasm and interest. *Ben is a **keen** football fan.*
interested involved or concerned with. *Peg is an **interested** committee member.*
antonyms: bored, indifferent

easy *adj.* not difficult. *Tad solved the **easy** puzzle quickly.*
simple not complicated. *Use a **simple** drawing of a few lines.*
uncomplicated not hard to understand, deal with, or solve. *We followed Dad's **uncomplicated** directions with ease.*
effortless easily done. *The athlete made weightlifting seem **effortless**.*
antonyms: complex, difficult, hard

effect *n.* something brought about by a cause. *The moon has an important **effect** on the ocean tides.*
consequence a direct outcome of something. *The fine performance was a **consequence** of practice.*
result something that happens because of something else. *The broken branches are the **result** of the storm.*
antonyms: cause, source

explore *v.* to look into or through closely. *Katie **explored** every inch of her closet for her missing shoe.*
study to examine closely and carefully. *Doris **studied** her notes before class.*
probe to search into thoroughly. *An investigator **probed** Rick's background.*
investigate to research carefully. *Who will **investigate** the jewel's disappearance?*

F

faithful *adj.* worthy of trust. *Ben knew his **faithful** friend would keep quiet.*
loyal offering constant support to a person, country, or cause. *The spy insisted that he was **loyal** to his country.*
true trustworthy and devoted. *Ariel was a **true** friend when I needed her.*
antonyms: changeable, treacherous, false

fake *n.* someone or something that is not what he, she, or it pretends to be. *We realized that the actor's moustache was a **fake**.*
fraud a person who lies about himself or herself. *That **fraud** claimed that he got us free tickets, but he did not!*
phony an insincere person. *Pete tries to act friendly, but he is a **phony**.*
impostor a person who pretends to be another person. *Was that woman really the queen or only an **impostor**?*

more ▶

Thesaurus Plus H91

How to Use This Thesaurus *continued*

Thesaurus Plus

fat *adj.* having much or too much body weight. *We put our **fat** dog on a diet.*
plump rounded and full in shape. *Her baby brother has **plump** cheeks.*
stout large and heavy in build. *Al is slim, but his brother Ben is **stout**.*
antonyms: skinny, slender, slim, thin

finish *v.* to get done. *When you **finish** cleaning, you may go for a bike ride.*
end to bring or come to the final moments. *The first half **ended** when the whistle blew.*
complete to get to the end of something. *I **completed** the test as the bell rang.*
stop to come to a halt. *The engine **stopped** when the car ran out of gas.*
conclude to be or cause to be over. *Ms. Wang **concluded** her speech.*
close to come to or bring to an end. *The play **closed** with a joke.*
antonyms: begin, commence, start

How Funny Was It?

funny *adj.* causing laughter or amusement.

1. somewhat funny: *amusing, droll, whimsical, witty*
2. quite funny: *humorous, laughable, comical*
3. extremely funny: *ridiculous, hilarious, sidesplitting, ludicrous, absurd*

antonyms: serious, sad, solemn, gloomy, depressing

further *adj.* added or other. *The news station released **further** storm bulletins.*
more greater in size, quantity, extent, or degree. *We need **more** ice for the bowl.*
additional extra. *Take **additional** socks in case one pair gets wet.*

G

gather *v.* to bring or come together in one place. *They **gathered** around the campfire and sang songs.*
assemble to bring or come together as a group. *The band members must **assemble** in the auditorium at noon.*
collect to bring things together. *Tina has **collected** twenty different baseball hats in only one year.*
antonyms: scatter, separate

get *v.* to receive. *Did you **get** any payment for your work in the garden?*
earn to gain by working or by supplying a service. *Jay **earns** five dollars a week by baby-sitting for families in his neighborhood.*
obtain to gain by means of planning or effort. *Carol took a test to **obtain** her driver's license.*
win to receive as a prize or reward. *Did Joe **win** a prize in the school essay contest?*
acquire to gain by one's own efforts. *Ed worked many hours to **acquire** his typing skill.*
buy to gain by paying a price for. *Ana used her allowance to **buy** a gift for her mother.*
antonym: lose

give *v.* to hand over to another. *Sara **gave** her sister a small music box for her birthday.*
offer to put forward to be accepted or refused. *Jan **offered** Ina half of her sandwich and apple.*
supply to make available something that is needed. *Blood **supplies** oxygen to the brain.*
present to make a gift or award to. *Coach Hart **presented** the trophy to the captain of our basketball team.*
antonyms: receive, take

Shades of Meaning

good *adj.*

1. well-behaved: *polite, obedient, well-mannered, courteous*
2. trustworthy: *honest, decent, honorable, law-abiding, upstanding, upright, moral*
3. aiding one's health: *healthful, nutritious, nourishing*
4. pleasant-tasting: *delicious, tasty, flavorful, mouth-watering, yummy, appetizing, luscious, scrumptious*
5. having much ability: *skilled, able, capable, talented, gifted, masterful, expert, qualified, experienced*
6. kind: *considerate, caring, thoughtful, generous, unselfish, friendly, loving, charitable*
7. better than average: *outstanding, excellent, fine, superior, praiseworthy, admirable*

antonyms: awful, unkind, harmful, bad, evil, wicked, disagreeable, disgusting, unworthy, cruel, mean, nasty, heartless, inferior, poor, second-rate

glance *v.* to look briefly. *I* ***glanced*** *at him quickly.*
glimpse to get a brief view of. *She only* ***glimpsed*** *the passing car.*
peek to look briefly. *He* ***peeked*** *around the corner.*

grateful *adj.* feeling or showing thanks. *The Smiths were* ***grateful*** *when their neighbors helped rebuild their barn.*
appreciative expressing or feeling gratitude. *The* ***appreciative*** *man thanked Lori for finding his cat.*
thankful showing an understanding of how fortunate one is. *Dad was* ***thankful*** *that no one was hurt.*

great *adj.* remarkable. *Pearl took* ***great*** *pictures of the baseball game.*
terrific excellent. *A* ***terrific*** *swimmer like Natalie should make the team.*
fantastic extraordinary. *There is a* ***fantastic*** *view of the ocean from here!*
wonderful astonishing. *This is a* ***wonderful*** *museum.*
marvelous notably superior. *Your speech was* ***marvelous****.*
antonyms: inferior, ordinary

Shades of Green

green *adj.* having the color of grass; a mix of blue and yellow.

olive: light yellowish-green, like green olives
lime: bright yellowish-green, like limes
kelly: bright green, like grass or clover
emerald: bright, slightly dark green, like emeralds
hunter: dark green, like pine trees and cucumbers

grow *v.* to become or cause to become larger. *Rain helped the plants* ***grow*** *tall.*
raise to promote the development of. *Kate* ***raised*** *her puppy with love.*
produce to bring forth; yield. *Kansas* ***produces*** *wheat.*
mature to develop fully. *Has the fruit* ***matured*** *enough to be picked?*
antonym: stunt

H

happy *adj.* showing or feeling pleasure or joy. *Tina was* ***happy*** *because she got the lead part in the play.*
cheerful being in good spirits. *It is pleasant to be near* ***cheerful*** *people.*
glad pleased. *Sam was* ***glad*** *to be home.*
antonyms: sad, sorrowful

healthy *adj.* free from disease or injury. *The* ***healthy*** *plants grew tall.*
fit being in good physical shape. *Drew feels healthy and* ***fit****.*

more ▶

Thesaurus Plus

Thesaurus Plus H93

How to Use This Thesaurus *continued*

sound having no damage or disease. *The old house still had a **sound** frame.*
well not sick. *Even during the flu season, Molly stayed **well**.*
antonyms: diseased, ill, sick

hide *v.* to keep or put out of sight. *The cat **hid** under the bed.*
conceal purposely to keep from being seen or known. *Allan **concealed** his sadness behind a happy face.*
bury to cover from view. *The dog **buried** another bone under the rose bush.*
antonyms: reveal, show

honest *adj.* straightforward; truthful. *The **honest** witness told the truth in court.*
direct to the point. *I will be **direct** and not waste time.*
frank free and open in expressing thoughts or feelings. *In a **frank** talk, I told Lina how I felt.*
antonyms: deceitful, insincere, misleading

J

job *n.* something that must be done. *Would you prefer the **job** of scrubbing or waxing?*
work things that must be done. *You have enough **work** to keep you busy.*
task an assignment or a chore. *Adam's **task** was to sweep the hall.*
employment an activity by which one earns money or to which one devotes time. *Teaching is a wonderful form of **employment**.*
antonyms: play, hobby, leisure

join *v.* to put together or attach. *We all **joined** hands to form a circle.*
connect to link things together. *A bridge **connects** the two cities.*
unite to bring together to form a whole. *The thirteen colonies were **united**.*
antonyms: part, separate

jump *v.* to rise up or move through the air. *The cow in the nursery rhyme **jumps** over the moon.*
hurdle to go over a barrier. *The horse **hurdled** the fence and galloped away.*
leap to jump or cause to jump quickly or suddenly. *Carl **leaped** away from the falling tree.*
spring to move upward or forward in one quick motion. *I **spring** out of bed when my alarm rings.*

L

last *adv.* after all the others. *Add the ice **last** so that it does not melt.*
finally after a long while. *After waiting two hours, the train **finally** arrived.*
at the end at the conclusion. *Flo stumbled **at the end** of her speech.*
antonym: first

Shades of Meaning

laugh *v.* to make sounds to express amusement.

1. to laugh quietly: *giggle, chuckle, titter*
2. to laugh in a mean or sly way: *snicker, snigger*
3. to laugh loudly: *cackle, chortle, guffaw, roar, shriek, howl*

antonyms: whimper, weep, cry, wail, sob, blubber

leave *v.* to go away from. *Please **leave** this dangerous place at once!*
abandon to go away from because of trouble or danger; to desert. *The crew **abandoned** the sinking ship.*
quit to depart from. *Phil wants to **quit** Seattle and move to Tulsa.*
antonyms: arrive, come, return

let *v.* to give permission to. *Ron took the leash off his dog and **let** her run free.*
allow to say yes to. *Please **allow** me to go to Jenny's party.*

permit to consent to. *The state law **permits** sixteen-year-olds to drive cars and motorcycles.*
antonyms: prevent, stop, hinder

little *adj.* not big in size or quantity. *Leroy is six feet tall, but he looks **little** next to that thirty-foot statue.*
tiny extremely reduced in size. *Dan could not read the **tiny** print without his glasses.*
small reduced in size. *I cannot wear this coat because it is too **small**.*
miniature reduced from its usual size. *Ella built a **miniature** city with toothpicks and glue.*
antonyms: enormous, large

lively *adj.* full of energy, active. *They were out of breath after dancing a **lively** polka.*
chipper full of cheer. *Ike felt **chipper** on this lovely morning.*
energetic full of strength and action. *The **energetic** children played on the swings all morning.*
spirited full of life. *Our team played a **spirited** game and won.*
antonyms: inactive, lazy

Shades of Meaning

look *v.* to focus one's eyes or attention on something.

1. to look quickly: *glimpse, glance, scan*
2. to look secretively: *spy, peep, peek, snoop*
3. to look long and thoughtfully: *gaze, contemplate, view*
4. to look steadily and directly: *stare, gape, gawk*
5. to look with anger or displeasure: *glower, glare, scowl*

antonyms: overlook, dismiss, ignore, avoid, shun

M

make *v.* to shape or put together out of materials or parts. *Mrs. Lewis **made** that rug from pieces of old clothes and curtains.*
build to put up something with materials or parts. *Dad **built** a tree house in our yard.*
construct to make by fitting parts together. *Will the town **construct** a bridge over the river?*
form to shape. *Ali **formed** a bird out of her piece of clay.*
manufacture to put things together with machines. *That factory **manufactures** many popular toys and games.*
antonyms: destroy, dismantle

many *adj.* adding up to a large number. *Jay learned to identify the **many** different birds on the island.*
several more than two but not a large number. *The power was out for **several** hours after the storm.*
numerous made up of a large number. ***Numerous** people lined up outside the factory to apply for a job.*
antonym: few

meaning *n.* the intended thought or message of something. *Ms. Clark explained the **meaning** of the poem to her puzzled students.*
significance the special message or intention. *What is the **significance** of the maple leaf on the Canadian flag?*
sense the many ideas implied by a word. *The **sense** of a word usually depends on its use in a sentence.*
antonyms: nonsense, pointlessness

moment *n.* a very short period of time. *Please wait just a **moment**, and a salesperson will help you.*
instant a second in time. *In an **instant**, before anyone could blink, the clown had disappeared.*

Thesaurus Plus

more ▶

Thesaurus Plus H95

How to Use This Thesaurus *continued*

N

necessary *adj.* having to be done. *It is* ***necessary*** *that you complete this form.*
essential very important, basic. *Regular brushing is* ***essential*** *to healthy teeth.*
required called for or needed. *The exam* ***required*** *careful thinking.*

nervous *adj.* shaken and jittery because of fear or challenge. *The* ***nervous*** *actor forgot his lines.*
anxious upset or fearful about something uncertain. *Olive feels* ***anxious*** *about her exam.*
edgy tense. *Bill was* ***edgy*** *the night before the exam and could not sleep.*
antonyms: calm, placid

new *adj.* never used, worn, or thought of before. *We finally bought a* ***new*** *car.*
fresh just made, grown, or gathered. *These are* ***fresh*** *beans, straight from Grandfather's garden.*
original not copied from or based on anything else. *The brilliant inventor came up with another* ***original*** *idea.*
novel strikingly different. *The detective's* ***novel*** *method of investigation was successful.*
antonyms: old, ancient, antique

Shades of Meaning
nice *adj.*
1. pleasing: *pleasant, agreeable, appealing, delightful, refreshing, lovely, charming, enchanting* 2. good: *fine, skillful, admirable, splendid, superb, excellent* 3. kind: *sweet, companionable, gentle, sympathetic, friendly, amiable, mild* 4. polite: *gracious, considerate, proper, well-mannered, courteous*
antonyms: insulting, offensive, displeasing, repellent, terrible, flawed, vile, mean, contemptible, vicious, rude, cold-hearted, crass

O

operate *v.* to run. *Can you* ***operate*** *a bulldozer?*
work to perform a function. *Who knows how to* ***work*** *the computer?*
use employ for some purpose. *Did you* ***use*** *my saw to build the bookcase?*

P

perfect *adj.* having no errors, flaws, or defects. *A* ***perfect*** *day for sailing is sunny and slightly breezy.*
ideal thought of as being the best possible. *Casey has an* ***ideal*** *job that allows her to travel.*
excellent of the highest quality. *The chef made our* ***excellent*** *meal from the freshest ingredients.*
delightful very pleasing. *A* ***delightful*** *breeze cooled the hot beach.*
antonyms: faulty, flawed

persuade *v.* to cause someone to do or believe something by pleading, arguing, or reasoning. *I* ***persuaded*** *Jim to clean my room for me.*
convince to cause someone to feel certain. *I* ***convinced*** *my mother that I was telling the truth.*
antonyms: dissuade, deter

Word Bank

pretty *adj.* pleasing to the eye or ear.

attractive	beautiful	radiant
cute	appealing	brilliant
charming	handsome	
dazzling	gorgeous	
ravishing	glorious	
stunning		
lovely		
glamorous		

antonyms: ugly, unattractive, homely, offensive, unappealing, disgusting, repulsive, revolting

price *n.* the amount of money asked or paid for something. *The **price** of this shirt is $10.95.*
charge a fee asked or paid, particularly for a service. *Is there a **charge** for washing the car windshield and windows, or is it a free service?*
cost amount of payment for a product or a service. *The **cost** of a concert ticket has increased ten dollars.*
expense something paid out. *Can we afford the **expense** of piano lessons?*

protect *v.* to keep safe from harm or injury. *Calvin wears a helmet to **protect** his head when he rides his bike or goes roller skating.*
guard to defend or keep safe from danger. *The police **guarded** the museum against theft.*
antonym: endanger

pull *v.* to apply force to in order to draw someone or something in the direction of the force. *I **pulled** the door toward me as hard as I could.*
drag to draw along the ground by force. *Jim **dragged** the heavy trash barrel across the lawn.*
haul to draw along behind, usually with great effort. *The horse **hauled** the heavy wagon up the mountain.*
tow to draw along behind with a chain or a rope. *With a strong rope, the big boat **towed** our canoe into the harbor.*
antonyms: push, shove

put *v.* to cause to be in a particular position. ***Put** your bike in the shed.*
place to lay something in a certain space. ***Place** your hands on your hips.*
locate to establish something in a certain area. ***Locate** your garden in a sunny place.*
set to cause to be in a particular location. ***Set** your books on the table.*
antonyms: remove, take away

Q

quick *adj.* done or happening without delay. *We took a **quick** trip to the store just before dinner.*
fast moving or acting with speed. *Traveling by plane is **faster** than traveling by car.*
hasty in a hurried way. *Jim scribbled a **hasty** note and then ran out the door.*
rapid marked by speed. *The **rapid** subway train zoomed through the tunnel.*
swift able to move at great speed. *You will need a **swift** horse if you want to get to the farm before dinner.*
speedy able to get from one place to another in a short time. *A **speedy** little rabbit outran my dog.*
antonym: slow

R

real *adj.* not imaginary, made up, or artificial. *This apple looks **real**, but it is wax.*
actual existing or happening. *Tory's visit to the palace was an **actual** event, not just a dream.*
true in agreement with fact. *Whether or not you believe it, the story is **true**.*
antonyms: artificial, fake

rough *adj.* full of bumps and ridges. *The carpenter sanded the **rough** wood.*
bumpy covered with lumps. *The **bumpy** road made us bounce in our seats.*
coarse not polished or fine. *The surface of sandpaper is **coarse**.*
uneven not level. *Because the floor was **uneven**, the table didn't sit straight.*
antonyms: smooth, polished

run *v.* to move quickly on foot. *Please do not **run** in the halls.*
dash to move with sudden speed. *We **dashed** out the door to get the mail.*
race to rush at top speed. *Leon **raced** to catch the bus.*
antonyms: walk, stroll

Thesaurus Plus

more ▶

Thesaurus Plus H97

How to Use This Thesaurus *continued*

S

same *adj.* being the very one. *This train is the **same** one that I rode last week.*
equal being alike in any measured quantity. *We got **equal** test scores.*
identical exactly alike. *The twins were **identical**; no one could tell them apart.*
antonym: different

Shades of Meaning
say *v.* speak aloud.
1. to say quietly or unclearly: *whisper, murmur, mutter, sigh, mumble, grunt* 2. to say in an excited or nervous way: *exclaim, cry, stammer, sputter* 3. to say loudly: *yell, scream, screech, shout, holler, bellow, roar, howl* 4. to say in an angry way: *snarl, snap, growl, bark, hiss* 5. to say in a complaining way: *whine, moan, groan, grumble, whimper, gripe*

scary *adj.* causing fear. *Your story was so **scary** that I was afraid to walk home.*
alarming causing a feeling of approaching danger. *The police siren was **alarming** to drivers.*
frightening causing sudden, great fear. *The **frightening** noise was thunder.*
terrifying causing overpowering fright. *The elephant made a **terrifying** noise.*

see *v.* to take in with the eyes. *Julie could not **see** the bird in the tree.*
notice to pay attention to. *Ron entered quietly, but we **noticed** he was late.*
observe to watch carefully. *The cat **observed** the bird in the tree.*
view to look at. *We **viewed** the city from the top of the mountain.*
antonyms: ignore, overlook

shake *v.* to move back and forth or up and down with short, quick movements. *The leaves on the oak tree **shook** in the wind.*
quake to move suddenly, as from shock. *The ground **quaked** when the herd of cattle moved by.*
shiver to move without control, as from cold or nervousness. *The child **shivered** in the cold rain.*
shudder to move with sudden, sharp movements, as from fear or horror. *Al **shuddered** when he read the story.*
tremble move back and forth gently or slightly, as from cold or fear. *My lips **trembled** as I began my speech.*

shiny *adj.* reflecting light. *Craig's **shiny** new bike sparkled in the sun.*
bright giving off strong rays of light. ***Bright** sun can be harmful to your eyes.*
gleaming glowing with light. *The **gleaming** runway lights showed the pilot where to land.*
glistening sparkling. *The sun turned the lake into a **glistening** pool of light.*
antonyms: dark, dim, dull

shout *v.* to call out at the top of one's voice. *The fans at the football game **shouted**, "Go, team, go!"*
yell to make a loud outcry, often in anger. *Helen **yelled**, "Your dog is eating my glove!"*
cry to utter a special sound or call. *Jeremy **cried** out in sudden pain.*
holler to call out to. *"Sue, come in for dinner!" I **hollered**.*
antonym: whisper

some *adj.* being an unspecified number or amount of. *Joanne invited **some** friends to play volleyball.*
few a small number of. ***Few** people today get enough exercise.*
several more than two but not a large number. *Carl moved **several** blocks away, but we can still walk there easily.*

start *v.* to take the first step in an action. *Joan turned to page one and **started** to read her book.*
begin to get a process underway. *I will **begin** my homework right after school.*
commence to perform the first part of an action. *The graduation ceremony **commences** at noon.*
antonyms: close, end, finish, stop

strange *adj.* different; unfamiliar. *I felt **strange** on my first day at the new school.*
weird odd or peculiar. *My brother has a **weird** sense of humor.*
odd out of the ordinary. *I read a story about an **odd** animal with three bumps!*
peculiar hard to understand or explain. *There is nothing **peculiar** about a green apple, but what do you think about a purple orange?*
unusual rare or different from what might be expected. *Her **unusual** name was hard to say.*
antonyms: normal, familiar, common, ordinary

surprise *v.* to cause to feel wonder because of the unexpected. *The sudden thunder **surprised** the picnickers in the park.*
amaze to fill with wonder or awe. *The skilled juggler **amazed** the crowd.*
astonish to startle greatly. *The unexpected news **astonished** the world.*
astound to strike with great wonder. *People were **astounded** by the speed of the new plane.*

T

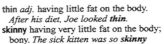

thin *adj.* having little fat on the body. *After his diet, Joe looked **thin**.*
skinny having very little fat on the body; bony. *The sick kitten was so **skinny** that we could see its ribs.*
slender having little fat or width. *The **slender** ballerina looked like a doll.*
antonyms: fat, plump, stout

Shades of Meaning

think *v.*

1. to use one's mind:
   consider
   evaluate
   reflect
   study

2. to have an opinion:
   feel
   judge
   assert
   believe

3. to suppose:
   imagine
   conceive
   dream
   speculate

antonyms: forget, ignore

U

unclear *adj.* not easy to see, hear, or understand. *Those complicated directions are **unclear**.*
fuzzy blurred. *The TV picture was too **fuzzy** to see any details.*
confusing mixed up. *The recipe was so **confusing** that we could not follow the steps.*
cloudy hazy; not clear. *The powder made the water **cloudy**.*
faint not distinct or bright. *The star was only a **faint** speck in the sky.*
antonyms: distinct, obvious, sharp

upset *adj.* sad or unsettled. *I was **upset** when I heard the bad news.*
worried uneasy because of fear. *Janet was **worried** about getting lost.*
nervous shaken and jittery because of fear or challenge. *Dean was **nervous** because he had to give a speech.*
troubled concerned because of pain, fear, or sadness. *Phil was **troubled** by his father's illness.*
disturbed being bothered or feeling

more ▶

Thesaurus Plus

Thesaurus Plus H99

How to Use This Thesaurus *continued*

unsettled. *They were **disturbed** by some noisy fire engines.*
antonyms: calm, comfortable, pleased, satisfied, composed

useful *adj.* being of service. *A rake is **useful** for cleaning up the yard.*
handy convenient, easy to use. *A wastebasket is a **handy** thing to have in each room of the house.*
helpful providing assistance. *I found this book **helpful** when I was looking for facts about the battle.*
antonyms: inefficient, useless, worthless

W

walk *v.* to move on foot at a steady pace. *Gabriel can **walk** to the store to get milk.*
march to move forward with regular and measured steps. *The band **marched** around the stadium as they played.*
stride to take long steps. *You **stride** so fast I cannot keep up with you.*
stroll to go forward in a slow, relaxed way. *Shall we **stroll** through the park after dinner?*
antonyms: run, stand still

How Wet Was It?

wet *adj.* covered or moistened with liquid.

1. extremely wet: *drenched, saturated, soaked, water-logged, sopping, flooded*

2. quite wet: *dripping, soppy, soggy, sodden*

3. slightly wet: *moist, damp, dank, dewy, wettish*

antonyms: parched, arid, dry, dehydrated

while *conj.* at the same period of time as. *I was waiting at the airport for Lois **while** she was waiting at the train station for me.*
as long as for an entire length of time. *We vowed to remain friends **as long as** we lived.*

wish *v.* to want, hope for. *What sights do you **wish** to see in the city?*
desire to want strongly. *More than anything else, Jan **desired** to travel around the world.*
crave to long for intensely. *The thirsty runners **craved** a cool drink.*

Glossary of Language Arts Terms

abbreviation a short form of a word.
action verb a word that tells what people or things do.
adjective a word that describes a noun and can tell what kind or how many.
adverb a word that describes a verb and tells how, when, or where.
apostrophe a punctuation mark (') that takes the place of any missing letters in a contraction and is used to form possessive nouns.
articles the adjectives *a, an,* and *the.*
audience person or people who read or listen to something.
brainstorm to think of different ideas.
cluster See **web**.
comma a punctuation mark (,) used to separate words in a sentence.
command a sentence that tells someone to do something. It ends with a period.
common noun names any person, place, or thing.
complete predicate includes all the words in the predicate.
complete subject includes all the words in the subject.
compound predicate made by using *and* to combine the predicates of two sentences with the same subject.
compound sentence two related, short sentences that have been combined, using a comma and the connecting word *and, but,* or *or*.
compound subject formed by using *and* to join the subjects of two sentences with the same predicate.
contraction a shortened form of two words joined together. An apostrophe replaces the missing letter or letters.
conventions the standard rules of spelling, grammar, usage, capitalization, and punctuation.
details exact facts or information.
direct quotation someone's exact words.
drafting the part of the writing process when the writer first attempts to put his or her ideas on paper in the form of a composition.
elaborate to give more details.
exclamation a sentence that shows strong feeling. It ends with an exclamation point (!).
future tense shows action that will happen.
helping verb a verb that comes before the main verb, such as *have, has, had.*
ideas thoughts that form the main points of a composition.
indent to begin the first line of a sentence a few spaces in from the margin.
irregular verbs verbs that do not add *-ed* to show past action.
linking verb a verb that joins the subject to a word in the predicate that names or describes the subject.
main idea the most important thought or point.
main verb the most important verb.
noun a word that names a person, a place, or a thing
negative a word that means "no."
order words words that signal sequence, such as *first, next, last, then, when,* and *later.*
organization the structure of a composition.
paragraph a group of sentences that tell about one main idea.
past tense a verb that shows action that has already happened.
phrase a group of words that does not have a subject or a predicate.
plural noun names more than one person, place, or thing.
plural possessive noun shows ownership. It is formed by adding an apostrophe to a plural noun.

more ▶

Glossary

Glossary of Language Arts Terms

Using the Glossary

This glossary provides an easy reference for the definitions of important language arts terms related to grammar, mechanics, usage, and writing that are introduced in the pupil book.

Draw students' attention to these pages. Encourage students to refer to the glossary whenever they need to review a definition or to understand instructions.

Glossary of Language Arts Terms *continued*

Glossary

possessive noun a noun that shows ownership. It is formed by adding an apostrophe and *s* to a singular noun.
predicate tells what the subject of a sentence does or is.
preposition a word that shows the connection between other words in a sentence, such as *at, for, with, after,* and *about.*
prepositional phrase a group of words that begins with a preposition and ends with a noun or pronoun.
present tense a verb that shows action that is happening now.
presentation the way in which writers show and share their compositions with their audience.
prewriting the part of the writing process when the writer chooses a topic and plans the composition.
pronoun a word that replaces one or more nouns.
proofreading the part of the writing process when the writing is checked for errors in grammar, usage, mechanics, and spelling.
proper noun a word that names a particular person, place, or thing and is capitalized.
publish the part of the writing process when writers make a final copy of their composition.
purpose the goal of a composition.
question a sentence that asks. It ends with a question mark.
quotation marks punctuation used before (“) and after (”) a direct quotation.
revising the part of the writing process when the writer tries to improve the working draft by adding, deleting, reorganizing, and rewriting.
run-on sentence has two complete thoughts that run into each other.
sensory words words that describe how something looks, sounds, feels, tastes, or smells.
sentence a group of words that tells a complete thought.
sentence fluency the structure and order of sentences so that a composition reads smoothly.
series a list of three or more words in a sentence.
simple predicate the main word in the complete predicate. It tells exactly what the subject does or is.
simple subject the main word in the complete subject. It tells exactly whom or what the sentence is about.
singular noun names one person, place, or thing.
statement a sentence that tells something. It ends with a period.
subject tells whom or what a sentence is about.
supporting sentences sentences that tell more details about a main idea.
tense the form of a verb that identifies whether something happens in the present, past, or future.
topic the subject of a discussion or a composition.
topic sentence a sentence that states a main idea about a subject.
transitional words words that connect sentences or ideas, such as *also, however,* and *for example.*
voice the use of words to show the writer's personality.
web words in connected circles that show how ideas are related.
word choice the selection of interesting, exact words.
working draft a composition that is still being revised or proofread and not yet final.
writing conference a discussion between a writer and a reader about the writer's composition.
writing process a series of steps (prewriting, drafting, revising, proofreading, publishing) that a writer follows to write a composition.

Index

Index

7. What do you find when you look up the term *Punctuation marks?* (a cross-reference to the specific types of punctuation)
8. What word would you look under to find information about the action parts of sentences? *(sentences)*
9. What word would you look under to find information about magazine titles? *(titles)*
10. On what pages would you find information about signal words? (272 and 284)
11. On what page would you find information about call numbers? (H21)
12. On what page would you find information about listening for enjoyment? (268)

Index

Lesson Objective

Students will:

- use an index

Focus on Instruction

- Explain that an index helps a reader find information in a nonfiction book. Unlike a table of contents, though, the index does not show the organization of the book. Tell students that the index lists the topics in the book. Ask students when they might want to use an index to find information. (when looking for facts about a particular topic)
- Point out the levels of entries, as indicated by indents. Explain that the entries are presented in an outline format. The words in dark type are main topics. Underneath many main topics are subtopics. In some indexes the subtopics are further divided.
- Have students look at the first page of the index. Ask students to notice in what order the topics in boldface are listed. (alphabetical order) Explain that the key words are alphabetized and that less important words and phrases are listed in alphabetical order after the key words they go with. Tell students that the numbers following the key words or less important words and phrases are page numbers. Call students' attention to the paragraph preceding the entries, and tell students that when they look up an entry they may first want to look at the pages whose numbers are in boldface.
- Have students find the entry *Business letters.* Tell students that this entry has a cross-reference. Explain that if students look for a term in the index and they don't find it, they should try to think of a closely related term.
- Have students use the index to find the following information.
  1. On what page would you find information about evaluating reasons? (458)
  2. What are the types of informative writing? (expository composition, instructions, and research reports)
  3. On which page are opinions first discussed? (115)
  4. What are the subtopics for the main topic *Instructions?* (following, giving, and writing)
  5. Where would you find information about direct objects? (page H73)
  6. What word would you look under to find information about parts of letters? *(letters)*

Index

L

M

Index

Index

Index

INDEX I-11

Index

Acknowledgments *continued*

"Knuckle Down That Taw!" by Beth Kennedy from *Highlights For Children* Magazine, January 1999 issu
Copyright ©1999 by Highlights for Children, Inc., Columbus, Ohio. Reprinted by permission of the publis

"A Play" from *Childtimes: A Three-Generation Memoir* by Eloise Greenfield and Lessie Jones Little. Copyright ©1979 by Eloise Greenfield and Lessie Jones Little. Used by permission of HarperCollins Publishers.

From *The Sea Otter* by Alvin, Virginia and Robert Silverstein. Copyright ©1995 by Alvin, Virginia and Rob
Silverstein. Used by permission of The Millbrook Press.

Poetry

"Keziah" from *Bronzeville Boys and Girls* by Gwendolyn Brooks. Copyright ©1956 by Gwendolyn Brook
Blakely. Used by permission of HarperCollins Publishers.

"A Matter of Taste" from *There Is No Rhyme for Silver* by Eve Merriam. Copyright ©1962, 1990 by Eve Merriam. Used by permission of Marian Reiner.

"My Name Is . . ." from *Silver Bells and Cockle Shells* by Pauline Clarke. Copyright ©1962 by Pauline Cla
Reproduced by permission of Curtis Brown Ltd., London.

"Penguin" from *The Llama Who Had No Pajama: 100 Favorite Poems* by Mary Ann Hoberman. Copyright ©1973 by Mary Ann Hoberman. Reprinted by permission of Harcourt, Inc.

Book Report

Little House on the Prairie by Laura Ingalls Wilder, illustrated by Garth Williams. Illustrations copyright 1
by Garth Williams, copyright renewed 1981 by Garth Williams. Used by permission of HarperCollins Publishers.

Student Handbook

Definitions of "floppy disk," "harbor," "mineral," "mingle," and "printer" from *The American Heritage®*
Children's Dictionary by the Editors of the American Heritage® Dictionaries. Copyright ©1998 by Hough
Mifflin Company. Reproduced by permission of *The American Heritage Children's Dictionary.*

Definition of "hard disk" from *The American Heritage® Student Dictionary.* Copyright ©1998 by Hough
Mifflin Company. Reproduced by permission of *The American Heritage Student Dictionary.*

Pronunciation key on page 25 from *The American Heritage® Children's Dictionary* by the Editors of the American Heritage® Dictionaries. Copyright ©1998 by Houghton Mifflin Company. Reproduced by permission of *The American Heritage Children's Dictionary.*

From "Robert Edward Lee" from *Collier's Encyclopedia,* Volume 14, page 440. Copyright ©1997 by Atlas Editions. All rights reserved. Used by permission.

Getting Started: Listening

Bees Dance and Whales Sing: The Mysteries of Animal Communication by Margery Facklam, illustrated b
Pamela Johnson. Illustrations copyright ©1992 by Pamela Johnson. Reprinted by permission of Sierra Cl
Books for Children.

Cricket Magazine, May 1999 issue, Volume 26, Number 9. Copyright ©1999 by Carus Publishing Compa
Reprinted by permission of *Cricket* Magazine.

One Minute Warm-up

4/1 *A River Dream* by Allen Say, published by Houghton Mifflin Company, 1988. Used by permission.

4/1 *The Great Yellowstone Fire* by Carole G. Vogel and Kathryn A. Goldner, published by Sierra Club Book
1990. Used by permission.

Acknowledgments

Sarah, Plain and Tall by Patricia MacLachlan, published by HarperCollins Publishers, 1985. Used by
mission.

Yang the Youngest and His Terrible Ear by Lensey Namioka, illustrated by Kees de Kiefte, published by
le, Brown and Company, 1992. Used by permission.

Cam Jansen and the Mystery of the Circus Clown by David A. Adler, illustrated by Susanna Natti,
blished by Puffin Books, 1983. Used by permission.

Radio Man: A Story In English and Spanish by Arthur Dorros, published by HarperCollins Publishers,
93. Used by permission.

The Secret Shortcut by Mark Teague. Copyright ©1996 by Mark Teague. Used by permission of
nolastic Inc.

The Story of the Olympics by Dave Anderson, published by William Morrow & Company, 1996. Used by
rmission.

Why Doesn't My Floppy Disk Flop? by Peter Cook and Scott Manning, illustrated by Ed Morrow. Text
pyright ©1999 by Peter Cook and Scott Manning. Illustrations copyright ©1999 by Ed Morrow. Reprinted
permission of John Wiley & Sons, Inc.

Akiak: A Tale from the Iditarod text and illustrations by Robert J. Blake, published by Philomel Books,
97. Used by permission.

Charlotte's Web by E.B. White, pictures by Garth Williams, published by HarperCollins Publishers, 1952.
ed by permission.

5 Carlos and the Skunk/Carlos Y El Zorrillo by Jan Romero Stevens, illustrated by Jeanne Arnold, published
Rising Moon Books for Young Readers, 1997. Used by permission.

5 Fables written and illustrated by Arnold Lobel, published by HarperCollins Publishers, 1980. Used by
rmission.

5 Justin and the Best Biscuits in the World by Mildred Pitts Walter, illustrated by Catherine Stock,
blished by Lothrop, Lee & Shepard Books, 1986. Used by permission.

5 Sadako by Eleanor Coerr, illustrated by Ed Young, published by G. P. Putnam's Sons, 1993. Used by
rmission.

6 A Llama in the Family by Johanna Hurwitz, illustrated by Mark Graham, published by Morrow Junior
oks, 1994. Used by permission.

6 Clambake: A Wampanoag Tradition by Russell M. Peters, photographs by John Madama, published by
rner Publications Company, 1992. Used by permission.

6 Creepy, Crawly Baby Bugs by Sandra Markle, published by Walker and Company, 1996. Used by
ermission.

7 The Sunday Outing by Gloria Jean Pinkney, pictures by Jerry Pinkney, published by Dial Books for Young
eaders, 1994. Used by permission.

tudent Writing Model Contributors
lizabeth Allen, Aimee Carney, Carolin Castillo, Wesley Crane, Asa Horvotz, Jeremy Jones, James Lee, Jessica
u, Colin McMillan, Jane Sawyer, Jillian Tully, Jack Welch, Andrea Zawoyski

Credits

Illustrations

Special Characters illustrated by: Sal, the Writing Pal by LeeLee Brazeal; Pencil Dog by Jennifer Beck Harris; Enrichment Animals by Scott Matthews.
Yvette Banek: 101
Mary Jane Begin: H14
John Bendall-Brunello: 23, 100 (top), 140, 471
Lisa Chiba: 244
Chris Demarest: 148, 220, 246, 269, 286, 306, 311, 349, 351, 427, H13
Eldon Doty: 37, 108, 204, 242
Rita Durrell: H92
Kate Flanagan: 114 (bottom), 141, 142, 146, 183, 186, 216
Jim Gordon: 240 (top)
Jennifer Harris: 100 (bottom), 166, 234
True Kelley: 208
Rita Lascaro: H17
Jared Lee: 144, 180
Rosanne Litzinger: 1-7
John Manders: 184 (bottom)
Patrick Merrell: 36 (top), 170 (bottom)
John Meza: 174
Laurie Newton-King: 70
Chris Reed: 38, 94, 114 (top), 170 (top), 218
Scot Ritchie: 112 (bottom), 240 (bottom)
Tim Robinson: 74
Ellen Sasaki: 184 (top)
Lauren Scheuer: 103, 118, 138, 248, 249 (center), 285, 287, 336, 358, 456, 460
Susan Spellman: H20, H25
George Ulrich: 44, 80, 106, 112 (top), 182, H88, H89, H91, H93-H96, H99, H100
Matt Wawiorka: 188 (center, bottom), 200, 307, 309, 379, 380, 408, 410, 423, 437, 438
Garth Williams: 9,10
Jean Wisenbaugh: 473
Amy L. Young: 36 (bottom), 209
Debra Ziss: 119 (bottom), 249 (bottom)

Photographs

iii © Lester Lefkowitz/The Stock Market. **iv** © Telegraph Colour Library/FPG International. **v** © Lori Adamski Peek/Tony Stone Images. **vi** © David Young-Wolff/PhotoEdit. **vii** © David Stewart/Tony Stone Images. **viii** © David Madison/Tony Stone Images. **ix** © Dewitt Jones/Tony Stone Images. **x** © Zigy Kaluzny/Tony Stone Images. **xi** (t) © Daryl Benson/Masterfile. (b) Courtesy NASA. **xii** © Lori Adamski Peek/Tony Stone Images. **xiii** (t) © Julie Habel/CORBIS. (b) © Nova Stock/FPG International. **31** © Lester Lefkowitz/The Stock Market. **32** © Barbara Filet/Tony Stone Images. **33** © Bob Calhoun; Clara Calhoun/Bruce Coleman/Picture Quest. **34** (tl) © David R. Frazier Photolibrary. (tr) © Len Rue, Jr./Animals Animals. (bl) © PhotoLink/PhotoDisc, Inc. (br) © R. Cetera/Mammoth Cave National Park. **35** © Jeremy Woodhouse/PhotoDisc, Inc. **38** (t) © PhotoDisc, Inc. (b) © M. Bridwell/PhotoEdit. **39** © PhotoDisc, Inc. **40** © Kurgan-Lisnet/Liaison International. **41** © Alan Pappe/PhotoDisc, Inc. **42** © Brian Bailey/Tony Stone Images. **43** © PhotoDisc, Inc. **44** Courtesy U. S. Space Camp, Mountain View, CA. **45** © CORBIS. **46** (t) © Culver Pictures. (frame) Image provided by MetaTools (b) © Jeff Greenberg/PhotoEdit. **47** © Albert J. Copley/PhotoDisc, Inc. **48** (l) © CORBIS. (c) © Michael Newman/PhotoEdit. (r) © Bob Daemmrich/The Image Works. **49** © Jeffry W. Myers/The Stock Market. **56** © Tom Benoit/Tony Stone Images. **57** © PhotoDisc, Inc. **58** © David Madison/Tony Stone Images. **59** (t) © Bachmann/Stock Boston. (b) © PhotoDisc, Inc. **60** © Joe Atlas/Artville. **61** © SuperStock, Inc. **63** © Telegraph Colour Library/FPG International. **64** © Jeff Greenberg/PhotoEdit. **65** © PhotoDisc, Inc. **66** © Nada Pecnik/Visuals Unlimited. **67** © Bettmann/CORBIS. **68** © Cartesia. **69** © The Granger Collection, New York. **70** © Jeff Lepore/Photo Researchers, Inc. **72** © Jane McAlonan/Visuals Unlimited. **74** © Donna Ikenberry/Animals Animals. **77** © James L. Fly/Unicorn Stock Photo. **78** (t) © PhotoDisc, Inc. (b) © SuperStock, Inc. **79** © PhotoDisc, Inc. **81** © Bettmann/CORBIS. **86** (l) © CORBIS. (r) © Coco McCoy/Rainbow/Picture Quest. **87** © Jim Cummins/FPG International. **88** © Stella Snead/Bruce Coleman, Inc. **89** © Corel Corporation. **90** © SuperStock, Inc.

·2 © Lee Snider/CORBIS. **95** © Lori ·damski Peek/Tony Stone Images. **96** © ·obert Brenner/PhotoEdit. **97** Image provided ·y MetaTools. **98** © Bob Daemmrich/Tony ·tone Images. **99** © PhotoDisc, Inc. **102** © ·hotoDisc, Inc. **104** © Jim Whitmer. **106** © ·im Cummins/FPG International. **107** © ·hotoDisc, Inc. **108** © Esbin/Anderson/The ·mage Works. **109** © Joseph Sohm; ·hromoSohm, Inc./CORBIS. **110** © Tony ·reeman/PhotoEdit. **111** (t) © PhotoDisc, Inc. ·) Image provided by MetaTools. **115** © ·igel Shuttleworth/Life File/PhotoDisc, Inc. ·**16** © Sonda Dawes/The Image Works. **121** · PhotoDisc, Inc. **125** © Wood ·abold/International Stock. **126** © David ·oung-Wolff/PhotoEdit. **127** © J. & P. ·egner/Animals Animals. **128** © Bonnie ·amin/PhotoEdit. **129** © M. Siluk/The Image ·orks. **130** (t) © Michael ·ewman/PhotoEdit. (b) © PhotoDisc, Inc. ·**31** © David Madison/Tony Stone Images. ·**32** © Mark Junak/Tony Stone Images. **133** · Horst Oesterwinter/International Stock. **134** · Myrleen Ferguson/PhotoEdit. **135** © Stuart ·estmorland/Tony Stone Images. **136** © ·ayne Kennedy/CORBIS. **137** © Adalberto ·ios Szalay/Sexto Sol/PhotoDisc, Inc. **139** © ·ORBIS. **141** © Glenn M. Oliver/Visuals ·nlimited. **142** © SuperStock, Inc. **143** © ·artesia. **144** © Arthur Hill/Visuals ·nlimited. **145** © Santokh Kochar/PhotoDisc, ·nc. **155** © SuperStock, Inc. **156** (b) © ·hotoDisc, Inc. **157** © John Giustina/FPG ·nternational. **158** (l) © Alan G. ·elson/Animals Animals. (tr) © Eye Wire, Inc. ·r) © Willard Luce/Animals Animals. **159** © ·yrleen Ferguson/PhotoEdit. **160** (t) © ·awrence Migdale/Tony Stone Images. (b) © ·euters Newmedia Inc./CORBIS. **161** Image ·rovided by MetaTools. **162** © CORBIS. ·**63** © CORBIS. **165** © Art Wolfe/Tony Stone ·nages. **168** © Doug Menuez/PhotoDisc, Inc. ·**71** © Myrleen Ferguson/PhotoEdit. **172** © ·aron Wolman/Tony Stone Images. **173** © ·laine Harrington, III/The Stock Market. **174** · Bill Bachmann/PhotoEdit. **176** © Steve ·tarr/Stock Boston/Picture Quest. **177** © ·igital Vision/Picture Quest. **179** (t) © PhotoDisc, Inc. (b) © Artville. **180** © SuperStock, Inc. **181** © Mark Newman/International Stock. **194** © Gerard Lacz/Animals Animals. **195** © National Portrait Gallery, London/SuperStock, Inc. **196** © Bob Daemmrich/The Image Works. **198** © American Museum, Bath, England/Bridgeman Art Library, London/SuperStock, Inc. **199** © Bob Trehearne/Stock Connection/Picture Quest. **201** © J. P. O'Neill/VIREO. **202** © Comstock, Inc. **203** © David Young-Wolff/PhotoEdit. **204** © PhotoDisc, Inc. **205** © Corel Corporation. **206** © PhotoDisc, Inc. **208** © Benn Mitchell/The Image Bank. **211** (tl) © David R. Frazier Photolibrary. (tr) © Don Lowe/Tony Stone Images. (bl) © Walter Chandoha. (br) © Lester Lefkowitz/The Stock Market. **212** © Walter Hodges/Tony Stone Images. **214** © Renee Lynn/Tony Stone Images. **215** © SuperStock, Inc. **217** (t) © CORBIS. (b) © David Young-Wolff/PhotoEdit/Picture Quest. **218** © Tim Davis/Tony Stone Images. **219** © Alan and Sandy Carey/PhotoDisc, Inc. **220** © PhotoDisc, Inc. **223** © PhotoDisc, Inc. **226** © Leonard Lee Rue, III/Animals Animals. **227** © Robert Lubeck/Animals Animals. **228** © Jeff Schultz/Alaska Stock Images/Picture Quest. **229** © Topham/The Image Works. **230** © Robert Maier/Animals Animals. **231** © PhotoDisc, Inc. **232** © C.C. Lockwood/Animals Animals. **233** © David Stewart/Tony Stone Images. **235** © Culver Pictures, Inc./SuperStock, Inc. **237** (tl) © Nigel Francis/ZEFA/The Stock Market. (tr) © Michael Andrews/Earth Scenes. (b) © Corel Corporation. **238** © ADAMSMITH/FPG International. **239** Courtesy of Special Olympics, Inc. **242** © Tony Freeman/PhotoEdit. **244** © Gayna Hoffman/Stock Boston. **247** © Randy M. Ury/The Stock Market. **248** © Walter Bibikow/FPG International. **251** Courtesy NASA/Finley Holiday Film. **255** © CORBIS. **256** (t) © SuperStock, Inc. (b) © Alvis Upitis/The Image Bank. **257** © PhotoDisc, Inc. **258** © Barbara von Hoffman/Animals Animals. **259** © Andy Sacks/Tony Stone Images. **260** © Bob Daemmrich/Stock

Acknowledgments *continued*

Boston. **261** © Bob Daemmrich/The Image Works. **262** © Ken Cole/Animals Animals. **263** © Richard During/Tony Stone Images. **266** © David Madison/Tony Stone Images. **266-7** © Dewitt Jones/Tony Stone Images. **267** (b) © Jerry Kobalenko/Tony Stone Images. **268** © PhotoDisc, Inc. **270** © Dennis O'Clair/Tony Stone Images. **271** © SuperStock, Inc. **272** © Inga Spence/Visuals Unlimited. **274** © David Madison/Tony Stone Images. **275** Courtesy Eloise Greenfield. **279** © Breck P. Kent/Earth Scenes. **297** © Jerry Kobalenko/Tony Stone Images. **310** © William Delzell/Tony Stone Images. **317** © *Carrie and Cocoa,* Robert Vickrey/Oklahoma City Art Museum. **328** © Zigy Kaluzny/Tony Stone Images. **328-9** © Daryl Benson/Masterfile. **329** (b) Courtesy NASA. **330** (l) © PhotoDisc, Inc. (r) © Daniel J. Cox/Tony Stone Images. **331** © Patti Murray/Animals Animals. **333** © Lester Lefkowitz/The Stock Market. **335** (l) © Rob Tringali, Jr./Sportschrome East/West. (r) © Lori Adamski Peek/Tony Stone Images. **338** © Zigy Kaluzny/Tony Stone Images. **339** © Kelly-Mooney Photography/CORBIS. **340** © Kelly-Mooney Photography/CORBIS. **364** (l) © Tony Freeman/PhotoEdit. (r) © Tony Hutchings/Tony Stone Images. **366** © Douglas Pebbles/Words & Pictures/Picture Quest. **368** Courtesy NASA. **369** © Kevin Schafer/CORBIS. **373** © Dani/Jeske/Earth Scenes. **381** © Art Wolfe/Tony Stone Images. **382** (l) © Gary Braasch/CORBIS. (r) © Wolfgang Kaehler/CORBIS. **392** (l) © Tim Flach/Tony Stone Images. (r) © Michael & Patricia Fogden/CORBIS. **393** © *Nino En Rojo,* Rufino Tamayo/ Christie's Images. **398** © Terry Vine/Tony Stone Images. **402** © Roger Ressmeyer/CORBIS. **404** © Lori Adamski Peek/Tony Stone Images. **404-5** © Julie Habel/CORBIS. **405** (b) © Nova Stock/FPG International. **409** © Lori Adamski Peek/Tony Stone Images. **412** © Lori Adamski Peek/Tony Stone Images. **413** © Paul Buchbinder. **414** (tl) © George Ancona. (bl) (r) © George Ancona/International Stock Photo. **415** © Leo Hsu. (inset) © George Ancona. **433** © *Black Camel with Blue Head and Red Tongue,* Alexander Calder (1898-1976), 1971. Sheet metal/cut, bent and painted (21 1/8 inches), National Gallery of Art, Washington/Gift of Mrs. Paul Mellon, in honor of the Fiftieth Anniversary of the National Gallery of Art. Photo by Philip A. Charles. **444** © Joseph Sohm; ChromoSohm, Inc./CORBIS. **446** © Nova Stock/FPG International. **447** © Joe McDonald/CORBIS **448** © Clive Druett; Papilio/CORBIS. **452** © Arthur Tilley/FPG International/Picture Quest. **458** (l) © PhotoDisc, Inc. (r) © Frank Siteman/Rainbow/Picture Quest. **469** © Bob Winsett/Index Stock Imagery/Picture Quest. **H8** © Spencer Grant, III/Stock Boston/Picture Quest. **H10** © Pablo Corral V/CORBIS. **H11** © Digital Vision. **H15** © EyeWire, Inc. **H17** © John Gerlach/Animals Animals. **H23** © PhotoDisc, Inc. **H31** (tl) © Comstock. (tr) (bl) © PhotoDisc, Inc. (br) © CMCD/PhotoDisc, Inc. **H46** (t) © Bettmann/CORBIS. (b) © Brown Brothers. **H51** © Telegraph Colour Library/FPG International. **H52** © Mark Newman/Stock Connection/Picture Quest. **H53** © Johnny Johnson/Animals Animals. **H72** © Wolfgang Kaehler/CORBIS. **H74** © Index Stock Photography. **H77** © CORBIS. **H78** Image provided by MetaTools.

Cover Photograph

Cover Stuart Westmorland/Tony Stone Images.